The Connoisseur's
Complete Period Guides

*to the Houses, Decoration, Furnishing
and Chattels of the Classic Periods*

The Connoisseur's Complete Period Guides

to the Houses, Decoration, Furnishing and Chattels of the Classic Periods

Edited by

Ralph Edwards and L. G. G. Ramsey

The Connoisseur
London

Designed and produced for The Connoisseur,
Chestergate House, Vauxhall Bridge Road,
London, SW1
by
George Rainbird Limited, Marble Arch House,
44 Edgware Road, London, W2.

Printed and bound by Grafoimpex,
Zagreb, Yugoslavia.

Contents

THE TUDOR PERIOD 1500-1603

THE STUART PERIOD 1603-1714

THE EARLY GEORGIAN PERIOD
1714-1760

THE LATE GEORGIAN PERIOD
1760-1810

THE EARLY VICTORIAN PERIOD
1830-1860

The Tudor Period

1500-1603

DIEV ET MON DROIT

Acknowledgments

Permission of the Controller of H.M. Stationery Office has been obtained for the reproduction of all photographs supplied by the Royal Commission on Historical Monuments.

The block on the title-page of this section has been made from the engraved title-page by Pieter van den Keere of John Norden's *Speculum Britanniæ*, part 1, 1593.

For the following illustrations acknowledgment is made to Picture Post Library: title-page, Plates 1B, 3, 4 and 91A.

The line blocks on pages 257 and 260 have been kindly loaned by Messrs Bernard Quaritch, Grafton Street, London W1.

The line block on page 253 is from *The Oxford Companion to Music* by Dr Percy Scholes, by kind permission of the Oxford University Press.

The line drawings in this section are by Mrs R. J. Charleston, Joan Drabwell, Audrey Frew, Helen McKie, Daphne Smith and John Wood.

The Tudor Age

JOEL HURSTFIELD

The turbulent and creative genius of Tudor culture grew and flourished amidst conditions of political and social instability. There was no decade during the sixteenth century when an English king or queen did not cast anxious eyes overseas at the gathering menace of foreign arms; while more than once the throne was rocked by a vigorous outburst of domestic discontent. What was true of the Crown was even more true of its ministers. It was not many paces from the council room to the block; and the Tower of London offered its cruel hospitality to the greatest in the land. Thomas Cromwell received in a short space an earldom and a death-sentence from his grateful master, Henry VIII. If instability was the climate of politics, the same was true of economic and social affairs. The traditional bases of English economy, corn and wool, were shifting under the uneven pressure of industry and trade; unemployment and poverty were the unyielding companions of expansion and progress. The brilliant prospects of an overseas empire brought, so far as the sixteenth century was concerned, occasional windfalls, cruel defeats, lasting disappointments and discredit upon its leading exponent, Sir Walter Raleigh. Yet, as in our own age, the very uncertainty of the times gave a stimulus and urgency to the inquiring mind, so that ecclesiastic and craftsman, statesman and poet exercised their skills in the buoyant atmosphere of fundamental change.

Peace and retrenchment

What kind of England was it that Henry VII won and ruled in 1485? Though it was licking its wounds after foreign defeat and civil war, the country as a whole showed in many ways the unchanging features of the medieval centuries. The population was small, perhaps not exceeding three millions, very small indeed compared with that of the powerful and wealthy France. The majority of English men and women lived in the country, as they were to go on doing for another three and a half centuries. Most men stood close to the plough and cultivated their scattered strips in a manner which would not have seemed strange to the administrators of William the Conqueror, four centuries before. But this was not invariably the case. Here and there a manorial lord or a prospering tenant was joining strip to strip and field to field in search of better techniques and richer yields. Apart from this, great tracts of England had never been broken by the plough. In Yorkshire and elsewhere Cistercian monasteries bred sheep where corn would not grow, as they had done since the twelfth century; and English wool won the golden opinions of all Europe and beyond. But not every Englishman tended his plough or watched his flock. In town and country alike a rising wool-textile industry was challenging the as yet superior products of continental skill.

In the north of England lay the frontier counties where English and Scots alike followed their traditional outdoor sports of cattle-raiding, arson, murder and rape. Further north still lay Scotland, where great lords disputed amongst themselves and with their king for mastery of an unruly land. Wales and Ireland, England's two other neighbours, displayed contrasting scenes. Over Wales,

Henry VII was king, and within half a century political assimilation would be completed. But good fortune, geography and the tenacity of a mountain people preserved the Welsh language and culture for the generations to come. In Ireland it was another story. No native prince and no English army succeeded in establishing a mastery over a treacherous and discordant land. Fleeting victories proved as costly as major defeats. Bloodshed and blunder sowed a wanton harvest whose fruits taste bitter even in our own day.

Within the British Isles, England was the dominant, though by no means irresistible, power; but in the eyes of Europe she was still economically backward and diplomatically insignificant. She had no army, no navy, no adequate merchant fleet. In trade and industry there were undoubtedly progress, expansion and ambition. But a good deal of her exports were still carried by the Hanseatic merchants trading with London and, indeed, still living as a flourishing and semi-independent community with their wharves, warehouses and residences on the north bank of the Thames. Southampton still looked forward each year to the visits of the Venetian galleys with their exotic Mediterranean products, in return for which they carried away the cloth of Hampshire, Wiltshire and elsewhere. Before the Tudor era was half over Hanseatics and Venetians alike were to lose their share in England's overseas trade, but for the present the Hanse merchants alone handled one-fifth of England's cloth export.

England was what would be known today as an under-developed territory, with all that euphemism may be taken to imply. She was a producer of raw materials: corn, wool, unfinished cloth, tin and a few other commodities. She was an importer of the manufactured products of other, and more advanced, nations: finished cloth, wine, armaments, luxuries. But the majority of her demands were satisfied in the home market. If she was to advance to the level of her neighbours – and in the warlike state of sixteenth-century Europe no nation could risk being dependent upon the finished products or arms of a foreign power – then she must cease to be a granary and a sheep-ranch. She must develop the new techniques of both light and heavy industry. She must also make use of the newer and more complex financial processes which the bankers and traders of western Europe had evolved. To do all these things England had to attract foreign skill and foreign capital; and, already since the fourteenth century she had, with foreign aid (soon to be augmented with Protestant refugees), made notable advances in one field – the textile industry, a good deal of whose products went to the overseas market, principally in the Low Countries. English cloth was usually exported 'white': that is to say, the finishing and dyeing were done abroad; while raw wool, in a diminishing proportion, continued to be funnelled through Calais, the last English possession on the continent.

If England's economic greatness lay in the future, the same was even more true of her role in international affairs. In the challenging pattern of European alliances England, possessing neither money, nor men, nor prestige, must walk warily. Peace and retrenchment were the most urgent needs and Calais must be regarded not only as a bridge-head but as an escape hatch. In religious affairs England seems to have recovered from the disordered heresies of the early fifteenth century; and in politics an exhausted nation needed a respite from the trials and errors which had sapped her strength for so long. Over such an England Henry VII came to rule.

A great deal of sterile polemics has been employed in the debate as to whether Henry VII was a medieval or a modern king. No historian now believes that the medieval world came to an end on that famous August day in 1485 when Henry picked up Richard III's crown on Bosworth field and placed it on his own head. Henry was not concerned to establish a new order or even a new monarchy. His ambitions can be much more simply expressed than that: he wished, like some of the uneasy rulers of modern states, to stay alive and at work. That in itself was a tremendous task. The crown he had won in battle could also be lost in battle. He had beaten the Yorkists at war and married a Yorkist queen; but Margaret of Burgundy was a Yorkist also, and from the Low Countries she fought a remorseless rearguard action against the usurping King. Lambert Simnel and Perkin Warbeck have become jokes amongst schoolboys, but Henry treated them with the seriousness that they deserved. Even more important to Henry than the destruction of their power in battle was the destruction of the conditions which made such risings possible. In other words, Henry had to restore the prestige of the English monarchy at home and abroad. To his own people he brought at last stable, inexpensive government, a healthy overseas trade and the hopes of tranquillity. Abroad he played a cautious, sensitive, waiting game, wasting neither men nor resources but using with finesse the weapons at his disposal – his native wit, financial strength and English wool – to press his claim for recognition and respect. At no stage in the sixteenth century was England strong enough to dominate European diplomacy. If Henry VIII and Wolsey ever dreamt that they could dictate conditions to the European powers, that dream soon became a nightmare. In this the father was wiser than the son. Henry VII's flexible and unadventurous foreign policy sought neither territory nor glory, but peace and recognition for the House of Tudor. The Wars of the Roses did not end in 1485 with Bosworth and Henry VII's accession. They ended in 1501, when Henry's eldest son married Catharine of Aragon. This marriage more than anything symbolized that the Tudors had at last arrived.

Church and State under Henry VIII

It is rare in English history for an eldest son to succeed his father as king. That young man of high promise, Arthur – whose name recalled memories of the Welsh ancestry of the Tudors and, beyond that, of the ancient and heroic kingship of Britain – died before his father and the succession passed in the year 1509 to Henry, the second son. Undoubtedly Henry VIII felt far more secure than Henry VII had ever been. The father's hope of uniting the warring houses was fulfilled in the person of his son, in whose veins flowed Yorkist as well as Lancastrian blood. Moreover, a generation had passed since Bosworth; and a throne captured in battle had been rebuilt upon the firm foundations of renovated institutions and of peace. If England could not speak first in the counsels of

Europe, she was by now at least entitled to be heard. Even so, with all this significant accretion of power and prestige, we find Henry VIII more than once looking over his shoulder at the tainted, but not extinguished, claims of rivals. It was this cunning and ruthless watchfulness which brought the Duke of Buckingham in 1521, and the aged Countess of Salisbury in 1541, to the block. There were no Warbecks and Simnels in Henry VIII's reign. The rebels who pressed down from the north in 1536, it is true, told Henry exactly what they thought of his government and what they would do to his ministers – but to Henry himself they affirmed from start to finish their utter loyalty. Henry did some terrible things to Church and State in the thirty-eight years of his rule, yet he always weathered his crises. It looks as though his father had built to last.

Yet no system is truly well-founded if it does not hold firm into the third generation; and of the third generation there was as yet no adequate sign. Henry's wife – Arthur's widow – had borne him only one surviving child, a daughter. A female successor filled the lawyers with doubt and the politicians with alarm, amply justified ultimately by Mary's performance on the throne. The King's mistress had indeed borne him a son, the Duke of Richmond, but not even the masterful Henry, though he had perhaps toyed with the idea, would dare supplant the legitimate female successor by an illegitimate male one. If he did, he would at once open the door to the Wars of the Roses, second series. No diplomatic or military victories of Henry and his minister, Cardinal Wolsey – and most of their victories, with the exception of Flodden, were transient ones – no victory could erase the darkening fear of the succession as Catharine grew past child-bearing and Henry past patience.

An early fear became with the passage of time dominant and obsessive; and it needed no conscious effort on the part of so self-centred a man to come to the conclusion that the doctrine of Leviticus, the laws of Christendom, the wisdom of the universities, nay, the voice of God enjoined that he should set Catharine aside. The curse of sterility – with only Mary left it was nearly that – which had descended upon his marriage was, he now saw, divine punishment for his transgression in wedding his deceased brother's widow. It is true that Anne Boleyn, as masterful as the King, was at hand, and with that lady, unlike her sister – who had for a time been Henry's mistress – it was marriage or nothing at all. This may have given point and urgency to the heart-searchings upon which the King had now embarked. But if the whole business is dominated by self-indulgence and hypocrisy, we must recognize that the King was thinking also in the national interest. Let us suppose that Henry had behaved with greater decorum and consideration to Catharine and that the brief marriage with Anne Boleyn had never taken place. After him would have come Edward VI and Mary – short and troubled reigns – and then …? Instead of half a century of consolidation and achievement under the daughter of Anne Boleyn, England would have entered upon a well-nigh hopeless quest for a new dynasty amidst turmoil and war. Much could be said against Henry VIII as a man, the least attractive of the Tudors, possessing neither the long-headedness of Henry VII, the pathos of Edward VI, the sincerity of Mary Tudor nor the wayward charm of Elizabeth. But when all that can be said against him has been said, we would do well to remember that, as a statesman, he made his dynasty safe enough to last out the century. France destroyed her sons and ruined her economy in eight increasingly bitter civil wars during the second half of the sixteenth century. 'We fought the first war like angels,' said a French Huguenot, 'the second like men, and the third like devils.' (Perhaps he did not live long enough to find appropriate terms to describe the eighth.) During this same period England went about her business at peace with herself.

So it came about – whether from lust or policy or a typically Henrician amalgam of both – that Henry reshaped both Church and State and, to achieve his purpose, broke with Rome. Here it is the son who outdistanced the father. If there was a new monarchy in the sixteenth century, and if it was the work of a royal founder and not his ministers, then Henry VIII has a better claim to the title than Henry VII.

The origins of the Reformation may then be found in the troubled conscience of a theologically minded monarch; and the issue, as far as he was concerned, may have been resolved when both Anne Boleyn and Catharine of Aragon were in their graves. But the King had opened doors which he could not shut, and through them there blew an easterly wind from the German plains and elsewhere which would sweep the King himself along with it, if he did not keep his feet planted hard on the ground. But the King set himself firmly against doctrinal change: a successful revolutionary inevitably becomes opposed to revolution – at least in his own country. Henry VIII always claimed to be a Catholic (apart from a certain *contretemps* with the Papacy); Thomas Cromwell claimed on the scaffold that he too was a Catholic. We may be a little uneasy about taking Cromwell at his word, but there is no reason to doubt the sincerity of Henry. In the matter of the mass, clerical celibacy, the structure of the Church, Henry stood where English kings had always stood.

This was not so of all his ministers. Cromwell's fall and execution may have been on account of the King's refusal to take the road along which his Protestant-minded minister was propelling him. But if Cromwell died, Cranmer lived. Henry VIII died but the strongly Protestant Edward VI succeeded him. Each year that passed was to show that Henry was not only the author of the breach with Rome but, no less serious, the breach within England. Henry belongs to the long line of mistaken despots who have imagined that you can start a revolution and then arrest it half way. What had been a widening breach under Henry VIII was made an unbridgeable gulf by his two successors, Edward VI and Mary: and they in turn transmitted to Elizabeth the intolerable situation of two embittered minorities prepared to destroy England for the sake of their immortal souls.

But the Reformation was, of course, not simply a movement of religion. If the soul of England was reshaped, so was her soil; for at least a fifth of it had passed into the possession of the Church. 'Mortmain' the lawyers called it – the dead hand – for land which had once passed to the Church by gift, bequest or purchase never returned. But the monasteries were also the bastions of the old order, though laxity and luxury had seeped in to soften the harsh discipline of a life of service. Upon this laxity Henry VIII and Cromwell fastened, publicized it, magnified it and used it, in a series of crushing blows, to break the hold of the Church upon the English shires. The blows were not as merciless as they used to be thought: some of the evicted monks went on drawing their pensions right through the sixteenth and into the seventeenth centuries, though the monasteries had fallen more than sixty years before. Nor was the King as prodigal as historians at one time imagined he was. It is true that some Court favourites and officials reaped a bounteous harvest of gifts of ecclesiastical estates, gifts which made their name and fame and which have now been in their families longer even than they were held by the monasteries from whom they came. But for the few whom the King delighted to honour, there were many who bought these confiscated lands for as high a price as the market would bear. And the children or grandchildren sometimes discovered, long afterwards and to their horror, that the King had attached to the monastic lands the ancient rights of feudal wardship, which imposed cruel conditions of guardianship and marriage upon those who had played no part in the original transactions. But whether the land came by gift or purchase, whether it was bought cheap or dear, the vesting of this confiscated property in the English landed classes gave them solid arguments for maintaining the Reformation settlement which Henry had made. Later, when Mary set about restoring the original Church system her faithful and flexible Commons told her that they would acquiesce in the restoration of the Papacy and Roman doctrine, that they would let the Protestant theology go, but the monastic lands would never return. What they had they held. More than a century later, when dark rumours were in circulation that James II was planning to restore both the Church and the lands, the great-grandsons of Mary's parliamentarians held as fast as had their predecessors to their Protestant inheritance.

We are inclined to believe nowadays that the agrarian effects of the Reformation were not so profound or widespread as at one time appeared. Many of the new owners had already been lessees of the lands of which they now obtained fuller possession. Others had acted as monastic stewards for the estates they now acquired. If a number of them turned out to be cruel and enclosing landlords, some of the abbots who preceded them could have taught them a sound lesson on how to go about the business. Here and there more progressive ideas could be applied, and a city businessman or an active country gentleman, with an eye to see, might begin to open up the rich coal seams often untouched by the monastic landlords. Sometimes the original servants and retainers of the ecclesiastical estates were, after the dissolution, let loose upon the countryside to join the bands of motley toughs who begged and bullied their way over England; if they were not hanged for a felony before they were half-way across. But the dissolution of the monasteries was not the cause of vagabondage, poverty and unemployment: and, in this respect at least, Henry can plead not guilty of an evil whose roots lay deep in the changing and complex economy of Tudor England.

Culturally the effects of the dissolution may have been more severe. Valuable manuscripts perished as the estates quickly passed from churchman to layman and from layman to layman. Wonderful products of medieval architecture decayed and collapsed as the vandals tore the lead from their roofs and carried away anything else upon which they could lay their hands. And then, under Edward VI, the chantry lands—bequeathed to provide a chantry priest to pray for the soul of the departed but used also to pay for the education of the living—went the way of the monastic lands. Some of the Edward VI grammar schools which are still with us were not those founded by Edward VI but those which escaped the rapacity of his ministers.

Inflation and the social revolution

The Reformation, then, was one of the two major destructive forces of the age. The other was inflation. Contemporaries and historians alike were aware that, during the sixteenth century, prices showed a sharp upward movement. But only we, who have endured two massive inflationary waves in forty years, can give to this movement the weight that it deserves. Moreover, unlike what is happening today, the change could be clearly seen: for the money literally changed colour. By reducing the silver content and adding alloy, the metallic currency took on a different and suspicious hue. Of this, Hugh Latimer, reformer, Court preacher and martyr, made great play in his sermon before Edward VI. The silver coins, he said, could easily be mistaken for copper ones – 'We have now a pretty little shilling indeed, a very pretty one: I have but one, I think, in my purse; and the last day I had put it away almost for an old groat.' Bad money (pumped into circulation by the government itself) was driving out good; and the reputation of the pound was sinking in the centres of international trade.

Meanwhile, after Henry VIII had done his worst to the English currency, the flow of silver from abroad, especially from Peru in the 1540's, gave the inflationary spiral a sharp upward twist. Under Edward VI in this, as in so much else, the situation still further deteriorated; a half-hearted attempt to reform the currency made confusion worse confounded. In 1561, under Elizabeth, a second and more resourceful scheme held firm. The value of sterling was forced up, both at home and abroad, and the country began to turn away from the treacherous optimism of cheap money. Deflation brought unemployment in its wake but, even so, the inflationary process was not wholly arrested. Though it never again during the century reached the severity of the mid-Tudor period, its dragging burden hung around the necks of Government and people alike.

We know also, from the living experience of our own century, that inflation is not simply an economic phenomenon the effects of which are felt merely when goods and money change hands. It is a revolutionary process as profound as the revolutions that men make in Parliament or in the streets. It was no less fundamental in the sixteenth century. Then, as now, it turned the balance heavily against those with fixed-money sources as compared with those who could move along the crest of the wave to higher incomes. Many landlords, for example, found that a good proportion of

their revenue was derived from rents on lands held by their tenants on long leases. In cases such as these, the tenant was protected against the effects of inflation by as powerful a shield as any raised by our modern rent restriction acts. Against him was the landlord who faced a rising cost of living with an income whose purchasing power – though not monetary value – was shrinking before his eyes. Worse still, considerable areas of the lord's land might be held by what was known as copyhold tenure, which in some cases, though by no means all, gave the holder full immunity to change in his rent, status or conditions. Not every tenant was so protected, nor was every landlord faced with a falling income throughout his estate. A shrewd lawyer or a bullying agent might induce a protected tenant to abandon his security out of fear, ignorance or illusory gain. Elsewhere the lord might still recoup himself by raising rents and premiums – entry fines as they were called – where the tenant's rent and status had no protection other than an expiring contract. Since well over fifty per cent of the tenants had little or no safeguard against the consequences of a rising price-level, it is clear that, as far as the landlord was concerned, the position was not as bad as it has sometimes been made out to be.

A progressive landowner had at his disposal another method by which he might trim his sails to the wind. As leases fell in, or as tenants were evicted by law or force, he, or some other lessee who took the land at a higher rent, could seize the opportunity, at one and the same time, to solve his labour problem (because sheep needed far less men than corn), increase his profits and meet a rising demand. He might convert his land from corn to wool; and as the sheep followed hard on the heels of the departing tenant, so the lord harvested the richer profits of the time. In the first half of the century there seemed no means of stopping the advancing flocks. We used to think that Thomas More exaggerated when, in his *Utopia*, he flayed the all-consuming sheep: 'Your sheep that were wont to be so meek and tame, and so small eaters, now, as I hear say, be become so great devourers and so wild that they eat up and swallow down the very men themselves!' As a result men were 'compelled to sell all: by one means therefore or by other, either by hook or crook, they must needs depart away, poor silly, wretched souls, men, women, husbands, wives, fatherless children, widows, woeful mothers with their young babies'. The picture may indeed be overdrawn, but in recent years new historical techniques have produced impressive evidence to show that, in some of the midland counties, the wool drove out corn so fast that whole villages were emptied as the plough gave way to the hoof. A booming textile trade – increasingly unhealthy in the middle years of the sixteenth century – put pressure on sheep just as they, in turn, put pressure on men. These developments were by no means universal; most men looked out upon an unchanging rural scene. But if only one family in a hundred were evicted from their holdings, they were taken to be a sign of the times, and the other ninety-nine stirred uneasily as they wondered where the next blow would fall.

The great curse of inflation is that its incidence is uneven. Those who were unprotected paid dearly for the shelter which accident and the law gave to their neighbours. In the same way an unskilled landlord, or one who dissipated his capital in luxury or litigation – sometimes litigation rather than luxury consumed a great estate – would be unable to stand the pace of economic progress and he too would have no option but to sell out and go.

For one landlord, the greatest of them, the situation offered the least freedom to manœuvre. By inheritance, conquest and confiscation, the Tudor monarchs were masters of vast estates. But, for reasons too complex to be considered here, they had even less economic elasticity than other great lords in adapting themselves to a climbing price-level. The real value of their rents and other incomes shrank at the very time when their mounting commitments were pressing heavily upon them. War, diplomacy, administration made unparalleled demands upon the Treasury and played their part in stimulating the desperate measures which the Crown sometimes took. Henry VIII's seizure of the ecclesiastical lands was merely one extreme example of how the Crown was forced to live on capital – other people's as well as its own. But when rents, customs and the rest proved inadequate for the Government to discharge its duties, what should it do? It must perforce ask Parliament for money. But these demands were known technically as 'extraordinary' and, to contemporary eyes, extraordinary they undoubtedly were. They were a sign that the Crown was not living within its normal means. It was not to be expected that the hard-headed lawyers, country gentlemen and business men would tamely respond to demands on an unprecedented scale. They usually granted less than they were asked, and they made speeches and offered advice, unsought for and unwelcome to the Crown. Finally they tried to impose terms as to the use of the money and on government in general. The day might indeed come when this policy would bring first deadlock in government, then civil war and then the transfer of power to the parliamentary classes. So it was that the second half of the sixteenth century and the first half of the seventeenth were played out against a double revolution in religion and society.

The Tudor crisis: Edward VI and Mary

Henry VIII had carried through a revolution in order to make his dynasty secure. Now he found it doubly necessary to safeguard his dynasty in order to make his revolution secure. Yet what was the position at the time of his death in 1547? His illegitimate son, the Duke of Richmond, was dead. His two daughters, Mary and Elizabeth, had each been declared illegitimate by King and Parliament. Only a boy of nine, Edward VI, remained to carry on his slender shoulders the heavy burden of Tudor rule. There survives, amongst other things, the boyish diary kept by the young King, and we know something also about his febrile precocity, especially displayed in theological intercourse. Here he was a true son of his father, but in matters of state, naturally enough, there was no sign yet of the Tudor skill. He accepted, ready-made, his opinions from the professional politicians who filled him with stories about the treachery of their opponents. It proved the most squalid period of the sixteenth century, with the carrion courtiers feeding upon the remains of Henry's system. The

Protector Somerset, Edward's first minister, tempered his greed with an idealistic concern for social welfare. His supplanter, Northumberland, had no such inhibitions. He suppressed the peasantry with the aid of German mercenaries and then set about pillaging the State in the name of the King, and the Church in the name of Protestantism. Finally, in his wild bid for power as the young King lay dying, he joined his name to the remote title of Lady Jane Grey and brought tragedy upon them both. His ill-fame fastened itself for the moment to the extreme Protestantism with which he had identified himself, with the result that he made England safe for Catholicism. Almost without opposition, Mary ascended the throne.

The mother of Mary was an embittered Spaniard. The mother of Elizabeth was the very English product of a native aristocratic household. Mary was half Spanish and married her Spanish cousin; Elizabeth was 'mere English'. Yet, if in their difference of temperament and outlook they owed so much to their maternal heredity, we should remember also that they were the daughters of the same father. To him they owed the tough, imperious will, the firm stand in a crisis, the ability on occasion to sense, express and shape the national mood. But from the age of sixteen Mary's whole outlook had been distorted beyond endurance as humiliations were piled upon her mother and herself. From the age of twenty, until her accession, Elizabeth lived in the shadows under the Catholic restoration of Mary. Elizabeth knew that her enemies were watching her every move in the hope of a false one; that her friends, in their enthusiasm, would make her into a second Lady Jane Grey. So Elizabeth learned to soften her father's passion with her grandfather's patience, and the result made her greater than them both.

Elizabeth was the focus of plotting and it could be said that Mary displayed a mistaken clemency when, as Queen, she did not put Elizabeth to death. On the contrary, if she had done so, she would have fully earned the soubriquet which has become attached to her name. For at no stage did Elizabeth supply a single word or deed to indicate treason. If she had, nothing could have saved her. But in the absence of evidence, to have executed her would have been plain murder. Even a bloodthirsty age would have shrunk before the execution by the Queen of her royal half-sister whose only crime was close kinship. And Mary was not a bloodthirsty woman. She must, of course, share the blame with her advisers for the burning of Protestant martyrs, but outside this narrow, fanatical channel of her mind she could be warm, humane, temperate. Neither her father nor her husband responded to her womanly love, and in the end her love turned sour within her: her death in 1558 did not come too soon either for herself or for her country. Blighted Mary she was, rather than Bloody Mary.

England under Elizabeth

The prospects for her sister were no better. Civil war, an attack from a Catholic power to stamp out once and for all the reviving English Protestantism, or human mortality itself might intervene to write *finis* to the reign and the dynasty. If the smallpox which she contracted in 1562 had completed its fatal cycle, then almost certainly the work of her father – and her grandfather – would have been undone. Then Mary Queen of Scots would have become Mary Queen of England and the disaster about to begin north of the border would have been re-enacted on a grander scale in the southern kingdom. But a resilient body was joined to a resilient mind and Elizabeth recovered. Instead of ruling for five years, she ruled for forty-five.

For long she, too, was insecure. It is a glib and baseless generalization to say that, at the accession of Elizabeth, half England was Catholic and the other half Protestant. No historical evidence is available – or likely to become available – to support this example of sheer speculation. What we do know, however, as the result of the masterly studies of Sir John Neale, is that a noisy minority of Members of Parliament, sustained by extremist exiles – who had spent the five years of Mary's rule drinking deeply from the pure fountains of continental Protestantism – joined to press on the Queen a harsh and extremist religious settlement, abhorrent to her nature. We know also that in the northern shires the older traditions held fast and that even the lukewarm political-protestantism of the Queen affronted their faithfulness to the Catholic ideal. To them, Mary Queen of Scots, for nineteen years an exile-prisoner in England, offered the treacherous prospect of a leader and a queen. Somewhere between the north and the south, the right and the left, were men like the Duke of Norfolk, whose religion and politics were elastic enough to open before him the dazzling vision of a marriage to Mary and a place beside her on the throne of two realms. The northern rebels of 1569 rose in vain. The Duke of Norfolk came to the capital not to be crowned but to be executed. These were not the last of the plots and rebellions but probably the last prospect of their success. After that new plots emerged: clumsy, fantastic, hopeless. Queen Elizabeth sometimes knew the next move of the plotters before they knew it themselves. In the end the Queen of Scots, in response to a tireless campaign by the parliamentary classes, received the just sentence for two decades of sedition.

Elizabeth did to her cousin Mary what her own sister had never done to her but, even after signing the death-warrant, she hesitated about the ultimate step. Whether she intended to rescind the warrant or not, her ministers anticipated that the woman in her might triumph over the queen. Hastily they sent off the death-warrant before the emotions of the night should have time to distort the reason of the day. When the news of the execution was brought to Elizabeth she hesitated for some terrible hours as to whether she should appease her own conscience and the anger of Europe by executing some of her principal ministers. In the end she was satisfied with the dismissal and imprisonment of a lesser scapegoat, her unfortunate Secretary of State, Davison. Yet, by a typical irony of the Tudor mind, she continued to pay him his salary while he expiated his crime.

The Elizabethan achievement

Elizabeth possessed a quality which was for a long time rare in the English monarchy, though she shared it with her great contemporary, Henri IV of France. She held no strong views on the subject of religion and rated the welfare of the present State above that of the eternal Church. Had it been necessary, she might, in the language of Henri IV, have said that London, like Paris, was worth a mass. But it was not necessary. What was desperately needed was to restrain the hotheads of both wings and seek to rally behind the throne the voiceless majority who, she believed, had had their fill of the ceaseless disputations of the theologians. In this more than anything else the secular minded Queen reached out beyond her own age to a re-united England she did not live to see. But she saw the first signs of it and rejoiced as much over one Catholic as over a thousand Protestants who stood fast at her side when Philip II launched his long-awaited crusade.

If the Catholics represented a waning danger as one plot after another collapsed in ignominy and there even emerged a body of Catholics who had discovered how to serve both God and the Queen, the threat from the extreme Protestants—Puritans, as they were coming to be called – could not be so easily exorcized. Here was a righteous remnant who would have established Calvin's intolerant Geneva throughout the length and breadth of the land, even though before the day came half England might have gone up in flames. To them Elizabeth represented the betrayal of the great cause, and, with their backs to the wall, they used the sounding-board of the House of Commons to tell her what they thought. 'Certain it is, Mr Speaker,' said the irrepressible Peter Wentworth, 'that none is without fault: no not our noble Queen ... Her Majesty hath committed great faults, – yea, dangerous faults to herself and the State'. 'Make you Popes who list', this same Wentworth had once retorted to the Archbishop of Canterbury, 'for we will make you none!' Here was the paradox. Wentworth in the name of liberty opposed the Queen. Yet she, in the name of liberty, opposed Wentworth and the Puritan minority. For their idea of freedom meant freedom to impose their intransigent creed upon the overwhelming majority of their fellow-countrymen. Puritanism would have ended the power of the bishops, reduced the power of the Queen and, with the bible in one hand and the sword in the other, have established the dictatorship of the godly

27

which would have tried even the patience of saints.

So the Queen stood fast, even when some of her most important ministers, like Leicester and Essex – for reasons of their own – flirted with the Puritans. It was a difficult and thankless task to which she committed herself, and some of it, later on, had to be done all over again. But when she, and those who shared her purpose, like the humane and scholarly Hooker, had done their work, an English church emerged which was neither Roman Catholic nor Puritan but, with typically English eclecticism, took the best from both worlds and built itself deeply into the life and language of the people.

The execution of the Queen of Scots in 1587 had marked the end of serious Catholic plotting. The hopeless rising of the Earl of Essex in 1601 had no religious basis. It smacks of the theatre and the tavern: disappointed youth hurling itself in vain against the sturdy pillars of wisdom and age. It hurt the Queen to have to destroy a young man of such high promise and such erratic and irresponsible performance. But he quite misunderstood the character of personal monarchy and he blundered too near the throne. In the main, the last fifteen years of the reign saw no fundamental cleavage within the nation.

Perhaps domestic peace made it possible for a united nation to face the darkening menace from abroad. Such unity was desperately needed in the last decades of the Queen's life. France was fighting a civil war of which the upshot might decide whether she stood with Protestant England or against her. The Netherlands were divided against themselves and Protestantism flickered on only in the northern provinces, fighting a well-nigh hopeless battle against Spain. If the Netherlands fell, or if France finally decided for pro-Spanish Catholicism, England's position would be more serious than in the darkest days of the Napoleonic Wars or of Dunkirk. Spain, the greatest Empire since the fall of Rome, closed in upon a desperate island. Yet a desperate island could inflict grievous blows in the Atlantic and even in Cadiz during the wearing years of undeclared war. The struggle with Spain was not to be completed in the glorious events of 1588. The battle with the Armada was no more than the brilliant overture to a long drawn-out, exhausting struggle of which the Queen did not live to see the end. It was left to her unromantic successor, James I, to come down from Scotland and bring the wearisome business to its overdue end.

Unity had been needed; but how long would it last? Would the commercial and landed classes be content to leave government in the hands of the monarchy, or would they make a bid for political power to match their rising economic power? In politics, religion, foreign policy their demands were rising, and Elizabeth more than once heard the tocsin sound for the approaching constitutional struggle. When James VI of Scotland succeeded to the English throne and had his first taste of the ways of Parliament, he looked upon it with astonished eyes.

End of an epoch

A recalcitrant and opinionated House of Commons was not the only thing which surprised James when he came to London to be crowned. (His coronation, indeed, had to be stripped of its pageantry because plague, a recurrent visitor throughout the sixteenth century, returned to participate in the rejoicings of the new reign.) It was a changing London that James I found, and he was not sure that he liked it. There were, it is true, many great and stately buildings, about which more is said elsewhere in this volume; but there existed cheek by jowl with them insanitary, overcrowded tenements of the worst kind. The drift to London was something which neither threat nor legislation could arrest. To the capital flowed the professional classes in search of wealth and advancement, with the help perhaps of the vast, unofficial network of contact men who knew or claimed to know, all the right people. Here also came the young men to study law at the Inns of Court; and the Members of Parliament, their wives and families for politics, the social round, prestige and a husband for an eligible daughter, for we have entered upon the period of the town house and the 'season'. The Tudor House of Commons has been compared by one historian to a matrimonial agency; and it may well be that the growing corporate spirit of the place owed as much to family ties as it did to politics. To London also came the drovers of cattle from the west country; corn, vegetables and dairy produce from the home counties in increasing volume; wool and cloth for consumption and export. From Newcastle by water there came an increasing supply of coal and, as the fashion for the new domestic fireplaces took hold, the Londoner looked up uneasily at the darkening sky as yet further pollution was added to his already fœtid air. To London also came the latest fashions from sophisticated Europe – 'apes and japes and marmosets', as one diatribe has it. To the city finally came the unemployed and the poor in search of work and relief: sometimes a veritable army on the march whose noise and clatter still echo to us through our memories of childhood rhymes of beggars who had come to town. They had a mixed reception –

> ' Some gave them white bread, some gave them brown,
> Some gave them a good horsewhip and sent them
> out of town.'

Yet it was in London, in the great livery companies, the city council and in Parliament that, after a century of experiments, some harsh, some humane, there emerged at last a social welfare system which endured for centuries.

The great diversity of the capital was reflected also throughout provincial England. There were the great ports like Bristol, Southampton, Hull and bustling satellite ports clustering round them like Chepstow, Poole, Chichester, Winchelsea, Yarmouth and scores of others. There were the fine Tudor mansions, lasting memorials to the affluent gentry of the shires; the sturdy yeoman cottages which mirrored the tough qualities of their inhabitants. But beside them could be seen the rough hovels of the peasantry or perhaps even, and especially in the midland counties, the deserted

relics of once prosperous hamlets. The textile industries of the north, the west country and of East Anglia had during the sixteenth century known both boom and slump, and there were many signs before the old Queen died that the sheep had outstayed their welcome and corn was reclaiming some of the acres it had lost to wool. The enclosure movement continued at a varying pace. But under changing market conditions the first passion for conversion to pasture had spent itself.

Indeed, other passions too seem, at least for the time being, to have passed away; though soon new and equally fierce ones would burn in their place. Yet it was not a humdrum age over which the old Queen presided. An adventurous spirit still sent her explorers to probe into the untenable Spanish Empire across the Atlantic which seemed to bar the way to the half-legendary, half-known riches of the Far East. Others had tried a north-east passage which, if it failed to get through to the east, at least got as far as the Russian capital and resulted in a treaty with its ruler – no mean achievement in any age. Others, like Hawkins, linked up the storehouse of labour in Africa with the storehouse of raw materials in America, with no little profit to himself. He did not always come through unscathed, but he pointed the way to one of the major developments of the seventeenth and eighteenth centuries. The age saw also the supreme literary adventure of Shakespeare who explored fields in literature, drama and the human soul as unknown and as rewarding as any sought by Frobisher, Chancellor or Drake. And, like them, Shakespeare moved in an impressive company. There were other achievements, in politics, religion, trade, which would have done high credit to any period. But it is with the arts that this book is concerned: and what we have said so far must serve simply as the backcloth · to the unfolding glories of a brilliant age.

Architecture and Interior Decoration

ERIC MERCER

In the hundred years between the completion of Richmond Palace in 1501 and the building of Hardwick Hall from 1590 to 1597 English architecture underwent a revolution and a long evolution. A comparison between the two buildings serves to illustrate this double process. The contrasts between the two are obvious: the lack of symmetry, the irregular massing, the broken and confused skyline, the gothic ornament and construction of the first, and the carefully and symmetrically balanced masses, the regular skyline, the classical columns of the second. Yet the similarities, although less remarked on, are also great; both are very big buildings with long facades, both make use of boldly projecting masses along the facade, both break up and emphasize the skyline with towers or pavilions (Pl. 5). Neither is a classical building, and the most striking feature of English architecture in the sixteenth century is that, for all its use of classical concepts of design, and of symmetry at all costs, it relies for its effect on traditional and unclassical elements. It is the paradox of this period, and the refutation of those who treat its problems as a matter of analysing and pigeon-holing foreign 'influences', that while Richmond might conceivably be mistaken for a foreign building, Hardwick, for all its use of imported classical ideas, could never be mistaken for anything but an English house.

Not only in the elements of design, but even in many details of ornament, the architecture of the sixteenth century continued along traditional paths, and although the history of that ornament is largely one of successive classicist forms, nevertheless in many houses, and particularly in the smaller houses, native forms of decoration continued to be used even into the seventeenth century. In such a house as Chantmarle, Dorset, of 1612, it is only the porch and the mature character of the design that betray the date; by its ornament the building could well be mistaken for one of a century earlier. In these smaller houses elements of design from the beginning played a bigger rôle, and details of ornament a smaller rôle, than in the houses of the very great. It must always be remembered, therefore, that although a discussion of the period may concern itself very much with varying forms of classical ornament, there was a great amount of building that had little or nothing of any one of them.

With that reservation in mind, the century may be divided into three main periods. The first, which may be taken to end with the death of Henry VIII in 1547, can be characterized as one in which great 'inward-looking' courtyard-houses are built, with a varying amount of applied renaissance motifs of quattrocento character and some symmetry of design. The second period begins in the reign of Edward VI and lingers into that of Elizabeth. It is mainly the work of a learned and radically Protestant circle around the two Seymours, and is distinguished by its purer and more restrained classicism and its completion of the transition to the 'outward-looking' house with carefully designed façades. The third period begins in the early years of Elizabeth's reign and does not wholly end before the Civil War. Its 'outward-looking' houses are designs in which bold related masses and structural features have the main rôle, and in which decoration of a very free and often debased classical character is used, not in its own right, but as an emphasis to the important elements in the design. It is a period which reaches its culmination and its most mature expression in the first twenty years of the seventeenth century.

The early years

It has recently been remarked by Mr Summerson that classical architecture made its way in England as a mode of decoration. This is, perhaps, not the whole truth, but certainly classical architecture entered England in that guise. It is not accidental that there are far more examples of early sixteenth-century renaissance ornament on tombs and screens than on buildings, and its most obvious early manifestation is in the form of applied decoration upon essentially gothic buildings. Wolsey's Hampton Court is a typical house of the period in the traditional style with little in its architectural features to distinguish it from many of fifty years before. In some of its ornament, however (the work of the Italian, Giovanni da Maiano), it marks an æsthetic revolution. On the main gateway are terra-cotta roundels with egg-and-dart and leaf-swag mouldings enclosing portrait-busts of figures in Roman costume. Within the courtyard is an achievement of Wolsey's arms with cherub supporters and flanked by classical composite columns on an egg-and-dart moulded plinth and beneath a lion-mask cornice. In themselves these are works of art, in their context they are irrelevancies that show how much renaissance ornament was liked and how little renaissance architecture was desired. Even more striking in this respect is the screen at King's College Chapel, Cambridge. It was completed between 1533 and 1535, and is the finest example of renaissance woodwork in England; it is also the most finely inappropriate in its setting within the chapel that is the culmination of late gothic architecture.

It might perhaps be suggested that in both these cases the ornament was added after tastes had changed and the men responsible did the best they could in difficult circumstances. But this cannot be said of Sutton Place, Surrey (Pl. 6A). There the elevations within the courtyard are lavishly decorated in terra-cotta with the familiar renaissance motifs; recessed rectangular panels with urns and vases, with running ornament and crudely modelled cherubs; a gallant English attempt, it might be thought, at being classical. But the placing of this ornament, side by side with the cusped tracery and mullions of the windows and the ornament in the spandrels of the four-centred doorway arch, reveals again the unclassical conceptions of the builder. At the almost contemporary Layer Marney in Essex such renaissance ornament is used not only within a gothic framework but in such a way as to produce a gothic effect. The windows have consoles at the heads formed by two dolphins placed back to back and reversed; but the classical console and the un-gothic dolphins combine to give an effect from a distance of window-heads with pure gothic ogees. At Hengrave Hall, Suffolk, of 1525 onwards, the gatehouse is given a typically late gothic oriel provided with classically moulded corbelling supported by cherubs. At Ford Abbey, in Dorset, classical and non-classical ornament are placed together upon a gothic building. In the smaller houses of the period, as at Sandford Orcas and Athelhampton in the same county, renaissance panels with a wreath-mould surround are placed upon otherwise wholly 'Tudor' buildings. At East Barsham Manor House in Norfolk a great number of Italianate terra-cotta plaques are used upon the exterior, but only a few have classical motifs (Fig. 1); at Great Snoring Rectory nearby are similar terra-cotta panels. The accidental and whimsical nature of classical ornament at the time is illustrated not only by the houses in which it jostles native ornament against a native background, but by those great houses – Thornbury in Gloucestershire, Tichfield in Hampshire are examples – in which it is not used at all. As long as classical feeling meant no more than a liking for renaissance ornament it was a mere matter of chance where or how it was used, and a medley of styles was inevitable.

Nevertheless there were already signs that classicism was beginning to mean more than a use of irrelevantly applied details; that it was influencing design. In the early years such signs are few, for so long as greater houses retained the medieval practice of building around a courtyard and turning their backs on the world, design was not of great moment. And nearly all the great houses of the period are of such a type; with decoration, and design if any, on the courtyard elevations, and the exterior elevations wholly uncared for. Hampton Court is a typical example, Kirby, Northants, of the 1570's, is a surprisingly late one. Even within the courtyard, however, some design was possible, and Sutton Place attempted it with a symmetrically designed Hall block. Symmetry is not peculiar to classical canons of design, but symmetry at all costs was a feature that England had never known before in domestic architecture. To achieve symmetry at Sutton Place the builders broke entirely with the old plan of a Hall, conveniently entered through a screens passage at one end, and placed the entry in the centre of the side wall, an inconvenience which later builders of symmetrical hall blocks tried very hard to avoid. As a piece of planning the hall block at Sutton Place was perhaps not ingenious, but it is important as an early example of disregard of plan and convenience in the interests of a design (Pl. 6A).

As long as the great courtyard houses remained 'introvert' such practices were rare, and it was in the smaller non-courtyard houses that design had its fullest fling. At Wharf House (now St Lucien's), Wallingford, a very careful symmetrical design was achieved, with a central doorway flanked by crenellated bay-windows and with the effect enriched with plaster decoration (Pl. 6B). Here again, as at Sutton Place and as at Winterborne Clenston Manor House in Dorset, the design is achieved by disregarding the traditional function of the hall. A comparison of these houses with such a late fifteenth-century manor house as South Wraxall in Wiltshire shows the extent to which convenience and traditional planning had to be subordinated in order to achieve a coherent design, and indeed most smaller houses of the period continued to be built in the convenient and asymmetrical medieval manner.

Their greater evidence of conscious design must not be ascribed to a greater æsthetic ability or a deeper classical feeling among the builders of the small houses, but to the difficulties that the building of great 'introvert' courtyard houses, meant to accommodate a whole community of dependants and guests, placed in the way of the greater courtiers. It is noticeable that in these smaller houses renaissance details are wholly absent. At Wharf House decoration is in the form of crenellations, and of geometrical patterns in the plaster-work; at Winterborne Clenston in the labels over the windows; at Barrington Court, Somerset – an early E plan house – in the 'barley-sugar' corner shafts and crocketing. The nature of their buildings allowed these men to achieve designs of a certain classical symmetry without any classical ornament; the nature of the houses of the greater men forced them into a manner of applying the classical ornament that they liked to non-classical buildings. Not until Nonsuch, begun in 1538, was a great house of an 'extravert' character erected, one which placed considerable decoration upon and attempted to make a regular and symmetrical design of the previously neglected exterior elevations.

The Sharington school

The accession of Edward VI in 1547 brought into prominence a group of men – Protector Somerset and his brother the Lord High Admiral, the Earl of Warwick, later Duke of Northumberland, Sir William Sharington, Sir John Thynne – with radical Protestant sympathies and a considerable interest in architecture. The first architectural book ever published in England, *The First and Chiefe Groundes of Architecture*, by John Shute, was the product of its author's visit to Italy at the expense of his patron or employer, Northumberland. Shute claimed that in his work he had mainly followed Vitruvius's precepts. The truth or falsity of the claim is less important than the fact of it, for the claim in effect states the architectural intent of the group to which Northumberland belonged. The work of these men reveals a revulsion against the gay and light-hearted quattrocento ornament that had been used in England until then. In its place is a form of architecture and decoration that is more correct by classical standards and even somewhat austere. The greatest monuments of this style are Sharington's work at

Lacock, Wilts, Sudeley, Gloucestershire, Dudley, Worcestershire, and Thynne's Longleat, Wilts, but the style is also found at Hill Hall, Essex, and the Gate of Virtue at Gonville and Caius College, Cambridge. The builders of these last two, Sir Thomas Smyth and Dr Caius, were not members of the Seymour circle, but they were both men of considerable classical learning. Echoes of the style are found farther afield at Moreton Corbet, Shropshire, at Deene Park, Northants and at Broughton, Oxon.

The earliest of all, that of the late 1540's and early 1550's at Lacock, Sudeley and Dudley, may be regarded as the work of the 'Master' of the school, Sir William Sharington, a typical renaissance figure; man of affairs, swindler and artist, and subject of a drawing by Holbein. The most striking feature of Sharington's work is its correctness and preciseness. His decoration is never lavish, but is mainly confined to such features as doors and windows. Where, as in the Conduit House at Bowden Hill near Lacock, he uses a decorative feature along the whole face of the building, it is a plain dentil course below the eaves. The elaborately decorated mullions of Layer Marney are avoided by Sharington who, instead, marks the main intersections of mullions and transomes with a plain roundel. The sills he carries correctly on plain brackets never before seen in England. He gives his windows consoles at the heads, but with no hint of the gothic outline of Layer Marney. His doorways are all flat-headed with classical entablatures carried on brackets. At Dudley the doorway is flanked by columns now very decayed, but probably similar originally to that in the courtyard at Lacock, of a very correct Ionic order on a podium and base, and with necking, echinus and bracket above. Such complete small buildings as the Conduit Houses at Sudeley and Lacock are built in a very plain style with very little ornament of any sort, but of classical intent. Above all, however, he drops the inconsequent motifs of the earlier years, and even where, as at Lacock, he builds a somewhat gothic tower, he attempts, with the use of balustrading and label-less flat-headed windows, to give it a classical air.

The mantle of Sharington fell upon his erst-while companion, Sir John Thynne, who, however, built many years later. That Thynne was Sharington's pupil seems certain, but the fact is obscured because Thynne lived longer and progressed farther. Thynne's first work at Longleat was either partly or wholly destroyed by fire in 1567, and the present building, apart from Wyatville's alterations, is the work of his mature years. It needs to be considered in some detail because it is the only surviving example of a great house in the true Sharingtonian manner. Thynne was a man of very precise æsthetic intent and was jeered at by his Wiltshire neighbour, 'Wild Will' Darrell, for his preoccupation with the details of design and his 'beating down windows for this or that fault, they knew not why or wherefore'. Longleat has been called 'the Momentary High Renaissance of English Architecture', and it is only by its mullioned and transomed windows that it betrays its Tudor origin. In all else it is a correctly classical design, and it could be so because it was a wholly extravert house, in which the exterior elevations were not determined by convenience or as the by-product of what went on in the courtyard, but were the object of conscious æsthetic thought. Nevertheless it is not this feature that marks Longleat as of the Sharington school, but the nature of its decoration. The windows along the main face have plain heads, and aprons below flanked by moulded brackets. The windows of the slightly projecting bays have circular niches below and are flanked on the ground, first and second storeys by Doric, Ionic and Corinthian pilasters that carry entablatures continued along the main face as plat bands. Doric columns, with an entablature and a broken pediment, flank the central door, and the roof-line is hidden behind balustrading. The decoration differs from earlier work in its correctness and austerity; it differs, as we shall see, from later work not only in its character, but also in its ubiquity (Pl. 7A).

Work that has an affinity with this learned architecture of Sharington and Thynne is that of Smyth and Caius. The courtyard at Smyth's house, Hill Hall, of about 1575, which appears to have preserved its original character, has attached columns of a Doric order below and Ionic above.

Despite the incorrect spacing of the triglyphs and metopes of the Doric order, the whole is an attempt at a correct and severe classical effect. The Gate of Virtue, built some time after 1565, is a severe and plain structure with little decoration other than the classically moulded angels in the spandrels of the arches. Neither of these buildings has even a hint of the gay decoration of the earlier years, and the transformation of Sutton Place's jolly cherubs into the would-be elegant angels of the Gate of Virtue is a measure of the change in mood of the later decoration of these men.

At the same time the influence of this style of ornament spread even among men who did not wholly understand it and who used its correct motifs as indiscriminately as their predecessors had used the gayer decoration of the quattrocento. At Gorhambury, Herts, Sir Nicholas Bacon built a porch with very correct detail, with well-proportioned superimposed Doric and Ionic columns and a finely moulded pedimented cornice adorned with statues; in itself a highly classic composition. But he clapped it onto a building with windows with four-centred heads to the lights and returned labels and with no hint of any classical ideas. At Broughton Castle in Oxfordshire the oriel of 1554 has superimposed Doric and Ionic columns of good proportion and carrying an entablature. In themselves they are quite correct, but they are used, as no classical column ever was used, as window-mullions. At Deene Park, built between 1549 and 1572, the east front has fluted columns similarly employed in a very broad window. Essentially this is the same practice, although the forms are different, as the use of flat mullions covered with elaborate early renaissance motifs in the windows at Layer Marney.

In many houses, of course, the manner of decoration that had been fashionable a generation before was still continued. Caius himself, on the 'Gate of Honour', which was completed after his death in 1572, used many of its most characteristic motifs – roundels in high relief, perspective masoned arches, decorated panelled pilasters – and he used them as his predecessors might have done, in association with an archway with a four-centred head. At Dingley Hall, Northants, the porch of 1558–60 has on the first and second floors central panels enriched with rosettes and human figures in the manner of the terra-cotta work of the earlier years of the century. At Kirby there are reminiscences of the earlier fashion on the decorated pilaster buttresses of the north face of the courtyard and on the porch of 1572.

And throughout the country, and particularly in the houses of less importance, there was, if anything, rather less classical ornament than in the previous period. It is noticeable that at Cowdray the work carried out by the Earl of Southampton before 1543 has some renaissance decoration, but the parts completed after the house had passed from his possession are in a wholly 'Tudor' style. Houses such as Loseley, Surrey (Pl. 7B), and Hoghton Tower, Lancs, both of the 1560's, are devoid of classical decoration and, indeed, of almost any decoration at all. Smaller houses such as Eastbury Manor House, Barking, and Chavenage, Tetbury of the next decade have decoration that is 'sub-gothic'. At Eastbury, for example, there are tracery daggers in the spandrels of the doorway and 'barley-sugar' shafts used as gable-finials. In their general lack of classical or any other decoration these houses contrast with many of the smaller houses of the first half of the century; they contrast even more strongly in their greater use of design.

The Elizabethan achievement

It is not accidental that design, the distinguishing feature of the later years of the century, begins in the smaller houses mentioned above which had turned earlier than the great houses to the H or half-H plan. This plan contrived most of the advantages of the great courtyard plan – space for a Long Gallery, a Great Chamber, suites of rooms – within a more compact and economical structure and with a far greater flexibility of space and convenience of access. Its form played a great part in determining the manner of design of the later houses of the period, and although that manner was used in courtyard houses as well, it was used more timidly, and with more difficulty.

The earliest of the great 'extravert' courtyard houses was Longleat (Pl. 7A), and it is necessary to consider why its 'High Renaissance' character was so momentary. Longleat differs from later houses in its very slight vertical emphasis, the shallowness of its projecting bays, and its achievement of effect by decoration. At Longleat not even the entrance is structurally emphasized. It is an attempt to build an Italian town-house in the English countryside. To Thynne this seemed a worth-while effort; to men less conscious of the refinements of classical architecture and more alive to their position in English society it was of little importance, and although Longleat was a famous house from its inception, its principles were rejected by later builders. When Cecil gave Burghley House, Northants, its present form after 1577 he used a great amount of broken planes and contrasting masses. The pavilions at the ends of the entrance front project deeply forward and are further emphasized by cupola turrets rising above the main roof-line. The entrance is heavily stressed with twin turreted towers, and, by contrast, the rest of the elevation is extremely restrained. The effect is achieved by the use of structural masses and not, as at Longleat, by refinement of decoration, and it is important to notice that Burghley's entrance front and the façades of those houses designed in the same manner have little decoration at all, and what decoration they have is concentrated at one or two carefully selected points. With the exception of Wollaton, Notts, no Elizabethan house has the amount and ubiquity of ornament of Longleat.

Different as Burghley was from Longleat, it was yet, because of its courtyard nature and a still strong aristocratic disdain for such vernacular features as gables and prominent chimneys, only a timid exponent of the ultimately universal method of design. In smaller houses the use of structural features and dominating masses begins earlier and is carried further. Barrington Court in the 1530's had been a very early, almost a freak, example. Loseley, however, in the 1560's was a herald of things to come. It has very little decoration at all, it has not even any regularity of fenestration, but it uses the projecting masses of the end bays and of the porch and the symmetrically varying sizes of the gables along the roof-line to achieve a coherent design. In some ways, particularly in the small size of the gables, it is, like Danny Park, Sussex, still

hesitant in its use of the new method, but the retention of the gable in smaller houses at a time when greater buildings were rejecting it was an important factor. In general, in the smaller houses gables played the part that terminal towers and pavilions played less well in the larger houses; and in time even the greater houses rediscovered the gable.

There were few courtyard houses built after Burghley, and the H or half-H plan, such as Montacute, Doddington, Condover, Hardwick and Wimbledon, became almost universal. Yet even in courtyard houses the use of terminal and central masses was developed; Brereton Hall in Cheshire with its great dominating central tower flanked at the ends of the façade by projecting bays and Longford Castle with its huge terminal bastions are bolder Burghleys. At Wollaton, which is formally on a courtyard plan, the manner is taken very far. At the ends of the façades two towers, higher than the main building, project boldly forward not from the main front but from projections from it. In the centre, above the recessed main face, the keep-like hall dominates all else and has its own corners emphasized by 'tourelles'. Whatever the relationship of the famous 'Architector' Smythson to Longleat and Wollaton may be, two more dissimilar buildings in their general design could not well be found.

In the H and half-H houses the use of flanking and central masses was made the easier by the projection of the wings, and the problem was little more than that of emphasizing the salient features of the plan. One method was to employ those terminal towers that some courtyard houses had used. At Castle Ashby, Northants, begun either in 1574 or 1584, on a half-H plan, the ends of the wings are raised one storey above the level of the rest of the range and have cupola turrets rising another storey higher. At Hardwick the ends of the elevations are emphasized by the pavilions that project from the main face and rise above the main roof-level. There were, however, other methods. At

Fig. 1, *opposite*. Brick Gatehouse at East Barsham, Norfolk, c. 1538. From a drawing by Edward Blore (1787–1879) in the British Museum.

Wimbledon, now demolished, the ends of the wings had the roof kept low and out of sight, giving the impression of a cliff-like mass. At Montacute, Somerset, and Doddington, Lincs, gables are used, but in a hesitant manner; at the first small curvilinear gables are used on the wings, and between them and above the porch are mere stone semi-circles. At the second, all the gables are treated as small semi-circles.

Such a treatment, rather similar to that of Loseley, contrasts strongly with that of the modest houses of Kingston Maurward, Dorset, and Bishop's Hull, Somerset; and of the more important Condover, Shropshire, where the large gables of the wings dominate the whole composition. At Bishop's Hull the impression of mass is accentuated by the absence from the wing-front of any fenestration at all, except for a small two-light window in the gable itself. Even in those smaller houses that were not built on an H or half-H plan, such as North Cadbury Manor House and Moyns Park, gables were used with increasing skill to obtain architectural effect. At North Cadbury, Somerset, of about 1581, the front is broken by two projecting bays and four small gables are used along the roof (Pl. 8A). At Moyns Park, Essex, three symmetrically placed bay windows are linked by the four gables flanking them. At Newton Surmaville, Somerset, of 1608–12 (Pl. 8B) the hesitant formula of North Cadbury has been turned into a design in which the two bay windows are related and dominated by the three great gables that occupy all the roof-line between and on either side of them. Even in a great house like Condover, of 1595, the wings are emphasized by enormous gables flanking smaller gables along the main front. By the early years of the next century, two almost stock formulæ had been evolved, and there are very few houses of the Jacobean period which are not a variant of the Kingston Maurward–Condover type or of the Newton Surmaville type.

This use of native features in a classically coherent design can be seen at its most obvious in the treatment of chimneys, always an embarrassment to doctrinaire English classicists. At an early house like Hampton Court they were content to be themselves and were placed wherever convenience demanded, although the stacks were always placed on the exterior and unimportant elevations. They were often highly decorated with cut brick patterns, as at Thornbury, or with early renaissance motifs, as at East Barsham. In the middle years of the century at Longleat, Kirby, Burghley, they were often designed as classical columns or hidden among a forest of turrets and cupolas along the roof-line. In the later years they were consciously used as an element in the design and massed together to form a feature of it. Cobham and Condover are early examples of this practice, which reached its highest point in the 'regiment' of thirteen chimneys that dominates the wings at Hatfield.

Decoration

The decoration applied to the architecture of this period is a consequence of the manner of design. It is a myth that Elizabethan and Jacobean architecture has, to quote a recent writer, 'a mass of extraneous ornamentation upon its exterior elevations'. Anyone who thinks so may look at the south front of Castle Ashby and compare the highly-decorated 'Palladian' screen of the 1630's with the restrained and austere wing-fronts of the Elizabethan building. The method of design forbade any great amount of scattered ornament; even a decorated frieze, although found at Montacute and Condover, is a rarity and the ubiquitous ornament of Wollaton is a freak. In many of the smaller houses despite such exceptions as Gravetye almost the only ornament is a cartouche of arms over a doorway or, occasionally, a pair of classical columns flanking an entrance. In the larger houses more ornament is apparent, but is used mainly as an emphasis to a structural feature that is playing its part in the design. This is particularly true of the famous 'frontispieces' of the period. They are often very heavily ornamented, but are also very often the only feature in the façade with any ornament at all. Giles de Witt's frontispiece at Cobham, and that at Gayhurst, Bucks, both of the later years of the century, are typical in this respect (Pl. 9). Whatever their ornament may be, it is not 'extraneous', for its richness is meant to contrast with the general plainness and emphasize the importance of the entrance. In earlier houses – Tichfield, Hampshire, and Layer Marney, Essex – that could be done by the sheer individual massiveness of the gatehouse towers; in these later houses, with their subtle use of related masses, the effect was achieved by a concentration of rich ornament on the chosen feature. Whatever the character of this ornament, its disposition is a logical result of the whole architectural design.

Indeed, the nature of the ornament used in the later years of the century is a matter of which too much can be made. A discussion of the architecture of the early and middle years of the century must largely concern itself with decorative details; in the later years these are of much less importance than design. In many cases these details are nothing but the English craftsman's version of classical decoration – the friezes at Montacute and Condover, the heraldic badges and floral ornament of the panels at Brereton – or else, as in the nail-head friezes of Montacute and Wakehurst, they are purely native decoration with no classical connotations at all. At Kirby, French motifs and motifs from Serlio's book on architecture can be isolated, and at Longford considerable French influence can be seen together with the use of coarse Flemish thermæ and strapwork. At Cobham, de Witt's porch is French in inspiration, but the strapwork cresting of the windows of the exterior elevations is more Flemish. At Wollaton the strapwork cartouches appear to be from Flemish sources, the 'tourelles' at the corners of the central tower to be French and the heads of the hall windows and the dies of the ground-floor pilasters to derive possibly from Venice. At Kingston Maurward pure Perpendicular features can be seen in the bases of the window-mullions; and at many houses the four-centred heads to doorways and lights and the returned labels above doors and windows can be called nothing but Tudor. This is also true of the use of diaper patterning in different coloured bricks, and of the practice, in later years, of contrasting the red brick of the walling, often deliberately heightened in colour by 'russeting', with the white stone, or sometimes white-mortared brick, of jambs, fascias and string courses.

Where ornament was of such a polyglot character it may well seem paradoxical to say that the style is patently Flemish. It is, however, a question not of motifs from this or that country, but of a style that mingles motifs from many countries and abandons all classical rules and feeling. In his book *Architecture*, a book that went through many editions in the late sixteenth century, Jan Vriedeman de Vries stated his and his compatriots' views quite plainly; that rules of art must accommodate themselves to national conditions. Such a viewpoint meant, in practice, the more or less rapid abandonment of all classical principles. Direct copying from de Vries's designs was rare in England; the application of his methods was almost universal, for those methods so exactly suited the needs of English architecture. By the end of the century that architecture had no classical feature except its conscious design, and that design was achieved by the use of native structural features and related masses. It needed little decoration, but what it did need had to be bold and striking. The delicate ornamentation of the early Renaissance had to give way to the coarser motifs that Flemish pattern books provided, and classic discrimination to a wholly unclassic medley, in which, as at Hardwick, Doric columns could be used in conjunction with a fretwork cresting made up of Bess of Hardwick's initials. The development of English architecture in the sixteenth century is largely a process in which design successively conciliates, supersedes and finally determines decoration.

Interior Decoration

Just as the new type of house-plan radically altered exterior design, so, to a lesser degree, it altered the internal decoration of houses. In particular, the decline of the hall led to the disappearance of the massive and highly decorated open roofs that had been a feature of so many buildings since the end of the fourteenth century. Often in the early years of the century an open roof, generally of hammer-beam or pseudo-hammer-beam construction, was still the greatest single feature of the hall, and as long as such roofs were built they changed only in the character of the decoration upon them. The roof in the Great Hall at Hampton Court, the work of an English carver, combines late gothic tracery with renaissance cherubs. Later roofs such as those of Middle Temple Hall and Wollaton differ only in their lack of gothic ornament. At such houses as Layer Marney and Kirby much less elaborate open roofs were built, and with the tendency of the hall to become a room one storey high they disappear from private building. Their disappearance is one aspect of the increasing importance of other rooms; such as the Great Chamber and the Long Gallery. In these decoration undergoes a development in which increasing emphasis on a coherent design is evident.

Chimney-pieces and overmantels

The most striking aspect of this is seen in chimney-pieces and overmantels. At first even when an important room had a chimney-piece it was rarely emphasized against the general decorative theme. In a highly decorated room such as Wolsey's Closet at Hampton Court the fireplace is merely a break in the wall surface, and the space above, that in later years became the overmantel, is taken in their stride by the linenfold panelling and painted frieze that run around the room. In the somewhat later Abbot's Parlour at Thame the same treatment is found. By the mid century, as at Sawston Hall, Cambs, or a little later at Littlecote in Wilts, some emphasis was given either by varying the form or manner of the panelling above the

fireplace opening or by breaking up the panelling with thin pilasters flanking the opening and the space over it. Although there are early examples of highly decorated chimney-pieces (that from Nonsuch now at Reigate Priory is one), it was only in later years that the chimney-piece attained a dominating place in the design of a room.

The chimney-pieces of the period from about 1580 onwards are characterized by their great size, in height, breadth and projection, and the richness of their decoration. They generally rise from floor to ceiling and have an overmantel in two, or occasionally, as at Burton Agnes, even in three stages. Laterally the overmantel is often divided by columns or thermæ into three panels framing some sort of ornamentation. The majority are in wood, and in consequence often have many of the characteristics of contemporary wainscot. Thus the use of inlays of different coloured woods that is occasionally found in panelling is found also in some overmantels. In 'The Old House' at Sandwich the overmantel of *c.* 1575 has inlaid scenes from the life of Samson, and that in the Senior Combination Room at St John's College, Cambridge, has swans on a lake in front of an architectural composition. Sometimes they were of stone, as at Condover, or of chalk, as at Loseley (Pl. 10A). Apart from the lesser or greater amount of intricate cutting that the material allowed their character in these cases differed little from wooden ones. In some cases, however, as at Cobham and at Knole, coloured marbles were used to form patterns, and very little carving or figure-work appeared.

Not surprisingly, the commonest subject of these 'storied stones' was one or more achievements of arms: sometimes the Royal Arms, but more usually those of the owner and his real or invented connexions. At Barlborough they are combined with the figures of the owner and his two

Fig. 2, *opposite*. A chimney-piece at Crewe Hall, Cheshire, no longer extant. From *The English Interior* by Arthur Stratton.

wives. Quite commonly whole scenes are portrayed; most frequently from the Bible, but often from classical mythology. 'Daniel in the Lions' Den' is shown at Stockton House in Wilts and 'Jupiter and Danaë' at Charlton. The overmantel of the Senior Common Room at University College, Oxford, has scenes from Aesop's fables. Often there would be nothing more elaborate than arcading or, in later years, a simple geometrical pattern within the panel.

Panelling

These great chimney-pieces were not, however, the only decoration of a room and were generally set off, at least in houses of any standing, against more or less richly decorated panelling. In smaller houses and in the lesser rooms of greater houses, however, there is throughout the period a great amount of wainscot, with plain stiles and uprights forming small panels. Such panelling is found at Cuckfield Place, Sussex, and Breccles Hall in the 1580's, at Quenby, Leicestershire, and Winterborne Anderson, Dorset, forty years later, and is not uncommon in some of the Oxford Colleges up to the Civil War. But against this somewhat unchanging background panelling of more importance underwent a development in which an overall and diffused patterning gave way to an architectural treatment that related the panels to the proportions of the wall-space. It has two aspects: an increase in the size of the panels, and a concentration of the decoration upon them. There are, of course, many instances of late panelling in which this new method is wholly absent, but the general trend is clear.

At Hampton Court or at the Vyne, Hants, the richest form of wainscot consists of innumerable small panels decorated either with the native linenfold or with early renaissance motifs. Just as classical forms appeared first upon English architecture in a Gothic setting, so in interior decoration they were fitted into a traditional framework (Pl. 10B). By their nature these motifs, for example the popular roundel with human heads in profile, fitted easily into a system of small panels and provided no æsthetic reason for breaking it up. In consequence although these early renaissance forms and the native linenfold died out by the middle of the century the use of small panels continued. There was apparently an early defection at Nonsuch, where the decoration would seem to have used the great cartouches and figured friezes and large panels of the Primaticcio and Rosso school of Fontainebleau. There is, however, no evidence that this had any wide repercussions at the time. It is in the last quarter of the century that the small oak panels give way to a larger and more elaborate panel, sometimes of deal. In some cases, as at Haddon Hall in 1579, panels of contrasted sizes are used. At Fenners in Great Yarmouth the wainscot of 1595 is in a few very large panels divided by squat pilasters; at Burton Agnes, Yorks, the panels are eight feet high and six feet wide, and those at the later Hatfield and Dorfold have similar proportions. With panels of such a size repetitive panelling disappears, and at Chastleton, Oxfordshire, in 1602 a single panel, as in the drawing-room, occupies the whole wide space between window-jamb and wall return.

Their greater size allowed, and indeed demanded, a different decorative treatment of panels, and such small-scale decoration as jewel-ornament and roundels gives way in some cases to the more diffuse strapwork, or to geometrical patterning, or to a large-scale motif within the panel. This latter form became increasingly common, and the culmination of Tudor panelling is revealed in the wainscotting of the chapel at Lincoln College, Oxford, with its range of perspective masoned arches, and in the blind windows with architrave and pediment of the White Room formerly at Holland House (Pl. 11A).

Plaster-work

Unlike joinery, plaster-work was not a highly developed native craft in England in 1500, and in many early houses was not in evidence. The wainscot often went from floor to ceiling and precluded a plaster frieze; and the ceiling in an ordinary room, as at Paycock's in Essex, was divided by the exposed beams and joists of the floor above. As late as the mid-century great men were asking one another for the loan of 'a cunning plasterer' several counties away. At first plaster ceilings were confined to people who were under the influence of renaissance feeling. One of the earliest such ceilings is that in the Chapel Royal at St James's Palace (reputedly by Holbein), with a rich and intricate geometrical design. By the 1550's such small Dorset houses as Mapperton and Melcombe Bingham had plaster ceilings wholly hiding the beams above them, and at Mapperton the overmantel had plaster decoration. These ceilings were generally covered with more or less intricate geometrical designs formed by moulded plaster ribs. Within the panels that the ribs created there might be other decoration; roses or fleurs-de-lys, or real or mythical beasts or cartouches of arms. At first these ribs were of deep projection, often with late Gothic mouldings upon them; later they tended to become flatter and broader and to have running decoration placed upon their under-surface (Pl. 11B). Coincident with this change there was a tendency for geometrical rib-patterns to give way to curvilinear and strapwork patterns. In some cases, as at Speke Hall, Liverpool, and at Gawthorpe, the ribs had the form of running tendrils and floral ornament. At Burton Agnes the Long Gallery ceiling was covered with six parallel series of scrolls of roses, and the Oak Room has a ceiling with a running pattern of honeysuckle. Quite often the ribbing had pendants at the main intersections. At Mapperton and Sizergh, Westmorland, such pendants are little more than decorated bosses, but they became more elaborate in time (Pl. 12A). At Winterborne Herringston and at Dorfold, both of the years around 1620, they take the form of delicate openwork lanterns, of plaster on an iron core, somewhat like the pendants of the great hammer-beam roofs of earlier years. As in panelling there is a general tendency for the panels, and the motifs within the panels, to become larger and less diffuse and, in the end, for a treatment to appear which is not far removed from the great compartments of the trabeated ceilings of the later years of the seventeenth century.

Friezes

Friezes developed in a manner very similar to that of ceilings. At first, as at Thame Park, the frieze is little more than a plaster copy of the wainscot below, divided into panels and covered with repetitive motifs. The enormous frieze of Hardwick at the end of the century with its moulded figures and rural scenes is exceptional, but in many houses running friezes of considerable depth and design can be found. Sometimes, as at Loseley, the family badges are displayed, or a series of arms and cupids and cartouches. In the Ballroom at Knole the frieze has a series of mermaids, dolphins and satyrs in high relief. At Gilling Castle, Yorks, the frieze of c. 1584 is in five courses, each with its own running pattern of flowers and fruit.

Painted decoration

All this ornament of chimney-pieces, wainscot and plaster-work was enhanced, and often superseded, by a great amount of painted decoration. It would not be very wrong to say that sixteenth-century interior decoration abhorred an unpainted surface of any material and covered whatever it could reach with bright and simple colours. The ribbing and other decoration of plaster ceilings was generally coloured, chimney-pieces, of whatever material, often had paintwork upon them and the wainscot was not infrequently painted. In most cases this painting meant little more than a colouring that emphasized prominent features, but sometimes an elaborate decorative scheme was imposed upon the original material. At the Royal Palace of Oatlands in 1597 the wainscot was expensively painted in imitation of marquetry. At Gilling Castle the frieze is painted with rural scenes and coats of arms, and similar work appears to have existed at Theobalds. Even some ceilings had a painted decorative scheme, often intended to represent a cloudy sky; and possibly intended as a cheap imitation of the famous ceiling at Theobalds, where various mechanical devices combined with painted decoration to turn the ceiling into a primitive planetarium.

Murals

In smaller houses, where wainscot or tapestry or painted cloths were not so common, the walls were often completely covered with painted decoration, generally in the form of patterning of one kind or another, but quite often with figure subjects. At first, as at High Sunderland, Halifax or at the Old Flushing Inn at Rye of 1547, elaborate foliage and animals in a very medieval manner are found. These tended to give way to an increasing use of 'antique work' – the general term of the period for all the commoner renaissance motifs – both in the main filling and in the frieze (Pl. 12B). The native tradition of naturalistic representation never wholly died, however, and in a house in the Cornmarket at Oxford the geometrical patterning of c. 1580 is enriched with delicate Canterbury bells and wild roses. As in plaster-work, geometrical patterning was in the later years largely superseded by strapwork and arabesque designs.

As textiles and painted hangings became commoner in houses of any distinction, the often very competent figure subjects of the first half of the century, such as those formerly at Carpenter's Hall and the spirited 'Jonah and the Whale' from a house at Waltham, disappeared. So great a painter as Holbein had been commissioned in 1537 to paint portraits of Henry VIII and members of his family upon the walls of the Presence Chamber at Whitehall. Where figure subjects are found in the later years they are nearly always small and generally confined to the frieze. Such a well-known painting as 'The Story of Tobit' in the 'White Swan' at Stratford-on-Avon is, in effect, a frieze, and the 'Four Ages of Man' at West Stow Hall, Suffolk, is above the fireplace opening. Their competence is not to be compared with those of the earlier years, and murals of that quality, with the exception of Hill Hall, Essex, – and I am not convinced that the paintings from there are of the late sixteenth century – do not again appear until the early seventeenth century at Eastbury and Rothamstead. The subjects of these paintings are generally biblical scenes, or moralities or such popular figures as the Nine Worthies. Classical references are rare before the end of the century.

Stained Glass

Stained glass, generally in the form of an achievement of arms, added its splendour to many houses. It is a medium that might have been especially designed for the simple charges and bright colours of heraldry, and its rich effect can still be seen in the hall windows of some of the Oxford and Cambridge colleges. Its development is almost a microcosm of the general development of classicist ornament throughout the century. Early examples have the achievement enclosed in a roundel made up of the candelabra and laurel-leaves of the contemporary terra-cotta work. Later ones, e.g. those by Bernard Dininkhoff at Gilling Castle, are enclosed in elaborate cartouches, generally of strapwork. In the very last years of the century the practice of enamelling was introduced and allowed the painting of complicated subjects upon a single sheet of glass. At Old Betley Hall in Staffordshire there is a series of twelve panels representing the characters of the May Day game. Such a window was exceptional, but whether stained glass or plain glass was used, the window was enriched by the often complicated geometrical patterns formed by the lead framing of the small quarries.

All these forms played their part in achieving the striking contrast between the austere exterior and lavish interiors of Tudor houses. In time, as interiors became more subdued, the contrast lessened and conscious design was applied nearly as much to separate rooms as to whole buildings. By the end of the century Robert Stickles, a clerk of works in the Royal service, was writing a memorandum in which the importance of designing rooms with correct proportions was stressed. The first step had been taken on a journey that was to end in Inigo Jones' double-cube room at Wilton.

Furniture

JOHN HUNT

In every household from manor-house and merchant's residence to princely palace in sixteenth-century England the pattern of domestic economy was approximately the same. The rooms followed the same order from hall door to attics, their relationship to one another was the same, and they were used for the same purposes. They were larger or smaller according to circumstances, and in the great houses the chambers in the private apartments were more numerous. The daily life of the inhabitants was not, of course, in every case ordered on precisely the same lines, yet it was arranged with increasing ceremony as the rank and wealth of the owner rose. It is therefore no matter for surprise that when we examine the inventories of the furniture of the houses of the middle and upper classes of this period we find the same pattern recurring again and again. Given any room and its dimensions, it is possible to say almost exactly how and with what pieces of furniture it would have been garnished. Joseph Nash's *Mansions of England* made an earlier generation familiar with the appearance of the interiors of Knole, of Hardwick and of Haddon Hall as they existed in the second quarter of the nineteenth century. But Nash furnished them very much to suit the romantic taste of his age. More people than ever before are now familiar with their present appearance. And by combining fact with fiction the film-screen has accustomed us to what producers fondly believe are typical Tudor interiors. Such reconstructions of the interiors of the greater houses may sufficiently serve their purpose, but it is very doubtful if a 'Tudor' or 'Elizabethan' room, in the sense meant

by the period furnishers of today, ever had any real existence in the homes of the sixteenth century. Apart from the built-in aumbries and the wall-seats, and the panelling – which were part of the house when it was first set up – the movables were an agglomeration brought together over a period of perhaps a hundred years. New pieces were added, or old ones were replaced as the need arose. The day when a Benedict brought his bride home to a house in which the principal rooms were filled with new furniture had not yet dawned.

The furniture in the principal rooms of an early Tudor house must have been a pleasing mixture of the late gothic and the early renaissance; but by the time that the then owner's grandson had come into possession, the gothic relics had no doubt been banished to the lesser rooms and the domestic offices, and what was left, with the addition of new pieces, must still have been a mellow hotch-potch of styles – early and late renaissance – set against the old panelling and its immovables.

Dr Andrew Boorde in his *Dyetorie or Regiment of Healthe*, 1547, recapitulates the principles to be observed when laying out a house. There is, however, nothing new in his plan, since it is the same one on which all houses from the franklin's farm to the baronial residence in the fourteenth century were arranged. 'Make the hall', he says, 'of such fashion that the parlour be annexed to the head of the hall, and the buttrye and pantrye at the lower ende thereof; the cellar under the pantrye sett somewhat at a base; the kechyn sett somewhat at a base from the buttrye and pantrye; coming with an entrie within by the wall of the buttrie; the pastrie house and the larder annexed to the kechyn.' But Boorde clearly envisages a much more ambitious building. After some words on the position of the gate-house, he goes on: 'Let the prevye chamber be annexed to the great chamber of estate, with other chambers necessary for the buildinge'. He is here thinking of such palatial residences as Hampton Court, wherein the functions of the hall and the parlour were split up among other chambers such as the presence chamber or great chamber of estate, the dining-room and the withdrawing room; the hall being used only for special festivities such as those of Christmas and Easter.

To illustrate the manner in which such a house was furnished there is the inventory of the contents of a moderately sized house, that of Sir William More of Loseley, the contents of which were scheduled in 1556. It was a typical house of the period in which the domestic economy system of the century had reached its complete development. The organization and arrangement of the house are clear-cut and sharply defined. They are not blurred by the ceremonial of a Hatfield nor reduced to the minimum as for example in the case of a working weaver's house at Biddenden in Kent, of which we also possess particulars.

The Interior of Loseley House

When the hall door shut behind the visitor he found himself in a long, narrow passage that crossed the house from side to side and led to the kitchen and domestic offices, one wall being one of the main walls of the house, while the other was a wainscotted screen, the 'spere' of the Middle Ages, pierced with two doorways usually one at either end, which opened into the hall. There was no furniture in this narrow passage-way, and it was unlit except by perhaps a pair of sconces or flambeaux.

On passing through one of the doorways in the screen the visitor entered the hall. Its arrangement and furnishing followed a common plan. Its most prominent feature was the large chair of the master of the house standing upon the dais or raised platform at the top of the room. Before this stood the high table, the table dormant of Chaucer's

franklin, while behind it, if the owner's rank warranted it, hung a cloth of estate embroidered with his coat-armour. To one side of the chair was perhaps a second and lesser one for the lady of the house, though in general she would be accommodated with a stool. And when the family dined, they and such guests as might be present at the high table were provided with stools. To one side of the dais stood a cup-board on which the appointments for the high table were kept. At the lower end of the hall, between the two doorways in the screen, stood a hutch table, the ancestor of the modern sideboard, acting as a serving-table on which the dishes or messes were placed as they were brought in from the kitchen, and from which they were distributed to those at the high and the other tables by servants. Against the wall opposite the windows were high-backed benches, which were garnished as necessary with bankers and cushions for comfort. Between them was the fireplace and perhaps facing it a settle.

As the entire household dined together, temporary tables, boards with supporting trestles, were placed in position down the hall, and the necessary forms and stools grouped about them. But by the early sixteenth century these removable tables were already tending to give place to fixed standing tables, with forms at the sides, while the stools were nested underneath them until required. At the side of the room stood one or more livery cupboards or hutches.

The only shortcoming in this pleasant scene of well-ordered domesticity was the floor of the hall. Erasmus, who lived for some years in England in the early part of the sixteenth century, and knew both great houses like that of Sir Thomas More in Chelsea and the Colleges at Cambridge, as well as those of lesser standing, had a very poor opinion of the way in which English halls were floored and the way in which they were generally kept. It is difficult to believe that the hall of the author of *Utopia* was of the kind he describes, but his findings were undoubtedly true of many another. They were, he says, laid with white clay and covered with rushes, of which the upper layers were renewed with reasonable regularity. The lower, however, remained undisturbed sometimes for as much as twenty years, and harboured in their depths the abominations that should by rights have been swallowed by the cess-pit. Much that in the then prevailing way of life should have been emptied into the kennels was spilt upon the hall floor, covered with fresh rushes, and the stench concealed as far as possible by a generous sprinkling of sweet-smelling herbs. But this was not so in the private chambers, where tiled floors were common on the ground level and boarded ones above. Such were the bare furnishings of the hall. But this somewhat austere picture must be completed by the addition of wall-paintings above the panelling, tapestries or painted cloths and stained glass in the windows. Portraits and other decorative paintings are dealt with elsewhere in this volume. 'Tables of the Royal Arms' are frequently mentioned in inventories, and were displayed not to bolster up a claim to kinship with the Sovereign but as a gesture of loyalty. Inventories make frequent mention of a few weapons in the hall, and these were undoubtedly kept there as a precaution against a forced entry; for every man in those days was his own constable and was prepared to meet violence with arms in his hands. But certainly relics of half-forgotten battles, or the ancient harness of an ancestor, might well be hung up for monuments, and they are described as being so displayed in the song *The Old and the New Courtier*.

The parlour

At the upper end of the hall and to the side of the dais a doorway opened on a short passage to the private rooms of the family. Out of one side of this passage was the staircase to the upper floor, and just beyond was the parlour, the sitting-room of the family. So far as can be judged from the rather bare record in the inventory, More's parlour was well furnished. Firstly there was 'a table of Chesnut wt a frame joyned to the same', evidently a fairly large table that could be used as a dining-table when Sir William wished to entertain his guests in private. There was 'one joyned cheyre' for Sir William and 'vj joyned stoles of chesnut' for the rest of his family or guests, with a supply of 'footstoles'. There was 'a lyttle joyned table' for occasional purposes, and 'a syde-table joyned',

which was possibly a so-called 'credence table'. There was also a chess-board.

Beyond the parlour were two small rooms, the closets respectively of Sir William and Lady More. The first was devoted principally to the business of the estate, and in many old houses such a room is still called the Justice Room, because in it were disentangled the many problems that arose between the master and his tenants and his household servants. It was the room in which tenants paid their rents, and those in charge of the affairs of the house and the home farm rendered their accounts. Its impedimenta, of which a very full list is given in the inventory, reflect these activities. Firstly there was a 'counter bord of chesnut tree', which was undoubtedly a counting table perhaps incised on the top with a chequer design on which the counters or jettons were shuffled in casting accounts. Unmarked examples when in use were covered with a green baize cloth embroidered with the necessary chequers. For smaller sums there was 'a slate to wryte in' with 'a pinne of bone to wryte wt', and 'a pene of yron' and two desks. No chair or stools are listed. It would seem these were brought in from the parlour when required. There are no presses or hutches to house Sir William's fairly extensive library of some hundred and thirty books. Some of these from their titles were evidently acquired for their usefulness in solving daily problems. Others hint at More's interest in history and geography, and the remainder are classics, or works of entertainment. Lady More's closet on the other hand was devoted to the domestic economics of the household, and was at the same time equipped to attend to minor ailments or accidents. Beside the bare necessities of a table and stool the only furnishings were shelves upon which stood flagons and jars of unguents and simples.

Beyond these rooms, if the size of the house and the position of the master warranted it, was the chapel, which generally occupied the end of one or the other wing of the house. It was generally two floors high, and on the upper floor the room behind it often lacked the wall between it and the chapel, so that a rail across the open side converted it into a watching chamber for the family.

Back from the chapel on the upper floor a

gallery led to the stairs, and off this were the great bedroom, that of the master, and beyond it that of the mistress. The movables in Sir William More's bedroom – 'The Chamber wherein I lye' – were not as numerous as one might have expected. The inventory merely lists a 'joyned bed', 'a square table of walnut tree', a 'lyttle joyned chayre', 'another joyend chayre', and 'iij joyned stoles of chesnuttree for women'. The table and one of the chairs stood normally at the head of the bed, one at each side, the one supporting the night-light or watch, a cup and a flagon of wine in case of need. In the morning they were no doubt moved to the centre of the room or over to the fireplace, where they joined company with the other chair and the stools, when the master in his night- or chamber-gown broke his fast in the company of his wife and her ladies.

Such a chamber usually also contained a chest for valuables placed at the foot of the bed, where it served as a seat, and a second one for clothes and linen

'In cypress chests my arras counterpoints,
Costly apparel, tents and canopies,
Fine linen, Turkey cushions boss'd with pearl,
Valance of Venice gold in needle work,
Pewter and brass, and all things that belong
To house or housekeeping.'
Taming of the Shrew, 1594–1600, Act II.

The utensils for washing were either a two-spouted hanging laver with its basin in an iron stand, or an ewer and basin which, when not in use, stood upon a cup-board.

Of immovables there were probably one or two wall-benches and perhaps a press for clothes set in the wall.

If not an aumbry, there was probably an alcove hidden behind a curtain with a bench or transverse rod from which garments could be hung, the ancestor of the modern built-in clothes cupboard.

The children's chamber at Loseley was apparently furnished purely as a night nursery. There was no table, or chair: not even a stool. The inventory lists only a 'bedsted joyned', for the nurse and her older charges, and 'a credell' for the youngest. 'A joyned cup-board' was doubtless used for the storage of any necessaries in the way of platters, an ewer, bason and so forth. Clothing and extra bed-linen was kept in the 'cofere with a lock' and the second 'cofere without a lock', which acted as seats when necessary. The furnishings were completed by 'ii little close stoles', evidently to meet the requirements of the children.

Back on the ground floor and in the Hall, through the screen and at the end of the entrance passage, were the pantry and buttery and the wine-cellar, and beyond them the kitchen with the still-room and dairy. Some of the male servants slept in the pantry and buttery on pallet beds, a practice that continued until the nineteenth century. Above were the attics where the servant-maids slept. Outside were the stables, with rooms above for the grooms, the coachman if there was one, and a store-room for saddlery, and the armoury. These domestic quarters would have been furnished with the discarded and broken furniture of previous generations. With the exception of rough and primitive tables in the kitchen, which would also have had racks for meat and a simple cupboard for bowls and pots, the furnishings would consist solely of the pallet beds or simple palliasses, a stool or two, and a few rush-light holders.

The smaller country house

Smaller country houses, occupied either by gentry of the standing of Chaucer's franklin, or by farmers or master weavers, were sometimes built on a more modest plan, a plan that would seem to have been that generally used in the house of well-to-do but not wealthy merchants. The focal centre of the house was again the hall, with the entrance in one of the long walls, but without the interposition of a screen between the body of the hall and the entrance, or with a screen with a central opening only. At one end, and forming the main wall of the building, was the chimney-stack accommodating two fireplaces back to back, one serving the hall, the other the kitchen. Over the kitchen, reached by a ladder or staircase, was the servant's bedroom. At the other end of the hall and behind a boarded partition was the parlour, furnished in rather different manner to the chamber of the same name in the larger country house. It took on much of the character of the small bed-sitting room so frequently seen in late medieval illuminations, which, in houses of the type under review, was also used as a counting-house. The house being of only moderate size and of a limited capacity, the parlour combined the functions of the parlour proper, the master's bedroom, and his closet or place of business. The movables and immovables therein would seem always to have been of the same character and number: a canopied bedstead with a chest at the foot of it, a settle and 'enclosed' table on which the master worked at his accounts with the aid of counters, and against the wall another settle or a built-in bench, with a hutch or aumbry upon legs bearing various pewter utensils. Above the parlour was a second bedroom.

The craftsman's house

In those domiciles in which some handicraft was carried on, it was not unusual for the boarded end wall to be pierced high up with a shuttered window overlooking the hall so that the work being done below might be supervised. If the entrance was dignified with a porch, the floor above it afforded space for a second room, frequently described today as an oratory; though its most probable use was that of a closet. But such an addition called for the insertion of a screen and would necessarily modify the entire arrangement of the interior. The hall itself, being half work-room, would be occupied with the looms or the tools of the master's trade, and the domestic movables would be limited to the master's chair, a stool for his wife, a table at which both family, workmen and apprentices sat for meals upon forms, and a hutch and benches along the walls, with perhaps a couple of chests beside a bed upstairs. Such a house would require far less furniture both movable and immovable than a building of the type previously described. Yet it must not be supposed that such houses lacked good and substantial furnishings. There is a particularly apposite passage in William Harrison's *Description of England*, 1577, which hints vividly at the furnishing of a house of this type: 'Manie farmers ... thinke his gaines verie small towards the end of his terme, if he have not six or seven yeares rent lieing by him, beside a fair garnish of pewter on his cupboard, with so much

more in od vessels going about the house, three or foure feather beds, so many coverlids and carpets of tapestrie, a silver salve, a bowle for wine, and a dozen spoones to furnish up the sute'.

The cottage

Architecturally and economically the cottage was a simplified and smaller version of the farm-house on which it was modelled. It consisted of one moderately large room for living purposes, combining the functions of hall and kitchen, with a chimney-stack at one end housing a fireplace and oven, and a two-floored annexe, for sleeping accommodation and store-room: and the cottager's furniture was as simple as his home. Of what these movables consisted we can do little more than guess, since they have not survived. They met with the roughest usage, and when no longer serviceable were broken up for kindling. Nor are there any pictorial records of English cottage interiors of the time. The old illuminators of manuscripts, who, in the fourteenth century, delighted in portraying the daily doings of the peasantry were no more. We must in our need then turn abroad for enlightenment, to Peter Brueghel the Elder and his brother interpreters of peasant life, whose permutations and combinations of the background essentials of the ever-recurring *Boors carousing in an Inn* give us a reasonably accurate picture of a cottage interior at the period.

The cottager's main concern was for utility, and if his home was but barely furnished, it was because he lacked both the means to better it and the space therein to house anything more than necessities. A box-bed for the good-man and his wife; straw mattresses upon the floor for others in the household; a chest or two; some stools and a form; a rough table and a hutch for food; would be about as much in the way of movables that it would contain.

There is, however, an interesting passage in Warner's *The Patient Countess*, c. 1587, which shows that one convention at least of the great house was observed even in the humblest home, that which decreed that the master of the house should sit in a cushioned arm-chair at his board. The Countess's husband, with whose one amorous adventure the poem deals, is described as finding himself benighted at a 'peakish graunge within a forest great'. He is made welcome by the cottager and his wife, who regale him with their best provender — 'browne bread, whig, bacon, curds and milk were set him on the borde'. And for his ease — 'A cushion made of lists, a stoole halfe backed with a hoope Were brought him, and he sitteth down beside a coupe'.

There can be little doubt that this stool, with its hooped half-back, was the half-round chair which figures frequently in the representations of cottage life in the Middle Ages. The furnishings of the cottage would consist of wooden or base-metal spoons, wooden bowls and crocks for the storage of food, skillets and an iron or latten pot on a crane over the fire. Roast meat was the privilege of the manor house and the farm, while boiled meat was proper to the cottage. Scattered about would be the implements of husbandry, or those of the cotter's craft or trade.

Colour in sixteenth-century furniture

An entirely false impression of the appearance of the movables in the better-class house of the sixteenth century is conveyed by the present condition of so many pieces preserved either *in situ*, in museums or in private collections. Except in the cottages of the peasantry, furniture throughout the earlier Middle Ages was almost invariably painted, initially no doubt as a preservative. Manuscript illuminations, ecclesiastical sculptures and a few surviving pieces of furniture on the Continent afford ample evidences of this treatment during the twelfth, thirteenth and fourteenth centuries. There are authorities who maintain that this practice was still universal in the fifteenth century. It is evident that the carved decoration upon the legs of tables and upon bed-posts, based upon the heraldic chevron motif, was sometimes given added variety and emphasis by the use of colours and gilding applied over a gesso ground. Traces of original colour have been found in the undercutting of carving of many early pieces. But the practice of polychroming was not universal.

In the inventory recording the goods and chat-

tels of Richard Tvocky, a well-to-do London grocer, drawn up in 1391, the hall of the house was furnished with the usual fixed wall benches — this may be deduced from the number of bankers and cushions listed — together with a large trestle table, a pair of tables of spruce — probably a chessboard — three forms and two chairs all unpainted, and 'a painted table', probably the high table, and 'a painted table for cups', a cup-board for the display of his plate. Illuminations depicting domestic interiors of the middle and second half of the fifteenth century very rarely show painted furniture. It was nearly always, even in the most exalted houses, of natural coloured wood. But with the 'thirties of the sixteenth century we find ample evidence of the return to favour of the use of colour on the domestic appointments. The Revels Accounts of this period show to what an extent colour was employed in important theatrical properties, provided by the Italian artist, Da Maiano, and the workmen of the Revels Office, for Hampton Court and the Palace of Placentia at Greenwich. Examples of such coloured work of about 1530 from Hampton Court are preserved in the Victoria and Albert Museum (*Guide 1*, No. 231). Thereafter the practice became general until, at the close of the century, upholstering in textiles replaced paint, and such pieces that were not so finished were just left with the surfaces wax polished.

The precise names of the movables and immovables in the foregoing summary afford the antiquary sufficient data on which to base a fairly accurate reconstruction of any room at the beginning, in the middle or at the end of the sixteenth century. In every form of applied art the period witnessed a more complete change than had ever happened before in England. In half a century, though the pattern of daily life did not alter to any marked extent, the trappings and accessories of that life underwent the amazing transformation implied by the substitution of the late renaissance ideals, designs and ornament for the gothic. In that momentous half-century furniture completely changed in its outward appearance. Some movables disappeared from fashionable use, though individual pieces survived, to moulder away in kitchens, offices and stables. Others, though retaining their original names, were so modified in their construction that they are almost unrecognizable. Most of our present knowledge of the furniture of the sixteenth century is drawn from the wills and inventories of this period, and in them a constantly recurring vocabulary of terms for pieces of furniture is found. But the co-relation of these terms with existing sixteenth-century pieces in many instances presents a difficult problem.

The matter is still further complicated by the retention by contemporary writers of words, originally employed to describe particular movables, but later applied to others, which, though derived from the first, were entirely different from them both in form and function.

Moreover, names in common use among collectors and dealers today have in some instances only a recent history, and their sixteenth-century application was put to quite a different use. Others are purely romantic appellations invented in the nineteenth century. Much valuable work has been done in recent years in identifying types of furniture, but a rigid typology is impossible. The following pages are accordingly devoted to brief definitive notices of the principal types of movables in use in the sixteenth century.

Aumbry

The earliest type of hutch for the storing of food or household necessaries, now called a cupboard, was the aumbry or ambry. The aumbry began as the almery, whereby its purpose is indicated as a box in which to keep broken meats from the table, which were later to be given as alms to the needy and starving. Often it was a recess in the wall closed by a door, but it cannot have been long before the fixed aumbry, one of the immovables of the medieval household, was for convenience converted into a doored box which might be hung up or stood in any convenient position. In the sixteenth century the word aumbry was applied to any small hutch or doored receptacle built into a larger piece of furniture such as a cup-board, as for example in 1527 'a wainscot cupboard, with two aumbrys and two tills.' However, in the early part of the century it is used equally with hutch for a large cupboard in the modern sense. One of the finest and most elaborate surviving example is that in the Burrell Collection (Pl. 19B). It has three doors, two above and one below, and two drawers or tills. A number of analogous pieces exist. There are two others in the Burrell Collection at Glasgow. The type seems to die out before the high middle of the century.

Beds

In the rooms in the private parts of the house the most important piece of furniture was the bed – whether of the post or boarded variety. During the sixteenth century both types, together with the truckle-bed, were in use. But their social standing was very different. The bed which in the later Middle Ages could have figured among the movables in the best room of a house of some distinction would have been of the usual stock type, a stout rectangular frame elevated on four legs, the sides and ends pierced with holes through which passed the cords which supported the mattress. It was quite unornamented, as it was draped with the bed-cover, and was normally quite invisible. Over it was suspended a tester or a rectangular framed canopy from which hung the bed-curtains, which at night could be drawn all round it to prevent draughts from reaching the occupant. During the day the curtains were drawn back so that the bed might be used as an extra seat, while the curtains at the foot were turned up and folded in upon themselves in such a way that they hung down like two swollen bags. Later a low panelled head was added.

The four-post bed which was *par excellence* the great bed of the sixteenth century had a similar bedstock, but the panelled tester was carried upon four posts, one at each corner. As the century advanced, the beds became larger and more elaborate, overburdened with ornament, caryatids and inlay. Some of the carving was enhanced with paint as in the illustration of the headboard of a bed in the possession of Mr L. G. G. Ramsey (Pl. 20).

In the late fifteenth and sixteenth centuries the type of bed usually found in poorer homes was the boarded bed. It was constructed in the fashion of a long open box with shallow sides, mounted on four legs. In this the straw mattress was laid. It was, however, a bed with an aristocratic ancestry, since in twelfth- and thirteenth-century illuminations it is shown as used by royalty, when the supports are usually represented as lions or fantastic monsters. By the sixteenth century, however, it had sunk in the social scale and was found only in farms and cottages, where it no doubt was regarded as the best bed, in the guest-rooms of inns of no great standing, and in the dormitories of the large residential schools. No examples of this early date are known to have survived. However, a print representing the dormitory of Westminster School included in the *Microcosm of London*, 1808, shows such beds still in use in the early nineteenth century. Each bed has a slightly elevated head provided with a narrow shelf on which a candle and books could be placed at need. And beds of exactly the same construction are still a feature of the dormitory of the Royal Hospital, Chelsea.

The truckle bed was, as its name indicates, a low bed or pallet upon truckles or solid wheels, which could be rolled out of sight under the great bed when not required. It was generally reserved for the use of a page or maid, who slept either in the master's or mistress's room or in the anteroom. They were still in use in palaces and the greater houses throughout the sixteenth century, but were not extensively in use in the average manor-house, which rarely possessed anterooms to the bedrooms. Those that survived were, like the box-bed, banished to the servants' quarters.

Chairs

Foremost among secular domestic chairs was the chair of estate, that which in gentle and noble houses was occupied by the master when he took his seat upon the dais in the hall behind the high table to preside at the daily assembling of his dependants at dinner. In houses other than palaces in the late fifteenth and early sixteenth centuries there was probably no more than one such chair, or two at the most, the second being of slightly lesser dimensions. The chair of estate like the table dormant was never moved from its commanding position since, with the cloth of estate on

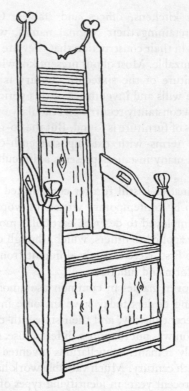

Fig. 1. 'Joyned' chair of framed and panel construction; gothic in type. Early sixteenth century.

the wall behind it, it was the visible symbol of the master. Its position was analogous to that of the throne in the throne-room of a palace. The earliest surviving English box-seated joined-chair is the Coronation Chair in Westminster Abbey. This type of chair was the normal chair of estate of the late fifteenth and early sixteenth centuries. It is the chair which Randle Holme, the Chester Herald and antiquary, describes in his *Accademie of Armoury* of 1688 as 'the settle chair ... having a kind of box or cupboard in the seat of it'. He adds, 'being so weighty that it cannot be moved from place to place, but still in its owne Station'. There is a fine example of about 1530 in the Victoria and Albert Museum (*Guide 1*, No. 328). An interesting variant, with a half-round panelled back, is in the Peter Gwynn Collection. This again, on account of its size and weight, must have occupied a fixed position. From inventories, however, we know that the parlour and master's bedroom also

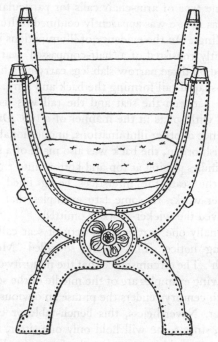

Fig. 2. Queen Mary's chair at Winchester Cathedral covered with blue velvet and garnished with gilt nails. The pommels and boss are copper gilt. c. 1550.

contained chairs, and examples of a more movable form, such as the so-called caqueteuse type, borrowed from France, were in vogue (Victoria and Albert Museum *Guide 1*, No. 327).

Another form of chair, of different origin to the boxchair, was the X chair. With a long history of royal and ecclesiastical use in palace and convent, it was a much more useful and movable object than the great wainscot chair, but much less able to stand rough usage. The earliest surviving English chairs of this fashion are those in York Minster and in Winchester Cathedral, the latter having been used at the marriage of Mary 1 to Philip of Spain in 1554 (Fig. 2). The other chair which must have been used at the same ceremony has never been traced.

Both chairs are assigned to about the same period – that is the middle of the sixteenth century – and there can be no doubt that this is correct of Queen Mary's chair. But there are excellent historical grounds for believing that the York chair is the best part of a century older, with which date

nothing in its construction or ornament is at variance. It is illustrated in Henry Shaw's *Specimens of Ancient Furniture*, 1836.

By the second half of the sixteenth century the X chair must have become comparatively common, and this and other types of upholstered chairs appear in the houses of the wealthier gentry and of the more prosperous merchants. By then two modifications in the appearance of this chair and in its construction had taken place. The arms had in general ceased to be provided with pommels at their extremities, and were so shaped that the ends projected beyond the front uprights (Fig. 3), as in Sir Antonio Mor's portrait of Queen Mary, where the Queen is sitting in a chair of this fashion. Before the close of the century such chairs ceased to have seats formed of a squab cushion resting on the cradle of webbing, but were fully upholstered, the cushion being an integral part (Fig. 4). Late in the century we meet with a square joined-chair, the back of which is, however, clearly modelled on that of the X chair. A splendid example, formerly in the Duke of Buccleuch's Collection and now in Exeter Cathedral, is polychromed in green, gold and cream with trails of flowers and possesses some of its original green cut velvet upholstery. The 'joyned' chair, the more usual type at the close of the sixteenth century, and which must have figured in most gentlemen's houses, carries the rectangular framing and scrolled arms carried by turned supports, with the back decorated with the Elizabethan floral and chequered inlays, and surmounted by a scrolled cresting with brackets at either side. In lesser houses the turned-chair, differing but little from its medieval prototype, continued in use. Preserved in the President's Lodgings at Queens' College, Cambridge, is a very beautifully proportioned and unique turned-chair, which tradition asserts, possibly correctly, was used by Erasmus during his residence at the University as Lady Margaret Professor of Divinity. Two other chairs of turned work, but of a less elaborate description, evidently intended for the use of schoolmasters of the sixteenth century, have survived at Westminster School.

It has never been suggested that these turned,

53

or, as they were usually known at the period, 'thrown' chairs were the products of one particular district. On the other hand, the usually triangular-seated so-called 'bobbin-frame chair', which represents the frenzy of turnery, has no parallel on the Continent, and would seem to have been confined to the Welsh Marches, the Severn Valley, and to Cheshire and Lancashire. This type of chair in its embryonic form was unquestionably known in the sixteenth century, though whether any of the more flamboyant examples, such as that in the Victoria and Albert Museum, which in the *Guide* is discreetly given to the sixteenth–seventeenth century, should be dated earlier than the commencement of the seventeenth century is doubtful. Until comparatively recently they were often ascribed to the reign of Henry VIII, an assumption based in all probability on the circumstance that one of the best-known examples of this type of chair was formerly preserved at Cheshunt Great House, where it was known traditionally as Cardinal Wolsey's Chair.

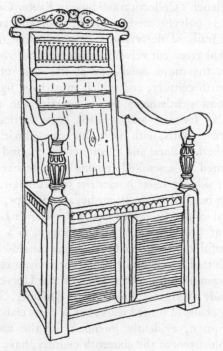

Fig. 3. An Elizabethan panelled chair of transitional design between a box seat and open frame.

One type of arm-chair calls for particular notice, as its use was apparently confined to humble dwellings. On the evidence of illuminations it apparently consisted of a 'half-compassed' seat supported on three narrow slab legs carrying a horse-shoe-shaped rail forming the back and arms. The space between the seat and the rail was usually filled with splats in the manner of a tub. On the evidence of other illuminations, unquestionably of English origin, the back was also made of a series of spindles passing at top and bottom into the rail and the seat, the interstices being filled with wicker-work. In some late examples that have survived the wicker-work is omitted.

Finally one particular variety of seat calls for passing notice. This is the so-called 'Monk's bench'. The circumstance that the majority of the surviving examples are of the middle of the seventeenth century renders the phrase an obvious misnomer. Nevertheless, this bench-table or chair-table, since some will hold only one sitter, has a very respectable ancestry, and a few examples are known of the turn of the fifteenth and sixteenth centuries.

Livery, court and close cup-boards

The cup-board, as the name implies, was the board upon which the cups – used loosely for all and any articles of plate which graced early dining-tables – were displayed in the hall for the envy and admiration of guests, when not in actual use. Such a display was not then thought of as ostentation. It was a gesture inspired by a wish to compliment an honoured guest. At ordinary times plate was securely locked away in chests and coffers. The unheralded visitor would be met by the sight of bare cup-boards, and his welcome would perhaps be limited to a friendly cup from the side-table, or a flagon from the livery hutch.

The cup-board itself in its early days was an open structure fitted with shelves, normally two or three one above the other, rising even to as many as six in the manner of that which, according to George Cavendish, graced Wolsey's Hall at Hampton Court – 'cup-board ... of six desks high full of gilt plate, very sumptious'. A similar arrangement may today be seen at Guildhall upon

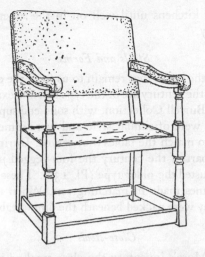

Fig. 4. A late Elizabethan chair with a beech frame. The back and the arms are covered with velvet.

State occasions. Since, however, the cup-board in the hall was for use as well as for display, it was customary, long before the close of the fifteenth century, to enclose part of the space below the board with panels at the ends and doors in front, and in the resulting close cupboard or aumbry to store the extra napkins and kerchiefs of pleasaunce that might be required during dinner. These are clearly the 'cup-boards with ambries' listed in the inventories of Henry VIII's funiture. Early examples of them can also be seen in the illuminations depicting domestic interiors which occur in manuscripts of the middle and second half of the fifteenth century. But it must be emphasized that the partial boxing-in of one or even two stages of the erection did not alter its nature: it still remained a cup-board (Pl. 16A).

No example of a sixteenth-century cup-board, *pur sang*, has yet been identified, and the difficulty of co-relating inventory entries with existing examples has been already mentioned.

Two constantly recurring types of cup-board are to be found throughout the second half of the sixteenth century. One type has two open stages or shelves with a pot-board below (Pl. 17, 18B). The other type is similar in appearance, but with an aumbry in the upper stage. The first type has

been identified as a court cup-board, and the second as a livery cup-board, terms made familiar by their constant use in documents of the sixteenth century.

The phrase livery cup-board is partially self-explanatory, since here livery was clearly the daily allowance of food and drink provided for every member of the household. Some authorities maintain that it was so named from the circumstance that it was used as a resting-place for dishes and messes on the way from the kitchen to the table and from which they were taken to the diners. They have accordingly identified this particular form of cup-board with the open shelved type. Here it should be noted that certain cup-boards made for Hengrave Hall, Suffolk, in 1587–8 were to be 'in the fashion of livery, that is without doors'. Other authorities will have it that the livery cup-board was an enclosed or partly enclosed one in which that part of the livery not consumed at the tables – cold meats, cheese, butter, bread and ale – was kept until required for an informal collation such as supper or after-supper. In this connexion it is worth noting that livery cup-boards make a regular appearance among the furnishings of bedrooms. The close cup-boards were of similar form, but with the lower portion below the central shelf enclosed by doors.

Desks

More's closet at Loseley also included two desks, but there is no indication as to their exact nature. One or both may have been of the lectern type, the medieval *armariola*, with a lid inclined at an angle on which a book might be laid for reading. Actual examples are rare. There is a fine fifteenth-century desk of this type in the Victoria and Albert Museum (*Guide 1*, No. 320). Another is the famous standing desk from King Edward VI Grammar School, Stratford-on-Avon, now displayed at Shakespeare's birthplace. But desks of this type would appear more appropriate to an academic or pedagogic setting than to that furnished by the closet of a country gentleman. It is more probable that these two desks were table-desks, similar to that shown in Dürer's engraving of Erasmus, which, when boxed-in, became the desk-box, miscalled bible-box, of the seventeenth century.

Press

The term press, from its first recorded appearance in Chaucer's *Millers Tale* of 1386 – 'His presse covered with a faldying reed' – would seem to have been used loosely to describe any tall, doored and shelved hutch used for storing napery, hangings or clothing. Like the word hutch-press, it was used in the sixteenth century to describe the small doored enclosure built into the upper stage of a cup-board, and in this sense it appears in a will made in Bury St Edmunds in 1552. The press proper, however, still maintained its pre-eminence as the largest type of hutch in the house, and when Master Ford (*Merry Wives of Windsor*, 1598, III iii, 226) is turning his house upside down in jealous fury at the Fat Knight, Sir Hugh Evans says that they have searched in the chambers, and in the coffers, and in the presses, the two last being the only pieces of furniture large enough to conceal a man. In the seventeenth century the press usually figures as the press cupboard – cupboard being used in its present sense – and in function it corresponded to the modern wardrobe (Pl. 19A).

Settles

Next to the spere or screen, the fixed bench was the most important of the immovables in the domicile of whatever description, and consisted in its most rudimentary form of a stout plank furnished at intervals along its fore or free edge with legs and braced at the back against the wall of the room. Other benches were affixed in the window recesses like modern window-seats. Still others were provided with backs and high ends. From this last developed the settle, which was merely a free standing bench that could be placed in any convenient position about the hall or chamber. The high-backed settle was a necessity in England, where screens to keep out draughts were unknown. In winter two or three grouped in strategic positions about the hearth made when desired a comfortable and cosy little room within the larger one. Settles of this nature continued to serve in farm-houses

and in kitchens until well on in the nineteenth century.

Stools and Forms

All the stools that remain to us from the earlier part of the century are of the type of a fine example in the Burrell Collection, with solid end supports. Forms were of similar style and were sometimes made to match the tables they served. During the latter part of the century the four-legged joyned stool ousted the older type (Pl. 13B). These were sometimes made in matching sets. When not in use they were packed beneath the dining-table.

Close-stools

In More's inventory the close-stool or secret-stool is only once mentioned: 'ij lettle close-stoles' are listed as in the children's chamber. The close-stool was a very necessary movable at a time when interior sanitation – at least in so far as the middle-class house was concerned – was in its infancy. In Tower Street, in the Parish of All Hallows, London – a street inhabited by wealthy merchants – it is recorded that in 1579 there were but three privies to meet the needs of near sixty houses. That great contemporary authority upon matters of health, Dr Andrew Boorde, urges that the common house of office of any domicile should be set over water or at the least at some distance from the house. We are, however, concerned more with close-stools than with jakes. An example which was at one time said to have belonged to Henry VIII is at Hampton Court. But upon examination it proves to be of a later age. Nevertheless the appearance, as in an example at Knole, probably approximates to that of the earlier article – a square box with a lifting lid covered with velvet held in place by gilded nails, and the top quilted for comfort.

Tables

In the first half of the sixteenth century, the principal table of the house and the position of its master's authority continued to be the medieval table dormant, the high table in the great hall. The trestle table was also still in use at Court. The secondary dining-tables for the servants and dependants may have also been fixed, or they may have been removable boards upon trestles after the old manner. But with the change of manners in the Elizabethan age and the decline of importance of the communal life of the great hall and the greater use of the private chambers, tables of another sort became the fashion. Draw-tables, where the board could be increased to almost double its length by the pulling out of the leaves below the top, were produced in large numbers, and though no doubt they were often used in the great hall, they were also to be found in the private chambers of the master and mistress. One of the earliest examples of the early part of the sixteenth century is the fine specimen in the Victoria and Albert Museum. But during the reign of Elizabeth they became very common. An unusual example in the Burrell Collection has the legs carved as figures instead of the more usual bulbs. An example with bulbs is in the Hart Collection (Pl. 15B).

Apart from the great tables in the hall, other lesser tables were scattered about the Tudor house and were used for various purposes, which can frequently be deduced from by their construction. In More's 'chamber wherein I lye' is listed what was evidently an occasional table which, as already indicated, may have stood at his bed-head at night and served as a breakfast table in the morning. A second type of table is that which usually passes under the name of a 'games table', a purpose which it may well have served. Like all free standing tables, they have all-round decoration. They are invariably furnished with a boxed upper section for the storage of dice, dice-boxes and the marked cloth that covered the table when in use. There is an interesting example at Penshurst; there are other examples in the Burrell Collection; and Mrs Hart's table here illustrated (Pl. 18c) is of exceptional character. The tops of these fold outward, and the legs are carved and stand upon stretcher feet in the fashion of the fifteenth century. All these tables, with the exception of Pl. 18c, are of the earlier part of the sixteenth century.

Hutch tables

There exists a class of table, of which about a score of examples are known, called, for want of a more scientific name, a hutch- or serving table. They have not so far been identified from inventories of the period, and take the form of a long, narrow side-table having a cupboard below, upon short legs. The top was often of the draw-type, but none with the original leaves *in situ* has yet been recorded. The best-known examples are those in the Victoria and Albert Museum and the collection of Lord Rochdale. A fine example in a private collection is illustrated (Pl. 13A). Some of the earlier examples evidently had tops which folded lengthways. The form is not found in later renaissance times; all the known examples are of the first half of the century.

One of the most celebrated and important from a documentary point of view is Sudbury's Hutch in St James' Church, Louth, Lincolnshire, though it has apparently undergone considerable restoration. The name is no piece of contrived archaism of the nineteenth century, since the phrase occurs in the churchwardens' accounts for 1586. The donor was one Thomas Sudbury, vicar of St James', whose incumbency began in 1451 and ended with his death in 1504. The hutch presumably originally stood in the hall of his Vicarage, as it is clearly domestic and is not an item of church furniture. It cannot antedate his death by many years, and its carved decoration proves that it was produced after Henry VII's accession in 1485. The principal motif is the Crowned Tudor Rose flanked by the heads of Henry VII and his queen Elizabeth of York.

Turned ware

Before concluding the subject of domestic furniture of the sixteenth century something must be said of the productions of the wood-turners, generally known to collectors as 'treen'. The Worshipful Company of Turners of the City of London possess no records of an earlier date than the Grant of their Charter in 1604. But in 1478, though charterless, they were nevertheless an established and important manufacturing and trading association of craftsmen, and their ordinances were accordingly submitted to, and in that year approved by, the Court of Aldermen. These ordinances supply a too brief list of the wares which the turners produced – 'shovels, scoopes, bushell trees, washing-bowls, chairs, wheels, pails, trays, truggers wares, wooden measures'. Only a few of these were actually turned, and only half of them can be legitimately regarded as domestic utensils. At best the list must be regarded as a catalogue of headings, under each of which many kindred articles were included. Wash-bowls cannot have been the only type of bowl for which the Turners were responsible. Wooden bowls of various sizes had throughout the Middle Ages been almost the only tableware of the lower orders, the journeymen and apprentices in the towns and the peasants in the country districts. They were easy to make, their initial cost was negligible, and when solidly made they were almost indestructible. Small bowls replaced the cups of the wealthy classes, and larger ones held the stews of bacon or rabbit and vegetables that were the staple diet of the labouring classes. Mazer bowls appeared on the boards of both private houses and of charitable institutions and colleges, while large bowls were used for the storage of bread, milk, curds and cheese, and the like. Chairs must have implied not only the halfround and square-seated chairs previously noted, but stools of the type now generally referred to as 'milking stools', together with the bases and uprights of spinning-wheels and embroidery frames and the frames of hour-glasses. The fact that the Turners produced pails and wooden measures shows that to some extent the Turners trespassed on the preserves of the Coopers. They must also have made cheese presses, of which the circular head of a very fine example incised with the arms

of Edward IV is in the Strangers Hall at Norwich, together with a second one incised with the sacred monogram I.H.S., the latter being probably of the early sixteenth century. They must also have turned wooden trenchers, when these replaced trenchers of bread, and those charming painted roundles known to collectors as 'fruit trenchers'.

Horn

In leaving the subject of turnery it will be convenient here to add a few words on the contributions of the Horners to the way of life in the sixteenth century. In the Middle Ages the horn was still one of the principal drinking-vessels, as it had always been; and in parts of the country, in Wales particularly, the *Hirlas Horn* still remained until the seventeenth century the ceremonial vessel, a draught from which welcomed a stranger on arrival and sped his departure. But for all ordinary purposes it had been replaced by the cup and the bowl. The day of the horn tumbler was yet to come. But glass being beyond the reach of all but the very well-to-do, sheets of horn were inserted in window-frames and in the sides and fronts of lanterns. Horn spoons appeared upon the tables of the farm-house and the cottage. And in the days before the standish was known, or was at least a rarity, the turned ink-horn appeared on most desks, accompanied by the penner of tooled leather, horn or turned bone. These and other minor objects were not of great moment, but they were invaluable in an age and society that was debarred from using metal by its cost and had not achieved the blessings of this present age of plastics.

Fig. 5. Late Elizabethan carved gadroon ornament.

Painting

DAVID PIPER

The fundamental inspiration of medieval art was religious, and medieval painting normally has close affinities with, on the one hand, a hymn, and on the other, a gloss or illustration of a Biblical theme. This was as true of English art as of that of any other European country, and the finest of the late medieval wall-paintings in England, in Eton College Chapel, were devoted to miracle themes and were finished three years after the first of the Tudors, Henry VII, took the crown unto himself after Bosworth, in 1485. Throughout his reign, and through much of that of Henry VIII, the decoration of churches, with wall-paintings, window-glass like that at York, at Fairford and at King's College Chapel, Cambridge, and rood-screens like those in East Anglia, was the over-riding concern of English painting. It is, however, a period of which our knowledge is extremely scanty: largely probably because the great majority of the paintings themselves were deliberately destroyed after the Reformation, but also in some part because their generally mediocre quality reduced their chances of survival. What does survive, with a few notable exceptions, goes to show that the vigorous, flat and linear native style was tending to succumb to a fashion that preferred the more spatial and naturalistic Flemish manner, even though purveyed in England by second-rank immigrant craftsmen.

When, after the Reformation, images were forbidden in English churches, English painting lost not only its subject-matter, but its market and its patron, and whole crafts almost withered within a generation from lack of support, including that of wall-painting and that of glass-painting. The painters, however, were not yet concerned with the dignity of art, and all of them, from Holbein downwards, would turn their hand to any kind of painting – settings for pageants and masques, decoration of barges and coaches, wall-decoration and even no doubt straightforward house-painting. Much of the painting throughout the Tudor period was ephemeral in nature, and some of their most brilliant *tours-de-force* must have had a life-span of only a few days, such as the fabulous decorations for the Field of Cloth of Gold. The prospects for more durable and more profound works of art, early in the sixteenth century, were not good; there was no constellation of princely Maecenases to offer patronage, as there was in Italy; there was no established tradition of domestic magnificence in which pictures were acknowledged and eagerly sought after as desirable house furniture. In the great houses of the land, wall-decoration was generally of tapestry, for which a form of painted or stained cloth often served as cheaper substitute; in lesser houses there was often no decoration at all, and certainly not pictures. Wall-painting, perhaps more frequent than the surviving fragments might suggest, was mostly purely decorative, tending to patterns like wall-papers. But there are exceptions, such as those from Carpenters Hall, showing carpenters at work. Occasional mythological or biblical subjects survive elsewhere. It took all of the sixteenth century to accustom even the topmost strata of English society to the habit of hanging paintings on their walls. Their value as decoration is questionable; in the first half of the century, at least, many pictures were provided with a curtain, which was drawn, presumably, only when they were specifically to be looked at. (There may be here a suspicion of the primitive fear of the magic of images; the object may have been to protect the pictures, but may also have been to preserve the owners from the images.) Even when the habit was more or less established it was confined mainly to one kind of picture: portraits. The English were accustomed to the idea of tomb-effigies, and much of Tudor portraiture conveys an impression as of effigies domesticated. This chapter will be primarily concerned with portraiture, but there are first some other kinds of painting to be considered.

Paintings other than portraits

The demand for religious paintings, of course, ceased, and there is little evidence that there was any sudden efflorescence of them in the brief Catholic dominance of Mary I in the 'fifties. There are, however, some sporadic examples later in the century of a curious religious-allegorical manner, of which a good specimen is reproduced (Pl. 23c)—a kind of visual tract. There seems again to have been a slight demand for mythological and to a greater extent for allegorical pictures. Professor Waterhouse has suggested that the *Ulysses and Penelope* of 1570 at Hardwick was painted in England, and mythological themes were a primary inspiration of painted hangings and tapestries. Allegory, however, was probably more popular for pictures, and was even amalgamated with portraiture by one considerable artist, Hans Eworth, in pictures ranging between 1550 and 1570 (cf. Pl. 22B). These suggest that quite a number of allegorical pieces in the Flemish Mannerist style, showing naked gods and goddesses with long and strangely arranged limbs, may have been painted in England by immigrant artists. In the last quarter of the century the allegorical method became extremely rarified, and will be discussed in the section dealing with the problems of Queen Elizabeth's portraits. Of true landscape painting there is hardly a sign in the Tudor period. There are some topographical views of royal palaces, drawings made by the Fleming A. van den Wyn-

gaerde on a flying visit about 1557, and the famous drawing of Nonsuch Palace by Hoefnagel, who was in England about 1568. The same artist's painting of the *Wedding at Horsleydown in Bermondsey* at Hatfield is almost the only genre-painting in England of the century, though others are hinted at in inventories, such as the Earl of Leicester's *A Butcher and Maid buying Meat*, by Hubbard. Instead of landscapes the Elizabethans had maps; at Lambeth, for example, in 1575 there were listed with the pictures about thirty maps, some framed, including English and European maps, 'a greate mappe of the peregrination of Christ', one of the 'Land of Promise', and one of America. The world was opening fast.

'Dynastic painting'

Another kind of painting may be isolated here, though as a category it melts into that of portraiture. It is the propaganda picture, religious, political or dynastic. Henry VII's consciousness of his position as the founder of a lineage is reflected in the magnificent chapel at Westminster and in his tomb. It is enlarged upon by his son in Holbein's great wall-painting that was in the Privy Chamber at Whitehall (and no doubt there strategically placed), which showed Henry VII and his Queen, Henry VIII and one of his (Jane Seymour, mother of the heir), and which was so impressive that it was said still to make people shake even at the end of the century (Pl. 24A). This was elaborated further, late in Henry VIII's reign, in the strange long picture now at Hampton Court, which shows Henry VIII enthroned with one of his Queens (again Jane Seymour, though long dead, as mother of the heir), and the Prince Edward at their side (Pl. 22A). At each extreme end of the picture, as though first and second reserves, stand the next in line, the Princesses Mary and Elizabeth. This picture was to be brought up to date in a revised edition of it painted by Eworth about 1570, in which Mary (now with Philip II of Spain) is attended by figures of War and Discord, while Queen Elizabeth is led forward to the centre of the stage by Peace (Pl. 22B). There were also straightforward anti-Papal paintings, most notably that at Hampton Court. This has recently been plausibly attributed[1] to Girolamo da Treviso, an Italian who worked for Henry VIII between 1538 and 1544, and it certainly belonged to Edward VI in 1547, when it was described as 'the bishop of Rome [i.e. the Pope] and the four Evangelists casting stones upon him'. But the most curious document of this kind unites the religious, political and dynastic themes, and is also as it were an icon of iconoclasm. It shows Henry VIII on his death-bed, handing on the Protestant Succession to the already enthroned Edward VI (Pl. 22B). On the right-hand side is the Protector Somerset with the Council of the protectorate, including Cranmer, and in the foreground the Pope, slumped in his seat, mortally sick, while two monks flee away. In the top right-hand corner, a domed church, presumably intended for St Peter's, founders in flames, while two armed men break up a statue of the Madonna on a column with lances. The picture must date from about 1547, the year when the major fury of the iconoclasts was released and so much of our medieval heritage of works of art was destroyed. Something of a dynastic consciousness like the Tudors' is discernible also in Holbein's (lost) family group of the More family of 1526 and the revised editions of it produced for descendants (and including themselves) in the fifteen-nineties, as in the National Portrait Gallery.

Portraiture and the Tudor collectors

The bulk, however, of Tudor painting that remains to us consists straightforwardly of portraiture. Realistic portraiture was known in England through the fifteenth century, if not much before. It was, however, a rarity, called upon mainly for specific occasions, generally either memorial or marital. Portraits were exchanged between royal houses during marriage negotiations, so that each side might see what the bargain looked like; and probably about the end of the century there seems to have become standardized a set of portraits of the kings of England. Portraits of a lesser rank than royal remain extremely scarce until after 1525, and it was only in Elizabeth's reign that it

[1] By P. Pouncey, *Burlington Magazine*, XCV (1953), pp. 208–10.

seems to have become customary for the heads of the most distinguished houses to have themselves recorded in paint, that they might preside not only over their present hearths but over the long generations of their descendants down the centuries to come. They put themselves on record in these portraits in much the same spirit as they built themselves their splendid tombs, standing in the full pride of their office and their blood, often, for the greater precision, showing their coat-of-arms.

To begin with, paintings had probably no place in less than Royal Tudor homes. The little information so far to hand suggests that the earliest private collectors of importance were amongst that group of humanists centred round Sir Thomas More. More himself had other paintings than the 'fine painted cloth with nine pageants and verses' which he had designed himself when a youth for his father, and the Holbein family group: and Sir Brian Tuke had a small but apparently choice collection, including a portrait by the Venetian painter, Antonio da Solario. The Royal collection is revealed as rich in quantity by inventories of 1542 and 1547, but the quality (apart chiefly from the Holbeins, and the Raphael of St George now in Washington) is difficult to assess, as so few of the pictures are now identifiable. There were, however, besides portraits, a high proportion of religious paintings. Clearly, the Protestant iconoclasm did not extend to private collections, although few new religious pictures were painted in England. The pictures seem to have been distributed through the Royal Palaces; the main concentrations being probably in the Long Galleries (at Greenwich there was even 'In the Jakes house a picture'). Protector Somerset, a great builder and keenly interested in the arts (he employed a French painter as drawing-master for his daughters) doubtless had a collection, but the great characteristic Elizabethan collections did not begin really to accumulate until the sixties. At that time the hoards of the Fitzallens, Earls of Arundel, of the Cecils, of Matthew Parker at Lambeth began to swell, but the largest were probably those of Leicester and of the heir of the Arundels, John, Lord Lumley. They were not truly art collections, but were specifically portrait collections. In Bess of Hardwick's collection in 1601 there were about seventy portraits (thirty-seven of them in the Long Gallery), as against less than ten other pictures. Leicester, in 1583, had at Kenilworth alone thirty-seven portraits, as against three subject pictures (excluding twenty-three maps and 'five of the seven planets painted in frames'). Lumley, about 1600, had some two hundred portraits, but only about thirty other paintings. The portraits were of relations, friends and colleagues, the kings of England and sometimes of Scotland, contemporary celebrities both English and European irrespective, to a remarkable degree, of political or religious sympathies (both Pole and Cranmer were represented at Lambeth). At Lumley Castle the subjects listed as portraits swept grandly from Adam and Eve onwards, including Julius Cæsar, not only Petrarch, but Dante, Raphael, Jane Shore, a complete set of Lumley's own ancestors made up to order, and 'old Tyme'. Many of these were naturally copies (the extent to which portraits of famous men were copied in the late sixteenth century is one of the factors that makes attributions so difficult a problem). The collections were of celebrities rather than of works of art, but, although the great collectors of the next century such as Arundel and Charles I were to winnow taste drastically, the predominant emphasis of English collections upon portraiture thereafter remained constant.

Early portraiture

It is time, however, to consider in more detail the artists who worked in England during this period. The sets of portraits of kings of England (as in the Society of Antiquaries of London) may represent a largely English style. They show (the earliest ones were much copied and revised through the sixteenth century) rather humble, less-than-life-size figures, half-length, in arched frames of black and gold like niches; the effect being somewhat of a line and wash drawing, delicate, linear, attenuated, a little pale and reserved in characterization. The style survives until well into the century, and a similar pallor and reserve will be characteristic of the Elizabethan portraits. One of the best early specimens is the portrait of the Countess of Salisbury of c. 1530-5 in the National Portrait Gallery (Pl. 26A). A portrait (also in the National Portrait Gallery) of Henry VII, 1505, probably by Michel Sittow, an international court-painter, is a stronger and much more vivid affair, though in the same tradition, representing the corresponding style current in North European courts. It can have had little effect in England, as it went abroad immediately, as part of a marriage bid for one of Maximilian's daughters. A different, though by no means novel, concept of portraiture is that of the English merchant Withypol, at Bristol, painted by Antonio da Solario, 1514 (Pl. 21A). It now seems very possible that this Venetian painter visited England in the second decade of the century.[2] This is a 'donor' portrait, showing the sitter in adoration before the Virgin, and is part of a triptych, destined probably as altar-piece for a church or chapel. Doubtless other similar paintings were commissioned, including portraits, but, being in churches, they almost all would have fallen victims to the Protestant iconoclasts later in the century.

The sixteenth century is liberally supplied with artists' names, culled from documentary records, but very meagrely supplied with paintings that can be attached with any certainty to those names.[3] Thus, in the first half of the century, we know that there was a considerable influx of Italian talent: the Neapolitan artist Volpe, in England between 1513 and 1536; Antonio Toto, here between about 1519 and 1555, and Serjeant-Painter; Nicholas da Modena, a considerable artist, here between 1537 and 1568; and the already mentioned Girolamo da Treviso, who arrived about 1542, and was killed in Henry VIII's service at the siege of Boulogne, 1544. There were others, but hardly anything of consideration in the way of paintings can be ascribed to any of them.

[2] See an article on this subject by Professor L. Bradner in *P.M.L.A.* (1956).
[3] The archival material for the whole period is very fully summarized by Dr E. Auerbach, *Tudor Artists*, 1954. The best general account of sixteenth century painting is in E. K. Waterhouse, *Painting in Britain, 1530–1790*, 1953.

In the same period, we know too the names of English painters like John Brown and Andrew Wright, Serjeant-Painters between 1512–32 and 1532–43: yet not a line of their work is known. There were also active in England between the 'twenties and 'forties various members of the Ghent family of painters, the Horenbouts (cf. *Miniature Painting*), and of one Fleming (?), Joannes Corvus, we have two reasonably certain works, one of Bishop Foxe, rather stronger and more sculptural in quality than the English manner.

Holbein

The only artistic personality who emerges from the early sixteenth-century mists, amongst the painters, is Hans Holbein (1497-8–1543) – but he with such stunning clarity that the work of all other painters in England throughout the century pales in contrast like ghosts. Holbein arrived in late 1526 (withdrawing from Bâle as a result of the drying-up there of patronage following upon the Protestant triumph). He was already a formed and mature artist, aware of the work of Raphael and of da Vinci, and he came bearing an impeccable passport from the great Erasmus to Thomas More. Within More's own circle, he was welcomed, and employed, and there he painted not only a number of individual portraits of the first order – including More himself, Archbishop Warham and Tuke – but his masterpiece, the More family group, which is now known only from copies. This, though it inspired no immediate fashion, was the first of English conversation pieces. Holbein's clientele, however, did not spread much wider, and he returned to Bâle early in 1528. Only on his second visit, from 1532 onwards, did he achieve real Court patronage, probably by way of the Norfolk family of the Godsalves and their patron, Thomas Cromwell. Henry VIII seems to have first sat to him about 1536, and thereafter Holbein, in the brief seven years left to him (he died of the plague in 1543), painted courtiers, was sent abroad to take likenesses of prospective royal brides (the Duchess of Milan in the National Gallery, and the Anne of Cleves in the Louvre) and produced the definitive account in paint of Henry VIII himself, including the great dynastic piece of Henry VIII, Henry VII, Elizabeth of York and Jane Seymour (Pl. 26D). He also made prolific designs for objects ranging from jewellery to chimney-pieces. Another source of employment was the German community in London, particularly the Hanseatic merchants of the Steelyard, for whom he painted not only portraits but two large allegories: the *Triumph of Poverty* and the *Triumph of Riches*, now only known from copies.

The quality in Holbein's work that must most have intrigued the English was its naturalism – illusionism. No painter in England before had had anything approaching this power to summon up, in a flat, two-dimensional image, the solid weight and living presence of a sitter. This depended equally on his fabulous skill and on the pictorial genius that could combine such acute recording of detail with an infallible grasp of plastic form and design. His sitters sat to him but briefly: as a rule probably only once, long enough for him to take a drawing of their heads (Pl. 26c) (possibly with the aid of some mechanical device of the nature of a *camera obscura*). From these – a famous series of them remains at Windsor – he built up his paintings, sometimes life-size, sometimes miniature, often somewhere between these two scales. Whole- or three-quarter-lengths seem to have been reserved for his most important clients, generally he shows half the figure or less. The portraits of his first English period (Pl. 26B) have a truly humane breadth and grandeur, fully consonant with the character of his chief patron, Sir Thomas More. In the second English period a more hieratic conception pervades, especially in his royal portraits, the figure being sometimes almost as if cut out against the empyrean background, at once glossy and marmoreal in their stiff grandness. With this goes an increased emphasis on surface texture and on the flat patterning of design (Pl. 26D). This was a trend foreshadowing the development of English sixteenth-century portraiture and carried to its logical extreme in the late portraits of Elizabeth.

The generation after Holbein

Scholars continue to be baffled by the problem of Holbein's studio. He must have had some extremely able assistants, yet none of them has so far been identified, and there is little work dating from immediately after his death that can be associated plausibly with them. A painter called John Bettes, by whom one portrait is known (Tate Gallery), is clearly very dependent on Holbein's style. Other painters of whom a little is known are all foreign, and fundamentally closer in style to continental trends than to Holbein, though they are not entirely free of his influence. Gerlach Flicke, a German, worked in England from 1547 or before until his death in 1558; Guillim Scrots, or Stretes, a Netherlander with experience of court-portraiture with Mary of Hungary, was here from about 1545 to 1553; the work of Hans Eworth, from Antwerp, ranges from 1549 or before until about 1574. Flicke, as in his portrait of Cranmer (Pl. 27A; see also Pl. 63), rivals Holbein in the bold clarity of his characterization, but is more brutal and blatant while far inferior in subtlety, close in mood and composition to painters of the Westphalian school. In a whole-length of Edward VI attributed to Scrots (Pl. 24B), there is a more refined blend of Holbein and of continental influences – the young king's pose is clearly based on that used by Holbein for Henry VIII, though more elegantly mannered. Very closely similar designs were used throughout Europe during the rest of the century for official royal portraits. Other portraits of Edward VI and of the Princess Elizabeth, of a less rigid but equally accomplished quality, are at Windsor. They are three-quarter-lengths and both are by unidentified artists. In Queen Mary's reign, at the time of her marriage with Philip II of Spain, Antonio Mor came over for a brief visit. No certain portraits, other than that of Mary (Pl. 27B), were painted in England by him, but later English portraiture has more in common with the continental style, of which Mor was the most accomplished exponent, than with Holbein. The characteristic formula, derived from designs by Titian in part, but cooler, the colour smoothly glazed, was a three-quarter-length – the sitter at once more polite, more detached, than with Holbein, and with a narrower design and character in contrast to his generally broad confrontation.

Hans Eworth

But the most interesting and various artist of the period was Hans Eworth: so various, indeed, that his works would be ascribed to three or more different hands, had he not had the admirable and only too rare habit of signing his paintings with his monogram: HE. His earliest known works, of 1549 and 1550, are entirely novel to English art: the exotic small-scale painting of a Turk on Horseback (Pl. 23A), and the two portraits of Sir John Luttrell and of Captain Wyndham. The Luttrell portrait is a curious composite of mannerist allegory and realistic portraiture, showing the sitter wading naked in a stormy sea, while a very classicized goddess leans to him from a cloudy heaven above. The whole picture is, in addition, liberally scattered with inscriptions and mottoes. The Wyndham portrait (Pl. 23B), on the other hand, is the first truly informal portrait in England, showing a soldier as though in a lull in battle, with gun and powder flask, leaning against a tree – burly, untidied, almost sweaty. But these three very different paintings do not seem to have caught on, and by 1554 Eworth was working for the Court. His portrait of Mary I is a very formal (though very successfully so) regal document, reminiscent of Holbein's Duchess of Milan, but with an impersonal emphasis on pattern and that cool aloofness that hints at Mor. Eworth's portraits of the later 'fifties and 'sixties all show a rich incrustation of detailed magnificence in costume, coupled with a curious inflated rotundity of flesh, the figures sharply lit and detached against the background; there seems to be a progressive flattening of the overall pattern, and, in the twin portraits of the Duke and Duchess of Norfolk, 1562 (Pl. 23D), the main elements of the late Elizabethan portrait are already visible. About 1569, we find Eworth reverting to his mannerist mixtures, but now in the special and apt case of Queen Elizabeth herself, for whom a simultaneous presentation in terms both mortal and divine was fitting. One example is the Tudor family piece (described above, Pl. 22B), and the other is the well-known painting at Hampton Court, also a revision, this time of the Judgement of Paris story. The Queen has

The Tudor Monarchs

(A) Henry VII (1485–1509), artist unknown. *The National Portrait Gallery.*
(B) Henry VIII (1509–1547), by Holbein. *Trustees of the Chatsworth Settlement.*
(C) Elizabeth I (1558–1603), artist unknown. *The National Portrait Gallery.*
(D) Edward VI (1547–1553), after Holbein. *The National Portrait Gallery.*
(E) Mary I (1553–1558), artist unknown. *The National Portrait Gallery.*

PLATE 1

The Opening of Parliament, 1523. From Wriothesley M.S., the Royal Library, Windsor Castle.
By gracious permission of Her Majesty the Queen.

PLATE 2

The Commons presenting their Speaker to Queen Elizabeth I in the House of Lords, from R. Glover's *Nobilitas Politica vel Civilis*, 1608.

PLATE 3

Queen Elizabeth I on the road to Blackfriars to attend the marriage of Anne Russell and Lord Herbert in
June 1600, engraved by Vertue after Gheeraerts.

PLATE 4

(A) Richmond Palace, Surrey, built for Henry VII 1499–1501: the front facing the Thames.
Engraved by Hollar, 1638.

(B) Hardwick Hall, Derbyshire, built by Bess of Hardwick, Countess of Shrewsbury, in 1590–7.
National Buildings Record.

PLATE 5

(A) The Hall Block with terra-cotta decorations in the Courtyard at Sutton Place, Surrey, 1522–5.
National Buildings Record.

(B) The garden front at St Lucien's, Wallingford, Berkshire: note the symmetrical composition.
National Buildings Record.

PLATE 6

(A) 'The momentary High Renaissance of English Architecture', Longleat, Wiltshire, completed after 1567. *National Buildings Record.*

(B) Loseley, Surrey; the unsymmetrical grouping of the less formal southern side. *A. F. Kersting.*

PLATE 7

(A) North Cadbury Manor House, Somerset, showing the early use of unrelated gables and bay windows. *W. H. Rendell.*

(B) Newton Surmaville, Somerset, showing the developed combination of gables and bay windows in an architectural relationship. *National Buildings Record.*

PLATE 8

Gayhurst, Buckinghamshire, the frontispiece as the only ornamented feature of the elevation.
Royal Commission on Historical Monuments.

PLATE 9   73

(A) Loseley, Surrey, the early seventeenth-century chimneypiece of chalk; typical in its ornate decoration, highly exceptional in its material. *A. F. Kersting.*

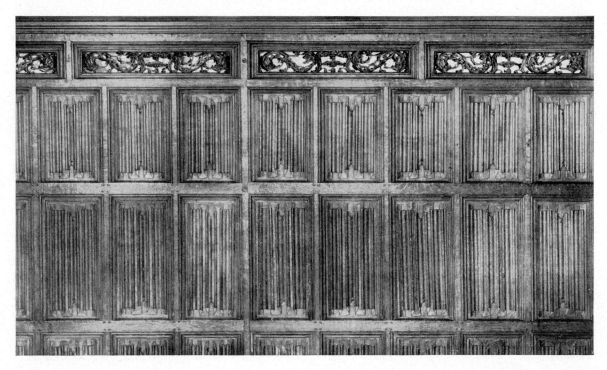

(B) Part of the early sixteenth-century linenfold panelling, from the Neptune Inn, Ipswich. *A. C. Cooper.*

PLATE 10

(A) The large panels with architectural motifs of the early seventeenth century: White Parlour at Holland House, London, destroyed during the Second World War.
Royal Commission on Historical Monuments.

(B) Geometrical patterning and animal and bird motifs on the ceiling at Melbury House, Dorset, early seventeenth century. *Royal Commission on Historical Monuments.*

PLATE 11 75

(A) Mid-sixteenth-century overmantel, frieze and ceiling at Mapperton Manor House, Dorset.
Royal Commission on Historical Monuments.

(B) Early seventeenth-century wall painting of 'Antique Work' at the Meeting House, West
Hanningfield, Essex. *Royal Commission on Historical Monuments.*

PLATE 12

(A) A hutch table of oak with doors carved with a tracery design, the centre panel carved with a floreated pattern. *Private Collection*.

(B) Carved oak joyned stool, of the late sixteenth century. *S. W. Wolsey*.

PLATE 13   77

Carved oak armchair inlaid with holly and bog oak, dated 1596.
S. W. Wolsey.

PLATE 14

(A) An early example of a sixteenth-century table with three trestle supports and stretcher rail.

(B) An Elizabethan table with drawing leaves and carved bulbous supports.
Hart Collection.

PLATE 15

(A) A five-sided cup-board with an aumbry, of the early sixteenth century.
Sir William Burrell Collection.

(B) English Oak counter or rent table, early sixteenth century.
Peter Gwynn Collection.

PLATE 16

Oak open court cup-board with two frieze drawers and carved heraldic animal and figure supports, late sixteenth century. *Sir William Burrell Collection.*

PLATE 17

(A) Small panelled oak cup-board with two doors. Late sixteenth century. *Peter Gwynn Collection.*

(B) A rare type of late sixteenth-century court or plate cup-board. *Hart Collection.*

(C) Small late sixteenth-century games table, with two folding extensions to the top. *Hart Collection.*

B

C

(A) Oak press cupboard ornamented with turning, carving and inlay. *c.* 1600. *Hart Collection*

(B) An oak early sixteenth-century aumbry with doors and drawers. *Sir William Burrell Collection.*

PLATE 19

Headboard of an oak carved and painted late sixteenth-century four-post bed; the acanthus-decorated frieze brackets in walnut. *L. G. G. Ramsey Collection.*

PLATE 20

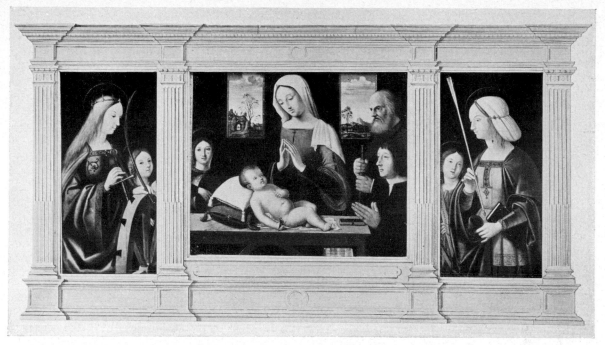

(A) ANTONIO DA SOLARIO, 1514. The Withypol Triptych.
Bristol Art Gallery (the wings on loan from the National Gallery).

(B) Artist unknown, *c.* 1547. Henry VIII on his deathbed, Edward VI and his council, and the Pope.
Private Collection.

PLATE 21

(A) Artist unknown, *c.* 1546. Henry VIII and his family.
Royal Collection (Hampton Court). Reproduced by gracious permission of Her Majesty the Queen.

(B) HANS EWORTH, *c.* 1565–70. Henry VIII and his family.
Mrs Dent-Brocklehurst.

PLATE 22

(A) HANS EWORTH, 1549. A Turk on horseback.
The Earl of Yarborough.

(B) HANS EWORTH, 1550. Thomas Wyndham.
The Earl of Radnor.

(C) Artist unknown, *c.* 1570. A Morality.
Derek Sherborn, Esq.

(D) HANS EWORTH, 1562. Margaret, Duchess of
Norfolk. *Audley End. Crown Copyright reserved.*

PLATE 23   87

(B) GUILLIM SCROTS or STRETES, c. 1550. Edward vi.
Royal Collection (Hampton Court).
Reproduced by gracious permission of Her Majesty the Queen.

(A) HANS HOLBEIN, 1537. Henry viii and Henry vii
(Cartoon for the Whitehall wall-painting).
Trustees of the Chatsworth Settlement.

PLATE 24

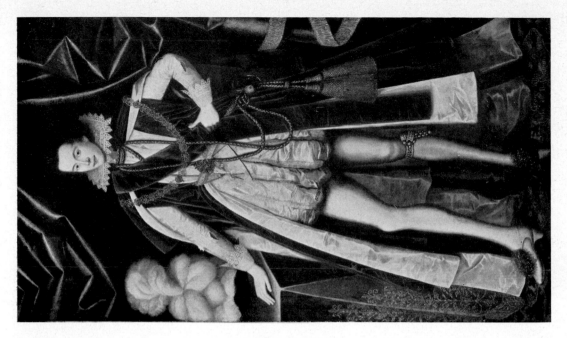

(B) Artist unknown, *c.* 1616. George Villiers, Duke of Buckingham. *National Portrait Gallery.*

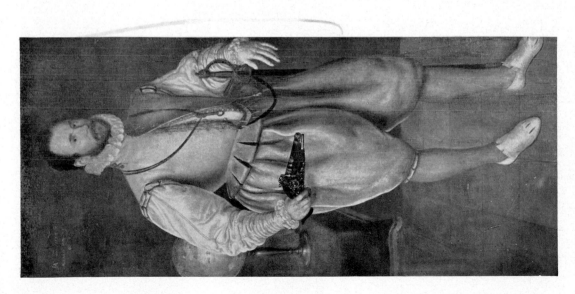

(A) Cornelius Ketel, 1577. Sir Martin Frobisher. *Bodleian Library, Oxford.*

PLATE 25

(A) Artist unknown,
c. 1530–35.
Margaret Pole,
Countess of Salisbury.
National Portrait Gallery.

(B)
HANS HOLBEIN,
1527.
Archbishop Warham.
Lambeth Palace.

(C) HANS HOLBEIN, *c.* 1538-40.
George Brooke, Lord Cobham.
*Royal Collection (Windsor). By gracious
permission of Her Majesty the Queen.*

(D) HANS HOLBEIN, 1536.
Jane Seymour.
Kunsthistorisches Museum, Vienna.

(A) GERLACH FLICKE, *c.* 1547. Archbishop Cranmer. *National Portrait Gallery.*

(B) ANTONIO MOR, 1554. Queen Mary I. *Prado.*

(C) FEDERICO ZUCCARO, *c.* 1574. Queen Elizabeth I. *British Museum.*

(D) Artist unknown, *c.* 1588. Queen Elizabeth I. *The Duke of Bedford, Woburn.*

PLATE 27   91

(A) (By or after) JOHN DE CRITZ, *c.* 1595. Robert Cecil, Earl of Salisbury. *National Portrait Gallery.*

(B) HIERONYMUS CUSTODIS, 1589. Elizabeth Bruges, Lady Kennedy. *The Duke of Bedford, Woburn.*

(C) SIR WILLIAM, or FRANCIS, SEGAR, 1590. Robert Devereux, Earl of Essex. *Irish National Gallery, Dublin.*

(D) GEORGE GOWER, *c.* 1577. Sir Thomas Cornwallis. *Audley End. Crown Copyright reserved.*

PLATE 28

Tomb of Lord Marney, Layer Marney, Essex. Early sixteenth century.
Royal Commission on Historical Monuments.

PLATE 29

Tomb of the Earl of Rutland, Bottesford, Leicestershire, by Richard Parker.
Courtauld Institute of Art.

PLATE 30

Tomb of Sir John Jefferey, Whitchurch Canonicorum, Dorset, *c.* 1611.
Royal Commission on Historical Monuments.

PLATE 31

Daughters of Lord Teynham on his tomb at Lynsted, Kent, by Epiphanius Evesham.
National Buildings Record.

PLATE 32

usurped the rôle of Paris, having awarded to herself the apple or orb as the most beautiful of them all, while the three claimant goddesses are routed in disordered acknowledgement of their better.

From the 'sixties and 'seventies, there survives a number of formal three-quarter-length portraits by unknown artists, monotonous in composition and rarely inspiring in quality. One known artist who painted such portraits was Steven van der Meulen, from Antwerp, naturalized in England in 1562; the John Lord Lumley, still at Lumley Castle, is certainly by him, 1563, and a considerable number of other portraits are very close in manner, though doubtless the work of several different artists. Typical examples, though of varying quality, are the Leicester, and the Sir William Petre of 1567, both in the National Portrait Gallery, and the portraits of Burghley and his wife at Hatfield, the last two verging on the style of Hans Eworth. They are dignified, but rather tame and anonymous in handling and represent a Court style that was international. Steven van der Meulen had painted also at the Court of Sweden, while the portrait of Sir Nicholas Throckmorton in the National Portrait Gallery, which dates probably from 1562 (another version is so dated), in which year Throckmorton was mainly in France, is very reminiscent of Clouet's portrait of Pierre Quthe of the same date in the Louvre. The Throckmorton may, however, have been painted either in England or in France. Rather later, the portrait of Sir Philip Sidney, 1577, seems perfectly consonant with English work, but was probably originated in the Low Countries. Less than life-size portraits, similarly posed, also remained popular. One unnamed painter, by whom several portraits are known, is the artist of the fiercely doll-like Hugh Fitzwilliam (Pl. 64A). Whole-lengths, like the Earl of Pembroke on loan from the Duke of Leeds to Lancaster House, are relatively rare, and generally follow in composition and atmosphere the example of Scrots' Edward VI.

The Portraits of Queen Elizabeth

In the 'seventies, the portraiture of Queen Elizabeth began to present its own specialized problem: that of reconciling the not entirely pristine appearance of an ageing woman with the concept of ideal, fadeless and beautiful majesty that she represented. Already, by 1563, her portraits were the cause of some concern, and action was meditated along the lines of standardizing a pattern portrait by some 'special cunning painter', whence satisfactory and inoffensive copies might be reduplicated. There was clearly a large demand for her portrait, and it was probably the first painting to hang in many English homes. In her famous interview with Nicholas Hilliard (presumably in, or before, 1572) she made clear her own views: especially that to model the figure by light-and-shade was wrong, that it should, on the contrary, be lit by a clear and even light, and scrupulously contoured and delineated – an idea exactly in line with the Italian theorists of Mannerism. It was also an idea that, with its apparent insistence on the presentation of the sitter under ruthlessly searching illumination, might seem to make the necessary compromise in her portraits almost impossible. The solution is however latent in a drawing (Pl. 27C) of her made by one of the most eminent of the Italian Mannerist painters, Federigo Zuccaro (who, in spite of the countless portraits ascribed to him in English houses and sale-rooms, was in England for less than a year, in 1574-5; no painting made by him in England is known to exist). The drawing is free and attractive in line – that was to be no part of the solution – but in the background is a column entwined with a snake. Both column and snake are fraught with symbolic significance, and it was to be through allegory and symbolism that Her Majesty was henceforth largely to be demonstrated in her portraits rather than by any accurate reflection of her physical presence. We find her withdrawn behind the richly jewelled and embroidered fabric of her incredible wardrobe: the red wig, the confection of lace, the bolstered sleeves, the iron V of the bodice planted in the great circular hoop of the skirt, the jewellery, the rigging of pearls (themselves symbols). Her face is represented by a summarized and expressionless mask, unwrinkled and ageless. Stiffly she stands, an all but religious image, for veneration. On and about her are the attributes of her majesty –

branches of olives, the sheathed sword, the crown, the claimed globe itself; jewels representing a phœnix or a pelican in its piety; or a map of England beneath her feet, thunderous storm and sunshine to left and right, or a whole rainbow clasped bodily in the hand; and, amongst it all, mottoes, even whole sonnets (Pls. 27D, 68B).

Late Elizabethan painters

This richness of emblematic lore is not entirely confined to Elizabeth's own portraits: it is indeed an essential idiom of Elizabethan imagination, and the literature is seamed and studded with it. Hilliard's miniatures are often conceived in that idiom, and it intrudes into and sometimes dominates other life-size portraits. It is symptomatic of a literary rather than a plastic approach to the arts. One may suspect that even the bodies in the portraits may be but emblems for man, or clothes-horses. But the clothes indicate rank and blood: hence, too, perhaps the Elizabethan indifference to visual coherence and to scale – life-size portraits are but blown-up miniatures in conception. The technique that served this curious intellectualism was also on the lines laid down by the Queen, tending to produce a rather flat figure, linear in quality, sharply defined in outline and in detail, yet with the individuality of the face summarized. Of the painters themselves, we again know as yet very little, but at least some of them, like Hilliard, seem to be native English. George Gower was one. He was well established by 1570 and Serjeant-Painter from 1581 to his death in 1596. The bust portrait of Sir Thomas Kytson (Tate Gallery), 1573, is certainly by him. A few other bust portraits are known, and a fairly certain three-quarter-length is the Sir Thomas Cornwallis at Audley End (Pl. 28D). His portraits have something of Hilliard's lucid modesty, but, in the simplified planes of the face, are more sculptural in feeling. Between about 1580 and 1600 we also know a little of Segar – Sir William Segar, also herald and Garter King-at-Arms, and his brother Francis. It may well be that they worked in partnership, and on a miniature as well as life-size scale. The Earl of Essex, 1590 (Pl. 28c), in Dublin, is a reasonably certain example of Segar's work, and this is very close,

though more gauche, to a life-sized exercise in Hilliard's manner. Hilliard himself is known to have worked on a large scale, but no certain example has been discovered, and until one is, his quality on that scale cannot be assessed. There were also active at the time a group of painters mainly of Flemish origin, settled in England: the de Critz and the Gheeraerts families, and, with them associated, an Englishman (?) Robert Peake, and also the miniaturist Isaac Oliver. As de Critzes, Gheeraerts and Olivers inter-married, and the families may have collaborated, some sort of joint studio is possible. At all events their work so far has resisted all attempts at disentanglement. A portrait by John de Critz (c. 1552–1642) is the Earl of Salisbury at Hatfield, being repeated in many versions and later re-dressed in Garter robes (Pl. 28A). Marcus Gheeraerts the Elder (in England 1568–77) was probably not a portrait painter, but an engraving by him of the Knights of the Garter in procession is in the British Museum. His son, also Marcus, who worked probably from the 'eighties until almost 1630, is recorded by various documents and a number of portraits so diverse in manner that the individuality of his style, if any, is far from apparent. The same applies to Robert Peake. The name 'Gheeraerts' is used in the art-market to cover almost any portrait of the late Elizabethan period, including no doubt many other painters' work as well. The outstanding achievement of the time, however, for part of which this group must have been responsible, is the series of splendidly decorative whole-length portraits that range from the 'eighties until almost 1630 (Pls. 66A, 68A and B, 25B). Jointless images, dressed in costumes of great brilliance, posed generally by a gold-fringed velvet chair under a canopy or tent of rich curtains, they are often as flat and almost as formal as the patterned Turkey carpets which most of them feature. The renaissance concepts of depth, of plasticity, of the *vraisemblable*, are here abandoned for an effect almost as though a Byzantine artist had turned his hand to fashion-plates. They are best seen in mass, as at Redlynch Park and there is a good single example in the Duke of Buckingham, c. 1616, in the National Portrait Gallery.

The end of the Elizabethan tradition

These whole-lengths constitute a remarkable and uniquely English departure from the mainstream of European painting. The European tradition, however, with its concern for a more naturalistic portraiture, had never been lost from sight in England, and Elizabethan portraiture as a whole steers somewhere between the more naturalistic art of the Netherlands and the extreme stylization of the 'Jacobethan' whole-lengths, the high fashion of the Court. A family like the Greshams, wealthy international merchants and financiers, shows an interesting pattern of patronage. Sir Thomas Gresham had a whole-length of himself, of remarkable dramatic flamboyance, painted perhaps abroad already in 1544. In the 'sixties he sat, probably in Flanders, to Mor. William Gresham, in 1579, sat like a sober Dutch merchant to the Dutch painter Cornelius Ketel, who was working in England between 1573 and 1581. Some of Ketel's portraits conform to the usual Court designs, but his Frobisher of 1578 in the Bodleian Library (Pl. 25A) irrupts, in spite of its damage, into the waxen canon of Court portraiture like a live bandit into Madame Tussauds. Burly and intransigent, here there is at last more of a suggestion of movement. Closer to the Anglo-Flemish manner is the Antwerp painter Hieronymus Custodis (Pl. 28B), active in England in the 'eighties and dead by 1593, by whom several signed and dated portraits exist. The unknown but outstandingly able painter of the Sir Henry Neville of 1582 (Bacon Collection) suggests an anglicized counterpart of a Dutch painter like Pieter or Aert Pieterz. It was the realistic European tradition that was in fact to prevail. The fading of Hilliard before the fleshier talent of Isaac Oliver in the first decade of the seventeenth century is symptomatic of the shifting taste, and in the second decade there arrived from the Low Countries some able and up-to-date painters, including van Somer and Mytens, and the stiff 'Jacobethan' formulæ began to melt. They were finally to be liquidated only by the arrival of Van Dyck and the Baroque in 1632.

Wood-cut tail-piece from *Caveat or Warneing for ... Vagabones,* printed by W. Griffith, London 1567.

Sculpture

ERIC MERCER

By the early years of the sixteenth century English sculpture, despite the skill and training of its practitioners, was barren of ideas. Its motifs were few and hackneyed, and its standard of carving, while still high, was well below the delicate accomplishment of a mid fifteenth-century work such as Humphrey of Gloucester's chantry at St Albans Sculptural stonework was largely disappearing from domestic building and the effigies and figures on tombs were becoming competently conventionalized. There was still an occasional liveliness and freshness of approach, as in the Last Judgement on a tomb at Kingston-upon-Soar and the Virgin and Child at Broadwater, both of about 1540, but such qualities were not to survive the Reformation and the advent of patrons who guarded their position in this world only a shade less jealously than their place in the next, and did not intend to have the one or the other compromised by boisterous genre scenes or by idolatrous saints and virgins.

In this situation the arrival of artists like Torrigiani and Giovanni da Maiano, trained in the schools of the Italian Renaissance, had a wide but not deep effect. Their work in sculpture stands out from that of their English contemporaries as Holbein's does in painting; not merely because they were greater artists, but because of the way in which they were greater. Torrigiani's tomb of Henry VII at Westminster and da Maiano's work at Hampton Court introduced into England a conception of sculptural modelling and of the human figure wholly unknown here before. They also introduced quite incidentally a new set of motifs.

English craftsmen, with their own ideas of the human figure but trained in motifs that they now used mechanically, borrowed the decorative detail and rejected the essential form of Italian Renaissance sculpture Before long on tombs, and much less frequently in private houses, renaissance or sub-renaissance details were surrounding wholly un-renaissance English figures. The Marney tomb at Layer Marney (Pl. 29) is an early example, the work of John Guldon of Hereford with its quattrocento motifs and its ill-proportioned human figures is a late one. On a domestic building such as Sutton Place of the 1520's, where an attempt was made at introducing renaissance cherubs, the result is merely a series of small naked figures, lively and amusing, but not removed in spirit or execution from late Gothic work.

This failure of an imported sculpture to take root in England occurred again in the third quarter of the century There is a series of tombs in Buckinghamshire and Bedfordshire distinguished by their severely correct classical detail and their sculptural modelling. The tomb of Sir Robert Dormer at Wing has well-proportioned Corinthian columns supporting a correct entablature and flanking a tomb chest in the shape of a Roman altar with finely carved bucrania and fruit-swags. The monuments of Anthony Cave at Chicheley and of Lord Mordaunt at Turvey are remarkable for their sculptured figures. Although those at Chicheley are, in fact, ill-proportioned, nevertheless they and the admirable figures at Turvey have great elegance and a remarkable freedom of pose. The reclining female figures in the spandrels of

Caius' Gate of Virtue at Cambridge, although less well carved, have the same elongated elegance. These examples are of importance not because they had, but because they had not, any influence. They emphasize the lesson of the earlier years, that in essentials English sculpture went its own way in the sixteenth century.

Funeral monuments

The direction of that way was largely determined by the restricted demand for sculpture, a demand that was mainly confined to funeral monuments for the wealthier classes. The best-known native school up to and beyond the middle of the century was that of the Midland alabasterers, but all the work of the period until the very last years of the century is essentially similar. It might use Renaissance or even occasionally Gothic motifs, the effigies might be on an altar tomb or beneath an architectural canopy, the ancillary figures of weepers or children might be standing or kneeling, the standard of execution might vary from the competent work of the Burton alabasterer, Richard Parker, to the crudity of the carver of the Poulet tomb at Hinton St George, but whatever their foibles or talent, its sculptors had two features in common: they gave their figures a stiffness of pose, and their standing figures a lack of proportion, generally in the direction of squatness, that distinguish them at once from the work of the Italians and from that of the sculptor of the Mordaunt tomb. The stumpy figures on Parker's tomb of the Earl of Rutland at Bottesford (Pl. 30), those on the Royleys' Fermor tomb at Somerton and on the Ernle monument at West Wittering are as ill-proportioned in one way as the lanky figures on the Duchess of Suffolk's tomb at Spilsby or on the Harford tomb at Bosbury are in another. The stiffness of pose was largely determined by the prevailing attitude towards funeral monuments, the proportions by the failure of the designers to solve the problems of relating human figures to classical architecture and by a general unconcern for the human form. In sculpture that was non-monumental but still placed in an architectural framework – the Nine Worthies along the second storey at Montacute, James I and his family at Trinity

College, Cambridge, the figures on the chimneypiece at Condover – the pose was very much freer, but the proportions were still squat. Less obviously this unconcern for the human form is revealed in the innumerable thermæ of wood and stone in domestic work, figures that were borrowed from abroad, no doubt, but which were seized on with relish because they allowed free play to a delight in facial representation, but set the carver no problem in physical proportions.

Portraiture

It was to the delineation of the human face that the sculpture of the time devoted its greatest skill and care. Although there is no certain proof, the variety of facial types in the alabaster monuments of the period up to 1550 suggests deliberate attempts at portraying individuals. In the later years the London or 'Southwark' sculptors were contracting to make the 'picture or similitude' of the deceased, and the inscription on the tomb of Sir Robert Watter and his wife at York boasts that their effigies are their 'true portraiture'. The increasing fashion from about 1580 onwards for bust monuments illustrates the tendency to dispense with the superfluities and provide the essential likeness. On the Suffolk tomb at Spilsby, where the figures are execrable, the busts are at least competent. In the much later tomb of Provost Murray at Eton the bust replaces an effigy as a central feature and is cut and modelled with great skill, while the cherubs above it have met with a more cavalier treatment. In those rare instances where sculpture had a domestic setting, as at Lumley Castle, the figures were nearly always busts or half-busts. But at Lumley the one full-length figure, standing upon a fountain, was undraped, well proportioned and freely posed. The female figure surmounting a fountain shown in a contemporary drawing among the Hatfield MSS, probably the figure of 'Justice' that was made for the courtyard at Hampton Court in 1591–2, is similarly well-proportioned and freely posed. These and the statues, generally of characters from classical mythology, that were placed in gardens and courtyards, were free of the limitations imposed by an architectural setting or by any intimations of mortality, and gave their sculptors the opportunity, if no more, of breaking the restrictive bounds that hampered the monumental sculptors and their associates.

The London school

In the later years of the century the Anglo-Flemish style of the London sculptors spread widely and either ousted or influenced the provincial craftsmen. Much has been made of this Flemish influence, but it too, like its continental predecessors, was at first mainly confined to detail. The funeral monuments were on a larger scale, their composition was even more architectural, they were often designed with a great deal of coloured stone and marble in geometrical patterns, they were covered with the conventional motifs of strapwork and of ribbon-scroll and they tended to have coarse mouldings, and especially the heavy belly-mould to horizontal features. In essentials of composition, however, and consequently in their attitude to the human figure, they differed but little from the more native tombs. Yet that little was to be important. One feature which they occasionally introduced was one or more figures of the 'Virtues', or other emblematical conceptions, placed upon the cornice of the monument and unconditioned, therefore, in their form and volume by any necessity to fit an already determined space. Such figures did not have their proportions determined by non-sculptural considerations, and because they were 'emblems' and not mourners, from whom a 'modest stillness and humility' in the presence of the mighty dead was demanded, could be given much freer poses.

The work of these men of the London or 'Southwark' school was, however, more a response to, than the originator of, a country-wide demand. The tomb of John Leweston of about 1584 in Sherborne Abbey – a tomb that is clearly not Southwark work or in any way derived from it – has six free-standing cherubs upon its cornice. What the Southwark sculptors did was to follow the age; they turned the provincial cherubs of Sherborne into the fashionable emblematic figures, and then used their superior skill to exploit to the full the new artistic freedom. By the second de-

cade of the seventeenth century the free-standing 'Virtues' and all their cousins were a necessary part of every sculptor's stock-in-trade and were being used, however clumsily, by local craftsmen in the remotest parts of England (Pl. 31).

The effigies themselves were not wholly immune from this development. Although the flat-on-the-back attitude never wholly disappeared, it was increasingly superseded by freer poses. The reclining effigy, of which the Hoby tomb at Bisham is a very early example, was soon accompanied by the kneeling effigy, a form which culminated in the seated 'Conversation Piece', to use Mrs Esdaile's phrase, of the figures of Sir Giles Mompesson and his wife at Lydiard Tregoze.

With this freedom of pose went, in some cases, a new freedom of expression, particularly noticeable in the work of the English sculptor, Epiphanius Evesham. Evesham was a pupil of the Southwark tomb-maker, Richard Stevens, and his tombs are little different from the general run in their composition; they are a portent of things to come in their emotional content. Previously the 'weepers' or the children and relations placed as accessory figures upon monuments had usually either stood stiffly, holding heraldic shields, or had knelt, equally stiffly, in conventional attitudes of prayer. In the one case they look like professional mutes, in the other like members of the family keeping up appearances. Nowhere is there any hint of grief at the ending of a personal relationship. In Evesham's work the expression of grief is obvious, even perhaps excessive. On the monument of Lord Teynham at Lynsted his daughters are shown in various poses, and are giving way to a great deal of distress and of unself-disciplined emotion at their father's death (Pl. 32).

Such an emotional approach was not confined to Evesham; the work of his fellow-pupil, Isaac James, is sometimes in the same spirit. The work of James' pupil, Nicholas Stone, belongs to another era, but its emotional content is foreshadowed in the work of these earlier men. It is the content of their work, and the figure sculpture of the later members of the Southwark school that marks the end of the austere and restricted sculpture of sixteenth-century England.

Silver

HUGH HONOUR

An Italian who visited England at the beginning of the sixteenth century said that all the shops of Milan, Rome, Venice and Florence put together could not provide such gold and silver as he had seen on sale in London. The supercilious foreigner would not be slow in pointing out the unpolished manners of the English or in drawing unfavourable comparisons between their art and architecture and the sophisticated modes of France and Italy. But he would be bound to confess his astonishment at, if not his admiration for, the national wealth expressed in vast loads of heavy plate. During the Tudor period a collection of silver was regarded principally as an ostentatious method of storing riches, and the finest pieces were intended for display or purely ceremonial purposes, rather than for daily use. The peer or prosperous merchant who sat at table with a huge and curiously wrought salt-cellar before him, who toasted his guests in a cup enriched with gems, whose hall was brightened by the light of torches held in great sconces of silver and reflected in gargantuan gilt plates, would eat with his fingers, as likely as not, off a wooden trencher well soaked with the rancid gravy of former meals. Indeed, the very shape of some of the most exquisite drinking-vessels was determined by the necessity of their being clutched in wet or greasy hands. Although the hundred and twenty odd years which separate the coronation of Henry VII from the death of Queen Elizabeth can have seen but a slight improvement in manners, they saw the dissemination of the use of silver throughout the upper and middle classes of society, until what had once been the prerogative of the few became the ambition of the many. Stylistically the period is for silver, as for the other arts, one of transition from the Gothic to an exuberant if somewhat vulgarized Renaissance style.

Domestic plate

Henry VII's accession to the throne in 1485 is of no particular relevance to the historian of English silver, but it marks the beginning of a dynastic epoch which may conveniently be taken as a point of departure. From testaments and inventories we know that the noble household of that date frequently possessed a considerable weight of silver On his death in 1459, Sir John Fastolf, who had augmented by a prudent marriage a fortune made originally in the French wars, owned 1,175 lb. troy of domestic and 110 lb. troy of chapel silver. The will of the 13th Earl of Oxford accounts for 1,116 lb. troy of domestic silver in his possession in 1509. Most noble households in the first years of Henry VII's reign must have contained a hoard of cups, some very large and used only on special occasions, some plain or in the form of mounted coconuts and made for personal use. There would also be several ewers and basins for the ablutions which took place before every meal and between its many courses, at least one ceremonial salt-cellar to stand to the right of the lord's place at the high table (Sir John Fastolf owned nine salts, eight of which were large), a number of spoons and, perhaps, such objects as table fountains. Lower down the social scale, in the house of a rich merchant or yeoman, one would expect to find a cup or two, possibly a small salt, silver-mounted mazer-bowls and some spoons which were acquired as the first emblems of gentility.

So few pieces of late fifteenth-century silver have survived that it is difficult to make any but misleading generalizations about their quality or style. Plate acquired as a means of storing wealth was sold in time of need, and as its value was rated by weight, many pieces must have been melted down in later years to be remade in a more fashionable style. It may, however, be presumed that extraordinary craftsmanship might save a very rich or curious vessel from the crucible, and it must not be imagined that all, or even a large proportion, of the objects whose disappearance we so much regret, were of the same high quality as the few remarkably fine pieces which have fortunately been preserved. It is significant that the only survivor of Queen Elizabeth's treasury of plate is the famous Royal Gold Cup (now in the British Museum), – a superb example of French craftsmanship of the fourteenth century (Pl. 33), though such richly bejewelled pieces as the 'Dream of Paris' cup were of too great an intrinsic value to be preserved in the 'Jewel-house'. On the other hand, the simple mazer-bowls and coconut cups survived because the silver on them was barely worth the melting.

No more than a whisper of the Italian Renaissance had reached the zenophobic shores of England at the beginning of this period: and it was not until the second decade of the sixteenth century that it affected the style of the English silversmiths. Late fifteenth-century plate, in its more elaborate manifestations, was comparable in style with the carvings of the then outmoded 'Decorated' period and such monuments as the Percy tomb in Beverley Minster: the ogee curve continued to nod in silver long after it had vanished from architecture. Cups, such as those described in the fourteenth-century alliterative poem, *Cleanness*, were still popular at the end of the next century; they were 'en-aumayled with azer', pinnacled and decorated with all manner of flora and fauna:

Pyes & papeiayes purtrayed with-inne,
As thay prudly hade piked of pom-garnades,
For alle the blomes of the bozes were blynkande perles,
& all the fruyt in the formes of flaumbeande gemmes.

Fig. 1. Font-shaped cup from Wymenswold, Leicestershire, 1512.

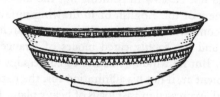

Fig. 2. Mazer-bowl, c. 1490. *Victoria and Albert Museum.*

Of this type, without the jewellery, was the hour-glass-shaped salt made towards the end of the fifteenth century and given to Corpus Christi College by Bishop Foxe. The same spirit is evident in the pinacled top and crocketed rim of a standing-cup which belongs to the Mercers' Company; though some of its ornament is later (Pl. 34). As specimens of a simpler, not to say ruder, style current between 1485 and 1520, the dumpy little font-shaped cups (Fig. 1) may be cited; though these vessels were sometimes provided with ogee-shaped covers which endowed them with a rustic grace.

The most popular form of drinking-vessel in use at the end of the fifteenth century was the mazer-bowl, so called from the spotted maple-wood of which it was made. Mazers were first introduced into England in the fourteenth century, and their popularity, especially in monasteries and

Fig. 3. Coconut cup with silver mounts, c. 1580. Height 8 in. *Victoria and Albert Museum.*

Fig. 4. Normal type of late 15th century chalice.

among the yeoman and merchant classes, persisted until the Reformation in England. (In Scotland they appear to have been made in the latter part of the sixteenth century.) Normally they were mounted in latten metal, silver or silver-gilt, with a wide band round the rim, which sometimes carried a sententious inscription, a circular medallion in the bottom of the bowl and some form of foot (Fig. 2); occasionally they were set upon baluster stems, which allowed more scope for decoration. Otherwise they vary only in the engraving of the medallion referred to as the 'print' or 'boss'. A very fine example of the more elaborate form of mazer – provided, as many were, with a cover – has survived in the possession of the Barber Surgeons' Company, but its bowl has been replaced by one of silver (Pl. 37A).

More highly esteemed than mazer-bowls were the cups made from ostrich eggs, contemporarily called griffin's eggs, and coconuts, which first appeared in England early in the thirteenth century. The Ironmongers' and Vintners' Companies possess examples of coconut cups dating from the early sixteenth century, with rich Gothic mounts, but no ostrich-egg cup made prior to the Renaissance is known to have survived. As the silver on these vessels is frequently unmarked, and as they were produced in England and the rest of Europe throughout the sixteenth century, those still in existence can seldom be assigned either a date or place of manufacture except on stylistic grounds (Fig. 3).

Ecclesiastical plate

Ecclesiastical plate was no less plentiful than domestic at the beginning of the Tudor period. Every parish church must have possessed at least one chalice and paten, whilst many of the greater ones had treasuries of immense value. The chalice commonly in use in the 1480's was a small hemispherical vessel on an hexagonal stem, ornamented in the middle with a knop, standing on a foot with six incurved sides (Fig. 4). Decoration was generally confined to the knop, which was frequently enamelled, and to one section of the foot, which was usually engraved with a Crucifixion. The mullet-shaped foot had been introduced at the beginning of the fourteenth century, and for a very short time between 1490 and 1500 its points were enriched with little sexfoil toes – later abandoned, presumably because they were found to catch in the altar-cloth. Early in the sixteenth century the form of the foot seems to have been changing to one that was basically circular, like that on the very fine chalice at Trinity College, Oxford. Patens were circular, some saucer-shaped and some with quatrefoil or sexfoil depressions: they seem to have been growing in richness of engraved decoration and enamelling up to the time of the Reformation.

Most of the gaudy, bejewelled censers, monstrances and reliquaries were destroyed at the outset of the Reformation, but some idea of the richness and high quality of the finest ecclesiastical silver may be obtained from the crozier made in about 1487 for Bishop Foxe (at Corpus Christi College, Oxford). Its shaft is decorated with a diaper of bands and crowned by two tiers of canopied niches, buttressed and crocketed, holding little saints. The volute of the crook is supported by an angel and encloses the figure of St Peter beneath a richly decorated canopy. Such a work is reminiscent of the elaboration of Bishop Alcock's Chantry in Ely Cathedral, which was begun in 1488, rather than the soaring simplicity of King's College Chapel, which was building at the same time.

The history of English church silver in the sixty years after the Reformation is so simple that it needs but a brief summary. Henry VIII's despoliation of the cathedrals and conventual churches was extended to the parish churches during the reign of Edward VI. The Commissioners were, however, instructed to leave 'in every parish churche or chappele of common re-

Fig. 5. Communion cup and cover, c. 1570. *Victoria and Albert Museum.*

sort one or two or more chalesses or cupes, according to the multitude of the people'. A few new Communion cups were made, of a simple pattern with a bell-shaped bowl on a waisted stem standing on a slightly domed foot. Yet most parishes must have continued to use chalices or secular vessels like that at St Mary's, Sandwich, which is clearly inscribed 'This is the Comunion Coup', lest there should be any mistake. Mary's reign called a temporary halt to the work of destruction, but the final establishment of the Anglican Church on the accession of Queen Elizabeth gave impetus to the work of transforming the old plate into new. At Wells it was ordained that 'the plate that beforetime were used to superstition shalbe defaced, and of the greatest challaice shalbe made a fayer Communion Cuppe', but usually more than one chalice went into the crucible to make a cup of the size needed for congregational communion. Elizabethan Communion cups in given areas almost invariably range round the same date: 1568 in Sussex, 1570 in Yorkshire, 1576 in Gloucestershire. In Yorkshire the date seems to have been determined by the appointment, in 1570, of Archbishop Grindal, who immediately required his clergy 'to minister the Holy Communion in no chalice nor any profane cup or glass, but in a Communion cup of silver, and with a cover of silver, appointed also for the ministration of the Communion bread'.

Whether they were made in London or the provinces, and however much they differ in size and engraved ornament, nearly all Elizabethan Communion cups are essentially of the same shape (Fig. 5). The bowl is in the form of an inverted bell, the stem has a knop, the foot is circular; a domed cover carries a flattened knop which could serve as a foot when reversed for use as a paten. Round the outside of the bowl, the foot and the cover there is generally an engraved band of foliage or strap-work. The wide use of this pattern, which is derived from Germany, is probably due to Archbishop Parker's desire for law and uniformity in the Church. Flagons were in general use only after the publication of Canon xx in 1603, and those which survive from before that date do not differ stylistically from domestic examples.

Later domestic plate

When the Reformation interrupted the history of ecclesiastical silver in England, the Renaissance style was gaining complete sway in the domestic field: nor does it appear to have been inhibited by any Protestant desire for plainness and simplicity. In the inventory of Henry VIII's plate, made in 1520, there is reference to a salt-cellar 'parcell gilte well wrought with A naked child with wingis on the knoppe', which is the earliest recorded piece of silver in England which seems to reflect the Renaissance style, though it may well have been of foreign origin. The Howard Grace cup (in the Victoria and Albert Museum), which was made in 1525 [1] to adorn an ancient ivory vessel,

has nothing to distinguish it from its purely Gothic predecessors save for three bands of decoration which embody urns and flowers of a distinctly Renaissance flavour. It is, in fact, a transitional piece embodying some of the motifs which the English silversmiths were to be using with uninhibited profusion within a few years.

It is hardly necessary to emphasize that as far as silver was concerned the Renaissance reached England by way of Germany and the Low Countries rather than from Italy direct. Hans Holbein the younger, who was in England from 1532 until his death in 1543, can be credited with a considerable influence on the work of English silversmiths, and although no examples of silver made to his designs have survived, his drawings for cups give the clearest indication of his style. There is no classical restraint about these designs for vessels bestrewn with foliage, encrusted with gems and hung about with pearls, but the patterns of leaves, the grimacing masks, the naiads and the *putti* are all in the 'antique' taste. Henry VIII's patronage of Holbein encouraged his courtiers to demand the same kind of work, and the silversmiths were forced to derive their designs from the many pattern-books which were being published in Germany. Yet the English craftsman appears to have been too conservative to follow foreign patterns in all the elaboration of their strange shapes, or, alternatively, in what he would have considered their bald simplicity. He preferred to copy points of detail on to his traditionally-shaped vessels. It is usually asserted that only the foreign silversmiths followed the pattern-books precisely, but too many vessels have vanished and too few of the Tudor makers' marks have been identified to permit such a generalization. Hans Brosamer's *New Kunstbüchlein*, published about 1545, includes designs which are almost identical with the famous Anne Boleyn cup (Pl. 36A) of 1535 and a beaker of 1545 which belongs to the church of St Margaret Pattens, London.[2] Furthermore, there are cups similar to his designs at Trinity Hall and Gonville and Caius College, Cambridge. But the

---

[1] As the hall-mark date letter is changed at the end of May a piece of plate may date from the latter seven months of one year or the first five of the next. The dates used in this chapter refer to the year in which the mark was initiated.

[2] The presence of a piece of silver in a church does not indicate that it was necessarily intended for ecclesiastical use.

Anne Boleyn cup and the St Margaret Pattens beaker are also similar in form to Venetian glasses of this period and both they and Brosamer's engravings may well have been derived from a common source. On the other hand, an engraving of a gourd-shaped cup by Paul Flindt, a silversmith of Nuremberg, seems to have set the pattern for a number of similar vessels made in England at the end of the sixteenth century.

Decoration

Foreign influences are more apparent in the decoration than in the forms used by Tudor silversmiths. The complicated bands of strap-work and floriated ornament with which many cups are engraved must frequently have been copied from German or Low Country pattern-books, but the sources can seldom be identified except where the decorations are distinguished by some peculiarity, like the sea-horses which Lambert Hopfer incorporated into his arabesques of foliage. It seems, indeed, that the engraver of the more complicated subjects was sometimes of foreign origin, and it is known that the set of spice-plates (now in the collection of Mr and Mrs Francis E. Fowler of Los Angeles)[3] made by Thomas Bampton in 1567 was engraved with the *Labours of Hercules* by Pieter Maas after prints by Heinrich Aldegraver (Pl. 39). Another of the few surviving sets of plates (in the Victoria and Albert Museum) is engraved with panels representing the story of Isaac, incongruously surrounded with borders of sea monsters after Adrian Collaert. The Elizabethan passion for allegory demanded that the more important articles of silver should be decorated with emblematic figures for which the engravings of Pieter Flötner were occasionally used, as on the Vintners' salt and the Queen Elizabeth salt in the Tower of London. Such evidence as a limited number of objects allows us to assemble is sufficient to suggest that the decoration of English silver was strongly influenced, if not controlled, by artists from Germany and the Low Countries, many of whom, as religious refugees, were living

in London after the Reformation. The departure of the Dutch towards the end of Queen Elizabeth's reign was, of course, compensated by the arrival of the Huguenots, but as the seventeenth century progressed foreign influence waned. In spite of the 'taste of the upper classes for foreign things alone', censured by Richard Mulcaster, the English silversmiths seem to have hesitated to indulge their patrons with the more absurd conceits of Nuremberg and Vienna. It was a combination of foreign fantasy and native reticence that produced most of the outstanding examples of Tudor silver. But, it need hardly be pointed out that any assessment of foreign influences must be based principally on the surviving pieces of silver, which represent but a fraction of what once there was.

The years between the advent of the Renaissance style and the death of Queen Elizabeth were marked by the rise of a wealthy middle class who set great store by the hoards of plate they were able to amass. In the 1530's the possession of considerable quantities of silver was still confined to the upper classes, and the amount displayed in a very grand household may be seen from Cavendish's *Life of Cardinal Wolsey*. In the Cardinal's dining-room 'There was a cupboard ... six desks high, full of gilt plate and of the newest fashions; and upon the nethermost desk of all garnished all with plate of clean gold, having two great candlesticks of silver and gilt most curiously wrought, the workmanship wherof with the silver cost three hundred marks, and lights of wax as big as torches burning upon the same ... The plates that hung on the walls to give light to the chamber were of silver and gilt, with lights burning in them'. Nor were the bedrooms less opulently furnished, each one having 'a bason and a ewer of silver, some gilt and some parcel gilt; and some two great pots of silver, in like manner, and one pot at the least with wine and beer, a bowl or goblet and a silver pot to drink beer in; a silver candlestick or two ...' Wolsey's household was of exceptional magnificence, but reflects the taste of the governing classes. Fifty years later the use of silver had spread, and William Harrison was able to write that 'the farmer thinks his gains very small towards the end of his term if he have not ... a silver salt, a bowl for wine (if not

---

[3] See *The Connoisseur*, October–November, 1953, p. 84, Pl. 1.

a whole neast) and a dozen of spoons to furnish up the suit'. Indeed, the more fashionable Elizabethans of Harrison's time considered silver a little vulgar: 'it is a world to see in these our days wherein gold and silver most aboundeth, how that our gentility, as loathing those metals (because of the plenty) do now generally choose rather the Venice glasses both for our wine and beer, than any of those metals or stone wherein before this time, we had been accustomed to drink'.

From Harrison's observations and from a wealth of inventories it is possible to form a picture of the collection of silver one would expect to find in a well-to-do Elizabethan home – a salt, a ewer and basin, a number of cups, some silver-mounted jugs and a collection of spoons. Cavendish's description, the noble inventories and, most illuminating of all, the list of plate belonging to Queen Elizabeth furnish us with some idea of the contents of a great house, but tease us with references to articles which have not survived. We do not know of any Tudor silver wall-sconces, candlesticks, trenchers, chargers, andirons or fountains, for these weighty objects were the first to go into the melting-pot in time of need. Nor is any Elizabethan silver chamber-pot known to have survived, though, with bald concision, they are mentioned in inventories. The principal survivors are the ceremonial salts, ewers and basins, jugs, various types of drinking-vessel, tazzas and spoons, which we may now consider in that order.

The salt-cellar

The important place the salt-cellar occupied on the table demanded that it should be of greater magnitude than was necessary for its function, and on it the silversmith was able to exercise his ingenuity in making an object of the utmost magnificence. At the end of the Gothic period it was usually shaped like an hour-glass, but fantastic shapes were also employed both then and later. A salt in the form of a dog graced the table of the Earl of March in the fourteenth century, those fashioned like dragons, falcons and castles formed part of the royal collection in the fifteenth century. Nor did the Renaissance diminish this craving for fantasy: Queen Elizabeth's collection included a

salt in the form of a Noah's ark containing a chess-board, and the Earl of Leicester owned a 'Salte ship-fashion of the mother-of-perle, garnished with silver and divers workes of warlike ensignes and ornaments, with xvi pieces of ordinance, wherof ii on wheles, two anchers on the forepart. ...' None of these, we may be sure, approached the splendour of Cellini's masterpiece, but all must have possessed a toy-like fascination. Curious and

Fig. 6. Bell-shaped salt. Height 9⅛ in. 1594–95. *Victoria and Albert Museum.*

elaborate as many of the surviving Tudor salts are, they seem mundane beside the tantalizing descriptions with which the inventories abound.

Two principal types of later Tudor salt have come down to us: the round and the square. An excellent example of the former, dating from 1586, is the Mostyn Salt, (in the Victoria and Albert Museum), which is as richly and closely decorated with lion masks, fruit, flowers, birds, monkeys and dogs as any object can be, resembling in style the heavily carved screens and chimney-pieces which were to be found in the greater houses. The square type is best illustrated by the Vintners' Company salt, which was made in 1569 and decorated with embossed panels of the cardinal virtues, after Pieter Flötner, flowers, fruit, shells and terms. Pillared-form salts also enjoyed great popularity, though few survive, the most notable being the Gibbon Salt belonging to the Goldsmiths' Company (Pl. 35). This remarkable piece has four Ionic columns around a central pillar of rock-crystal which supports the receptacle for the salt and contains a figure of Neptune, who consequently appears to be submerged – a charming conceit which would have appealed to every Elizabethan. It will be noticed that the columns are mounted on pedestals and stand, not in the corners, but in the middle of each side, reminding one of the cavalier use of classical motifs, and even the sacrosanct *orders*, in Elizabethan architecture. None of these magnificent salts, it should be added, was made for a public corporation or, as far as may be ascertained, for an exceptionally wealthy nobleman. They all stand at least twelve inches in height (the Mostyn Salt is over sixteen inches), but not all surviving examples are of the same grandeur. Some, no more than six inches high, were intended for the lower places on the table of a great house or for the homes of the less affluent. A simpler type, shaped like a bell, appears to have been popular throughout the second half of the sixteenth century, though the only examples to survive date from the end of the period (Fig. 6). It was in fact a double cellar surmounted by a perforated dome to act as a castor.

Ewers and basins

'My house within the city', claims Gremio in *The Taming of the Shrew*,

Is richly furnished with plate and gold,
Basons and Ewers to lave her dainty hands.

The hand-washing ceremony played an important part in the strange ritual of Tudor life, not least at table, where the ewers and basins were vessels of great magnificence. But they were usually weighty, and for that reason have vanished. Two principal types of ewer have survived, the earlier, having a body that is either polygonal or shaped

like an orthodox Communion cup with a wedge-shaped spout (Pl. 36B), has an air of characteristically English angularity about it. The other kind is vase-shaped with a cursive-handle sometimes formed out of a demi-woman or a beast, and may well have been introduced by Huguenot craftsmen. Basins were large and usually decorated in the centre and occasionally around the rim with strapwork, fruit and heraldic or allegorical devices.

Flagons

Covered flagons intended to hold wine or beer, and kept on the sideboard, were no smaller than the ewers with which they are sometimes confused, but many more have survived. Generally speaking, they are without either spout or lip, sometimes enriched with chased decoration. An unusual pair of flagons composed almost entirely of shell motifs (Pl. 40C) was made in London in 1597, and shows the elegant fantasy with which such vessels might be treated. Flagons were wholly of silver only in the richer houses, according to the invaluable Harrison, who states that other households possessed 'pots of earth of sundry colours and moulds whereof many are garnished with silver'. Stoneware jugs finely mounted with silver enjoyed great popularity; most were of the so-called tiger-ware, but some were more elaborate, like that decorated with amusing scenes of everyday life which belonged to Sir Richard Knightly, son-in-law to the first Duke of Somerset (Pl. 40A). In the houses where silver was thought a little demodé Chinese or Turkish pottery jugs, exquisitely mounted with English silver, might be found to decorate the sideboard.

Drinking-vessels

In considering the advent of the Renaissance style, reference has been made to the Howard Grace cup, a vessel intended for ceremonial toasting rather than deep potations. Such cups were of great importance in the Tudor household, and those that have been preserved demonstrate the whole range of the Tudor silversmith's art. In decoration they varied from the dignified simplicity of the fine example which belongs to the church of St Mary, Plympton, Devon to the elaboration of the Sir Peter Gleane cup made in 1573 (in the church of St Peter Mancroft, Norwich). The Gleane cup, with its profusion of highly finished decoration – the Meeting of David and Abigail, a crowd of attendant Virtues and emblematic figures emerging from festoons of fruit – is an exceptional fine example of this type of vessel, but its shape conforms to a general pattern which, towards the end of Elizabeth's reign, was giving way to a form of cup with an egg-shaped bowl and a cover terminated by a spire or steeple. One of the most handsome of the latter sort is the magnificent cup, decorated with an overall pattern of shells, which was made in 1599 and now belongs to the parish church of Charing in Kent (Pl. 40D).

As the more elaborate standing-cups were used solely for ceremonial purposes, their makers were frequently able to indulge a pleasant strain of fantasy in their creation. The Glynne cup (Pl. 38B), on loan to the Victoria and Albert Museum, is in the form of a pelican in her piety. Once it was even richer and stranger; for its body was made out of a nautilus shell. Other precious or rare materials were used for the bowls of cups, both in England and the rest of Europe; rock-crystal was particularly favoured, as it was believed to act as a poison detector, and various hard stones were also employed. In the Victoria and Albert Museum there is a small agate cup on a singularly rich mount amusingly decorated with snails at the base (Pl. 38A). Although the æsthetic value of most of these extravaganzas is slight, there are some which have a strange beauty, such as that made in the form of a pomegranate with one section open to display the pips, on a spiral stem enriched with curly tendrils. Probably least satisfying are the gourd-shaped cups on stems made to resemble tree trunks, which were based on a German pattern and, to judge from the number that have survived, were of considerable popularity.

Personal drinking-vessels were simpler and owe many of the elements of their design to the ruder cups which preceded them, though one must not be too Darwinian in seeking to find some natural shape for the prototype of each kind. Those most popular were goblet-shaped, conic like Venetian glasses, or plain beakers, their surfaces decorated in innumerable ways according to taste. A strange little beaker with rings of cabling round it (in the church of Honington, Lincolnshire) may have been designed to resemble a nest of cups, but it is more likely that the rings were intended to prevent it from slithering out of greasy or unsteady fingers. Most drinking-cups were provided with covers which necessitated an almost sacerdotal ritual outlined by Hugh Rhodes in *The Book of Nurture* (1568): 'at the degree of a Knight ye may set down your cup covered, and lift off the cover

Fig. 7. Silver-gilt Tazza. Height 6 in. 1579.

and set it on again, and when he listeth to drink and taketh off the cover, take the cover in thy hand and set it on again'. Servants must have blessed the tankards with hinged covers (Pl. 37B) which were introduced from Germany in the 'seventies, and obviated much of this complicated business. At about the same time the plain beakers also seem to have become popular, more probably for their convenience than for their chaste elegance (Pl. 40B).

Although few Tudor plates [4] and no trenchers have survived, a number of little dishes, usually called tazzas, have been preserved, principally because they were given to churches, where they

[4] The use of silver plates seems to have been confined to the very rich throughout the Elizabethan period. Sir Francis Drake's habit of eating off silver even while at sea was commented on by his contemporaries.

were used as patens. Their name is derived from the Italian word for a cup, and should, strictly speaking, be reserved for shallow drinking-vessels on stems, which some have seen as the ancestors of the champagne glass. Most of the objects so described are, however, standing dishes, probably intended for sweetmeats or what Rhodes terms 'conceits'. They stand on baluster stems and are enriched in the centre of the bowl with an embossed medallion, usually bearing an armed Roman head (Fig. 7).

Smaller objects

There remain to be mentioned some of the smaller silver objects to be found in sixteenth-century England. First among these are the spoons which altered little in shape between the middle of

Fig. 8. Apostle Spoon: St James the Less 1602.

the fifteenth century and the Restoration; the bowls were fig-shaped and the stems either circular or polygonal. Variations are to be found only in the decoration of the knops, which were fashioned like seals, acorns, female heads, whole human figures, heraldic devices or, quite simply, diamond points. Among the most popular were the Apostle spoons (Fig. 8), some of which were made in sets of thirteen with Christ on the master-spoon, but individual spoons of this type must frequently have been made, for they were often given as christening presents. Other small objects that have survived include little scent-bottles (Fig. 9), spice-boxes and a pair of snuffers which formed part of the furnishing of the Privy Council chamber in the reign of Edward vi, and is now in the Victoria and Albert Museum.

The silversmith

In this necessarily brief survey little has been said of the Tudor silversmith, who is an elusive

figure indeed. The London guild to which he belonged was a proud body ranking its members above mere tradesman, and although it was never large, it was very powerful, as may be judged from the fact that before 1524 it had provided the City with seventeen lord mayors. In the fifteenth and early sixteenth centuries it included many foreigners (in 1477 they numbered more than a fifth of the total), who were freely admitted until their strength grew apparent and the native craftsmen complained of their competition. In 1575 the Goldsmiths' Company barred its members from accepting apprentices who were not the children of English parents. It is therefore clear that many silver articles bearing the London hall-mark are the work of foreign craftsmen living in England. It would be sufficiently difficult to distinguish these vessels from those of the native silversmiths without the additional task of identifying certain pieces which may have been made abroad and hall-marked in England.

The laborious task of identifying makers' marks has failed to reveal any outstanding personalities, rather for lack of objects than lack of names, and, by the irony of circumstance, most of the finest pieces bear on them a mark which is to be found on few others. For example, the maker of the fine ewer at Guildford (Pl. 36B) is otherwise known only by a number of orthodox Communion cups. One of the few craftsmen to whom a substantial number of vessels may be attributed signed himself *R D* and was identified by Sir Charles Jackson as Robert Danbe. He made a clumsy, shallow-bowled cup now in the church at Deane in 1551, a very graceful standing cup belonging to the Armourers' and Braziers' Company in 1553, a fine covered salt belonging to Corpus Christi College, Cambridge, in 1562, a flagon belonging to the Armourers' and Braziers' in 1567 and a number of orthodox Communion cups in the 1570's. Not even the most clairvoyant historian of art could piece together an artistic personality from such evidence. The maker of the fine Charing steeple-cup (Pl. 40D) was also responsible for a number of gourd-shaped cups almost identical with another, which bears a different maker's mark. As far as may be seen, the designer had a more potentially interesting artistic personality than the silver-smith, but still less is known about him.

If we cannot generalize about Tudor silversmiths, we can, from a study of such of their works as remain, form some estimate of the taste of their patrons. It seems that their first demand was for magnificence, which could be expressed in the size of vessels which we know only from inventories, in profusion of decoration and in gilding – few of the pieces illustrated here are ungilt. Many an Elizabethan would have shared the day dream of Jonson's Alchemist,

> My meat shall all come in, in Indian shells,
> Dishes of agat set in gold, and studded
> With emeralds, saphires, hyacinths and rubies....

But few of the semi-barbaric extravaganzas made to satisfy such ambitions have survived. The taste for allegories and conceits in poetry and painting extended also to silver-work, and is responsible for much of the decoration of the larger vessels, helped out by heraldic devices which also served as marks of ownership. Towards the end of the century English table manners were undergoing a change, partly by contact with Italy, whence Coryat brought back a fork which, he discovered, could make eating a cleaner business, though such foppish notions could not win acceptance for many a year. At the same time there seems to have been a tendency towards simpler forms and less over-crowded decoration as the desire for fantasy waned.

BIBLIOGRAPHY

Charles Oman: *English Domestic Silver*, 1947. This is the best general introduction to the subject.

Sir C. J. Jackson: *An Illustrated History of English Plate*, 2 vols. 1911.

Sir C. J. Jackson: *English Goldsmiths and their Marks*, 1921. Both these works are indispensable for a thorough study of the subject.

W. W. Watts: *Old English Silver*, 1924. A monumental work of considerable value.

A. J. Collins: *Jewels and Plate of Queen Elizabeth I*, 1955. An invaluable study of the hoard of plate which belonged to Queen Elizabeth.

There are excellent and informative catalogues of the plate belonging to the City Companies, and the Universities of Oxford and Cambridge. In many counties catalogues of the plate in the possession of the churches have been published by the local antiquarian societies. Mention should also be made of the catalogues of certain exhibitions of outstanding importance, notably those devoted to *The Historic Plate of the City of London* (1951), the *Corporation Plate of England and Wales* (1952) both at Goldsmiths' Hall, and *Silver Treasure from English Churches* (1955) held in Messrs Christie's auction rooms in aid of the Historic Churches Preservation Trust.

Fig. 9. Scent-bottle. Height 4¾ in. 1546. *Victoria and Albert Museum.*

Pottery, Porcelain and Glass

R. J. CHARLESTON

Lead-glazed wares

The characteristic medieval pottery of England was lead-glazed earthenware of plain red or buff clay, the glaze either brown or yellow in tone, or stained a leaf-green by the addition of copper. These green-glazed wares were taken up and improved during the Tudor period, to become perhaps the most characteristic indigenous pottery of the sixteenth century, at least in the south-eastern parts of England. The most notable development of the period was in the direction of an all-round refinement. For the body a whitish clay was used, on which the green glaze, itself improved in depth of colour and in brilliance, showed up to far greater advantage. This improvement in quality was accompanied by a great extension of the forms for which pottery was used. The medieval pottery shape *par excellence* was the large jug. Such jugs, although they are known to have been ordered for Royal use, were probably employed only in the cellar and buttery. The actual table-furniture would be of other materials – wood, silver, horn or glass. With the Tudor period, pottery finds its way on to the table. Henry VIII had 'green plates of earth for spice and fruit', and in the excavations of Eltham Palace during the 1930's there was found a green-glazed dish decorated with the Royal Arms supported by the dragon and greyhound – a version of the Arms which must antedate the accession of Queen Elizabeth I (Pl. 41C). This decoration is taken from a mould, while the rim of the dish is ornamented with a *guilloche* design freely incised with a pointed instrument. Com-

parable with this dish is a much-damaged flask in the British Museum. This bears moulded on one side the same coat-of-arms, which, taken in conjunction with other devices and the inscription DNE SALVVM FAC REGEM REGINAM ET REGNUM ('O Lord, save the King, the Queen and the Kingdom'), makes it virtually certain that the flask was made in the reign either of Henry VII or of Henry VIII. The same may be said of a fine cistern in the Victoria and Albert Museum decorated in moulded relief with the Royal Arms supported by the English lion and the Welsh griffin, as borne by Henry VII (Pl. 41A). This achievement is accompanied by the rose and lily and the initials H R and E R, for *Henricus Rex* and *Elisabetha Regina* (Elizabeth of York, consort of Henry VII). Flanking the ornaments already described are pilasters delicately moulded with a design of symmetrical plant-forms springing from a slender gadrooned urn, a characteristic motive of the Italian Renaissance. Any Renaissance influence on English art, however, is extremely rare before 1515, and almost unthinkable before 1509. It therefore seems more likely that the cistern was made after Henry VII's death, and probably as late as 1525 or 1530. The survival of the emblems of a previous reign can be paralleled in the windows of King's College Chapel, Cambridge, where the tracery-lights contain both the initials H E (Henry VII and Elizabeth) and H K (Henry VIII and Katherine of Aragon). Work did not begin on these windows until 1515 at the earliest.

The cistern just described is perhaps the most important surviving piece of Tudor pottery, but there are numerous other green-glazed pieces which are akin to it in that they bear the Royal Arms or initials and are themselves of a semi-architectural nature. These comprise wall-sconces to hold candles, and large hollow tiles and other components of glazed stoves of German type. The candle-sconces (one of which is traditionally said to have come from Hampton Court) bear the initials E R and may well be of the reign of Edward VI. If they are, they form, with the similarly decorated stove-tiles already referred to, a bridge between the cistern of Henry VIII's reign and other pieces which are indisputably of the Elizabethan period (such as a tile-fragment bearing the recognizable portrait of the Queen). These hollow stove-tiles, which are about 13½ in. by 10 in. in size, have been found in a number of different places, a fact which suggests that tiled stoves of the sort familiar from Germany and Switzerland enjoyed a vogue in Tudor England. William Harrison, in his *Description of England*, written in 1577 and revised in 1587, says: 'As for stoves, we have not hitherto used them greatly, yet do they now begin to be made in divers houses of the gentry and wealthy citizens ...' Had such stoves remained in use in England, they would have provided a comfort for Englishmen the absence of which Lady Mary Wortley Montagu was to lament some two hundred years later. The fact that the custom was never established in England, and the close similarity between English and Continental tiles, suggest that they were manufactured by immigrant potters.

It is clear from what has been said above that green-glazed pottery was manufactured throughout the Tudor period, and that it had even found its way on to the royal table by Henry VIII's reign. It is not, however, so certain that its use in this way was widespread. In a description of an election feast of the Drapers' Company in 1522, occurs the passage: 'At the said High board were ... green pots of ale and wine, with ashen cups set before them at every mess; but they had gilt cups for red wine and ipocras.' Here the 'green pots' may have been jugs rather than drinking-vessels. In the records of the Inner Temple, however, occurs in 1559–60 the order: 'that from henceforth there

shall not any ashen cups be provided, but the House to be served in green cups, both of winter and summer'. A number of fragments and complete pieces of green-glazed pottery have been found on the sites of the various Inns of Courts, and one now in the British Museum is mounted with a silver collar inscribed 'Found in a Vault under the Steward's Office, Lincoln's Inn, 1788' (Pl. 41B). These pots, being of too small capacity for jugs, must be the 'green cups' of the Inner Temple records. Other table-wares in the same type of pottery include finely shaped lobed cups; circular saucer-dishes; and candlesticks (one of these is stamped with the Pegasus badge of the Inner Temple, Pl. 43B). Objects of humbler use include chafing-dishes; kitchen-mortars; feeding-dishes for chickens, formed of a series of concentric raised ridges; and turnip-shaped money-boxes, or 'thrift-boxes', the subject of a popular conceit in the immediately succeeding period – as in Mason's *Handful of Essaies*, 1621: 'Like a swine, he never doth good till his death; as an apprentice's box of earth, apt he is to take all, but to restore none till hee be broken.'

In the excavation of the sites of several Yorkshire Cistercian abbeys at the end of the last century there were found numerous fragments of a hard pottery of dark-red body and an almost black, metallic glaze. From the circumstances of their finding, these wares were dubbed 'Cistercian' wares, and they must in general date from before the Dissolution of the monasteries in 1540. A characteristic shape in this pottery was a tall mug of trumpet shape, with two handles ('tyg'), and it is a significant coincidence that the *Regulations of the Order of Cistercians of the Strict Observance* lay it down that: 'Each religious has for his own use a wooden spoon and fork, a knife, a two-handled cup, and a napkin.' This rule dates back at least to the early twelfth century. Mugs of this same form, however, continued to be made long after the Dissolution, as an example dated 1599 in the British Museum clearly proves (Pl. 43A). Some tygs found on the sites of the Yorkshire abbeys had four, or as many as eight, handles; and this multiplicity of handles remained a feature of English pottery right into the eighteenth century. Mugs of inverted bell-shape, with three handles, were made in the vicinity of Abergavenny, in Monmouthshire; and other potteries producing these hard, dark-glazed wares were situated at Babylon, near Ely; at Tickenhall in Derbyshire; at Wrotham in Kent, and possibly also in Bristol. Most of this pottery was plain (Pl. 43F), but occasional telling use was made of horizontal ribbing, and some of the Yorkshire (and possibly also the Tickenhall) wares were decorated with pads of white 'slip' under the glaze (Pl. 43C, D). These were cut in the form of small roundels, rosettes or the like, and occasionally, as on a series of covered porringers from the monastic sites, formed into overall designs of different types.

Tin-glazed earthenware

One of the great inventions in the history of pottery was the discovery of a glaze suitable for decoration by means of painting. This was obtained by adding oxide (ashes) of tin to a lead glaze, thus providing a beautifully smooth and dense white surface. Originally discovered in the Near East as long ago as the ninth century A.D., it passed in the late fourteenth century, by way of Spain, to Italy. In the Italy of the High Renaissance, that forcing-ground of painters, painted pottery of this type ('maiolica') reached its zenith during the fifteenth and sixteenth centuries. The demand for maiolica in other parts of Europe ensured that the art of making it spread in the course of the sixteenth century to the Netherlands, the Germanic lands, France and England. The agents of this diffusion were usually migrant Italian potters. One of them, a certain Guido di Savino (of Castel Durante, in the duchy of Urbino), set up a pottery in Antwerp not later than 1512. In the Netherlands he was referred to as Guido Andries, and various members of his family were engaged in potting both in Antwerp and elsewhere. England at this time had very close connexions with the Netherlands, and a proportion at least of the Flemish 'maiolica' of the early sixteenth century found its way to England, including perhaps some of the many pieces in Henry VIII's inventories described as 'of gally-makynge' – an expression commonly used of tin-glazed pottery in the sixteenth

and seventeenth centuries. A number of pieces dug up in London and elsewhere suggest by their style a Netherlands origin, and a series of tiles found in England undoubtedly came from the same source. It was no doubt this ready demand for Netherlands maiolica in England which encouraged two potters to come here at the time of the persecution of Protestants in the Netherlands after 1566. Stow's *Survey of the Cities of London and Westminster* (in Strype's edition of 1720) records: 'About the Year 1567, Jasper Andries and Jacob Janson, Potters, came away from Antwerp, to avoid the Persecution there, & settled themselves in Norwich; where they followed their Trade, making Gally Paving Tiles, and Vessels for Apothecaries and others, very artificially. Anno 1570 they removed to London ...; & desired by Petition, from Queen Elizabeth, that they might have Liberty to follow their Trade in that City without Interruption; and presented her with a Chest of their Handy-work ...' Jasper Andries, who must have been related to Guido Andries, appears to have remained in East Anglia, but Jacob Janson settled in the Liberty of Catherine Creechurch in Aldgate, and appears to have attracted to himself a number of other potters of Flemish extraction. It was perhaps at this pottery that was made the only inscribed and dated piece of English 'maiolica' which can be definitely attributed to the Tudor period – a dish in the London Museum bearing the inscription THE ROSE IS RED THE LEAVES ARE GRENE GOD SAVE ELIZABETH OUR QUEENE, and painted in blue, purple, green, orange and yellow with what may well be meant for a representation of the Tower of London hard by (Pl. 42C). This dish is dated 1600. A number of small cylindrical drug-jars (perhaps the 'Vessels for Apothecaries' of Andries' Petition) and of bulbous-bodied jugs with cylindrical necks, apparently copying the contemporary Rhenish stonewares, may have been made, as well as found, in London. But it is naturally impossible at this period to distinguish between Flemish imports and pieces made in London by Flemings in their native style. There is, however, one class of wares which seems to be exclusively English. This comprises jugs of the bulbous-bodied type referred to above, often mounted in precious-metal mounts. The earliest dated example bears the London hall-mark for 1549–50 (Pl. 42B). These jugs are covered with a tin-glaze coloured blue or green, or dappled in tones of blue, purple, yellow, brown and green, in different combinations. A number of them have Kentish associations (the class as a whole is referred to as the 'Malling' jugs, from the village of that name), and two examples which closely resemble them, but which have a mottled brown lead-glaze (Pl. 42A), have been regarded as the possible forerunners of the later pottery made at Wrotham, in the same county. Since two of the potters who joined Jacob Janson in Aldgate had previously been settled at Sandwich, a Kentish origin for this family is by no means out of the question. Of their English manufacture there can be no doubt.

Foreigners remarked of the English that they were wont to mount their cups in silver or silver-gilt. Thus, Stephen Perlin, a Frenchman, visiting England in 1558, writes: 'They consume great quantities of beer, double and single, and do not drink it out of glasses, but from earthen pots with silver handles and covers, and this even in houses of persons of middling fortune; for as to the poor, the covers of their pots are only pewter ...' These silver-mounted cups no doubt formed part of the 'garnish' of plate which a butler laid out on his 'cupboard' (or sideboard) –

'than emperialle thy Cuppeborde [lay] with
    Silver & gild fulle gay'.

A manuscript work of the late fifteenth or early sixteenth century, entitled 'Ffor to serve a lord', lays down instructions for the due preparation of a banquet: 'Thenne the boteler shall bryng forth basyns, ewers, and cuppis ... redressing all his silver plate, upon the cubbord, the largest firste, the richest in the myddis, the lightest before.' This no doubt refers to silver cups, but a passage from William Harrison makes it clear that mounted pottery cups too were displayed on the 'cupboard': 'As for drink, it is usually filled in pots, goblets, jugs, bowls of silver in noblemen's houses; also in fine Venice glasses of all forms: and, for want of these elsewhere, in pots of earth of sundry colours and moulds, whereof many are garnished with silver,

or at the leastwise with pewter, all which notwithstanding are seldom set on the table, but each one, as necessity urgeth, calleth for a cup of such drink as him listeth to have, so that, when he has tasted of it, he delivered the cup again to some one of the standers by, who, making it clean by pouring out the drink that remaineth, restoreth it to the cupboard from whence he fetched the same. By this device ... much idle tippling is furthermore cut off ...'

Examples of English pottery mounted in silver-gilt or pewter have already been quoted: of far greater moment than these indigenous wares, however, were the pottery and porcelain imported from abroad.

Chinese porcelain

Isolated examples of Chinese porcelain began to reach Europe in the fourteenth and fifteenth centuries, and are recorded as great treasures in the inventories of princes and potentates. It was probably not, however, until the Portuguese made direct contact with China, in 1514, that this precious commodity began to reach Europe in appreciable quantities: and of these, only a small proportion percolated to Northern Europe. When pieces of porcelain did come to England, they were naturally treated as great rarities, and were mounted in precious metal mounts, to be kept in treasuries or 'cabinets of curiosities'. New College, Oxford, possesses a small bowl of the grey-green Chinese porcelain known in latter days as 'celadon', mounted in silver-gilt with broad bands round the rim and foot connected by openwork hinged straps (Pl. 44A). It was given to the College by Archbishop Warham, and although the mount is not dated, it must have been made not later than 1530, when the bowl was left to the College. The porcelain itself is probably considerably older. The earliest mounted piece with an English hall-mark is a small bowl in the David Foundation, University of London (Pl. 44B). It is of white porcelain with incised decoration on the outside, and on the inside painting in blue on the white ground. The silver-gilt mount bears the London date-letter for 1569–70. The decoration on the inside of this cup gives a foretaste of things to come; for from this date onwards, the porcelain *par excellence* for the European market was blue-and-white. It began to issue in considerable quantities in the course of the reign of the Chinese Emperor Wan Li (1573–1619). But the full exploitation of the European market did not occur until the seventeenth century was well under way. Numerous pieces of Wan Li blue-and-white porcelain with English silver or silver-gilt mounts are known, but of these the most famous are those which by a trustworthy tradition are reputed to have come from Burghley House, one of the seats of Lord William Cecil, Queen Elizabeth I's Lord Treasurer (Pl. 44C). The interest of the Cecil family in porcelain is confirmed by the list of New Year's gifts offered to the Queen in 1587–8. These include –

> Item, one porrynger of white porselyn, garnished with gold, the cover of golde, with a lyon on the toppe therof; all geven by the Lord Threasorour, 38 oz..
>
> Item, one cup of grene pursselyne, the foote, shanke, and cover silver guilte, chased lyke droppes. Geven by Mr Robert Cecill, 15 oz.
>
> Item, one cup of pursseline, thone syde paynted red, the foote and cover sylver guilt. Geven by Mr Lychfelde, 14 oz.qᵃ.

A bowl of the type perhaps indicated by the last item is now in the collection of Judge Untermyer, in New York. The porcelain, probably of the Chia Ching period (1522–66), is coral-red on the outside, with a faint decoration of gold scrolls; whilst in the interior is a medallion enclosing chrysanthemums in underglaze blue (Pl. 45A). The mount probably dates from the 1570's. By the end of the century, porcelain had become sufficiently common to have passed beyond the prerogative of great lords. In 1599 the German traveller Thomas Platter remarked in the house of a certain Mr Cope, the owner of a cabinet of curiosities, 'Earthen pitchers from China' and 'Porcelain from China'.

Chinese porcelain, along with other exotic rarities such as coconut-shells and ostrich-eggs, imperatively called for precious-metal mounts, both for protection and embellishment. So too did the gaily painted Turkish pottery of Isnik, of which a few pieces appear to have reached England in the course of the sixteenth century (Pl. 45B). Far less rare, but of considerable ceramic distinction, was the German salt-glazed stoneware. This stoneware was mainly manufactured in the Rhineland. At Siegburg, near Bonn, was made a greyish ware of considerable charm, even when left unglazed, as was often the case. It was usually decorated with applied moulded relief-designs (Pl. 45C), but an effective technique of cutting a diaper pattern of interlocking lozenge-forms was also practised. Far more common than these wares in England, however, were those made at Cologne and later at the neighbouring Frechen. These, owing to the use of an iron-bearing clay, fired to a rich brown colour which shines most handsomely in a silver mount (Pl. 45D). The jugs most favoured in England during the second half of the sixteenth century were roughly globular in shape, with low footrim and short cylindrical neck, and a simple, strong strap-handle, to which the mounts of rim and cover were attached. It is possible that these were made especially for the English market. The jugs selected for mounting were commonly plain, and in this were chosen with great discrimination. Other jugs, however, were simply decorated with applied moulded reliefs – most frequently with the effigy of a bearded man applied below the neck in front. These are commonly called 'Bellarmines' being supposedly made in derision of the Cardinal of that name, who, as a counter-Reformation controversialist, incurred the odium of Northern Europe. The face on the front of the bottle must have taken on life in the wine-fevered fancy of many an English tippler, like the carouser in Ben Jonson's *Bartholomew Fayre*, who had 'wrashled so long with the bottle here, that the man with the beard hash almosht streck up hish heelsh'.

German stoneware was certainly imported into England in considerable quantities during the sixteenth century, although by no means all of it was worthy of mounting in silver-gilt, some of the bottles being possibly no more than commercial containers of the Rhenish wine. However that may be, the importation was sufficiently large to suggest the thought of a native stoneware manufacture. In the reign of Queen Elizabeth I, a certain William Simpson, in petitioning for a monopoly to import the German wares, undertook to 'draur to the making of such like pottes into some decayed town within the realm, wherebie manie a hundred poor men may be sett at work'. It is not known, however, what became of this project, and no certainly English stoneware pot of this period has been identified.

Glass

After the Saxon period there is a great gap in the knowledge of glass in England. It is certain, however, that by the thirteenth century glass was being manufactured here. This industry, situated in the well-wooded country of the Weald which supplied it with all the timber needed for its furnaces, was mainly devoted to the making of window-glass. The blowers, however, were certainly also capable of blowing simple vessels; and fragments of such vessels, of a thin green glass, have been found on the Wealden glass-house sites. Impure green glass of this sort, however, was probably restricted to humble domestic rôles, being made into lamps, bottles, urinals and the like. Glasses for table use were imported from abroad, mainly from Venice, the greatest glass-making centre in the world. Records of the glass used in England during the first half of the sixteenth century are in general not easy to find. But an ample existing inventory attests the considerable quantities of fine glass-ware owned by Henry VIII at the time of his death. His 'Glasse Housse' at Westminster contained over six hundred pieces, the forms including bottles and flagons, basins and bowls with ewers, cups, cruses, spice-plates, candlesticks, and other less common shapes. These enviable chattels seem to have been made in most of the techniques known to the time. We read of 'glasse iasper colloure', which must be the opaque glass coloured and streaked in imitation of natural stone and called by the Venetians 'calcedonio'; of glass of many different colours, frequently 'p[ar]tely guilte'; of glass with 'white worke nette fashion', which must refer to the glass with elaborate decoration of crossing opaque-white threads called by the Venetians 'vetro di trina' [or 'lace-glass'.]

Along with the simpler items are described important pieces which must have served as centre-pieces for tables, or as 'verres de parade' for side-boards – such as the 'faire glasse the foote and cover garnished w[ith] silver and guilte upon the Toppe of the Cover A woman holdinge A skutchine in thone hande and A snake [?] in thother hande.' Many of the glasses were, like this one, mounted in silver-gilt. One of these is referred to as 'a glasse like a potte paynted and garnished aboute the brym[m]e w[ith] silver and guilte w[ith] a cover w[ith]out garnishinge'. The use of the word 'pot' probably implies a shape like that of the 'maiolica' and stoneware mugs already discussed, and there is in the British Museum a small mug of this form decorated with vertical stripes of white and mounted with a silver-gilt rim and cover which bear the date-mark for 1548 – one year after the preparation of this inventory (Pl. 47A). The use of the word 'Paynted', however, as in the description of the 'pot' just mentioned, is surprisingly rare, and this absence of references suggests that glasses with enamelled decoration had by this time gone out of fashion. At least one important enamelled Venetian glass, however, is known which has been in England ever since the sixteenth century (Pl. 46B). It was stated by the owner, when he bequeathed it in 1631 to the Founders' Company, to have formed part of the booty brought from Boulogne when it surrendered to Henry VIII in 1546. With this date the mark on the silver-gilt foot (a replacement) accords well enough.

Harrison, writing in 1577, says: 'It is a world to see in these our days, wherein gold and silver most aboundeth, how that our gentility, as loathing those metals (because of the plenty) do now generally choose rather the Venice glasses, both for our wine [Pls. 46, 48B] and beer, than any of those metals or stone wherein before time we have been accustomed to drink; ... and such is the estimation of this stuff that many become rich only with their new trade unto Murana (a town near to Venice, situate on the Adriatic Sea) from whence the very best are daily to be had. ... And as this is seen in the gentility, so in the wealthy communalty the like desire of glass is not neglected, whereby the gain gotten by their purchase is yet much more increased to the benefit of the merchant. The poorest also will have glass if they may; but, sith the Venetian is somewhat too dear for them, they content themselves with such as are made at home of fern and burned stone ...'

This increase in the import of Venetian glasses was reflected in the formation of a Glaziers' Company, which received arms in 1588.

In the meantime, however, a far more important event had taken place. This was the start on English soil of glass-making in the Venetian manner. It began effectively probably in 1570, and was given official support by the grant in 1575 of an exclusive patent for the manufacture in England of Venetian-type glass. The patentee was one Jacob Verzelini, a Venetian who had migrated to this country by way of Antwerp. Roughly a dozen glasses can with reasonable probability be attributed to the period of Verzelini's monopoly (which was cut short in 1592), and of these all but three are decorated with diamond-point engraving. This technique (which covers the glass in fine spidery lines) was one widely used at the time on the thin glass of Venetian type. The English examples, however, are characterized by the division of the field of decoration (normally the bowl of a drinking-glass) into arabesques alternating with panels left plain, to be subsequently filled with the devices, initials or names of the persons ordering the glass, and frequently with the date (Pl. 46c). These range from 1577 to 1586. One glass, dated 1590, is decorated with similar devices and inscriptions, but the decoration is carried out in gilding instead of diamond-point engraving (Pl. 46A). Verzelini's monopoly was taken up after 1592, and only one English glass made between this date and 1603 is certainly known – the wine-glass in the Victoria and Albert Museum dated 1602 and inscribed with the name 'Barbara Potter' (Pl. 46D). In decoration, even if not in shape, it obviously belongs to the family of Verzelini's glasses. That this family should be decimated by time was only to be expected. It is nevertheless evident that by the end of Queen Elizabeth's reign glasses of this sort, many of them probably made in Verzelini's glass-houses at the Crutched Friars and in Broad Street, were common in the houses of the rich.

Thus, in the residence of the Earl of Leicester at Kenilworth, in 1588, there were:

Ffyve plaine bole glasses, without covers.
Ffyve indented bole glasses, two graven bole glasses; twelve beare [beer] glasses of severall fashions,[1] iii with covers; two plaine taper glasses with covers; two other ribbed taper glasses; an embossed glasse with a cover; two glass ewers.

Glasse Dishes

Tenne glasse dishes gilte, with the sinque foyle on the brims.
Eight graven dishes of glasse aboute the brims.
Twelve greate standing indented bole glasses for creame.
A deep standing glasse, with a cover.
Ffyvteen glasses brode brimed and narrowe bottoms.
Ffowertene greate deepe glasses, viii of them plaine.
A dozen of dishe glasses of one sorte.
Two dozen and iiii dishe glasses of another sorte.'

That these were of 'Venice making', or the English surrogates, went without saying in a household of this pretension. In humbler homes, the possession of a piece of Venetian glass was worthy of special remark. Thus, in the inventory of a house at Cockesden, taken in 1610, occurs the entry: 'In the Tapestrie Chamber' – 'Item, there is the great Venise glasse...'

Venetian and Venetian-style glasses, however, were by no means the only, nor the commonest, glasses in use, as Harrison notes in the passage quoted above. The substitute glass was the humble green material made in the woodland glass-houses already referred to. The source of alkali in these forest houses was obtained by burning fern and other vegetable-matter and utilizing the lixiviated ashes. This was not so pure an alkali as the imported *barilla* (soda obtained from burned marine plants) used in Venetian glass-making; nor were the sources of silica so carefully selected, being often tainted with iron impurities which gave the glass a green tone. The resultant glossy green material nevertheless has æsthetic merits of its own, and the simple beakers, cups and bottles made in the English country glass-houses form a family which, although unpretentious, is well worthy of attention.

The impetus in the Wealden glass-manufacture

[1] cf. Pl. 48A.

Fig. 1. Reconstruction of a beaker with mould-blown design and thread-foot. Woodchester, Glos. c. 1600. Ht. 4¾ in.

Fig. 2. Reconstruction of a beaker with threaded decoration. Woodchester, Glos. c. 1600. Ht. 4½ in.

during the Middle Ages had come from France, probably from Normandy and Poitou. In the middle of the sixteenth century, the same enterprising spirit which had established Venetian glass-making in London brought into the Sussex–Surrey industry an infusion of new blood – mainly from Lorraine, but also perhaps from the Flemish glass-houses. During the last quarter of the sixteenth century the country's dwindling resources of timber gave increasing concern, and the glassmakers of the forest-houses were forced – sometimes by actual shortage and sometimes by local hostility – to uproot themselves and settle wherever they could be assured of timber supplies. The wanderings of the Lorrainers from the Weald took them via Hampshire into the Border country and into Staffordshire, and the traces of their migration are to be found in church-registers, place-names and occasional glass-house sites. Most of these sites yield scanty information. At Woodchester, in Gloucestershire, however, excavation has provided fragments which enable us to form a clear picture of the work done in these forest-houses (whose staple, it should not be forgotten, was normally window-glass).

The glasses made at Woodchester fall into two main classes – drinking-glasses and bottles. The drinking-glasses were tall tumbler-like beakers of two types. The first kind were straight-sided and almost perfectly cylindrical, being made stable by the addition of a coil of glass round the foot and by the pushing-in of the base in a slight conical 'kick' (Fig. 1). The second of the taller beaker-shapes was made by pushing in the bottom of the vesicle of glass whilst still soft, and thus making a low pedestal of double thickness, above which the body of the glass rose in the form of a slightly everted cylinder (Fig. 5). This method of fashioning the foot, which was characteristic of French glass-making, was also used in making goblets, the second main group of drinking-glasses. Here the pedestal base was constricted and extended to form a foot and 'stem' (Fig. 3). Drinking-glasses were also made in the shape of a boot (Fig. 4) – a trick-form favoured in the Netherlands which survived in England until at least the eighteenth century.

The bottles made at Woodchester were quite small (the only intact example measures 5½ inches in height), and were normally hexagonal in section

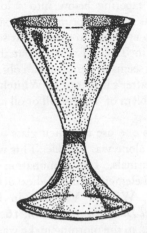

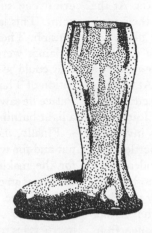

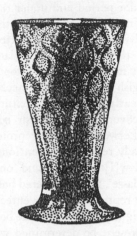

Fig. 3. Reconstruction of a wine-glass. Woodchester, Glos. c. 1600. Ht. 5½ in.

Fig. 4. Reconstruction of a drinking-vessel in the form of a boot. Woodchester, Glos. c. 1600. Ht. 4¾ in.

Fig. 5. Reconstruction of a beaker with mould-blown design. Woodchester, Glos. c. 1600. Ht. 6 in.

(Pl. 47c). One exceptional fragment, however, came from a flattened spherical bottle of German type, decorated with ribs blown in a mould and then 'wrythen' to produce a diagonal patterning (cf. Pl. 47D).

Mould-blowing, indeed, was the most favoured method of decorating the glasses found on this site. The moulds imparted either a honeycomb pattern (Fig. 5) or a design of vertical ribs which could be twisted on withdrawal from the mould, to give the 'wrythen' effect described above. Another favoured decoration was a trail of glass laid round and round the glass, either in a spiral (Fig. 2) or in a series of horizontal bands. In the latter case, the trails were sometimes combined with small applied blobs of glass stamped with a design like the pips of a raspberry. Similar 'prunts' were worked, whilst still plastic, into the form of rosettes.

Of all the simple forms made, the beaker is by far the commonest, and there can be little doubt that these glasses were used by the commonalty for drinking beer. A writer at the end of the six-teenth century could say: 'Take a Beer glasse of six or eight inches in height and being of one equal bigness from the bottome to the top', which admirably describes their general cylindrical form.[2]

Although the bottle fragments at Woodchester were not so numerous as those of beakers, there must have been in the late sixteenth and early seventeenth centuries a vast output of small green bottles for a variety of purposes (cf. Fig. 6). Small cylindrical phials, presumably used by apothecaries, are very commonly found in excavations in towns in this country, and are often mistaken for Roman glass. But fragments of bottles of square section or with globular bodies are also often found, and such convenient small receptacles must have had a number of uses. Thus, in an inventory of 1605, the following glass objects are noted (amongst others more easily identifiable): '2 glasses w[i]th Balsamum …', 'one big conserve glasses', '3 little Conserve glass, one hath sugar Candy', '4 little Conserve glass w[i]th oyles'. These were almost certainly bottles of one sort or another (the word 'glass' at this period meaning 'bottle', as well as the modern 'glass').

Bottles of larger capacity seem to have gone

[2] Sir Hugh Platt: *Jewell House of Art and Nature*, (1st edn. 1594). London, 1653, p. 76.

through a transitional phase at the end of the Tudor period and under the first Stuarts. At the beginning of the sixteenth century, they were probably mostly of imported Venetian glass, and had the common Venetian form of a spherical body mounted on a low foot, and surmounted by a longish slightly everted neck (Pl. 47B). At latest by the early seventeenth century it became customary to cover these thinnish bottles with leather or wickerwork for their protection: the inventory already referred to mentions '2 glasse bottles couerde w[i]th leather' and 'one great wanded bottle of glasse'. Such wickered bottles are almost invariably represented in seventeenth-century paintings as slightly flattened in the body, although it cannot at present be determined when the change from the spherical to the flattened body took place. So long as bottles were made of thin and fragile glass, the advantages of this shape were obvious. When, at a later date, bottles began to be made of stout green glass, they resumed the circular section — presumably for reasons of economy in making.

Of the many other domestic uses to which glass was put, lighting was undoubtedly one. Green glass fragments of what were certainly lamps are not infrequently found in the excavations of English cities, and probably date from the later Middle Ages. The form of these lamps was that of a cylindrical cup suddenly tapering below into a long point. This lamp was intended primarily for suspension. There is no evidence to show what sort of lamps were used in Tudor England, but that they could be of glass seems evident from an observation of Thomas Platter's in 1599. In Whitehall Palace he saw an emblem of 'a glass full of oil and a light burning in it'.

Finally, there was one use to which glass was put and for which it alone was suitable. This was for the making of urinals. The examination of urine was an essential element in the medical diagnosis of the period. William Vaughan in his *Naturall & Artificial Directions for health*, 1602, instructs his reader: '... in the morning make water in an vrinal: that by looking on it, you may ghesse some what of the state of your body...' In Henry VIII's possession at Westminster were 'vii cases of wicker twoo of theym p[ar]telye guilte w[i]th vii brode mouthed Urynalls in theym w[i]th laces of thrid to eache of theym'. This tradition continues, and in the inventory of 1605 mentioned above there occurs the item: 'one Ewrinall w[i]th the case hanging at thend [i.e. the end] of that Cupborde'. Thus housed, it was no doubt readily available for use.

Fig. 6. An itinerant glass-seller of the mid-16th century, from a wood-cut.

Domestic Metalwork

G. BERNARD HUGHES

The Tudor home, whether of noble or merchant prince, knight, gentleman, yeoman or farmer, depended for much of its newly-won comfort upon the accessories and utensils created by craftsmen in metal. Most important was the ironwork forged by the blacksmith; the hammered latten and turned brass of the brassworker; the tableware of the pewterer and tin caster; the lead cisterns and outside water-leeds of the plumber. Every room in the house possessed some metal accessories, but the majority was to be found in the living-room and kitchen.

The household inventory of Sir Thomas Ramsey, Lord Mayor of London in 1577, taken immediately after his death in 1590, totalled £1,454 11s. 7d. Included were fifty-eight candlesticks of brass valued at £2 13s. 4d.; 2,201-lb. pewter, £45 16s. 1d.; latten, brass, and copper vessels £24 0s. 3d.; lead cisterns £11 3s. 4d.; miscellaneous kitchen ironwork £3 18s. 4d., altogether valued at £87 11s. 4d.

The glowing, gleaming tones of brass and latten brought much colour to the Tudor home: inventories distinguish between the two metals. Brass was the cast alloy of copper and calamine,[1] usually finished by turning in the lathe and filing; brass ingots hammered into tough, close-textured plates were known as latten. The term brass was a medieval misnomer for the harder, brownish bronze made from copper and tin. Wrought goods of latten in 1545 were assessed at more than twice the value of similar domestic ware in brass. These

[1] Zinc was first used in brass under James Emerson's patent of 1780.

metals were used for a wide range of articles, including chandeliers and candlesticks, warming-pans, curfews, cauldrons and cooking pans with heavily tinned interiors.

English brass was not made in commercial quantities until 1585: earlier it was mainly imported from Flanders and Germany in the form of yellow ingots. Mid-Tudor inventories entered this metal as yellow, such as 'one yolloe candel-stycke iiijd', thus distinguishing it from bronze. English brass of the late Tudor period was described by the Founders' Company as being 'hard, flawy, scurvy and difficult to work'.

Lighting in the Tudor home might consist of a chandelier in the hall, a candlebeam and wall-sconce in each of the principal chambers, and table branches and candlesticks. These were usually of latten, although brass or gilded copper might be used: pewter and iron were less expensive.

Candlesticks and snuffers

The chandelier or hanging candlestick was an elaborate pendant fitting with sockets for as many as a dozen candles (Pl. 49A). The somewhat less elaborate candlebeam was composed of two or three crossed beams, carved and gilded, fitted with sockets and drip-pans, the latter known as 'bills'. Chandelier and candlebeam alike were suspended by two or more chains to a rope passing over a pulley-wheel so that the whole fitting could be lowered two or three times an hour for snuffing. The candlebeam might be supplemented in a large house by wall-lights or sconces fitted with reflectors behind the candles. These were generally inventoried as 'plates for candles' or 'plate candle-sticks'.

A branch candlestick for the table was defined by Huloct in 1552 as a 'candlestycke with thre brannches of lights'. The term branch was also used for the bracket or arm carrying a socket and fixed to the centre of the chimney-breast. Table candlesticks were often very elaborate, and occasionally might be of gilded copper. A fine example would be modelled as an heraldic beast, a wood-wose, a lance knight or a man armed cap-a-pie with outspread arms supporting two candle-sockets.

Less ornate table candlesticks of the fifteenth century followed the Flemish style. The design included a high, circular foot resembling an inverted mortar with its upper rim encircled by deep moulding to form a drip-pan: this supported a short cylindrical stem. By the 1520s the stem might be lengthened and ornament added in the form of from two to five matching and equidistant knife-edge knops. Instead of being brazed directly to the foot it rose from a high cone placed in the centre of the drip-pan (Pl. 49B). The tapered socket was of the cage type.

New patterns of candlesticks were being made by the mid-sixteenth century, including bell- and spool-shaped feet in variation. Baluster stems were now usual and continued fashionable throughout the Tudor period. The socket became fully developed and tapered less than formerly. The horizontal aperture cut in its lower half was tending to be replaced, by the 1550s, with a vertical slot cut in each side, sometimes below a small circular hole: the two might be joined, forming a cusped opening. In some Tudor candlesticks a long socket was set on a ring brazed to the centre of the drip-pan. Ringed sockets might also be supported by stems modelled in the form of human figures, and the knight in armour was a favourite form, the ringed socket being held by his uplifted head.

The most popular style of Elizabethan latten candlestick was made with a highly domed foot and a spirally fluted or horizontally corrugated stem. This was fitted immediately above the dome with a flat drip-pan, its upper surface sometimes decorated with floral ornament in re-poussé. Such candlesticks were known as 'flow-ered'.

Candle-snuffing was a delicate operation in Tudor days: only if properly carried out would illumination be increased, and the awkward candle-snuffer was liable to damage clothing and other textiles. Throughout the Tudor period candleshears were used. These consisted of a pair of plain scissors with loop handles and with the lower blade dished to receive the smouldering snuff. A dozen of these in iron cost thirty shillings in 1604.

Those who could afford them used the more elaborate candle-snuffers with a wick container on each blade. These were still a comparative novelty and appeared in precious metals, brass and iron. At first each container was semi-heart-shaped, a complete heart being formed when the sharp blades closed upon the charred end of the wick, leaving the snuff loose and smouldering in the box. The handles, forming a U when closed, were bent to form a pair of scrolled loops. The boxes on brass candle-snuffers were often of latten ornamented in repoussé with all-over classic themes, and to accommodate designs such as the 'Labours of Hercules' they tended to be made extravagantly large. Coats of arms are also found. By the mid-sixteenth century handles had become straight, terminating in circular bows and one of the blades was extended into a round projecting spike, its purpose being to lift the end of the wick from the melting wax before snuffing. By the middle of the century the spike had become further extended and flattened (Pl. 50B).

The douter or out-quencher was an equally necessary adjunct to candle-burning, used to prevent smoke or fumes when the light was extinguished. Early specimens might be *en suite* with candle-snuffers. These douters bore a basic resemblance to snuffers, but in place of a box and press-plate the arms of the scissors terminated in flat discs between which the wick might be nipped.

Warming-pans

Warming-pans made from latten are entered in inventories of the rich throughout the Tudor

'The Royal Gold Cup of the Kings of France and England', probably French work of the fourteenth century, with scenes in enamels from the legend of St Agnes on the exterior of cover and bowl. The one identifiable survivor from Elizabeth I's plate, recorded (Item no. 48) in the inventory published by the British Museum, 1955. *British Museum.*

PLATE 33

Standing cup and cover, silver, gilt and enamelled, 16 in. high, 1499. *The Mercers' Company.*

PLATE 34

The Gibbon Salt; silver gilt, 12 in. high, 1576.   *The Goldsmiths' Company.*

PLATE 35

(B) Ewer, silver parcel-gilt, 9 in. high, 1567.
The Corporation of Guildford, Surrey.

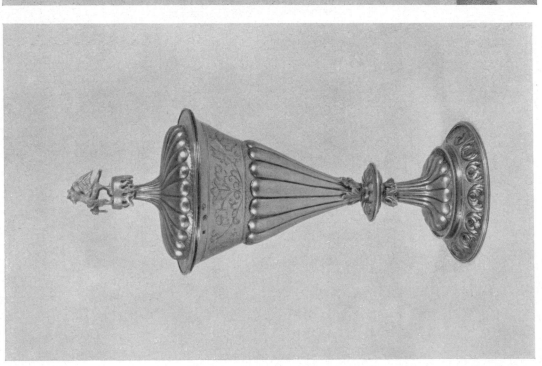

(A) The Boleyn cup; silver gilt, $12\frac{3}{8}$ in. high, 1535.
Cirencester Parish Church.

PLATE 36

(B) Tankard; silver parcel-gilt, 7¼ in. high, 1579.
The Goldsmiths' Company.

(A) Standing mazer, silver gilt, 10½ in. high, 1523. Altered
in 1540. *The Barbers' Company.*

PLATE 37

(B) The Glynne cup; silver gilt, 15½ in. high, 1579–80.
C. A. Gladstone, Esq.

(A) Cup; oriental agate and silver gilt, 7⅞ in. high, 1567.
Victoria and Albert Museum.

PLATE 38

Two of a set of twelve parcel-gilt plates. London, 1567, by Thomas Bampton, engraved by Pieter Maas with the 'Labours of Hercules'. *Collection of Mr and Mrs Francis E. Fowler, Jnr, California.*

PLATE 39

135

A   B

(A) Jug; stoneware and silver, 10 in. high, jug dated 1597, mount made in Hull.
Messrs Hicklenton and Phillips, London.

(B) Beaker; silver parcel-gilt, 7 in. high, 1591.
The Church of St Giles without Cripplegate, London.

(C) *Left.* One of a pair of Elizabethan silver-gilt flagons, $12\frac{1}{4}$ in. high. London, 1597–98.
Collection of Judge Irwin Untermyer, New York.

(D) *Right.* Standing cup and cover; silver-gilt, $19\frac{1}{4}$ in. high, 1599.
The Parish Church of Charing, Kent.

(A) Cistern of green lead-glazed earthenware, with Royal Arms of England as borne by Henry VII, and initials of Henry VII and Elizabeth of York. English, about 1525–30. Height $12\frac{3}{4}$ in. *Victoria and Albert Museum.*

(B) Mug, green lead-glazed earthenware. English, third quarter of sixteenth century. See p.118. Height $4\frac{7}{10}$ in. *British Museum.*

(C) Dish of green lead-glazed earthenware, with Royal Arms of England, from the site of Eltham Palace. English, about 1540. *H.M. Office of Works.*

PLATE 41

137

(A) Tankard, brown lead-glazed earthenware, in English embossed and engraved silver-gilt mount. London hall-mark for 1547–48. English, about 1545. Height 7⅝ in. *Victoria and Albert Museum.*

(B) Tankard, tin-glazed earthenware ('Malling jug') with silver-gilt mounts bearing the London hall-mark for 1549–50. Made in London or Kent; about 1545–50. Height 6⅕ in. *British Museum.*

(C) Dish, tin-glazed earthenware. Made in London, dated 1600. Diameter 10⅛ in. *London Museum.*

PLATE 42

A   B   C

(A) 'Tyg', dark-brown lead-glazed earthenware ('Cistercian' ware). English, dated 1599. Height 5⅗ in. *British Museum.*

(B) Candlestick, green lead-glazed earthenware, with the Pegasus badge of the Inner Temple impressed. English, late sixteenth century. Height 5⅜ in. *Victoria and Albert Museum.*

(C) Two-handled cup, dark-brown lead-glazed earthenware with white 'slip' decoration. Probably found and made in Yorkshire; middle of sixteenth century. Height 6⅜ in. *Yorkshire Museum, York.*

(D) 'Tyg', dark-brown lead-glazed earthenware ('Cistercian' ware), with white 'slip' decoration. English, sixteenth century. Height 3 in. *Victoria and Albert Museum.*

(E) Tankard, dark-brown lead-glazed earthenware ('Cistercian' ware). Found at Youlgreave and probably made in Derbyshire, sixteenth century. Height 11½ in. *Fitzwilliam Museum, Cambridge.*

(F) 'Tyg', dark-brown lead-glazed earthenware ('Cistercian' ware). Found and probably made at Tickenhall, Derbyshire; sixteenth century. Height 4⅜ in. *Victoria and Albert Museum.*

D   E   F

PLATE 43

(A) Bowl, celadon porcelain with incised decoration, set in an English silver-gilt mount. Chinese, period of the Ming dynasty (1368–1643). Height 4¾ in.
By courtesy of the Warden and Fellows of New College, Oxford.

(B) Cup of white porcelain decorated outside with incised designs, and inside with blue-painting, and mounted in embossed and engraved silver-gilt. London hallmark for 1569–70. Chinese, period of Chia Ching (1522–66). Height with cover 6 in.

(C) Ewer and bowl of blue-and-white porcelain, mounted in silver-gilt by a goldsmith working about 1583–90. Originally in the possession of Lord Treasurer Cecil. Chinese, period of Wan Li (1573–1610). Height of ewer, 13⅝ in. *Courtesy of the Metropolitan Museum, New York.*

PLATE 44

(A) Cup, porcelain with coral-red glaze, decorated with gilt scrolls. English silver-gilt mount of about 1570. Chinese, middle of sixteenth century. Height 7½ in.   *Courtesy Judge Irwin Untermyer, New York.*

(B) Jug of pottery in blue, green and red, and mounted in an English silver-gilt mount of about 1580. Turkish (Isnik); middle of sixteenth century. Height 10¼ in. *Victoria and Albert Museum.*

(C) Ewer of unglazed greyish stoneware, by the potter Christian Knütgen, with English silver mounts. German (Siegburg); dated 1590. Height 10¾ in. *Victoria and Albert Museum.*

(D) Tankard of mottled brown salt-glazed stoneware, with English silver-gilt mounts bearing the London hall-mark for 1579–80. German (probably Cologne); about 1575. Height 10¼ in. *Victoria and Albert Museum.*

PLATE 45   141

(A) Wine-glass with gilt decoration including two coats of arms (one that of the Vintners' Company) and the name Wenyfrid Geares. English, dated 1590. Height 7½ in.
The Duke of Northumberland.

(B) Goblet, enamelled glass set in silver-gilt foot bearing the London hall-mark for 1547–48. Venetian, early sixteenth century. Height 9 in.
The Founders' Company and the Goldsmiths' Company.

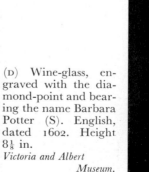

(C) Wine-glass, engraved with the diamond-point, perhaps by Anthony de Lysle. Decorated with the Royal Arms as borne by Queen Elizabeth I, and the names JOHN JONE *Dier*. English, dated 1581. Height 8⅛ in.
Victoria and Albert Museum.

(D) Wine-glass, engraved with the diamond-point and bearing the name Barbara Potter (S). English, dated 1602. Height 8⅛ in.
Victoria and Albert Museum.

PLATE 46

(A) Mug of glass with *latticinio* stripes, the silver-gilt mounts bearing the London hall-mark for 1548. Venetian, *c.* 1540. Height 5⁴⁄₅ in. *British Museum.*

(B) Detail from portrait of Erasmus by Holbein, showing (top right) a glass bottle, perhaps Venetian, the adjacent book gives the date 1523. *The Earl of Radnor.*

(C) Bottle of hexagonal section, in green glass. Found and made in Woodchester, Glos., about 1600. Height 5½ in. *City Museum, Gloucester.*

(D) Flask of green glass with 'wrythen' ribbed decoration. Said to have been excavated in Oxford. Perhaps English, *c.* 1600. Ht. 4⅜ in. *Victoria and Albert Museum.*

PLATE 47

(A) 'A Financial Transaction', oil-painting by Lucas Cranach, the Elder (1472–1553), showing a colourless glass beaker of about 1530, probably made in the Netherlands. *Nationalmuseum, Stockholm.*

(B) 'Family Group', oil-painting probably by Maarten van Heemskerck (1498–1574), showing a wine-glass probably made in Venice or perhaps in the Netherlands during the second quarter of the sixteenth century. *Staatliche Kunstsammlungen, Kassel.*

PLATE 48

(A) Bristol Cathedral: a rare latten chandelier which hangs in the Berkeley Chapel. Flemish, sixteenth century.

(B) Brass candlestick of the early sixteenth century: a development of earlier Flemish styles. Height 6¾ in. *Victoria and Albert Museum*.

(C) Wrought-iron lock and handle: early sixteenth century. Height of lock 5⅝ in. *Victoria and Albert Museum*.

PLATE 49

(A) Fireback with radiated design in the centre, known as a 'carboncle', part of the coat of arms of Anne of Cleves. Additional prints include Tudor roses and fleur-de-lis. About 1540.

(B) Silver-gilt snuffer, the box chased with the arms and initials of Edward VI: the handle stems are inscribed GOD SAVE THE KYNGE EDWARDE WYTHE ALL HIS NOBLE COUNCIL, *c.* 1550. *Victoria and Albert Museum.*

(C) Lock, chiselled with the arms and supporters borne by Henry VII and Henry VIII. From Beddington House, Surrey. First half of the sixteenth century. *Victoria and Albert Museum.*

PLATE 50

(B) A Gothic hearth carved with ST GEORGE and the Dragon. The three-panel fireback with arched top and cable twist borders is dated 1588. The pair of cast-iron fire-dogs are of the same period.

(A) The only known pair of HENRY VIII andirons, in the Great Hall at Knole House, Sevenoaks, Kent. These bear the arms of HENRY VIII and Anne Boleyn. These are made of iron, except the crests, which are of bronze.

PLATE 51

(A) Three late sixteenth-century steel knives struck with the bladesmith's marks: handles and blades forged in a single piece and riveted with wooden scales. Excavated in London. *Victoria and Albert Museum.*

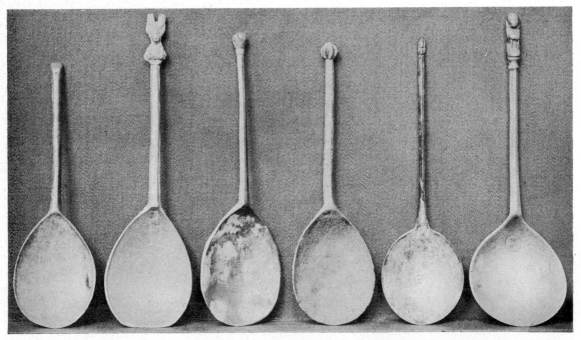

(B) Pewter spoons of the fifteenth and sixteenth centuries, their terminals being slipped-in-the-stalk; female bust with horned head-dress knop; writhen ball knop; ribbed ball knop; notched finial; lion-sejant knop. *Victoria and Albert Museum.*

PLATE 52

Tapestry Hanging, woven in the Netherlands about 1580 for Robert Dudley, Earl of Leicester.
Burrell Collection, Glasgow.

PLATE 53

Section of a tapestry hanging, showing part of Surrey, woven on Sheldon looms about 1588.
Victoria and Albert Museum.

PLATE 54

A

B

(A) Tapestry cushion cover, with figures of Faith, Hope and Charity, woven on Sheldon looms;
late sixteenth century. *Burrell Collection, Glasgow.*

(B) Part of a tapestry hanging, with Biblical and emblematic subjects among flowers; woven on
Sheldon looms; late sixteenth century. *Sudeley Castle.*

PLATE 55

Embroidered hanging, English, about 1580. *Victoria and Albert Museum.*

PLATE 56

Hanging of green velvet, with embroidered panels by Mary, Queen of Scots, and Elizabeth, Countess of Shrewsbury; about 1570. *Oxburgh Hall, Norfolk.*

PLATE 57

A

B

(A) Cushion with applied embroideries, about 1600. *Victoria and Albert Museum.*
(B) Cushion cover, embroidered in silk and gold thread, made for the Earl of Leicester
or the Earl of Warwick, second half of the sixteenth century. *John Wyndham, Esq.*

PLATE 58

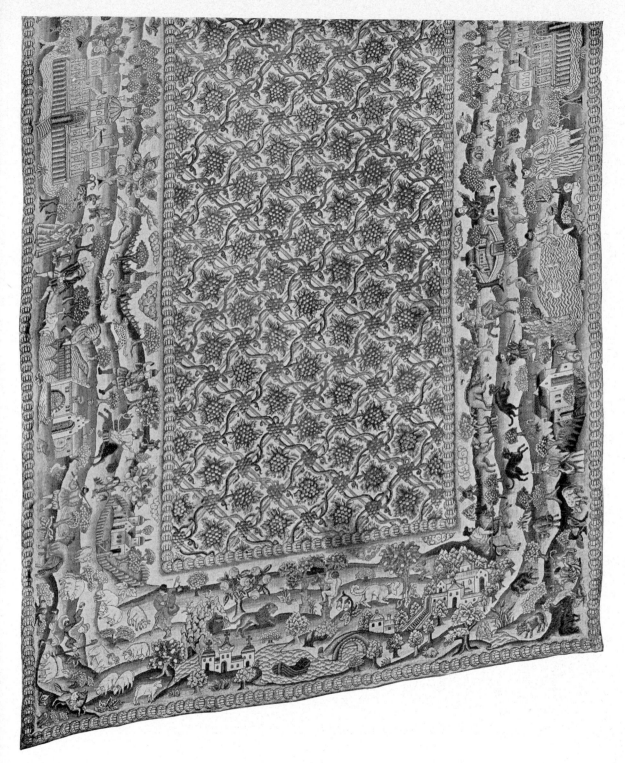

Embroidered table cover, about 1600. *Victoria and Albert Museum.*

PLATE 59

(A) Cushion cover with the arms of Henry Sandys; middle of the sixteenth century.
P. V. Barker-Mill, Esq.

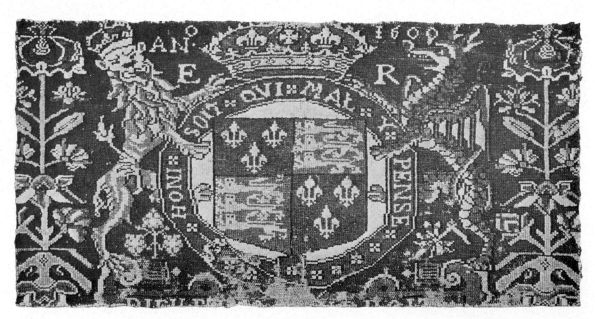

(B) Carpet with Royal Arms, dated 1600. *Victoria and Albert Museum.*

'The Noble Life' tapestry, 1500–1510. The man in gown with full sleeves; bonnet with turned-up brim. Long hair and clean-shaven. The woman on his left: trained gown with wide sleeves, the tight kirtle sleeve showing at the wrist. Girdle. Draped hood. *Victoria and Albert Museum.*

PLATE 61

157

(A) Sir Richard Vernon tomb (1517). Medium-long gown with full wide sleeves, over doublet with low neck showing shirt above. Small round cap with crown moulded into lobes. Square-toed shoes with ankle straps. *Courtauld Institute of Art.*

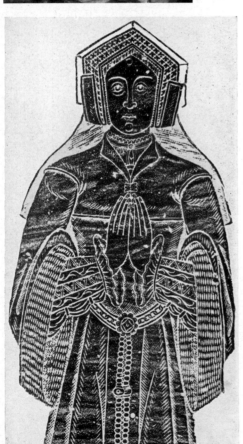

(B) Panel from a Flemish tapestry, at Norwich, *c.* 1530. The Lady has a 'bongrace' on the head, trained gown. *Castle Museum, Norwich.*

(C) E. Perepoynt brass, West Malling, 1543. English ('gable') hood with sides turned up, and back curtain hanging loose. Kirtle with over-sleeves and large turned-back cuffs; under-sleeves with back seam open showing edge of chemise. Jewelled belt. *Victoria and Albert Museum.*

PLATE 62

Lord Grey de Wilton in 1547. Leather jerkin paned to the waist, with a pinked yoke above it.
Pinked codpiece. Doublet sleeve, pinked, on right arm; left covered by gown sleeve. Small Court
bonnet. *National Gallery of Scotland.*

PLATE 63

(B) Sir Edward Hoby in 1578. Tall crowned hat with plume and metal ornaments. Closed ruff. Slashed doublet. *Lady Vansittart Neale.*

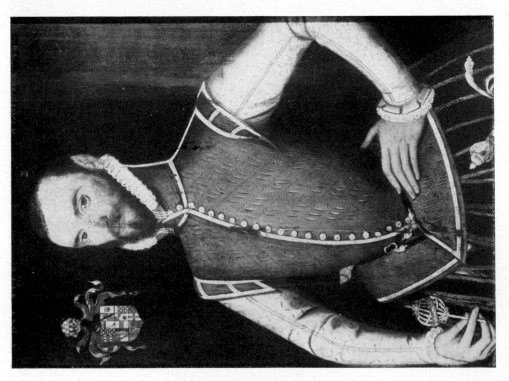

(A) Hugh Fitz-William, of Sprotborough, in 1568. Pinked sleeveless jerkin with high collar. Open ruff and band-strings. Short skirt flared over distended trunk-hose. Doublet sleeves tabbed at the wrist in 'pickadil'. Hand ruffs. *Peterborough Museum.*

period, and seldom more than one to a household. The extensive 1590 inventory of Sir Thomas Ramsey shows him to have possessed a single example valued at eleven shillings. They were mostly importations until about 1588, when heavy ember pans were made from English latten by the battery process, introduced a few years earlier from Germany. A beater might use as many as twenty different hammers, the marks being removed later by turning in a lathe. These ember pans were sold to small masters who fitted them with three-foot wrought-iron handles, and ornamental covers made from thin Dutch latten plate of best quality.

Curfews and hearth furniture

Associated with the warming-pan was the curfew, produced by the same group of metal-workers. Fire hazard from the household hearth was reduced during Tudor times by a curfew regulation requiring the fire to be covered over or extinguished at night. At first it was customary to lift the stone or cast-iron slab which lay in front of the hearth as a day-time protection against falling embers, placing it vertically against the fireplace recess, thus effectively preventing danger from sparks.[2] When wrought-iron sheets could be afforded a quarter sphere cover was made with a handle extending from top to lower rims. This was placed over the embers and pushed against the fireback, thus excluding draught and retaining sparks. Such covers were also made in latten and copper and might be ornamented with elaborate repousse designs. A latten example owned by Sir William More was inventoried as 'a pan to cover the fyre, iij^s iij$_d$'. The term 'curfew' associated with these fire covers seems to date no earlier than 1620.

In the Tudor home the hearth furniture was a major item, consisting of fireback, firedogs, shovel, tongs, poker and, in the kitchen, spits, crane and hooks. Here wrought-iron work was splendidly displayed. Our Tudor ancestors took for granted that convected heat was a fuel-saver, for the cast-iron fireback radiated heat into the room, instead of allowing it to be absorbed by the stone and

[2] The John Every Catalogue at Lewes Museum.

bricks. Its basic purpose, of course, was to protect the walls of the deep, wide recess of the down hearth from the ravages of wood fires burning on the hearth.

Massively rectangular, its width twice its height, and with plain rough surfaces, it was known as a 'fireplate'. Founders experienced no difficulty in casting these large flat plates if the section were thick enough to prevent warping while cooling. The result was that firebacks were heavy, weighing about fifteen to the ton. The face of the plate became a field for clear-cut cast ornament in which the Elizabethans attained a high standard of design (Pls. 50A, 51B).

Early Tudor decoration consisted of a cable-twist border enclosing a variety of individual stamps such as the Tudor rose, heraldic lion, portcullis, the fleur-de-lys arranged in threes with butts pointing downward, and also homely little reliefs of dogs, sheep and human figures. Such decoration continued in use until mid-Elizabethan times.

Firebacks during the reign of Elizabeth 1 began to echo the extravagance of prosperity. Simple rectangles gave way to clipped corners and stepped heads, but the stamped decoration continued, being placed symmetrically. By the 1570s the arched head had become fashionable and single-piece, all-over patterns were designed. At first the pattern was divided into three vertical panels, the central one extending the width of the arch, displaying topical or personal motifs, and the two side-panels containing flowers and foliage.

The 1590s saw the introduction of the armorial fireback, an expansive coat of arms surrounded by scrolls and floral motifs, the whole composition being enclosed in a moulded rim. Obviously these armorial firebacks were commissioned, and they usually bear the original owner's initials and the date of first casting. The original wooden casting might continue in use through several generations.

Andirons

In the great chamber of a large establishment a pair of handsome andirons in silver, bronze, brass or polished iron would flank the hearth: on the stone hearth itself stood a pair of serviceable firedogs with a pair of low creepers between them. Thomas Fuller, in 1662, described their purpose: 'The iron dogs bear the burthen of the fuel, while the brazen andirons stand only for state, and the little creepers bear up all the heat of the fire.' The short-necked creepers, known also as 'middle dogs' and 'chenets', were usually much reduced copies of their accompanying firedogs.

Andirons – the end irons in a set of six – became fashionable in the reign of Henry VIII: Cardinal Wolsey possessed fifty-seven pairs in different designs at Hampton Court in 1547, many displaying his coat of arms. Eight pairs were in bronze, the remainder in wrought iron, some with finials of the Tudor rose in red and white enamels, others with 'bawles of latten and libbardes heddes upon the staukes'. Colourful andirons, contrasting vividly with the polished grey of the firedogs, were made in considerable numbers from the 1580s.

Tudor firedogs (Pl. 51B) were seldom more than rugged castings faced with relief ornament copying such carved oak furniture motifs as strapwork and guilloche on standard and arch, with terminals modelled in the round. The arch was usually cusped in the Gothic style and the arch-standard junction concealed beneath a cast shield displaying coat of arms, crest, cypher or other personal motif. Alternatively such a motif might form the finial. Many firedog standards terminated in heads or demi-figures. At first a face was made fitting squarely into the front of the finial: soon this was expanded into a bust, and finally a demi-figure with arms held close to the body and occupying about half the height of the standard. Animals were similarly used. A lion's head might be placed below a demi-figure and again on the face of each foot.

In the kitchen fireplace stood a pair of tall firedogs known as 'spit-dogs'. Spit-turning mechanism had not been developed at this period, the wheel being operated by a boy turn-spit. Hooks for supporting the spit were welded to the standards, which had a slight backward curve to the flames. Their finials were forged, usually into skeleton cresset or cup-like forms with encircling rims which could support and keep warm vessels filled with soup or spoonmeat. In some instances their depth and diameter suggest their use as supports for pewter flatware.

Within the chimney, secured to the back wall, was a crane, hinging with a lateral motion and inventoried variously as a cobrel, tramell, jib-crook, hanger or hanging iron, and in the south as a cotterel. Pot-hooks hung from the horizontal bar of the crane, terminating in one with a central swivel. Also hanging from the crane was an adjustable pot-hanger with a vertical serrated plate so that the cooking-pot could be raised or lowered as required.

The tinder-box

Essential detail in all the laborious Tudor ritual of providing heat and light was the tinder box. This usually consisted of a latten box containing 'fyre yrons, flynte stones, Tinder, and Brimstone', and a damper to extinguish the tinder after the match had been lighted. The cutler-made fire steel, a blade with a loop or hook handle entirely devoid of ornament, was held in the left hand a few inches above the tinder. It was struck a sharp blow with the flint. This broke off a spark of red-hot steel which fell upon the tinder causing it to smoulder. A sulphur match touched to this at once burst into flame.

Wheel-lock tinder-boxes were made throughout the sixteenth century by the gunsmiths. A small piece of pyrites, held in by a cock, was pressed down on the roughened edge of a steel wheel. When the trigger was pulled the spring-actuated wheel revolved rapidly, producing sparks which ignited gunpowder. This was used to set the tinder smouldering. The spring was wound each time with a key.

Clocks

Clockmakers on the other hand were of comparatively minor importance to the average Tudor home, for Tudor clocks were costly pieces of mechanism and poor timekeepers. The balance had no natural period of vibration and in consequence never swung freely. When accurate time was needed indoors the hour-glass was preferred. Sir John Paston as early as 1469 owned a clock and Henry VIII owned many, one of them now in the Royal Collection at Windsor. No more than half a dozen Tudor clocks are known to remain, however, including a fine spring-driven bracket clock by Bartholomew Newsam, Clockmaker to Elizabeth I. This is now in the British Museum.

The majority of Tudor clocks were crudely constructed of brass or iron with uniform characteristics of thirty-hour running time and a single hour-hand. Two trains were fixed one behind the other, the striking one at the rear. Regulation was by a vertical verge controlled by a horizontal balance called the 'foliot'. The portrait of the family of Sir Thomas More, painted in 1593 and now in the National Portrait Gallery, shows such a clock enclosed in a long glazed case hung high on the wall, with holes in the base through which hung the essential plaited cords and weights supplying the driving force. There was, of course, no pendulum.

Locks

For delicate metal craftsmanship in the Tudor home one turns, rather, to the work of the locksmiths who brought about technical and artistic improvements in their craft, although the wearing quality of steel continued poor. Stock locks for doors continued plainly practical but remarkably secure. Plate locks, then completely boxed in metal locks for use on inner doors, accommodated themselves to the carved panelling they were intended to accompany.

The decoration of plate locks might tell the story of the house and its founder. These locks of iron and steel, displaying Gothic ornament, coats of arms and so on, might be enriched with gold leaf and brightly hued paints. The cases and movements of fine locks were almost invariably of steel until late in the sixteenth century, when they were sometimes of latten, decorated with a wide range of simple designs composed of vari-sized points, circles and lines applied by means of punches. Both stock and plate locks could be operated from within (Pl. 49c).

Lock bolts at this time operated on two principles. The majority were warded, fixed obstructions preventing a false key from throwing back the bolt; the remainder operated with tumblers,

immovable except to the right key which lifted them to predetermined heights and shot the bolt. The stock lock, set into a stock or hollowed rectangular block of oak, was held to the inner surface of the door by bolts and banding.

The clicket lock was a form of plate lock used extensively upon coffers, aumbries and cupboards to provide greater security than that afforded by a simple latch, bolt or snib. Twenty-seven clicket locks, each with three keys, were bought for All Souls College, Oxford, in 1439. Such a lock consisted of a rectangular or hatchet-shaped plate of wrought iron to which the action was riveted, either exposed or boxed within a small circular framing. The action was sunk into the wood and the plate fixed against it. The iron bolt worked in slides.

Inner doors were secured by wrought-iron latches. To open, the latch was lifted by a thumb-lever passing through the door or by a double cam attached to the inward end of the spindle from which the closing ring depended, both latch and ring being usually of curved outline, the latter continuing the Gothic feeling in its stirrup outline.

Until the Elizabethan period a caller made his presence known by beating the door with a stick, or by using the closing ring as a knocker. By the 1570s the 'hammer' or knocker had been devised. Higins in 1585 referred to 'the ring or iron hammer wherewith we knocke at the door'. In 1611 Cotgrave referred to 'the ring, knocker, or hammer of a dore'. Thereafter knocker was the only term used.

The Blacksmith

The blacksmith, who worked his own bars from the billet, strengthened Tudor outer doors by providing hinges, bolts, door-plates and nails. Hinges were of the strap T-ended type in strong wrought iron, further strengthened by the use of branching strapwork curving beneath them in ornamental scrolls. The central strap was usually elaborately expansive. Interiors of outer doors were also strengthened within by scrolling branches of ornamental strapwork. J. Starkie Gardner, in *Ironwork*, 1892, noted that towards the end of the period branching ironwork grew less elaborate: because of the destruction of forests the establishment of new furnaces was forbidden and wrought iron for domestic purposes became scarce.

The Plumber

As important as the blacksmith to the outward appearance of the Tudor house was the plumber who supplied lead water-cisterns, gutters, pipe-heads, down pipes, perforated lozenges for ventilation, and roof covering. The plumber, who worked directly from English-mined lead ingots carried to the premises, gave his finished sheets a beautiful white appearance by tinning the outer surface.

Rain-water was conveyed from the roof to a lead cistern ornamented in relief and enriched with gilding and the householder's livery colours.[3] Tudor water-cisterns are rare, but an Elizabethan example was illustrated and fully described in *The Builder*, 1862. Its front was cast with ornament in the style of a contemporaneous three-panelled fireback. The front rims of leaded gutters were cut into ornamental outlines, and short lengths of pipe directed running water to the square or rectangular pipe-heads leading to the down pipe, always made square to permit expansion during frosty weather. The pipe-heads might be small and plain or large and over-decorated, with side-flaps for attachment to the building. Pipe-heads were made from sheet lead with cornices beaten to shape over a hardwood pattern. A funnel-shaped section below joined the pipe-head to the down pipe. There are several lead pipe-heads at Windsor Castle bearing applied cast Tudor roses, the royal cypher and the date 1589. Some of these have an outer casing of lead with fine tracery panels pierced through it which show bright against the shadow. At Knole in the 1590s the lead was decorated with patterns in bright solder. The down pipes were flat rectangles in section, usually ornamented only at the collars. The fixing flaps were cut long enough for them to be folded back over the nail-heads.

[3] *Leadwork*, by W. R. Lethaby, 1895.

Kitchenware

For the minor items of metal-work, for the innumerable small wares that made the Tudor house a home, one turns instinctively to the records of its kitchens. The inventory of Ralph Ewrie, yeoman, Bedbourne Park, Edgnolle, County Durham, taken in 1586, lists a wide range of kitchen metal-work, valued at £4 19s. Detailed kitchen inventories are rare, and this example helps one to visualize the array of tools available to the domestic staff of the late Elizabethan housewife.

Iron, tin, pewter, latten and brass were used in the Ewrie kitchen: '2 iron racks, 2 spits, 1 little dripping pan, 1 frying pan, 1 fire shovel, 2 pairs of tongs, 3 racken crookes,[4] a broiling iron, 2 pairs of pot hooks and a trivet, all valued at 10s. 8d.; a basin and ewer of tin, 2s. 6d.; one liverie pot of tin 2s. 6d.; 1 quart pot, 2 pint pots, 6 flower pots, 2 salts, 2 candlesticks, pottingers, and 4 trencher plates of tin 11s. 4d.; 12 tin spoons, 12d.; 3 chamber pots of tin, 3s. 8d.; 4 platters of pewter, 8s.; 4 pewter dishes, 8 sawcers, 1 pie plate and one hand basin, 17s.; 5 candlesticks of latten, 2 chafing dishes, 3 scomers, a basting ladle of brass, 1 other brass ladle, 5s. 4d.; 3 pots, 3 kettles and 4 pans of brass, 30s.; brass mortar and an iron pestle, 5s.; 2 cleavers, 2 mincing knives, and a breadgrate of tin, 2s.' A considerable amount of unspecified pewter was stored in the parlour press.

Pewter

Plate pewter was really toughened tin, hammered or planished to give rigidity and compactness of texture. This could be distinguished from cast and turned pewter by its bell-like ring when struck. When newly bought, domestic pewter was highly burnished with a lustre resembling silver. It was a requirement of the Pewterers' Company throughout the Tudor period that the interior of all domestic ware should be burnished.

The inventory of Thomas Hall, a Durham farmer, detailed the pewter flatware in his press during 1586. From this it has been possible for the first time to compute the weight of single pieces: great chargers, $5\frac{3}{4}$ lb.; chargers, $4\frac{3}{4}$ lb.; lesser

[4] A crook for raking or stirring ashes.

Fig. 1. A composite figure of a worker in wood, stone and iron, with a *dolabre* or adze in his left hand, a hammer in his right hand, and a trowel at his girdle. A blacksmith's anvil and tongs are seen to the left. Woodcut from William Caxton's *The Game and Playe of the Chesse*, printed in Bruges, c. 1475. *British Museum.*

chargers $3\frac{1}{2}$ lb.; great platters, $3\frac{1}{2}$ lb.; platters, 3 lb.; lesser platters, $2\frac{1}{2}$ lb.; doublers, 3 lb.; lesser doublers, $2\frac{1}{4}$ lb. Special purpose flat-ware was also itemized: custard plates, $1\frac{3}{4}$ lb.; spice plates, $1\frac{1}{2}$ lb.; pudding dishes, $1\frac{1}{4}$ lb.; pie and paste plates, 1 lb.; egg dishes, 1 lb.; banquet dishes, 14 oz.; large saucers, $\frac{1}{2}$ lb.; plate trenchers, 14 oz. to 9 oz.

Doublers and trenchers

Doublers were flat-bottomed, deeply-bouged plates with slightly uprising rims, used for serving the many semi-liquid spoonmeats of the period. The banqueting dishes, measuring about six inches in diameter, were for the service of sweetmeats, at the fruit and wine repast served between meals and known as the banquet. Spice plates or trays were for the service of dried fruits, such as raisins, currants and figs, and not for the pungent spices then used for flavouring under the name of sauces, which were served in deep rimless saucers, about six inches in diameter. The basin and ewer entered in the Ewrie and many another inventory was intended for washing the hands at the end of a course. Queen Elizabeth 1 dined in gloves to avoid this continual washing, changing into a fresh pair with each course, thus setting a fashion that continued until the introduction of table-forks. For washing in the bedroom there would be a hanging laver with its basin and iron stand. The laver was a two-spouted cauldron suspended by a loop handle from a bracket over the basin. By tipping up one spout the water was shot from the other into the basin. These were common in the early Tudor period

Trenchers were for individual use, and might be round, square or slightly rectangular, rimless or with wide, low, rounded rims, a type termed plate trenchers. Trenchers quickly became disfigured by knife-marks. This, in large establishments, brought about the occupation of trencher scraper and pewter scourer for work that was done by one of the maids in a smaller household. Knife-marks were removed from the trenchers after each meal with a specially designed tool.[5] Polishing was done with horse-tail rush or pewter-wort.

Spoons and cutlery

Everyone used a spoon at meals, the majority being in pewter, the bowl hammered into shape so that it would withstand the wear of everyday use (Pl. 52B). A decorative knop was cast separately and soldered into a V-shaped notch on the end of the hammered stem. This knop might be gilded.

The amount of cast tin domestic hollow-ware inventoried during the Tudor period is surprising. When turned and highly burnished it was virtually indistinguishable in appearance from sterling silver. Tin casting had become a recognized London trade by 1515.

The cutler was responsible for the steel knives of various sorts necessarily possessed by every household (Pl. 52A). The blades of Tudor table-knives resembled elongated and widened spear heads, the upper edge thick and heavy, tapering to a finely ground cutting edge, and fitted to a haft. In a wealthy establishment the guests at the high table were provided with knives protected by a decorative case of cuir bouilli, from which each guest helped himself. The case used by the Earl of Leicester at Kenilworth represented an equestrian figure of St George overcoming the dragon. Guests at the lower tables brought their own knives, which they sharpened on a whetstone hanging by a string at one side of the door.

In other households pairs of knives were carried suspended from the girdle in decorative sheaths. One was designed for cutting meat, the other for bread. The carver used a special cutting-knife with a long, wide blade sharpened on both edges, and a long, broad, square-ended serving-knife with a rounded edge. Such knives were stamped with the bladesmith's mark, the majority being registered in London or Sheffield. The tang head of a table-knife was forged into a decorative knop and baluster outline. One inexpensive form of table-knife had a blade and handle forged from a single strip of steel, to which wooden plates known as 'scales' were riveted to form a grip.

The Tudor coppersmith appears to have produced little domestic ware, being engaged almost entirely on large goods for brewers, soap-makers, dyers and the like. The many-paged inventory of Marketon taken in 1545 contains not one reference to copper, and the extensive inventory of Sir Thomas Ramsay, 1590, only one: 'A copper kittle, poiz xxx lb at 8^d per pownde xx^s.' Nevertheless, that most companionable vessel has become the very symbol of the big, noisy, untidy, but, as regards metalwork, decoratively and effectively equipped Tudor home.

[5] *History of the Worshipful Company of Pewterers*, by C. Welch, 1902.

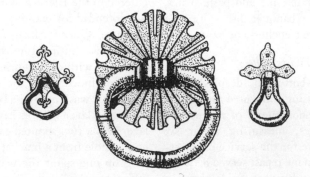

FIG. 2. Three Tudor wrought-iron door-knockers.

Textiles

DONALD KING

The Reformation stands astride the Tudor age like a gateway from medieval to modern times. Interlinked with the changes in religion, a multitude of other changes, political, economic, social and psychological, combined to transform English life. For good or ill, men came to believe that the fruits of this world were of more immediate moment than the rewards or penalties of the next. The wealth which in former times they had devoted to the construction and worthy furnishing of God's house they now applied to the pursuit of private ends, to the adornment of their own persons and the greater comfort of their own homes.

The textile arts, many of whose finest products had hitherto been consecrated to the service of the Church, now contributed lavishly to secular ease and ostentation, a change of rôle which is curiously underlined and exaggerated by the hazards of survival. For when we survey the textile remains of Tudor England before the Reformation, we find that, apart from a small number of tapestries, they consist almost exclusively of the copes and chasubles of priests and the rich palls with which guilds and confraternities were wont to honour the coffins of their departed members. Post-Reformation textiles, on the other hand, are almost all articles of secular dress or household furnishings.

The subject of costume is dealt with elsewhere in this volume. As for furnishings, it will be appropriate, before proceeding to details, to introduce here some brief general comments on the main uses of decorative textiles in the Tudor, and especially the Elizabethan, house. Firstly, the walls of the principal chambers were hung with tapestries, or with embroidered or painted hangings. Window-curtains, however, were by no means common, and if used, they were nearly always purely utilitarian and without decorative pretensions, though they were sometimes paned (i.e. composed of strips of materials of contrasting colours). In the more luxurious establishments, carpets might be found on the floors, but commoner floor-coverings were plaited rush-matting and, particularly in the earlier part of the period, the strewn rushes whose accumulations of filth appalled Erasmus. Carpets were seen just as often on tables as on floors, though for this purpose fine woven and embroidered cloths were also used. The long, rectangular cup-board cloths which, laid on the shelves of open cup-boards, served to set off the display of plate, might also be of carpet, of tapestry or of woven or embroidered stuffs. All these materials were likewise used as covers for loose cushions on wooden chairs and benches as well as on the seats and backs of the less common upholstered chairs. The principal article of Tudor furniture, the four-poster bed, had a particularly lavish textile equipment. Its four, five or six curtains could be drawn so as to enclose the sleepers completely. Valances were hung from the upper frame and often from the lower frame also; in the latter case they were known as bases. If the bed were not of the more elaborately panelled variety, it might also have a roof-piece and a head-piece of fabric. For all these hangings the richest materials were employed – silks, velvets and fine embroidery, trimmed with fringes and with gold and silver braids. In addition, the coverlet and pillows were often of fine woven and embroidered stuffs. Apart from the major articles of furniture it must be remembered that the use of decorative textiles extended also to a great variety of minor objects of household use, such, for instance, as embroidered cases for table-knives, and book-covers in needlework or silk tapestry. It cannot be doubted that the rich textures and hues of all these furnishings, and the flowers, animals and emblems with which many of them were luxuriantly adorned, nourished and stimulated the Elizabethan imagination that had conceived them.

The details of this short sketch can readily be filled in by reference to inventories of the great houses of the period. At Hardwick Hall, indeed, it is still possible to see many of the textiles in their original setting. But it must not be imagined that the new comfort and luxury were restricted to the uppermost social levels. In a well-known passage of his *Description of England* (1577), William Harrison testifies to the revolution which had taken place in the living conditions of the middle and lower classes within the space of a generation, so that 'even ... the inferiour artificers and manie farmers ... have for the most part learned also to garnish their cupboards with plate, their ioined beds with tapistrie and silke hangings, and their tables with carpets and fine naperie.'

Bibliography. The following are some of the more important published inventories for the study of textiles in the Tudor period: Dame Agnes Hungerford (1524) in *Archaeologia*, XXXVIII, 1859, 323 ff. Henry Fitzroy, Duke of Richmond (1528) and Queen Katherine of Aragon (1536), both in *Camden Miscellany*, III, 1854; Scottish royal property (1539, 1542, 1561-4, 1578) in T.Thomson, *A Collection of Inventories and Other Records*, Edinburgh, 1815; Robert Dudley, Earl of Leicester (1588), contents of the London house in *Archaeologia*, LXXIII, 1923, 28 ff., and of Kenilworth Castle in J. O. Halliwell, *Ancient Inventories*, London, 1854; Sir John Petre (1600), partially published as *Ingatestone Hall in 1600*, Essex Record Office Publication No. 22, 1954. The inventory of Hardwick Hall taken in 1601, particularly important since many of the objects are still *in situ*, is as yet unpublished.

Woven Stuffs

As the leading European producer of wool, and a considerable producer of flax, England was in a favourable position to support a weaving industry. And indeed English weaving, financed and organized by great cloth-magnates, did flourish exceedingly in Tudor times. Cloth of many types and qualities was made in a large number of weaving centres – in East Anglia, Yorkshire, the West of England and elsewhere – in quantities sufficient to supply not only most domestic needs but also to leave a huge surplus for export overseas. English kerseys and broadcloths were exported throughout Europe, and even beyond. They formed a major item in the Hanseatic trade to the Baltic ports and in the Venetian trade to the Near East. Nevertheless, despite the fine quality of many of their products, the English weavers seem to have been relatively uninventive, and slow to develop the higher skills of their craft. The very varied 'new draperies', which became fashionable in the Elizabethan period thanks to their novel and superior finish, were largely the work of Flemish immigrant weavers in East Anglia. Even these were cloths of rather simple character, and throughout the Tudor period most of the more elaborate types of patterned woollens and linens were imported from the Netherlands, while the majority of silks came from the Italian centres of silk-weaving, of which the chief were Florence, Venice, Milan and Genoa.

The sheen and richness of silk fabrics were appreciated for themselves and many of these imports from Italy were plain unpatterned stuffs – taffetas, sarcenets, satins and velvets. These, like the humbler English woollens and linens, were often enriched, both for dress and furnishings, with embroidery, with gold and silver braid and with spangles. Alternatively – and this was fashionable particularly for costume – they might be pinked or slashed, mutilations by which the rich displayed their aristocratic contempt for the sumptuous materials on which they squandered a considerable part of their fortunes. For these silk stuffs were by no means inexpensive. Henry VII, for example, paid about 14s. a yard for black satin, 26s. 8d. for crimson, £3 6s. 8d. for ordinary cloth of gold and £6 2s. a yard for richer varieties – figures which must be multiplied at least thirty-fold to obtain approximate modern equivalents.

Still higher prices were attained by some of the many varieties of patterned Italian silks which were also in use for costume and furnishing. Of these the main types were the silk damasks, with designs in a single colour, the brocades and brocatelles with designs in two or more colours, often enriched with gold, and the patterned velvets. The last-named attained in the fifteenth and sixteenth centuries a technical perfection which has never been surpassed. With remarkable ingenuity the weavers contrived in them a richness of relief rare in textile art. The background of the patterns is often of gold; above it rises the sumptuous silk pile, woven in two or three levels to render the details of the design, and above this again rise groups of gold loops which provide the final accents. Such velvets, combining fine materials, masterly technique and superb design, were indispensable accessories of Renaissance luxury and pride.

The designs of these Italian silks and velvets were, for the most part, variants of a relatively small number of types. In the early part of the period the most popular of these were based on large lobed leaves of ogival form in association with conventional flower-sprays. As the sixteenth century advanced such patterns tended to become more rigidly organized, often assuming the form of a curvilinear trellis, but towards the end of the period this discipline was relaxed and materials with a loose powdering of naturalistic plant-forms came into favour. At the same time the strongly massed reds, golds, and rich blues and greens tended to lose ground to more broken colour or softer, more muted tones, such as mauves, pale blues and greens, fawns and browns. Such trends, however, must not be exaggerated; it is possible to find textiles of every imaginable hue in Tudor inventories.

The patterned linen and woollen cloths which were imported into England from northern Europe were strongly influenced by the designs of the Italian silks, and in many cases were simply reproductions of them in another material. But a certain number of the fine white linen damask tablecloths and napkins woven in the Netherlands are of particular interest, since the English coats-of-arms and other devices which appear on them indicate that they were woven specifically for the English market. A napkin of about 1500 in the Victoria and Albert Museum shows the royal arms with supporters, while small hunting scenes appear in the borders. Another design, of which examples exist in a number of museums and private collections, dates from the second half of the sixteenth century and includes the royal arms, St George overcoming the dragon, the falcon device of Anne Boleyn and a half-length portrait of Queen Elizabeth.

Bibliography. Fanny Podreider, *Storia dei tessuti d'arte in Italia*, Bergamo, 1928.

Tapestry

Throughout the Tudor period vast numbers of woollen tapestries, the more expensive of them enriched with details in silk and gold, were imported from the Netherlands, where the chief centres of the manufacture were Brussels, Antwerp and Oudenarde. The warmth and comfort of these thick woollen fabrics were almost indispensable in inadequately heated Tudor houses, and they were used not only as wall-hangings but also as hangings and coverlets for beds, as covers for tables, court-cupboards and benches, and for cushions. Even quite humble households would possess a few pieces, while the furnishings of a great house might include many dozens. The inventory of King Henry VIII enumerates more than two thousand tapestry wall-hangings, of which a small but important remnant may still be seen at Hampton Court.

The tapestry process, unlike most other weaving techniques, which produce repeating patterns, is by its nature adapted to pictorial representation, and the world of images which it created in the Tudor home was no insignificant factor in the imaginative life of the period. Some of the most popular designs were those known under the generic title of 'verdures'. They comprised all kinds of tapestry in which leaves and flowers, often represented with remarkable naturalism, were the major elements of the design; birds and beasts might lurk amongst the foliage, and heraldic shields and other devices were often introduced. A related class of design, likewise extremely common, was that of landscape tapestries, the 'park work' or 'forest work' of the inventories, which were frequently enlivened with scenes of hunting and other country pursuits. Thus the Tudor family could surround itself, even within doors, with the sights, pleasures and pastimes of the countryside.

Large numbers of hangings with figure subjects were also imported from the Netherlands. The sets of Brussels tapestries with elaborate theological or allegorical programmes, such as the 'Triumphs of Petrarch' or the 'Seven Deadly Sins', which were popular in the early part of the period, fell from favour as the sixteenth century advanced. But Scriptural subjects, especially sets relating the histories of Old Testament characters – Joshua, Jacob, David, Solomon, Esther and Judith were among the most usual – continued in use throughout the period. Subjects from classical myth and history – the stories of Jupiter, Vulcan and Venus, Hercules, Paris and Helen, and Julius Cæsar among others – had long been favoured, and tended to become more and more numerous. It is perhaps worth noting that there are also many tapestries of this period whose subjects are not readily identifiable, and it is clear from the inventories that they not infrequently remained unsolved riddles even for their original owners.

In the course of the Tudor period these Netherlandish figure tapestries underwent a fundamental change of style. The late Gothic tapestries of the late fifteenth and early sixteenth centuries are packed from top to bottom with elongated figures; the element of surface ornament is strong and there is a minimum of plasticity and pictorial recession. This older manner did not long survive the arrival in Brussels in 1516 of Raphael's cartoons for the tapestries of the Sistine Chapel. On the basis of Raphael's figure style, Barent van Orley and his successors evolved a new tapestry style in which linear and surface values were combined with more plastic and monumental figures and with a considerable degree of pictorial depth. They also incorporated much of the Italian repertory of classical and grotesque ornament. There can be no doubt that the massive importation into England

of tapestries in this Netherlandish Renaissance manner profoundly affected English pictorial style and taste.

A few sixteenth-century tapestries bear heraldic evidence of having been woven expressly for English patrons. These include tapestries with the arms of the King and of Cardinal Wolsey (Hampton Court), a hanging with the royal arms on a floral ground (Belvoir Castle), a table-cover with the Luttrell arms (Glasgow, Burrell Collection) and another with the Lewkenor arms (Chawton Manor), a set of verdure hangings with the arms of Robert Dudley, Earl of Leicester (Glasgow, Burrell Collection) (Pl. 53), a cushion with the arms of Lord Burghley and a landscape background (Hatfield House), and a hanging with a grotesque design and the arms of William Herbert, Earl of Pembroke (Victoria and Albert Museum). These tapestries, in a variety of styles, are more or less closely related to contemporary Netherlandish work. Some may conceivably have been made by immigrant tapestry-weavers who fled from religious persecution in the Low Countries to settle in the eastern counties of England; they are known to have settled, among other places, at Sandwich, Canterbury, Norwich and York. The balance of probability, however, is that most of these tapestries were woven to order in the Netherlands.

In addition to the refugees from abroad, we know the names of a considerable number of arras-workers (as the tapestry-weavers were called) of English nationality, who were active during the Tudor period. But the products of these craftsmen, who probably concentrated mainly on repair work or on small objects such as cushion-covers, remain obscure. The only English tapestry manufactory to which a body of work may confidently be attributed is that founded by William Sheldon on his estates at Barcheston (Warwicks) and Bordesley (Worcs) shortly after 1560. The works of these establishments are generally known, in commemoration of their founder, as Sheldon tapestries (Pls. 54, 55).

William Sheldon's enterprise, as we learn from his will, was a deliberate attempt to introduce a new industry which would provide employment for Englishmen and at the same time stem the tide of English wealth which flowed into foreign hands in exchange for imported hangings. He himself died in 1570, but the weaving establishments continued to be fostered by his son, Ralph Sheldon, who died in 1613. The weaving was directed by Richard Hyckes, who is referred to in the elder Sheldon's will as 'the only author and beginner of this Art within this Realm'; according to the seventeenth-century Oxford antiquary Anthony Wood, he had learned the craft under a Dutch weaver in Holland. His son, Francis Hyckes, was likewise a skilled weaver; in addition to their commitments with Sheldon, the two men were successively head of the royal arras-workers 1584–8 and 1588–1603. Richard Hyckes lived until 1621 and Francis Hyckes until 1630, but there is at present no evidence that the weaving continued after Ralph Sheldon's death.

The best-authenticated work of the Sheldon looms is a set of county maps woven as wall hangings, which are known both in the fragments of the sixteenth-century originals (mostly in the possession of the Bodleian Library, Oxford) and in copies of the middle of the seventeenth century (belonging to the York Philosophical Society). On them appear the names of Richard and Francis Hyckes, the arms of Ralph Sheldon and the date 1588. There can be little doubt that the original set was commissioned by Ralph Sheldon for the new house which he built at Weston in that year. The maps, which are based on those of Christopher Saxton, include one of Worcestershire, one of Warwickshire, one of Gloucestershire and one of Oxfordshire and Berkshire. In their minute pictorial renderings of town and village, park and woodland, they reflect the authentic charm of the Shakespearian countryside.

A series of hangings and cushions, formerly at Chastleton House, near Barcheston, and now dispersed among various collections, bears the date 1595 and the initials of various members of the Jones family, who are known to have been close friends of the Sheldons. The presumption is strong that these tapestries also are of Sheldon weaving. The figure subjects, from Ovid (one hanging) and from the story of Judah (four hangings), are confined to a small cartouche in the centre of the tapestries, while the remainder of the field is occupied by flowers. A similar arrangement, with figures symbolizing the Virtues in small medallions on a floral background, occurs in two tapestries at Sudeley Castle. The impression arises that the weavers, though well able to deal with floral subjects, lacked confidence in their ability to render the human figure; even on the small scale to which they voluntarily restrict themselves, the figure-drawing is notably unconvincing.

Only in one set of tapestries, attributed on stylistic grounds to Sheldon looms, do large-scale figures appear. These are the four 'Seasons' at Hatfield, which bear the arms of Sir John Tracy of Toddington in Gloucestershire and the date 1611. The designs, adapted from engravings by Martin de Vos, though clumsy in drawing and overloaded with accumulations of flowers, fruit and animals, possess a good deal of quaint charm. In the borders, a large number of small medallions contain emblematic designs, of which a number are derived from Geoffrey Whitney's *Choice of Emblems*.

Large wall-hangings, however, were probably relatively rare in the Sheldon output, and it is likely that the weavers worked for the most part on small looms. Some minor pieces, such as book-covers and glove-gauntlets, are perhaps of their weaving, while a considerable number of cushion-covers show convincing stylistic analogies with details of the large tapestries. These cushions, in the standard sizes of Elizabethan and Jacobean square and long cushions (19 × 19 in. and 19 × 38 in.), generally have scenes (e.g. the story of Susanna and the Elders) or single figures (e.g. Virtues) beneath arcades, surrounded by borders with fruit, flowers and little hunting scenes. Though æsthetically undistinguished, they are furnishings of an attractive and homely type, delightful in colour and in their rendering of plants and landscape.

Notwithstanding the typically English appeal of its work, it must be admitted that Sheldon's manufactory, though the only one in the country whose activity can be identified, was of local rather than of national importance. Most of its more important commissions seem to have come from local squires, and the remainder of its production suggests that its status approximated to that of a cottage industry. It is significant that the official commission for a set of ten tapestries illustrating the defeat of the Spanish Armada (the tapestries were destroyed in the burning of the Houses of Parliament in 1834, but the designs are recorded by the engravings of John Pine's *The Tapestry Hangings of the House of Lords*, 1739) was given not to Sheldon's or to any other English factory, but to the Delft workshop of François Spierincx. Thus Sheldon's brave enterprise failed in its primary endeavour to stem the flood of imported tapestries. As was discovered both in England and in France during the seventeenth century, only factories supported by royal subventions on a lavish scale could compete with the inherited skills and organization of the tapestry-weavers of the Netherlands.

Bibliography. W. G. Thomson, *A History of Tapestry*, London, 1930; W. G. Thomson, *Tapestry Weaving in England*, London, 1914; E. A. B. Barnard and A. J. B. Wace, *The Sheldon Tapestry Weavers and their Work*, in *Archaeologia*, LXXVIII, 1928, 255 ff.

Painted and printed cloths

Cloths with painted designs were used as cheap substitutes for wall-hangings of tapestry or embroidery. William Harrison writes: 'The walls of our houses on the inner side be either hanged with tapisterie, arras worke, or painted cloths, wherein either diverse histories, or hearbes, beasts, knots and such like are stained.' There are frequent references to them in Elizabethan literature, and the triteness of the moral saws with which they were inscribed was evidently proverbial. Common enough to serve as decoration for the walls of alehouses, they were used also, as may be seen from the inventories, in the mansions of the rich, but there they seem generally to have been relegated, at least in the later years of the sixteenth century, to the less important chambers and to the servants' quarters.

Being common, relatively cheap and no doubt often crude in workmanship, they were little valued, and only a very few specimens have survived. The most imposing of these is the set of hangings with subjects from the Acts of the Apostles at Hardwick Hall, which are frank imitations of tapestries in another medium. The composition of the figure scenes is congested and ungraceful; the floral borders include the large ES monogram, surmounted by a coronet, of Elizabeth, Countess of Shrewsbury. Two other English painted hangings, one of Susanna and the Elders, the other of Esther and Ahasuerus, with the personages dressed in the height of Elizabethan fashion, are in a Norwegian collection. Other subjects recorded in contemporary sources are the Nine Worthies, the Rape of Lucrece and the Prodigal Son.

The nature of the distinction between the 'stained cloths', which were common in the Middle Ages and down to the reign of Henry VIII, and the 'painted cloths', which seem to replace them in inventories thereafter, has never been satisfactorily explained. They certainly did not differ in function or subject-matter, and both types were evidently painted in the present sense of the word; according to one theory, the former were painted in distemper or water-colours, the latter in oil-colours.

Probably a good many workshops, up and down the country, were capable of producing these more or less rough paintings on canvas; 'stainers' are recorded, for example, in London, Norwich and Ipswich in the sixteenth century. But by the end of the Tudor period foreign competition and the decline in popularity of painted hangings had brought the craft almost to extinction. In 1601 it was said that 'Painting of Cloths is decayed, and not an hundred yards of new Painted Cloth made in a year here, by reason of so much Painted Flanders pieces brought from thence'.

In the 1581 charter of the Painter-Stainers Company of London we read also of other types of cloth prepared 'with patterns, print, stencil or otherwise'. This reference is perhaps to be brought into connexion with certain linen cloths, printed in black from woodblocks or engraved plates, with plants, animals and scrolls (Harrison's 'hearbes, beasts, knots and such like'). These designs are very close to those of contemporary English embroidery, and some of them, at least, may have been made as patterns for the embroideress; one or

Fig. 1. Design for embroidery by Thomas Trevelyon, beginning of the seventeenth century. *From a MS book, early seventeenth century, in the Folger Shakespeare Library, Washington, U.S.A.*

two specimens exist in which the printed outlines have been worked over with the needle.

Bibliography. Oliver Baker, *In Shakespeare's Warwickshire*, London, 1937, pp. 127 ff.

Embroidery

Embroidery is the one textile art at which the English have excelled at almost all periods of their history, and in this respect the Tudor age was by no means the least distinguished. Tudor embroidery did not perhaps enjoy the same international repute as the great ecclesiastical needlework, *opus anglicanum* or 'English work', as it was called, of the late thirteenth and early fourteenth centuries, but there can be no doubt that, particularly during the reign of Queen Elizabeth, it compared very favourably with the best work produced abroad, while at the same time evolving a fresh, original and peculiarly English style.

The professional embroiderers of the early part of the Tudor period were the heirs of a long and still vigorous tradition. Their surviving work, however, cannot be said to be especially distinguished in quality. The seraphim, the fleurs-de-lis, the thistles and other motifs with which they powdered the velvet surface of copes and chasubles, the saints standing beneath arcades which they strung together as orphreys, are too clearly mass-produced by the quickest and most economical methods to give much pleasure to a critical eye. Nevertheless, the general level of competence remained high, and even the relative coarseness of the work when compared with the exquisitely minute needle-paintings of an earlier era is not without its justification, since these later vestments still make a magnificent decorative impression from the distance at which, in church, they are normally seen. From the numbers of them which survive, both in England and abroad, it is clear that their qualities were generally appreciated and they were the object of a considerable export trade.

Some rather finer work is found on the early Tudor funeral-palls, of which a number are still in the hands of the City companies for which they were made. They consist normally of a panel of the richest type of Italian velvet, from which em-broidered velvet borders hang down on all four sides. A particularly fine example is the pall of the Confraternity of St John the Baptist, sometimes known as the Fayrey pall, which belongs to Dunstable parish church. The embroidered borders, showing St John the Baptist preaching to members of the confraternity, date from about 1525 and are finely executed in coloured silks stitched over parallel lines of gold thread.

The Reformation marks the watershed in the history of English needlework. The late medieval traditions of embroidery came to an abrupt end, and were replaced by new styles, new techniques and new conditions of work. Vestments no longer required embroidered imagery, and the professional workshops were forced either to disperse or to turn their hands to costume embroidery or other secular work in the Renaissance taste. Their activities were further circumscribed by the fact that for much of the embroidered costume and furnishings which the new luxury and comfort of the time demanded, many households became self-supporting. In the great houses a resident professional embroiderer might be employed to design, organize and add finishing touches, but the bulk of the actual work was carried out by the mistress of the house and her relatives and servants. Thus the embroideries at Hardwick Hall are a monument to the skill and industry of Elizabeth, Countess of Shrewsbury, of her ladies and of her illustrious captive, Mary, Queen of Scots. Ladies of humbler station could take their designs from some of the numerous embroidery pattern-books published on the Continent and in England, or they might have recourse to the services of a professional pattern-drawer such as Thomas Trevelyon, whose manuscript book of embroidery designs, compiled shortly after 1600, is now in the Folger Shakespeare Library, Washington. The work of these amateur needlewomen is remarkable for its technical skill and high quality; indeed, it is impossible, in the Elizabethan period, to distinguish the work of the amateur from that of the professional.

One of the first types of Renaissance ornament to become popular in English embroidery was the internationally fashionable arabesque style. This makes its appearance in the Court portraits of Holbein in the 1530's, and formed the subject of the first English embroidery pattern-book, *Morysshe and Damashin renewed and encreased very profitable for Goldsmiths and Embroiderars* (i.e. Moorish and Damascene patterns, etc.), by Thomas Geminus, published in 1548 (Fig. 2). One of the very rare surviving examples of this style is a bed-valance in the collection of Sir William Burrell; the design, executed in black velvet cut to shape and stitched on to white satin, consists of arabesques interspersed with the letters H and A, for Henry VIII and Anne Boleyn.

This technique, in which the pattern is formed by patches of cloth of one colour applied to cloth of another colour, can be adapted to most types of design. It was popular in continental embroideries of the Renaissance, and was probably in common use for furnishing fabrics in this country, though few specimens have survived. Some fine curtains and valances with formal floral patterns in black velvet, applied to red woollen cloth, come from the castles of Linlithgow and Lochleven and have been associated with Mary, Queen of Scots. The same colour arrangement recurs in a fragment with a vine-stem design, from Berkeley Castle, now in the Victoria and Albert Museum. A more ambitious employment of this technique appears in a set of large wall-hangings at Hardwick Hall. These, executed in cloth of gold and other fabrics on a ground of black velvet, show classical heroines with attendant Virtues standing beneath arcades. In the Hardwick inventory of 1601 they were noted in the 'withdrawing chamber' as 'ffyve peeces of hanginges of cloth of golde velvett and other like stuffe imbroidered with pictures of the vertues, one of Zenobia, magnanimitas and prudentia, another of Arthemitia constantia and pietas, an other of penelope prudentia and sapientia, an other of Cleopatra fortitudo and justitia, an other of Lucrecia Charitas and Liberalitas everie peece being twelve foote deep'. The persistence of this appliqué technique into the early years of the seventeenth century is exemplified by its use in a strapwork design in two colours of velvet on upholstered chairs at Knole.

A different type of applied work embroidery is found in a set of wall-hangings (later converted to bed-hangings) at Oxburgh Hall in Norfolk. To a ground of green velvet have been applied many small panels worked with coloured silks in *gros point* and *petit point*. These panels, some of which are signed with the monogram of Mary, Queen of Scots, and others with that of Elizabeth, Countess of Shrewsbury, show plants, animals, birds and fish, taken from the woodcuts of contemporary books of natural history, principally from Conrad Gesner's *Historia Animalium*. In the centre of each hanging a larger panel contains some personal emblem of one of the two ladies; one, for example, has a hand pruning a vine and the motto VIRESCIT VVLNERE VIRTVS (Virtue is strengthened by a wound), a favourite emblem of Mary, Queen of Scots. One of the panels is dated 1570, and it may well have been of these very embroideries that Mary spoke in 1569, saying that all day she 'wrought with hir Nydill, and that the Diversitie of the Colors made the work seem less tedious' (Pl. 57).

Many another lady of the period, besides the unfortunate Queen, found diversion in inventing colour schemes for the animals and plants whose outlines the designers had sketched in ink on the embroidery canvas. It appears from the inventories that small motifs of this type were worked in great numbers and stored until required. When the time came, they were cut out from the canvas, usually following the contours of the embroidered forms, and applied to plain silk, velvet or woollen cloth, for use as hangings, cushion-covers or upholstery. Heterogeneous motifs are juxtaposed at random, insects may be as large as horses, and the total effect, if unsophisticated, is very gay and charming. There are good examples of this class of work at Hatfield, Hardwick, the Victoria and Albert Museum and in various other collections.

These motifs for applied work are invariably worked in silk on loosely woven linen canvas in the so-called canvas stitches, cross stitch and tent stitch, or, as they are generally known, *gros point* and *petit point*. This technique, which combines rich and even pictorial effects with simple and rapid methods of work, had rarely been used in the Middle Ages, but it was characteristic of post-

Renaissance secular embroidery all over Europe. In England it was used not only for the small pieces already mentioned, but also for work on the largest scale, so extensive in some cases that the intervention of professional hands seems almost certain. Such is the case with a very large table-cover from Melchbourne Park, now in the Victoria and Albert Museum. This piece, dating from the middle of the sixteenth century, bears the arms of Gifford among small geometrical ornaments inspired by Oriental carpet patterns. It is signed with a number of minute initials, remote in spirit from the self-advertisement of contemporary amateur signatures such as those of Bess of Hardwick, which are frequently several inches high. Two other embroidered table-covers of comparable size, dating from about 1600, are also in the same museum. One of them, likewise from Melchbourne Park, shows the arms of St John of Bletso among vine-scrolls. The other, from the collection of the Earl of Bradford, has a vine-trellis in the central panel, while the border is filled with charming scenes of country life.

The same technique, and designs of similar character, were used also for cushion-covers. An example of about 1550, wonderfully fresh in colour, with green vine-scrolls on a scarlet ground and the arms of Sandys of the Vyne, is in the collection of Mr Barker-Mill (Pl. 60A). Another, dating from the end of the sixteenth century, with the arms of Queen Elizabeth, belongs to Lord Hastings.

Another group of embroideries, also worked in canvas stitches on an impressive scale, comprises wall-hangings and bed-valances with elaborate mythological and scriptural subjects, in which the characters appear tricked out in the most extravagant forms of late sixteenth-century fashion. While a number of these pieces come from English houses, their origin remains in some doubt, and it cannot be said that they show entirely convincing analogies with authenticated types of English embroidery. Many examples also exist in Scotland and in France, and it is not impossible that this group represents the professional work of some continental centre.

Perhaps the most typical class of Elizabethan embroidery, though in fact its vogue continued well into the Stuart period, is that in which the design consists of endless running scrolls, containing within their convolutions a host of flowers and fruits, sometimes conventionally rendered, sometimes exquisitely naturalistic. An early form of this kind of pattern is seen on the embroidered cuffs of Catherine Howard, painted by Holbein in 1540, and it long continued to be popular for certain types of costume, particularly for the coifs, the undress jackets and the detachable sleeves of the ladies, and for the so-called nightcaps (really informal day-caps) of the men. For furnishing purposes it found its principal use in ornamental pillow-covers (the 'pillow beres' of the inventories) and in certain long covers, about eight feet long and three feet wide, which were perhaps associated with the pillow-covers in some way which is as yet unexplained. Both the costume and furnishing pieces in this style were almost invariably executed on fine white linen. The popular variety known as blackwork, often worn by Queen Elizabeth in her portraits, had the pattern worked entirely in black silk. This is well exemplified by a set of two pillow-covers and one long cover, acquired by the Victoria and Albert Museum from the collection of Lord Falkland; the pattern of vine-scrolls, with its leaves covered with ingenious filling-patterns, is a model for students of fine embroidery. Another variety of this scroll-pattern embroidery achieves effects of sober magnificence with a combination of black silk and gold thread. A third and more lively type has the scrolls in gold and the flowers in polychrome silks. A fine early specimen of this last group is a cushion-cover at Petworth (Pl. 58B), which, from the heraldry, appears to have been made either for Ambrose Dudley, Earl of Warwick (d. 1589), or for Robert Dudley, Earl of Leicester (d. 1588). Other good examples are in the collections of Sir John Carew-Pole and Lady Richmond, as well as in various museums.

This flower-scroll embroidery is without parallel abroad, and it may be said, indeed, that nearly all English secular embroidery of the sixteenth century, with its predilection for familiar plant and animal forms, for scenes of hunting and other country pursuits, was a highly characteristic and vivid expression of the native genius.

Bibliography. M. Jourdain, *English Secular Embroidery*, London, 1910; A. F. Kendrick, *English Needlework*, London, 1933; Victoria and Albert Museum, *Catalogue of English Domestic Embroidery of the Sixteenth and Seventeenth Centuries*, London, 1950.

Carpets

It was during the Tudor period that the Oriental carpet became a familiar adjunct of English domestic life. Recent discoveries have proved beyond doubt that carpet-knotting was practised in the East long before the birth of Christ, and though there is no direct evidence, it is not unreasonable to assume that a few specimens of such fabrics must have found their way to these remote northern islands in the course of the Middle Ages by way of trade, gift or crusader loot. But it was certainly not until the sixteenth century that carpets began to be commonly seen in great English houses.

Even then, the older English fashions in floor-coverings died hard. As late as 1598, the German traveller Hentzner noted that Queen Elizabeth's presence-chamber at Greenwich was strewn with hay, and the household accounts of Naworth Castle in Cumberland suggest that the change from strewn rushes to plaited rush mats was not made there until the 1620's. Naworth, however, was evidently behind the times. The first secure evidence for the presence of Oriental rugs in England dates from over a century earlier and is connected, characteristically enough, with Cardinal Wolsey. It appears from Venetian diplomatic correspondence that, as a price for showing favour to certain Venetian requests on matters of trade, particularly relating to the repeal of the duty on Candian wine, Wolsey demanded large gifts of carpets. Accordingly, in 1518, the Venetian merchants in London presented him with seven very handsome Damascene carpets, and a further consignment of sixty, the gift of the Signoria of Venice, was accepted with evident signs of satisfaction in 1520.

In the latter part of the reign of Henry VIII the evidence for the use of carpets begins to multiply in both paintings and inventories. The latter, however, must be interpreted with care, since the word carpet was not by any means confined to carpets of the Oriental knotted type, but was applied indifferently to any substantial fabric, knotted, woven or embroidered, whether laid on the floor or used as a covering for a table or a court-cupboard. If a knotted fabric is meant, the word Turkey was generally added ('a turkie carpet', 'a quition of turkie work'), not implying necessarily that the object was of Turkish origin, but that it was made in the manner of a Turkish carpet. It is nevertheless true, as may be seen from the carpets which are depicted lying on floors and tables in portraits of the period, that the great majority of knotted carpets in use in England in the sixteenth century belonged to certain familiar Turkish types, principally to the types known as 'Holbein carpets', from their frequent occurrence in the works of that painter. These have either angular arabesque designs, or else rows of strapwork figures, alternately octagonal and diamond-shaped, rather like the patterns of modern Bokhara rugs; in both varieties the strong Turkish reds are very prominent.

Inventories make it clear, however, that some of the carpets were of English manufacture. The inventory of the property of the Earl of Leicester at Kenilworth Castle in 1588, for example, includes the item 'A Turquoy carpett of Norwiche work', while that of Bridget, Countess of Bedford, in 1602 mentions 'one Turkey Carpet of Englishe makinge' and 'two Wyndowe Turkey Carpettes of my owne makinge thone of them being wrought with Roses and Marygouldes'. These entries seem to imply that the knotting of carpets was carried on both as an organized manufacture and, for smaller pieces, as a domestic craft, in Elizabethan England. A fine, long, knotted carpet, dated 1570, in the collection of the Earl of Verulam at Gorhambury, is undoubtedly an example of this English work. It displays three coats-of-arms – those of Queen Elizabeth, of the Borough of Ipswich and of the Harbottle family – surrounded by a somewhat angular floral diaper pattern; the border has a typically English naturalistic honeysuckle trail. An important group of four carpets in the possession of the Duke of Buccleuch at Boughton House, of which three have the arms of Sir Edward Montagu in the borders and two have dates, 1584 and 1585, were long considered to have been woven to order in Turkey. Their designs are, indeed, almost exact reproductions of those of Turkish Ushak and 'Holbein carpets', but their peculiarities of colouring and technique, together with the presence of inconspicuous initials – presumably those of the weavers – worked into the carpets, leave no doubt of their English origin. A carpet in the Victoria and Albert Museum, with a design rather freely adapted from one of the Holbein type, is likewise completely un-Turkish in colouring; woven into it are the arms of Sir Edward Apsley (knighted in 1603) and the inscription 'FEARE. GOD. AND. KEEPE. HIS. COMMANDEMENTS. MADE. IN. THE. YEARE. 1603.'

Apart from the larger carpets, the inventories are full of references to the use of knotted-pile fabrics on cushions and upholstered furniture. 'A quition of turkie worke ... a chare of turkie worke ... a stoole of turkie worke' are entries which appear repeatedly, for instance, in the Hardwick inventory of 1601. Most, if not all, of these were probably of English manufacture, and probably many, like the Countess of Bedford's window-carpet with roses and marigolds, were home-made in the floral style of contemporary embroidery. A number of examples survive of turkey-work cushion-covers and upholstered furniture with floral motifs, but they are attributable rather to the early Stuart than to the Tudor period. One piece in the Victoria and Albert Museum, however, which was perhaps a long cushion-cover, bears the royal arms and the date 1600 (Pl. 60B).

Bibliography. C. E. C. Tattershall, *A History of British Carpets*, Benfleet, 1934.

Fig. 2. Engraved arabesque designs by Thomas Geminus, 1540–50. *Victoria and Albert Museum.*

Costume

C. WILLETT CUNNINGTON

Fashions in costume reflect changes in popular taste. Spread over an epoch we have, as it were, a theme and variations, the theme representing the general spirit of the times, the variations expressing the passing moods. Sometimes the basic formula of the predecessors is accepted and fresh variations on it are composed by the new generation; sometimes a profound change of outlook dictates an original theme. The sixteenth century was such a moment: Europe was in a turmoil and the medieval attitude of mind was disintegrating.

A generation clothed in new ideas assumed a new shape and their costume, abandoning the slender Gothic line, expressed a broadening outlook, heavy and emphatic. England, whose population of four millions had at last replaced the losses caused by the Black Death, was emerging from the frittering waste of civil war; its people, governed by a strong hand, valued the new stability.

The social structure had undergone a radical change. At the top the 'Court circle', whence fashions arose, was new. The old nobility, decimated in the Wars of the Roses, was being replaced by newcomers, often of middle-class origin, who elbowed their way to the front, aided by a lavish display of wealth. The monarch's own position depended largely on popularity; no Tudor sovereign could risk being insignificant; it was essential to demonstrate power by impressive pageantry. Fashions emanating from such a source would be likely to have certain characteristics. There would be a good deal of borrowing from better established Court circles abroad, and there would be a swaggering note about the male modes. We should not expect suave elegance or subtle undertones, and so it was. Tudor costume was nothing if not blatant.

We must recollect of course that outside the fashionable circle, which after all was numerically small, was the substantial middle class, comprising the merchant in the town, the country squire and the yeoman farmer, most of whom were concerned in one way or another in England's staple industry, wool. That group was aware of the fashions of the time, though perhaps not those of the day: and beneath them were the manual labourers in town and country, dressed often in traditional garments indicative of their respective occupations.

As a fashion spread from the centre in widening circles there was a vast time-lag: the country squire and his wife might be clinging to styles of dress dating back to their youth. The fashion-ripple finally ceased to be perceptible at the level where it interfered with practical needs: the Elizabethan yokel must often have seen the gentry wearing ruffs, yet it would not have occurred to him to do likewise.

A feature of Tudor costume was its well-defined class distinction. When Thomas Lupset (*temp.* Henry VIII) wrote 'Now you see there is almost no man content to wear cloth here made in our own country, neither linen nor woollen; but every man will wear such as is made beyond the sea', referring to silks and cottons, he was speaking of the fashionable folk only. Such strictures did not apply even to the more prosperous middle class. Similarly the much-quoted comments from Philip

Stubbes, Harrison and Nashe, who were lashing the follies of fops.

Fops have their uses: they caricature the modes of their day and draw our attention to the salient features, but they are never typical portraits.

What then did the 'typical' Tudor man and woman look like? There are portraits, most of those surviving belonging mainly to persons of rank, whose faces we scrutinise to read, if we can, the essential Tudor character. We glimpse in the male face a cold efficiency and merciless mouth; in the woman's a deadly calm, the youthful eye expectant but without tenderness and in the aged an unmelting reserve. We may see a Beatrice or a Lady Macbeth, but no Ophelia or Desdemona.

The successful merchant and his wife are presented in church brasses and effigies wearing sober versions of the fashions of their time. But those solemn effigies are not portraits. We cannot understand the meaning of their costume unless we can picture them as they were, alive, like ourselves choosing to wear what they considered appropriate to their 'point of view'.

For there was a distinctive Tudor 'point of view'. It saw life as a harsh reality, a dangerous adventure, or a grim ordeal. Furnished with lusty appetite and brutal humour, the Tudor mind was wholly lacking an element which we have come to regard as 'the typical English characteristic'. It was markedly unsentimental. (It is significant that girls' names with a soft-sounding last syllable – the so-called 'feminine ending' – were rarer in the Elizabethan period than ever before or since. Parents gave their daughters hard incisive names like Magret, Katrin, Emmot, Sabine, Gartright; and appropriately no Tudor young woman ever wore clothes that were 'dainty' or 'pretty'.) Such were the people of England in the sixteenth century.

In the houses of the wealthy, rooms were becoming larger and better lighted. Harrison in 1577 wrote: 'Now only the clearest glass is esteemed' for windows; white-washed ceilings aided indoor visibility while candles gave fair illumination at night. Consequently coloured fabrics and intricate patterns could be appreciated. It became possible in Elizabethan days to use black as a fashionable colour.

As a feature of class distinction the sixteenth century introduced into the costume of both sexes an unnatural degree of rigidity. In women's portraits especially we see how every joint in the body was constrained and held as in a vice. In this respect the Tudor fashions accepted the European. We also notice a significant change appearing about the middle of the century. During the first half, with England ruled by kings, and in Europe the prominent figures of Francis I and the Emperor, the male fashions seemed to overshadow the female. During the second half of the century, with England ruled by Queens, and nearby the figures of Catherine de Medici and Mary of Scotland, the role was reversed. Feminine modes expanded into an aggressive immensity while men's shrank and became even effeminate. That, at least, is the impression given by portraits of the period. To appreciate their costumes more fully, however, we have to explore other sources of information, such as domestic bills, inventories, and wills. These reveal the extent of the wardrobe, the nature of the materials used and their relative values, for persons of different social classes.

We learn, for example, from wills that garments were not only handed down to the next generation but from one relative to another. Thus in 1522 a merchant left to his brother 'my marieng gowne furrd with blacke lambe, with my best dublet and jaket', and 'to the vicar a gowne of medley tawny unlined'.

Evidently second-hand garments were acceptable gifts. Servants commonly received such items as 'my old russet gown', or 'as much cloth as will make him a syde cotte, a paire of hosse and a dublet'.

Inventories of wardrobe contents expose some significant gaps: nightshirts appear to have been worn only by the higher ranks. For the rest, their inventories suggest that men and women slept in their day shirts or smocks or else were naked in bed.

But all classes wore night-caps, and these are often bequeathed by will: thus, in 1557, 'to my father my beste velvet nighte cappe'. Usually this necessary protection against the dangerous night air was red, Dr Andrew Boorde (1557) advising

'Let your nyghte capp be of scarlet, to be made of a good thycke quylte of cotton', while another recommended 'Let your nighte cappe have a hole in the top through which the vapour may go out'. Humble folk made do with

'A knit night cap of coarsest twine,
With two long labels buttoned to the chin'. (Hall's *Satires*, 1598)

Bills give us prices of materials, and records of the Quarter Sessions often tell of garments stolen from persons of all classes. A *silk* shirt stolen in 1582 (Essex Quarter Sessions) must have been owned by a gentleman of rank. The day shirt, in fact, was one of the most indicative garments of class distinction, and Philip Stubbes in *The Anatomie of Abuses*, 1583, bemoans their extravagance, costing even 'some ten pounds apiece which is horrible to hear'.

A similar wide range of values applied to the woman's smock, from the fine lady's 'cambric smock wrought in black silk and edged with bone lace of Venice gold' – a suitable birthday gift to Queen Elizabeth, down to the countrywife's plain garment of lockeram.

Chance records suggest that the more elaborate – and uncomfortable – garments worn by persons of rank were discarded in the privacy of domestic life. The Tudor gentleman might at such times relax in his waistcoat, without a doublet. The Elizabethan ruff and farthingale could, in homely seclusion, be omitted, but naturally their portraits were not painted with them in such deshabille so that we do not see them except in full finery.

It will be more convenient to consider the fashions of each half century separately.

1500–1550

The male costume presented a markedly top-heavy appearance, with an exaggerated breadth of shoulders. Over the shirt was worn a doublet, close-fitting, quilted within, and shaped to the waist. Its square-cut neckline added to the burly look. At first the doublet was without skirts, but these were always present after 1530. Its sleeves, often detachable, were excessively full. Over the doublet was the jerkin, close-fitting, and knee-

length. Its sleeves were full to the elbow or in the form of 'hanging sleeves'. Over this was the gown, loose ankle length, broad-shouldered, and with a flat collar. Gradually the gown was replaced by the cloak, the former becoming worn only by the learned professions or the elderly.

A loose jacket or 'cassock', sometimes sleeveless, was an occasional garment. The lower half was clothed in the hose, this being breeches and

Fig. 1. c. 1530–40. Jerkin with wide U opening over doublet slashed and puffed. Full skirt hiding upper stocks. The doublet sleeves emerge from the gown sleeves. Bonnet with halo brim. *Drawn from the miniature carving of Henry VIII in the manner of Hans Holbein, owned by Mrs Dent-Brocklehurst.*

stockings in one. The trunk portion was close-fitting and a conspicuous feature was the protruding codpiece. The significance of this, inherited from the previous century and not banned as indecent until towards the end of the Tudor period, ought not to be ignored by the social historian: nor the fact that it seems to have provoked no feminine disgust, which throws light on the Tudor woman's attitude to sex relations. The stocking portion of the hose was known as the nether stocks, and the whole garment was cut on the cross with a seam down the back. The surface garments were decorated with extensive slashing revealing the material beneath.

Shoes, flat-heeled, were square in the toe becoming extraordinarily broad in front, and the surface was slashed. Hats, worn indoors as well as out, were large, low in the crown and decorated with a plume. Bonnets and caps, flat and wide, often with the brim turned up with side flaps, gave the head a massive breadth. One sees bonnets with halo

Fig. 2. c. 1540. Bonnet with halo brim and feather. Sleeveless jerkin with short stand collar, over doublet with full slashed sleeves. *Drawn from the painting Darnley of Lennox, 1567.*

brims and flat caps 'couched fast to the pate like an oyster'. With the bonnet an under-cap or coif of linen was worn.

Early in the century the hair was long to the shoulders, becoming somewhat shorter, and at first the face was clean-shaven. With the shorter hair of the head a beard, moustache, and whiskers became the fashion.

The Tudor man in such a garb was heavily impressive to the eye; and we must assume that its brutal masculinity exercised a dangerous fascination on the Tudor woman.

The woman's costume, in the first half-century, comprised gown and kirtle. The former was voluminous, moulding the figure to a high waist and then expanding over the hips in massive folds trailing on the ground in a long train. Its sleeve expanded at the wrist into a wide opening. A girdle or belt was worn round the waist, and the front borders of the gown were commonly trimmed with velvet. The kirtle, worn under the gown, was a simple frock with a full skirt and fastened down the front. The sleeves, close-fitting, reached the wrist. The square-cut decolletage was edged with lace and the bodice portion of the kirtle fitted the figure. Under the kirtle was the shift emerging at the neck and wrists. In addition a woman might wear a cloak in the form of a full mantle, open in front.

Head-dresses were low and worn over an under-cap. The hood, draped over the head with a curtain hanging behind, had various forms. In the early years of the century the English hood was gable-shaped with a pointed arch above the crown of the head. Later the French hood, much smaller and built on a stiff foundation, was worn far back exposing the front hair. Bonnets with halo brims and worn over a coif were less usual.

The Lettice cap, with side-pieces covering the ears, was popular and ladies of rank wore crespins (hairnets) worked in gold. A feature of the period was the bongrace, a flat piece of velvet worn flat on the head and projecting over the forehead. This, associated with the French bonnet, served to protect the face from the sun.

Hair was mostly concealed, almost entirely by the Gable hood, but much more exposed with the

French bonnet. It was worn smooth and straight with a centre parting. After 1540 it became waved. Long hair flowing loose down the back was worn by brides, young girls and by queens at their coronation. The feet were concealed from view by the gown and shoes resembled in style those of men. The general effect of a woman's costume was suggestive of a static pose; by contrast to the man's she appeared to be a dignified spectator, impressed no doubt by the huge magnificence of the male.

1550–1560

In the second half of the century the appearance of each sex was very different. The feature of the male costume was 'bombast'. This was padding by means of horsehair, flock, wool and the like. 'They shew the swellings of their mind in the swellings and plumping out of their apparel' (Nashe, 1593).

The effect was made the more remarkable by the fact that the male waist was rendered as small as possible by tight-lacing and tight clothing. The doublet, close-fitting with tight waist, was pointed below, the body of the doublet being padded and stiffened by buckram so as to resemble a kind of armour. It now possessed a standing collar and the skirt was shortened to a mere border. Its sleeves, with 'wings' over the shoulder-joints, were either close-fitting or wide ('leg-of-mutton' or 'cannon' shapes) or full to the wrist. The garment was decorated with slashing, pinking or embroidered. Over the doublet was a jerkin or jacket, commonly of leather, having a collar and often sleeveless. The gown, knee- or ankle-length, was now a garment for the elderly or worn indoors as a negligée.

The height of fashion was the cloak, circular in cut and flaring out from the shoulders. The length was variable and sometimes it possessed sleeves. The mandilion was a loose, hip-length jacket with standing collar and hanging sleeves which were often sham. The fashionable mode was to wear it awry or 'Colley-westonwards'. An alternative garment was the cassock, a loose hip-length jacket with full sleeves.

It was the neckwear, however, which caught the eye. At first this was a 'falling band' (turned-

Fig. 3. 1598. Late type of trunk hose with canions and no codpiece. Sleeveless jerkin with wings with a gorget over upper part of the chest. A lovelock hangs on the shoulder. *Drawn from the painting of Henry Wriothesley, 3rd Earl of Southampton, at Welbeck Abbey.*

down collar) of embroidered linen attached to the top of the shirt and turned down over the top of the doublet. By 1560 the frilled edge of the top of the shirt had developed into the ruff. This, starched and goffered, became so large by 1570 that it was thenceforth a separate article. Tied by 'band-strings' under the chin, it expanded to such dimensions that by 1580 it was appropriately known as the 'cartwheel ruff'. By then it needed the support of a wire frame, the ruff itself being made of linen, lawn, lace, etc, stiffened by starch.

(The gentleman has habitually worn round his neck something sufficiently uncomfortable as to make it unlikely that the manual worker will imitate him. But no such symbol of class distinction has equalled the Elizabethan ruff in significance or discomfort.)

The lower half of the body was clad either in 'whole hose' (breeches and stockings in one), in which case the trunk-hose portion was ballooned into the shape of a huge pumpkin, or by being cut across below the level of the hips, into that of a cottage-loaf, with an extension down the upper thighs known as 'canions'. Alternatively the breeches might be separate from the stockings: the breeches being either tight knee-length 'Venetians', or wide and baggy, known as 'slops'.

Shoes had rounded or bluntly pointed toes, and the boots for riding were thigh-length with the tops turned down. Hats and bonnets were worn indoors and at meals, and headgear was low and rather flat up to 1570: thereafter rising in height, 'some pearking up like the shaft of a steeple, standing a quarter of a yard above the crown of their heads', wrote Stubbes in 1583. A favourite was the 'Copotain' hat, the shape of a sugar-loaf. Expensive beaver hats, often worn tilted, decorated the dandy, and inferior imitations in felt sufficed the unfashionables. The hair was closely cropped or brushed up stiffly from the temples and forehead. Exquisites favoured curls all over the head, or with hair reaching to the shoulders and a curl on the forehead. Beards, too, had become fashionable. Of various shapes, they were long and pointed, short and pointed, or spade-shaped: and with the beard, a short or long moustache.

The Elizabethan fop deserves notice as a straw indicating the way of the wind of fashion. He shunned too masculine a shape, cultivating a narrow waist and swelling hips as though his ambition was to resemble a girl in male dress. Bishop Hall in one of his *Bytyng Satyres* (1598) depicted those 'comely striplings' who:

> 'weare curl'd periwigs and chalk their face,
> 'And still are poring on their pocket-glass,
> 'Tyr'd with pinn'd ruffs and fans and partlet strips,
> 'And busks and verdingales about their hips
> 'And gripe their waist within a narrow span....'

Fig. 4. c. 1560. Slashed sleeves, close-fitting to the wrist. Small ruff open at the throat. Gown open in front displaying forepart. *Drawn from the painting of Princess Elizabeth Tudor by Sir Antonio Mor, owned by Lord Milford.*

And a few years later Barnabee Rych was asking: 'Whence cometh this wearing and this imbrodering of long lockes, this curiositie that is used among men in freziling and curling of their hair, this gentlewoman-like starcht bands so be-edged and be-laced, fitter for Mayd Marion than for him that should be a gentleman?' A far cry from the emphatic virility of the early Tudors. The more usual Elizabethan man appears to us to have been mainly concerned to demonstrate his social rank by his costume. But we must also suppose that its fantastic discomfort was effectively captivating; just as the boxed-in young woman of his day suggested a locked casket of delights.

The Elizabethan woman's dress was not only

Fig. 5. c. 1545. The English variety of French hood and jewelled 'billiment'. Bodice with high neck and Medici collar; oversleeves with wide hanging cuffs, the undersleeves with embroidered bands and aiglets. Spanish type of farthingale. *Drawn from the painting of Princess Mary Tudor, owned by Sir Bruce Ingram.*

more conspicuous than the man's but its design was more original: and whenever the art of costume invents something really original (which is seldom) we may take it that the sex wearing it is inspired by some progressive impulse. The woman of the mid-sixteenth century introduced the dress with bodice and skirt as separate garments. There had been a hint of this as early as 1470, when the gown appeared to have been made with a seam at the waist. But once the skirt had detached itself and started a separate career, there was nothing to prevent its indefinite expansion as a symbol of social importance. The invention is highly significant of a change in woman's position.

The bodice (spoken of as a 'body') was rigid and corset-like, stiffened with busks of wood or whalebone, descending to a low pointed waist. Its lower border was often edged with scallops or tabs known as 'pickadils'. The neck was either high with a standing collar open in front or a low square decolletage and a partlet 'fill-in'. The sleeves, up to 1560, were funnel-shaped, and later, close to the wrist, the shoulders being puffed out or covered with 'wings'. From 1580 the front lengthened and was covered with a 'stomacher', a separate piece of stiff material in the shape of an inverted triangle, pinned in place. At the same time the sleeves became 'bombasted' with buckram or whalebone, tapering to the wrist.

The separate skirt was now known as the 'kirtle', and its shape was given it by the farthingale beneath, which was indeed the distinctive feature of the whole costume. The farthingale or underskirt was made of some brightly coloured material (scarlet was usual) distended by hoops of whalebone, wire or cane. The Spanish farthingale (from 1545) was funnel-shaped, domed or bell-shaped, the material gored so as to slope stiffly from the waist to the ground. It might have a front opening filled in by a separate panel ('forepart') and for ceremonial wear a train. From 1560 the new fashion was the French farthingale in the shape of a tub. A padded bolster (known as a ' bum roll') tied round the hips gave the farthingale a slight tilt up at the back.

A still more aggressive shape appeared in 1580 – the 'wheel farthingale', in which the wire or whalebone, covered with material, resembled a horizontally placed wheel round the waist. Over this the skirt was carried outwards for some four feet and then fell vertically to the feet. By 1590 a circular frill of material began to decorate the edge of the top. The whole structure, rigid and unbending, gave the impression of a solid block, as broad as it was high, out of which emerged a portion of a petrified woman.

'Alas poor verdingales must lie in the street,
'To house them no dore in the citie may meet,
'Since at our narrow doores they in cannot win'.
(Heywood, 1599).

In such a costume Queen Elizabeth danced: and Melville observed that Queen Mary of Scotland 'danced not so high'. Over the dress was worn a gown, either loose or fitting the figure, and round the neck a ruff resembling the man's. This, a separate article from 1560, was worn with the high-necked bodice or the high-necked fill-in, being left open at the throat. In 1580 it became the 'cartwheel ruff' (in the opinion of Stubbes, 'cartwheels of the Devil'). This immense structure, worn with either high or low-necked bodices, was shaped and wired to stand up round the back of the head. For the unmarried a fan-shape was correct, and for that reason worn by the Virgin Queen.

Headgear had many forms. There was the 'Mary Stuart' hood, small and curving down into a dip in the centre of the forehead: sometimes the back of the hood was turned up to lie flat on the crown. By 1590 the hood was increasing in size, with huge arched hoods worn out of doors or for mourning. The 'Court' bonnet was flat and small, worn over a jewelled caul, and in fashionable circles a small brimless beret over a hair-net was the mode. Indoors, a linen coif or a reticulated caul was general. Out of doors the hat with a tall crown decorated with a plume was usual. 'English burgher women usually wear high hats covered with velvet or silk' (1599, Platter, *Travels in England*). Another foreign visitor, in 1575, observed that: 'Married women only wear a hat, both in the street and in the house; those unmarried go without a hat'.

Waved in front from a centre parting or turned back over a pad, was the usual hair style. It was nevertheless more impressive to have it raised over a high wired support (a 'palisadoe'). The back hair, plaited or coiled behind, was generally hidden by the head-dress. The lady of fashion employed false hair, wigs and hair dyes, and decorative borders to the front of the built-up coiffure.

Shoes were similar to the men's, but the heel, as we know it, was not introduced until the seventeenth century.

When we examine the records to learn what materials were used in Tudor costumes we discover a singular feature of class distinction. Although wool was the staple industry and English woollen textiles were already famous, the highest ranks refused to wear them for surface garments.

They preferred foreign imports, silks, satins, velvets, lace and lawn. To encourage the wool trade, the Elizabethan Parliament passed a law that all women below the rank of nobility must wear at least one petticoat made of wool. The garment was popularly known as a 'Statute Petticoat'. But as the law omitted to appoint inspectors courageous enough to see that it was obeyed, this unique attempt to legislate on feminine underwear proved a failure.

The prices of imported silks and velvets were often staggering. In the trousseau of Sir William Petre's daughter (1559) we find: '6 yards white satin at 10/8 a yard for a trained kirtle lined with white sarcenet; a crimson satin kirtle lined with crimson sarcenet at 6/- a yard; 10 yards black velvet at 22/4 a yard; a farthingale of red worsted; a gown of damask costing £81, and a riding saddle at £61.13.4' (Essex Record Office, *Petre Accounts*). It would be difficult to translate those prices into their modern equivalents; yet it is sufficient to say that at that time the daily wage of a labourer was fixed at threepence and that of a skilled artisan at fivepence or sixpence. In 1572 a butcher was summoned for paying his man-servant 'great and excessive wages' of two shillings a week, contrary to the Statute (*Essex Quarter Sessions Records*).

It was all very well for Nashe to describe the England of 1593 as 'the player's stage of gorgeous attire, the ape of all nations' superfluities, the continual masquer in outlandish habilments'. But this did not apply as one descended the social scale. The wardrobe of an Exeter merchant in 1589, for instance, comprised 3 gowns, 2 cloaks, 1 coat, 2 doublets, 1 leather jerkin, 2 pair of hose, 2 pair of stockings, 1 hat and 1 cap. The garments were either of wool or leather.

A widow in the same city (1587) possessed 4 cloth gowns, 4 petticoats, 3 hats, 9 aprons (one of taffeta) 26 kerchiefs 'and other trumpery'. The Essex Quarter Sessions Records throw light on what was worn by the smaller tradesman and country-folk, through descriptions of stolen garments. An occasional silk article such as 'a sarcenet tippet worth 20/-' in 1559 was doubtless a goodwife's Sunday best. In 1580 there was stolen 'knytt sleeves being not full finished with the knytting pynnes', showing that by that time knitting was common even in some rural districts.

The superior merchant favoured gowns edged with fur, and in 1570 an Exeter cordwainer possessed two such, together with three cloaks, two doublets, two caps, one pair of hose and a hat. In 1590 we meet 'a pedlar apparelled in a Spanyshe lether jerkynne with large cuttes and a payre of canvas Venetians'. The pedlar, travelling about the country with the latest materials and dress accessories, played an important part in spreading fashion news.

In towns the tailor made the clothes for both men and women, but his skill in cut and fit was still primitive. A bill of 1594 informed the customer: 'for the other gownes your measures were so ill taken that the taylor says he cannot tell what to make of them'. Some light on the habits of the time are revealed in a trial in 1594. A tailor states that the accused came to his house 'about 12 o'clock in the night with certain stuffs to make him a pair of hose and a doublet and would have him to take the measure of him'. The accused then extracted out of his sleeve 'half a pound of bacon, two hens, and a cock which this examinat did suspect that he had stolen'.

The Elizabethan Statutes of Apparel limited the use of silk to the nobility, though the more prosperous middle class certainly employed some silk when they could. As a substitute for velvet there was fustian, a velure of cotton or of flax and wool, and by the end of the century 'the wearing of fustian has lately grown to greater use than ever before', much of it being made in Norwich.

But in spite of legal restrictions there was throughout the Tudor period a persistent encroachment by those who could afford it, on those materials reserved for the nobility. Cotton, imported from India, made calico a luxury; Spanish merino wool came into use in the West of England cloths by the middle of the century, improving their quality. All through the reign of Queen Elizabeth I the English cloth trade expanded, aided by Protestant weavers from abroad, and 'the new draperies' were enjoyed by the middle classes.

As yet the fashionables disdained their use. For them the more lustrous surface of silk was the material of choice which, to be rendered still more conspicuous, was slashed so as to exhibit a different colour beneath. It was the age of elaborate embroidery, sometimes of black silk in all-over patterns (known as 'black work') and bold tree-like designs worked generally upon linen. Lace (in the modern sense of the word) was introduced in the middle of the century.

By such means the costume did not present plain surfaces but exposed glimpses of different layers, each varying in colour. The aim of the fashionable Tudor man or woman was to exhibit a picture in depth, rendered still more conspicuous by its unnatural outline. George Gascoigne's description (1589) is but objective:

'Thy bodies bolstered out,
'With bumbast and with bagges,
'Thy roales, thy ruffs, thy cauls, thy coifes,
'Thy jerkins and thy jagges'.

But what was the essential spirit which inspired that strange disguise? We get a hint perhaps from the comment of Richard Verstegan written at the sunset of Tudor glory: 'When your posterity shall see our pictures they shall think wee were foolishly proud of apparel'.

Portrait Miniatures

GRAHAM REYNOLDS

The art of portrait painting in miniature was developed in Europe during the early sixteenth century and was introduced into England in about the year 1525. It received so immediate a welcome that Holbein, the chief painter of large-scale portraits in England in the next decade, was induced to give some of his time and energies to practising and perfecting this newly invented art: and so sure were the foundations laid by him and his contemporaries that this specialized form of portraiture did not lack for gifted exponents or adequate patronage until the invention of photography in the mid-nineteenth century.

The place of origin of the portrait miniature has been much in dispute; but it has never been claimed to be England. At one time the claims of France, based as they were on the miniatures of the Preux de Marignan painted by Jean Clouet in a manuscript of *c.* 1519, seemed to be well established. But more recently Dr Colding [1] has traced a direct line of succession for the earliest portrait miniatures from the book illuminations of the Ghent–Bruges school: that is, the works of that group of painters of whom the most important are the Master of Mary of Burgundy, Simon Benninck and Gerard Horenbout.

The word miniature is derived from *minium*, or red lead, the pigment in which initials were rubricated in medieval manuscripts: it has no connexion with minuteness, though the fact that most miniatures are in fact not of large compass had led to the current use of the word as synonymous with small. The portrait miniature, or limning – as it was more generally called in the sixteenth and seventeenth centuries – took not only its name but its technique of opaque and transparent watercolour on vellum from the practice of the book illuminators. It may be that these small portraits would never have been emancipated from the bound pages of a book to lead an independent life of their own but for the example of the medieval small portable jewellery with religious motifs for decoration and the intimate portraiture in the round of the Renaissance medal. Certainly the miniature owes its interest, both to its contemporaries and to us, to the quickened insight into human personality fostered by the rebirth of learning. The portrait was no longer a sacred, stylized ikon, a representation of saint or king, with personal idiosyncrasies suppressed in favour of an ideal of divinity or royal power; it was the examination of a man's character as reflected by his external appearance.

To this interest in the individual, common to large- and small-scale portraiture alike at this time, was added the Flemish insistence on naturalism which the illuminators of the Ghent–Bruges school derived from Van Eyck, Memling and Van der Goes, and transmitted to the earliest portrait miniaturists. Dr Otto Pächt [2] has traced the origins of the separate *genres* of still-life and landscape painting to the practice of the Ghent–Bruges

[1] *Aspects of Miniature Painting*, Copenhagen, 1953, Chapter IV.

[2] *The Master of Mary of Burgundy*, London, 1948, pp. 32, 39.

illuminators: in the same way, the portrait miniature may be regarded as a specialization and canalization of one element of their art.

Luke Horenbout

No English portrait miniatures are known as early as those produced by Jean Clouet in 1519 for Francis I. Though it is evident from his style that Clouet was brought up and trained in Flanders, the early details of his career are quite unknown. But a direct link can be established between the earliest English miniaturists and the Ghent–Bruges school; for Gerard Horenbout, himself a leading member of that group, came to England soon after 1520, bringing with him his daughter Susannah and also Luke Horenbout, probably his son. Both Gerard and Luke were in the service of Henry VIII by 1528, the first year for which accounts are available; and it is significant that Luke had the higher salary. Taking this fact in conjunction with the record of Carel van Mander, writing in 1604, that Holbein was taught the art of portraiture in limning by one *Master Lukas* at the Court of Henry VIII, it is fair to deduce that this *Master Lukas* was Luke Horenbout and that he was the King's leading miniature painter at that time. It is true that his supreme position cannot be taken entirely for granted, since his sister Susannah was evidently also a gifted limner. Dürer bought a religious illumination by her in Ghent in 1521 and praised her competence in warm terms in his diary; and Vasari and Guicciardini, writing about 1567, speak of her skill and the favour in which she was held at the English Court. Since, however, no official payments to the sister are recorded and she was not called on to teach Holbein the technique of limning, we may well prefer to regard Luke, the highly salaried Court retainer, as the most prominent limner of the Horenbout family.

Henry VIII, in inviting the Horenbout family to his Court, was evidently continuing his policy of emulating at Whitehall the richness and splendours of the European Courts, and in particular that of his nearest neighbour and rival, Francis I. Francis took into his service, at one time or another, Benvenuto Cellini, Leonardo da Vinci, and Primaticcio; Henry responded by taking Holbein

into his service. Francis employed the Fleming Jean Clouet to paint miniature portraits of himself and his Court; therefore Henry VIII must invite the Horenbouts to do likewise. The part which small portraits – even if they were not necessarily miniatures – already played in the diplomacy of the times is well illustrated by the letter of 1527 in which Henry VIII is informed of the reception by Francis I of the likenesses of himself and the Princess Mary: 'The French King liked them singularly well, and at the first sight of Henry's phisonamye took off his bonnet, saying he knew well that face, and further, "Je prie Dieu qu'il luy done bone vie et longue". He then looked at the Princess's, standing in contemplation and beholding thereof a great while, and gave much commendation and laud unto the same.'

Only recently has there arisen any body of belief in the possibility that any work at all might plausibly be attributed to Luke Horenbout. But once a single miniature has been found which is likely to be by him, others with an equal claim can be grouped with it. The key piece in the case of Horenbout is the portrait of Henry VIII at the age of thirty-five, in 1525 or 1526, set in a surround of censing angels, which is now in the Fitzwilliam Museum, Cambridge (Pl. 69A). To this may be added virtual replicas – two of the King's head in the Royal Collection at Windsor Castle; and probably also another of the King's head in the collection of the Duke of Buccleuch. In one of these Royal miniatures the King is shown bearded; in the other he is beardless; and there are various small differences in the inscriptions. Both the miniatures at Windsor and that in the Buccleuch Collection were in the collection of Charles I, having been given to him by the Earl of Suffolk. To the same hand may plausibly be attributed the portrait of Henry, Duke of Richmond (Henry VIII's illegitimate son), also at Windsor; the portrait of a man said to be Thomas, Earl of Essex, sold from the Sotheby Collection in October, 1955 (Pl. 69c); and the portrait of an unknown man in a private collection (Pl. 69B).

The seven or so miniatures thus grouped together have, beside their underlying unity of style, some external and inessential features in common.

Taking the minor points first: they are on vellum, the natural support for a book illuminator, stiffened by being laid on card;[3] they are all circular, with the exception of the miniature in the Fitzwilliam Museum, in which the portrait of the King is nevertheless itself circular; the background is ultramarine blue; the inscriptions, where they exist, are in gold capitals and with portions written horizontally across the background; and the sitter is posed three-quarters right to give the full articulation of his profile. All these points are of interest if the artist is correctly believed to be the founder of the English school of miniature painting, because their example was to be felt, even if not slavishly followed, well into the seventeenth century.

In point of style the miniatures here grouped together under the attribution to Luke Horenbout agree in being painted with a relatively broad brush and with a well-defined method of rendering the shadows under the eyelids, eyes and nose. Some flatness of presentation, especially about the royal portraits, is noticeable when the miniatures are compared with the works of Holbein. All are pervaded by a certain gravity of outlook and an unforced search for complete truth of representation. Already some hint of the national characteristic of reserve seems to affect the foreign-born artist's style, as it was to influence Holbein himself and, in a later generation, van Somer and Van Dyck.

Apart from the apparent distinction between the style of these miniatures and Holbein's, there is quite other evidence to show that some at least could not be by him; for the age of the sitter given on some of the portraits of Henry VIII shows that they were painted in either 1525 or 1526. Holbein did not enter the King's service nearly so early as this: not, in fact, until about 1532. These portraits of the monarch, sufficiently prized to be repeated for distribution, were no doubt by the King's chief limner, and, for the reasons already cited, Luke Horenbout must be regarded as having occupied this position.

[3] Miniatures by François Clouet are known which are on thick vellum which has not been laid down on card.

The set of miniatures of Henry VIII by Horenbout are of all the more interest because there is no authentic miniature of the King by Holbein himself. Holbein's intense and forbidding image of the King at Whitehall, from which the miniatures attributed to him are usually derived, was painted twelve years later. Horenbout's portrayal is only ten years from the time when the Venetian ambassador could write of Henry: 'His Majesty is the handsomest potentate I ever set eyes on; ... his complexion very fair and bright, with auburn hair combed straight and short in the French fashion, and a round face so very beautiful, that it would become a pretty woman, his throat being rather long and thick.' That Horenbout should have been entrusted in 1533 with the portraiture of the King's illegitimate son, at the time when Henry was bringing him forward for the succession, confirms our impression of his high standing at Court.

Hans Holbein

Hans Holbein took over all the elements of Horenbout's art, refined them, and added to them his inimitable subtlety of vision and finesse of drawing. Where Horenbout's line is coarse, Holbein's is fine; where his shading is broad, Holbein's is modulated by almost imperceptible gradations. As Van Mander put it in 1604: 'in a short time he far excelled Lukas in drawing, arrangement, understanding and execution, as the sun surpasses the moon in brightness'. That is not to decry Horenbout's art; had Holbein not come to England or not painted miniatures his works would have provided an admirable foundation for the school. Indeed, it could be argued that, in spite of all Hilliard's professed self-education through the limnings of Holbein, his style, in its breadth and its flatness, is closer to that of Horenbout. Be that as it may, the difference between Horenbout and Holbein amounts in the end to a difference in quality: the distinction between great talent and genius.

The determination of the exact number of known miniatures authentically Holbein's is necessarily a difficult task. Many inferior or dubious works representing persons of the reign of Henry

VIII have been fathered on to him from the early seventeenth century onwards. With the possible exception of two disputed self-portraits, no miniatures which purport to be by him are signed. The existence of a drawing or painting of the sitter by Holbein is not sufficient to establish the authenticity of a similar miniature, since many of such miniatures are clearly contemporary or later copies by another hand. Only the merit of the miniature itself can proclaim whether it comes above or below the line dividing true from false or an authentic work from a school piece. In the most satisfactory application which has so far been made of this principle, Mr Carl Winter [4] has concluded that between nine and twelve of the miniatures in question may be confidently accepted. Judging by photographs, the miniatures of William and Margaret Roper which have recently been acquired by the Metropolitan Museum, New York, may be added to this short list.

Fortunately the authenticity of the two most accessible to visitors in England could not reasonably be challenged: that is, the portraits of Anne of Cleves and of Mrs Pemberton in the Victoria and Albert Museum. Alike as they are in the supreme mastery of their execution, these miniatures form an interestingly assorted pair. The miniature of Anne of Cleves (Pl. 70B) is the outcome of Holbein's official visit to Düren to take her portrait, so that Henry VIII might decide whether to marry her. His previous journey on a similar mission produced the full-length panel of the Duchess of Milan in the National Gallery. During his actual visit to Düren in 1539, it is believed, Holbein confined himself to making drawings of Anne and her sister Amalia; and he painted subsequently the panel portrait of Anne in the Louvre and the miniature now in London. These remain as a perpetual challenge to the onlooker, to decide for himself whether Holbein flattered the looks of one whom her husband described as a 'Flanders mare', bearing in mind that many once-famous beauties look plain to our eyes in their portraits and that the reverse may

apply: and in fact that in a great portrait it is the character of the sitter rather than his or her degree of beauty which survives the years. Holbein's contemporaries considered the likeness excellent. Dr Wootton wrote to the King: 'Your Grace's servant Hanz Albein hathe taken th'effigies of my lady Anne and the Lady Amalye [who was also being considered as a possible bride for Henry] and hath expressed theyr imagyes very lyvelye'.

The miniature of Mrs Pemberton (Pl. 70A) represents a person in a much more retired station of life; indeed, it is by no means certain that the sitter has been correctly identified as Margaret, wife of Robert Pemberton of Rushden, though the heraldry on the reverse of the frame shows that she is one of the members of that family. This portrait is pervaded by a poise and an intensity of vision which cause it to stand unsurpassed even by Cooper's work in the later course of English limning. As Mr Winter says: [5] 'It is incontestably the greatest miniature ever painted in England.'

We must hope that there are yet other miniatures by Holbein awaiting discovery. But the collector is more likely to increase our knowledge of Tudor miniatures by adding to the number of works which can be attributed to Horenbout and other contemporaries. There is a fairly plentiful group of miniatures from this period, representing Henry VIII himself, Sir Thomas More (Holbein's first patron), Jane Seymour and Thomas Cromwell. Many of them have been claimed at one time or another, though unjustifiably, for Holbein. It may be that in some of them is to be discerned the hand of a member of the Horenbout family disguised somewhat as a copyist of Holbein: others must be by those contemporaries recorded by Hilliard: 'Yet had the King in wages for limning divers others'. Certainly such full-face portraits of Henry VIII as those at Windsor and in the Buccleuch Collection (from Charles I's collection) are copied by a contemporary hand from the Whitehall fresco by Holbein. Nor did the practice of copying his portraits cease with Holbein's death: miniatures after them are known by Hilliard, by

[4] *The Burlington Magazine*, Vol. LXXXIII, 1943, pp. 266-9.

[5] *The British School of Miniature Painting*, British Academy (Hertz Lecture), 1948.

(B) Sir Henry Unton in 1586. Hat with high crown trimmed with cypress hat-band; jewel and ostrich tips topped with osprey. Large cartwheel ruff. Marquisette beard. *E. Peter Jones Collection.*

(A) Earl of Leicester in 1579. Gown faced with fur. Striped doublet with slight 'peascod belly'. Paned trunk-hose. Small bonnet and feather. Falling band. Spade beard. *University College, Oxford.*

PLATE 65

(B) Portrait of a lady thought to be Lady Elizabeth Sydenham, in 1583. A Court bonnet, early form of cartwheel ruff. The bodice with stomacher front and flounced skirt worn with a French farthingale. Sleeves of the demi-cannon shape. Feather fan. A turned-back cuff replaces the wrist ruffle. *The National Maritime Museum.*

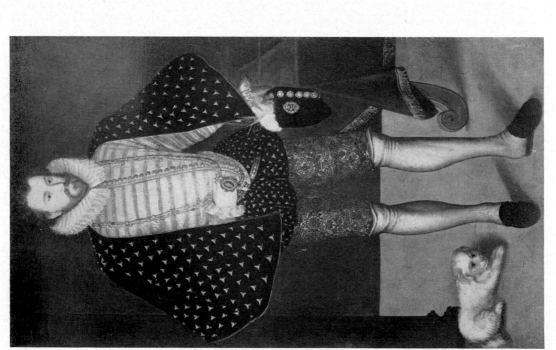

(A) Sir Christopher Hatton in 1582. Trunkhose over canions. Stockings drawn over them. Doublet with slight 'peascod belly', under a collarless cloak. Pantofles worn over shoes with high tongues. Court bonnet. Pickdevant beard.

Lady Spencer tomb, Great Brington, Northamptonshire, 1586. Great arched hood trailing to the feet, worn over the hair. Puckered trunk sleeves. Kirtle rolled up. No farthingale. *Courtauld Institute of Art.*

PLATE 67   195

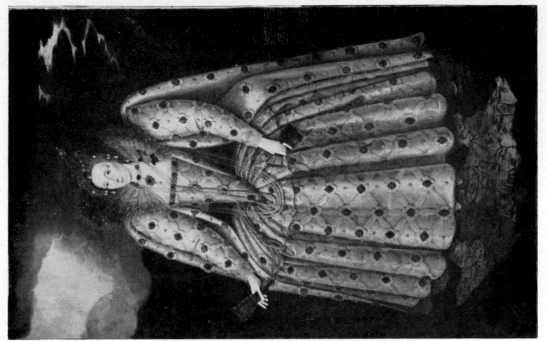

(B) Queen Elizabeth in 1592. Bodice with long stomacher, front dipping to a point. Flounced French farthingale-skirt. Trunk sleeves and hanging sleeves. Fan-shaped ruff and wired head rail behind. *The National Portrait Gallery.*

(A) Lord William Russell in 1588. Slashed doublet with unbuttoned slit sleeves. Slashed Venetians with stockings drawn up over them. Large cartwheel ruff. Pickdevant beard. *The Duke of Bedford, Woburn.*

PLATE 68

A

B

C

(A) Ascribed to Luke Horenbout (d. 1544). Henry VIII, aged 35 in 1525–6. *Fitzwilliam Museum, Cambridge.*

(B) Ascribed to Luke Horenbout. An unknown man aged 35. *Private Collection.*

(C) Ascribed to Luke Horenbout. An unknown man. *Formerly in the Collection of the late Major-General F. E. Sotheby.*

PLATE 69

A

B

C

(A) HANS HOLBEIN (1497?–1543). Mrs Pemberton. *Victoria and Albert Museum.*
(B) HANS HOLBEIN. Anne of Cleves. *Victoria and Albert Museum.*
(C) HANS HOLBEIN. Catherine Howard. *In the Collection of the Duke of Buccleuch.*

PLATE 70

NICHOLAS HILLIARD (1547–1619). Robert Dudley, Duke of Northumberland.
Nationalmuseum, Stockholm.

PLATE 71

A

B

C

(A) NICHOLAS HILLIARD. Queen Elizabeth I. *Ham House.*
(B) NICHOLAS HILLIARD. Mary, Queen of Scots. *In the Collection of Mrs Doris Sassoon.*
(C) NICHOLAS HILLIARD. An unknown woman. *Victoria and Albert Museum.*

A

B

C

(A) NICHOLAS HILLIARD. An unknown man, 1572. *Fitzwilliam Museum, Cambridge.*

(B) NICHOLAS HILLIARD. Sir Francis Drake, aged 42 in 1581. *Kunsthistorischesmuseum, Vienna.*

(C) NICHOLAS HILLIARD. Leonard Darr, aged 37 in 1591. *In the Collection of the Duke of Portland.*

PLATE 73

A

B

C

(A) NICHOLAS HILLIARD. An unknown Youth. *Fitzwilliam Museum, Cambridge.*

(B) NICHOLAS HILLIARD. An unknown man against a background of flame. *Victoria and Albert Museum.*

(C) NICHOLAS HILLIARD. George Clifford, Earl of Cumberland. *Formerly in the Collection of the late Major-General F. E. Sotheby*

PLATE 74

A

B

C

(A) Isaac Oliver (died 1617). Self-portrait. *In the Collection of the Earl of Derby.*
(B) Isaac Oliver. An unknown man, aged 37. *Nationalmuseum, Stockholm.*
(C) Isaac Oliver. An unknown man. *In the Collection of the Duke of Portland.*

PLATE 75   203

(A) Unknown artist.
William Hawtrey.
Chequers.

(B) Unknown artist. An unknown lady.
National Gallery of Victoria, Melbourne.

PLATE 76

(A) *Above*. Portrait of Queen Elizabeth, known from the jewel upon her breast as 'The Pelican Portrait': *presented by Peter Jones, Esq., to the Walker Art Gallery, Liverpool.*

(B) *Below*. Henry VIII and his son, Prince Edward. Ascribed to Richard Astyll. *Reproduced by gracious permission of Her Majesty the Queen.*

PLATE 77

A

B

A

C

C

D

(A) St Thomas More's pendant with St George on the obverse and the Resurrection on the reverse. *By permission of the Rector, Stonyhurst College.*

(B) A gold enamelled hat-badge of the Tudor period, *c.* 1550, the medallion depicting Our Lord at Jacob's Well with the woman of Samaria. *British Museum.*

(C) Mary Queen of Scots cross. Inscription round side: BEHOLD WHO SUFFERE WHAT AND FOR WHOM HE SUFFERED. Length 2 3/16 in. *John Hunt Collection.*

(D) The reverse side of the heart-shaped Lennox and Darnley Jewel. *Reproduced by gracious permission of Her Majesty the Queen.*

PLATE 78

(A) Early sixteenth-century Italian pendant: in the centre a fine Byzantine cameo of the sixth or seventh century, surrounded by various heads contemporary with the setting. *Reproduced by gracious permission of Her Majesty the Queen.*

B

C

(B) Cameo: portrait of Queen Elizabeth I, probably the finest known example of a large cameo of the Queen, an oriental sardonyx in three strata. *Reproduced by gracious permission of Her Majesty the Queen.*
(C) Philip II, King of Spain, possibly by Jacopo da Trezzo of Milan (*c.* 1515–1589), probably given by Charles I in 1637. *Reproduced by gracious permission of Her Majesty the Queen.*

PLATE 79

(A) Pectoral Cross with relics of SS Augustine, Gregory the Great and Thomas of Canterbury. Note likenesses to 'Mary Queen of Scots' cross. Inscription round side: ECCE UT IMITERIS COM PATERE UT CON REGNES. *John Hunt Collection.*

(B) A Niello crucifix of St Thomas More at Stonyhurst.
By permission of the Rector, Stonyhurst College.

PLATE 80

(A) Coffret, or forcer, of wood covered with tooled hide. Perhaps Flemish, late fifteenth century. *Museum of Leathercraft.*

(B) Paten box, *cuir bouilli*, finely decorated with moulding, punching and incising. Sixteenth century. *Victoria and Albert Museum.*

(C) Prayer-book casket, of *cuir bouilli* with modelled and punched ornamentation, lined with red sheepskin, fifteenth century. *Museum of Leathercraft.*

(D) Standard or large travelling trunk, nearly five feet long, of solid oak covered with shaved hide and iron banded, with two large locks and original medieval padlock. Fifteenth or sixteenth century. *Woodbridge Church, Suffolk.*

PLATE 81

209

A   B

C   D

(A) Leather lanthorn with horn window, of Tudor pattern. Illumination is provided by a candle. *Museum of Leathercraft.* (B) Flask or bottle of moulded leather (*cuir bouilli*) of unusual form and small gunpowder flash. *Museum of Leathercraft.* (C) Saddle of doeskin ornamented with appliqué leather and brass nails. *Royal Ontario Museum of Archaeology.* (D) Two forcers of inferior quality (one with a secret compartment in the lid, shown open) but still covered with hide rather perfunctorily tooled. Also a knife-sheath with a design impressed by a single plate. *Museum of Leathercraft.*

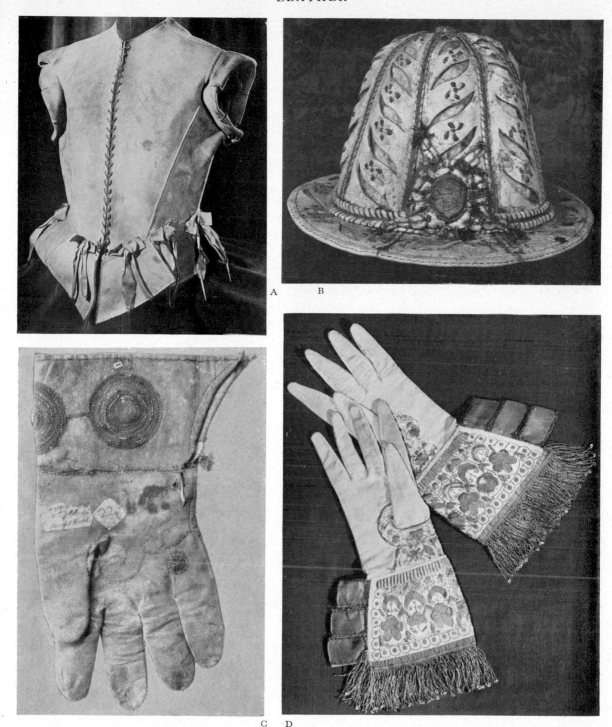

(A) Buff tunic, late sixteenth century, with leather lacing, butt-joint seams and decorative 'points' of silk ribbon with brass 'aigulets'. *Museum of Leathercraft*. (B) Man's hat of shamoyed, buff-colour leather, probably doe-skin, slashed to reveal salmon-coloured silk, embroidered badge. Elizabethan. *London Museum*. (C) Henry VIII's hawking glove made of shamoyed leather embroidered with red and blue silk and silver wire. *Ashmolean Museum*. (D) Men's gauntlet gloves of white doeskin, embroidered in silver-gilt thread, the cuffs lined with plum-covered silk. Elizabethan. *Museum of Leathercraft*.

PLATE 83   211

(A) An English blind-stamped binding of *circa* 1500; stylistically gothic. A number of the tools are close copies of twelfth and thirteenth century tools.

Westminster Abbey Library.

(B) The only known example of a leather 'carpet', probably a bed cover, forming part of the seventeenth-century furnishings of the Queen's Room, Ham House (discarded in the eighteenth century). Of shaved hide, silvered, embossed and painted, the background in opaque light grey, flowers and foliage in transparent glazes through which the silver still gleams. This particular example is probably of the mid-seventeenth century, Dutch, but leather carpets are mentioned as early as 1423. *Ham House, Richmond, Surrey.*

Lady Mary Sidney, holding a bass lute of the largest size, chiefly used for accompanying. *The Viscount de l'Isle and Dudley, Penshurst.*

PLATE 85

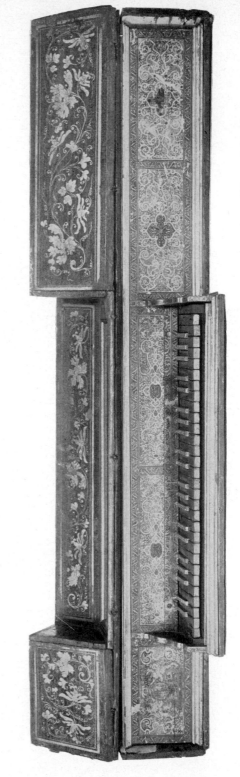

'Queen Elizabeth's virginals.' Open and closed views of an unusually decorated small harpsichord of a design properly known as 'spinet,' and bearing the arms and device of Queen Elizabeth. Venetian mid-sixteenth century. *Victoria and Albert Museum.*

214   PLATE 86

Combined organ and harpsichord. English, 1579, made by Ludovic Theewes. Both instruments are controlled from the same keyboard. *Victoria and Albert Museum.*

PLATE 87

A

B

Murals at Gilling Castle, Yorkshire, showing (A) a tenor violin and a cittern, and (B) a treble violin and a pandore. These are genuine violins of early date, though not of standard shape. *By courtesy of the Abbot of Ampleforth and Methuens Ltd.*

216   PLATE 88

A   B

Two small English viols (A) an alto by J. Strong, late sixteenth century. The shape and soundholes are unusual, and (B) a treble, late sixteenth century, probably by Henry Jay, of classical shape and detail.

PLATE 89

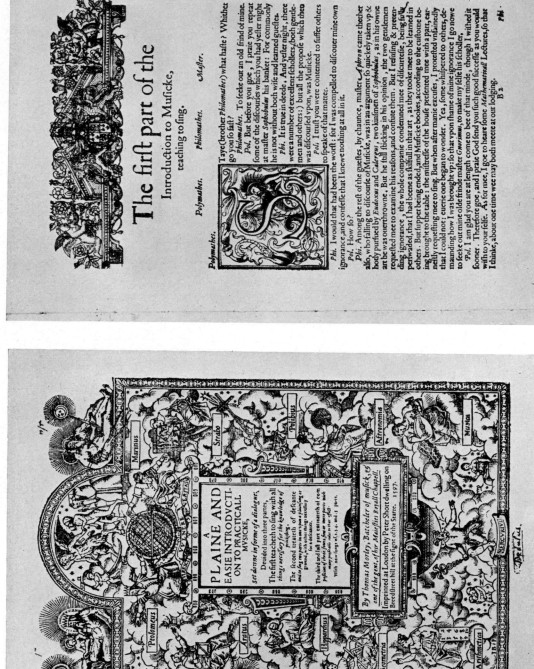

PLATE 90

Title-page and page 1 of Thomas Morley's famous text-book, published 1597, used throughout the seventeenth century and republished in 1771 (3rd edition edited by R. Alec Harman, Dent, 1952). The title-page block was previously used for *The Cosmographical Glasse* in 1559 (*see* p. 259 below).

(A) Woman with lute, engraved by Crispin de Passe (c. 1550–1643).
British Museum.

(B) Woman at virginals, from the engraved title-page to *Parthenia*, the first printed collection of English virginal music, and one of the first English musical publications from engraved plates. 1612 or early 1613, but contents by composers already active under Queen Elizabeth. Engraved by William Hole.
British Museum.

PLATE 91

'A Broken Consort', accompanying the masquers at Sir Henry Unton's marriage, late sixteenth century. These instruments – treble violin, flute, cittern, ? pandore, base viol and lute – formed a very fashionable combination at this date, and Thomas Morley, amongst others, composed for them.
The National Portrait Gallery.

PLATE 92

Bible in embroidered velvet binding presented by the printer, Christopher Barker, to Queen Elizabeth I on New Year's Day, 1584. *Now in Bodleian Library.*

PLATE 93

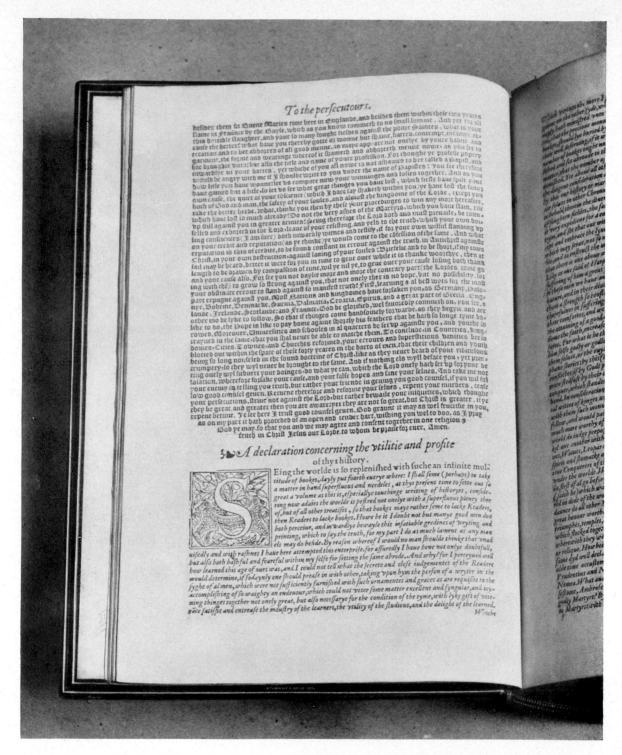

Foxe s 'Book of Martyrs', printed by John Day in 1563, showing black letter, italic and roman type. *Messrs B. Quaritch.*

PLATE 94

(A) An opening of Foxe's 'Book of Martyrs', showing a woodcut illustration. The columns of type are in black letter, with roman for the headlines, caption, etc.

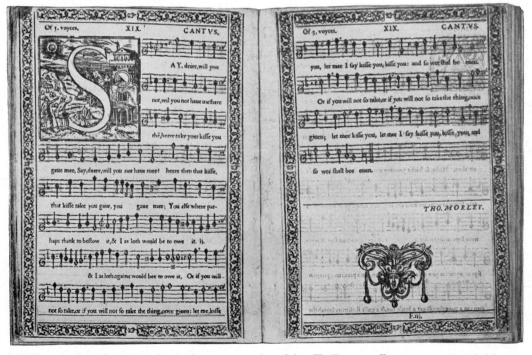

(B) An opening from Morley's *Canzonets*, printed by T. East or Este, 1593. *British Museum*

PLATE 95   223

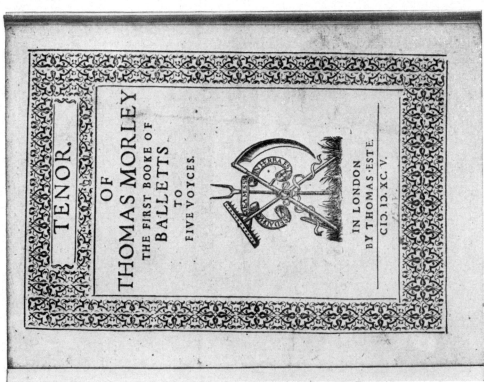

Decorative Elizabethan typography: title-pages of song-parts printed by Thomas East or Este. *British Museum.*

Hollar in the seventeenth century and by Vertue in the eighteenth.

Horenbout to Hilliard

Holbein died in 1543, and Luke Horenbout in 1544. Little is known about English miniature painting between this date and the time when Hilliard attained recognition and the full maturity of his powers: that is, about 1570. It is true that there are some documentary references: engravings in stone were made after limnings of royal portraits by John Bettes the elder in 1547, and he or his son is referred to elsewhere in this volume as the painter of an oil miniature of Queen Elizabeth. John Shute and Gwillim Stretes (Scrots) are believed to have painted miniatures, but the two known sixteenth-century miniatures which appear to be signed S cannot certainly be ascribed to either of them. The most interesting name among the recorded limners is that of Levina Teerlinc, who, as the daughter of Simon Benninck and grand-daughter of Sanders Benninck, was the heiress of a great tradition. She received an annuity of £40 per annum – a substantial wage – from 1547 till 1576, the year of her death, and therefore was a favoured royal servant of Edward VI, Queen Mary and Queen Elizabeth. Yet so far there has been no convincing ascription of a miniature to her. The portrait which she is known to have made of the Princess Elizabeth in 1551; her New Year gifts to the Crown, such as 'a small picture of the Trynite', 'A carde with the Queen's ma^tie and many other personages': all these still await identification.[6]

Actual miniatures dating from the reigns of Edward VI and Queen Mary are as sparse as the names of miniaturists. A favourable example is that of an unknown young woman in a fur-trimmed dress, dated 1549, in the Victoria and Albert Museum. A miniature of the same period, but not apparently by the same hand, is in the Royal collection; another is in the art trade. An oil miniature of Mary, Queen of England, which, when in the collection of Charles I, was attributed to

[6] Erna Auerbach in *Tudor Artists*, 1954, gives valuable particulars of the artist's career, including these entries.

Antonio Mor, and is certainly of exceptional merit, is now in the Buccleuch Collection.

The mood of English portraiture alternates between the serious and the elegant, the direct and the poetical. Whereas it took a full century for the solemn baroque of Samuel Cooper's portraiture in miniature to give place to the rococo of Jeremiah Meyer and Richard Cosway, it took only one generation to replace the grave naturalism of Horenbout and Holbein by the Elizabethan lyricism of Nicholas Hilliard. Many ages have been fortunate enough to find in their leading portrait painters their interpreter and mirror. The Commonwealth and the Restoration are reproduced for us in all their diversity by Cooper and Lely; the 'Age of Elegance' by Reynolds, Gainsborough and Cosway. Just so Hilliard embodies the spirit of the Elizabethan age, in its contrasting moods of adventure and frivolity, extravagance and spiritual insight.

Nicholas Hilliard

He was able to enter into these variant moods because he himself took full part in the wide-ranging, full-blooded Elizabethan life. Fortunate not only in his native endowment of skill, he was the son of a goldsmith, Richard Hilliard of Exeter, and married into the family of another goldsmith, John Brandon. Soon after we first hear of him – as a member of the Goldsmith's Company – we learn that he is prospecting for gold in Scotland with two fellow limners, van Brounckhurst and Devosse.

In 1577 he went to France in the service of the Duc d'Alençon, then suitor for Queen Elizabeth's hand; there he found fresh patronage and won the friendship of Ronsard and other distinguished men. Such was his reputation abroad as a painter of small portraits that he was called upon to supply engraved portraits, cut in wood, of the Duc de Nevers and his Duchess, to replace two in a large title-page which had been bungled by the French engraver. In addition to this occasional activity as a wood engraver, or designer for engravings, he practised as a goldsmith; though in this field his output must have been mainly ornamental lockets and settings for his own miniature portraits, or gold medals which resembled those portraits. A far more important piece of goldsmith's work entrusted to him was Queen Elizabeth's Second Great Seal which he designed and engraved in 1584.[7] He was also asked to supply designs for a third Great Seal: and portions of these, or of his models for the Second Seal, were found in the luggage of one Thomas Harrison, a suspected atheist and confessed alchemist, in company 'with such poison as hath endangered the apothecary's man that did but put it to his tongue'. Equally typical of the times is the report of an informer that the English Catholics abroad were trying to get a portrait of Lady Arabella Stuart by him to further a Romish succession to the English throne.

The succession of James seems to have quenched some of the energy and gaiety of Elizabethan times, and removed much of the splendid dash of Hilliard's style. But he remained an adventurer still; in 1610 he was canvassing his friend and patron, Robert Cecil, on behalf of a fellow goldsmith who claimed to be able to repair highways at half the existing cost. He had been harassed by money troubles almost all his life – indeed, he accepts this as a necessary consequence of the artistic temperament: 'Such men are commonly no misers, but liberal above their little degree, knowing how bountiful God hath endowed them with skill above others.' His affairs ultimately came to an acute crisis when, two years before his death, in 1617, he was imprisoned for debt.

Clearly Hilliard participated in a wide range of activities. He moved as a fellow adventurer among the men and women of the Court who sat to him for miniatures, and numbered Sidney, Hatton, Cecil and Bacon among his friends. Unfortunately oblivion has triumphed over the names of many of the men and women he painted. If we exclude his many repetitions of his Court portraits of Queen Elizabeth, King James and his family, far less than half his extant miniatures have an even remotely plausible identification: in some cases, of course, corroborative evidence for a traditional description

is unobtainable. None the less, a fairly well-populated portrait gallery of prominent Elizabethans can be formed from his works; there are many gaps which we should like to fill, but we may be reasonably content with what remains.

First in point of interest, if not of style (for he was at his best in the never-to-be-repeated single portrait of a private sitter), in such a gallery must be one of his portraits of Queen Elizabeth. He was her servant for well over thirty years, and was called on during that time to paint a great number of portraits for the Queen to give to ambassadors and favoured courtiers. He begins with one of her in her coronation robes, doubtless painted before he was out of his 'teens, and ends with portraits of her old age when she sought to distract attention from the ravages of time by elaboration of costume, false hair and cosmetics. The version illustrated here (Pl. 72A) is one of the most elaborate of his later portraits of her, showing her seated in a costume and ruff bespangled with jewels real and false: which, indeed, have even spread to the glove in her left hand.

Hilliard is said first to have painted Mary Queen of Scots when she was eighteen. If the story is true she can only just have returned from France to Scotland and he was only fourteen years old. This unfortunate lady has been accorded some of the veneration of a cult, and her portraits have been studied to more purpose than those of Queen Elizabeth. The miniature illustrated here (Pl. 72B) is of considerable interest, not only as an authentic portrait of her by Hilliard (there is a replica by him at Windsor), but as the probable original of the notorious Sheffield type of full-length oil painting, many versions of which are by inferior hands. Mary's secretary, Claude Nau, wrote from Sheffield in 1577 about sending a portrait of her to France. It was to go with his next letter. Now though it has been argued that this could as easily refer to an oil painting as a miniature (since even bedsteads had been sent to Mary from France), it is intrinsically more likely that the miniature, which has all the quality of an *ad vivum* portrait, should have been sent, rather than an oil which in any of the known versions is an inferior though contemporary copy.

[7] For the story of its proposed replacement see Noel Blakiston: 'Nicholas Hilliard and Queen Elizabeth's Third Great Seal', *The Burlington Magazine*, Vol. XC, April, 1948.

Strangely enough, there are no known portraits by Hilliard of Lord Burghley or the Earl of Salisbury, who were his constant friends and patrons and to whom most of his surviving correspondence is addressed. The names of Hilliard's children – Lettice, Penelope, Francis and Robert–have suggested to some commentators that there was a special link between the artist and Robert Dudley, Earl of Leicester: and Mr Noel Blakiston, who has added so much to our knowledge of Hilliard's life, has recently shown that this was so. It is not therefore surprising to find that Hilliard painted full-length miniatures on the grand scale of Leicester and of his natural son Sir Robert Dudley, later Duke of Northumberland (Pl. 71). Among Hilliard's known miniatures – perhaps 150 to 200 in number – are some half-dozen whole-length figures. His most famous miniature of all is among them: the young man amongst roses, in the Victoria and Albert Museum, a magical embodiment of the spirit of the age in its extravagance, lovelornness and gallantry. Yet it must be confessed that this is a happy exception on a scale in which Hilliard did not usually shine so well as in his smaller head-and-shoulders portraits: and of the rest, that of Robert Dudley is most successful.

Dudley made his voyage to the West Indies and was on the expedition to Cadiz. Therefore he leads our thoughts to that most typical of all Elizabethan activities – naval adventuring. In this field Hilliard, born at Exeter, was thoroughly at home, finding many fellow Devonians amongst the great naval heroes of the reign of Elizabeth. Such was the fame of Drake and Raleigh beyond the seas that the Archduke Ferdinand of Tirol commissioned portraits of them for his very small portrait gallery of distinguished Englishmen; such was the fame of Hilliard's portraiture that it was from his miniatures that the copies were made for the gallery. A fine miniature by Hilliard of Drake, which is still in Vienna, was the original from which one of these copies was made (Pl. 73B). George Clifford, Earl of Cumberland, a representative figure in his mixture of pirate and gambler, commissioned no less than five portraits of himself from Hilliard. The full-length representation in the

habit of Queen's Champion in the National Maritime Museum at Greenwich is the most ambitious, but that formerly in the Sotheby Collection, showing him against a sky lurid with an emblematic thunderbolt, is certainly the best (Pl. 74C).

In the Elizabethan age the pictorial arts were never far from the literary. The young man seen supporting his head on his hand, with an open book and his glove on the grass amid the daisies, is clearly an admirer of the poets, and perhaps a poet himself (Pl. 74A). For there is a much larger portrait of the same youth, showing him recumbent at full length by an enclosed garden and with the emblem of a pen weighed in the balance against the world, signifying the supremacy of the poet's art. And in the portrait of the passionate lover holding the miniature of his mistress in a locket at his breast, the background of flames against which he is drawn is the visual equivalent of a metaphor for the torments of love consuming him (Pl. 74B).

The countenances of all these lights of his age, and those of less notoriety, such as Leonard Darr (Pl. 73C) (believed to be a Tavistock merchant) Hilliard rendered with a certain elongation and foreshortening: that is with such of the 'manner' of contemporary European mannerism as he had imbibed from the prints of Goltzius, Lambert Suavius and Rosso. But his was an essentially English vision, expressed in a characteristically English way with a flowing line and a delicate perception of the nuances of fresh complexions. He remained convinced that: 'Rare beauties are ... more commonly found in this isle of England than elsewhere'.

Hilliard's pupils

Hilliard, who had taught himself limning by studying the miniatures of Holbein, passed on the knowledge of his craft to a number of pupils. Haydocke said of him that his 'true and lively Image' was 'more than reflected upon the mirrors and glasses of his two scholars M. Isaac Oliver for limming and Rowland Lockey for Oyle and Lim: in some measure'. Hilliard's third son, Laurence, also followed his father's calling and obtained the reversion of his post of Royal Limner. But his known career lies entirely in the reign of James I

K

and, being outside the scope of this essay, is dealt with in the next period covered by these volumes.

Rowland Lockey remains as conjectural a figure as Levina Teerlinc and John Bettes. If, as there is some not entirely decisive reason to believe, he painted the limned copy of Sir Thomas More and his family (now in the collection of the Rev. and Mrs J. E. Strickland), then he might also be the author of two or three pieces in a similar style, among which is the interesting three-quarter-length portrait of a woman in the National Gallery of Victoria (Pl. 76B). At least two other definite hands could be sorted out of the Elizabethan miniatures which are of the school of Hilliard and Oliver without being by either of them. The artist more often met with, among these anonymous miniatures, has as one of his chief works the portrait of William Hawtrey (Pl. 76A). Hawtrey reconstructed the house of Chequers in 1565, one of a long line who lived there, and this portrait is still at Chequers.

But the accomplishments of Laurence Hilliard and the unnamed artists just mentioned are frail compared with those of Isaac Oliver, who rose to eclipse his master's renown in his own day. His parents had fled to England from religious persecution in Rouen in 1568; he was probably a young baby at the time and therefore about twenty years younger than Hilliard. The accession of James I cut his career into approximately equal halves, each with its distinct style. Oliver remained an unassimilated foreigner in the midst of Englishmen, known to the end of his life as 'the Frenchman', and his style, in spite of Hilliard's instruction, remained essentially Continental in inspiration. His natural bias in this direction was reinforced by his travels; the fruits of his visit to Italy are evident in his later, Jacobean works. Yet in his earlier style the predominant impress is that of the Low Countries. His sense of the dramatic is apparent in the way he lights up and poses his figures, and is nowhere more evident than in his swaggering, narcissistic self-portraits (Pl. 75A). The full opportunity for deploying his talent and up-to-date style came with the accession of James I. Shortly afterwards he was taken into the household of Prince Henry Frederick and was extensively employed at

Court. Before that change in his fortunes his sitters are largely unidentified, but a notable exception is found in his well-known portrait of the Earl of Essex, of which the best version is in the possession of Her Majesty the Queen.

The chief mark of Hilliard's success is to be found in comparing the status of the portrait miniature at the end of Queen Elizabeth's reign with that at her accession, or in the neighbouring Court of France. Holbein had elevated the art to a status comparable with that of easel painting, but we cannot believe that he and Horenbout and their contemporaries painted miniatures in large quantities. In France, although Jean Clouet had the start over Horenbout and trained his son François in limning, the total number of surviving miniatures from the sixteenth century is remarkably small. But by the end of Queen Elizabeth's reign in England the miniature virtually challenged the supremacy of the larger panel portrait. It was the fashion for diplomatists to make play with the Queen's miniature, which they displayed on their dress, and lovers carried their mistress's picture half privately, half ostentatiously. A seventeenth-century writer noted that: 'Cavaliers ... are ever more earnest to have their Mistresses picture in limning than in a large draught with oyle-colours'. This change came about during Hilliard's career and as a result of his singular happiness in combining skill of hand with his evident sympathy for his sitter's character and appearance.

The wearing of miniatures

There are many contemporary references to the wearing of miniatures as articles of dress. Queen Elizabeth even snatched from Lady Derby's bosom a portrait of young Cecil and tied it to her shoe. Of miniature portraits as wall-decorations or objects about the Tudor or Elizabethan home we know next to nothing. So large a rectangular portrait as Hilliard's 'George Clifford, Earl of Cumberland' at the National Maritime Museum, Greenwich, may well have been intended for hanging on a wall. But if any English courtier arranged a room of small portraits like the twenty-four by Bronzino behind a door in the Palazzo Vecchio which are described by Vasari, we have yet to learn of it. Indeed, the small size and portability of miniatures made them unsuitable for leaving loose about a room. In the time of Henry VIII they were commonly housed in a turned ivory box with a closely fitting lid, and these thin roundels, about two inches in diameter, were probably kept in a cupboard or cabinet when they were not actually being looked at. Hilliard explicitly says that miniatures 'are to be viewed in hand': that is, to be held in the hand to be properly seen at not more than arm's length.

For Queen Elizabeth's own manner of keeping her miniatures we have the interesting description of Sir James Melville, who had an interview with her on behalf of Mary Queen of Scots in 1564: 'She took me to her bed-chamber, and opened a little cabinet, wherein were divers little pictures wrapped within paper, and their names written with her own hand upon the papers. Upon the first that she took up was written "My lord's pic-

ture". I held the candle and pressed to see the picture so named; she appeared to be loath to let me see it, yet my importunity prevailed for a sight of it, and I found it to be the earl of Leicester's picture. I desired that I might have it to carry home to my queen, which she refused, alleging that she had but that one picture of his. I said, Your majesty hath here the original, for I perceive him at the furthest part of the chamber speaking with the secretary Cecil. Then she took out the queen's picture, and kissed it, and I adventured to kiss her hand, for the great love evidenced therein to my mistress.' There is no reason to suppose that other owners housed their miniatures much differently, though, fortunately for their preservation for posterity, they were generally in lockets or ivory boxes rather than loose in paper. It was not until the seventeenth century that the growth in the size of collections, and their more public nature, led to more formal methods of display.

Wood-cut headpiece from Holinshed's *Chronicles*, printed by Henry Denham, London 1579.

Jewellery

CHARLES R. BEARD

Throughout the Middle Ages the extent to which jewellery was worn by those whose birth entitled them to wear it or whose circumstances enabled them to afford it was governed by the requirements of their dress, their standing among other men and their spiritual needs. The first and the last necessities were common to all. Buttons and brooches of brass served the common man to hold the various parts of his array together; a pair of beads of wood, bone or horn helped him to tell his Aves and Paternosters; a leaden badge representing his patron saint aided him in his devotions; they served him as well as might those of gem-set goldsmithry his overlord. It was only in the emblems of rank that precious metals and stones of price were a necessity, in the girdles and collars of knighthood, and in the circlets and coronets of nobility. The embellishment of costume was in general confined to the enrichment of those accessories which might legitimately be enhanced by chasing, overlaying, enamelling and gem-setting.

The use of jewellery was neither an end in itself, nor was it for the display of the wearer's wealth, or as a sop to his vanity. It was a visible indication of his standing in the world about him. However rich and colourful the accessories of medieval costume might be, they were invariably subordinated to the purpose of the ornament worn. A man wore a livery collar or chain about his neck to indicate by its fashion and adornment that his allegiance was to some overlord; a prince or noble wore a coronal about his hat or upon his headpiece to indicate his rank; and he wore a ring upon his finger that therewith he might affix his signet

to such documents as he might find necessary to sign. His girdle was an indication of his rank and supported his sword and dagger or his purse with its pouch-rings. Buttons, aiglettes, brooches and buckles held the various components of his dress together. And the same general practices applied to women's costume. Rich but not gaudy was the key-note. The many sumptuary laws on the Statute Book bear this out; these were designed, as we read them, not to curb exuberance in apparel and ornament by all and sundry, but to prevent one class from using the materials and assuming the ensigns and other visible emblems which were proper to the ranks above them.

The liking for jewellery in the Middle Ages increased with the passage of time, and culminated at the Court of Burgundy, at which extravagance in this particular direction reached phenomenal heights; and it was probably from Burgundy, with which our relations were intimate if not invariably cordial, that this taste spread to England.

A comparison between the inventory of the jewels of King James III of Scotland, which also lists some of those belonging to his Queen, drawn up in 1488, and that of the jewels of King Henry VIII of 1530 and of Queen Mary in the Palace of Westminster produced just after her death, is very informative. The first lists the King's jewels as collars, both chivalric and purely decorative, with their appropriate badges and 'hingars' or pendants, neck-chains, a sarpe, or collar of extra length worn diagonally across the body, mounted corses or girdles, ouches or brooches, rings in such numbers that the clerk did not bother to count them, a few accessories such as two gold tooth-picks and an ear-pick, and amulets such as four 'serpents tongues' mounted in gemmed gold, and 'a stone of the pillare', a precious relic of the Flagellation. The Queen's jewels consisted of collars, chains, pairs of beads, two bracelets, a frette and two 'edges' or borders to head-dresses, later known as 'habilaments'. Except for their quantity, there is nothing in the foregoing to suggest that the use of jewellery was extravagant.

In the sixteenth century matters were very different. A new order of society had come into being. Birth and long descent meant little when the grandson of a Welsh gentleman of small estate but great ambitions sat in St Edward's Chair; one whose only claim to be of the Blood Royal lay in his mother's bastard descent from John of Gaunt and his mistress Katherine Swinford, all of whose offspring, though legitimated by Act of Parliament, were by that self-same Act expressly barred from the succession. Fortunately for Henry of Richmond the rite of election or 'Recognition' continued to be practised, albeit formally, and he was elected King by his victorious troops on Bosworth's bloody field, an election that Parliament hastened to ratify, the Church to sanctify and Henry to consolidate by marrying Elizabeth of York. But a King with so insecure a seat in the saddle – there were three Yorkist insurrections in his reign – and whose Court was graced by half a score of individuals who could set forth real claims to the Crown, needed men about him who owed all that they were to his favour and generosity. A man was henceforth to be what the King chose to make him, or what commerce might lift him up to be. And to indicate his standing in this brave new world of *parvenus* such a man was compelled in order to receive the deference due to his new-found condition to load his person with gemmed gewgaws which he hoped would be accepted as indications of the merits of the man beneath.

The inventory of Henry VIII's jewels drawn up in 1530 is evidence of a small increase in the number of types of ornaments worn by men. It lists hat-brooches, of the type generally known by the name of *enseignes*, carcanets and valentines – the earliest use of this word to describe a jewel pre-

sented as an indication of affection for the recipient on St Valentine's Day – but the list of collars and chains is a very long one, and it is quite apparent from their numbers that the sets of buttons and aiglettes were primarily intended for trimmings and not for use. The inventory of Queen Mary's jewels drawn up some thirty years later in their quantity and variety bear witness to the great increase of the practice of wearing purely ornamental jewels by the fair sex, and foreshadow the extravagance that reached its culmination in the reign of her sister.

Tudor jewellery design

To turn from the general sociological aspect of the subject to the more particular one of the art forms employed by the goldsmiths of the turn of the century and during the early part of the sixteenth century, very little jewellery of this period and of British provenance has survived. The bulk was undoubtedly melted down in the middle and second half of the century and remade in the fashion then popular, from which circumstance it may be legitimately deduced that jewellery, like costume as a whole, still retained many characteristics of the medieval. Funeral sculpture, the few surviving portraits of this period and existing English table-plate would seem to support this deduction; while the so-called 'Crown of Bruce' among the Honours of Scotland, a work of the very highest artistic quality, which, if we ignore the arches, belongs to the reign of James IV of Scotland, who died on Flodden Field in 1513, completely confirms it. Foreign influences may well have made some impression on the work of English craftsmen, especially those working for Court circles. Spanish and German techniques were probably reflected in their work, German certainly in the second quarter of the century, and Spanish, French and Low-Country inspiration is to be detected in the works of the middle and second half of the century. This internationalism in jewel forms was, however, common to all western Europe from the middle of the sixteenth century onwards. This was due to the pattern books which disseminated art-forms and decorative motifs throughout the Continent. Durer and Holbein were past-masters at designing jewellery, but they are not known to have produced pattern-books; their designs were invariably executed to the orders of a particular patron. On the other hand, the German artists Virgil Solis and Hans Brosamer, Frenchmen like Etienne Delaulne, and the Netherlander Hans Collaert of Antwerp, produced books of designs, which were used throughout Europe. It is therefore possible to identify the school to which a particular jewel belongs, but such identification is not necessarily an indication of the country of its origin.

Henry VIII as patron

Henry VIII treated all the craftsmen who worked for him with the easy familiarity that characterized the conduct of the Emperor Maximilian in similar circumstances. But those whom Henry patronized would never seem to have achieved that intimacy which had existed in the late fifteenth century in Italy between popes, princes and magnificos and the artists who worked for them, a relationship that sprang from the ready and general acceptance of the artists' pre-eminence. This was perhaps due to the attitude adopted towards their patrons by the artists themselves, who, if we can accept the many anecdotes in Vasari's *Lives* and Cellini's autobiography at more or less their face value, regarded themselves as the equals of the most exalted in the land, and firmly believed that they were conferring a favour upon their patrons when they supplied them with works of art. Time and again it is stressed that the artist on presenting his latest creation received a more than commensurate gift in return. He never descended to commerce, or sold what he had produced. The transaction was always an exchange of gifts between equals. Henry VIII, on the other hand, was at all times a generous employer, but the craftsmen who worked for him were his stipendiaries, and Henry insisted upon the most meticulous accounts being kept. There were no perquisites to be had. Every ounce of gold, whether in leaf or filings, had to be accounted for. This relationship probably explains to a very large extent the anonymity of the many great craftsmen who undoubtedly worked for him. The King reduced their individualities to mere names in a ledger. A contributory cause of the anonymity of the English goldsmiths was the circumstance that the functions of the designer and the executant, except among the later craftsmen such as Nicholas Hilliard, who was both, were kept separate and distinct. On the Continent many of the outstanding goldsmiths were also painters, and in their portraits they delighted to immortalize their own masterpieces. Italian portraiture is an illustrated catalogue of the artists' own productions.

Holbein

Holbein designed for Henry VIII many jewels of the most elaborate description in which the balance between the gems and the mounting is most nicely calculated. The metal-work and the gems are of almost equal importance, though, as in all early work following the medieval tradition, the design of the metal-work is the artist's first consideration, the stones being used with supreme discretion to heighten the effect of the complete jewel. There is, however, no evidence that he ever carried out his own designs, the execution of which called for a craftsman of the first rank. Holbein found him in the celebrated John of Antwerp, who was employed by Thomas Cromwell, Henry VIII's all-powerful minister, to make neck-chains, rings and Collars of the Garter. John also produced jewellery for the King, and an interesting instance of the joint work of artist and executant is afforded by the design of a pendant, preserved in the British Museum, and a painting of the completed jewel which appears on the neck of Katherine Howard in her portrait in the National Portrait Gallery.

Renaissance jewellery

The revived interest in the Classics and in works of art of classical antiquity was largely reflected in the jewels of the Renaissance.

The collection of classical antiquities and works of art became a passion, which infected all classes during the late fifteenth and sixteenth centuries. The medallic records of the Roman Republic and the Empire first attracted the attention of scholars, and it was not long before their decorative value was appreciated, when they made regular appearances in cap-brooches, and in the pommels of sword-hilts. Antique cameos and intaglios were however more suitable for use in jewellery. Throughout the Middle Ages they had played an occasional and very minor part among the many gems, precious and semi-precious, employed in the embellishment of jewellery. With the advent of the Renaissance they returned to a pre-eminent position that they had not held since the fall of the Roman Empire. But the supply of authentic cameos was limited, with the result that the demand was met at first by copies of gems of the classical period or by variants of them, and later by cameos which reflect the mannerisms and conventions and frequently portray individuals prominent in the period to which they belong. They show a delightful freshness and originality even when the basis of the design is a classical subject. Popes and the princes of the Church, the despots and magnificos of Italy made collections of cameos and vied with each other for the possession of gems of the highest quality. Even damaged and fragmentary cameos did not come amiss if of superlative quality, the fragment being built up by the goldsmith into a complete gem by replacing the missing portions in chased gold.

Cameos

To what extent cameos figured among the Royal jewels in the early part of the sixteenth century cannot be determined. Probably hardly at all, if the inventory of 1530 can be accepted as complete; for among the many hundreds of items listed there occurs only a brooch 'with a man of white jasper' on a white velvet bonnet, and a second 'with a head and breast of jacinth' on a bonnet of black velvet. Whether these were antiques or sixteenth-century reproductions cannot be known, but no classical cameo would seem to have entered the collection until the purchase by James I of the collection formed by Straham de Goorle of Delft after the latter's death in 1609. Henry VIII, however, clearly admired such classically inspired works, and the Royal Collection at Windsor includes one magnificent cameo (Pl. 77B) in oriental sardonyx in which Henry is represented with his left arm about the shoulder of

the very young Prince Edward, afterwards Edward VI, and a no less interesting portrait of the King alone. These have been attributed, probably correctly, to the artist Richard Astyll or Atsyll, who is known to have worked about the middle of the sixteenth century. Queen Mary also patronized (or at all events contemplated patronizing) cameo cutters, as a third gem at Windsor representing her profile but left unfinished was, in the reign of her successor, converted into a portrait of Queen Elizabeth I, who was very frequently portrayed by the cameo cutters. Probably the finest, the work of Atsyll or maybe of Julien de Fontenoy or of Coldore, perhaps, who were attached to the Court of Henri IV, is also at Windsor (Pl. 79B). Other examples are preserved in the British and Victoria and Albert Museums, in the Kunsthistorisches Museum at Vienna, and in the Cabinet de Medailles, Paris.

Indeed throughout the century ingenuity and fantastic imagination were two of the qualities most valuable to an enterprising goldsmith. Designing a setting for table-cut or *cabochon* [1] stones was a comparatively simple matter, but to find a use for and to evolve a harmonious mounting for large irregularly shaped baroque pearls was a much more difficult matter and tested the artist's inventive faculties and his whimsicality to the full. The more bizarre the shape of the pearl the greater the stimulus to the artist and the greater the ultimate pleasure of the patron, when the grotesque gem had been built up into the likeness of a mermaid, a triton, a sea-horse or some other monster. Regularly shaped gem-stones were, however, frequently used in the same way, being used for the bodies usually of creatures of a symmetrical form—parrots, falcons, spread eagles, pelicans in their piety, and phoenixes. These were for the most part inspired by the *impresi* that were so popular at the time, or by the symbolical meaning of the creatures, or their supposed attributes.

The mounting of gems

The gems were chosen for their colour, and even what are now considered to be flaws did not

---

[1] *Cabochon* = polished, but not cut into facets or shaped.

detract from their artistic value in the eyes of the renaissance craftsman. They were mostly fashioned *en cabochon*, and were generally mounted in collet or openwork settings. In the later sixteenth-century stones *en cabochon* very generally yielded to those which were table cut, a form which still ensured the preponderance of colour over sparkle. The mountings are generally of gold cast, embossed and chased and enriched with enamel. Opaque colours, other than white and black, were rarely used. The enamel might be used to cover the entire surface of the jewel, as in the case of those representing animal or bird forms, or considerable areas of the jewel, especially when the framing was built up of scrolls or ribbon work; or it might be used as a filling for arabesques in the manner of Etienne Delaulne against a ground of burnished gold, both treatments being admirably illustrated by the Lennox Jewel of about 1575 in the Royal collection (Pl. 78D).

Masculine jewellery

The masculine personal ornaments of the period are not very numerous. The girdle built up of great *charnons* from which the knightly sword and dagger had been suspended vanished in the middle of the fifteenth century to be replaced by a simple strap garnished with an ornamental buckle and pendant and bars at the fancy of the wearer; and in the early sixteenth century, when the sword was no longer worn as an adjunct to civilian dress, the dagger was usually worn suspended from a ceint or narrow scarf about the waist garnished with a 'Venetian tassel', for so the great fringed bullion tassel was named; and when the girdle finally reappeared in civilian dress about 1540 in company with the continental rapier it was still a leather textile-covered strap and hangers embroidered to the fancy of the wearer, with hooks and buckles of a purely utilitarian nature. The most prominent masculine ornament on account of both its size and richness was the collar which hung in a deep sweep from shoulder to shoulder. It was primarily a livery collar in that the motifs that ornamented it indicated the wearer's attachment to the sovereign, either as a Knight of the Most Noble Order of the Garter, or as an

official of the Household, as was the case with the Collar of Esses. Other collars were worn by those who could afford such costly baubles, but they had no official standing and were merely indications of the wearer's wealth and new-found nobility. Others of simpler design, usually heraldic in their motifs and of silver or silver gilt, were worn by the waits attached to City Corporations and to mercantile Livery Companies. Neck-chains were worn by gentlemen, nobles and merchants also as an indication of their social standing and as a convenient way of carrying portable wealth about with them, since a link or two broken from a chain could be converted into money at a moment's notice by any goldsmith. Silver gilt chains with a heraldic pendant were generally worn by domestic officials such as chamberlains, porters and gentlemen ushers in the houses of the great.

The brooch

Next in importance was the brooch worn on the up-turned brim of the hat, or bonnet, usually referred to by collectors as an *enseigne*. This was a circular medallion bearing some device or 'word' personal to the wearer, or figures or emblems indicative of his devotion to the Three Persons of the Trinity or to some particular Saint. When Henry VIII landed in France in 1514 Edward Halle, the chronicler, evidently using some eyewitness account, says that the King wore a brooch of St George in the fold of his hat. This was almost certainly the 'round brooch of a George on horseback' listed in the inventory of Henry's jewels drawn up in 1530, and the so-called 'Holbein George' still in the Royal Collection at Windsor. It is south German work of about 1510, and may well have been a gift from Maximilian to King Henry. It clearly owes nothing to Holbein, and its designer may have been Lucas Cranach or Hans Burgkmair. It is interesting to compare the iconography of this medallion with that of the rather later and undoubtedly English George pendant of St Thomas More at Stonyhurst (Pl. 78A). For in the former the Saint is represented as a German knight of the period, wearing a base-coat over his armour; in the latter he is garbed in the pseudo-classical style,

which has from that day to the present characterized all the representations of the Saint in either
the Greater and Lesser Georges of the Garter, or
on the coinage. An equally magnificent gold and
enamel hat-brooch of about the same date has
recently been acquired by the British Museum
(Pl. 78B). The subject represented is Our Lord
and the Woman of Samaria at Jacob's Well. On
the upstanding mouth of the well is the English
inscription in niello '✠ Of a trewthe ✠ thow art
the trew Messias.' Only two other objects of
enamelled goldwork of this period bearing English
inscriptions are known. One is the 'Girdle'
Prayer-book, which recent research suggests almost certainly belonged to Queen Elizabeth I.
This is also in the British Museum. The second is
a small crucifix which belonged to Mary Queen
of Scots, now in the collection of Mrs John Hunt
(Pl. 78c). Along the sides runs the inscription –
'Behold who suffere what and for whom He suffered.' Both these latter objects are considerably
earlier than their known or reputed ownership
would suggest, and Mrs Hunt's crucifix may very
well have first belonged to Queen Mary's grand-
mother Margaret, the widow of James IV and
Henry VIII's sister.

A second hat-brooch, almost certainly of English origin, is that in the Wallace Collection which
is charged with a representation of Judith in the
tent of Holophernes; a third is in the collection
of Lord Wharton, which like that in the British
Museum represents Our Lord and the Woman of
Samaria.

The list of the King's jewels of 1530 includes
other hat-brooches, one of which bore the emblem
of the Pillar – that at which Christ was scourged.
In Scotland they were known as 'targets', and
brooches or targets are constantly mentioned as
both masculine and feminine hat ornaments until
well into the seventeenth century, when they
were generally used to secure the aigrette of
feathers in the hat.

Buttons and aiglettes

Buttons and aiglettes, the metal finials attached
to the free ends of the points holding the parts of
the dress together, had in the Middle Ages been of
a utilitarian character, though they had been enriched according to the capacity of the wearer's
purse. But in the sixteenth century they were employed in a purely ornamental capacity, hats and
garments being trimmed with a profusion of buttons and aiglettes, and the garments on which they
were worn cut and slashed merely as an excuse for
the metallic trimmings. Buttons and aiglettes were
accordingly made very large and richly ornamented
and gem-set, since ornamentation was their purpose and not utility.

It was also a frequent practice, at least during
the second half of the sixteenth century, to wear
round the neck a thin gold chain on which was
strung the wearer's signet ring together with his
tooth-pick, the latter usually a bittern's claw
mounted in gold and enamel, or an imitation of
one made in gold and enamel.

Rings

The finger-rings worn in the sixteenth century
were of the same general types that had become
fashionable during the preceding hundred years.
Signet rings of an armorial character for those who
were armigerous and cut with a mark for those
whose avocations were commercial remained a
necessity. Posy rings, with their often blunt pro-
testations of devotion or amorous intention in
French or Latin and later in English, were common, especially as they would appear to have been
generally used as betrothal or wedding rings.
Posies such as 'In thee my choice I do rejoice' and
'Thou hast my heart till Death doth part' may indicate either one or the other. But 'I kiss the rod
from thee and God' can only have been worn by a
married woman with a very real appreciation of a
husband's right to chastise; and that bearing 'If I
survive I will have five' – husbands being understood – could scarcely have been given by a man to
his spouse unless he were possessed of an abnormal
sense of humour. Gimmal or double rings were
mainly used as betrothal or wedding rings, as the
necessary interlocking of the two rings before they
could be worn typified the union of man and wife.
The best known of such rings is the wedding ring
of Martin Luther, which bears the initials of the
Reformer on one of its components and those of

Katherine von Bora, his ex-nun wife, on the other. Its pedigree is irreproachable. Of the same nature are the puzzle rings consisting of anything up to half a dozen rings which have to be adjusted together before the resultant wide ring can be worn. Decade rings, of which the perimeter was garnished with ten knops and a bezel, were used in place of 'a pair of beads', the knops representing Aves and the bezel the Paternoster. Memorial rings make their appearance in the sixteenth century, and are frequently of the most magnificent character, quite unlike the sombre memorials of a later date. The best known of English rings of this character are the Gresham rings, which are all charged on the inside of the hoop with Sir Thomas's emblem, the green grass-hopper. Poison rings, with which novelists of the cloak-and-dagger school make play, are vouched for by contemporary references to them, but how effective they were for murder or self-destruction is another matter. Toxicology was in its infancy. The famous reputed poison of the Borgias, *cantarella*, was merely a distillation of cantharidin or rather a powder of cantharides; and though the drug can be fatal, it is to be suspected that the crude preparation was used only as an aphrodisiac. Even the potent and never-failing *Aqua Tofania* which won so grim a reputation in the days of Louis XIV had to be taken in large quantities before the desired result could be achieved. It is very doubtful if any poison was then known so powerful that a fatal dose could be concealed behind the diamond in a ring.

Feminine jewellery

This difference between the taste of the fifteenth century and the wild exuberance of that which followed is even more noticeable in feminine dress. In the Middle Ages jewellery is conspicuous by its absence. As in masculine dress, the use of gew-gaws was limited by necessity. Buttons and brooches were worn where they were called for; the girdle or ceint and the demi-ceint supported the pouch, the pair of beads and the book-of-hours, rings adorned the fingers, and a caul or frette or other head-dress confined the hair, and was replaced upon occasions of ceremony by a circ-let or coronet if the rank of the wearer demanded such an ornament. But as the sixteenth century waxed and waned the wearing of jewellery by the fair sex became oriental in its display and barbaric in its quantity. The neck and bosom were festooned with chains, collars, necklaces and carcanets, the arms were wreathed with bracelets, while the lobes of the ears were pierced to support earrings and pendulets, which had hitherto been the mark of the gipsy and the Moor. The customary ornaments for the head were increased in number; the simple 'edges' became the upper and nether habiliments of the newly introduced and very popular French hood; the bonnet was garnished with brooches and aiglettes, and we meet with constant mention of the puzzling 'frosepaste'. To the impedimenta suspended from the girdle were added pomanders, feather fans or flaps with gem-studded handles, and looking-glasses framed in goldsmithry. For warmth a narrow strip of sables or ermine was worn about the neck and shoulders, of which the animal's head and paws were reproduced in precious metal set with gems. The hair was intertwined with strings of pearls, and the entire dress trimmed with pearls and set with ornamental buttons, brooches and pendants.

In the almost complete absence of actual jewels of the sixteenth century that can be proved to be of English or British origin, or which are known to have been associated with English families since that period, it is very difficult to make an appraisal of the work of the native jewellers merely from the delineations of their presumable work in portraits. The Collar of Esses worn by the Lord Mayor of London is ostensibly the work of an English goldsmith of about 1520, but our knowledge that John of Antwerp was responsible for so many Garter Collars of this period, to which it bears a very close resemblance, may mean that it is actually a production of the Low Countries. The achievements of English goldsmiths as manifested in articles of princely and less exalted domestic plate, however, afford us some measure of their capabilities, which were not inferior to those of the great continental craftsmen. The fashion of the objects they produced, however, rather prejudices any attempted appreciation of their work as jewellers. Queen Elizabeth's great Salt among the Regalia is one of the few objects that may be regarded as jeweller's work rather than that of a goldsmith producing table plate. Another object from which an even clearer appreciation of their capabilities, though not of their originality, may be obtained is the silver gilt hilt of the Pearl Sword of the City of London, which we may feel assured is that made in 1554. This is the equal of if not superior to anything produced by the great hilt-makers of Germany and Italy at the period, and unlike their work which has a tendency to de-

teriorate into flamboyant jewellery, as in the case of the hilts of the *Epee de la Religion* and its companion dagger, the unknown artist responsible for the Pearl Sword never lost sight of his object, to produce a two-handed sword that should be symbolical of the wealth and power of the metropolis and the wisdom of its rulers, but should yet remain a sword. Unfortunately there is no feature of the ornament, with which it is almost overloaded, that can be regarded as English. Every detail is evidently borrowed from German pattern books of the period.

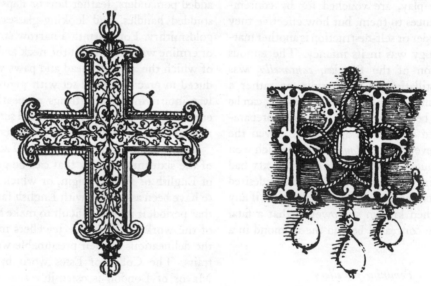

Two designs for jewellery by Hans Holbein, c. 1530: *left*, the back of a cross; *right*, a pendant with the initials R.E. From Joan Evans' *A History of Jewellery*, 1100–1870, published by Faber and Faber.

Leather

JOHN WATERER

Leather, using the word as indicative of animal skins dressed by any method from the most primitive to the most highly developed, has been indispensable to man from so remote an age that it comes as no surprise to find it still an essential and conspicuous ingredient of the social context of Tudor times. There was still a large and experienced body of craftsmen (at least fourteen different gilds concerned with leather were listed in 1422)[1] skilled not only in the preparation of leather but also in the working of it into a great variety of everyday products. Moreover, its use was common to all classes. It is interesting to note that leather has always been used primarily because it was the best – and in some instances the only suitable – material for a given purpose. It was therefore utilized in an essentially practical manner, and only occasionally was it treated merely as a medium for the decorative arts. The leather craftsmen seem to have developed quite early an instinct for appropriate form whose inherent beauty needed no decorative embellishment; although when required this could be provided with artistry and skill fully the equal of that found in other fields.

Leather hangings

Conspicuous among the furnishings of the richer homes in Tudor times were the so-called 'Spanish leather' hangings. Although originating in Spain, perhaps as early as the eleventh century, this type of decorative leather, varying in detail, was eventually made in all the principal European countries.

England apparently excelled in the making of gilded, embossed and painted panels for mural decoration,[2] but there is no record of any organized craft of leather gilders. It therefore appears probable that only a handful of craftsmen were concerned with this somewhat exotic product; and those not much before the early years of the seventeenth century. Earlier hangings must therefore have been imported, probably chiefly from France and the Low Countries. Leather hangings were not purely decorative: they were esteemed because they were not affected by damp or insects, could be cleaned by sponging and retained their brilliance indefinitely. An article in the *Illustrated London News* for 11th October, 1851, states: 'About 1531 or 1532, Henry VIII built a manor-house near Eastham Church in Essex, with a high square tower, that during her sort of year of probation, Anne Boleyn might enjoy the prospect of the Royal Park at Greenwich. This tower had hangings of the most gorgeous gold leather, which remained until fifty years since, when the house coming into the hands of a proprietor with no especial love for the memory of the Bluff Harry, nor the sad hauntings of the fate of Anne Boleyn, nor the old art and workmanship of leather decoration, but a clear perception that in so many yards of gilt leather there must be some weight of real gold, had the tapestries [*sic*] torn down, sent to the goldsmith's furnace, and some £60 of pure gold gathered from the ashes.' Whilst real gold-leaf

---

[1] Brewers' Company, London.

[2] Fougeroux de Bondaroy in a report to the Academy of France, *Description des Arts et Métiers*, 1762.

was undoubtedly used on occasion, usually the effect was produced by covering the leather with silver or tin-foil and then applying successive layers of yellow varnish. The decline of leather hangings seems to have resulted in part from changing fashions, and in part from the introduction of the cheaper embossed paper wall-coverings, to the earliest of which the leather gilders turned their hands.

Leather for furniture

Although leather appears not to have been used for upholstery prior to the middle of the seventeenth century, it played an important part in other ways for furniture. At an early date, for example, it was employed for 'sling' seats, as in the X chair, and for backs, Spanish leather being sometimes so employed. Leather 'carpets', that is to say covers for furniture such as beds and tables, are mentioned as early as 1423 in an inventory of the wardrobe of Henry VI, being made of Spanish leather. But no example was known to have survived until one was found in the attics of Ham House, Richmond, dating from the Restoration period (Pl. 84B). Examples of another use of leather came from the same rich storehouse, namely leather covers for a pair of globes. Although the Ham House examples are of seventeenth-century date, there is little doubt that such things were made earlier. The technique employed for ornamentation is interesting and unusual. Natural (undyed) sheepskin was placed over patterns cut in relief on wooden blocks, and subjected to a rubbing, probably with a wood or bone 'slicker'. This bruised the surface of the leather where there was contact with the raised design below, leaving charming patterns in brown on the biscuit-coloured leather. Gilt leather piping and tassels enhanced the effect.

Containers

In many homes would be found examples of small containers, in great variety, either made entirely of leather or in the making of which leather played an important part: of these, large numbers still exist (Pl. 81, 82). The finest were individual cases into which the objects for which they were specifically made fitted snugly, and the majority, to judge from those still extant, were imported from France and Italy. They were made to hold precious books, reliquaries, jewels, knives and scissors, daggers, clocks, astronomical instruments and Church plate such as chalices, patens and pyxes. In France such containers were produced by the *gainier*, both the word and the craft itself having no precise equivalent in England. Such cases as were made here bear no distinguishing name and were possibly the work of the Pouch-makers, who, when they were absorbed by the Leathersellers in 1517, were responsible for an extraordinarily wide range of products. There were three distinct types: leather-covered pre-formed wooden boxes, cases moulded by building up layers of thin leather over a pre-formed wooden block the shape of the interior, and the process anciently known as *cuir bouilli*.[3] This consisted of softening vegetable-tanned cattle-hide in water and then shaping it over wooden blocks, or by means of a plastic core of clay or wet sand inserted into a sewn-up 'bag' approximating to the required shape and then beating it into the final form. Decoration, by boning, modelling, punching and incising would be carried out whilst the leather was still pliable, and the article was then 'set' by the application of moderate heat, when it would retain its shape permanently, almost as though carved in wood (Pl. 81, 82). This method is the most interesting because it notably exploits the

[3] *Cuir bouilli*: the term is misleading, for no leather made before modern times could be boiled in water. Suggestions have been made that it was boiled in oil or wax. The former would soften, not harden it; the latter is possible but unlikely. Whilst special measures may have been adopted for particular purposes, all observed results could have been obtained by the process still used, namely soaking vegetable-tanned hide in cold water, leaving it to drain ('samming') and then, whilst soft, moulding and decorating it. The final setting can be achieved by drying in controlled heat, and this process can be accelerated by plunging the object momentarily into very hot water – perhaps the origin of the term. All bottles and drinking vessels are lined with pitch or resin, which would be unnecessary had the leather been impregnated with such substances as part of the moulding process.

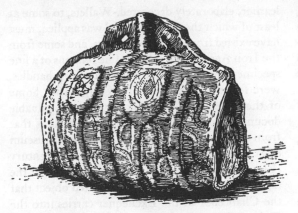

Fig. 1. A very large leather 'bottel' (16 inches long) with relief designs that include the Tudor Rose and pomegranate, which may indicate that the bottel belonged to Henry VIII or his elder brother, Prince Arthur.

Fig. 2. Typical leather 'bottell' with round holes for carrying cord: it is thought this feature indicates a date from the seventeenth century onwards.

unique fibrous character of leather. Protective armour was an early use of this process and, although leather body armour had been superseded by metal armour in the reign of Elizabeth, leather helmets continued in use until the seventeenth century.

Leather jacks

A familiar sight in the homes of both rich and poor, as well as in community establishments and taverns, were the black jacks, the larger of which (some holding as much as four gallons) were termed 'bombards', from a fancied resemblance to a cannon of that name. It was a monster jug such as this that Shakespeare had in mind when he caused Falstaff to be spoken of as 'That swol'n parcel of dropsies, That huge bumbard of sack' (*I Henry IV*, II. iv.) or when, in *The Tempest*, Trinculo says 'another storm brewing ... yond same black cloud, yond huge one, looks like a foul bombard that would shed his liquor' (II. ii. 21). Black jacks, also sometimes known as 'pottes' (although this term was also applied to vessels of metal and wood) or 'leder kannes', have a respectable pedigree. One of the earliest references to jacks is dated 1414, when New College, Oxford, purchased 'four leather jacks', two holding a gallon each and two a pottle each, the four costing 4s.

8d.[4] But the earliest representation in the familiar form is to be seen on an early fourteenth-century misericord in Malvern Church. A fragment of a Saxon ancestor, in simpler form with silver mountings, was excavated in Buxton in 1848,[5] and another, cruder and certainly much earlier but not, alas, well documented, belonging to the Syer Cuming Collection (and at present on loan to the Museum of Leathercraft) is believed to be Neolithic. Jacks with pewter linings and silver mountings date from the Stuart period, and whilst silver-mounted jacks would not be impossible in the Elizabethan era, alleged examples must be regarded with scepticism. The writer has seen one jack, the mounting of which was certainly Elizabethan, but equally certainly not made for the leather jack to which it is now affixed. Shakespeare has a number of references to black jacks, including the pun in *The Taming of the Shrew* (IV. i. 51): 'Be the jacks fair within, the jills without?'.

Jacks were made by the *cuir bouilli* process. The body, complete with handle, was cut in one piece (see Fig. 1), the round, flanged bottom being

[4] Quoted by Thorold Rogers in *A History of Agriculture and Prices in England*, II, 547. He also mentions jacks bought by Eton College in the same year at prices ranging from 2s. 4d. to 3s.
[5] Thomas Bateman: *Ten Years' Diggings*, 1861.

241

separate. They were moulded over wooden blocks, sectionalized to facilitate withdrawal, and sewn with waxed thread whilst still damp. After 'setting' by heat, molten pitch or resin was swilled round inside to prevent liquor soaking into the leather.

Sheaths and pouches

Leather sheaths for knives, daggers and swords, made by methods which can be traced back to Neolithic times and still used, would have been common in the Tudor home, many of them finely decorated. There was a gild of Sheathers, but they were absorbed at an early date by the Armourers. It would appear that they made little else: perhaps their products were pirated by other gilds, as so frequently happened in the Middle Ages. Bags, pouches and purses of many different kinds, made by the Pursers and Pouchmakers, were universally used, and many were of leather; but actual examples from the Tudor period are very rare, and most of what is known of types and designs has been gleaned from carvings in wood or stone, paintings and engravings. Many pouches were elaborate, often suspended from hinged metal frames which were sometimes elaborately ornamented, usually having two main compartments and, in addition, on the front, three small circular purses closing with draw-cords. Often these would be suspended from the girdle, which might be of

Fig. 3. Budget from the ninth-century Breac Moedoc shrine, probably made for carrying religious books.

leather, elaborately decorated. Wallets, to some at least of which the name 'budget' was applied, must have existed from prehistoric times, and some from the Iron Age are still extant. The remains of a fine specimen, of fluted leather with silver handles, were found in the Sutton Hoo ship-burial. Some of these were made specifically to hold valuable documents and books. A notable example is that from the Breac Moedoc shrine (National Museum of Ireland, Dublin), which is of the ninth century (Fig. 3): and perhaps the latest actually to bear the name 'budget' is the rather dilapidated object that the Chancellor of the Exchequer carries into the House of Commons on a notable occasion. The present model, however, being a rigid case, does not follow the ancient tradition. An interesting representation occurs in one of the sculptured figures, that of St James the Great, in the Henry VII Chapel, Westminster Abbey. These realistic carvings, which date from the early years of the sixteenth century, throw much light on the details of dress, footwear and a variety of personal, portable objects of the early Tudor period. The habit of keeping important documents in leather bags is also exemplified by a number which still perform their original function, now in the Public Record Office, London. All examples known to the writer are of white alumed sheepskin and are usually marked with particulars of the contents. Similar bags were used to hold tallies. But wooden boxes, covered with sheepskin or shaved hide, were also used to hold seal moulds and for the storage of important documents. Also in the Public Record Office is a fine wooden case covered with hide and elaborately tooled with designs that include the Rose and Portcullis, made to hold deeds connected with Henry VII's Chapel: it has a drum-shaped annexe to accommodate the Great Seals.

Bookbindings

Legal documents continued to be written on parchment or vellum (not technically leather, as they had not been 'tanned', but first-cousin to it). These materials also continued to be important, in the early Tudor period, for sacred and secular manuscripts, in spite of the rapid expansion and

Figs. 4 and 5. Litters consisted of a light wooden framework over which shaved hide was stretched and held in position by close nailing with brass nails. Early coaches followed the same technique.

cheapening of book production that followed the invention of movable type. A consequence of this expansion was an increased demand for bookbinding, which caused considerable changes in method (Pl. 84A). Calf, sheepskin, deerskin, parchment and vellum were the principal materials, and ornamentation took the form of patterns built up by the impressions of various small metal stamps, some beautiful in themselves, together with a number of ruled lines. Coloured morocco leather appeared about the same time as gold stamping and tooling, the introduction of which into England occurred during the reign of Henry VIII. The process itself was older, having perhaps originated in North Africa, at least as early as the middle of the sixteenth century; then being developed by Moorish workers in Spain, eventually spreading, by way of Naples, to Venice. The bookbinder's technique, employing both blind and gold tooling, was also employed for small leather goods, perhaps by the same workmen using the same tools.[6] An interesting form of binding, typically medieval although still known, if not actually used, in Tudor times (for a representation occurs on one of the early sixteenth-century sculptured figures in Henry VII's Chapel, Westminster), is the girdle binding in which the leather cover is extended at the bottom of the book and gathered into a large ball that could be tucked under the girdle.

[6] G. D. Hobson: *English Bindings before 1500*, 1929.

Games

Leather also played an important part in other forms of recreation and in sport. It covered bladder or rag-core to make balls, since tennis-balls, covered with white alumed leather, have been found in the rafters of Tudor tennis-courts. For dog-leashes, hawk hoods and jesses, falconer's gloves and mittens, it was indispensable. It even helped in the making of music, as well as providing the inevitable covering for wooden carrying-cases for musical instruments. The shrill-toned cornett with a conical bore but octagonal exterior derived some of its peculiar tone from the leather covering which was usually ornamented with tooling. The magnificent gittern in Warwick Castle, which Queen Elizabeth gave to the Earl of Leicester in 1578, already an antique dating from the fourteenth century or earlier, has a leather case that possibly dates from Tudor times.

Travel

Travel was no simple matter. The wealthy, who travelled from one great house to another, moving on when all the stored provisions had been consumed, took with them much household equipment, including important articles of furniture. These had to be provided with suitable portable containers known as coffers and standards. The distinction, if any, between these two terms, is not clear, but it is usual to refer to the great, heavy, three-panel sloping lid objects with heavy iron banding, such as that still to be seen in Woodbridge Church, Suffolk (Pl. 81A), as 'standards', while the term 'coffer' is applied to the lighter form with arched lids and quantities of brass nails which served to keep the leather covering in place and were also charmingly used as decoration particularly in the seventeenth century (Pl. 81D). But there is a record of Cofferers being regulated as early as 1272: the word 'trunk' does not appear to have been used before the end of the fifteenth century. Other forms of luggage included males, clothes-sacks and gardeviaunces. These are known only by name, but the probability is that they were limp leather containers.

Leather played an important part in harness and saddlery, although not all saddles were covered with leather. These still followed the medieval pattern, with very high pommel and cantle offering a firm seat, first introduced for jousting. Packhorses provided the principal means of moving goods about, but great lumbering wagons, the leathern covers of which were called 'barehides', were employed for royal and other 'progresses'. The coach, which could only be used in and around the principal cities, is believed to have been first introduced in England for Queen Elizabeth, and consisted of a light wooden framework over which shaved hide was stretched and secured by close nailing. The litter, which was similarly constructed, was used much earlier (Pl. 82c and Figs. 4, 5).

Clothing

The importance of leather clothing is indicated in one of the petitions against a monopoly for searching and sealing granted in 1593 to one Edmund Darcy, where protest was made that the monopoly was 'a great unnecessary taxing of all the commons in the realm and especially of the poorest sort whose chief wearing leather is'.[7] Leather breeches were common long before Tudor times and portions of interesting jerkins from this period have been excavated in London. They were rendered flexible and ventilated by a close

[7] Lansdowne MS 74 No. 42.

244

pattern of slits, a method used in ancient Egypt at least as early as the fifteenth[8] century B.C. But the rich man had his doublet of buff leather, superbly made, the parts joined together with the craftsman's 'split-seam closing', the stitches going through only half the thickness of leather, his sugar-loaf hat, of chamoised leather, gaily ornamented with elaborate embroidery and slit to reveal coloured silk, magnificent gloves and his gaily-coloured but relatively insubstantial shoes (Pl. 83).

Footwear

Medieval footwear was, on the whole, very different from the sturdy types to which we are accustomed today. Women's shoes, of course, were subject to the vagaries of fashion then, as now. It was the military campaigns of the seventeenth century that stimulated the design of really robust boots and shoes. The fantastic long-toed shoes, poulaines or cracowes (introduced, it is said, by Anne of Bohemia, wife of Richard II), the ancestors of which can be traced in Hittite sculpture,[9] were still in use towards the end of the fifteenth century, but were superseded, during the period under review, amongst the fashionable by the broad-toed shoes, often slashed, familiar in portraits of the period (Fig. 6). Heels appeared during Elizabeth's reign, which also saw the introduction, from Venice, of the chopine or stilt-shoe referred to by Shakespeare in the words: 'Your ladyship is nearer Heaven than when I saw you last, by the altitude of a chopine' (Hamlet, ii. 2): and the altitude could be twelve inches or more. Some were beautifully made, covered, for example, with white kid with pierced designs through which showed a coloured backing. As usual, fashions adopted by the aristocracy descended the social scale and affected the design of even the humblest shoes, of which examples have frequently been excavated in London. These workaday shoes, although usually black and made of cattle-hide rather than gaily-coloured but delicate cordwain, display all the

[8] Tomb of Rekh-mi-rē at Thebes.
[9] At Carcemish. Illustrated in J. W. Waterer, Leather in Life, Art and Industry, 1946, Pl. XLVI.

principal features – pointed, horned or duck-bill toes, often slashed to reveal coloured stockings – of the fashions of the day. Clogs were worn to protect the fragile footwear of the upper classes (for example, the women's shoes of white kid were embroidered with silk and pearls). These clogs were sometimes of wood, perhaps hinged with leather, and sometimes consisted of several layers of thick leather sewn together, anticipating the thick soles of the seventeenth century.

Gloves

Gloves were more common than has been supposed. Drawings in the Luttrell Psalter show, as early as 1341, gloves and mittens, almost certainly of leather, worn by agricultural workers. But surviving Tudor gloves are, in the main, richly ornamented, and on that account have been carefully preserved. One pair is believed, with some probability, to have belonged to Shakespeare. Of grey leather ornamented with gold embroidery and fringes,[10] they are now in America. Another, plainer, pair, also claimed to have been Shakespeare's, and said to have been presented to Garrick by the Mayor and Corporation of Stratford in

1769, are ornamented with stitching in red and gold, and yellow ribbon, a border of punched leather being superimposed on the edges of the cuffs.[11] The ownership of many fine extant gloves is ascribed to a number of famous people, but such ascriptions, although not improbable, cannot be unreservedly accepted. In the Ashmolean Museum, forming part of the original Tradescant Collection, is a hawking glove said to have belonged to Henry VIII, and also a fine pair of white kid gloves, embroidered with silver, presented to Queen Elizabeth (who imposed a ban on imports of gloves that lasted for 261 years) on a visit to Oxford (Pl. 83). They were perhaps made at Woodstock, a famous glove centre. A particularly magnificent pair, now in the Victoria and Albert Museum, is stated to have been given by Henry VIII to his friend and Privy Councillor Sir Anthony Denny. These gloves, of cordwain leather, have cuffs covered with white satin with couched work, silk embroidery, gold and silver thread and seed pearls.[12] Gloves for both men and women were at this period frequently scented ('Those gloves the Count sent me, they are an excellent perfume':

[10] W.B. Redfern: *Royal and Historic Gloves and Shoes*, (1904) 29 & Pl. XVIII.

[11] S. W. Beck: *Gloves, their Annals and Associations*, 1883, 122.

[12] Illustrated in J. W. Waterer *op. cit.* (10) Pl. LXI.

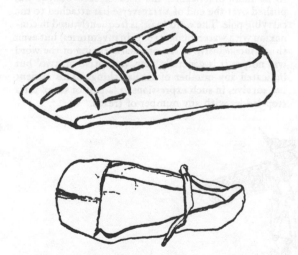

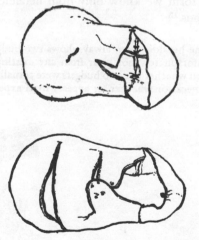

Fig. 6. Top left-hand shoe is of dyed cordwain (goat-skin) of Henry VIII's time. Bottom left is a working-woman's shoe of the early sixteenth century; right-hand shoes are boys' workaday footwear, same period.

Much Ado about Nothing, III, iv). In 1532, according to Privy Purse accounts, there was 'paied to Jacson, the hardwareman, for a dousin and a halfe of Spanysshe gloves 7s. 6d.'. These were probably scented. But, according to Stowe, it was not until Elizabeth's time that such conceits were made in England: once introduced, however, the habit of using perfume spread apace, and we hear of 'sweet' bags, gloves, cuffs and jerkins.

Fans

The folding fan was probably introduced into England from the Far East during the sixteenth century. It was usually of quadrant shape, and frequently was made of parchment or vellum with elaborate geometrical cut-out designs, attached to ivory sticks.

Fire-buckets

Fire was an ever-present and terrible hazard. An outbreak in larger establishments would bring into use the black leather buckets, kept for the purpose, which were moulded into shape by the ancient process, stitched together and strengthened round the mouth with a withy ring. In the cities, at least in early Tudor times, an alarm would bring the water-carriers running to the scene with their primitive water-budgets or byttes, the English version of the ubiquitous water-skin, whose form we know only from heraldic representations.[13]

[13] The heraldic form always shows two budgets but it is unfortunately not clear from any existing representation whether the two budgets were actually joined by the necks or whether, as appears from experiments

Fakes

While it is frequently difficult to assess the precise age of a piece of leathercraft without assistance from such features as datable metal or other components, or decorative motifs (these are often not reliable, as some motifs – e.g. the fleur-de-lys – and certain tools, such as stamping dies, remained in use for long periods), it should not be difficult to detect modern 'fakes'. It is probably true to say that the expert is rarely deceived. There was no motive for 'fakes' prior to the latter part of the nineteenth century, since when there has been some faking of black jacks, most of which are very crude. In the same period jacks and bombards were actually made – not deliberately to deceive and with no suggestion of artificial ageing, but for the amusement of those with a hankering after the medieval – by a firm that had actually made them for Greenwich and Chelsea Hospitals and some public schools, in the course of trade, up to the early years of the nineteenth century, and still possessed the original tools. Old leather acquires a texture and, particularly in the case of moulded objects, a 'feel', a patina and a 'set' of stitching, cuts, cracks and incised ornamentation that cannot be successfully simulated.

---

to be more practicable, the neck of each budget was pushed over the end of a transverse bar attached to the carrying pole. The word 'pair' is frequently used in connexion with water-budgets (e.g. in inventories) but even this is inconclusive as the original meaning of the word was not, as it is generally now, indicative of 'two' but indicated any number of similar things. This ancient use survives in such expressions as 'a pair of steps' for a step-ladder with any number of treads.

Fig. 7. An itinerant shoemaker carrying thirty-two pairs of shoes.

Music and Musical Instruments

ROBERT DONINGTON

A musician at the Court of Henry VII would have left no great mark behind him unless he was a church musician. Under Henry VIII, his chances of making a largely secular reputation were already much increased. Here is a pointer to the great changes both of spirit and of substance undergone by English music under the Tudor dynasty.

Consider the distance between sacred and secular music in the Middle Ages: the former a skilled mystery, a written art, a main subject in education; the latter unsystematized, unwritten, unrecognized officially, and flourishing by tradition and improvization. Consider, too, the distance between sophisticated and unsophisticated music at the present time, with popular dance-tunes striking the specializing minority as unbearably banal and great contemporary masterpieces like *Wozzeck* overshooting the majority by a wide margin.

But in Tudor England these distinctions between pious and pleasurable, and 'highbrow' and 'lowbrow', were reduced to a minimum of importance. It was not only that the same skill, from the same hands, now went into motets and into madrigals; it was not only that Byrd could incorporate tavern melodies or that Dowland could compose tunes which every theatre audience in London got to know by heart. The very concept of an opposition between different branches of the art would have seemed unnatural.

Psalms

There were, of course, gradations. One of the most general of all Tudor musical activities was simply singing psalms. (We know this from the astonishing number of editions which the Tudor metrical psalters ran through – close on a hundred in the reign of Elizabeth.) That is a very straightforward form of music if the tune is sung unaccompanied, and a not very elaborate form if sung in parts; but it is music of real feeling and artistic value, and was enjoyed as such.

> The Psalter of David newly translated into Englysh metre in such sort that it maye the more decently, and wyth more delyte of the mynde, be reade and songe of al men [runs the title of Crowley's four-part musical version of 1549].

That is typical of the whole long series, designed, in the even more explicit words of Henry Lawes' Psalter a century later (1648), for 'such as desire to joyne Musick with Devotion'.

A musical age? A devout age? Both, of course; but the striking feature is the rare union of these two aspects in a kind of joyous exaltation expressed through the act of making music.

'In Churches', says the Sternhold Psalter preface of 1566, 'and moreover in private houses' ... And I have no doubt they made the rafters ring:

Motets and Anthems

What psalms were to Everyman – namely an outlet for his lungs, his piety and his musicality at the same time – motets and anthems were to an always numerically restricted class, the class of those who have cultivated the skill of music as a special interest.

Exceptionally musical as Tudor England was, we must not dismiss the gradations as if they were of no significance. Everyman is naturally musical, and in that age he had opportunities which our present confusion of artistic purpose perhaps denies him; but although simple music can be good music, not all good music is simple, and music which is not simple calls for unusual aptitude and unusual application.

There will always be a minority who have gone much farther into music than Everyman can follow, even if he wants to, which he probably does not. In Tudor England it was this minority which sang elaborately polyphonic motets in private chapels and living-rooms with the same attractive blend of devoutness and musicality as Mr Everyman, his wife and children showed at their psalms; but with a more cultivated skill.

The history of the Tudor motet was an eventful one. Like all English sacred music it was influenced profoundly by the Reformation.

The earliest Tudor sacred music is so complicated in its polyphonic construction that the words stand little chance of being distinctly heard. Their syllables may be greatly prolonged; their phrases

Fig. 1. Page from Sarum Processional, 1502 (reduced).

overlap as the fugal entries weave together. And Taverner at the beginning of Henry VIII's reign was writing, under the influence of Flemish church music, not less but more fugally than Fayrfax under Henry VII.

'Modern Church music', wrote Erasmus in a famous letter, 'is so constructed that the congregation cannot hear one distinct word'. The reformers, who replaced Latin by the vernacular so that the words should be understood, were certainly determined that they should be heard. Archbishop Cranmer advised Henry VIII in a letter of 1544 that church music should 'not be full of Notes, but as near as may be, for every syllable a note, so that it may be sung distinctly and devoutly'. For some years (with a respite, of course, under Catholic Mary) there was a real danger that the main achievement of early Tudor music, namely its superb church counterpoint, would decline to simple, and indeed beautiful, but exceedingly restricted, part-writing of the note-against-note kind called homophony. But in this as in other matters, Elizabeth insisted on a reasonable compromise, which presently proved to be a compromise interpreted still more liberally than its actual terms suggested.

For the service itself, her Injunctions of 1559 permitted 'a modest distinct songue, so used in all partes of the common prayers in the Church, that the same may be as playnely understood, as yf it were read without syngyng, and yet neverthelesse, for the comfortyng of suche that delyght in musicke', what we call an anthem could be appended 'in the best sort of melodie and musicke that maye be conveniently devised, having respect that the sentence of the Hymne [anthem] may be understanded and perceyved'.

In practice, both Short Services in largely homophonic style and Great Services in freely contrapuntal style were produced by Elizabethan composers, of whom Tye and Tallis, Whyte and Byrd, Morley and Gibbons are the leading names. And motets were produced in great numbers, of which many are not only elaborately contrapuntal, but set with Latin words, thus proving that they were intended partly for college and school chapels specially licensed to use this language on the grounds of its being well understood there; but still more for private use.

Two circumstances really saved the situation for our Tudor tradition of fine and complex sacred music. One was certainly the character of Elizabeth herself. She loved music as genuinely as she hated extremes. To have a reigning family as musical as the Tudors is a rarity, and it made a difference. Henry VIII, in his younger days, was the composer of some instrumental chamber music for viols, the best of which is well worth playing; Elizabeth played the virginals excellently, even allowing for the element of flattery in the contemporary descriptions. As patrons of music they were more than well-meaning; they were knowledgeable and sincere.

The other saving factor was the quiet insistence of that sizable minority of good families for whom fine and complex music was a natural part of life, and therefore of religion in an age to which it had not yet occurred to separate the two. Motet-singing to an Elizabethan meant delighting in the cunning workmanship of the music and at the same time delighting in offering to the Almighty anything so finely wrought: a dual pleasure of which the ingredients were not divorceable.

The Madrigal

Nevertheless the spirit, and especially the Renaissance spirit, moves just as freely in what we please to call purely secular directions. The secular counterpart to the motet is the madrigal.

The lighter madrigals are gay, not to say frivolous, and their counterpoint is appropriately sketchy, casual and impertinent. Yet the most light-hearted of madrigals is still contrapuntal, without having caused anyone any uneasiness on the grounds of being 'highbrow'. The difference is only one of degree; the gradation is still continuous. The more solemn madrigals are truly secular motets in form and substance alike, which was no doubt what Orlando Gibbons had in mind when he entitled his volume (1616) of exclusively secular madrigals: *The First Sett of Madrigals and Motets*. Martin Peerson called his secular set of 1630: *Mottects or Grave Chamber Musique*.

Part-songs were always familiar in Tudor Eng-

Fig. 2. Page from Crowley: Psalter, 1549 (reduced).

land, but the true madrigal reached us mainly from Italy. In *Musica Transalpina* (Pl. 96B), a book of Italian madrigals published in 1588 (the year of the Armada), Yonge wrote of the 'great number of Gentlemen and Merchants of good account' who came for 'the exercise of Musicke daily used in my house ... with Bookes of that kinde yeerely sent me out of Italy and other places'. And as the fashion waned in Italy, so it waxed in England. Byrd, Morley and others were producing fine but Italianate madrigals in the latter years of Elizabeth: at the very end of her reign the generation of Wilbye and Kirbye was transforming that Italianate style into a remarkably English, and remarkably impassioned, idiom which had no close parallel elsewhere.

The structure of the English madrigal, being contrapuntal along sixteenth-century lines, was already old-fashioned on the standards of contemporary Italy, where dramatic monody stood for modern music. But the harmony and the mood were forward-looking. Nothing could surpass the force and maturity of the best examples.

It was at the very end of Elizabeth's reign, too,

249

The Base.   The, cxxxii. pfame.   W.P   103

Remember Dauids troubles Lord, how to ye lord

he fwore, & vowd a vow to Iacobs God, to kepe

forever more, I will not come within my houfe, nor clime vp to my bed,

nor let my temples take their reft, or the eyes in my bed.   Remember

Fig. 3. Page from John Day's Psalms, 1563 (reduced).

that Dowland was perfecting the true English Ayre, a species of part-song in which the top voice took the predominant melody, while the other voices (which could be replaced by melodic instruments), though still of some contrapuntal interest, were unmistakably subordinate to that melody. Indeed, the most characteristic way of performing ayres was for solo voice with lute accompaniment; Dowland himself being the most celebrated English lutenist of his day, at home and abroad.

The poet-composer Thomas Campion and his friend Rosseter, in the unsigned preface to their joint *Booke of Ayres* of 1601, wrote that 'what Epigrams are in Poetrie, the same are Ayres in musicke, then in their chiefe perfection, when they are short and well seasoned'. They called the Ayre 'a light song'; but within this lightness and brevity a wonderful intensity of feeling could be

achieved. Dowland's best are among the most moving songs in all music.

No doubt the profoundest madrigals and Ayres, like the noble motets, had a limited currency even in Elizabethan England. Yet we find a tune like Dowland's famous *Lacrimae* mentioned in numerous passages in the popular plays of the day. It must have been familiar to the entire populace of London; whistled in the streets; played by hack musicians not only in the theatre but in the taverns, at weddings and festivities and on all the other multifarious occasions of common music-making. With all that, it is one of the great and enduring tunes of musical history.

Folk Music

The common people of Tudor England had in addition their own musical resources. Folk-dance

250

and folk-song were living arts. Mayings and Morrises, Sword Dances and Country Dances are described by many contemporary authorities in terms which leave us in no doubt that remnants of their ancient ritual and mythological significance still lingered. The tunes themselves were still in process of that creative modification, which is the mark of folk-music. Tradition was their native setting, of course; but we meet them from time to time where they were adopted by composers who incorporated them in written works.

The number of popular Elizabethan tunes which survive in this way is very great. By no means all of them are folk-tunes; there was an intermediary region of ballad melodies and the like which are anonymous and unsophisticated, but in no sense communal in origin. As usual in Tudor music, the gradation is continuous, with none of our harsh distinctions between popular (and largely commercial) idioms on the one hand and highly specialized cultured idioms on the other hand.

Some, though not all, of the country-dance tunes published in Playford's seventeenth-century editions are obviously, from their style, of Tudor date or older, and quite a few favourites, like *Greensleeves* and *Sellenger's Round* were Tudor bye-words.

> Every troublesome and laborious occupation [wrote Case in his *Praise of Music*, 1586] useth musick for a solace and recreation, and hence it is that wayfaring men solace themselves with songs ... that manual labourers, and mechanical artificers of all sorts keepe such a chaunting and singing in their shoppes – the tailor on his baulk – the shoemaker at his last – the ship-boy at his oar – the tinker at his pans – and the tiler on the house-top.

And if Everyman could take Dowland's *Lacrimae* to his heart, Dowland in his turn preserved *Greensleeves* in several of his lute manuscripts. Byrd used it in one of his big contrapuntal fantasies for viols, and it occurs in many other settings. These instances are very typical of the mutual interchange between popular and cultivated music throughout the Tudor period.

Keyboard Music

Curiously enough, it is in one of the most cultivated achievements of late Tudor music that we find the greatest use of popular tunes as the themes of elaborate variations. This is the astonishing school of English keyboard music of which Byrd was the main founder, Gibbons and Farnaby the next generation of masters, and John Bull the brightest ornament, with Tomkins as the last great exponent of the style in Stuart England.

Idiomatic keyboard music evolved all over Europe during the sixteenth century, mainly in the form of variations on dance music, vocal music and popular melodies. The Englishmen were undoubtedly influenced by the general movement; as with the madrigal, our national achievement came a little late, but made up for that by superb quality. In fact, with the keyboard music it is not too much to say that we surpassed all contemporary rivals. By the end of the century, Englishmen were writing for the virginals, the harpsichord and the organ in a highly individual national style. The virtuosity of our late Elizabethan and early Stuart keyboard music is often impressive on any standards – and not only for its brilliance. The best of this music is suffused by feeling, with a directness of impact comparable to that of the Romantic period.

The virginals is in fact the same instrument as the harpsichord, but with more restricted resources. The strings are plucked, and the resulting clarity was exploited so idiomatically by the best composers that the piano is incapable of doing them justice. A great many good families possessed a virginals, and some of them a small chamber organ in addition. The lute, with its beautifully coloured and expressive tone, was another highly favoured plucked instrument; it acquired a large literature both as a soloist and as an accompanist, particularly of songs. The cittern, flat-bodied where the lute is the shape of a half-pear sliced down the stalk, was the poor man's lute, and hung in many barbers' shops for the customers to pass the time with while waiting for their turn.

Wind and string instruments

Of wind instruments, the recorder, which is a variety of flute; the shawm, which is a more pungent relative of the oboe; the cornet, which is nearest to a very refined variety of horn, and nothing like the modern instrument of the same name; the sackbut, which is a trombone – all these were in common use among church musicians, theatre musicians, strolling players and to a lesser extent cultured amateurs. But apart from the virginals and the lute, the most serious amateur instrument was the viol.

The violin was just coming in as a popular dance-instrument, much as the rebec had been from time out of memory (the rebec, unlike the viol, is an ancestor of the violin, with an astonishingly assertive and ringing tone). But the viols were a long-established family and an aristocratic one among Renaissance instruments: a complete chamber group occupying a position like that of the string quartet in the late eighteenth century and subsequently. The tone is less powerful but more sharply etched than that of the violin, thus giving great clarity to the motet-like counterpoint characteristic of the sixteenth-century repertoire. The quality in the hands of a good performer (but not of an indifferent one) is warm, satisfying and expressive.

There are Tudor chamber-works for the viols by Byrd which are of a cheerful disposition; but most of the Tudor output in this field is too close to vocal counterpoint in style for a very lively effect. The chief exceptions are dances, particularly pavans and galliards. But at the end of the century, the vitality and symmetry of dance-music merged with the contrapuntal solidity of the

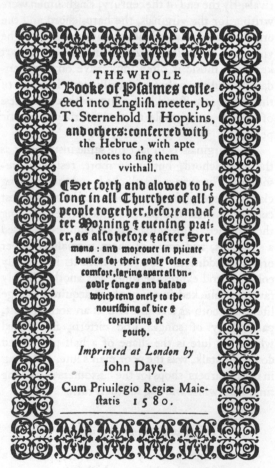

Fig. 4. Title and page from Sternehold's *The Whole Booke of Psalmes*, 1580 (reduced).

motet style to produce a genuinely instrumental idiom – largely, as with the madrigal, under Italian stimulus. One John Cooper returned from a visit to Italy as Giovanni Coperario, virtually to found an English school of chamber-music for the viols which the next generation made genuinely national, and as unique in its way as the great keyboard school.

Developing just a little later than the English madrigal, and continuing some decades longer than that meteoric apparition, the genuinely instrumental chamber-music of the viols was a product of Stuart and Commonwealth and not of Tudor England. But plenty of enjoyable though not very idiomatic music was performed on viols in the sixteenth century, partly transcribed from vocal sources, partly imitated from them, partly straight dance-music. We know from the inventories of great private houses, like Hengrave Hall with its long list of viols, lutes, instrumental and vocal part-books, how active a share was taken in this direction too by cultured amateurs.

Cultured amateurs from royalty to yeoman farmers; professionals from church organists to theatre musicians, and from municipal bands to tavern touts; popular balladry; equally popular psalm-singing; living folk music – all this had not necessarily a wider range than our own BBC, TV, Lyons Corner House, Jive, Covent Garden, Westminster Abbey and the Royal Festival Hall, but it was united by something much more like a common language. No modern composer

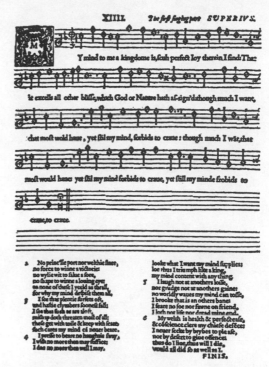

Fig. 5. Page from Byrd: *Psalmes, Sonets and Songs*, 1588 (reduced).

can help envying the Elizabethans that favourable state of affairs, when he compares it with his own virtual certainty of not being understood beyond a rather narrow and self-conscious circle of adepts. But possibly the neo-Elizabethan generation of Britten and Tippett has taken some first steps towards a new meeting-ground.

Fig. 6. Teaching the elements of music by 'the Guidonian hand'. *From John Day's Whole Book of Psalms, 1563.*

Printing

RUARI McLEAN

Much Tudor printing has been lost, and many interesting books survive only in a fragment, or as a sheet of printers' waste inserted to strengthen a binding; but what remains is enough to give us a clear general picture.

An ordinary book, in Tudor times, would come from the printer in flat sheets, as it does today, and go to the binder for folding and then sewing in quires. It might then be merely covered in paper, to save the expense of binding; but the normal binding would be vellum, tied up with tapes, and with a flat spine. The title of the book might be written on the spine or front of the binding. Kings and rich men had their books bound in leather: but Queen Elizabeth I liked her books bound in embroidered velvet (Pl. 93), which explains why more leather bindings survive from the time of Henry VIII and Mary. The best English bindings of the Tudor period are, in general, less skilful than the best work then being executed on the Continent. This subject, however, awaits fuller investigation and documentation than it has yet received.

The first printer in England was Caxton. He had spent his life as an English merchant in the Low Countries, became the 'Governor of the English Nation' in Bruges, and then, at the age of fifty, learned the art most probably in Cologne, and set up England's first printing-press at Westminster in 1476.

He printed over a hundred books, many of them large folios. The type he used (in all, eight kinds of 'black-letter') and some of the woodcut illustrations came from the Continent. As specimens of printing the books are not impressive, for Caxton did not learn from the best masters. But what matters is that he printed, for the first time in English, *The Morte d'Arthur*, *The Canterbury Tales*, *Æsop's Fables*, *Reynard the Fox*, *The Golden Legend*: great literature which we know he loved and which, when the originals were in French or German, he had laboured to translate himself into English until his eyes were 'dimmed with ouer moche lokyng on the whit paper'. England owes very much to William Caxton.[1]

Before Caxton's death in 1491 various other presses had been set up in England, probably all by foreigners. Books were printed by an unknown schoolmaster in St Albans between 1480 and 1486, by Theodoric Rood of Cologne at Oxford between 1478 and 1486, and in the city of London by Lettou (probably a Lithuanian) and de Machlinia, a Belgian. But most English books were printed in the Low Countries and imported. It has been estimated that while about 360 books were printed in England before 1500, nearly 2,000 were printed in the Low Countries and imported during the same period, mostly liturgical books; and that it was not until about 1550 that the country's printed needs were being satisfied by her own printers.[2]

[1] See W. J. B. Crotch, *The Prologues and Epilogues of William Caxton*, O.U.P., 1928, and L. A. Sheppard, 'A New Light on Caxton and Colard Mansion': *Signature 15* (New Series), London. 1952.

[2] M. E. Kronenberg: *Notes on English Printing in the Low Countries in the early XVIth Century*, London, The Bibliographical Society, 1928.

Caxton's own material and presses passed, on his death, to his foreman Wynkyn de Worde, of Alsace. To examine every publication from de Worde's presses would be a labour indeed, for he lived until 1535, and over 700 items with his imprint have been listed.[3] Many of these were reprints and booklets, and not a few may have been printed on other men's presses, but nevertheless his output was formidable. His chief rival was Richard Pynson, a Norman, the first printer in England to be appointed 'King's Printer'. Pynson may have taken over de Machlinia's business; he was active from before 1492 to his death in 1530.

De Worde and Pynson between them printed about three-quarters of all the books printed in England up to 1530. In 1500 de Worde left Caxton's house in Westminster and joined Pynson in Fleet Street. Caxton's patrons had been, first, Margaret, Duchess of Burgundy, at Bruges, and then her brother, King Edward IV of England, and members of his Court. De Worde had neither Caxton's friends, tastes, nor literary gifts and, to make his living, he had to move to the famous street in London which was even then the centre of the printing trade. 'If the characteristic work of Caxton is the large folio,' says H.S.Bennett, 'running to hundreds of pages, the typical volume of de Worde is the quarto of 24 or 32 pages'[4] – and its subject probably religious and homiletic. Pynson specialized in law books.

An examination of de Worde's and Pynson's books reveals nothing so well printed as, say, the contemporary work of Aldus in Venice or the Estiennes in Paris. Compared with Italy and France, England was still a fairly primitive country, with glass, for example, only just coming in for windows, and knives and forks for eating. Books were set in rough-looking types, mostly black-letter; and the crisp contrast between black ink and white paper, which marks fine printing, and can be seen in the earliest work of the German and Italian master printers, is lacking.

The sources of the types, all of continental origin, have been convincingly analysed in F. Isaac's *English Printers' Types of the Sixteenth Century*, O.U.P., 1936. The woodcuts used for illustrations, too, are copies of foreign originals, or the originals themselves. Wood-cut blocks were as valuable then as photo-engraved blocks are today, and had a longer life. In the course of having many editions run off them, and travelling, as they did, from country to country, they deteriorated; and the deterioration helps to establish the dates of editions. Every crack is carefully measured, and even the worm-holes have been counted.[5]

Sometimes the origin of a design can be traced exactly. For example the elaborate title-page border used in a book printed by Pynson in 1521 is in fact a crude copy of a block designed by Holbein for Froben in Basle. The subject of the illustration in the bottom half of the woodcut is the story of C.Mucius Scaevola and Lars Porsena of Clusium, which has no connexion at all with either the book Pynson first used it for, or the twelve or so books it was later used in, which include Froissart's Chronicles and the New Testament.

Among the books we might pause at, in de Worde's output, are Higden's *Polychronicon*, 1495 (Fig. 1), the first book in which music was printed from type in England; and his song-book of 1530, the first actual music-book printed in England. The words of the songs are set in black-letter. On the Pynson shelves we should look at *Sermo fratris Hieronymi de Ferraria* of 1508, in which roman type appeared for the first time in an English book. In 1518 Pynson was printing books entirely in roman type: but black-letter continued to be used for normal reading-matter all through the century. It was used, for example, for the text of the first edition of Hakluyt (1599 and 1600), although the introduction to these volumes was in roman; yet *Venus and Adonis*, 1593, the first known printing

[5] See McKerrow & Ferguson's *Title-page borders in England and Scotland 1485–1643*, London, 1932, which reproduces and records the history of over 300 of these blocks.

Fig. 1 *opposite*. Page 101 from Higden's *Polychronicon*, 1495, set in a black-letter type of continental origin, and showing the first music printing in England.

---

[3] H. S. Bennett: *English Books and Readers 1475 to 1557*, C.U.P., 1952.
[4] H. S. Bennett: *Ibid*.

de of twelue/the thyrde of eyght/the
fourth of .ir. as this fygure sheweth.

Dpapaſon   Dpapente   Dpateſſeron   Duplex diapaſon

¶Whan theſe
accordes were
foūdey pictago
ras paf hem na
mes . And ſo þ
he called iy nō
bre double / he
called iy ſow,
nes Dyapaſon.
And þ he called
iy nōbre other
halfe he called
iy ſowne Dya
pente. And, þ þ
iy nōbre is cal,
led all e þ thyr
de dele/hete iy ſones Dyateſſeron/e
that þ iy nombres is called all e the
eyghteth dele / hete iy tewnes double
Dyapaſon.As iy melodye of one ſtrē
ge/yf the ſtrynge be ſtreyned enlonge
vpoy the holowneſſe of a tree / e de,
parted euey a two by a brydge ſette
there vnder iy eyther parte of þ ſtren
ge/the ſowne ſhall be Dyapaſon/yf
the ſtreng be ſtreyned e touched.And
yf the ſtreng be departed euey iy thre
e the brydge ſette vnder/ſo that it de
parte bytwene the twey deles e þ thyr
de/than the lenger dele of the ſtreng
yf it be touched ſhall yeue a ſowne cal
led Dyateſſeron.And yf it be depar,
ted iy nyne/and the brydge ſette vn,
der bytwene the laſt parte and the o,
ther dele / than the lenger dele of the
ſtrenge yf it be touched ſhall yeue a
ſowne/that hete Tonus/for nyne cō
teyneth eyght/and the eyght parte of
eyght as iy this fygure that foloweth

¶Je,
ronim⁹
contra Ruf.Many of pictagoras dyſ
cyples kepte her mayſtres heeſtes iy
mynde and vſed her wytte and myn
de iy ſtudye of bookes / and taught
that many ſuche prouerbes ſhall kyt,
te and departe ſorowe from the bo,
dye/vnconnynge from the wytte/le,
cherye from the wombe/treaſoy oute
of the lyte / ſtryfe out of the houſe
Incontynence and haſtyneſſe oute of
all thynges.Alſo all that frendes ha,
ue ſhall be compyn . A frende is the o,
ther of tweyne . Me muſt take hede
of tymes . After god ſothneſſe ſhall
be worſhypped that maketh mey be
next god. ¶Yſydorus libro octauo ca
pitulo ſexto.

¶Capm̄   .xii.

The name of phyloſophres
hadde begynnynge of picta,
goras. for olde Grekes cal,
led hyy ſelfe ſophiſtris that is wyſe/
But pictagoras whay me axed what
may he was/he anſwerde and ſayde
that he was a phyloſopher / that is a
louer of wytte and of wyſedome for
to calle hyy ſelfe a wyſe may/it wol
de ſeme grete booſt e pryde.Afterwar
other philoſophres hadden her names
of her auctours.And ſo they that hel,
de pictagoras looze/were called pic,
tagozaci . And they that heldey pla,
toos looze / were called platonici .
¶Pot.libro prī⁹ Some phyloſophres
haddey names of contrees / e ſo they
þ heldey pictagoras looze were called

of Shakespeare, was set wholly in roman. Black-letter in fact survived for poetry and romances into the seventeenth century, for Bibles and prayer-books until the end of the seventeenth century, and was still being used for legal books in the eighteenth century.

In 1523 an Act was passed requiring alien craftsmen to take only English-born apprentices, and not have more than two alien journeymen. In 1529 it was enacted that no foreigner could start a new press, but existing presses were in no way interfered with. A more restrictive Act was passed in 1534, returning foreigners in printing to the same footing as foreigners in other trades (they had been specially privileged since 1484). A further enactment prohibited the importation of books from abroad except in unbound sheets.

The remaining years of Henry VIII's reign were a particularly unsettled period for the book trade: Duff, the authority on English printers of this period, has written 'the printers themselves seemed hardly to know what might or might not be printed and even the most important were continually in trouble'.[6]

In 1538 a proclamation was made which, R.B. McKerrow says, 'seems to be the first attempt to establish a regular censorship'.[7] But it was not till 1549 that the Privy Council decreed that no printer should print or sell any English book unless it were licensed. In May, 1557, the last year of Mary's reign, the history of the English printing trade really begins with the incorporation of the Stationers' Company; an arrangement which made it much easier for the authorities to control the press.

All through the century English printers remained far behind the best Continental printers both in artistry and technique. However, the first known example of a copper-engraved title-page – an important innovation in book design – appeared in England. This was Thomas Geminus's *Anatomy*, printed by J. Herford, London, in 1545.

Geminus (a surgeon and scientific instrument-maker in the service of Henry VIII) also engraved a handbook of arabesque ornaments for Goldsmiths and Embroiderers in 1548, of which only one copy is now known to exist, in the Landes-museum, Münster, Westphalia (see Fig. 2, p. 112 above).

Up to 1600 only about twenty books appeared in England with engraved titles, whereas after 1610 it was rare for an important book to appear without one. The normal way to decorate a book, all through the century, was with woodcut blocks and typographical ornaments. Most of the blocks and ornaments were direct copies from Continental models, but some fine ones were designed and cut in England. Holbein, who settled in England in 1532, probably designed the title-page for the first English edition of the Bible in Coverdale's version, printed secretly abroad in 1535; almost certainly he did not design the title-page of the Great Bible of 1539, often ascribed to him; but he probably designed the charming device of boys robbing an apple-tree used by the printer Renold Wolfe (Fig. 4), and a handful of other small initials and engravings mostly used by that printer. It is believed that most, if not all, of these blocks were engraved in Basle.[8]

A striking block that first appeared on a title-page of Calvin's Sermons printed by Binneman in 1574 (and additionally familiar because it was copied by Pickering and Whittingham and used for their edition of *Holy Dying* in 1840) bears the initials N.H., who is 'almost certainly'[9] Nicholas Hilliard; and one other title-page has been ascribed to him. The former block also bears the initials C.T., which appear on three other title-page blocks of the same period, and may stand for one Charles Tressell, Treasure, or Tressa, a Dutch 'graver of letters' and 'carver to the printers'. That is the nearest we can get to ascribing any of the important Tudor title-pages to individual artists. McKerrow and Ferguson state that the cutters

[6] E. Gordon Duff: *A Century of the English Book Trade 1457–1557*. London, 1905.

[7] R.B. McKerrow: *A dictionary of Printers and Booksellers 1557–1640 in England, Scotland and Ireland*. London, 1910.

[8] Campbell Dodgson: *Woodcuts designed by Holbein for English Printers*, Walpole Society, Vol. 27. Oxford, 1939.

[9] See A.M. Hind in *Engraving in England in the 16th and 17th Centuries*, Part 1. Cambridge, 1952.

were not in most cases professionals, for there was not enough work: it was probably a sideline of the engraver and chasers of metal (e.g. on guns and armour).

When Pynson died in 1529 he was succeeded, as Royal printer, by Thomas Berthelet, who was perhaps a Welshman. Berthelet died in 1555, with upwards of 350 publications to his name.[10] At this time there were about a dozen printing firms in London: there were only twenty-three in 1583.[11]

When Queen Elizabeth I came to the throne in 1558 there was immediately a general improvement in English book production, typified by the work of John Day, the chief printer of the Elizabethan period. Day had been printing since 1546, had been imprisoned in the Tower in 1554 'for printing of noythy bokes',[12] and had found it necessary to go abroad during Mary's reign, where he certainly saw, and studied to good purpose, the best printing of the time. When he returned to England he received patronage and informed encouragement from Matthew Parker, Elizabeth's humane and literary-minded Archbishop, who liked the 'new Italian letter' (i.e. italic type) so much that he made Day import specially an excellent fount of it.

Now, for the first time, we can find books printed in England which do not suffer so greatly when compared, not with masterpieces like Tory's *Champfleury*, but with the ordinary work of the great Continental firms like Plantin at Antwerp.

This is partly due to an increased use of good roman and italic types, and to a more careful printing of them. No original designer of types worked in England, either at this period or for many years to come, but better types were now available, particularly the Garamond and Granjon letters. In some cases the types themselves were imported, but more usually the matrices were brought over, cast in England, and sold to various printers. There was, at the time of the accession of Queen

Elizabeth I, says F. Isaac, an influx of refugee printers and type-founders from the Continent, who would all tend to raise our standards.[13]

One of Day's finest books was *The Cosmographical Glasse*, 1559, one of the earliest English works on practical mathematics and of considerable importance to Elizabethan seamen and surveyors. The allegorical woodcut title-page (which may be by the miniaturist, John Bettes, as it bears the initials I.B.) was probably designed for this work, but was used again for six more books by Day (including the first English edition of Euclid, 1570), and for at least ten more books (including Morley's *Introduction to Practicall Musicke* and several editions of Dowland's *Songs and Ayres*) by other printers up to 1613. It is illustrated on Plate 90.

Perhaps Day's most famous book is John Foxe's *Actes and Monuments of these latter and perillous days, touching matters of the Church*, 1563, better known as Foxe's *Book of Martyrs* (Pl. 94). This was set in double columns of black letter, but the Dedication to the Queen was set in a fine italic with a magnificent woodcut initial 'C' depicting Queen Elizabeth being waited on by three bearded gentlemen; the one in the middle looks like John Day himself.[14]

In all, about 275 publications are credited to Day, who died in 1584. In 1583 he had four presses. Of the twenty-two other printers in London at that time, only one other, H. Denham, had four, and one, Christopher Barker (the Queen's Printer) had five. Most of the other printers had one or two only. These are the figures on the records of the Stationers' Company. For John Wolf the entry runs: 'iij presses and ij more since found in a secret vaut'. Bibliographers have to contend with many falsifications of dates and imprints during this period: some are obvious, like 'Printed at Jerico in the land of Promes by Thome Truuth' (actually London, 1542), but others used more probable imprints and even those of their fellow-printers. The key to such problems was, at the time, the examination of the printer, but now (and

[10] H. S. Bennet: *English Books and Readers 1475 to 1557*, C.U.P., 1952.
[11] *Records of the Court of the Stationers' Company 1576 to 1602*, Bibliographical Society, London, 1930.
[12] F. Isaac: *English Printers' Types of the 16th Century*, Oxford, 1936.
[13] F. Isaac: *Ibid.*
[14] This page is well reproduced in Sir Francis Meynell's *English Printed Books*, London, 1948.

CHARI TAS.

Fig. 2. Device used by the printer Renold Wolfe, probably designed by Holbein (see p. 172).

more reliably) of his types. The whole story of the illicit printing trade in England and the Low Countries, including the printing and smuggling of the first English New Testaments and Bibles, and under Elizabeth, the secret Puritan and Catholic Presses, is too long to be told here.

Another fine Elizabethan printer, about whom too little is known, is Thomas East or Este, *c.* 1540–1608, of first-rate importance in the history of English music. He was the assigne of William Byrd, and printed and published nearly all the early books of madrigals. The title-pages of these song-books are masterpieces of typography (Pl. 96), and the inside pages no less beautiful. East was also a considerable printer of other books, and over 250 items are credited to him in the *Short Title Catalogue.*

The way the early printers prepared their MSS, set up their type and corrected their proofs is of the greatest importance to modern textual criticism and the establishing of what authors actually wrote. Various manuscripts still exist which are known to have been used as copy by English prin-

ters, even as early as Wynkyn de Worde, besides corrected proofs of all periods. A detailed account of the subject is given in Dr Percy Simpson's *Proof Reading in the 16th, 17th and 18th Centuries* (London, 1935), and particular instances are described in various issues of *The Library,* e.g. Fifth Series, Vol. VIII, No. 4 (Dec., 1953).

Besides books, there was much printing, from the earliest times, of ballads and broadsheets. There is a scene in *The Winter's Tale,* Act 4, in which a shepherdess-customer says: 'I love a ballad in print, a life, for then we are sure they are true'; and the pedlar says: 'Here's another ballad of a fish that appeared upon the coast, on Wednesday the fourscore of April, forty thousand fadom above water ...' 'Is it true too, think you?' – 'Five Justices' hands at it, and witnesses more than my pack will hold' ... and so on. These ballads are now extreme rarities, but examples are possessed by, for example, the British Museum and the Society of Antiquaries in London. Another kind of ephemeral Elizabethan printing is described in E.F. Bosanquet's *English Printed Almanacks and Prognostications* (to 1600) (London, Bibliographical Society, 1917).

In 1586 came the final and worst Star Chamber decree restricting printing in Elizabeth's reign. It confined all printing to London and the two Universities, and forbade the setting up of any new printing business, 'till the excessive multitude of Printers having presses already set up be abated, diminished, and by death given over ...' [15] No books could be printed, except by the Queen's Printer (and apart from Law Books), without being licensed by the Archbishop of Canterbury and the Bishop of London. The red light of censorship was to gleam unhelpfully on English printing all through the coming century.

[15] J. R. Tanner: *Tudor Constitutional Documents,* Cambridge, 1930.

The
Stuart Period
1603-1714

After Hollar, 1644.

Acknowledgments

The title-page of this section has been adapted from an etching by Wenceslaus Hollar, dated 1644, which forms the frontispiece to *Aula Veneris*, a series of plates etched and mostly drawn by Hollar of women's costumes of the period. The line block is enlarged to about twice the size of the original.

For the illustrations on pages 379 and 420 acknowledgment is made to the Bodleian Library, Oxford.

The two engravings on Plate 1 of this section and the line illustration on page 276 are reproduced by kind permission of the Fellows of Magdalene College, Cambridge.

The original photographs for Plate 95A and B were kindly lent by A. F. Johnson, Esq.

The fount of Union Pearl on page 508 was kindly supplied by Stephenson Blake and Company Limited of Sheffield.

For the illustration on page 504 acknowledgment is made to the British and Foreign Bible Society.

For the following illustrations acknowledgment is made to Picture Post Library: Plates 2, 3, 4, 83 and the tail-pieces on pages 442 and 500.

The line drawings in this section are by Susan Bader, Mrs R. J. Charleston, Sheila Cheese, Audrey Frew, Elizabeth Hammond and Judith Spero.

The Jacobean Age

PETER LASLETT

When the great Queen Elizabeth died at Richmond on the 24th March, 1603, the most glorious English age had come to an end. Never again was so English a person to wear the English crown. No longer was Shakespeare's little, little land to be the land of the English alone, for with her successor, James I, begins the era of Britain and the British, England, Scotland, Wales and Ireland. No longer could the English look upon their country as the westernmost European community, an island off the great historic continent. It was not to be an outpost, but a centre. By the year 1714, at the time of the death of Queen Anne, great-granddaughter to James I, it was indeed a centre: it was fast becoming the centre of the world.

An age of influence from outside

For this period of some one hundred and ten years the name of the Royal Family was Stuart, and it is often called the Jacobean age because in Latin James becomes Jacobus. In the history of Europe as a whole, this century – the seventeenth century – is sometimes referred to as the century of greatness, intellectual greatness. The British peoples shared to the full in this triumph of the European intellect: indeed, at the end of the epoch our great men were perhaps the most distinguished of them all. Although for most of the time we lived to ourselves and apart from the Continent, these were generations of pervasive influence on the English from outside the English borders. Scottish James was getting on for forty when he came to the throne, and he brought with him a Scottish Court and Scottish favourites. His second son, Charles, was only three years old when he came to England. But this weakly child, born at Dunfermline and intended for the Church, was to die on the scaffold at Whitehall as Charles I, King of England, Scotland and Ireland. High tragedy of the great Shakespearian sort is associated with him, but from our point of view his successful marriage is almost as important as his terrible death. His wife was Henrietta Maria of France: she herself was quintessentially French, and with this determined lady, the mother of Charles II and James II, there came into England a strong and persisting pressure from the most cultivated and successful nation in the world.

Seventeenth century Europe, in fact, came to be dominated by the French, militarily and politically, but above all in the arts. The English Royal Court, like all the rest of them, took to French manners, French furniture and decoration, French literary and artistic modes, and with the Court, as always, went the great nobility and those within the fashion. But it was not only from France that the alien winds blew upon the society of Stuart England. European commerce and finance were governed not from Paris, but from Amsterdam, Rotterdam and the other large cities of the United Provinces of Holland. The British Isles were set for much of the century in a Dutch seascape, and a strong sea-breeze from Holland blew through the huge city of London and over the whole English commercial and industrial community. When the House of Stuart gave way for a while to the rule of the Protector Cromwell in the

1650's, this Dutch influence became stronger still, and naval and commercial rivalry with Holland a dominating theme. From then on the French and the Dutch pulled a tug-of-war over England, and at the Glorious Revolution of 1688 the Dutch were the winners. From that year until his death in 1702 the English king was a Dutchman: William III, Stadtholder of Holland and leader of the European coalition against the mighty Louis XIV of France. Our houses, our painting, our books, many of the articles of our ordinary use showed plainly enough this Dutch economic and political infiltration.

Neither Holland nor France at this time was the simple national community which we think of when we call to mind the England of William Shakespeare. Through the high culture of France, the cultivated Englishman was brought into contact with the world of ancient Greece and Rome, with Turkey and the Middle East, even with the far Orient of India and China. Through the merchants of Amsterdam, and to an ever-increasing extent through those of London and Bristol, the English men of business caught their first glimpses of the primitive peoples of Africa and the Americas. Strange, wild but rich landscapes, far indeed from the English counties, but important for the future of the English peoples. These travellers' tales told the clergymen and the philosophers of men without the idea of a God, of peoples undreamt of in the Bible and the Christian revelation. Something of the world as it really is, the world as we now know it, was beginning to be dimly seen, and it was through English eyes that it was to be first seen as a complete whole.

The seeds of Empire

For if they were so much under the pressure of forces from outside, the English people of the Stuart age were nevertheless themselves a great and growing force upon Europe and the world. It was the arrogant Tudor, Henry VIII, who had first proclaimed that 'this realm of England is an Empire', and it was under his daughter Elizabeth's rule that the English first set foot in the American continent. But it was not until the time of the Stuarts that the first English colonies sprang up

and that the Englishman first felt himself a member of an imperial race, where Empire meant something very different, something close to what we mean by it now.

Our imperial mission began at home, in the unfortunate country of Ireland. By the end of the century the English dominated the other countries in the British Isles far more completely than they had ever done before. Along the western seaboard of the North Atlantic those British colonies which were so soon to become the United States of America were already flourishing. Not only in the Atlantic, but also in the Mediterranean, in the Indian and China seas, English seamen, English merchants and slave-traders were everywhere to be found. There was no longer one English community, but many: the English at home, the English elsewhere in the British Isles and especially Ireland, and the English overseas, especially in America.

All this meant wealth and power. The money and the rulership went to the merchants who exploited this vast hinterland, and to the noblemen who were given the task of administering the areas which were conquered and settled. But the booty, the silks, the spices, the precious metals and the jewels, the tropical timber, the tobacco, the sugar, the industrial raw materials – the big English share of Europe's sack of the rest of the world – these things went to English society as a whole. They came not simply by crude piracy and loot, which had been the pattern under Elizabeth, but by the part we played in the growth of European trade: the Atlantic trade routes wound about the English seas, but we found our way into the trading lines with Russia, India and China also. Ours was already a rich country, well up to the rest in the development of agriculture, industry and commerce. The new wealth intensified the process of economic change, and in the end it helped to bring about the growth of modern industrialism, though the Stuart age was not one of uniform economic progress. What interests us is how the English used the wealth which was coming to them. Some of it – a great deal more than might be expected – went into houses, furnishing and gardens. Indeed, it was the men of the Stuart age who first thought of England as we still would like to think of her—as a garden, or as a stately house set in a garden.

The growth of England's foreign trade and her wealth generally has a more obvious bearing on our subject. It was because of this opening up of the world's markets and resources that it became possible to use Virginian walnut for desks and tall-boys, to put Indian tea and Arabian coffee into china cups, instead of small beer into pewter flagons. It was because so many people could afford to live substantially that so much was created to enable them to do so, by the silversmiths and the potters, the iron-masters and the glaziers, the girdlers, the haberdashers and the cordwainers, as well as the carpenters, painters and architects. But the proportion of their income which people will be prepared to spend on things like these will depend on who they are and what their standards have to be. The historian, then, must explain what sort of people they were, these English nobles, gentry and merchants who used all these things, as well as saying why it was they could afford them. But before we look more closely at English society at this time, and the way it was arranged so as to require the things which are the subject of this book, it is necessary to remind ourselves of what happened to the English and the British under the Stuarts—the doings of the kings, the battles, the revolutions and so on.

Elizabethans and Jacobeans

James I reigned for nearly a generation, from 1603 to 1625. These were twenty-two years of marked political decline for the English throne: from being just about adequately rich, effective at home and respected abroad, and above all immensely popular under the last of the Tudors, it became, under the first of the Stuarts, dangerously impoverished, less efficient in governance and noticeably less beloved. Nevertheless the life of the country as a whole did not change very much with the change in the surname of the sovereign. When, indeed, the English Bible was published in 1611, its preface talked of 'that Bright *Occidental* Star, Queen Elizabeth' as if the afterglow was still to be seen in the sky. The shining constellation was still above the horizon when James himself

died: Shakespeare lived until 1616, and it was for the subjects of James I, not Elizabeth, that many of his plays were staged; Bacon lived until 1626, and Ben Jonson till the year 1637, the very eve of the climacteric of the whole Jacobean epoch. The aesthetic life of these first forty years of the new century was very little different from what had gone before.

But there were two changes of fundamental importance going forward, one religious and the other constitutional and political. A great and growing body of powerful religious opinion, the Puritans and Puritanism, was becoming more and more hostile to the official organization of the English or Anglican Church, the Tudor Establishment. Now the Church and its bishops were part of the State itself, and in demanding the abolition of the office of bishop, the Puritans were threatening the whole political fabric. Meanwhile James I was finding it more and more difficult to get on with the English Parliament, both because its members tended to be Puritan sympathizers and also because they were beginning to take a view of the proper constitution of the country somewhat different from what had been previously assumed. The Crown, on its side, was also developing a constitutional attitude which Parliamentarians could feel was new, unjustifiable and autocratic. In this way the basic social and political linkage—that between the Crown (the Government) and the country at large—was being progressively weakened. The great debate of the Jacobean age was well on its way.

Under James himself neither of these issues became extreme. Religious uniformity was maintained somehow, and both Puritan and Catholic dissidents kept under control: after the Gunpowder Plot of 1605 the measures against the Catholics began to look ugly. As the reign went on, successive Parliaments became successive crises. The inflation of the previous century continued, and its political results became evident. The fixed income of the Crown grew smaller and smaller in proportion to the growing cost of government. All attempts to supplement the royal revenue from parliamentary taxation tended to break down, because the members tried to get their grievances redressed before they would grant the money, and grievances began to include the foreign and religious policy of the Crown, which James would not allow to be the concern of Parliament. He bullied, cajoled and complained in what was to be the Stuart fashion. It was not only Parliament which he had to treat so, but the common lawyers who found his financial expedients and his ideas on the extent of the royal prerogative to be against English legal precedent and practice.

For the rest, James I filled up the English peerage, to some degree, with his own Scottish favourites, and he created a new order, the order of baronets. Baronetcies were sold, and so were knighthoods too: suitable candidates were impelled to take them. This was done because the fees helped the royal revenue, and the titles made it clear where political and economic influence lay – among the English gentry. He made peace with Spain, and pursued a weak and ineffective policy abroad: he could scarcely afford anything else. One incidental result of this was that English gentlemen began to travel abroad and see for themselves how cultivated Frenchmen and Italians lived.

Charles I and the Puritan upheaval

When Charles I succeeded in 1625 the position of the Crown was such that unless some sort of settlement could be reached with Parliament, government of the country along the traditional lines would no longer be possible. But the gentlemen of the House of Commons, Puritans and lawyers as so many of them were, were no more prepared to trust son than they had been to trust father: from the beginning they suspected Charles of Catholic leanings, and they hated his Catholic French wife. He had inherited a disastrous military policy and an even more disastrous favourite, Buckingham, to carry it out. He summoned three new parliaments in his first four years, so difficult had his financial position become: in return he got not supplies, not even those which his father had been given and which were regarded as the traditional right of the Crown, but a classic statement of the Parliamentary championship of the rights of the people, the Petition of Right of 1628. After this Charles I resolved to rule without Parliament,

and in respect of some of his taxation at least, to rule outside the law. There succeeded the famous interlude known as the Eleven Years' Tyranny, though this title suggests a despotism far harsher than the mild inefficiency of a Stuart ruling alone.

It lasted from 1629 to 1640, and these were perhaps the most placid and prosperous years of the whole century. Money was raised by the revival of obsolete royal dues, and so successful was this policy at a time when nothing expensive was undertaken that financial disaster was avoided. This was the period of Strafford and Laud, Strafford being Chief Minister and overcoming opposition with his policy of 'Thorough', and Laud the Archbishop of Canterbury, putting down the Puritans. It looked as if England was going the same way as most other European monarchies, where the Estates of the Realm (or Parliaments) were disappearing for want of being summoned, and monarchs were ruling alone, as despots. But the English gentry were forging weapons of resistance unknown to Frenchmen or to Spaniards, and when John Hampden of Buckinghamshire refused to pay Ship Money, the most famous of the royal impositions, in 1635, the end of early Stuart despotism was in sight.

It would not have ended unless Charles and Laud had blundered into war, war which could be paid for only by something more substantial than arbitrary impositions. In 1637 they decided to require the clergy of Scotland to conform to a liturgy of the Anglican, episcopal type, and within a very few months Charles found himself fighting his own native kingdom. The royal expedition to punish the rebellious Scots was a dreary fiasco, and Charles summoned Parliament at last early in 1640, as it had traditionally been summoned to meet a national emergency. The response of the outraged members was so discouraging to the Royal policy, that Charles sent them all away once more. But by this time his position was desperate, and the only way of buying off the invaders was to summon Parliament once again, and to agree at long last to some redress of religious and political grievances. In September 1640 the Long Parliament – the longest in our history, for it was not to be finally and legally dissolved until

1660 – was summoned to Westminster. This Parliament brought about revolution.

For two years the gentlemen of the House of Commons had their way with the royal policy, the royal ministers and the governmental institutions. Led by John Pym, a clear majority voted to remodel everything which they found obnoxious, unchristian in their definition of Christianity or unconstitutional: there was no one but the King and his Court to oppose them, because until 1642 no Royalist party existed, at Westminster or in the country at large. But Englishmen had yet to teach themselves that permanent, acceptable change cannot be brought about except by compromise and in gradualness: Pym was running his country into civil war. In 1642 it came, and it was nearly won for the Crown in the first few months by the strength of traditional loyalties and the inexperience of Parliament in anything else but legislation and debate. But on the Parliamentary side were ranged first the earnest mass of the Puritans and second the wealthier half of the kingdom, London and the south-east. The eastern counties brought into being a New Model Army, organized and financed in a way quite different from the armies of the King or any other army before. The man who commanded it was a gentleman from Cambridge and the Fenland, a sober, convinced Puritan of the extremer wing: his name was Oliver Cromwell.

When Cromwell won the first Civil War at the battle of Naseby in the year 1645 the English people broke with their traditional past. For the first time in the history of Europe an army claiming to be the army of the people as a whole had defeated and made helpless a legal sovereign; in their own eyes, and in the eyes of their supporters then and ever since, moreover, they had vindicated for the first time and in the most conspicuous fashion the principle of government by the consent of the governed. But the political problem, the problem of who should govern England and how, had not been solved: it was to take forty-five years to solve it. A whole complicated series of negotiations had to take place with the defeated King, a second Civil War had to be fought, an extraordinary interlude had to be faced in which the common man was to be seen for the first time at the centre of

political decisions, before the next stage could come about. This was the stage at which it became inevitable that a court should be set up to try Charles Stuart, King of England, and find him guilty. He was executed on the 30th January 1649. The future of the country now lay not with the representatives of the people in Parliament, which had been so purged that it was hardly recognizable, but with Cromwell and his generals.

The problem of government

It was not until 1653 that Oliver Cromwell was made Lord Protector. By that time he had conquered Ireland, defeated Scotland and raised the military fame of his country to a height which it had not reached for two hundred years. Once again the English had a foothold on the Continent, in the French seaport of Dunkirk; the Protector's navy was victorious in home waters and in the Indies. But the changes which had come about since 1640 were far wider than the establishment of a new political regime and an outburst of patriotic fervour. The English Church was stripped down and the Anglicans turned into a persecuted minority. In obedience to Puritan principle the theatres were closed, and the stream of dramatic writing – the peculiarly English literary activity – was interrupted. The whole ambience of English society was changed. The settled rule of the squires in the countryside was almost replaced by direct military command, in the form of Cromwell's major-generals: the trauma about a standing army sank deep into the national consciousness. But for all his strength and success, the political problem defeated the Lord Protector. After his death in 1658 and the short rule of his son Richard in his place and with his title, the Cromwellian system collapsed with dismal suddenness. With it went the ideal of the first British Commonwealth, a republic with Irish delegates in an assembly made almost representative. In 1660 the Stuarts were restored, and to the stern countenance of the Lord Protector succeeded the clever, good-humoured face of Charles II; Old Rowley, the hero of the sporting gentry and the darling of the ladies of the theatres, flourishing once again.

B

In the popular memory, then, the reign of Charles II, from 1660 to 1685, and the whole Restoration period up to 1688, is a time of rejoicing and of licence. A carefree and loose-living Court we still remember, a country doing its best to believe that the 1630's had returned: Milton, once Cromwell's Latin secretary, at work on *Paradise Lost*, blind, ageing and despised. Perhaps it is true that the Restoration was a period of social relaxation and excess. The dingy rule of the Saints was expiated on Newmarket Heath, at the Royal Sport of racing horses, and in many a gentleman's hall, where the brimming Stuart silver flagons were hoisted in damnation to the enemies of Church and King. But the most important date in English history between 1660 and 1688, perhaps of the whole Stuart Age, was not marked by a war, or a revolution, or anything conspicuous or violent, but by something much more sudden and final. This was the year 1687 when *Principia Mathematica* by Mr Isaac Newton was published, and the problem of the physical world was solved – finally solved, or so it seemed to an astonished England and Europe.

For the gay courtiers and ministers around Charles II were 'natural philosophers', members of his own most enduring creation, the Royal Society. And there was another development of the less exciting but permanently influential sort – that of religious toleration. The Puritans who were driven from political influence and religious control in 1660 did not disappear before the victorious Anglicans. In the counting-houses of the merchants, in the colonial enterprises – and this is the time when the growth of the American colonies and of foreign trade in general was becoming really formidable – the Puritans flourished and got rich as the Dissenters, tolerated in their religion if excluded from politics. Their persistence and their influence helped to intensify the problem of the distribution of political power.

Philosophy, parties and revolutions

The instability in the foundations of English political and constitutional life showed itself vividly enough in the events of the last few years of Charles II, when civil war and revolution came very near to the surface once again. Fear of Catholicism and the power of the Pope had been a national neurosis for three generations, and Charles himself was a crypto-Catholic; James, his brother and heir, was an open convert. For all his suave ingenuity, Charles had been incautious enough in 1670 to sign a secret treaty with that almighty Catholic, King Louis XIV, promising – with some cynicism, no doubt – the conversion of England. The ablest and most vigorous of his ministers then was Lord Ashley, a champion of the Dissenters and of Toleration, and within a few years he was at the head of a nation-wide opposition movement. When Shaftesbury – Ashley's final title – ferreted out the truth of Charles's promises to France, he was outraged and furious: furious that he had been tricked, for he was no inept trickster himself, and outraged as a patriotic, Protestant Englishman. In 1678 the master card fell into Shaftesbury's hand. Titus Oates, the nastiest liar in our history, a man whose morals were too low for life aboard ship, 'revealed' a Popish plot to kill the King and put his Catholic brother on the throne; a few days later a conspicuous champion of Protestantism was mysteriously murdered. Shaftesbury made out of the coincidence of this with the informations of Oates a full-scale Parliamentary campaign to exclude James from the succession, and between 1679 and 1681 England looked the same as she had in 1639–41: on the eve of an insoluble conflict and bloodshed. It was perhaps mainly because the terrible memory of the Civil War was so close to everyone that Shaftesbury failed, and died an exile in Holland in 1683. A year later James the Catholic did succeed to the throne, on a surprising wave of popularity for the Stuart Crown.

It did not last for long. By 1688 it was James II who was in exile – in France and not in Holland, for out of Holland came the expedition which dethroned him. With his successors, William and Mary, we approach the last phase of the Stuart story, but before we go into it we might look for a moment at the new generation of Englishmen who had grown up since the Puritan Revolution. We may take Shaftesbury himself as our example, together with his 'assistant pen',

John Locke, one of the cleverest Englishmen who ever lived. They were both originally Puritans, and they were both born in the 1630's into the ranks of the English gentry of the south-west. Shaftesbury was rich and ambitious, endowed with every attribute for success in politics and in the vital business of making money out of trade and the colonies. He was successively a soldier for Charles 1; a general, then a minister for Cromwell; one of the engineers of the Stuart Restoration; a baron; Chancellor of the Exchequer; the chief mover in the settlement of the colony of Carolina; Lord Chancellor, an Earl and a Whig – the founder of the Whig party, in fact. 'Sagacious, bold and turbulent of wit', John Dryden, the Poet Laureate, was paid to call him, and by his shrivelling satire blasted his reputation for ever. 'Resolved to ruine or to rule the State.' Dryden was a Tory – these imperishable party names were coined at this time – and Dryden, like Shaftesbury, was a turncoat and a Fellow of the Royal Society. Conspicuously able they both were, but their outlook and experience were nevertheless typical.

John Locke wore chamois-leather pants beneath his splendid, silken Jacobean breeches. These details are worth recording because they remind us that we have at last reached the time when we can begin to know about men in enlarged detail – almost talk with them, in fact – which we could never do before. He loved oranges, and had a man specially posted to tell him when the fleet from Spain was coming up the river to London, so that he could get them fresh. But his favourite fruit was a true exotic, one that Englishmen had only just got to know about: the noble pineapple from the Indies. He went to Westminster School as the son of a modest gentleman, and was there, within earshot of the frightened crowd, when Charles 1 was beheaded. From Westminster to Christ Church, Oxford, from there to Shaftesbury's political household in London, then to France for an extensive residence among the highly intellectual; back to London for the Popish Plot, then away after his dead master to Holland to exile with the rest of the hard core of the Whigs in 1683. He was in Holland when the

Glorious Revolution of 1688 was brought about by a combination of exasperated Tories and Whigs.

The gentry of England, of all opinions, could no longer endure James 11 as a catholicizing king, nor face the prospect of a Catholic Stuart heir in the baby boy who was born to him in that year. Locke was not there in November 1688 to hear the young mothers of England singing over their cradles

> Hush-a-bye baby on the tree-top,
> When the wind [1] blows the cradle will rock,
> When the bough breaks the cradle will fall,
> Down will come baby,[2] and cradle and all.

But Locke came back in the very ship which brought in that unfortunate infant's elder half-sister Mary to reign as co-sovereign with William. It was only in the changed air of the final Stuart reigns that Locke could settle down to publish the theories of knowledge, of politics, of education, economics and religion which set the mould of English intellectual life, at home and in America, for hundreds of years to come. But he had worked them out in the years which saw the society of Milton and Cromwell change into the society of Newton and Sir Christopher Wren.

Political stability and war

Under William and Mary there was a state of political and constitutional equilibrium in England which has never since been upset. From being the least effective of the greater European countries, always liable to revert to civil strife and never able to put out her true strength for any length of time because her Government did not have the whole resources of the country behind it, England became the most stable, the best organized and, for her size, the most formidable of them all. It came about because after 1688 we were something quite new – not a despotism, not a republic, but a Parliamentary monarchy. The Crown accepted the rule of law and Parliament accepted political responsibility. These were years

[1] This wind was the Protestant wind which was to blow in William, the Protestant successor.
[2] This baby was the young Stuart who lived to be the Old Pretender.

of war against France. King William commanded a coalition of Protestant European powers against her, and led their armies in the field. The method of raising money for this prolonged conflict was also new, and also most important; for in 1694 the Bank of England was founded to help in government finance. National administration began to change in the direction of our own standard of efficiency, and meanwhile Parliament was passing a great code of statutes to sanction the classic English freedoms: freedom of the Press, freedom of the person, freedom of worship. Mary died in 1694, and William ruled alone for eight more years. When he died in 1702 neither the struggle against France nor the Revolution Settlement was finally complete.

William was succeeded by another daughter of James II: Queen Anne, the last of the Stuarts. In fact not one, but three people took over the task from him: Anne herself, and John and Sarah Churchill, Duke and Duchess of Marlborough. The Duke commanded the Protestant armies of Europe and the Duchess dominated the Queen, her bosom companion. The twelve years of Anne's reign were a story of glorious military success – Blenheim (1704), Ramillies (1706), Oudenarde (1708) – and of complicated strife between factions around the person of the sovereign. The Marlboroughs and the party for war against France were finally ousted by Robert Harley and the Tory peace party, acting in concert with an intriguing woman, unique in our annals, Abigail Masham. She rose from being Queen Anne's chambermaid to take Sarah's place in her affections and policy. But the work of saving Europe from French and Catholic domination was already done. The last important act of the Stuart dynasty was the signing of the Treaty of Utrecht in 1713, when Louis XIV at last admitted that the English, the Dutch and the others had their rights in Europe and in the expanding European world overseas. Parliament – and after 1707 it was an Anglo-Scottish assembly of a united kingdom – had provided for a Protestant successor in George, Elector of Hanover, great-grandson of James I in the female line. When he came to the throne in 1714, the name of the Royal family was not Stuart, but Guelph. Georgian England had begun.

The English people and the English gentlemen

We have told the story of the Stuart century much as our school books told it, from the point of view of the King, as if the person on the throne and what he did were the things that mattered most. But we have been forced from time to time, and this increasingly towards the end, to talk about the English people, in particular the English gentlemen, as if they were the real actors in the drama. It may seem surprising that for the word 'people' it is in fact possible to read the word 'gentlemen'. Of the five or six million persons living in England at the end of the Stuart period, there were some 50,000 gentlemen, and yet for practically all historians' purposes, and particularly for our purpose in this volume, this one per cent of the population is really all that mattered.

It was the gentlemen – including of course the nobility, though there were scarcely two hundred of them – who took all the political action. It was for them, above all, that the houses were built, the pictures were painted, the glassware, the silverware, the carpets, the tables, the chairs and the cabinets were made. Only these people were either educated or cultivated enough to know much of style, or indeed rich enough to be likely to possess anything which is to be found today in our houses, museums, or shops as an 'antique'. The whole of the rest of the population, except the considerable merchants – counted as gentry in any case for these purposes – lived under the direction, and even as the dependants, of this ruling minority. The great mass of the yeomanry, or farmers as we might call them, and of the trades-folk, with the far, far greater mass of those who worked for them, have very little to do with an account of English art and decoration.

The gentleman's family

How, then, did the gentle-folk live? The answer here is simple: they lived in families – large families: much larger than the family we think of. In the 1690's one of our early statisticians calculated that the 160 peers of his day lived in families of forty people, the 800 baronets had families of sixteen, the 20,000 gentlemen proper had families of eight to ten. This was not because there were more children in each family: certainly many more were born than now, and more into each of these families than in those below them in the social scale; but so many died that this is not what made them big. It was the fact that grandfathers, uncles, aunts and cousins tended to live together with father, mother and children, especially when death had broken up the families from which they came. Moreover the family was not confined to those related to each other: it included the servants. They lived in – not simply the cooks and housemaids and the gentlemen's valets, but even the farm-hands and gardeners, at least until they were married. Of the thirteen people reckoned by the same writer to live in each knighted household, seven, eight or even ten would be servants, though the definition of servant was wider than it is now. For the Stuart family had many more social and economic functions than ours has: it could be anything from a commercial establishment to the headquarters of a political party, at the same time as being a household as we know it.

The first thing such a large family needed was a house, big enough to accommodate all these people and grand enough to express the status of the family head. Nothing indicates more clearly that this period was one of insistence on the importance of the individual family than the fact that by the middle of it – between the beginning of Elizabeth's reign and the Civil War – an impressive proportion of all the houses in the country had either been built new or remodelled and extended. This building and rebuilding went on throughout the century and all over the country, and their connexion with architecture, furniture and decoration is perfectly obvious. Very often the alterations were confined to ceiling over the raftered rooms on the ground floor – the only floor – to make bedrooms upstairs, and opening out the roof to provide windows for them. The motive for this was psychological: a consciousness of a need for privacy which was offended by the previous habit of sleeping in the parlour, often the only second living-room in the house. Here we seem to be faced with a change in fundamentals; but the urge to build bigger, and with more rooms for each

person to live on his own, is connected with another historical movement: the one known as the rise of the gentry. But before we consider the relevance of this to our purposes, we may go a little further into the general shape of society.

A society of families

From what has already been said a simple picture of rural England can be drawn, and the country was seventy or eighty per cent rural. It was a landscape of villages each and every one of them with only one house of any size: the house of the local gentle family. Everything else and everyone else in that little locality were dominated by that house and household. This simple picture is familiar enough, and of course it is much too simple, though there were villages which conformed exactly to it, where every male inhabitant of military age would be described in the muster rolls as a 'servant' of the resident family. But the number of gentle houses in any village was frequently more than one, and there were also hamlets in which no gentleman's house was to be found. Each gentle family could have more than one house, often many miles apart. It made a considerable difference to the whole atmosphere of the community if the great family kept its main establishment at another house, or resided elsewhere for long periods.

But what was inside those houses is not much affected by these complications. What did affect it was the wealth and importance of the gentle family concerned, right down to the particular personality of its head. If he were a rich and successful nobleman, especially a nobleman who spent much of his time at Court or in the royal service, then he would have furnished and decorated his house in the village in imitation of the royal palaces he knew. He would have been abroad, and himself have seen the Flemish wall-hangings, the Venetian glass, the French cabinets, the Dutch printing the King had round him. And he might have bought such things for himself. He would certainly see that what was made for him showed signs of these foreign influences.

The number of these highly successful noble families was naturally small. We have in mind such surnames as the Cecils of Hatfield House, Earls of Salisbury and ministers to Elizabeth and James I; or the Wentworths of Wentworth Woodhouse under the Earl of Strafford, minister of Charles I; or the Ashley Coopers, of Wimborne St Giles, Earls of Shaftesbury, whom we have already mentioned; or the Osbornes of Yorkshire, whose fortunes were founded by Sir Thomas Osborne, successively minister to Charles II, James II and William and Mary and successively Earl of Danby, Marquess of Carmarthen and Duke of Leeds. We might add the family of Sir Winston Churchill, Comptroller of the Green Cloth to Charles II, and his son John Churchill, who ended as Duke of Marlborough and who has had some notable descendants. For the importance of this little knot of families was not confined to the Jacobean age.

The spread of fashion

Tiny as it was, this little group contained the key men in the process whereby the tone of the English style was struck. The high, cosmopolitan taste of the Court, varying as it did from king to king and influenced as it was from France, Holland and the rest of Europe, found its way from the royal residences to the country houses through this channel. The other nobles in the county where such a man had his seat could not fail to take note of what he imported, or had built, or had made for his splendid establishment, and the baronets, the knights and the gentry at large in that area would admire, envy and imitate too. This was how the high taste of the few became the fashion for the many. This is what it means to say that English decoration was to some extent inspired by France and by Holland in the seventeenth century. We must not forget that some of these men were foreigners by birth, like the Keppels, Earls of Albemarle, founded by a Dutch minister of William III.

The great country house, then, especially the new one set up by a family newly risen in the world, was the centre of growth and change, if only because its style both inside and out was necessarily new. But the extent to which it changed the taste of a local community – a county, above all, since the English gentry lived in county communities – depended on the personality of its owner. He might be a virtuoso himself – most of them were – with his own critical appreciation and an enthusiasm for the newly beautiful, but he might also be merely following a fashion he could not appreciate. The same thing applies with much more force to his neighbours, on his own social level and beneath. The anciently established noble house had a choice before it. It could keep the house and the accoutrements it had inherited, or it could rebuild and restock; it depended on the policy, taste and resources of its head at any one time. With the mass of the gentry, the choice was often even more difficult, and the variation greater. For them it was above all a matter of money – money possessed or money which must be made. A young gentleman could ruin himself and his family soon after he succeeded by spending too much on a new seat and new possessions. Or he could be content with what his ancestors had left him, improve his estate and let his descendants catch up with the times.

Stuart London

The process, then, was very irregular and uneven: whether a particular part of the country came under the influence of the newer forms of decoration depended on what great houses there were in the neighbourhood, and the attitude of their owners, together with the attitude of the local gentry to them and to the world at large. But there is one constant we must not overlook. All the gentry of Britain, especially those seated in the south and east, but even as far away as Northumberland and Wales, Cornwall and Ireland, and the American Colonies, had their connexions in London. They nearly all had occasions to visit London, on legal business most often, but also to go to Westminster to sit in the House of Commons. They nearly all had relatives there to stay with, since London was a tenth of the kingdom, and they reckoned kinship to the third or fourth remove of cousin. There, in the 'season', which began in early Stuart times, the gentry foregathered to make their marriage alliances and talk politics. And London, as we have said, was a cosmopolitan city, a European capital, fast becoming a world capital. The country gentleman during his stay in town met every day with the artifacts of continental Europe, and of the other continents too. He could, if he were rich or extravagant enough, order his next suit of clothes or a Tompion clock or a new set of chairs in the workshops of the best and most fashionable craftsmen in the country. He might well meet the Sovereign himself. The sights these men saw must have had a direct influence on many a remote manor-house: they were quite literal when they claimed on their return that they had seen the world.

London had always played this part in English life, and in the succeeding century it was even more important. But two things happened to London in the Jacobean age which intensified its effect on English cultural life, both of them of high interest to our subject. In 1666 the city was burnt. This gave Sir Christopher Wren his opportunity, as we all know, but the rebuilding which this disaster brought about would have transformed English architecture even if no presiding genius had been there to take advantage of it. The new style of domestic and church architecture of the reviving city was there in abundance for all the City to see in the three last decades of the seventeenth century. All these new buildings and houses needed new furniture and decoration: there is no need to dwell on the stimulus which this gave to the cabinet-maker and designer, or all the trades associated with the creation of new houses for the richest and largest city in the kingdom. The other development was much more gradual. It was the slow divergence of the social environment of London from that of other towns. Something of our own shopkeeping, commercial society, class-conscious in quite a different sense from the one we have been using, was already becoming apparent in London.

The bulk of what is to be surveyed in this volume has come from the houses of the gentry, or their London cousins. The contents of the great noble houses, the masterpieces and the museum exhibits, were important for their influence, but very few in number: far fewer than we should think from the proportion of things surviving, for it is natural that the very best should be preserved. But it is from the houses of the gentlemen that the vast majority of Stuart settles, stools, beadwork baskets and bedstead hangings have come, not from royal and noble households. The most important thing about the English gentry at this time is, in a sense, their number. Not only did they outnumber the nobility by hundreds to one, but their collective wealth was greater than that of the rest of the society put together – nobility, Crown and all. The general social process going on throughout the century, though most marked in the earlier generations, was the growth in the number and importance of the gentry, in social and economic weight as well as in political supremacy. This was what historians call the 'rise of the gentry'. It was not simply the sudden success of mere gentlemen, who, like Sir Thomas Osborne and Sir Anthony Ashley Cooper, became great nobles, but the persistent promotion of men of lower status to the status of gentry, in trade and industry as well as in agriculture.

The 'rise of the gentry'

It is important to realize what this meant. It distinguished English society from that of France and the rest of continental Europe. There the nobles were more powerful and the gentlemen much more subordinated to them, and those below far more distant, far less likely to rise into the gentle class. There also the merchants lived in their towns, apart from the nobility of the countryside. It was the ease with which families could move upwards into gentry and into and out of the towns in the society of Stuart England that gave it its relatively modern flavour. The climb up the rung in the social ladder from below into the gentle class was critically important. It is especially significant to us, because directly a Stuart family had reached the condition of wealth and distinction which made it fit to undertake the social responsibilities of gentle conditions, then it had to accept them.

It had to accept them even if its money was made in industry or commerce and in the towns. It had to turn its money into a manor-house with all its accoutrements, it had to send its sons to the university, it had to live a life of relative leisure – not actually working in the fields or at the bench, as the richest yeoman could do. It was obliged, in fact, to 'bear the port and mien of a gentleman'. Inevitably, then, the paraphernalia of living the gentle life were multiplied among us. Is it, then, surprising that so many houses were rebuilt at this time, or that there is so much Stuart furniture and utensils, as compared with what we have from earlier periods? Not only did the family have to acquire these things, and replace them with better and more fashionable ones when the neighbours or relatives did so, but it also had to maintain them. The family had to go on, and it could not go down; hence the placing of the younger sons in commerce or colonies, hence the great struggle to get into Parliament or into offices under the Crown.

This brings us back to the point where we began our consideration of Stuart society as it can be seen reflected in the material things which have survived to us. This period, from the age of Elizabeth to the age of George I, we have said was the great age of the family, and the family was, typically, the family of hundreds and thousands of Stuart country gentlemen. All these families, and all at the same time, had to put glass into the windows of their houses when it became accepted that a gentleman's residence was glazed. All of them had to possess and even to read books, when the possession of books and an interest in them became one of the distinguishing marks of life in a gentle household: this meant bookcases and what we call 'Bible boxes', and later bureaux. They had to replace benches and joint stools with chairs for the same purpose, or cloth hangings with panelling, or rushes on the floor with carpeting – carpeting which is to be seen in so many contemporary pictures of Dutch interiors, not on the floor, but still on the tables. All these things had to be done to maintain the family in the way of life to which it had become accustomed. Wealth was growing fast enough to make these things possible, and therefore the relatively large number of Elizabethan and Stuart family possessions which still survive.

The people who worked

Something of the same kind was at work among the yeomen in the countryside and the smaller trades-folk in the towns, only there the compulsion to live up to a certain standard was not so much the issue. Indeed, it was still true that for a man or woman of that quality to dress as their superiors did or to surround themselves with things which their superiors used was a social offence. 'Aping your betters' is the phrase we still use for it, but it must be recognized that this was wrong only if the family concerned refused to undertake the burden of actually becoming a unit in the superior order. But when it comes to less conspicuous things like furniture or bed-linen, the line was not firmly drawn. Many a wealthy yeoman family was eating as well as the gentlemen, and its articles of everyday use might be exactly the same. Indeed, it was said even before Stuart times that,

> A Knight of Wales
> A Gentleman of Cales [perhaps Calais]
> A Laird of the North Countrie [Scotland]
> A Yeoman of Kent
> With his yearly rent
> Will buy them out all three.

But this was the prosperous yeoman, frequently with resources outside his own little holding of land. Often a yeoman could not read; he might live on a pressed-earth floor, in a house with no upstairs: even at night he was among his cattle, if not in the same room (as he was in Holland as late as 1690), yet under the same roof. It was no disgrace for him to live like this, as it would be for a gentleman to live below his condition. Most yeomen were obliged to do so. Theirs was a life of working and getting, and from such surroundings as these nothing of elegance to interest us could possibly come. Far less so could it come from the much greater number even worse off than the yeoman. These people, the workers in the country and in the towns, were housed in flimsy hovels under conditions which we can only compare to those we know of in Asiatic countries. That is, when they were able to live at home, for these were the servants of their betters, and many of them lived as part of the families in the houses.

Not that they are unimportant to our subject. They made all the things we are interested in, and on their craftsmanship everything we prize depended. Moreover, they carried on the folk traditions of decoration, celebration and so on which survived unaltered, though perhaps diminishing, throughout the Jacobean age – but these things belong to folklore and folk museums rather than to our present purpose. But neither the yeomen nor they were likely to be able to afford many things elaborate enough to become the sort of 'antique' which we collect, though their candlesticks and warming-pans still interest us. In the richer cities it was different and particularly in London, whose differences from the rest of the country we have already hinted at.

Nine stools for nine children

There is much more that should be said about the family in the Stuart age and the way in which its development and maintenance gave rise to our modern conceptions of what a house should contain. There is a great deal of evidence about it, evidence which is only now beginning to be used by the historian. When the ruling head of a family of gentry died and his property had to be disposed of according to his will, an inventory of his possessions had to be made. There are thousands and thousands of these, and they cover many yeomen, and people we have had no occasion to mention so far, like the clergy, as well as the gentry. From them we learn, for example, that a gentleman of the rich county of Kent who died in 1629, and who had had nine children, possessed nine joint stools for them to sit on. We also know how many beds he had and everything else the family used, including the instruments in his dairy and brewhouse – all part of the household establishment, of course. All that we can do is to mention such lists here. There are many more sources open to the use of people who want to know about the material possessions of that society in order to understand its domestic environment and style of decoration. There are lists of things ordered from home by settlers in the colonies, for example: the gentleman whose stools we mentioned was sent such a list every year by his brother in Virginia, ordering all the things which were necessary to stock his house in its tobacco plantation just as the Kentish manor-house itself was stocked.

Such, then, is the significance for the structure and development of English society in Stuart times of the objects of beauty and of use which this volume describes. When he looks at what remains of Jacobean architecture and decoration, the social historian interprets them in terms of the rising and consolidating gentry of that age. He thinks of rivalries between families, and all that it meant to politics, local and national; he thinks of the struggle to maintain each family, as generation gave way to generation, in the proper style of comfort and elegance, and the rebuilding and refurnishing which were necessary; he thinks of the expedients these gentlemen used to that end, and this brings in trade, colonies and the law. Above all, he has in mind what was being created: a way of living for a large community of substantial people, not nobles, but not men at work, not even a middle class, since that term has such deceptive overtones; but independent, small-scale gentry living indoors and outdoors in the classic English fashion.

Accident or design?

We must end with a word or two in justification of our claim that it is the life of the gentleman's family which explains what we want to know. Like the nobility, the gentlemen themselves decided how far they should modify the household equipment to keep pace with the changing times. The result of all the changes made by so many people was something which might be described as a conscious policy, a policy of arranging things in just the way which would make the life of the family as convenient and dignified as English standards required. The innumerable squires and squires' wives who made these changes were, of course, not themselves aware that they were creating a way of life, a particular environment. But there were exceptional men among them who did realize just this. Of the considerable number of them, we can mention only one: John Evelyn, of Sayes Court, in Deptford. Evelyn, as his well-known diary and famous books make clear, had an attitude to these things which is almost exactly what we understand when we see 'House and Garden' on the cover of a magazine. He took the whole tradition of gardening and planting as it had been practised in Europe and elsewhere since the fall of Rome. In his books and in his own garden at Sayes Court he blended it into that manner of creating a secluded and beautiful home which is the most conspicuous element of leisured life in England to this day. For some generations now a large part of the world has been trying to live as the English country gentry lived and live. They do so because of what happened in our island under the reign of the house of Stuart.

uyn cancun ens peut tomber sur celuy, qui es fondemens de la sapience, aura jette la temperance et continence, deux pilliers sur lesquels l'homme ayant poss'e toute son esperance ne peut estre ebranle de la fortune.

A copperplate engraving (reduced) from a Stuart writing-master's book, *Calligrapho Technia* by Richard Gething, dated 1619. From Samuel Pepys's collection in Magdalene College, Cambridge.

Architecture

MARGARET WHINNEY

'Houses are built to live in and not to look on; therefore let use be preferred before uniformity, except where both may be had.' Bacon's essay *Of Building*, which opens with these words, was written after 1612 and published in 1625, but its views were already largely out of date. For Jacobean houses reveal a consistent attempt at symmetry (i.e. uniformity) in their exterior design, though in most cases the interior was not symmetrically arranged. The great hall, entered through á screen at one end, still dominated the plan, and at Hatfield House, finished in 1611, it is still balanced on the other side of the entrance by a series of smaller service rooms. Experiments were being made, however, at for instance Charlton House, Greenwich (1607–12) (Pl. 5A) with placing the hall across, and not along, the main axis of the house, and thus permitting a more symmetrical arrangement of the rooms on either side of it. Lord Bacon's statement is, however, of interest for the attitude it reveals. Symmetry is agreeable, but use, or convenience, is more important. And even though most patrons in his day might have been reluctant to destroy the appearance of a house by unbalanced wings, they were very willing to vary the shape and size of their windows to suit the character and use of the rooms behind them. At Charlton House, where there is a saloon on the top floor over the hall, a great window, far larger than any other on the front, is uncomfortably placed on the upper storey of the porch. It is convenient, for it gives a good light in the big room behind it, but not happy in its relation to the rest of the façade, and is the clear result of designing from within outwards. It, and all the windows in houses of this kind, are divided into many lights, and are the direct descendants of medieval windows of the Perpendicular period. Their size can be varied at will by the addition or omission of some of the lights.

The new style of Inigo Jones

Four years after Charlton was completed, the first house in England which attempted the discipline of fitting the interior to the exterior was begun. This was the Queen's House at Greenwich (Pl. 5B), designed by Inigo Jones, who had recently returned from the last of his journeys to Italy. There he had learnt the theory of the great Italian architects of the Renaissance, a theory based on a system of strict mathematical proportions controlling plan, elevation, and indeed every detail of the house. Windows are no longer of varied shapes and sizes, but run in an even and scarcely broken rhythm along the front. The building is compact (it consisted originally of two rectangular blocks behind each other and joined by a bridge), simple and clear-cut in its outlines, with no projecting porches or bay windows, and no towers breaking the skyline. The rooms within are planned in small suites, each room carefully proportioned to the next, and the hall, which is a perfect cube, is no longer a living-room, as in the traditional English house, but has become something of a grand entrance vestibule. Inigo Jones's revolution in English architecture was not limited to the Italian character of his designs. He was, indeed, a new kind of man, a professional architect in the modern sense instead of a craftsman. Before his time, though a master mason or possibly a surveyor might have designed a house, he would not have been responsible for exterior and interior alike. The other craftsmen, carpenters, plasterers and smiths, would have made their separate contracts with the patron, and no one designer would have controlled the whole undertaking. Jones, who had absorbed Italian views about the prestige of an artist, was the first to introduce into England the idea of an architect as the single controlling mind, dominating the entire work. He is therefore a vitally important figure in the history of English architecture, and though little of his work has survived unaltered, the Queen's House, the Banqueting House, Whitehall (now the United Service Museum), and the Queen's Chapel at St James's, are enough to reveal his quality.

His position as a country-house architect is more difficult to assess. Many houses have been attributed to him on slender grounds, for since his reputation, particularly in the eighteenth century, was great, almost all Italianate building, good or bad, of the early seventeenth century, was ascribed to him. Some knowledge of Italian forms was, however, by now available even for Englishmen who had not been to Italy, for in 1611 a translation of the architectural treatise of Sebastiano Serlio was published by Robert Peake. Moreover, English gentry travelled to Italy more freely in the seventeenth than in the sixteenth century (though the number who did so was still small); many more became interested in Italian and French books on architecture. The Flemish books which had been mainly used as pattern books when James I came to the throne were gradually recognized as lacking in taste, for their florid designs were seen to be a distortion of the best Italian models. Such a work as the Italianate entrance front of Castle Ashby, Northamptonshire, built probably about 1630, may well be the result of an intelligent study of Italian books, though since it is fairly accomplished it may possibly have been built under the advice of Jones or someone who had worked with him. Much of Jones's time was taken up with work for the Crown, both on buildings and Court

masques, and it has recently become known that even so important a member of the Court circle as the Earl of Pembroke could not command his full attention. For the south front of Wilton House was almost certainly built by a Frenchman, Isaac de Caux, in consultation with Jones. The executed building is only part of a larger design for a very long Italianate palace with a great columned portico in the centre.

These examples prove clearly enough that the new Italian manner fostered by Jones had caught the fancy of the builders of great houses by the 1630's. He also had an effect on more modest buildings. For there is little doubt he was responsible for the introduction of a new kind of house (Fig. 1): a simple box-like building with a sloping roof sharply separated from the walls by a deep projecting cornice, with plain rectangular windows all similar in design, running in straight rows across the front, with plain chimneys rising above the roof, and often with a balustraded platform between them. Unfortunately Chevening in Kent, which was probably designed by Jones himself about 1630, was altered in the eighteenth century, but the type is recorded in his drawings and was frequently copied and adapted by other architects. Thorpe Hall in Northamptonshire, built by Peter Mills, Bricklayer and afterwards Surveyor to the City of London in 1654, and Ashdown House in Berkshire (Pl. 6B), designed by an unknown architect probably after 1660, are variants of the same pattern. It was indeed to become the most usual type of medium-sized house in the middle years of the century, and persists almost to the end of the Stuart period, for Nether Lypiatt in Gloucestershire is as late as about 1700. Other late modifications of the type can be seen on Figs. 2 and 3.

The idea, as almost always in Jones's work, is derived from Italy, though it does not come, like the Queen's House, from the Venetian villas of Palladio or Scamozzi, nor from the works of Serlio, but almost certainly from Rubens's book, the *Palazzi di Genova*, published in 1622.

Sir Roger Pratt

The most beautiful house connected with the type was Coleshill in Berkshire (Pl. 7A), built by

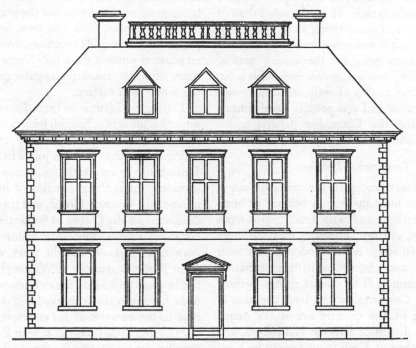

Fig. 1. Inigo Jones's new type of house; perhaps first used at Chevening, c. 1630.

Sir Roger Pratt between 1649 and 1662 and burnt in 1952. Pratt was a different kind of man from Jones, who came from artisan stock. The son of a country gentleman, he travelled widely on the Continent during the years of the Civil War, living in Rome for a time with John Evelyn, whose famous *Diary* tells us so much about seventeenth-century art. Pratt, like many men of his class, had a taste for architecture; he looked at foreign buildings with an intelligent and critical eye, and the notes which he made about them and about his own ideas of good and practical designing suggest that he may have been planning a treatise on architecture which was never completed.

On his return from Italy in 1649 he eagerly undertook the supervision of his cousin's new house at Coleshill, though Inigo Jones and his assistant John Webb were also in some degree concerned with it. Coleshill is a longer house than the Chevening type already discussed, but the

general pattern is similar. It shows, however, skill and sophistication in the handling of the nine windows in each storey, for though they are regular in size, monotony has been avoided by varying the spacing, the three in the centre being set more widely apart than those on either side of them. And the great chimneys, rising high above the sloping roof, are carefully proportioned with the same restraint and beautiful cutting of the mouldings which characterize the whole house. The interior decoration was equally fine, and will be discussed later.

Most of Pratt's other houses have disappeared, though Kingston Lacy in Dorset still exists much altered. He was an influential figure just after the turn of the century, and the house which he built for Charles II's chief minister, Lord Clarendon, in Piccadilly was freely copied by other country-house architects. Clarendon House itself was a development of the Coleshill pattern, with a pediment

279

above the entrance, and two wings projecting in front of the main façade. It was closely followed at Belton House, Lincolnshire, as late as 1684. Here the architect is unknown, and there may not indeed have been one, for the master mason, William Stanton, was a London man with a big business, making tombs as well as carrying out building contracts, and was possibly capable himself of adjusting the Clarendon pattern to his patron's, Sir John Brownlow's, requirements.

Traditional buildings

The new ideas of complete symmetry in design, with elevations built up from a balance of horizontals and verticals and with detail copied from Italian sources, did not, however, oust the older tradition immediately. Many modest houses built between 1630 and 1650 show little appreciation of the new manner. The curved gables, derived from the Low Countries, which were common at the beginning of the century are still a major feature of the design of Broome Hall, Kent, and the Dutch House at Kew (now known as Kew Palace), which date from about 1630. Swakeleys in Middlesex (Pl. 6A), begun in 1638 for Alderman Sir Edmund Wright, is a good example of the more conservative taste of the merchant classes. The traditional hall and screen are retained; on the outside the picturesque skyline, the gables running up and masking the division of wall and roof, the windows of varying shapes and sizes, all afford the strongest possible contrast to the simple, clear-cut lines of the Chevening type. A similar conservatism can be seen in many Cotswold houses, a good stone-producing district where tradition was clearly handed on from father to son, and where it is often hard to date a house with any precision. In East Anglia, too, the Dutch gable survives very late, and in buildings of the almshouse type appears right up to the early eighteenth century.

Interior decoration

Changes in interior decoration in the first sixty years of the seventeenth century were as great, and perhaps even more complete, than those already discussed in exterior design. At the beginning of the Stuart period rooms were wainscoted, generally in oak, and the panels were small, their width being governed by the size of the plank that could be cut, vertically, from the tree. Sometimes the panels were arranged in sections, divided by wooden pilasters running the whole height of the room; more often the small rectangular panels covered the whole wall surface.

During the lifetime of Inigo Jones, and perhaps under his influence, English joiners increased their practice of cutting wood across the grain and fitting it together with fine joints in larger panels. Unfortunately very little decoration by Jones has survived, for nothing remains of his wall treatment at the Queen's House, and the rooms he redecorated for the Queen at Somerset House were destroyed in the eighteenth century. His many drawings, however, and the work which he and John Webb carried out at Wilton (Pl. 9A) after a fire in 1647 prove that the richness of his interiors must have provided a marked and deliberate contrast to the restraint of his exteriors. Richness of interior decoration was not new in England. Jacobean houses are notable for the overloaded decoration of their chimney-pieces, with motives taken from Flemish, German and occasionally French pattern books, thick curling strap-work, grotesque herms at either side, and occasionally a scene carved in stone or moulded in plaster. Jones introduces a new elegance. His fireplaces have a picture frame above (occasionally as at Wilton flanked by figures), the mantelpiece is usually supported on consoles, and there is sometimes a finely designed band of carving below it. Such fireplaces were in use in France in the reign of Louis XIII (the brother of Queen Henrietta Maria) and it seems almost certain that here Jones looked to French rather than to Italian models.

Ceiling design also changes. The all-over patterns of interlacing strap-work of the Jacobean age disappear, and ceilings take on a more architectural quality. Simple geometrical patterns are traced by heavily moulded beams, with a flat interlace on the underside, and there is often a circular or oval wreath in the centre of the ceiling composed of a tightly packed rope of fruit and flowers. The surfaces of the ceiling between the beams are plain, though Jones sometimes planned to fill them with painted canvases. His full intention can be judged from the ceiling, with Rubens's splendid paintings glorifying the Stuart dynasty, still in the Banqueting House at Whitehall. Other drawings for ceilings for Wilton show an increasingly free decoration of acanthus scrolls in high relief. Indeed, the Double Cube Room at Wilton (Pl. 9A) proves that by the end of his life Jones had established an entirely new form of interior decoration. The large panels with carved palms at the top are designed for the series of portraits by Van Dyck and his school, and are separated not by pilasters but by drops of fruit and flowers in tight bunches joined by ribbons. The cornice is richly carved, the coved ceiling is painted and the door is framed by columns carrying a broken pediment. Rich in white and gold, with the reds and blues of the ceiling, and the fine eighteenth century furniture, it is without doubt the most splendid room now remaining of the first half of the seventeenth century, and the only place where Jones's ideas of interior decoration can now be judged.

It is less easy to assess his influence on staircase design. By the time he began to work, English craftsmen had developed a type of wooden staircase with richly decorated newels, running up in straight flights round the sides of a square staircase hall. Jones's only remaining staircase, that at the Queen's House, departs completely from this tradition, and is a circular stone stair, unsupported in the centre, with a fine iron-work balustrade. It does not seem to have been copied elsewhere, but London workmen who were certainly influenced by him in ceiling and panel design, employed the open wooden stair at Ham House, Surrey, in 1637 (Pl. 8B), but instead of the flat balusters and decorated newels of the Jacobean staircase they introduced pierced panels of carved trophies below the rail. This type of staircase was further developed in the middle years of the century: many examples can be found in which the trophies are replaced by a beautiful scrolling acanthus.

Coleshill was discussed as an especially accomplished elaboration of a Jones type of house. Its interior decoration was no less beautiful than its exterior, and since we know that Jones's pupil, John Webb, produced at least one drawing for its

decoration in the 1650's, it is reasonable to assume that it carries on some of Jones's ideas, though the novel staircase (Pl. 8A) is almost certainly due to Sir Roger Pratt. It rises on both sides of the entrance door, running up the sides of the hall to a balustraded landing crossing the hall at first-floor level. It was extremely Italian in character and was probably derived from Baldassare Longhena's staircase in the Convent of S. Giorgio Maggiore in Venice, which bears the date 1643, and which Pratt is likely to have seen when he was in Italy. The whole decoration of the staircase hall, with its antique flavour given by the busts of Roman emperors in roundels, its simple and finely designed door-cases, its beautiful plaster-work with wreaths in very low relief beneath the landing, and its ceiling, which echoes that of the Banqueting House, was in the best Jonesian tradition.

After the middle of the century the motives used by Jones are copied by other designers, though sometimes mixed with older traditions. For instance, the saloon at Forde Abbey (Pl. 9B) in Dorset has a picture-frame fireplace, but the ceiling has pendants and Old Testament scenes in high relief in a manner Jones would surely not have tolerated. Thorpe Hall has at least one ceiling based on a John Webb drawing for Wilton, and panelling which can also be paralleled in his drawings. In the mid 1660's he was designing a palace for Charles II at Greenwich, his fireplace designs being similar to those he used at Drayton and Lamport, both in Northamptonshire, while a small room at Stapleford Hall, Leicestershire, has decoration which is very close to the Greenwich drawings.

Restoration architecture

By now, however, new trends were appearing in English architecture and decoration. During the eleven years of the Commonwealth Charles II and his supporters had spent their exile partly in France, but mainly in Holland, and their taste had shifted from the Italianism of Jones. Partly perhaps for this reason, but chiefly because Charles II rewarded his supporters by the grant of public offices, Webb was not given the post of royal Surveyor which had been promised to him by Charles I.

The appointment went to Sir John Denham, the poet, who, like most of the gentry (according to Webb), had 'some knowledge of the theory of architecture, but none of the practice'; Webb was made his Assistant and the Paymastership (that is, the second senior post in the Office of Works) was given to Hugh May. May, a friend of Sir Peter Lely the painter and cousin of Baptist May, Charles II's Keeper of the Privy Purse, had certainly been in the Low Countries, and his most complete remaining country house, Eltham Lodge in Kent (1663–65) (Pl. 7B), bears evidence of his knowledge of Dutch architecture. For the Chevening pattern is transformed into something new. The house is of fine brick-work, with giant stone pilasters carrying a pediment in the centre of the front. The angles of the house are no longer emphasized by stone quoins, as was the case at Chevening itself, Ashdown, and even Coleshill. The roof, which is not a straight slope, but which sags a little, rises from a cornice decorated with wood modilion blocks. Shallow niches in the brick-work are a feature of the ends of the house. All these motives can be found in Dutch architecture of the middle of the seventeenth century; all are characteristic of the type of house which is commonly, but wrongly, called 'Queen Anne'; and the Dutch influence which is generally associated with the reign of William III is in fact far stronger in the early years of Charles II.

Grinling Gibbons and interior decoration

The somewhat flat surface treatment which is Dutch rather than Italian, and which is characteristic of Eltham, is also to be seen in stone in the work May carried out for Lord Clarendon at Cornbury Park, Oxfordshire. His most important private house, Cassiobury Park, Hertfordshire, no longer exists, though some of its interior decoration is now in the Metropolitan Museum, New York. Its interest lies partly in the fact that it was probably the first house in which Grinling Gibbons worked as a decorator. Born in Holland of English parents, he had been discovered working near Deptford by John Evelyn the diarist in 1671. Evelyn's quick eye was caught by the technical brilliance of the young carver's work, and an in-troduction to the King followed. In spite of Evelyn's hopes this seems at first to have proved fruitless, and it may have been Sir Peter Lely and not Evelyn who persuaded Hugh May to employ him. In the dining-room at Cassiobury Park the tight festoons and bunches of the Jones type of decoration had been replaced by trails of fruit and flowers, cut in the round and applied to the ground, treated with the utmost naturalism and rich in their profuse variety. It is hard to find carving of such extreme realism in Holland itself, though there are hints of it in the Royal Palace at Amsterdam. Gibbons must have known and deeply admired Dutch flower paintings, for his carvings closely parallel them in wood. Both arts appear to be an artless arrangement of natural forms; both are equally deceptive, for the grouping is most carefully planned.

From now until the end of the century many houses were decorated in the new manner, though in relatively few cases is there any documentary proof that the work is by Gibbons himself. Indeed it seems probable as Sir Christopher Wren was later to note that: 'English Artists are dull enough at Inventions but when once a foreigne patterne is sett, they imitate soe well that commonly they exceed the originall.' While it would be going too far to say that English carvers exceeded Gibbons in virtuosity, there is evidence enough to show that they could produce a close imitation of his work, and it is therefore necessary to be cautious in attributing carving to his hand. At Belton House, which has already been discussed as an example of conservatism in exterior design, the carving (Pl. 10B) is in the manner of Gibbons, though there are no payments to him. Moreover, it is not only in the woodwork that Belton shows the new advance in decoration. The fine plaster ceilings echo the naturalism of the carving. The controlled forms and tight wreaths of the Jones school have been superseded by a freer, looser type of decoration, like Gibbons carving worked in the round and applied to the ground. Although some of John Webb's drawings for Greenwich Palace suggest that work in very high relief was contemplated there, the naturalistic flowers do not appear and would probably not have appealed to him, for it is

Fig. 2. Stansted, Sussex; built in 1686 perhaps by
William Talman. From J. Kip's *Britannia Illustrata* (1707).

likely that here, as in other arts such as silver, the inspiration for this rich naturalism comes from Holland.

The influence of France in the reign of Charles II was less widespread than that of Holland. Indeed it appears mainly in two royal undertakings, the new Apartments at Windsor built by Hugh May between 1675 and 1683, and the Palace at Winchester begun by Sir Christopher Wren in 1683, but never completed. The importance of the work at Windsor was very great in the development of the baroque style in England. The great painted interiors, St George's Hall and the Chapel Royal with wood carving by Gibbons (which is now re-used in the Waterloo Chamber), can more properly be discussed with the history of decorative painting, but the first appearance of painted staircases is part of the history of architecture. The Queen's Stair was of the usual pattern of straight flights running round the sides of the staircase hall, but was covered by a painted dome; the King's Stair, with flights running off to right and left, was of an entirely new pattern based on the Escalier des Ambassadeurs recently completed at Versailles. In both there was a new sense of display, and in the Queen's a dramatic movement from a dark columned vestibule to the spacious and richly coloured staircase hall which can, alas, now be deduced from descriptions only, since both staircases were swept away by George IV.

One other minor fact concerning Windsor is of interest. It seems to have been the first English building to have sash windows. Before then all windows had been of the casement type, usually divided into two large and two small panes by a transom cutting the central mullion at about two-thirds of the height of the window. Most early seventeenth century buildings have had their windows altered to sashes, but occasionally the original effect can still be seen.

Baroque developments

Although Wren's work at Winchester Palace, where the plan is linked with that of the original Versailles and much of the detail was French, was less immediately influential than Hugh May's work at Windsor, it was not without significance, for here and at Chelsea Hospital of about the same date, Wren was making his first experiments in large-scale planning, using great blocks of buildings ranged round three sides of a court, with strong accents given by giant porticoes or small cupolas, at the sides and centre. Schemes of grouped buildings were to occupy much of Wren's time during the next twenty years, though he was hardly ever able to carry them out as he desired. The early scheme for Hampton Court with a 'Grand Front' on the entrance side surmounted by a dome; the first scheme for Greenwich Hospital with long blocks of buildings running back to a hall and chapel with a domed vestibule between them closing the vista; the elaborate layout (which included a Parliament House) for Whitehall Palace after the fire of 1698 are clear enough evidence of his increasing desire to plan on baroque lines, with a cumulative effect rising to the major focal point. None of these belong, strictly speaking, to the story of English domestic architecture, but the development of the great baroque houses designed by Sir John Vanbrugh and Nicholas Hawksmoor at the end of the Stuart period cannot be understood without reference to them, for Wren's ideas clearly meant much to the younger men. He himself, with his vast programme of ecclesiastical, royal and public building, had little time for domestic architecture, but the impetus given to craftsmanship, as well as to large-scale planning, by his undertakings must not be forgotten.

William Talman

The first steps towards the baroque house appear to have been taken by William Talman. His training is unknown, but since in his first house, Thoresby in Nottinghamshire (now destroyed), he seems to have taken ideas for interior design at least from Hugh May's Windsor, it is possible that he had some connexion with it. His next and most famous house, Chatsworth in Derbyshire (Pl. 11A), where he worked from 1687 to 1696, introduces a new theme. For instead of the plain walls, sloping roof and dormer windows of Belton, begun only a few years earlier, the south front (Talman's most important contribution) has a new

Fig. 3. Uppark, Sussex; probably by William Talman about 1690. From J. Kip's *Britannia Illustrata* (1707).

monumentality. The two-storied façade, set on a rusticated basement, is adorned with giant pilasters at both ends, and the whole is topped by a straight balustrade. The idea is almost certainly borrowed from Bernini's last design for the east front of the Louvre, and indeed throughout his career Talman was to make free use of French engravings. The interior of Chatsworth, which is confused in plan owing to the Earl of Devonshire's method of rebuilding his house piecemeal, also shows a development towards the baroque. The chapel (Pl. 13A) combines architecture, painting and sculpture in a single, rich entity, though the figures by Caius Gabriel Cibber are static and a little dull compared with Continental standards. The great stone staircase leading to the State Rooms on the upper floor has a fine iron-work balustrade, the work of the Huguenot smith, Jean Tijou. The State Rooms themselves are adorned with painted ceilings by Louis Laguerre and carving in the manner of Gibbons, executed by a local craftsman, Samuel Watson (Pl. 10A).

It was no doubt Talman's success at Chatsworth which obtained for him in 1689 the Comptrollership of the Office of Works, vacant since Hugh May's death in 1683. In spite of his quarrelsome nature he seems to have got on well in King William's circle, and the exterior design of Dyrham Park, Gloucestershire, built for Mr Blathwayt, William's Secretary at War, is almost certainly his. Like Chatsworth it is a massive block, ending in a straight balustrade. It is less grand, for there are no giant pilasters, but much of the detail seems to come from French engravings. The clearest example, however, of Talman's dependence on France lies in the little hunting-lodge – a kind of *Trianon* – which he designed, but never executed, for King William at Thames Ditton, across the river from Hampton Court. Here both the plan, with its small oval vestibule, and the exterior design can be traced almost exactly to French engravings. Some of the interior decoration which appears in the drawings is from a slightly different (though ultimately French) source, for it follows designs carried out for William in Holland by Daniel Marot, a Huguenot refugee whose influence can be seen elsewhere in certain types of English furniture. Sometimes, however, Talman designed houses which are more traditional in type, and are indeed developed from the houses of Jones and Pratt. The engravings from Kip's *Britannia Illustrata* (1707) of Stansted and Uppark (the latter now the property of the National Trust) (Figs. 2 and 3) show two such houses; many of these houses contained formal gardens, which are typical of the landscaping of the period.

Hawksmoor and Vanbrugh

It was perhaps Talman's use of the pilastered house at Chatsworth (or its appearance in French engravings of Louis XIV's building at Marly) that influenced Nicholas Hawksmoor in the design of his beautiful house at Easton Neston in Northamptonshire. It is dated 1702 on the parapet, but had been under consideration in Wren's office since at least 1686. Hawksmoor was Wren's chief assistant, and the commission was probably passed on by Wren. A wooden model still in the possession of the owner shows a house in two sharply separated storeys, with small superimposed columns as a porch. The executed design has giant pilasters right along the front; and the sense of scale is enormously increased. The handling of the detail and the cutting of the mouldings is extremely fine; the arrangement of the staircase in a confined space is masterly, and by skilful introduction of mezzanine floors Hawksmoor has managed to insert a considerable number of rooms into a relatively small space.

Easton Neston is the only house which Hawksmoor carried out independently. By the time the exterior was completed the support of his sound architectural training and long practical experience was being given to that gifted amateur, Sir John Vanbrugh, in the evolution of Castle Howard, Yorkshire (Pl. 12A). Lord Carlisle, the patron, had at first employed William Talman, who had produced two fine plans and an interesting lay-out for a different design composed of linked blocks. Talman, however, asked inordinately high fees, and by 1699 Vanbrugh, a playwright with no experience of architecture, was providing a model for the house. It is likely that the drawings for this were made by Hawksmoor, and that the scheme consisted of a balustraded centre block decorated with giant pilasters, and side blocks joined to it by quadrant arcades. The final design, in which it is known that Vanbrugh and Hawksmoor collaborated, was far more spectacular. The pilastered centre block was retained, but was surmounted by a cupola on a high drum. The side buildings were greatly increased, spreading round subsidiary courts, and in the engraving which shows the full conception (which was never completed) many smaller cupolas break the skyline, and echo in little the dominant accent of the central dome. The compact rectangular central block has given place to a far more complex building, with long, low wings running off from the centre on the garden side, and quadrant colonnades leading forward to the massive side blocks. There is a new sense of display hitherto unknown in English country-house design, and only so far seen in England in Wren's palace designs. But this building, with its heavily rusticated side courts, its rich surface decoration on the main block, its broken and exciting skyline, is more dramatic, and therefore more fully baroque, than any of Wren's buildings. That a new powerful imagination is here brought to bear on English architecture is certain; and that the conception is Vanbrugh's seems almost sure. It is, however, an open question whether, at this early stage of his career, he would have been able to translate his ideas into stone without the assistance of Nicholas Hawksmoor.

The novelty is not on the exterior alone. Within the centre block is a great hall (Pl. 13B), flanked by staircases, with a saloon behind looking on to the garden. A state suite is contained in each of the long wings running off from the centre, with a corridor on its inner side, so that the rooms at the end of the wings could be reached without passing through those nearer the hall. This corridor is new in English planning (though something like it appears in some of Talman's drawings) – and indeed it is hard to find its counterpart abroad – for in all great houses of the late seventeenth century it was normal to pass from room to room, and privacy and convenience were little considered. The other

major innovation lies in the character of the hall, for it is no longer panelled in wood, in the English traditional manner, but is entirely of stone, with the painted cupola above (destroyed by fire in 1940), and has something of the grand monumentality of Roman baroque architecture.

Not long after Castle Howard was begun, Vanbrugh, who was favoured by the Whig aristocracy, superseded Talman as Comptroller of the Office of Works. In 1705 he was given the greatest commission of his life, the creation of the palace to be presented to the Duke of Marlborough by a grateful nation. At Blenheim Palace (Pl. 12B) Vanbrugh attempts, and indeed achieves, heroic architecture. The scale is vast (too vast to please the Duchess), the forms are massive, and though the age in which he lived compelled Vanbrugh to express his ideas of the heroic by using the forms of classical architecture, he uses them with a unique effect of strength. The whole conception is grander than that of Castle Howard; it does not build up to the centre in the same way, but depends on the grouping of the massive towers, on the sheer extent of the masses of honey-coloured stone, on the constant emphasis on weight and solidity. The rich surface carving which gives a certain elegance to Castle Howard has disappeared; the motive of a contrast between plain and rusticated wall surfaces, which he was to develop still further in his later houses, is chosen to give a greater impact of strength. The house was never completed according to his conception, for only one of the side courts flanking the great forecourt was built, and he fell out so irrevocably with the formidable Duchess that the later stages of the house were left to Hawksmoor. To him is due the beautiful library in the west wing of the house and probably much of the detail elsewhere, but the force which created the most original of the great houses of England is certainly Sir John Vanbrugh.

After Blenheim, Hawksmoor was mainly engaged on work in London and at the Universities, and Vanbrugh designed several houses without his help, Kings Weston near Bristol, Eastbury in Dorset, Seaton Delaval in Northumberland and a new wing at Grimsthorpe in Lincolnshire being the most important. All show an increasing control of his medium. They are much smaller than Castle Howard or Blenheim, and are relatively compact in plan. Eastbury no longer exists, and Seaton Delaval was burnt in the early nineteenth century and is only a shell. Even so, it is of incomparable grandeur. Vanbrugh had before this made it clear, in letters and in a variety of small houses that he built at Blackheath, that he was strongly attracted by medieval architecture. As early as 1707, when he altered Kimbolton, he 'thought it best to give it something of the castle air, but at the same time to make it regular'. At Seaton Delaval he manages to combine medieval angle turrets and side towers containing circular staircases with his great Doric entrance columns. At Grimsthorpe the medieval element is less obvious, but the composition depends for its effect on the balance of small towers on the entrance screen with the great towers of the wings, and in the façade itself, on the contrast between smooth and broken surfaces. Within Vanbrugh's wing at Grimsthorpe is a single great hall (Pl. 14B) in which the maximum emphasis is laid on the simplicity of the stone, and the minimum on decoration.

Vanbrugh's influence can, however, be seen in a number of houses, some of them undoubtedly created by men who had worked under him. He is perhaps the most original of all English country-house architects and his romantic, individual interpretation of baroque was to be admired by Robert Adam and Sir Joshua Reynolds, and detested by Horace Walpole.

His contemporary, Thomas Archer, betrays more immediate dependence on seventeenth century Roman models, though little of his work has survived unaltered. Heythrop Hall, Oxfordshire, a great Roman palazzo, has been rebuilt, though it follows the original design. The north front of Chatsworth has also been mutilated, and the charming oval windows surrounded by a rich cartouche have disappeared. The basic baroque motive of a curved front can, however, still be seen. Several other buildings – Chettle House, Dorset, Marlow Place, Buckinghamshire, and Chicheley Hall (Pl. 11B) in the same county – have been attributed to Archer, largely on their resemblance to his designs for houses that no longer exist. The last, even if it is not by him, can be taken as a good example of the baroque theme modified to suit a brick-and-stone house of medium size. The bold proportions, the great pilasters, the treatment of windows and door, the curves sweeping up to the centre – all these are baroque, and form an interesting contrast with the treatment of Eltham Lodge, built some fifty years earlier. Other houses – Frampton Court in Gloucestershire, which is as late as 1730, Duncombe Park and Gilling Castle in Yorkshire (Pl. 14A) – betray the influence of Vanbrugh. The last two were carried out by William Wakefield, though perhaps not from his own designs. In both, however, the interior decoration combines something of Vanbrugh's monumentality with a new richness of plaster-work. The next chapter in the history of English architecture, which is purely Georgian, shows on the one hand the dramatic baroque exteriors replaced by the dry elegance of the new Palladian manner, while interior decoration, under the influence of William Kent and the Italian plasterers, becomes increasingly lavish.

SHORT BIBLIOGRAPHY

The best general text-book is: J. Summerson, *Architecture in Britain, 1530–1830* (2nd edit. 1955). For a general discussion of the architecture of the period, see M.D.Whinney and O.Millar, *English Art, 1625–1714* (1957). Fine photographs and good descriptions of most of the houses discussed will be found in: H.A.Tipping and C. Hussey, *English Homes*, Period IV, Vols. i and ii (1920, 1928). For contemporary engravings, see J.Kip, *Britannia Illustrata* (1707), details of two plates from which, chosen mainly for their reproductive quality, have been used as Figs. 2 and 3. For individual architects, see H. Colvin, *Dictionary of British Architects, 1660-1830* (1954).

Two illustrations from *The Genteel Habits of England*, a book of engravings by Sir Edmund Marmion, *c.* 1640. They show a great lady first at her toilette, and then singing with her gallant. The table of her bedroom is heavily draped, and her dressing-box with its mirror lid is set upon it, but the floorboards are bare. The bosom-revealing fashion of the time was a sore point with the Puritans.
Pepysian Library, Magdalene College, Cambridge.

PLATE 1

Banquet of Charles II and the Knights of the Order of the Garter in St George's Hall, Windsor. Such feasts were costly. Archbishop Laud's quadrangle for St John's, Oxford, was built for £5,087: the Royal feast at its opening cost him £2,226. *Wenceslaus Hollar.*

A contemporary engraving of the Great Frost Fair on the Thames, 1683–4, an extraordinary sight for the gentry up from the country. In one of the booths they could get their names printed on a dated ticket. Bull baiting is going on at Q. *British Museum.*

PLATE 3

Illustration to *Wit at Several Weapons* by Beaumont and Fletcher, published by N. Rowe, 1711: a lively and grotesque picture of Jacobean dramatics. The orchestra is above the stage—music always came from above, even in the great halls. Underneath at each side are the gentlemen playgoers with their ladies in the stage boxes.

PLATE 4

(A) Charlton House, Greenwich (1607–12). A Jacobean house with windows of many sizes.
Royal Commission on Historical Monuments.

(B) INIGO JONES. The Queen's House, Greenwich (1616–35). An Italianate villa with a regular façade.
Ministry of Works.

PLATE 5

(A) Swakeleys, Middlesex (1638). Built in a conservative style for Alderman Sir Edmund Wright. *Royal Commission on Historical Monuments.*

(B) Ashdown House, Berkshire (after 1660). A variant of an Inigo Jones type. *A. F. Kersting.*

PLATE 6

(A) Sir Roger Pratt. Coleshill, Berkshire (1649–62, burnt down 1952). The assimilation of Italian ideas. *Country Life.*

(B) Hugh May. Eltham Lodge, Kent (1663–65). Showing strong Dutch influence.
Royal Commission on Historical Monuments.

PLATE 7

(A) SIR ROGER PRATT. Coleshill, Berk-shire (1649–62, burnt down 1952). The Hall, with Italian influence in design and decoration. *Country Life*.

(B) Ham House Surrey (1637). The Stair-case, with carved and pierced panels instead of balusters. *National Buildings Record*.

PLATE 8

(A) INIGO JONES. Wilton House, Wiltshire (1649–52). The Double-Cube Room, the only surviving interior by the architect. *National Buildings Record.*

(B) Forde Abbey, Dorset (1658). The Saloon, showing new trends in woodwork, but an older type of ceiling. *Royal Commission on Historical Monuments.*

PLATE 9

(A) Chatsworth, Derbyshire. The State Dining-Room, painted by Louis Laguerre -and carved by Samuel Watson (about 1690). *National Buildings Record.*

(B) Belton House, Lincolnshire (1684). The Hall, with naturalistic carving and plaster work. *Country Life.*

PLATE 10

(A) WILLIAM TALMAN. Chatsworth, Derbyshire (1686–96) The South front, baroque in its sense of mass. *National Buildings Record.*

(B) Chicheley Hall, Buckinghamshire (*c.* 1703–21). A modified baroque theme. *A. F. Kersting.*

PLATE 11   299

(A) SIR JOHN VANBRUGH. Castle Howard, Yorkshire (begun 1699). *Country Life*.

(B) SIR JOHN VANBRUGH. Blenheim Palace, Oxfordshire (begun 1705). Heroic in theme and treatment. *A. F. Kersting*.

PLATE 12

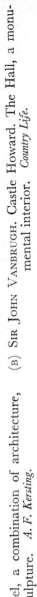

(B) Sir John Vanbrugh. Castle Howard. The Hall, a monumental interior. *Country Life.*

(A) Chatsworth. The Chapel, a combination of architecture, painting and sculpture. *A. F. Kersting.*

PLATE 13

(B) Sir John Vanbrugh. Grimsthorpe, Lincolnshire (1723). The Hall, which stresses the simple grandeur of stone. *Country Life.*

(A) Gilling Castle, Yorkshire (c. 1715). The Hall, with some echoes of Vanbrugh's style. *Country Life.*

PLATE 14

(B) Oak press cupboard, the recessed upper part containing two cupboards, separated by pilasters framing a central panel with carved round-headed arch, and the lower part a cupboard with shelf, enclosed by panelled doors. Dated 1610.
Victoria and Albert Museum.

(A) Oak press cupboard, with drawers below, and panelled sides. Late seventeenth or early eighteenth century. *Private Collection.*

PLATE 15

(A) 'Folding' table of oak, with one movable gate. *c.* 1650. *Hart Collection.*

(B) Hanging livery or food cupboard, enclosed by doors each with a row of turned balusters above a panel decorated with lozenges; the frieze carved with guilloche ornament. Mid-seventeenth century. *Private Collection.*

(C) Draw table, the legs of bulbous form, tied by plain stretchers. Length (unextended) 6 ft 9 in. Second half of seventeenth century. *The Oak House Museum, West Bromwich, Staffs.*

PLATE 16

(A) 'Farthingale' chair of walnut, the front legs of columnar form. Height 3 ft; width 1 ft 10 in. First quarter of seventeenth century. *Victoria and Albert Museum*. (B) (*right*) Carved and turned oak chair, Lancashire type. Dated 1641. *Victoria and Albert Museum*.

(C) Chest, panelled and elaborately carved with conventional ornament. Height 2 ft 5½ in.; width 5 ft 6 in. From Lincolnshire, dated 1637. *Victoria and Albert Museum*.

PLATE 17

(A) Settle-table, the lower part in the form of a chest. The table top is attached to the backs of the arms by wooden pegs, and serves, when raised, as a back to the settle. Length 5 ft 11 in. Mid-seventeenth century. *Victoria and Albert Museum.*

(B) Oak armchair, the panelled back inlaid with a floral arabesque design within a carved arch and surmounted by a heavy scrolled cresting; the framing uprights decorated with applied split balusters, flanked by scrolled 'ear-pieces', the front legs and arm supports turned. Mid-seventeenth century. *V. and A. Museum.*

(C) Oak chest of drawers, on a low stand with twist-turned supports tied by stretchers; the drawer fronts decorated with panels of raised mouldings. Height 4 ft 4½ in. Late seventeenth century. *Victoria and Albert Museum.*

(A) Walnut gate-leg table, the oval top supported on turned legs with shaped feet. Height 2 ft 4 in. Late seventeenth century. *Victoria and Albert Museum.*

(B) Carved and gilt table with decoration of gilt gesso. Height 2 ft 6½ in.; length 3 ft 6 in. About 1700. *Victoria and Albert Museum.*

(C) Walnut side table, decorated with arabesque marquetry and fitted with one long drawer in the frieze; twist-turned legs tied by flat curved stretchers with an oval marquetry panel in the centre. Last quarter of the seventeenth century.

PLATE 19

(B) Burr mulberry bureau bookcase, with inlaid pewter stringing lines. Attributed to Coxed and Woster. Early eighteenth century.

(A) State bed, upholstered in red and gold brocade. From Wroxton Abbey, Oxfordshire. Late seventeenth century. *Aston Hall, Birmingham.*

(A) Mirror frame, overlaid with incised oriental lacquer. c. 1675. *Victoria and Albert Museum.*

(B) Dressing glass, japanned red and gold. The sloping front of the base is hinged and opens to disclose an arrangement of small drawers and pigeon holes, with central cupboard. Height 3 ft. 3 in. Early eighteenth century. *Victoria and Albert Museum.*

PLATE 21

A

B

C

(A) Walnut winged armchair, upholstered and covered with silk needlework; the cabriole front legs, carved on the knee with a shell, are hipped and finished in modified hoof feet. Early eighteenth century. *Formerly in the Hart Collection. Now at Colonial Williamsburg.*

(B) Upholstered chair with walnut framework; the high back surmounted by a foliated cresting carved in openwork; the turned legs are joined by shaped cross stretchers with a finial. End of the seventeenth century. *Victoria and Albert Museum.*

(C) Cane settee of double chair design, supported in front by scrolled legs joined by deep scrolled rails; the uprights to the back and the stretchers are of turned baluster form, *c.* 1700. *Hart Collection.*

PLATE 22

Artist unknown. Henry, Prince of Wales.
Courtesy The Hon. Clive Pearson, Parham. (Canvas 92¼″ × 88″).

PLATE 23

Artist unknown. Philip, 4th Earl of Pembroke.
Courtesy The Hon. R. H. C. Neville. (Canvas 84″ × 49½″).

PLATE 24

DANIEL MYTENS. Charles I (1623?).
Courtesy The Hon. Clive Pearson, Parham. (Canvas 71″ × 56″).

PLATE 25

(A) CORNELIUS JOHNSON. Spencer, 2nd Earl of
Northampton (1633).
Castle Ashby. (Canvas 30¾″ × 25½″).

(B) SIR PETER LELY. James, Duke of York (1647).
Syon House. (Canvas 28¼″ × 23¾″).

(C) SIR ANTHONY VAN DYCK. Anne, Countess of
Bedford.   *Petworth. (Canvas 53⅝″ × 43¼″).*

(D) MARCUS GHEERAERTS. Mrs Anne Hoskins
(1629).   *Courtesy Capt. C. E. H. Master.*
(Panel 44″ × 32½″).

PLATE 26

SIR ANTHONY VAN DYCK. Thomas, 1st Earl of Strafford.
Courtesy the Earl Fitzwilliam. (Canvas 90½″ × 56¼″).

PLATE 27

WILLIAM DOBSON. Henry, 2nd Earl of Peterborough (1644).
Drayton House. (Canvas 97″ × 64″).

PLATE 28

SIR ANTHONY VAN DYCK. Mary, Duchess of Richmond, with Lord Arran.
North Carolina Museum of Art. (Canvas 83″ × 40″).

PLATE 29

317

(A) WENCESLAUS HOLLAR. Shipping on the Thames.
British Museum. (Pen and watercolour $4\frac{1}{2}'' \times 11\frac{1}{4}''$).

(B) WILLIAM DOBSON. James, 3rd Earl of
Northampton.   *Castle Ashby. (Canvas $45\frac{1}{2}'' \times 36\frac{1}{4}''$).*

(C) SIR PETER LELY. Robert, 2nd Earl of
Sunderland.   *Knole. (Canvas $48\frac{1}{2}'' \times 39\frac{1}{4}''$).*

(A) SIR PETER LELY. Barbara, Duchess of
Cleveland.   *Courtesy the Earl Spencer.*
(Canvas 50″ × 40″).

(B) JACOB HUYSMANS. Elizabeth, Countess of
Orkney.   *Courtesy the Earl of Jersey.*
(Canvas 50″ × 40″).

(C) JOHN RILEY. Sir William Coventry.
Courtesy the Marquis of Bath. (Canvas 50″ × 40″).

(D) GERARD SOEST. John Bulwer.
Courtesy R. Leon, Esq. (Canvas 50″ × 40″).

PLATE 31

(A) JOHN MICHAEL WRIGHT. Lady Elizabeth Stonor. *Stonor Park. (Canvas 28⅞″ × 24″).*

(B) SIR GODFREY KNELLER. Antonio Verrio. *Burghley House. Country Life. (Canvas 28⅞″ × 23¾″).*

(C) JONATHAN RICHARDSON. The Artist and his Son in the Presence of Milton. *Capesthorne Hall. (Canvas 25″ × 30″).*

PLATE 32

Furniture

RALPH FASTNEDGE

Introduction

Stylistically, English seventeenth century furniture falls into two main groups: first, joined furniture, which developed slowly on established lines from that in use during the Elizabethan period, comprising useful, solid, enduring articles, such as long tables, press cupboards, settles and joint stools, made usually of oak or indigenous woods; and secondly, post-Restoration furniture, the design of which was strongly influenced by contemporary models from France and Holland. This latter furniture, first made for the Court in London, resulted from the revolution in taste which followed the restoration of the monarchy in England in 1660. Some reaction against forms which had had their being under the Commonwealth was perhaps inevitable. There was a demand for luxury evidenced by the introduction of new specialized pieces, such as the scrutoir and bureau, dressing-glass and candle-stand. Fashionable post-Restoration furniture represented a break with tradition and was the work of new craftsmen, many of whom were Huguenot refugees, employing new techniques (veneering, marquetry, japanning and subsequently gesso) and new woods – in particular, walnut. Their productions were decorative and their standard of skill very much higher than that possessed by the native joiners. Their presence here was quickly felt. 'Joyners, cabinet-makers, and the like ... from very vulgar and pitiful artists', wrote Evelyn, in a familiar passage, 'are now come to produce works as curious for the fiting, and admirable for their dexterity in contriving, as any we meet with abroad.' [1] Such furniture, however, was not in general supply under the late Stuarts. The provincial or country joiner was but little affected at this date by London fashions in furniture; he worked by usage and was incapable of making pieces other than those of familiar design and construction. Thus, much surviving furniture of late seventeenth-century date is in the style of the preceding period. Compare the oak box (Fig. 1), inscribed 'I.S. 1682', decorated simply and in

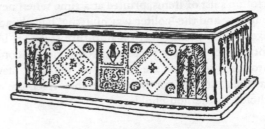

Fig. 1. Box of oak, with punch work ornament.
Dated 1682.

accordance with tradition, with punch work and gouge carving (at the ends), with a veneered walnut and marquetry counterpart of comparable date. The disparity of style and execution is remarkable.

A reliable account of the proper furnishing of a provincial gentleman's house in the late seventeenth century is provided by a contemporary

[1] *An Account of Architects and Architecture*, by John Evelyn. *The Miscellaneous Writings of John Evelyn*, ed. by William Upcott, 1825, p. 361.

writer, Randle Holme.[2] His *Academy of Armoury*, published at Chester, contains definite instructions on this matter, as much else. The dining-room, he stated, is to be

> 'well wanscoted about, either with Moontan [3] and panells or carved as the old fashion was; or else in larg square panell.
>
> The Rome hung with pictures of all sorts, as History, Landskips, Fancyes, &c.
>
> Lang table in the midle, either square to draw out in Leaves, or Long, or Round, or oval with falling leaves.
>
> Side tables, or court cubberts, for cups and Glasses to drink in, Spoons, Sugar Box, Viall and Cruces for Viniger, Oyle and Mustard pot.
>
> Cistern of Brass, Pewter, or Lead to set flagons of Beer, and Bottles of win in.
>
> A Turky table couer, or carpett of cloth or Leather printed. Chaires and stooles of Turkey work,[4] Russia or calves Leather, cloth or stuffe, or of needlework. Or els made all of Joynt work or cane chaires.
>
> Fire grate, fire shovell, Tongs, and Land Irons all adorned with Brass Bobbs and Buttons.
>
> Flower potts, or Allabaster figures to adorn the windows, and glass well painted and a larg seeing Glass at the higher end of the Rome.'

Holme's list of items, printed at a time when new building and the 'politer way of living' had already exercised a great effect on furniture styles, is informative. He was prepared, seemingly, to compromise between the claims of old and new fashions and to allow considerable freedom of choice to the householder.

[2] *The Academy of Armory, or, a Storehouse of Armory and Blazon*, by Randle Holme, Chester, 1688. Roxburghe Club edit., 1905, Vol. II, pp. 15–16. The MS. is dated 1649, when Holme completed his 'first colleccions and draughts' for the work.

[3] *Mountan* or *Muntin*. A vertical member of the framing of wainscot or other panelled woodwork.

[4] A coarse wool needlework, made in imitation of a Turkey carpet.

[5] *The Lumley Inventories* by Lionel Cust, and *A Lumley Inventory of 1609* by Mary F. S. Hervey, *Walpole Society*, Vol. VI, 1917–18, pp. 15–35, 36–46.

[6] Francis Cleyn was born at Rostock in 1582. He studied in Rome and Venice. Court Painter to Christian IV of Denmark. Cleyn was in England from 1625, and died in London, 1657–58.

I. FURNITURE OF PRE-RESTORATION CHARACTER

The great houses: the Lumley inventories

Surprisingly few varieties of domestic furniture existed in England at the beginning of the century, even in the richest houses. This is sufficiently clear from the inventory of the possessions of John, Lord Lumley, taken by his steward of household, one John Lambton, in 1590.[5] The inventory is of considerable length and details the 'monumentes of Marbles, Pictures and tables in Paynture, with other ... howseholde Stuffe and Regester of Bookes' at Lord Lumley's three houses – Nonesuch Palace, the London house on Tower Hill, and Lumley Castle. The pictures may here be disregarded, as also the statuary. The fantastic marble objects (tables, screens, and fountains), which are recorded by the several pages of drawings prefacing the inventory, have not survived. (It is likely that these pieces were the work of Italian craftsmen.) A table, now at Aston Hall, Birmingham, with polychrome marble top inlaid in an elaborate perspective design, is, however, representative of this small but fashionable class of Italian or Italianate furniture; the table is certainly of Italian inspiration, although its square wooden frame, carved with strapwork decoration, is English work of about 1600. The unusual and interesting chair reproduced in Fig. 2 is, too, strongly Italian in style. There is good reason to suppose that it was made to the design of the elder Francis Cleyn,[6] master of the tapestry works for Charles I at Mortlake. Cleyn is known to have been in Italy for some four years. The chair is almost identical with those 'carved and gilt, with large shells for backs' which were noted by Horace Walpole as being in a room decorated by Cleyn at Holland House, and remarked as being 'undoubtedly from his designs, and evidences of his taste'.[7]

[7] *Anecdotes of Painting in England*, by Horace Walpole; 1st edit. Strawberry Hill, 1762–71.

See *English Decoration and Furniture of the Early Renaissance*, by Margaret Jourdain, 1924, wherein C. J. Richardson's lithographs of Holland House are reproduced, Figs. 16, 127, and *The Baronial Halls ... of England*, by S. C. Hall, F.S.A., 1858, Vol. I, p. 7.

Fig. 2. Painted arm-chair, made probably from the design of Francis Cleyn, after an Italian model. Height 3 ft. 7½ in. *c.* 1625.

It is difficult now to conceive a true idea of the splendid character of the furnishing of the rooms of these houses: their brilliance derived largely from valuable fabrics, and gold and silver plate. Many 'sutes of hanginges of arras, sylke and tapistre' (fifty-seven), 'Turkye carpettes of sylke' (eleven) and 'other Turky Carpettes' (ninety-five) were listed in the Lumley inventory, with 'carpettes of velvet for tables and wyndowes' (twenty-five) and 'coveringes and Quyltes of sylke' (forty). There were 'quisshins [cushions] of clothe of gold, velvet and sylke' (one hundred and nine); indeed many chairs (seventy-six) and stools (eighty) were covered with these materials, and a few with red Spanish leather, or with crewel needlework. The essential wooden, and un-upholstered, furniture by comparison showed small variety and comprised only chairs (seventeen), stools (one hundred and seventy-five), forms (twenty), tables (seventy-five) and cupboards (fifty-two), which were distinguished as of 'walnuttre and Markatre' (walnut decorated with an inlay of woods), of 'walnuttre' and of 'Waynskot' (imported oak). Oak furniture, of course, preponderated over walnut, but not to the extent that was general in most houses. Bedsteads were 'gylt' (four), 'of walnuttre and markatre' (twenty-three) and 'of weynskot' (forty), and there were, besides, the 'pallet beddes with their bolsters' and 'lyvereye beddes' which were in common use. Curiously, there is no mention of

the chests, which must have been numerous; they were not here valued.

A second Lumley inventory taken for probate in 1609 ('a trew Inventarie of all such moveables as were found in Lumley Castle after the decease of the Lord John Lumley ...') is as to furniture more explicit. We have such entries as these: 'Itm two long drawinge[draw] tables of walnottree one folding table of wainscott & a little table of wainscott'; 'Itm two fyne merketree cupbords & two livere cupbords'; Itm x square oake & elme tables & liverie Cupbords sutable'; and 'Itm one old iron chist & a firre chist'. This inventory applies only to Lumley Castle; consequently the number of entries contained in it is greatly reduced.

Upholstered seat furniture

Upholstered seat furniture of a luxurious character existed in quantity by the earlier seventeenth century in many of the great houses of England. This furniture, because of its perishable nature, has almost entirely disappeared. (Knole, Kent, where early upholstered chairs, stools, and couches remain still in untouched condition, if sadly worn and faded, provides a notable exception.) [8] The 1590 inventory, it may be noticed, listed as many as seventy-six 'Chares of Clothe of gold, velvet and sylke' but seventeen only 'of walnuttre and markatre' (i.e. Joined Chairs, see below).

These pieces, which were the products of the upholsterer,[9] were in general 'covered all over' (i.e. all exposed surfaces were covered with fabric), 'garnished with nails', and 'fringed with gold'. They were constructed with frames of beechwood – a wood particularly liable to attack by worm. It is probable that numerous suites of upholstered seat furniture were made under the early Stuarts, comprising chairs, couches and stools. At this time the single chair, or 'back-stool', with stuffed seat and back first emerges. The low-backed farthingale

[8] See *The Upholstered Furniture at Knole*, by R. W. Symonds, *The Burlington Magazine*, May and July 1945. The illustrations include a chair of early X-shape design, one of rectangular form with low stuffed back, and couches.

[9] And, at first, of the coffer maker.

chair, said to have been designed to accommodate ladies wearing the farthingale, which attained extravagant proportions under James 1, was too made without arms and is distinguished by a wide and very high, stuffed seat (Pl. 17A). It was supported usually on columnar legs and covered frequently in 'Turkey work'.

Comparatively few upholstered stools have survived, although they would seem once to have been plentiful. According to Sir John Harington, writing in the later sixteenth century, upholstered stools were to be seen 'in every merchant's hall'. Indeed, men could 'scant endewr to sitt upon' the hard plank forms and wainscot stools 'since great breeches were layd aside'.[10]

At the time of the Commonwealth, leather coverings were introduced; strips of hide were strained over seat and back panel and secured by large brass-headed nails.

Joined chairs, stools and benches

Joined chairs are listed in most early seventeenth century inventories, and evidently were owned by all but the poorest sections of the population. They were not numerous, at least in the houses of yeomen and country tradesmen, and were reserved for the master of the house and his guests. John Osburne, for example, a yeoman of Writtle, in Essex, whose goods and chattels were appraised in 1638, kept: 'In the Hall – one great ioyned table, eigght stooles and one forme, 1 *li.* 10s.; one litle ioyned table, 2 stooles and one great ioyned chayer, 8s.; one cubbard & one settle with 3 boxes in it, 1 *li.*' While Robert Jackson, also of Writtle, the inventory of whose goods was taken that same year, possessed: 'In the Hall One table, 2 formes, one Joyned stole, 1 *li.* 6s. 8d.; 2 little tables, 2 chayres, 8s.; 1 bench bord, 4 cushens ... 13s.;' and, 'In the Porler – One Joyned bedsted with all that belongeth to it, 5 *li.*; 2 chayers, 1 little table and one Joyned stole, 1 Cuberd, one warming pan, 1 *li.* 15s.'[11]

[10] *Nugae Antiquae*: being a collection of original papers in prose and verse by Sir J. H. and others, 1804 edit., Vol. 1, p. 202.
[11] *Farm and Cottage Inventories of mid-Essex, 1635–1749*, ed. by F. W. Steer, 1950.

At the beginning of the century, joined chairs with open arms and panel backs were still of very substantial construction. They were at that time rarely made of walnut. Ordinarily, the back panels were arched and, in some finer specimens, decorated with a floral inlay. Such inlay was of holly, bog oak, box, yew, the fruitwoods and other woods, such as ash and poplar. The legs were baluster turned or of columnar form, and tied by moulded stretchers.[12] Chairs tended to be more lightly made as the century advanced. Certain stylistic changes may be remarked: first, in later chairs, the downward slope of the arms is more pronounced; secondly the top rail of the chair back (which bears a scrolled cresting) later often rests on the uprights, and is not contained within them, and pendant brackets, or 'ear-pieces', are attached at the sides, below the cresting; and, finally, the thin wooden seat, conforming to a lighter pattern of chair, is narrower (Pl. 18B). In many post-Restoration chairs of this panel back type the decorative area of the back is thinly but profusely carved with strapwork, scrolls or floral arabesques. Such features as the foregoing provide some indication of the date of construction. But panel back chairs were supplied to farmhouses and cottages at least until the middle of the eighteenth century; and modifications in their design made over many years in any one locality were often slight. The variety to be found in surviving chairs is due in large part to the stylistic differences which existed between the furniture of one region and another. The carved oak single chair, dated 1641, which is illustrated in Pl. 17B, is, for example, from the north country. The influence of region on furniture style was considerable.

Joined stools and benches were in common use as seats, particularly at the dining-table, and innumerable sets of stools, and benches, were made; they were often 'sutable' (i.e., designed *en suite*) to the table. (Stools were ranged under the table when not in use, and rested on its stretcher rails.) Stools, like chairs, developed towards lightness,

[12] See *The Dictionary of English Furniture*, revised edition by Ralph Edwards, 1954, Vol. 1, p. 231 – *Chairs*, Figs. 18, 19 and 21.

and the somewhat massive carved and fluted legs found in late Elizabethan examples, were, too, succeeded by those of columnar or turned baluster form. These supports were slightly splayed, so as to give stability to the seats (Fig. 3). Three-legged or 'cornered' joined stools were also made. Benches and forms, less used in the seventeenth century, developed on similar lines, being, by construction, no more than heavy elongated stools, purposed to seat several persons.

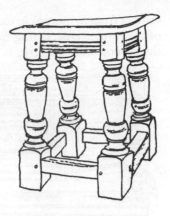

Fig. 3. Oak 'joint' stool; the seat has a moulded edge and is supported on turned legs united by plain stretchers. Height 1 ft. 9 in. Mid-seventeenth century.

Settles

Settles resembled in form contemporary chairs, but were made with very high backs. They were either movable or fixed; and were extremely popular pieces, particularly in poorer households, where they offered comparative comfort as seats, both by virtue of a position by the fireside and as providing protection against draughts. Most late settles, supplied to farmhouses and cottages, were of a serviceable and composite nature. In many, a locker was contained beneath the seat, which was hinged and opened as the lid of a chest. Some settles, constructed with a hinged back, combined the functions of seat and table (Pl. 18A).

Cupboards

Cupboards figure prominently in inventories of the period, but seldom are particularized, and while it is clear that cupboards of several types existed in most houses of substance, and were to be found in hall, parlour and bedrooms, it is yet difficult exactly to identify the purpose served by many of the numerous surviving specimens.[13]

The court-cupboard, introduced by the third quarter of the sixteenth century, or earlier, and possessed by manors and the larger farmhouses by about 1600, had, however, a definite place in the dining parlour and was used for the display of plate and as a service table. (Those which were made under Elizabeth and James I were often of walnut and were richly carved and inlaid, as befitted ceremonial pieces.) The function of the court-cupboard remained the same throughout the course of the century. It was specifically listed by Randle

Holme[14] in his work of 1688, as being among those 'things necessary for and belonging to a dineing Rome'. The court cupboard was of open construction, in three tiers, and rarely exceeded 3 ft. 10 in. in height. The tiers were supported at front, at the corners, usually by bulbous columns. These were a distinctive feature, and were at first of pronounced 'cup and cover' form, but later modified and attenuated, and, towards the end of the century, undefined, except sometimes by grooving. Drawers were contained behind the upper and middle friezes, and 'carpets' or cloths were laid on the shelves. The late court-cupboard, particularly after 1700, is usually of comparatively poor quality, the design stinted, and the character of the carved decoration inferior. It was at that time the unfashionable product of the country joiner, and had been superseded by the side table.

Two other types of cupboard, related closely structurally to the open court-cupboard, but each formed with an enclosed upper stage, were also in common use. First, a splay-fronted cupboard, with central door, which presumably served much the same purpose as an open 'cup-board' (there is adequate room for the display of 'flaggons, cans, cups, and beakers' on the shelves) and may also have been described as a 'court cupboard'. Its dimensions are much the same; and, often both friezes open as drawers. And secondly, a straight-fronted cupboard enclosed by a door or doors above and flanked by panels, which, although of similar proportions to the court-cupboard, must be regarded as a piece

<hr />

[13] See Edwards, *op. cit.*, Vol. II, pp. 156 ff.

[14] See Holme, *op. cit.*, Vol. II, p. 15.

distinct from it, more akin to the press. An example of the former type, dating from the second half of the seventeenth century, is illustrated in Fig. 4.

Fig. 4. Cupboard of carved oak, in two tiers; the upper part containing a recessed central cupboard with canted sides. Second half of the seventeenth century.

Here, bulbous columns in front have given way to vase-shaped and squat baluster turned supports. The flat posts at the back corners are standard as, too, is the moulded edge to the central shelf. The carving, decorating the upper frieze and bordering the panels of the front of the enclosed stage below, is shallow and recessed – another late feature. Sunk or recessed carving was much employed on post-Restoration provincial oak furniture, and was utilized by the country joiner as a comparatively easy method of carving. Often, the ground was punched, so as to throw the design into relief.

The press or 'close' cupboard was to be found throughout the century in the living-rooms and bedrooms of most houses, large and small. The press was an extremely useful piece of furniture, and plain specimens of oak or a native wood were made in country districts well into the eighteenth century. Many late presses are dated. In some, the upper stage was recessed; the frieze was supported by turned bulbous columns (which later were replaced by pendant bosses) framing the upper doors and resting on a narrow shelf (Pl. 15B). The large cupboard doors of a substantial lower stage were often divided into one horizontal panel with two vertical panels below. Other presses, with a plain front, and fitted with shelves, were designed for use in the bedrooms, or as storage pieces. There survive also a number of interesting specimens which were made with cupboard doors and drawers in the lower portion; the combination was not unusual (Pl. 15A). In general, presses were between 5 and 6 ft. high, and tended to develop towards greater width. They were not fashionable by the late Stuart period, and it is significant that few walnut or marquetry examples have survived (but see Fig. 5). Three-tiered cupboards – distinctive in appearance and of Welsh origin – are known as *tridarns*.

Small hanging cupboards, for food, enclosed by doors each with one or more open rows of turned spindles, which provide the means of ventilation, date for the most part from the first half of the century (Pl. 16B). Later examples are more roughly made, but sometimes still very decorative.

Long tables

The long framed tables and draw tables of this period were substantially made; and were, by Evelyn's phrase, 'as fixed as the freehold', intended to endure and give service to many generations. They were used for dining, and were to be found in hall and parlour; and they have survived in large numbers, often in good condition. Some smaller varieties of table, however, which are listed in most contemporary inventories, and which must have been plentiful from an early date (since they would be required for many different purposes), are comparatively scarce. Indeed, a 'square table', of which there is frequent enough mention, is not certainly to be identified with a known existing type. Small round and oval tables, and tables with octagonal or polygonal tops, of sixteenth century date, are known, and specimens are often of very decorative appearance, with an elaborately arcaded underframing. Many tables were constructed with a folding half-top and some form of gate support, and from these latter derived the small gate-leg tables with hinged flaps ('falling' tables), made in increasing numbers, and size, under the Stuarts (see *Gate-leg Tables* below).

Fig. 5. Clothes press of walnut; door, drawer fronts and sides veneered and decorated with herring-bone inlay and cross-banding. Height 6 ft. 7 in. Early eighteenth century.

Most of the long framed tables of seventeenth century date which remain are of oak or, less commonly, of elm or yew; walnut was rarely used at this period. During the reign of James I these tables were supported on columnar legs or on massive carved legs of an exaggerated bulbous form, and were tied by moulded stretchers. The supports are a distinctive feature. The bulb, Flemish or German in origin, built up from several sections and sometimes ornately carved with acanthus and gadroons was of a well-defined 'cup and cover' form, with ionic capital above a thin turned neck. The bulb became much modified in the course of the first half of the century. Some later tables had a graceful vase turned leg, but a coarse form of turning (reminiscent of bobbin turning) was to be found in many of those

made during the Commonwealth, or the period immediately succeeding.

Tables were frequently of great length, and many of those with fixed tops had six or eight legs and intermediate cross stretchers. Draw tables, however, which were fitted with two subsidiary leaves (attached to raking bearers and situated under the main board), and might be extended to almost double their length, were supported only at the four corners.[15] Their height, when closed, was generally about 2 ft. 9 in. Draw tables and long tables with fixed tops were made contemporaneously and their stylistic development followed a parallel course.

A draw table now at the Oak House Museum, at West Bromwich (Pl. 16c) is a good late specimen and, characteristically, is simple in design, with a mimimum of carved decoration. The frieze, which noticeably in many earlier tables dating from the first third of the century was used as a field for a decoration of inlay, often of chequer pattern, or was elaborately carved with strapwork, with flutings, gadroons or lunettes, is here plain. The bulbous supports of the table are much attenuated and their 'cup and cover' form is barely defined by a carved grooving. There are ring mouldings above and below the bulbs. The top consists of two narrow boards, set in a mitred surround. The length of the table, unextended, is 6 ft. 9 in.; and with both end leaves fully drawn out, 11 ft. 6 in. As is so often the case with these tables, the feet, which finished in square blocks, have been cut by some 2 or 3 in. The table stands now at 2 ft. 7 in.

Long tables with fixed tops, the friezes of which are decorated on one long side only, clearly were designed for use as side or serving tables. Tables of trestle construction, which were still made in the seventeenth century, may have been put to the same use.

Gate-leg Tables

Gate-leg tables are among the most useful and pleasing pieces of seventeenth century furniture

[15] See Edwards, *op. cit.*, Vol. II, p. 130 – *Construction*, Fig. 7.

readily to be acquired by the collector. Tables of this class have survived in surprisingly great variety, and are dissimilar in construction, size and shape, and in the character of supports and stretchers. Gate-leg tables when extended were round, oval, square, oblong or polygonal; and the number of supports ranged from three to twelve. They were jointed by mortice and tenon, secured by dowel-pins. Most of these tables were made in the post-Restoration period, when the habit of dining at separate small tables became fashionable, and when a very considerable demand existed.

The early type of gate-leg table (a 'folding' table) was of semi-circular form, with a single gate. It was designed to stand against a wall when closed, and was supported on three legs tied by a semi-circular stretcher. One of the two back legs was halved vertically and framed to the stretcher (also halved) so as to form a single swinging gate. The table when open was circular and was then supported at four points. In other types with hinged double tops, the gate was formed as a complete section. Tables with a triangular framing and a semi-circular overhanging top often were constructed with four legs, one of which was attached to the gate, and was movable. A number of tables of this sort, with a triangular top (which opened to a square form), were intended to stand in the corner of a room. This is evident from the fact that the side to which the gate was attached, and the gate itself, frequently was decorated with carving. Tables of polygonal form were often provided with four fixed supports, in addition to those of the movable gate. The 'folding' table, with carved and arcaded underframing and gate supported on a ground shelf, which is shown in Pl. 16A, is of this description. The character of the decoration, in particular the applied ornament, suggests that the piece dates from the middle years of the century.

Oval tables with 'falling' tops and a gate on either side made their appearance early in the century. The centre portion of these tables was fixed, and usually was supported either by solid trestle uprights pegged into a base-board at each end, or by turned balusters, finishing in trestle feet, tied

by a double stretcher, or by turned legs at each of the four corners (Pl. 19A). The last type is that most commonly to be seen. The legs on either side, four in number, two of which compose the gate, were baluster turned or twist turned, and the stretchers, square or turned; the hinged flaps of the fixed top were upheld by the gates. Often a drawer was fitted in the underframing. Some of these tables which were made after the Restoration were of exceptional size (between 7 and 8 ft. long) and provided with four gates; they were therefore furnished with twelve legs. However, these tables did not provide a satisfactory solution to the problem of seating a large number of people at one table, because of the lack of leg room, and few consequently were made; but they are very handsome pieces of furniture. Occasionally they were made with square tops.

An ingenious and singularly attractive type of small gate-leg table, with a single pivoting gate, so constructed as to uphold both flaps, was also made.[16]

Gate-leg tables were generally of oak, particularly the larger specimens, but yew and the fruit-woods were employed with good effect by country craftsmen. Walnut is found used in some tables made after the Restoration.

Beds

The Elizabethan and early Stuart great bed was of very substantial proportions. The panelled head-board, usually of architectural character, with arcaded decoration and pilasters sometimes in the form of terminal figures, was elaborately carved and inlaid with floral ornament. The massive bulbous foot-posts, supported on pedestals of square section, were free standing (i.e. were clear of the bedstock), and served to carry a heavy, panelled tester. The hangings were of velvet or other rich materials. Beds of this type were of considerable consequence and were handed down from one generation to the next.

'Joined' beds figure largely in inventories of the time. They are not in general to be identified with

---

[16] See Edwards, *op. cit.*, Vol. III, p. 239 – *Tables, gate-leg*, Fig. 20.

the great beds of the foregoing description, but rather with beds of box-form, with panelled head, foot and canopy, which in construction resemble those made contemporaneously on the Continent (many, presumably, were fitted with enclosing side curtains); or with the low 'stump' beds, of panelled construction, with short corner-posts and an open foot which were in common use, and which continued to be made throughout the seventeenth and eighteenth centuries.

Chests

The very numerous chests made throughout this century were mostly of framed and panelled construction. 'Boarded' chests (i.e. chests wherein the solid front is rebated into the ends, which form the supports) were comparatively rare.

Many early seventeenth century chests were decorated with a floral inlay used in combination with carved ornament. Some specimens were arcaded in front, the stiles framing the arches being carved with conventional ornament, or, occasionally, faced with terminal figures. An all over decoration of carving in low relief is often found in chests dating from the second quarter of the century, particularly those coming from northern and eastern districts (Pl. 17c).

2. THE POST-RESTORATION STYLE

Veneered cabinet furniture

From the reign of Charles II, new methods and materials were largely employed in the making of cabinet furniture. The period from the Restoration to the reign of George I is distinguished by an extensive use of walnut, both in the solid and as a veneer. *Juglans regia*, the English variety, pale brown in colour, with brown and black veining, and *Juglans nigra*, the 'black wood', which resembles mahogany, were both being grown in England by the later seventeenth century, but in insufficient quantity to meet the increased demand. 'Were the timber in greater plenty amongst us', remarked Evelyn, 'we should have far better utensils of all sorts for our Houses, as chairs, stools, Bedsteads, Tables, Wainscot, Cabinets, etc., in-

stead of the more vulgar beech, subject to the worm, weak and unsightly: — I say if we had store of this material we should find an incredible improvement in the more stable furniture of our houses. ...'[17] The scarcity of walnut was met in part by importations from the Continent (especially from France) and from Virginia, and by the use of other decorative woods such as olive ('highly in request' as a veneer), laburnum and kingwood (then described as 'princes wood'). The cuts of these woods possessed the variety and richness of figure desired by the veneerer.

Veneering 'whereby several thin slices or leaves of fine wood of different sorts are applied and fastened on a ground of common wood',[18] hitherto had been practised to a very limited extent in England. From the Restoration, however, veneered furniture, inspired by foreign example, and workmen, became fashionable. Veneered work was the product of a cabinet maker. Veneers were laid by means of glue on the flush prepared surfaces of a carcase wood. Panel construction, long employed by the joiner, was by this technique in the main discarded. Joiners, of course, and craftsmen in the country, continued to make pieces in 'wainscot', that is in imported oak; and some attempted to adapt their designs to new fashions. And 'wainscot furniture', of joined construction and unveneered, was cheaper and popularly supplied to all classes throughout the 'Walnut period'.

Equally, many of those workmen employing new styles and techniques were dependent to a more or less considerable extent on tradition. The walnut clothes-press (Fig. 5), a rare and interesting piece dating from the early eighteenth century (the design of its cornice and convex frieze is characteristic, and is found on the veneered walnut and marquetry 'scrutoirs' fashionable under the late Stuarts), illustrates the complexity and variety of production throughout the period. Compare this piece with the oak press of framed construction (Pl. 15A).

[17] *Sylva*, by John Evelyn, 1664.
[18] *New and Universal Dictionary of Arts and Sciences*, 1756.

Lacquer and japanning

Soon after 1660, oriental lacquer furniture was imported in quantity by the East India Company, and offered for sale in many of the 'curiosity' shops at that time existing in London. Oriental lacquer was of two varieties: incised lacquer, known as 'Bantam work', which was shipped in the form of screens, or plain boards, often subsequently made up into mirror frames (Pl. 21A), table-tops or cabinets, sometimes with curious effect; [19] and a lacquer with raised gilt ornament on a hard, smooth, polished ground, in colour generally black. (The numerous lacquer cabinets of late seventeenth century date, and later, which have survived are of this latter sort; they were mounted on decorative carved and gilt stands of English manufacture.) By the 1680's the 'Indian' wares, as they were called, were being very commonly imitated in England, both by professional workmen and by amateur decorators, and a *Treatise of Japaning and Varnishing* produced by John Stalker and George Parker in 1688, which gave instruction in the art, enjoyed markedly substantial success. Certainly, the directions given by the authors of this work are technically sound and would seem to have been followed closely by contemporaries. The European imitations of oriental lacquer (see Pl. 21B and Fig. 6) properly are to be termed 'Japan' rather than 'lacquer' and were produced by a method which was akin to varnishing. [20] This distinction however was not observed in the seventeenth century; the term 'Japann' was then applied indiscriminately to furniture of Eastern origin or home manufacture.

[19] The mirror frame (Pl. 21A) was carelessly constructed, and illustrates the contemporary statement that 'Bantam work' was 'obsolete, and out of fashion ... no person fond of it ... except some who have made new Cabinets out of old Skreens. And from that large old piece, by the help of a Joyner, made little ones ... torn and hacked to joint a new fancie ... the finest hodgpodg and medly of Men and Trees turned topsie turvie.' *A Treatise of Japaning and Varnishing* ... (1688) by J. Stalker and G. Parker.

[20] Japanning consists in 'covering bodies by grounds of opake colours in varnish; which may be either afterwards decorated by painting or gilding, or left in a plain state. ...' (Robert Dossie, 1758).

Fig. 6. Chair of beechwood, japanned green and gold on a red ground. Height 3 ft. 9 in. Early eighteenth century.

Gesso

Gilt furniture enjoyed considerable popularity at this period. The fashion for gilding first appears under Charles II in the many floridly carved and gilt stands which were made for imported oriental cabinets, and in elaborately decorative side-tables, mirrors and stands dating from late Stuart times. These latter are magnificent pieces, strongly influenced by French models.

Gesso furniture, which may be regarded as a subsidiary branch of gilt furniture, is found in England after about 1690. The technique is distinctive. Gesso ornament is executed in very low relief and follows the lines of an intricate and symmetrical traced pattern, usually 'arabesque' in nature. The gesso, a composition of chalk and parchment size, was applied in successive thin coats to the surface (already roughly carved) of the piece to be decorated, and when hardened was re-carved, sanded or punched, and gilded. Gesso was most suitable for the decoration of large flat surfaces, such as table-tops (Pl. 19B). During the reign of Anne, gilt gesso was frequently applied to the mirror frame.

Marquetry

Furniture of 'markatre' is recorded in numerous inventories of early seventeenth century date. The term 'markatre' then was descriptive of inlaid furniture. Marquetry, however, as we now know it, was not introduced into England from the Continent until shortly after the Restoration. (Evelyn, in *Sylva*, which was first published in 1664, refers to certain exotic woods used in marquetry decoration.) The technique was distinct from that of inlay, and comparable with veneering. Small veneers of different coloured woods, cut to various shapes, were assembled, according to a prepared design, and set in a veneer ground. This composite veneer overlaid the carcase wood. Patterns were usually floral, or of flowers with birds, and at first were brightly coloured. Certain of the woods used for the patterns (these included fruitwoods, yew, beech, holly or sycamore) were stained. The marquetry decoration was in many cases reserved in panels, usually oval in shape.

'Seaweed' or arabesque marquetry, which was a later development, particularly fashionable in the first years of the eighteenth century, was conceived on a smaller scale and was subdued in colouring. The delicate and intricate scrolling patterns were executed in two woods only – box, or sometimes holly, on a walnut ground. In the character of the decoration the influence of André Charles Boulle and other French artists working under Louis XIV is clearly discernible. The woods of the pattern and the ground were sometimes reversed, as in the *partie* and *contre partie* of Boulle. 'Seaweed' marquetry was used sometimes in conjunction with parquetry.

Many of the small walnut tables with twist – or baluster-turned legs which came into favour after the Restoration were decorated with marquetry. The 'little table with a drawer' illustrated in Pl. 19c is characteristic in design of this type. The panels of arabesque marquetry of the table top are bordered by broad bands of oyster-shell veneer; and the supports are tied by a flat stretcher with Y-shaped ends connected by an oval platform. The stretcher, like the edge of the top, is veneered in cross-banded walnut.

Cane furniture

Cane chairs first were produced in England early in Charles II's reign, as is evident from the wording of a petition to Parliament by the cane-chair makers in the 1680's, wherein it was stated:

'... That about the Year 1664, Cane-Chairs, &c. came into use in *England*, which gave so much Satisfaction to all the Nobility, Gentry, and Commonalty of this Kingdom, (for their Durableness, Lightness, and Cleanness from Dust, Worms and Moths, which inseparably attend Turky-work, Serge, and other Stuff-Chairs and Couches, to the spoiling of them and all Furniture near them) that they came to be much used in *England*, and sent to all parts of the World. ..' [21]

The early examples resembled in form, if not in materials, leather covered chairs in use under the Commonwealth; and indeed for some years the two types were produced contemporaneously. The low square back, set rather high above the seat rail, and the seat itself, were filled with a coarse-meshed caning; the legs, uprights and stretcher rails were twist turned; and the arms were flat, very slightly shaped, and horizontal (Fig. 7). At this time the frame bore no carved decoration save for an incised lozenge pattern which is sometimes found.

Cane chairs were not expensive, and in London within very few years there was a strong demand for them, usually in sets comprising perhaps two armchairs with six or more single chairs. Construction was in the solid. Polished French walnut was used for the frames of the finer chairs; while beech, painted or japanned, or stained to resemble walnut, served as a (cheaper) substitute wood. (The manufacture of cane chairs, even at a late stage of their development, when they were no longer fashionable, would seem largely to have

[21] Quoted in full in *English Cane Chairs – Part I*, by R. W. Symonds, in *The Connoisseur*, March 1951.

Fig. 7. Arm-chair of turned walnut with caned back and seat. *c*. 1665.

been confined to London. Defoe, in a well known passage, describing the furniture of a country tradesman, stated: '... The chairs, if of cane, are made in London; the ordinary matted chairs, perhaps in the place where they live.') [22]

The stylistic development of cane chairs is complex, and was very rapid. By about 1670 the height of the back was increased, and a broad flat top rail, or cresting, which was carved in low relief, was tenoned between the uprights. Then a deepened front stretcher rail was carved to correspond with the cresting, and the framing of the back panel was similarly enriched, usually with a decoration of scrolls, flowers and foliage. The device of cupids supporting the crown was particularly popular and the description 'carved with Boyes and Crowne' figures repeatedly in contemporary accounts. The motif, although associated with the Restoration of the monarchy was, in fact, in fashion until as late as about 1700. Arms were swept, and finished in deep scrolls, and an exuberant S-scroll form was incorporated in the design of front legs. By the end of the reign of Charles II, the carving was frequently pierced and executed in comparatively deep relief, with great gain in effect. Baluster turning was re-introduced as a popular alternative to twist turning. The mesh of the caning was finer, and some chairs were dished for flat squab cushions. Some of these features are exemplified in a cane seat in the form of two chairs in a private collection (Pl. 22c). This piece, nevertheless, was perhaps made about 1700: the design of the undulating crestings, and matching front rails, in particular, and of the baluster turned uprights, suggest a comparatively late date of origin. Seats of this description, which presumably were often supplied as part of a large set of seating furniture, are now extremely rare. This is an unusual and pleasing example. Designs were influenced by foreign fashions. It is significant that a number of chairs supplied to the Royal Palaces by Richard Price in the early 1680's were 'turned of the Dutch turning'. Generally, Dutch chairs may be distinguished from English by the character of the twist turning.

The Dutch turning is thicker; the hollow is less pronounced. Moreover, two varieties of turning are sometimes found on the one chair. There is also in the great majority of cases a difference of construction: the stretcher which unites the back legs is placed high on English chairs — about midway between the seat rail and the ground; while in Dutch chairs it is either non-existent or is at the level of the side stretchers.

Under William and Mary the chair back was made even taller, and was narrower and surmounted by an elaborate cresting. The rake of the back was much increased; and the seat was smaller. The form of the cresting frequently matched that of the arched front stretcher rail; it was not, as formerly, secured between the uprights by means of mortice and tenon but rested on them and was attached by dowel-pegs. Dowel jointing was used also to secure the front legs, which were pegged to the base of the arm supports or, in the case of the single chair, to the underside of the seat rail. Structurally, these features are weak. The uprights were sometimes of baluster form, and occasionally fluted, and the arch of the cresting was repeated in the filling of the back which was caned in exceedingly fine mesh. Alternatively, the back was open-carved with a design of foliage and interlaced scrolls. The seats of many chairs of this latter type were upholstered. Covering materials included fine damasks and Genoese velvets. By the end of the century straight taper legs were introduced as a fashionable alternative to those of scroll form. These were of square moulded or round section, and finished in octagonal, spherical or 'Braganza' scrolled feet. Pear- or mushroom-shaped cappings were a distinctive feature of the taper leg. The carved front rail was replaced by moulded diagonal stretchers of serpentine form meeting in a centre piece which was usually surmounted by a turned finial (Pl. 22B). The stretchers, ornamental in character and associated with chairs of fine quality, gave little additional strength to the legs. Tall upholstered single chairs of this ornate character were sometimes gilded.

Soon after 1700 the fashion for cane furniture declined. The industry nevertheless was securely established in London, and 'Cane-Chair Shops',

[22] *The Complete English Tradesman* (1745), by Daniel Defoe; edit. of 1841, Vol. I, p. 266.

particularly those in St Paul's Churchyard and the near neighbourhood, continued to thrive. Cane chairs, stools, couches and tables, were supplied in quantity to innumerable households in England and were also exported to the Continent and to the American Colonies. Many pieces were based on models fashionable under William and Mary. They were simplified versions of these models, incorporating some new features. Cane chairs still figure in the Royal accounts under George I, although certainly they were not required for the private apartments. The cane furniture trade flourished until about 1740. In great part the continued wide popularity of cane furniture is to be explained by its cheapness. Chairs of beech were sold at a few shillings apiece. The claims of the chairmakers too had had much to recommend them: as stated, cane chairs were light and clean, and quite durable. But cane furniture was not readily to be obtained in all parts of the country. Communications were bad and many districts were almost completely isolated for long periods at a time. As a consequence country chairmakers had a market for chairs, of cane-chair pattern, which were upholstered in leather or cloth – as well as for rush-seated chairs with slatted backs. The former are interesting on two counts: first, by the not unattractive blending of new and old features of style and construction (such chairs are nearly always later in date than would appear at a glance) and secondly by evidence that they may provide as to the time-lag in fashion in the provinces. The plainly made chair illustrated in Fig. 8, now at Dennington Church, Suffolk, is reminiscent in general appearance of a type fashionable in the late seventeenth century. The tall back and shaped cresting, and the turned front stretcher rail, have the form and grace peculiar to the cane chair of that period, without its richness of ornamentation. The front legs are pegged to the bottom of the seat. The uprights to the back, however, are moulded and not turned, and the back panel and the seat upholstered simply with leather. The front supports, which are of hybrid cabriole form, and roughly shaped, are unusual; they point to a date of construction probably as late as the second quarter of the eighteenth century.

Chests of drawers

Veneered chests of drawers dating from the last quarter of the century are to be found in a variety of decorative woods – in figured walnut, kingwood, yew, burr elm and in a parquetry of oyster shells of walnut or laburnum, with a geometrical inlay of holly or boxwood.[23] Sycamore was often used as a banding wood. Marquetry chests of drawers first appeared about 1680, and japanned examples a few years later.

The chest consisted usually of three long drawers, graduated in depth, with two short, shallow drawers above, and was supported on shaped bracket feet, or alternatively on ball or bun feet. The projecting ovolo moulding at the top of the chest was frequently repeated, inverted, at its base, immediately below the bottom drawer. Many chests were mounted on low stands, with four, five or six legs, tied by stretchers. The stands, also, frequently contained drawers. Chests on stands rarely exceeded 5 ft. in height. The mouldings surrounding the drawer fronts, marking the divisions between drawers, were at this date applied *to the carcase*. A half-round moulding was commonly used on pieces dating from the end of the century; and was succeeded shortly after 1700 by a double half-round moulding. Mouldings were cross-banded. The carcase of the piece was usually of yellow deal, and drawer linings of oak or deal according to its quality. Normally, the grain of the wood of the bottom boards of the drawers ran from back to front and not from side to side of the piece. In many chests the sides were unveneered. The double

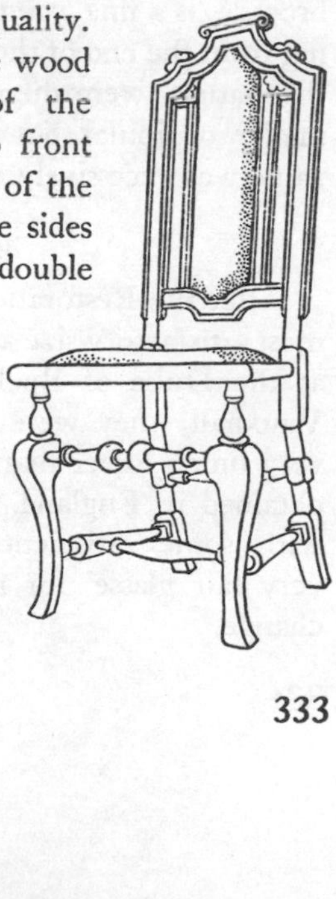

[23] See Edwards, *op. cit.*, Vol. II, p. 33 – *Chests of Drawers*, Fig. 29.

Fig. 8. Chair at Dennington Church, Suffolk. Early eighteenth century.

chest or tallboy would seem not to have been made in England much before about 1710.

The oak chest of four long drawers illustrated in Pl. 18c, although dating from the post-Restoration period, is joiner's work, and has therefore little in common with these fashionable specimens. Stylistic features of mixed date are interestingly combined in this piece. The legs of the low stand, while spirally turned, are tied by plain moulded stretchers of a type which had long been in general use. The distinctive decoration of the front of the chest, with raised panels of geometrical design, mitred and in strong projection, is in the style of the mid century. The brass escutcheon plates, and drop handles, are of a form introduced in the late seventeenth century.

Beds

By the late Stuart period, fashionable beds were taller, and luxuriously upholstered. The value of the four-post bed then lay almost entirely in its often very costly 'clothes and hangings' – curtains and fringed valances of rich materials, and tester head-cloth; silk or linen inner curtains; blankets, rugs, quilts and counterpane; and flock, feather or down mattresses. Its wooden framework, the bedstead itself, was almost completely invisible. The bedposts were slender and, like the shaped headboard and tester, were covered with material. The state bed from Wroxton Abbey, now at Aston Hall, Birmingham, upholstered in red and gold brocade, is a fine example of this type of bed, dating from the end of the century (Pl. 20A). Beds of this nature, were the products not of the cabinet maker or joiner but of the upholsterer. Their value was excessively high.

Mirrors

After the Restoration, looking-glass plates of a most satisfactory size and quality were being made at the Duke of Buckingham's Glass House at Vauxhall; they were sold at prices which were very much lower than those which formerly had obtained in England. Pepys for example bought with some satisfaction in December 1664 'a very fair glasse' for five guineas at the Old Exchange.

The mirror frame at this time was of square or rectangular proportions, and was surmounted by a semi-circular hood, sometimes pierced (which in many cases has not survived, having become detached from the body of the piece). The frame was broad, and of pronounced convex section. It was made by the cabinet-maker, or joiner, and was constructed of deal, veneered with cross-banded walnut, an oyster-shell parquetry of walnut, laburnum or olive wood. Various marquetry and japanned specimens still exist; these, being very decorative, must have been popular. Materials such as tortoiseshell and the imported incised lacquer were also occasionally employed for this type of frame (Pl. 21A).

Pier glasses

The pier glass, which was designed to be hung between windows above a side table of matching workmanship, was introduced towards the close of the century. It was sometimes 7 or 8 ft. high, and consequently of very tall proportions. Mirror and accompanying table were regarded as an interior architectural feature of the room. The pier-glass frame was flat, moulded and comparatively narrow, and was often decorated in gilt gesso. Sometimes the moulded frame was itself of glass.

Dressing mirrors

The dressing mirror on box stand (Pl. 21B) was a most serviceable introduction of the late seventeenth century; specimens of this small piece in veneered walnut, or japanned, were in general use within a few years.

A Queen Anne interior

The Tea-Table, a print which was published at London in or about 1710,[24] provides some evidence as to the appearance of a contemporary interior. Therein we see 'Thick Scandal

[24] *The Tea-Table*, a print measuring $6\frac{1}{4} \times 5\frac{3}{8}$ in., published *c.* 1710 and sold by John Bowles of 13, Cornhill, London. See *Catalogue of Prints and Drawings in the British Museum. Division I: Political and Personal Satires*, Vol. II, 1873, No. 1555.

circulate with right Bohea'.[25] The room is richly but sparsely furnished. There is a foot carpet, which was an article of some scarcity at the beginning of the century, and an open alcove cupboard which apparently contains small pieces of china – 'a neat booffett furnish'd' perhaps 'with glasses and china for the table'[26] or with collectors' specimens of Chinese porcelain or Delft ware. The ladies in the room are seated in high-backed cane chairs at a gate-leg table of conventional design. Significantly, the chairs are of a type more often associated with the period of William and Mary than that of Anne. By contrast, the gesso wall mirror which hangs to the right of the fireplace is in the newest style.

3. THE QUEEN ANNE STYLE

Furniture which was in fashion under Queen Anne is characterized by a new restraint of form and ornament, and by a seeming simplicity. Enrichment of surface was gained by the use of figured veneers of walnut, and other woods, rather than by carved ornament or marquetry decoration. The flamboyant taste of the immediately preceding period – an expression of the first phase of English Baroque – underwent a sudden and considerable change about 1700, due in large part to the introduction of the cabriole support and to improving standards of craftsmanship. The cabriole rapidly superseded the scroll and the 'Marot type' leg and was applied to chairs (Pl. 22A and Fig. 6) and settees, tables, tripods, stands and other articles of furniture, with decisive effect on design, and construction. On fine pieces, stretchers were often dispensed with, not to be re-introduced until the beginning of the second half of the eighteenth century. In no other article of furniture, perhaps, is design so finely and nicely adjusted as in the developed 'hoop-back' single chair, the well-defined serpentine curves of which, by nature ornamental, are governed by structural purpose – the vase or fiddle-shaped splat, enclosed by undulating uprights and shaped to the form of the user's back, and the seat rail, often rounded in front, supported on graceful cabriole legs finishing in club feet.

An appreciable increase in domestic comfort in this reign was due in part to the introduction of new and useful pieces, and to the development of those but newly adopted.

Small walnut bureaux on open stands with turned legs were made first towards 1700. (Extant specimens, which are now exceedingly scarce, are usually of very fine quality and workmanship.)[27] Bureaux on chests (pieces constructed with a base of two or three long and two short drawers, or with a base containing a central kneehole) were in general production in the early eighteenth century, particularly in a 'stock size' of 3 ft. 6 in., and have survived in comparatively large numbers, together with tall bureaux in two stages, or bureaux bookcases, which in form are closely related to them. The cupboard doors of the upper stage of these latter pieces were faced often with mirror glass, and the surmounting cornices were alternatively straight, hooded or pedimented. The bureau bookcase illustrated in Pl. 20B is a fine specimen and of striking appearance. It is veneered with the burr wood of mulberry, decorated with cross bandings bordered by inlaid pewter stringing lines. The technique is distinctive and the bureau bookcase may be attributed to John Coxed, or to Coxed and Woster, working at the White Swan in St Paul's Churchyard, London, in the early eighteenth century, on the basis of its close similarity in form and materials to other known (labelled) pieces made by this firm.[28]

This cabinet is significant of the rapid development of the cabinet-maker's craft which had come

---

[25] Tea had been introduced into the country from Holland about the time of the Restoration, and was at this date drunk in private houses only by the well-to-do. It was still very expensive, and the Bohea was priced at more than 30s. per lb.

[26] *The Journeys of Celia Fiennes*, ed. by Christopher Morris, 1947, p. 345. A house at Epsom (London and the Later Journeys, c. 1701–3).

[27] See *English Furniture Styles*, by Ralph Fastnedge, Pelican Books, 1955, Pl. 23.

[28] John Coxed was succeeded by G. Coxed and T. Woster (*fl. c.* 1710–36). After Woster's death in 1736, these famous premises were occupied by Henry Bell. See *Georgian Cabinet-Makers*, by R. Edwards and M. Jourdain, 1954, for fuller details.

about within a generation, and evidence of technical skill.[29] The reticent character of much early eighteenth century case furniture is to be seen in the walnut chest on stand which is illustrated in Fig. 9. The chest is distinguished by fine proportions, and by its quality of workmanship; and the matched, figured veneers of the front provide the main enrichment. By the early eighteenth century foreign styles had become assimilated and naturalized. The best walnut furniture of the Queen

Anne period is direct and unaffected in character. The sets of chairs and upholstered settees with open arms, side and dressing-tables, card tables and bureaux, made for the upper and middle classes have consistently a purity of style hitherto unrealized in England.

SHORT BIBLIOGRAPHY

1. *A Treatise of Japaning and Varnishing ...* (1688) by J.Stalker and G.Parker.
2. *Furniture in England, from 1660 to 1760*, by Francis Lenygon, 1914; revised by Margaret Jourdain, 1925.
3. *English Decoration and Furniture of the Early Renaissance (1500–1650)*, by Margaret Jourdain, 1924.
4. *The Dictionary of English Furniture*, by P.MacQuoid and Ralph Edwards (3 vols., 1924–7); revised by Ralph Edwards (3 vols., 1954).
5. *Furniture-Making in Seventeenth and Eighteenth Century England*, by R.W.Symonds, 1955.

[29] Smaller cabinets, with fall-fronts, which were inspired by foreign models and were known as 'scriptors' or 'scrutoirs', enjoyed great popularity during both the late Stuart and Anne periods. These cabinets, which are found often veneered in burr walnut or decorated with floral marquetry, were supported either on a base of drawers or on an open stand, and rarely exceeded 5 ft. 9 in. in height. Some cabinets were constructed with a pair of hinged doors in place of the fall-front.

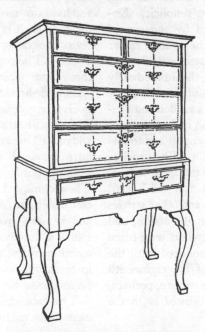

Fig. 9. Walnut chest of drawers, on stand containing one long drawer, supported on plain cabriole legs, the drawer fronts veneered with figured walnut and bordered by herring-bone bandings. Early eighteenth century.

Painting and Portrait Miniatures

OLIVER MILLAR

The age of the Stuarts is a rich and fascinating period in the history of painting in England and the development of English connoisseurship. In its earlier years the number of private collections of any size was limited almost entirely to the Court circle. The motives behind the formation of these collections remained predominantly, as they had been in the previous century, iconographical, historical and dynastic. Pictures had not yet come to be valued as works of art in their own right or as sources of aesthetic delight to their owners, and tapestries or painted hangings were the accepted form of decoration in a private house. Even in the large and rapidly increasing collection of pictures in the royal palaces there was a preponderance of contemporary and historical portraits, topographical views and maps: Charles I, the most enthusiastic and discerning of all royal patrons and collectors, wholly transformed the Crown collections, but likewise assembled a very large and varied collection of portraits of his family and ancestors, of earlier and contemporary European rulers, of his closest friends and of the artists he admired or who had worked for him. In the other great and lesser collections which grew up in the seventeenth century there was the same continuing interest in the portrait and some patrons even commissioned painters to concoct gratifying sets of 'ancestors'. The most significant example of an historical portrait gallery was assembled by the Earl of Clarendon at Clarendon House as a commentary on his famous *History*, but something of the flavour of these collections can still be felt at Woburn, where the portraits assembled by the Earls and Dukes of Bedford survive fairly intact; at Welbeck, with its remarkable concentration of likenesses of the Cavendish, Vere, Holles, Harley, Wriothesley and Bentinck families; at Althorp, where a series of portraits of the Spencers and their relatives (a series of consistently high quality) runs from the sixteenth to the twentieth century; at Gorhambury, Drayton, Penshurst, Hardwick, Arbury, Boughton, Belvoir and Knole; at Euston, which still houses the remains of the collection of family and historical portraits formed by the Earl of Arlington; in such Scottish houses as Penicuik, Drumlanrig and Leslie House; and throughout the British Isles, where a steady succession of family portraits forms the backbone of numberless country-house collections.

By the time of the Hanoverian succession, however, taste in this country had undergone a radical transformation. In the reign of Charles I, and indeed in the last years of his father's reign, there had been a sudden flowering of connoisseurship in the King's immediate circle and an awakened interest in the arts of the Renaissance and contemporary Europe. The Grand Tour had become an increasingly important and regular part of a gentleman's education and some Englishmen had undergone an even deeper experience of European civilization. The structure of patronage, collecting and taste that we associate with the age of Hogarth and Reynolds was already formed in the age of Anne, and there was already a strongly cosmopolitan flavour in the 'state of the arts' in the days of the later Stuarts. The great collections of European pictures that were formed in this country in the century after the Peace of Utrecht were anticipated by such travellers and collectors of taste and discernment as the Duke of Shrewsbury, the fifth Earl of Exeter, the second Earl of Sunderland and Sir Thomas Isham: the three last, for instance, had grafted on to their hereditary collections at Burghley, Althorp and Lamport pictures which gave a Mediterranean lustre to their English walls. The same susceptibility to European influences is of fundamental importance for the growth of landscape painting and the lesser genres in England in our period, and an admiration, even in severely Protestant minds, for the full baroque style of Italy, France or Flanders bore fruit in the reflection of continental baroque and early rococo in the work of decorative painters on the walls and ceilings of many English palaces, castles and houses.

Nevertheless, the primary concern of English patrons was still with their 'own dull counterfeits', and here the seventeenth century, which had witnessed, among so many upheavals, this quiet revolution in taste, saw a no less revolutionary turning-point in the development of the English portrait: the arrival of Anthony van Dyck in London in the spring of 1632.

Jacobean portraiture still presents a most complex problem. A large number of portraits was produced in the first two and a half decades of the century and we know the names of many painters who were then at work. Within this rather narrow context there is a considerable variety of quality and style and some of the grandest Jacobean pieces are truly impressive (Pl. 23), but we are unable to link the most splendid of them (or, indeed, many of those whose appeal is gentler and less spectacular) with safety to any of the available painters; the slightly more familiar painters, such as Marcus Gheeraerts the younger, John de Critz, Paul van Somer, and even Daniel Mytens in his earlier English period, are still very inadequately defined. The most sumptuous Jacobean portraits (Pls. 23, 24) seem to represent a belated and distinctively English form of the mannerist style that was current in the Courts of Europe in the sixteenth century. The painters who created them concentrated on an elaborate and often highly polished surface-pattern; the designs are rigid, the figure is often narrow and attenuated; and the decorative value of costume, accessories and setting was thought more important than an attempt to evoke more fully the sitter's personality. The effect of a set of these magnificent Jacobean full-lengths hanging in the Long Gallery of a palace or of a great Jacobean or late Elizabethan mansion (one can perhaps imagine the series, painted for the Earl of Suffolk and now at Redlynch, in the Earl's new house at Audley End) must have been most spectacular, although 'when your posterity shall see our pictures they shall think wee were foolishly proud of apparel'.[1] The cumbersome splendours of the Jacobean age are no less clearly reflected in the miniatures of Isaac Oliver (Pl. 81), who provides an exact parallel, on a tiny scale, to the most ornate forms of Jacobean portraiture 'in large'. His over-confident, full-blooded style, with its naturalism, sculptural modelling, fine finish and polished surface, is predominantly Netherlandish in origin and the antithesis of Hilliard's delicacy and lyricism, but it represents most vividly the heavy exoticism of King James's Court.

In the second decade of the century we can sometimes detect tendencies towards restraint and a more sensitive understanding of the character of the sitter: tendencies that can be guardedly described as English. The pieces in which they are most clearly seen could perhaps be very tentatively associated with John de Critz, Robert Peake or Marcus Gheeraerts: certainly Gheeraerts's portraits of the 1620's (Pl. 26D) have a reserve and simplicity that can be seen in a rather different form in the less attractive work of Paul van Somer, but which are associated particularly with Daniel Mytens and Cornelius Johnson.

Mytens and Johnson were profoundly influenced by contemporary portrait-painting in the fashionable studios of Miereveld and Ravesteyn in Delft and The Hague: Mytens was trained in The Hague and was established in London by 1618, but Johnson, who came of Netherlandish

[1] Verstegen, *Antiquities concerning the English Nation* (1605): quoted by C. W. and P. Cunnington, *Handbook of English Costume in the Seventeenth Century* (1955), p. 11.

stock, had been born in London, and his portraits have an indefinably English delicacy in mood, close though they are in design to the Dutch school from which both painters derived. The Anglo-Netherlandish style, of which Mytens and Johnson were the main exponents, but which can be seen in the work of such less familiar or more migratory painters as Abraham Blyenberch, Geldorp, Johann Priwitzer or the monogrammist VM, marks a great advance on the flamboyant earlier 'Jacobethan' manner: simpler and more worldly, more sensitive in technique and with a feeling for texture which is wholly Dutch. These qualities, and Mytens's grave sense of character, can be seen in his earliest and rather timid English full-lengths (Pl. 25); but in his latest English portraits, the most distinguished that were painted in this country before Van Dyck's arrival, they are enhanced by a new elegance and swagger, manipulated with complete assurance, and enriched by sophisticated colour and broad, free handling.

Cornelius Johnson was a more limited painter and was most at ease with heads and shoulders, often set within the painted oval which he did much to popularize in this country. His earliest pieces, which are usually painted on panel, are tentative and insubstantial, though they have a Jacobean richness of texture; but his style became broader and softer, with a delicacy of colour and touch exactly suited to his tender, perceptive vision (Pl. 26A). He never seems to have worked for as illustrious a *clientèle* as Van Dyck or Mytens and for some years he was painting portraits for the country families of Kent and Sussex which provide a charming commentary on life in the smaller country houses in the years before the outbreak of the Civil War. In the work of Peter Oliver, who succeeded to his father Isaac's fashionable practice as a miniaturist, we find the same gentle sense of character and soft fullness of form. The style of Johnson and Peter Oliver could with safety be called increasingly English, and Mytens was painting at the English Court portraits that could hold their own with any comparable portraits being painted at that period on the Continent; but the potential development of English portraiture along the lines laid down by Mytens and Johnson was shattered by the impact of Van Dyck.

As a very young man Van Dyck had spent a few months in England in the service of James I, and since then his name must have been much in the minds of the collectors and patrons at the English Court. Charles I already owned pictures by him and was prepared to give him, on his arrival in London, a warm and generous welcome: a gesture for which history has richly rewarded him, for we shall always see through Van Dyck's eyes the King, his family and his courtiers. Our conception of the social life at the Caroline Court is deeply coloured by our knowledge of Van Dyck's commentary upon it. King Charles was not only, in Rubens's words, 'the greatest amateur of paintings among the princes of the world': he had set himself to attract distinguished foreign artists to his Court. A number of lesser painters (such as Keirincx, Poelenburgh and Pot) worked for him for short periods; Gentileschi, Honthorst and Rubens came to London in the 1620's; and in Van Dyck the King found a portrait-painter admirably suited to his services: of wide experience, distinguished in person and manner and accustomed to moving in the most illustrious circles. He was a new phenomenon in English society.

As a painter Van Dyck provided for his successors a source of inspiration and a series of patterns and conventions which have still not been exhausted. From his earliest years as Rubens's most privileged student and assistant in Antwerp he had been a painter of rare brilliance, with a refinement and nervous delicacy that enabled him later so admirably and so subtly to record the transient security and fragile elegance of King Charles's Court. At his studio in Blackfriars he had to cope with an increasing fashionable practice. Many of Van Dyck's portraits show the lassitude of an over-wrought painter, and he was compelled to organize a team of assistants to turn out a large number of canvases by methods of production that were to be developed and perfected by Lely and Kneller.

Van Dyck's portraits with their changing moods must have given the King and his more sensitive courtiers the intensest pleasure. Where the subject required it, Van Dyck's touch could be nervous and incisive and his sense of tone (especially in his lovely silvers and pinks) appropriately light and delicate; on other occasions his paint is rich, juicy and direct. He could create a state portrait, rich in echoes of Titian, with all the formal accessories of baroque portraiture perfectly controlled and inter-related (Pl. 27); in his portraits of women and children (Pl. 29) Van Dyck could evoke, in a subtly aristocratic mannered style, a fragile charm which only Gainsborough was fully to understand. There is in almost all his English portraits an air of infinite remoteness, but he was sometimes inspired to paint, of such patrons whom he knew well as the King or Lord Strafford, a penetrating and sympathetic analysis of character. His spectacular double portraits and groups have a magnificent air of parade and his interest in landscape (which is shown in a handful of exquisite drawings) enabled him on occasion to set his sitters wholly within an open-air context (a form of portraiture which was to be developed in the eighteenth century) instead of placing them against the conventional backcloths of Van Somer or Mytens. The Countess of Bedford at Petworth (Pl. 26c) draws on her glove; the royal children and their little gestures are frozen into immobility for a moment; the Earl of Strafford wields his baton of authority and caresses the 'bigg white irish dogg' (Pl. 27); Northumberland as Lord High Admiral stands contemptuously on the sea-shore; Lord Denbigh in oriental costume lurches into a glade with his fowling-piece and starts back as he sees a brightly-coloured parrot. It is this new understanding of the relation of the sitter to a chosen context, and a new ease, informality and variety of pose that set Van Dyck off so entirely from his predecessors and potential rivals in England and make him the immediate precursor of Reynolds and Gainsborough.

The impact of Van Dyck's style on painters working in England was instant and profound and the years immediately after his death in 1641, on the eve of the Civil War, produced a very large number of portraits cast in his patterns and painted in an almost invariably crude imitation of his handling. Even during his lifetime painters who had worked in the Anglo-Netherlandish manner were overwhelmingly influenced by the brilliant sophistication of Van Dyck's mature style. Johnson's later full-lengths, in particular, show an unashamed and oddly incongruous attempt to take over Van Dyck's conventional accessories and mannerisms; and Adriaen Hanneman, a gifted young Dutch painter who had worked in London since 1626, was back in The Hague in 1637 and imported into Holland an exaggeratedly Van Dyckian style. Among English painters Robert Walker, who was paradoxically the favourite painter of the Parliamentarian party during the Civil War and Interregnum, showed the most slavish dependence on Van Dyck; a certain angular sincerity only partly conceals the paradox of portraits of the regicides in patterns borrowed directly from Van Dyck's images of the King and his supporters.

To set William Dobson as the normal antithesis to Walker is to do him an injustice. His working life as we know it was pathetically short (nothing is known of his work before 1642 and he died in 1646), and he worked in the unsettling atmosphere of the war-time Court at Oxford. Nevertheless he was the most arresting and individual native portrait-painter 'in large' in the Stuart period and probably the most distinguished English painter before the advent of Hogarth. His debt to Van Dyck was limited and controlled, and he had clearly studied the *tenebristi* painters of Italy and the North and the Venetian pictures in the great Caroline collections. He was a gentleman by birth and he was interested in problems which appealed to no other English painter in the century. His most elaborate compositions (Pl. 28) are sometimes over-ambitious and his learning (in, for example, the use in his backgrounds of reliefs which would point to his sitter's tastes or occupation) is sometimes a little ponderous; but he painted for the royalist officers the only truly English baroque portraits: direct and uncompromisingly English in mood, filled with allegory and allusion, painted in a full-blooded, virile technique; rich in colour; and charged with a sense of the tragedy which they so vividly evoke (Pl. 30B).

His portraits, and their indication of the influences that he had been able to absorb, give us a glimpse of the effects which the enthusiasms of the 'Whitehall group' of patrons and collectors might have had on painting (and indeed on architecture and sculpture) in this country if the Civil War had not shattered the brittle fabric of the Caroline Court where those enthusiasms had been stimulated. In landscape painting neither the Dutch painters, such as Keirincx, Poelenburgh and Stalbempt, who had worked in England in a form of Italo-Netherlandish, late Mannerist, style, nor Rubens and Van Dyck, who were among the most modern landscape painters in Europe, had formed a school of landscape painting in England; and throughout the Stuart period a predominating passion for topography, though it produced much very interesting material, prevented painters from exploring the English scene more deeply. In the field of decorative painting, however, Charles I's employment of Gentileschi, Vouet and Rubens, and his collection of Italian *cinquecento* pictures, bore fruit in the decorative schemes initiated, for example, by his courtiers William Murray, at Ham House in the 1630's, and the fourth Earl of Pembroke at Wilton in the closing years of the Civil War. In the Green Closet or Miniature Room at Ham, and even more in the Double Cube Room at Wilton, painting is made to play its part, with architecture and sculpture (or carving), in the evolution of a sumptuous baroque interior. The painting is far more ambitious and modern (with its clumsy echoes of Raphael, Polidoro and Rubens) than the monotonous repetition of standard decorative motives with which English homes and palaces had formerly been embellished.

The painters who have so far been discussed were employed in the main by patrons of the highest rank, and their work, with the partial exception of Dobson, has in varying degrees a strongly continental quality. There were, however, a number of much less distinguished painters at work in London and the provinces, painting portraits which lack the sophistication of the work of their more successful and cosmopolitan contemporaries. Such painters as Thomas Leigh, John Souch, Gilbert Jackson and Edward

Bower spent a considerable part of their careers in the provinces. Their portraits have a *gaucherie*, a naïve decorative quality or an archaizing flavour, even when they show the influence of Johnson, Mytens or Van Dyck, which enhance the ingenuousness and lack of affectation or technical skill with which the sitter's personality is set before us. And their portraits clearly represent the forms of painting which were available to all but the richest or most cultivated patrons. It was only at the Court, moreover, that a painter such as Van Dyck was commissioned or encouraged to paint subject pictures, and the Civil War inevitably hardened the 'transalpine barbarous neglect' with which English patrons were inclined to regard any other form of painting than the portrait.

With sympathetic contempt for this neglect the poet Lovelace tried to console his young friend Peter Lely, who had apparently met with little success in painting, on his arrival in this country from his native Holland (probably *c.* 1645), '*Landtschapes*, with small *Figures* and *Historical Compositions*' in a nostalgic Dutch manner with strong reminiscences of Poelenburgh and Both. Lely was not the man to work unprofitably and thereafter he wisely concentrated on portraiture. By 1647 he was working for some of Van Dyck's former patrons; he was already described in 1654 as 'the best artist in England'; and by the time of the Restoration, when he officially inherited Van Dyck's position at Court, his reputation was made. Until his death in 1680 he remained the leading fashionable portrait painter in England.

In Lely's portraits the influence of Van Dyck was very strong, but although his vigorous handling and fine sense of colour set him, after the death of Dobson, above any other painter working in England, he did not fully assimilate his great predecessor's example until the eve of the Restoration. At that time he produced his finest portraits (Pl. 30c): with a Van Dyckian ease at last fused with his innate Dutch feeling for volume, and of an entirely personal richness and purity of tone. They are the most distinguished reinterpretations of Van Dyck to be painted in this country in the seventeenth century.

Lely's practice was considerably larger than

Van Dyck's and from the early 1660's he relied increasingly on the highly organized team of assistants who worked with him in his studio in Covent Garden and who could repeat over and over again, for different sitters, the patterns, with their increasing artificialities, which Lely evolved. The extreme familiarity of Lely's female beauties (Pl. 31A), who, with perennial fascination, seem to recapture the jaded splendours of the Court of Charles II and were eagerly sought after for their houses and galleries by collectors in Lely's lifetime, has eclipsed the greater qualities in Lely's achievement: his ability, in the freshness and timidity of his earlier portraits (Pl. 26B) and in some of the more deeply felt portraits of his maturity, to present a sympathetic or attractive analysis of his sitter's personality, and his great powers as a technician. In his compositions he was almost invariably content to rely on the heritage of Van Dyck, but in his later years his handling became more impressionist, and his last portraits are painted in a technique which was the fruit of many years' experience and which no pupil or imitator could wholly understand.

John Greenhill, a young English painter of some promise, was perhaps Lely's most interesting pupil, and his understanding of character (Pl. 33E) remained unmistakably English even after he had come completely under Lely's sway; and the Dutchman, Willem Wissing, was the pupil best qualified to inherit Lely's fashionable *clientèle* and to serve them with repetitions of the mannerisms and affectations that Lely had evolved in his later Court style and were common to all fashionable painters in London in the 1680's. Lely's most formidable rivals were probably those with the least ability, the French or Italian painters who were so popular in the open or latent Catholic atmosphere of the Courts of Charles II and James II: the Vignon brothers, Simon Verelst or Henri Gascars, whose work represents the nadir of contemporary French Court portraiture but was very popular with the Francophile element at Court; or Benedetto Gennari, the nephew of Guercino, who was a *protégé* of Mary of Modena and produced for a most distinguished circle of patrons at Court religious and mythological canvases and

tastelessly elaborate portraits of unpleasant texture. Jacob Huysmans (Pl. 31B) may also, for a short time, have been a more formidable rival. He was a Catholic and was taken up by Catherine of Braganza; his more ambitious canvases are almost as unpleasant and vapid as Gennari's, but he was capable of greater sincerity with less intimidating or exigent clients.

Two painters stand outside Lely's orbit: his fellow-countryman Gerard Soest and the Scotsman Michael Wright. Soest was an individual and penetrating portrait-painter, but quite unfitted by temperament to answer the demands made by fashionable clients; Wright, a less distinguished craftsman, remained essentially an amateur with interests outside his work as a painter, but a number of years spent in Rome and elsewhere on the Continent often gave to his canvases an educated cosmopolitan air. Soest's unusual sense of colour, his mannerisms in drawing, and his grave, introspective heads are sometimes reminiscent of Terborch, and, although he was never at ease with conventional society patrons, he could, when faced with a more interesting and sympathetic sitter (Pl. 31D), produce a portrait of a haunting individuality beyond the powers of the more cynical Lely. Wright's sense of character remained, despite his travels, unmistakably British and he never entirely overcame a provincial inability to assemble more than the simplest form of composition. There is a charmingly unspoilt freshness in his presentation of character (Pl. 32A). Neither Soest nor Wright had Lely's technical abilities, but their handling is unmistakable: Soest's thin and shadowed and creating strange inflated masses of draperies; Wright's cooler and drier, but light and liquid in the treatment of details.

Michael Wright was almost certainly a Catholic and was much patronized by Catholic families: Bagots, Howards, Arundells of Wardour and Stonors are to be found among his sitters. But his religion was probably a grave liability at the time of the Revolution, and he had been directly associated with James II's schemes for reunion with the Church of Rome when he went as chief steward to the Earl of Castlemaine on an unfortunate embassy to Innocent XI in 1686. There can be no doubt that the difficulties of his later years were made no easier by the increasing success of the arrogant young German, Godfrey Kneller.

Kneller had been extremely fortunate in the premature deaths of Wissing in 1686 and John Riley in 1691. The unhappy Riley, indeed, seems to have made little mark before Lely's death in 1680 and later to have been outshone by Kneller. He was not so capable a painter as his foreign rivals, and was often content to make use of their patterns; he was only rarely (and then in a very arresting manner) wholly at ease at compositions grander than a head and shoulders, and on a larger canvas he relied, at one period, on the facile collaboration of Closterman; but his individual cool silvery colour, light touch and gentle, ingenuous sense of character are at times reminiscent of Cornelius Johnson and the temper of his portraits is wholly English (Pl. 31C). He handed on these qualities of tone, character and touch, and an engaging provincialism, to his followers, Thomas Murray, Jonathan Richardson (Pl. 32C) and (to a lesser extent) Sir John Medina. Murray and Richardson remained almost unaffected by Kneller and, like their master, are seen at their best, with very rare exceptions, in portraits on a small scale; Murray was a much weaker painter than Riley and Richardson's portraits are often clumsy and coarse. But Richardson, as something of a scholar, and as a professional critic and theorist, did much to enhance the dignity of his profession (of which he was inordinately conscious) and has the distinction of being at the source of one of the streams that were to be an inspiration to the young Joshua Reynolds. John Baptist Medina, who was of Spanish origin and probably arrived in England in 1686, came under the influence of Riley and Closterman, but after he had been persuaded to seek his fortune in Scotland his style became increasingly a slick and effective imitation of Kneller.

Godfrey Kneller was admirably qualified for the great position he held as the leading portrait painter in England, and one of the most successful in Europe, from the Revolution until his death in 1723. As a very young man in Holland he had come into contact with Bol, and possibly with Rembrandt himself, and in Italy, where he may have met Maratti and Bernini, he is said to have had some success as a portrait painter. By 1677, soon after his arrival in this country, he had gained introductions into the most illustrious circles and his success may well have been a formidable challenge to Lely in his last years. There is in Kneller's earliest English portraits a confusion between French, Dutch, Roman and Venetian influences and he also made use of Lely's patterns. His early portraits are dry and thin and tend towards a brownish monochrome. By the early and mid-1680's, however, his canvases show a new directness in modelling, and in his best portraits of this period there is a lean, austere informality (Pl. 34B) which must have been very refreshing to patrons who had for so long been accustomed to Lely's lush, full-blown style.

Towards the end of his long and active life Kneller was fulsomely praised by Addison, who evokes a procession of Kneller's State-portraits, 'in their robes of state arrayed, the kings of half an age displayed'. He had painted Charles II and produced the official portraits of English sovereigns from James II to George I and his heir; many distinguished foreign visitors and European sovereigns, among them Louis XIV and Peter the Great, had sat to him in London, Paris and Flanders; and a monument in Westminster Abbey, embellished with an epitaph by Pope, crowned a career rich in worldly success. The organization of a small army of specialized assistants was perfected by Kneller in his studio in Great Queen Street, but the steady output under his authority of a mass of competent but perfunctory work has done almost irreparable harm to his later reputation. Nevertheless, he deserved the position which he held in his own day, and not only because he was by temperament so well equipped to sustain it. Many of his portraits are irredeemably dull and stereotyped, but his best are varied, penetrating, original and, in many cases, brilliantly painted (Pl. 32B). He was never so fine a colourist as Lely, but in his best pieces his touch was fresh and incisive and his sense of tone pure and silvery. He was not afraid of painting portraits on a scale far more ambitious than Lely had attempted, and his full-lengths and equestrian portraits show a range unknown in England since the death of Van Dyck. And in a comparatively small number of portraits, some of them from his earlier years, Kneller broke away from the conventions which Van Dyck had established or popularized and to which Lely had remained almost consistently faithful, and, with an economical technique and unexpected powers of getting at the mind of his sitters, produced portraits of a new vigour or sympathy which would do credit to Hogarth or of a noble reserve which anticipates Reynolds.

In the reign of James II and the earliest years of William III Kneller's portraits still had something of the rich colour and the elaborate stage-craft that ultimately derive, through Lely's latest style, from Van Dyck's most formal English portraits; in the 1690's his more ambitious pieces sometimes have a sombre grandeur that may contain a reminiscence of his Roman years; but in the early years of the eighteenth century there is a new and rococo atmosphere in his portraits: light and silvery in key, gay and light-heartedly affected in design, soft and loose in handling. The same mood is felt in the portraits of his most talented rival, the Swede Michael Dahl. Kneller's portraits of the Kit-Cat Club proclaim that he was, at least intermittently, a Whig: Dahl was a favourite painter in Tory families. His more stereotyped female portraits are often unblushing repetitions, in a few standard patterns, of the most tiresome affectations of an age which saw the nadir of the Van Dyck tradition, but his feeling for character ranges from the weather-beaten old heads of his admirals, which hang beside those of Kneller at Greenwich, or rather wistful portraits of children (Pl. 35A) and young women. His later portraits are painted in soft, pastel-like tones of pink, silver, light blue and grey, and their fluttering movement and lightness of touch come near to the more completely rococo painters, such as Mercier and Vanloo, in the reign of George II.

It would be impossible in so short a survey to analyse in any detail the host of minor portrait painters who could turn their hands to a variety of tasks, some of a very humble nature, in London and the provinces during the second half of our period. There is, indeed, less temptation to do so than in its earlier years: some native painters such as Thomas Sadler or John Wollaston worked in a naïve manner which shows practically no advance from the days of Jackson and Bower. The fashionable conventions of portrait painting in the big London studios can be tiresome enough with painters as skilled as Lely or Kneller, and are irredeemably depressing in the hands of their imitators. It is only important to realize the debt to Lely of painters who flourished in the provinces, such as Matthew Dixon or Mr. Comer, or of the hardworking but uninspired amateur, Mary Beale, in London, and to recognize the influence of Kneller on such lesser contemporaries as Jacques D'Agar or Thomas Gibson. None of the painters who remained rather outside the influence of Lely and Kneller (such as the two Kersebooms or the later members of the Verelst family) produced work of quality.

Dixon and D'Agar seem to have had a circle of clients in Northamptonshire and Comer was working in York for a number of years. Local patriotism probably caused the Corporation of Salisbury in 1673 to commission from Greenhill a portrait of Seth Ward, Bishop of Salisbury, and led the Shaftesbury family at St Giles's House to patronize him rather than the more illustrious Lely. Wissing was a favourite painter in country houses in the neighbourhood of Stamford and died at Burghley while he was at work on a large family group of the Cecils in hunting costume in which he 'Seven-Times one great Perfection drew';[2] Michael Wright found time to spend some months in the 1670's working for the Bagots in Staffordshire and talked of his 'kind remembrance at the syllabubs and staghunting' and of the 'Invitation I had to two other Countyes';[3] and even Lely 'spent some time at Gentlemen's houses' in the neighbourhood of Bury St Edmunds. In these country houses and in the capital,

[2] Matthew Prior, *Dialogues of the Dead ...*, ed. A. R. Waller (1907), p. 32.
[3] W. J. Smith, 'Letters from Michael Wright', *Burlington Magazine*, Vol. xcv (1953), pp. 233–6.

drawing and painting were becoming, in the hands of such enthusiasts as Mrs Pepys, the minor poetess Anne Killigrew, Lady Bathurst or the Princess of Orange, one of the favourite accomplishments of ladies of leisure that it has remained ever since. The only amateur painter of distinction in the Stuart period was the country gentleman, Sir Nathaniel Bacon, whose few surviving and arresting portraits are closely related to the Anglo-Netherlandish style of Johnson or Mytens.

The purest expression of the English spirit in painting in the seventeenth century is perhaps to be found in the miniatures of Samuel Cooper, the most famous English painter of the day in continental minds and the greatest native portrait painter of the Stuart period. He stands supreme with Hilliard among English miniaturists. He studied under his uncle, John Hoskins, whose early miniatures have the reticent charm of Cornelius Johnson; but Hoskins's later miniatures (Pl. 33A) already reflect, in a new breadth of handling and realization of character, the work of his brilliant nephew. Hoskins had been deeply influenced by Van Dyck and had produced a number of copies in miniature, many of them for distribution by the sitter, of Van Dyck's portraits; but it was an influence that he could not quite assimilate. Cooper, on the other hand, had by 1640 absorbed from Van Dyck a new spontaneity and a baroque sense of design which he adapted perfectly to the small scale of his portraits and which mark a complete break with the formal limitations and conventions within which the Olivers, Hoskins and their lesser contemporaries had worked. By these methods, and with a most beautiful sense of tone, Cooper, 'un piccinetto', as he was described, 'tutto spirito e cortesia',[4] produced again and again portraits which bring us face to face, with an almost painful directness and as no other portraits of the century can do, with English men and women of that turbulent age. His powers of analysis and sympathy are equally remarkable with attractive, light-hearted women and girls (Pl. 33B), with the rakes and ladies of the Restoration Court

or with sitters of an austerer, Puritanical mood, whose personality comes across to us with an intensity that only Soest, in rare moments of inspiration, could equal (Pl. 33C). After the Restoration and when his reputation was at its height, Cooper tended slightly to enlarge the scope and scale of his miniatures (Pl. 33D): in these last years his technique becomes softer and finer, but his modelling loses nothing of its breadth and his colour remains as pure and subtle as before.

After his death in 1672 there was a steady decline in miniature painting in this country until the time of Cosway and Engleheart. Thomas Flatman, who was essentially an amateur at a craft which was much recommended as a pleasant diversion for gentlemen, had something of Cooper's moving understanding of character, but lacked his great technical accomplishment; and the work of Nicholas Dixon and Laurence Crosse and their successors into the eighteenth century was too closely related to contemporary portraiture 'in large' to deserve separate treatment. Miniatures had hitherto been painted on parchment in opaque water-colour, a method established in England in the previous century by Hans Holbein: the dullness of miniatures in the late seventeenth and early eighteenth centuries was not relieved by the experiments that were being made increasingly in enamelling and painting on ivory.

By the end of the Stuart period miniatures were much sought after by collectors. In their earlier history they had been painted for very personal reasons. As portable likenesses, often in richly jewelled or enamelled settings, they served as presents and as tokens of a special and intimate affection. They can sometimes be seen in portraits, prominently displayed over the hearts of widowed ladies. In a more official context miniature portraits of Stuart sovereigns, and even of Oliver Cromwell during the Interregnum, were given to visiting ambassadors or dispatched overseas as presents to foreign rulers. Charles I, however, had built up a remarkable collection of contemporary and sixteenth century limnings which had been kept in his Cabinet Room at Whitehall in 'shutting Cases with Locks and Keyes' and had included, as well as a great many ancestral and

[4] A. M. Crinò, *Rivista d'Arte*, Vol. xxix (1954), 148–55.

family portraits, a number of specially painted copies in miniature of famous Italian master-pieces. The popularity of these little reproductions is shown by the Duke of Newcastle's purchase in 1708 of seventy such limned copies by Dixon. In 1717 James Sotheby, a less illustrious collector, acquired from Thomas Bridgwater 'a Little Wallnut Tree Cabinet, gilt lock & Hinges & lin'd with green Velvet' [5] for his growing collection of miniatures.

The qualities that we find in the English miniaturists of the Stuart period can be seen no less clearly in portrait drawings in black chalk, coloured pastels or plumbago in the later half of the century. The renewed interest in this slight but charming form of portraiture may have owed something to the popularity of such French draughtsmen as Claude Mellan and Robert Nanteuil, who had drawn John Evelyn and his family in Paris during the Commonwealth. No English school of portrait draughtsmen was formed and the number of portrait drawings in any medium between 1660 and 1700 is small. But it was a form of artistic expression particularly suited to informal and intimate portraiture and it thus appealed to the amateur artist, and it was also part of the routine practice in some studios in the production of a painted portrait: the finest English portrait drawings of our period were produced by Lely and members of his circle such as Greenhill (Pl. 33E) and Tilson. The pastel technique was developed in a more painterly manner by Edward Lutterell and Edmund Ashfield: Ashfield's portraits are especially rich in colour and free in handling. William Faithorne provides the closest parallel to Robert Nanteuil in France. His drawings are perhaps less accomplished than Ashfield's, but his portrait engravings, whether from his own studies *ad vivum* or after Van Dyck, Dobson, Lely or Soest, are vigorous and sensitive and illustrate the rapidly increasing output in the seventeenth century of original or reproductive engraved portraits. Many of Faithorne's portraits were drawn to be used as frontispieces. His best

engravings were in line, in face of the growing challenge of the mezzotint, and David Loggan, who was the last important line engraver of portraits in the same tradition, produced a number of rather timid little plumbago portrait drawings of much charm and in a technique that was carried to greater refinement by Thomas Forster, John Faber and Robert White.

The excellence and the limitations of the Stuart miniatures and portrait drawings are essentially English: for the appearance and temperament of English men and women of the Stuart period we should turn to Cooper or Loggan rather than to Lely or Kneller. A more cosmopolitan glamour was occasionally given to a family's growing collection of portraits when its members brought back from their travels portraits of themselves that had been painted abroad. There is a fascination in seeing on the walls of an English house portraits of English travellers and diplomats painted in Holland by Miereveld, Lievens, Maes or Netscher; in France, especially if they were attached to the exiled Stuart Court at St Germains, by such French painters as Belle, Rigaud or Largillierre; and in Italy by Massimo Stanzione, Salvator Rosa, Carlo Dolci or Carlo Maratti (Pl. 35B). The less transitory experiences in Rome early in the eighteenth century of such young English artists and noblemen as William Kent, Lord Burlington and Thomas Coke were to be of profound significance for the structure of patronage and the history of the arts at home; but already, before the stricter standardization of tastes and enthusiasms in the Hanoverian age, classical influences had affected the outlook of the more sensitive Englishmen on the Grand Tour and found expression in pictures painted for them in England. The third Earl of Shaftesbury, a distinguished philosopher who devoted much of his life and thoughts to the formulation of an æsthetic theory in which artistic and moral issues were closely interwoven, found in the adaptable Closterman (who had formerly worked with Riley) a painter who could express something of the loftiness of Shaftesbury's unyielding classicism. Closterman could paint equally easily in a Flemish or Spanish idiom, but he was sent to Rome by

[5] MSS. formerly at Ecton, and now at the Victoria and Albert Museum.

Shaftesbury in 1699 and on his return produced portraits of his patron, in the full Roman manner, that could well serve as illustrations to the *Characteristicks* (Pl. 34A).

This cosmopolitanism was by no means a universal element in English taste. Lord Shaftesbury would not have enjoyed a visit to James Sotheby's collection and would not, for example, have approved of the tastes in pictures of William Blathwayt or William III. The continuing patronage of foreign painters, the importation of pictures from abroad and an admiration for continental painting that may often have been imitative and fashionable rather than thoughtfully formulated, and was to be so savagely attacked by Hogarth, were already resented and opposed by such reactionary bodies as the Painter-Stainers' Company. Their efforts to vindicate native talent were triumphantly successful only at the very end of our period, when, early in the reign of George I, Sir James Thornhill wrested from his more facile and gifted foreign rivals the two leading commissions for decorative painting. Previously, in the reign of Charles II, such English decorative painters as Isaac Fuller and Robert Streeter had played second fiddle to their foreign rivals and had spent much of their time painting scenery for the stage.

The scope and quantity of decorative painting in this country between the reigns of Charles II and George I, and Thornhill's achievements in this context, are most significant for the English attitude to the full baroque style of the Continent and for the effect of the Grand Tour on the tastes which English patrons wished to gratify in their own homes. Extensive painting on walls and ceilings was of course primarily required in public buildings, such as the Hospitals at Greenwich and Chelsea, or in the royal palaces. Private patrons would often be content with a limited area of painted decoration, on ceiling, wall or staircase, enclosed in a raised carved or moulded framework: Laguerre and a team of interior decorators worked in this way for George Vernon on the ceilings of the Parlour, Saloon and staircase at Sudbury Hall between 1691 and 1694, and there are earlier examples of the same practice in the Duchess's Bedroom and Queen's Closet at Ham

House. The full baroque panoply of painted ceilings and walls, often throughout a suite of rooms, on a staircase or in a private chapel, was almost invariably (though Thornhill's work at Stoke Edith was a remarkable exception) commissioned by patrons from a very limited class: by such noblemen of taste and discrimination as the fifth Earl of Exeter, who wished to recreate at Burghley (Pl. 36) some of the splendours which he had admired on his travels, or by such great subjects as the first Duke of Devonshire and the Duke of Marlborough, who found in the full baroque style of Rome or Versailles the perfect means of decorating their magnificent new houses with an expression and a glorification in paint of the great achievements of their country or of their own parts therein (Pl. 37B).

In England the first complete example on a considerable scale of the full baroque interior, relying on the close co-operation of architect, sculptor and decorative painter, was initiated at Windsor Castle by Charles II, partly in emulation of his cousin's activities at Versailles. The painted decoration, which contributed greatly to the lavish brightness of the new interiors, was entrusted in the main to the Leccese painter, Antonio Verrio, who first brought to this country a new repertory of decorative conventions and motives. He arrived here soon after he had been enrolled in the Académie Royale in Paris in 1671. He was a Catholic, painted for a number of patrons in the Court circle, and after the flight of James II found it convenient to settle at Burghley. There he painted for Lord Exeter, whose payments to Verrio and his team run from 1687 to 1698, in six of the rooms in the Earl's new apartments and left unfinished the great staircase at the end of them. His work at Burghley is perhaps his finest achievement: gay and festive and a most attractive embellishment of a fine set of late seventeenth-century interiors. His work retains an Italian lightness of mood and tone, but the devices by which Verrio extended in the imagination the actual space defined by the walls and ceilings of the rooms are predominantly French in inspiration. Verrio, and to a greater extent Laguerre, were deeply influenced by the methods evolved by Le

Brun for the decoration of the Louvre, Vaux-le-Vicomte and, above all, Versailles: methods that in turn owed much to such Italian baroque painters as Pietro da Cortona and Romanelli. Verrio's two principal means of piercing a ceiling and its coving, to open a vista to the sky above, can be traced back to Le Brun. But an Italian prototype should perhaps be sought for his most ambitious device, in such rooms as the 'Heaven' Room at Burghley (Pl. 36), where the entire surface of the room is painted with an elaborate feigned architectural structure, through, above and around which Verrio's gods and goddesses pour and tumble. The actual construction of Verrio's feigned prosceniums and painted architecture is always convincing; his imitation gilt, bronze and stucco are thoroughly effective; and his assistants were competent painters of still-life and flowers. It is only in the actual figure compositions that Verrio's draughtsmanship proves to be lamentably inadequate for the lavish and ambitious inventions of which he was so prodigal.

Louis Laguerre, who probably came to England in 1684, had been apprenticed to Le Brun and much of his work, such as the Ball Room at Burghley or the Grand Stairs at Petworth, has the dully academic competence of that school; but his finest work, which he executed for the Dukes of Devonshire and Marlborough, could hold its own with any of the painted decoration by Le Brun and his team at Versailles. In the Saloon at Blenheim (1719–20) Laguerre painted a grandiloquent, arid reinterpretation of Le Brun's designs for the walls and ceiling of Louis XIV's *Escalier des Ambassadeurs*. Between 1689 and 1694 he had been working for Devonshire at Chatsworth and his ceilings in four of his patron's five state rooms are closely integrated in the decoration of these nobly sumptuous interiors: with great ingenuity and carefully evolved illusionism Laguerre built up on the coving a feigned sculptural, architectural and painted support for the big painted framework, on the ceiling itself, within which his mythological scenes are enacted (Pl. 37A). Laguerre's work at Chatsworth is more restrained, but richer, more ingenious and more convincing in its illusionism than any of Verrio's decorative schemes.

Thornhill was closely influenced by his two continental predecessors: one of the earliest rooms that he painted, probably in 1706–7, was the Sabine Room at Chatsworth. But there is perhaps a lightness of touch and a new delicacy of form, even though he worked within the conventions that Verrio and Laguerre had brought to England. The rococo elements in Thornhill's style are possibly due to the Venetian painters who came to London in the early years of the eighteenth century. On a very different scale Thornhill showed himself to be a charming draughtsman who left behind him more drawings than any other painter working in England in our period: drawings that reveal, like his sketches in oil (Pl. 37B), a teeming invention and a light and facile touch. These are qualities that were inevitably lost when his ideas were eventually transferred on to a wall or ceiling: at Blenheim, for example, Wimpole or Easton Neston.

In 1708 the Earl of Manchester returned from his embassy in Venice and brought back with him two of the principal decorative painters of the city whose music and painting had so greatly charmed him: Giovanni Antonio Pellegrini and Marco Ricci. They were joined later by Marco's uncle, Sebastiano Ricci. These Venetian painters were attracted to the country by the prospect of such important commissions as the painting of the dome of St Paul's Cathedral, and they must have presented a formidable challenge to Laguerre and such other decorative painters as Gerard Lanscroon or Louis Cheron, whose work at Powis, Drayton or Boughton was faithful to the older Anglo-French tradition. Marco Ricci was mainly employed in painting landscape overdoors, in a rich and picturesque style, at such houses as Castle Howard, but his uncle and Pellegrini covered the walls and ceilings of their patrons' houses in a style which discarded the older decorative conventions, with their elaborate architectural basis, in favour of a much more dramatic presentation or of a bright, unhampered sunlit fluency. Sebastiano Ricci's design for the first Duke of Portland's chapel at Bulstrode show, in the words of George Vertue 'a Noble free invention, great force of lights and shade. with variety & freedom. in the composition of the parts'.[6] Pellegrini's most important work was for the Whig noblemen, Manchester and the third Earl of Carlisle, in the houses that were being remodelled or built for them by Sir John Vanbrugh at Kimbolton and Castle Howard. His painting in the Chapel and Boudoir, and especially on the staircase and little landing at Kimbolton, or in the Hall and two of the burnt-out rooms at Castle Howard, has a wholly rococo quality and charm. Pellegrini and Sebastiano were in the forefront of the Venetian renaissance in which Tiepolo was to be the most prominent figure and which owed so much to a renewed appreciation of Veronese: there are characters on Pellegrini's walls at Castle Howard and Kimbolton who could have stepped down from the walls of the Villa Maser, and the presence of these painters in England sets this country within the range of one of the most important and seductive movements in eighteenth century painting.

The influences that brought about this most spectacular phase in the history of English decorative painting came entirely from the Catholic countries of Europe: from Paris, Rome, Naples or Venice. The full baroque style, in which architecture, painting and sculpture could proclaim the greatness of an absolute monarch such as Louis xiv or the unbending doctrines of the post-Tridentine Catholic Church, would obviously have excited the admiration and envy of Charles ii and his openly Catholic brother, and at Windsor and Whitehall the secular and religious iconography which was produced for them by painters and sculptors would not have been out of place in Rome, Versailles, Vienna or Madrid. Lord Exeter had Jacobite leanings, but the other patrons of Verrio, Laguerre, Thornhill and the Venetians were loyal Protestants and the most lavish of them were to be found among the Whigs and the most convinced opponents of Louis xiv. The Dutch influence in this period, however, though it was less spectacular, was more deep seated and productive and perhaps more congenial. And under the later Stuarts it was primarily the visiting Dutch and Flemish painters who laid the foundations of the English achievements in the eighteenth century in the genres of landscape, marine and sporting painting.

These genres were considered by such strict classicists as Lord Shaftesbury to be less honourable than history painting and they were of course much less popular than the portrait. In the Stuart period, moreover, they were often used to serve a purely subsidiary purpose: landscapes of various kinds, sea-pieces, battle-pieces and still-lifes were frequently painted to be set into the panelling of a room, over a door or mantelpiece, and thus to fulfil a decorative function in the design of an interior. Examples of this practice can be seen at Drayton, Sudbury Hall and Ham House. At Sudbury George Vernon commissioned from Jan Griffier a number of curiously lit landscapes with ruins and odd piles of sculptural fragments. The second Earl of Peterborough set over the doors and fireplaces in his newly decorated rooms at Drayton a most interesting series of canvases: classical landscapes, probably by the Dutchman Hendrick Danckerts and including a view of the Tiber and the Castel Sant' Angelo; mountainous landscapes with picturesque torrents in the manner of Beerstraten; a very interesting set of topographical pieces that includes Greenwich and the Monument and, further afield, Pontefract, Edinburgh Castle, Holyroodhouse and the Bass Rock; two groups of birds by Francis Barlow; and a remarkable set of equestrian medieval knights in armour against classical backgrounds. The careful heraldry in these strange pieces indicates that they were inspired, like the series of ancestral portraits in the King's Dining Room at Drayton, by Peterborough's inordinate pride of race. The Duke and Duchess of Lauderdale commissioned in the 1670's a more familiar and accessible series of overdoors and overmantels for their new rooms at Ham House.

Danckerts was perhaps the first professional landscape painter to work for a considerable period in England: turning his hand with equal facility and moderate competence to straightforward topography or to classical landscapes (Pl. 40B) which combine a Claude-like nostalgia with recollections of the buildings and prospects that Danckerts had studied in Italy and which were often intended

[6] *Notebooks*, vol. iv, Walpole Soc., vol. xxiv (1936), pp. 47–8.

to be set into panelling. Such purely decorative landscapes, or more exciting scenes in the tradition of Jacob Ruysdael or Salvator Rosa, were painted for English houses by Adriaen van Diest, Gerard van Edema and Marco Ricci. Their canvases, and the use to which they were put, anticipate the pieces painted in the eighteenth century for houses such as Saltram, Harewood, Osterley or Bedford House by Zucchi, Zuccharelli or Gainsborough.

Landscape painting in the Stuart period was still almost synonymous with topography: Danckerts's topographical views of England or Italy were very popular with patrons from Charles II and the Duke of York to Samuel Pepys, and Wenceslaus Hollar, whose vast output of drawings and etchings throws such light on the interests of educated Englishmen of that time, devoted much of his energies to topographical prints and drawings (Pl. 30A). But the two most interesting topographical painters were the Dutchman Leonard Knyff and the Fleming Jan Siberechts. The patient and industrious Knyff drew an extensive series of bird's-eye views of English royal and country houses; they were engraved by Johannes Kip for the *Nouveau Théâtre de la Grande Bretagne* (1707–8) and are an incomparable source for the architectural historian and the student of garden design. Knyff also painted on a much larger scale panoramas of English buildings in their surroundings: his particularly attractive view of Clandon (1708) provides a charmingly naïve anecdotal picture of the day-to-day life of a country house. Siberechts was a much more individual artist. His approach to the English scene and his treatment of country people, their dwellings and occupations remained fundamentally Flemish; his grander views of the English countryside and of houses, such as Longleat or Wollaton, have great charm, but are constructed in a standard topographical formula that was constantly exploited on the Continent and especially in France by Van der Meulen or the Martins in their views of the French king's houses and campaigns. In subjects where he was perhaps less controlled by a patron's need for an accurate record of the house and garden, Siberechts created a freer and more sensitive impression of the English

countryside: the spacious views from Richmond Hill or along the Trent, or a glade on a hillside with a glimpse of a great house below (Pl. 38). And his water-colour drawings of the Peak District (1694 and 1699) are, with Francis Place's later drawings (for example those of Scarborough and Knaresborough), the most important premonitions of the English supremacy in this technique in the following century.

Kip, Knyff, Siberechts and a number of lesser and mainly anonymous painters enabled the landed classes to secure drawn, painted or engraved records of their houses and estates. At Badminton a particularly interesting set of views survive of the first Duke of Beaufort's house and of his other possessions and castles: a series that must have given special pleasure to so great a territorial magnate and to his Duchess, who later, in her widowhood, secured Knyff's services in showing 'what a noble place my deare Lord has left'. In a tentative manner these canvases at Badminton foreshadow the more sophisticated views of English castles and country houses by Canaletto, Richard Wilson or Marlow. The liveliest picture of social life in an English seventeenth century village was provided by Gillis van Tilborch's fascinating *Tichborne Dole* (1670), where the villagers await the distribution of the hereditary charity at the hands of Sir Henry Tichborne, who stands surrounded by his family, retainers and servants in front of his Tudor house (Pl. 39B).

When Celia Fiennes visited Sir Edward Blackett's mansion at Newby in 1697, she saw in the pantry 'a picture of the dimensions of a large ox that was fed in these grounds'. The owners of country estates were becoming increasingly desirous of portraits of their animals as well as of their houses and themselves, and the origins of the sporting piece, a peculiarly English genre that was to achieve such rich expression in the eighteenth century, are to be found in the Stuart period. The only English painter to work for the Lauderdales at Ham (appropriately in the Volary) was Francis Barlow, the earliest professional English animal painter, who as early as 1652–53 was specializing in birds and fishes. He never acquired more than a limited sense of composition; his subjects and sense of narrative have an engaging provincialism; and he was technically a less distinguished painter of animals than Knyff or Abraham Hondius. But Barlow's creatures are most carefully and lovingly observed and his many drawings, some of them appropriately for an edition of Aesop's *Fables*, are the first sensitive studies by an Englishman of wild and domestic animals: his studies of hunting scenes, some of which were etched by Hollar for *Severall Wayes of Hunting, Hawking and Fishing* (1671), recapture something of the sylvan charm of the *Compleat Angler*. His drawings (Pl. 39A) also provided Barlow with the material for his large canvases, such as those he painted for Denzil Onslow's house at Pyrford. These, which hang today at Clandon, are a direct anticipation of the series of huge canvases of hunting scenes with which Wootton decorated the halls of Longleat, Althorp and Badminton in the time of George II.

John Wootton was a more accomplished painter and of much greater importance in the development of the English sporting piece. The greater part of his *œuvre* lies beyond our period, but he had already, by 1715, produced a number of life-size portraits of horses (at Clandon, Welbeck and Chatsworth) and one or two large, spacious and ambitious hunting scenes: Lady Henrietta Harley hawking and hunting and Lord Conway drawn up with his fellow-huntsmen on a vast canvas (1714) at Ragley. The most important precursors of these canvases are the huge portraits of horses that were painted, traditionally by Abraham van Diepenbeeck, for that great horseman the Duke of Newcastle and survive at Welbeck. Wootton's more mature sporting pieces are on a lesser scale and his smaller pictures, which are of such value as documents in a great age of horse-breeding, established conventions which survived to the days of Stubbs, Ben Marshall and beyond. Peter Tillemans, as a topographical and sporting painter, had a lighter and more rococo touch (Pl. 40A), but his compositions are less closely integrated than Wootton's.

It was not until comparatively late in his career, paradoxically, that Wootton seems to have come under the influence of Gaspar Poussin, Claude or Jan Wyck. Jan Wyck, who is recorded in Lon-

don in 1674 and worked at Ham, painted battle-pieces in the manner of Wouwermans and a number of hunting scenes in a fluent style which directly foreshadows Wootton's (Pl. 40c). He also specialized in little equestrian portraits (a genre which had been neglected since the time of Van Dyck) which were of no less significance for his successors. His little portrait of Monmouth seems to have been accompanied by a set of canvases depicting moments in the Duke's career as a soldier in Scotland and the Low Countries (there are similar canvases by Wyck at Drayton). And, probably in 1672, there arrived in this country from Holland the two most distinguished naval painters of the age: Willem van de Velde, father and son. They were given a warm welcome by the King and his brother and for nearly thirty years worked in partnership to provide the royal brothers and naval commanders with records of their ships and the engagements in which they had taken part: the dining-room at Ombersley Court, for example, is hung with the pictures of the Earl of Orford's flagship and actions which the Van de Veldes painted for his house in Cambridgeshire. These dramatic compositions and their spacious 'calms' (the younger man painted examples of both moods for the Lauderdales soon after his arrival in London) were of profound importance for such painters as Samuel Scott in the succeeding period. The Van de Veldes were indeed the fathers of marine painting in this country.

The importance to English painting of the Dutch influence in the lesser genres can hardly be over-estimated. Dutch pictures had been admired in England since at least the time of Charles I, who had owned works by Rembrandt, and in the later Stuart period certain types of Dutch painting were gaining a popularity which they have never lost: the microscopic realism and fine finish of the Dutch flower-piece and the exciting illusionism of perspective painting caused painters like Simon Verelst and Samuel van Hoogstraaten to be much admired. Flower painting was already a favourite pastime for ladies and was developed professionally as a highly decorative genre, admirably suited for overdoors, by the prolific Frenchman Jean Baptiste Monnoyer, who worked almost exclusively for the first Duke of Montagu, and by the Hungarian Jakob Bogdani. Bogdani also specialized in animal and bird painting in the style of Hondecoeter: his fascinating record of the aviary formed in Windsor Park by Admiral George Churchill was bought by Queen Anne after the Admiral's death in 1710 and is now at Kew.

Although they were anathema to Lord Shaftesbury there is no doubt that 'waggish Collectors, and the lower sort of *Virtuosi*' delighted in the subject-matter of pictures by Brouwer, Adriaen van Ostade or Jan Steen. The Dutch painter Egbert van Heemskerck worked with success in this vein at the end of the century: there is an instructive set of pieces by him at Birdsall which were probably painted for Sir Thomas Willoughby. His satirical pieces were to influence Hogarth's choice of subject-matter. In a different social context, hesitant efforts were being made at the conversation piece, a genre which Hogarth was to develop and which was to be so popular in the eighteenth century, by painters in the seventeenth century such as Joan Carlile and Stephen Browne.

'In growing and enlarging times, Arts are commonly drowned in Action.' [7] The Stuart period was this country's 'growing and enlarging time' and the political, economic, social and religious upheavals of the age inevitably affected the development of the arts. For the fundamental issue is this: the ability of a country where religious and national prejudices were so strong, to realize and to absorb influences from the Continent. The enthusiasm and cosmopolitan tastes of Charles I attracted to this country the greatest of all baroque painters and, in prompting Van Dyck's decision to work here for a number of years, entirely altered the development of the English portrait by laying before English patrons new and infinitely sophisticated idioms which were to be a continuing source of inspiration. The arts of the Caroline Court evoked the hostility of reactionary and more simply Protestant minds, but by the end of the century, although there were iconoclastic outbreaks in 1688, increasing religious toleration

and first-hand acquaintance with the arts of the Continent had done much to break down these older prejudices: Whig and Tory patrons could employ Catholic artists on Catholic subjects with no twinge to their consciences.

In English taste and in English painting the seventeenth century is a watershed. By 1700 engravings had brought a knowledge of the arts to circles far wider than those to which they were accessible in 1603. The lack of the regular and organized academic training, through which young Continental painters could pass, gave even to the finest native painting, the portraits of Cooper and Dobson, a freshness and independence and something of the amateur's unspoilt vision. Much English painting is exceedingly provincial and the native painter was often eclipsed by his more accomplished foreign rival: Greenhill or Riley could never achieve the facility of conception and execution of Lely, Wissing or Kneller, and only Thornhill had the experience to equal Verrio or Laguerre. But it was the foreign portrait painters, Mytens, Lely, Kneller, the foreign artists in the lesser genres, and above all Van Dyck, who brought to England continental experience and technical methods of a high order and who thus divide the archaisms of the Jacobean age from the achievements of Hogarth, Wilson, Reynolds, Gainsborough or Stubbs: achievements which were made possible by their predecessors under the Stuarts and by a growing realization that English painting could only thrive if patrons and artists alike were prepared to open their minds to the inspiration of European art.

SHORT BIBLIOGRAPHY

The most recent accounts of painting in England under the Stuarts are to be found in: Ellis Waterhouse, *Painting in Britain 1530–1790* (1953), and Margaret Whinney and Oliver Millar, *English Art 1625–1714* (1957). Both books contain full bibliographies for further study. The best guide to miniature painting is Graham Reynolds, *English Portrait Miniatures* (1952). Among works of importance that have appeared since the above were written are Henry V.S. and Margaret S. Ogden, *English Taste in Landscape in the Seventeenth Century* (1955), A.M. Hind, *Engraving in England* ..., Part II (1955), and the catalogue and illustrated souvenir of the exhibition, *British Portraits*, R.A., 1956–7.

[7] Sir Henry Wotton, preface to *Elements of Architecture* (1624).

Sculpture

MARGARET WHINNEY

English sculpture in the Stuart period, though great in quantity, is much less distinguished in quality than either architecture or painting. Moreover, its scope is limited very largely to tombs. The rich figure decoration of saints and angels of seventeenth century continental churches was not approved in England and, until late in the century, there is relatively little external sculpture on secular buildings. Tomb sculpture had, however, a special appeal to Englishmen, for, like the painted portrait, it fostered the interest in the individual and the emphasis on the family. All classes of men, great landowners, scholars and merchants, ordered tombs either in their wills or before their death; they are to be found in countless country churches and they range from sumptuous architectural structures with many figures, through the simpler types with only an effigy of the owner, to wall tablets (often beautiful in design) which record a burial near by. From them a wonderfully clear picture can be obtained of changes in taste throughout the century.

At the beginning of the century tomb sculpture was largely in the hands of foreign craftsmen, Dutch and Flemish, most of whom had come to England as refugees during the sixteenth century Wars of Religion. They established workshops (generally in Southwark on the south bank of the Thames) which often lasted for two or three generations. Tombs made there were sent all over England. The work is usually competent, and the designs, broadly speaking, fall into two groups, one showing the effigy of the patron and his wife lying on their backs, with their hands joined in prayer, beneath a simple architectural canopy, the other having kneeling figures. The tomb of Sir Roger Aston at Cranford, Middlesex (d. 1612), by William Cure (Pl. 41A), rich in coloured alabaster, is only one of a great number of the second type. Both patterns were to last down to the middle of the century, but gradually the handling and often the materials change. Nicholas Stone (1583–1647), about whom we know a great deal – his Note Book and Account Book have survived and show the daily working of his studio – was trained in one of the foreign workshops and later in Holland, but in 1619 he was made Master Mason at the Banqueting House at Whitehall, and so came into close contact with Inigo Jones. His tomb of Thomas, Lord Knyvett (Pl. 41B), at Stanwell, Middlesex, for which he was paid £215 in 1623, is quieter in colour and more refined in its handling of architectural detail than the Aston tomb, and the modelling of the figures is more sensitive and gracious. Stone had an enormous practice and made tombs of many different types. His best work has fine quality, but he employed many assistants and the 'workshop pieces' are often a little dull. His association with the Court brought him into touch with the new Italian taste and also aroused his interest in the antique sculpture bought by Charles I. His monument to Francis Holles (d. 1622) in Westminster Abbey, the first to show an Englishman as a Roman hero, is modelled on Michelangelo's tomb of Guiliano de' Medici and several of his later works show figures with soft, clinging draperies imitating the antique.

Other contemporary sculptors, however, were little influenced by new ideas. Edward Marshall (1598–1675), who, like Nicholas Stone, was also a mason and became Master of the Masons' Company in 1650, made the lovely quiet figure of Elizabeth, Lady Culpeper (d. 1638) at Hollingbourne, Kent (Pl. 43A), following the traditional pattern, though since she lies easily with one hand on her breast there is a greater naturalism and intimacy than in the effigies of the earlier generation, whose hands are joined in prayer. Maximilian Colt, who came from Arras, and whose real name was Poultrain, was made Master Sculptor to the Crown by James 1 and executed for him the tomb of Queen Elizabeth 1 in Westminster Abbey. His most original work, however, is the tomb of the first Earl of Salisbury at Hatfield, Hertfordshire (Pl. 43B), made in 1614. This with the effigy on a black-marble bier supported on the shoulders of four Virtues, and a skeleton beneath, follows a foreign pattern which never became popular in England, though the simple contrast of black-and-white marble, of which this is probably the first example, was to be very widely adopted. Colt's Virtues are static figures heavily and roundly modelled in a manner that could be paralleled in France almost a hundred years earlier. It is not, therefore, entirely surprising that though Colt remained Master Sculptor throughout the reign of Charles 1, his style was evidently regarded as too conservative to please the more sophisticated taste of the Court, and he appears to have been employed mainly on minor decorative work.

Charles 1 had been fortunate in attracting to his Court one painter, Van Dyck, of European reputation. Rubens also worked for him, and though Inigo Jones is hardly an artist of equal rank, he was at least a man of great gifts and wide knowledge. The King was less lucky in the sculptors he employed. Hubert le Sueur, a Frenchman who first appears in England in 1625, had been in contact with distinguished Italian artists in France, but thought he had learnt something of their methods, his own work is strangely dull. He is, however, of some importance in the history of English sculpture, for he brought new forms and new techniques. From about 1520 until the time of Le

Sueur's arrival nearly all sculpture in England had been in alabaster or stone (though very occasionally marble was used). Le Sueur was a skilled worker in bronze; indeed he is far more accomplished as a craftsman than as a designer. His statue of the third Earl of Pembroke, now in the Schools Quadrangle at Oxford (Pl. 42A) is pompous in pose and empty in the modelling of the head, but the detailed treatment of the armour is finely done. The same insensitive modelling appears in his best-known work, the statue of Charles 1 on horseback at Charing Cross. Le Sueur was also responsible for the development of the portrait bust as part of the furnishing of a house. The English mason-sculptors, Nicholas Stone and Edward Marshall, had made monuments which showed a bust generally in a roundel, with the shoulders cut by the frame. Stone's monument of 1615 to Sir Thomas Bodley in Merton College Chapel, Oxford, is a good example of a fairly common type. Le Sueur also made monuments with busts (for instance, the Lady Cottington in Westminster Abbey), but the form is different, for his busts stand on a small pedestal, and are therefore independent works of art. And he made too a number of busts which had no connexion with monuments. The Charles 1 in antique armour, now at Stourhead (Pl. 44A), stood in the Chair Room at Whitehall Palace; his bust of Archbishop Laud belongs to St John's College, Oxford. All his work has the same smooth modelling of the features, giving almost no feeling of the texture of the skin or of the precise form of the bony structure beneath it; the pose is always stiff and frontal, lacking vitality. Both the other foreign sculptors who worked for Charles 1, Francesco Fanelli (who made the Diana Fountain in Bushey Park) and Francois Dieussart, were better artists, but neither was anywhere near the first rank, and the one major piece of sculpture connected with the King, his bust made by Bernini in Rome in 1636, perished in the fire at Whitehall in 1698.

The mason-sculptors of the first half of the century had many of them established workshops which passed to their sons or nephews, and much sound if rather uninspired work was done. After the Restoration, however, a new type of man appears, who describes himself as a 'statuary' rather than a carver, and who had generally travelled. The first, and in some ways the most important, of these was John Bushnell (c. 1630-1701). Trained at first in an English workshop, he was forced because of domestic trouble to flee to the Continent. Several years were spent in Italy before his return in the late 1660's. During this time he saw, and clearly admired, Roman baroque sculpture with its drama and movement, its deeply undercut draperies, its brilliant exploitation of expression and of materials. His first works, the Stuart kings and a queen still on Temple Bar, or the statues of Charles I and Charles II from the Royal Exchange, now in the Old Bailey, make a valiant, though not completely successful attempt to reproduce the Italian manner. His monument to Lord Mordaunt (d. 1675) in All Saints, Fulham, (Pl. 42B) is perhaps his finest work. It is new in its use of a lively standing figure, and in its rejection both of an architectural frame and of all suggestion of Christian piety. Mordaunt is vigorous and alert, in white marble against the curved black background, his gauntlets and coronet on pedestals at the sides. The dramatic turning pose, the sweep of the cloak wrapped round the figure and deeply undercut, all proclaim its baroque intention. A comparison of this figure with Le Sueur's Pembroke (Pl. 42A) reveals at once the change of style. Bushnell's first works in or near London must have been a revelation to many English craftsmen; it is sad that he never fulfilled his early promise. As early as 1675 in the Ashburnham tomb at Ashburnham in Sussex, he is already showing an inability to convey the structure of the body; his work becomes progressively weaker, his mind deteriorated, commissions were left unfinished, and he died insane. He is also recorded as a maker of busts, and there is good reason to believe that the portrait of Charles II, of which the finished marble is at Melton Constable, Norfolk, and the preliminary terra-cotta (Pl. 44B) in the Fitzwilliam Museum, Cambridge, is his. The twist of the head, the rich and lively treatment of the curled wig and lace cravat, are again clear evidence of a knowledge of baroque art, and stress the contrast with the more conservative work done for Charles I (Pl. 44A).

Busts were evidently becoming more common, and not only among the great, for Pepys records how, on the 10th February, 1669, he had a life-mask taken, and the bust of his wife on her monument in St Olave's, Hart Street, is almost certainly by John Bushnell. Not a large number, apart from monuments, has survived, but among the finest are the few made by Edward Pierce, who was one of the Master Masons of St Paul's Cathedral. His bust of Sir Christopher Wren in the Ashmolean Museum, Oxford, of 1673 is baroque in form, broad across the shoulders, with a loop of drapery falling over the chest, though the head is still frontal. The Thomas Evans (Pl. 44C) of 1688, belonging to the Painter-Stainers' Company, London, is more vigorous in pose, with the head slightly turned and lifted. It is broadly and fully modelled, and indeed in its description of the features and its perception of the planes of the face, is superior to the Bushnell. Many monuments scattered up and down the country have good busts, but few are signed. Some, such as the Withers monument at Arkesden, Essex, come close to Edward Pierce; others may perhaps be from the workshop of William and Edward Stanton, whose recorded works reveal a very large practice.

A rather different continental tradition is represented by the sculpture of Caius Gabriel Cibber (1630-1700) and Grinling Gibbons (1648-1721) for they are far less Berninesque than Bushnell or Pierce. Both use modified baroque types and draperies, but their figures (especially their female figures) are often heavily built with heads following the classical tradition. It seems probable that both were influenced by the work of the studio of Artus Quellin in Amsterdam, and it should perhaps be recalled that there is much Dutch influence to be found in England in other arts in the reign of Charles II. Cibber, a Dane by birth, had visited Italy, but almost his whole working life was spent in England, which he reached during the Commonwealth, and is first recorded as foreman in the workshop of John Stone, Nicholas Stone's son. He is known to have been in Holland with Stone, who had Dutch relations. His most ambitious work is the relief on the Monument, in London, an allegorical piece showing Charles II succouring the City after the Great Fire of 1666, but his most appealing is certainly the Sackville Monument (1677) at Withyham, Sussex (Pl. 45B). This is, in one way, a transformation of the old type of monument with kneeling figures, but instead of men and women kneeling in prayer, the parents are now shown on either side of a free-standing tomb, mourning their young son, who reclines between them. The spectator is inevitably drawn to join in their grief, and to this extent the conception is baroque; but there is none of the rhetoric of Bushnell's work, and the smoothly cut rounded figures are very Dutch in handling. Cibber was also responsible for garden figures at Belvoir and Chatsworth (a few garden figures, but not many, are known to have made earlier in the century), and in the latter house he played his part in the ensemble of the chapel (Pl. 13A). The statues above the altar of Faith and Justice are his, but compared with the adoring saints, or angels alighting from rapid flight, of Italian baroque art, they are markedly static in pose. He had, before he went to Chatsworth in 1688, made a fountain showing Charles II above the Four Rivers of England for Soho Square (parts of which survive), and the figures of Raving and Melancholy Madness, with their unforgettable realism, which adorned the gate of Bedlam Hospital, and are now in the Guildhall Museum. His last work was architectural decoration for Sir Christopher Wren: the south pediment of St Paul's with the phœnix rising from ashes and the more important pediment on the garden front of Hampton Court Palace, showing the Triumph of Hercules, an allusion to William III's victories over Louis XIV. His career, therefore, gives clear enough evidence of the increased range of opportunity open to sculptors in the later years of the century, and though his work is seldom very distinguished, it never falls below a fair standard of competence.

Grinling Gibbons is a more controversial figure. His brilliance as a wood-carver has been indicated in the chapter on architecture and it was certainly here that his chief strength lay. But much sculpture of very varied quality was also produced by his studio. Some of it, for instance, the bronze statue of James II now outside the National Gallery, is very fine; other figures, for instance the Duke of Somerset in the Library of Trinity College, Cambridge, are almost grotesque in their clumsiness. Judging from an account written by George Vertue at the time of Gibbons' death, it was generally recognized by his contemporaries that he had no great ability in bronze or marble, and that most of such work was carried out by assistants. The most important of these was Arnold Quellin, the son of the sculptor at Amsterdam, who worked with Gibbons from about 1681 until his early death in 1686. Most of the best large-scale figure sculpture which came from Gibbons' studio dates from these years, and it may be that such quality as it has was due to Quellin, who in his monument to Thomas Thynne in Westminster Abbey proves that he had considerable ability as a designer. The tomb of Baptist Noel, Viscount Campden (Pl. 45A), erected in 1686 at Exton in Rutland, is the most lavish example of the work of these years. Like many tombs of the period, there is no direct Christian sentiment; Lord Campden and his wife, both in classical dress, stand on either side of an urn (always an emblem of mortality), while above is a tent-like drapery. The children, instead of kneeling below or beside their parent, as in the tombs of the first years of the century, are shown in conversation or at play in reliefs on the two flanking obelisks, and below the main figures. The latter have neither the vitality of Bushnell's Mordaunt, nor the sincerity of the parents in Cibber's Sackville tomb, but in their slightly theatrical poses are very typical of the work of Gibbons' studio at its best. His later tombs – Lady Newdigate at Harefield, Middlesex, or Sir Cloudesley Shovell in Westminster Abbey – are far more clumsy in their treatment of the figure, and it is a relief to turn to a smaller work, the monument to Robert Cotton (1697) at Conington, Cambridgeshire (Pl. 46A), which was more within the artist's capacity. The wreath of flowers which surrounds the portrait of the boy is comparable to Gibbons' best woodcarving, and it may well be that he was proud of it, for it is one of the few monuments which he signed.

Another foreigner linked with this studio was Jan van Ost (or John Nost as he came to be called), who married Arnold Quellin's widow. Although he made a few tombs, he is chiefly known for his lead garden figures. Some, like those at Rousham, Oxfordshire, have a strange angular quality which is highly personal; others, at Melbourne, Derbyshire, or on the gateposts at Hampton Court, are charming chubby boys, based on good Italian models. And at Hampton Court also, Nost may be seen in a different vein in the elegant relief of the Car of Venus (Pl. 46B) from the overmantel in the Cartoon Gallery.

A purely English sculptor whose best work has considerable merit was Francis Bird (1667–1731), but he too was trained abroad, first in Brussels and then in Rome. The dates of many of his tombs are uncertain, but the Dr Busby in Westminster Abbey (probably of about 1703) is greatly superior, both in design and cutting, to any marble monument by Gibbons. It would seem that Sir Christopher Wren also had a good opinion of Bird, since he chose him to make his daughter's monument, and also to carve the dramatic scene of the Conversion of St Paul on the west front of the Cathedral. This is difficult to see, much weathered, and is therefore usually under-rated. Bird also appears to have made tombs of a wide variety of types. The Sir Orlando Gee (c. 1705) at Isleworth, Middlesex, shows him continuing the tradition of the bust monument, but giving it a baroque liveliness and at the same time displaying considerable skill in portraiture. His later and more ambitious works, such as the tomb of the Duke of Newcastle in Westminster Abbey, made from the designs of James Gibbs, fall outside our period.

Several other English sculptors of ability – Richard Crutcher, Thomas Green of Camberwell and Thomas Stayner – were producing work of good quality in the early years of the eighteenth century, and there were also competent men in the provinces. In the case of many elaborate, ambitious tombs the artists are still unidentified. And, in addition, there is a great quantity of attractive work on a more modest scale. The innumerable wall tablets, without figures, though often with beautifully designed shields, drapery, cherubs' heads, skulls or flowers, bear witness both to the good level of English craftsmanship and also to the wish for commemoration felt by men of all classes.

SHORT BIBLIOGRAPHY

There is no good general survey except K.A.Esdaile, *English Monumental Sculpture since the Renaissance* (1927), which is now somewhat out of date. M.D. Whinney and O.Millar, *English Art, 1625–1714* (1957), Chapters VI and X give a rather fuller account of Stuart sculpture than has been possible here. For individual sculptors see R.Gunnis, *Dictionary of British Sculptors, 1660–1851* (1953).

Two cherubs' heads carved in wood by Grinling Gibbons in Trinity College, Cambridge.

Monument to Tobias Rustat (d. 1693),
in Jesus College Chapel, Cambridge,
probably by the workshop of Grinling
Gibbons.

Silver

N. M. PENZER

With the death of Elizabeth I and the end of the House of Tudor we move from a period of rugged splendour, domestic upheaval and the protracted strain of foreign wars, to one of peace and comparative safety, a much-needed breathing-space before the Great Rebellion was to cast its shadow over the land and destroy so much that was rare and beautiful. So far as social, economic and artistic England was concerned, the early Stuart era was merely a continuation of the Elizabethan. The union of the Crowns meant little more than that a Scottish king now sat on the English throne, but the two countries remained as distinct and aloof from one another as ever. In the north the end of the Border war was gradually to replace the fortified castle with the manor-house, and a period of peace at home was to encourage the spread of domestic architecture and the pursuit of all that formed part of a gentler mode of life.

James had exchanged a poor country for one rich and prosperous, and he was determined to do all in his power to see that it remained so. His first act, then, was to make an official end of the war with Spain, and this he did in 1604 by concluding a peace treaty with the Constable of Castile, Don Juan Fernandez de Velasco, Duke of Frias, envoy of Philip III. On such occasions an exchange of plate or jewels was customary, but in this case James saw an opportunity of stressing the sincerity of his peaceful intentions in no uncertain manner. The treasures of the Tudors lay in the Jewel-house – and at his mercy – and without qualm or compunction he removed for the grati-

fication of the Constable over 29,000 oz. of priceless bejewelled gold cups and gilt plate, including the famous Jane Seymour ewer and basin, and the Royal Gold Cup of England and France, which had been the cherished possession of royalty for over two centuries.

But James had previously caused drawings of the gifts to be made, and on seeing the bare shelves of the Jewel-house immediately ordered his goldsmith, John Williams, to make replicas, never realizing that such a thing was impossible.[1] However, before the end of 1611 he had paid Williams over £90,000 – an enormous sum – for new plate, which all too soon was to be used to alleviate financial embarrassment. In the latter part of James' reign the royal collection was regarded not as plate, but as treasure to be melted down, sold or pawned as occasion demanded. Such a regrettable course of action had been forced on Elizabeth in 1600, and in future it was to become a precedent, until finally in 1649 misguided Puritan zeal was to destroy anything that was left. But we need not dwell further on this distressing subject.

The gradual change

The English goldsmiths still used German sheets of ornamental designs, but a lighter touch was soon to be detected, and although the sideboards of the rich still groaned under a mass of highly decorative plate, great changes were about

[1] A. J. Collins, *Jewels and Plate of Queen Elizabeth I*, 1955, pp. 137, 138.

to commence. These were caused by a new activity, a general 'movement', an urge to create which only a settled state of peace could engender. It first affected all branches of architecture, industry and commerce, and so in turn was to dictate change and innovations in both the style and decoration of plate.

Although such great Jacobean houses as Audley End, Bramshill and Hatfield still retained many features noticeable in Elizabethan houses like Longleat, Burghley, Theobalds, Wollaton and many more, the position of the Great Hall had changed. Instead of being lengthwise to the main front, it was now built at right angles to it, and so became, except on special occasions, a reception hall, rather than a banqueting hall, and the earlier parlours were to become the dining-room and withdrawing-room. Such rooms, being of only one storey in height, tended to create a much greater feeling of privacy and homeliness than had ever been possible in the lofty raftered Great Hall, constantly filled with guests, retainers and servants. As a consequence of this change, ceremonial plate, especially the Great Salt, Cups of Assay and elaborate centre-pieces, gradually became out of fashion, and the smaller rooms demanded smaller and more personal types of plate, unpretentious silver rather than garish gold and silver-gilt.

At the same time James kept his palaces well supplied with plate, for he revelled in his newly-acquired pomp and circumstance, of which lavish entertainment formed an important part. The new Banqueting House at Whitehall, built by Inigo Jones, had its own 'great gilt cupboard of estate', in which was kept a sufficient quantity of plate both for use at table and also to furnish the cupboards and side-tables with an imposing array of the more striking and decorative pieces. Included among the plate were doubtless examples of cups and salts surmounted by an obelisk or steeple, which have been described as typically English, and quite unknown elsewhere. As these vessels are interesting from many points of view, and because the great majority of extant specimens date roughly from 1602 to 1619, we shall make them the first subject of discussion.

The steeple-cup

From the earliest times the steeple, pyramid or obelisk had been a symbol of greatness, power and achievement, a symbolism observed in such great Tudor houses as Montacute, Burghley and Wollaton Hall. It was a favourite ornamentation in the screens of the halls at the Universities, it was cut to shape by lovers of topiary and was woven into tapestries, while it is very familiar on monumental statuary in Westminster Abbey, and in many parish churches. No wonder, then, that James I, a firm believer in the Divine Right of Kings, should look with favour on the steeple. Although the steeple appeared on drinking-cups and bowls before 1559, and Sir Nicholas Bacon presented one in gold to Elizabeth in 1573, so far as existing examples are concerned the earliest appears to be that of 1593 at Creeting St Mary, Suffolk. As a chalice the steeple-cup was suitable in shape and size, while the cover, if still used, formed an attractive and not unecclesiastical ornament. This may partly account for the fact that nearly fifty steeple-cups are to be found in British parish churches. Those belonging to Livery Companies and Corporations bring the number to well over a hundred. Of the sixteen examples at the Kremlin, nine lack covers, but the number includes two very fine specimens presented by James I. There are four characteristic features. These are: (1) The egg-shaped bowl and cover. (2) The short baluster stem with attached grotesque brackets bounded by horizontal collars. (3) The trumpet-shaped foot with spreading base. (4) The cover, which completes the ovoid outline, with a solid or pierced steeple, usually three-sided, resting on curving caryatid brackets set on a low reel-shaped platform. The forms of embossed or engraved decoration include the usual acanthus foliage, both on the stem and as a calyx to the bowl, fruit, flowers, plain strapwork, trefoils, fleurs-de-lis, scallops, gadrooning and fluting. Less often we find a Dutch motif of rippling sea and the heads of marine monsters, as on the 1627 Tait Cup at the Victoria and Albert Museum (M. 80–1921). Apart from the usual egg-shaped pattern, two other types should be noted. The first is gourd-shaped, elaborately engraved, with a calyx of acanthus leaves, the bowl supported by a forked and twisted tree-trunk. Good examples occur at Hutton Buscel, Yorks (1611) and at the Armourers' and Braziers' Company (1608), both of which have solid steeples surmounted by a finial of a Roman soldier. The second type is globular, and very rare. The best example is that of 1604, with a replaced cover of 1677, belonging to the City of Westminster (Pl. 47c).[2] Only six others are known – two at the Kremlin (1605 and 1608), two at Guisborough, Yorks, one at Trinity College, Cambridge (1615) and the last at Canongate, Edinburgh – neither of the last two having covers.

The steeple-salt is much less common than the steeple-cup. Such examples as exist have a circular body with a base resting on claw-and-ball feet, with usually one, and more rarely two, salt containers protected by covers supported on scroll brackets. There was a good example of the former in the Swaythling Collection, while the Victoria and Albert Museum has a double-container type of 1614 (Pl. 47B). The only other type of salt usually considered as 'Jacobean' is the bell-salt. Actually they date back to the time of Henry VIII, while seven are mentioned in the 1559 inventory. The bell-salt consists of two bell-shaped containers, the upper and smaller one fitting closely into the lower and larger one, which latter rests on ball-feet. The conical cover is surmounted by a perforated knop or ball for use as a pepper-caster. The reason for the popularity both of the steeple-salt and the bell-salt at this time is explained by the fact that they were both small types of standing-salts, as compared with those of mid-Tudor days, and were indicative of the passing of the Great Hall.

The only remaining type of standing-salt to make its appearance, before the more personal trencher-salt was to supplant it entirely, was the scroll-salt. It appeared, apparently from France, about 1630, and lasted nearly to the end of the seventeenth century. The chief feature was the three, and later four, brackets or arms which terminated in scrolls and stuck out from the rim of the salt cavity in an outward curve. There were several varieties, the earliest being circular and reel-shaped, to which the term 'pulley-salt' was given at Goldsmiths' Hall. Others are drum-shaped, or square. The object of the arms was not to hold a napkin, but to support a bowl to hold dessert. In describing the Seymour Salt, Pepys made this quite clear and both French and Dutch engravings and paintings prove it conclusively.[3]

Apart from steeple-cups, most of the other standing-cups produced in Jacobean times, such as the coconut and ostrich-egg cups, were merely repetitions or revivals of Tudor types, and do not concern us here. The true Jacobean standing-cup had a conical bowl with a bell-shaped foot surmounted by a baluster stem either with or without brackets. If there was a cover, which was not always the case, it was either conical and produced an ovoid outline to the whole, as with the steeple-cup, or else it had a slightly domed cover with a somewhat elaborate finial, as in the example of 1611 at the Victoria and Albert Museum (Pl. 48B).

The ewer and basin

The only other large pieces of ceremonial plate which call for notice are the ewer and basin, in constant use since the Middle Ages, and to become decorative pieces for the sideboard when the introduction of the fork rendered their use redundant. They are usually spoken of as if they formed an inseparable and matching pair, but the inventories of Tudor sovereigns show that the ewers – or 'lairs' as the more ornate ones were called – outnumbered the basins by nearly two to one.[4] Moreover, no attempt was made to keep a matching pair together, and the ewer was presented to one envoy or ambassador and the basin to another. A further interesting fact revealed by Tudor inventories is that the well-known 'helmet'

[2] It is known as the Pickering Loving Cup. See *Insignia and Plate of the Corporation of the City of Westminster*, Cambridge, 1931, pp. 9–13.

[3] *Apollo Annual*, 1949, pp. 48–53.
[4] See A. J. Collins, *op. cit.*, p. 52.

type of ewer was known before 1521 – the date of an inventory which lists no less than eleven made 'helmet fation'. Until the death of Elizabeth the decoration of the basins was confined to the broad rim and the raised central boss with its surround, but in Jacobean times an 'all-over' ornamentation was introduced, covering the depressed portion, which had previously been left plain, whereby much of the former beauty of contrast was lost. Existing ewers can be classified under four types:

1. The prototype is the 1545–46 ewer, with matching basin, at Corpus Christi, Cambridge – a really lovely object. It has a slightly swelling octagonal body, the sides of which are alternately engraved and plain, as is also the scotia of the round, low foot, but in counter-changed order. The plain, partially rounded handle is angular, while the four-sided spout extends to the entire height of the body. The flattened domical cover, with double 'C' thumb-piece, is enriched with spiral flutings shaped like the heraldic *goutte*, matching those on the basin. Later examples are cylindrical with horizontal bands of ornamentation. The cover is domed, the handle an S scroll, while the foot is often convex, surmounted by a reel-shaped stem.

2. Vase-shaped, of Italian renaissance style. It has a narrow neck with shaped lip and gadrooned mouth. In some cases the shoulder is decorated, in others the entire surface is elaborately engraved and embossed. The tall, curved handle varies from a plain S scroll to a highly ornate terminal figure or animal's head. The stem has a gadrooned collar and spreading foot, often decorated with ovolo moulding. Examples can be seen at the Victoria and Albert Museum, Sidney Sussex College, Cambridge, Eton College, Norwich Castle Museum, Windsor Castle, etc.

3. The chief feature of this type is its absolute plainness. It extends from the reign of Charles I, through the Commonwealth, to that of Charles II. The earlier examples are deep, plain, beaker-shaped, with a long spout stretching nearly the entire length of the body, a curving lip, plain scroll handles and trumpet-shaped stem with a circular foot. Good examples are at Trinity College, Cambridge (1635), and the Barbers' Company (1657).

After the Restoration the long spout is replaced by little more than an indentation in the plain rim, while the handle is usually harp-shaped. The body is encircled by a plain rib-moulding, and there is usually a calyx of cut-card work. See Queen's College, Oxford (1668), Drapers' Company (1674 and 1678), King's College, Cambridge (1675), Clothworkers' Company (1676), etc.

4. The 'Helmet' type was revived at the end of the seventeenth century by such Huguenot goldsmiths as Pierre Harache, David Willaume and and Pierre Platel. Apart from the inverted helmet shape, other features are the terminal figure handles, often of great magnificence, masks under the spouts and elaborate calyces of floral design. Owing to their great ornamental value, they persisted long after the introduction of the fork, and when not in actual use, remained as decorative pieces on the sideboards of Livery Company or College Halls.

Drinking utensils

Turning to drinking utensils, mention may first be made of the beaker. Strange to say, the true rôle of the beaker in later Tudor times, and after, was not as a secular drinking-cup, but as a chalice. This was due to the trading between the Netherlands and the east coast towns of England, especially Norwich, and to similar trade communications between the Low Countries and Scotland – especially Aberdeen. The plain type of Dutch beaker appealed strongly to the Scots, and even today nearly a hundred are still used in Scottish kirks in the north-east part of the country. Secular Dutch beakers, with appropriate engraving, were imported for sale in this country, and it is these which from time to time find their way into the sale-rooms. Large quantities of beakers were used by the Puritans of New England, and when Jones [5] made his survey of American churches, he found that no fewer than 577 silver beakers, mostly plain or chastely engraved, were still in use. In England the beaker as a secular vessel never entirely disappeared,

[5] *The Old Silver of American Churches*, Letchworth, 1913.

partly because of its æsthetic appeal, and partly because of its handy form for easy stacking, whether for hunting parties or for use in college halls.

Apart from the beaker, the only Stuart drinking-vessels needing brief consideration are the wine-cups and the tankards. Made for individual use, the charming Jacobean wine-cup is found in various shapes and styles of decoration. They can be conveniently classified under five main types as follows:

1. Shallow, nearly hemispherical bowl, slender baluster stem, trumpet-mouthed or cymbal-shaped foot.
2. Ovoid bowl, similar stem and foot.
3. Bell-shaped bowl, similar stem and foot.
4. Octagonal straight-sided bowl, slender baluster stem with applied open scroll-brackets surrounding upper knop. Feet as above.
5. Beaker-shaped bowl, thick baluster stem, trumpet-shaped foot with convex base.

Some of the above shapes may be based on Venetian glass of the sixteenth and seventeenth centuries, but further research is needed on this subject. A few further notes on these five types are necessary.

1. This type is called 'tazza-shaped' by Jackson, but in view of the constant misuse of this word it should be entirely avoided. The bowl forms a shallow section of a sphere, and exactly resembles the Victorian and Edwardian champagne glasses. Two varieties occur in Stuart times, one quite plain and the other having a network of squares. The plain variety, of which there are twelve (1631–1633–1640) at the Armourers' and Braziers' Company, has a very shallow bowl with a rather flat base, a spindle-like baluster stem and a plain round spreading base. The other variety is deeper, and the lip is left plain for about half an inch, below which a line of depressed dots marks the beginning of a granulated design of punched quadrilaterals resembling Venetian lace glass – *Vetro di Trina*. Usually there is no further decoration, but examples occur in which three large *fleurs-de-lis* alternate with three plain straps ex-

tending from the dotted line to the juncture of the plain baluster stem and the base of the bowl.

2. This type is conical or ovoid in outline, often resembling a steeple-cup without its cover. Except in rare cases, the bowl is chased with a broad band of bold floral design on a matted ground occupying the entire central surface, leaving only a plain rim above, and a calyx below, which usually consists of radiating lobes also on a matted ground.

3. The bell-shaped cup has straighter sides and a more rounded base than type 2. Though sometimes plain, the bowls usually have a narrow line near the lip-band, with conventional trefoil pendants, while the calyx displays elaborate *repoussé* ornamentation of fruit and flowers. The plain baluster stems are slender and graceful, the circular, spreading, cymbal-like foot being engraved with motifs taken from the calyx.

4. Each of the eight sides is decorated with a large open flower on a tall, vertical stalk, from which leaves protrude laterally. The design is flat chased, and arranged in bands on a matted ground. The lip is left plain. In several cases a shield is substituted for a flower in one of the panels. The calyx is embossed with fruit and flowers, and the bowls are supported by three open brackets applied to the top of the slender baluster stem. The spreading, cymbal-shaped feet are usually chased with acanthus leaves on a matted ground.

5. This beaker-shaped type is quite plain, and is typical of Charles I and the Commonwealth. The bowl has gently sloping sides with a nearly flat base. It rests on a sturdy baluster stem, which merges into a round foot of the usual cymbal form. In most cases the foot is moulded. There is a fine set of four (1640) belonging to the Leathersellers' Company.[6]

The tankard

The Stuart wine-cup was ousted from its place on the table by the wine-glass, but once the tankard had been introduced it came to stay. Sixteenth century tankards had a cylindrical body tapering upwards from the base, which was usually

[6] *Cat. Historic Plate of the City of London*, Goldsmiths' Hall, 1951, No. 97 and Pl. XLII.

decorated with lozenge-like ornament and an egg-and-tongue base-moulding. They were comparatively small in size, both in respect to their height and diameter. Other features to be noted are the decorations on the body, or drum, which may be engravings of fruit and flowers and medallion heads, or flat chased strapwork, arabesques, etc., divided into sections by horizontal bands. The handle is a recurving or S-shaped scroll, while the low, domed lid, which is hinged to the handle, is embossed with fruit or chased arabesque work. The finial is vase- or baluster-shaped, and the thumb-piece occurs in a variety of designs. It was this type (Pl. 48A) which extended into Stuart times, and contemporary with it was a perfectly straight-sided type as shown in Jackson, *History*, Fig. 980. A fine example is that of 1602 belonging to the Guildford Corporation.[7]

The next ten or fifteen years seems to have been a transition period, and examples are very scarce between 1610 and 1630. The Victoria and Albert Museum has two serpentine tankards, one *c.* 1620 with a high, domed lid and pointed finial (M. 52–1912), the other from the Jackson collection, of *c.* 1630, mounted in plain silver-gilt, with a flat lid, chased with concentric rings and a broad thumb-piece (M. 92–1914). Of the typical plain Charles I tankard, with the flat lid pointed in front, plain scroll handle and tapering cylindrical body, excellent examples are the 1635–36 one at Trinity Hall, Cambridge, and the matching pair of 1639, and the single one of 1667 among Christ's Hospital plate.[8] A most unusual example is that in the collection of Earl Beauchamp. It has three royal portraits engraved round the cover, and a flat, cushioned lid bearing the arms of Charles I. It stands on three claw feet, and is dated 1643.[9]

The Cromwellian tankard is recognized by its low, flat-topped cover in two stages, and the wide splayed or skirted base. Several fine examples were to be seen at the Park Lane Exhibition in 1929.[10] The Carpenters' Company has a beautiful specimen of 1653 (no. 411 and Plate XXIX of the 1927 Victoria and Albert Exhibition of Livery Company Plate); while still another equally fine one of 1655, formerly at Barnard's Inn, Holborn, is now in the Earl of Rosebery's Collection (see Jackson, Fig. 988). What Jackson describes as a 'freak' tankard is that of 1649 at Winchester College. It is made in imitation of a slightly tapering cylindrical barrel, with chased vertical lines representing the joints between the staves and two grouped sets of horizontal lines representing the hoops. It has a flat cover with a two-lobed thumb-piece and a short C-shaped plain handle.[11]

With the Restoration the tankard was made in increasing numbers, and to this period we can assign those ordered by Livery Companies and Corporations, as well as by colleges of both Universities. Although the flat lid was retained, it usually had a larger projecting flange with a serrated edge, and the lid was often in two stages, with a convex member separating them. The thumb-pieces were chiefly twin-lobes, scrolls and volutes (such as were later to figure on the 'Onslow' spoon in the mid-eighteenth century). The general shape of the tankard was somewhat squat, drum-like and slightly tapering. Although the great majority were plain, some are embossed with acanthus or palm leaves, and later with cut-card work from the base to nearly half-way up the side of the tankard. Others, from about 1670 to 1685, have the entire surface covered with beautifully engraved trees, birds and flowers in *chinoiserie*. In some instances, from the late seventeenth century to the early years of Anne, the ordinary thumb-piece was replaced by fine cast figures of animals, such as the hedgehog at Balliol (1669), where the tankard is supported by three lions-couchant, or, more usually, the lion-couchant, as at Christ's

---

[7] A second similar tankard is 1619. See Oman, *Apollo*, September 1948, pp. 56, 57.

[8] H. D. Ellis read a paper on Christ's Hospital plate at a meeting of the London and Middlesex Society in April 1900, but dated the tankards incorrectly.

[9] See *Cat. to the Park Lane Loan Exhibition*, 1929, No. 283 and Pl. XXIII.

[10] *E.g.*, Nos. 91 (1649), 31 (1651), 691 (1654) and 680 (1655).

[11] See *Burlington Magazine*, July 1903, p. 163 and Pl. V. A very similar one, but with a larger handle, was made by Louisa Courtauld and George Cowles in 1772 (Gerald Taylor, *Silver*, Pl. 19d).

(1678), King's (1701), and Queens' (1703) Colleges at Cambridge, or Jesus College (1701) at Oxford.

Towards the end of the seventeenth century a distinct change in tankards began – the cover was domed and the lower part was spirally fluted, like the contemporary candle-cups which had become so popular. Although the flat-top type persisted into Anne's reign, we always think of a domed lid when we refer to a Queen Anne type of tankard. In some instances (as in the 1708 gallon tankard of the Founders' Company) the lid has a large button finial, while in others (as in the 1713 example of the Ironmongers' Company) both finial and lion-couchant thumb-pieces are retained, and the tankard is supported on four more lions. The sides are slightly bulbous, a feature that at this time began to make its appearance.

In concluding these brief notes, reference should be made to two varieties of tankard of which the prototypes were imported direct from Scandinavia. The first of these is rather squat, with a flat, slightly domed lid, often with a twin-lobe or lion-couchant thumb-piece. It can be quite plain, or completely covered with engraving or embossing. The chief feature, however, is the three ball feet, usually in the form of pomegranates, and fixed to the tankard by applied scroll leaves. They were made chiefly in Hull and Newcastle (the Victoria and Albert Museum has one of c. 1670 – Pl. 53B) and also in London.[12]

The other variety which was introduced direct from Denmark to Hull, and found chiefly with York marks about from 1657 to 1675, is the peg-tankard.[13] Although the earliest Danish vessel with pegs is not a tankard at all, but a large, two-

[12] For Danish examples see Boesen and Bøje, *Danish Silver*, Nos. 15a–21.

[13] The phrase 'to take one down a peg' has nothing to do with the peg-tankard, as has been repeatedly stated. The phrase is nautical in origin and refers to a ship's colours which used to be raised and lowered by pegs, the higher the colours the greater the honour, so that to take a person down a peg was to award less honour. Although the pegs were usually inside the tankard, this was not always the case. See *Cat. Festival Exhib. ... Silver*, Cheshire Standing Joint Committee, 1951, No. 61 and Pl. XV.

handled cup of 1577, it was the ordinary peg-tankard which came over to England. Examples with Hull, Newcastle, Edinburgh and London marks are known, but it was John Plummer of York who seems to have specialized in them (Pl. 50A).

Two-handled cups

Just as the massive Great Salts of the Tudor period were replaced by less pretentious types, and later the Jacobean silver wine-cup had been superseded by that of glass, so also the Hanaps, or Standing Cups, were replaced by the two-handled cups. Although certain rare types appeared in the sixteenth century, such as the vase-shaped renaissance-style covered cups of 1533 at Corpus, Oxford, and of 1555 and 1570 at Corpus, Cambridge, they apparently had no progeny. The so-called 'college' or 'two-eard' cups, confined almost entirely to Oxford colleges, were of peculiar shape (Pl. 50B) – a truncated pear-shaped outline on a low concave base with a moulded rim and two hollow, thick ring handles projecting vertically from the shoulder of the bowl just below the neck – and were never universally adopted. The two-handled cups that were to vary in size and shape and achieve great popularity after the Restoration first appeared in the middle of the seventeenth century. They were usually straight-sided, or very slightly tapering, but sometimes, as with the silver-mounted mother-of-pearl cup of c. 1650 at the Victoria and Albert Museum, they were of basin- or semi-circular shape on a low trumpet foot, with ornate cusped caryatid handles. Such handles, often of fine workmanship, are found on most two-handled cups of this period, but plain scroll handles also occur.

From about 1660 the cups appear in two main forms – those with a bulge in the lower part of the body, showing both in this respect and in the embossing of fruit and flowers strong Dutch characteristics, and those with straight sides. To the former the names caudle- or posset-cups have become attached, while the latter are usually known as porringers. Such names are quite arbitrary and applied largely because they appear in inventories and wills, and it has been assumed that it is to these cups that such terms refer. While it is clear that such cups would be used for all domestic purposes, including the drinking of caudle and *eating* of posset, it seems clear that the larger ones were still used as loving-cups. But with the use of the term *porringer* matters are quite different. This word means simply a vessel to hold pottage, and although largely applied to simple vessels of wood and pewter, was also given to elaborately ornamented ones of silver. From a study of the descriptions of the nine porringers mentioned in the 1574 inventory, it is clear that such vessels had two ornamented horizontal handles, and were shallow dishes. In fact, they corresponded very closely with the French *écuelle*, and were used for the same purposes. It is not surprising, then, to find that in his French–English dictionary of 1611, Randle Cotgrave renders *porringer* as *escuelle à oreillons*. It should be realized, however, that both *écuelle* and porringer were also made for personal use. It is interesting to note that one *écuelle* was used by two people, each holding a handle with one hand and a spoon with the other.[14] One imagines that considerable tact and discrimination would have to be shown by the hostess when placing her guests!

Although no two-handled English silver porringer exists from the fourteenth or fifteenth centuries, we can clearly see one in the hands of a servitor in one of the dinner scenes (folio 208) in the fourteenth century Luttrell Psalter. It would appear that when the larger dish-porringer was supplanted by the smaller personal vessel, the second handle became superfluous, and all existing examples have but one handle. It should be noted

that the piercing of this handle acts as a heat insulator as well as affording a simple means of suspension when not in use.

As the pewter porringer was naturally much more common than that of silver, many more have survived, and we can learn much from them that helps considerably in our understanding the different uses to which porringers were put. First and foremost we see that the term *porringer* is still universally retained by all collectors of pewter, while for some quite unexplained reason (unless Cripps is to blame) we have, in the past, called such objects in silver by the thoroughly unattractive name of 'bleeding-bowls'. It is satisfactory to note that the Victoria and Albert Museum 'Small Picture Book, No. 17', *Charles II Domestic Silver*, Charles Oman shuns such terms as 'caudle cup' and 'posset cup' and calls them all merely 'cups', while the single horizontal-handled 'bleeding-bowl' is at last correctly called a porringer. Incidentally, confusion also exists with regard to the 'taster', which E. Alfred Jones was inclined to regard as the original of the so-called 'bleeding-bowl'. Reference to the records of the Worshipful Company of Pewterers, however, clears up most of these difficult points. In 1556 this type of vessel was referred to as 'eare dysshes' and continued to be used until July 1596, after which identical pieces hitherto called 'eare dysshes' were henceforth called 'porrengers'. In 1571 'smal pewter Tasters' are mentioned, confirming the use of small porringers for sampling wine. Early silver wine-tasters, however, were very possibly used in place of the assay-cup lid for tasting the wine for poison.[15] Now the first mention of 'blood porringers' is made in 1659, and when the Company laid down tables of weights in which porringers of various sizes were to be made in future, apart from 'smale' and 'greate' porringers, reference is made to 'Ordinary blood porringers' at $1\frac{1}{2}$ lbs per dozen. This works out at 2 oz. apiece, and would indicate small pewter vessels of approximately 3 in. in diameter. Thus it is quite clear that wine-tasters and blood porringers were made *as such*, and of

14 H. Havard, *Dict. de l'ameublement*, Vol. II, col. 310.

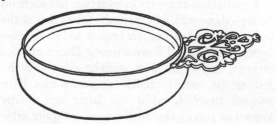

Fig. 1. Porringer, London hallmark for 1684–5. Maker's mark R.P. Width $6\frac{7}{8}$ in. *Victoria and Albert Museum.*

15 See Richard Warner, *Antiquitates Culinariae*, 1791, pp. 93–106.

the required size, but that the ordinary food porringer constituted the main product of the Company. In Randle Holme's *Academy of Armory* of 1688 and Dionis' *Course of Chirurgical Operations* of 1733 we see wood-cuts of the blood porringer, but when on 29th May 1661 Pepys slipped six spoons and a silver porringer into his pocket, and *carried them about all day*, we can be quite sure that it was the typical food porringer like the 1684 example (M. 420–1922) shown in the Victoria and Albert 'Small Picture Book' mentioned above. It is obvious, then, that the only safe name to give to all vessels of this period with vertical handles, whether bulbous or straight-sided, is 'two-handled cups', while the term 'porringer' should be applied only to the shallow vessel with the flat, pierced horizontal handle. When the early settlers in New England took the porringer with them it became the most popular domestic vessel in Boston households, and to this day the name has never been altered.

The more ornate, two-handled cups stood in the depressed centre of broad-brimmed and heavily-embossed round salvers. In many cases these salvers stood on a foot and presented a most striking and important piece of plate for the centre of the table. See, for instance, the Gloucester set of 1672 in Jackson, *History*, plate facing page 238. Salvers were also included in elaborate toilet sets, as in the Calverley toilet service (240m–1879) of 1683 at the Victoria and Albert Museum (*Charles II Domestic Silver*, Nos. 17 and 21). As the word in its original Spanish sense testifies, the salver was formerly used to hold the cup of assay. After the *salva* (lit. 'preservation') had been made, the cup was presented on a flat dish to which the term *salva* was also applied. The Spanish expression *hacer la salva*, 'to drink one's health', conveys the hope of preservation.[16] In English, by analogy with such words as *platter*, *trencher*, etc., we substituted the -er ending in place of -a. It is interesting to see that the connexion between the assay cup and salver is shown as late as 1721, when the

royal inventory records 'One Salver and one Essay cup, gilt, 18 ozs'. Circular salvers were followed by square and octagonal ones, and later still by those of oval shape, but these are outside our period.

The punch-bowl

Apart from new types of vessels created for tea, coffee and chocolate, mention should be made of the punch-bowl and the monteith. Punch had been introduced in England about 1630, and doubtless was made largely in china bowls, and two-handled cups. It was sufficiently well known to appear in such Carolean cookery books as Hannah Woolley's *The Queen-like Closet* of 1670. Owing to the chance introduction about 1680 of a scalloped silver vessel to cool the bowls of glasses in – the passage in Anthony à Wood is almost too well known to quote [17] – the silver punch-bowl made its appearance earlier than otherwise might have been the case. The monteith, as this glass-cooler was called, was soon considered to be an unnecessary luxury, especially as its size was most convenient for serving punch. The scalloped edge was unsatisfactory because the lemon-strainer could not rest comfortably on its edges. The difficulty was overcome by making the rim or collar detachable, but many Livery Companies and Colleges preferred the plain even-rimmed punch-bowl. So far as is at present known, the earliest existing punch-bowls [18] date from 1680 or a little

[16] Thus our word *credence* means nearly the same thing – a *belief* that the food or drink is safe and free from poison.

[17] 'This yeare [1683] in the summer time came up a vessel or bason notched at the brim to let drinking glasses hang there by the foot so that the body or drinking place might hang in the water to cool them. Such a bason was called a 'Monteigh' from a fantastical Scot called 'Monsieur Monteigh', who, at that time or a little before, wore the bottome of his cloake or coate so notched: ∪∪∪∪.' See *Life and Times of Anthony Wood, antiquary, of Oxford, 1632–1695, described by himself*. Ed. Andrew Clark, Oxford, Vol. III, 1894, p. 84. The identity of 'Monsieur Monteigh' remains undiscovered. He may have been an Oxford host or innkeeper.

[18] Owing to an unfortunate mistake, Jackson (*History*, p. 797) speaks of three bowls of 1666 belonging to the Skinners, but they have only two and they are dated 1685. It was the Salters who had three (now only two) and these are *c.* 1716.

Fig. 2. Tea-pot with stand and lamp, London hallmark for 1705–6. Maker's mark Simon Panton. Ht. 5⅞ in. *Victoria and Albert Museum.*

Fig. 3. Gilt tea-pot, about 1685. Maker's mark RH. Ht. 5¾ in. *Victoria and Albert Museum.*

earlier, while several monteiths of 1684 (e.g. Lord Beauchamp and King's College, Cambridge) can be quoted. These are decorated in the *chinoiserie* style and are without handles. In the following year, although the type persists (J.P. Morgan), other examples (Drapers' and Skinners' Company) have a lion's-mask head with round·or shaped swing handles. About 1699 (Mansion House, Hearst Collection, etc.) the collar was decorated with foliage and cherubs' heads, and this type remained popular until their disappearance about 1720.

The tea-pot

Just as punch was first made in already existing vessels until a suitable silver bowl had been evolved, so also the same thing appears to have happened in the case of tea-pots. Although Pepys took his first cup of tea in 1660, we have no idea of the shape of the pot from which it was poured but we can make a pretty good guess. It would have been a tall tin or pewter pot with a high conical lid copied from the slightly earlier coffee-pot of the same type. Even the first silver tea- and coffee-pots are hard to distinguish as those of 1670 and 1681 respectively at the Victoria and Albert Museum prove. The tea-pot is so called only because George Berkeley, the donor, had no suitable example to copy. Consider the date of the gift. The East India Company had shipped its first lot of tea in 1669, and as a new member Berkeley supposedly wished to ingratiate himself by the presentation of a tea-pot, but the small stoneware ones were too small, so he gave them a coffee-pot and called it a tea-pot! But while the shape of the coffee-pot remained much the same, except for the conical lid, the tea-pot developed from the red stoneware tea-pots made at Yi-Hsing near Soochow, sent over from China with the tea, to suit Dutch methods of infusing rather than pouring boiling water on the leaves in a small handleless bowl. The tea-pots were copied by such Delft potters as Arij de Milde and Jacob de Coluwe, and it is from these that the famous and lovely Queen Anne tea-pots were gradually evolved. At first the shapes were largely based on the Chinese wine-pots and water-pots. An example made about

1690 by Benjamin Pyne (Jackson, Fig. 1262) is hexagonal, with a curved spout, domical lid and half-hoop handle. A very similar one by Richard Hoare of also *c.* 1690 can be seen at the Victoria and Albert Museum (M. 48–1939). The pear-like shape of these pots persisted, but somewhat more squat in outline, into the reign of Queen Anne, the age of lovely tea-pots. The body was perfectly plain and either rounded or polygonal, with curving 'duck's neck' spout, domical lid hinged to the upper of the two silver sockets into which the C-shaped wooden handle fitted. Stands with lamps were also made, but are now very rare. The Lipton collection contains a fine example of such a tea-pot and stand, the former by Benjamin Pyne and the latter by Isaac Liger; the date is 1707. Another perfect type of Queen Anne tea-pot is the globular or 'skittle-ball' type. It has a straight, tapering spout, a base rim or low moulded foot, a removable lid and a scroll wooden handle fitting into plain silver sockets. The globular pot on a tall foot seems to have been confined to Scotland. Apart from the well-known one by James Ker of Edinburgh made in solid gold, Jackson (Figs. 1270, 1271) shows one of 1708 also of Edinburgh make, and another of later date with the Glasgow mark. Many globular tea-pots were made in America by such well-known silversmiths as Jacob Hurd, Paul Revere (senior) and Nathaniel Hurd, but in all cases the spout was of 'duck's neck' shape.

Space will not allow us to deal in any detail with coffee- and chocolate-pots, which resembled each other very closely in their earlier forms. They were tall and mostly cylindrical and tapering with a high-domed cover, hexagonal ones being of rarer occurrence. In the case of chocolate-pots the handles were usually set at right angles to the curving spout, and although they are also found in coffee-pots the handles and spout are usually in a straight line. The most unusual type of chocolate-pot, claimed as the earliest recorded, appeared at Sotheby's on 20th June 1935. It was of inverted pear shape on a moulded base, a swan-neck spout, large wooden C-shaped handle in silver sockets and a low, domed lid with cut-card ornament surmounted by a removable terminal for the

insertion of the *molinet* for breaking up and stirring the chocolate. It was made by George Garthorne in 1686.

Lighting appliances

Turning now to lighting appliances – candlesticks and sconces – we find that with the single exception of a two-branch candlestick of silver and rock-crystal (Jackson, Fig. 1105) no examples of either exist prior to Stuart times, and even then they are of great rarity. The destruction of these objects must have been enormous for they occur in quantity in the 1574 inventory of Elizabeth I – both socket and pricket variety – while numerous references are found in wills as well as in many other inventories. We can only guess at the shape of the early Stuart candlestick, but judging by early seventeenth century examples in base metals, apart from later examples in silver, we can conclude that it would consist of a plain, cylindrical barrel with a grease-pan placed low down protecting the hand. The base would probably be either cymbal-shaped or resembling an inverted bowl. In 1663 Charles II sent, among other vessels, a pair of candlesticks of that date to the Czar Alexis.[19] The cylindrical bands, embossed with tulips and foliage, have a projecting convex band some 3 in. from the plain flat nozzles. The broad-spreading foot is embossed with animals and fruit, while midway up the barrel is a wide, flat grease-pan also heavily embossed. The candlesticks are 17 in. in height and have a base diameter of 14⅜ in. Other types of candlesticks found during the reigns of Charles. II, James II and William and Mary include those based on the Doric column, the clustered column and the baluster-stem. The broad bases may be shaped, square or octagonal, either plain or gadrooned. The nozzles are usually fixed, and the grease-pan has disappeared. The thick wick of only semi-combustible material led to the use of snuffers with a scissor-like action and small attached container to receive the candle-wicks. They either rested on a plain rectangular or shaped pan (called a 'slice' by Pepys), or fitted into a vertical

[19] See E. Alfred Jones, *Old English Plate of the Emperor of Russia*, Pl. XXV.

Fig. 4. Sconce, one of a pair. Silver, made by John Rand of Lombard Street. English, London hallmark for 1703–4. *Victoria and Albert Museum.*

receptacle with a handle. Excellent examples of both types (1682 and 1696 respectively) can be seen at the Victoria and Albert Museum (Pl. 52B).

The cast candlestick came in about 1700, and during Queen Anne's reign flourished in all its plain simplicity and beauty. Full advantage was taken of the use of plain faceting by which reflection was shed on the other table silver, imparting to it that soft loveliness and charm that only candlelight can give. Wall sconces, known in Tudor days as 'hanging candle-stickes', 'candele-plates' or 'candelsticke plates' appear in the Elizabethan inventory, already cited, under the general heading of 'Chaundellors'. The candle-holders could be either of the socket or pricket variety, or even interchangeable, while the back-plates were both plain and, later, highly embossed and engraved. They lasted throughout Anne's reign, and the inventory of George I (1721) shows that 195 still existed in the royal palaces. Probably the finest collection of sconces dating from the times of Charles II and James II is that now open to public view at Knole. The term 'branches', found in

inventories, means chandeliers, but in late Georgian days it was used to mean the arms of a sconce. The usual extinguisher was conical in shape, being attached to a rod for sconces and chandeliers, while it was hooked on to hand candlesticks, for which the flat-plated scissor-like douter was also used.

The spoon

And now we come to the consideration of that piece of plate which is at once the oldest and most personal of all – the spoon. As we are concerned only with the forms it took in Stuart times, there will be no need to deal with the early fig-shaped bowl and its contemporary types of knop. At the same time it must be realized that in speaking of the spoon during any particular period we are dealing with two totally different things – spoons still in use from earlier times, and spoons of a type that had not appeared before. Thus spoons used in Jacobean times were very largely Elizabethan, if not earlier, for a silver spoon was a precious thing, and once acquired was treated with the greatest care and affection, to be handed down from father to son, as is proved in wills all over the country. In the ordinary way people used spoons of latten, pewter or brass [20] so a silver spoon – usually the first, and often the only silver object that many a family possessed – was an acquisition of which a man might well be proud, for it bespoke a certain standard of prosperity, if not of affluence. The spoon formed the ideal christening or wedding gift and could be a single one – perhaps surmounted by the finial of an apostle corresponding to the name of the child – or a whole set, if a wealthy family was concerned. The apostle spoon then, apart from its religious significance, had a wide appeal which assured for it a long popularity well into Stuart times. Other forms of finial, such as the diamond-point, the acorn knop, the wrythen knop, the hexagonal knop etc. had disappeared long ago, while for some reason or other slip-tops, seal-tops, baluster-seal tops and lion sejants lasted into the seventeenth century. As to bowl form, the early fig-shape almost imperceptibly merged

[20] See F. G. Hilton Price, *Old Base Metal Spoons*, 1908.

into the less elongated and broader shouldered pear-shape which remained popular well into Jacobean times. The early hexagonal stem gradually gave place to one with wider back and front facets, while, especially in smaller spoons, the stem became thinner. The flattened stem of the seventeenth century appears at its fullest development as the thin, flat Puritan spoon.

Turning to types of spoons that first appeared in Stuart times, we can mention the stump-top of James I, the Puritan and its variants from the latter part of the reign of Charles I to the end of the Commonwealth, and the trifid of the Restoration which was to become the type from which all later spoons developed. The chief distinguishing feature of the stump-top is the long tapering octagonal stem which is rounded at the end like a broom-handle. As with London slip-tops the date-letter is struck near the top of the stem. The bowl is oval, but whereas in examples of about 1630 the greatest breadth is just below the centre of the bowl, in those of about 1660 it has moved nearer the juncture of the stem and bowl, and a more perfect oval is formed.

The well-known Puritan spoon first appeared in England about 1643. It was probably imported from the Continent, where flat spoons had been made at an earlier date than in England. It was pure chance that it happened to reach England at a time when its severe plainness so well suited Puritan taste. After the Restoration this plain stem formed an excellent surface to take a running pattern of scroll foliage, while a short rat-tail, if there was one, could be made very ornate by the addition of engraved acanthus leaves. The bowl of the average Puritan spoon can be described as oval, but in some examples it is nearly round. The flat stem tapers slightly as it reaches the bowl, which it joins with only a very small drop. The top of the stem is sometimes referred to as a 'stump end', but in view of the stump-top spoon, the term is to be avoided. It might be described as having a square-top or straight-top. As can be seen in both French and English examples, the straight-top was often broken by one or two notches, suggestive of the cleft end of the trifid which was soon to follow the Puritan. Although the London Puritan type ended

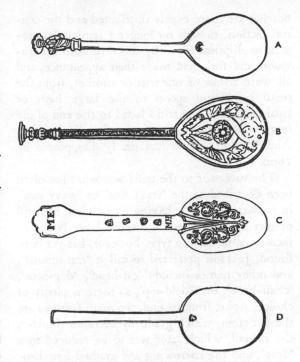

Fig. 5. Four English silver spoons. (A) Apostle type, London hallmark for 1610–11 (?). (B) Seal-top type, Exeter hallmark, seventeenth century. (C) Rat-tail type, Taunton hallmark, second half of seventeenth century. (D) Puritan type, about 1660. *Victoria and Albert Museum.*

about 1670, examples are found in the Provinces for at least another ten years, many of them having decorated stems.

The trifid, or double-notched spoon, appears very soon after the Restoration and shortly replaced all other types. As with the Puritan spoon, the trifid appears to have come from France. Its chief features, apart from the trifid top, are the flat stem often slightly tapering, but sometimes with practically parallel sides, the oval bowl with level edges set just below the level of the stem, and the rat-tail with a ridge in the middle, and a pointed channel either side. In early examples the two clefts or notches are cut very near to the sides of the stem, thus producing a broad central section, semi-circular in outline and usually turned up in the direction of the bowl, while the two lateral sections are very small. In later examples the

371

notches are more evenly distributed and the central section, though no longer a semicircle, projects in elliptical form. By this time both the teaspoon and fork had made their appearance, and all were trifids of one sort or another, from the small condiment spoon to the large hash or basting-spoon. The trifid lasted to the end of the reign of William III and is occasionally found in Anne's reign, but it had nearly disappeared by 1690.

The successor to the trifid was what has often been described as the 'wavy line' or 'wavy end', in consequence of it having no notches, but still preserving the projecting central lobe. No satisfactory name for the type, however, has yet been found. Jackson preferred to call it 'transitional', and other names include 'cat-head', 'dog-nose', 'chair-back', or 'shield-top', so there is plenty of choice. Apart from its end, the main features are the flat stem, which gradually becomes rounder, the rat-tail, which later was to be reduced to a 'drop', and the narrowing and gradual lengthening of the bowl. In some late examples the projecting lobe has been bent right back to form a kind of hook. When this bent-over portion ceased to be free, and became welded to the main part of the spoon, the extra thickness so produced led to the appearance of a central ridge with lateral concavities sloping towards the edges, and the outline of the top is a perfect semicircular curve. To this type of spoon the name 'Hanoverian' has, not altogether happily, been given. Although rare before the time of Queen Anne, the marrow-scoop handle makes its first appearance about 1697. Apart from apostle spoons,[21] which do not really concern us here, among others with human finials appearing in Stuart times are the so-called Maidenhead, popular in the sixteenth century, the rare 'Virgin-and-Holy-Heart' finial, as How calls it, which appears as late as 1606, the 'Moor's head' or 'head-and-neck' finials, and the curious half-length nude female finials found on spoons considered to have been made by John Quyche of

Barnstaple, c. 1590–1630. Their origin is problematical, but they would appear to be derived from German prototypes.[22]

In conclusion mention should be made of a spoon which appears to have been introduced about 1630, or possibly a little earlier, known, owing to its Oriental form, as a Buddha-, Krishna- or Vishnu-knop. They were made, it seems, only in Plymouth and Barnstaple. Whether they are merely a variant of other terminals made as a curiosity by certain enterprising West Country goldsmiths, or whether, as Jackson suggested, they had some connexion with the trade that was carried on between England and the Orient in the sixteenth century, seems to be entirely unknown.

From the spoon it is only natural to pass on to the fork, although hundreds of years separates their first introduction on the English table. We may well ask why it was that so obvious and useful a utensil as a fork never came into general use until the Restoration. The answer, if not altogether satisfactory, seems to be that with meat and poultry cooked until it fell from the bone, and the smaller knife of the *écuyer tranchant* used to steady the joint in cutting, there was no need for the individual fork. It was not, however, a change in cooking that caused its introduction. It was the gradual knowledge and popularity of the fork that not only altered the style of cooking, but also banished the basin and ewer from the table. It has been customary to ascribe the use of forks mentioned in early inventories to the eating of green ginger, pears, mulberries, etc., but when we find no less than seventy-three listed in the 1574 inventory, we can but conclude that many of them, especially those which fitted into canteens, were for use at 'banquets', the course of sweetmeats, fruit and wine which followed the principal meal. Apart from the flat two-pronged fork of 1632 at the Victoria and Albert Museum, the earliest existing set is apparently that of nine three-pronged forks by I.K. (possibly John Keech) with the date-

---

[21] For these we can now consult the *magnum opus* of the late G. E. P. How, *English and Scottish Silver Spoons ...*, 3 vols., 1952—.

[22] See Charles Beard's article in the catalogue of the Ellis spoons, Sotheby's, Nov. 14th, 1935, No. 158–60. Very similar finials occur on a set of knife, fork and spoon in the Zschille catalogue, No. 87.

letter for 1667–68 (Pl. 54B). They belonged to the Earl of Mount Edgcumbe,[23] formerly of Cotehele, Cornwall. The collection also contained a rare three-pronged marrow-scoop fork and a set of six trencher salts by the same goldsmith. The former bears only the maker's mark, but the salts are also 1667. Owing to the fact that nearly every book on silver [24] deals with the New,

or Britannia Standard of silver, which was compulsory from 25th March 1697 to 1st June 1720, and thereafter optional, it has been considered unnecessary to go over the same ground again. So too the history and effect of the Revocation of the Edict of Nantes in 1685, resulting in an influx of skilled Huguenot goldsmiths who were to do so much to raise the standard of English craftsmanship, need no emphasis here.

While many articles in use during late Stuart times have not been discussed – such as all accessories to the serving of tea, mustard and pepper pots, cruets, standishes, furniture, toilet sets, baskets, vases, wine-coolers, fountains, snuffboxes, etc. – they all extend into Georgian times, and concern a later volume of the present series.

[23] They were sold, together with the marrow-scoop fork, the trencher salts and other plate on 24th May, 1956, at Sotheby's. See the illustrated catalogue, Pls. IX–XI.

[24] But see especially Jackson's *English Goldsmiths and their Marks* (Chapters II to VI); and J. P. de Castro, *The Law and Practice of Hall-marking Gold and Silverwares*, 2nd edition, 1935.

Fig. 6. The lid of a snuff-box, *c.* 1685. Maker's mark I.H. between two stars. Width 3¾ in. *Victoria and Albert Museum.*

Fig. 7. A Goldsmith's workshop in the reign of Charles II. From
A new Touch-Stone for Gold and Silver Wares, London, 1679.

Pottery, Porcelain and Glass

R. J. CHARLESTON

Lead-glazed earthenware

Lead-glazed earthenware has had a continuous history in England from at least Anglo-Saxon, and probably from Roman, times. In the seventeenth century, however, it takes on a special character. Whereas in the sixteenth century the potters had had recourse, in much of their best work, to a glaze coloured green with copper and to decoration formed by moulding, in the seventeenth century other forms of ornamentation come to the fore. The first hints of these developments are to be seen in the sixteenth century, when, particularly in some of the northern potteries, a dark-bodied earthenware was decorated by means of pads of white clay cut into designs and applied to the vessel. This technique was taken up and greatly developed during the succeeding century. The earliest large and coherent body of wares decorated by this means, however, is to be credited to one of the southern counties. At Wrotham, in Kent, a brickworks was already at work towards the end of the sixteenth century, and on the site a number of wasters have been found of the hard-fired red pottery with a dark glaze which, if of sixteenth century date, would be called 'Cistercian' ware (cf. *The Tudor Period Guide*). Pottery of this sort was still made in the seventeenth century, however, and the Wrotham wasters are no doubt those of the common everyday pots made for purely utilitarian purposes (cf., however, Pl. 55A). Of far greater interest is the large series of pieces decorated with white 'slip' (clay of a creamy consistency) which can be associated with the Wrotham potters. The

earliest of these usually take the form of a 'tyg' – a mug with slightly outsplayed sides, with three or more handles disposed at equal intervals round the perimeter of the pot (Pl. 55C). Such early pieces (the first dated example is of 1612) are usually sparingly ornamented with pads of white clay bearing simple impressed devices such as rosettes, plant-sprays, fleurs-de-lis, lions rampant and the like: the double-loop handles are frequently decorated with a twist of red-and-white clay let into the upper loop, which is surmounted by a white cottage-loaf finial (Pl. 55C). Towards the middle of the century the decoration becomes more elaborate, with liquid white slip being applied from a spouted can in dots and dashes, or forming simple decorative motifs and inscriptions. The dashes were frequently used in conjunction with the applied pads in such a way that the latter looked as if stitched on to the pot. The red clay used was of two tones – a darker showing deep-brown under the glaze, and a lighter showing up as reddish-brown – while the white slip appeared of a cream or yellowish tint owing to the iron impurities in the glaze. The pots were frequently stamped with initials (Pl. 55A), and these can in many cases be connected with potters known to be working in Wrotham at the time. The dated series continues until at least 1739.

It is evident that the elaborately decorated wares described were not ordinary productions, but must have been made especially for weddings, christenings, betrothals and the like. They often bear, in addition to the potter's initials, those of the intended recipient. In one case the initials are

375

those of the potter and the girl whom he is known to have married. The forms most frequently found, apart from the 'tyg' already described, are globular cups with a single handle of the double-looped form, elaborate four-nozzled candlesticks, jugs, puzzle-jugs and, very rarely, large dishes. These last are remarkable, not only for their rarity and large size, but also because they are decorated in an exceptional technique. The dish was first coated with a layer of 'slip', and the design was then cut through this layer to the red clay below, showing up in red on cream (*sgraffiato* technique).

Far less ambitious and fanciful than the Wrotham wares, but overlapping them in date, is a kind of slipware which is frequently found in the London region and must have been made there. These wares, usually jugs, mugs (Pl. 55B) and cups, are decorated in a rather thin cream-coloured slip on a light red ground. The majority of dated examples fall in the second quarter of the seventeenth century, and this fact and the circumstance that many of them bear pious inscriptions (such as 'Remember God' or 'For Earth I am') suggest that this pottery was made either for Puritans or to conform with the canons of propriety expected in a predominantly Puritan city. The same considerations may have dictated the somewhat impoverished style of decoration which is common to most of them. This consists of little more than one or two feathery stylizations of acanthus leaves, groups of dashes, wavy lines and the like. The absence of later dated pieces has prompted the suggestion that the potteries which made this ware were destroyed in the Fire of London in 1666.

Of much greater consequence were the slipwares made in Staffordshire. Here in due course practically every possible combination of the potentialities of slip-decoration was triumphantly exploited. This whole class of slipwares has sometimes been called 'Toft' ware, from a name which appears frequently on some of the finest examples of this pottery. These are normally large dishes, some 17 to 22 in. in diameter and 3 in. deep, with a flat base and a broad, flat rim (Pl. 56A). Such pieces are normally coated with a layer of white slip (showing up rather yellowish under the lead-

glaze), and the design is then drawn on with a darkish brown slip, any areas required to be of a solid colour being filled in with a slip of a redder tone. The rim was decorated with a trellis pattern of contrasting lines of the two red slips. Finally, the design in the well of the dish was picked out with dots of a white slip, which endow it with a lively sparkle. The motifs most popular on these dishes include loyal portraits of Charles II and Catherine of Braganza, the royal and other arms, and emblems, such as the Pelican in her Piety and the Mermaid combing her hair. Signed Toft pieces are known dated 1671 and 1674, whilst a third piece may have been made before 1680. These great dishes were almost certainly not the routine productions of the potters who made them, but, like the Wrotham wares, commemorated special events in the lives of the people who commissioned them; and they would have stood on dressers for show, rather than have been exposed to risk in use. The same may be said of the large and elaborate many-handled posset-pots (cf. Pl. 56D) of a slightly later date, and of the model cradles, often of a considerable size, which were made to commemorate the birth of a child (Pl. 56C). To this circumstance we no doubt owe the survival of a surprisingly large number of these fine pieces.

To the technical repertory of the potters of the great slipware dishes (Pls. 56A, B), the latter part of the seventeenth century made a number of additions. Notable among these was the use of slip-combing, in which trails of slip, contrasting in colour with the surface of the piece to be decorated, were laid on in parallel lines and then 'combed' into feather patterns by drawing a point across the lines so made (Pl. 55D). Slightly dished oblong trays with patterns produced in this way have continued to be made in country potteries from that day to this.

Another way of handling slip-trailing was to lay on the lines of contrasting slip and then, by jogging the dish, to cause them to run into patterns somewhat resembling those of marbled papers. The Staffordshire (and other) potters also availed themselves of the *sgraffiato* technique already referred to, which also exploits the contrasting colours of dark and light clays. Finally, the second half of the seventeenth century saw the introduction of a method of decoration which was fraught with significance for the future development of the pottery industry in Staffordshire. This was the use of convex moulds of hard-baked clay, into which designs had been incised while it was still soft. Over these were pressed thick sheets of clay, the design being thereby transferred in raised outline. Into the depressions so formed, clay of contrasting colours could be poured to obtain the necessary chromatic effects. This technique was the first portent of the mass-production methods which were, in the eighteenth century, to make the pottery industry one of the leaders in the Industrial Revolution.

Staffordshire, however, although coming in the course of the seventeenth century to a prominence which it never subsequently lost, was only one of many centres in which lead-glazed pottery was made. Dark-glazed pottery had been made in Derbyshire in the previous century, and Tickenhall in particular is credited with a type of ware in which designs were cut out from pads of white clay and applied on a dark ground: less plausible is the attribution to this centre of a number of the types of slipware already here ascribed to Staffordshire. It seems reasonable, however, to credit the Derbyshire potteries with some of the particularly hard pottery with dark, almost metallic, glaze which seems to carry on the Tickenhall characteristics of the sixteenth century in shapes of the seventeenth century, or even later. Somewhat similar pottery, with dark-brown glaze shading off into various tones of purple and green, was made at a variety of centres in our period. In Wiltshire, somewhere in the vicinity of Salisbury, a red-bodied pottery, usually with a dark purplish-brown glaze, was decorated by means of incised or applied inscriptions (Pl. 56D), sprays of foliage, interlaced ornaments and so forth. Somewhat similar wares were made at Buckland, in Buckinghamshire, from 1701 onwards. At Gestingthorpe, in Essex, in the course of the eighteenth century, was made an analogous red-bodied pottery, covered with a yellow glaze flecked with dark brown, and decorated with incised inscriptions and rough sprays of flowers: since there was

a brick-works here in 1693, it is reasonable to infer that pottery of this type was made in our period also.

All the pottery so far described owes its decoration solely to the use of various coloured clays under the yellowish lead-glaze of the period, or to incised ornaments. At other centres, however, advantage was taken of the possibilities of staining the glaze itself by means of copper- or manganese-oxide. At Donyatt, in Somersetshire, were made 'tygs', posset-pots, dishes and other shapes, decorated by scratching through a white slip to the red clay, and by staining the otherwise yellow glaze with a green mottling produced by means of brass or copper filings. Many of these pieces bear dates in the second half of the seventeenth century. To Fareham, in Hampshire, is ascribed a type of posset-pot made of a light-red clay and decorated with simple designs and inscriptions formed from notched strips of light-coloured clay, often stained purple or green with manganese or copper. These mostly bear dates in the opening years of the eighteenth century.

Stoneware

Stoneware is a type of pottery made of a clay sufficiently resistant to withstand firing at very high temperatures – so high that the clay vitrifies. Such a substance is in itself impervious to liquids. To improve its appearance, however, a glaze was often used on it. This was obtained by shovelling into the kiln, at the height of the firing, quantities of common salt. This volatilised, and combined with the constituents of the clay to form a glassy surface-layer on it. Salt-glazed stonewares of this type had been imported into England from Germany in quantity during the sixteenth century, and even in Queen Elizabeth I's reign there appears to have been an attempt to replace this costly import by a home-manufacture. Nothing is known of the fate of this venture. The same tale is repeated in the seventeenth century. In 1626 a patent was granted to Thomas Rous and Abraham Cullen to 'use, exercise, practise, and put in use the arte and feate of frameing, workeing, and makeing of all and all manner of potte, jugge, and bottele, commonly called or knowne by the name or names of stone potte, stone jugge, and stone bottelle. ...' Nothing is known of the stoneware, if any, made by this partnership, and the same is true of another joint patent granted in 1635 to three capitalists seeking to exploit the coal-firing process for, among other things, the 'Makeinge and Dyeinge of all sortes of Panne Tyles, Stone Juggs, Bottles of all sizes ... and other Earthen Comodityes within this our Realme, which nowe are made by Straungers in Forraigne Partes; ...'

The commonest form of stoneware, as these quotations show, was the wine-bottle or -pot, the former most frequently being decorated with a bearded head in applied moulded relief. Such bottles are usually referred to as 'Bellarmines' after the Cardinal of that name who, by his unremitting opposition to the reformed religions, made himself obnoxious to northern Europe. The bottles are supposed to satirize his short stature, his full figure and his hard countenance. That they were referred to by contemporaries as 'Bellarmines' is certain, since in Ben Jonson's play *The Ordinary* occurs the passage:

'Or like a larger jug that some men call A Bellarmine ...'

At a later date, however, as has been pointed out by Mr Martin Holmes,[1] 'the man with the beard' came to be identified with the great Duke of Alva, another anti-Reformation personality well hated in northern Europe. Evelyn the diarist wrote in 1697 of Alva: 'Of whom there are a Thousand Pictures (not on medals only, but on every Jugg-Pot & Tobacco Box) showing a most malicious, stern and merciless aspect, fringed with a prolix and squalid Beard, which draws down his meager and hollow Cheeks, Emblems of his Disposition.' Whoever was represented, the 'jug faced with a beard' was a commonplace of seventeenth-century literature: and the innumerable fragments of such bottles which are excavated in this country bear witness to their almost universal employment. Most of them were probably made in the Rhine-

land, although some may be the unrecognized products of the kilns of Rous and Cullen. When we come to the second half of the seventeenth century, however, we are on safer ground.

In 1671 a patent was granted to a certain John Dwight for 'the Mistery of Transparent Earthenware, Comonly knowne by the Names of Porcelain or China, and Persian Ware, as alsoe the Misterie of the Stone Ware vulgarly called Cologne Ware'. In 1676, and again in 1677, John Dwight entered into contracts with the Company of Glass Sellers to supply them with stonewares. On the site of Dwight's pottery at Fulham were discovered in the nineteenth century a certain number of stoneware bottles which must have been of his making (Pl. 58A). They reveal certain differences from the normal German stonewares, to be seen in the details of the medallions applied to the body of the bottles, and in the technical peculiarity that they do not appear to have been cut from the wheel with a string, and therefore do not show the elliptical string-marks on the base which are a common feature of German stoneware pots. Dwight's fine stonewares, however, were of quite a different order. Dwight himself had been an ecclesiastical lawyer, and was a characteristic man of the late seventeenth century – many-sided, interested in the arts and sciences, and above all of an experimental frame of mind, like a true member of the Royal Society. As the terms of his patent show, he imagined himself to have discovered the secret of making porcelain. It is evident, however, from his recipes, some of which have come down to us in transcripts from his own notebooks, that what he made was a whitish salt-glazed stoneware, often so thinly potted as to be translucent. The drab, mouse-coloured and brown colours at his disposal were skilfully exploited by Dwight to produce a variety of decorative effects. White and mouse-coloured clays were kneaded together to produce a marbled effect; white reliefs were used on a brown ground; and occasionally oxide of cobalt was employed to stain a white clay blue. By these means were produced bottles and mugs of a very high ceramic quality. Far more important, however, were the figures made in the same

[1] Martin Holmes, "The So-Called 'Bellarmine' Mask on Imported Rhenish Stoneware", *Antiquaries' Journal* XXXI (1951), pp. 173 ff.

A Decantor
A Carved Teapot
A Capuchine
A Mogg
A Flower-Pot
A Carved Jug
Such as have Occation for these Sorts of Pots commonly called Stone-Ware, or for such as are of any other Shape not here Represented may be furnished wth them by the Maker James Morley at ye Pot-House i Nottingham

Fig. 1. Copperplate advertisement of the Nottingham stoneware potter, James Morley, about 1700. *The Bodleian Library, Oxford.*

materials. These are usually regarded, and rightly so, as representing a zenith in English pottery. Not only did the material lend itself admirably to modelling, its tightly-fitting glaze in no way obscuring sharpness of detail, but the figures were made by an artist of great skill. It is not known who he was, but it may have been Dwight himself; his fellow-member of the Royal Society, Dr Plot, said of him that he had 'so far advanced the *Art Plastick* that 'tis dubious whether any Man since Prometheus have excelled *him*, not excepting the famous *Damophilus* and *Gorgasus* of *Pliny*.' The Dwight figures include Royal portraits and mythological personages, but the most eloquent of all are undoubtedly the effigies of the potter's own daughter, Lydia, one showing the child recumbent on her death-bed, the other showing her rising in her shroud to meet the Resurrection (Pl. 58B). They reveal a very strong feeling in the artist.

In 1693–94 John Dwight brought actions against a number of other potters for infringing his patent of 1684, which confirmed and extended the patent of 1671. Among those named were

Aaron, Thomas and Richard Wedgwood, of Burslem, in Staffordshire, and James Morley, of Nottingham. Little is known of stoneware-potting in Staffordshire at this date, but it is an interesting fact that in a list of Staffordshire potters working about 1710, drawn up by Josiah Wedgwood considerably later in the century, Dr Thomas Wedgwood is shown as making 'brown stone', whilst others made 'stone' and 'freckled' ware. These literary references are supported both by fragments of stoneware excavated in Staffordshire and by intact pieces of almost certain Staffordshire origin. Of the former class are fragments of mugs decorated with bands of horizontal reeding and applied relief-sprigging of characteristic seventeenth century type: some of them bear the crowned cipher AR, and come from mugs of certified capacity. Although these initials are not always to be taken at their face-value, in this case there is no reason to think that the mugs were not made in the reign of Queen Anne. Furthermore, in the Enoch Wood Collection (assembled in Staffordshire in the early nineteenth century, before the trade in antiquities had properly begun) were three small mugs which are relevant in this context. One is in buff stoneware with a broad brown band round the top: the other two are of virtually identical shape, but of a mottled lead-glazed earthenware. It is reasonable to assume that the first is of the 'dipped white stoneware' referred to by Wedgwood, while the others are of the 'freckled' ware. Either category, but especially the first, might be classed as the 'brown mugs' of Dwight's law-suit.

The case of James Morley is simpler. Stonewares of a lustrous light-brown surface are known with inscriptions which connect them with Nottingham, and with dates commencing in 1700. These pieces, often decorated with incised designs or with ornaments pierced through the outer layer of a double-wall (Pl. 58D), frequently agree in shape and style with those represented in Morley's own trade-card, now preserved in the Bodleian Library, Oxford (Fig. 1).

Of greater ultimate importance than either the Wedgwoods or James Morley, however, were two other potters indicted at the same time in Dwight's suit. These were John and David Elers, then of Fulham, who were accused of infringing the patent as regards 'brown muggs and red theapotts', corresponding to the 'Cologne' wares and the 'Opacous, Redd, and Dark coloured Porcellane or China and Persian Wares ...' of Dwight's patent. These red teapots imitated the stoneware teapots of Yi-hsing, which were at this time being imported into England by the East India Company (see p. 101 below). Probably as a result of Dwight's litigation, the Elers withdrew to Staffordshire, and set up a pottery at Bradwell Wood, near Newcastle-under-Lyme. The scientist Martin Lister wrote in the *Philosophical Transactions* for 1693: 'I have this to add, that this clay, *Haematites*, is as good, if not better than that which is brought from the *East Indies*. Witness the *teapots* now to be sold at the potters in the *Poultry* in *Cheapside*, which not only for art, but for beautiful color too, are far beyond any we have from *China*; these are made from the *English Haematites* in Staffordshire, as I take it, by two Dutchmen, incomparable artists.' The work of the Elers has been reasonably well determined. It consists of unglazed red teapots, globular mugs (Fig. 2), reeded straight-sided mugs, cups and saucers, and tea-bottles (small caddies). Most of these pieces are decorated with sprays of flowers and leaves moulded in relief, but some have figural decorations in relief on recessed panels, the latter being, in one instance, backed with gilding. One or two examples of the Elers' work are known which are decorated with simple enamelling. This is perhaps the first enamelling carried out on European ceramics, and is noteworthy for this reason, if for no other. The Elers were apparently silversmiths by training, and the transference from metal-work to pottery of a technique hitherto exclusive to the former may well have occurred more readily to them than to more ordinary potters. This jewel-like enamelling (Pl. 58c), mainly in white, may well have a continuous history in England from the Elers' time down to the middle of the eighteenth century. A dated example of 1706 shows that it survived the Elers' period of activity in Staffordshire, for they are known to have returned to London by 1700 at the latest. Their importance resides in the fact that by the fineness of their work they set a standard hitherto undreamed of in Staffordshire. It was destined to inspire the potters there during the vital formative period of the industry in the first half of the eighteenth century.

Tin-glazed earthenware ('delftware')

The expression 'delftware' is something of a misnomer in so far as the greater part of the tin-glazed pottery made in England during the seventeenth century is concerned, for the industry was well established in this country long before Delft rose to eminence as a city of potters. In fact, the making of tin-glazed earthenware, as was shown in *The Tudor Period Guide*, was transplanted here from the Spanish Netherlands. They had in turn received it from Italy, the fountain-head of this painted pottery (there called *maiolica*). English 'delftware' potteries are known in the late sixteenth century both in East Anglia and in Aldgate, London. Although some 'delftware' was made in Norwich during the second half of the seventeenth century, however, the emphasis throughout the Stuart period is on London. Here, apart from the Aldgate pottery already mentioned, two factories existed in Southwark in the first half of the seventeenth century – in the parishes of St Olave's and

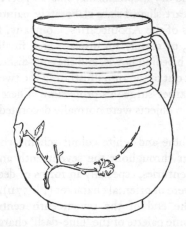

Fig. 2. Unglazed red stoneware mug with relief decoration, mounted with a silver band round the lip. Staffordshire (Bradwell Wood, factory of the brothers Elers), *c.* 1700.

St Saviour's. To the certainly English pottery of the period 1600–60 it is therefore more accurate to give the label 'Southwark' or 'London', rather than the more usual 'Lambeth'; since it was not until the period 1660–80 that one or more potteries making 'gallyware' (as it was called by contemporaries) began operations at Lambeth. The position is complicated by the fact that potters from Southwark migrated about the middle of the century to Brislington, near Bristol, and founded a pottery there: this in turn hived off a factory in Bristol itself (the Temple pottery) in 1683. In evidence given before a Committee of the House of Commons in 1698 it was stated that 'there are 7 White Earthen-warehouses about *London*: Two at *Bristoll*; and One at *Norwich*, which is since broke'. To the potteries of the London area already mentioned should be added at least one, and probably two, at Vauxhall; while at the very end of our period (in 1710) the manufacture of delftware was begun in Liverpool.

Tin-glazed pottery is a lightly-fired earthenware covered with a lead-glaze made an opaque-white by the use of oxide (ashes) of tin. Its virtues reside in the beauty of the dense white glaze itself, and in the possibilities which it opens up of decoration by painting. Painting on ware of this type, however, offers its own special difficulties. The pottery is first fired to a porous 'biscuit' condition, in which state it readily soaks up the glaze mixture (ground glaze suspended in water) into which it is dipped. On this somewhat rough base the painter has to carry out his designs without benefit of rubbings-out or *pentimenti*. These exacting conditions demand of the practitioner sureness of touch, and the chief virtues of delftware-painting are directness and boldness. The pigments used have to be such that they stand up to a considerable degree of heat in the second firing, when glaze and painting are developed together by the fire. The range of these metallic pigments is therefore limited, being restricted in practice to cobalt-oxide for blue, manganese-oxide for purple and brown tones, copper-oxide for green, antimony for yellow and iron for red.

The 'delftwares' made at the beginning of our period were probably mostly in the general style of the contemporary Netherlands wares, with their echoes of Italian *maiolica*, being painted in the blue, purple, green, yellow and orange palette favoured at the time. Very little pottery of any pretension survives from the first two decades of the seventeenth century, however, and it is not until the founding of the Southwark potteries that an individual English style develops. At first it is most apparent in the shapes used. Typical among these is a small barrel-shaped mug (Pl. 60D), and although of these one of the earliest (1628) is decorated with no more than an overall speckling in manganese-purple, while a later example (1642) still displays the polychrome ornamentation of grotesques derived from the *maiolica* of Urbino, a small number of such mugs, of dates about 1630, are decorated in an entirely new way. Between borders of lines or conventional ornament are painted figures of birds standing on rocks amidst flowers and foliage, with an occasional insect flying in the interspaces (Pl. 60D). Both border-patterns and bird motifs are clearly copied from the imported Chinese porcelain of the Wan Li period (1573–1619),[2] but they are painted with a naive charm of their own. One finds similarly decorated straight-sided mugs, spouted covered posset-pots, and wine-bottles of the same general shape as Dwight's stonewares (p. 96 above). As important as the decoration is the Chinese-inspired palette in which it is carried out – soft blue on the (sometimes pinkish) white of the glaze. This cool colour-scheme was extended to the embellishment of a range of wares which owed nothing else to imported porcelain – plates, posset-pots, porringers, candlesticks and wine-bottles decorated with nothing more than a coat-of-arms or a cartouche containing the owner's initials and a date; or, in the case of the wine-bottles, little more than the name of the wine, the date and a calligraphic scroll below them in the manner of the flourished signatures of the period (Pl. 60E). This beautiful pottery was made from the 1630's until the 1680's. The dense white glaze which constitutes its chief charm was occasionally left to speak for itself on pieces entirely undecorated by painting.

[2]See p. 383 below.

The delftwares so far described were all made for use. Contemporaneously, however, the London potters were turning out ambitiously painted dishes which were solely for decoration, to be displayed on the court-cupboards where richer people would range their plate. These pieces preserve the polychrome palette of an earlier period, and, from the circumstance that the great majority of them have a border of slanting blue brush-strokes, are familiarly known as 'blue-dash chargers'. The subjects chosen to decorate the centres of these showy pieces included biblical scenes, fruits and flowers, ships, coats-of-arms and representations of the Kings of England. Four types in particular were constantly repeated, and these form the most characteristic 'Lambeth' and 'Bristol' polychrome delftwares of the second half of the seventeenth century. These four are the chargers painted with the story of the Fall (Pl. 57A), with a spray of tulips and other flowers (Pl. 57B), with representations of the reigning monarch (whether mounted, standing or half-length), or with vigorous formal designs of scrolls and curved strokes.

Apart from the decorative and functional pieces already described, mention should be made of the numerous vessels made for medical use. These consist mainly of spouted jars on pedestal feet, and of cylindrical pots, used to contain respectively liquid and dry medicaments; smaller pots for ointment, heart-shaped slabs elaborately painted with the arms of the Apothecaries' Company, for rolling pills, or merely for display; and, finally, one-handled bleeding bowls, and shaving-dishes with a segment out of the rim, illustrating the two aspects of the barber-surgeon's profession. These mainly utilitarian objects were normally decorated in blue only.

The blue-and-white colour-scheme continued in favour throughout the seventeenth and eighteenth centuries, especially in forms of decoration which were of oriental character (Pl. 57D); but towards the end of the seventeenth century the polychrome palette of the 'blue-dash' chargers was discarded in favour of rather more sober schemes, in which blue, manganese-purple, red and green played a dominant part (Pl. 57C).

Oriental porcelain

Porcelain had reached England in only very small quantities during the sixteenth century, and was accordingly treated with the greatest respect, as its evident superiority to any European pottery warranted. It was normally mounted with gilt metal mounts, both to preserve it and to call attention to its importance – and occasionally to adapt it to European usage. This reverential attitude to Chinese porcelain is evident in the early part of the seventeenth century. In the inventory of Lettice, Countess of Leicester, 'prized the viith day of January, 1634' was 'Item, one pursland boule, with a guilt footte and a guilt cover. xlvs.' (a considerable sum in those days). This may have been a treasured possession from an earlier period, for in the same inventory occurs the more casual entry 'Item, six pursland fruit dishes': but the practice of mounting porcelain still continued at this time, as is shown by Pl. 59c – indeed, many pieces of this type were especially manufactured in China for mounting in Europe, the lid being made separately.

The most usual imports of porcelain during this early period were of bowls, dishes and vases (although smaller items were already being made to suit European taste – in 1638 Lady Brilliana Harley made a present to a friend of 'two cruets of chinna, with silver and gilt covers, and bars and feete ...'). Thus, when some East India commodities were 'put to sale by the candle for readie money' in London in 1618, the porcelain consisted of three 'greate deepe bason(s)'; and when the Dutch wished to make a present to Charles I in 1635, they selected 'two large basins of China earth'. This emphasis tended to shift somewhat with the introduction of the oriental beverages – tea and coffee – into this country. In Holland, the Directors of the Dutch East India Company could write to their factors in Batavia in 1637: 'As tea begins to come into use by some of the people, we expect some jars of Chinese as well as Japanese tea with every ship'; but the earliest printed reference to tea in England seems to be a well-known advertisement in the *Commonwealth Mercury* of September, 1658. Of coffee, Evelyn

wrote in his *Memoirs* for 1637: 'There came in my tyme to the Coll: one Nathaniel Conopios out of Greece. ... He was the first I ever saw drink coffee, whch custom came not into England till 30 years after.' In this Evelyn was ten years or so out, for from about 1652 that drink ('blacke as soote, and tasting not much unlike it', as an earlier writer had said) was to be had of Pasqua Rosee in St Michael's Alley in Cornhill. For exotic drinks, exotic cups were fitting; and from about the middle of the century wares for the tea-table assume a greater importance. In 1637 the Dutch East India Company ordered 25,000 tea-cups from its factors, and from that date tea-wares formed a constant and important item in their porcelain requisitions. This change of emphasis is paralleled in England. At a supper-party given by Lady Gerrard in 1652 there is mention of cups and saucers of porcelain, as well as of plates, all in considerable quantities. The saucer, from being a little plate for sauce, as its name implies, was now to become the inseparable adjunct of the tea-cup. Tea was extremely expensive at this period, costing anything between 25s. and three guineas per pound, and it was in consequence no doubt drunk weak in the Chinese manner, and in small quantities.

Most of the porcelain so far described would have been of the blue-and-white ware made at the great pottery-centre of Ching-tê Chên, in the Kiangsi province of China. For the brewing of tea, however, 'porcelain' of another sort was deemed appropriate. This was the unglazed red stoneware of Yi-hsing, in Kiangsu, which was highly esteemed by the Chinese themselves for the purpose: in Europe it was sometimes, through confusion with a superficially similar Spanish ware, called *boccaro*. Thus, in 1681 a Treasury Warrant issued to the Customs Commissioners to permit the landing of 'some pictures, pourcellin and Boucaros'. The small teapots made from this red ware were usually decorated with sprays of prunus-blossom in relief (Pl. 59D), and it is to such ware that an advertisement in the *London Gazette* of 14th to 18th February 1695, refers: 'At the Marine Coffee House in Birchin-lane Cornhill, on Friday the 1st of March at 3 after Noon will

H

be exposed to Sale by the Candle, fine red figured and flowered Tea Pots, Chocolate Cups, and other Curiosities. ...' The red teapots, chocolate-cups, saucers and tea-bottles were copied by the potters in Holland, and in England by John Dwight and the Elers brothers (see p. 380 above).

The porcelain hitherto described has been mainly of a utilitarian character, however exalted the uses to which it was put. At the same time, however, porcelain vases and bowls were being used for purely decorative purposes, as one may occasionally see them represented in the contemporary Dutch paintings of interiors. Wycherley in his *Plain Dealer* (1674) makes Olivia say of porcelain that it is 'the most innocent and pretty furniture for a lady's chamber'. Hitherto most of the porcelain which had reached England had come via Holland. About this time, however, it began to be imported by the English East India Company, although considerable imports direct from China do not seem to have begun much before 1700. As to the scale of the trade at this date we have not only the records of the East India Company, but the words of a contemporary seaman, a certain Barlow, who was serving as chief mate and China pilot on the *Fleet Frigate*: '... And having all things ready, on Monday the 1st day of February 1702-3, we set sail from a place called "Whampow" in the river of Canton in China, praying God for a good passage to England, being a full ship and laden with goods, namely: 205 chests of China and Japan ware, porcelain ... and a great deal more loose China and Japan earthenware, which was packed up on board ....' The great quantities, often running into tens of thousands of pieces, which suddenly flooded the market as the East Indiamen reached home, caused the prices of porcelain to fluctuate violently. Thus it stands on record that in 1699 'the price of chinaware is fallen 12s. in the pound'. Normally, however, the demand for porcelain was greater than the supply, and in years of war prices might rise to three times the normal. In addition to the inherent high cost of a rare commodity brought from so far away, the English customer had to pay duty on his porcelain at the rate of 33 per cent.

Despite high prices, however, enormous quantities of porcelain were absorbed by Europe during the second half, and particularly the last quarter, of the seventeenth century; and it began to be used purely for decoration in a way hitherto undreamed of. This fashion was given in England the supreme impetus of being taken up by the Queen. Already whilst still in Holland, Queen Mary had contracted a passion for porcelain, and in her country residence of Hunsslardiek, near The Hague, she had an audience chamber which was described in 1687 as 'very richly furnished with Chinese work and pictures ... The chimney-piece was full of precious porcelain, part standing half inside it, and so fitted together that one piece supported another'. This interior must have been the modest counterpart of certain rooms in German palaces, where every available space was filled with great pyramids of porcelain of every shape and size. This conception, on a more modest scale, was carried to England when King William III and his Queen began to rebuild and redecorate Hampton Court in 1689. The traces of this provision for porcelain are still to be seen in the shelf-topped corner fireplaces in many of the rooms, and much of Queen Mary's Chinese and Japanese porcelain is still to be found there (Pls. 59A, B). Defoe wrote in his *Tour thro' the Whole Island of Great Britain* (1724–27): 'The Queen brought in the Custom or Humour, as I may call it, of furnishing Houses with *China*-Ware, which increased to a strange degree afterwards, piling their *China* upon the tops of Cabinets, scrutores, and every Chimney-piece, to the Tops of the Ceilings, and even setting up Shelves for their *China*-ware, where they wanted such Places. ...' This was indeed the China-mania, of which we hear already in Wycherley's *The Country Wife* (first acted 1672 or 1673), when Lady Fidget says: 'What, d'ye think if he had had any left, I would not have had it too? for we women of quality never think we have china enough.'

As has already been said, the vast majority of the pieces brought home from China were blue-and-white, and these display the changing styles of the time, from the Wan-li (1573–1619) plates and dishes, with their birds on rocks, deer and other

(A) JOHN HOSKINS. Unknown
Man (1657).
Royal Collection, Windsor Castle.
Reproduced by gracious permission of
Her Majesty the Queen. ($2\frac{5}{8}'' \times 2\frac{1}{4}''$).

(C) SAMUEL COOPER.
Sir William Palmer (1657).
Victoria and Albert Museum.
($2\frac{1}{4}'' \times 1\frac{3}{4}''$).

(B) SAMUEL COOPER. Unknown Woman.
The Fitzwilliam Museum, Cambridge. ($2\frac{5}{8}'' \times 2\frac{1}{4}''$)

(D) SAMUEL COOPER. Frances, Duchess of
Richmond.
Royal Collection, Windsor Castle. Reproduced by gracious
permission of Her Majesty the Queen. ($4\frac{7}{8}'' \times 3\frac{7}{8}''$).

(E) JOHN GREENHILL. Sir Robert Worsley (1669).
Courtesy Sir Bruce Ingram. (*Pastel* $9\frac{1}{2}'' \times 7\frac{1}{4}''$).

PLATE 33

(B) SIR GODFREY KNELLER. Hugh Hare (1685).
Courtesy the Earl of Radnor. (Canvas 95″ × 60″).

(A) J. B. CLOSTERMAN. Anthony, 3rd Earl of Shaftesbury, and his
brother Maurice (?1702). *Courtesy Lord Shaftesbury. (Canvas 92″ × 56″).*

386   PLATE 34

(B) CARLO MARATTI. Sir Thomas Isham (1677).
Lamport Hall. (Canvas 58" × 47½").

(A) MICHAEL DAHL. Unknown Boy.
Drumlanrig Castle. (Canvas 53" × 39½").

PLATE 35

387

ANTONIO VERRIO. The 'Heaven' Room, Burghley House.
Country Life.

PLATE 36

(A) Louis Laguerre. The State Bedroom. *The Trustees, the Chatsworth Settlement.*

(B) Sir James Thornhill. The Duke of Marlborough in Triumph.
Blenheim Palace. (Canvas 25″ × 30″).

PLATE 37

389

Jan Siberechts. Huntsmen near Longleat (1684).
Musées Royaux des Beaux-Arts, Brussels. (Canvas 86″ × 51″).

PLATE 38

(A) Francis Barlow. Southern-Mouthed Hounds.
British Museum. (Pen and watercolour $5\frac{5}{8}'' \times 8''$).

(B) Gillis van Tilborch. The Tichborne Dole (1670).
Tichborne House. (Canvas $46'' \times 81\frac{1}{2}''$).

PLATE 39

(A) PETER TILLEMANS. John, 2nd Earl of
Ashburnham. *Courtesy the Rev. John Bickersteth.*
(Canvas 51¼″ × 38¾″).

(B) HENDRICK DANCKERTS.
Classical Landscape (167–).
*Royal Collection, Windsor Castle. Reproduced by gracious
permission of Her Majesty the Queen.*
(Canvas 75¼″ × 46½″).

(C) JAN WYCK. The Stag Hunt.
Thomas Agnew and Sons Ltd. (Canvas 42½″ × 67½″).

PLATE 40

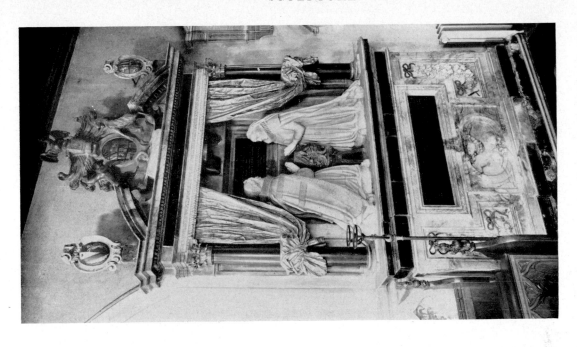

(B) NICHOLAS STONE. Tomb of Thomas, Lord Knyvett, 1623, at Stanwell, Middlesex. More refined in detail and cutting. *Royal Commission on Historical Monuments.*

(A) WILLIAM CURE. Tomb of Sir Roger Aston, died 1612, at Cranford, Middlesex. Southwark work, rich in colour, but coarse in handling. *Royal Commission on Historical Monuments.*

PLATE 41

(A) HUBERT LE SUEUR. William, 3rd Earl of
Pembroke, *c.* 1629, Schools Quadrangle, Oxford.
Continental influence in the use of bronze.
Dr Pamela Tudor-Craig.

(B) JOHN BUSHNELL. Tomb of Lord Mordaunt, died
1675, at Fulham Parish Church, London. A lively
baroque design. *Courtauld Institute of Art.*

PLATE 42

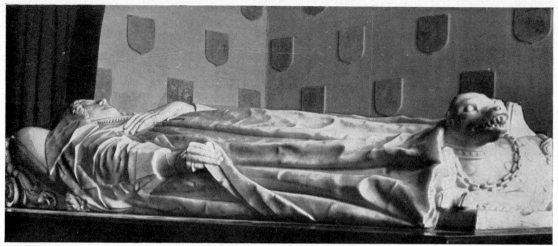

(A) Edward Marshall. Tomb of Elizabeth, Lady Culpeper, died 1638, at Hollingbourne, Kent. A traditional recumbent effigy.   *Dr Margaret Whinney.*

(B) Maximilian Colt. Tomb of Robert Cecil, 1st Earl of Salisbury, 1612, at Hatfield, Herts. A foreign type in black and white marble.   *Photo Precision Ltd.*

PLATE 43

(A) HUBERT LE SUEUR. Charles I, at Stourhead, Wilts. Smooth and empty in modelling.
The National Trust and A. C. Cooper.

(B) JOHN BUSHNELL. Charles II. Terracotta, baroque in design and handling.
Fitzwilliam Museum, Cambridge.

(C) EDWARD PIERCE. Thomas Evans, 1688. Vigorous in pose and modelling. *The Painters' Company.*

PLATE 44

(A) GRINLING GIBBONS. Tomb of Viscount Campden, 1686, at Exton, Rutland. Figures in classical
dress.   *The Rev. H. V. P. Nunn.*

(B) CAIUS GABRIEL CIBBER. The Sackville tomb, 1677, at Withyham, Sussex.
A baroque transformation of a traditional type.   *National Buildings Record.*

PLATE 45   397

(A) GRINLING GIBBONS. Detail of monument to Robert Cotton, 1697, Conington, Cambridge. Beautiful, decorative work. *Edward Leigh.*

(B) JOHN NOST. The Car of Venus, 1700, detail of overmantel in the Cartoon Gallery, Hampton Court Palace. An elegant late baroque design. *The Warburg Institute.*

PLATE 46

(c) The Pickering Loving Cup, silver-gilt, the bowl engraved with a scroll of foliage, daisies, etc. London hall-mark for 1604–5. Height 16¼ in.
Westminster City Council.

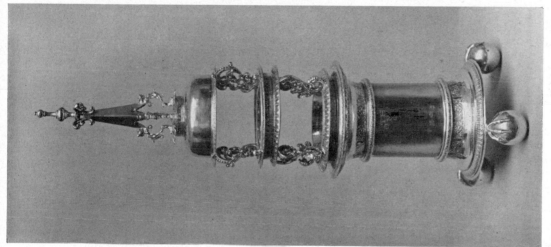

(B) Standing Salt, silver-gilt. London hall-mark for 1614–5. Height 16⅛ in.
Victoria and Albert Museum.

(A) Steeple Cup, silver-gilt, chased and repoussé. Inscribed 'Mr Richard Chester his gift Beinge Mr of the Corporacion in Ano: Dmo: 1615'. Made by F. Terry. London hall-mark for 1626. Height 17.2 in.
Victoria and Albert Museum.

PLATE 47

399

(B) Standing Cup, and Cover, gilt. London hall-mark for 1611–2. Height 18⅝ in. *Victoria and Albert Museum.*

(A) Tankard, silver-gilt, chased and repoussé. Maker's mark R.M. London hall-mark for 1607–8. Height 8.3 in. *Victoria and Albert Museum.*

(B) Beaker, gilt inside. Mark P.S. Dated 1648. Height 5¼ in. *Victoria and Albert Museum.*

(A) Waiter, gilt, with chased ornament after Jean le Pautre (1618–82). Engraved with the arms of Sir William Courtenay of Powderham Castle, Devon. Maker's mark of Benjamin Pyne. London hall-mark for 1698–9. Width 9½ in. *Victoria and Albert Museum.*

PLATE 49

401

(A) Peg-tankard, silver, engraved with flowers and the arms of Sayer. Maker's mark of John Plummer, York hallmark for 1657. Height $7\frac{1}{4}$ in.
Victoria and Albert Museum.

(B) College Cup, Merton College, Oxford. Inscription recording gift by Henry Knapp with date 1657 (date of donor's matriculation). Arms of donor and of College. Known in the College inventories as an 'ox-eye' cup. Maker's mark ET, a crescent below in a shield. 1661. Height 5 in.
Merton College, Oxford.

PLATE 50

(A) Salt cellar, silver, chased and repoussé. London hall-mark for 1664–5. *Victoria and Albert Museum.*

(B) Salver on foot, silver chased and repoussé, the centre engraved with the arms of Rokeby impaling Danby. London hall-mark for 1664–5. Diameter 14.5 in.
Victoria and Albert Museum.

PLATE 51

(B) Candlestick. Maker's mark R.M. monogram. London hall-mark for 1682–3. Height 7 in. *Victoria and Albert Museum.*

(A) Ewer, gilt. Maker's mark of David Willaume. London hall-mark for 1700–1. Height 8⅛ in. *Victoria and Albert Museum.*

PLATE 52

(3) Tankard. Maker's mark of William Ramsey. Newcastle hall-mark *c.* 1670. Height 7 in. *Victoria and Albert Museum.*

(A) Chocolate-pot. Maker's mark of William Fawdery. London hall-mark for 1704–5. Height 10 in. *Victoria and Albert Museum.*

PLATE 53

(A) Cup and cover. Maker's mark I.B. with a stag. London hall-mark for 1683–4
Height 7⅛ in. *Victoria and Albert Museum.*

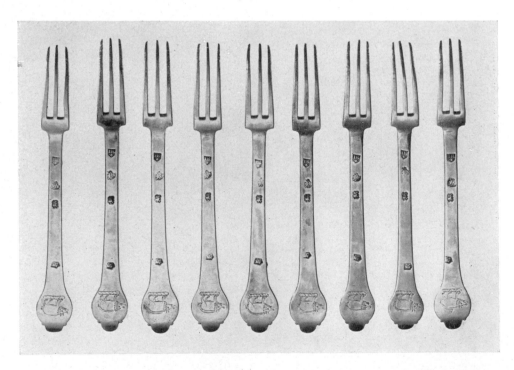

(B) Nine Charles II three-prong trifid forks, engraved at the terminals with a contemporary crest. Maker's mark I.K., rose and two pellets below. 1667.
Formerly in the Mount Edgcumbe Collection.

PLATE 54

(A) Jug of dark lead-glazed earthenware with applied relief decoration. By the potter John Ifield of Wrotham, Kent, dated 1674. Height 12⅜ in. *V. and A. Museum.*

(B) Tankard, lead-glazed earthenware with slip decoration. Probably made in London, mid-seventeenth century. Height 7⅘ in. *London Museum.*

(C) 'Tyg', lead-glazed earthenware with impressed and trailed slip decoration. By the potter John Livermore, of Wrotham, Kent, dated 1649. Height 6¼ in. *Victoria and Albert Museum.*

(D) Mug, lead-glazed earthenware with trailed and combed slip decoration. Staffordshire, dated 1701. Height 4¼ in. *Victoria and Albert Museum.*

PLATE 55

(A) Dish, lead-glazed earthenware with slip decoration. By Thomas Toft, of Staffordshire, about 1675. Diameter 17¼ in. *Victoria and Albert Museum.*

(B) Dish, lead-glazed earthenware with trailed slip decoration. Staffordshire, late seventeenth or early eighteenth century. Diameter 13 in. *Northampton Museum.*

(C) Model of a cradle, lead-glazed earthenware with trailed slip decoration. Staffordshire, dated 1700. Length 16 in. *Fitzwilliam Museum. Cambridge.*

(D) Posset-pot, greenish-brown lead-glazed earthenware. Inscribed 'William and mary Goldsmith'. S. Wilts, dated 1697. Height 8¾ in. *Fitzwilliam Museum, Cambridge.*

(A) **Charger**, polychrome delftware. London, dated 1635. Diameter 19 in. *Victoria and Albert Museum.*

(B) **Charger**, polychrome delftware. Lambeth, about 1680. Diameter 13¾ in. *Victoria and Albert Museum.*

(C) **Bowl**, polychrome delftware. Perhaps Bristol, early eighteenth century. Diameter 12 in. *Victoria and Albert Museum.*

(D) **Posset-pot**, delftware painted in blue. Lambeth, dated 1685. Height 13½ in. *Fitzwilliam Museum, Cambridge.*

PLATE 57

409

(A) Wine-bottle ('Bellarmine'), salt-glazed stoneware with applied moulded relief decoration, about 1680. Found on the site of John Dwight's factory at Fulham. Height 8 in. *Victoria and Albert Museum.*

(B) Figure of Lydia Dwight, salt-glazed stoneware. By John Dwight, Fulham, about 1673–4. Height 11¼ in. *Victoria and Albert Museum.*

(C) Teapot, brown salt-glazed stoneware with enamelled decoration. Staffordshire, about 1700. Height 5½ in. *Victoria and Albert Museum.*

(D) Mug, brown salt-glazed stoneware with incised decoration. Probably by James Morley at Nottingham, about 1700. Height 3⅞ in. *Fitzwilliam Museum, Cambridge.*

PLATE 58

(A) Covered jar, porcelain painted in underglaze blue. Chinese, second quarter of the seventeenth century. Height approx. 13 in. *Hampton Court, by gracious permission of Her Majesty the Queen.*

(B) Covered jar, porcelain painted in polychrome enamels in the 'Kakiemon' style. Japanese (Arita), late seventeenth century. Height 12½ in. *Hampton Court, by gracious permission of Her Majesty the Queen.*

(c) Tankard, porcelain painted in underglaze blue, mounted in a contemporary English silver mount. Chinese, second quarter of seventeenth century. Height 7½ in. *Victoria and Albert Museum.*

(D) Teapot, unglazed red stoneware with moulded decoration. Chinese (Yi-hsing); late seventeenth or early eighteenth century. Height 4⅛ in. *Victoria and Albert Museum.*

(E) Mug, porcelain with enamelled decoration. Chinese (Tê-hua), late seventeenth century. Height 3¾ in. *Victoria and Albert Museum.*

PLATE 59

(A) Wine-glass, English or Venetian for the English market, middle of the seventeenth century. Height 6 in. *Victoria and Albert Museum.*

(B) Wine - glass, English, early eighteenth century. Height 7⅛ in. *Victoria and Albert Museum.*

(C) 'Flute'-glass, engraved with the diamond-point. Arms of England and Scudamore. English, c. 1650. Ht 13½ in. *London Museum.*

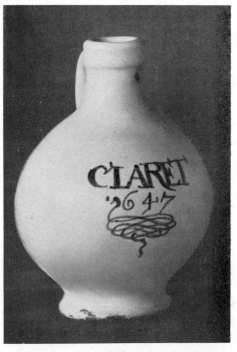

(D) Mug, delftware, painted in blue and inscribed: 'IOHN POTTEN & SVSANNA 1633'. Southwark. Ht. 5⅜ in. *Fitzwilliam Museum, Cambridge.*

(E) Wine-bottle, delftware, inscribed in blue. London, dated 1647. Height 4¾ in. *Victoria and Albert Museum.*

PLATE 60

(A) Posset-pot, glass. English, about 1685. Height 12¼ in. *Courtesy Donald H. Beves, Esq.*

(B) Jug, glass. Probably made at the Savoy glasshouse of George Ravenscroft, about 1680. Height 10⅞ in. *Victoria and Albert Museum.*

(C) Roemer, glass, with applied impressed 'prunts'. London, about 1680–85. Height 7⅞ in. *Victoria and Albert Museum.*

(D) Goblet, glass, the hollow stem enclosing a sixpence of King William III, dated 1690. English, last decade of the seventeenth century. Height 9 in. *Victoria and Albert Museum.*

PLATE 61

(A) Oil-painting by WILLIAM DOBSON, said to show Prince Rupert and Col. Murray persuading Col. Russell to rejoin the Royalists. In the wine-glass a red wine.
Courtesy Lord Sandys.

(B) Detail from still-life in the manner of E. COLLIER, showing a silver tankard bearing the English hall-mark for 1688, a wine-glass, and a black glass bottle. English, late seventeenth century. *Victoria and Albert Museum.*

PLATE 62

A weight-driven alarm clock of brass, signed and dated 'Edward Webbe in Church Stoke, 1676'.
Victoria and Albert Museum.

PLATE 63

(A) Curfew made from latten decorated with heads enclosed in laurel wreaths and floral ornament. 16 in. high, 24 in. wide. Late seventeenth century. *Victoria and Albert Museum.*

(B) Bronze mortars and pestles, *c.* 1625–50. *Science Museum.*

PLATE 64

motives, through the 'Transitional' period (Pl. 59A) consequent upon the breakdown of Ming power, to the classic period of K'ang Hsi (1662–1722), when the power of the Manchu dynasty was stabilized upon the Imperial Throne. Occasional pieces in other modes of decoration, however, reached Europe. Queen Mary possessed late-Ming wares with purple- and green-dappled glazes, and the East India Company records make reference to other types of coloured wares. Japanese porcelain, particularly that from Arita, exported by the Dutch through their trading centre near Nagasaki, was much favoured; and at Hampton Court are some splendid pieces in the Kakiemon style from Queen Mary's collection (Pl. 59B). Side by side with such pieces in decorative *ensembles* might be found figures and vessels in the creamy *blanc-de-chine* porcelain made at Tê-hua, in Fukien (Pl. 59E).

Glass

During the sixteenth, and the greater part of the seventeenth, centuries European glass was dominated by Venice. The fine thin glass-metal (dubbed 'cristallo', from its approximation to natural crystal in appearance), and the extraordinary dexterity of the Venetian workmen, combined to produce glasses of unrivalled elegance and fantasy. An English traveller writing in 1648 about Murano (the glass-making island close to Venice) says: 'Here continually ... are Fornaces to make Glasses, which for the variety of the worke, and the Chrystall substance, exceed all others in the world, and are transported to all parts: out of which merchandise *Venice* drawes infinite summes of money.' Potentates all over Europe tried to set up in their own dominions glass-houses working in the 'façon de Venise', and many were successful, despite the fact that severe penalties were exacted by the Venetian state from any glass-worker who left Murano and revealed its secrets abroad. An account has been given in *The Tudor Period Guide* of the setting-up in England of a glass-house manned by Italians and making glass of the Venetion kind. Glass nevertheless continued to be obtained from Venice sporadically throughout the seventeenth century, sometimes by special licence

(as when, in 1619 and 1635, the import was otherwise specifically forbidden), sometimes through such agencies as were empowered to import it. It does not seem to have been in practice very difficult for anybody with influence in high places to get hold of Venetian glass. Such people would probably be more particularly anxious to obtain the highly-wrought goblets, with fantastic stems and finials, which were the delight of seventeenth century glass-making. No doubt such a glass is referred to in an inventory taken at Marston Hall in 1605: 'It. – one great knotted glasse *wth* a Couer called Charynge Crosse' (cf. Pl. 61A).

Glass-making in England during the first half of the seventeenth century was, like other industries, characterized by the system of monopolies. A somewhat confusing structure of privileges, apparently to some extent overlapping, was cleared away by an edict of 1615 which forbade the use of wood for firing glass-furnaces. The control of the glass industry was thereby effectively put in the hands of a combine which had at its disposal a successful method of coal-firing. This combine included among its members a certain Sir Robert Mansell, an Admiral and erstwhile Treasurer of the Navy. After a tour of naval duty in the Mediterranean in 1620, Mansell successfully set about buying out the other members of the company, and in 1623 obtained from the King a new grant of letters patent to 'use exercise practise sett up and putt in use the arte feate and misterie of melting and makeing of all manner of drinking glasses broade glasses windowe glasses looking glasses and all other kinds of glasses, bugles bottles violls or vessels whatsoever made of glass of any fashion stuff matter or metal whatsoever with sea cole pitt coale or any other fewell whatsoever not being tymber or wood'. This complete control of the glass industry was exercised by Mansell until at least the period of the Civil War, and during the Commonwealth the industry was still sufficiently flourishing to be a fruitful source of revenue. Whether it remained so completely under Mansell's control during this period, however, is uncertain, and Mansell himself died four years before the Restoration of Charles II in 1660.

No glass certainly made in England between

417

the accession of James I and the end of the Commonwealth is known, but there are two sources of information which throw light on the types made. The first is Mansell's own list of his products, supporting a petition to the House of Lords, probably in 1639. From this it appears that he made principally wine-glasses and beer-glasses in three different types of material – 'ordinary' and two sorts of 'cristall', of which one was somewhat more expensive than the other. Apart from these, he made 'mortar-glasses' (probably small bowl-like lamps), looking-glasses and 'Spectacle-Glasse Plates', window-glass and green glass of all sorts. The wine-glasses were no doubt in the main stemmed forms, the beer-glasses being cylindrical beakers on a low pedestal foot, of the type described and illustrated in *The Tudor Period Guide*. We can fill in details from the second source of our information concerning the glass-making of this period – fragments excavated on English sites. These occur in considerable quantities, and often have a character which seems to mark them off from Venetian products of the same period. In the first place, their metal is frequently somewhat inferior, being rather thick and relatively lacking in translucency and lustre (these may represent Mansell's second-quality 'cristall'): in the second, their shapes and decoration often diverge from the Venetian norm. The parts of wine-glasses most frequently found, because most robust, are the stems, and of these (apart from the normal Venetian type of pear-shaped stem moulded with lions' masks and festoons) two patterns occur particularly frequently – those with a ladder-design moulded on a pear-shaped stem, and those which are plain with a profile varying from that of a fairly squat pear to that of a finely tapered 'cigar'. Occasionally a stem occurs which shows the complex treatment of coiled threads or of applied wrought 'wings' familiar in the Netherlandish and Venetian glass-making of the time. This decoration is referred to in the Mansell list as 'of extraordinary fashions'. The English glass-houses of this period were still partly manned by Italian workmen, some of whom are known to have been capable of this work. The rather subdued character of this decoration may have been due either to the sobriety of English taste, or to the modifying effect of English workmen's collaboration in their making. Wine-glasses, and cylindrical beer-glasses, are occasionally decorated by means of applied threads of opaque-white glass. The 'ordinary Drinking-Glasses' of the 1639 list were no doubt of common green or greenish glass of the type made, for example, at the Woodchester glass-house and described in *The Tudor Period Guide*.

After the Restoration there was a return to a modified system of patents and monopolies, in which the Duke of Buckingham played a leading part, if only as a figurehead. For the first ten years of the period, however, imports of glass from Venice were permitted, and of greater significance than the monopolists in the evolution of glass in England were two new factors. The first of these was the rise of the Glass Sellers' Company, incorporated in 1664: the second was a gradual movement in European taste away from the light and fantastic qualities of Venetian glass towards a conception of glass as a surrogate of rock-crystal. The Glass Sellers' Company was a powerful and active organization, and by its position as intermediary between glass-house and customer, was able to influence the design of glass for the English market. Some of its members regularly obtained their supplies from Venice, and the orders of one of them, accompanied by detailed drawings, have fortunately been preserved, enabling us to form an idea of current taste in glass (Fig. 3; cf. Pl. 60A). These orders were sent by the firm of Measey and Greene to the house of Allesio Morelli at Murano, between 1667 and 1673. Minute instructions as to quantities and quality were given, and among these specifications occurs the significant phrase 'verry Bright cleer and whit sound Mettall'. This illustrates the second formative influence referred to above – the striving after a solid and clear glass resembling rock-crystal. In 1660 a Frenchman, John de la Cam, had signed an agreement with the Duke of Buckingham for the making of 'Cristall de roach (cristal de roche) for and during the continuance of the Terme of Tenne yeares'. The agreement did not run its full term, and in 1673 a more important project was set afoot, when a certain George Ravenscroft, who had been en-

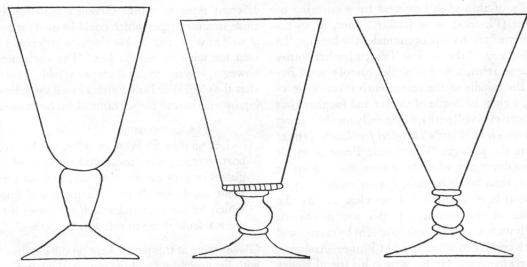

Fig. 3. Drawings for wine-glasses from amongst those
sent by John Greene to accompany his orders for glass
to Allesio Morelli in Venice, *c.* 1670. *British Museum.*

gaged in the Venetian trade, started a glass-house in the Savoy. Within a year Ravenscroft applied for a patent for 'a particular sort of Christalline glass', and in 1674 he signed an agreement to supply glasses to the Glass Sellers' Company. This first type of glass suffered from a defect due to excess of alkali in the composition and known as 'crizzling' – a proliferation of tiny gleaming hair-lines in the body of the glass, often accompanied by a roughening of the surface. Ravenscroft, how-ever, continued his experiments, probably under the ægis of the Glass Sellers' Company, and finally evolved a revolutionary new type of glass contain-ing oxide of lead. This happened in about 1675, and the new metal was signalized by the use on vessels made from it of a seal impressed with a raven's head (from the Ravenscroft crest). At least seventeen such sealed vessels or frag-ments are known, and include bowls, bottles, jugs (cf. Pl. 61B), globular mugs, posset-pots, and wine-glasses of two forms.

The use of lead-oxide in glass spread through-out the 'white' glass-houses in the country before the end of the seventeenth century, and the ratio of lead was continuously increased until, by about

1700, the metal took on a dark and 'oily' brilli-ance. In Ravenscroft's glasses, and more markedly in the great covered goblets and posset-pots (Pl. 61A) of some ten years later, the traces of Italian workmanship are clearly to be seen, albeit modi-fied to an anglicized idiom. Towards the close of the century, however, and particularly in wine-glasses, there emerged a style which was wholly English. This concentrated on the stem of the drinking-glass, in which it worked innumerable variations by different combinations of balusters and bulbs and flat discs. In all these a just propor-tion is observed between the bowl, the stem and the foot of a glass, and the sobriety and harmony of this style accord well with the taste of the 'Queen Anne' epoch (Pls. 60B, 61D, 62B).

Apart from the 'white' glass made for the table, green glass was made at a number of glass-houses up and down the country. Windows and wine-bottles formed the main produce of these houses, but small globular and cylindrical bottles for apothecaries, and scientific and medical glasses of many sorts were also made. The typical wine-bottle of the late sixteenth and early seventeenth centuries had a flattened spherical form, and was usually of thin glass protected by a covering of wicker (Pl. 62A) or of leather. Thus, in an inventory of 1610 there occur under the heading 'In the Buttery ...' the entries: 'Item, 4 leather bottles of glasse. Item, 2 wicker bottles, one of glasse'. Before the middle of the seventeenth century, however, a globular bottle of thicker and tougher glass had been evolved, perhaps originally for the storing of beer. In H. Platt's *Delightes for Ladies* (1644) occurs the passage: 'When your Beere is ten or twelve dayes old, whereby it is growne reasonable cleere, then bottle it, making your corkes very fit for your bottles, and stop them close ...' By the middle of the century, bottles are mentioned which were tough enough to be sent by carrier and which contained wine: in 1651 Phineas Andrews, in Berkhamsted, Herts., sent to his friend Henry Oxenden, in Kent, 'two doussen glasse bottles of the best Canary Dick Weeden hath'. The earliest dated bottle bears a seal stamped 1657, and from now on we are able to follow accurately from dated and datable seals the evolution of the bottle shape (cf. Pl. 62B), right up to the appearance of the modern wine-bottle. Cork-screws are not known before 1686, and the binning of wine cannot have been practised much before this date. Mineral waters, however, were already being bottled, and Celia Fiennes in her *Journal* says of Tunbridge Wells (1697): '... they have the bottles filled and corked in the well under the water and so seale down the corke which they say preserves it ...'

In the seventeenth century there was little distinction between the shapes of glasses used for different types of drink. Greene's drawings include stemmed types which could be used for beer as well as wine, and beaker shapes which could be used for wine as well as beer. The distinction, however, was rigorously observed at table. Shortly after the Civil War Lord Fairfax issued the following instructions to the servants of his household:

'The Cup-board.

Let no man fill beere or wine, but the cup-board-keeper, who must make choice of his glasses or cups for the company, and not serve them hand over heade. He must also know which be for beer and which for wine; for it were a foule thing to mix them together.'

Glasses were at this period kept on the cup-board, both for decoration and for use; in the latter case they were handed to the diners as called for, the glass being held by the foot (cf. Pl. 62A), and not by the bowl or stem. One exception to the indiscriminate use of glasses for different drinks seems to have been provided by the 'romer' (German 'Roemer'), a glass with a globular bowl, a wide, hollow stem decorated with applied patterned blobs of glass, and a conical foot. This glass, which was made in England (compare Pl. 61C), was reserved for Rhenish wine; it is always seen in the Dutch still-life pictures of the seventeenth century. It is possible also that the tall tapering 'flute' glass (Pl. 60C, cf. Pl. 62A) was used mainly, if not exclusively, for Spanish wines. Thus Richard Lovelace, writing in 1649, speaks of 'Elles of Beare, Flutes of Canary'.

Edward Cocker's signature in a *trait* from *Penna Volans*, 1661.

Domestic Metalwork

G. BERNARD HUGHES

The Stuart home differed little from the late Elizabethan in its domestic metalwork until followers of Charles II introduced a new elegance during the 1660's. Technical accomplishments were for the most part held in leash by powerful politicians possessing the sole right to manufacture and sell articles of commerce. The result was that prices were kept at artificially high levels until the early 1690's, domestic accessories and utensils being made from metals differing little in quality from that available to late Elizabethans. Brassworkers, for instance, were compelled to import plates of Flanders latten because English-made plates were of poor colour, lacked brilliance, were variable in texture and contained numerous air-bubbles which showed as surface flaws on finished work. They were liable to split, too, during manipulation.

Clocks continued down to about 1660 to be poor timekeepers needing frequent repair (Pl. 63). Records show that a simple weight-operated clock in gilded copper cost £10 – equal to about £150 in present-day values. Two such clocks included in the Earl of Northampton's inventory taken after his death in 1614 were each entered as a 'chamber watch with an Alarum', the second being further described as of 'copper and guilte in a case'. Its second-hand value was £4. The Earl also possessed a watch, inventoried as 'a clocke of golde and crystall sett with rubies and diamonds, £45'. This was accompanied by a small jewelled hour-glass to check its time-keeping, additionally valued at £13.

Sir William Ingilby of Ripley, Yorkshire, paid £10 for a striking clock in 1616, and in 1629 the household accounts of Lord William Howard, Naworth Castle, record the purchase of 'a clocke for My Lord, bought of Mr Jo. Charleton'. Shortly afterwards 'a waynescott frame for my Lord's new clock' was bought for 1s. 6d. and a 'glasse for the clock case' 2s. 6d. Subsequently Rauphe Smith, clocksmith and sun-dial maker, was called upon to mend the clock, charging 6s. 8d. for three days' work and travelling expenses. Entries of 'one dosen yeards of lyne for clock stringes for my Lord, ij vj' were frequent.

The pendulum as a clock regulator was invented by Galileo in 1641, but overlooked by clockmakers until 1656. Pendulum clocks provided a greatly improved standard of timekeeping and were first made in England by Fromanteel of London during 1658. Soon both clock and pendulum were enclosed within a tall wooden case, thus forming the long-case or 'grandfather' clock.

Little change was made in domestic door-locks during the first half of the Stuart period apart from minor improvements in the mechanism. Cases of Flanders latten were made, except between 1660 and 1675, when its importation was prohibited and English plate was used. Such locks displayed a flawed surface and a dull lustre.

Rim-locks now began to be made in suites, often with a different key for each lock and a master key capable of opening the entire series, no matter how extensive. Such a suite of locks was fitted to the doors of Marlborough House when it was built, and they still operate perfectly. From the 1680's high relief decoration was cast in

A to E   Keyhole escutcheons of bloom iron hammered into plate with filed outlines and sawn piercing.

F   Strap hinge in wrought iron, common in the seventeenth century.

G, H   Casement latches of wrought iron such as were made by seventeenth century iron workers.

I   Brass candlestick with adjustable slide, third quarter of the seventeenth century.

J   Double cock's head H-hinge.

K   Door latch in wrought iron.

L   Adjustable candleholder in wrought iron, thirty inches long when open.

Typical of mid-seventeenth century ironwork

All in Victoria and Albert Museum

'prince's metal', a brass alloy resembling gold, invented by Prince Rupert. This ornamental plate was riveted to the lock face, extending across the latch end: often a coat of arms was used here. By 1700 the top plates were cast throughout in 'prince's metal' with all-over decoration in relief, chased and engraved. Delicate filigree work was associated with beautiful reticulated lace-like perforations laid over plates of blued steel. Locks were now sold with matching hinges, catchplates and key escutcheons. The corners of the brass cover and the keyhole surround were enriched with applied steel ornament cut in delicate designs.

Interior door-hinges were now usually of the H-type, the ends of their long, narrow plates following the arching outlines of the period. In later hinges the plates were curved and terminated in matching 'cock's head' outlines such as a crowing cock with the beak open or closed, the comb exaggerated or omitted, and the breast full or almost flat. Others might display serpents' or griffins' heads.

Illumination was considerably increased in rich households by including a reflecting sphere in chandelier design, and by using candles of wax and tallow clarified by an improved method. Fine chandeliers of latten followed Flemish patterns, several socketed arms extending from a boldly-shaped baluster stem, terminating beneath in a large burnished reflecting sphere of Flanders latten. Following the introduction of finer English latten at the end of the seventeenth century the branches might be brazed directly to the reflecting sphere, gadrooned ornament also being incorporated as an additional aid to reflection.

Such a chandelier was usually suspended by a chain: more rarely it hung from a suspension rod of wrought iron centred from a large ceiling rose and lavishly ornamented with flowers, leaves and scrollwork, enriched with gilding and colourful paints. Chandeliers less costly than either were produced by village blacksmiths in simple patterns such as several socketed branches curving outward from a plain central stem.

Brass candlesticks until the 1690's were made by late Tudor methods, English brass being used almost exclusively. Improvement in the quality of bought candles brought about a reduction in the size of the drip-pan, which now became separated from the foot. This was at first set high above a trumpet-shaped foot, a style revived from early Tudor days. The stem might be plain or horizontally corrugated and might have a cushion knop. This style had been abandoned by the mid-seventeenth century in favour of a cylindrical stem rising from a low, wide, slightly concave circular foot. The neck-ring which had encircled the stem immediately below the socket had become emphasized into a bold knop by the 1600's. The brass candlestick foot of the late seventeenth century was usually domed, supporting a baluster-and-knop stem. By 1690 the drip-pan had been abandoned in favour of a socket rim expanded into a saucer-shaped nozzle. The oblong aperture in the socket gave way early in the seventeenth century to a small circular hole, and by the end of the Stuart period no aperture was considered necessary.

Improvements in brass-casting techniques during the 1690's facilitated production. Lead was added to candlestick metal making it softer and smoother, more pliable, rather yellow. The introduction of greater furnace heat at this time drastically reduced the number of tiny gas-bubbles in its texture. Stem and socket could now be cast in separate halves and brazed together, leaving the centre hollow.

So far brass candlestick design had been little affected by the silversmiths, but in the 1690's for the first time brass founders copied characteristic forms in Carolean silver. Circular feet might be highly domed or deeply concave, thus providing greater reflecting surface, the central rise supporting a baluster stem in which the knops might be gadrooned.

The Tudor candle-snuffer with its airy double-pan was superseded in the early years of the 1600's by a new type with a single open-sided semicircular box attached vertically to the underblade. To the upper blade was fixed a flat press-plate fitting into the box. When the snuff was cut from the wick the plate forced it against the inner wall of the box, where it was at once extinguished.

These snuffers were lavishly ornamented until the late 1640's. Stems were then connected to the bows with S-shaped scrolls, and a smaller box was fitted, now rectangular with incurved corners. A fine quality example would pair with a rectangular dish upon which the snuffers lay when not in use.

Midway in Charles II's reign there began a vogue for snuffer trays following the silhouette of the snuffers themselves. This was followed by the upright snuffer stand with a vertical socket to receive the snuffer box, and standing on a short baluster stem, and was in silver, succeeded by brass and fine steel. Attached was a narrow vertical loop to receive the hook of a cone-shaped extinguisher. Such stands continued fashionable until early Georgian years.

Whale oil was less costly to burn than candles and most houses supplied this odorous illuminant in servants' and working quarters. When Charles Butler was describing the duties of a maid in 1609 he included making wicks and preparing for use the open-flame oil lamps known as 'sluts'. This lamp consisted of a flat-based circular oil-container hammered from latten or iron and fitted with a small handle or suspension rod. From this evolved the better-known crusie during the early Stuart years. The open-bowl crusie was oval and pointed at one end to support the wick. Fumes were minimized by hanging a water-soaked sponge above the burning flame. This was succeeded late in the seventeenth century by the double crusie, designed to collect the drips that fell from its wick.

From about 1700 a tubular wick holder was fitted into the wick channel, guiding excess oil back to the reservoir and making it possible to dispense with the drip-pan. Oil reservoirs were then enlarged and some lamps furnished with two wicks.

Rushlights, surprisingly, date no earlier than early Stuart days. These inexpensive tallow-covered illuminants, measuring about one-quarter inch in diameter, should not be confused with standard sized candles burning rushes as wicks which caused a writer in *British Apollo*, 1708, to express wonder that 'a Rush Candle should burn longer than a cotton one'.

Because the rushlight was too slender to stand in a socket unsupported, it was held in a pair of iron nippers kept tightly closed by either a weighted lever or a spring. These were spiked and driven into a heavy block of oak which formed a foot. Table rushlight holders from about 1700 might consist of wrought iron throughout, rising from a plain tripod, the tops of the spreading legs being bent to form flat feet.

In the private apartments of houses in districts where mineral coal could be won from outcrops or shallow shafts, coal-burning grates might stand in the wall down hearths. As early as 1580 the household inventory of Daniel Hochstetter, Keswick, included '2 cradles for seacoal fire', the coal costing eightpence a horse load. Coal-burning increased as supplies of wood lessened during the seventeenth century. A four-barred rectangular iron basket grate might stand on four legs or the back might be left barless and the grate placed closely against the fireback.

The Howard household accounts for 1612 first record the acquisition of 'an iron grate xiiijs' at a time when iron cost 2s. 4d. a stone. The inventory of Sir William Ingilby's domestic possessions at his house in the coal-bearing region of Dighton, Yorkshire, shows that the more important rooms such as Sir William's chamber, the dining and outer parlours, hall and kitchen were fitted with coal-burning iron grates. Relegated to the loft were 'four payre of andyrons'. The fireplace ironwork in the dining parlour consisted of 'one range, fire shovel and tonges, and a fire porr [poker] and two skrenes, one greate one and a little one, a toasting iron and a payre of snufferes xlll[s]lV[d]'. In the yard lay sea coal worth £12 and charcoal valued at £1 6s. 8d.

Firebacks under the name of iron chimneys continued to be made in large numbers throughout the Stuart era, many a specimen displaying a coat of arms surrounded by scrolls and floral motifs, the whole composition enclosed within a moulded rim (Pl. 65B). Commonwealth firebacks were designed with restraint: this was the period of the 'family' fireback when a border of severely plain moulding enclosed the owner's name, the date and various crosses.

The 1660's saw the introduction of firebacks enriched with pictorial design, the Bible, mythology and current history being the chief sources. In newly built houses there was a tendency for fireplaces to be built much narrower than formerly, with the result that fashionable firebacks became taller and narrower with elaborate crests extending upward from their arched tops. Towards the end of the century hearths became perceptibly smaller. Firebacks to fit could be cast thinner than formerly, but the relief work was necessarily lower than in their massive predecessors. Ornament was more graceful and intricate, and bordered with flowering scrolls of foliage and festoons of fruit.

Andirons (Pl. 68), firedogs and creepers followed Elizabethan styles until the 1640's. Figures and demi-figures, often nude, were popular, favourites being cupids with arms lifted high and supporting ornamental finials such as shields of arms. Each foot of the semi-circular arch might be scrolled. During the Commonwealth the earlier ornament was usually lacking, and the arched base became a plain semi-circle with standards relieved only by shields displaying coats of arms or other personal motifs.

London-made bronze andirons 'garnished with silver' became fashionable during the reign of Charles I. The Restoration brought even greater lavishness, sterling silver being used by all who could afford it.

With the flat iron bars available from the 1660's blacksmiths produced symmetrically scrolled and curved work, much lighter in weight than castings and so designed that little welding was necessary. Elaborate cast andirons were made in bronze and brass and cast-iron standards might be faced with fretted and perforated brass or copper sunk into a narrow frame of steel. These might be enriched with finely fretted convex roundels in latten. The steel and brasswork were highly burnished (Pl. 68D).

Andirons of William III's reign naturally reflected Dutch influence (Pl. 68c). Slender, tapering standards of brass or steel rose from heavy iron bases, with elaborate urn- or flame-shaped finials, or with simple acorns or balls which might be flattened or gadrooned. The triangular base, box-like with gadrooned walls, became fashionable, hand-made from latten plate and supported by two scrolled wrought steel feet at the front and a billet bar behind. The standards were composed of three vase-like units, each differing in form, one above the other, all of cast and turned brass, gadrooned and hand-finished.

As fireplaces decreased in size, andirons and firedogs were gradually abandoned in favour of larger creepers, or adapted to support the barred fire-basket. A hole was drilled into each return bar, fitted with an iron peg, thus securely fixing the grate. Creepers were brought to the front of the hearth and used as supports for fire irons.

In some rooms the only metalwork was the fireside equipment, most of it in wrought iron and consisting of fire-shovel, tongs, poker and, for wood fires, a fire fork. The Howard household accounts suggest that these were bought singly and not in matching sets. The shovel, as shown in two woodcuts illustrating the *Roxburgh Ballads* consisted of a round-headed pan, longer than wide, welded to a straight stem terminating in a round eye. The tongs were straight-armed, their ends hammered into flat discs, or, when intended for wood, welded to four-pronged claws. At the top each arm was shaped into a semi-circle, both hinging with a spring into a short tapering square handle with a ball finial.

The down hearth was still protected at night by a fire-pan or curfew measuring about 2 ft. in width and costing 1s. 10d. to 2s., in hammered iron and as much as 30s. in Flemish latten chased with a complicated all-over design (Pl. 64A). The grate fire was protected with a wire screen consisting of a wrought-iron frame of the eighteenth century cheval-screen type, filled with the closely woven wire mesh then recently introduced following the speedy production of wire by means of drawplates.

Typical of the metalwork to be found in the kitchen of an early Stuart home was that belonging to William Middleton of Stokeld, Yorkshire:

'Kitchin irne – two payr of yrn racks, 1 galibake [a bar or beam in a chimney from which pot hooks hang], 5 crookes, 3 pothucks, xxxiij^s iv^d; 12 broches [spits] xx^s; 5 dripping pans, xv^s; 2 gridiarns, iij^s; 3 laddles, 2 yrne forks, 5 chopping knyves, 1 frying pan, 1 skimar, vij^s vj^d; total iiij^{Li}xviij^s x^d. Brasse – 60 uld pots, xxxvj^{s}viij^d; 3 other pottes, 1 posnett, iv^{Li}; 2 brazen mortars, 2 pestells, xiij^{s}iv^d; 2 kettels, 7 pannes, 1 yrn band, 1 coper caldren, 1 chofing dysh, xxxxvj^s; total, viij^{Li}xvj^s. Pewter – in waight, 8 ston and a halfe, iv^{Li}iij^s.'

In cottage homes of the seventeenth and eighteenth centuries simple baking and cooking on a down hearth was carried out by means of a baking-iron or dough grate. This resembled a two-legged trivet with a lengthy handle which might extend horizontally or be bent into a high semi-circular arch. The trivet was pushed into a blazing fire, and upon it was placed either a small portable iron oven or a covered iron cooking-pot to be used as an oven. A portable oven cost about 6s. in the early Stuart period (see also Pl. 68A).

Wafer irons, although used in the previous century, were far more common during the Stuart and early Georgian periods. They cost about 8s. in the mid-seventeenth century and were substantial tongs with each arm ending in a large circular disc which might be ornamented with a complicated intaglio pattern. They were used with wood or charcoal fires; ordinary coal was found to taint the wafers which were made from a thick spiced batter. This was poured on one of the heated discs and the other closed down over it. When baked the wafer was rolled off the iron around a stick, and when cold was very crisp.

Warming-pans hung in every well-found household during the Stuart period (Pl. 69A). They were less weighty than formerly with thin, tapering iron handles measuring from 27 to 30 inches in length and terminating in loop finials for hanging on the wall when not in use. From about 1625 the handle might be in turned brass with a loose shackle on the finial for hanging. The stem was decorated at both ends and in the centre with turned baluster-and-knop ornament.

During the second half of the seventeenth century handles of brass continued, but considerable numbers consisted of two 15-in. lengths of square or round iron fitted into three brass mountings of baluster and knop formation. From the 1660's handles might be of oak or other hard wood carved with flutes and terminating in large knops. These received polished finish only.

Straight, almost vertical, sides were standard for the ember pan in the brass warming-pan until about 1720. This measured about $3\frac{1}{2}$ in. deep and $8\frac{1}{2}$ in. in diameter with the addition of a flat, 1-in. rim. In later examples the outer edge of this rim might be bent downwards to conceal the iron ring into which the pan was fitted. Thin Flanders latten of fine colour was used for the lid, which measured about a foot in diameter and swung loosely over the ember pan. Lids were highly convex in late Stuart examples.

Warming-pan lids received ornament in the form of punched decoration and low relief work. The design might be encircled with one or two rings of closely spaced holes of $\frac{1}{8}$-in. or $\frac{1}{16}$-in. diameter. In Charles II's reign fine warming-pans were elaborately pierced with fret-cut designs, but the majority were now smoothly plain.

On New Year's Day 1663 Samuel Pepys, invited to the Lord Mayor's banquet, wrote in his diary that only the tables reserved for the principal guests were furnished with knives. Although the food and wine were good and plentiful Pepys complained: 'we had no napkins nor change of trenchers, and drunk out of earthern pitchers.' Trenchers at this time were often of hard battery copper and tinned, thus providing greater resemblance to silver than pewter, and also more resistance to knife-marks.

Otherwise pewter domestic ware resembled that of the late Tudor period with occasional slight differences of form. Plates, for instance, were given a deeper bouge with a less abrupt fall. The wide horizontal beaded rim was encircled with two closely-spaced chased lines, the space between them being slightly concave. From 1660 to the 1690's the rim, now given a slight rise, might be half as wide as formerly, its edge strengthened with oval beading. These beadings prevented careless servants from bending the brims when scouring the plates. A third type, which continued until the end of the period and beyond, had a wide horizontal rim bordered with triple reeding and a beaded edge oval in section, or simple moulding twice as broad as the reeding and a beaded edge of circular section.

Among the new additions to pewter table-ware were dish rings, inventoried at Northwick House in 1705, mazarines and flagons. Mazarines were for serving ragouts – then diced meats stewed with vegetables and highly seasoned. Andrew Marvell in 1673 writes, 'What Ragousts had you to furnish the Mazarines on your table?' Kersey's *Dictionary*, 1706, defined mazarine as 'a kind of little Dishes to be set in the middle of a large Dish for the setting out of Ragoo or Fricassies'.

Another newcomer to the ranks of Stuart domestic metalware was the cistern containing iced water for cooling wines immediately before drinking. These cisterns were in hand-beaten Flanders latten, copper or pewter, and from the 1660's in silver. The Howard household accounts for 1629 show that £2 3s. 4d. was paid for 'a little copper sesterne to sett flaggons in, in the greate chamber, weighinge 30 poundes and a halfe; one pewter Sesterne, weighing 35 poundes and 3 quarters at 15d a pound; and 2 pewter flaggons weighing 25 poundes and a half at 14d a pound'.

The wine was taken directly from the cask into the flagons, which, contrary to popular conception, were for serving rather than for drinking from. These pairs of 'greate flaggons', tall, weightily massive vessels of thick metal, with slightly conical straight-sided bodies, and hinged lids, stood in a cistern of iced water. In 1667 Pepys commented, 'I see the price of a copper cistern for the table, which is very pretty, and they demand £6 or £7 for one.' This records the introduction of the table wine-cooler made to contain a single bottle of wine.[1]

[1] There is a painting in the National Gallery, Dublin, showing such a single-bottle wine-cooler in silver: this still exists, the writer believes, and was made for Lord Santry in 1700 by Anthony Nelme of London. The writer has also seen two other contemporary illustrations.

The wine-cistern, however, still continued in use, its iced water now receiving bottles of wine instead of a pair of flagons. Wine might now be served from a wine fountain of silver, or tin-lined latten or copper, and containing an ice-chamber. This vase-shaped vessel might hold two gallons of wine drawn off by means of a tap.

Throughout the Stuart era Sheffield was a source of inexpensive hard-wearing blades. A dozen could be bought retail for as little as 8d. Special purpose knives are noted in household accounts, such as oyster knives at sixpence; mincing knives 1s. 10d.; voider knives 1s.; 'a pair of knives' such as were carried by women 1s. 3d. (see also Pl. 67).

Spoons beaten from latten or cast from brass were tinned and burnished so that at a casual glance they would be mistaken for silver. When cast terminals were brazed on the ends, these were gilded. The majority of Stuart spoon stems in pewter, tin or tinned brass made before the 1660's were of the type known as 'slipped-in-the-stalk', the end of the stem being finished with a slanting cut from the front of the spoon. Then came the trifid-end spoon, its finial hammered into a semi-circle which was cut vertically with two deep notches near the sides, dividing the terminals into three sections. From the mid-1670's both sides of the terminal were covered with low-relief scroll decoration. By the 1690's the spoon end was expanded into a series of small arcs, the central larger arc having an upward curve; this was known as the cat-head stem.

SHORT BIBLIOGRAPHY

Decorative Ironwork, by Charles Ffoulkes, 1913.
Iron and Brass Implements of the English House, by J. Seymour Lindsay, 1927.
English Ironwork of the XVIIth and XVIIIth Centuries, by J.Starkie Gardner, 1912.
History of the Ironmongers' Company, by J.Nicholls, 1886.
Metalwork, by M.Digby Wyatt, 1852.
English Metalwork, by W.Twopenny, 1904.

The engraved backplate of a clock, by Joseph Knibb, *c.* 1675. Described and illustrated in *Furniture Making in Seventeenth and Eighteenth Century England* by R.W.Symonds (1955).

Textiles

DONALD KING

The textures, colours and patterns of textiles are always an essential part of the picture which man makes of himself by his dress, and of the environment which he creates around him by his furnishings. Unquestionably this was true of the Stuart period, which we see in its portraiture as a world rustling in silks and satins, in love with bright colours and the breaking of light on shining stuffs, yet not unmindful of the effects of matt surfaces and monochrome sobriety.

In the home, as in dress, the chief uses of textiles remained substantially the same as in the Tudor period, though with some modifications. Walls continued to be hung with tapestries, but the use of these tended to decline as alternative materials – gilded leather, printed stuffs, wallpapers – became available; silk fabrics also were increasingly used for this purpose, and for window-curtains. The bed, with its woven, embroidered or painted coverlet and hangings, was still the most important article of furniture. Upholstered chairs and settees became commoner and loose cushions were less used. Pile carpets were still seen as often on tables as on floors, and the same material was also used to cover upholstered furniture.

The patterns of textiles inevitably followed the wider artistic movements of the time. Fabrics which suited Hatfield or Audley End would not harmonize with Blenheim. The small repeated motifs of the renaissance patterns fashionable at the beginning of the seventeenth century were caught up into larger baroque rhythms, which, after a period of turbulence, settled into stately symmetries. As always, textiles were among the most effective vehicles in the international diffusion of styles, carrying ideas not only from the continent of Europe, but also from the Near East and from India and China.

Bibliography. Among the household inventories which provide interesting details of seventeenth century furnishing textiles are those of Henry Howard, Earl of Northampton (1614), in *Archaeologia*, XLII, 1869, pp. 347 ff.; Dame Anne Sherley (1622), in E. P. Shirley, *Stemmata Shirleiana*, 1841; Sir Thomas Fairfax (1624), in *Archaeologia*, XLVIII, 1884, pp. 136 ff.; Lettice, Countess of Leicester (1634), in J. O. Halliwell, *Ancient Inventories*, 1854; Edward Sackville, Earl of Dorset (1645), in C. J. Phillips, *History of the Sackville Family*, 1929, I, pp. 353 ff. For smaller establishments, see also F. G. Emmison, *Jacobean Household Inventories*, 1938, and F. W. Steer, *Farm and cottage inventories of mid-Essex, 1635-1749*, 1950.

For the early part of the century, the *Household Books of Lord William Howard of Naworth* (Surtees Society, Vol. LXVIII, 1877) include some useful information. Among narrative sources of the later Stuart period, Celia Fiennes showed a keen eye for textiles in the houses she visited (*The Journeys of Celia Fiennes*, edited by Christopher Morris, 1947).

Woven stuffs

Throughout the Stuart period England remained a large importer of woven materials. Woollen cloth, it is true, continued to be produced in sufficient quantities to supply most domestic needs and was, in addition, one of the country's major exportable commodities. For most types of linen goods also, home production was adequate, though for the more elaborate patterned linens England depended on cloth imported from Flanders. Linen damasks for tablecloths and napkins (the latter called 'towels' in the inventories) came almost exclusively from this source; they have survived in considerable numbers and generally have designs with figures – biblical scenes, or commemorative subjects with portraits of Kings and Queens woven expressly for the English market. Such cloths were not inexpensive; Lord William Howard's steward expended £12 10s. on '25 yardes of damask for table cloathes.' For cotton cloth England depended almost entirely on supplies brought from India by the newly founded East India Company. As to silk, besides James I's abortive attempt to naturalize the silkworm, a certain amount of raw silk was imported for weaving in England. Following the influx of French Protestant weavers resulting from the Revocation of the Edict of Nantes in 1685, this silk-weaving industry, centred on the Spitalfields district of London, made rapid strides, but throughout the Stuart period a large proportion of the silk materials used were imported, chiefly from Italy, but also from France, and from India and China.

Many of these woven stuffs were naturally plain, unpatterned materials. Chairs, for instance, were commonly covered in plain velvet, and the portraits of Van Dyck and Lely leave no doubt that plain satins were among the most admired fabrics for costume. Both plain and patterned materials were enriched in various ways, by slashing or pinking (common in costume until the middle of the seventeenth century), by stamped designs, and by embroidery. Sumptuous effects were obtained in the late seventeenth and early eighteenth century by applications of galon and tasselled fringes; examples may be found among the furniture designs of Daniel Marot, and numbers of beds and chairs decorated in this way still survive.

Among patterned silks, dress and furnishing materials differed chiefly in the scale of their designs, dress patterns being frequently very minute. In both cases, however, the historical evolution of the designs was much the same. The principal line of development may be summarized as follows. The designs of late sixteenth and early seventeenth century are for the most part orderly arrangements of fairly small, fairly naturalistic, independent floral units, either standing alone or in a trellis pattern. As the century advances, naturalistic features are abandoned in the search for rounded, full-blown, rolling forms; powerful, undulating lines, moving diagonally, knit the designs together in dense, exuberant baroque effects which reach a peak about 1660–70 (Pl. 71A). Thereafter the tempo slackens, the plant forms become flabbier, and a splendid, dignified, somewhat pompous symmetry is achieved, which, for furnishing textiles, persists far into the eighteenth century. Alongside this, however, is a gayer, more inconsequent style, in whose asymmetrical designs floral forms mingle with strange, bizarre shapes. It owes something to oriental ideas, but a recent attempt to attribute these silks to India [1] is certainly erroneous; they are undoubtedly European. Imported Indian silks seem generally to have been plain or striped. Of the artistically more interesting Chinese silks, a good example is the white floral damask used about 1695 for the magnificent state bed of the first Earl of Melville, in the Victoria and Albert Museum.

Most of the silks used for furnishing purposes were, however, of Italian origin. They included velvets, damasks and various kinds of polychrome silks, including stuffs brocaded with gold and silver – these last especially popular towards the end of the period. 'Genoa damask' and 'Genoa velvet' are frequently mentioned in the records, but are perhaps type-names rather than indications of provenance. The state-canopies of William III at Hampton Court still show the 'rich Crimson Genoa Damask ... at 24/- per yd.' which was bought for them in 1699; a piece of this material is illustrated on Pl. 71B. Also at Hampton Court are some pieces of a red and yellow silk with trophies of arms, royal crowns, the mottoes 'Dieu et mon droit' and 'Je maintiendray', an unidentified monogram 'SC', and 'JJ 1700', the latter indicating the date and the name of the mercer John Johnson, who charged 16s. 6d. per yard for the material in that year. Evidently this silk was woven to order, perhaps at Spitalfields. In 1714 the same firm of mercers also supplied '321 yards $\frac{1}{8}$ of white crimson and yellow figured velvet for a

---

[1] V. Slomann, *Bizarre Designs in Silks*, 1954.

standing bedd compleate, three pairs of large window curtains, vallance and cornishes, a large arm chair and 8 square stools at 42/- per yard'. This very elaborate material was stated in the *English Connoisseur* (1766, Vol. II, p. 199) to have been woven at Spitalfields, and the design of arches and flowers does in fact resemble those of other silks and wallpapers of the period which are fairly certainly of English make. The quality and variety of the patterns of the Spitalfields silks of the time are shown by the surviving designs of James Leman (active 1706–37), many of which are of the bizarre type mentioned above. Unfortunately no silks woven from these designs have yet been identified.

Despite the existence of this active industry at Spitalfields, Italian silks were often preferred. The Duchess of Marlborough, in 1707–8, ordered prodigious quantities of damasks and velvets through the Earl of Manchester at Venice. Special designs could evidently be woven to order in Italy, since at one point in the correspondence she observes: 'My Lord Rivers has two pieces making of yellow damask. He sent the pattern from England drawn upon paper. The only difference is that if it is a new pattern they must be paid for setting the loom.' The majority of these Italian furnishing stuffs, however, were fairly stereotyped in design. The velvets, in particular, persist in sumptuous, symmetrical floral patterns from the end of the seventeenth to the middle of the eighteenth century. The Duchess of Marlborough specified 'figured velvet without any mixture of colours', but equally, if not more, popular were polychrome velvets such as those 'figured crimson, green, several coullers in one', which Celia Fiennes observed on beds at Burghley. Many such velvets are still to be seen in country houses and museums.

Bibliography. Fanny Podreider, *Storia dei Tessuti d'Arte in Italia*, 1928; G. F. Wingfield Digby, *Damasks and Velvets at Hampton Court*, in the *Connoisseur*, CIII, 1939, pp. 248 ff.; Frank Lewis, *James Leman*, 1954.

Tapestries

Despite political upheavals, the Netherlands maintained throughout the seventeenth century the pre-eminence in tapestry-weaving which they had enjoyed since the Middle Ages, but the period was notable for certain new developments which contained the seeds of future decline. The first half of the century saw the foundation, in rapid succession, of a number of important factories in other countries – often under royal patronage. They included, among others, that of Munich in 1604, Paris in 1607, Mortlake in 1619 and Rome in 1633. These drained away some of the most highly skilled Flemish weavers and reduced the number of tapestries of fine quality ordered from the Netherlands. The output of the new factories, however, was both expensive and limited in quantity, and for most grades of work offered no serious competition to the Flemish industry, with its great reservoir of craft-skill and extremely efficient commercial organization. More dangerous was the remodelling of the French industry under the auspices of Louis XIV, whereby one after another the Gobelins (1662), Beauvais (1664) and Aubusson (1665) were put on a new and more efficient footing. These state-aided French factories, weaving designs by the finest decorative artists of the day, were able to withstand the decline in the demand for tapestries in the eighteenth century, while the Flemish factories withered and died. In the seventeenth century, however, the dynasties of tapestry-weavers established in Brussels, Antwerp, Oudenarde and other towns defied all competitors and their tapestries continued to be exported in vast quantities to the whole of Europe.

In 1678, tapestry imports into England were estimated to be running at a value of £100,000 per annum, the bulk of which was undoubtedly accounted for by Flemish tapestries. Even today, Flemish seventeenth century hangings are probably the commonest type of tapestry to be seen in England. In quality, most of them are adequate for their purpose, but hardly distinguished. Many are verdure or landscape tapestries, sometimes enlivened with hunting scenes, in prevailing tones of green, yellow and blue. Others are classical or Biblical subjects, in a hotter range of colours, and with a massive, plastic figure-style which owes something to the painting of Rubens. Later in the century many landscape-tapestries were woven with peasant scenes in the manner of Teniers, a style which persisted down to the middle of the eighteenth century and which seems to have been popular in England.

Compared with this large influx of Flemish tapestries, the output of the English industry, despite the fact that the seventeenth century was its most active period, was on a modest scale. But its history is not without interest, and the work of the Mortlake factory, at least for the short period between 1620 and 1635, was unequalled in quality anywhere in Europe.

Tapestry-weaving was no novelty in England. The skilled workers of the Great Wardrobe had long been engaged in the repair and maintenance of the magnificent tapestry collections of the Crown, and from time to time other tapestry-weavers had been active in various parts of the country. The looms which William Sheldon had established, in Queen Elizabeth's time, on his estates in Warwickshire and Worcestershire, were still working during the early years of the reign of James I; their somewhat provincial productions have been discussed in the preceding volume. The Mortlake factory, however, represented a completely new departure, in that it was conceived as an instrument of royal prestige, and the Crown was prepared not only to commission from it tapestries of the most luxurious kind, but also to give it financial support as a matter of policy. The documents relating to its foundation show that it was deliberately modelled on the tapestry factory which Henri IV, with very similar aims, and founded in Paris in 1607.

The Mortlake factory was fortunate in its first director, the experienced courtier and Chancellor of the Order of the Garter, Sir Francis Crane. (A fine tapestry portrait of him, woven at Mortlake after a painting by Van Dyck, is in the possession of Lord Petre at Ingatestone Hall.) As soon as the project was agreed upon in 1619, Crane set himself energetically to the task of collecting a team of highly qualified weavers, some of whom he recruited directly from the Netherlands, while others, including his chief weaver, Philip de Maeght, were won over from the Paris factory.

These negotiations were conducted with speed and secrecy, and by 1620 the authorities in the Low Countries were alarmed to read, in diplomatic dispatches from London, that some fifty Flemish weavers were already assembled at Mortlake. Crane's conduct of the factory, terminated by his death in 1636, seems to have been eminently successful, though on more than one occasion he was accused of enriching himself at the King's expense. No doubt his operations were materially assisted by the fact that during his tenure of office Charles I, who both as Prince of Wales and as King took a keen interest in the factory, was sufficiently supplied with funds to exercise a generous patronage.

It was for Charles that the first tapestries were woven on Mortlake looms between 1620 and 1622. This was a set of nine hangings with scenes from the story of *Vulcan and Venus*; some of these tapestries, identified by the Prince of Wales's feathers and interlaced C's in the borders, are at St James's Palace, while others are dispersed in museums and private collections (Pl. 72). Part of another set, made for the Duke of Buckingham, is in the Swedish royal collection, and the series was subsequently re-woven on a number of occasions for private patrons. The second group of tapestries to leave the looms, in 1623–24, was a set of *Twelve Months*, which was begun for Charles but transferred later to the Duke of Buckingham's account. This set likewise was repeatedly rewoven down to the beginning of the eighteenth century; examples are at Buckingham Palace, Ham House and elsewhere. It is noteworthy that the designs of both these series are of a somewhat archaic character, for they are based on Flemish tapestry cartoons which go back to the middle of the sixteenth century, or even earlier. Indeed this use of old designs for the main subjects, often in conjunction with new and ingenious baroque designs for the borders, is characteristic of much Mortlake work, and may perhaps be connected with Charles's taste as a connoisseur of Renaissance art. It was he who in 1623 acquired for the Mortlake factory the most famous of all tapestry designs, Raphael's *Acts of the Apostles*, which had exercised so decisive an influence on Flemish tapestry style over a century before. These magnificent cartoons still form part of the English royal collections and are exhibited at the Victoria and Albert Museum on loan from H.M. the Queen. Of the tapestries woven from them at Mortlake, part of the royal set is now in the French national collection; among the many sets woven for private patrons – for the *Acts* were naturally one of the most sought-after of Mortlake sets – those at Chatsworth, Boughton House and Forde Abbey may be mentioned.

In 1624 Mortlake acquired its own designer in the person of Francis Cleyn, a native of Rostock, who, after studying in Rome, had been court painter to Christian IV of Denmark. He was at once granted an annuity of £100 in respect of his duties at Mortlake, which he continued to perform until his death in 1658. His principal contributions to the repertory of Mortlake cartoons were the story of *Hero and Leander* in seven scenes, a series of eight classical subjects known as the *Horses*, and a set of the *Five Senses*. Charles I's set of the *Hero and Leander* tapestries, magnificently woven and rich with gold, is now in the Swedish royal collection. Cleyn was not an artist of great distinction but the curiously hesitant and tongue-tied proto-baroque style of his tapestry cartoons has considerable charm.

With the death of Sir Francis Crane in 1636, and the King's increasing financial embarrassments, Mortlake entered a more difficult period from which it was never fully to recover. Under a succession of directors the work was carried on, for private patrons, but it was generally of a simpler and less luxurious kind. The Commonwealth Government took measures to support the factory, and in 1657 commissioned the weaving of a new set of tapestries based on Mantegna's paintings of the *Triumphs of Caesar*, which Charles I had bought with the Gonzaga Collection from Mantua; some hangings with this subject are in the collection of the Duke of Buccleuch. Designs by Giulio Romano, perhaps also from Mantua, formed the basis of another popular series, showing *putti* playing among foliage, and known as the *Naked Boys*.

The history of tapestry-weaving in the later Stuart period is a tangled skein which has not yet been completely unravelled. The Mortlake factory was not finally wound up until 1703; it is known to have been selling tapestries to the Crown and to private patrons in Charles II's time, but no serious effort seems to have been made to arrest its decline and it was probably inactive for some years before its eventual demise. For most of this period effective control of the factory seems to have been in the hands of Lady Harvey, acting on behalf of her brother, the Earl of Montagu. The situation is complicated by the fact that the Earl of Montagu was simultaneously Master of the Great Wardrobe, where tapestries were also being woven, and it is impossible to be sure, for example, whether the set of tapestry table-covers with his arms in the possession of the Duke of Buccleuch, were made at the Great Wardrobe or at Mortlake. Furthermore, while some of the old Mortlake weavers were transferred to the Great Wardrobe, others apparently set up on their own account. As all these establishments continued to weave the Mortlake designs and to use the old Mortlake mark of a St George's cross on a shield, their products can be distinguished only if they are signed, or if documentary evidence is available. The former Mortlake weaver, William Benood, apparently operating independently at Lambeth, is known to have woven a set of five hangings of the *Vulcan and Venus* series for the Countess of Rutland in 1670–71; these are at Haddon Hall. A tapestry in the Victoria and Albert Museum, inscribed 'Made at Lambeth', is presumably also from Benood's workshop; it reproduces one of the designs of Cleyn's *Horses*. The signature of Stephen de May, a surname borne by several Mortlake weavers, is also found on tapestries; in 1701 he was engaged on weaving a series of *Months* for Lord Nottingham. Tapestries with subjects taken from the *Metamorphoses* of Ovid have recently been shown to be English work, but it is not known in which workshop they were woven.

The production of the weavers associated with the Great Wardrobe, which was situated first in Hatton Garden and subsequently, from 1686, in Great Queen Street, can be distinguished a little more clearly. The signature of Francis Poyntz, who bore the title of 'His Majesty's Chief Arras-Maker' appears on three hangings representing the *Battle of Solebay* (1672), which were woven in 1677-78, perhaps after designs by Willem van der Velde the Elder. He also signed a set of *Naked Boys* at Hardwick, and a curious tapestry with full-length portraits of James I and Charles I, their Queens, and Christian IV of Denmark, at Houghton. On his death in 1685, a kinsman, Thomas Poyntz, seems to have succeeded to the business, and his signature appears on sets of the *Solebay* designs and on tapestries of the Mortlake *Months* and *Naked Boys* series; he is known to have been weaving a set of *Months* for the Queen's bedchamber at Windsor in 1686. In 1689 John Vanderbank succeeded to the position of chief arras-worker at the Great Wardrobe, where he continued until 1727. Much of his time was inevitably occupied with the cleaning and repair of the royal tapestries, but he also wove a considerable number of new sets, both for the palaces and for country houses. Among these were designs after the fashion of Teniers, and a series of *Elements*, adapted from the designs made by Le Brun for the Gobelins, of which the set at Boughton House was woven for the Earl of Montagu before 1705. Vanderbank's name is, however, more particularly associated with another kind of tapestry, lighter and more frivolous in effect than any of its predecessors, and representing a radical departure from the heroic themes hitherto traditional to the medium. These are the tapestries now known as *chinoiseries*, but which Vanderbank himself described, when he delivered a set of them for Kensington Palace in 1690, as 'designed after the Indian manner' (Pl. 73). They show groups of small figures, in Indian or Chinese dress and surrounded by a variety of exotic accessories, standing on little strips of landscape which are distributed over the whole field of the tapestry without regard to continuity or perspective. The scenes are invariably in light tones on black, dark blue or brown backgrounds, and although they may owe something to the painted cotton hangings imported from India, their effects are much more closely related to those of the lacquer objects which were also carried in the East India Company's ships.

It has recently been suggested that the designs of these hangings may have been the work of Robert Robinson (active 1674-1706), a decorative painter of *chinoiserie* subjects, but they do not seem to show any decisive affinities with his style. Vanderbank seems to have specialized in tapestries of this type and several examples with his signature are known; another signature which occurs is that of M. Mazarind, who is not otherwise identified. The best-known set of the kind, which is however unsigned, are the four from Glemham which once belonged to Elihu Yale and are now preserved at the American university which bears his name.

All these English tapestries of the later Stuart period, though decorative in design and competent in weaving, are nevertheless not tapestries of the highest class. The major official commissions of the period went to Flemish factories. Hence it was the interconnected workshops of Le Clerc, De Vos, Van der Borcht and Cobus, in Brussels, who wove the fine armorial tapestries of William III, who recorded his successes against James II, and who celebrated, in a series of ten hangings at Blenheim, the victories of the Duke of Marlborough.

Of smaller works in tapestry, it may well be that some of the early eighteenth century covers for chairs and settees, woven with floral designs, are of English workmanship, but this subject has not yet been adequately explored.

Bibliography. W. G. Thomson, *A History of Tapestry*, 1930 (2nd edition); W. G. Thomson, *Tapestry Weaving in England*, 1914; H. C. Marillier, *English Tapestries of the Eighteenth Century*, 1930; H. C. Marillier, *Handbook to the Teniers Tapestries*, 1932; G. Wingfield Digby, *Late Mortlake Tapestries*, in the *Connoisseur*, CXXXIV, 1954, pp. 239 ff.

Painted and printed textiles

The pictorial hangings of painted canvas, which had been extensively used as a relatively cheap substitute for tapestries during the fifteenth and sixteenth centuries, were already in the late Elizabethan period chiefly associated with ale-houses. In Stuart times they no longer formed part of the furnishings of an elegant house, though rustic examples continued to be painted far into the eighteenth century. Their place was taken by decorative oil-paintings set into the panelling of rooms, but these belong to the history of painting rather than to that of textiles.

Printed fabrics, on the other hand, were made in considerable quantities in England, though surviving examples are extremely rare. Floral patterns printed on linen for the use of the embroideress show that textile-printing from both wood-blocks and engraved plates was practised at the beginning of the century. For furnishing purposes, however, the decorative value of the technique was limited by the fact that most of the printing was done in black only; other colours, added with block or brush, were pale and impermanent. Block-printed wall-hangings of this type were nevertheless made, and were presumably stuck to the wall like a wallpaper. Some linen fragments in the Victoria and Albert Museum show figures of a lady and gentleman of about 1680 against a background of trees, printed in black in a broad style, and washed with colour. A few other block-prints of the same kind, possibly English, have floral patterns reminiscent of contemporary wallpapers.

More effective than this type of work were the wall-hangings of flock-printed canvas which were the predecessors of flock papers. The technique of printing an adhesive on cloth and dusting it with flock (the process could be repeated to obtain polychrome designs) was one which had been practised on the Continent since at least the fifteenth century. In 1634, one Jerome Lanyer took out a patent in London for the manufacture of a material of this type, which he proposed to call 'Londrindiana'. It is not known whether his material ever reached the production stage. If it did, it may conceivably be represented by a set of flock-printed panels recently discovered in a Yorkshire house and now in the Victoria and Albert Museum; it must be admitted, however, that their formal baroque designs, somewhat reminiscent of the patterns of gilded leather, in no way differs from contemporary continental examples in the same technique.

These somewhat unexciting creations of the English textile-printer were outclassed in every respect by the Indian painted quilts and hangings which, in the Stuart period, were one of the staple commodities of the East India Company's trade. In the course of many centuries the Indian craftsman had perfected a complex method of painting and dyeing designs on cotton cloth; he had a range of blues, reds, pinks and purples which could be dyed fast, and with another more fugitive dye he could add yellows and greens. It is not surprising that these finely textured cottons, each one an individual work of art, executed in brilliant colours which no amount of washing could remove, were enthusiastically received in England. In addition to their other advantages, they were not excessively expensive. In 1631 the London price of Indian hangings sufficient for a room was about £30; in 1650 two sets of bed-hangings sold for £17 and large quilts cost £2 10s. each. At first the exotic quality of the style was one of its principal attractions and there was a demand for pictorial hangings of the type made for the Indian home market; of this kind were those noted by Evelyn at Lady Mordaunt's house in 1665, 'full of figures great and small, prettily representing sundry trades and occupations of the Indians, with their habits'. Later, as prices fell and the demand became more generalized, the Company sought to modify the designs to suit English taste, and after 1662 it became usual to send out designs in a hybrid Anglo-Indian style, for copying in India. Despite its relative cheapness, the material was much used even in the finest houses. In his *Tour through Great Britain* Defoe notes Queen Mary's 'fine chintz bed' at Hampton Court and 'a bed hung with Atlass and Magglapatan chintz' at Windsor. Apart from furnishing, chintz with small floral patterns was increasingly used for dress, initially among the lower classes and later, in the 1680's, by a reversal of the usual rule that modes descend through the strata of society, this was eagerly taken up by the fashionable world and, as the Company observed with satisfaction, by 'ladies of the greatest quality'. Examples of these seventeenth century painted cottons from India may be seen in museums (Pl. 76A).

Cloth-printers in Europe made strenuous efforts to emulate this work. The Indian method, complex though it was, could hardly be kept secret from the Europeans working in India, and accounts of it were soon transmitted to interested persons at home. The major difficulties in the way of adapting it for purposes of European manufacture were the laborious and lengthy nature of the processes and the degree of artistic skill necessary for the hand-painting, both of which made it uneconomic under European conditions. From 1676 onwards, however, various patents were taken out in London for printing in the Indian manner, and it seems likely that a simplified version of the method had by then been adapted to the European practice of block-printing. For a century thereafter the English cloth-printers remained technically and artistically in advance of their European competitors. A more dangerous rival was excluded in 1701 by the banning, as a result of agitation by English weavers, of further imports of Indian chintz. Unfortunately, no examples of English printing 'in the Indian manner' from the late Stuart period have yet been discovered.

Bibliography. G. P. Baker, *Calico painting and printing in the East Indies in the Seventeenth and Eighteenth centuries*, 1921; J. Irwin, *Origins of the 'Oriental Style' in English decorative art*, in *Burlington Magazine*, XCVII, 1955.

Embroidery and lace

Embroidery has been assiduously cultivated at most periods of English history, but it may be said that standards of domestic needlework have never been higher than they were in Stuart times. The amateur worker was trained from childhood in all the techniques of the needle, and her deficiencies with the pencil were supplied by a considerable industry engaged in drawing or printing designs for her use, either directly on silk or linen, or in books whence they could be traced or pounced. It is true that the combination of technical virtuosity and naïve pictorial design led, for instance in the stump-work of the Commonwealth and Restoration periods, to effects which, at best quaint and curious, are too often merely absurd; but it must be remembered that these were show-pieces, the first-fruits of the newly acquired skills of small girls. Embroideries made by their elders for prac-

tical use and display in the home are generally characterized by simple and bold decorative effects and perfect discretion in execution. In design, the keynote of all this domestic embroidery is informality, except for the rare occasions when a woven fabric is directly copied with the needle. Nearly always it is concerned with animals and plants, more or less naturalistically rendered. The manner in which these motifs are organized naturally follows the wider stylistic evolution of the period. The repeated units, characteristic of the early part of the period, are caught up, by the middle of the century, into larger schemes characterized by strong, undulating, diagonal movements, which subside at the end of the period into more sedate patterns, often enlivened by the frivolous intrusion of orientalizing motifs. Throughout these changes of fashion, however, the work is marked by its delight in the motifs, naturalistic or exotic, for their own sake, its refusal to exaggerate them or to submit them to any kind of rigid formal pattern, and its strongly national character.

In contrast, such of the English professional embroidery as survives belongs to the international baroque style and cannot be distinguished from contemporary continental work. An embroidered panel of the *Adoration of the Shepherds* in the Victoria and Albert Museum, one of a series formerly at Corby Castle, bears on the back the signature 'Edmund Harrison Imbroderer to King Charles made theis Anno Doni. 1637'. This picture, of a decidedly Flemish character in design, is worked by shading with coloured silks over parallel lines of gold thread, a delicate technique which had long been favoured for pictorial work by professional embroiderers on the Continent. Harrison, besides being a prominent member of the London Broderers' Company, was embroiderer to James I, Charles I and Charles II, and in 1660 he petitioned the latter monarch for arrears due to him in respect of embroidering two hundred and fifty coats for the yeomen of the chamber and others. It was no doubt in this kind of livery and heraldic work, and in the more formal kinds of furnishing and costume embroidery, that the members of the Broderers' Company and their fellow

Fig. 1. Sheets of designs for needlework from *A schole-house for the needle*, published by Richard Shorleyker, London, 1624. *Victoria and Albert Museum.*

professionals were chiefly engaged. Surviving examples (e.g. herald's tabards, military scarves, embroidered doublets, gloves, etc.), though often of impressive quality, are generally less interesting than the productions of the amateurs.

The domestic embroidery of the early Stuart period is in many respects a prolongation of the Elizabethan style. In general, the same articles continued to be embroidered in the same ways. A few of the most ambitious types of Elizabethan embroidery do, it is true, seem to have fallen into disuse, notably the great table-carpets and the large pictorial wall-hangings and bed-valances worked throughout in tent stitch with Biblical or mythological scenes. But the persistence of the

closely related tradition of tent-stitch cushions is shown by two examples in the Victoria and Albert Museum, one with the royal arms, the initials I R, and the ostentatious amateur's signature MARY HVLTON, the other with the arms of Hereford and a Latin inscription recording that it was made for the mayor of that city in the second year of James I (Pl. 74A). The latter cushion shows the characteristic plant-scroll ornament of the Elizabethan period, with each convolution enclosing a single flower or fruit. The same pattern continued in use for small articles such as purses and book-covers. It persisted also for fine embroidered linen, particularly for pillow-covers and the long covers associated with them, for the 'night-caps' (really

437

informal day-caps) of the men, and for the coifs, bodices and jackets of the women. In these, the linen ground is left exposed, the coiling stems are generally of gold thread, while the flowers may be worked in a single colour – silver, black or red – or in polychrome silks.

An alternative pattern for most of these articles omits the coiling stems and disposes naturalistic plant and animal motifs in rows across the field (Pl. 74B). The arrangement then approximates to that of applied work, another Elizabethan technique which retained its popularity under James I. In applied work, plant and animal motifs which had been worked on canvas in *gros point* or *petit point* were cut out round their outlines and sewn on to a plain ground, often of velvet, for use as cushions or hangings. The Stuart embroideress could draw on a rich treasury of these naturalistic motifs in the various pattern-books published in London by Shorleyker, Johnson, Stent and Overton. The rare surviving copies of the books show signs of hard use, with the designs pricked for pouncing and many leaves torn out. It is surprising therefore, and perhaps indicative of how small a fraction of the vast output of Stuart needlewomen has come down to us, that the existing embroideries hardly ever show a motif which can be traced to a pattern-book. It is by a rare chance that a number of motifs embroidered on a lady's shift of about 1630 in the Victoria and Albert Museum are found to reproduce designs in Shorleyker's pattern-book of 1624.

The naturalistic motifs, the coiling stem and other related designs are also found on the samplers of the first half of the seventeenth century. By the 1630's, however, the standard type of Stuart sampler was common and it is exemplified by many signed and dated examples down to the end of the Stuart period. It consists of a long, narrow strip of linen, embroidered in coloured silks with row after row of narrow border-patterns, ornamental alphabets, etc., in a variety of stitches. It is without pictorial ambitions and was not meant to be framed and hung, but served on the one hand as a certificate of a girl's proficiency and on the other as a reference-sheet of patterns and stitches for her future use. Sometimes as a part of this sampler, but

more often on a second independent sampler, she worked exercises in whitework, i.e. embroidery in white linen thread, in lacis or darned netting, and in needlepoint lace.

At this point a few words must be introduced on the subject of lace. Many English amateur needlewomen were competent in lace-making and considerable quantities of lace were also made professionally in England. But throughout the Stuart period the great commercial centres were, for bobbin-lace, Flanders, and for needlepoint lace, northern Italy and, later in the century, France. The majority of the finer laces used in England for costume and bed-linen were probably imported from these centres. It may be noted in passing that the *gros point de Venise* fashionable in the Charles II period presents in particularly pure form the fleshy, stylized plant-growth, with undulating and spinning movements, which is also found in the embroideries and woven stuffs of the time. Lace-design was very international in character and it may well be that some of the pieces classed as Italian or Flemish may actually have been of English workmanship. The English needlewoman had ready access to continental designs for lace and lacis through English editions of continental pattern-books; Boler's *The Needle's Excellency*, for example, which had reached its twelfth edition by 1640, was a compilation from the pattern-books of Sibmacher, originally published in Nuremberg. Lacis or darned netting, 'network' as it was known at the time, was probably a good deal used in early Stuart homes, but little has survived. A small example of unknown use in the Victoria and Albert Museum is dated 1633 and has figures symbolizing the Five Senses; it is shown to be English by the moralising doggerel which accompanies them:

> So keep your senses that they be
> As innocent as these you see
> So pure your heart as if it were
> In breast of network to apeare.

Having worked her samplers, the young needlewoman turned her attention to more entertaining tasks, generally to some pictorial work – covers for a book of devotion, an embroidered picture which

Fig. 2. Sheets of designs for needlework from *A schole-house for the needle*, published by Richard Shorleyker, London, 1624. *Victoria and Albert Museum.*

could be framed and hung, or panels to be made up as a work-box or a frame for a mirror. The subjects chosen (the designs in this case were invariably bought ready sketched on the material to be embroidered) were usually the more piquant episodes of the Old Testament – David and Bathcheba, Solomon and the Queen of Sheba, Susanna and the Elders – occasionally varied with scenes of classical myth or courtly life, figures of the Seasons or Senses, and portrait busts. During the first half of the century these little pictures were normally embroidered all over in *petit point*; in Commonwealth and Restoration times, however, it was more usual to work on a white satin ground, which was left exposed, while the figures stood out

against it in relief – the bodies padded, the heads often finely modelled (Pl. 75). The variety and skill of the stitchery are astonishing, and if the final effect is more amusing than artistic, it should be recalled that these objects are essentially toys, which no doubt gave the young needlewomen a great deal of innocent entertainment as they plied their needles. The progress of one of these young ladies is succinctly recorded in a group of objects belonging to Lady Gerahty: Martha Edlin, who was born in 1660, worked her coloured sampler in 1668, her whitework sampler in 1669, and her stumpwork work-box, which contains an armoury of pin-cushions, needlecases, etc., also worked by herself, in 1671. In addition the Victoria and

Albert Museum possesses a large trinket-box worked by her in coloured beads in 1673. This beadwork was a popular alternative for stumpwork and was similarly used for pictures, work-boxes, mirror-frames and small cushions; its most characteristic use, however, was for beadwork baskets, with openwork sides, and a biblical or courtly scene worked on the bottom of the tray.

In contrast with the small size and minute execution of the work just described, another of the chief types of seventeenth century embroidery is notable for the boldness of its scale. This is crewel-work, in which the designs are worked in coloured wools (or crewels) on a background of tough white twill sheeting of mixed linen and cotton. This kind of embroidery, though it occurs in a variety of articles such as workbags and ladies' bodices and skirts, was primarily used for sets of bed-hangings, comprising the valances and bases which hung round the upper and lower frames of the bed and the three or four curtains which completely enclosed the sleepers. In a few cases the design of these is based on those of woven materials. In others, dating from the reign of Charles I, it is a variety of the coiling stem pattern. Later, thicker stems flourish more wildly, undulating and interlacing diagonally across the curtains and bearing colossal curling leaves reminiscent of Flemish tapestries of the large-leaf verdure type (Pl. 76B). These designs are executed in monochrome green wool, or in a restricted range of colour shading from indigo to yellow; the leaves are worked in outline, with linear veining or abstract filling patterns. In the last decades of the century the powerful rhythms subside and the vegetation becomes lighter and less robust; slender stems or semi-naturalistic trees, growing from hummocky ground, bear leaves and large flowers worked solidly in bright polychrome wools; birds and animals are often introduced, and both flora and fauna show orientalizing or chinoiserie characteristics. There is an obvious relationship between these hangings with their exotic tree-designs and the imported painted hangings or palampores from India, which were used for the same purpose. The embroidered hangings were certainly influenced by the painted ones but, as has been mentioned above, the latter were themselves based, in this period, on designs sent out from England. The influence was doubtless mutual, and both types contain elements of East and West.

Oriental embroideries also reached England, though in much smaller quantities than the painted pieces. There is a fine Indian coverlet of the sixteenth century at Hardwick. In 1614 similar pieces were selling in the East India Company's London auctions at between £10 and £30 apiece. In the same year the inventory of the Earl of Northampton's property includes 'A china quilte stitched in chequer worke with yealowe silke, the ground white', an item which recalls a popular style of English quilting which was still fashionable a century later. Hardly any English embroidered coverlets exist which can be dated before the last decades of the seventeenth century. At that time the most popular designs showed a light sprinkling of *chinoiserie* motifs, worked in coloured silks, often on white satin, as in the twin coverlets of Mary and Sarah Thurstone, dated 1694 (Fitzwilliam and Victoria and Albert Museums, Pl. 77).

A number of furnishing embroideries in *gros point* and *petit point*, and other canvas stitches have survived from the later seventeenth and early eighteenth centuries. The most ambitious example is a set of six wall-hangings from a house in Hatton Garden (Victoria and Albert Museum); worked in coloured wools, they show an arcade about which twine leaves and flowers like those of crewel-work hangings, together with animals reminiscent of stumpwork; they probably date from the early years of the reign of Charles II. The chairs, settees and firescreens for which these techniques were more often used are all rather later in date. A few have designs derived from the more pompous type of woven textiles; others show *chinoiserie* motifs and strange shapes probably suggested by silks of the bizarre type; others again show figure-scenes, classical or pastoral subjects or peasants in the manner of Teniers. Whole rooms were decorated in this way, like that observed by Celia Fiennes 'hung with cross-stitch in silks ... the Chairs Cross-stitch and two stooles of yellow mohaire wth cross-stitch ... an Elbow Chaire tent-stitch'. Her notes on the Queen's Closet at Hampton Court suggest the use of a kind of crewel-work for the same purpose: 'the hangings, chaires, stooles, and screen the same, all of satten stitch done in worsteads, beasts, birds, images, and fruites all wrought very finely by Queen Mary and her Maids of Honour'. Queen Mary's industry with her needle was notorious. Nor were her hands idle even when needlework was impossible, for we are assured by Sir Charles Sedley that the Queen

> When she rode in coach abroad
> Was always knotting thread.

This knotted thread was applied in formal patterns to chairs and coverlets in the same way as galon; there are yellow silk chairs, decorated in this way with red knotted thread, at Ham House. The technique, like that of cross stitch and tent stitch for furniture, had a considerable development in the following reigns; both will be more fully dealt with in the next volume.

Bibliography. M. A. Jourdain, *English Secular Embroidery,* 1910; Victoria and Albert Museum, *Catalogue of English Domestic Embroidery of the Sixteenth and Seventeenth Centuries,* 1950 (2nd edition); F. B. Palliser, *History of Lace,* 1902 (4th edition).

Carpets

The use of carpets of oriental type, i.e. of knotted pile, as coverings for floors, tables and court-cupboards and for cushions and upholstery, had made rapid strides in the Tudor period and became still more common under the Stuarts. The 1614 inventory of the Earl of Northampton's property, like others of the period, includes many carpets: for example, '... a wallnuttree cupboarde with a Turkie Cupboorde clothe ... two small tables with two Turkie carpettes ... fowre Turkie cushines ... two small Turkie carpettes, whereof one is upon the ground ... two large Persian carpettes ... 12 stooles of Turkie worke billed red white and blue with cruell fringe'. In such entries the word Turkey denotes the technique only, and is not an attribution of origin.

Nevertheless, the portraiture of the period shows clearly that most of the carpets used on floors and tables were, in fact, Turkish. Those depicted almost always show the geometrical patterns of 'Holbein',[2] Transylvanian, Bergama and other traditional types of Turkish rug, with their characteristic robust colour-schemes of red, blue, yellow and white. Persian carpets occur relatively rarely in the inventories and are generally specified as of large size. They were shipped from time to time by the East India Company, who did not, however, find the trade profitable. Examples of this period in English houses (e.g. at Ham House and in the collections of the Duke of Buccleuch) are chiefly of the Herati pattern, with leaves and flowers, softer in colour and more finely woven than the Turkish rugs. The Company also traded, to a small extent, in carpets of somewhat similar character made at Lahore and Agra. These were sold at the London sales of 1616 at prices ranging from £2 11s. to £30, according to size. Two such Indian carpets which survive were specially made for officials of the Company. One, commissioned by Robert Bell in 1631 for presentation to the Worshipful Company of Girdlers of London, shows the arms of donor and recipient among foliage ornament; the other, of about the same date, has the arms of William Fremlin interspersed with flowers and fighting animals (Victoria and Albert Museum).

Armorial carpets were also made in England, where the craft of carpet-knotting, already firmly established in Queen Elizabeth's time, continued to flourish. The Earl of Northampton's inventory, quoted above, contains a reference to 'a longe Turkie carpett of Englishe worke with the Earl of Northampton his armes, being 5 yeardes and 3 quarters longe'. There are two carpets of about 1610 at Knole which have English floral patterns; another, in the possession of Sir Westrow Hulse, is dated 1614 and, with its design of naturalistic flowers and fruit on an apple-green ground, stands still closer to contemporary needlework (Pl. 78A). This last carpet makes more comprehensible the homely phrases of Dame Anne Sherley's inventory (1622): 'My Turkey carpet of

---

[2] Conventional name for a type of rug which often appears in Holbein's paintings.

cowcumbers. My cabbage carpet of Turkey work.' Even if, as is likely, some of the larger carpets were made in professional workshops, there is no doubt that many of the smaller pieces for cushions and upholstery were made at home. Those of the first half of the seventeenth century generally have open repeating patterns of naturalistic flower-sprigs like those used by the embroideress. In the second half of the period, again as in embroidery, the flowers become more exotic and more densely packed; one large carpet of this type is known, bearing the date 1672 and the arms of Sir John Molyneux of Tevershall (Victoria and Albert Museum; Pl. 78B). A number of armorial cushions of about the middle of the century have a more polished and professional air; they include sets of cushions at Brasenose and Pembroke Colleges, Oxford, and another set presented to the Corpora-tion of Norwich by Thomas Baret, Mayor in 1651. Norwich seems to have been especially concerned with the craft; already in 1588, the Earl of Leicester's property included 'a Turquoy carpett of Norwiche work'.

The households rich enough to use pile-carpets on their floors were not very numerous in Stuart times. Elsewhere strewn rushes and plaited rush matting remained in use, and there is evidence to show that the stout double-cloth weaves of Kidder-minster were also utilized for this purpose. The 1634 inventory of the Countess of Leicester's property, for instance, includes '4 carpets of Kidderminster stuff.'

Bibliography. A. F. Kendrick and C. E. C. Tattersall, *Handwoven Carpets, Oriental and European,* 1922; C. E. C. Tattersall, *A History of British Carpets,* 1934.

Girl making bobbin-lace. From an engraving by Wenceslaus Hollar, 1636.

Costume

C. WILLETT CUNNINGTON

If English portraits of the early seventeenth century are compared with those of a hundred years later the most striking change in costume is to be seen in the male dress.

The earlier portraits present surfaces of various depths, differing in colour and texture; the later have begun to present smooth surfaces mostly on a single plane, a process destined in following centuries to develop still further.

To the modern eye that Jacobean technique of displaying glimpses of garments through gaps in their coverings, as in slashing and paning, so that it is not always easy to determine to which particular layer of clothing a visible part belongs, appears to savour of 'fancy dress', an illusion heightened by the fact that many of the garments do not appear to have been made to fit the wearer.

But with the dawn of the eighteenth century the whole spirit of male costume has changed; his clothes, especially those for day wear, are in process of becoming subordinate to the man wearing them. They may seem to us, sometimes, to smack of the theatre, but they no longer suggest a carnival.

This insidious change, which affected men's fashions long before women's, is associated with other social changes. Thus, from the beginning of the seventeenth century the English gentleman began to adopt woollen textiles for his day suits, and these were materials which lent themselves to the tailor's art of cut and fit; gentlewomen, on the other hand, did not wear woollen dresses (except riding habits) until much later.

In addition the seventeenth century saw a lowering of those social barriers which had formerly hedged about the aristocracy, separating them from the minor gentry. Indeed, by the middle of that century one who declared 'I was by birth a gentleman, living neither in any considerable height nor yet in obscurity' had become Lord Protector of England.

It was this infiltration into the upper ranks from the minor gentry and merchant class that helped to raise the status of woollen cloth and gave a gentleman's suit a simpler construction.

It seems that a Puritan of the upper class was hardly to be distinguished by his dress from a Cavalier of the same social standing. *The Memoirs of Colonel Hutchinson* inform us that 'the leaders and their wives were as well dressed on the one side as the other', and the fact that many Puritans wore 'sad' colours (meaning dark tints) was because these were the ordinary cloths worn by the less fashionable gentry.

The distinction in dress which separated the middle class from the mass of the people remained as rigid as formerly; for these latter must needs wear clothes adapted to their various manual occupations. In the fashionable world, which always borrows freely from foreign countries, the seventeenth century saw a steady decline in Spanish influence and the dominating influence of France. In addition, Charles I's queen was French and Charles II spent much of his formative youth in France. Fashions, at least at Court, could hardly escape this French influence.

The Stuart period was split in two by the Civil War, and the Restoration of 1660 came almost exactly midway between the accession of James I

443

and the death of Queen Anne. It will be convenient therefore to consider the costumes of these two phases separately.

Male fashions, 1603–60

Until about 1630 the Jacobean modes were in effect a continuation of the late Elizabethan. The doublet, close-fitting and long-waisted, had a front stiffened with buckram; its skirt, divided into tabs, flared out over the breeches, which were attached by 'points' or ties passing through visible eyelet holes in the tabs or through concealed holes under the skirt.

The sleeves were usually plain and close-fitting, or else full and 'paned' from shoulder to elbow. Wings concealed the shoulder seams and slashing persisted.

From 1630 to 1645 the doublet became easy-fitting and high-waisted; the corset-shape disappeared and the skirt tabs lost the pointed effect. The sleeves, loose and shorter, with a turned-back cuff revealed the ruffled shirt-sleeve. The wings shrank and disappeared after 1640.

The breeches were now attached by hooks and eyes instead of points, and the skimpy doublet became so short that between it and the breeches a gap allowed the shirt to protrude. (It was in fact becoming the 'waistcoat' of later times.)

The doubtlet throughout preserved a standing collar, while the jerkin worn over the doublet, disappeared by 1630 except when serving as a military garment of stout leather.

The Mandilion, known after 1620 as a 'Manderville' and then used for livery only, was a loose, thigh-length overcoat with standing collar, and its loose sleeves usually worn as hanging sleeves.

The Cassock, somewhat shorter and widening towards the hem, often had no standing collar after 1620. Its sleeves had turned-back cuffs.

The Riding Coat was sometimes hooded. The Gabardine, worn by all classes and both sexes, was a long loose overcoat with wide sleeves.

Cloaks were very fashionable; mostly circular in cut and matching the doublet and breeches, though velvet was a popular material. The 'French cloak', reaching the knees and with or without a flat square collar, was commonly worn over one

shoulder and gathered up over the arm. The 'Spanish cloak', short, full and hooded, together with the 'Dutch cloak' with wide hanging sleeves, both became rare after 1620.

The Gown, a long loose garment open down the front, had by the seventeenth century become the formal attire of officials and the elderly.

Neckwear was of two kinds, the Band or collar, and the Ruff. The Band, tied round the neck with tasselled strings, was either in the form of a 'standing band', semi-circular and supported by a wire 'under-proper' (1605–30), or as a 'falling band' (to 1670's) in the form of a deep turned-down collar.

The Ruff, usually closed all round, was composed of goffered bands supported, if large, by a wire frame; the upright stiffened frame attached to the back of the doublet collar and edged with horizontal tabs which supported the ruff, was known as a Pickadil. Both ruff and band were of linen, lawn and lace, matching the hand-ruff or 'ruffle'.

The widespread use of 'starch' (actually starch mixed with size) for ruffs, bands, etc., by all classes above the labourer is indicated in a complaint (Essex Quarter Sessions) in 1614 against a starchmaker of Stratford whose business caused 'such a stink and ill-favour so that liege subjects are not able to come and go along the highway without great danger to their lives through the loathesome smell'.

Legwear

The term 'Hose' continued to include breeches, and was not transferred to the stockings until after 1660.

The 'Trunk Hose' or 'trunk slops' comprised breeches, and nether stocks un ed (to 1610), or trunk hose with short extensions ('canions') down the upper thighs (to 1620). The breeches portion was distended with 'bombast' (wool, flock, hair, etc.).

Knee-breeches continued in the mode of the previous century, as a separate garment, to 1630, when the fashion changed to 'Spanish hose', in which the legs extended well below the knee. There was also the open breeches unconfined at the knee, somewhat resembling modern 'shorts',

Fig. 1. Skimpy doublet with tabbed border, sleeves turned up at wrists, falling bands. Note love-locks and facial patches. Breeches with gaping front opening. Turned-down boot-hose and bucket-topped boots.

From a contemporary caricature of a fop, 1645.

a style appearing at the beginning of the century and revived from 1640 to 1670.

Breeches had a front closure with about ten buttons not concealed by a fly, though more or less hidden by the skirts of the doublet, to which the breeches were attached by hooks and eyes (from 1630).

Footwear

The toe, rounded to 1635, then became tapering to a square toe for the rest of the century. Raised heels, starting from 1600, soon became moderately high with a square base.

A feature of the shoe was the huge rosette or 'shoe rose' adorning the shoe from 1610 until the Restoration. Even more conspicuous were the boots of the period; long, with cup-shaped tops which about 1635 became 'bucket tops' from which the frilled 'boot-hose tops' might emerge.

The 'butterfly' spur-leathers spread widely across the foot (from *c*. 1635), and fashionable pedestrians enjoyed wearing spurs that jingled as they walked. 'You that weare Bootes and Ginglers at your heeles' was a taunt of 1604.

Cloth stockings in that century were being replaced by knitted woollen or worsted ones, and embroidered clocks on them were commonly seen. To protect those of the better quality an over-stocking or 'boot hose' was worn over the stocking inside the boot.

'A pair of green silk stockings 19/-', (1647) and 'a pair of half silk stockings 9/6' (1646) suggest a range of qualities, while the poor wore stockings 'Kersie to the calfe and t'other knit' (1609).

The garters tied in a large bow below the knee on the outer side were often elegant affairs fringed with gold. £1 a pair was a not unusual price. Cross-gartering had become unfashionable early in the century.

Headgear

Men wore hats indoors, at meals and in church up to about 1680, when the size of the wig made a hat indoors a superfluity.

During the first half of the century hats with moderate crowns and wide brims turned up at one side, or the Copotain (sugar-loaf shaped), were the usual types, the former, enriched with a feather, becoming associated with the Cavaliers, and the latter with the Puritans; but neither style was limited to one political party.

The hair, in flowing locks reaching to the shoulders and a forehead fringe brushed to one side, was often adorned with a single 'love-lock' brought forward from the nape of the neck to fall over the chest, where it might be tied with a ribbon bow. It was perhaps as much the name of the 'love-lock' as the thing itself which so exasperated and shocked the Puritan as savouring of carnal delights.

The face was commonly clean-shaven, though a Vandyke beard might be worn or the T-shaped.

> Strokes his beard,
> Which now he puts i' th' posture of a T,
> The Roman T; your T beard is in fashion
> (1618, Fletcher and Massinger, *Queen of Corinth*.)

The fashionable dandy was beginning to wear a periwig and to employ dyed and scented hair, false hair, paint and patches. 'Neat combed and curled, with powdered hair, with long love-lock, a flower in his ear, perfumed gloves, rings, scarves, feathers, points' (1621, Burton's *Anatomie of Melancholy*). Gloves with gauntlets elaborately embroidered or with short tabbed cuffs and heavily perfumed, were the mode. And, as always, the fop, thus adorned, excited scornful comments. So, in 1617 we have, from Henry Fitzgeffery,

> the spruce coxcombe ...
> That never walks without his lookinge-glasse,
> In a tobacco box or diall set,
> That he may privately confer with it,
> How his band jumpeth with his pecadilly,
> Whether his band stringes ballance equally
> Which way his feather wags. ...

But it was not merely the fop whose clothing was expensive; we can gather from bills and inventories some notion of the vast difference in values between the costume of the gentleman and that of his social inferiors, ranging from the labourer up to the petty tradesman. Thus at the beginning of the century a gentleman was paying for ash-coloured satin for his doublet, 14s. a yard; cloth for his cloak at 11s. a yard; taffeta at 7s. and a pair of silk stockings cost 25s. A black beaver hat, lined, with gold band cost £3 4s. while a felt hat was 16s.[1]

Towards the middle of the century a country gentleman was paying 15s. a yard for brown cloth for his suit; holland for shirts at 3s. a yard; pair of worsted stockings 6s. 6d., and Spanish cloth, for his cloak, at 23s. a yard.[2]

It is difficult to estimate the modern equivalent of these prices, but they may be contrasted with those values given in the Essex Quarter Sessions Rolls of items stolen, presumably from village folk and tradesmen. Such a man, in 1609, was described as wearing 'a black stuff doublet, pair of pleated fustian hose, white frieze jerkin, black hat with a band, and ash-coloured knit stockings'; and about the middle of the century there was a theft of 'a black stuff doublet worth a penny, a pair of black stuff breeches, and one of woollen, each worth one penny and a pair of broadcloth breeches worth sixpence'. We may assume these garments to have been well-worn; of a better quality would have been 'a dublett worth 5/-; a paire of breeches worth 5/-' and 'a paire of hedginge gloves worth sixpence'.

Higher up the social scale we find in an inventory of 1620 that a prosperous alderman of Exeter owned 8 gowns; 12 cloaks; 2 tippets; 3 suits of satin; 6 pairs of silk stockings – 'good and bad' – silk garters, a muff and a head-brush amongst his wardrobe.

Among Lord Scudamore's domestic accounts for 1632 are such items as 3½ yards of kersey for the footman's suit at 4s. 6d. a yard, 2¼ yards of broadcloth at 9s. a yard for the groom's coat and '4½ yards at 2/2 the yard to make the foole a coat'.[3] Apparently the fool was breechless.

(All these prices may be multiplied by 12 to 15 to get their approximate modern equivalents.)

Male fashions from 1660 to 1714

After the Restoration the 'old style' of dress survived for some ten years; the short skimpy doublet with tabbed border was worn with either the wide open breeches or, among the fashionables, the Rhinegrave, otherwise known as 'petticoat breeches'. The feature of this garment was the immensely wide legs pleated into a waistband and descending to the knees, so voluminous as to resemble a short petticoat and trimmed with a mass of dangling bunches of ribbons.

'A fine silken thing which I spied walking th'

---

[1] 'The Jervois Archives', *The Ancestor*, 1902.
[2] 'James Master, His Expense Book' (*Archeol. Cantiana*, Vols. XV to XVIII).

[3] F. C. Morgan, *Steward Accounts of John, first Viscount Scudamore.*

other day through Westminster Hall that had as much ribbon about him as would have set up twenty country pedlars'. (1661, J. Evelyn, *Tyrannus or the Mode*). But about 1665, with most men the jerkin and doublet began to be replaced by the coat and waistcoat, the prototype of the modern costume.

The essential change was the growing attention paid to cut and fit of the garments, a feature which the man of fashion came to regard as distinctive of his class.

For a few years the Court circle experimented with a loose flowing version of 'vest' reaching below the knees, with a tunic or surcoat, also loose and somewhat shorter than the vest. But by 1670 the coat was becoming a garment fitting above and hanging loose below the knee level. Its skirt had deep back and side vents, and was fastened down the front by buttons. It had no collar.

Pockets, set very low, were without flaps until 1690.

The sleeves, elbow length, had deep turned-back cuffs, buttoned up to the sleeve in front and open behind.

As the tailor's skill improved a closer fit became a desideratum and thus established the new symbol of class distinction. The well-cut garment presently meant a close-fitting one, and this distinguished the gentleman for the next couple of centuries. It indicated one who had no occasion to engage in degrading activities such as manual work. Here was the first stage towards an entirely novel conception in dress; that superior rank could be demonstrated by the tailor's skill instead of by the display of lavish ornamentation.

The waistcoat (formerly an undergarment) now came to the surface, reaching below the knees, with sleeves but no collar. After 1690 it scarcely reached to the knee.

As the eighteenth century opened the outline of the whole costume became more rigidly defined; the coat skirts, stiffened with buckram, flared out from the waist level, as though to match the lady's hooped petticoat, and the sides and back had deep pleated vents, without which it would have been difficult to sit; the flapped waistcoat, equally stiff, concealed the thighs, and incidentally

the front opening of the close-fitting knee-breeches.

It was the mode for the waistcoat to be fastened by a few buttons at the waist only, so that the ruffled shirt edged with lace might be exposed to view. 'His new silk waistcoat which was unbuttoned in several places to let us see that he had a clean shirt on, which was ruffled down to his middle' (1711, *The Spectator*).

For outdoor wear over such a costume the Restoration introduced the Brandenburg, a large loose overcoat with turned-down collar and wide

Fig. 2. Slightly waisted coat with double vertical pockets, cocked hat trimmed with ribbon. Shoes with high square tongues. *Roxburgh Ballads*, 1680–90.

447

sleeves; and gradually the cloak became shorter. Thus in 1660 Pepys informs us of his intention ' to change my long black cloak for a short one, long cloaks being now quite out'.

But the most conspicuous feature from this time on was the decoration of the head and neck, to which the man of fashion devoted extraordinary attention.

The falling band, deep and bib-like, became replaced by the more exquisite cravat of lace elegantly fringed, and the various modes of tying it indicated niceties of taste. Thus, a twisted form known as a 'Steinkirk' (1690–1730) had the ends passed through a button-hole. Others expanded over the chest. 'His cravat reached down to his middle and had stuff enough in it to make a sail for a barge. A most prodigious cravat-string peeped from under his chin' (1700, Tom Brown, *London Amusements*).

There were even contemptible fellows who would wear made-up cravats fastened at the back of the neck.

But it was the periwig which transformed the wearer into a personage and gave the epoch a distinctive symbol of magnificence. Worn over a shaven head, the periwig no longer imitated the natural hair, but assumed the proportions of a gigantic head-dress. The large French wig, known as the 'full-bottomed', was a mass of curls framing the face and falling on to the shoulders. A centre parting divided the front, which rose up like horns high above the forehead. The Campaign or travelling wig, full but shorter, ended in one or two corkscrew curls or 'dildos' sometimes tied back on the neck in a queue.

The full-bottomed was a ponderous affair heavily powdered. 'His perriwig was large enough to have loaded a camel and he bestowed upon it at least a bushel of powder' (1702, Tom Brown, *Letters from the Dead to the Living*). The cost was no trifle; a Surrey gentleman in 1705 records 'a full-bottomed wigg £22' (in modern money, say £200).

The wig with a queue or lock of hair hanging down behind, and tied with a ribbon, dated from 1700 and developed from the discomfort and heat of the full-bottomed. 'The smart tye wig with the black ribbon shows a man of fierceness of temper', we learn from Steele. Less fashionable folk would be content to wear a plain 'bob wig', without a queue and more or less imitating natural hair.

The fashion for wigs necessarily affected the fashion in hats; the tall-crowned 'sugar-loaf' Copotain was replaced by 1670 either with a wide-brimmed flat-crowned 'boater' or with the brim cocked in a variety of positions, such as the 'Monmouth cock' which Pepys described in 1667: 'a brisk young fellow with his hat cocked like a fool behind, as the present fashion among blades is'.

By 1690 this settled down and persisted for the next hundred years as a tricorne hat symmetrically cocked to form an equilateral triangle with point in front and trimmed with a fringe of ostrich feather.

Boots became less fashionable after the Restoration and were worn chiefly for riding. Shoes, usually black, tapered to square toes with heels high and square. The uppers ended in squared tongues which were high in front of the ankle, a mode copied from the military. 'I took him for a captain ... he has tops on his shoes up to his mid leg' (1707, G. Farquhar, *The Beaux' Stratagem*).

The stockings, from 1690 on, were drawn up over the breeches and turned down in a flat roll above the knee, concealing the garters. Hence they were known as 'roll-ups', a device not employed by the working-class man.

As the eighteenth century opened gentlemen cultivating the art of elegance developed the functions of the 'negligée'. Though called a 'nightgown', this resembled a superior kind of dressing-gown in which the wearer could receive visitors informally.

A specialized version, brought back from India and becoming known as a Banyan, was a garment with a wrapping front reaching the knees which could be worn out-of-doors. Steele in 1713 comments on the custom at Bath, where 'the men of dress in shewing themselves at the Pump in their Indian nightgowns without the least decorum'.

The description of 'a satin nightgown, striped red and white and lined with yellow' reminds us that in the modern dressing-gown we are preserving a tradition of man's liveliest garment.

(A) Cast-iron fireback with arched top and moulded border, and with an all-over design of the Boscobel oak and royal crowns. Stock pattern from soon after the Restoration. *The John Every Collection, Lewes Museum.*

(B) Armorial fireback with shaped top and bearing the coat of arms of the Trevor family, *c.* 1625-50. *Private Collection.*

PLATE 65

Single-branch wall-sconce of cast brass with reflector; signed
"Edward Gore, 1706". *Victoria and Albert Museum.*

PLATE 66

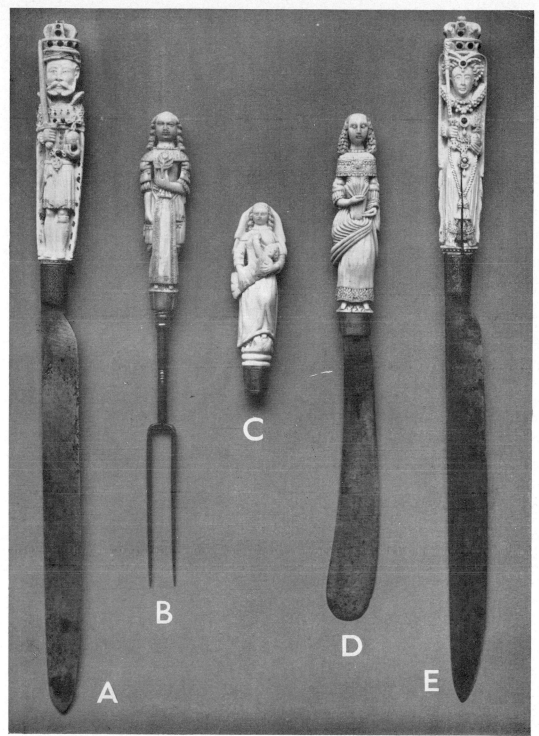

Steel knives and forks with English-carved ivory handles: (A and E) figures of Henry VIII and Elizabeth I set with jewels and dated 1607, ferrules ornamented with damascene scrollwork designs. Part of a set of fourteen knives representing monarchs from Henry I to James I. (B and D) handles carved with ladies in Restoration period dress, the silver ferrule of the knife engraved 'Anne Doyley'. *Victoria and Albert Museum.*

PLATE 67

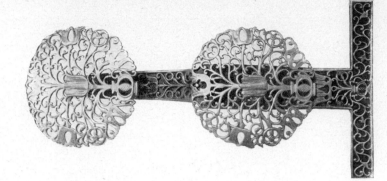

(D) Steel andiron ornamented with perforated facings and fretted convex roundels in latten. Late Charles II. *Private Collection.*

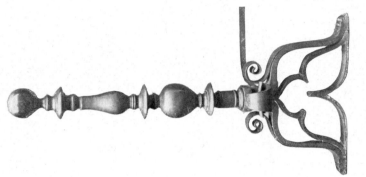

(C) A William and Mary andiron with turned cast brass standard and wrought iron base. *Courtesy the Duke of Rutland.*

(B) Andiron with cast brass standard on low spreading foot of wrought iron, billet bar fitted with wrought iron peg for securing firebasket. At Hampton Court. *By gracious permission of Her Majesty the Queen.*

(A) Wrought iron pot hanger, 4 ft. 8½ in. long. *Victoria and Albert Museum.*

PLATE 68

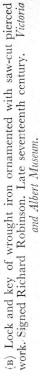

(B) Lock and key of wrought iron ornamented with saw-cut pierced work. Signed Richard Robinson. Late seventeenth century. *Victoria and Albert Museum.*

(A) Warming pans with brass pans, latten covers and wrought iron handles. (*Left*) engraved with the arms of the Clothworkers' Company, *c.* 1610; (*centre*) with Royal Arms without supporters, 1619; (*right*) with punched decoration, mid-seventeenth century. *London Museum.*

PLATE 69   453

A latten rim lock chased with flower and foliage scrollwork. 7¼ in. long. Late seventeenth century. *Victoria and Albert Museum.*

PLATE 70

(B) Red silk damask, from Hampton Court. Italian, end of the seventeenth century.
Victoria and Albert Museum.

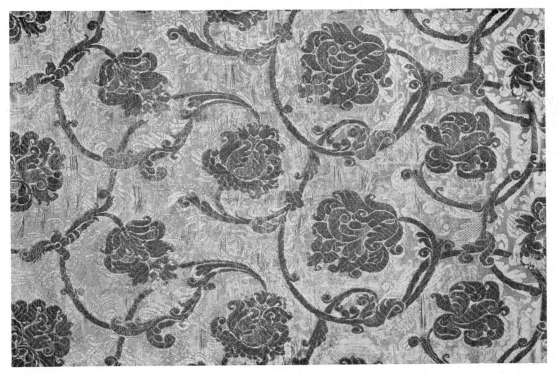

(A) Pink and white silk tissue, brocaded with silver and silver-gilt thread. Italian, third quarter of the seventeenth century.
Victoria and Albert Museum.

PLATE 71

455

Tapestry; the Gods discovering the Amours of Mars and Venus. English (Mortlake),
1620-2. One of a set of *The History of Vulcan and Venus* woven for Charles I as Prince
of Wales. Coloured wools and silks and silver and silver-gilt thread. Signed with the
monogram PDM, for Philip de Maecht.   *Victoria and Albert Museum.*

Tapestry; Oriental subjects. English (Great Wardrobe), late seventeenth or early eighteenth century. Woven in coloured silks and wools. Signed IOHN VANDREBANC FECIT.
Victoria and Albert Museum.

PLATE 73

(A) Long cushion cover, with inscription recording that it was made for the mayoral chair of Hereford in the second year of James I (1604). Embroidered in wool and silk in tent stitch on linen canvas.   *Victoria and Albert Museum.*

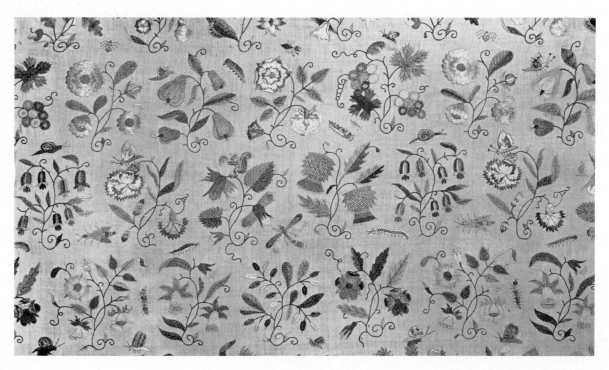

(B) Part of a long cover; English, early seventeenth century. Embroidered in silk on linen. *Victoria and Albert Museum.*

PLATE 74

(A) Needlework cabinet, containing a miniature garden; English, third quarter of the seventeenth century. Scenes from the story of Abraham embroidered in coloured silks and metal thread.   *Victoria and Albert Museum.*

(B) Embroidered picture. The Story of David and Bathsheba; English, signed MY 1656 Coloured silks and metal thread on white satin.   *Victoria and Albert Museum.*

PLATE 75

(A) Painted and dyed cotton hanging; Indian, late seventeenth century. *Victoria and Albert Museum.*

(B) Bed curtain; English, third quarter of the seventeenth century. Cotton and linen twill embroidered with wool in shades of green. *Victoria and Albert Museum.*

PLATE 76

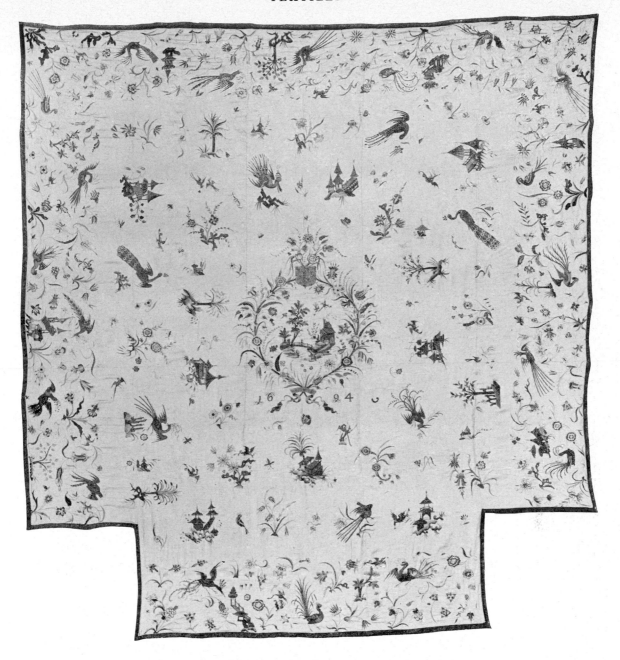

Coverlet; English, signed SARAH THVRSTONE 1694. Embroidered in coloured silks and
silver thread on white satin.   *Victoria and Albert Museum.*

PLATE 77   461

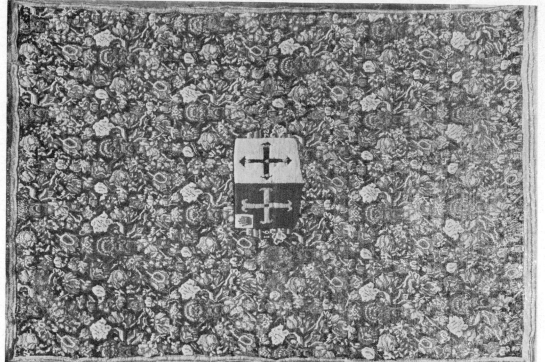

(B) Carpet; English, dated 1672. Arms of Molyneux impaling Rigby, for Sir John Molyneux of Teversall. *Victoria and Albert Museum.*

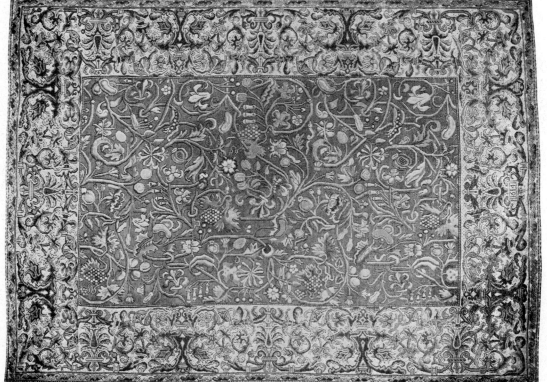

(A) Carpet; English, dated 1614. *Courtesy Sir Westrow Hulse, Bart.*

PLATE 78

(B) Lady Arabella Stuart, c. 1610. Cornet and standing-falling ruff, jacket and bodice, no farthingale. Draped mantle. *Temple Newsam House, Leeds.*

(A) Lady Isabel Rich, c. 1615. Wearing a standing band ('golilla'), embroidered jacket and full gathered embroidered skirt, worn without a farthingale. Tight sleeves with turned-back cuffs. Shoes with large roses. Note extreme decolletage.

PLATE 79

Margaret Laton of Rawdon, 1620–5. On the head an embroidered cornet or shadow, edged with lace, lace falling ruff. Note earrings and ear-string. Embroidered jacket under a loose gown, apron to the waist. *Courtesy Colonel Headborn.*

PLATE 80

The Earl of Dorset, by Isaac Oliver, 1616. Standing band and gorget. Doublet with wings and short tabbed skirt. Paned trunk-hose. Embroidered stockings. Shoes with roses and heels. *Victoria and Albert Museum.*

PLATE 81

465

The younger sons of the 3rd Duke of Lennox, by SIR ANTHONY VAN DYCK, 1639. Young man on left wears loose-fitting doublet open to show the shirt, wide falling band, long-legged breeches fringed below with ribbon loops. Boots with bucket-tops, butterfly spur leathers, lace boothose tops. Young man on right wears velvet cloak trimmed with lace and lined with silk. The doublet sleeve is turned up above the wrist. Note gloves and clogs.

Courtesy the Countess Mountbatten of Burma.

PLATE 82

Gowns with hanging sleeves, having upper and lower openings. The left-hand figure wears a falling band,
the right-hand figure a ruff. Large broad-brimmed hats. From *Essayes by Sr. William Cornwallyes,* 1632.

PLATE 83   467

(B) Sir Horace Vere, 1625. Winged jerkin with false hanging sleeves, standing-falling ruff. 'Cloakbag breeches', embroidered down the seams. Turned-down boot-tops. Spur leathers. *Christchurch Mansion, Ipswich.*

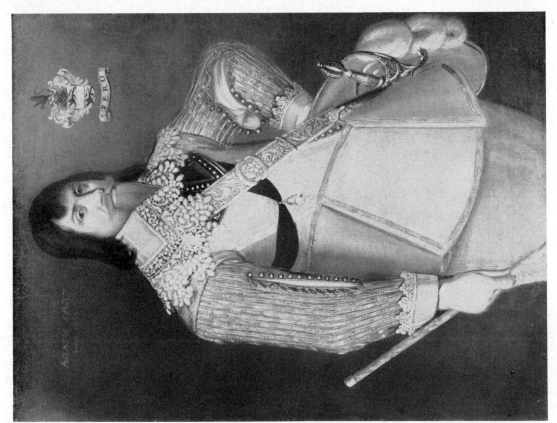

(A) Sir Daniel Goodricht, 1634. Leather jerkin with stuff sleeves probably attached under the wings, no underlying doublet. Broad laced falling band over military gorget. Shoulder belt for sword. Full breeches. *York Art Gallery.*

PLATE 84

(B) Portrait of a Lady, by GERARD TERBORCH, *c.* 1670. Tight boned bodice sloping to a deep point, low neckline finished with a lace falling whisk. Short sleeve with ruffled chemise sleeve emerging. Long skirt open over embroidered underskirt. *Edinburgh Art Gallery.*

(A) Catherine Gage, *c.* 1660. Gown with low circular decolletage, the openings closed by jewelled clasps. Hair style of the early Restoration period. *Christchurch Mansion, Ipswich.*

PLATE 85

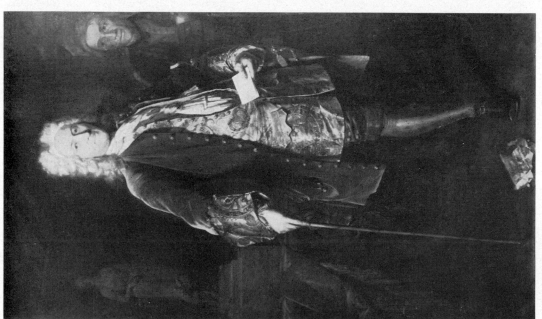

(A) William Leathes, 1705–10. The collarless coat, low in the neck, is buttoned from top to hem. Embroidered waistcoat, open above to display the Steinkirk. Roll-up stockings, shoes with blocked toes and massive heels. Full-bottomed wig. *Christchurch Mansion, Ipswich.*

(B) Portrait of a Gentleman, *c.* 1705–10. Full-bottomed wig. Collarless coat cut low, short sleeves with medium-sized cuffs and protruding lace-ruffled shirt sleeves. Long embroidered waistcoat open to the waist. Steinkirk cravat. *Christchurch Mansion, Ipswich.*

PLATE 86

(A) Miniature portrait of Elizabeth, daughter of James I, later Queen of Bohemia, by Nicholas Hilliard, about 1610. See page 496. *Victoria and Albert Museum.*

B

C

D

(B), (C) and (D) Designs for an earring and pendant set with diamonds, and an aigrette set with rubies and emeralds, by Arnold Lulls, jeweller to Anne of Denmark; first quarter of the seventeenth century. *Victoria and Albert Museum.*

PLATE 87

471

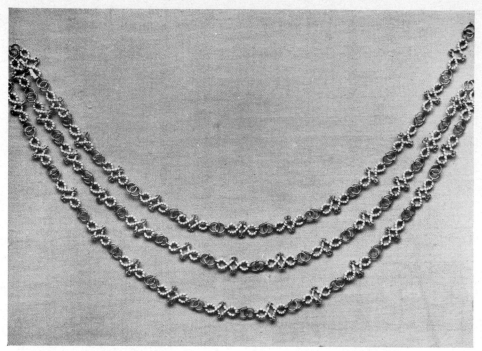

(A) Chain of gold, enriched with white enamel, from the Cheapside Hoard; early seventeenth century. *Victoria and Albert Museum.*

(B) Miniature portrait of a lady after Samuel Cooper: the necklace, earrings and hair adornment of pearls, corsage jewel in the form of a large table diamond set in enamelled gold with a pendant pearl, other jewels composed of diamonds set in gold. About 1640. *Victoria and Albert Museum.*

(c) Miniature case of enamelled gold set with table-cut rubies, formerly containing a miniature portrait of James I; first quarter of seventeenth century. *Kunsthistorisches Museum, Vienna.*

PLATE 88

(A) Part of a chain, enamelled gold, set with paste medallions bearing a cypher; first half of the seventeenth century. *Victoria and Albert Museum.*

(B) Dress ornament, enamelled gold set with seed pearls, first quarter of the seventeenth century. *Victoria and Albert Museum.*

(c) Scissors case, gold enamelled with naturalistic flowers; late seventeenth century. *Victoria and Albert Museum.*

(D) Corsage jewel, gold enriched with black and white enamel and set with table-cut diamonds; second quarter of the seventeenth century. *Victoria and Albert Museum.*

PLATE 89

(A) Watch case of gold, enamelled in colours, given probably by Charles I to the Earl of Monteith; second quarter of the seventeenth century. *Victoria and Albert Museum.*

(B) 'Lesser George' of the Order of the Garter, enamelled gold; about 1640. *Victoria and Albert Museum.*

(C) Reverse of a 'Lesser George', enamelled with a miniature of Raphael's St George, the front set with paste roses; second half of the seventeenth century. *Windsor Castle, reproduced by gracious permission of Her Majesty the Queen.*

(D) Miniature portrait of a lady wearing a necklace of pearls, and brooches of rose diamonds and pearls in silver settings. Attributed to Richard Gibson, about 1680. *Victoria and Albert Museum.*

PLATE 90

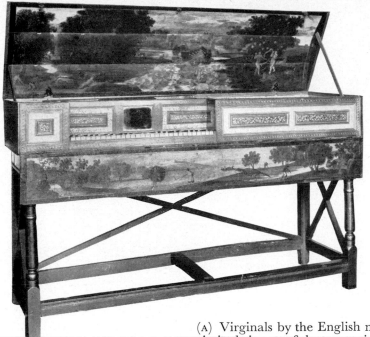

(A) Virginals by the English maker JOHN LOOSEMOORE, 1655. The virginals is one of the two main forms of miniature harpsichord, the other being the spinet (see Pl. 92B). *Victoria and Albert Museum.*

(B) John Bull, by an unknown artist. *Faculty of Music, Oxford.*

(C) Henry Purcell, 1659–1695, attributed to KNELLER. *National Portrait Gallery.*

PLATE 91

475

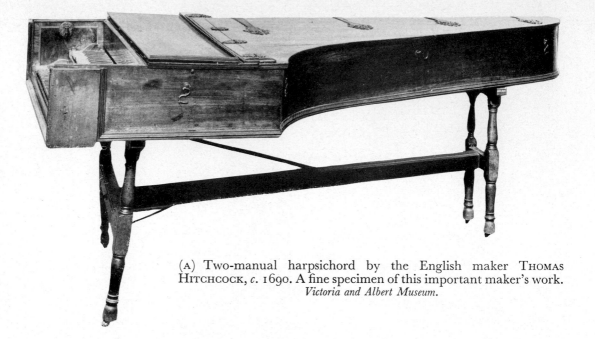

(A) Two-manual harpsichord by the English maker THOMAS HITCHCOCK, *c.* 1690. A fine specimen of this important maker's work.
Victoria and Albert Museum.

(B) Spinet by the English maker JOHN PLAYER, *c.* 1680. See Pl. 91A.
Victoria and Albert Museum.

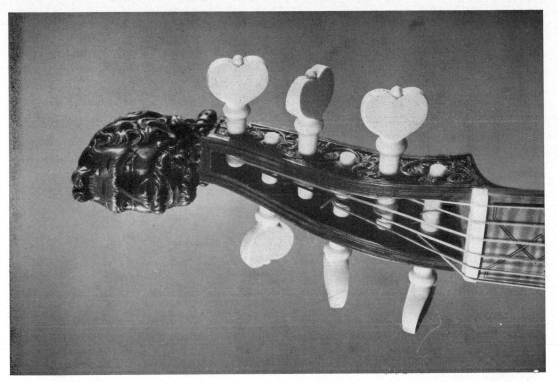

(B) The carved head and peg-box of the Barak Norman gamba. The carved work is original; the ivory pegs are modern.

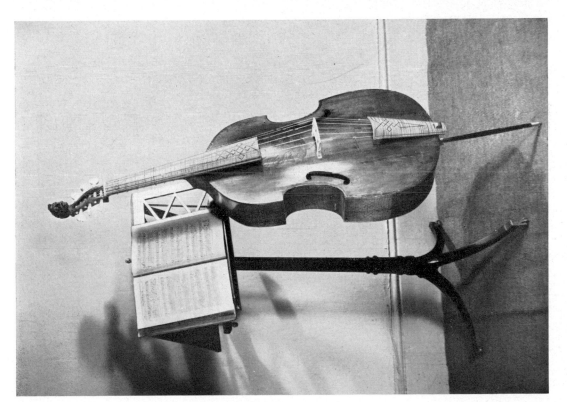

(A) Bass viol (viola da gamba), dated 1696, made in London by BARAK NORMAN, the best and most famed English maker of viols. Still in regular concert use. *Author's Collection.*

PLATE 93

477

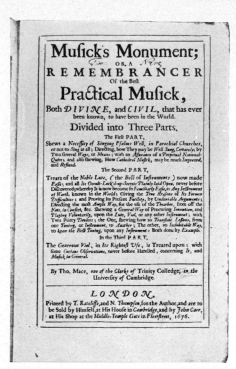

(A) The title-page of one of the most extensive and valuable instruction books in the history of the lute and an important one for the viol (1676). Thomas Mace was a conservative musician, and his nostalgic account of the then declining chamber music of the viols is particularly informative. *Author's Collection.*

(B) A page from Christopher Simpson's *Compendium of Practical Music* (1667), a straightforward and unacademic musical treatise of the mid-seventeenth century. Simpson was probably the most celebrated virtuoso performer of his day on the bass viol (viola da gamba). *Author's Collection.*

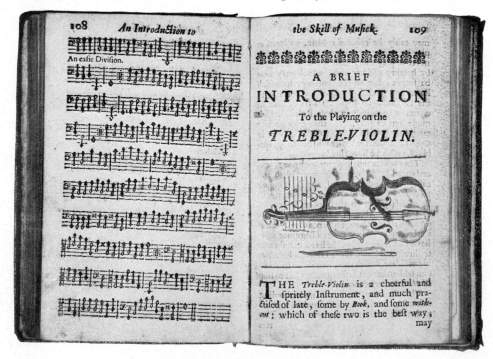

(c) Two pages from Playford's elementary but useful treatise on music (1654) etc.; the left-hand is *An Easie Division* (i.e., set of variations); the right-hand speaks for itself, but the representation of instrument and bow is crude and inexact. *Author's Collection.*

PLATE 94

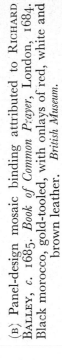

(B) Panel-design mosaic binding attributed to RICHARD BALLEY, *c.* 1685. *Book of Common Prayer*, London, 1684. Black morocco, gold-tooled, with onlays of red, white and brown leather. *British Museum.*

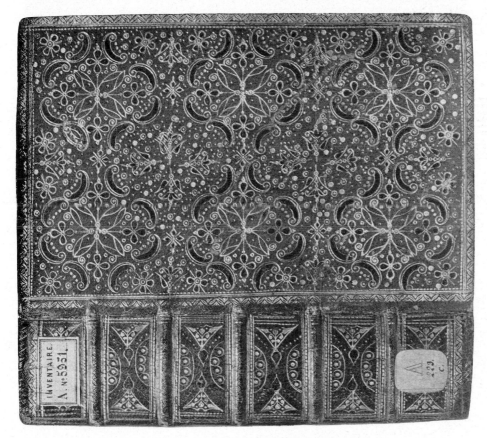

(A) 'All-over' style binding with drawer-handle tools, *c.* 1676. *Holy Bible*, London, 1676. Red morocco, gold-tooled, with details in black paint. *Bibliothèque Nationale, Paris.*

PLATE 95

479

Two copperplate engraved title pages (both much reduced), typical of Stuart book production, both engraved by John Payne. *A Guide to Godlynesse* was published in 1622, and Gerard's *Herball* in 1633.

Women, 1603–1660

The Jacobean woman inherited from the late Elizabethan a shape strangely unfeminine; a rigid figure embedded in a gigantic tub and presenting an outline from which flowing lines where wholly excluded.

From this hard, ungraceful form the Stuart woman had to remould herself into a seductive creature with palpitating undulations. It is true that woman's costume has seldom suggested her real shape and the flow of a trailing gown is perhaps as disguising as a farthingale; but to the male eye the former seems to express, in the perpetual inconstancy of its curvatures, a more feminine quality; and it is significant that only after the flowing gown had replaced the stiff farthingale did poets discover how:

> A sweet disorder in the dress
> Kindles in clothes a wantonness;
> ... A winning wave (deserving note)
> In the tempestuous petticoat. ...
> Do more bewitch me, than when Art
> Is too precise in every part. (Herrick, c. 1650.)

Until 1625 the late Elizabethan modes continued, woman's dress comprising a bodice, known as a 'body', with the skirt known as a 'petticoat'. The term 'kirtle' was already old-fashioned.

The Gown made in one piece was worn, if worn at all, over the bodice and skirt.

The low-necked bodice, corset-like and busked, with long pointed waist and triangular stomacher (which was becoming less usual after 1620), presented a neckline square, round, or U shaped. The extreme decolletage often exposed the whole of the breasts in the unmarried. 'Eye those rising mounts, your displayed breasts, with what shameless art they woo the shamefast passenger' (1641, R. Braithwait, *The English Gentleman and the English Gentlewoman*).

The married woman filled in the decolletage with a partlet, and when no stomacher was worn the neck of the bodice might be considerably higher.

The 'cannon sleeve', projecting above the shoulder, was distended with buckram, narrowing at the wrist; and immense hanging sleeves were

Fig. 3. High-waisted, tabbed, basqued bodice, full sleeve to the elbow and long gloves. Note hair style with forehead fringe of the period. From an engraving by Hollar, 1640.

often added. In the twenties a gigot shape became fashionable.

The French farthingale, either wheel-shaped under a tub-like skirt, or a roll farthingale was worn, the latter being a padded roll tied round the waist like a lifebelt with a gap in front, and commonly known as a 'bum roll'.

The skirt might be open in front, displaying an ornamental apron or 'forepart'.

The gown, fitting the shoulders and thence hanging in loose folds to the ground, had either a standing collar behind or a flat collar all round the neck. Its sleeves were either short, straight, and slit

481

up in front, or as long hanging sleeves open from the shoulder; or the gown might be sleeveless.

The Nightgown was a form of negligée without the corset-like underbodice. It could be worn out of doors. 'I went to church in my rich night-gown and petticoat' (1617, *The Diary of Lady Anne Clifford*: Heinemann, 1923).

With the coming to the throne of Charles I in 1625 there seemed, to some earnest-minded folk, a moral decline in the fashions and habits of both sexes. Thus S. Rowlands in 1628 lamented:

> 'Your gallant is no man unless his haire be of the woman's fashion, dangling and waving over his shoulders; your woman nobody except (contrary to the modesty of her sex) shee be halfe at least of the man's fashion; she jests, she cuts, she rides, she sweares, she games, shee smoakes, shee drinkes, and what not that is evil?'

Doubtless the awful result of discarding the farthingale; for such masculine groans always arise whenever woman gets rid of a restricting garment.

Her costume now reverted to the high waist, the bodice commonly without basques, with bal-looned sleeves often short, and a full skirt reaching the ground in folds, the front open to expose an underskirt. (Here was a dress in which the seated woman could be graceful, a thing impossible in a farthingale.)

The ruff in its various forms had ceased to be fashionable by 1630, its place being taken by some form of 'falling band' or flat, cape-like collar. The decolletage was filled in with a tucker.

The cloak, reaching the ground, had a turned-down collar, and for winter wear there were loose outer coats, hip-length and usually furred. It had become the fashion to go bareheaded, though the late Elizabethan hoods and cornets were not quite extinct.

A more distinctive mode of this period was the head rail, a large square of material pinned around the back of the head. The sugar-loaf hat worn over a white coif and the wide-brimmed 'Cavalier' hat, with or without a plume, were worn for travelling or riding.

The hair was brushed up high over a 'roll' or pad or wire support; the back hair, which in the reign of James I had been coiled into a flat 'bun'

high on the occiput, persisted in that form, while from about 1620 a forehead fringe began to de-velop. Then after *c.* 1645 the front hair was brushed back, with two side partings and cork-screw curls falling to the shoulders.

Shoes, similar in shape to the men's, had com-monly high heels of cork, but after 1625 the longer skirt concealed the feet from view. It was a period when elaborate make-up was in fashion; paint, powder and patches, together with rouge, adorned the face and 'for a penny a chambermaid will buy as much ochre as will serve seven years for the painting of her cheeks' (1641, H. Peach-am, *The Worth of a Penny*).

Night-masks were worn to protect the com-plexion 'to supple wrinkles and to smooth the skin.' Gloves were heavily perfumed, and jewel-lery, in the form of bracelets, necklaces, rings, ear-rings, and chains, was lavishly worn up to the middle of the thirties.

The march of Fashion, checked somewhat during the Civil War, developed at the Restora-tion a more sensual quality. Tight lacing became a marked feature, and the bodice, once more long-waisted, sloped down to a deep point in front, sometimes with short tabs flaring out over the hips.

A low horizontal decolletage encircled the bust and bared the shoulders, while its edge revealed the frill or lace of the top of the chemise. Below this, across the bodice, was a broad lace bertha known as a 'whisk'. The shape of the bosom was thus skilfully emphasized, being in fact the feature of sex appeal in the costume of that period.

Elbow sleeves ended in ruffles, and the volu-minous skirt gathered in small pleats at the waist hung in loose folds to the ground. It was usually open in front to display the petticoat, the front edge of the overskirt either falling naturally or turned back to exhibit a rich lining. The train be-came very long by 1680, when a bustle was adopted with the trained overskirt hitched up over it. From that date an alternative was the Gown, comprising a close-fitting bodice joined to a full gathered and trained skirt which was open in front. The front of the corsage might be em-bellished with an embroidered stomacher ending in a point at the waist.

The sleeves were short and straight, ending just above the elbow where the frilled sleeve of the chemise emerged. After 1690 that frill was generally replaced by single or multiple lace ruffles sewn on. The underskirt or petticoat was very ornamental, often trimmed with three or four lace flounces or a single deep flounce or a reversed flounce at the waist.

The Nightgown at this period was known as a Mantua, and resembled the gown though looser. It might be bound at the waist by a sash. 'Your black crape Manto to dress you in when the mornings are cold' (1681, *Verney Memoirs*), on the one hand and 'Your frugal huswifery Miss in the Pit at a Play, in a long scarf and Nightgown' (1677, Aphra Behn, *The Town Fop*) suggest a wide range of uses.

Growing attention was being paid to the head; thus the Cornet, fitting the occiput, now had long lappets hanging down each side of the face, while from 1690 to 1710 a complicated structure decorated the summit. A wired-up erection of stiff frills of linen towered one storey above another on the head; the wire frame was the 'commode'; the 'tower' was the mass of false curls building up the edifice known as the fontange'.

For Tour on Tour and Tire on Tire,
Like Steeple Bow or Grantham Spire
        (1690, J. Evelyn, *Mundus Muliebris*.)

Similarly the hair itself, lavishly strained, curled, wired, and fortified, developed a swarm of modes, the curls variously nicknamed 'Favourites' 'Confidants', 'Heart-breakers', etc., with ribbon bows or 'knots' placed in appropriate spots.

The Restoration introduced for ladies a shoe tapering to a blunt point with high Louis heel and high instep tongue; likewise mules with short uppers, pointed toes and high heels. For full-dress shoes were elaborately embroidered.

For outdoor wear the Mantle persisted into the eighteenth century; this, a garment entirely different from the Mantua, was a long tent-like cloak reaching the hem of the gown; it had a flat turned-down collar and was worn with a hood. Velvet was a fashionable material. 'A musk-coloured velvet mantle lined with squirrel skins' is mentioned by Steele in 1710.

Fig. 4. Large-brimmed hat and oval ruff, bodice with stomacher front. Full elbow sleeves from which the frilled sleeves of the chemise emerge, ornamental apron. From an engraving by Hollar, 1640.

An elegant wrap was the Scarf, rounded in shape, at waist level behind and lower in front. 'My new scarf from London .... 'tis all extravagance and fancy; I believe there's six thousand yards of edging in it; such an enchanting slope from the elbow!' exclaims a lady in Colley Cibber's play *The Careless Husband*, 1704. Its trimming with furbelows was a feature.

We gather from *The Tatler* that at the beginning of 1709 'the figure of a woman in the present dress bears the figure of a cone which is the same

483

with that of an extinguisher with a little knob at the upper end'. But now a transformation was to take place, for in the following year the Hoop had returned to fashion, at first dome-shaped with petticoat and overskirt enlarged to fit over it.

And presently Swift was writing to Stella in Ireland: 'Have you got the whalebone petticoats among you yet? I hate them; a woman here may hide a moderate gallant under them'.

It is not very surprising, too, that Swift complained how seldom English ladies took active outdoor exercise on foot. Riding, however, was fashionable, and *The Spectator* of 1711 describes the costume: 'Hair curled and powdered hung to a considerable length on the shoulders and tied in a scarlet ribbon; coat and waistcoat of blue camlet, trimmed and embroidered with silver; a cravat of the finest lace; and wore, in a smart cock, a little beaver hat edged with silver ... and made more sprightly by a feather ... a petticoat of the same

Fig. 5. Gown with trained overskirt turned back to show the petticoat. Embroidered stomacher and modesty piece. From a contemporary woodcut, *c*. 1700.

with the coat and waistcoat'. The coat and waistcoat, cut on masculine lines, gave the wearer a mannish air.

The fashionable taste in colours was sometimes for matching that of gown and petticoat, though contrasts were more general. Thus we read of a costume composed of 'a black silk petticoat with red and white calico border, cherry-coloured stomacher trimmed with blue and silver, and a red and dove-coloured damask gown flowered with large trees, and a yellow satin apron trimmed with white' (1709).

For the lady of leisure the task of dressing had become an arduous occupation, and to be successful she required, it seems, to be versed in the indoor arts of elegance. The intricacies of make-up were never more studied. 'By help of paint, powder, and patches they were of a waxwork complexion', comments Ned Ward in 1698, and Henri Misson in the same year informs us, 'I have often counted fifteen patches or more upon the swarthy wrinkled phiz of an old Hag of three score and ten upwards'. Cork balls or Plumpers were worn in the cheeks to produce a roundness, and the face was heavily coated with red and white paint, applied with Spanish wool impregnated with the colouring matter. From William King's *The Art of Love*, 1708, we learn:

Of French pomades the town is full,
Praise Heaven! No want of Spanish wool!
Let them look flush'd, let them look dead,
That cant afford the white and red.

Lead combs were employed to darken the eyebrows, while the more skilful used artificial eyebrows made from strips of mouse-skin. Reddened lips and finger nails, a contemporary poet warns his readers, distinguish 'the Modern Maid'.

Lovers, beware! To wound how can she fail
With scarlet finger and long jutting nail?

SHORT BIBLIOGRAPHY

Historic Costume, by Kelly and Schwabe, 1929.
Histoire du Costume, by Leloir (Volumes 8 and 9), Paris 1939.
English Costume in the Seventeenth Century, by C.W. and P.Cunnington, 1955.

Jewellery

JOHN HAYWARD

This section cannot, for the reasons discussed below, be confined to jewellery made in England by English-born jewellers, but covers, without regard to provenance, the type of jewel worn in England in the seventeenth century. Though there were many highly skilled jewellers working in England at the Court of James I and subsequently of Charles I, and though many of them had English names, it is no longer possible to identify their works, if any have, in fact, survived. With the exception of certain special types, such as mourning rings or badges of the Order of the Garter, there are no particular features in seventeenth century jewellery that can be described as specifically English. There is, on the other hand, no shortage of information about jewellery worn in seventeenth century England; with the exception of the Commonwealth period, persons of quality or wealth wore jewels in profusion, and we have in the innumerable seventeenth century portraits an excellent guide as to the course of fashion. The jewels worn by the sitters in English portraits do not differ from those represented in portraits of persons of similar rank painted in north-west Europe. It was not until the wearing of jewellery ceased to be confined to the aristocracy and the merchant classes that recognizable local types developed. Those who wore jewellery in the seventeenth century were aware of fashions abroad and were interested in remaining abreast of them. Just as the materials of jewellery, gold and precious stones were the subject of international trade, so also highly skilled jewellers wandered from Court to Court bringing the newest fashions with them.

Great fortunes were made by the merchants and bankers who dealt in precious stones: personalities like Sir John Spilman or Sir Paul Pindar. The latter, merchant, adventurer and diplomat alike, after serving for many years as Consul in Aleppo, was sent by James I as English Ambassador to Turkey, whence he eventually returned with a fabulous stock of precious stones. James I used to borrow from Pindar for wear on State occasions a particularly fine jewel set with diamonds, which was valued at one time as high as £35,000; it was eventually purchased, though not paid for, by Charles I in the year of his accession for £18,000. Sir Paul Pindar's jewels also accompanied Charles I in 1623 when, as Prince of Wales, he went with Buckingham to Madrid to negotiate the Spanish match. Pindar, who as late as 1638 negotiated the purchase of a diamond by the King for £8,000, suffered great losses as a result of the Civil War. The façade of his town house, which once harboured precious stones of such immense value, is still preserved in the Victoria and Albert Museum, London.

Jacobean jewels

The accession to the throne of James I in the year 1603 did not mark any new development in dress or the jewellery that adorned it. The immense display of jewels on head, breast, shoulders and indeed on any part of the dress to which they could be conveniently attached continued unabated during the early decades of the century. A foreign observer, writing of Queen Elizabeth in 1597, had said of her: 'She wore innumerable jewels on her person, not only on her head, but also within her collar, about her arms and on her hands, with a very great quantity of pearls round her neck and on her bracelets. She had two bands, one on each arm, which were worth a great price'.

The miniature portrait of James I's daughter, Elizabeth of Bohemia (Pl. 87A), shows a similar profusion of precious stones on her person. On the back of her head is an openwork gold circlet composed of seven members, each of triangular shape threaded with pearls. From the central member hangs down towards the forehead a pendant of gold with a large pearl in the centre, and two large ruby drops. Her earrings are each composed of a large diamond, from which hangs a pear-shaped pearl drop. Around her neck is a necklace of pearls from which hang at intervals six pendants of enamelled gold set with diamonds, rubies and pearls. In the centre of the corsage is a large gold bow set with a ruby, from which hangs a pendant formed of a large table-cut diamond surrounded by two rubies and six smaller table-cut diamonds with a pear-shaped pearl drop. At each corner of the corsage is a further gold bow brooch set with ruby, en suite with that in the centre, but lacking the pendant. On the right shoulder is another jewel, the top of which is concealed by the lace collar. It appears to consist of a group of table-cut diamonds from which hang three pear-shaped pearl drops. Finally, slung over the right shoulder and reaching to the waist, is a magnificent chain of heavy gold links, probably set with diamonds. All these jewels are painted with the greatest fidelity, but their richness and variety are by no means exceptional for the period, and it would be possible to cite many other portraits of noblewomen by Hilliard wearing jewels of comparable splendour.

Royal purchases of jewellery

The State papers of James I's reign show that the Queen, Anne of Denmark, was very extravagant in her purchases of jewellery, and immense debts were incurred by the Crown to the consortium of bankers and jewellers who supplied her. Thus on 18th December 1609, a warrant was issued for the payment of £20,500 for jewels etc. provided for the Queen to the Court

jeweller, George Heriot, Sir John Spilman and others; that the money was not available to meet the warrant is shown by the offer to pay £10 per cent. to any persons prepared to advance the requisite sum. The costliness of her jewels can be measured by the sum of £1,550 paid to Arnold Lulls, another Court jeweller, for a diamond jewel with pendant pearls and two dozen buttons, given her by James I at the christening of Princess Mary in 1605. The cost of a jewel of more modest character is indicated from a warrant dated 20th April 1610, for the payment of £60 to George Heriot in respect of a jewel of gold set with diamonds, a wedding present to one of the ladies of the Queen's Bedchamber.

Anne of Denmark's jewels

The typical renaissance jewel was made in the form of an animal, monster, ship or a little temple with figures; though such jewels became less fashionable as the seventeenth century advanced, they were still worn by Anne of Denmark and the ladies of her Court. The inventory of the Queen's jewels lists many of them, including a ship, a heart entwined by a serpent, a flower *de luce*, a frog, an anchor, a horn of abundance, a burning heart, a parrot, a corselet, a bayleaf with a lizard, etc. That such jewels were already becoming unfashionable we know from the design book of the jeweller and goldsmith, Arnold Lulls, referred to above. This book, which is preserved in the Victoria and Albert Museum, contains designs for jewels of various types, of which three are reproduced here (Pl. 87B, C and D). Whether these designs were ever executed is not known, but they are believed to have been prepared for the Queen and for Henry, Prince of Wales. It will be seen at once that they differ greatly from the so-called renaissance jewel. Whereas in the latter the central feature was usually some exquisite piece of goldsmith's work, enriched with polychrome enamelling, in Lull's designs pride of place is given to the precious stone, and in particular to the diamond. Figure-work is hardly represented, and even enamel is used only to enrich the narrow settings of the large stones of which most of the jewels are formed. Another significant development is the setting of small stones in very narrow collets in such a way as almost to conceal the setting altogether. The illustrations show a pendant, one of a pair of earrings, and an aigrette, a hat or head ornament in the form of a conventionalized feather. The stones used are diamonds, emeralds and rubies with pear-shaped pearl pendants. Lulls' designs doubtless represent the vanguard of fashion, and jewels of this type were still being worn until the Commonwealth put an end for a time to displays of jewellery.

Whereas the wearing of dress that is out of fashion has always been scorned, jewellery has usually had a somewhat longer lease of life, though eventually fine stones have always been reset. If the tradition that the enamelled and jewelled gold pendant in the Soane Museum, London, was worn by Charles I at the Battle of Naseby be true, then he was, with remarkable lack of concern for fashion, wearing a piece that was at least forty years old.

Jewellery was not confined to women's dress during the seventeenth century, though the amount worn by men decreased in the course of that period. The hat-badge grew to large proportions in the early seventeenth century, becoming a far more splendid thing than the medallion worn during the reigns of the Tudors. In 1613 we find a payment of £4,000 to George Heriot for a chain and a hatband set with diamonds made for the late Prince (Henry of Wales). This was probably the same hatband that was included amongst the presents taken on the Spanish embassy in 1623. It was then described as being composed of 'twenty fair diamonds set in buttons of gold in manner of Spanish work, whereof eight are four-square table diamonds, two large six-square table diamonds, two four-square table diamonds cut with facets, two large pointed diamonds, one fair heart diamond and three triangle diamonds'. The finest hat-badges were of aigrette design, similar to Arnold Lulls' drawing (Pl. 87D). Other forms of jewellery worn by men included jewelled buttons and buckles, chains and, more rarely, sword and dagger hilts. A peculiar fashion for men which persisted from Elizabethan days until the middle of the century was the wearing of earrings or of one earring only. Charles I always adhered to the

fashion and hung a large pearl from his left ear; the one he wore on the scaffold in 1649 is still preserved. It is pear-shaped and some ⅝-in. long.

The Cheapside Hoard

If fine jewellery of the seventeenth century is rare, even more uncommon is the thinner and cheaper jewellery worn by the wives of the merchants and richer tradesmen. By a remarkable chance an extensive collection of English early seventeenth century jewellery has been preserved intact. This collection, known as 'the Cheapside Hoard', was discovered in 1912, when a house in Cheapside was being demolished. With the exception of a watch set in a large emerald, the objects in the hoard were not of high intrinsic value and were evidently intended for a middle-class rather than an aristocratic market. The most notable feature of the pieces is their lightness of construction, in marked contrast to the massive character of the typical renaissance jewel. This lightness was evidently dictated by economic rather than æsthetic considerations, and the preservation of this collection enables us, just for the first decades of the seventeenth century, to speak with authority about English second-quality jewellery. It includes most of the categories of jewellery in use at the time, and in view of its extent must have been the stock of a jeweller. Most of the types are familiar from contemporary portraits; the most interesting group is the series of chains, or carcanets to give them their seventeenth century name. The effect of the chains in the Cheapside Hoard (Pl. 88A) does not depend on any particular originality of design or quality of workmanship, but on their attractive colour combinations achieved by the juxtaposition of precious or semi-precious stones and coloured enamel. The majority are composed of little flowers in gold, enamelled white or green, with emerald or diamond centres, alternating with emeralds, garnets, lapis-lazuli panels, etc. One of the most attractive is composed of white-and-gold Tudor roses linked with green leaves. The introduction of an English feature such as the Tudor rose is not paralleled in other surviving jewellery of this period. Some of the gold ornaments that were sewn to dresses

L

during the earlier decades of the century were also enamelled; the example in Plate 89B is very light, and instead of being enamelled with properly fired colours, is decorated in cold enamel, that is with unfired painted colours.

The rose-cut

Precious stones had in the sixteenth century usually been table-cut, a treatment which did not bring out the potential brilliance of the stone. Little refraction of light was to be seen in the diamond, and the effect of the latter was not greatly enhanced by the black varnish with which the back of the stone was painted. Towards the latter years of the sixteenth century various fancy cuts were devised which provided a larger number of facets on the stones, and so increased their brilliance. This development culminated in the rose-cut, based on a hexagon divided into equilateral triangles. The perfection of the rose-cut is usually attributed to certain Dutch lapidaries commissioned by Cardinal Mazarin, but a version of it was already known in England at the beginning of the seventeenth century. Thus a ring supplied by George Heriot for Anne of Denmark was set with a diamond cut in the form of a rose, and the famous Lyte jewel, presented by James I to Thomas Lyte in or before 1611, is set with rose-cut stones. Such technical advances in the cutting of stones doubtless contributed to the change of fashion in favour of precious stones rather than goldsmith's work.

The most easily recognizable English jewellery of the early seventeenth century are the miniature cases of enamelled gold set with precious stones, such as the Lyte jewel referred to above. Their English origin is proved beyond doubt by the miniatures they contain. In spite of their large proportions, they were worn as pendants around the neck; a portrait of Elizabeth Vernon, Countess of Southampton, at Welbeck Abbey shows her wearing two of them, one attached to a chain around her neck and the other pinned to her bosom. The finest work of the English seventeenth century jewellers is to be found in these miniature cases. The example illustrated (Pl. 88c) from the Kunsthistorisches Museum, Vienna, is less familiar than the Lyte jewel or those in the Victoria and Albert Museum, but it is unsurpassed in quality. It originally contained a miniature of James I, but was subsequently used as a frame for a classical cameo. Though described in the 1619 inventory of the Emperor Matthias' collection as 'French work', it must have been a gift from James I to the Habsburg Emperor and was surely the work of one of his Court jewellers.

Influence of dress on jewels

During the third decade of the century a change took place in female dress; the farthingale skirt was abandoned and clothes became altogether looser and less formal. There was at the same time a great passion for lace. The wearing of much lace about the neck and bosom left less space for the display of jewellery, but when in the 1630's lace in turn went out of fashion, there was no return to the almost barbaric profusion of jewellery of the early years of the century. The effect of the change can be seen in the miniature of an unknown lady of about 1640 in Pl. 88B. The contrast is most striking; just as the renaissance jewel was replaced by the jewel composed mainly of diamonds, in which the setting played a very secondary and mainly functional role, now the latter has given way to a lavish display of pearls. The extensive décolletage worn by the ladies of Charles I's Court provided the ideal frame for the restrained beauty of lustrous pearls. Not only was a rope of large pearls *de rigueur* around the neck, but pearls were entwined in the hair, whence indeed they were never finally evicted until the more practical days at the end of the eighteenth century. Pearls were also worn as earrings and as pendants from brooches and clasps, and finally as a girdle about the waist.

The portraits of fashionable ladies of the period immediately preceding the Civil Wars, painted by Van Dyck and his school, show an extraordinary conformity of dress. There is almost invariably a large jewel in the centre of the corsage, and the open sleeves are held together over the shoulder and down the arms with a number of clasps. It is evident from the portraits that these jewels were composed of large stones with plain settings. The absence of any particular artistic merit in the settings has led to their being broken up and reset;

as a result such jewels are considerably more rare than those of the early seventeenth century. A fine brooch of the type worn in the centre of the corsage is illustrated in Plate 89D. Its form is derived from that of a knot, and similar knots are to be seen in many portraits, composed of ribbons in the case of the less wealthy sitters, and of enamelled gold in the case of the rich. A jewel of this type belonging to Lady Warwick just before the Restoration was described as a 'fair knot of gold enamelled with tulips and set with diamonds'. A knot or bow of some sort was the favourite form of corsage ornament during the remainder of the seventeenth century, and continued to be so until well into the following century. The pattern books of jewellery designs published in Paris about the middle of the seventeenth century already include a number of the large open bow brooches or pendants of the type subsequently known as the Sévigné. The most influential of these pattern books, both inside and outside France, was that published by the Parisian jeweller, Gilles L'Egaré, who was jeweller to Louis XIV. Published in 1663, it contains, besides various types of Sévigné, girandole earrings, cross pendants and miniature frames set with table- and rose-cut stones. The designs for the backs of the jewels in the form of baroque floral compositions are amongst the most pleasing that the seventeenth century produced. The enamelled gold scissors case in Plate 89C shows something of the effect of the L'Egaré designs, though the flowers are more formally arranged than would be the case in a L'Egaré jewel.

In addition to jewels worn around the neck and shoulders, the lady of the first half of the seventeenth century wore a variety of more or less decorative objects attached to her girdle, which was itself probably of enamelled gold, or of silvergilt. The links from a chain illustrated in Plate 89A, which is of gold set with pastes, might have served equally well as a necklace or a girdle. To the girdle were attached a pomander, a scissors case (Pl. 89C), a key ring, a case containing knife and fork, and in some cases a small mirror and a prayerbook enclosed in a jewelled gold binding (girdlebook) as well. These various articles were often suspended from long chains and must have greatly

encumbered movement. The equipage might well be completed with a watch, the latter worn around the neck or attached to the girdle. The English watch case illustrated in Plate 90A, which was given by Charles I to the first Earl of Monteith, bears out the claim that the English jewellers of the first half of the seventeenth century were the equal of those working in foreign capitals.

Enamelled decoration

Next to miniature cases, watch-cases are the most useful source of information as to the versatility of the English jeweller in the seventeenth century. The presence of an English signed movement, if not an absolute guarantee that the case enclosing it is English, makes it exceedingly likely, and we can, therefore, recognize all the forms of jewellers' work on such cases as English. Besides the usual enamelled gold of the type shown in Plate 88C we find painted enamels, *champlevé* enamel and a rare and difficult technique known as *émail en résille sur verre*, in which cells were cut in the surface of a glass panel, lined with foil and then filled with coloured enamel that fused at a lower melting point than the glass ground. The same technique is also found on a locket in the Victoria and Albert Museum which is thought to be of English origin. Though jewellery of the highest quality was certainly produced in this country, it seems that fashions were probably derived from abroad. No pattern books of jewellery were published in England during the seventeenth century, and it must be presumed that the jewellers relied on books imported from France for new ideas. Though the individual jeweller would doubtless have been capable of drawing up a design for a client, he would have had to look to Paris to learn something of new developments in fashion. Charles II's appointment in 1666 of a Frenchman, Isaac le Gomme (or Gouse), as Jeweller to the Royal Household in succession to the deceased Englishmen, Francis and John Simpson, is not insignificant in this connexion. Such was the dominance of the French jewellers that the type of jewel decorated with opaque enamels in black and white or in light blue and white, which was so popular during the second half of the century, is

Fig. 1. Two designs for miniature cases, each set with a rose diamond. From *A Book of Severall Jewellers Work* made by J.B.Herbst, London, 1710. *Victoria and Albert Museum.*

still generically known as 'Louis Treize', though many of them were made outside France.

While the jewels of the first quarter of the century were mainly enriched with translucent enamels applied by the *champlevé* technique, by the middle of the century the cheaper technique of painted enamel was employed for the decoration of the backs even of the better-quality jewellery. The technique of painted enamel was most effectively developed by members of the Blois family of goldsmiths and watch-case makers, Toutin. Painted enamel of other than purely conventional design is rarely found on jewels, where there was little space available for the representation of figure-subjects such as those painted by the watch-case enamellers. Miniature cases, on the other hand, were frequently decorated with painted enamel.

One further group of identifiable English jewels remains to be described – those of the Order of the Garter. The jeweller who made them was restricted to a uniform design, but was able to introduce variety by using differing materials and settings. The jewel illustrated in Plate 90B belonged, according to tradition, to the Earl of Strafford and dates from before the Commonwealth. Plate 90C shows the back of a 'lesser George' in the Royal collection at Windsor Castle, enamelled with an attractive miniature after Raphael. The front is set with a cameo of St George and the Dragon within a ring of paste brilliants.

The Civil War

The twenty years between 1640 and 1660 wrought great havoc as far as jewellery was concerned. During the Civil Wars innumerable jewels were broken up in order to contribute towards the military chest of one side or the other; not only were all the Crown Jewels broken up and sold, but many private families sacrificed their jewels as well. Subsequently during the Commonwealth there were few commissions to produce fine jewels, and the craftsmen must have been hard put to it to find enough work to earn their bread. The Commonwealth did not, however, discontinue the long-established custom of rewarding foreign envoys with a fine jewel, and the few references to commissions given to jewellers in the State papers at this time refer to presents for diplomats. Charles II ran up heavy debts to the Royal jewellers, Francis and John Simpson, in respect of the cost of jewels presented to ambassadors. In a petition dated as early as February 1662 we find the firm of Simpson asking for the payment of the sum of £15,595 in respect of jewels supplied for the

King's Service. We do not, however, encounter such immense sums as were expended during the reign of Charles II's grandfather. In September 1658 the Protector paid £350 for a jewel for the French ambassador, and ten years later, in June 1668, Isaac le Gomme received £530 for a jewel, the destination of which was not specified.

Restoration fashion in jewellery

The absence of any progress in jewellery design during the Commonwealth becomes noticeable when one turns to the fashions of the Restoration (Pl. 90D). No change can be seen as against those of Charles I's reign. The beauties painted by Lely wear the same loose robes with deep decolletage, the same open sleeves, the same pearl necklaces and earrings as the generation which had sat to Van Dyck. The jewels in these Lely portraits are not painted with the careful detail that we find in the Elizabethan portraits. Their treatment was so far standardized that what appear to be the same jewels are represented in a whole series of portraits. The Restoration gave rise to a large trade in Stuart commemorative jewellery; lockets, rings, pendants, cuff-links and buttons were all produced with minute portraits of the Martyr King. Much of this jewellery, which was of quite low intrinsic worth, has survived to the present day, and it is by far the commonest type of English jewellery of the period existing. It owes its survival as much to its sentimental appeal as to its low value.

Though the lady of the latter years of the seventeenth century wore considerably less jewellery than would have been normal some fifty years before, it would not be correct to think that anything like the sobriety of the Puritan interlude had persisted. The oft-quoted lines from Evelyn's *Mundus Muliebris* or *Voyage to Marryland*, published in 1690, which gives a rhyming catalogue of a fashionable lady's toilet convey an idea of its extent:

> Firstly the chatelaine
> To which a bunch of onyxes,
> And many a golden seal there dangles,
> Mysterious cyphers, and new fangles.
>
> Diamond buckles too,
> For garters and as rich for shoe.

> A manteau girdle, ruby buckle,
> And brilliant diamond rings for knuckle.
>
> A sapphire bodkin for the hair,
> Or sparkling facet diamonds there:
> Then turquois, ruby, emrauld rings
> For fingers, and such pretty things;
> As diamond pendants for the ears
> Must needs be had, or two pearl pears,
> Pearl necklace, large and oriental
> And diamond, and of amber pale.[1]

The brilliant-cut

Evelyn refers to 'brilliant diamond rings', but it is not clear from the context whether he is referring to the 'brilliant-cut' or merely describing the effect of the precious stones. The 'brilliant-cut' (a double cone with its top truncated to form a flat, eight-sided table, the upper and lower slopes cut into a series of triangular facets) was invented by the Venetian, Vincenzo Peruzzi, about 1700, and it seems unlikely that Evelyn would already have been familiar with it. The importance of the discovery can hardly be exaggerated, for it transformed

[1] One type of jewel not mentioned by Evelyn is the 'Brandebourg'. These were in fact frogs, copied from those worn by Polish gentlemen but executed in diamonds instead of in cord. A series of them graduated in size were worn down the front of the bodice.

Fig. 2. Two designs for scissor cases, set with rose diamonds. From *A Book of Severall Jewellers Work* made by J. B. Herbst, London, 1710. *Victoria and Albert Museum.*

the diamond and brought out its qualities to the full. It did not, however, by any means displace the rose-cut completely, and roses were still produced and set, though not in the most expensive jewels, throughout the eighteenth century.

During the first half of the seventeenth century enamel, either translucent or opaque, had been used to enrich the back of many jewels and also to add touches of colour to the front as well. Those jewels that were mainly composed of precious stones offered little scope for the enameller, but there was another type of jewel, including such objects as miniature and scissor cases (Figs. 1 and 2), scent-flasks and étuis, which was more suitable for enamelled ornament. An example is illustrated in Plate 89c; the painting of the flowers on the scissors case, though doubtless copied from a pattern book, is most effectively adapted to the space available.

Late Stuart jewels

Such pieces are, however, no more than by-products of the jeweller's art, and late Stuart jewellery must be judged by the major pieces which can now be studied only in portraits. The jewels are more remarkable for their large size than for their design; they usually consist of large square stones with pearls or smaller gems set at the angles. The portraits of ladies of the Charles II period show the rather uninteresting character of this late seventeenth century jewellery. This can scarcely have been due to lack of imagination on the part of the artists. Confirmation for the view that the jewellers were responsible can be found in the ledger of Sir Francis Child, who supplied jewellery to the Crown from 1689 to 1696. This ledger contains rough sketches of the various jewels that passed through his hands, and the designs seem excessively stereotyped.

To judge by the Royal accounts that have been preserved, the banking house of Child mainly supplied jewellery intended to be passed on as rewards for foreign ambassadors. Unfortunately the books give no details as to the appearance of these presents, but they do give the prices. For the most part, a ring costing between £200 and £400 was adequate, but the more important ambassadors received miniatures of the King and Queen set in jewelled frames and these were extremely costly. Thus five jewels with miniatures for the Dutch ambassadors in October 1689 cost £5,000, while two jewels for the Venetian ambassadors cost £1,600 in May 1696.

Looking back at the seventeenth century jewellery as a whole, one of the most remarkable features is the persistence of enamelled enrichment, in spite of the development of new methods of cutting precious stones and the increased range of effect obtainable with stones. It was not until the end of the century that enamel was finally banished to the back of the setting, and not until the eighteenth century that its use was generally abandoned.

SHORT BIBLIOGRAPHY

Inventory of the Jewels and Plate of Queen Elizabeth I, by A. J. Collins, 1956.
English Jewellery from the fifth century A.D. to 1800, by Joan Evans, 1921.
A History of Jewellery, 1100–1870, by Joan Evans, 1953.
English Watches (Victoria and Albert Museum), by J.F.Hayward, 1956.
The Cheapside Hoard of Elizabethan and Jacobean Jewellery, London Museum Catalogues, No. 2, 1928.
Jewellery, by H. Clifford Smith, 1908.

Design for an aigrette, signed by M.Gunter, Amsterdam, 1711. Röhsska Museum, Göteborg.

Music and Musical Instruments

ROBERT DONINGTON

Early Stuart England musically an island

The chief musical development which coincided with the Stuart age in England first gathered impetus in Italy. It was a development in the art of writing music melodically, as opposed to contrapuntally.

Melody is itself a more ancient art than counterpoint. It is, so to speak, a primary art, whereas counterpoint is the secondary art of combining melodies. The combination results in harmony; but harmony can arise on other foundations than a contrapuntal foundation.

It is indeed perfectly possible to write music in which harmony plays no part at all. Primitive melody is of this kind. True folk music, which is by no means necessarily primitive, has usually remained devoid of harmonic implications.

Melody as we in the modern West conceive it, on the other hand, has harmonic implications whether we intend it or not. In all really harmonic music there is a pressure which one chord exerts in the direction of the next; and it is very often this harmonic pressure which is the essential driving force. The tune which seems to be taking us along is shaped by the chords and not the other way about.

The third force in music is rhythm; but this has the distinction of being necessary to both the other two, while they are not necessary to it. The length of notes in melody and the timing of chord changes in harmony are aspects of rhythm whose importance it would be impossible to exaggerate. But the beat of a drum can stir the heart without a suggestion either of melody or of harmony.

Now good tunes there have always been, that is obvious: what is perhaps less generally known is that tunes have been harmonized, in the straightforward sense of having chords added to them, long before the rather sophisticated technique of counterpoint. There is a fascinating early Stuart manuscript in the British Museum which gives unexpected evidence of this. It is a collection of Welsh music for the harp. The contents are older than the manuscript; some of them as old as the twelfth century, having been passed down as a jealous tradition of hereditary Bardic material. But the Welsh harp was a fashionable instrument at Court: after all, the Tudors had come from Wales; and the music was undoubtedly still in use when this copy of it was made, in about 1613.

What is so remarkable about this most unusual written collection of works in a style normally traditional, and for the most part long since forgotten, is that, as comes very naturally to the harp, the music is melody accompanied by good fat chords carefully spaced out for either hand. In other words, it is vertical harmony largely dating from a period at which the more old-fashioned histories of music still do not recognize that vertical harmony had been invented. But it had been invented: not, as the old-fashioned belief was, in the late sixteenth century as a derivative of the horizontal harmony produced by counterpoint, but demonstrably in the twelfth century when counterpoint was still something of a novelty; and inferentially far earlier when counterpoint was still to come. For the Bardic tradition of Celtic harp music at the time of these earliest surviving medieval specimens of it was already an art of the periphery, elbowed out of the main centres of European civilization. At the centre the novel art of producing harmony by weaving melodies together horizontally, i.e. contrapuntally, was all the fashion.

The block chords which were the harmony of the Celtic harpists and the interwoven melodies which were the harmony of the medieval contrapuntalists have nevertheless one essential characteristic in common. They never seriously modulate: they remain, as we should describe it, virtually in one key. There is plenty of urgent movement from one chord to the next; yet all this movement takes place around a stationary centre of tonal gravity.

It was the composers of the Renaissance who to the best of our belief first evolved the art of modulation. Little by little their chords began to progress not merely around a stationary centre of tonal gravity but around a centre which is in itself in motion. As we should describe it, they made a journey through the keys in course of the music. And all this they undeniably did by means of counterpoint.

By the sixteenth century the situation was that melody and harmony had been brought to a state of almost perfect balance. You could not say that the living tissue of contrapuntal melodies was itself moulded by the urgent movement of the harmony, as you can certainly say of the eighteenth century counterpoint of Bach or Handel. You could not say that the expressive requirements of the melody outshone the movement of the harmony in interest and significance, as you can say of the dramatic Italian music of the early seventeenth century. You could only say that the interest was evenly distributed – and not merely evenly distributed, but so blended that the pattern of melody and harmony is quite exceptionally unified.

This exceptional degree of unity and balance is not confined to the technical characteristics so far described. It extends throughout sixteenth century music, and in some ways throughout the sixteenth century mentality. Sacred and secular music, and for that matter high-brow and low-brow music, merged at their boundaries with an easy familiarity we in modern times are the poorer for having lost.

The relative unity of sixteenth century music had its geographical as well as its mental aspects. Our Tudor musicians as a whole lay in the main European stream. Tallis and Byrd compare with Palestrina or Lassus not only in merit, but also in style.

That is no longer the case with the Stuart music of the seventeenth century. During the first half of this century our musical situation was that of an island substantially, though not of course wholly, cut off from the mainland of European development. During the second half of the seventeenth century traffic was resumed across the Channel, though much more in the incoming than the outgoing direction. Our musical history then revolved around a series of more or less successful assimilations of continental influence, each somewhat paradoxically revealing the profound inner strength of our native tradition of music. Not until the death of Purcell did this tradition more than temporarily falter, and not until the English sojourn of the German-born but Italian-adapted Handel did our native genius for music pass into a long eclipse.

Modern technique in late renaissance music

Before tracing the two stages of our Stuart musical history in a certain amount of detail, let us consider what were the new factors in continental music – for present purposes almost synonymous with Italian music – which during the first half of the sixteenth century were substantially rejected by English musicians, though not so during the second half.

I have called them a development in the art of writing music melodically as opposed to contrapuntally. But since melody is much more ancient than counterpoint and even than harmony, the novelty of the development – and it really had elements of extreme novelty – clearly did not lie merely in the fact that the melody was made more significant and interesting than the harmony, and that the contrapuntal element was so exiguous as to become virtually non-existent. The novelty lay in a quite conscious and deliberate attempt to put both melody and harmony at the service of the human passions.

The attempt, of course, late though it arose in the history of the Renaissance, was a typically renaissance undertaking. The predominant music of the sixteenth century was sacred counterpoint: in so far as art can ever be called impersonal, the art of Palestrina is impersonal. A better description might be that it expresses as no other style of music has ever quite expressed the most numinous and universal of all the great archetypes deep within the human soul. The swift play of passion lies more visibly on the surface: in reality it is just as archetypal and its sources lie just as deep; but by contrast with the serenity of Palestrina, we can readily see that the quicksilver flexibility of Caccini, Peri, Monteverdi and the other pioneers of the Italian new music at the turn of the sixteenth and seventeenth centuries stands for everything that historians of the Renaissance mean by Humanism.

Let us put it, then, that the new factors in the modern music of late renaissance Italy were first: melody of a singularly flexible yet unpretentious outline moulded to every outline, both phonetic and emotional, of a highly dramatic and expressive verbal text; and second: harmony of great simplicity, in a sense even of great crudeness, but also very often of quite extraordinary boldness, power and unexpectedness, equally subordinated to dramatic and expressive need.

All this arose at first from the ambition of a small and select circle of aristocrats and connoisseurs, together with their professional protégés, to recreate what they fondly imagined to be the musical style which accompanied the great mythological dramas of classical Greece – another and direct link, of course, with the renaissance ideal. What came Venus-like from a good deal of inevitable preliminary froth and foam was in fact the early Italian opera of Monteverdi; but that was only the most obvious and immediate outcome. No music, I think, could be of greater genius; but the style in its first form did not last long nor produce numerous masterpieces. On the other hand, the general influence of its particular brand of directly expressive melody and support-ing harmony can hardly be exaggerated. It was the very germ-seed of the succeeding baroque period of music.

By far the most typical structure of a baroque work of music is a tuneful melody on top; a strong supporting bass-line at the bottom; and in between, the chords filled in so as to provide the harmony, but with a certain indifference as to the texture with which they do so, and not necessarily any contrapuntal working at all. Sometimes the melody itself may, as it were, go into duplicate: instead of one tune there are then two tunes, but more or less at the same pitch, and intertwining as they go along. This is, of course, technically a kind of counterpoint, but to the ear the effect is really that of a twin melody with the usual supporting bass-line and filled-in harmonies. This form, when for instruments, is known as the trio-sonata, the two melodic instruments and the bass instrument being separately counted to add up to three, but not the keyboard instrument which doubles the bass-line and fills in the harmonies.

The modern technique not characteristic of early Stuart music

Now let us turn to the English musical scene in 1603 as Elizabeth ended her long life and eventful reign, to be succeeded by the first of England's Stuart kings.

Who were then our most reputable musicians? There was Byrd, elderly but with much creative activity still in front of him, the doyen of English composers. There was Morley, already ailing; and Gibbons, young, but destined for a somewhat early death; there was Tomkins, in old age the last survivor of the post-Elizabethan school – he did not die until 1656. These were primarily vocal composers, though also very productive for the harpsichord and organ and to a lesser extent for viols. Between them they continued the Elizabethan tradition of sacred counterpoint, adding to it (particularly Gibbons) the new and rather less traditional verse-anthem, with its solo interludes. They founded and carried on our English variety of madrigal, an importation from Italy when there already on the verge of decline, but here acclimatized for a brief, belated and somehow unmistakably English decade or so of brilliant efflorescence. But they did not respond perceptibly to the Italian new music of Caccini, Peri and Monteverdi in its monodic development. They neither avoided counterpoint nor subordinated the musical texture to the words.

Nor did the men do so whose chief work lay with the secular madrigal, like Kirbye and Wilbye. Not even Dowland, Campion or Rosseter (composers whose music includes some of the world's great songs and whose Ayres have a most direct and flexible melody) chose to dispense with counterpoint in their accompaniments, which were played on the lute or on viols, sung by other voices, or given with a combination of these methods. In comparison with Byrd, or even with Gibbons, we may regard them as the modernists of late Elizabethan and early Stuart England; but even so they did not construct their music on the new Italian model.

At this same date, John Bull was establishing on the keyboard, like Dowland on the lute, an international reputation as a virtuoso instrumentalist. He composed perhaps the greatest of all the keyboard music of the great English school, to which Farnaby was meanwhile contributing some of the tenderest examples. This, too, was in a modern style, and one in which England actually excelled the Continent, but it is not the monodic style of Monteverdi, being, in fact, as elaborate in musical construction as it is effective in performance.

So, too, Giovanni Coperario – who was christened plain John Cooper – visited Italy at the turn of the century, and came home to enliven the Tudor chamber music of the viols with the classic grace of the Italian fantasias; but that had not much to do with the modern Italian style of the day, being, on the contrary, highly contrapuntal and in the best sense of the word abstract. His immediate successors were two Englishmen of genuinely Italian extraction. Thomas Lupo was a felicitous composer of loosely contrapuntal fantasies for viols; Alfonso Ferrabosco the Second was a very profound one, with a versatile idiom embracing great brilliance at the one extreme and a most intimate serenity at the other.

These Jacobeans were followed by two Caroline composers most interestingly contrasted. William Lawes was a tempestuous figure who got himself almost gratuitously killed at the siege of Chester in 1645. His inspiration, too, was tempestuous. In boldness of harmony he is one of music's perennial moderns – rather like Purcell, on whom his influence can be most clearly traced. He arrived at his romantic harmony through counterpoint of six parts in his finest fantasies for viols: just the opposite of the Italian monody which was modern music to his continental contemporaries. It is worth mentioning that this William had a brother Henry who was one of the few Englishmen actually to experiment with the monodic method; but he was a much lesser man, and neither his nor the other English experiments in this kind yet led very far.

John Jenkins was the opposite of William Lawes in every obvious way but degree of talent. A most equable man in private life, he lived on in his old age well into Purcell's time. His five-part fantasies for viols are many of them masterpieces in a warmly lyrical mood conveyed through graceful but resourceful counterpoint. His later works for violins show Italian influence and belong to the second phase of Stuart music rather than to the first.

We may sum up the story thus far as follows. The structure of all the important English music of the early seventeenth century remained in more or less degree traditionally contrapuntal: that is to say, from the viewpoint of the music of the future as it was already developing in Italy and elsewhere, old-fashioned. Yet the mood is somehow not old-fashioned at all: it is forward-looking. This forward-looking mood is conveyed chiefly in the harmony.

It was a most paradoxical position. Right down to Purcell's death the harmony of the best English music remained more striking, warm and feelingful than any on the Continent but the finest of the Monteverdi school. Yet even when the channels were fully opened up again later in the century, it was England which accepted the continental influence rather than the other way about. It was the characteristic of Stuart music as a whole – not excluding Restoration Stuart music – to be far more valuable in itself than as a legacy to the immediate future.

The amateur still well served in early Stuart music

The character of English society did not change with the death of Elizabeth. Certainly there were forces of disruption at work which were presently to break into open conflict; but on many levels Jacobean and Caroline England remained, what Elizabethan England had long become, an exceptionally united nation.

This was markedly the case between class and class. 'A follower of a great lord was wont to say', wrote John Robinson (*Observations*, 1625) 'that he had in effect as much as his lord, though he were owner of little or nothing, considering how he had the use of his lord's garden and galleries to walk in, heard his music with as many ears as he did, hunted with him in his parks, and ate and drank of the same as he did, though a little after him; and so for the most part of the delights which his lord enjoyed.' His lord's music might include a resident master of the stature of John Wilbye, for example, at Hengrave Hall, where surviving inventories of instruments point to everything from light music played professionally at meals, on the one hand, to lute songs, madrigals and viol consorts performed among the family, their friends and their relations, on the other.

This was, no doubt, an ideal setting; but the conditions for amateur music remained generally favourable in early Stuart England. And it must be realized that equal-voiced counterpoint has these great advantages for the amateur: each part is of equal interest; and none is of especial technical difficulty. The English fantasies for viols include some of the profoundest instrumental chamber music ever to be designed specifically for amateur enjoyment.

Although in many outward respects the viols are very similar to the violins, both families being string instruments played with the bow and of basically the same construction, their musical effect is decidedly contrasted. The viols are made of much thinner wood and are much more lightly strung. Their tone is consequently less robust; but it is singularly free and colourful. When several viols are played together, the sound of each is heard very distinctly from its neighbours. It is for this reason that they are so admirably suited to the contrapuntal chamber music of early Stuart and Commonwealth England. The viols were given preference over the violins so long as that style of chamber music remained fashionable.

Thomas Mace, a great teacher of the lute and the viol in his day (see Fig. 1, p. 162, and Pl. 94A), tells us something of the spirit in which he and his musical associates enjoyed their chamber music:

'We had for our Grave Musick, Fancies of 3, 4, 5, and 6 Parts to the Organ; Interpos'd (now and then) with some Pavins, Allmaines, Solemn, and Sweet Delightful Ayres; all which were (as it were) so many Pathettical Stories, Rhetorical, and Sublime Discourses; Subtil, and Accute Argumentations; so Sultable, and Agreeing to the Inward, Secret and Intellectual Faculties of the Soul and Mind; that to set Them forth according to their True Praise, there are no Words Sufficient in Language; yet what I can best speak of Them, shall be only to say, That They have been to my self (and many others) as Divine Raptures, Powerfully Captivating all our unruly Faculties, and Affections, (for the time) and disposing us to Solidity, Gravity, and a Good Temper; making us capable of Heavenly, and Divine Influences. ...
And These Things were Performed, upon so many Equal, and Truly-Sciz'd Viols; and so Exactly Strung, Tun'd and Play'd upon, as no one Part was any Impediment to the Other. ...'

Apart from these grave and complex chamber works, which must always have appealed chiefly to amateurs with a strong inclination towards serious music, there was plenty of light, tuneful music being enjoyed both on the viols and the violins; on the lute, with its soft but extraordinarily sonorous and poetical tone; on the cithren, a brighter and more popular alternative to the lute; and on the brilliant harpsichord, which ranged from the smaller spinets and virginals up to the full double-manual instruments of 7 or 8 ft. in length (see Pls. 91A, 92). But to judge from the numbers of surviving manuscripts, no instrumental music had such vogue during most of the seventeenth century in England as the contrapuntal music of the

Effigies Tho: Mace
Trin: Coll: Cantá: Clericus.
Ætat: Suæ 63.

Fig. 1. Portrait frontispiece of Thomas Mace in his *Musick's Monument*, engraved by W. Faithorne. See also Plate 94A.

viols. Even as late as 1728 the septuagenarian Roger North was still nostalgically describing his youthful enjoyment of it, adding that:

'The fantazia manner held thro his reigne [*i.e.* through Charles 1 after James 1] & during ye troubles & when most other good arts languished musick held up her head, not at Court nor (In ye cant of those times) profane theatres, but In private society, for many chose rather to fidle at home, then to goe out & be knockt on ye head abroad; and the enterteinment was much courted & made use of not only In country but citty familys, In which many of the Ladys were good consortiers and in this state was musick dayly Improving more or less till the time of (in all other respects But musick) the happy restauration.'

As the viols went out the violins came in; and it is not without interest that the first commercially organized concerts of which historians have record took place in London under the Commonwealth. The most unified age in English social history was passing away, and it seems more than a coincidence that the happiest of all ages for serious amateur musicianship was passing too.

The modern technique acclimatized in later Stuart music

The split in English society, which was only latent under Elizabeth and no more than subterraneously preparing under the first two Stuarts, became an open rift in the Civil War, when father took arms against son and brother against brother until all that was best in our native spirit became divided. The great houses where the viols and the madrigals had flourished were largely ruined, their scions flocking to London at the Restoration in the attempt to restore their broken fortunes. The music of the cathedrals and the big parish churches had been actually prohibited under the Commonwealth, and a choral tradition once interrupted is not easily recovered. In other respects the Puritans were not in the least inimical to music; but the incidental disorganization was immensely so, and it is not surprising that new influences found a ready entry.

The first to arrive was naturally the French, since it was in France that Charles ii had spent his most impressionable years. He liked music, we

are told, to which he could wag his head in time; he had little use for counterpoint. He formed a French-style band of four-and-twenty violins, and sent young Pelham Humphrey to study French composition, which, though distinct from Italian, was a half-way house to it. The direct Italian influence was not long in following.

Yet the English tradition soon showed its power of recovery. The irascible Matthew Locke, one of the liveliest talents of the early Restoration, with some genuinely operatic music to his credit as well as much for instruments, roundly declared that he knew no foreign music worth an Englishman's copying save for a few French dances. He and the still more talented John Blow and others soon had English church music on its feet again. But it was English church music with a great difference. In place of equal-voiced counterpoint there were rousing tunes and choruses and brilliant accompaniments and instrumental interludes. The style was – there is no other word for it – operatic: operatic in the sense in which Italian opera had by then developed, which was some distance from the intimate yet impassioned style of Monteverdi. The grain was coarser; the effects were more obvious; the appeal was shallower but wider. Within these limitations much excellent music was composed.

It is against this background that we must set the supreme genius of Stuart music, and one of the supreme geniuses of the entire musical galaxy, Henry Purcell. Entering with a will into the frankly operatic style just described, he produced church anthems, welcome odes and the like, with the best of them; and fine compositions many of these are. He wrote many long songs and scenas like the famous *Blessed Virgin's Expostulation*, which are a blend of genuinely monodic declamation as by then developed in Italy, on the one hand, with jaunty Restoration rhythms and catchy melodies, on the other. He wrote some typical dance-suites for harpsichord. In *Dido and Aeneas* he gave English opera itself a send-off which it is one of the sad enigmas of history that we proved as a nation unequal to continuing at the time. In his solo violin sonata and his two great sets of trio-sonatas for two violins, gamba and keyboard accompaniment, he set himself deliberately, as he tells us in one of his own prefaces, to imitate the best Italian masters of his day; and he does so with masterly accomplishment; but it is not for this that these sonatas are so particularly interesting. What is most interesting about them, over and above their superb musical value, is once again their uncanny Englishness.

Purcell had studied the old English music of the great days before the Civil War, as his own autograph copies of some of its masterpieces show; indeed, the Tudor church music was to some extent

being heard again. He himself wrote a series of splendid contrapuntal fantasies for viols in what was by then, even in England, a quite superseded technique; but he very shortly followed them with his first set of trio-sonatas in the modern Italian idiom. And here it is that we see the conditions of early Stuart music almost exactly reversed. For the form and structure of these trio-sonatas are up-to-the-minute in technique; it is their mood and their harmony which look back to the burning passion and intrepid freedom of Lawes and Dowland.

Lady playing a small portable virginals. From an engraving by Hollar, 1635.

Bookbinding

HOWARD M. NIXON

At the beginning of the seventeenth century the majority of the books in an English library would be bound in limp vellum. This grew unfashionable, however, and by the end of the century sheep or calf was almost always used. Except for pamphlets, which were stitched in paper wrappers, full binding was the rule, although the library of Samuel Pepys, who died in 1703, contains some attractive half-bound books with patterned paper sides.

The reigns of the first two Stuarts saw English decorative bookbinding beginning to develop specifically national characteristics. The period has not yet been closely studied, and little is known about the London binders of these reigns. John and Abraham Bateman were appointed binders to King James 1, but the extant bills for the Royal Library and that of Henry Prince of Wales for the first fifteen years of the seventeenth century are for bindings supplied by John Norton and Robert Barker. Both Norton and Barker were important booksellers and printers, and we have no evidence (though it is not impossible) that either possessed his own binding staff.

The first sign of change in the new century was the introduction of new materials. In Elizabethan England the majority of the finest bindings had been executed in embroidered fabrics, the Queen herself having a marked taste for velvet bindings. Elaborate gold-tooled leather bindings were not very common and had always been of calf. At the beginning of James 1's reign, morocco, in various shades of brown and green, began to replace calf for the best work and gold-tooled limp vellum

also became popular. The normal design at the start of the reign was still that misnamed 'Lyonese', with large centre- and corner-pieces blocked in a press, which had been in common use all over Europe for the previous quarter of a century. The centre ornament often consisted of arms, as on most of the royal bindings of James 1's reign, or of a cartouche containing a badge or initials, as on bindings by Williamson of Eton, some of which have Queen Elizabeth's falcon badge and others the initials of Sir Charles Somerset. The corner ornaments were usually of formal design and semi-circular or L-shaped, although on the standard library bindings executed for Henry Prince of Wales in about the year 1610 they were replaced by huge and rather ugly lions, fleurs-de-lis, roses and ostrich feather badges.

At the start of the century small tools were largely confined to the portions of the covers not decorated by the centre- or corner-pieces where a diaper or 'semis' was formed by a single tool such as a thistle or fleur-de-lis. Some of the presentation bindings in the library of Prince Henry, who died in 1612, however, have corner ornaments made up of small tools, and from about 1620 onwards their use greatly increased. French influence still persisted in the designs of some London bindings which were direct, if not very close, imitations of the Paris 'fanfare' bindings with interlacing ribbons outlining small compartments of varied shapes. Simultaneously, however, distinctively English bindings began to appear with the addition to the earlier centre- and corner-piece design of an outer frame, usually decorated with repeated impressions of large tools, the most common being wedge-shaped blocks of conventional foliage ornament. This style flourished in the 1630s with the centre- and corner-pieces of the panel within the frame gradually being replaced by small tools similarly arranged or by a lozenge-shaped band of ornament recalling a favourite arrangement of blind-tooled rolls on London bindings of the sixteenth century. A diaper of small tools over the whole cover was also frequently employed in the 1630's, some of the designs evidently copying French models, but a distinctively English variation being found with alternations of small lozenges and slightly larger circles, each containing a small floral tool. Another repeating pattern, with a series of gold-tooled rectangles placed one inside another like Chinese boxes, was used mainly on Cambridge work, but the most typical Cambridge bindings of the 1630's still have the decoration concentrated on a central circle and quarter circles at the corners. The best of these bindings are probably the work of Henry Moody and Daniel Boyse. They used a number of distinctively Cambridge tool-patterns only found elsewhere on the amateur work of Nicholar Ferrar's female relations at Little Gidding, who were taught by a Cambridge bookbinder's daughter 'that bound rarely'. Onlays of different coloured leather appeared on some white vellum bindings of the late 1630's which may also be Cambridge work, and in the next decade coloured onlays and tools engraved *au pointillé* (i.e. with a dotted outline) began to infuse variety and grace into the better class work.

Surprisingly enough, the supposedly drab days of the Commonwealth period saw the growth of the use of brighter-coloured moroccos, particularly the red 'Turkey leather' which was to prove so popular for the next hundred and fifty years. A Cambridge binder, who was probably John Houlden, and the Londoners Stephen and Thomas Lewis of Shoe Lane and Henry Evans of Wood Street, were producing by 1660 polychrome bindings with onlays of coloured leather which clearly foreshadowed the glories of the Restoration period – the greatest age in the history of English bookbinding. From 1660 until the end of the seventeenth century the best bindings from London, Oxford and Cambridge were unrivalled in Europe for originality and charm, variety and gaiety. Many of the tools used were clearly copied from French originals, and the tooling was never quite as good as that of the best French finishers of the day. Some French influence persisted also in design, echoes of the 'fanfare' style still being found on some English bindings of the 1670's and 1680's. The majority of the designs, however, were new and distinctively English. The rectangular panel, often with onlaid corner-pieces of leather of contrasting colour, was fashionable at the time of Charles II's return, and continued in use to the end of the century. Possibly inspired by designs on Persian rugs, it was being used by Fletcher in 1661 on a Prayer Book bound for the future King James II and in the last fifteen years of the century by Richard Balley, a binder who, in Bagford's words, 'hath contrived to bind a book that at sight you could not know the fore-edge from the back, both being cut and gilded alike' (Pl. 95B—an example with a normal back).[1]

The most characteristic design of the Restoration period, however, and one that is peculiarly English, is the so-called 'Cottage style'. In this the central panel is no longer rectangular, but has a broken pediment at head and foot. The name is based on a vague resemblance to the roof of a cottage with overhanging gables, but the broken pediment was a favourite architectural motif of the period, particularly on carved woodwork. It probably made its first appearance on another binding by Fletcher, the copy of Foxe's *Book of Martyrs* presented by the Stationers' Company to King Charles II in 1660, but the majority of the more elaborate 'cottage' bindings seem to come from the shop of Samuel Mearne. Mearne (to whom in the past all bindings of this period have been uncritically attributed) was one of the leading members of the Stationers' Company and a wealthy stationer and bookseller. He had, however, been apprenticed to a bookbinder and there

[1] John Bagford, who died in 1716, compiled some notes (now in the British Museum) on the history of bookbinding in which he refers to a number of the leading English binders of his day.

is no doubt that he had binders working in his shop. Two of his apprentices, William Willis and Robert Steele, subsequently became master binders, and we learn from Bagford not only that one Suckerman 'perhaps one of the best workmen that ever took tool in hands ... commonly worked for Mr. Mearne', but also that Richard Balley who 'contrived' the backless bindings, was trained under Suckerman 'at Mr. Mearne's'. Balley occasionally used the 'cottage style' himself, as did Roger Bartlett, a native of Oxfordshire who learned his trade in London, but returned to pursue a somewhat chequered career in Oxford after the Great Fire. To him may be safely attributed a very homogeneous group of bindings which usually have a number of *pointillé* volutes disposed along the pediments.

Equally characteristic and numerous are the bindings in the 'all-over' style decorated with repeating patterns of 'drawer-handle' tools. These tools are also architectural in origin, being no doubt suggested by an Ionic capital. The finest bindings with this design have been attributed to an unidentified craftsman, termed the Queens' binder, but they appear to come from several shops employing close copies of one another's tools and working in this manner between about 1670 and 1690 (Pl. 95A) Similar in style, but more easily distinguished, are the tools used by another anonymous craftsman, the so-called 'Devotional binder', which were larger and bolder in outline and included a characteristic sunflower and an unusual tubby little bird.

Thanks to Bagford's notes on the bookbinders of the day, compiled for his projected history of printing and the book trade, and the notes on his bookbinders to be found in Dunton's *Life and Errors*, more information has been available in the past on this period than on any earlier and many subsequent ones. The names of eighty-two binders appended to the 1669 agreement on the prices of binding, together with Mr Ellic Howe's researches in the records of the Stationers' Company, have further increased our knowledge. In addition to the names already mentioned, we can identify the work of Mearne's erstwhile apprentice, Robert Steele, and there is a group of bindings which include in their tooling a vase decorated with a leopard's head which may be safely assigned to Alexander Cleeve. On the other hand, although Nott, whose work was much admired by Pepys, is known to have been Clarendon's binder, the existing bindings with the Clarendon arms appear to be presentation bindings from a number of different shops; there is only one binding very doubtfully attributed to Baker, binder to the Archbishop of Canterbury; and we know nothing that can be connected with Tatnam, classed by Bagford with Nott among 'others that have deserved well and ought to be remembered in after ages'. It is among these names, perhaps, that we shall identify eventually those responsible for the best bindings of the 'Queens' binder' group, the work of the 'Devotional binder' and that of the 'Naval binder', which includes some of the finest English bindings of that or any other age.

Printing

RUARI McLEAN

There is no great English printer during the Stuart period, for the times did not allow it. English printing during the seventeenth century was poor in quality, hardly profitable, and heavily persecuted.

In 1586 the Star Chamber had decreed that

no new printing press was to be set up 'till the excessive multitude of Printers having presses already set up, be abated' – and no printing was allowed anywhere in the provinces, except at Oxford and Cambridge; a degree of censorship without parallel in any other country, which was maintained for almost the whole century.

In 1615, by a Stationers' Court decree, only twenty-two printers were allowed in London. In 1637 a Star Chamber decree enacted that when vacancies arose, new master printers could only be appointed by the Archbishop of Canterbury or the Bishop of London; and a new press could not be constructed without official sanction. At this time twenty-three printers and four foundries were permitted in London. The number of printers gradually increased, during the Civil War and Interregnum, until in 1660 Sir Roger L'Estrange wrote that there were sixty printers in London, and the number ought to be reduced to twenty. This he was soon able to set about implementing, when he was appointed 'Surveyor of the Imprimery and Printing Presses'; he made one less, for example, when John Twyn was hanged, drawn and quartered for printing *A Treatise on the Execution of Justice*. L'Estrange's ravages were followed by those of the Plague (1665) and the Fire (1666), which ruined many in the book trade.[1] Nevertheless, in 1662 York became the fourth place in England where printing was permitted.

In addition to censorship, there was a system of monopolies in the different kinds of printing, which made the monopoly-holding printers themselves interested in restriction. None of these conditions was conducive to good printing.

Copper-plate engraving

Perhaps the most characteristic feature of Stuart book-production in general is the copperplate title-plate. After 1600, for about a hundred years, nearly every English book had to have one;

and the woodcut title-page characteristic of Elizabethan books disappeared. These engraved title-pages are comparable to modern book-jackets, and, indeed, many of them have been adapted for that purpose during recent years. A selection of them is shown in A. F. Johnson's *A Catalogue of Engraved and Etched English Title-pages ... to ... 1691* (Oxford 1934): but many of the best are not by English artists, or are copies of designs which first appeared in earlier, foreign editions (see Pl. 96).

No English-born engraver of the first rank emerges during the Stuart period; but England was fortunate in receiving the great Czech engraver Wenceslaus Hollar. He had left his native Prague as a refugee from war and oppression in 1627, and came to England in 1637 in the service of Thomas Howard, the Duke of Norfolk and Earl-Marshal. As a protégé of the Court circle, Hollar moved back to Amsterdam in 1644, but returned to London in 1652, where he died in 1677. Perhaps the best-known of his work is his bird's-eye views of London before and after the Great Fire, and his engraving of Ogilby and Morgan's Survey made immediately after the Fire. His views of Windsor, Richmond, Greenwich, Albury in Sussex (where Howard had his country seat), Hull and, above all, London and Westminster, are of exquisite beauty and verisimilitude.

Hollar, whose output was prolific and of great variety, does not seem to have produced any books of engravings like, for example, the books of bird's-eye views of Oxford (1675) and Cambridge (c. 1690) by David Loggan, the *émigré* from Danzig who was certainly inspired by Hollar's style.

At the beginning of the Stuart period the general style of engraved title-pages was conventional and architectural. The doorway, or arch, was the obvious way to provide an imposing frame for the title of the book. Well-known examples are Hooker's *Ecclesiastical Politie* (1611), Drayton's *Poly-Olbion* (1612), and Ben Jonson's *Workes* (1616), all engraved by William Hole, and Raleigh's *History of the World* (1614), engraved by Renold Elstrack. This style sometimes degenerated into an overloading of ornamentation which surpassed the worst efforts of the Victorians,

---

[1] See H. R. Plomer, *A Short History of English Printing*, London 1900, p. 207, where L'Estrange is quoted as writing that 80 printers died of the Plague; but only eight printers are said to have been actually ruined by the Fire.

and was in addition complicated with symbolism that was often highly obscure even to those who were expected to understand it.

There were, however, plenty of other ideas in title-page design: for example, Francis Bacon's *Instauratio Magna* (1620), engraved by Simon van de Passe, shows two free-standing columns through which a ship is sailing; and *All the Workes of John Taylor the Water Poet* (1630), engraved by Thomas Cockson, has its title lettering displayed on a small sail tied between two oars.

In the second half of the century the composition of the engraved title-pages became freer. The famous title-page to Hobbes's *Leviathan*, unsigned (1651), is formal but no longer architectural, and the designer has used an arrangement which gives him full scope for an imaginative picture of the royal Leviathan (the body ingeniously formed from a crowd of his subjects) rising over a landscape which is not English – probably because it was drawn by a French or Dutch artist while Hobbes was on the Continent.

Hollar engraved (but he may not have designed) some of the most attractive title-pages of the period. His title-pages for *An Embassy ... to ... China* (1673), and Ogilby's *Britannia* (1675), are straightforward illustrations, in a style recaptured and transmuted by the late Rex Whistler. Another illustrative title-page is that in Scarron's *Comical Romance of a Company of Stage Players* (1676), which vividly portrays a performance by strolling players on a temporary stage. It is by William Faithorne, who had been a pupil of Hollar's, and in whose house Hollar lived when he first returned from Antwerp in 1652.

Copper-plates, besides being used for title-pages, were also frequently used for head- and tail-pieces, and initial letters in the text. But a copper-plate cannot be printed at the same time, or even on the same press, as type: every sheet with such an illustration must be put through a different press, which greatly increases the cost. Copper-plate engravings are also sometimes open to criticism on artistic grounds, as not harmonizing with the pages of a book printed from type. They can always be identified by the mark of the plate, unless this has been trimmed off.

The writing-masters

It is perhaps surprising that the writing-masters, or scriveners, did not influence book or type design during the Stuart period. No publisher, apparently, employed a penman to design a simple and purely calligraphic title page; yet many of the writing-masters were men of outstanding artistic and intellectual ability.

Our knowledge of the Stuart writing-masters owes much to Samuel Pepys' interest in the subject: he made an alphabetical list of sixty-four writing-masters alive in England (mostly in London and Westminster) in 1699, and collected specimens of English and foreign calligraphy which are now in the Pepysian Collection in Magdalene College, Cambridge. Pepys knew the prolific Edward Cocker (1631–76), the writing-master whose name is perpetuated in the phrase 'according to Cocker' from the best-selling *Cocker's Arithmetick*, of which, however, Cocker was not probably the author.[2] Cocker was one of the ablest penmen of his day in England, and published at least twenty-four copybooks, which were printed from copper-plates (see Fig. on p. 420).

Printing the Bible

The greatest technical achievement of the London printing trade during the seventeenth century was the Polygot Bible, (1654–57), edited by Brian Walton; a work of enormous complexity, since each opening presents 'some ten or more versions of the same passage ... so set that each comprehends exactly the same amount of text'.[3] It was printed by Thomas Roycroft in six folio volumes, in about four years; and although the Plantin Polyglot of 1572 and the Paris Polyglot of 1645 are far handsomer, the London Polyglot is said to be the best arranged and of the most use to scholars, which was, after all, its chief function. The Polyglot Bible was published, apparently successfully, by subscription. It is stated by T.B. Reed

[2] See Sir Ambrose Heal and Stanley Morison in *The English Writing Masters and Their Copy-Books*, Cambridge, 1931.

[3] T.B. Reed and A.F. Johnson, *The Old English Letter Foundries*, London, 1952.

that the price was £10, and that £9,000 was sub-scribed four months before the first volume was put to press; the cost of the six volumes being £7,500, and the number of each volume printed about 1,000.

Mention must be made of the first publication, in 1611, of the King James version of the Bible, still today the 'Authorized', and the most popular text. It was a folio, printed by Robert Barker, the King's Printer, and may be supposed to represent the best London printing of the time, although the King's Printer had then no competition. The text is set in black-letter (Fig. 1), with interpolated words, notes and headlines in roman. It is a plain and open page, but shows little sense of typo-graphic artistry. It has a fine engraved title by an Antwerp-born engraver, whose only known work in England this is; and some pages contain wood-cut embellishments.

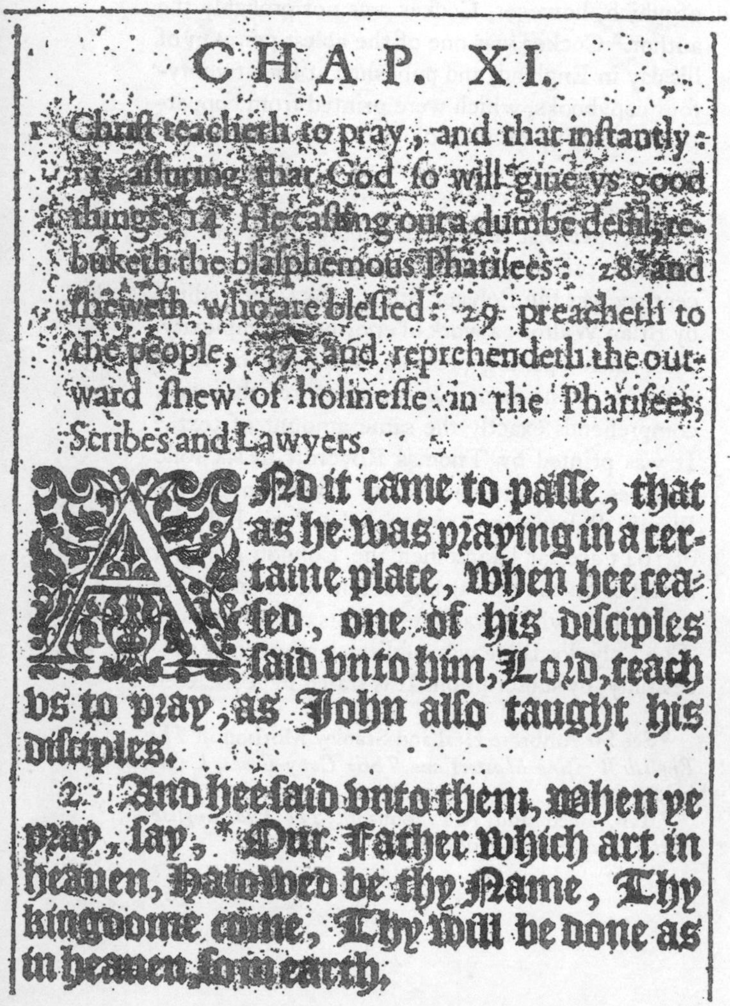

Black-letter was still the more formal and 'im-portant' type-face, generally used for the Bible, official proclamations and legal works. But roman type was already the type-face for literature and such ordinary matter as news-sheets and pamphlets. Roman was used, for example, for the first print-ing of Shakespeare's plays in 1594 (by a pirate publisher), the quartos and the First Folio in 1623. Typographically, the first Folio is finer than most volumes of its period,[4] and its title-page, with type as well as engraving, is unusual.

If the King's Printer had no competition in Bible-printing in 1611, it was not long that he had to wait. The opposition came from Oxford and Cambridge, where a constant battle was waged during the whole century with the Station-ers' Company of London over printing and pub-lishing privileges, of which the Bible privilege was the most valuable. Cambridge produced its first Bible in the Authorized King James version in 1629, and Oxford not until 1675; yet the right of the Universities to print the Bible was contested by the Stationers' Company all the time. The Ox-ford side of the dispute is fully described in John Johnson and Strickland Gibson's *Print and Privi-lege at Oxford to the year 1700.*[5] Around 1680 there was a price war between Oxford and Lon-don which brought the prices of Bibles down to less than half of what they had been and greatly increased the number of Bibles in circulation 'to the great benefit of Souls, and their advantage in Christian Knowledge', as a hopeful contemporary wrote.

In the latter half of the century Oxford printing had a champion who brought to England types whose value is perhaps only now being fully realized. This was Dr John Fell, Dean of Christ Church, Bishop of Oxford and from 1666 to 1669 Vice-Chancellor of the University. Besides pro-moting and upholding the rights of the University

[4] See A. Sampson, 'The Printing of Shakespeare's Plays', *Signature* 15, New Series, 1952.
[5] Oxford, 1946.

Fig. 1. *Left.* Part of a column from The King James Bible of 1611 (actual size).

CHAP. XI.

Christ teacheth to pray, and that instantly: 11 assuring that God so will giue vs good things. 14 He casting out a dumbe deuil, re-buketh the blasphemous Pharisees: 28 and sheweth, who are blessed: 29 preacheth to the people, 37 and reprehendeth the out-ward shew of holinesse in the Pharisees, Scribes and Lawyers.

And it came to passe, that as he was praying in a cer-taine place, when hee cea-sed, one of his disciples said vnto him, Lord, teach vs to pray, as John also taught his disciples.

2. And hee said vnto them, when ye pray, say, * Our Father which art in heauen, hallowed be thy Name, Thy kingdome come, Thy Will be done as in heauen, so in earth,

Press, he made – partly by purchase and partly by commissioning – a collection of punches and matrices for Greek and roman types, mostly in Holland, so that by 1672 Oxford had the best-equipped type foundry in England. Some of the smaller 'Fell' roman types are believed to be original Garamond or Granjon designs; the larger sizes, down to 'English' (= 14 pt), are of seventeenth century Dutch design. These unique types are all still in use at the Oxford University Press.

In 1702–4 the University Press issued the folio volumes of Clarendon's *History of the Rebellion*. Clarendon presented the copyright to the University (which it still holds, confirmed by the Copyright Act of 1911), and from the profits that accrued the University built the first 'Clarendon Press' building – hence its name. The *History*, printed in the 'Fell' types, is a monumental piece of book production, one of the finest of the whole eighteenth century.

At the end of the century efforts were also being made to improve the equipment and output of the Cambridge University Press. The chief instigator of change was Dr Richard Bentley (1662–1742), the classical scholar, and Master of Trinity College; like Fell, he re-equipped his Press with types from Holland.[6]

Publishing

Towards the end of the seventeenth century the pattern of modern publishing economics begins to emerge. Dryden (1631–1700) has been called our first 'eminent man of letters', because he earned his living by writing for the booksellers; and Jacob Tonson (1656–1736) the first 'eminent publisher'. They quarrelled. Yet, then as now, neither publisher nor author could go far without the other.

Tonson cared, as any real publisher must, for the appearance of his books, which are better than most of his time; but good printers and good type-founders did not yet exist in London. On at least one occasion, in 1703, Tonson had

to go to Holland himself to procure good types. Two of his notable books published within our period are the first illustrated edition of *Paradise Lost*, 1688,[7] and Dryden's complete translation of Virgil, 1697. In William Bowyer (1663–1737), who started in business on his own in 1699, Tonson did at last find a printer of ability. Bowyer's son, whose work is mentioned in the next volume of this series, was perhaps the first printer of intellectual stature in England since the Elizabethan John Day.

Technique of printing

The technique of printing, type-founding and paper-making remained basically unchanged throughout Europe during the Stuart period. An improved hand-press was invented by Blaeu in Amsterdam in 1620, which slightly increased production; but it was not generally adopted in England.

Newspapers

The first regular printing of news [8] seems to have begun in Germany in 1609, in the form of 4- or 8-page pamphlets, whose pages were just like the book-pages. The next stage was the issuing of single sheets, known as 'corantos', in Amsterdam in 1618. The earliest extant newspaper in English was published by Pieter Van den Keere in Amsterdam in 1620. The printing of news in England was at that time forbidden by King James I, but there was a considerable circulation of Dutch-printed news in England, followed probably by news-sheets with Dutch imprints secretly printed in London. Eventually the King decided to control what he could not suppress, and on 2 September 1621 there appeared the earliest extant dated newspaper in English, headed *Coranto*, printed and published under licence in London. The

[6] See S. C. Roberts, *The Evolution of Cambridge Publishing*, 1956.

[7] See C. H. Collins Baker, 'Some Illustrators of Milton's *Paradise Lost*', *The Library*, June 1948.

[8] All the information following is contained in *The Origins of the Newspaper*, a lecture delivered by Stanley Morison at the St Bride Institute, London, in 1954 and privately printed by *The Times*; see also the same author's *The English Newspaper*, 1932.

publishers, or licensees, were Nicholas Bourne and Thomas Archer, with a licence dated 13th August 1621. Thomas Archer lost his licence on 20th September, but seems to have regained it soon afterwards, for his name appears on many subsequent newspapers.

The early English newspapers were set in rough-looking roman types on quarto size pages (about the size of the present volume). Owing to Star Chamber restrictions, only foreign news could be printed: but in 1632 the Star Chamber prohibited newspapers altogether, a ban which remained for six years and was celebrated by Milton's biting pamphlet for the freedom of the press, *Areopagitica*, published in 1638.

In 1641 the Star Chamber was abolished, and it became possible, although not prudent, to print domestic news. The Parliamentarians were no more anxious to allow themselves to be criticized than the Royalists, and the life of a publisher of news continued to be vexatious and precarious.

Not until 1783, for example, were reporters allowed to take notes in the House of Commons.[9]

The first English daily newspaper was *The Daily Courant*, appearing for the first time on Wednesday, 11th March 1702. It ran for over 6000 issues. The reign of Queen Anne saw the founding of *The Tatler* (1709), *The Spectator* (1711), and many other names still familiar; in the lists of their contributors occur the first great names in English journalism, including Addison, Swift, Steele, Arbuthnot (the creator of 'John Bull') and Defoe.

In 1695 the Licensing Act lapsed, and the printing trade was at last freed from its worst limitations. Presses immediately began to be established in provincial towns; and a new age began with the new century.

[9] See A. Aspinall, 'The Reporting and Publishing of the House of Commons Debates, 1771–1834', in *Essays Presented to Sir Lewis Namier*, 1956.

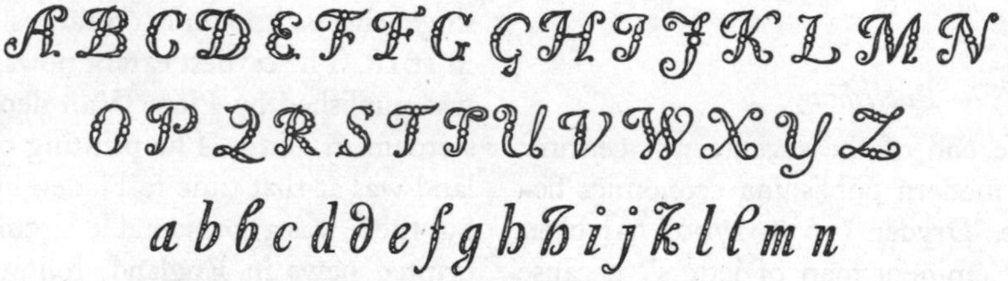

Fig. 2. Complete fount of Union Pearl, cast by the Grover Foundry at the end of the seventeenth century. This is believed to be the first decorated typeface produced in Europe, although no contemporary examples of its use have been found. The original matrices still exist and are owned by the typefounding firm of Stephenson Blake of Sheffield. The typeface is in commercial use today.

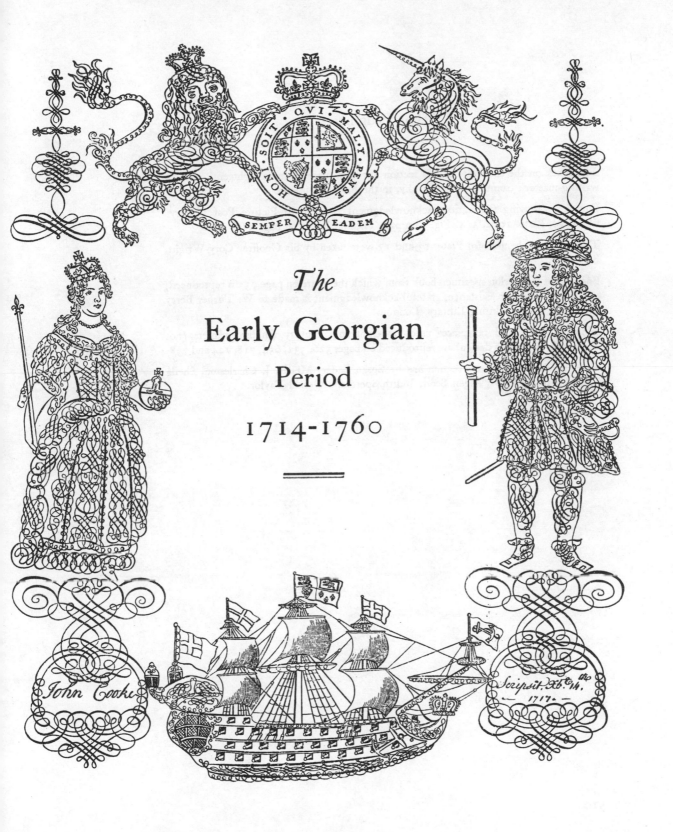

The
Early Georgian
Period

1714-1760

John Cooke

Scripsit Xbr 14
1717

Acknowledgments

The block on the title-page of this section has been made from an eighteenth century writing-master's example of calligraphy, in the British Museum.

For the following illustrations acknowledgment is made to Picture Post Library: title-page, Plates 1C, 2, 3, 4, Fig. 1 on page 515 and Fig. 2 on page 517.

The photographs used for Plates 13 and 17 were taken by Sir Geoffrey Cory-Wright, Bart.

For loan of the Caslon specimen book from which the figure on page 753 is reproduced, and for much other assistance, grateful acknowledgment is made to W. Turner Berry and the St Bride Printing Library, London.

Woodcut head and tail-pieces used by eighteenth century English printers (not necessarily of English design) are reproduced on pages 526, 532, 654, 718, 724 and 738.

The line drawings in this section are by Susan Bader, Mrs R. J. Charleston, Sheila Cheese, Audrey Frew, Asgeir Scott, Judith Spero and Gerald Taylor.

Early Georgian England

JEAN LINDSAY

The year 1714, 'when George in pudding time came o'er', marked the beginning of a new epoch in the politics, but not in the economic history of England. Economically the most important change was one which had been taking place gradually since about the middle of the seventeenth century.[1] From that time both the volume and character of international trade had altered most spectacularly. In 1716 French exports had been worth 120 million livres; by 1789 they were worth 500 million. British exports increased in value from £8 million in 1720 to £15 million in 1763. Not only did the amount of trade grow prodigiously but the re-export of colonial products such as sugar, tobacco, dyestuffs and rice became increasingly important. It also became clear that in this commercial expansion the Dutch, who in the mid-seventeenth century had had a fleet twice that of England and nine times that of France, were gradually being overtaken by France and England. By the middle of the eighteenth century, these two countries emerged as the greatest commercial powers, and in the later eighteenth century they came into conflict for commercial and colonial supremacy. At home the commercial prosperity was reflected in peace, social stability and, at least for the upper classes, a high standard of living.

Already in the first half of the eighteenth century the increased volume of international trade

owed something to technological progress. In England in the early eighteenth century there was a great demand for coal, as supplies of timber showed signs of exhaustion. There was a good deal of prospecting, but the new seams were not enough to meet the demand and make good the surface seams which had by now been exhausted. The answer was to work the deeper seams, but this was difficult because of the danger of flooding, until in 1712 Newcomen perfected a steam pump which was one of the fundamental technical advances preparing the way for the Industrial Revolution in the second half of the century. Another development of great importance for the future was the discovery by the Darbys of Coalbrookdale of a method of using coke to smelt iron. As early as 1713 they were using this fuel to replace the dwindling supplies of charcoal, and they had perfected the process by the 'thirties. Gradually furnaces shifted from the forests to the coalfields, and the fuel proved most valuable in the process of manufacturing such iron goods as nails, chains, tools, locks and other metalware which made up an important part of English exports. In the textile industry the demands of more sophisticated urban markets on the one hand and of tropical markets on the other encouraged producers to improve their products. Skilled workmen from Norwich were borrowed to help Yorkshire manufacturers change over from producing the heavier woollens to the smoother worsteds. Dyeing and finishing were improved, so that by 1750 English work in this field was as good as anything that the Dutch could do. But the most spectacular

[1] This point is developed by C. H. Wilson in his chapter on Economic Conditions in Volume VII of the *Cambridge Modern History*. I am indebted to him for much of the material on economic developments in England.

technical development in the textile industry, which caught the imagination of contemporaries, was the introduction of a machine to spin silk yarn. In 1716 John Lombe went to Italy and managed to steal the secret of spinning silk by machine. He and his brother Thomas set up a factory in Derby which became one of the sights of England. John died, but his brother made a fortune of £120,000, was knighted, and when, in 1732, his patent lapsed he was given £14,000 by Parliament. His career demonstrated the value of mechanization and factory organization, a lesson which his contemporaries were not slow to learn.[2]

The England in which these commercial developments were taking place [3] and in which the industrial experiments were beginning was a small country still very largely rural in character. The population was only about 6 millions, as compared with 19 millions in France, 20 millions in the Holy Roman Empire, 6 millions in Spain, perhaps 14 millions in Russia and 2 millions each in Holland and Prussia. More than half the population lived south of a line drawn from Worcester to the Wash, and a twelfth lived in London. In the country districts life went on as it had done for generations and methods of cultivation were largely unchanged until the second half of the century. Jethro Tull, who died in 1741, claimed that he 'introduced turnips into the field in King William's reign; but the practice did not travel beyond the hedges of my estate till after the Peace of Utrecht'. Lord Townshend did not begin his farming experiments seriously until he retired from politics in 1730, though by his death in 1738 he had been so successful that he had earned the nickname of 'Turnip' Townshend. A few men learnt from these pioneers and made large fortunes. In thirty years the rent of one farm rose from £180 to £800 and another farm which had been let to a warrener for £18 was let to a farmer for £240. But, in general, farmers remained conservative in their methods, and outside Norfolk

'classed turnips with rats as Hanoverian innovations, and refused their assistance with Jacobite indignation'.[4] Breeding remained unselective, and Bakewell, that Toby-jug figure in his loose brown coat and red waistcoat, did not begin his experiments until about 1745. Only after 1750 did the number of Enclosure Acts begin to increase rapidly, but even the few enclosures that were made before 1750 tended to ruin many agricultural labourers who had relied on common rights and had not the capital to afford to enclose their few acres. Several small yeomen suffered also, though a few were retained as tenants by the large land-owners. Rural poverty became more serious. The Game Laws were more strictly enforced. In 1723 Parliament passed an act allowing several parishes to combine to set up a workhouse. Yet though for the poor people of the countryside the first half of the eighteenth century was a time of growing anxiety, for the large landowners it was a period of great prosperity. Farming methods might be old-fashioned but large profits could be made, for there was a great demand for wool and a government bounty on corn.

Conditions favoured the large estate, and these tended to grow even larger. Some English peers were wealthier than many German princes. The Duke of Newcastle had estates in twelve different counties: the Dukes of Bedford were even richer. Part of this wealth the great land-owners spent on building, and such magnificent country-houses as Castle Howard, Wentworth Woodhouse and Houghton were the monuments to an age when 'men were so confident of themselves that they designed for their children's children. Europe first, and Asia next, were ransacked for treasures' [5] for these great houses. Trees, shrubs and flowers were brought from the ends of the earth to ornament their gardens. The weeping willow, the acacia, the fuchsia and, later in the century, the dahlia were among these treasures. As the wealth and social importance of the magnates increased, so did their political influence. A Lord Lieutenant of a county

[2] See J.H.Plumb, *England in the Eighteenth Century*.
[3] For an up-to-date survey of England in the 18th century see the chapter by W. Brock on England in Volume VII of the *Cambridge Modern History* (1957).

[4] Lord Ernle, *English Farming Past and Present*, p. 175.
[5] J.H.Plumb, *England in the Eighteenth Century*, p. 109.

was normally a peer with ministerial rank, or a high office at court, and as such he was courted by any one who wanted a place or a pension. He also controlled the appointment of Justices of the Peace, who were normally local squires. The justices were responsible for almost all local administration and summary justice in the rural areas. The basic unit of administration was the parish, but as parishes showed little initiative, or even competence, the burden of government fell increasingly on to the shoulders of the justices. Sitting alone or with one or more colleagues, they exercised summary jurisdiction, and the more serious cases were tried by a larger body of justices at Quarter Sessions. These quarterly gatherings provided very useful opportunities to discuss local and national business, and one meeting in the year tended to become the most important, when political questions would be discussed and it was customary for all the justices to be present. But apart from the great magnates and their supporters, some of whom might represent their county in Parliament, there were a good many of the lesser gentry who found that as the power of the great land-owners increased their own importance diminished. Some of these men, whose fathers had welcomed the revolution of 1688, turned Tory, though their Toryism was rather a 'country' attitude as opposed to a 'court' one. They objected to a standing army and high taxes, pensioners and placemen, excise and 'Hanover rats'. They disliked Dissenters and suspected the influence of the City. These Tory gentlemen were particularly strong in the west and north between the Bristol Channel and the Border. The country gentleman might be a great magnate, like the Duke of Newcastle with an annual income of £40,000, or a squire, like Nicholas Blundell of Lancashire, whose estate was worth only £482 12s. 2½d. a year; he might be a kindly, cultured, eccentric gentleman like Sir Roger de Coverley or a boor like Squire Western, who, though he had an income of £3,000 a year, had the rough manners of a yokel, saluted all company with a view-holla, blasphemed, talked bawdy and got drunk every evening. He might, like Sitwell of Renishaw in Derbyshire, have an excellent library, with Homer

and Aristotle, most of the Latin classics and the works of Christian Fathers beside Oughtred's *Trigonometry* and Evelyn's *Silva*. Private libraries were numerous in England, and many country gentlemen kept elaborate diaries and letter-books as well as account-books. Some kept commonplace books to record their reading. Some squires had very beautiful gardens with yew hedges, sundials, fish-ponds and fine trees. In fact, though many squires might be old-fashioned and seldom leave their country homes, many travelled up to London fairly often and when there bought silver and books, as Sitwell did. Others took great pride in improving their houses or building new ones. Some were interested in furniture, even if much of this was made only by local craftsmen. Some patronized portrait painters to record their own likenesses and those of their family and favourite animals. Hunting, the bottle, farming and local business might sum up the interests of many of the eighteenth century country gentlemen, but there were always a certain number who appreciated and patronized fine craftsmanship.

In the towns, and especially in London, the eighteenth century saw the emergence of a very fine culture. The towns were very small by modern standards.[6] London, which was far larger than any other city, had a population of about half a million, and though Smollett and Horace Walpole were horrified at the mania for building, in their days no part of the town was more than twenty minutes' walk from the country. On the west the town began at Tyburn, on the south at St George's Hospital. 'Portland Place was bounded on the north by a wooden railing with a stile in the middle, beyond it were fields.' Snipe were shot in the marshes of Pimlico; Camberwell and Dulwich were in the open country. Other towns were even smaller. Bristol had just outstripped Norwich, and may have had a population of 50,000; Norwich itself, though it was still one of the chief cities of eighteenth-century England, had not outgrown its medieval walls. Liverpool, which Defoe in the 'twenties thought 'already the next town to

---

[6] For further particulars about town life see Dr D. George, *London Life in the Eighteenth Century*.

Bristol' and which in 1773 had a population of about 34,000, in 1700 had only about 4,000 inhabitants. Manchester seemed to Defoe 'one of the greatest, if not the greatest mere village in England'. But these little towns, and especially London, had a very real urban character. One of the original achievements in north-western Europe, and especially in England, during the eighteenth century was to evolve a special kind of urban architecture.[7] Inigo Jones in the early seventeenth century had shown the way to design town houses as part of a coherent architectural scheme. Much of London had been rebuilt after the Great Fire, and as during the eighteenth century London developed towards the north and west, the houses were designed as parts of squares and streets. The inhabitants were very proud of these houses with their sash windows and classical proportions. The life in the towns was one which encouraged what was most original and characteristic in contemporary literature. By 1713 there were something like 3,000 coffee-houses in London, and in 1732 Berkeley wrote of them, " 'I'll undertake, a lad of fourteen, bred in the modern way, shall make a better figure, and be more considered in any drawing room or assembly of polite people, than one of four and twenty, who hath lain by a long time at school or college. He shall say better things, and in a better manner, and be more liked by good judges.' 'Where doth he pick up all this improvement?' 'Where our grave ancestors would never have looked for it, in a drawing-room, a coffee-house, a chocolate-house, at a tavern ...' "[8] In such a tavern met the Club founded by Johnson and Reynolds in 1764. It was in the coffee-house and tavern that gentlemen read the journals which even before the abolition of the press censorship in 1695 had been numerous and which throve after the censorship had ended. In 1704 Defoe had brought out a weekly review containing a section devoted to literature. Steele's *Tatler* after its eighty-third number ceased to carry

political news at all. In 1711 Addison launched the daily *Spectator*, which was to contain no 'single word of news or reflection on politics'. The natural description of characters and incidents of ordinary life in these journals prepared the way for another very characteristic and original literary form of the eighteenth century – the novel, which made its appearance in 1741 when Richardson wrote *Pamela*. In 1748 Smollett and in 1749 Fielding followed where Richardson had shown the way. This urban life was founded on the prosperity of the landed gentry, who came to London, or Bath or some provincial centre such as Bristol, and of the great merchants, who spent most of their working lives in the cities. The early eighteenth century was a period of growing prosperity, and especially among some of the greater merchants who controlled the chartered companies and the Bank of England. It was characteristic of eighteenth-century England that money was cheap. In no other country could money be borrowed so easily. The National Debt rose from £1 million in 1688 to £150 million in 1761, but it was possible for the Government to reduce the rate of interest from 5 per cent. in 1717 to 4 per cent. in 1727 and to 3 per cent. in 1749. The figures are an indication of the sound prosperity which provided the foundation for the fine houses and good talk, new books and elegant furniture which could be found in the towns of early eighteenth-century England.

But there was another side to urban life which earned for the towns the grim description of 'the graves of mankind'.[9] The population of the towns increased, but only because there was a steady influx of people from the country. It was estimated that in the early part of the century only one child in four born in London survived. In the rapidly growing towns in the north the number may have been even lower. After 1740 conditions improved. The population steadily increased, largely because of a small but perceptible decline in the death rate, especially in the mortality among infants. Perhaps this was due, as Dr Plumb suggests, to the im-

[7]See the chapter by Sir A. Richardson on the Arts and Imaginative Literature in Volume VII of the *Cambridge Modern History*.

[8] From Berkeley's *Alciphron*, quoted by J.Butt, *The Augustan Age*, pp. 31–2.

[9] This point is particularly stressed by J.H.Plumb in his *England in the Eighteenth Century*.

Fig. 1. Liverpool in the mid-eighteenth century, from a contemporary engraving.

provements in midwifery brought about by such men as Hunter, Pringle and Smellie of the Edinburgh medical school and partly to the establishment of more lying-in hospitals and orphanages. The increase in the numbers of the lower middle class may have been one of the causes which contributed to the industrial development later in the century, but at first the increase in population only led to the further growth of the towns which for the poor were horrible places. Disease was rampant. It was estimated that in London there were 15,000 cases of smallpox a year, that 60 out of every 100 people caught the disease at some time and that of those 20 died of it, while many of those who survived were horribly marked. It was quite usual in an advertisement for a maidservant to say that she must have had smallpox. The absence of fresh meat in the winter and a widespread prejudice against fresh fruit and vegetables made scurvy by no means uncommon. Typhus, sometimes known as spotted fever and sometimes as gaol fever, decimated the prison population and was endemic among the poor. Hydrophobia was a real danger and produced such horrible suffering that the patient's end was generally hastened. Ague, or marsh fever, was common even in London, for the Essex marshes were as yet undrained. Consumption was still a terrifying scourge. But the amount of disease is not surprising in view of the fact that nearly all the water supplies in towns were dirty; that the sanitary arrangements were almost non-existent, and that the dead were sometimes buried in such conditions as to pollute all the houses in the vicinity of the graveyard. In 1722 the Fleet ditch was called 'a nauceious and abominable sink of nastiness'. In view of the poverty, squalor and very real danger of early death, it is not surprising that the urban poor were often rough, violent and depraved. There was much drunkenness. London in the middle of the eighteenth century had 17,000 gin-shops and England, with a total population of 6 millions, consumed 11 million gallons of spirits in 1750 and 1751. There was much gambling, whether on bull-baiting, cockfighting or crown and anchor. There was also much violence in towns, which had hardly any public lighting and no force more efficient than a

few parish constables to keep order. The lean, hard faces of the poor appear in many of Hogarth's pictures of London life. These people were always ready to join in a riot in hopes of loot. The danger of violence made the Government use savage penalties in an attempt to check crime. In 1740 a child could be hanged for stealing a handkerchief. After the Gordon Riots in 1780 boys of fourteen were hanged; of them one observer wrote: 'I never saw boys cry so much.'

One reason which was suggested by contemporary observers for the increase in crime noticeable during the course of the eighteenth century was the decay of religion. A decline seems to have started after the death of Queen Anne. In 1736 Montesquieu found that, though in France he was thought not to be sufficiently religious, in England he seemed excessively devout. One reason for the decay may have been the extreme poverty of many of the country clergy. In 1731 Swift said of the country parson, 'He liveth like an honest plain farmer, as his wife is dressed no better than Goody. He is sometimes graciously invited by the squire, where he sitteth at humble distance. If he gets the love of his people they often make him little useful presents. He is happy by being born to no higher expectation, for he is usually the son of some ordinary tradesman or farmer. His learning is much of a size with his birth and education.' [10] But the lower clergy had been poor for a long time, and in the eighteenth century the values of benefices tended to increase as the whole country grew more prosperous. Something new must have happened to weaken religious conviction, and there appear to be two reasons. One cause was the growing scepticism which was associated partly with the triumphant achievements of human reason in the sphere of the natural sciences and which, though it found its completest expression in the work of French philosophers about the middle of the century, did also affect opinion in England. The other cause was the ex-

[10] *Considerations on Two Bills relating to the Clergy of Ireland* (1731), quoted by W.E.H.Lecky, *History of England in the Eighteenth Century*, (1892 ed.) Vol. I, p. 95.

Fig. 2. Hogarth's picture of *Gin Lane* (1749, reduced) is a shocking comment on the effects of drinking spirits. The houses are ruinous except for that of the pawnbroker. The people are in rags. One man is so hungry he is taking a bone from a dog. An emaciated ballad seller has no shirt and is in the last stages of famine yet holds a glass and bottle of gin. A drunken, half-naked, diseased woman is so stupefied with drink that she lets her child fall into an area. And so on.

tent to which office in the Church came during the eighteenth century to be the reward not of learning and piety, but the recognition that the man appointed was connected with someone who had parliamentary interest. The departure of the non-jurors had deprived the Church of some learned and pious men; their places were too often filled by men whose chief merits were political. Between 1715 and 1722, as Tory bishops who had been appointed by Queen Anne died, their places were filled by sound Whigs. If a man hoped for promotion from a poor bishopric, such as St Asaph or Oxford, to a rich one, such as London, Durham or Winchester, he had to prove his devotion to the Government by assiduous attendance at the House of Lords and a careful management of the electoral interest in his diocese. Outspoken criticism of Government policy could keep a man like Watson at Llandaff all his life, though Watson had little reason for complaint. He enjoyed tithes from two churches in Shropshire, two in Leicestershire, two in his diocese and three in Huntingdonshire, which brought him in £2,000 a year, and he lived in Westmorland, farming fairly profitably. By 1736 the Duke of Newcastle had secured control of clerical patronage, and thereafter clerical appointments tended to be made for political reasons. During the century more and more young men of good family tended to find their way into Holy Orders, until in 1752 Bishop Warburton could write, 'Our grandees have at last found their way back into the Church. I only wonder they have been so long about it.' These younger sons of the nobility and gentry favoured pluralism, so that they could collect an income comparable to that of their brothers. With bishops who were often primarily politicians, and a lower clergy discreet and worldly, it is not surprising that the Church lost its hold on the public. This restrained, formal, conventional religion was of no use to the poor of the London slums or in the growing towns such as Birmingham or Manchester or Liverpool. It was one of the great achievements of Wesley that he reached and won large numbers of the poor.

The death of Queen Anne in August 1714 marked the beginning of a new period in English politics, for the accession of George I brought the Whigs to power, where they remained until the early years of George III. In 1714 there had been fears that the Jacobites might make a serious attempt to seize the throne for the Pretender. This came to nothing, and some Tories, especially Bolingbroke, hoped faintly that the new King might be brought to rely on them or, at least, choose his ministers from both parties, but they were disappointed. When the names of the Lords Justices, who were to govern the kingdom till George arrived, were made known it was clear that all eighteen were prominent Whigs, though Sunderland, Marlborough's brilliant son-in-law, was not among them. When the list was read, Sunderland looked very pale. When King George reached England, his preference for the Whigs continued. Lord Townshend, who had acted as a mediator between the Whig Junto and the Elector and had the support of the Hanoverian statesmen Bothmar and Bernstorff, was made Secretary of State, and his colleague as Secretary of State for the Southern Department and leader of the House of Commons was James Stanhope, another of those who had helped to prepare the way for the accession of King George. Sir Robert Walpole, Townshend's brother-in-law, was given a minor post and Pultney was made Secretary for War. Marlborough was made Commander-in-Chief, but Sunderland was made only Lord Lieutenant of Ireland, which was nothing but dignified banishment.

At home the election of January 1715 returned a Whig majority. Bolingbroke and Ormonde fled abroad, which gave the Whigs good reason to brand every Tory as a Jacobite. There seemed no hope for the Tories except armed insurrection. In September 1715 the Earl of Mar led a revolt in Scotland, but by 1716 it had collapsed. Its effect was still further to discredit the Tories. Unfortunately there were bitter personal feuds among the Whigs themselves, and from 1716 to 1721 there was a struggle to see which of the Whig gentlemen was to be supreme. In 1717 Sunderland won over Stanhope and managed to discredit Townshend and Walpole, but by 1720 both the brothers-in-law had resumed office. The return of

Walpole was of vital importance, for in 1720 the Government was confronted with a major crisis as a result of Sunderland's financial policy. After the War of the Spanish Succession the National Debt stood at £54,145,363 and the annual interest on it was £3,351,358 in an average Budget of £10 million. Many people thought that this meant impending national bankruptcy. Before his fall in 1717 Walpole had started a Sinking Fund to redeem the Debt, and this had had a good effect on national credit. In 1720 the South Sea Act was passed to enable the South Sea Company to carry through what was in effect a conversion of the National Debt to a lower rate of interest. The Company had to persuade the public to subscribe, and there were wonderful rumours that the King of Spain would grant the Company gold and silver producing districts in the Indies. Gambling was very generally popular in the eighteenth century, and the public welcomed this chance to gamble on a large scale. By the end of June 1720, £100 South Sea stock stood at £1,060. Other speculators took advantage of the readiness of the public to invest, and even fantastic schemes for importing 'Spanish jackasses for unspecified purposes to unsuitable regions' [11] or 'for carrying on an undertaking of great advantage, but nobody to know what it is' [12] gained support. The South Sea Company unwisely prosecuted the promoters of some of these wildcat schemes, for operating without a charter. The exposure of the small frauds shook public confidence, and the South Sea Bubble itself burst, bringing ruin to many people and disgrace to the Government. Though Stanhope admittedly did not understand finance and was not guilty of any kind of dishonesty, he, as chief minister, bore the brunt of the attack, and after he had been particularly savagely attacked in the House, died of apoplexy. Aislaibie, the Chancellor of the Exchequer, was found guilty of being bribed. Craggs committed suicide and the younger Craggs died of smallpox. Sunderland was acquitted, but public opinion forced him to resign.

The one man who could save the country in the financial crisis of 1720 was Walpole. [13] He relieved the Company of £7 million it had undertaken to pay the Government and caused £2 million of the directors' private property to be distributed among the shareholders. He saved the Government and for the next twenty-one years he dominated English politics. 'In private life he was good-natured, cheerful, social; inelegant in his manners, loose in his morals.' [14] His notorious association with his mistress even during the life of Lady Walpole was supposed to have been satirized by Gay in 1727 when, in The Beggar's Opera, [15] Macheath is shown tormented at once by Polly Peachum and Lucy Lockit. Indeed, a good many passages in the opera were taken to refer to Walpole. Among the ruffians recorded in Peachum's books was one called 'Robin of Bagshot, alias Gorgon, alias Bluff Bob, alias Carbuncle, alias Bob Booty', who was said to spend his life among women. On the first night that the opera was produced the audience enthusiastically encored the song, 'When you censure the age', and looked pointedly at the stage box where Sir Robert was sitting. He, however, was not to be put out of countenance and immediately encored the song a second time himself, which earned him a cheer from the audience. He deprived Gay of his rooms in Whitehall, but was not otherwise vindictive. Chesterfield described him as having 'a hearty kind of frankness, which sometimes seemed impudence, and which made people think that he let them into his secrets, whilst the impoliteness of his manners seemed to attest his sincerity'. He was 'an artful rather than an eloquent speaker', seeing 'as by intuition, the disposition of the House'. 'So clear in stating the most intricate matters, especially in the finances, that, whilst he was speaking, the most ignorant thought that they understood what they really did not.' Chesterfield thought him 'both the best Parliament-man, and the ablest manager of Parliament, that I believe ever lived'.

At first Walpole's authority was not completely

---

[11] Quoted by C. Grant Robertson, *England under the Hanoverians*, p. 39. [12] *Ibid.*

[13] See Volume I of J. H. Plumb's *Sir Robert Walpole*.
[14] Lord Chesterfield, *Letters*, (1892), Vol. II, p. 473.
[15] See W.E.Schultz, *The Beggar's Opera*, Chap. 17.

paramount. But in 1722 Sunderland died. In 1724 the brilliant, masterful and ambitious Carteret, whom Sunderland's influence had made Secretary of State in 1721, came into conflict with Walpole and was transferred to govern Ireland. In 1730 even Townshend, having come into collision with Walpole, retired from public life. For the next nine years Walpole was undisputed master.

At home, after the collapse of the South Sea Bubble, Walpole was able to put through fiscal reforms which materially helped trade. His policy was enunciated in the King's Speech of 1721: 'To make the exportation of our own manufactures and the importation of the commodities used in the manufacturing of them as practicable as may be'.[16] Between 1721 and 1724 the customs system was reorganized. Duties were removed from most manufactures exported and from the import of raw materials. The rates of duties were reduced and simplified. Some bounties were given for the re-export of colonial products such as hemp. A system of bonded warehouses was introduced for tea, coffee and chocolate.

The death of George I in 1727 had threatened Walpole's authority, for the new King was known to think very little of his father's ministers. Townshend he thought a 'choleric blockhead', Newcastle an 'impertinent fool' [17] and Walpole he had called both rogue and rascal. But Sir Spencer Compton, whom George II would have liked to put in direction of affairs, was manifestly 'a plodding, heavy fellow with great application and no talents, his only knowledge forms and precedents',[18] who even had to consult Walpole to draw up the King's Speech. Compton had also offended the Queen by cultivating the King's mistress. Walpole was ready to increase the Civil List, and the administration in fact continued almost unchanged with Compton, now Lord Wilmington, as President of the Council and Walpole in effective control, as his treatment of Townshend in 1730 made abundantly clear.

The disappearance of Townshend inaugurated a period when Walpole himself was responsible for directing foreign policy, and, though this period was one of peace and growing prosperity for England, it saw the breakdown of the Anglo-French Alliance, which had been concluded by Stanhope in 1716, and the resumption by France of an independent and highly successful foreign policy which by 1738 had greatly increased her influence in Eastern Europe. The War of the Polish Succession, which broke out in 1733, was another trial of strength between the Bourbon powers and the Emperor, and traditional Whig policy would have been for England to intervene on the side of the Emperor. Some members of the Cabinet favoured such an intervention, the Opposition was loud in its attacks on Walpole's weakness, the King was eager for an opportunity to win martial glory. But Walpole would not fight. War would increase taxation and might damage trade, and Walpole could feel well satisfied when he said to Queen Caroline, 'Madam, there are 50,000 men slain in Europe this year, and not one Englishman'. He also feared that the secret alliance of 1733 between France and Spain might develop into an effective anti-British coalition if England were to take part in the war, whereas if she did not, the difficulties with Spain might once again be solved by diplomacy.

Walpole managed to keep England out of war in 1733, but from that time his influence gradually weakened. In 1733–34 his attempt to continue his fiscal and commercial reforms by introducing a general system of excise was defeated, and as a result of this struggle several Whigs went over to the Opposition. Up till that time the Opposition had been very weak. The Tories were divided and, though only some were still genuinely Jacobite, all were discredited by being spoken of as Jacobite. After 1723 Bolingbroke, though he had not been allowed to resume his place in the House of Lords, served the Opposition well with his pen. After Walpole's decision not to give office to Pultney in the ministerial reshuffle after the South Sea Bubble, he too joined the Opposition, and by 1725 his quarrel with Walpole had become acute. As Chesterfield said of him, 'resentment made him

[16] Grant Robertson, *England under the Hanoverians*, p. 54.
[17] *Ibid.*, p. 57.
[18] *Ibid.*, p. 57.

engage in business. He had thought himself slighted by Sir Robert Walpole, to whom he publicly vowed not only revenge but utter destruction. ... He was a most complete orator and debater in the House of Commons; eloquent, entertaining, persuasive, strong, and pathetic, as occasion required,' [19] but 'the warmth of his imagination, joined to the impetuosity and restlessness of his temper, made him incapable of conducting it long with prudence and steadiness'.[20] Together Pultney and Bolingbroke built up a group of 'Patriots', and from 1726 their criticism of Walpole was expressed in *The Craftsman*. The Opposition ranks were augmented by Chesterfield in 1726 and by Carteret in 1730. Carteret had 'wonderful quickness and precision in seizing the stress of a question', and 'a most uncommon share of learning for a man of quality', but 'he had been bred up in high monarchical ... principles of government, which his ardent and imperious temper made him think were the only rational and practicable ones'.[21] After the struggle over the excise, the Opposition was increased by some Whig peers such as Cobham, and this nucleus tended to attract aspiring young politicians such as Grenville, Lyttelton and William Pitt. The power of the Opposition was much increased by the support of the Prince of Wales, who from 1734 was openly opposed to his father. As the power of his enemies increased, Walpole's own influence weakened. The election of 1734 reduced the governmental majority to fifty. In 1737 the death of Queen Caroline robbed Walpole of one of his most steady and valuable supporters.

The final blow to Walpole came in the form of a dispute with Spain over illicit trade in the West Indies. Many merchants valued the profitable trade with Old Spain more highly than the largely illicit trade with Spanish America, but enough merchants clamoured for war to alarm the Duke of Newcastle. England rang with the story of Captain Jenkins, who was supposed to have had an ear cut off by Spanish *guarda costas*. The Directors of the South Sea Company chose this moment to refuse to accommodate their long-standing grievances with His Catholic Majesty. In 1739 in spite of all Walpole's efforts war broke out.[22] In 1740 England was also confronted with a war between her traditional ally Austria and Frederick of Prussia, who, on the death of the Emperor, had invaded the Habsburg province of Silesia. The elections of 1741 still further reduced Walpole's powers in the Commons, and when in 1742 the Government had been defeated by sixteen votes on an election petition, Walpole accepted a peerage and resigned.

At home the chief problem after the fall of Walpole was who was to succeed him. It was characteristic of the fluid state of parties and of constitutional practice in the eighteenth century that, though Walpole had been defeated, his colleagues Newcastle and Pelham remained in office, and between them continued to control affairs till the reign of George III. Even out of office Walpole still retained considerable influence, and used this to reduce Pultney's influence by getting him to accept an earldom. The ablest of the new ministers was Carteret. Walpole's influence prevented him becoming First Lord of the Treasury, but he became Secretary of State, and for a brief period was able to practise the diplomacy which was his 'joy and his genius. In 1743, when the titular head of the administration died, Walpole and Newcastle secured the post for Henry Pelham, who retained it almost without a break till his death in 1754. After Carteret's fall in 1745 the Pelham brothers reorganized the Ministry and gave office to two of Cobham's 'Patriots', the cousins Lyttelton and Grenville, but they were not able to give office to Pitt, whose outspoken and early attack on Hanover had made him personally displeasing to the King. It was not until 1746, when, in the midst of the Scottish rebellion, the Pelhams resigned in protest and when Pultney and Carteret found it

---

[19] Chesterfield, *Letters*, Vol. II, p. 471.
[20] *Ibid.*
[21] *Ibid.*, p. 475.

[22] One of the few English victories, Admiral Vernon's capture of Portobello, provided two popular names for English public houses. In 1752 *The Adventurer* in an article asked why should 'the brave Admiral Vernon retail flip?' See J. Larwood and J. C. Hotten, *English Inn Signs*, p. 14.

impossible to form a government without a majority in the House, that on their return to office the Pelhams were able to bring in Pitt. These ministerial reshuffles could be made by the Pelhams because the Duke of Newcastle had a special interest in electioneering politics, and from 1724, when he joined Walpole's administration, had controlled government patronage for nearly forty years. The Septennial Act of 1716 made seats far more valuable than they had been when each Parliament lasted for only three years. Newcastle made sure that government influence was exploited to the furthest extent. 'He made certain that the meanest government official in the Customs and Excise, or in the service of the Admiralty or the Post Office, had to use his vote, if he had one, in accordance with instructions or lose his job.' [23] From 1727 Newcastle began to make direct grants from the secret service funds in return for the right to nominate members. £1,500 was the figure generally accepted as the value of a nomination. Election contests tended to disappear, especially in the constituencies with very small electorates. The government machine in combination with the greater patrons could be certain of victory in a general election. All that the Opposition could do was to try to win over some of the patrons, provoke a ministerial crisis and then capture the Treasury. This was why Walpole took pains to prevent Carteret obtaining the Treasury in 1742, and he and the Pelham connexion made every effort in 1743 to secure the Treasury for Henry Pelham. Control of government patronage meant that from 1742 to 1762 was in domestic affairs the Age of the Pelhams, but in foreign policy the dominating geniuses were first Carteret and then Pitt.

Carteret's main interest was diplomacy, and the field in which he was particularly well informed was northern and central Europe. His embassy to Sweden in 1719–20 had been conspicuously successful, not only could he talk German, but he had a unique understanding of the intricacies of the constitution of the Holy Roman Empire. From 1742 to 1744, when he was Secretary of State for the Northern Department, he put a new energy into English foreign policy. Carteret wanted to preserve 'the liberties of Europe', and in 1742 these seemed to be threatened by an aggressive France. Where he misunderstood the situation was in his belief that the balance of power ought to be preserved on the Continent. As he once admitted, he had no ambition for conquests outside Europe,[24] yet at this time commercial and colonial rivalries between England and France were becoming more keen, and the surest way to have revived English prestige would have been, as Pitt realized, to challenge France in Africa, in the New World and in India. Carteret misread the situation and preferred to concentrate his attention on building up a coalition in Europe, but this only drove France to declare war on England in 1744 and encourage a Jacobite revolt. Carteret was held responsible for reverses. In October 1744 he fell. The Jacobite rising was defeated, but otherwise the war went badly for England. Pelham was alarmed at a National Debt which was now £78 millions, and in 1748 Britain made peace at Aix-la-Chapelle on terms which were a triumph for France.

But though the Government had been unsuccessful abroad, Pelham and Newcastle continued in direction of affairs until Pelham's death in 1754, and at home the period after the peace of 1748 saw a series of important social reforms, some of which were directly attributable to the great Lord Chancellor Hardwicke. Hardwicke, who held the post of Chancellor for nearly twenty years from 1737 to 1756, was most highly esteemed as a lawyer. Lord Mansfield, Burke and Wilkes all agreed that when he pronounced his decrees 'wisdom herself might be supposed to speak',[25] but as a minister of State he also played a very important part harmonizing difficulties within the Cabinet, and his steadiness, keen-sightedness and sound judgement did much to counteract Newcastle's weakness and eccentri-

[23] J.H.Plumb, *England in the Eighteenth Century*, pp. 39–40.

[24] Quoted by B.Williams, *Carteret and Newcastle*, p. 125.
[25] W.S.Holdsworth, *History of English Law*, Vol. XII, p. 253.

city. Hardwicke was particularly influential in domestic affairs, and his experience as assize judge, Chief Justice and Lord Chancellor had given him first-hand knowledge of many of the social evils of the time. After the Jacobite Rebellion it was Hardwicke who was largely responsible for the legislation which civilized the Highlands of Scotland. In 1753 he secured the enactment of legislation which ended the scandal of impetuously hasty marriages by requiring that all weddings should normally be performed by a clergyman of the Church of England in a regular place of worship and after banns had been cried in the parish churches of both parties for three successive weeks. In 1751 the Ministry passed an Act to try to regulate the drinking of gin, which had become a social evil of the gravest kind since the import of foreign spirits had been prohibited in 1688 and the trade of distilling had been opened to anyone on the payment of certain duties. In 1684 it had been estimated that home-distilled spirits amounted to only 527,000 gallons, as compared with 12,400,000 barrels of beer brewed in 1688. But by 1714 the gallons of spirits distilled had risen to 2 million, by 1727 the number was 3,601,000 and by 1735 it was 6,394,000 gallons. Between 1750 and 1751 11 million gallons were consumed by a population of only 6 millions. The evils of this widely spread addiction to spirits were vividly recorded by Hogarth in his *Gin Lane*. The general drunkenness affected the health of the people; in 1750 it was stated that in London alone there were 14,000 cases of disease directly attributable to gin drinking. Drunkenness increased poverty and was a potent cause of increased violence and crime. The Act of 1751 imposed a fine of £10 on distillers who retailed spirits themselves or sold them to unlicensed retailers, permitted the issue of retail licences only to fairly substantial householders and increased the penalties for selling spirits without a licence. The Pelham administration also tried to check the crime which in the mid-eighteenth century forced decent citizens to travel 'even at noon as if one were going to battle',[26] which allowed

notorious robbers with a price on their heads to ride openly through crowded London streets, which exposed respectable women to the risk of assault and which made outbreaks such as the Porteous Riot in Edinburgh or the various riots provoked by the attempts to curtail the unlicensed sale of gin an ever-present threat. The creation of the Bow Street runners was the beginning of an effective police force and did much to reduce the menace of street robberies. It was under the Pelham administration too in 1752 that the English Calendar was reformed and brought into line with the Gregorian system which had for centuries been used in Catholic Europe. The reform was obviously sound, and had the support of Lord Hardwicke, but was bitterly opposed by some ignorant people who rioted and clamoured to be given back their eleven days when these were cut from the month of September.

In March 1754 Henry Pelham died, and for three years there followed a bitter personal struggle for office made specially serious because for most of that time England was living under the threat of foreign war and even of invasion. The man left in control of affairs on Pelham's death was his brother, the Duke of Newcastle, who had held office of some kind since 1724, and who was determined to continue to do so, though his character made him completely unsuitable to direct affairs. 'His confused, tangled, unconnected talk, his fulsome flattery, his promises made on the spur of the moment and almost instantly forgotten, his childish exhibitions of timidity, ignorance, fretfulness and perplexity, the miserable humiliations to which he stooped rather than abandon office, his personal oddities, and his utter want of dignity and self control made him at once one of the most singular and one of the most contemptible figures of his time.'[27] Newcastle 'was good-natured to a degree of weakness, even to tears upon the slightest occasions. Exceedingly timorous, both personally and politically, dreading the least innovation, and keeping with a scrupulous timidity in the beaten track of business as having

[26] Horace Walpole to Sir H. Mann, 23 March 1752, quoted by Lecky, *History of England in the Eighteenth Century*, Vol. II, p. 108.

[27] Lecky, *History of England in the Eighteenth Century*, Vol. II, p. 347.

the safest bottom.' 'His ruling, or rather his only, passion was, the agitation, the bustle, and the hurry of business ... but he was as dilatory in dispatching it as he was eager to engage in it. He was always in a hurry, never walked but always ran. ... His levées were his pleasure, and his triumph; he loved to have them crowded, and consequently they were so. There he generally made people of business wait two or three hours in the ante chamber, while he trifled away time with some insignificant favourite in his closet. When at last he came into his levée room, he accosted, hugged, embraced and promised everybody, with a seeming cordiality, but at the same time with an illiberal and degrading familiarity.' [28] Newcastle was at first reluctant to share the control of affairs with any of his brilliant junior colleagues and provoked angry attacks from two of them. Henry Fox was later reconciled to Newcastle, but the old Duke completely alienated a far more brilliant man, William Pitt, who became harshly critical of the Government's diplomacy and in November 1755 was dismissed from office.

The international situation, while ministerial offices were being reshuffled at home, was becoming steadily more dangerous. The peace of Aix-la-Chapelle had left the frontiers of English and French settlements in America very vague, and in the summer of 1755 armed hostilities between English and French began in the New World. The diplomacy of Newcastle's Government at this juncture was completely inadequate, and by its very inconsistency provoked a reversal of alliances which has come to be known as the Diplomatic Revolution. In January Frederick of Prussia concluded a treaty with England, and by May 1756 France and Austria had concluded the first Treaty of Versailles. This diplomatic revolution, which brought France into alliance with her traditional enemy Austria and which made England the ally of Prussia, indicated two things. It stressed the emergence of Prussia and Russia as major powers. It also showed how deeply separated were the conflicts of the Maritime and the Central European powers.

In May 1756 England declared war on France. At home the Government was weakened by the defection of Fox and by the decision of Murray, one of the most eloquent speakers in the Commons, to become Chief Justice of the King's Bench. Newcastle, weakened by the loss of his two ablest supporters and discredited by his inept foreign policy and the disastrous course of the war, could not remain in office, in spite of all his skill as a 'manager' of elections, and resigned in November 1756. The King invited Fox to form a ministry, but he failed, and in December 1756 for a few months a government was formed under the leadership of the Duke of Devonshire with Pitt as its most able member. Unfortunately Pitt was incapacitated during most of the winter by gout and the King disliked and distrusted him.[29] In March 1757 the Government acquired much undeserved unpopularity when the King, refusing to listen to Pitt, insisted on the execution of the unfortunate Admiral Byng, who was held responsible for the loss of Minorca. The next month Pitt was dismissed, and the Ministry crumbled to pieces. For eleven weeks in the middle of a major war England was without a government, but in June 1757 Newcastle returned to office with Pitt as one of the Secretaries of State.

The man who now dominated English policy was a most remarkable genius. A poor young man with no influential family connexions, who from an early age had been tormented by cruel attacks of gout, William Pitt became one of the greatest war ministers England has ever known. Without ever stooping to corruption he acquired a considerable fortune, and though he had at the outset of his career incurred the dislike of the King, his natural brilliance and immense popularity with the nation carried him into office and earned him an earldom. Pitt had many faults, but he had genius. He was vain, supercilious, unbending and ostentatious. Under-secretaries were never allowed to sit in his presence. He exhorted his son to avoid being so undignified as to laugh. He was theatrical, his

---

[28] Chesterfield, *Letters*, Vol. II, pp. 483–4.

[29] *Waldegrave's Memoires*, pp. 95–8. Quoted by Lecky, *History of England in the Eighteenth Century*, Vol. II, p. 372.

crutch or his sling were carefully arranged even for a private interview. He was inconsistent, taking office under Pelham and Newcastle, though he had attacked Walpole and denounced corruption, and acquiescing in the use of Hanoverian troops by Pelham though he had denounced the same policy when pursued by Carteret as one which had made 'this great, this powerful, this formidable Kingdom, [to be] considered only as a province to a despicable electorate'. But he had qualities which far outweighed these defects. He understood the people. He loved freedom. He was blazingly patriotic. He was courageously independent, so that though he had only just returned to office and his ministry was pitifully weak, he risked the displeasure of the King and the hatred of the people by pleading against the execution of Admiral Byng. In the same way he later denounced the very popular Wilkes as 'a blasphemer of his God, and a libeller of his King',[30] and when the American colonists broke into rebellion he rejoiced at the Americans' courage in defending their liberties. He had high political principles and knew how to rouse other men to share them. As a speaker in the House of Commons he was one of the greatest orators that assembly has ever known. Contemporaries who knew both said that in grace and dignity he was the equal of Garrick. His powers of denunciation and invective were unsurpassed, and he could silence and stun an opponent and overawe the whole House. He had a gift for memorable and picturesque phrases, so that, though reporting was most inadequate, many of Pitt's sayings are still familiar. Above all, and in spite of his theatricality, he had a spontaneity which never failed to fire his hearers, for his speeches revealed a mind capable of formulating great policies and a personality even greater than the policies.

Till 1761 Pitt directed British foreign policy and the conduct of the war, and England achieved resounding victories. From the beginning of his career in Parliament,[31] Pitt had devoted much

time and study to French commercial and industrial statistics, and this had convinced him that France was the only serious rival Britain had to fear. To beat this rival Pitt believed that England must become supreme at sea and must seize trading-posts so as to gain control of the chief branches of French foreign trade. During the Seven Years' War Pitt pursued this policy with single-minded determination and great success. He used sea-power to blockade the French fleet in Brest and Toulon and then launched a series of combined operations to gain control of French trade. The capture of Louisbourg in 1758, Quebec in 1759 and Montreal in 1760 won control of the trade in fish, fur and naval stores from Canada. The capture of Dakar in 1759 secured the African trade in slaves and in gum. The capture of Guadeloupe in the same year won a great part of the French sugar trade, and though some City merchants feared that this might glut the market and ruin the British West Indies, the American colonies proved able to absorb the sugar from Guadeloupe, and within a year the income from the island's customs duties had risen by 50 per cent. and had paid for the expedition which had been sent to capture the place. In India Clive won the battle of Plassey in 1757, Sir Eyre Coote took Masulipatam in 1759 and in 1760 the French were defeated at Wandewash. The conquest of Manila in 1762 secured the China trade in tea. When the French fleets did venture out to sea in 1759 with the intention of launching an attack on England, Boscawen smashed the Toulon fleet off Lagos and Hawke destroyed the Brest fleet in Quiberon Bay. On the Continent, in spite of the genius and dogged determination of Frederick II, the war did not go so well for England and Prussia, but in a position of strategic stalemate Frederick managed by sheer military genius to retain tactical mastery.

But in spite of the genius of Pitt and the heroism of Frederick II, the war ended less well for the allies than appeared likely in 1759. In that year the pacific and Anglophil King of Spain was replaced by his half-brother Charles, who disliked England and favoured a close alliance with France, and in 1760 the English throne passed to George III. At this time Pitt was hoping to prosecute the

[30] Quoted by Lecky, *History of England*, Vol. II, p. 391.
[31] For this analysis of Pitt's policy see J.H.Plumb, *England in the Eighteenth Century*, pp. 109 *et seq*.

war with such energy that England would be able to compel France and her allies to acknowledge that they had been defeated as decisively in Europe as in North America and India and on the high seas. But the new King and his adviser Bute wanted peace. In 1761 Pitt urged the Cabinet to declare war on Spain, arguing that the new Spanish King certainly meant to join France and that the best method of defence was attack. Though Spain had, in fact, secretly concluded an alliance with France in August 1761, the British Cabinet did not believe that the Spanish danger was serious, and refused to declare war. Pitt at once resigned. Within three months the safe return of the Spanish treasure fleet and the publication of the Franco-Spanish alliance compelled England to declare war, in January 1762. However, fortune favoured England and Prussia, and England proved more than a match for Spain, capturing Havana and Manila. The death of the Tsarina Elizabeth in January 1762 brought to the throne of Russia Peter III, who had a great personal admiration for Frederick II and wanted to be free of the war against Prussia so as to press dynastic claims in the Baltic. The Tsar stopped hostilities against Prussia, and Frederick II was saved. At sea England won further successes against France, capturing Martinique, Granada, St Lucia and St Vincent. But Bute was not able to conclude a triumphant peace. In order to secure a speedy peace he abandoned Martinique, Havana, the West Indian islands and Manila. The tragic results of Bute's statecraft became apparent twenty years later. But the next twenty years were the beginning of a new epoch in English history. The death of George II had opened a new phase in English constitutional development. The Seven Years' War and Pitt's inspired policy of commercial and colonial aggression had made explicit rivalries and ambitions which had been only dimly apprehended before 1757. At home technical and other industrial developments were soon to change the face and the social structure of England. The end of the reign of George II marked a watershed dividing the age of Walpole, Pelham and Newcastle, of the great Whig families, of peace or at worst of limited wars with limited objectives from the age of the Pitts, of winning and losing empires, of economic and political revolutions and of great wars.

Architecture and Interior Decoration

JOHN FLEMING

During this short period of forty-five years we cross the great watershed of British architecture, for the rise and fall of Palladianism are very conveniently contained between 1715 and 1760. Of course several other styles and tendencies were evident and even flourishing at the same time – Wren and his Board of Works were still in power in 1715, Vanbrugh undertook Eastbury and Seaton Delaval in 1718 and Grimsthorpe in 1723, while James Gibbs prolonged our flirtation with baroque into the 1730's; and by the mid-century the neo-Gothic, the Chinese and other fancies had already begun to stir. Nevertheless, Palladianism dominates the whole period and Lord Burlington emerges as the central figure in the early Georgian architectural scene (cf. Hogarth's engraving, *The Man of Taste*). To his influence and that of his circle, which was widely exerted through their lavishly illustrated books, we owe not only the rational splendour of the great seats but the elegant refinement of innumerable smaller houses and the trim discipline of the streets and squares of London, Bath and many provincial towns.

Of the less spectacular forces which went to the moulding of early eighteenth century domestic architecture the most important were the speculative builders of London and their more humble followers in the country districts. The type of small town-house devised by these men dates back, in plan at any rate, to the Restoration. The limitation of the narrow street-fronted sites had compelled builders to an almost standard design, which needed but slight modification to conform with the Building Acts of 1707 and 1708 and, some few years later, with the Palladian rules expounded by Lord Burlington. The Building Acts are of great importance. They were directly responsible for many of those features by which we recognize an eighteenth-century house – the parapeted fronts concealing the roof, the set-back sash-frames and the segmental topped window-openings. Most of these small houses were built of grey or yellow stock bricks, instead of the red bricks of Queen Anne's reign, and this new fashion for more quiet and delicate colouring is symptomatic of the general trend of taste towards restraint and refinement. Isaac Ware remarked that although there were 'many very beautiful pieces of workmanship in red brick ... this should not tempt the judicious architect to admit them in the front walls of the building.

'In the first place, the colour is itself fiery and disagreeable to the eye; it is troublesome to look upon it; and, in summer, it has an appearance of heat that is very disagreeable.'

From the same authoritative writer, who was of course a Palladian, we obtain the best account of the typical small town-house of the period (Fig. 1):

'The general custom is to make two rooms and a light closet on a floor, and if there be any little opening behind, to pave it ...

'In common houses the fore-parlour is the best room upon the ground-floor: the passage cuts off a good deal from this, and from the back parlour; this usually running straight into the opening, or garden as it is called, behind; but it is a much better practice to make the back parlour the better room.

'The first floor in these common houses consists of the dining-room, over the hall or parlour; a bed-chamber over the back parlour, and a closet over its closet.

'The closet is usually a corner added to the building, and continued to the second story, not to the garrets.

'In houses something better than the common kind, the back room upon the first floor should be a drawing-room, or dressing-room, for the lady; for it is better not to have any bed on this floor.

'The two rooms on the second floor are for bed-rooms, and the closets being carried up thus far, there may be a third bed there.

'Over these are the garrets, which may be divided into a larger number than the floors below, for the reception of beds for servants.

'Such a house as we have been here speaking of is to be built for six or seven hundred pounds, or it will cost upwards, according to a little more extent of ground, and a little more than usual ornament. The common builders of them work jointly, one doing his share of business in the other's house, according to their several subordinate professions.'
(*Complete Body of Architecture*, 1756.)

English Palladianism

Palladianism is of such capital importance during this period that we must deal at some length with its inception and theory before describing the buildings it created. Lord Burlington was unquestionably the central figure both as theorist and practitioner, but he did not inaugurate the movement. He seems to have been indifferent to Palladio during his first Grand Tour and did not see the light until after his return to London in 1715. This coincided with the publication of Leoni's *Palladio* and the first volume of Campbell's *Vitruvius Britannicus*, which contained an attack on the licentious extravagance of Italian baroque and an eulogy of 'the great Palladio who has exceeded all that has gone before him and surpassed his contemporaries'.

It is significant that the Palladian revival should have begun not with building but with literary production and theory. Burlington espoused the cause without, so far as we know, having examined in detail a single example of the master's work and his interest was to remain, as it had begun, rigidly fixed on questions of artistic principle. Pope called him a 'positive' man, and both the strength and

weakness of Palladianism derived ultimately from his obsession to preach and establish absolute classical standards in architecture.

Vitruvius Britannicus, however, was not confined to theory. Campbell included among the engraved plates his designs for Wanstead (Fig. 2), which was to be the first important essay in the new style and the prototype of innumerable Palladian country-houses and palatial town-houses. As may be seen from the engravings (the house was demolished in 1824), Wanstead consisted of a somewhat cumbrous, elongated block with a rusticated ground-floor and *piano-nobile* above, the whole adorned with motifs drawn exclusively from the Palladian repertoire. An imposing hexastyle portico (the first to be erected in Britain according to Campbell) was the principal feature of the façade. Burlington was evidently captivated by this example of the new purism, for he immediately commissioned Campbell to take over the rebuilding of Burlington House. Not content with

Fig. 1. Characteristic house of the period 1740–63. 'Grey' brick, cornice and stone bands. From *Georgian London* by John Summerson.

the role of patron, however, Burlington set off again for Italy, and this time went straight to Vicenza to study Palladio at first hand. He returned in 1719 accompanied by a struggling young Yorkshire artist, William Kent, with whom he was to form one of the happiest and most fruitful partnerships in the history of architecture.

English Palladianism is a curious phenomenon in eighteenth century taste. At the precise moment when the light, elegant and frivolous rococo was emerging on the Continent, England embraced a rigid and austere classicism. The singularity of this contrast is best appreciated when we remember that in 1713 William Kent and Cosmos Damian Asam were fellow students and prize-winners at St Luke's Academy at Rome, and that twenty years later Kent was completing the august solemnities of Holkham Hall while his former companion was adding the final rococo curl to the Johann Nepomuk Kirche at Munich.[1]

It is not altogether surprising, of course, that Palladio's sober classicism should have appealed to the solid commonsense country-gentry of England rather than the wayward exuberance of a Borromini or the wanton frivolity of the rococo. Palladio was the one Italian architect who had designed buildings which approximated in size and purpose to the requirements of an English country-house and, moreover, his villas appeared to recapture the spirit of the ancient Roman house (then known only from literary descriptions) which made a strong appeal to the English upper-classes with their classical education. The strength of the Burlington school was indeed largely founded on the support it derived from the new Whig aristocracy, who had come into power with George I, and in this way Palladianism can be re-

[1] Equally significant for the student of English taste at this juncture is the fact that two very brilliant Italian architects came to London between 1714 and 1720, but failed to obtain a single client. Alessandro Galilei, the architect of the facade of St John Lateran at Rome, spent five fruitless years in England where he prepared designs for several country and town houses as well as for a Royal Palace at Whitehall. An even greater architect, indeed a genius, Filippo Juvara, experienced the same lack of appreciation for his work when he came to London in 1720.

lated to political history. The Whigs were naturally disposed to find the architecture of their Tory predecessors as misguided as their politics, and had therefore turned their backs on Wren, Vanbrugh and the Board of Works. The Burlingtonians were welcomed as the restorers of true architecture and, more specifically, of true British architecture, for they had returned not only to Palladio but to Inigo Jones.

That true politeness we can only call,
Which looks like Jones's fabrick at Whitehall

wrote J. Forrester in 1734, and Colin Campbell went so far as to doubt 'but an impartial judge will find in the Banqueting Hall and the Queen's House all the regularity of the former (Palladio) with the addition of beauty and majesty, in which our architect is esteemed to have outdone all that went before'.

What then were the principles which Palladio had first formulated and which were now to change the face of England? In his *Quattro Libri del Architettura* he laid down ratios of 'harmonic proportion' whose subtleties can have been grasped by few, if any, of the Burlingtonians, though they did employ the more simple formulas for the dimensions of particular rooms and their components. The influence of Palladio's book was exerted mainly through its numerous illustrations and not by the erudite and long-winded text. From these engraved plates the Burlingtonians equipped themselves with that limited but homogeneous system of forms and motifs by which their buildings may now be so easily recognized – the Venetian Window, for example (Fig. 3), or the heavy pediments over doors and windows, or the doors and windows framed by mouldings with superimposed blocked quoins, or the ubiquitous classical temple front – columns carrying a large pediment – a motif which Palladio introduced as a prominent feature into domestic architecture and which was employed by his English followers in all their major works, beginning with Wanstead (Fig. 2). The over-all impression of a Palladian country-house is typified by the clear, balanced and wide-spaced alternation between plain wall and openings and by the adoption of the Italian *piano-*

C

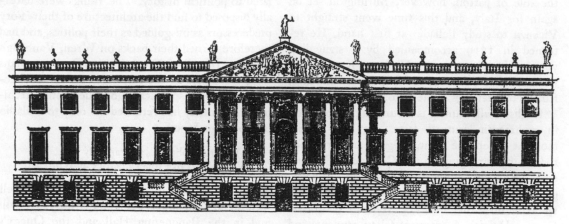

Fig. 2. The first design of the West Front of Wanstead, 1715.
From *Vitruvius Britannicus, Vol. I*, by Colin Campbell.

nobile at first-floor level with a rusticated base below and a small attic storey above. Palladio's influence was less pronounced within doors, where the Burlingtonians turned more readily to Inigo Jones for guidance.

Lord Burlington and William Kent

It is difficult to assess accurately the individual contribution of Lord Burlington and William Kent, but Horace Walpole probably summarized the position correctly by calling Burlington 'the Apollo of the Arts' and Kent 'his proper priest'. In architecture proper the Earl was certainly the guiding brain, but it seems equally certain that Kent was responsible for the exuberantly rich interiors of their joint works, such as Chiswick and Holkham.

Lord Burlington returned from Italy in 1719, and there followed a quick succession of buildings, now destroyed or largely rebuilt, until in 1725 he began his most influential work, Chiswick House. This remarkable construction consists entirely of state-rooms, being intended purely as an ornamental villa for the display of its owner-architect's taste and collections. Superficially an imitation of Palladio's famous Villa Rotonda, it reveals the Earl's cold and intellectual approach to his Venetian master, for when compared with its

supremely light and elegant prototype it appears distinctly squat and stocky, typically English, if not indeed broad Yorkshire (Pl. 32A). As might be suspected, it resembles the engravings in Palladio's book more closely than his building. Colin Campbell, who never went to Italy, so far as is known, came much nearer in feeling to Palladio in his version of the Villa Rotonda at Mereworth (Pl. 6B). Chiswick is uncompromisingly square and block-like, and the sudden and slightly awkward prominence of the dome, together with the spacing of the over-emphasized windows and niches, reveal that *staccato* quality which Professor Wittkower has shown to be the outstanding characteristic of Burlington's style. By *staccato* is meant that emphasis on each individual feature which gives an abrupt, jerky effect to the elevations and which arose from Burlington's habit of visualizing each motif separately – a symptom, no doubt, of his formula-loving and compartmented mind.

As might be deduced from Chiswick, Lord Burlington's style developed towards an increasingly dry and puritanical classicism, eventually reaching its full and well-nigh perfect expression in the York Assembly Rooms of 1730. This dogmatic building, with its stately Corinthian colonnades (an exact model of Palladio's Egyptian Hall, based on Vitruvius) and its facade, which alas no longer exists, reminiscent of the architecture of imperial Roman baths, is the most mature example of pure classical architecture in England and would alone suffice to establish Lord Burlington as an architect of European importance. However, we need not assess his achievement solely on the evidence of his two surviving buildings, for there is little doubt that he was responsible for much that is distinguished and forceful in Kent's work as an architect.

Kent was a man of happy temperament. Whimsical, impulsive, unintellectual and indeed all but illiterate, he was in many ways the antithesis of his patron. But he submitted dutifully to the Earl's guidance in all his major buildings, though remaining an eclectic at heart. He could be Roman, he could be baroque, he could be gothic, he could be fantastic almost in the manner of the Elizabethans and, as might be expected of one so volatile and capricious, his talents found an easier outlet in interior decoration than in architecture proper. As a designer of furniture he excelled; and it was perhaps as a landscape gardener that he made his most original and fruitful contribution to the arts.

His early essays in architecture were, rather surprisingly, in the neo-gothic manner, but his first important commission was Holkham Hall, begun in 1734 (Pl. 6A). This great palace, for it is too grandiose and princely to be called a country-house, consists of a rectangular block with corner pavilions raised into low towers, attached at the angles to form other blocks, each with a high pedimented centre and lower sides, also pedimented. Nowhere is Burlington's [2] *staccato* sense of design more evident than in this austere yet powerful conception, which imposes itself on the spectator as much by the ruthless logic of its closely knit composition as by its monumental scale. Each section, each separate feature is firmly and deliberately isolated (the Venetian windows, for example, are framed within relieving arches, a favourite

trick of Lord Burlington), so that no repetition of window or opening is allowed to set up a unifying rhythm. It is pre-eminently the design of an intellectual, and if it is also slightly forbidding, we may see in this a reflection of the Earl's aristocratic reserve – though it must be remembered that Holkham suffers greatly from the lack of glazing-bars which were originally gilded and must have brightened the exterior somewhat.

Of Kent's other buildings the most important are a charming and slightly Vanbrughian pavilion at Badminton, the King's Mews and the Treasury in London, No. 44 Berkeley Square and, finally, the Horse Guards, which was built to his designs after his death. This is closer to Holkham than anything else in his *oeuvre*, for the broken composition, with its isolated elements and the play of Venetian windows, are essential characteristics of both buildings. But remarkable though these great constructions are, they represent but one facet of Kent's versatile genius. He was least himself when striving dutifully to follow the Earl's Palladian precepts, and to see Kent at his best we must go inside his palatial houses, where he was evidently allowed a freer hand.

Grandeur, splendour, sumptuousness are the keynotes here. So thickly hung are they with rich brocades and Genoa velvets, so heavily carved and gilded or even, as in the famous hall at Houghton, sculptured throughout in marble, that they come much nearer in feeling to Italian baroque than the Earl would have cared to admit. There is nothing very austere about Kent's great saloon at Houghton (see dust-jacket) or his hardly less grandiloquently seigneurial drawing-room at No. 44 Berkeley Square (Pl. 9) with its heavily coffered and painted ceiling. The entrance hall at Holkham (Pl. 5) is perhaps Kent's masterpiece both as architect and interior decorator. Palladian themes were here exploited in an imaginative and theatrical manner, an Egyptian Hall being combined with a Roman basilica of which the apse contains a flight of steps leading up dramatically through a colonnade to the exedra and into the saloon beyond. Even more unrestrainedly baroque is his famous staircase at No. 44 Berkeley Square. But these daring compositions were something of

[2] Professor R. Wittkower has discussed Burlington's share in the designs for Holkham in *Archaeological Jnl.*, cii, 1945.

a *jeu d'esprit*. Normally his interiors are as static as they are rich and ponderous.

The spread of Palladianism

The Palladian movement began, as we have seen, with literature and theory. It precipitated an avalanche of weighty architectural tomes and engraved folios, beginning with those sponsored by Lord Burlington, such as Kent's *Designs of Inigo Jones* (1727), Castell's *Villas of the Ancients* (1728) and Burlington's *Fabbriche Antiche* (1730). These expensive and beautifully produced books reached only a small though influential audience, but the Palladian doctrine soon spread to a wider public through the books of such men as Roger Morris and Isaac Ware and, later still, of William Halfpenny, Batty Langley and others whose popular productions were directed specifically at the country builder and artisan. By these means the Palladian movement permeated to the small provincial towns of England, to the wilds of Scotland and even to America, where Roger Morris had considerable influence through his admirer Thomas Jefferson. In England the success of all this propaganda was complete by 1731, when Alexander Pope ridiculed Lord Burlington's followers, in his famous lines:

> Yet shall (my Lord) your just, your noble rules,
> Fill half the land with Imitating Fools;
> Who random drawings from your sheets shall take,
> And of one beauty many blunders make:

This is, of course, rather too severe, and certainly cannot be applied to the accomplished architects in the Earl's immediate entourage – William Kent, Colin Campbell, Giacomo Leoni, Isaac Ware and Henry Flitcroft – or even to such smaller fry as Roger Morris, William Adam and John Vardey. Colin Campbell we have already mentioned as the author of Wanstead and Burlington House, but he designed a dozen or more important buildings before his death in 1729. The most notable of these are Sir Robert Walpole's ostentatious palace at Houghton (redeemed by Kent's splendid interiors), the idyllic interpretation of Palladio's Villa Rotonda at Mereworth (1723, Pl. 6B), and the charming pavilion at Ebberston near Scarborough. Despite the picturesque appeal of such houses, posed in settings which evoke the arcadian landscapes of Claude and Poussin, Campbell's work now seems rather dry and academic. But he had great influence in his own day, principally through the wide circulation of *Vitruvius Britannicus*, in which his own buildings were naturally given a prominent place.

Giacomo Leoni, a Venetian by birth, was, like Campbell, both architect and author, and his editions of *Palladio* (1715) and *Alberti* (1726) are fundamental to the history of Burlingtonianism. His buildings are always accomplished (Lyme Hall, for instance), but he was occasionally unorthodox and daring, as at Clandon Park, and at Queensbury House in London he created a precedent which was to have far-reaching repercussions in town-house and street design (see page 26).

Isaac Ware and Henry Flitcroft both began as humble artisans, were taken up by the Burlingtonians and eventually reached clerkships in the Office of Works. Ware is now remembered chiefly for his translation of *Palladio* (1738) and his *Complete Body of Architecture* (1756), an invaluable compendium of knowledge on all aspects of the building trade of his day. But the unimaginative competence which was the making of him as an author robbed his buildings of any great distinction. Wrotham Park (1754) is cumbrous, though scrupulously correct, and Chesterfield House (demolished 1937) was remarkable chiefly for the French rococo interior for which Lord Chesterfield probably deserves more credit than Ware. The exterior followed Jones's Chevening with the addition of Doric colonnades.

Henry Flitcroft, or 'Burlington Harry', had even less originality than Ware and his best-known work, Wentworth Woodhouse (1734–68), perhaps deserves the lash of Pope's satire. The facade of this colossal mansion, which sprawls along no less than 606 ft, is a good example of the empty pomposity into which Palladianism ultimately declined. However, if the monumental scale renders the exterior absurd, it lends dignity to the princely apartments within, where rich plaster-work, marble floors, *scagliola* columns and copies of Graeco-Roman statuary abound.

Fig. 3. Venetian window of the Ionic order, 1739.
From *Treasury of Designs* by Batty Langley.

Though an ardent Palladian, Roger Morris was detached from the Burlington group. His patron was Lord Pembroke, an amateur architect whose contribution to their joint works it is now impossible to determine. The Palladian Bridge at Wilton is their masterpiece and perhaps the masterpiece of English Palladianism as a whole – a successful adaptation of classical precedents to create a new and wholly original work of art. This cannot be claimed for Marble Hill at Twickenham (Pl. 7A) – 'some prefer sweet Marble Hill, though

sure 'tis somewhat flat' – but it deserves a prominent place in the history of early Georgian architecture as a good example of the unpretentious excellence which could be obtained by the intelligent application of 'the rules'.

So much for the architects who initiated the Palladian revival. From the 1740's onwards the movement was consolidated by an ever-widening group of disciples, most of whom had no direct contact with the leaders in London. They included a variety of talent – spirited amateurs such

533

as Sir Thomas Robinson and Sanderson Miller (better known perhaps for his work in the gothic style); professionals such as James Paine in Yorkshire, William Adam in Scotland, Richard Cassels in Ireland; and a host of smaller fry in the provincial towns of England, often the local mason turned architect, like Francis Smith of Warwick or the anonymous author of White's House, Chippenham (Pl. 8A). Mention of a few works produced by such men will suffice to indicate the high quality attained in the lower ranks of Palladianism.

The Assembly Rooms at Doncaster and Heath House near Wakefield, both by Paine, are perhaps above the average standard, although Heath House displays a few of those peculiarities of Paine's style which must have caused some raising of polite eyebrows at Burlington House. But such impurities would have passed almost unobserved in the presence of William Adam's robust and individual handling of Palladian motifs. At Duff House near Banff (Pl. 7B) we see provincial Palladianism at its vigorous best. Undeniably wild and woolly when compared to the sleek and well-groomed façades of the London architects, it may yet be thought that Adam came closer to the spirit of actual buildings of Palladio than did the theory-ridden exponents of Lord Burlington's inner circle. His uninhibited use of rustication for dramatic effect, his reckless admixture of motifs drawn from Vanbrugh and Gibbs, gave his buildings a richness of texture which corresponds in an uncouth way to the more sophisticated and mannerist effects of Palladio. Adam's works were engraved and published posthumously as *Vitruvius Scoticus*, which had, rather surprisingly, a considerable influence in America, particularly in Virginia, where several of the more important mansions were based on Adam's engravings.

Palladian town-house and street design

An aspect of Palladianism to which we have barely referred hitherto now deserves special mention – town-house and street design. The Restoration type of London town-house persisted almost unchanged until the Palladians devised a new formula based on the old houses in Lincoln's Inn Fields and Queen Street, then thought to be by Inigo Jones. The general arrangement of the traditional small town-house has already been described (page 527): externally it was characterized by uniform fenestration on all floors, by the use of key-blocks to all windows, bands at the principal floor levels, a modillion eaves cornice and a wooden door-case of classical design (Fig. 4). The Palladian formula introduced a major emphasis at first-floor level (corresponding to the *piano-nobile* adopted for country-houses), the ground floor being treated as a podium and the upper floors embraced by a classical order – either expressed in pilasters or, more often, merely implied. In the latter event a broad band is used to mark the first-floor level, room being left between the lintels of the top windows and cornice for the missing architrave and frieze.

The best example of the Palladian town-house with order implied is No. 44 Berkeley Square, while Leoni's Queensbury House (now the Bank of Scotland) exhibits the expressed order style. It very conveniently leads us to a consideration of Palladian street design, since Leoni's great composition controls the proportions of the other houses in Old Burlington Street, where they meet its return façade. The principal of uniformity in street design, which accounts for so much of the charm of Georgian London, reached its first full expression in Grosvenor Square, designed in the 1730's, but now, alas, destroyed. The east side of seven houses was treated as a unity and given the character of a single palatial building by emphasizing the centre house with rusticated quoins and a pediment, and by marking off the end houses in a similar way. On the north side of the square the builder-architect Edward Shepherd treated the entire block as if it were a great Palladian villa, like Wanstead, rusticating the ground floor and erecting upon it an attached portico of six Corinthian columns.

This remarkable innovation reached its climax in Bath, where, from 1725 onwards, John Wood devoted his extraordinary talents to the creation of one of the most beautiful town-plans ever to be realized in Britain. Beginning with Queen's Square (Pl. 8B, 1729–36), which carried on the theme of Shepherd's Grosvenor Square, Wood indulged his dream of endowing Bath with the character, and

Fig. 4. Corinthian door, 1739. From *Treasury of Designs* by Batty Langley.

even the individual monuments of its ancient Roman predecessor, including a Forum, a Circus and an 'Imperial Gymnasium'. The result of this quixotic ambition was not only of great beauty but of great importance for the future development of town-planning. The Forum came first, and was never completed, but the Circus was a great success. This truly original conception consisted in turning the Colosseum inside out to serve as the frontispiece of thirty-three standard town-houses of moderate size. John Wood's work at Bath was continued by his son, whose great invention was the Royal Crescent, an enormous semi-elliptical block, which was repeated *ad nauseam* in the towns of England until well into the nineteenth century.

The decline of Palladianism

Lord Burlington died in 1753, and his closest associates had all predeceased him, so that we may say that the force of Palladianism was spent by the turn of the century. However, a second generation of architects, conservative and unenterprising men for the most part, carried on the style for several decades. The first intimations of its decline were

sounded by Isaac Ware as early as 1756, when he demonstrated, in his *Complete Body of Architecture*, that Palladio himself could err, and even went so far as to deny the existence of pre-established rules in architecture.[3] Although insisting that the ideals and 'science' of the ancients must control the 'licentiousness', Ware advocated what he called judicious variety, and in his section on interior decoration 'ventures to lead the student into all Fancy's wildness'. The Earl must have turned in his grave at such heresies from a former disciple. And it is perhaps worth remarking here that in the same year, 1756, the rising star of the next period, Robert Adam, had already asserted his independence from the Palladian rules and was writing from Rome, 'I dispise our famous Inigo ... and even Palladio is much to be criticized'.

But if Palladianism developed ultimately into a constricting and stultifying academicism, its innovations in one field, that of interior planning, proved wholly beneficial and fertile. By their free use of classical forms, derived chiefly from Palladio's plans of the Roman thermae, the Burlingtonians opened up the possibilities of space composition in domestic architecture – possibilities hitherto exploited only in church building. The full expression of this new concept was not to be attained until the second half of the century, but already by the 1750's the more varied and ambitious planning of the Palladians had introduced curved forms (elliptical halls, bow-windows, apses in dining-rooms, etc.) in place of the monotonous rectangular room shapes of an earlier period. The importance of this development for Robert Adam and his followers can hardly be exaggerated, and indeed it may be regarded as the most valuable legacy of Palladianism.

It is difficult to sum up adequately the Palladian achievement. Was it even a true style? Its defence against a charge of plagiarism is valid, provided of course that it succeeded in breathing new life into

[3] Of course criticism of Palladio was never completely silenced. In the 1730's, when Lord Burlington's influence was at its height, Robert Morris gave an important series of lectures in which he endeavoured 'to show you his (Palladio's) Blemishes as well as his Perfections'. *Lectures on Architecture*, 1734.

the ancient forms and motifs employed. This we must allow the Burlingtonians to have done, even if more by accident and misunderstanding than by conscious design. For they used the classical apparatus in an unprecedented way, far removed from anything Italian, and translated the cubic and functional motifs of Palladio into decorative and linear surface patterns. The Venetian window, for example, which had in Italy a clearly assigned place in the logical structure of a building, emerged in England as a purely decorative feature. Thus whereas Palladio's buildings must be judged for their plastic and functional values, an English Palladian country-house should be seen from a distance, like a picture. By this picturesque re-interpretation of their classical models the Burlingtonians created a new architectural idiom, expressive of the mood of the Augustan era. It is a noble and temperate style, devoid alike of dramatic splendours and unexpected fancies, so that it seems to echo the stately periods of Bishop Berkeley's and Dr Johnson's prose and the suave urbanities of Pope's and Gay's poetry.

Interior Decoration

'Having ascended a grand flight of steps, you come under a Doric portico, whose pediment extends 62 feet, with pillars 46 feet high; from thence you enter a noble hall, adorn'd by statues and busts, the saloon painted olive, the ornaments, as the cornice, etc. rich gilt; the sofas in this apartment are very fine tapestry. On one side the saloon is the common dining and drawing room, on the other the best drawing room, hung with and furnished with cut velvet; the state bed-chamber, hung with crimson velvet furniture; the same, the bed with gold, and lin'd with a painted India satin; the dressing room hung with green satin.

'The *Managareth* or Chinese bedroom and dressing room in the attic storey is excessively droll and pretty, furnish'd exactly as in China, the bed of an uncommon size, seven feet wide by six long.'

This description of Eastbury in 1760 by Mrs Lybbe Powys gives a good general impression of interior decoration during our period. It will be observed that the Palladian rules were considerably relaxed inside the house – even to the length of permitting a Chinese bedroom. But, quite apart from such extravaganzas, the Burlingtonians were distinctly more eclectic and adventurous as decorators than as architects. William Kent was the leading practitioner, and it is significant that his decorative style approaches that of James Gibbs, who was otherwise anathema to the Palladians. Kent regarded each room as a separate work of art for which every detail, including the furniture must be specially designed and, according to Horace Walpole,

'his oracle was so much consulted by all who affected taste, that nothing was thought compleat without his assistance. He was not only consulted for furniture, as frames for pictures, glasses, tables, chairs, &c. but for plate, for a barge, for a cradle. And so impetuous was fashion, that two great ladies prevailed on him to make designs for their birth-day gowns. The one he dressed in a petticoat with columns of the five orders; the other like a bronze, in a copper-coloured sattin with ornaments of gold.'

The antiquarian tastes of the Whig aristocracy, assiduously cultivated on the Grand Tour, affected not only the decorative style but the lay-out and whole conception of the great houses of the period. The Library and Sculpture Gallery replaced the earlier long-galleries and shared the honours of the house with the saloon, so called after the Italian *salone*. Similarly the reception-rooms were arranged enfilade, opening out of each other to afford *vistos* along the whole length of the *piano-nobile*.

Splendour and sumptuousness are the keynotes of early Georgian interior decoration, and the costliest materials were prodigally used in order to obtain the desired effect of opulent grandeur – brocades, satins, Genoa velvets, marbles, semi-precious stones and, of course, gilding, of which there could never be too much. Kent's masterpieces at Houghton, Holkham and No. 44 Berkeley Square display the style at its expensive best, though several no less magnificent examples have been destroyed. At Brandenburgh House, Hammersmith, for instance, there were doorcases of lapis-lazuli, and the columns of the saloon were monoliths of Sicilian jasper. As might be expected of so exuberant a style, it was sometimes in danger of falling into the gaudy and vulgarly showy – from which, indeed, it was often saved only by the superb quality of the craftsmanship and materials.

Kent was criticized for his 'constant introduction of pediments and members of architecture over doors and within rooms', and the passion for such features (derived from Inigo Jones) characterizes the whole period – coffered ceilings, pedimented alcoves, consoles carrying busts, richly carved and gilded tabernacle frames to doors and windows and, the focal point of every room, the bulging sculptural chimney-pieces (Pl. 35). These epitomize the style. They were of one or two storeys – the simple or continued type, to use Ware's terms. The simple type was thought best for rooms hung with paper or silk, while the continued type was reserved for the great stuccoed hall and other grand apartments. This normally had an upper structure of wood or stucco, continuing the lower structure of marble, and contained a picture or low-relief. The whole was surmounted by a pediment, often broken to contain a bust or to carry baroque *putti* modelled in the round (Pl. 11B). Combined with the equally ponderous door-cases and window-frames, these Cyclopean chimney-pieces give the Palladian interior its stately and slightly pompous solemnity, which might become uncomfortably oppressive were it not for the ebulliently Italian stucco-work. This introduced a less formal and haughty note into the Kentian harmonies. Stucco was generally by foreign artists whereas chimney-piece sculpture was rarely imported. All the leading sculptors, except Roubiliac, made reliefs for chimney-pieces, and their work looks distinctly neo-classic when compared with the exuberant baroque flourishes of the stuccadors.

Painted decoration on walls, as popularized by Verrio, Laguerre and Thornhill, gradually went out of fashion during the early eighteenth century, though it lingered on for a time as monochrome arabesques or *trompe l'œil* statuary. Natural wood-panelling also disappeared, and since wainscots were universally painted or grained, we find that deal and pine had replaced oak by the mid-century. Stucco took the place of panelling and painted decoration on walls, and of course it continued to be widely used for ceilings. The leading stuccadors were nearly all Italians, who appear to have imported not only their traditional techniques, but also their native designs, for they were allowed a completely free hand by their architect employers. The occasional incongruity of their Italian baroque manner in a sober Palladian interior has already been remarked, but if this was sometimes discordant, it more often added a piquancy and zest to the whole, as, for example, at Hall Place, where the swirling forms of the Venetian baroque dolphins are enhanced by their juxtaposition to the upright lines and sharp rigidity of the door-cases.

The best stuccadors were more than craftsmen. They were artists who made their own very individual contribution to early Georgian interior decoration, and their collaboration with all the famous architects of the day accounts for the similarity in most of the important decorative schemes. Artari and Bagutti, the best-known stuccadors, worked (either singly or together) for Kent at Houghton, for Campbell at Mereworth, for Gibbs at Ditchley and Orleans House (Pl. 10) and perhaps for Leoni at Clandon (Pl. 11A). Of their colleagues, Vassali and Serena were perhaps the most notable. Vassali introduced a light rococo style in his decoration of the drawing-room at Hagley, which he enriched with long festoons and drops of flowers with trophies of musical instruments. The Anglo-Dane Charles Stanley was more eclectic, and could be gay and whimsical (Kirtlington Park), rich and heavy (Honington Hall) or more Venetian than the Venetians themselves (Hall Place). These gifted artists were followed by a host of English imitators, only a few of whom attained an original style of their own. But we must mention Thomas Stocking, whose floral decorations in stucco at the Royal Fort, Bristol, are as fresh and as unmistakably English as the hedgerow flowers on which they were based.

Although stucco rather than painted decoration is the characteristic of our period, the painted ceiling demands a few words. At Rousham and Kensington Palace, William Kent employed 'grotesques' based on Raphael's loggie in the Vatican – a light and airy style which the Adams developed and refined in the second half of the century. Kent also carried out several important ceilings in his 'mosaic' manner – i.e. panels and medallions inset between gilded stucco ribs and painted in *grisaille* with scrollwork, *putti* and other motifs from

Roman decorative art. This drawing-room ceiling at No. 44 Berkeley Square is a good example of this style.

The French rococo style known as *singeries* is occasionally found, and should be mentioned, if only for its rarity. François Clermont carried out schemes in this manner at Kew and at Monkey Island, Bray, where the ceiling was enlivened with monkeys fishing and shooting, but perhaps the best example is a ceiling at Kirtlington Park, Oxfordshire, which Clermont painted in 1745.

James Gibbs

The importance of James Gibbs is emphasized by his isolation. He was a Scot, a Tory and a Roman Catholic. Alone among the prominent architects of his day, he resisted the doctrinaire influence of Lord Burlington, and clung tenaciously to the eclectic style of Sir Christopher Wren and to the principles of Italian baroque and mannerist architecture which he had imbibed at first hand in Rome. He is, indeed, unique in having studied under a distinguished Italian architect, Carlo Fontana, whose pupils included von Hildebrandt and Fischer von Erlach. Gibbs was therefore in the main stream of European architecture – and nothing could have cut him off more sharply from his contemporaries in England. It is significant that Campbell inserted a slighting reference to Fontana in the first volume of *Vitruvius Britannicus*.

Gibbs returned from Rome to London in 1709, when the Vanbrugh–Hawksmoor school was still in the ascendant, and his first important commission, St Mary-le-Strand, is one of the outstanding examples of baroque architecture in England, albeit of a very personal variety. He was then taken up by Lord Burlington, only to be dropped in favour of Campbell, who replaced him as architect of Burlington House. Thereafter Gibbs made some prudent though half-hearted efforts to trim his style to the prevailing winds of doctrine, but he never became a true Palladian, and had no further contact with Burlington or with Whig thought and influence. He remained faithful to Wren and his Italian masters, while absorbing into his style many diverse strains, in-

cluding a few Palladian features. Indeed, he had employed the Venetian window some years before it was popularized by the Burlingtonians.

Gibbs will always be remembered primarily as the architect of St Martin-in-the-Fields, which became an accepted model for the Anglican parish church throughout the English-speaking world. But his public buildings display his lively and unorthodox style to better advantage – the Senate House and King's Fellows' Building at Cambridge and, most remarkable of all, the Radcliffe Camera at Oxford, in which the principles of 'mannerist' ambiguity were exploited for the first and last time in England. Compared with these achievements his domestic architecture is uniformly sober to the point of tameness. Beginning with Cannons (1713, demolished 1747), a princely mansion of pronounced baroque tendencies, followed by Sudbrook Lodge, in which he indulged a passing whim for French motifs such as *œil-de-boeuf* windows, Gibbs's domestic style gradually declined in vigour and originality until we reach the country-houses of his middle years, of which Ditchley is the best example. This might almost pass for the work of a Palladian. Almost, but not quite; for all the windows, including those of the attic, are given equal emphasis by architraves and keystones – a lack of discrimination which Lord Burlington would have deplored.

As a decorator, Gibbs is perhaps of more significance to us, for if, as seems probable, he imported the stuccadors Artari, Bagutti and Serena, then he must be given credit for introducing into England their ebulliently Italian style of plaster decoration which, as we have already remarked, was to enliven the interiors even of the strictest Palladians. Gibbs's own interior decoration was unashamedly baroque and is seen at its best at Orleans House (Pl. 10), an octagon conceived in the same gay and festive spirit as animated the garden pavilions of the great continental palaces. Artari and Bagutti carried out the superbly rich and fully modelled stucco-work and Rysbrack probably made the female figures reclining on the chimney-piece. Pale blue-grey panels on white set off the gilding and the whole, with its gleaming black-and-white chequered floor, is as accomplished and sonorous as a Handel *concerto grosso*.

Gibbs exerted a considerable influence through his *Book of Architecture* (1728). Apart from engravings of his own works, he included many designs drawn from a wide range of English, French and Italian sources which proved an admirable antidote to the constricting influence of Palladian literature. The book was intended as a pattern book, and as such had an immediate success, for the designs could, as Gibbs said, be executed 'by any workman who understands lines'. In addition, he had his own personal admirers and imitators, of whom Thomas Ivory of Norwich is the most notable.

The gothic, Chinese and other fancies

Some cry up Gunnersbury,
For Sion some declare,
And some say that with Chiswick House
No villa can compare:
But ask the beaux of Middlesex
Who know the country well,
If Strawberry Hill, if Strawberry Hill
Don't bear away the bell.

This merry jingle by the Earl of Bath appeared in the *Gentleman's Magazine* for April 1756 and neatly expresses the swing in taste away from pompous formality towards something more gay and frivolous. Thus the rococo made its tardy but sprightly entrance into England, stepping somewhat gingerly at first in a neo-gothic disguise. William Kent is usually credited with the invention of Georgian gothic, a whimsical, playful interpretation of gothic motifs (very different from the solemn drama of Vanbrugh's medievalism or the matter-of-factness of survival gothic), and in 1729 he adorned the Tudor Gatehouse at Esher Place with quatre-foils and ogee-arched windows. Kent's fondness for the elegant double curve of the ogee-arch should be noted, for it closely resembles the shapes favoured by French rococo designers.

By 1736 'the modern gothick' was being praised for its delicacy and whimsicality, and in a few years the fashion had spread all over England. Particularly popular with the amateur architect and provincial builder, the style was mainly used

Fig. 5. Gothic Chimney-piece, 1742. From *Gothic Architecture Improved* by Batty Langley.

for decorative features, such as window-frames, chimney-pieces (Fig. 5), porches or garden follies (Fig. 6). And since Georgian gothic tended towards the flimsy, few of its works have survived. The style is therefore best studied in the pattern books – Batty Langley's *Gothic Architecture Improved* (1742) or William Halfpenny's

Rural Architecture in the Gothic Taste (1752). These reveal the essence of the style to have been a free adaptation of gothic motifs to titillate a classically trained taste. Langley even went so far as to gothicize the Five Orders!

The most distinguished practitioner of Georgian gothic was, appropriately enough, a Warwickshire squire and amateur architect, Sanderson Miller, whom we have already mentioned as a minor Palladian. His gothic career began in the 1740's with a sham castle and tower, complete with drawbridge, which he built on his estate at Edgehill. This started a fashion among his dilettante friends, for whom he was soon building other ruins such as that at Hagley (Pl. 12A), of which even Horace Walpole approved, declaring it to have 'the true rust of the Barons' wars'. His masterpiece, however, was Lacock Abbey, which he enlarged for Ivory Talbot in 1753. This charming and elegant affair was carried out as a light-hearted extravaganza, in the Kent tradition of Georgian gothic, for the medieval detail, including a 'Rose Window', was applied symmetrically as if dressing-up a Palladian façade.

But Strawberry Hill is of course the best-known example of eighteenth-century gothic. This elegant 'phantasy' was devised by various hands under the presiding genius of its owner, Horace Walpole, who bought the property in 1747 and devoted the next forty years to its enlargement and adornment. Walpole's approach to gothic was at first typically rococo and frivolous. He talked of the 'charming venerable Gothick' and called his staircase 'so pretty and so small that I am inclined to wrap it up and send it you'. But his attitude soon changed. Where he had come to mock he stayed to pray, and before long he was endeavouring to make his gothic detail accurate – an attempt which Kent and Langley would have thought ludicrously pedantic. Thus Walpole's book-cases (Pl. 12B) were copied from a screen from Old St Paul's and the chimney-piece in the Holbein Chamber from the tomb of Archbishop Warham at Canterbury. His gothic scholarship went only skin-deep, however, for he evidently saw nothing incongruous in using a cathedral monument for a villa fireplace.

Most of Walpole's taste and ingenuity was lavished on the interior decoration of Strawberry Hill, but the exterior, if less elegantly modish, is perhaps of greater importance in the history of architecture. In his additions and extensions Walpole imitated the fortuitous effects which groups of ancient buildings sometimes give, and thus he opened the door to the architecture of the Picturesque which was to blossom many years later under Wyatt and John Nash. It must be emphasized, however, that Strawberry had little immediate influence. Its contemporary importance lay in the social and artistic *cachet* which its aristocratic owner gave to neo-gothic.

'A few years ago everything was Gothic', wrote Whitehead in *The World*, XII (22 March 1753). 'According to the present prevailing whim, everything is Chinese.' And three years later J. Shebbeare wrote:

> 'Every chair in an apartment, the frames of glasses and tables must be Chinese: the walls covered with Chinese paper fill'd with figures which resemble nothing in God's creation, and which a prudent nation would prohibit for the sake of pregnant women. ... Nay, so excessive is the love of Chinese architecture become, that at present foxhunters would be sorry to break a leg in pursuing their sport in leaping any gate that was not made in the eastern taste of little bits of wood standing in all directions.' (*Letters on the English Nation*: 1756.)

Chinoiserie was essentially a decorator's fashion, satisfying that need for variety and the exotic which is so typical of the rococo. It was seldom carried to the length of an actual building (the Pagoda at Kew is one of the few examples, dating from 1757–62), and indeed the style was generally restricted to the decoration of one of the less important rooms, usually a bedroom, as in the house described above by Mrs Lybbe Powys. Few complete rooms in the Chinese taste have survived, and to find a good example we have to go slightly outside our period, to Claydon, where a carpenter, Mr Lightfoot, 'with no small spice of madness in his composition', created an extraordinary Aladdin's Cave of a room for the delectation of his patron. This was carried out entirely in carved

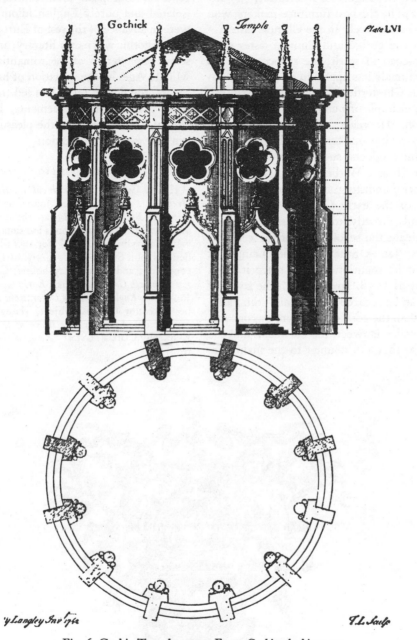

Fig. 6. Gothic Temple, 1742. From *Gothic Architecture Improved* by Batty Langley.

wood, in which Lightfoot's virtuosity is unequalled except by the best furniture-makers, who of course indulged freely in the Chinese taste.

Although the gothic and Chinese tastes were essentially rococo in spirit, the rococo style appears to have made less appeal in its pure and undiluted form. Chesterfield House, now destroyed, was the only example of a complete rococo scheme of decoration. However, the style was often employed by cabinet-makers and other craftsmen whose elegant products, such as the over-mantel at Peckover House, Wisbech (Pl. 11c), enliven many otherwise undistinguished rooms.

The last of the early Georgian revivals, the Grecian, leads directly to neo-classicism which was to dominate the second half of the century. Nevertheless, James Stuart's Doric Temple at Hagley must be mentioned here, since it dates from as early as 1758. In a sense all the styles of our period can be regarded as revivals – the Palladian no less than the gothic. But there was one important difference between the Palladians and the rest. Whereas they ran counter to the main currents of European architecture, producing an isolated and purely English idiom, the gothicists were in advance of the rest of Europe. The attraction of gothic was partly literary, and in their conscious exploitation of the romantic appeal of the Middle Ages by the imitation of historical monuments, the gothic revivalists led the way towards those architectural movements, both here and abroad, which practised the pleasures of historicism and evocative imitation.

SHORT BIBLIOGRAPHY

H. M. Colvin's *Biographical Dictionary of British Architects: 1660–1840* and John Summerson's *Architecture in Britain 1530–1830* are the authoritative works on the subject. Summerson is less detailed but includes valuable stylistic analyses. For town-house and street design, John Summerson's *Georgian London* should be consulted; and for country-houses, Christopher Hussey's *English Country Houses: Early Georgian*. Margaret Jourdain's *English Interior Decoration: 1500–1830* is the best account of this subject, though it should be supplemented by her *The Work of William Kent*. Sir Kenneth Clark's *Gothic Revival* is also essential reading.

Furniture

E. T. JOY

In order to appreciate fully the general character of English furniture-making in the period 1714–60, it is necessary to examine it against the social and economic background of the time. This was the period of the ascendancy of the Whigs, whose careful commercial and financial policy led to increased prosperity, especially for merchants and the landowning classes. Wealthy people were often anxious to spend lavishly on new houses and furniture which would embellish or raise their social status, and to meet this demand the furniture industry expanded considerably. The centre of the industry was, of course, London, which, as well as being the capital and the principal port, was of more importance and influence in relation to the rest of the country than it has been since. This is explained by its great size; in the middle of the century, while Bristol and Norwich, the next two largest cities, had some 50,000 inhabitants each, London had well over half a million. Here were found the largest single area for the production of furniture, and the main source of new ideas and styles. To London were attracted craftsmen of ability and ambition from the provinces, and from London the best furniture which was then being made in this country was sent to wealthy people throughout the kingdom, both by land and sea. A considerable export trade in every kind of furniture to world-wide markets was also developing during this period.

But, apart from the great capital city, England was still predominantly a country of villages and hamlets, of a society essentially rural in character; its towns were small by modern standards, though some were growing. The static and isolated nature of rural life is largely explained by the poor state of inland communications, for the great era of road improvements and canal-building did not begin until after 1760. In this kind of society most of the furniture used by all classes of the people, except the rich, was made locally. In the villages the furniture of cottages and farm-houses was made by the householder himself, or by the village joiner, who worked on traditional lines and paid little heed, if any, to the changing fashions of the towns. In the provincial towns the best cabinet-makers, some of whom were very capable craftsmen, supplied the lesser gentry and middle classes with good, well-made furniture which reflected something of the latest fashions from London; the less-skilled cabinet-makers, catering for ordinary townspeople, made unpretentious furniture which might be humbler adaptations of pieces that had been fashionable years – often many years – previously.

Furniture-making in London

In London there was a tremendous diversity in the nature of the shops, in the types of goods which they sold and in the skill of the craftsmen who made the furniture. It is clear that there were significant changes in shopkeeping. Some shops were notably growing in size, and required considerable capital to stock them. The furniture of the highest quality came from the shops where an eminent craftsman (or two craftsmen, for partnerships were common) controlled the business; but other large shops were directed by a shopkeeper who was not a craftsman at all, and did not even employ craftsmen on his premises to make the furniture, but obtained his goods for re-sale from outside craftsmen. Dealers of this kind had existed for a long time in the furniture trades, but during this period the scope of their business was widening appreciably. An anonymous writer in 1747, discussing London trades, described cabinet-makers as follows: 'Many of their shops are so richly set out that they look more like Palaces and their Stocks are of exceeding great Value. But this Business seems to consist, as do many others, of two Branches, the Maker and the Vendor; for the Shopkeeper does not always make every sort of Goods that he deals in, though he bears away the Title.' The same writer noted that turners could be divided into two classes: the 'Real Mechanics' who were the craftsmen, and a 'Set of Shopkeepers, many of them in a very large way [who] engross, as to the buying and selling part, all the produce of the real Turners and many Trades besides.' [1]

- The more fashionable craftsmen tended to work in the same area. In the earlier part of the century the chief centre was St Paul's Churchyard, but by about 1750 many of the leading craftsmen, among them Goodison, Hallett, Chippendale, Vile and Cobb, were working in St Martin's Lane and Long Acre. Some of their premises were very imposing. 'The corner house of Longacre,' wrote J.T.Smith in 1828, 'formed a small part of the extensive premises formerly occupied by that singularly haughty character, Cobb, the Upholsterer.' [2] The secret of the fine furniture which came from these shops lay in the great skill of the craftsmen who worked in them, each man specializing in a particular branch of his craft. This division of labour was carried on to a greater degree in London than elsewhere. The workman in furniture who had no specialist training was regarded as of very inferior status – 'no more than a cobbling Carpenter or Joiner'. To illustrate this specialization, the comments of the writer of 1747, already quoted, on the subdivisions of one single craft, that of chair-making, are worth not-

ing: 'Though this Sort of Household Goods is generally sold at the Shops of Cabinet-makers for all the better kinds, and at the Turners for the more common, yet there are particular Makers for each. The Cane-chair-makers not only make this Sort (now almost out of Use) but the better Sort of matted, Leather-bottomed and Wooden Chairs, of which there is great Variety in Goodness, Workmanship and Price; and some of the Makers, who are also Shopkeepers, are very considerable Dealers, employing from £300 to upwards of £500 in Trade. The white Wooden, Wickers and ordinary matted Sort, commonly called Kitchen-chairs, and sold by the Turners, are made by different Hands, but are all inferior Employs. Those covered with Stuff, Silks, etc., are made and sold by the Upholsterers.' Other kinds of craftsmen employed in chair-making could be added to this list, such as chair-carvers, gilders and japanners.

Oversea trade

London was the main centre of the export trade in all kinds of furniture and upholstery which were sent throughout Europe and to the colonies. Most of the emigrants who left this country to settle permanently in the colonies took some household furniture with them. Richer people, such as merchants, planters and colonial governors, took a great deal of furniture of the best quality. An interesting example of this practice is shown in Pl. 16, a view of the Supper Room in the Governor's Palace, Williamsburg, Virginia, as it was in the mid-eighteenth century. The furniture, brought from England by successive governors, is mainly of the Queen Anne and Chippendale periods.[3] These wealthier people frequently had other supplies of furniture sent out to them from home. Cabinet-makers in the American colonies also imported fashionable furniture from England to sell with their own products.

London was the chief importing centre for a whole range of goods which were required by the furniture industry. These included the many kinds of timbers and the raw materials of the uphols-

[1] *General Description of All Trades*, Anon., 1747.
[2] *Nollekins and his Times*, by J.T.Smith, 1828.
[3] *Williamsburg: a Restored Colonial Capital*, by H. Comstock, Connoisseur Year Book, 1954.

(A) Robert Walpole, 1st Earl of Orford, by
J. B. Van Loo, 1740.
National Portrait Gallery.

(B) Caroline Wilhelmina of Ansbach,
queen of George II, studio of C. Jervas,
1727. *National Portrait Gallery.*

(C) Dean Swift, engraving after Jervas.

(D) Sir John Vanbrugh, by Sir Godfrey
Kneller, from the Kit-Cat Collection.
National Portrait Gallery.

PLATE 1

Interior of the Rotunda, at Ranelagh, by CANALETTO, 1751. *National Gallery*. The Rotunda was built for concerts after the grounds, laid out by Lord Ranelagh, had been thrown open to the public in 1742 as a place of amusement.

PLATE 2

Taste in High Life, engraving after HOGARTH, 1742. This painting ridicules some of the most conspicuous follies of the mid-eighteenth century; the enormous, impractical hooped skirts and cripplingly high heels, which are again attacked in the picture on the middle of the back wall, the foppish dandy with his muff, absurdly exaggerated wig, and his useless little sword. The monkey with his quizzing glass and bag wig stresses the monkey like, unnatural appearance of the human beings. The old lady and old fop are in ecstasies over an absurd cup and saucer, which refers to the passion for collecting china. The monkey is reading a bill of fare made up of all sorts of exotic and unsubstantial dishes. In one corner is a tower made of packs of cards. Beside it is a bill for cards of £300. One of the pictures ridicules operatic ballet. The firescreen ridicules travel by sedan chair.

PLATE 3

547

The Distressed Poet, engraving after HOGARTH, 1740-1. Some of Hogarth's most biting pictures deal with the sufferings of the poor. Here the poor poet in a garret, trying to write while his wife repairs his one decent suit, is interrupted by one of the tradespeople who has come in person to demand settlement of her bill. This is not the degrading poverty such as Hogarth portrayed in *Gin Lane*, but the bare boards of the floor, the cracked plaster, the sparse, clumsy furniture and the poet's meagre library of three books provides a telling contrast to the carpets, curtains, mirrors and elegant occasional furniture shown in Plate 3.

WILLIAM KENT. The Hall at Holkham, Norfolk, designed in the early 1730's.   *Country Life.*

PLATE 5

(A) Lord Burlington's dogmatic Palladianism as expressed in his and WILLIAM KENT's Holkham Hall, Norfolk (1731–64).   *A. F. Kersting.*

(B) COLIN CAMPBELL. Mereworth Castle, Kent (*c.* 1722–1725) represents a more picturesque interpretation of Palladio.   *A. F. Kersting.*

PLATE 6

(A) The smooth manners of a London Palladian architect contrasted with, below, the rugged individualism of a provincial follower: ROGER MORRIS. Marble Hill, Twickenham (1728–29)   *Country Life.*

(B) WILLIAM ADAM. Duff House, Banffshire (1720–45).
Ministry of Works, Crown copyright reserved.

PLATE 7

(A) White's House, Chippenham (demolished 1933 and re-erected at Bath) exhibits the country-builder's Palladianism at its best.
Society for the Protection of Ancient Buildings.

(B) John Wood the Elder. Palladian street-design, based on a country house façade, at Queen's Square, Bath (1729–36). *A. F. Kersting.*

PLATE 8

WILLIAM KENT. The Drawing Room of 44 Berkeley Square, London (1742–44).
Country Life.

PLATE 9

JAMES GIBBS. Baroque interior decoration in the Octagon Room, Orleans House, Twickenham (1720), with stucco by Artari and Bagutti. *A. F. Kersting.*

PLATE 10

(A) *Above*. Italian-baroque stucco decoration, probably by Artari, on the hall ceiling at Clandon Park, Surrey, by Giacomo Leoni (1733).
A. F. Kersting.

(B) *Left*. The Palladian two-storey chimney-piece at Marble Hill, Twickenham (*c.* 1730) *Country Life*, contrasted with (C) the elegant rococo over-mantel made by an unknown craftsman for Peckover House, Wisbech (*c.* 1750). *Country Life*.

PLATE 11   555

(A) SANDERSON MILLER. Sham medieval ruin at Hagley Park, Worcestershire (1747–48). *A. F. Kersting.*

(B) Horace Walpole's Gothic Library at Strawberry Hill, Twickenham (1754). It displays his light-hearted antiquarianism. *A. F. Kersting.*

556   PLATE 12

The Stone Hall, Houghton, Norfolk, showing furniture designed by William Kent, *c.* 1725.

PLATE 13

(A) Mirror in gilt gesso frame, with shell ornament on the cresting, c. 1715.
Hart Collection.

(B) Walnut bureau-cabinet, c. 1725.
R. H. Heathcoat Amory, Esq.

PLATE 14

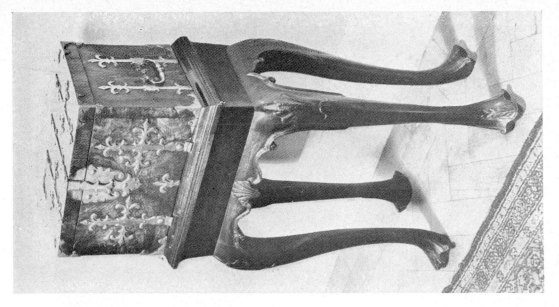

(B) Late seventeenth century walnut brass-bound casket (Flemish) on a George II period carved mahogany stand. *Private Collection.*

(A) Mahogany tea-table with scalloped top and tripod base, *c.* 1745. *Hart Collection.*

PLATE 15

The Supper Room, Governor's Palace, Williamsburg, Virginia, with English furniture, *c.* 1710–60, taken to America by Colonial Governors.

PLATE 16

Mirror in a carved and gilt frame in the rococo taste, *c.* 1755, reflecting an overmantel mirror in a frame designed by William Kent, *c.* 1725. *Courtesy the Marquess of Cholmondeley.*

PLATE 17 561

One of a pair of pier tables (*c.* 1710–20), of silvered gesso work, the top decorated (*see below*) with the entwined cypher —H.W. or W.H.—of the original owner. These tables are highly exceptional because they are silvered and not gilded, there being very little silvered gesso furniture extant. The silvering of gesso work instead of gilding was practised by the carvers and gilders of the time of Queen Anne and George I in order to give furniture the appearance of being made of real silver. James Moore (16? – 1726). who, in partnership with John Gumley, was one of the Royal cabinet-makers to the Crown in the reign of George I, appears to have specialized in the making of gesso furniture. At Hampton Court and Buckingham Palaces there are some gesso stands and tables of high quality which bear his signature on the top.

Hart Collection.

PLATE 18

(A) Mahogany serpentine-fronted commode, with rococo influence in the carving and handles, *c.* 1750. *Christie's.*

(B) Mahogany side table with marble top, *c.* 1745. *Victoria and Albert Museum.*

PLATE 19

(A) Mahogany chair with latticework back in the Chinese taste, *c.* 1760.

(B) Windsor chair with turned bars in back, *c.* 1750.

(C) Mahogany armchair, *c.* 1755.
Frank Partridge, Inc., New York.

(D) Upholstered walnut armchair with four finely carved cabriole legs, *c.* 1745. *Needham's Antiques, New York.*

PLATE 20

Mahogany bookcase, attributed to Thomas Chippendale *c.* 1760.   *The Lord Herbert.*

PLATE 21

(A) Japanned black and gold dressing commode, probably by Chippendale. *c.* 1750. *Victoria and Albert Museum.*

(B) Walnut card table with folding top, *c.* 1750.   *Hart Collection.*

PLATE 22

(A) Mahogany cabinet and
writing table, with carved
rococo ornament, *c.* 1760.
Messrs. Ackermann.

(B) Mahogany pedestal library table, *c.* 1750.

PLATE 23

Mahogany bureau bookcase with carving in the rococo taste, attributed to Thomas Chippendale, *c.* 1760.   *The Lord Herbert.*

(A) GAWEN HAMILTON.
'An Artists' Club'
(1735), showing, from
left to right,
George Vertue,
Hans Hysing,
Michael Dahl,
William Thomas,
James Gibbs,
Joseph Goupy,
Matthew Robinson,
Charles Bridgeman,
Bernard Baron,
John Wootton,
Michael Rysbrack,
Gawen Hamilton
and William Kent
*The National Portrait
Gallery.*

(B) WILLIAM
HOGARTH. The
Levée, the fourth
scene from the
Marriage à la Mode
Series (1743–5).
The Tate Gallery.

PLATE 25   569

(A) JONATHAN RICHARDSON. The 5th Viscount
Irwin and his Wife (*c.* 1718).
Temple Newsam House, Leeds.

(B) CHARLES JERVAS. Alexander Pope
(*c.* 1730).
The National Portrait Gallery.

(C) THOMAS HUDSON. Lady Oxenden
(*c.* 1750).
National Art Gallery, Sydney, Australia.

(D) GEORGE KNAPTON. The 3rd Earl of
Burlington (1743).
The Trustees, the Chatsworth Settlement.

PLATE 26

WILLIAM HOGARTH. Captain Coram (1740).
The Governors, the Thomas Coram Foundation for Children.

PLATE 27

(A) CHARLES PHILIPS. The Finch Family (*c.* 1732). *Charles Thornton, Esq.*

(B) ARTHUR DEVIS. Sir George and Lady Strickland (1751). *The Rev. J. G. Strickland.*

PLATE 28

(A) ALLAN RAMSAY. Ann Bayne, the artist's first wife. (c. 1739) W. R. Law, Esq.

(B) JOSEPH HIGHMORE. Samuel Richardson (1750). The National Portrait Gallery.

(C) JOSEPH HIGHMORE. Mr Oldham and his Friends (c. 1745). The Tate Gallery.

PLATE 29

(A) JOHN WOOTTON. Landscape with Figures (c. 1730). *Capt. M. V. Wombwell.*

(B) JACOPO AMIGONI. Jupiter and Io (1732). *Rickmansworth Urban District Council.*

(C) RICHARD WILSON. Rome and the Ponte Molle (1754). *National Museum of Wales.*

574

PLATE 30

(A) PHILIP MERCIER. Frederick Prince of Wales and his Sisters (1733).
The National Portrait Gallery.

(B) FRANCIS HAYMAN. The Dance of the Milkmaids (c. 1750), one of the paintings executed for Vauxhall. *Victoria and Albert Museum.*

PLATE 31

575

(A) GEORGE LAMBERT (with figures by another hand). Lord Burlington's villa at Chiswick (1742). *The Trustees, the Chatsworth Settlement.*

(B) SAMUEL SCOTT. The burning of Payta (1741).
The National Maritime Museum, Greenwich.

PLATE 32

terers – brocades, velvets, feathers for beds, etc. – as well as foreign articles (carpets, pictures, etc.) which were sold in some of the shops.

Kent and the Baroque

In the second quarter of the century the great figure in furniture design was William Kent (1685–1748), the first English architect who included furniture as an integral part of his interior decoration. His versatility as a designer was thus described by Horace Walpole: 'He was not only consulted for furniture, as frames for pictures, glasses, tables, chairs, but for plate, for a barge, for a cradle.' [4] He was the leading exponent of the Palladian revival which was sponsored by his patron, the Earl of Burlington, the 'Apollo of the Arts'. In the great Palladian house of the period, of which Raynham, Holkham and Houghton are celebrated examples, as well as in those parts of the royal palaces which he helped to furnish, Kent made free use of the rich and ornate baroque style which he had studied during his travels in Italy. He emphasized the bold and massive treatment of furniture, employing large, elaborately carved festoons, mouldings and masks, in soft woods richly gilt, or in mahogany parcel-gilt. Monumental side-tables, with large marble tops imported from Italy were his speciality. His furniture may be criticized as extravagant and florid – 'immeasurably ponderous', according to Walpole – yet it is perfectly in place with the particular settings for which it was designed, and in relation to which it should always be judged (Pl. 13). It was made for a small privileged group of wealthy clients, but the influence of its style is noticeable in the general architectural character of much of the best furniture made by leading cabinet-makers after 1725. In 1740 Kent's style was adapted to furniture of the middle classes by the Langley brothers in their trade publication (see *Design Books* below).

The Kent period was the great age of English gilding, and much furniture was gesso-gilt. Gesso was a mixture of whiting and parchment size which was applied in layers on a basis of soft woods. When the composition was hard, a pattern

[4] *Anecdotes of Painting*, by H. Walpole, 1762–71.

was formed in relief by working away the ground; the whole surface was then gilded or, more rarely, silvered (Pls. 14A, 18).

The mid-century styles

The reaction against the Baroque set in towards the middle of the century and took the form of a medley of styles: the Rococo, Chinese and Gothic. It is important to remember that these styles had quite different histories and that it is inaccurate to consider the Rococo as the parent of the other two. But in many respects there were affinities between them which do much to explain their vogue. They stressed the lighter treatment of furniture decoration and gave themselves to fanciful, capricious ornament in which their respective contributions could be blended. At this point some of the observations of Hogarth in his *Analysis of Beauty* (published in 1753) are interesting. He exalted waving and serpentine forms. 'The waving line', he wrote, '... is a line more productive of beauty than any of the former (i.e. straight and circular lines) ... for which reason we shall call it the line of beauty. The serpentine line hath the power of super-adding grace to beauty.' Together their beauty and grace produced intricacy in form – 'that peculiarity in the lines which compose it, that leads the eye a wanton kind of chace'. He also wrote of 'infinite variety' as an apt summary of beauty. Though he expressed approval of the Gothic ('have not many gothic buildings a great deal of consistent beauty in them?'), he decried both the Palladian and Chinese styles. He was also a bigoted anglophil in his prejudices against French influences, and it must be admitted, as Walpole wrote, that his views 'did not carry the conviction nor meet the universal acquiescence he expected'. But, all things considered, his ideas might be said to amount to a tacit approval of the Rococo taste, and they certainly reflected something of the prevailing mood.

Rococo

Rococo decoration in English furniture sprang from the French *rocaille*, among the outstanding creators of which were Pierre Lepautre with his transformation of baroque material about 1700, and J.A. Meissonier and Nicholas Pineau, who gave the movement a new phase about 1730. Lepautre employed delicate linear ornament in slight relief. To this Pineau's *genre pittoresque* added asymmetrical decoration in intricate curves and C scrolls. Thus the new style was in marked contrast to the baroque accentuation of plastic forms. In France the principal sphere of this movement in its early stages had been interior decoration, but 'in England, where classicism was so strongly entrenched, the fire of the French rococo made but small inroads, chiefly in furniture'.[5] It appeared in its most characteristic form in this country on sconces, mirrors, picture-frames and console tables, all elaborately carved and gilded by specialist craftsmen (Pl. 17). These pieces were closely related to French models, but in case furniture (unless French furniture was being deliberately copied) a more independent approach was evident; the ornament became less exuberant and usually took the form of delicate carving. The credit for introducing the style to furniture here belongs to Matthias Lock, in whose pattern-books, published from 1740 onwards, rococo decoration was applied to various small pieces of furniture of a limited range. The new mode was catching on in the late 'forties, and in 1754 it became the predominant style with the publication of Chippendale's *Director*, in which the 'modern taste' was applied to domestic furniture of all kinds. It was still the prevailing form in the third edition of the *Director* in 1762, but by then it was giving way to Robert Adam's neo-classical style.

Chinoiserie

In the 'forties there was a revival of the enthusiasm for *chinoiseries* which had been prevalent in the later seventeenth century. The extent of the revival was thus described, with some exaggeration, by a writer in *The World* in 1753: 'According to the present prevailing whim every thing is Chinese, or in the Chinese taste; or, as it is sometimes more modestly expressed, "partly after the Chinese manner". Chairs, tables, chimney-pieces, frames for looking-glasses, and even our most vulgar utensils are all reduced to this new-fangled standard.' He went on to note how freely Chinese designs had been adapted by English craftsmen: 'Our Chinese ornaments are not only of our own manufacture but, what has seldom been attributed to the English, of our own invention.' This interest in oriental fashions had been renewed to some extent by travel books, the chief of which was du Halde's description of the Empire of China, translated from the French in 1741. On furniture, *chinoiseries* took many forms: mirrors had pagodas, long-necked birds, icicles and small oriental figures; chairs had pagoda crestings and lattice-work backs; and other pieces – tables, cabinets, bookcases, etc. – had frets, open or applied, in a continuous geometric pattern (Pl. 20A). Japanned furniture, which had not previously gone out of fashion so much as other *chinoiseries*, was now very popular (Pl. 22A). The more bizarre aspects of the vogue were much criticized by contemporaries, as the above passage shows. In 1756 Angeloni (in reality J. Shebbeare writing as an Italian) complained that 'the simple and sublime have lost all influence almost every where, all is Chinese or gothic; every chair in an apartment, the frames of glasses, and tables, must be Chinese: the walls covered with Chinese paper fill'd with figures which resemble nothing in God's creation, and which a prudent nation would prohibit for the sake of pregnant women'.[6] The craze was on the decline by 1765, but while it lasted it had a great deal in common with the Rococo and was often skilfully blended with it.

Gothic

The 'Gothic Revival' of the mid-century will always be connected with Horace Walpole and Strawberry Hill, which he began to turn into a gothic villa in 1750, and of which the first stage in the transformation was complete in 1753. But it must be stressed that Walpole was not entirely a pioneer, for interest in the gothic style had long pre-dated Strawberry Hill. There was still a living tradition of gothic building and decoration which had persisted since medieval times, in spite of the

[5] *The Creation of the Rococo*, by F. Kimball, 1943.

[6] *Letters on the English Nation*, by B. Angeloni (J. Shebbeare), 1756.

Fig. 1. Chippendale China case, pl. CXXXV of Thomas Chippendale's
The Gentleman and Cabinet-Maker's Director, 1754.

Reformation and the classical Renaissance. This, however, had little influence on Walpole's ideas. Preceding Walpole, too, was a strong 'gothic' trend in literature, while the gothic work of architects of the classical school, as late as Hawksmoor and Kent, had further stimulated interest in medieval forms. What Walpole did was to make a particular contribution to the movement. He was the first patron of the Gothic who copied original medieval work for interior decoration, and his social position ensured that his new fashions would be widely imitated among the upper classes. He adapted gothic motifs in accordance with prevailing taste and turned them into a 'Rococo Gothic' which he himself described as 'more the works of fancy than imitation'. In the *Director* this gothic mode appeared in various forms on furniture, usually as carved crocketed pinnacles, carved and fretwork arches and arcading, and arched glazing bars. The style was considered by *The World* in 1753 as unfashionable ('a few years ago everything was gothic'), but this judgement was altogether too premature, for gothic pieces and decoration were illustrated in the third edition of the *Director* in 1762, and indeed the gothic taste (like *chinoiseries*) found some favour during the rest of the Georgian period.

The design books

The fourth and fifth decades of the century saw the publication of many books of engraved furniture designs. At first these designs were incorporated in pattern books produced by architects, builders and artists, and not by craftsmen, and the relatively few furniture plates which were shown were part of general decorative schemes and were of very varied merit. One of the earliest books of this kind was Batty and Thomas Langley's *City and Country Builder's and Workman's Treasury of Designs*, published in 1740 (with plates dated 1739). It was mainly concerned with architecture, but included designs for side-tables with marble tops, table-frames, a chest of drawers, a medal case, a dressing-table and several bookcases. In most of these pieces the baroque style of the Kent school was clearly evident; there were, however, a few designs of French tables (one of them

after Pineau) with rococo influences. As has been pointed out, the pioneer of the Rococo in England was Matthias Lock, who produced several design books between 1740 and 1752. In this latter year, in which he published *A New Book of Ornaments* in collaboration with Henry Copland, the Rococo had been applied to carvers' pieces, notably mirrors, pier-tables, clock-cases, stands and wall-lights. The Chinese taste was catered for by several pattern books which appeared in the 'fifties, particularly by Matthias Darly, and by William Halfpenny and his son John. The Halfpennys published some plates with Chinese chair designs in their *Rural Architecture in the Chinese Taste* in 1750-55, and Darly had a few illustrations of furniture in his *New Book of Chinese Designs* in 1754. An attempt – not a very successful one – to apply to seat furniture the various styles of the time was made by Darly in 1750-51, in the *New Book of Chinese, Gothic and Modern Chairs*.

Chippendale's Director

A landmark was reached in English furniture history with the publication of Thomas Chippendale's *The Gentleman and Cabinet-Maker's Director* in 1754, for it was the first pattern book to be devoted entirely to furniture, and the first to be published by a cabinet-maker. A second edition (virtually a reprint) appeared in 1755, and a third in 1762; and it was followed by a number of similar publications. It has made Chippendale's name a household word, and practically synonymous with the rococo style of the mid-century. But although Chippendale's signature appeared on the plates, it seems that he cannot claim sole credit for all the designs, for it is now known that he employed Lock and Copland as his 'ghosts' to help him.[7] He must, however, be given his fair share of praise both for his keen business sense in turning to good account the growing popularity of the rococo style, and for applying it to all kinds of furniture, including articles for ordinary domestic use. As a practical craftsman his knowledge and experience must

[7] *The Creators of the Chippendale Style*, by F. Kimball and E. Donnell, Metropolitan Museum Studies, 1929.

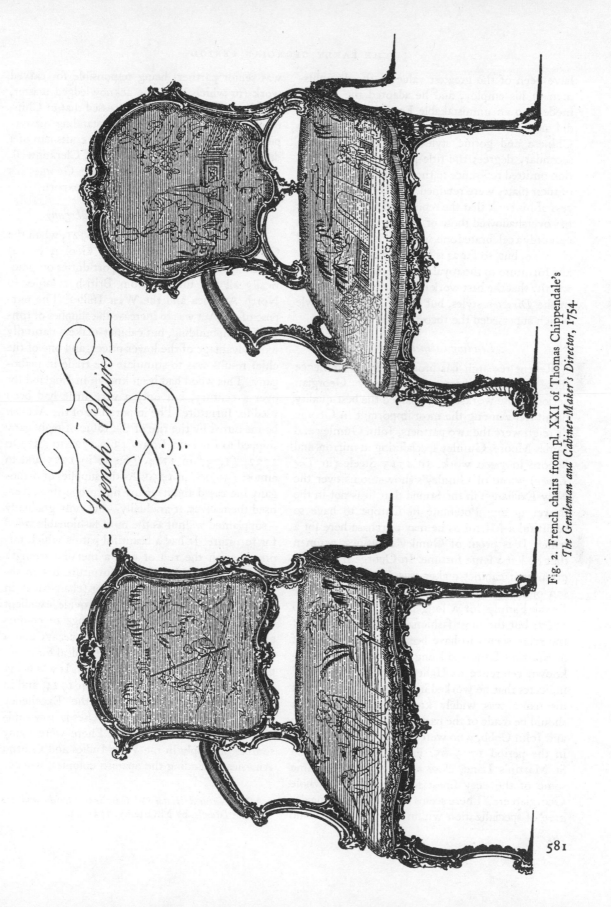

French chairs

Fig. 2. French chairs from pl. XXI of Thomas Chippendale's
The Gentleman and Cabinet-Maker's Director, 1754.

have been of the greatest value to the draughts-men in his employ, and he adapted the French mode into an unmistakable English version, and did not merely imitate it. In the *Director* the Chinese and gothic styles were exploited to a secondary degree; the title-page of the third edition omitted reference to these styles, though some of their plates were retained. It is through the success of his book that the reputation of Chippendale has overshadowed those of his rivals. His firm was certainly a celebrated one, with a rich and influential clientèle, but, so far as is known, he did not supply any furniture to the royal household, and it is noteworthy that the best work of his firm was done, not in the *Director* styles, but in the neo-classic style which superseded the rococo in the 'sixties.

Leading cabinet-makers

Recent research has brought into prominence those cabinet-makers of the early Georgian period whose workshops produced the best-quality furniture. Among the most important in George I's reign were the two partners, John Gumley and James Moore, Gumley specializing in mirrors and Moore in gesso work. In 1715 Steele (in *The Lover*) wrote of Gumley's show-rooms over the New Exchange in the Strand that 'it is not in the Power of any Potentate in Europe to have so beautiful a Mirror as he may purchase here for a trifle'. It is proof of Gumley's business acumen that he left a large fortune. In George II's reign a prominent cabinet-maker was Benjamin Goodison of Long Acre, who made furniture for the Royal Family for a long period, from 1727 to 1767; but the most fashionable cabinet-maker of the reign seems to have been William Hallett of St Martin's Lane and Long Acre. Walpole's well-known reference to Hallett's 'mongrel Chinese' indicates that he worked in that style and also that his name was widely known. Special mention should be made of the partnership of William Vile and John Cobb, who were the foremost craftsmen in the period 1755–65. From their premises in St Martin's Lane, close to Chippendale's, came some of the very finest furniture of the whole Georgian era. There seems to have been some degree of specialization within the firm, Vile (who

was senior partner) being responsible for carved work (in which he is the acknowledged master, for his work in the rococo surpassed that of Chippendale). Reference to some outstanding masterpieces of this firm is made below. A craftsman of a different kind was Giles Grendey of Clerkenwell, who made good furniture during George II's reign, including japanned pieces for export.

Woods: the introduction of mahogany

A significant event occurred in 1721, when the Government passed an Act (8 Geo. 1, c. 12) which abolished the heavy import duties on practically all the timbers from British colonies in North America and the West Indies. The purpose of the Act was to increase the supplies of timber for shipbuilding, but cabinet-makers naturally took advantage of the lower prices, and one of the chief results was to stimulate the trade in mahogany. This wood had been known in England for over a century, but only a very little had been used for furniture. The importance of the Act can be measured by the rise of the value of mahogany shipped to England, from £43 in 1720 to £277 in 1722, £1,237 in 1724, £6,430 in 1735 and to almost £30,000 in 1750. As the supplies of mahogany increased and its many fine properties advertised themselves, it gradually – but only gradually – supplanted walnut as the most fashionable wood for furniture. It had a beautiful patina which improved with the rub of use; a metallic strength which considerably affected furniture design towards the middle of the century (chair-backs in the rococo and Chinese styles provide excellent example of this); an attractive range of colours and figures; a strong resistance to decay; and a great width of board which made it ideal for table-tops, cabinet doors and similar pieces. It was being used by the royal cabinet-makers in 1724, and in 1743 Mark Catesby wrote that the 'Excellency of this Wood for all Domestick Uses is now sufficiently known in England'.[8] There were many sources of supply in the West Indies and Central America, including the Spanish colonies, whence

[8] *The Natural History of Carolina, Florida and the Bahama Islands,* by M.Catesby, 1731–43.

the timber was smuggled here via the British settlements to avoid the duty on foreign wood. At first San Domingo mahogany was chiefly used – a hard, dense wood with little figure. About 1750 it was generally superseded by the Cuban variety, which was easier to work, and had a dark, rich colour and fine figures; this meant more use of veneers instead of solid work, common with San Domingo wood. Honduras mahogany, lighter in weight and colour, was mainly used in the second half of the century.

It has been frequently stated that cabinet-makers turned to mahogany because walnut was in short supply. This is inaccurate, for there was no lack of supplies of good European walnut for veneers or of American ('black' or 'Virginia') walnut for work in the solid. Much furniture veneered with European walnut was made throughout the first half of the century, but considerable amounts have perished through worm, and it is this fact which has led to the supposition that walnut was replaced by mahogany earlier than in fact it was. Between 1725 and 1750 walnut and mahogany were perhaps equally fashionable in London (cf. Pl. 22B).

Other woods

In 1747 Campbell quoted the typical London timber merchant as 'furnished with Deal from Norway; with Oak and Wainscot from Sweden; and some from the Counties of England; with Mahogany from Jamaica; with Wallnut-Tree from Spain'.[9] This was a fair sample of the timber stocks which might be found in a fashionable cabinet-maker's yard, but the list of their places of origin could be enlarged. Yellow deal from the Baltic was used as carcase work for veneers, but after about 1750 red deal from North America came into more general use for this purpose. Good imported oak was used for drawer linings. Among other imported woods mention can be made of rosewood, sometimes used for solid work, and padouk, which was occasionally used after 1725. For gilding and japanning, carcases of deal, beech, lime and sometimes pear were employed, while chair-frames for this purpose were usually of

[9] *The London Tradesman*, by R.Campbell, 1747.

beech. Beech was also common for the cheaper kinds of chairs.

The country craftsmen worked with native woods, such as oak, elm, ash, birch, beech and fruit woods. For Windsor chairs the woods commonly found were yew for frames, beech or ash for spindles, and elm for seats.

Fashionable furniture: chairs

The chairs designed by Kent for his wealthy clients were usually of walnut or mahogany parcel gilt, or of soft woods entirely gilt, and had a great deal of mask, foliage and shell ornament (Pl. 13). But apart from these the design of chairs in the early Georgian period followed the Queen Anne tradition and was very little affected at first by the coming of mahogany. The cabriole leg with either the club foot or, on finer specimens, the ball-and-claw or lion's paw, continued to be fashionable throughout the first half of the century. After about 1725 carving became more elaborate and often took the form of the lion-and-satyr mask, or shell and pendant on the knee-piece and centre of the seat, and of the eagle's head at the end of the arms. Chair-backs, however, began to show more distinct changes from the earlier examples; the solid splat was replaced by an open design which at first was in the form of vertical piercing, and the hoop shape of the top rail became flatter and almost square at the corners.

As mahogany became more widely used its great strength led to daring carving and piercing on chair-backs and considerable changes in design had taken place by 1750. Chairs in the rococo style had carved open-work splats with much delicate ornament, which were generally varieties of C and S scrolls under a top rail of serpentine ('cupid's bow') form. The cabriole leg was retained, but the scroll foot was now often employed. (Fig. 3). Among the most celebrated examples in this style were the 'ribband-backs' which were introduced in the *Director* and had interlaced ribbon designs intricately carved, sometimes joining the side uprights. On some chairs of this period the straight leg was used and stretchers were re-introduced (though they were unnecessary from the structural point of view) after a lapse of some fifty years.

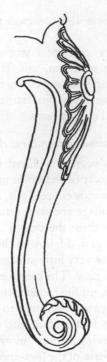

Fig. 3. Chair leg with scroll foot and cabochon ornament on knee, fashionable *c.* 1750.

Chinese chairs had large-scale latticework in the backs (Pl. 20A) and in the space between the arms and seats, and they often had a pagoda shaping for the top rails. Their legs were generally square in shape with frets, either in low-relief carving in the solid, or pierced. Another of their distinctive features was the use of brackets, fretcut, in the angles between the legs and seats. Gothic chairs had interlaced pointed arches in the centre splat or in the whole space between the uprights (Fig. 4).

Upholstered chairs of the early Georgian period normally had plain overstuffed backs and seats, and some arms were padded on the horizontal member (Pl. 20D). The *Director* shows several examples of 'French' upholstered armchairs with stuffed backs, arms of various shapes, and light, graceful versions of the cabriole leg. Carved motifs, among which the acanthus leaf was prominent, are found on the knees, seat rails, arms and cresting rails (Pl. 20C).

584

Chests of drawers, commodes, tallboys

Two main types of chests of drawers can be distinguished in this period – the plain, rectangular kind of traditional design, and the more elaborate variety influenced by the French commode. During the first half of the century there was little change in the former class; walnut continued to be the chief wood employed in making them, with some mahogany after 1730, and the usual construction was of four or five drawers of full width, and bracket, or, more occasionally, cabriole-form feet. Mouldings were now to be found on the edges of drawers, and not on the rails between drawers. At first drawer edges had the lip moulding which had come into fashion about 1710, but after 1730 it was gradually replaced by the cockbead, which was almost exclusively used from about 1745 until the end of the century. After 1750 taller chests of drawers became fashionable, with five or six drawers, of which two, of half width, were at the top. When mahogany veneers were used, they were generally put on a carcase of deal, and drawer linings were of good-quality oak.

Commodes became popular when the full impact of French influence was felt. In fact, 'commode' was the name applied about the middle of the century to all kinds of decorative furniture fitted with drawers, so much so that 'chest of drawers' was rarely used in the trade catalogues of the period (it is mentioned only once – on Plate CXIII – in the third edition of the *Director*). For convenience, commodes can be taken here to refer to the fashionable drawing-room pieces showing unmistakable French character.

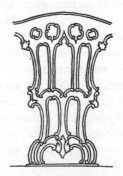

Fig. 4. Gothic back chair.

These early commodes were of mahogany enriched with carving on the frieze, feet, corners and drawer fronts. In the period 1740–50 some extremely fine examples have been attributed to William Vile. Pl. 19A illustrates a less elaborate specimen in the rococo style. It is serpentine fronted and has handles in the French taste; the carving appears on the canted corners, on the rail beneath the top drawers and on the plinth. In other pieces of this kind the edges of the top were often gadrooned. Some commodes were japanned, especially those intended for bedrooms in the Chinese taste in large houses. A fine example, formerly at Badminton House, is shown in Pl. 22A; besides the japanning, it has the pierced fret and latticework typical of this style.

Tallboys or chests-on-chests followed the same lines as the plainer chests of drawers. The large cavetto moulding on the cornice remained until about 1735, after which date the flat frieze came into fashion. This frieze was often decorated with applied frets, as were the canted corners (or the latter might be fluted). Feet, handles and drawer-edge mouldings were similar to those on the chests of drawers described above.

Tables

The large number of different kinds of tables in use at this time may conveniently be reduced to the following main categories: dining-, side-, tea-, card- and library.

Early in George II's reign, dining-tables, in walnut or mahogany, were still constructed on the gate-leg principle and had, in the larger examples, six cabriole legs, of which two – one on each side – could swing out to support the flaps. Usually the tops were oval or circular in shape. About the middle of the century another and more convenient version of the large table came into use. This was a composite piece of three units: a centre gate-leg table with rectangular flaps, and two semi-circular side-tables which could be fitted to the centre when required. There are no illustrations of dining-tables in the *Director*, presumably because they allowed little scope for showing the decorative features of the fashions then in vogue.

The term side-tables may be taken to refer to the ornamental tables which stood against the walls of the best rooms of the larger houses of the period, and they include console-tables, which were normally supported by two brackets but had no rear legs, and pier-tables, which occupied the pier or wall between two windows. In the earlier part of the century, preceding the baroque phase, but showing traces of the same kind of decoration, appeared some attractive gesso side-tables, one of which, dating from the period *c.* 1710–20, is shown in Pl. 18. This is an excellent example of the kind of work done in gesso, but it is unusual in that it is silvered and not gilt. The top of this table has the monogram of the original owner carved in the centre.

The carved and gilt side-tables designed by Kent were perhaps the best example of his work in the baroque style, and were influenced by the pieces which he had seen in the palaces of Venetia. Monumental in size, they had scroll legs with acanthus, scale and guilloche decoration, or the supports might be female figures, animals, etc., joined by swags of leaves, fruit and flowers. For the tops, in addition to marble (whence the description 'marble tables'), gesso, mosaic or scagliola were used. The latter was an artificial composition of plaster of Paris and glue into which small pieces of marble were worked; the whole could be coloured and highly polished. The friezes of these tables were carved with classical motifs, among which the Vitruvian scroll was prominent.

As the rococo style replaced the baroque the massive side-tables gradually went out of favour. After 1740 a more restrained treatment was generally evident, even though some early rococo examples carried a certain amount of lavish ornament. A mahogany side-table of *c.* 1745 is illustrated in Pl. 19B. It has a marble top, a mask in the centre of the frieze and female heads on the scrolled legs. Rococo-style side-tables in the *Director* keep the cabriole legs, while those in the Chinese and gothic tastes have straight legs. The Chinese varieties have fretwork on the frieze and legs (pierced in some cases on the latter). Marble remained in great demand for the tops of these tables.

Console-tables (or 'clap'-tables, as they were

Fig. 5. Console table with marble top, Vitruvian scroll on frieze and eagle support decorated with gilt gesso, *c.* 1730.

then called) were introduced into this country from France early in the century. In the baroque phase some elaborate specimens were produced, with supports in the form of an eagle with outstretched wings, or of a pair of intertwined dolphins (Fig. 5). There were also ornate examples in the later rococo taste, giving full rein to the prevailing asymmetrical decoration. None that were made, however, seems quite to have matched the highly intricate designs which are presented for these tables in the *Director*, where they go by the name of 'Frames for Marble Slabs'.

Card-playing for money was a popular pastime in high society in the early Georgian period, and in consequence many fine card-tables were produced by the cabinet-makers. From early in the century the most usual type was that with a folding top on cabriole legs. At the beginning of George I's reign the folding frame, with a concertina action, replaced the former method by which one leg was swung out to support the flap. The corners of the tables were at first rounded and were dished to hold candlesticks; they also had extra wells for money or counters. In some examples there were separate candle-brackets which swung out from the frieze. About 1730, when mahogany was coming into use for tables of this

kind, square corners were introduced, and remained popular until about 1760. Early mahogany tables had lion heads carved on the knee-pieces, and occasionally the frieze was serpentine. Rococo decoration took the form of carved coquillage and acanthus leaves on the frieze and legs, gadrooning on the borders (Fig. 6) and a more graceful cabriole leg, often with a scroll foot. Pl. 22B shows an example of *c.* 1750 on which the ball-and-claw foot is retained. It also illustrates the square corners of the period, and is a late example of the use of walnut, for it has figured walnut veneers on an oak carcase. Other card-tables often had Chinese and gothic motifs, and in these cases, as with side-tables, the legs were straight.

The custom of tea-drinking had been spreading rapidly since the end of the seventeenth century. In George II's reign the many tea-gardens which had sprung up in and around London fell into disrepute among people of fashion, who consequently carried on the habit in their own homes – an example which was soon copied by other classes. Hence the development of small 'china-tables', as tea-tables were then called, of which two main varieties can be distinguished: those with oblong tops, and those with round tops on a pillar and claw, i.e. tripod base. The oblong tops were frequently mounted on dainty cabriole legs with ball-and-claw feet, or on straight legs, often pierced, if in the Chinese taste (Fig. 7). Little galleries, which were in many cases fretted, ran round the edges of these tables. Tripod tables had either similar galleries, or scalloped and carved ('piecrust') edges. These raised edges were to prevent the fragile tea-things from being swept off. Pl. 15A illustrates a mahogany tripod table of *c.* 1745 with the characteristic turned and carved pillar and ball-and-claw feet. The small platform beneath the 'piecrust' top is wedged to the upper part of the pillar; this wedge can be removed to enable the table-top to be lifted off. Two designs in the *Director* bear the description: 'Tables for holding China, and may be used as Tea-Tables'. These tables were oblong in shape with serpentine edges. One design has cross stretchers with rococo carving, and both have galleries which could be either plain or fretted.

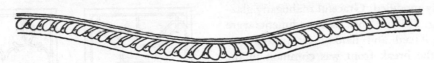

Fig. 6. Gadrooning, a carved ornamental edging in
vogue *c.* 1750.

Large pedestal library tables came into general use in the second quarter of the century for the libraries of the great Palladian houses. Tables of this type had already appeared in the late seventeenth century, and were modelled on the French pieces which had been made in the reign of Louis XIV, but they did not attempt either the intricate Buhl work or the ormolu work which distinguished the finest French examples. Instead, they were made of mahogany with lavishly carved mouldings and terminals which were sometimes gilded. The centres of the tables were left open, or occasionally contained a cupboard; the pedestals had drawers and cupboards; and particular care was taken over the decoration, as they were designed to stand in the middle of the library. The elaborate terminals were seldom found after about 1740, and a lighter kind of carving then became more usual. In the Chippendale period library tables were very much in demand, for the third edition of the *Director* shows eleven examples, all of the open pedestal type, compared with six in the first edition. Various forms of rococo, Chinese and gothic decoration are illustrated. Rococo influence is evident in the contemporary example in Pl. 23B.

Throughout the whole of this period the smaller knee-hole writing-table, with drawers on each side of the central recess, continued in favour. Two of this type are illustrated by Chippendale under the name of 'commode-buroe' tables.

Bookcases

In the early Georgian period the extreme simplicity of Queen Anne bookcases gave way to treatment of pronounced architectural character, with broken pediments, pilasters and classical cornices as favourite motifs. Batty Langley in the *Treasury of Designs* (1740) regarded a proper understanding of architecture as essential for cabinet-makers. ''Tis a very great Difficulty,' he observed, 'to find one in fifty of them that can make a Book-Case etc. indispensably true after any one of the Five Orders without being obliged to a Joiner for to set out the Work, and make his Templet to work by.' About 1745 two further developments occurred: the introduction of the bookcase consisting of a centre piece and two wings, and the addition of rococo carving. The most magnificent example of this kind of work – though it was made at a date, 1762, when the Rococo was on the wane – is the very beautiful bookcase made by William Vile for Queen Charlotte. It is in the classical style, but has rococo carving of a superb quality, and altogether it must rank as one of the finest pieces of furniture made in this country.

In the mid-century the architectural character

Fig. 7. Mahogany 'china' or tea table with fretwork gallery, *c.* 1750.

was generally modified. Graceful mahogany glazing bars (Fig. 8) were now used; pediments were sometimes pierced and flanked by fretted galleries; and the break-front was common in the larger examples. The importance which bookcases had attained is clearly shown by the fact that the *Director* of 1762 gives no less than fourteen designs under this heading, all but one having solid bases. Among them are some gothic examples, but their designs are so fanciful that it is unlikely that they were ever actually made, certainly not without a great deal of alteration. On other bookcases of the time the glazing bars, the designs of which varied considerably, were in the gothic taste, but rococo features were also evident in the carving.

Pl. 24 shows a remarkably fine bookcase at Wilton which can be assigned to Chippendale and is one of the best pieces of case furniture made by him in the rococo style. Its date is *c.* 1760. It has a musical trophy in the central section instead of glazing bars. The inlaid stars are noteworthy. They also appear on another bookcase at Wilton (Pl. 21) which lacks the rococo carving, but has the same kind of swan-neck pediment as the former.

Bureaux

The term 'bureau' was somewhat loosely used in the early eighteenth century to apply to several kinds of writing furniture. It included what is understood by a bureau today, i.e. the chest-of-drawers type with a writing-flap. This kind developed on the same general lines as the plainer chest of drawers of the period. But an older type of writing-piece was also being made – the desk on stand, which now had cabriole legs and club or ball-and-claw feet, and in some cases a richly carved underframing. This type seems to have been made for ladies' use, which is further indicated by the fact that some of them were surmounted by a mirror.

The scrutoire was not a very convenient piece of furniture, and it had already been modified into the bureau-cabinet, the bureau in two stages or, as it was then called, the 'desk and bookcase'. Some fine examples of the latter were produced, either decorated with japan, or in walnut, which re-

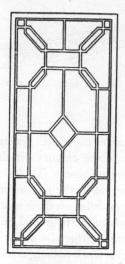

mained for a long time the most fashionable wood for bureaux. A notable specimen of a walnut bureau-cabinet of *c.* 1725 is illustrated in Pl. 14B. It has a broken pediment with gilt-metal mounts, carved wood finials and a central figure of Mercury on a plinth. The mirror is flanked by pilasters which are partly reeded and fluted and have gilt-metal ionic capitals. The interiors of pieces of this kind were fitted with small drawers, pigeon-holes, etc., arranged with great ingenuity, and they often contained secret receptacles.

During the early Georgian period mahogany bureau-cabinets made for large houses tended to be of greater size; they were enriched with baroque carving and had serpentine mouldings around the glazed doors. But about 1750 there was a return to the less ornate decoration of the earlier pieces, and the main features were delicate carving, fretted galleries on the cornices and unglazed doors which were panelled in long, thin mouldings. Several varieties of the 'desk and bookcase' appear in the *Director*. In general, they continue on traditional lines but add typical rococo carving. There is, however, one design in the Chinese taste which shows a little pagoda crest, a pierced fret gallery and icicle carving. And another innovation which is apparent on some of the designs is the division of the upper part into a central piece flanked by two smaller wings.

The outstanding example of this kind of furni-

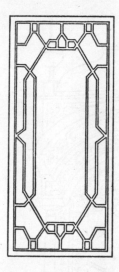

Fig. 8. Bookcase doors designed by T. Chippendale.

ture is another masterpiece by Vile – Queen Charlotte's bureau, made in 1761. It has a *bombé* base with beautiful rococo carving, and an upper part enclosed with delicate latticework in the Chinese taste, surmounted by a graceful canopy with a crown.

Cabinets

During this period there were several varieties of cabinets used for display purposes, mainly for china or for the collections of curios or 'curiosities' (jewels, coins, medals, etc.) which had been a hobby of the upper classes since the later seventeenth century. Those cabinets which had glazed upper parts were very similar to contemporary bookcases in design, so much so, in fact, that it is often impossible to distinguish the exact purpose for which they were intended. On the other hand, there were still examples of the type of cabinet fitted with small drawers and mounted on a stand which had been fashionable in Stuart times. The stands were now made with cabriole legs.

All types of cabinets were influenced by the strong feeling for architectural forms which marked furniture of this kind in the second quarter of the century, but after 1750 this treatment was modified. Chippendale presented designs for both cabinets and china cases in the prevailing styles, with a preference, which was most clearly and understandably discernible in the china cases,

for the Chinese taste. Many of these pieces were japanned. There was also much free blending of Chinese and rococo decoration. Pl. 23A shows how delicately, on occasions, this could be done, and it further illustrates one of the many kinds of combined pieces – in this case a cabinet and writing-table – which were made at the time. Small hanging cabinets for displaying china were also popular; they often had fretwork doors and sides.

An example of the enclosed cabinet on stand is Queen Charlotte's jewel cabinet supplied by Vile and Cobb in 1761. It is made of mahogany, with rich rococo carving, inlays of ivory, and veneers of various choice woods, all executed with consummate skill.

Mirrors

Considerable changes occurred in the design of mirrors at this time, particularly in that of pierglasses, for their prominent position on the wall between the windows in reception-rooms called for special decorative treatment. Three main trends can be distinguished. Until about 1725 elegant mirrors of carved and gilt wood and gesso were fashionable. A fine example is shown in Pl. 14A. Here the gilt gesso frame, five feet four inches high, has a shaped and scrolled cresting ornamented with a shell, and a shaped base. Mirrors of this kind usually had candle-branches attached to the base, as had the smaller hanging mirrors of the same period. The latter were generally square in shape and had similar gesso ornament of shells, scrolls and eagles' heads, but some simple and attractive ones were made in walnut with shaped crests which contained a central gilt decoration.

After about 1725 pier-glasses acquired an architectural character. The moulded frames were surmounted by a broken pediment which centred in a shell, plinth or cartouche; the sides were often enriched with floral ornament or draperies; and the bases were either curved, with a shell or similar decoration, or were straight and had a classical motif such as the Vitruvian scroll or the egg-and-dart. The usual materials were gilt soft woods and gesso, or walnut and mahogany veneers with gilt mouldings and ornament. In larger houses, where the whole of the decoration of the interior was directed by the architect, the mouldings of pier-glasses often matched those on the window archi-traves, doorways and cornices, and console tables were specially designed to harmonize with the mirrors beneath which they stood.

After 1745 this architectural form gave way to the rococo taste which found in gilt mirror-frames perhaps its freest expression. C scrolls gradually replaced straight lines until at length highly ornamental open-work carving was the mode. Intricate arrangements of scrolls, curling leaves and *coquillage* were mingled with chinoi-series – mandarins, birds, icicles, pagodas, etc. Chippendale exploited the new trends to the full. Two other prominent contemporary designers of mirrors in this style were Lock and Thomas Johnson, but some of the latter's designs were so extravagant as to be impracticable.

In Pl. 17, which illustrates some typical forms of the decoration employed by Chippendale, the fusion of styles is exemplified by the crest of *coquillage* surmounted by a bird. This mirror is of interest because an overmantel mirror in the ear-lier architectural style is reflected in it; the two mirrors thus show the changes which had occurred during the second quarter of the century. Over-mantel mirrors were frequently divided into com-partments and a number of them had brackets for displaying china. The carving of mirror frames had now become a highly specialized craft. 'This business,' wrote Collyer in 1761, 'which has lately been carried to great perfection, requires much ingenuity, a lively and elegant fancy, skill in drawing with great neatness foliages, fruit, flowers, birds, heads, etc., a good eye, and a steady hand.' [10] Good carvers were rated highly and were among the best paid of the London craftsmen.

Clock-cases

Clocks as pieces of furniture allied the crafts of the clock-maker and of the case-maker. Both these crafts had reached a very high standard in the late

[10] *Parent's and Guardian's Directory*, by J. Collyer, 1761.

Fig. 9. Upper portion of long-case clock, showing dome and finials, *c.* 1725.

seventeenth century, and this was maintained un-der the first two Georges. For the decoration of long-case clocks marquetry went out of fashion and the best cases were decorated with finely figured walnut veneers or with japan. Walnut cases show the figure to great advantage, and if they seem somewhat plainer than the intricate marquetry pieces of the preceding period, this really accentuates their elegant proportions and excellent workmanship. Cases tended to increase in height as rooms became larger. The clock dials had arched tops decorated with brasswork and were surmounted by arched hoods completed with domes and finials. Carving was seldom employed, and then only for minor details such as crestings, finials and, more rarely still, feet; for all these de-tails soft woods were used, either stained to match the walnut, or gilded.

Japanned long-case clocks, with various forms of oriental designs (Fig. 9), enjoyed great popularity during this period. The more usual background colours were green, black, red and blue, but yellow and scarlet were also found. Bright colours were used for the cases exported to what was then called the South Europe and Mediterranean trade – Spain, Portugal, Italy and Turkey – where there was a brisk demand for English clocks and watches.

For some twenty years after 1740 long-case clocks were less popular than the smaller bracket or table clocks, and the wall variety known as cartel clocks. One reason for this was that smaller clocks were more suitable for the elaborate carving and decoration of the rococo phase. Cartel clocks were made of soft woods carved and gilt; for bracket clocks, however, mahogany was coming into general use. The *Director* has illustrations of bracket clocks in both the rococo and Chinese tastes, and both the carving and the details like pagoda domes and fretwork show that the traditional designs of these clocks had now been considerably modified. When, about 1755, the long-case clocks began to return to favour, close-grained mahogany was chiefly employed, enriched with carving and fretwork, and some of the graceful proportions of the earlier cases were lost, for the bodies tended to become shorter and broader.

Country furniture

The kind of furniture which could be found in villages and hamlets depended on many variable factors among which, to name but a few, one might put the nearness to a town or port, the skill of the local craftsmen, and the poverty or prosperity of the community concerned. In isolated areas, such as Devon and Cornwall, the furniture in cottages seems to have been both scanty and primitive, consisting of a table, chairs (or, more likely, a form and stools), a chest and perhaps a bedstead. This state of affairs was confirmed at a much later date by Louis Simond's description of the interiors of Devon cottages during his travels in England in 1810–11.[11] But elsewhere cottages and farm-houses could have more comfortable

[11] *Journal of a Tour & Residence in Great Britain, 1810–11*, by L.Simond, 1817.

equipment. In most villages the joiner supplied, besides tables, chairs, chests and beds, such pieces as settles, hanging and corner cupboards and dressers. The last-named deserve special mention. Their prototypes had been found in the halls of medieval houses and had continued to be fashionable until the seventeenth century, when they were relegated to the kitchen and replaced by walnut and later mahogany side-tables. About 1750 oak cottage dressers, which had resembled long tables with cupboards, often had an upper stage of shelves to display earthenware and pewter. Occasionally there were details of ornament and construction which were influenced by fashionable furniture, but such modifications were retained long after they had gone out of fashion in London. Cabriole legs, for instance, were adapted to dressers during this period and continued in use until the end of the century.

Contemporary inventories of cottage furniture were so rare that special interest attaches to one which was drawn up in 1768 by the parish authorities of New Brentford, Middlesex. It shows that the furniture which had been in the possession of the occupier – he was described as a labourer, but his effects indicate that he was of a higher status, probably an artisan or craftsman – provided more than a modest degree of comfort. The bedroom furniture included feather beds and bolsters, 'a four post Bedstead with Green Harrateen Furniture', and 'a half Tester turn up Bedstead with Green Furniture'. There were five

Fig. 10. Hoop-back Windsor chair, first half of the eighteenth century.

tables, two of the type described as 'wainscott Dining Table', four cane and five rush-bottomed chairs, and 'a leather Covered Elbow chair'. Also on the list were 'a Deal Cloths Chest ... a wainscott Chest with Drawers veneered in Front ... a Mahogany Tea Chest ... eight Prints ... two small looking glasses'. There was a certain amount of old furniture in the garret.[12]

Though most country furniture was made locally, some cottages had articles which came from London. Defoe wrote the following (probably exaggerated) account in 1726: 'it is scarce credible to how many counties of England, and how remote, the furniture of but a mean house must send them ... the chairs, if of cane, are made at London; the ordinary matted chairs, perhaps in the place where they live. ... Tables, chests of drawers etc. made at London; as also looking-glass.'[13] Such goods would be distributed from the ports in the south and east which could be readily reached in the coasting trade from London.

Many cottages and farm-houses had Windsor chairs, the making of which became well-estab-lished during this period. The chief centre of manufacture was Buckinghamshire where in time High Wycombe became the focus – there is nothing, incidentally, to connect these chairs, despite their name, with the town of Windsor. In the Chilterns, where there was abundance of beech, the craftsmen or 'bodgers' turned the spindles which gave the chairs their characteristic 'stick-back' form. Chairs of this type were also made in London as well as in other rural areas. At first 'fan' and 'comb' backs were popular, but the well-known 'hoop' or 'bow' (Fig. 10) became usual after 1750. Belated traces of fashionable styles sometimes modified the traditional lines. Pl. 20B shows another type, sometimes known as the 'wheel back'.

SHORT BIBLIOGRAPHY

For further study of this period two indispensable works are the *Dictionary of English Furniture* by P. MacQuoid and R.Edwards (3 vols., revised edition by R. Edwards, 1954), and *Georgian Cabinet-Makers* by R. Edwards and M.Jourdain (revised edition, 1955). Good studies of styles of the period can be found in *The Work of William Kent* by M.Jourdain (1948), and *The Gothic Revival* by Sir Kenneth Clark (1928). There are also various reprints and abridgements of Chippendale's *Director* which well repay study.

[12] Middlesex Sessions Books, (Middlesex Guildhall), No. 1229, 1768.

[13] *The Complete English Tradesman*, by D.Defoe, 1726.

From Bickham's *The Universal Penman*, 1742.

Painting and Sculpture

HUGH HONOUR

'We are now arrived at the period in which the arts were sunk to the lowest ebb in Britain', wrote Horace Walpole of the reign of George I. It was with greater complacency that he entered upon 'a more shining period in the history of arts' which opened with the accession of George II, for, though painting 'made but feeble efforts towards advancement. ... The reign was not closed when Sir Joshua Reynolds ransomed portrait painting from insipidity.' Walpole was writing with the critic's usual contempt for the taste of the previous generation, but his assessment of the age may still be accepted. In 1714 Kneller was at the height of his popularity, and within a year he was awarded the baronetcy which proved to be the highest honour conferred upon a painter until Leighton was ennobled. Before the period had closed Reynolds, Wilson and, less conspicuously, Gainsborough had given clear indications of their ability. Essentially an age of transition, it spans the career of only one painter of outstanding importance, William Hogarth, whose complex personality reflects all the conflicting currents of the time. It must be admitted at the outset that from the point of view of the historian of painting, the early Georgian period is confused, and the most expert geographer of art, the most thorough student of *zeitgeist*, would be hard put to find any clear underlying principle beneath it.

Sir Godfrey Kneller's importance in 1714 can scarcely be exaggerated and his declining influence lasted throughout the period. Even so late as 1752 John Ellis, the King's painter, is said to have exclaimed, on seeing a portrait by the young Reynolds. 'This will never answer. You don't paint in the least degree in the manner of Kneller. ... Shakespeare in poetry and Kneller in painting, dammee.' The heavy periwigged style persisted for a generation of official portraiture which might well be dubbed the age of pomposity, though, at the same time, a contrary spirit of naturalism was stirring. The first artist to make a fortune out of painting portraits in Britain, Kneller was as ostentatiously successful as lordly manners, fine carriages and an army of attendants could show, and those who wished to emulate his social achievement followed his artistic practices. Perhaps his worst effect on English painting was in his establishment of a staff of assistants, not students, highly qualified to execute the different parts of a portrait – the peruque, the lace cravat, the coat, the background curtain – while the master confined his attention to the face. Only three of the notable portrait painters of this period – Hogarth, Highmore and strangely enough John Ellis – eschewed this business-like practice. Joseph Van Aken, the most widely employed drapery painter, consequently assumed an important role in the history of portraiture, leading Horace Walpole to remark that 'as in England almost everybody's picture is painted, so almost every painter's works were executed by Van Aken'. Occasionally the process was, so to speak, reversed; John Wootton employed a face-painter to complete equestrian portraits and George Lambert relied upon associates for the figures in his landscapes.

It would, however, be mistaken to assume that Kneller's influence was wholly unfortunate. His worldly success did much to raise the social standing of the artist who could, when sufficiently prosperous, move on terms of familiarity with the professional classes. The Academy he founded was responsible for training many painters of note, including Hogarth, and was the ancestor of the Royal Academy schools. But his most important legacy was in his rich, sensuous handling of paint which distinguished his followers from men like Richardson, Ramsay and Hudson who preferred a smooth texture.

Foreign influences

Foreign influences on English painting persisted throughout the eighteenth century, but their nature changed towards the end of our period. The early eighteenth century painter went abroad to study under a master from whom he might learn some 'tricks of the trade', to copy Old Masters for his patron's gallery and to acquire that diploma of fashion which foreign travel alone could give. William Kent studied under Benedetto Luti and Francesco Solimena, Allan Ramsay under Solimena and Imperiali, but when Reynolds went to Italy in 1750 he turned a blind or unappreciative eye on his contemporaries and gave his undivided attention to the earlier painters, to Raphael, whom he parodied in a caricature, to Michelangelo, to Albano and Guido Reni. In so doing he was merely following the aristocratic taste of the time, which had grown steadily more antiquarian as the century proceeded, and he would have been in full agreement with those travellers who based their standards on Jonathan Richardson's useful guide to the *Statues, Bas-reliefs, Drawings and Pictures in Italy*. It was indeed the writings of Richardson that had fired him with the ambition to be more than an 'ordinary painter'.

Contemporary foreign influence came principally from France, and its elegant refinement, popularized by the engraver, Gravelot, flourished in the work of Philip Mercier, himself a German of French extraction, Hayman, the young Gainsborough and, to a limited extent, Hogarth. Moreover a number of foreign artists set up their studios in England – the history painter Jacopo Ami-

goni, the portrait painters J.B. Van Loo and Andrea Soldi, the bird painters Pieter Casteels and Hondecooter, the *vedutiste* Canaletto and Antonio Joli – providing native artists with formidable rivals for the favours of the fashion-conscious patron. Influences from the past were more varied and derived principally from Holland and Italy. Claude Lorraine, Salvator Rosa and Gaspar Poussin exerted an almost crushing influence on decorative landscapes. The Dutch tradition of marine painting as practised by the Van de Veldes was followed by Peter Monamy and Samuel Scott. Dutch, as well as Italian landscapes, informed Richard Wilson, who confessed a debt to Cuyp, while Gainsborough learned from and copied Ruisdael and Wynants. Nor were Dutch genre pictures without their influence on Hogarth, whose attitude to the old 'dark' masters, whose names he found hard to pronounce was ambivalent. While he travestied several of their famous figures in his prints, satirized their cult (Pl. 25B) and painted *Sigismunda* to prove that a modern Briton could equal a seventeenth-century Italian, he was not above plundering their works more slyly to add dignity to a historic picture or even a portrait.

The British school

Out of this mixture, this 'ragout' of foreign styles and influences, there slowly emerged the British school of painting the growth of which was largely determined by two factors, a spirit of nationalism and a desire for greater truth to nature. In the literary and artistic history of the early Georgian period no movement is more important than that of nationalism, or rather growing national self-consciousness, which found its most notable expression in the novels of Fielding, the paintings of Hogarth, the architecture of the Burlingtonians and, finally, the gothic revival. It accounts to a great extent for the change which came over landscape painting when it was realized, in Horace Walpole's words, that 'because Virgil gasped for breath at Naples, and Salvator wandered among Alps and Apennines', there was no reason why 'our ever-verdant lawns, rich vales, fields of haycocks and hop grounds' should be neglected by poet or painter. Its least attractive form is found in the arrogant, Squire Westernish attitude displayed by Hogarth when he advised the student to beware of Italy because it would seduce him from nature. But Hogarth was not alone in this opinion, and the more moderate George Stubbs declared that he went to Italy in 1754 only 'to convince himself that nature was and always is superior to art, whether Greek or Roman – and having received this conviction, he immediately resolved upon returning'. The nationalist movement was best expressed by those artists who eschewed the airs and graces of the continental schools for the ideal of 'nature'. In part they continued the native tradition of John Riley, in part they reacted from the baroque style of Kneller. Portrait painters like Hogarth, Highmore and, at times, Richardson approached their subjects with less formality and greater directness; landscape painters like George Lambert began to abandon the decorative variations of Gaspar Poussin for scenes derived from the English countryside.

In direct opposition to the antiquarian taste of the aristocracy, the naturalist movement owed much of its success to the increasing patronage of a middle class enriched by the years of Whig supremacy. Many of the best portraits executed during the period were of middle-class sitters, and the conversation piece was established mainly because of its popularity with those who could neither afford nor house larger works. Above all, William Hogarth displayed both the merits and the prejudices of the middle-class, on whose patronage he principally relied for his portraits and prints of modern moral subjects. The growing popularity of prints is itself a symptom of a widening appreciation of the arts. John Smith and the younger John Faber appear to have found a not inconsiderable market for mezzotints after fancy pieces and portraits of celebrities. Like Hogarth's moral subjects, Highmore's illustrations to *Pamela* (Fig. 1) – the epitome of middle-class values – and most of Mercier's late works were painted primarily for reproduction in engravings. Such prints found their way into all manner of houses, from the great Palladian mansions to the small town house and country box.

In the greatest houses old masters, whether original or copies, were the rule which was broken only in favour of such works as the ancients could not supply: that is to say, portraits, topographical views of the owner's domains and decorative paintings which might take the form of vast ceilings or small landscapes let into the walls above doors and chimney-pieces. The relative importance given to such works is exemplified by the catalogue Horace Walpole made of his father's pictures at Houghton in 1743. Expatiating at length on the unequalled collection of works by Carlo Maratta, Guido Reni, Claude, Domenichino and others, he mentions portraits mainly with reference to their subjects and remains all but silent about William Kent's ceilings.[1] The great house would usually contain a fairly large number of portraits, some decorative views and a few topographical landscapes by English painters. In smaller homes the pictures would be limited almost exclusively to portraits which were mainly the work of itinerant journeymen.

Prices

As portraiture was the most popular form of art, so it was the most remunerative. Much as they might complain of lack of patronage and foreign competition, the successful painters seem to have enjoyed a solid bourgeois prosperity, indicated in Gawen Hamilton's painting of an artists' club (Pl. 25A). Thomas Murray, who specialized in portraits of academics and clerics, accrued thereby a fortune estimated at £40,000 on his death in 1735. Indeed, it is probable that foreign artists were attracted to England mainly because of the high prices obtainable. In 1718 Jonathan Richardson charged 10 guineas for a head and 20 guineas for a half-length, which was about the same as Jervas and twice as much as Dahl, but by 1730 he had doubled these figures and was asking 70 guineas for a whole length. When Allan Ramsay arrived in London in 1738 he charged 8 guineas for a head, but by 1751 he was commanding 12 guineas for a head and 42 guineas for a whole length, the same as Thomas

[1] It should, however, be remembered that Horace Walpole had a just contempt for Kent's paintings.

Hudson and Joshua Reynolds (who had begun at 5 guineas a head in 1743) were asking at this time. As a horse painter, John Wootton was paid at about the same rate, receiving some 40 guineas for a large and 20 guineas for a small picture. In 1721 he was paid £31 10s. for an equestrian portrait of Mrs Warde, whose face was filled in by Gibson, who received 6 guineas.[2] Smaller prices were paid for work in other genres, and for the six *Marriage à la Mode* pictures Hogarth received but £120, from which £24 must be deducted as the cost of the frames.

William Hogarth

Before proceeding to the various types of painting executed in this period we must consider the work of William Hogarth, who essayed all of them except landscape. No single artist reflects the various aspects of the period more clearly, and yet none, in his total achievement, was more revolutionary. When his borrowings from, and parodies of, Italian masters have been painstakingly detected, when his xenophobic attitude has been examined, when his moralism has been analysed and his æsthetic theory discounted, the artist remains, perplexing, alluring, always one of the most popular and sometimes one of the best of English painters. Truculently emerging from his apprenticeship as an engraver in 1728, he quickly made a name for himself, but never secured the highest patronage; unquestionably the best English and one of the best European artists of his time, he founded no school and his subsequent influence has been spasmodic.

The keenness and directness of Hogarth's vision are evident in all his work, in portraits no less than genre scenes. Although by no means the first artist to abandon the social mask for portraiture, no one had before combined a truth to nature so ruthless with psychological penetration so deep. Whether vain, techy, simple or sweet, there is never a shadow of doubt about the characters of his sitters. His one grand portrait, the full length

of Captain Coram (Pl. 27) which he presented to the Foundling Hospital in 1740, was based on a baroque portrait by Rigaud,[3] but has nothing grandiose about it; the kindly, beaming philanthropist has been painted in such a way that he is neither undignified nor standing on his dignity. It is one of the great landmarks in the history of English painting, for, as Professor Waterhouse has remarked, Captain Coram 'is no longer a type with individual features, but an individual in his own right, whose character is reflected in those features'. All his portraits are of individuals, not least the group of his servants (National Gallery) which he painted with such rare tenderness and understanding. But his frankness and keen perception of character did not recommend him to the wealthier patrons, who demanded a modicum of flattery. Even in the group of David Garrick and his wife (the Royal Collection) he has made no effort to disguise, or emphasize, the slightly vulgar staginess of his sitters.

While his best portraits, mostly those of acquaintances, suggest a long and careful study of his sitters' characters, his genre scenes owe their success to a rapid 'snapshot' technique. Figures are caught in the action of a moment – the coxcomb admiring himself in a glass, the drunkard toppling over, the debauchee ogling, the cat arching its back, the dog sniffing the contents of its master's pocket. Delighted by such incidents, Hogarth sometimes overcrowded his pictures with them to fill out the story and point the moral more forcibly. His details, however minute, are seldom irrelevant. In the fourth scene of *Marriage à la Mode*; *The Levée* (Pl. 25B), the Viscountess, far advanced on the path of fashionable extravagance, sits sipping her coffee as she listens to the endearments of her lover while foreign songsters warble and a negro page unpacks a newly acquired collection of *virtu*. Having taken the opportunity of satirizing the cult for antiques, one of the many vices into which the couple has fallen, he has carefully bound this theme to the main action by hanging a picture of Jupiter and Io above the Viscoun-

[2] This information is derived from an early eighteenth century MS. catalogue in the possession of Col. Warde of Squerries Court, where the portrait remains.

[3] The portrait of Samuel Bernard which he may have known from an engraving by Drevet.

Fig. 1. Pamela telling Nursery Tales, by Joseph Highmore, engraved 1745. *British Museum.*

tess and the lawyer, a Ganymede above the *castrato* singer, and by placing a bronze of the horned Acteon in the hands of the grinning page.

Brilliancy of handling, an almost French delight in *matière*, is the quality which distinguishes Hogarth from all his contemporaries, and is evident even in his earliest pictures of a scene from *The Beggar's Opera* of which he executed several versions between 1728 and 1729. The paint is applied *con amore* in rich rococo scrolls and suggests some intimate knowledge of French painting, though how he came by this technique is a mystery. It is seen at its best in the *Marriage à la Mode* series (Tate Gallery), in several of the intimate portraits and, at its most astonishing, in *The Shrimp Girl* (National Gallery), a virtuoso performance in which delicacy of touch and glancing caressing brush-strokes approach the refinement of a Degas pastel sketch. Unfortunately such happy marriages of hand and eye are rare in his work; there is little of it in the majority of conversations, less in *The Rake's Progress* (Soane Museum) and none whatever in the great canvases with which he so perversely hoped to establish his fame as a history painter.

Portraits

In 1731 George Vertue remarked that Dahl, Richardson and Jervas were the 'three foremost old masters'; Kneller had died eight years before and no one had succeeded to his commanding position. Michael Dahl, a Swede, had settled in England in 1689, and although he continued to paint until 1740, he had done his best work before this period began and long outlived the fashion for his portraits. Of his two chief rivals, Jonathan Richardson is the more interesting and not without historical importance as the pupil of John Riley, and thus the heir to an English tradition. If his heavy jowled, pompous men and hoydenish women are boring, at least they are so in the beer-sodden, fox-hunting, manner of the English squirearchy and not in any affected foreign fashion. 'The good sense of the nation is characterized in his portraits,' wrote Walpole; 'you see he lived in an age when neither enthusiasm nor servility were predominant.' The solidity of his style is demon-

strated by a ponderous life-size group at Temple Newsam (Pl. 26A); a forthright self-portrait (in the National Portrait Gallery) shows him at his best but least characteristic. Charles Jervas is principally remembered for the portraits of the literary friends with whom he associated, and it is ironical that the sparkling genius of Swift and of Pope (Pl. 26B) should be represented by such a dunce of an artist. Both Jervas and Richardson had visited Italy and both were fervent admirers of the *seicento*; the former copied old masters, the latter collected their drawings and wrote influential books about them, but neither seems to have learned much from the Italian school, possibly because they lacked humility. Upon finishing a copy of a Titian, Jervas was heard to exclaim, 'Poor little Tit! how he would stare.' Other portrait painters working in London at the same time included John Vanderbank, who initiated the fashion for dressing female sitters in Rubens costume, and William Aikman, a Scot who moved to London on Kneller's death with the hope, no doubt, of profiting from such a reign of dunces.

It was on this scene of almost 'Universal Darkness' that the bright light of Hogarth burst in the late 1720's. But he was not the only representative of a freer, lighter style, for Joseph Highmore emerged at about the same time. Like Hogarth, he painted with great directness, was sensitive to French influence, which he probably derived from Gravelot, and was most successful in portraits of the middle class from which he sprang (Pl. 29B). In a remarkable life-sized group of *Mr Oldham and his Friends* (Tate Gallery) (Pl. 29C), sedately tippling punch, he achieved a sense of spontaneity, naturalness and repose unparalleled at the time. He is said to have painted more family pieces than any of his contemporaries, but few have been identified. Bartholomew Dandridge also painted family pieces which play a part in the development of the Conversation, but most of his ordinary portraits are dreary exercises in the manner of Vanderbank — distinguishable by the long-nosed, sullen faces with which he endowed his sitters — though he could rise to an occasion as when he painted the amiable countenance of the great 'Signor' William Kent.

Fashionable portraiture seems to have been the prerogative of foreign artists, of whom the most interesting was Philip Mercier, who arrived in London in the mid-1720's and was able to give his sitters a mondaine French elegance. For some ten years he enjoyed the patronage of the Prince of Wales and then fell from power; in 1738 he appears in Leicestershire and in 1742 in Yorkshire, where he painted a number of life-sized portraits. Among the most notable are the full lengths at Temple Newsam, which are not without grace, refinement and, where children are included, a certain playfulness, but they have the air of enlargements. In 1737 the artistic dovecotes of London were fluttered by the arrival of a less able but more successful French painter, Jean Baptiste Van Loo, who had already made a reputation for himself in Paris and Turin, and thus arrived with a *cordon bleu* of continental approbation. Without being unduly frenchified, he was a little less dull than Richardson, whose power was on the decline, and he stayed five years enjoying the prosperity of the most fashionable practice which he shared with two other foreigners, Rusca and Andrea Soldi.

Thomas Hudson, the pupil and son-in-law of Richardson, was the only native painter capable of putting up any effective opposition to this invasion. Principally remembered as the master of Reynolds, he has been praised far above his deserts. Occasionally he excelled himself in female portraiture but he generally appears as little more than a fashionable painter able to essay the 'serious and the smirk', his gentlemen have a solidity and strength occasionally reminiscent of Dahl, but his ladies tend to be too feathery and coy, especially when dressed *à la* Hélène Fourment. In his female portraits the rendering of stiff silks and satins is often felicitous, for which credit is due to the indispensable Van Aken. Another minor artist who attracted a fashionable clientèle was George Knapton, a foundation member of and official painter to the Society of Dilettante. A portrait of Lord Burlington (Pl. 26D) shows his ability to combine the new natural style with an air of grandeur.

In 1739 a young Scottish painter, Allan Ramsay, who had just returned from Italy, settled in London, and within a year he was able to claim,

'I have put your Vanloos and Soldis and Roscos to flight and now play the first fiddle myself'. He mentioned no English rival, and there was indeed none to compare with him for the sure-handed elegance or delicate sensitivity which he was to refine through the years. As may be seen from the full length of the great collector Dr Mead, which he presented to the Foundling Hospital in 1746, he had learned enough from baroque portraiture to adapt the style successfully to an English sitter without giving him a foreign air. He had also learned to adapt poses from the Antique and painted the twenty-second Chief of MacLeod pacing the strand in the attitude of Apollo Belvedere, thus anticipating the attitude of Reynold's *Commander Keppel* by five years. As Professor Waterhouse has indicated, 'the marriage of the Italian grand style to British portraiture was primarily the achievement of Ramsay'. But he was not limited to the grand manner and could with equal facility depict the quiet, the thoughtful and the reticent (Pl. 29A). Although he made use of a drapery painter – he could not otherwise have satisfied the number of his sitters – he gave clear instructions on how the work was to be done and was well able to do it himself, as the lovely portrait of his second wife (now in Edinburgh) testifies.[4] In 1755 he visited Rome again and modified his style by contact with Pompeo Batoni, A.R. Mengs and the French pastellists. After his return in 1757 he painted some of his best works, including the portrait of Dr Hunter (Pl. 33B), but his appointment as Court painter on George III's accession involved him in a tedious routine of official portraiture which robbed the country of a notable artist.

It is probable that Ramsay's second visit to Italy was precipitated by the rising fame of Joshua Reynolds, who had returned thence in 1754. Five years later Walpole wrote, 'Mr Reynolds and Mr Ramsay can hardly be rivals; their manners are so different. The former is bold and has a kind of tempestuous colouring, yet with dignity and grace; the latter is all delicacy. Mr Reynolds seldom suc-

[4] This portrait was painted in Rome where he would not presumably have had the assistance of a drapery painter. *The Connoisseur*, vol. CXXXVII, No. 552, p. 82.

ceeds in women, Mr Ramsay was formed to paint them.' The greater solidity and forthrightness of Reynolds' style at this moment, as shown in the portrait of Admiral Holburne and his son (Pl. 33A), are certainly more masculine than Ramsay's, but he had yet to prove himself the great all-round portrait painter. Working in the provinces during these years and beknown to few, Thomas Gainsborough was developing a style more individual and revolutionary. Untouched by the Mediterranean tradition, he imbibed French influences from Gravelot, under whom he worked for a brief spell. Like Reynolds, he more properly belongs to the classical age of English painting, but before George II had died he had already executed some of his most masterly works, the picture of his daughters chasing a butterfly (National Gallery) and the portrait group of Mr and Mrs Andrews (Pl. 33C), which have a morning freshness and innocence he was never to recapture.

Conversation pieces

Deep as its origins may lie in the history of European painting, the conversation piece – a small-scale group of figures placed in a more or less informal arrangement – was first developed in England into an independent genre in the first half of the eighteenth century. The initial popularity of conversations may be attributed to the fashion for a relatively new type of portrait group; their natural appearance appealed to an age tiring of courtly formality, their small size and cost recommended them to middle-class patrons. Philip Mercier seems to have been responsible for the introduction of the genre which he handled with a gallic lightness of touch especially noticeable in the first painting he is known to have executed – *Viscount Tyrconnel and his Family* (1725–6, Belton House) and *Frederick Prince of Wales and his Sisters* (Pl. 31A). The greatest practitioner of the conversation piece was William Hogarth, who contrived to give it a freshness few of his contemporaries achieved, though he rarely succeeded in bridging the gulf between informality and awkwardness. In the 1730's and '40's the younger Marcellus Laroon painted a few and drew more (Fig. 2, p. 606), in which he made only the most

perfunctory attempts at compositional arrangement; his works have the air of being representations of life at its least formal. Gawen Hamilton and Charles Philips paid more attention to composition, perhaps at the cost of naturalness. Hamilton may be illustrated by the *Artists' Club* (Pl. 25A), Philips by the group of thirteen doll-like members of the Finch family in a little picture which also finds room for a crumbling triumphal arch, a bright new Palladian temple, statuary, and a landscaped vista terminating on an obelisk, to exemplify their architectural taste (Pl. 28A). The mode was also, though less frequently, employed by Bartholomew Dandridge, whose most notable contribution is *The Price Family* (Washington).

Most of the artists who painted conversations found the genre too unremunerative, but Arthur Devis clung to it and produced a vast number between the early 1740's and his death in 1787. 'His pictures are all of a sort', wrote Lord John Cavendish in 1764; 'they are all whole lengths of about two feet long; and the person is always represented in a genteel attitude, either leaning against a pillar, or standing by a flower pot, or leading an Italian greyhound on a string, or in some other such ingenious posture.' Genteel his figures certainly are, but they have a melancholy *naïveté* which has endeared them to collectors in recent years. A good and representative example, painted in 1751, shows Sir George and Lady Strickland enjoying the carefully contrived rustic charms of their park (Pl. 28B). The costumes, the backgrounds, and the accessories change with the taste of the years, for fashion is an essential of the genre, but Devis's style shows no recognizable development. Much of his work was executed in the reign of George III, after Zoffany had applied his sharper eye and abler brush to such paintings, but he belongs essentially to the earlier part of the century.

Fancy pictures

Like the conversation piece, the fancy picture was of French extraction, and was popularized, if not introduced by Philip Mercier. In a valiant and characteristically confused attempt to define the new form, Vertue said the pictures were 'pieces of some figures of conversations as big as life; conceited plaisant fancies and habits; mixed modes really well done – and much approved of'. Faber in 1739 engraved nine such works after Mercier, who, profiting from the example of Hogarth seems to have conceived his pleasant fancies – *A Venetian Girl at a Window*, *A Recruiting Officer* and the like – with an eye to the growing market for prints. The most notable English practitioner of the genre was the versatile Francis Hayman, who began his active career by working with Gravelot on the plates for Sir Thomas Hanmer's edition of Shakespeare which was published in 1744. At the same time he began the large fancy pictures of pastoral and Shakespearean subjects to decorate the boxes of the Vauxhall Pleasure Gardens (Pl. 31B). These works were strongly tinged with Gravelot's French influence but they remained English in conception and execution. The charm is always a little rustic, the comedy a little heavy-handed, the texture more than a little coarse. Like the pictures painted for reproduction in prints, they were intended to please a predominantly middle-class public. Historically they are of importance as the most frequently seen contemporary paintings in London and because they look forward to the fancy pieces of Gainsborough and the Shakespearean illustrations commissioned by Alderman Boydell. To our eyes they seem little more than cumbrous translations of French comedies into an English dialect.

History painting

A period which begins with Thornhill's commission to decorate the cupola of St Paul's and ends with Hogarth's *Sigismunda* and the first of Gawen Hamilton's vast neo-classical machines,[5] might appear to be one of singular importance in the development of history painting. It is, however, very difficult to discern any clear process of evolution. As far as this period is concerned, Sir James Thornhill is of greater importance as the father-in-law of Hogarth, who derived several ideas from him, than as a decorative artist, for, although he continued active until the late 1720's,

and much of his most important work was done in the reign of George I, he belongs stylistically to the previous epoch.

While Thornhill was intriguing for the St Paul's commission, William Kent, a young Yorkshireman, startled the artistic world of Rome in 1713 by winning the Pope's medal for painting. He was even allowed to paint the ceiling of a Roman church, at his own expense. But Kent's early promise to be *Raphael Secundus* was not fulfilled after his return home, and there must have been few besides his devoted patron, Lord Burlington, who could trace in his productions 'Titian's strong fire and Guido's softer grace'. His mythological ceilings were uncommonly ponderous save in the 'grotesque' decoration of their surrounds, and even Lord Burlington modified his opinion as soon as Kent discovered a genuine talent for interior decoration, the designing of furniture and landscape gardening. Much of his popularity as a painter may well have depended on his nationality, and it is not without significance that the first minister, Sir Robert Walpole, chose him to decorate Houghton. Of the few other English artists who indulged the declining taste for painted ceilings, Francis Hayman was probably the most notable.

Thornhill's success at St Paul's seems to have stemmed the invasion of Venetian artists who specialized in decorative histories, though the last of these visitors, Jacopo Amigoni, arrived in 1730 and left in 1739. His series of paintings illustrating the story of *Jupiter and Io* at Moor Park is with little doubt the most accomplished example of rococo art executed in England (Pl. 30B). Unlike his predecessors, Amigoni painted on canvases which were let into the wall, and he found a satisfactory market for large mythological subjects, though he was finally forced to turn his hand to the remunerative task of portraiture, in which he made unstinted use of the history painter's properties.

When the fashion for large decorative mythological paintings in the house had declined, it may well have seemed that all demand for history pictures was dormant. Generally speaking, the Church neither encouraged nor even welcomed

[5] See E. K. Waterhouse: *The British Contribution to the Neo-Classical Style in Painting*, 1955.

paintings, though Vincenzo Damini executed some of saints in Lincoln Cathedral in 1728, and James Parmentier an altar-piece for Holy Trinity Church, Hull, and there were others of less note. Hogarth, who had aspirations to be a great history painter, solved the problem by presenting large Biblical scenes to hospitals. He gave St Bartholomew's Hospital two vast canvases, *The Pool of Bethesda* and *The Good Samaritan* in 1736, and in 1745 he persuaded three other artists, Hayman, Highmore and the Rev. James Wills, to join him in presenting histories to the Foundling Hospital. This important institution was the first place in London, where contemporary paintings might regularly be seen by the general public. No doubt Hogarth's gift was partly activated by his usual desire for self-advertisement, but it appears to have borne fruit in one commission only, the *Paul before Felix*, which he painted for Lincoln's Inn in 1748. In 1756 he painted a large triptych for St Mary Redcliffe, Bristol, and in 1759 the notorious *Sigismunda*, which was in deliberate imitation of a picture by Furini (then believed to be by Correggio) and was greeted with howls of execration, though it might have been received enthusiastically had he passed it off as an Old Master.

Landscapes

The most important early Georgian landscape painter was John Wootton, who was capable of working in both the current traditions: the topographical based on the Anglo-Dutch painters of the seventeenth century, and the decorative which depended on Claude, Gaspar Poussin and Salvator Rosa. Probably the pupil of Jan Siberechts (with whom he appears to have been working in 1694), he achieved fame as an animal painter; but the topographical aspect of his training is evident in several of his hunting pieces and a view of Newmarket, in which he devoted no less care to the accurate rendering of the landscape backgrounds than to the horses. Under the patronage of the third Duke of Beaufort, he went to Rome in the early 1720's and formed an addiction to

Whate'er Lorraine light touch'd with softening hue
Or savage Rosa dash'd, or learned Poussin drew.

His decorative paintings (Pl. 30A) reveal an eye for fine gradations of greens and browns and suggest that his attitude to the works of Gaspar Poussin may have been modified by his knowledge of the parks landscaped by William Kent. When his work is considered as a whole, he has the best claim to the hotly disputed title of the 'father of English landscape'. His pupil, George Lambert, was also capable of attractive imitations of the Franco-Italians, but is more notable for the topographical views in which he used his experience as a theatrical scene painter to impose some art on the depiction of the English countryside – as in his views of Chiswick (Pl. 32A).

In 1746 another influence was introduced by the arrival of Canaletto, who had presumably felt the dearth of English grand tourists occasioned by the War of the Austrian Succession. Spending some nine years in England, he painted views of London and a number of English parks all bathed in a mellow or sparkling Venetian light. He attracted the imitation, and probably the assistance, of Samuel Scott, who had hitherto been a marine painter working very ably under the influence of the Van de Veldes (Pl. 32B). It is not inappropriate to mention here that marine painting enjoyed a limited popularity throughout the period. One of its most notable exponents was Charles Brooking, who died young in 1759, but had already shown signs of breaking away from the Van de Velde tradition, which was otherwise predominant.

As the reign of George II drew to its close, two greater English landscape painters emerged, Thomas Gainsborough and Richard Wilson. The former had indeed done much of his best work in this genre before 1760 and as early as 1748 painted the picture known as *Gainsborough's Forest* (National Gallery), welding the elements of the Suffolk countryside into a purely Dutch composition. In the same year he presented his more revolutionary view of the Charterhouse to the Foundling Hospital – a delightfully fresh treatment of a topographical subject in which every element is equally important and subordinated to the pictorial intention. He appears in a different light in 1755, at Woburn Abbey, painting two overmantels of pastoral scenes which are derived, through Gravelot, from France, and anticipate his fancy pictures.

There was nothing revolutionary about the topographical views which Richard Wilson presented to the Foundling Hospital in 1746, but in 1750 he departed on his momentous journey to Italy, where he remained some seven years, absorbing not only the styles of Gaspar and Claude, but the very light and spirit of the Italian scene. In contrast with the artists who merely imitated the Franco-Italian painters, he derived inspiration from them, and never condescended to the execution of pastiches, possibly because he had also been influenced by Dutch art. Like Claude, he invested the Campagna with a melancholy beauty no Italian has ever represented, expressing the nostalgic yearning of the northerner for the south. Most of his best work, including many of the Italian views which were painted in London from sketches made on the spot, falls outside this period, but the prospect of *Rome and the Ponte Molle* of 1754 (Pl. 30c) is sufficient to record the advance he made in landscape painting. This lyrically evocative composition is in the manner of Claude, but as distant from him as is *The Castle of Indolence* from *The Faery Queen*: Wilson has, so to speak, employed a Claudean stanza. It is an independent work of art, neither a mere topographical view nor an insignificant furniture piece.

Sculpture

The market for sculpture during this period was considerably narrower than that for paintings, and although it increased slightly, it never spread beyond a relatively small section of the aristocracy. Because of this more exclusive patronage, sculpture remained immune from those social forces which introduced a spirit of naturalism into painting. The isolation was also due to the dominant position held by the trio of foreign sculptors – Rysbrack, Roubiliac and Scheemakers – whose sepulchral monuments adorned with periwigged statesmen, full-skirted ladies, weeping loves, fates, skeletons and angels of doom, introduced the last reverberating trumpet notes of the baroque into our cathedrals and churches. But if the extravagant continental style of these artists was allowed to flourish in church, classical manners were alone tolerated in the private house. The patrician residences of this period might contain a small collection of antique marbles augmented by modern copies of the more famous Roman statues, a few busts and some heavy chimney-pieces in which low-relief carvings were sometimes set. Plaster copies of classical statuary, busts of notabilities and terracotta statuettes of monumental figures by Rysbrack and Roubiliac were, of course, cheaper and might be found in the homes of the less affluent *virtuosi*.

On account of its material, sculpture was expensive, though not much more expensive than fashionable portraiture. Rysbrack's lowest fee for a marble bust was thirty-five guineas, according to Vertue, who goes on to say that Scheemakers 'wd and dos for near ten gns. less; but that is the difference every one can distinguish tho in point of skill, likeness etc., there is difference sufficient to those who know better'. In 1744 Rysbrack was paid £220 for a statue of Dr Radcliffe at Oxford, in 1756 £300 for his Hercules and in 1761 £400 for a Flora at Stourhead. For Mr Bedford's 'busto in clay', Roubiliac asked ten guineas and promised 'for 30 guineas more to do the same in marble'. Sir Henry Cheere, the most notable native sculptor of the period, seems to have been more modestly remunerated; he was paid £135 a piece for the three Portland stone statues he made for Queen's College, Oxford, in 1734, and but £42 for a statue of the same material which he carved for Sir Thomas Lee of Hartwell in the next year. He received £284 for three marble chimney-pieces at Ditchley. Lead figures for gardens were, of course, less costly and a list sent by Andrew Carpenter to the Earl of Carlisle in about 1720 shows that his prices varied from £25 for a figure of Narcissus 7½ feet high to £7 for a Cleopatra 5 feet high.

Busts

A writer in *The London Tradesman* remarked in 1746 that 'the taste for busts and figures prevails much of late years and in some measure interferes with portrait painting. The nobility now affect to have their busts done that way'. Whole length figures in marble were rarely to be met with outside public buildings (among the most notable are Roubiliac's *Newton* at Trinity College, Cambridge and Scheemakers' *Shakespeare* in Westminster Abbey), but the popularity of busts increased apace, partly because three notable sculptors were available to execute them. The first of the foreigners to arrive in England was Michael Rysbrack, who settled in London in 1720 and won an almost immediate success. From the first his busts demonstrated a classicizing tendency, derived from François Duquesnoy through Van der Voort, but although they are often dressed in togas, they are not without realism. Even that of George I (Pl. 34c), crowned with laurels and attired in antique armour bearing the insignia of the Garter, is full of strength and character. In treating that most difficult of sculptural problems, the full-bottomed wig, he contrived to make it appear a part, and never an overshadowing part, of the classical composition, as is particularly notable in the bust of Sir Hans Sloane (British Museum). In contrast, Louis Francois Roubiliac, who settled in London in about 1732, worked solely in the rococo style. Whereas Rysbrack's busts look one calmly, squarely and perhaps coldly in the face, Roubiliac's sometimes give one no more than a glance as the head turns away to assume some characteristic attitude (Pl. 34B). Although cast in a classical mould, Roubiliac's bust of Pope (Pl. 34A) reveals his prepossession with the mood and appearance of a moment. Peter Scheemakers, who settled in London in about 1730, has usually been relegated to the third place in this group, but he was an artist of no mean ability. His busts are closer in style to those of Rysbrack than Roubiliac (Pl. 34D). Unlike his greater contemporaries, Scheemakers employed a number of assistants to work his marble, and it is significant that nearly all prominent late Georgian sculptors, including Joseph Nollekens and Thomas Banks, learnt their art in this way.

The fashion for busts was not confined to those of living notabilities, but extended to Roman writers and British poets, philosophers and kings. It seems probable that the desire to commemorate

Francis Bacon, Spenser, Shakespeare, Milton and John Locke, and enshrine their busts alongside those of Virgil and Cicero in library and temple sprang from the spirit of nationalism that is so marked a feature of the period. Roubiliac executed a series of ten marble busts of notable British writers, scientists and scholars for Trinity College, Cambridge, Scheemakers a group of four English poets for Hagley Hall, and Rysbrack seems to have made a speciality of this type of work, carving busts of such diverse figures as Raleigh, Cromwell, King Alfred and Milton. These busts were carefully modelled on such portraits as were available, and the sculptors took great pains to be correct in the details of dress. British worthies were not the only ones to be commemorated and Rysbrack executed busts of Michelangelo, Palladio, Duquesnoy, Rubens and Van Dyck, but they do not appear to have enjoyed the same popularity.

Recent authors might be allowed to stand beside the classics in the library, but living artists could hardly be given a footing among the ancients, and the original works of modern sculptors were rarely admitted to the collection of marbles. The copies of Roman statues which filled the niches in the saloon were frequently the work of Italian hands, but towards the end of our period two young British sculptors, Joseph Wilton and Simon Vierpyl, supplied such works for Wentworth Woodhouse, and Vierpyl executed similar figures for Lord Charlemont. Independent works for the house were of a purely decorative nature. Rysbrack, Scheemakers, Delvaux (who worked in England for a short time), Sir Henry Cheere and others were not too high-minded to stoop to the execution of chimney-pieces, many of which were of great size and magnificence, supported on heavily carved consoles, severe terms or buxom caryatids, garlanded with fruits or entwined with vine leaves and surmounted by low-relief panels (which were more frequently in stucco). The low reliefs – like those Rysbrack executed for Clandon (Pl. 35), Houghton and Woburn Abbey – were predominantly classical in feeling to accord with the pedimented door-cases and other Palladian features. Roubiliac alone seems never to have executed such works, possibly because his rococo style was thought to be unsuitable, though gay Italian stucco work was admitted on walls and ceilings.

Of the few large independent figures executed for private patrons in this period, that of Hercules which Rysbrack carved for Stourhead in 1756 is, with little doubt, the most important (Pl. 36A). Horace Walpole tells how this athletic statue, which he terms 'an exquisite summary of his (Rysbrack's) skill, knowledge and judgement', was modelled on the head of the Farnese Hercules and otherwise 'compiled from the various limbs of seven or eight of the strongest and best made men in London, chiefly the bruisers and boxers of the then flourishing amphitheatre for boxing, the sculptor selecting the parts which were most truly formed in each'. This figure marks an important stage in the history of English sculpture, for it was commissioned as a statue and not a mere piece of household or garden furniture, it was an original work derived from the antique but modelled on nature and, furthermore, it was placed among casts of the most famous Roman statues in the Pantheon at Stourhead. Roubiliac's large figures were nearly all portrait statues, the most important exception being that of *Religion* which he executed for Gopsal in 1761 (Pl. 36B); finely and sensitively wrought, like all his works, it is in the tradition of Roman late baroque sculpture and strikingly representative of his *retardataire* tendency. The earliest, and in many ways the best, of his statues was that of Handel, which he executed for the Vauxhall Pleasure Gardens in 1738. It shows the composer rather untidily dressed, having taken off one of his slippers and sitting back in an easy posture to strum the lyre which, like the *putto* at his feet, strikes an incongruous note in this otherwise realistic work.

Garden statuary

Outside the house, on the balustrade, the terrace and in the garden, sculpture was more generally popular than within doors. Trumpeting Fames, tip-toe Mercuries, shivering Venuses, monitory Apollos, dying Gauls, wrestling youths and leering satyrs abounded amid the beeches, oaks and willows of the English park. At the beginning of our period the days of the formal garden were numbered, but even William Kent was not averse to introducing statuary into his more natural lay-outs. Many sculptors seem to have specialized in such works, and the famed 'gods of Athens and of Rome' that jostled each other in the Hyde Park Corner yard of John Cheere were mostly intended as ornaments for the outside of the house or the garden. Most of these figures were based on well-known Roman statues, but the moderns – notably Giovanni Bologna – were also copied and adapted. Wholly original works were rarer, though John Cheere adorned the grotto at Stourhead with a crouching river-god and Rysbrack made stone figures of Inigo Jones, Palladio and Duquesnoy to stand guard over Lord Burlington's villa at Chiswick. In deference to the English climate, such works, were made of lead or rough stone, and were seldom of high quality. No less an authority than William Shenstone suggested that they should not be too fine, remarking: 'A statue in a room challenges examination and is to be examined critically as a statue. A statue in a garden is to be considered one part of a scene or landskip. ...' The same writer commends the use of sculptured urns, saying that they are 'more solemn if large and plain; more beautiful if less and ornamented. Solemnity is perhaps their point, and the situation of them should still co-operate with it'. The heyday of the great sculptured urn was over by 1714, but Cheere and others provided more modestly decorated and thus more solemn vessels ranging in design from the heavily baroque, popular at the beginning of the period, to the more chaste and classical favoured at its end.

SHORT BIBLIOGRAPHY

The essential book for the study of early Georgian painting is: *Painting in Britain 1530–1790* by E. K. Waterhouse (1953). A fuller account of the Conversation Piece gènre is contained in: *Early Conversation Pieces* by Ralph Edwards (1954). The best account of Hogarth's work is in *Hogarth* by R. B. Beckett (1949).

A Dictionary of British Sculptors 1660–1851 by Rupert Gunnis (1953) is the only full account of sculpture in the period. More detailed accounts of individual sculptors are contained in *The Life and Works of Louis Francois Roubiliac* by K. A. Esdaile (1928) and *Michael Rysbrack* by M. I. Webb (1954).

F

Fig. 2. A Concert at Montagu House in 1736, by Marcellus
Laroon, reproduced from a pencil drawing. *British Museum.*

Silver and Plate

GERALD TAYLOR

The patrons of the goldsmiths during the Whig supremacy, as the reigns of George I and II have been characterized, were, as they are at all times, people of ample means: peers and commoners, landowners and men of affairs, Whigs and Tories alike, who spent according to their needs and to their tastes. Some of those who amassed plate during this half-century had been born into families accustomed to its lavish use in magnificent surroundings; others felt the need, or discovered the pleasures, of acquiring it as their status improved. Indeed, in this period of expansion of both trade and empire, punctuated though it was with disturbances at home and abroad, there were many patrons who rose from modest circumstances to the possession of great wealth, or at least of moderate fortunes, but they were far outnumbered by those who began their lives in comfortable circumstances, and in contact with the ruling oligarchy or its fringes. Of the pieces illustrated here, the ewer and basin (Pl. 41) was made for a peer of little political importance, Algernon, sixth Earl of Mountrath; the castor (Pl. 42A) for Charles Fitzroy, second Duke of Grafton, and Lord Chamberlain; both the punch-bowl (Pl. 38A) and the toilet-service (*cf.* Pl. 37C) were commissioned from Paul de Lamerie by George Treby, one-time Secretary at War, and the large salver (Pl. 40) was commissioned by Sir Robert Walpole, the great Whig leader, from the same goldsmith after the death of George I. Indeed, it may be assumed that most plate was bought by those successful in the spheres of trade, war, politics or administration.

Yet the commissions of the various corporations and churches should not be forgotten, because together they must have constituted an important fraction of the goldsmiths' output. Not only the livery companies of London and other towns, but also municipal corporations and the colleges of Oxford, Cambridge and Dublin, required replacements of worn plate, while new plate was from time to time added to their possessions. At Goldsmiths' Hall itself are still preserved some of the pieces ordered from Paul de Lamerie in 1740 to replace plate which had been melted down in 1671 and 1711; notable among them are the ink-stand made to hold the bell given to the Company by Sir Robert Vyner in 1666, and the gilt ewer and dish which are not unlike in weight and quality, motifs and elaboration, those shown here in Plate 41. From the plate of one Oxford College, Merton,[1] may be selected at random two examples, the coffee-pot of 1727 made to replace a vessel, probably a tankard, given by Robert Jenison in 1657, and the set of four candlesticks of 1723 given by Hoby Stanley, who received his degree of Master of Arts in that year. The many lists of church plate published show that there must have been a steady production of communion cups, patens, almsdishes and flagons, both for replacement of worn, lost or damaged plate in existing parishes, but also for the equipment of the new places of worship that were being built in the growing towns.[2]

Many private patrons were enabled to travel

---

[1] E.A.Jones, *Catalogue of the Plate of Merton College, Oxford,* 1938, *passim.*

[2] In general, see C.C.Oman's history of Church Plate, published in 1957.

607

abroad, whether in the leisurely pursuit of culture, the peaceful interests of commerce or in the prosecution of war. The Grand Tour was becoming part of the education of a nobleman and of many gentlemen; some of these travellers were able to continue the tradition of bringing back all kinds of works of art from Europe or from even further afield; some few were in constant touch with their agents in Italy and elsewhere. While a small number of British artists, men such as Reynolds and Wilson (1750), were able to travel abroad, especially to Italy, to learn more about the works of those artists who were acknowledged supreme, the continuance of a reverse flow of artists from abroad seeking employment in Britain was occasioned by Britain's gradual rise towards economic preeminence. Besides painters such as Watteau (1719), Mercier (about 1726), Canaletto (1746–55) and Cipriani (1755), several craftsmen came to London; Nicholas Sprimont from the Netherlands who worked as a silversmith, evidently in close collaboration with the Huguenot Paul Crespin, in the early forties, or Jan Schuppe who specialized in silver cow-creamers in the 'fifties and 'sixties. This constant reciprocal exchange of artistic ideas between Europe and the British Isles was greatly furthered by means of books and engravings.

This two-way flow of artists served to reinforce the influence of the small but well-established group of Huguenot silversmiths; the obviously foreign designs of their early plate had not influenced greatly the work of their London rivals, who resented the intrusion, and they had in any case been much modified by the inaccessibility of up-to-date designs or models from Paris and elsewhere on the Continent, as well as by the less discerning taste of their British patrons. Nevertheless the Huguenots of the second generation, and especially their doyen, Paul de Lamerie, were still able to command many of the most lucrative commissions in plate that had been so swiftly captured by their predecessors of the first generation during the reigns of William and Queen Anne.

In the artistic sphere, therefore, England was far from being isolated, nor was it entirely provincial, as far as London – by far the greatest centre of

the manufacture of plate – and the most influential families – who divided their time between London and their country houses – were concerned. As a corollary, of course, it will be found, as must be expected, that most of the plate made in other, remoter centres does betray more or less of provincialism, in that it is either behind the times or lacking the quality in design and finish that was expected in the capital.

That throughout these two reigns there followed a succession of changing fashions in plate may be deduced from the arguments just set out, and is indeed confirmed by the numerous, one might say innumerable, pieces which have been preserved. While, on the one hand, some few approximate very closely indeed to the contemporary products of various centres on the Continent, and others are very practical interpretations in silver of essentially useful wares, the majority of pieces betray in their shape and ornament a mixture of foreign influences, from both Europe and the East, yet harmonized in such a way that their essential Englishness can be recognized.

From time to time decoration, or more occasionally some forms, of plate have been closely related to contemporary architecture. Yet the Queen Anne style, which for the purposes of plate may be considered to have predominated from the outset of her reign until about 1720, in spite of a basis of simplified classical ornament that is common to the later Palladian Renaissance in British architecture, seems to have no pervasive architectural inspiration behind its forms. Only a few comparisons can be drawn; courses of applied mouldings (Pls. 42A, B, C, D), baluster finials (Pl. 42A) and occasionally some vessel, for example a rectangular tea-canister shaped like a pedestal. On the other hand, the domed lids of tea-pots (Fig. 1'), tea-canisters (Pl. 38B), kettles and coffee-pots may well have been intended to reflect in miniature the conception and triumphant conclusion of the dome of St Paul's the daily progress of which must have been watched with interest by the goldsmiths of Cheapside and Foster Lane.

For the first six years of the reign domestic plate was essentially simple, practical, symmetrical and of good solid metal. Covered vessels were de-

(A) Sir Joshua Reynolds. Admiral Holburne and Son (c. 1756).
The National Maritime Museum, Greenwich.

(B) Allan Ramsay. Dr William Hunter (c. 1758).
The Hunterian Museum, Glasgow.

(c) Thomas Gainsborough. Mr and Mrs Robert Andrews (c. 1749).
G. W. Andrews, Esq.

PLATE 33

(A) L. F. ROUBILIAC. Alexander Pope (1738).
Leeds Art Gallery.

(B) L. F. ROUBILIAC. Handel (1739).
Reproduced by gracious permission of H.M. The Queen.

(C) MICHAEL RYSBRACK. George I (*c.* 1727).
Christchurch, Oxford.

(D) PETER SCHEEMAKERS. Sir Justinian Isham
(1737)
Sir Gyles Isham, Bt.

PLATE 34

MICHAEL RYSBRACK. Chimney Piece at Clandon Park, Surrey, *c.* 1729. *A. F. Kersting.*

PLATE 35

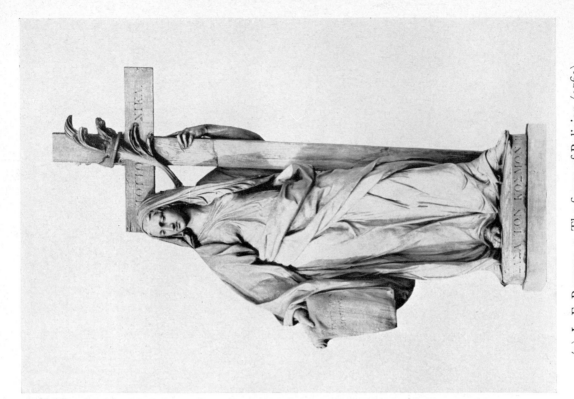

(B) L. F. ROUBILIAC. The figure of Religion (1761).
Leicester City Art Gallery.

(A) MICHAEL RYSBRACK. The model for his Hercules (1744) at Stourhead. *The Courtauld Institute of Art.*

PLATE 36

(A) JOHN WHITE. Coat-of-arms of the Bulteel family engraved on a salver, one of a set of three, 1720. *Ashmolean Museum.*

(B) PAUL DE LAMERIE. Canting coat-of-arms of the Mills family engraved on a tray, 1734. *Ashmolean Museum.*

(C) PAUL DE LAMERIE. The central ornament on the lid of one of a pair of rectangular caskets from the Treby toilet service, 1724. *Ashmolean Museum.*

PLATE 37

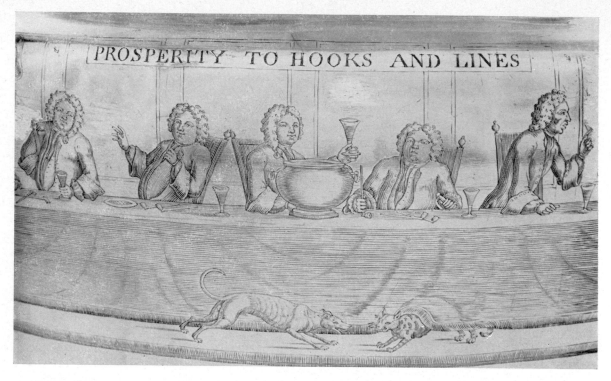

PROSPERITY TO HOOKS AND LINES

(A) PAUL DE LAMERIE. A detail from one of the two friezes of figures engraved round the Treby punch-bowl, 1724.
Ashmolean Museum.

(B) A detail from a painting by an unknown artist of about 1725 showing a family at tea.
The plate is of the period 1705-25. *Victoria and Albert Museum.*

(A) ANTHONY NELME. One of a pair of tea-canisters, 1716; note his mark, imperfectly struck and upside down near the base. Arms: Shore. Ht 3¾ in.; weight 6 oz. *Messrs. Crichton.* (B) SAMUEL TAYLOR. Sugar-vase and tea-canister, 1752. Ht 5½ in. *Ashmolean Museum.*

(C) PAUL DE LAMERIE. A tea-set, 1735. Ht of cream-jug 4 in. The tongs are certainly by a different maker, but the remainder of the flat-ware, though apparently only marked with a foreign control stamp, is probably also by de Lamerie; the knife handles correspond to those of an unmarked set in the Ashmolean Museum. The mounts of the mahogany case and its key are of silver. *Messrs Asprey.*

PLATE 39

PAUL DE LAMERIE. The Walpole Salver, 1728. Width 19¼ in.; weight 135 oz.
Victoria and Albert Museum.

PLATE 40

PAUL DE LAMERIE. Ewer and basin, 1742. Height of the ewer 18½ in.; diameter of the basin 29 in.; combined weight 442 oz. *Messrs Christie, Manson and Woods, Ltd.*

PLATE 41   617

(A) DAVID WILLAUME. Castor, 1735. Ht 8½ in.; wt 20 oz. Arms of Charles Fitzroy, 2nd Duke of Grafton, K.G. *Messrs. How of Edinburgh.* (B) BENJAMIN PYNE. One of a pair of sauce-boats, 1723. Engraved crest of Thomas Howard, 8th Duke of Norfolk. Length 9 in.; wt 18 oz. *Messrs. Burfitt.* (C) DAVID WILLAUME. One of a pair of sauce-boats, 1733. Engraved unidentified crest. Ht 5⅛ in.; wt 18 oz. *Ashmolean Museum.* (D) JOHN CHAPMAN. Warwick frame containing three small castors and silver-mounted oil and vinegar glasses, 1734. Engraved arms and crest of Cleve or Clive of Walford, Co. Salop. Ht of castors 5¼ in. and 7¼ in.

PLATE 42

A

B

C

D

E

(A) PAUL DE LAMERIE. Blade of a fish-slice, pierced and engraved with fishes, 1741. Width of blade $4\frac{1}{2}$ in. *Ashmolean Museum*. (B) BENJAMIN GODFREY. Top of a soap-box, *c.* 1735. The pattern of the perforations of scrolls and diapers are broken to preserve the engraved but unassigned crest. Diameter 3 in.; wt 9 oz. *Ashmolean Museum*. (C) MATTHEW COOPER. One of a pair of candlesticks, 1715. Ht $7\frac{1}{4}$ in.; wt 10 oz. *Captain H. D. Clark Collection*. (D) CHARLES KANDLER. One of a pair of candlesticks, 1730. The detachable nozzles are later additions by William Cafe, who entered his mark in 1757 and is probably the son of John Cafe, also a candlestick maker, who entered his mark in 1742. Height $8\frac{3}{4}$ in.; weight 30 oz. *Messrs. Carrington*. (E) JOHN CAFE. One of a set of four candlesticks, 1753. Ht 11 in.; wt 43 oz. *Formerly A. P. Boissier Collection*.

PLATE 43

CHARLES KANDLER. Wine Cistern, 1734. Width 5 ft 5 in.; weight 8,000 oz.   *The Hermitage, Leningrad.*

(A) Plate, delftware, painted in colours. Lambeth, 1737. Diameter 8½ in. *Victoria and Albert Museum.*

(B) Tray, delftware, painted in blue. Probably Bristol, 1743. Diameter 14 in. *Victoria and Albert Museum.*

(C) Bowl delftware, painted in colours. Lambeth, about 1760. Diameter 12 in. *Author's Collection.*

PLATE 45   621

(A) Plate, delftware, painted in blue on a sprayed manganese-purple ground. Wincanton, 1738. Diameter 8¾ in. *Fitzwilliam Museum, Cambridge.*

(B) Plate, delftware, painted in 'Fazackerly' colours within a *bianco-sopra-bianco* border. Probably Bristol, about 1750–60. Diameter 10⅛ in. *Victoria and Albert Museum.*

(C) Puzzle-jug, delftware, painted in blue. Bristol, about 1760. *Bristol Art Gallery.*

(D) Food-warmer, delftware, painted in blue. Probably Bristol, first half of eighteenth century. Ht of stand 5 in. *Victoria and Albert Museum.*

PLATE 46

(A) (*Left*) Plate, lead-glazed earthenware with moulded rim and patches of colour in the glaze. 'Whieldon-type'; about 1760. Diameter 9¼ in.

(B) Teapot, unglazed red earthenware. Staffordshire, about 1750–60. Ht 5 in.

(C) Teapot, 'agate-ware'. Staffordshire, about 1740. Ht 4 in.

(D) (*Right*) Figure of lead-glazed earthenware, the glaze dappled with colours. Staffordshire, about 1740. Ht 7 $\frac{9}{16}$ in.
All Victoria and Albert Museum.

PLATE 47

(A) Jug, lead-glazed earthenware, with the decoration incised through the dark to the light clay. Staffordshire, 1726. Ht 5⅞ in. *Fitzwilliam Museum, Cambridge.*

(B) Teapot, dark lead-glazed earthenware with white relief-decoration. Staffordshire, about 1740. Ht 6 in. *Victoria and Albert Museum.*

(c) Teapot, coffee-pot and jug of 'Astbury-Whieldon' type and 'Jackfield' jug. Mainly Staffordshire, about 1740–50. *Victoria and Albert Museum.*

PLATE 48

(A) Group of a Chinaman and Boy, porcelain. Derby, about 1755. Ht 9¼ in. (B) Figure of a carpenter, porcelain, painted in colours. Chelsea, about 1755. Ht 7¾ in. (C) Figure symbolic of Spring, porcelain, painted in colours. Chelsea, about 1755. Ht 5¼ in. (D) Figure of Neptune, porcelain. Bow, about 1755. Ht 6¼ in. *All Victoria and Albert Museum.*

PLATE 51

(A) Vase, porcelain, painted in colours. Bow, about 1755. Ht $7\frac{7}{8}$ in. (B) Dish, porcelain, painted in colours in the 'Kakiemon' manner. Bow, about 1755. Diameter $9\frac{1}{2}$ in. (C) Dish, porcelain, painted in colours in the Meissen manner. Chelsea, about 1755. Diameter $16\frac{1}{4}$ in. (D) Model of a dovecot, probably a pot-pourri, porcelain, painted in colours. Chelsea, about 1755. Ht $14\frac{1}{2}$ in. *All Victoria and Albert Museum.*

PLATE 52

(A) Jug, porcelain, painted in colours. Longton Hall, about 1755. Ht 8¾ in. (B) Tureen in the form of a rabbit, porcelain, painted in colours. Chelsea, about 1755. Length 14¼ in. (C) Tureen, porcelain. Bow, about 1750–5. Ht 7½ in. (D) Coffee-pot, porcelain with black transfer-print, 'L'Amour', by R. Hancock. Worcester, about 1765. Ht 8¾ in. *All Victoria and Albert Museum.*

PLATE 53   629

A   B   C

(A) Sweetmeat glass with cut decoration. About 1730–40. Ht 6 in. (B) Bowl engraved with arms of the Ferguson-Davie family, about 1760. Diameter 8½ in. (C) Sweetmeat glass, second quarter of eighteenth century. Ht 4⅝ in.

D   E   F

(D) Wine-glass, about 1725. Ht 6⅞ in. (E) Candlestick, glass with shouldered stem. About 1740. Ht 10½ in. (F) Toastmaster's glass with deceptive bowl. Early eighteenth century. Ht 6⅛ in. *All Victoria and Albert Museum.*

PLATE 54

A

B

C

(A) Drawn-stem wine-glass with engraved border. About 1735. Ht 6⅝ in. (B) Ale-glass with opaque-white twist stem. About 1760. Ht 9 in. (C) Wine-glass, the pedestal stem moulded with the words GOD SAVE KING G. About 1715. Ht 6⅛ in.

D

E

F

(D) Wine-glass with air-twist stem and bulb enclosing 2d piece of George II dated 1746. About 1750. Ht 6⅞ in. (E) Cruet-bottle, cut-glass. About 1740. Ht 7½ in. (F) Wine-glass with air-twist stem, engraved with portrait of Prince Charles Edward and motto AUDENTIOR IBO. About 1750. Ht 6¼ in. *All Victoria and Albert Museum.*

PLATE 55

A   B   C

(A) Decanter. About 1730–40. Ht 9 in. *Victoria and Albert Museum.* (B) Jar of opaque-white glass painted in enamels, perhaps in Staffordshire. About 1760. *Ashmolean Museum, Oxford.* (C) Decanter for Port, engraved on the wheel. About 1760. Ht 11 in. *Victoria and Albert Museum.*

(D) Portrait of the Duke of Newcastle and the Earl of Lincoln by SIR GODFREY KNELLER, *c.* 1718. *National Portrait Gallery.*

PLATE 56

(A) Toilet table box of black japanned iron enriched with gilding, lid mounted with English painted enamel plaque. The lid has a metal mirror on its interior surface. 7½ in. × 5¼ in. One of a set of three *c.* 1750. *National Museum of Wales.*

(B) Toilet service tray in English painted enamel, decorated with pastoral scenes *c.* 1760. *Messrs Christie, Manson and Woods.*

(C) (*Right*) A Battersea plaque transfer of Prince George, eldest son of Frederick, Prince of Wales, and later George III, printed in brown, lightly touched with brushwork in the same tint. *By gracious permission of Her Majesty the Queen.*

PLATE 57   633

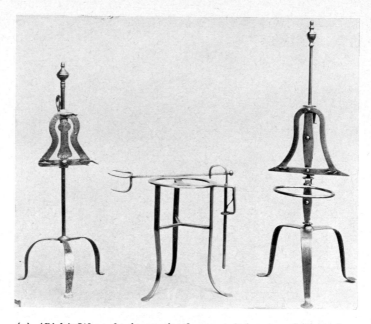

(A) (*Right*) Wrought iron spit: framework has two forks and a plate ring, both of which have springs for adjustment purposes; (*centre*) trivet with toasting fork; (*left*) an adjustable toaster on tripod foot.

(B) Trivets and (*centre*) a footman with curved perforated front. *All Victoria and Albert Museum.*

PLATE 58

A

B

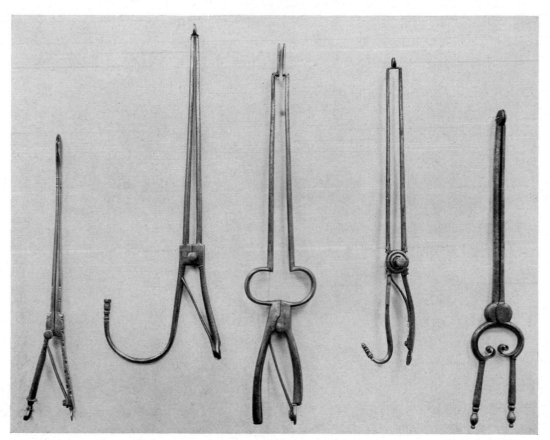

C

(A) Wrought iron plate warmer with revolving frame to hold a pile of plates in front of the fire.
(B) A four-legged footman with brass plate and apron pierced and engraved. (C) Smoker's tongs for
lifting charcoal embers from braziers. *All Victoria and Albert Museum.*

PLATE 59

635

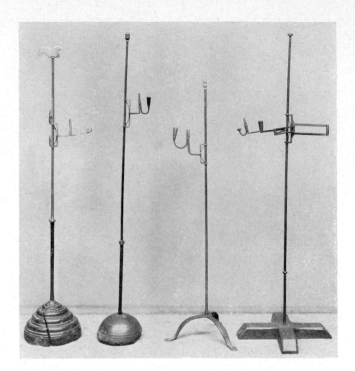

(A) Floor standard rushlight holders of wrought iron with spring adjustable clips and candlesticks. Nrs 2 and 4 measure 4 ft 8 in. in height. 1715–1740.

(B) A mid-eighteenth century brass candlestick flanked by earlier Georgian specimens in gunmetal. *All Victoria and Albert Museum.*

PLATE 60

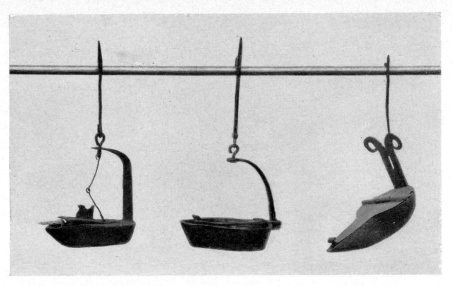

(A) Single valve crusies fitted with lids and wick holders, sometimes known as 'betty lamps'. *Science Museum, London.*

(B) Mid-eighteenth century circular hall lantern in brass with bells. Height 2 ft 4 in.; diameter 14 in. From Highcliffe Castle, Hants. *Pratt and Sons Ltd.*

(c) Mid-eighteenth century pendant lantern of iron with convex top and domed smoke cowl. Height 19 in.; width 12 in. *Mallett and Son Ltd.*

PLATE 61

(A) Mid-eighteenth century pewter wine measure with volute thumbpiece and *fleur-de-lys* lid attachment. Handle with bulbous tail and inserted strut. Height 5⅓ in.

(B) Tankard with double-domed lid and hollow cast handle with dolphin tail finial. Body encircled with an applied strengthening rib. Marked inside W.E. with hour-glass, the touch of William Edon, Master of the Pewterers' Company 1732 and 1737. *c.* 1720. *Both Victoria and Albert Museum.*

(C) An early Georgian full-skirted pewter flagon with double domed lid, double curved handle and struck with the X crowned mark and pseudo-silver marks.

(D) Early Georgian domestic still such as was used in the still-room for making cordials: copper, heavily tinned inside. *White Hart Hotel, Salisbury.*

PLATE 62

(A) Detail of upper portion of a walnut long-case clock by Richard Peyton with arched dial cut from brass plate, containing moon-phase attachment and calendar aperture.

(B) Detail of upper portion of mahogany long-case clock with brass movement by Edward Clarkson, Stockport. Arch contains indicator for four bell tunes, and moon-phase attachment.

(C) Interior of clock by Joseph Antram, clockmaker to George II, showing engraved back plate and bell mechanism.

(D) Brass-bound mahogany food voider with loose lining of hammered brass, 1750s and later. *All Mallett and Son Ltd.*

PLATE 63

(A) A mid-eighteenth century coppersmith's workshop and retail counter, showing a selection of domestic ware. From an English engraving reproduced in Diderot's Encyclopédie, 1751–3.

(B) A lockmaker's forge of the mid-eighteenth century, showing the iron rods being hammered into lock plates. From an English engraving reproduced in Diderot's Encyclopédie, 1751–3.

PLATE 64

signed on simple geometrical plans, based on the circle, rectangle, polygon or occasionally the triangle (Pl. 39A), the sides being straight or curved. Open vessels were similarly based on circular, oval, square or rectangular designs; the incurved corner was beginning to appear (cf. Pl. 40); the only common applied ornaments were horizontal mouldings, or vertical straps of simple design, often alternately palmate and arched. Engraved ornament was limited, generally to crests, armorials in ornamental surrounds or inscriptions (Pls. 37A, 39A).

During the following decade (1720–30) the gradual tendency to elaborate both shapes and ornaments went on; spouts and handles became more complicated; relief ornament was more frequently employed, in the forms of elaborated straps or of panels, stamped, cast and chased or chiselled (Pl. 37C); engraved ornament became more elaborate (Pl. 40) and was supplemented or replaced by the revived technique of flat-chasing (Pl. 37C), which produces a linear pattern superficially like that of engraving in its effect, but from which it can be distinguished; whereas the engraver's scorper removes the metal from the furrow, the chaser's tools merely depress a furrow in the metal, driving up a ridge on the reverse and smaller ridges on each side of it.

One of the most successful architects, James Gibbs (1684–1754), associated with the baroque and Palladianism, had also travelled on the Continent, and has left in his *Book of Architecture* (1728) some engravings that reflect ideas then current also in goldsmiths' work, particularly of ornamental cartouches to surround engraved coats-of-arms. It was perhaps during this decade that the standard of engraving of inscriptions, armorials and figure-scenes reached its highest peak (cf. Pls. 37C, 38A, 40). Speculation about and research into the problem of Hogarth's position as an engraver of arms on plate have yielded little positive information. It is known that he was apprenticed to learn this trade to Ellis Gamble, who was a retailer rather than a manufacturer in the strict sense, but that he declared his intention of giving up this work in 1720. Hogarth has been suggested as the engraver of the decorative friezes on the Treby punch-bowl (Pl. 38A) and the central roundel of

Fig. 1. Tea-pot, c. 1735.

the Walpole salver (Pl. 40), and has been associated without any real justification with the type of decoration round coats of arms like those illustrated in Pls. 37A and 39A. While there is no reason to suppose that he might not have changed his mind and undertaken just such work at a time when his reputation as an illustrator was still to be made, there is not yet enough evidence, external or stylistic, to warrant anything more than speculation. In short, the identities of the numerous engravers on plate seem to have been lost, though there is some possibility that detailed examination of some of their outstanding works, with reference to the dates and the goldsmiths concerned, may yield some framework from which inferential conclusions could be reached. There is, after all, a great affinity between engraving on copper and on silver, nor is it unreasonable to suppose that the same engravers may have turned to either material as opportunity offered.

At the beginning of the fourth decade (1730–40) there may be observed an almost universal adoption in London of some of the motifs of the international rococo style. The French court was still the most brilliant in Europe, and its members led the fashions throughout Europe. It was in Paris that the search for new and lighter decorative ideas, in keeping with the fanciful and delicate ornaments of Watteau (d. 1721), occupied the minds of many designers. But to three foreigners, Gilles-Marie Oppenort (1672–1742), Thomas Germain (1673–1750) and Justin-Aurèle Meissonier (1675–1750), all of whom had spent several of their formative years in Italy and had witnessed some of the attempts to lighten the heavy symmetry of baroque in the region of Genoa, is due the actual introduction of the light asymmetrical abstractions that came to be known as rococo. It appears that the haphazard and unending variety of forms assumed by rock formations which showed all the capricious irregularities of which nature is capable and can yet result in a harmonious whole, without any repetition of detail, as Ruskin later rediscovered, provided the inspiration for their development of the idea into a man-made style. The French word *rocaille* appears to have given rise to the universal expression rococo. The new ideas were eagerly taken up by decorators in Paris and in other capitals and centres on the Continent, and are principally concerned with lightness and asymmetry, being manifested by the use of rough, rock-like ornament interspersed with C- and S-scrolls. In theory these forms were equally suitable to ornament in three and two dimensions, and could be employed architecturally, notably in the grottoes which were constructed by certain English *dilettanti*, among them Alexander Pope, as well as ornamentally in interiors on a small or large scale. Though there are few fine rococo interiors in England, much use was made of rococo motifs in plate and other useful wares. To the motifs already mentioned were added, in baroque guise, figures from the repertoire of classical mythology, with emphasis on marine subjects, particularly the dolphin and scallop shell. The tea-kettle and stand of about 1727–37 in the Victoria and Albert Museum by Charles Kandler provides an unusually elaborate example.[3] Flat-chasers and engravers became equally accustomed to its use, as may be seen from the arms in Pls. 37B and 39. But in spite of this revolution in ornament, many of the forms of the last decade continued with little or no modification, though the double-scrolled handle became almost universal (cf. Figs. 2 and 7). Nor did the rococo forms of ornament by any means find their way on to all plate; indeed, as at all times, there

[3] Repr., *Mid-Georgian Domestic Silver* (Small Picture Book, No. 28), plate 2.

Fig. 2. Two-handled cup and cover, c. 1735.

was much useful ware made that bore little ornament (Pls. 42A, C, D) or was quite plain, conforming to current fashions only in form. But it must not be supposed that lightness of ornament in every case involved lightness in weight, for some of these graceful vessels are of very thick and solid metal (Pl. 42A).

By the fifth decade (1740–50) the rococo style was well established and some extension of the basic motifs was required. The most notable introduction was *chinoiseries* in relief, not long after Julienne's publication of Watteau's *Oeuvre*; oriental figures, sometimes in the round (Pl. 43E), oriental scenes or flowers were clearly derived, if somewhat fancifully, from the scenes painted on Ming wares or other importations from the East. These Chinese motifs, which are frequently combined with others of European origin, were used by goldsmiths almost as extensively as by furniture-makers and potters. One of the principal features of English plate in the mid-eighteenth century is eclecticism; designers united in a single piece, elements from the rococo style, the most anti-classical of all, with figures of classical deities (Pl. 41); or else introduced oriental motifs into rococo plate, and even in occasional instances

Fig. 3. Tankard, c. 1745.

Fig. 4. Sugar-basin, c. 1730.

Fig. 5. Sugar-basin, c. 1750.

combined all three elements.[4] Further elaborations can be seen in the general outline of many classes of vessels, by the use of undulating lines in the elevation (Fig. 5; Pl. 39B). Whether or not this trend was connected consciously with Hogarth's line of beauty, a serpentine or ogee outline appears in many vessels, which is most simply demonstrated by reference to the development shown in a sugar-basin (Figs. 4 and 5; or Pls. 38B, 39B). Perhaps it was no more than a reflection of the poverty of the rococo vocabulary that some rather impractical and even bizarre shapes were devised for vessels of all kinds from the group of elaborate large covered cups by Paul de Lamerie[5] with handles formed as naturalistic serpents (so very different from the meagre handles of wire twisted into the forms of snakes that may be found on some plate of the reign of Charles II, as well as on French plate contemporary with it) to the class of more common vessels like that already mentioned. Another feature of this decade is the elaborate open-work of pierced scrolls and diaper patterns that produce an appearance of lightness on all forms of baskets, épergnes and on the dish-rings that were to become such a feature of the Dublin silversmiths of the next generation.

The last decade of George II's reign (1750–60) can hardly be characterized as other than a time of transition when some of the features of earlier years overlap some of those which were to disappear before the rapid change from rococo to neo-classicism. While flat-chasing was still employed on rather small panels of imbrication or diaper, embossing with repoussé work was being developed, and in some cases no boundary between the two techniques can be descried. The conception of linear patterns, so strong in the 'twenties and 'thirties, had almost disappeared, and most ornament was of three dimensions. To such an extent was this sculptural interweaving of scrolls and volutes developed that in many vessels there is no straight line to be seen save that at the base, nor any regularly curved portion that is not further animated by shallow troughs and low ridges, curving and recurving in irregular lengths beginning at one motif and ending in a scroll, that invite the eye endlessly to follow them round the vessel and out of sight. Small bases, below bulged and undulating forms which are often elongated in proportion to their width, make many vessels seem poised so precariously that they could be handled only by those with a delicate touch. Of the definable motifs that were embossed, two stand out — flowers and *chinoiseries*; flowers, be they in sprigs, garlands or posies (*cf.* Pl. 39B), are a frequent and delightful theme, treated with more delicacy than those on Restoration plate, and may be compared with those on Chelsea and other porcelains of the period.

Other sources of natural ornament were tapped besides flowers. Branches were introduced into the engraved decoration round a coat-of-arms;

[4] *Cf.* the set of three canisters illustrated in Messrs. Christie's Catalogue of 26th October 1956, lot 156.

[5] See C. J. Jackson, *Illustrated History of English Plate*, 1911, p. 731; Catalogue of the Exhibition of Historic Plate of London, 1951, No. 225; and Catalogue of the Christie Sale of 27th June 1956, lot 124.

elaborately curled leaves in high relief were applied round the surbase of a cup or a tureen. A bird or animal, with heraldic allusion, might be cast and chased to form a finial. Apart from the cow-creamers of Schuppe,[6] there were no animal parallels in silver to the Chelsea tureens in the form of rabbits or birds. But sea-shells, crabs and other crustaceans were modelled, or more probably cast direct from nature, into salts or applied as ornament to other vessels, a fashion reintroduced by Nicholas Sprimont and his associate Paul Crespin in the 'forties.

Throughout these two reigns the names and some dry facts were recorded about all the goldsmiths, whereas almost nothing is known about the engravers and the designers. Numerous books and sheets of designs by many foreign artists were produced, and many are still preserved, for plate of all kinds; in England the list is small and the examples rare.[7] If at one extreme such an elaborate vessel as the Kandler wine-cooler (Pl. 44) is known to have been carefully designed and at the other many simple vessels could be made up without much thought, yet in between lies a great field where designers and modellers must have been required. Both de Lamerie and Kandler were outstanding as craftsmen and innovators, yet it is unlikely that they themselves were sculptors enough to have modelled the original figures from which casts were made for the vessels in Pls. 41 and 44.

Although Rysbrack was employed by Kandler for the massive cistern, one can only speculate about the latter's relationship with Johann Joachim Kaendler, the sculptor employed at Meissen from 1731 onwards, and the many other artists who must have fashioned figures for plate.

Only five London goldsmiths have so far been mentioned, of whom not one was British by birth. Yet comparatively few of those recorded by Sir Charles J. Jackson [8] and Sir Ambrose Heal [9] during this half-century bore foreign names, and most of the plate recorded carries the marks of makers with British names. While some, like Anthony Nelme, Benjamin Pyne, John White, George Wickes, James Gould and Thomas Heming, produced quantities of finely wrought useful plate, and while the standard of workmanship in design and finish was generally high, there is hardly an outstanding piece from among them all that can be compared with the bold and imaginative work of the foreigners. Perhaps we should not count their work as British, yet it was made in London, and much of it was commissioned, and most bought, by Britons.

This period almost coincides with the long and successful working life of Paul de Lamerie,[10] deservedly the most renowned London silversmith of the century. Himself of French parentage, he was apprenticed to another Huguenot, Pierre Platel, in 1705, and entered his mark in 1712. His early works were conventional and of a quality matched by many another maker: it was not until the early 'twenties that he began to develop into the outstanding master who produced the pieces shown here on Pls. 37c, 40 and 41, or could successfully innovate figure-engraving on a large scale (Pl. 38A) or introduce such a wealth of new ideas as are revealed by the Goldsmith's inkstand,[11] his series of large serpent-handled cups or, on a more modest scale, the fish-slice of 1741 (Pl. 43A). His death without a successor in 1751 did not at once put an end to his influence and type of work, for several cake-baskets of the scallop form, with figured handle and dolphin feet which he introduced in the 'forties, were made after his death by Phillips Garden, who had evidently purchased the moulds at the sale of de Lamerie's effects. A representative collection of his work may be seen in the Ashmolean Museum, and many fine individual specimens in the Victoria and Albert Museum and elsewhere.

The Goldsmiths' Company itself, though its affairs were reported to have been in a decline

---

[6] G.B.Hughes, *Country Life*, 7 January 1954, p. 26.
[7] Joan Evans, *Pattern in Western Europe*, Vol. II, p. 95, note 2.
[8] C. J. Jackson, *English Goldsmiths and their Marks*, 2nd ed., 1921 (reprinted 1949).
[9] A.Heal, *The London Goldsmiths: 1200–1800*, 1935, *passim*.

[10] P.A.S.Phillips, *Paul de Lamerie*, 1935; a full account of his life and works.
[11] J.B.Carrington and G.R.Hughes, *The Plate of the Worshipful Company of Goldsmiths*, 1926.

since 1683, seems to have begun to prosper with the rest of the country. Between 1713–14 and 1717–18 the amount of silver assayed showed a slight but irregular rise from just over 50,000 lb. to nearly 53,000 lb.; [12] expressed in other terms, the craft enjoyed an annual turnover of well over £300,000, nearly double the sum granted to build Blenheim Palace for the first Duke of Marlborough and his Duchess. The number of apprentices, who were fined 4s. (the value of an ounce of silver) on being bound for seven years, varied year by year, as did the number of journeymen, who were fined 8s. on admission – whereas the fine paid by a freeman called upon livery was £20. In the year ending on St Dunstan's day 1718, seventy-eight apprentices and forty-four journeymen were admitted; two years later, fifty-four of the former and fifty-five of the latter; in 1725 the total number of apprentices was 433. In 1761 the Company consisted of a Prime Warden and three other Wardens, with ninety-eight assistants and a livery of 198 members. The number of journeymen employed was probably about 2,000.

Two statutes should be briefly mentioned; the first, of 1719, was important because the Old, or Sterling, standard was thereby restored and the New, or Britannia, standard was made optional. The differences between the metals of these two standards is not apparent to the eyes of a layman, but was made distinguishable by the different series of stamped marks. All the makers' marks were at the same time changed to the initials of the first and surname; they were all broken and re-designed according to similar rules as a result of the second statute, which became operative in 1739. As a result of these two acts confusion is often caused by the many different marks used by Assay-masters and makers during this half-century. If London was unquestionably pre-eminent in the craft, with Dublin probably in second place and Edinburgh in third, it is nevertheless interesting to recall that the English assay offices of York, Exeter, Bristol, Chester, Norwich and Newcastle-upon-Tyne are mentioned in that order in the

latter act. York's long-established eminence in the north was being challenged by the silversmiths of Newcastle; of Bristol little is known, while Exeter and Norwich were fast declining. In Sheffield and Birmingham toy-makers were founding the trade that was to give the last-named city its eventual lead over all others in weight of silver and gold assayed.

Many similarities between wares made in such different fabrics as ceramics and silver are constantly to be observed – and some have already been remarked – not only in shapes but also in decorative motifs: tureens, tea-pots, bowls, salt-cellars, sauce-boats, plates, dishes, candlesticks and many other useful wares common to the potter and silversmith show obvious correspondences and a close relationship in their developments. The properties of the precious metals allow greater precision, thinness of material, strength and fineness of finish than do earthenware (whose thick glaze conceals so much detail), stoneware or even porcelain. In all branches of ceramics the potter faces the hazards of the fire and irreparable breakage, but he has the inestimable advantage of colour. In linear patterns the metal-worker was never able to make up for lack of this by his skill in engraving, flat-chasing and embossing, which rely for their effects on reflections, on light and shadow and on contrasts of tone. In modelling and reliefs, however, there is little to choose between the effects of their two skills. It is probable that the goldsmith – working in the more precious material – generally gave the lead to the potter, but this was by no means always the rule. Cow-creamers were produced in both plate and ceramics, as were shells for salt-cellars. On the other hand, a small tea-pot of 1748 by J. Wirgman in the Victoria and Albert Museum [13] seems to have been inspired by examples in salt-glazed stoneware, while taper-sticks in the form of Harlequin figures may have derived their immediate inspiration from their Meissen counterparts, though the human form was at nearly all periods a part of the silversmiths' repertoire.

It is useful to classify objects made of plate into

[12] W.S.Prideaux, *Memorials of the Goldsmiths' Company*, 2 vols., 1896–7, *passim*.

[13] *Mid-Georgian Domestic Silver*, plate 17.

Fig. 6. Mug, *c.* 1720.

Fig. 7. Mug, *c.* 1760.

convenient groups and those selected by Mr C.C. Oman [14] will here be followed: (*a*) the dinner service; (*b*) plate used in the service of wine and beer; (*c*) plate used in the service of tea, etc.; (*d*) lighting appliances; (*e*) miscellaneous plate about the house.

The group of matching vessels understood at the end of the eighteenth century to constitute a dinner service did not exist at Queen Anne's death. Indeed, the only wares remaining from the beginning of her successor's reign are circular plates, chargers (some are of massive size), castors, with slightly curved sides and tops pierced with panels of scrolls (Pl. 42A), small octagonal or oval salts, and flat-ware. An early tureen (*terrine*), that made by de Lamerie in 1723 (Duke of Bedford), foreshadows the *bombé* shape that was later to be freely elaborated, with feet and carrying handles, into one of the most ornate of the rococo vessels. Analogous covered serving-dishes are the low *écuelle*, for vegetables and the *mazarine*, with a pierced strainer, for fish (the fish-slice was a later refinement (Pl. 43A)): it is curious

[14] C.C.Oman, *English Domestic Silver*, 3rd ed., 1949.

that all three names are borrowed from the French. Double-lipped and -handled sauce-boats (Pl. 42B) were introduced, often in pairs, at about the same time, and were later developed in great variety. They were followed by single-lipped boats (Pl. 42C) on bases or on three or four legs, with all manner of fantastically contrived handles. There may be doubt whether such a vessel was intended to be a sauce-boat or a cream-jug; reference to Pls. 42C and 39C suggests that the latter vessel, when of a similar shape, is considerably the smaller.

The épergne was a form of centre-piece for the table introduced in the 'thirties and equipped with detachable baskets; some of the later examples were extremely complex, perhaps with a pagoda in the centre, small and large baskets, as well as castors and sauce-bottles. The baskets themselves, with their elaborately pierced sides, at first had a handle at each end, later a swing handle across the centre. The simple moulded forms of salt-cellar were developed and followed by circular bowls either on legs or on a similar but inverted bowl, plain or with a variety of light ornament, and by shells. Circular or octagonal castors mainly of the types shown in Pls. 42A and D, could be infinitely varied by applied ornament and piercings. They were usually made in pairs, but were as well combined in sets of three with two silver-mounted glass bottles for oil and vinegar on what is termed a Warwick frame (Pl. 42D). Sometimes just the two bottles were provided with a silver frame. Early Georgian mustard-pots are very rare.

Knives were generally pistol-handled (*cf.* those in Pl. 39C), with curved blades of steel for meat and of silver for dessert. The three-pronged fork became established, its Hanoverian, Old English or Onslow handle matching that of the companion spoon.

With the exception of tankards and mugs (Figs. 3, 6, 7), glass seems to have replaced silver as the fabric used for personal drinking-vessels, a trend which may be explained by its cheapness and by the increased consumption of wines and spirits. For communal use a two-handled cup (*cf.* Fig. 2) was no doubt handed round with much the same ceremonies as it is today. Its formal use at corporate dinners, or its value as a race-cup, ensured that it would be given every kind of ornament and modified into many shapes. From a rather squat vessel with plain scrolled handles it was developed into something much more imposing with double-scrolled handles, a high-domed cover surmounted by a large finial (Fig. 2), and considerable weight of metal. Its most remarkable transformations in the hands of Paul de Lamerie have been mentioned above. Silver jugs, similar to that in Fig. 8, but without the cover, were used for beer and other cold drinks. For hot beverages the brandy-warmer, a silver saucepan with a wooden baluster handle, was a common and attractive vessel. On a larger scale the punch-bowl, already distinguished by its unbroken horizontal rim from the monteith, was a large container set out after dinner as illustrated in the scene from the Treby punch-bowl itself (Pl. 38A).

In Pl. 38B is shown some of the silver that might have been found on a merchant's tea-table about 1725. The pear-shaped tea-pot (cf. Fig. 1), on its four-legged stand, with baluster handle and lamp, the fluted bowl, the shaped oval tray with spoons and tongs, the covered jug, the tea-canister, the sugar-bowl with its lid, may cover a period of about twenty years, from 1705 onwards. The more elaborate and much larger tea-kettle, of similar shape to the tea-pot, with a swing handle hinged above the lid, and a more substantial stand with two drop-handles, hardly lasted into the 'twenties. Both vessels were commonly circular or octagonal. During that decade both were superseded; the former by the bullet-shaped tea-pot (Fig. 9), which after the middle of the century developed the 'dropped-bottom' line (cf. Fig. 4) and was raised on a slightly higher foot. It was paralleled by a tea-kettle, smaller than its predecessor, which was frequently given much elaborate ornament. The simple pear-shaped cream-jug of George I's reign was developed into a great variety of shapes, both plain and lavishly decorated. In the accompanying illustrations may be seen some of the equally numerous varieties of tea-canister (Pls. 38B, 39A, B, c) and sugar-basin (Pls. 38B, 39B; Figs. 4, 5). The side-handled coffee-pot and chocolate-pot were displaced by those with an op-

Fig. 8. Jug, c. 1725.

Fig. 9. Tea-pot, c. 1720.

posed handle; the domed cover became lower and moulded, the straight-sided body elongated and pyriform.

The most elaborate form of lighting appliance, the chandelier, is scarcely represented during this period. Its rarity is more than compensated by the abundance of candlesticks, the development of whose form and ornament is reflected in the smaller taper-stick; simple angular and facetted designs gradually gave place to sticks with surface ornament and more complex shapes (Pls. 43c, D, E); the branched candlestick or candelabrum became more common after the middle of the century, and the detachable nozzle was often a later addition. Chambersticks retained a functional simplicity.

Of the miscellaneous plate about the house it is only necessary to mention that the inkstand, or standish as it was then known, was provided with its detachable containers for ink, sand and wafers, a depression for the pen, and often a taper-stick and bell.

Salvers and trays were made in many shapes and sizes, with a variety of moulded rims and ornaments; their open surfaces were especially suited to the work of the flat-chaser and engraver. The two most common outlines are that illustrated in Pl. 40, and later that with a 'pie-crust' moulding Of the several toilet sets that remain, the finest on public exhibition is that by Paul de Lamerie in the Ashmolean Museum; part of the ornament from the lid of one of the jewel caskets is illustrated in Pl. 37c.

Fig. 10. Slightly enlarged detail from an engraving of 1741 by A. and I. Kirk, aged 14 and 13, which shows some of the various skills used in a goldsmith's shop. They are from left to right: *Top row:* filing castings; turning casting on a lathe worked by a treadle and spring rod; hammering spoonbowls into a doming-block; polishing; *second row:* chasing a cup (note the sauce-boat, candlestick and kettle); wire-drawing; *third row:* engraving (note spoons, tea-pot, coffee-pot, tankard, sauce-boat, etc.); filing, small work, etc.; *fourth row:* hammering out sheet of silver. *Ashmolean Museum, Oxford.*

Pottery, Porcelain and Glass

R. J. CHARLESTON

Delftware

The making of tin-glazed earthenware was practised in England already in the sixteenth century, and by the second half of the seventeenth century there were a number of factories at work, both in the London area and in Bristol and the neighbouring Brislington. During the eighteenth century new factories sprang up (notably in Liverpool, where by the end of our period a dozen or so were active), whilst a few of the older-established works were forced to close down. In the London area there were manufactures near the Hermitage Dock, Wapping (until at least 1724); at Southwark, where one pottery in the parish of St Olave's and St John's continued working until late in the eighteenth century, whilst a second, in the parish of St Saviour's, appears to have closed down before the middle of the century; at Lambeth, where two factories were at work for the greater part of our period; and at Vauxhall. The Brislington pottery had disappeared by 1750, but there were three factories at work in Bristol itself – the Temple pottery, St Mary Redcliffe's and Limekiln Lane, of which the last-named had ceased production in 1754. Delftware was also manufactured at Wincanton, in Somerset (Pl. 46A). Apart from the English potteries, there were more or less short-lived enterprises in Glasgow, Dublin and Limerick.

The late seventeenth century had seen the supercession of earlier types of delftware by pottery almost exclusively inspired by Chinese porcelain, of which very large quantities were imported at the time. Apart from the blue-and-white colour-scheme, which, from the second quarter of the century, had symbolized the ascendancy of oriental wares, a bright polychromy of red, blue, green and yellow mimicked the enamelled wares of the late Ming and K'ang Hsi (1662–1722) periods. In this palette were painted not only more or less direct copies of Chinese designs and more fanciful *chinoiseries*, but boldly brushed-in patterns of purely European inspiration, such as a windmill, a fish (Fig. 1), a swan swimming or a cock in a landscape. In the eighteenth century, as in the seventeenth, delftware was a useful outlet for the expression of political sentiment (Pl. 45A). Towards 1750 a gradual change comes over the colours used by the English delftware painters; they grow paler and softer, and in general conform to the changed colour-sense characteristic of the rococo, as opposed to the baroque, movement in art. About the same time, a form of plate characterized by a low foot-rim, taken over from imported Chinese porcelain, was universally adopted (Pls. 46A, B; Fig. 2). This plate is the commonest of all forms in delftware during our period, but the first half of the century saw the evolution of many shapes unknown in the seventeenth century, catering for most domestic needs. For drinkers of strong drinks there were punch-bowls (Pl. 45C), tankards (sometimes with glass bases), monteiths, wine-labels and puzzle-jugs (Pl. 46C). For tea-drinkers, despite the unsuitable nature of the material, which did not stand up well to sudden changes of temperature, there were tea-cups and saucers, tea-pots, sugar-bowls, cream-

Fig. 1. Plate of blue-painted delftware, Bristol, c. 1730.

jugs and tea-trays (Pl. 45B); for those who favoured coffee, coffee-cups and pots. For the service of the dinner-table, apart from the plates and dishes, there were sauce-boats, tureens, and even gravy-argyles; and in apartments other than the dining-room there were bowls with perforated tops to hold flowers; rectangular 'bricks' similarly pierced for the same purpose, or in some instances adapted as inkstands, with a central large hole for the ink-well; and candlesticks copied from silver models. For the sick-room or nursery there was the food-warmer, in which the food was kept hot by a small lamp, the cover being fitted with a candle-holder (Pl. 46D); whilst in the bedrooms the exiguous toilet of the eighteenth century was catered for by a small basin and a water-bottle scarcely larger than a modern carafe.

The bold, simple forms of decoration of the

Fig. 2. Cross-section of plate common to the English delftware factories from c. 1725–30 onwards.

early eighteenth century gave way during its second quarter to a softer and more elegant style better attuned to the changing taste of the period. Ladies and gentlemen in contemporary costume stroll through European landscapes (Pl. 46c), and delicate *chinoiserie* scenes evoke some of the qualities of space and atmosphere which are characteristic of true Chinese painting, and which in England may look forward, as one authority has pointed out, to the achievements of the English School of water-colourists (Pl. 45c). On a different plane were the many designs, painted with far less sophistication, which reproduced naïve *chinoiseries*, versions of Chinese porcelain bird- and flower-painting, or simply rather artless European subjects of figures or flowers (Pl. 46A, B, D).

The English delftware potters of the eighteenth century were responsible for a number of innovations, not all of which were entirely original. The powdered grounds of Chinese porcelain were copied in cobalt-blue and manganese-purple (Pl. 46A), whilst a sponge charged with colour was often used to dab in the foliage of trees. One technique which in the eighteenth century was almost exclusive to England was the use, on a glaze tinged bluish or greenish, of designs drawn in opaque-white (*bianco-sopra-bianco*), a method of decoration which had its technical roots in the Italian *maiolica* of the Renaissance, but which may have owed its immediate inspiration to the incised designs on some Chinese porcelain (Pl. 46B). The use of over-glaze enamelling and gilding on a tin-glaze, so widely familiar in the contemporary faïence of the Continent, is extremely rare in England, and is found only on some Liverpool delftware. Uncommon too, although characteristically English, was the employment of transfer-printing, found occasionally on Liverpool (and Irish) pieces.

Lead-glazed earthenware

English lead-glazed pottery of the early Georgian period is characterized by a striving after refinement. Although in many parts of the country 'slipwares' of the types described in *The Stuart Period* continued to be made, their use was confined to the humbler orders of society. Meanwhile, in North Staffordshire, where the most interesting slipwares of the seventeenth century had been made, great changes were afoot. Although pieces made in the old techniques certainly survived into the period under discussion, even they reveal in many instances an elegance not distinguishable in the earlier wares (Pl. 48A). This tendency can be traced to two causes – the growing awareness of the qualities of imported Chinese porcelain (with which was included the unglazed red stoneware of Yi-hsing), and the memory of the Elers brothers. The Elers brothers had moved in the last decade of the seventeenth century from London to Bradwell Wood, and had there produced teapots, mugs and so forth in imitation of Yi-hsing stoneware. These wares were fastidiously potted and neatly decorated with stamped relief designs in the general manner of the Chinese originals. The quality and finish of this pottery must have made a most forcible impression on the contemporary Staffordshire makers, and borne in on them the realization that such things were possible for them too. The unglazed redwares continued to

be made throughout the eighteenth century (Pl. 47B), but the trend away from the more primitive wares of the past is to be more clearly seen in other forms of pottery, and in other techniques.

Perhaps the earliest variant is a type of ware which still employs the brown-and-white colour-scheme of slipware, but which also uses the newer technique of decoration by means of reliefs stamped from pads of white clay and applied to the brown body of the piece (Pl. 48B). This type of pottery has traditionally been attributed to John Astbury (1686–1743), but it was certainly also made by Thomas Whieldon (1719–1795), at Fenton Low, and probably by other potters too. Astbury is also credited by tradition with two innovations which were of crucial importance at this stage of the industry. These were the use of Devonshire white clay as a surface-wash to darker clays; and the introduction of calcined flint into the body of wares, to make them whiter and lighter. The latter innovation is alternatively attributed to Thomas Heath, of Lane Delph, Staffs; but the whiteness of calcined flint was at this period familiar in the glass industry, and would naturally recommend itself as a possible ingredient to potters looking for materials in which to imitate the whiteness of porcelain. This practice seems to have been introduced during the 1720's, and although the use of calcined flint was more immediately appreciated in the manufacture of white salt-glazed stoneware (see p. 654 below), its use in earthenware bodies made possible the development of the coloured lead-glazes discussed below. The 'Astbury–Whieldon' phase of the industry's development is perhaps best illustrated by the group of pieces shown in Pl. 48c. Here are the colour contrasts familiar from the earlier wares – the white of handle and spout against the warm brown or buff of the body – accompanied by one or two technical innovations. Instead of the stamped relief-decoration of the 'Astbury' wares (cf. Pl. 48B), the ornament was obtained by 'luting' to the surface of the pot previously moulded relief-motives, and by connecting these with 'stems' formed of threads of clay rolled out thin between the hands. This whole process was known as 'sprigging'. A pointer to things to come is the use of dabs of colour to enliven the leaves and flowers of the sprigged decoration. The use of metallic oxides to produce colours is familiar in England from medieval times, but it here makes its first appearance in Staffordshire. Coloured decoration had to await a further technical improvement before it could be used to its greatest advantage. This improvement consisted in the substitution of liquid-glazing for the older method of dusting with a powdered sulphide of lead (galena). By the newer technique, the piece, fired once to the 'biscuit' condition, was dipped into a mixture of powdered glaze and water, which it soaked up evenly. This smooth glaze, when laid on the improved white body, was a perfect medium for the development of decoration by means of colouring oxides. Yellow, green, purplish-brown, and particularly a slate-blue and -grey, were used in patches laid on without any particular pattern. At their best, particularly when the grey is used with one or two other colours, the pieces so decorated have a softness and charm peculiarly their own: sometimes, however, as when the yellow and green are used in an 'egg-and-spinach' combination, the effects are far less pleasing. Perhaps the most charming of all pieces made in this style are the artless figures, or 'image-toys', of the 'Astbury–Whieldon' phase. These, although perhaps inspired ultimately by porcelain, are, with some exceptions, original in conception and execution. Such are the little figures of seated musicians, or of men and women on horseback (Pl. 47D), or the grotesque adaptation of the classical *spinario* taking a thorn out of his foot, entirely changed in character by the substitution of an enormous lolling head. On the earlier members of this family some details are picked out in clays of contrasting colours, in addition to the coloured glazes, and these form a bridge between the figures of the 'Astbury–Whieldon' class, and those of the 'Astbury' group, in which all the colour contrasts are obtained solely by the use of clays of different tones.

Other wares made by the potters of this period include a pottery with a dense black glaze, and 'agate-ware'. The former, often called 'Jackfield' pottery (from the place of that name in Shropshire), was certainly also made in Staffordshire and

at Newcastle. The pieces with a dense black glaze and relief decoration are probably to be attributed to Staffordshire, whereas the true Jackfield wares are usually smooth of surface, browner in colour, and decorated with unfired painting or gilding. They are usually later in date (third quarter of the eighteenth century), and there can be no doubt that the art of making this pottery was transplanted there from Staffordshire. 'Agate-ware' was made by mixing together dark and light clays (and frequently also a white clay stained blue with cobalt), to produce a marbled effect. This material would tolerate a minimum of handling, and could not therefore be used in thrown shapes, teapots and the like being made by pressing the clay into two-part moulds (Pl. 47c). This 'true' agate-ware was at a later date imitated by means of a marbled surface-wash imparted to a plain clay base.

The technical improvements so far described have all been in the direction of refining the materials of body and glaze. One further, and vital, innovation affected the formation of the pot itself. This was the introduction of the plaster-of-Paris mould. The use of moulds as a speedy way of duplicating shapes or decoration had already been appreciated by the makers of the earlier slipwares. In this phase, a convex mould with an incised design was prepared in clay and fired hard. On this a slab of red clay was pressed, producing a hollow dish with an outline pattern in relief. Into the cells so formed a white slip was poured, thus producing a design in white on a dark ground, with a minimum expenditure of time and skill. These dishes continued to be made until about the middle of the eighteenth century, but in the meantime the practice of moulding had been greatly extended. The plates with dappled glazes, for instance, often have borders moulded in the form of basket-work and the like (Pl. 47A): these were formed by pressing a slab of clay down on a plate-shaped mould which had this design on its upper surface and which was fixed to the head of the wheel. The plate was then 'thrown' in the normal way, the back and foot being profiled as desired. The crowning innovation in this movement towards labour-saving, however, was the plaster mould. First a master-mould was prepared in alabaster or the like, in the exact semblance of the body of the finished pot. From it a cast was taken, and from the cast a clay 'block' was pressed. This was fired to stoneware hardness, to become the working model, and from it the plaster moulds were pulled. These moulds were made up in two or more sections, the design being in negative on the inside of the sections. Into the composite mould so formed, the clay was poured as a thin slip. The water was absorbed by the porous plaster, leaving a thin film of clay adhering to the inside of the mould. When this skin was of the desired thickness and the clay was sufficiently dry, the mould was taken apart, leaving the pot ready for the next stages of manufacture, with the decoration sharply defined on its surface.

Although used to a far great extent by the stoneware potters, this technique was also employed at the end of our period to produce relief-decorated hollow-wares with colour-glazes. Some of the best of these are amongst the earliest productions of Josiah Wedgwood when working on his own account. His famous 'cauliflower' and 'pineapple' wares (teapots and so forth made in those forms), with their strong green and yellow glazes, were produced by this technique.

Salt-glazed stoneware

When in 1693 John Dwight brought his famous lawsuit in protection of his patent rights, he sued (besides the Elers brothers) potters in London, Nottingham and Staffordshire. Stoneware continued to be made in the London area in the eighteenth century, not only at Dwight's Fulham factory after his death, but also at Southwark, Lambeth Marsh and Mortlake. Some white stoneware was undoubtedly made, presumably in styles more or less resembling those in vogue in Staffordshire (see p. 654 below), but the majority must have been brown wares of a more or less utilitarian character. The most ambitious of them were large mugs decorated with drinking- or hunting-scenes in relief (Pl. 49B), or smaller isolated motifs, such as a head of Queen Anne, trees, rosettes and the like, of a sort familiar from the Fulham stoneware of the previous century. These mugs were usually of a buff body, the upper half being coloured a rich brown by means of a ferruginous wash applied before the piece was fired. They were frequently made to order for a particular publican, whose name is then found incised in the clay of the body.

Of a similar brown colour was the stoneware made at Nottingham throughout the eighteenth century. This pottery, however, far surpassed that made in the London area by dint of its lustrous surface, the fineness of its potting, and the fresh style of decoration with which it was most often embellished. Apart from repetitive designs made by stamping or rouletting, this ornamentation often included flower-sprays and the like freely incised when the clay was soft (Pl. 49A). A rarer, but charming, technique of decoration was the use of a 'resist', whereby a design was protected from the surface wash, and therefore stood out in a lighter tone on the warm brown ground. Reliefs were also used, but far more sparingly than in either London or Staffordshire, and a not particularly attractive application of shreds of clay, giving bands of ornament resembling 'rough-cast' (particularly favoured on the joke jugs made in the form of a bear, where the shreds of clay simulated fur). A very similar stoneware was produced at Crich, in Derbyshire.

Of far greater consequence than any of the wares so far dealt with, however, was the stoneware made in Staffordshire. Amongst the defendants in Dwight's lawsuit had been members of the Wedgwood family, and it is possibly to the son of one of them, 'Dr' Thomas Wedgwood of Burslem, that were due the great improvements which took place in the manufacture of salt-glazed stoneware in the eighteenth century. The wares complained of by Dwight were probably mugs of a buffish stoneware, the upper parts dipped in a brown wash, technically very like the Fulham mugs already described; and the earliest 'white' Staffordshire stonewares were probably only more or less purified varieties of this buffish body. The use of imported West Country clay and calcined flint, however, affected the manufacture of salt-glazed stoneware no less than that of lead-glazed earthenware, many of the potters being in fact

Fig. 3. Bell in the form of a woman, salt-glazed stoneware, Staffordshire, c. 1740. Ht. 5¾ in.

makers of both. Comparable in technique and quality with the 'Astbury–Whieldon' pottery decorated by means of contrasting clay-colours (see p. 651 above and Pl. 48c) was a type of stoneware traditionally and plausibly associated with the younger 'Dr' Thomas Wedgwood. This consisted of a drab-coloured body decorated with neat reliefs in contrasting white, the rusticated spout and 'crabstock' handle being often also made in the same white clay. The white reliefs, which mingled wyverns and figures of Bacchus with delicate scroll-work in the general manner of the 'Bérain' style, were sometimes also ephemerally gilt by an unfired process (Pl. 49c). Thomas Wedgwood died in 1737, and the style of these wares is consistent with this date. Possibly slightly later than these wares, but overlapping them chronologically, was the pure white stoneware made of the improved body incorporating white clay and

calcined flint. The appearance, on some of the pieces made in this material, of reliefs commemorating the capture of Portobello in 1739 (Pl. 50D), suggests that it was perfected during the 1730's; although isolated examples are known with dates as early as 1720. The earliest of the mature white stonewares are, like the contemporary earthenwares of the 'Astbury–Whieldon' phase, decorated by applied moulded reliefs and 'sprigging' (sometimes gilt or picked out with blue). The greatest development, however, took place on the introduction of the techniques of moulding described above (pp. 652-3). These were enthusiastically taken up by the stoneware-potters, perhaps because their process, involving no glaze-dipping, favoured the making of very thin-walled vessels. The earliest moulded pieces are 'open' shapes made by pressing a sheet of clay into a metal or alabaster mould, and little pickle- and spoon-trays were made by this means with decoration of a beautiful sharpness of definition. Of much greater significance, however, was the adoption of slip-casting in plaster-of-Paris moulds (see above, p. 652). From about 1745 onwards the Staffordshire potters poured out an unceasing stream of fine hollowwares made in this way – teapots, coffee-pots, cups, sauce-boats, tureens, tea-caddies, basins and many more. These are usually remarkable, not only for their fineness, but also for the force and humour of the relief decorations. These were often by no means 'correct' or in any known style, being frequently a curious hotch-potch of motifs drawn from different sources – chinoiseries, European figures, tree- and plant-forms, shells, heraldic animals and so forth, combined in a naïve but often effective way. This unconventionality often extended to the form of the vessel itself (Pl. 50A). The authors of this very English manner were the men who made the original blocks from which the plaster moulds were ultimately taken. Prominent among them were members of the Wood family, notably Aaron Wood (1717–85), to whom have been attributed also the vigorous and amusing saltglaze 'Pew Groups', modelled in the round and representing a man and woman courting, a pair of musicians, etc. (and cf. Fig. 3). These far surpass in originality and power the numerous contemporary small figures made in two-part moulds and representing the Chinese deity Shou Lao or such historical figures as Doctor Sacheverell and Maria Theresa. These figures are often embellished with touches of cobalt-blue, a pigment which is also used to enliven the small figures of cats moulded in brown-and-white 'agate-ware' (see p. 652 above), and the group of so-called 'scratch-blue' wares. These comprise mugs (Pl. 50B), loving-cups and jugs, with incised decoration into which the cobalt pigment was rubbed before firing. The wares of this class are frequently dated, the years ranging between 1748 and 1776. Their shapes differ from those of most of the types of salt-glazed stoneware hitherto described, and it is possible that they were made in separate factories. Much, however, remains to be learned about them. It is certain, for example, that Whieldon made 'scratch-blue' wares, although no intact example has been certainly identified.

This mild flirtation with colour, however, was of little significance beside a style of polychrome ornamentation which was both incomparably more effective and far more widely practised. This consisted of painting the surface of the finished pot with enamel pigments which had to be subsequently fired in a 'muffle' kiln. A simple and restricted form of enamelling was being carried out on 'Elers' and other stoneware in the early years of the eighteenth century, and it is possible that the process was exploited continuously in Staffordshire from then onwards. The course of its development in the second quarter of the eighteenth century is obscure, but in its mature manifestations Staffordshire enamel-painting is clearly recognizable. It is marked by a violent palette which included turquoise-blue and leaf-green, pink, purple, red and yellow. These clamorous colours were used to embellish scenes derived from Boucher, *chinoiseries*, flower-sprays with great pink roses, landscapes (Pl. 50A), topical motives (such as portraits of the Young Pretender) and so on. In these wares the ambitions of the Staffordshire potters to rival porcelain were at last realized, and it may well have been to a piece of enamelled salt-glazed stoneware that the poetaster referred when he wrote:

To please the noble dame, the courtly Squire
Produced a Tea Pot made in Staffordshire.
So Venus looked, and with such longing eyes
When Paris first produced the golden prize.
'Such works as this', she cries, 'can England do?
It equals Dresden, and excels St Cloud.' [1]

Porcelain

Chinese porcelain, which in the Middle Ages and the sixteenth century had been treated much as a precious stone and set in silver mounts, began to enter Europe in increasing quantities during the seventeenth century. Whereas Charles I had been content to acquire single pieces of it, Louis XIV, at the end of the century, had ordered a whole service, consisting of hundreds of (presumably matching) pieces. Before Louis' death, however, France, already had two factories of her own, making 'soft-paste' porcelain – that is, a porcelain made essentially of white clay compounded with ground glass, as opposed to the true 'hard-paste' porcelain of oriental type, made of china-clay and china-stone fused at a far higher temperature. These French factories were Rouen (making porcelain from 1673 until probably 1696) and Saint-Cloud, which received its letters patent in 1702. Very little porcelain was made at Rouen, and until the foundation of the Meissen factory in 1709, St Cloud was the only porcelain manufacture in Europe. Its fame long survived its effectual eclipse by Meissen, as the verse quoted above shows. In England, in the early part of the eighteenth century, Saint-Cloud porcelain was still sought after. Lady Mary Wortley Montagu, writing to the Countess of Mar in June, 1721, says: 'My little commission is hardly worth speaking of; if you have not already laid out that small sum in St Cloud ware, I had rather have it in plain lutestring of any colour.' By this date, however, Meissen had long since taken the lead as Europe's foremost manufacture. Not only was its porcelain true 'hard-paste', but its artists, both modellers and painters, were evolving a truly European and original style which was destined to become the model for all the factories which succeeded it. At the same time, however, Meissen was obliged in

[1] Sir Charles Hanbury-Williams, *Isabella* (1740).

many things to copy closely the oriental wares which were, when all was said and done, the popular criterion of what porcelain should be. When the English factories were started, they found themselves bound by the same considerations, and were constrained to follow the models supplied by the Far East and by Meissen. The first of these factories were Chelsea (in production by 1745 at latest), Bow (perhaps started in 1744, certainly by 1748) and Bristol (founded in 1749 and transferred to Worcester by 1752). The Derby factory was in production by 1750, and a manufacture was founded about the same time at Longton Hall, in Staffordshire. All these factories made 'soft-paste' porcelain, but two of them used bodies which differed from those evolved in France. Bow used the ashes of calcined bones, a strengthening element in the paste which was subsequently taken up at Chelsea and Derby, and which ultimately became the distinguishing feature of a specifically English type of porcelain – the 'bone-china' of the nineteenth century factories. The Bristol–Worcester concern added to its paste an admixture of soapstone (steatite), which produced a body better able than the normal soft-pastes to resist sudden changes of temperature. This was an obvious advantage in the production of tea- and coffee-wares, and a writer of 1763 already realised this clearly when he wrote: 'I have seen porcelain of all the manufactures in Europe. Those of Dresden in Poland, and Chantillon (sc. Chantilly) in France, are well known for their elegance and beauty: with these I may class our own of Chelsea, which is scarce inferior to any of the others; but these are calculated rather for ornament than use, and if they were equally useful with the Oriental China, they could yet be used but by few, because they are sold at high prices. We have indeed, here, many other manufactories of porcelain which are sold at a cheaper rate than any that is imported; but, except the Worcester, they all wear brown, and are subject to crack, especially the glazing, by boiling water: the Worcester has a good body, scarce inferior to that of Eastern China, it is equally tough, and its glazing never cracks or scales off.' [2] Soap-

stone porcelain of the Worcester type was made later also at Liverpool.

Of all the English factories, Chelsea, as the above quotation suggests, was held in the highest esteem, then as now. Apart from the beauty of its white paste and glaze, which have a quality all their own, its painters and modellers were of the highest class, and its manager a man of originality as well as of taste. Although Japanese designs were freely copied (sometimes perhaps from the Meissen copies!), and sometimes Chinese *famille rose* patterns, in a palette wholly unknown to that class of porcelain; and although the factory's first European flower- and figure-subjects (Pl. 52c) were closely derived from Meissen, it also made porcelain in styles entirely its own (Pl. 52D). The proprietor and manager, Nicholas Sprimont, was a silversmith by training, and a number of early Chelsea designs were such as might equally well have been executed in silver (and some were): in this, the factory shared a source of inspiration with Meissen, without in any way being dependent on it. To the naturalistic flowers which evolved at Meissen from the more formal European flowers in the manner of Klinger (cf. Pl. 52c), Chelsea added a decoration of large-scale flowers and plants derived from actual botanical examples (known by contemporaries as 'Sir Hans Sloane's Plants'). Tureens in the form of animals, birds or vegetables are a commonplace in the porcelain and faience of the eighteenth century, but none excel in humour of conception or beauty of execution the tureens made at Chelsea (Pl. 53B). Lastly, the Chelsea factory produced innumerable small *bibelots* or 'toys' which have no equal in the work of any other manufacture. These, mainly scent-bottles (Fig. 4), *étuis*, seal-hafts, patch-boxes and *bonbonnières*, seem to have been made pre-eminently as gifts, witty tokens in the elaborate game of eighteenth century love-making. As such, their subjects are slily chosen. Cupid as kettle-drummer plays on a pair of breasts; minute *amorini* work away at a scent-flask made in the form of a forge of hearts; or the ubiquitous Cupid, seated on a pedestal, holds a globe inscribed JE TIENS LE MONDE, and so forms a haft for a carnelian intaglio inscribed FIDELLE. These little trifles frequently

[2] *Annual Register*, 1763, p. 104.

bear such inscriptions, often in amusingly mis-spelled French – JE VOUS COFFRE (for 'l'offre') or JE LE 'N PORTERAI.

The Bow factory, less accomplished, neverthe-less produced porcelain which at its best is of high quality (Pl. 53C). Apart from its numerous copies and adaptations of Japanese 'Kakiemon' designs (Pl. 52B), it evolved a charming, characteristic palette of its own, and a style of soft flower-paint-ing which is peculiar to it and very pleasing (Pl. 52A). Beyond this, it takes the credit for being the first English factory to introduce over-glaze print-ing into its decorative repertoire, although this process only developed fully at the Worcester fac-tory (Pl. 53D). The obvious advantages of this process in the quick production of repetitive de-signs was quickly realized, and transfer-printing became common for the decoration of Liverpool porcelain and cream-coloured earthenware of all sorts during the third quarter of the century. The Derby factory was more remarkable for its figures (see below, p. 658) than for its table-wares, whilst the Longton Hall factory, although capable of charming and individual work (Pl. 53A), was too short-lived, and on the whole too dependent on Chelsea and other styles, to encompass any very notable achievements.

By a sequence of historical accidents, European porcelain in the eighteenth century was more than a mere material in which to make pleasing and convenient table-wares. It had been the custom in Germany, from as early as the fifteenth century, to deck out the tables at banquets with allegorical and symbolic scenes, the figures and properties of which were modelled in wax or in sugar confec-tionery. This vogue continued throughout the sixteenth and seventeenth centuries, and survived well into the eighteenth. It was therefore almost inevitable that an attempt should be made to sup-ply these adjuncts of the table in the same material as that used for the table-wares. This natural im-pulse was brought to its full realization mainly by the genius of one man, the modeller J.J. Kaendler, who from 1731 onwards exercised an ever-grow-ing influence at the Meissen factory. The develop-ment of porcelain figure-making, both technically and artistically, was extraordinarily rapid. From

Fig. 4. Scent-bottle in the form of a lady dancing, porcelain mounted in gold, Chelsea, *c.* 1755. Ht. 4 in. *Schreiber Collection, Victoria and Albert Museum.*

the small stiff and doll-like early figures on the one hand, and the slightly later large effigies of ani-mals, saints and so forth on the other, there was during the 1730's a swift improvement in the modelling of smaller figures suitable for table de-coration. By the time the English factories came on the scene, in the 1740's, there were innumer-able Meissen models available for copying, and it is known that Sir Charles Hanbury-Williams, who had been English Ambassador at Dresden, in 1751 lent pieces of Meissen porcelain to the Chel-sea factory for this purpose. It is certain that a number of the Chelsea models of the 'red-anchor' period (about 1755) are direct imitations of Meis-sen prototypes. By 1754 the Chelsea factory was able to insert in the *Public Advertiser* a notice: 'To be sold by Auction. ... The large, valuable, and entire Stock of the CHELSEA PORCELAINE, brought from the Manufactory there and the

Warehouse in Pall-Mall; consisting of Epargnes and Services for Deserts, beautiful Groups of Figures, etc. ...'

In 1748 Sir Charles Hanbury-Williams had drawn up a list of 'Figures to adorn the Middle of the Desert', in which different types of figures were systematically set out. The first fifty-four items were of a pastoral character, the next thirty-four had to do with hunting, the next four with everyday occupations; then came thirty-two figures of an allegorical character, followed by ten of foreign types. English figures very largely reflect these groupings, and a study of the Chelsea *Catalogues* of 1755 and 1756 shows how frequently figures within the different groups were lotted up together. Amongst the commonest types were 'abstractions' of all sorts – the *Continents*, the *Elements*, the *Senses*, the *Seasons* (Pl. 51c) and so on, but Chelsea in particular evolved a beautiful series, partly original, partly copied from Meissen, in which figures of everyday life were portrayed (Pl. 51B). Mythological (Pl. 51D) and allegorical figures were common, whilst characters from the Italian comedy and representations of foreign peoples (Pl. 51A) appealed to the contemporary taste for the exotic. The final result, when from the store of figures available a grand assemblage was laid out, is brilliantly brought before our eyes by Horace Walpole in an essay written for *The World* of 8 February 1753:

'Jellies, biscuits, sugar-plumbs, and creams have long given way to harlequins, gondoliers, Turks, Chinese, and shepherdesses of Saxon China. But these, unconnected and only seeming to wander among groves of curled paper and silk flowers, were soon discovered to be too insipid and unmeaning. By degrees whole meadows of cattle, of the same brittle materials, spread themselves over the whole table; cottages rose in sugar, and temples in barley-sugar; pigmy Neptunes in cars of cockle-shells (Pl. 51D) triumphed over oceans of looking glass or seas of silver tissue, and at length the whole system of Ovid's metamorphosis succeeded to all the transformations which Chloe and other great professors had introduced into the science of hieroglyphic eating. Confectioners found their trade moulder away, while toymen and china-shops were the only fashionable purveyors of the last stage of polite entertainments. Women of the first quality came home from Chenevix's laden with dolls and babies, not for their children, but their housekeeper. At last even these puerile puppet-shows are sinking into disuse, and more manly ways of concluding our repasts are stablished. Gigantic figures succeed to pigmies; and if the present taste continues, Rysbrack, and other neglected statuaries, who might have adorned Grecian salons, though not Grecian deserts, may come into vogue.'

Glass

English glass in the eighteenth century took a course of its own which marked it out from that of the rest of Europe. The invention of lead-glass in 1675 had resulted, by the end of the seventeenth century, in a heavy glass 'metal' with a high degree of light-refraction, brought about by the increasing use of lead oxide in the composition. This glass, although brilliant, was often also dark in tone, probably as a result of excessive 'de-colourizing'. The new English 'crystal' was both heavier in substance than the Venetian 'cristallo' which had been the universal clear metal of seventeenth century European glass-making, and took longer to cool while it was being worked. The light and fantastic touches which were both the effect and the inspiration of Venetian glass-making *legerdemain* were inappropriate to this more ponderous and glutinous substance. Although many tricks of Venetian ornamentation – frilled and pincered open-work stems and finials and the like – survived in the repertory of English glass-making, they were at first used only for elaborate 'bespoke' work, and finally became entirely subordinated to the plain and monumental style in which lead-glass finally found its true soul. This was the period of the great 'balusters', in the last years of the seventeenth and the opening years of the eighteenth centuries, when the thick, dark, yet brilliant, glass was ponderously wrought into goblets and wine-glasses with plain straight-sided bowls, deeply 'folded' feet, and solid stems compiled of various knops and baluster-shaped elements.

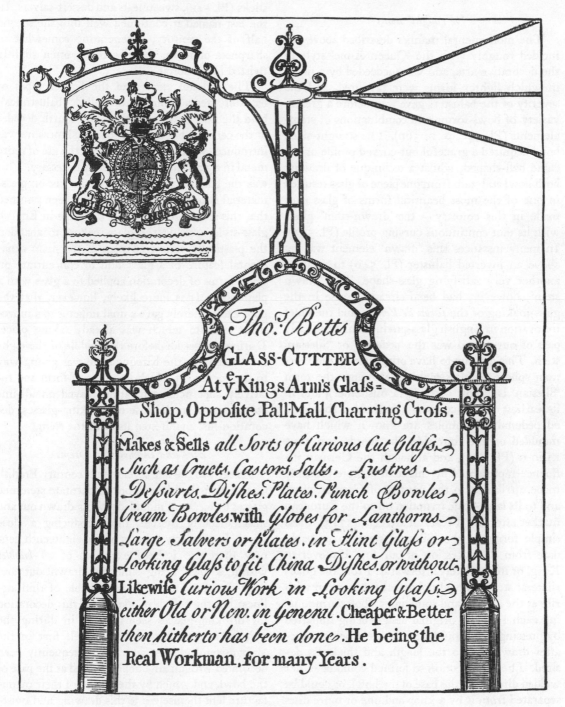

Tho: Betts
GLASS-CUTTER
At y.e Kings Arm's Glass=
Shop. Opposite Pall-Mall. Charring Cross.

Makes & Sells *all Sorts of Curious Cut Glass.*
Such as Cruets. Castors. Salts. Lustres
Desarts. Dishes. Plates. Punch Bowles
Cream Bowles with *Globes for Lanthorns*
Large Salvers or plates. in Flint Glass or
Looking Glass to fit China Dishes. or without.
Likewise *Curious Work in Looking Glass.*
either Old or New. in General. Cheaper & Better
then hitherto has been done. He being the
Real Workman. for many Years.

Fig. 5. Trade card of Thomas Betts, London, about 1740–50.

659

'Wrought' stems

The monumental manner described above co-incided roughly with the 'Queen Anne' style in the decorative arts, and was succeeded by a phase in which lighter forms were favoured, and the severity of the balusters gave way before a greater variety of bowl-forms and combinations of stem-elements (Pl. 54C, D, F; 56D). The straight-sided bowl acquired a graceful out-curved profile or became bell-shaped, whilst a technique of drawing both bowl and stem from one piece of glass resulted in one of the most beautiful forms of glass ever made in this country – the 'drawn-stem' glass, with its taut continuous curving profile (Pl. 55A). In many instances this 'drawn' element was set above an inverted baluster (Pl. 54D) to produce another very satisfying glass-shape. The 'drawn stem', however, had been already in use in the glass-making of the *façon de Venise*, and the chief innovation in English glass-production in the early part of our period was the 'pedestal' or 'Silesian' stem. This appears to have originated in the German sphere of glass-making (although the term 'Silesian' is almost certainly a misnomer), and in its earliest form occurs as a four-sided shouldered pedestal. Examples are known which have moulded on the four sides the words GOD SAVE KING G (Pl. 55C), and although the German influence represented by this stem is more probably to be attributed to the prestige of German glass, and to its large-scale irruption on to the European market after the Treaty of Utrecht (1713), these simple forms of the 'Silesian' stem do probably date from the accession of our first Hanoverian King, or immediately afterwards. From the quadrilateral stem evolved polygonal types, often with ribs at the angles (and sometimes a boss surmounting each rib), the original design being imparted by pressing in a mould, and the stem being thereafter drawn out to the length and thickness desired. The stem-section so formed could be either welded directly to the base of the bowl, or could be separated from it by a knop and one or more discs of glass. Towards the middle of the century this stem-form began to fall out of use for wine-glasses and to be taken up in other forms, notably candle-sticks (Pl. 54E), sweetmeats and dessert-salvers. In the last-named it continued well into the second half of the century, degenerating somewhat in sharpness of form, the ribs being often slightly twisted into a spiral.

The pedestal stems and the lighter types of baluster stems (sometimes called 'balustroids') held the field during the third and fourth decades of the century, but in 1745–6 a fiscal measure was introduced which militated against the use of more metal in a glass than was absolutely necessary. This was the glass excise, which levied a tax on glass-material *by weight*. It has sometimes been assumed that this alone brought about a change in English glass-style, causing the glass-makers to abandon the plastically conceived stem as the main ornamental feature of a glass, and to concentrate on other forms of decoration applied to a glass with a plain stem. It is more likely, however, that the glass excise merely gave a final impetus to a movement in taste which was already taking place. During the decade before the middle of the eighteenth century the baroque style was giving way to the rococo, in which lightness of form and relatively superficial decoration played an all-important part. In the case of drinking-glasses, decoration first manifested itself in the stem.

Air- and enamel-twist stems

As early as the late seventeenth century English glass-makers had been wont to decorate stemmed glasses by means of moulded ribbing drawn out and simultaneously twisted, thus producing a close spiral. In the early decades of the eighteenth century there are isolated examples of *air-bubbles* within a glass being similarly drawn out and twisted to produce an internal cable of thin air-lines: but the full development of this decoration for drinking-glasses seems to set in during the 1730's. It probably suggested itself first in the 'drawn-stem' glasses, which had frequently been decorated with an air-bubble trapped at the base of the bowl, and which by the nature of their manufacture lent themselves to this drawing and twisting process. With increasing proficiency, however, the glass-maker was able to extend the use of air-twists to stems with one or more baluster-like swellings (Pl. 55D, F). Somewhat before the middle of the century, the columns of air trapped within the stem were occasionally replaced by rods of opaque-white (or 'enamel') glass, these rods being stood in a circular mould and 'picked up' on a blob of glass in which they were then incorporated, the whole being drawn out and twisted as before. Occasionally, air-twists are used in conjunction with enamel-twists, and sometimes the white enamel canes were replaced by canes of coloured transparent or opaque glass. The 'enamel', 'mixed' and 'coloured' twists were usually made in lengths which could be cut up and used to make a number of straight stems (Pl. 55B).

All these decorative techniques were practised in the glass-house and were intrinsic to the glasses themselves. During the period under consideration, however, a number of other methods of ornamentation came into vogue. Without exception, their technical origins may be sought in Germany, from which country both workmen and ideas reached England under the favourable conditions provided by the settlement of 1713 and the presence on the English throne of a German sovereign.

Engraved and cut glasses

Of these imported techniques, two are closely related. Both consist of grinding away the surface of the glass by means of a rapidly revolving wheel on to which is fed a stream of abrasive suspended in a liquid. In the first (engraving) the small copper wheels vary in profile and can be rapidly interchanged in the chuck of the power-shaft to suit the needs of the work in hand; in the second (cutting) the wheels, of iron or stone, are large, and in the eighteenth century were somewhat blunt of profile, either flat, rounded or mitred. A skilful engraver can render intricate devices or delicately modelled forms of great fineness, whilst the cutter grinds away planes and surfaces in such a way as to enhance the play of light and multiply images in his transparent medium. In Germany and Bohemia the seventeenth century produced complete masters of both techniques, and at the accession of George I German prestige in this art was supreme. Glasses with engraved inscriptions and coats-of-

arms are known from the reign of Queen Anne, but they are rare, and the circumstances in which they were engraved are unknown. The engraving of such armorial or propaganda glasses to order continues through the first half of the eighteenth century, but is supplemented (probably from the 1720's onwards) by the use of decorative borders which, in their technical competence and in their display of characteristic German baroque ornamental motives, reveal the hand of the immigrant artist. This border-style is transformed by the middle of the eighteenth century, the neat formality of the ornament being replaced by freer and less coherent designs of scrolls and leaves and flowers (Pl. 55A). These betray an English taste, if not necessarily an English hand, although English engravers were certainly at work by then. Well before the middle of the century, too, these same flowers and leaves had strayed from the borders to occupy the bowl of the glass. Amongst these 'flower'd' glasses are to be found the not uncommon wine-glasses, engraved with Jacobite symbols, beloved by the treasonable societies of the mid-eighteenth century, and by the glass-collector of today (Pl. 55F). Figural engraving is not common on English glass, but occasionally renders pleasantly the *chinoiseries* of the French engravers of decorative prints; or the more English landscapes with ruins, or vignettes of country life, as we know them on contemporary porcelain. This work belongs mainly to the 1760's and 1770's, and, in all of it, German correctness and refinement were modified to suit the less formal and exacting, and often more bucolic, taste of the English gentleman (Pls. 54B; 55A, D; 56C).

Glass-cutting had a similar early history in England, but was far more significant than engraving for the future development of English glass. In the main, it was a German technique grafted on to the indigenous art of the plate- and mirror-grinders, who had already flourished in England in the seventeenth century. In the second decade of the eighteenth century, cut sconces were being advertised in London, and a German craftsman, John Akerman, had already settled there. As early as 1722 a Scottish visitor remarked on 'a high scaloped glass' seen during the dessert-course at a fashionable dinner; in 1728 the same visitor observed sweet-meat glasses with 'cornered brims'. This early cutting was restricted when possible to the thickest and most easily accessible parts of a glass. Thus the edge of a sweetmeat glass might safely be notched into a scalloped or serrated border, while its stem could be cut into flat vertical flutes or alternating hexagonal facets (Pl. 54A). On the thinner parts of a glass the cut motives were at first shallower and more hesitant (Pl. 55E). By the middle of the century, however, the skill of the cutter had ripened to a point where he could cover the whole of a vessel with cut motives, including asymmetrical lunate 'slices' formed by presenting the glass at an angle to the cutting-wheel; diamonds in low relief; and scalloped edges of far greater complexity than hitherto.

Coloured, enamelled and gilt glass

The glass-makers of the early eighteenth century, confident of the superiority of their own glass-material, seem to have scorned the use of metallic oxides to colour it. Already by about 1725 or 1730, however, green and blue glasses with air-twists and engraved borders were being made, and

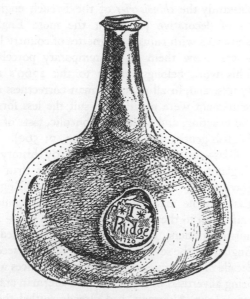

Fig. 6. Bottle of blackish-green glass, with seal impressed 'T. Ridge, 1720'. Ht. 7⅝ in. *Victoria and Albert Museum.*

to these colours was added in 1754 a ruby-red invented by a German immigrant named Mayer Opnaim. Probably also of German origin was the practice of enamelling on glass, which appears to have begun in England about the middle of the eighteenth century. Although later in the century colourless glass was decorated by means of enamelling, the art was most commonly practised on opaque-white glass. This material was already known to English glass-makers in the late seventeenth century, and, after a brief eclipse in the early eighteenth century, seems to have come into its own again about 1730. From then until about 1770 there was a continuous production of decorative vessels (jars and beakers for garnitures, tea-caddies, candlesticks, mugs, cruet-bottles and salt-cellars) often decorated in fine enamel-colours (Pl. 56B). The heyday of this painting seems to have been about 1755–65, and it clearly coincides with the rage for porcelain enamelled on a white ground which obtained at this time. With the introduction of Sèvres styles about 1760, the opaque-white glass probably declined in favour *vis-à-vis* blue glass with gilt decoration. Gilding, also a German process, was employed both on clear glass and on coloured. Its use, however, was rare in the period under discussion, and it was usually limited to simple sprays of flowers, vine-leaves and grapes, or hops and barley, in the manner of the contemporary engraved glasses.

The uses of glass

Glass in the early Georgian period, as in most others, was pre-eminently for the service of the drinker. The shapes of wine-glasses were dictated mainly by fashion rather than function, for the age of the specialized wine-glass was yet to come. Possible exceptions to this rule, however, were provided by champagne-glasses, which, it is often implied, were glasses of special shape – probably with a tall, narrow bowl derived from that of the tapering 'flute-glass' of the seventeenth century. A similar bowl form, but on a smaller scale, was shared by the 'ratafia' and other cordial-glasses, from which the potent liquors of the still-room were drunk; and by the ale and perry glasses, with their more generous capacity (Pl. 55B). Tumblers were used for drinking strong drinks perhaps more frequently than is generally realized (cf. Pl. 29c), and in 1717 Lord Cardigan laid in a stock of three dozen of them. Punch-bowls (Pl. 54B) and monteiths (wine-glass coolers with notched edges from which the glasses hung down in water) were also occasionally made in glass. The decanter of the early part of our period followed roughly the form of the plain green-glass bottle (cf. Pl. 56A and Fig. 6). About the middle of the century, however, two new forms evolved. The first (Pl. 56c) again followed the form of the sloping straight-sided glass bottle of the period; the second was a shouldered form, broader at the top than lower down (Fig. 7). Both, like the wine-glasses which they accompanied, and which were often *en suite* with them, were frequently decorated by means of cutting or engraving (Pl. 56c and Fig. 7).

Glass was almost as essential to the dessert as it was to the drinking-party. The slender bell-shaped 'syllabub' and jelly-glasses were ranged in order on glass salvers – broad, circular trays with a raised edge, set on a stem and foot. Frequently a medium-sized salver was set on a large one, and itself surmounted by a smaller. This structure was termed a 'pyramid', and, decked out with the appropriate jelly- and sweetmeat-glasses, and with little bottles containing flowers, often formed the decorative *pièce de résistance* of a dessert. The whole was surmounted by a sweetmeat-glass (Pl. 54A), often containing preserved fruit, and sometimes therefore called the 'orange' (or 'top') glass.

English glass, with its high refractive index, made it peculiarly suitable for the manufacture of candlesticks (Pl. 54E) and candelabra. The most splendid lighting, however, was provided by the chandelier, which at first closely followed the shape of the contemporary brass chandelier, with S-shaped arms radiating from a central stem decorated with one or more globular elements strung on it. It was soon observed that cutting was a decorative treatment particularly well suited to chandeliers, and by about the middle of the century almost every part of the chandelier was cut in the 'flat' style of the period. By the accession of George III the rococo chandelier was at the height of its glory, with richly cut canopies echoing the

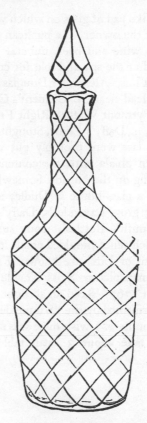

Fig. 7. Glass decanter with all-over facet-cutting, about 1760, Ht. about 11 in.

Chinese taste and hung with drops cut in any number of fanciful shapes, and with pinnacles formed like spires or fleurs-de-lis or star-topped wands.

All the glass hitherto described has been of more or less high quality, made in the 'white glass-houses'. Throughout the period, however, there were also 'green glass-houses', making mainly window-glass, and 'bottle houses'. The wine-bottle in the reigns of the first two Georges evolved from a low, onion-shaped flask (Fig. 6), through a phase corresponding to the 'slope-shouldered' decanter (Pl. 56c), to a cylindrical form which was in all essentials that of the modern wine-bottle. This could be binned on its side to obviate 'corking instead of being stored neck-down, as was sometimes done with the 'onion'-shaped bottles. Wine-bottles were often equipped

663

with a seal-like pad of glass on which was stamped the name of the owner, of a publican or the like. Apart from wine and beer, mineral waters also were bottled at the spa and sold for consumption elsewhere. Thus, 'Alexander Douglas Chymist at Glauber's Head near St. Clement's Church' sold 'Spaw and Pyrmont Waters, Right French Hungary Water, ... Daffy's Elixir, Stoughton's Drops, &c.' These last were probably put up in small mould-blown phials with the contents noted in relief lettering on the outside. Somewhat later in the century a glass-house at Dudley advertised a stock of '43 gross Lavender's, Daffy's, Turlington's and Smith's Bottles'; many surviving examples of such relief-moulded phials for Turlington's 'Balsam of Life' are known. From such a bottle one may picture Sylas Neville taking his daily dose in 1767: 'Read an account of some of the cures performed by the "Baume de Vie" since its publication here. I wish mine was added to the number. I take about 3 small table-spoonfulls every day.'

SHORT BIBLIOGRAPHY

Pottery and Porcelain.

Bernard Rackham, *Catalogue of the Glaisher Collection*, 2 vols., Cambridge University Press (1934).

W.B.Honey, *English Pottery and Porcelain*, Black (1947).

Pottery.

Bernard Rackham and Herbert Read, *English Pottery*, Benn (1924).

F.H.Garner, *English Delftware*, Faber (1948).

Bernard Rackham, *Early Staffordshire Pottery*, Faber (1951).

Porcelain.

W.B.Honey, *Old English Porcelain*, Faber (new ed., 1948).

J.L.Dixon, *English Porcelain of the 18th century*, Faber (1952).

Glass.

Francis Buckley, *History of Old English Glass*, Benn (1925).

W.A.Thorpe, *A History of English and Irish Glass*, 2 vols., Medici Society (1929).

W.B.Honey, *English Glass*, Collins (1946).

W.A.Thorpe, *English Glass*, Black (1949).

Domestic Metalwork

G. BERNARD HUGHES

The first twenty years of the early Georgian period saw little change in domestic metalwork. Stuart processes and patterns continued until technical achievements of the late 1720's brought about improvements in the quality and colour of metals, prompting merchants and shopkeepers to develop more attractive-looking articles. There was greater efficiency, and skilled work was speeded up immeasurably, making it possible to put less costly articles on the market. Domestic metalwork was thus carried into homes where wood had predominated. Plate-workers in copper, brass and iron now followed the three-century-old lead of the pewterers and made domestic wares in ranges of standard sizes and weights.

Tin-plate became silvery white throughout its substance; copper and brass smoother of surface and more attractive in colour; pewterers made their flat-ware much harder, in defiance of their Company's regulations; iron and steel were far more ductile and in consequence simpler to manipulate. The number of London master craftsmen engaged as sheet-metal workers, blacksmiths, braziers and coppersmiths increased three-fold between 1730 and 1747.[1]

The inventions by which it became possible to enlarge the scope of domestic metalwork were four:

1. Abraham Darby's process for smelting iron with coke. This iron was more ductile than any formerly made for commercial use, and

[1] *The London Tradesman*, 1747.

was found ideal for rolling into plates. It also produced a free-running metal from which clearly and deeply moulded castings could be made.

2. In 1728 John Cook of the Pontypool Ironworks patented a rolling machine in which compression springs were incorporated, enabling iron, copper and brass to be rolled more efficiently and evenly.

3. Pontypool then evolved a method of dipping iron plate into tin which penetrated completely, giving the plate a white colour throughout its texture. Such plates, measuring 2 feet by 4 feet, were first sold in the early 1730's, thus founding the Welsh tin-plate industry. Formerly only the surfaces of iron plates had been tinned.

4. George Moor in 1725 patented a process of refining and purifying copper at one operation. Under the Hawkesbee–Lund patent of 1728 further purification became possible. Copper was now made of a rose-pink colour, a soft, smooth texture, and ductile enough to be rolled into flawless plate.

The new tin-plate was enthusiastically welcomed by certain of the plate-workers who, as the newly established craft of tin-plate workers, issued a wide range of everyday domestic ware for kitchens and servants' quarters. This included such articles as basins and drinking-cans, candle-boxes and chamber candlesticks, kitchen flour-dredgers and scoops, dripping-pans and funnels.

The new tin-plates were a boon to japanners,

who had long laboured to overcome the defect of their japan peeling from surface-tinned iron plate. Japanned metal in brilliant colours enriched with gold- or silver-pencilled ornament was already in use (Pl. 57A). Gumley and Turing of the Strand, London, for instance, supplied George I with 'four fine large tin plate receivers japanned in red with neat drawings in silver and fixing them up with silver chains to large double-branched plate [wall] sconces'. These receivers were receptacles to catch the hot wax that might fall from burning candles.

Pontypool japan ware

The new plates, tinned throughout their texture, enabled Edward Allgood of Pontypool to perfect his outstandingly fine japan ware, costly because of the large number of japan coatings involved, each one fired separately and smoothed by hand. This japan with its intensely rich coloured grounds – at first in black, chocolate, crimson and tortoiseshell – was to be found in every home of importance. When Bishop Pococke visited the Allgood japan factory at Pontypool in 1756 he described the productions as being 'adorned with Chinese landscapes and figures in gold only, and not with colourings as at Birmingham. ... They also japan copper boxes, or any other thing made in copper which they cannot work well in iron.'

Allgood enhanced his reputation with magnificent tea-trays and waiters so toughly japanned that hot kettles and teapots made no mark upon them. These set a century-long fashion for displaying the porcelain tea-service accompanied by japanned tea-canisters and tea candlesticks, and even, at first, by a japanned teapot, for early English porcelain could not withstand the impact of boiling water.

Baskerville's japan ware

John Baskerville of Birmingham was a competitor on a more ambitious scale, making a gross of inferior articles to one of Allgood's finer quality. In 1742 he invented a combined rolling and grinding machine which made his untinned plates as 'level as the best joyner could perform in wood'.[2]

2 Patent No. 582, 1742.

He had need to give them only two or three coats of japan, but failed to overcome flaking. Baskerville made japanned iron to resemble 'fine glowing Mahogany, a Black in no way inferior to India goods, or in Imitation of Tortoiseshell, which greatly excels Nature itself in Colour and Hardness'. In iron japanned to resemble mahogany he made sets of knife-boxes, wine-cisterns, tea-trays, and screens in shapes closely resembling those of the cabinet-makers. There were also voiders defined in Bailey's dictionary 1730 as 'Table-Baskets for Plates, Knives and Also a Japanned and Painted vessel to hold Services of Sweetmeats'.

Baskerville appears to have been the first japanner to have enriched his ware with oil-paintings in full colours, following the lead of enamellers at Battersea and Bilston. Trays were centred with landscapes or figure groups, bellows became bright with portraiture, coal-scuttles displayed flower-sprays. The early Georgian home-furnisher might also buy a pair of urn-shaped chestnut servers, an oval monteith for cooling wine-glasses, tea-chests in which were locked two or three canisters containing tea, smoker's charcoal braziers on trays or even a toilet table set. Every considerable room in a house possessed its table or mantel snuff-box, which might be of japanned iron.

Battersea enamels (Pl. 57C) became vigorous though short-lived competitors with small japanned ware such as table and pocket snuff-boxes, technically more brilliant and with a greater range and delicacy of colour. Meanwhile in South Staffordshire japanning had been carried on since the time of Queen Anne, and after Battersea closed in 1756 this region became the centre for painted enamels built over a basis of thinly rolled rose copper, and with much of the hand-coloured ornament applied over transfer-printed outlines. White-enamelled candlesticks sparsely painted with flower-sprays might ornament the table; on the side table there might be a pair of knife-boxes with perhaps a kettle; a pair of cassolettes (vases with perforated covers for burning perfumes) would find a place on the mantelshelf; and on the walls might hang portrait plaques of celebrities enamelled in full colour or merely transfer-printed in black or red. For the toilet table there were sets of large japan boxes, their lids mounted with enamel plaques painted with scenes in full colours, the black japan-work enriched with complicated borders of gold lines (Pl. 57A).

Copper and brass

The making of movements for domestic clocks was a considerable early Georgian craft. Every medium-sized town supported several clock-makers – for instance in 1750 there were four in Wolverhampton. The majority fitted their movements into cases supplied by cabinet-makers. Improvements in brass-making ensured that the surfaces of dials were less flawed than formerly. The arched dial by 1720 had become accepted in fashionable lofty rooms (Pls. 63A, B and c). By 1730 the clockmaker's ingenuity had produced mechanical figures to fill the arch and by the 1750's Thomas Ogden of Halifax had made such a name for clocks with rotating moons that these became known as Halifax clocks.

The range of domestic copper and brass ware was immeasurably extended from the 1730's. One side of a well-equipped kitchen was now a-gleam with burnished copper and brass cooking-vessels, the number in a large establishment exceeding five hundred and necessitating the full-time services of a cleaner, whose duties included also the polishing of the hard pewter, now seldom in need of scraping.

Georgian copper from the early 1730's was more attractive in colour, seldom revealed surface flaws and was much easier to work than formerly. The metal could now be worked into warming-pans without danger of splitting. Four sizes of warming-pan were standardized, measuring from $12\frac{1}{2}$ inches to $10\frac{1}{2}$ inches in diameter. The ember-pan remained vertical-sided, but now seldom exceeded $\frac{1}{16}$ inch in thickness. The lid, shaped like a beefeater's hat, with a short sloping rim fitting over the beaded rim of the pan, was usually free of ornament, but might be sparsely embossed or engraved. Hinges were narrow and often three-jointed, although the stronger five-joint was preferred. Brazed or riveted to the ember-pan was a strong, tapering socket of cast-brass fitted with a handle of polished or japanned wood.

Kitchen shelves displayed saucepans in ten sizes, with uprising handles of hardwood; pottage pots in fourteen sizes from one to fourteen gallons; straight-sided soup pots in a design with a flat, sunken cover fitting tightly over the rim of the pot and containing the pewter plates set to warm; stew-pans; fish-kettles with plates and covers; pudding-pans from 6 to 15 inches in diameter; slow-burning charcoal braziers for keeping foods warm on their journey to the dining-room; jelly moulds; preserving pans; chestnut roasters; frying-pans, now with half-hoop handles; ale-warmers. All these were heavily coated inside with pure-grained tin, to combat health hazards, real or imagined, associated with copper as a container of liquid foods. Cookery books of the period advocated the use of untinned pans by those who liked their vegetables bright green. Still-room appliances were usually of copper, such as the domestic stills for preparing cordials (Pl. 62D) and sets of measures.

In brass plate or latten were coffee-pots and chocolate-pots with stands and waiters, made in four sizes of from one to three pints, and tea-kettles with stands and waiters varying from three pints to one gallon. These were of wine capacity: all other domestic hollow-ware conformed to Winchester measure.

Until early in the eighteenth century coffee was made by boiling whole beans that had been roasted in a perforated cylindrical iron vessel turned like a spit over a charcoal fire.[3] The coffee-mill was then evolved from the spice-grinder. This squat, box-like mill operated on the principle of horizontal millstones with a vertical iron shank revolving upon a fixed corrugated-iron plate. Until about 1740 the ground coffee was collected upon a waiter placed beneath; then a drawer was designed to receive the fragrant powder. The outer case of the coffee-mill was of iron plate which might be gilded, japanned or painted.

Illumination

Brass added colourful and often costly brilliance to Georgian illumination also (Pl. 61B). Globe chandeliers of burnished brass hung in the entrance

[3] *All About Coffee*, William H. Ukers, 1922.

halls and reception-rooms. From the 1730's the globe tended to be displaced by a fluted and gadrooned vase-shaped stem, increasing the burnished reflecting area. The spreading branches encircled the widest diameter of the stem, two or three tiers of diminishing spread being frequent, carrying in all thirty-six wax candles. Instead of hooking to the stem, as formerly, branches were now secured by screwing them into position. The upper finial might be merely a plain loop or an ornamental casting, chased and burnished, such as a figure, a bird or a flame.

On occasions when dusk was falling and the candles on several chandeliers had to be lighted whilst guests were present, it was a fashionable conceit for the candles on all the chandeliers to be lighted simultaneously. Slender threads of cotton wool, almost invisible to the eye, saturated with sulphur of saltpetre and other ingredients, were arranged to carry the flame rapidly from one candle to another.[4] When such an arrangement was skilfully prepared, hardly a single candle failed to take fire. Hall chandeliers were enclosed in glazed lanterns (Pl. 61B) to protect the candles in such draughty situations. At first these were usually in wrought iron; from about 1740 in brass. The ornamental head contained swivel and pulley (Pl. 61C) and was suspended from the ceiling by means of four colourful cords.

Brass candlesticks were made in ever-increasing numbers, the unworked casting costing 1s. 2d. per lb. at the foundry. The hollow stem continued from late Stuart days with an octagonal foot supporting a slender octagonal and faceted stem. During the 1720's alternate angles of the octagonal foot might be recessed to form a square with hollow angles. In the late 1730's this style changed in favour of a lobed foot, at first with four and then with six lobes. Later lobes in this period were made to appear more prominent by grooving the surface of the foot and shaping its edge: scalloped edges date from the late 1750's (Pl. 60B).

Chamber candlesticks, which might be in brass, copper or japanned iron, came into considerable use during this period, designed as expansive saucers with low-set sockets. Their purpose was to light the way from room to room, and the stairs, and to serve generally where a temporary, safely portable light was required. Formerly special non-drip candles had met this need – tallow candles thickly coated with scented virgin wax so that they could be carried around without contaminating the fingers. From 1720 a chamber candlestick might be equipped with a cone-shaped extinguisher. Some were designed to carry a pair of snuffers in a slotted support beneath the socket.

In large establishments a boy known as the 'snuffer' was employed to snuff burning candles.[5] His snuffers of plain iron hung from his waist by a chain or cord. Domestic snuffers might be in silver, cast-brass, lavishly ornamented cut steel, pewter, iron or, from the 1740's, in japanned iron. These were for individual use, and when not in action rested on a long rectangular snuffer-tray. Early Georgian snuffers for the most part continued the rectangular wick box of Stuart days, but oval, lozenge, semi-circular, and barrel shapes, fluted, engraved or plain, were also made. The undersides of snuffers rested flat upon the tray until about 1750, when three short feet were added making it simpler to lift the finger loops from the tray.

Snuffers possessed one serious defect: the greasy snuff, often still smouldering, was liable to fall from the container when the blades were reopened to snuff a second candle. Benjamin Cartwright, of the Strand, London, patented a preventive device in 1749. This controlled the movement of the blade by means of a coiled spring so arranged that the snuffers automatically closed and were kept closed after use. The blade cut off the red-hot snuff and crushed it against the side of the wick box and immediately extinguished it, thus preventing the unpleasant smouldering smell associated with dying snuff. In these snuffers the pivoting joint and coiled spring were concealed by a convex boss often cut and engraved with rosette ornament. In some iron snuffers bows and stems were close-plated to resemble silver. No further change in snuffer design was made until 1810.

---

[4] *Letters of César de Saussure*, 1729.

[5] Boyer's *Dictionary Royal*, 1722.

Floor-standard rush-light holders were used in many small houses and servants' quarters of the period. The 4-foot stem might be spiked and driven into a heavy block of oak which formed the foot or might be supported on a wrought-iron tripod foot. The lower portion of a spiked stem was thicker than the upper, the extra weight ensuring stability. A combined rush-light clip and candle-socket was fitted to a sliding carrier which gripped the stem by means of a friction spring. A stop prevented the carrier from slipping unnoticed to the floor, when the flame might cause a fire (Pl. 60A). Pendant rush-light holders with central swivel joints were used in outhouses.

The hand lantern became a more frequent domestic accessory in this period. Many forms were designed to the whims of individual craftsmen: the majority were square, and when in brass might be decorated with repoussé ornament. Glazing consisted of either a horn plate or a bull's eye, a by-product of contemporary window glass-houses. Ventilation perforations might be saw-cut in attractive patterns.

Fully enclosed open-flame oil-burning spout-lamps illumined innumerable small homes from the 1720's in brass, copper, tin-plate and iron. The cylindrical reservoir was fitted with a straight, tubular wick-holder sloping forward from the base. Oil-drips from the wick were caught in a channelled gutter and collected in the lower part of the reservoir for use again. The lamp burned a round, plaited wick and emitted a yellowish light about equal to that of two ordinary candles. Crusting of the wick made necessary the use of a slender iron wick-pick, which hung by a chain from the lid. A table-lamp was usually supported by a thick, hollow stem rising from a spreading foot: both were weighted with sand to give stability.

Oil-burning bedside lamps from which the time could be read during the night were made from the late 1720's. The *Craftsman* in 1730 illustrated an example. The oil was contained in a tall glass tube fitted into a brass case, the wick holder protruding from one side at the top. The time was indicated by the sinking of the oil in the tube, which was marked in hour degrees.

Pewter

Early Georgian pewterers working in plate abandoned the use of the old soft metal in favour of a harder, more utilitarian pewter, in contravention of the four-hundred-year-old regulations of the Pewterers' Company. The Company's resolute refusal to permit master craftsmen to raise their standards, and so compete with Staffordshire salt-glazed stoneware, was directly responsible for its decline from the status of a powerful guild.

Pewterers' trade-cards from the 1720's placed emphasis on 'superfine metal', such as 'Fine White Hard Metal Dishes and Plates, call'd French Pewter', and 'Superfine French Metal'. Knife-blades did not cut into this pewter as into ordinary hammered pewter, and therefore it did not require scraping after each meal, so that its useful life was considerably lengthened. By the 1760's even this pewter fell beneath competition from the cleaner, smoother, pleasant-looking, cream-coloured earthenware.

The hard pewter was distinguished from the soft by marking it with X crowned (Pl. 62c). An early Georgian list of 'Pewterers' Goods' records that dishes were made in eighteen sizes, 28 inches to $10\frac{3}{4}$ inches in diameter, and six sizes of plates, $9\frac{3}{4}$ inches to $7\frac{3}{4}$ inches in diameter, with soup dishes and soup plates in the same sizes, only deeper. Flat ware also included pie-plates, fish-plates and cheese-plates with foot-rims or three small feet.

Pewter plates until the 1740's were broad brimmed with single reeding and wide, thin, oval beaded edges. These were succeeded by narrow rims, the majority of flat ware now being cast and turned instead of hammered, in an effort to reduce cost. By 1750 plates and dishes might be octagonal, at first with plain rims, then with borders double or treble reeded, gadrooned, or in a combination of beading and reeding. Wavy-edged plates in pewter copying contemporary shapes in silver were made: these might be five-lobed, reeded, gadrooned or plain; five-lobed with scroll and shell decoration; eight-lobed; plain, single or double reeded.

Early Georgian pewter hollow-ware was entered in the list of 'Pewterers' Goods' as being

Tho. Scattergood
PEWTERER
at the Blackmoors head near the South Sea House in Bishops-gate street LONDON
Makes & Sells all sorts of Pewter Wholesale & Retail at reasonable Rates

Fig. 1. London pewterer's trade card, *c.* 1730.

made from a less costly metal then termed 'trifle'. This included candlesticks, casters, salt-cellars, jugs, sauce-boats, tea canisters, herb-boxes, tureens, porringers, standishes, tobacco boxes and snuff-boxes, and teapots in five sizes ranging from half-pint to one quart with hardwood handles. 'Lay metal', then described as being almost as coarse as lead, was seldom used for domestic work. Drinking vessels, of course, were still made from fine quality pewter, consisting mainly of tin (Pl. 62A and B).

Table-ware

Pewter spoons made early in the Georgian period were hand-worked as formerly. A new shape came into use, known to collectors as the 'Hanoverian pattern'. This had a gracefully curved stem and a thicker, rounded finial with an upward curve. From the finial, extending nearly half way up the front of the stem, was a tapering central ridge resembling the rat-tail on the back of an oval-shaped bowl. By 1750 the spoon bowl was made egg-shaped, tapering towards the tip: such spoons might be cast in gun-metal moulds. Spoons and forks were made from the 1730's of cast-iron, too, close-plated with silver, but these were not very successful.

Table knives in the early Georgian period varied little from the scimitar form, but from about 1740 the finest were hand-forged from the harder, sharper steel invented by Benjamin Huntsman: scissors and razors were made from the same steel. Because of its scarcity – only a few pounds weight could be made in a single crucible – table knives continued to be made from common steel and highly burnished. Among the new types of knife-blades which became fashionable were those for oysters, onions and cheese. Sharpening steels replaced whetstones in the dining-room under the name of 'knife sharpening instruments'.

Sets of knives and forks with matching hafts became fashionable early in the period. These might be in silver, gilded copper, gilded princes metal or steel, in heavy patterns. Weight was reduced considerably by 1760. The most frequent shapes were reeded, plain with a shell finial, and in the pistol-butt curve.

For the table, too, were hand-bells, already used for two centuries or more to summon a servant into the room, but only widely adopted when it became possible to cast them by brass-founding methods – entirely different from complicated bell-founding. Such hand-bells came into frequent use during the 1720's, measuring from 4 to 7 inches wide at the mouth, and fitted with turned ivory, bone or hardwood handles. A familiar design of this period was cast and chased in the form of a serving-woman wearing a wide skirt and apron, her hands clasped before her. Such table bells were usually gilded. Voiding pails of brass and copper, into which waste food fragments were scraped from plates by servants in the dining room, became fashionable, replacing the shallow rectangular trays formerly used for this purpose. By the mid-eighteenth century the pail might be enclosed within brass-bound mahogany (Pl. 63D). A matching pail was introduced for carrying away the used plates: this was widely slit down one side enabling the plates to be placed flat within it. Before the meal the dinner plates were warmed in a wrought iron plate warmer with a revolving frame (Pl. 59A).

The fireplace

Andirons and firebacks continued to be made throughout the early Georgian period by those who had not yet replaced their down hearths with coal-burning grates. Darby's freely running metal produced firebacks with designs clear-cut in high relief and costing only one penny a pound at the foundry. These lighter plates made it possible to construct grates from flat cast plates, such as the well-known duck's-nest grate. Three-barred portable grates, fitted with tall, narrow firebacks of thin section, rested on low firedogs, the andirons being brought forward as fire-iron rests. In some instances a pair of imposing andirons in brass stood at each side of the fireplace, in which the jambs might be lined with blue-decorated delftware. It was often necessary in these adapted down-hearth fireplaces to raise a coal-burning grate upon four tall legs to prevent smoke from escaping into the room. In new buildings the fireplace opening was made smaller.

Fenders or fend-irons became an essential safety device as boarded floors were made to approach the fireplace more closely than formerly and as yet were seldom carpeted. The fender was first shaped from a long, flat strip of rolled iron set up on edge with returned ends and welded into a wrought-iron base to give stability. These fenders, like the grates themselves, were always kept highly polished. From the 1730's fenders were decorated with saw-cut ornament. With the increasing use of sea-coal, coal-scoops and scuttles became important decorative details of the hearth-side.

Coal-burning grates brought into living-rooms a considerable range of attractively designed, well-finished domestic fireplace equipment in brass and iron. Trivets were made small and might be entirely of cast brass, or worked from latten and saw-cut, or constructed from an openwork brass plate and iron supports (Pl. 58B). The small standing trivet with two flat vertical hooks at the rear by which it hung from the top bar of a grate dates from the 1750's.

Standard and trivet toasters of wrought-iron designed for use with grates now replaced the earlier low-standing toasters. The vertical standard, rising from a tripod, was fitted with a sliding fork of steel, held firmly in position by a spring and adjustable both vertically and horizontally. Brass trivets might also be fitted with sliding toasters of steel held firmly by friction springs (Pl. 58A). Less simply (Pl. 58A) the standard might support a bell-shaped frame with three sets of steel prongs attached: these might serve as spits for roasting small birds. There were also firebar toasters.

Improved grid-irons came into use at this time: each grill was grooved to drain liquor into a deep trough welded to the outer rim of the iron. Here the meat-juices were collected instead of being lost in the fire and might be poured off for gravy through a spout at one end. The two near feet were forked to fit over the top firebar.

The smoke-jack for turning spits in the kitchen, although first made in the late Stuart period, was increasingly used in the early eighteenth century. Its power was derived from the upward rush of hot air from the fire, which operated a chimney rotor, this in turn moving a vertical shaft geared to a horizontal shaft. The cog wheel often turned in what in later years was patented as an 'oil bath'.

Fire was an ever-present hazard and inventories for centuries refer to brass hand squirts for extinguishing fires. Made from rolled latten they were much lighter in weight and more efficient than when made from battery brass. Water-baskets of leather were now commonly replaced by fire-buckets of tin-plate painted with coat of arms or cypher. These, accompanied by a couple of such squirts, each containing a bucketful of water, became commonplace on every floor of the early Georgian home.

Locks

Domestic locks from about 1720 began to be enclosed in cases of cast brass, with plain or raised edges. Formerly brass cases had been hand-made from battery plate. By the 1740's the outer plate might be cast with designs in relief, chased and double gilded. The finest of this work was in an alloy of the pinchbeck quality. Thick, solid mahogany doors of the period prompted the introduction of the mortice lock, concealed from view by inserting it into a rectangular recess sunk into the edge of the door. In most early mortice locks only the brass knob was visible against the polished mahogany, and the keyhole masked by a swinging escutcheon. Decoration might be added in the form of an ornamental end-piece matching the adjoining striking plate: these might be engraved, pierced, or cast and chased, often displaying the owner's coat of arms or cypher. Emphasis of security was laid upon ward locks. Iron locks continued to be made in ever-increasing quantities for lesser homes (Pl. 64B).

Doors might now be fitted with cast brass hinges with 'a secret joint so designed that the door would slowly close if not propped open'. The hinge was cast with its pin running through the loops of the joints, surrounded by cast metal and entirely hidden.

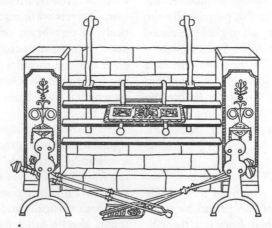

Fig. 2. Cast-iron firegrate with hobs, wrought-iron bars and bar trivet with brass plate, c. 1750. In the dining room at Astley Hall, Stourport.

(A) Italian silk damask, first half of the eighteenth century.   *Private Collection.*

(B) Italian silk velvet, first half of eighteenth century; red, green and yellow pile on cream ground.   *Victoria and Albert Museum.*

PLATE 65

Silk and wool tapestry. English (Soho), by Joshua Morris, about 1720–30.
Courtesy Viscount Cobham, Hagley Park.

PLATE 66

Silk and wool tapestry: 'The Fruit Gatherer'. English (Soho), by Bradshaw after Watteau, about 1730–50.
Ham House

PLATE 67

Woollen pile carpet. English (Exeter), by Claude Passavant dated 1757.
Victoria and Albert Museum.

676

PLATE 68

Needlework carpet in silk and wool. English, first half of the eighteenth century.
Private Collection.

PLATE 69   677

(B) Back of an armchair, in silk and wool needlework. English, first half of the eighteenth century. *Victoria and Albert Museum.*

(A) Back of an armchair in silk and wool needlework. English, first half of the eighteenth century. *Victoria and Albert Museum.*

PLATE 70

(A) Coverlet, silk and wool embroidery on linen. English, early eighteenth century. *Victoria and Albert Museum.*

(B) Bed curtain, wool embroidery on linen. English, about 1729. *National Museum of Wales.*

PLATE 71

(B) Coverlet, block printed linen. English, by George Ormerod at Wallington, Surrey, dated 1752. *Philadelphia Museum of Art.*

(A) Coverlet, silk and gold embroidery on linen. English, about 1715. *Courtesy John Vyvyan, Esq.*

PLATE 72

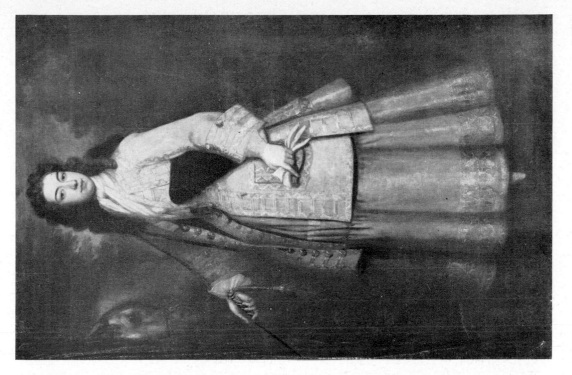

(B) The Countess of Mar, by Sir Godfrey Kneller, 1715. Riding habit, the coat and waistcoat cut on masculine lines. Steinkirk, tricorne hat and wig. *Courtesy The Earl of Mar and Kellie.*

(A) Unknown man, 1710–20. Collarless coat with buttons from neck to hem, flared skirts. Tricorne hat. Shoes with high tongues and small buckles. Full-bottomed wig. *Private Collection.*

PLATE 73

681

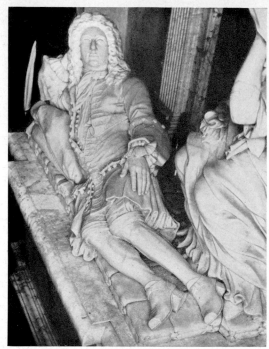

(A) Sir Charles Bloir, *c.* 1725. Coat fitting the neck, medium turned-back cuffs. Shoes with round toes and square buckles. Smaller wig with centre parting. *Christchurch Mansion, Ipswich.*

(B) Marble effigy of Sir R. Jennens, Acton Church, Suffolk, 1722–5. Fashionable dress showing full-bottomed wig, Steinkirk, rollups, shoes with blocked toes and high tongues.

(C) Mary Pettus, *c.* 1740–5. Wearing a wrapping gown over an oblong hoop. Tucker; elaborate double ruffles. *Norwich Castle Museum.*

(D) Sir George Wynn, 1727. Fringed waistcoat open to display the long cravat. Huge turned-back cuffs nearly up to the elbows. *Private Collection.*

PLATE 74

The Bull Family, by ARTHUR DEVIS, 1740–2. The man in a frock, the women in mob caps with kissing strings. Note handkerchief round the shoulders, laced bodice, turned-back cuffs with ruffles. *Harris Art Gallery, Preston.*

PLATE 75

(B) Colonel Charles Ingram and children, by P. MERCIER, 1741. The son in coat with 'mariner's cuffs' (slit vertically and buttoned); breeches buckled over the stockings. The father in laced coat and waistcoat and rollup stockings. The daughter in back-fastening gown, apron with bib, pinner on the head. *Temple Newsam House, Leeds.*

(A) Seated Lady, by ARTHUR DEVIS, *c.* 1740. Small round-eared cap without lappets, handkerchief and long apron, laced, to match. The ruffled chemise-sleeves protrude from the gown sleeves. *City of Birmingham Art Gallery.*

(B) Henry Ingram, 7th Viscount Irwin and his wife, by P. MERCIER, c. 1742. He wears coat with round cuffs, embroidered waistcoat with buttons ending at the waist, clocked stockings, shoes with round toes and rectangular buckles. She wears a back-fastening gown over a domed hoop. The edge of the decolletage is unusual. *Temple Newsam House, Leeds.*

(A) Miss Fenton, by ARTHUR DEVIS, 1743–5. Open robe over oblong hoop, plain short robings, corset front, winged cuffs, quilted petticoat. Round-eared cap and bergère hat. *Private Collection.*

PLATE 77

685

(A) Mrs Birch and daughter, by JOSEPH HIGH-MORE, 1745. The mother in a wrapping gown with edge-to-edge closure. The daughter's coiffure shows a *tête de mouton* and on the head a pompon. *The Fitzwilliam Museum, Cambridge.*

(B) Seated Gentleman, by ARTHUR DEVIS, *c.* 1740–5. Wearing a coat with open cuffs looped to a button. Stockings gartered below the knee. Laced waistcoat buttoned up to the neck. *City of Birmingham Art Gallery.*

(c) Seated Gentleman, by FRANCIS HAYMAN, *c.* 1750. A toupee wig. Breeches buckled above the knee; note shoe buckles. *Hon. Michael Astor.*

(D) Charles Tottenham, M.P., *c.* 1748. Frock with flat collar, sleeves with closed cuffs falling away from the arm, laced waistcoat closed for riding. Heavy jackboots. *The National Gallery of Ireland, Dublin.*

PLATE 78

(A) The Gascoigne Family, by FRANCIS HAYMAN, *c.* 1745. The standing man on right in frock and double-breasted waistcoat; the two younger women (right) wearing early form of round-eared caps; the two older women (left) with mob caps and kissing strings. The standing man (behind) wears a coat and a wig with the beginning of a toupée. *Leggatt Brothers, London.*

(B) The Grant Family, by FRANCIS HAYMAN, *c.* 1745. The man in a frock with slit sleeves; shoes with large, oblong buckles. The woman in open robe, the bodice with robings; turned-back elbow sleeves; round-eared cap. *Hon. Mrs Basil Ionides.*

PLATE 79   687

(B) A Lady, by THOMAS HUDSON, *c.* 1750. Closed robe with plain robings; criss-cross lacing over stomacher. Low decolletage. Note long gloves and high-heeled shoes. In the hair a pompon. *Bristol City Art Gallery.*

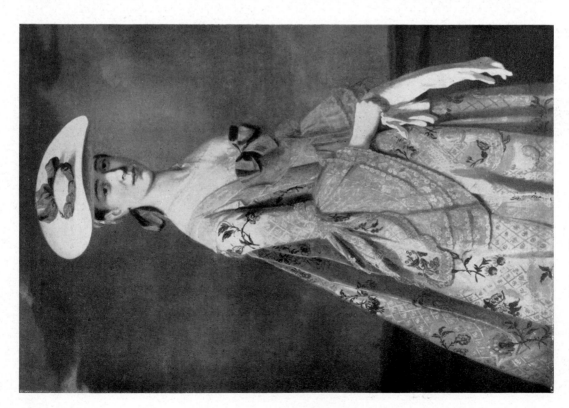

(A) Elinor Frances Dixie, by HENRY PICKERING, 1750–60. Sack gown as an open robe. Tight sleeves with treble flounces, turned up at bend of elbow, deep treble ruffles. Handkerchief secured by breast-knot. Bergère hat worn over an under-cap. *Nottingham Art Gallery.*

A

B

C

D

(A) CHRISTIAN RICHTER (1678–1732). An Unknown Lady, signed and dated 1715. *Private Collection.*
(B) BERNARD LENS (1682–1740). Self-portrait, signed and dated 1721. *National Portrait Gallery.*
(C) BERNARD LENS. Sarah Churchill, Duchess of Marlborough, signed and dated 1720. *Victoria and Albert Museum.*
(D) ANDREW BENJAMIN LENS (1713?–after 1779?). Miss Dering, signed. *Private Collection.*

PLATE 81   689

A

B

C

D

(A) PETER PAUL LENS (1714?–1750?). A Ragged Boy, signed and dated 1744. *Victoria and Albert Museum.*
(B) CHARLES BOIT (1662–1727). The Earl of Pembroke, enamel, signed. *The Lord Herbert.*
(C) CHRISTIAN FRIEDRICH ZINCKE (1684?–1767). Lady Bayly, enamel. *Victoria and Albert Museum.*
(D) CHRISTIAN FRIEDRICH ZINCKE. A Man, said to be Robert Lee, 5th Earl of Lichfield (1706–76), enamel. *Victoria and Albert Museum.*

PLATE 82

A

B

C

(A) GERVASE SPENCER (d. 1763). Lady Mary Wortley Montagu (1689–1762), in Turkish costume, enamel, signed and dated 1755. *Victoria and Albert Museum.*

(B) GERVASE SPENCER. An Unknown Young Man, enamel, signed and dated 1749. *Victoria and Albert Museum.*

(C) NATHANIEL HONE, R.A. (1718–84). The Duchess of Hamilton, enamel, signed and dated 1750. *The Lord Herbert.*

PLATE 83

A

B

C

D

E

(A) LUKE SULLIVAN (1705–71). An Unknown Lady, signed and dated 1760. *Victoria and Albert Museum.*

(B) PENELOPE CARWARDINE (1730?–1800?). A Lady, probably a member of the family of the Earl of Stamford, signed and dated 1759. *Victoria and Albert Museum.*

(C) WILLIAM PREWETT (fl. 1735–50). Mr James Newsham, enamel, signed and dated 1736. *Victoria and Albert Museum.*

(D) SAMUEL COTES (1734–1818). Miss Brougham, signed and dated 1760. *National Gallery of Victoria, Melbourne.*

(E) GUSTAVUS HAMILTON (1739–75). An Unknown Man, signed and dated 1768. *Victoria and Albert Museum.*

PLATE 84

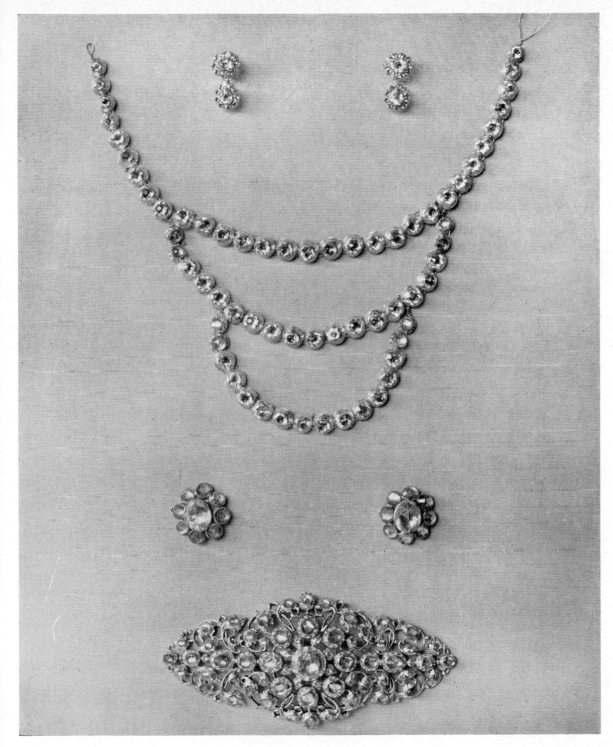

Parure of silver set with crystals from the funeral effigy of Frances Stuart, Duchess of Richmond. About 1702. *Westminster Abbey.*

PLATE 85

(A) Garter Jewel presented to the Duke of Marlborough by Queen Anne, enamelled gold set with rose diamonds. Early eighteenth century.
Wellington Museum.

(B) Brilliant bow set in silver, one of a graduated set, perhaps English, mid-eighteenth century.
Victoria and Albert Museum.

Plate 87 (opposite)

(A) Pendant, silver set with rose diamonds and topazes. Second quarter of the eighteenth century.

(B) Earring, silver and gold set with diamonds and rubies, mid-eighteenth century.

(C) Girandole brooch, silver set with pastes. About 1760.

(D) Bow brooch and pendant, silver partly gilt, set with diamonds and rubies. Early eighteenth century.

All in Victoria and Albert Museum.

A

B

PLATE 86

A

B

C

D

(For caption see opposite page)

PLATE 87

695

London Jeweller's trade card, mid-eighteenth century.
British Museum.

PLATE 88

Burkat Shudi and his family, painter unknown, *c.* 1745
Captain Evelyn Broadwood.

PLATE 89

697

'Handel's' Harpsichord, by Joannes Ruckers. Although made in the seventeenth century, this harpsichord has always been associated with Handel, and may be the one possessed by him and bequeathed by him to his friend Christopher Smith. *Reproduced by gracious permission of H.M. Queen Elizabeth the Queen Mother.*

698   PLATE 90

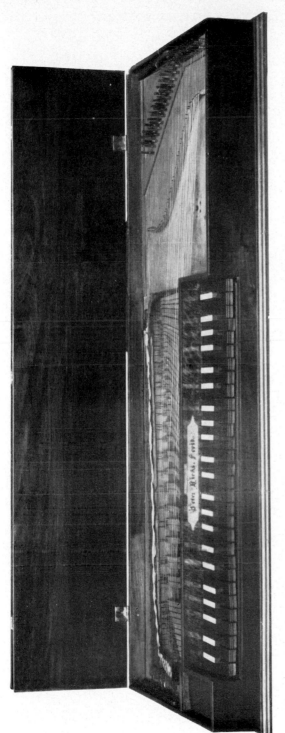

(A) An English clavichord, by Peter Hicks, *c.* 1720.
Victoria and Albert Museum.

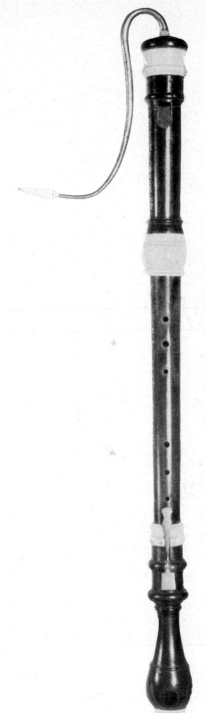

(B) Bass Recorder in E flat. English, *c.* 1750.
Victoria and Albert Museum.

PLATE 91   699

George Frederick Handel, by B. DENNER.
National Portrait Gallery.

PLATE 92

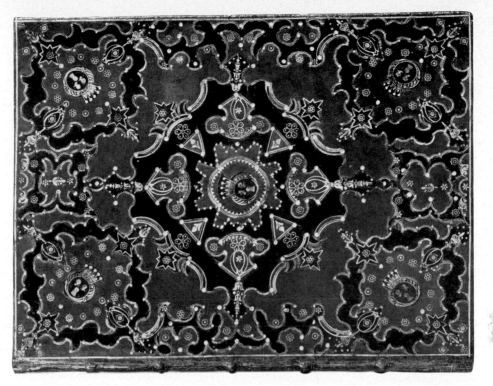

(B) A London mosaic binding, 1743. Faerno, *Fabulae Centum*, London, 1743. Red morocco, with onlays of blue and the arms of the Earl of Cholmondeley. *British Museum.*

(A) A Cambridge binding in the Harleian style, attributed to Moore. T. Rutherforth, *A System of Natural Philosophy*, Cambridge, 1748. Red morocco, gold-tooled. *British Museum.*

PLATE 93

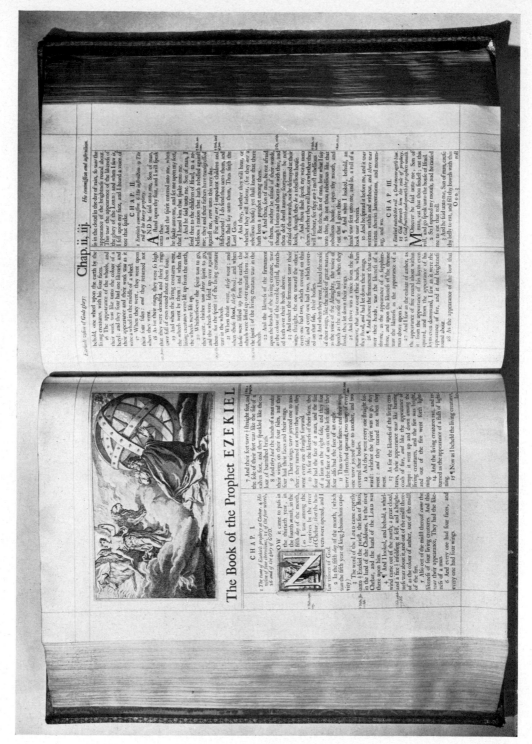

An opening of the fine 'Vinegar' Bible printed at the Oxford University Press, 1717. The illustration and initial are printed from copperplates.

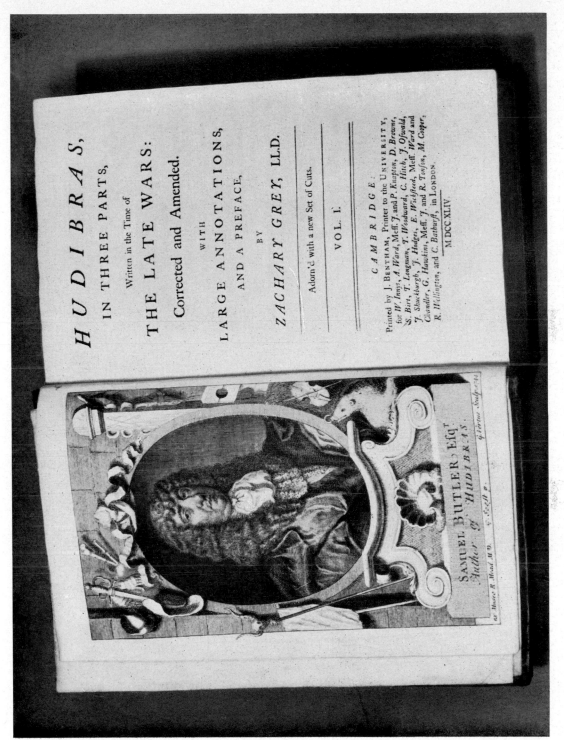

Title-page opening of an edition of *Hudibras* printed at the Cambridge University Press, 1744, with a copperplate frontispiece.

PLATE 95

703

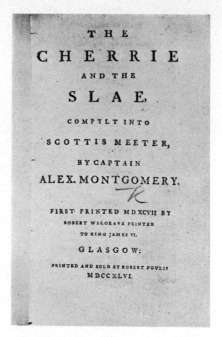

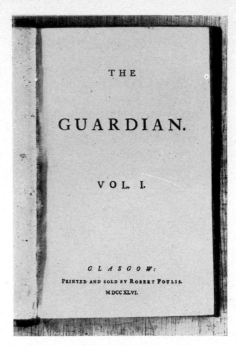

(A) Two Foulis title-pages of 1746, showing Foulis's use of capital letters only, unusual at that date. *The Guardian* title-page is, for its simplicity, in advance of its time.

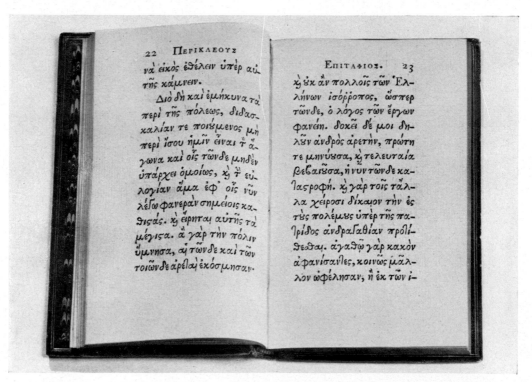

(B) Opening of *The Funeral Oration of Pericles*, from Thucydides, printed by Robert Foulis at Glasgow, 1755.

PLATE 96

Textiles

DONALD KING

After the tumults and revolutions of the Stuart century, English political and social life under the first two Georges was marked by a new stability. The abortive Jacobite attempts of 1715 and 1745 served only to cement the Whig supremacy. The prudent policies of Walpole and Pitt combined strength abroad with prosperity at home. Trading interests were consolidated in all parts of the world. The mercantile and landowning classes were well content, and the gulf between rich and poor did not, in this period, give rise to acute social pressures. Average wealth per head was rising, and the industrious apprentice had good cause to hope that solid commercial virtues would make his fortune.

This vigorous, stable, complacent society decked its homes and its persons in textiles which reflected the qualities and faults of its character. It made much use of good, plain materials in sober colours. It also displayed a taste for ostentatious luxury, in silks which glittered with a massive burden of gold and silver threads. It preferred colour harmonies which were simple, powerful and brilliant, but which are now too often falsely mellowed by the ravages of time. Patterns, too, were positive and definite, with a tendency towards heaviness and stolidity which was checked by frequent injections from foreign sources of style. The influence of French design and technical skill is often apparent. The formal curves and counter-curves of Italian baroque patterns underline the grandiloquence of Kent's interiors. Exotic motifs reflect the continuing fascination of the Far East. And English taste manifests itself in the undisciplined riot of naturalistic flowers – single flowers, massed flowers, flowers in pots and flowers in baskets. They are the characteristic, ubiquitous motif of the period. People clad in flowers sat on chairs of flowers in rooms which seemed flower-gardens.

The uses to which textiles were put in the early Georgian period did not differ markedly from those of the preceding age. In interior decoration they were expected to contribute strong patterns and pictorial interest. Tapestry, though gradually declining in importance, continued to be much used for wall-hangings, carpets, upholstery and fire-screens. The even, tapestry-like effects of embroidery in cross and tent stitches (*gros point* and *petit point*) were utilized for the same purposes. Silk embroidery on linen or silk was used, like painted and printed stuffs, chiefly for bed-furnishings and costume. Silks, velvets and cheaper woven stuffs were used for dress, upholstery, bed-furnishings, window-curtains and wall-hangings. Knotted-pile fabrics served both for carpets and for upholstery.

Bibliography. Something of the effect of textiles in interiors of this period can be seen in the illustrations of Christopher Hussey, *English Country Houses: Early Georgian* (1955). For the use of textiles in upholstery, consult the illustrations of Ralph Edwards, *A Dictionary of English Furniture*, Revised edition 1954, svv. Beds, Chairs, Screens, Settees, Stools.

Woven textiles

Though our interest lies primarily with patterned textiles, it must not be forgotten that, as in all periods, unpatterned materials were extensively used. Plain English woollens, the best in the world, were woven in prodigious quantities for home consumption and for export. Plain leather was frequently employed for upholstery, as in the chairs covered in green leather which were supplied for the New Treasury Offices in 1739; and plain silk mohair, plush and velvet, generally in shades of red, blue, green and yellow, were all used in the same way. A bed of about 1755 at Corsham Court is covered and hung with plain yellow velvet; plain green velvet, trimmed with silver braid, is used for chairs at Houghton. Watered silks or, more often, the watered woollen stuff known as moreen, were also in use; a bed from the Victoria and Albert Museum, exhibited at Ham House, has red moreen hangings.

For richer effects, silk damasks were favoured. These monochrome stuffs, usually in much the same colours as the plain materials, retained throughout the period the stately, symmetrical patterns of large, conventionalized plant forms which were already in use under the later Stuarts (Pl. 65A). Indeed, most furnishing textiles showed, in contrast with the rapidly evolving patterns of dress materials, a marked conservatism in design. On chairs and settees few original damasks have survived, and those generally in a state of extreme dilapidation; in most cases they have been replaced by reproductions of late date. Damask wall-hangings survive in some houses, as, for instance, the green damask in the old Drawing Room at Clandon Park and the crimson damask in the Claude Room at Holkham. Of beds with damask hangings, there are two good examples at Hampton Court, a magnificent one of 1715 and a smaller one of about 1725, both made for George II. The earlier, made for him as Prince of Wales, is of particular interest, since the accounts relating to it are still extant. It formed part of a suite comprising 'a standing bed of State all compleat, the furniture of a Crimson Damask and a counter paine of the same and two pair of window curtains, cornishes and vallances, two armd. chairs, eight[n] square stools, all stuffed and covered the damask as the bed and all trimmed with a rich arras silk lace suitable and a case curtain to the bed of Crimson taffaty ...' The walnut stools and chairs and the elaborately carved oak bed cost £149 15s., where-

as the bill for the silk materials, bought from the mercers John Johnson and Company, who had earlier provided the materials for the beds of William III and Queen Anne, amounted to £934 4s. 3d. This was accounted for by 'one hundred twenty-six yards of rich broad crimson damask @ 28/-, five hundred seventy three yards of rich crimson damask @ 23/- and one hundred seventy nine yards and three quarters of crimson taffeta @ 11/-.' Nor was this all, for the bed was trimmed with crimson silk braid (then known as lace), in respect of which William Weeks, laceman, rendered an account for 'six hundred seventeen yards and a halfe of very broad rich Crimson ingraine silk arras lace @ 3/3, two thousand seven hundred forty yards and a quarter of narrower ditto @ 2/6 ... etc., etc. ...' This formidable expenditure was by no means unique among the great beds of the period. The cost of the gold braid and embroidery applied to the green velvet covers and hangings of Kent's State Bed at Houghton amounted to no less than £1,219 3s. 11d. in 1732. As for bed-furnishings of a more practical nature, the Hampton Court bed was equipped with 'a very large down bed and bolster in Dimity case, three large ffustian mattresses, one of them covered with white sattin, a holland quilt covered with white sattin, a set of down pillows and bolster covered with white satin, ... a pair of large white sarcenett blankets, [and] a pair of fine large fflannell Blankets bound with ribbon'.

Apart from damasks, the materials chiefly used for the more sumptuous styles of furnishing were the patterned velvets. Their bold designs, effects of relief and rich colourings (most often deep reds and greens on white or cream grounds – Pl. 65B) made them especially suitable for interiors in the style of Kent, and they may be seen in use, as hangings for beds and walls and as covers for stools, chairs and settees, in the principal rooms of Houghton, Holkham and other great houses of the time. Their designs tended to be even more conservative than those of the damasks and throughout the period consisted almost exclusively of symmetrically radiating compositions of large, fleshy, conventionalized plant forms. They are commonly referred to in contemporary documents as Genoa velvets, and the damasks similarly are often called Genoa damasks, as in the case of the 'Green genoa damask' used for wall-hangings, window-curtains, chairs and stools in the Queen's Withdrawing Room at Hampton Court in 1737. The word sometimes appears, as above, without a capital letter, and it may well be that it indicated a type of design rather than a place of origin. None the less, most of these fine velvets can be paralleled in Italian houses, and there can be little doubt that they were woven in Italy, though not necessarily in Genoa. A few velvets of different character, such as that which is said to have hung on the walls of the Velvet Room at Ditchley since 1738, resemble in colour the velvet used for Queen Anne's bed, at Hampton Court, in 1714; these may possibly have been woven at Spitalfields. The design of the Ditchley velvet, showing the many-armed Indian dcity Shiva seated on a lotus flower, is striking, but it is hard not to feel some sympathy with the comment made by Mrs Lybbe Powys in 1778 – 'crimson and yellow velvet, all pagoda, very ugly'.

The silk-weaving industry of Spitalfields, which had been reinforced by the arrival of large numbers of French refugee weavers at the time of the Revocation of the Edict of Nantes in 1685, was at the height of its prosperity during the early Georgian period. For the evaluation of its work, the most important surviving document is the series of several hundred original designs for patterned silks, preserved in the Print Room of the Victoria and Albert Museum. Many of these bear the precise date on which they were delivered to the weaving-shop, and together they provide an almost complete year-by-year sequence extending from 1717 to 1756. The earliest group, running from 1717 to 1721, continues the series of designs by James Leman, which have been referred to in the preceding volume. The main series is associated with the name of Anna Maria Garthwaite, but undoubtedly represents the work of several different hands. One group of drawings is specifically marked as French. There are many French names – Lekeux, Ogier, Sabitier, Vautier – as well as English – Baker, Carr, Turner – among the proprietors of the weaving firms, some of which

employed as many as a hundred looms, and the existence of the French drawings is an interesting confirmation that the Spitalfields industry remained in direct contact with French sources of design. The great majority of the drawings, however, were undoubtedly produced in London.

They include relatively few designs for velvets or damasks; nearly all the drawings are for silk tissues or brocades, often enriched with gold and silver. This may be mere chance, but it may well signify that Spitalfields pattern-weaving was chiefly concentrated on dress materials. Tissues and brocades were not in common use for furnishing purposes; among the rare exceptions is a pair of love-seats of about 1720, formerly at Glemham, which are covered with a gold-and-silver brocade. From the point of view of design, the drawings show the evolution of a vigorous tradition. The extraordinarily bizarre, exotic and fantastic character of some of the early eighteenth-century patterns is softened after the death of Queen Anne. But *chinoiserie* designs recur, and the drawings of the 1720's retain in general a profiled, flattened quality, often in conjunction with angular shapes. Under the influence of French patterns, the 1730's reacted strongly against this style, and most of the designs of the decade abound in ripe curves and plastically conceived forms; massive fruits and flowers, rendered with naturalistic chiaroscuro and rich polychromy, hang in dense swags and bunches, sometimes framing little landscape vignettes. The 1740's and '50's are marked by increasing elegance. The naturalistic flowers, though still plastically treated, become smaller, and are scattered singly or in little posies, linked by curving stems or twisted ribbons; their bright colours stand out sharply against white backgrounds enlivened with flush patterns of rococo character. It is chiefly in this phase, about the middle of the century, that surviving silk textiles can be recognized as originating from Spitalfields looms, and some charming examples are preserved in English and American museums. Spitalfields silks of the earlier styles have yet to be disentangled from their continental parallels, but it is hoped that further study of the designs may make this possible.

The patterns of the silks were imitated and simplified in cheaper materials, but practically nothing of this kind has survived. Linen damasks, for table use, were largely imported from Germany and the Low Countries. Numerous examples commemorating George I and George II, as well as many continental sovereigns of the period, still exist in English houses; generally the monarch is shown as an equestrian figure, with an identifying inscription and a view of his capital city. Linen damasks with floral and armorial designs were also made in some parts of the British Isles, chiefly in Scotland and Ireland.

Bibliography: F.J.Rutherford, *The Furnishing of Hampton Court Palace: 1715–37*, in *Old Furniture*, Vol. II, 1927, pp. 77–86; J.F.Flanagan, *Spitalfields Silks of the Eighteenth and Nineteenth Centuries*, Leigh-on-Sea, 1954.

Tapestries

Although tapestries were gradually losing their former importance as an element of interior decoration, most of the great houses of the early Georgian period still had tapestry hangings in at least one of their principal rooms. As in earlier periods, most of these hangings were imported from Flanders, and the chief Brussels workshops of the first half of the eighteenth century – those of De Vos, Leyniers, Reydams, Van der Borght and Van den Hecke – are well represented in English country-houses. Typical of many fine examples are the *Bacchus and Ariadne* set and the De Vos set of *Venus and Adonis* after Albani, both at Houghton, the De Vos *Vulcan and Venus* at Ditchley, the Leyniers-Reydams *Don Quixote* set at Compton Place, the Van der Borght *Four Continents* at Mereworth, the Van der Borght *Achilles* and *Sportsmen* and the Van den Hecke *Kermesse*, all at Nostell Priory. The most popular subjects were scenes from classical history or mythology, hunting scenes or peasant scenes after the manner of Teniers. The treatment is entirely pictorial, and the woven borders not infrequently simulate carved picture-frames; the style shows little or no development over that of later seventeenth-century hangings. In point of fact, tapestries of the seventeenth century were frequently used even in the grandest of early Georgian houses, as, for instance, the Poyntz *Kings and Queens* at Houghton and the Brussels *Months* and *Continents* at Holkham. Seventeenth-century baroque tapestries were not felt to be in any way discordant with current English styles of decoration.

The newer, and infinitely gayer, French tapestries, with their lighter palette and their emphasis on the ornamental rather than the pictorial aspects of design, were little used in England. An interesting set of *Grotesques*, hung at Chevening after the house had been bought (1717) and altered by the first Earl Stanhope, harks back to the older style of Bérain; these tapestries, though they resemble Beauvais hangings, were actually made by French weavers of the Royal Tapestry Works in Berlin, and were presented to the Earl by Frederick I of Prussia. As for the many delightful new designs which were woven at Beauvais and the Gobelins during the early part of the eighteenth century, it is difficult to find evidence that any were seen in an English house before 1765, when the Duke of Richmond, then ambassador in Paris, bought for Goodwood House a Gobelins set of *Don Quixote*, after Coypel's designs.

Though the production of tapestries in England was never comparable in scale with that of the French and Flemish factories, it was none the less fairly active in this period, and by no means negligible in quality. Several workshops were operating, but for want of documentary evidence it is difficult to distinguish their products, and even signed examples are not always free from problems. English tapestries of the eighteenth century are commonly known by the generic title of Soho tapestries. This is not, however, strictly accurate. The most distinguished tapestry weaver in England at the beginning of our period, John Vanderbank, was from 1689 until his death in 1727 chief arràs-worker of the Great Wardrobe, which was situated in Great Queen Street, beyond the boundaries of Soho. His tapestries, comprising Teniers Peasants, *Elements* after Le Brun, *Venus and Cupids* after Albani, and the especially characteristic *chinoiseries*, are referred to in the preceding volume. The tapestries of Joshua Morris, on the other hand, can properly be called Soho. The *Daily Journal* for 26th November 1726, announced that on 1st December 'A Large Quantity of Curious, Fine, New Tapestry Hangings are to be Sold by Auction, by Mr Joshua Morris, Tapistry-Maker, at his House in Frith Street, near Soho-Square'. The only other biographical detail recorded of him (in *Biographical Anecdotes*, 1785) is that he commissioned Hogarth to make a tapestry design of *Earth* and, disliking the result, took the matter to law. Morris, like Vanderbank and others, essayed the *chinoiserie* style. His signature appears on a set of *chinoiseries* at Up-Ottery Manor, Honiton (formerly at Erleigh Court, near Reading). But his name is chiefly associated with sets of hangings known, for no very good reason, as *Arabesques*. One such hanging, from a set formerly at Perrystone Court, is signed I. MORRIS and dated 1723; a fine set at Hagley Park (Plate 66) is similarly signed, and another at Grimsthorpe (formerly at Normanton Park) is said to have been made in 1721. These differ from most other tapestry hangings in use in England at the time in that their designs are not pictorial, but ornamental; they show vases and baskets of flowers, parrots and other exotic birds, combined with strapwork and acanthus scrolls to form light-hearted but beautifully organized and distributed decorative compositions. The weaving is good, the colours are light and brilliant, and these are among the few English tapestries that need not fear comparison with hangings in the contemporary French idiom. The explanation of this phenomenon has been provided by Mr Croft-Murray, who suggests that the designs are due to the French decorative and flower-painter Andien de Clermont, who was active in England from about 1716 until 1756; the announcement of his sale of pictures, held in Frith Street in 1740, refers specifically to designs for tapestry and embroidery.

Compositions of vases, flowers and scroll-work are found also in tapestry covers for chairs, settees and screens (e.g. chairs at Harewood House and the Victoria and Albert Museum), alongside other, typically English, designs consisting of uninterrupted masses of naturalistic blooms (e.g. settees and chairs from Glemham, later at Waldershare Park; one settee of this set is in the Victoria and Albert Museum). It may well be that numbers of workshops producing this kind of small-scale upholstery work have left no other records of their existence. One such small workshop, which is by chance recorded, is that set up in Chelsea about 1723 by J. C. Le Blon, the pioneer of the three-colour mezzotint process; it seems to have been short-lived, and its only known production is a profile portrait of Christ which exists in a dozen or more copies (Victoria and Albert Museum, Spalding Gentlemen's Society, Warwick Castle, etc.). Another workshop, set up in Westminster in 1750 by two French weavers from the French national carpet factory of the Savonnerie, was subsequently directed by Peter Parisot, first at Paddington, and later at Fulham, under the patronage of the Duke of Cumberland. Additional workers were recruited from abroad, and for a time the establishment numbered as many as a hundred persons. In 1753 Parisot published a prospectus of his enterprise under the title *An Account of the New Manufactory of Tapestry after the manner of that of the Gobelins and of Carpets after the manner of that at Chaillot*, and Bubb Doddington, visiting the works in the same year, noted in his diary that both kinds of work were 'very fine but very dear'. For unknown reasons, this hopeful enterprise came to an untimely end in 1755, when the entire contents of the factory were offered for sale by auction. The catalogue of the sale is of some interest. It includes one set of tapestry hangings with subjects of the Teniers type, but most of the tapestries are small pieces for chairs or fire-screens. The following are typical examples: '3 patterns for screens with a Flowerpot and a Parrot ... 1 ditto with 3 Beautiful India Birds, another with Apollo and Daphne. ... A pattern for a screen or chair with the fable of the Stork and the Fox. ... Similar items of the Wolf and the Stork, the Fox and the Grapes, the Monkey and the Cat, the Stag and the Lamb. ... 11 large chair seats with curious Baskets of Flowers ... A large and magnificent State-chair, the back with Beautiful Fowls and the seat a Landskip ...' This represents almost a complete repertory of tapestry designs found on English chairs and fire-screens of the period. Although no tapestry from Parisot's factory has been positively identified, it seems likely that some of the more

French-looking specimens in English houses, often attributed to Beauvais, were actually woven at Fulham.

There were undoubtedly other factories producing similar designs. A settee of about 1720, formerly at Belton House, has a tapestry cover with pots of flowers, parrots, fowls in a landscape and a small mythological scene; it is ostentatiously signed STRANOVER BRADSHAW. A tapestry hanging with a hunting scene, reminiscent of the paintings of Wootton, bears the same signature inverted: BRADSHAW STRANOVER. This belongs to a group of tapestries with similar hunting subjects (e.g. in the Hunting Room at Clandon Park) which, with their little huntsmen, horses and dogs in wide, airy landscapes, are modest but not unattractive English cousins of Oudry's superb Gobelins series, the *Chasses de Louis XV*. Not unlike these tapestries in general pictorial character, and with similar narrow borders, are the pleasant hangings composed of excerpts from paintings by Watteau; there are sets of these at Ham House and Holkham, and one of those at Ham bears the signature BRADSHAW (Pl. 67). All these Bradshaw tapestries are of good quality and are evidently products of an active and efficient workshop. The identity of the signatories, however, remains mysterious. STRANOVER could be Tobias Stranover (1684–after 1724), a Czech painter of birds, flowers and still-life who was the pupil and son-in-law of the Hungarian painter James Bogdani in London; nevertheless, it must be admitted that a designer's name rarely achieves such prominence on tapestries. For BRADSHAW there are two possible candidates. He may have been William Bradshaw, who was active as a furniture-maker and upholsterer between 1736 and 1750; in 1737 he provided a tapestry carpet (not necessarily of his own making) for Longford Castle. Alternatively, the signature may be that of George Smith Bradshaw, active as a furniture-maker and upholsterer from 1756 onwards. He seems late in date for Tobias Stranover and the Belton settee; on the other hand, he was in partnership with the tapestry-weaver Paul Saunders between 1756 and 1758,

when their firm was supplying tapestries and textiles for Holkham, and it is presumably to him that Matthew Brettingham refers (*Holkham*, 1773, p. 14) when he states that the Vanderbank tapestries of *Venus and Cupids* at Holkham were supplemented by two pieces 'manufactured by the late Mr Bradshaw'.

Brettingham (*ibid.*, p. 8) also notes that the Flemish *Continents* in the State Bedchamber at Holkham were supplemented by tapestries made 'by the late Mr Paul Saunders', thus distinguishing between the work of the two members of this partnership, which had its headquarters in Greek Street, Soho. Saunders' tapestries at Holkham comprise panels of *Sleep* and *Vigilance* and three pieces (of which one is signed P. SAUNDERS, SOHO) of a *Turkish Pilgrimage to Mecca* after Zuccarelli, who was paid for the designs in 1758. Saunders evidently specialized in these Oriental subjects; the Duke of Northumberland has a similar set signed P. SAUNDERS, SOHO, 1758, and there is another signed set at Petworth. They are competent but undistinguished work, chiefly notable for their curiously dreamy, nostalgic atmosphere, reminiscent of the romantic Orientalism of William Collins' *Persian Eclogues*. From 1760 until his death in 1770 Saunders was working for the Great Wardrobe and, apart from some minor official commissions, seems to have been chiefly occupied with the cleaning and repair of the royal tapestry collection.

With Bradshaw and Saunders, the English tradition of tapestry-weaving came to an end. The newer, lighter styles of interior decoration which made rapid progress after 1760 were unfavourable to pictorial hangings, and the rare English commissions for tapestries in the later eighteenth century were executed by the infinitely more accomplished weavers of the Gobelins.

Tapestry-weaving in Ireland requires a brief reference. Of a set of six tapestries intended for the Irish House of Lords, only two, the *Defence of Londonderry* and the *Battle of the Boyne*, were in fact delivered, about 1732, by the official upholsterer Robert Baillie; they still hang in the building for which they were made, now the Bank of Ireland. Baillie's chief weaver in Dublin was the

Fleming John Van Beaver. In 1738 the latter wove a tapestry portrait of George II (Messrs Atkinsons, Dublin), and there is evidence that he and other weavers continued to produce small-scale tapestries in Dublin for some years, in one case as late as 1768. A few tapestry carpets were also made there.

Bibliography: W.G.Thomson, *Tapestry Weaving in England*, London, 1914; H.C.Marillier, *English Tapestries of the Eighteenth Century*, London, 1930; Ada Longfield, articles on Irish tapestry-weaving in the 18th century, in *Journal of the Royal Society of Antiquaries of Ireland*, LXVIII, 1938, pp. 91–105; LXXVI, 1946, pp. 171–75, LXXXI, 1951, 34–36.

Carpets

Any fabric that has sufficient weight and strength can be used as a floor-covering. The principal materials used for this purpose in the early Georgian period included *gros point* embroidery, knotted pile fabrics and various types of woven stuffs.

Woven carpets are unlikely to survive two centuries of wear, and it is perhaps not altogether surprising that no example of this period has yet been identified in an English house. There can be no doubt, however, that they were in common use at the time. There is documentary evidence for the use of carpets woven by the tapestry method (e.g. the carpet supplied for Longford Castle in 1737, as mentioned above). At Kidderminster there was a flourishing manufacture of double-cloth carpets (i.e. carpets composed of two cloths of different colours woven together in such a way that first one and then another appears on the surface, thus forming a pattern). About 1740, through the initiative of Lord Pembroke, the manufacture of Brussels carpets, woven with a looped pile like a terry velvet, was introduced at Wilton; Kidderminster began using the same process in 1749. The cutting of the pile loops, resulting in the familiar texture of the modern Wilton carpet, was probably introduced very shortly afterwards. In the absence of examples, nothing can be said at present with regard to the patterns of these various types of woven carpet.

Of knotted-pile carpets, there is no doubt that the great majority continued to be imported from the Near East. The 1735 inventory of Canterbury Cathedral, for instance, includes 'A Pertian Carpet and a Turkey Carpet ... a very large New Turkey Carpet and Two Small carpets ...' Here again no existing example has been positively identified as having been acquired for an English house during the early Georgian period, but it can be said with complete certainty that the designs were of the traditional Oriental types, not unlike those of many of the older Oriental carpets in use today.

In 1765 the Duke of Richmond acquired a Savonnerie carpet for Goodwood, along with his Gobelins tapestries, and it is possible that a few other knotted carpets may have reached England from the same source.

The Oriental technique of carpet-knotting had been widely practised in England during the Elizabethan and Stuart periods, both as a domestic and as an industrial craft. Many small pieces for upholstery, as well as a few larger specimens, have survived (see *Connoisseur Period Guides*, Vols. 1 and 2). There is evidence that this tradition of turkey-work, as it was called, persisted to some extent in the early eighteenth century. Large numbers of 'Turkey-worked chairs' were ordered for both Houses of Parliament in 1739. Strangely enough, however, no early eighteenth-century English chair with original turkey-work covers seems yet to have been identified. The only tangible evidence of English carpet-knotting in the first half of the eighteenth century is a small carpet now in the George Washington Mansion at Mount Vernon, U.S.A. Its design of a flowering tree is reminiscent of contemporary needlework and, like the embroidered carpets, it has been made, for convenience of working, in two halves, which have been subsequently joined. It is signed in bold capitals, ANN NEVILL AND PARNEL NEVILL 1746, and is obviously domestic work.

Commercial carpet-knotting of high quality seems to have been reintroduced into England by the two *émigré* workers from the Savonnerie at Chaillot, near Paris, who have already been referred to in connexion with tapestries. The work of Peter Parisot's Fulham factory, which developed out of their enterprise, is known only from the sale catalogue of 1755, which includes some floor-carpets, described as 'rich and beautiful', and a number of small panels, chiefly for chairs, stools and fire-screens, of which the following are typical specimens: 'A Pattern for a screen, with a Beautiful Basket of Flowers ... a beautiful Rich Pattern for a screen, 2 Chinese Figures, Flowerpot and trees. ... Another with a Beautiful Chinese Pheasant, a Parrot, and a King's Fisher in a Landskip. ... A Picture of the King of France, most exquisitely done ... in a frame and glass. ... A superb State-chair, the back with a Parrot eating fruit and the seat a Landskip.' A panel signed PARISOT was sold at Christie's in 1913, but no other example has been positively identified, and it is probably almost impossible to distinguish these small panels from the similar pieces made at the Savonnerie.

The Fulham factory was subsequently acquired by Claude Passavant, a native of Basle, but within a short time he removed to Exeter, no doubt carrying some of the Fulham workers with him. In 1758 he competed for the premium which the Royal Society of Arts, in an endeavour to encourage the industry, was offering to makers of hand-knotted carpets, and he shared the prize with Thomas Whitty of Axminster. The carpet which he submitted was described as of very fine quality and was priced at £85. Three carpets are known which bear the mark EXON, and these are without doubt products of Passavant's Exeter factory. The first, dated 1757, is in the Victoria and Albert Museum; its parrots, flower-baskets and acanthus scrolls recall the tapestries of Joshua Morris, but the central feature, a spaniel dog curled up on a tasselled cushion, perhaps intended as a *trompe-l'œil* effect, looks oddly Victorian (Pl. 68). Another carpet, dated 1758, at Petworth, is more formal: its acanthus scrolls are enlivened only with a chequer pattern and a few flowers. The third example, dated 1759, at Dumfries House, Ayrshire, is said to resemble the 1757 carpet.

Bibliography: C.E.C.Tattersall, *A History of British Carpets*, Benfleet, 1934.

Embroidery

Early Georgian carpets in needlework have survived in fairly considerable numbers. Worked chiefly in cross stitch (*gros point*) on coarse canvas, they employ wool and a little silk in many brilliant shades, which are generally set off by dark tones in the backgrounds. An example belonging to Lord Barnard, said to have been worked by Lady Grace Fitzroy, whose marriage to the first Earl of Darlington took place in 1725, has an imposing design composed entirely of conventional ornament – strapwork and acanthus, with a mask as the central feature. Such formal patterns, however, are rare among embroidered carpets, in which both field and border are usually densely strewn with large naturalistic flowers – a decorative idiom which persists in English needlework with very little change from the reign of Charles II (e.g. Hatton Garden hangings in the Victoria and Albert Museum) down to examples dated as late as 1765. A typical floral design, balanced, but asymmetrical and non-repeating, is seen in a fine needlework carpet at Hatfield. The great blooms run riot over the entire surface, unconfined except by the narrow bands of ribbon ornament which mark the limits of the border. Sometimes a slightly more formal effect is produced by the introduction of a central medallion and corner quadrants with backgrounds of a contrasting colour (Pl. 69). Occasionally this central field may be occupied by a pictorial subject; more often the great flowers flourish wildly both inside and outside the compartments, as in a carpet of 1743 in the collection of Judge Untermyer, New York. The effect of these carpets is honest rather than elegant, but they impress by the richness of their colour and the tumultuous energy of their design.

Designs of similar character occur in the panels of *gros point* and *petit point* needlework which were used for fire-screens, sconces, card-tables, stools, chairs and settees down to the period of Chippendale (Pl. 70). These smaller pieces show rather more varied treatment. The flowers may be scattered broadcast, they may be confined by scroll-work or other formal ornament, or more decorously arranged in urns or baskets. Birds and animals are introduced, sometimes for their own sake, sometimes to illustrate fables. Exotic ornament and *chinoiserie* subjects are not uncommon. Mythological scenes were evidently popular, likewise landscapes and country scenes, peasant subjects and scenes of genre and of gallantry. An interesting set of chairs belonging to Lord Hastings depicts incidents from family history. There is ample evidence to show that most of this eighteenth-century furnishing embroidery was the work of amateur needlewomen and the question arises as to the manner in which they obtained their very varied designs. A few especially talented ladies perhaps drew their own patterns. Original studies and designs by Lady Barbara North (died 1755) were preserved at Glemham until round about the beginning of the present century and are said to have been connected with the fine embroidered covers, with naturalistic birds and flowers, which she worked for a set of chairs formerly at Glemham (later at Waldershare Park). But the majority of the needlewomen were doubtless content to contribute their effects of colour and stitchery to designs drawn by another hand. Sometimes they could enlist the help of some local character whose skill with the pencil was available in return for a suitable reward. The schoolmaster of Mayfield in Sussex, Walter Gale, noted in his diary for the winter 1750–51, among other similar entries: 'I finished the bed-quilt after five days' close application. It gave satisfaction, and I received 10s. 6d. for the drawing. ... Went to Mr. Baker's and did the drawing for Miss Anne's handkerchief. I took for my reward a pint of strong.' Most of the designs, however, exhibit a fluent yet stereotyped character indicative of a professional hand and there can be little doubt that they were supplied, ready drawn on the embroidery canvas, by specialists working in London and other centres. The sources on which these designers drew for their purely floral designs are difficult to trace, but they certainly made good use of collections of flower-prints, and publishers of such collections (e.g. Robert Furber, *Four Hundred Curious Representations of the Most Beautiful Flowers ...*, 1734) specifically recommended their usefulness for embroidery purposes. In the case of figure-subjects, it is sometimes possible to find the prototype on which the design was based. An early eighteenth-century armchair in the Victoria and Albert Museum and the top of a card-table at Penshurst both show subjects derived from the engravings of John Ogilby's *Virgil* of 1658, while a fine set of chairs formerly in the possession of Mr Russell Palmer has subjects taken from Kent's and Wootton's illustrations to Gay's *Fables* of 1727.

Sets of wall-hangings, sometimes of very large size, were also similarly worked in tent and cross stitches, and must represent a prodigious labour on the part of their industrious authors. Some, like the carpets, show massed flowers; of this kind are those at Wallington Hall, Northumberland, which were worked by Julia Blackett, wife of Sir Walter Calverley; one of the panels is dated 1717. Another group has compositions of ornament surrounding landscape panels; those at Aston Hall, whose grotesque designs include views of Aston and Brereton, were worked together with a carpet by the third daughter of Sir Charles Holte, and one of them bears her signature: *Mary Holt, Spinster, aged 60, 1744. Chinoiserie* designs are also found. Two small examples at the Victoria and Albert Museum show scattered groups of Oriental figures like those of the *chinoiserie* tapestries of Vanderbank and others. Hangings with country scenes are usually treated in a purely pictorial manner; those from Stoke Edith, now at Montacute House, Somerset, depict fashionably dressed people walking in a garden with statuary, fountains, orange trees, topiary-work and formal flowerbeds.

The early Georgian period was pre-eminently a period of embroidery made for practical use, and although many of the pieces worked for furnishing purposes were pictorial in design, the embroidered picture made for its own sake, with a view to its being framed and glazed, was less prominent than in the preceding or succeeding periods. Nevertheless, numbers of them were worked, both in tent stitch on canvas and in satin stitch on white silk grounds. Scriptural subjects, country and garden scenes, and portraits of English kings and queens were among the most popular subjects. At the same time, youthful needlewomen seem to have developed decorative ambitions for their samplers, and some of these, too, were evidently intended for framing. The older tradition of the sampler as a reference-sheet for a variety of stitches and patterns did not disappear, but a new type of sampler developed, in which pious texts and little pictures, worked in cross stitch, are neatly and symmetrically arranged within a floral border.

Some of the more practical samplers have insertions in needlepoint lace, generally the 'holly point' which was chiefly used for trimming baby-linen. Many amateur needlewomen could make simple needlepoint lace of this kind, and in addition bobbin laces were very extensively made in various parts of England as a cottage industry. None of this English lace, however, could compare in design or quality with the best continental laces, and most of the fine lace which adorned the costume of both ladies and gentlemen was imported from Flanders; the Brussels and Mechlin types were especially favoured. As a substitute for lace, fine lawn with whitework and drawn-thread embroidery was often used for ruffles, flounces and ladies' aprons. White embroidery of a stouter kind was used for men's waistcoats.

Monochrome white embroidery was also in use for bed-hangings and coverlets. One popular type was the knotted work which had become fashionable in the later Stuart period; it consisted of knotted linen threads, sewn down in floral or other patterns on a linen ground. A quantity of such work made by Princess Amelia, daughter of George II, is in the possession of Lady Chichester, and the Victoria and Albert Museum has an armorial coverlet of this type which is dated 1738. Quilting, too, was much used for bed furniture and for ladies' costume.

A number of characteristic styles of silk embroidery worked on linen grounds are found on coverlets and the informal jackets and petticoats worn by ladies. One large class, which generally has vermiculate or foliage patterns, often with exotic birds, is worked in back stitch with yellow silk only, or, less often, in red or green silk. Designs worked in a restricted range of yellow and brown silks were also very popular, but the majority were executed in a great number of rich and brilliant colours (Pl. 71A). The designs are almost always of leaves and flowers, sometimes naturalistic, sometimes more or less conventional-

ized, and Oriental motifs are not uncommon. Much of this work is undoubtedly from the hands of amateurs, but some of it is of such exquisite technical perfection that it can hardly have been produced otherwise than in professional workshops. This is particularly true of the sets of embroidered bed-furniture – comprising coverlet, bolster-cover and pillow-covers of various sizes – which often include great quantities of gold thread, and are sometimes worked not on linen but on a white silk ground; they were clearly meant for display, rather than for use. A splendid set belonging to Mr John Vyvyan, with conventional floral ornament of baroque character is traditionally dated 1715 (Pl. 72A). Another fine set, in the Victoria and Albert Museum, with baskets of naturalistic flowers, is associated with the marriage of Sir John Dolben and Elizabeth Digby at Sherborne Castle in 1720; there are related sets at Blickling Hall and at Longleat. Work of a somewhat similar type is found on some of the so-called Queen Anne aprons, many of which are in fact of the early Georgian period, and on the ladies' embroidered dresses of the 1730's which vied with the contemporary woven silks in the massiveness of their fruit and flowers and the fantasy of their landscape views. Dresses of this kind are described at length in the correspondence of Mrs Delany. There is a good example in the Victoria and Albert Museum.

Bed-hangings in this period were of various kinds, but among the commonest were the crewel-work hangings, executed in coloured wools (called crewels) on white linen. The old tree designs, so popular for this class of work in Stuart times, survived into the Georgian period, with brighter colours and attenuated forms of a *chinoiserie* character. Designs of large naturalistic blooms scattered thickly and indiscriminately over the whole curtain are also found. The commonest type, however, shows a regular sprinkling of floral sprays, within formal borders; one of the hangings of a set of this kind (divided between the Victoria and Albert Museum, the Royal Scottish Museum and the National Museum of Wales) is inscribed *yt was begun April 22 1729* (Pl. 71B).

Oriental motifs occur in a great many English embroideries of the period. Most of them are doubtless no more than the decorative commonplaces of the time. It is worth remembering, however, that actual Oriental embroideries were not unfamiliar in England. Embroidered coverlets imported from Persia seem to have influenced the style of English embroidered coverlets. And embroideries from India and China were likewise included in the cargoes of the East India Company's ships. The State Bed of about 1730 at Houghton has hangings of Indian embroidery, worked in a European design with birds and baskets of flowers, while the splendid angel bed of 1720 at Erthig Park has a coverlet and hangings of Chinese embroidery, with figure-scenes. A Chinese floral embroidery in the Victoria and Albert Museum includes the arms of the first Duke of Chandos, and suggests that this type of work could be made to order.

Bibliography: M. Jourdain, *English Secular Embroidery*, London, 1910.

Printed textiles

Textile imports from China included also silks with painted floral patterns, which were used in England for both costume and furnishing purposes. Imports of chintz, the painted and dyed cotton material from India which had achieved extraordinary popularity in the Stuart period, were banned by Act of Parliament in 1701. Nevertheless, it seems to have been possible to some extent to evade this prohibition. It is certain, at least, that all through the early Georgian period Indian craftsmen continued to make their characteristic coverlets and bed-hangings for the European market. Many of these retain the tree-patterns current in the seventeenth century, but others, with cornucopias, swags and baskets of flowers, are clearly based on models newly arrived from Europe. A chintz coverlet in the Toronto Museum, for example, has floral motifs derived from designs by Peter Casteels, which appeared in Robert Furber's *The Twelve Months of Flowers*, 1730. It is interesting to note that Casteels also acted as designer for English textile-printers, first at Tooting and subsequently at Richmond.

The primary purpose of prohibiting the import of Indian chintz in 1701 was to protect the English weaving industry. But the fashion for printed cottons, both for dress and furnishing, was not so easily discouraged, and the chief beneficiaries of the ban were in fact the English textile-printers, who in the late seventeenth century had succeeded in combining the Indian technique of fast-dyed patterns with the European tradition of block-printing. In response to renewed agitation by the weavers, during which some ladies suffered the embarrassment of having their print gowns torn from their backs, the government laid a tax on English printed cottons in 1712, doubled it in 1714, and finally prohibited printing on cotton entirely in 1720. Undeterred, the printers began to use fustian (a mixture of linen and cotton) and, despite further pressure from the weavers, their right to do so was vindicated by the so-called Manchester Act of 1736. Eventually, in 1774, Richard Arkwright, representing the rising English cotton industry, engineered the repeal of the 1720 act, and printing on cotton was resumed.

The English print-works were almost all, in this period, situated in and around London, on the banks of the Thames or its tributaries Wandle, Lea and Cray. They seem to have been in flourishing condition – the Mitcham works of the Huguenot family of Mauvillon, for example, employed 150 hands in 1719 – and the design and technique of their products were the admiration and envy of their continental competitors. Unfortunately, these English block-printed stuffs of the early Georgian period have succumbed almost without trace. They seem to have included both floral and figure patterns and the colours, as in Indian chintz, were chiefly reds and blues. The most important surviving examples are two block-printed coverlets signed by George Ormerod, whose factory was at Wallington in Surrey. One of these, in the possession of Lord Stanley of Alderley, shows flowers, urns, birds and figures of Fame, within floral borders. It bears a dedicatory inscription to Sir Edward Stanley, Bart., and is dated 1751. The second piece, dated 1752, is in the Philadelphia Museum. It was made for the East India merchant John Vandermersch, and uses many of the same blocks, with the addition of elephants, lions and figures of Indians (Plate 72B).

In addition to block-printing, a method of printing fast-dyed patterns from engraved plates was introduced at the end of the period. Francis Nixon, whose factory at Drumcondra in Ireland was employing this method as early as 1752, transferred his activities to Phippsbridge, near Mitcham, in 1757. The fine printed stuffs produced in this manner, forerunners of the better-known *toiles de Jouy*, are discussed in the next section of this Guide.

Bibliography: Muriel Clayton and Alma Oakes, *Early Calico Printers around London*, in Burlington Magazine, XCVI, 1954, pp. 135–39; K.B.Brett, *An English Source of Indian Chintz Designs*, in Journal of Indian Textile History, I, 1955, pp. 40–53.

(A) Design for woven silk, London, 1717. (B) Design for woven silk, from a Spitalfields weaver's pattern book, *c.* 1727. (C) Design for woven silk, from a Spitalfields weaver's pattern book. The design bears the name of Anna Maria Garthwaite, *c.* 1733–34. (D) Design for woven silk, from a Spitalfields weaver's pattern book, 1744.

Costume

C. WILLETT CUNNINGTON

Ancestral portraits from the reigns of George I and George II seem at first sight to present a certain sameness; a row of incredible creatures in pompous wigs and hoops. There have been epochs when fashions changed but sluggishly, and to a casual glance those two reigns suggest an example. But a portrait gallery can be deceptive, and for the first half of the eighteenth century there are other sources of information such as printed matter, much of which has only recently come to light, from which we discover that those staid ancestors were quite human in their love of change. Details of the newest modes were for them matters of moment. A reader of *The Weekly Messenger* in 1735 writes: 'I shall be all amazement if your paper does not become the favourite of the Ladies as it gratifies their inclination of knowing the prevailing fashions', and writers from the country inquire eagerly of the latest cut or trimming and whether last season's novelty is 'now totally exploded'.

At this distance we cannot always detect evidence of those explosions, though many resound in the contemporary essay and social comedy. The Court, elderly and foreign, no longer supplied fashion-leadership; instead, the Stage was beginning to provide models. Mrs Oldfield as Lady Betty Modish or Lady Townly taught audiences the genteelest manner of wearing the newest modes; dressmakers' 'moppets' or dolls wearing Parisian fashions were constantly imported, and news of them spread far and wide over the country, 'where the newest fashions are brought down weekly by the stage-coach and all the wives and daughters of the most topping tradesmen vie with each other every Sunday in the elegance of their apparel. ... The same genteel ceremonies are practised there as at the most fashionable churches in town. The ladies, immediately on their entrance, breathe a pious ejaculation through their fan-sticks and the beaux very gravely address themselves to the Haberdasher's bills glewed upon the linings of their hats'.[1] The former conventions which used to distinguish the dress of one social class from another were being over-run. 'A laced coat, waistcoat or trimming are so common that they are indifferently worn by the Master and the servant, nor is it easy to distinguish the Chambermaid from the Mistress.'[2] Snobbery was in full blossom. The prosperous merchant and the nabob returning from India laden with spoils were equally intent on pushing into the world of fashion, and round the outskirts of it were grades of would-be gentry, the Spruce Fellow, the Smart, the Flap, the Dapper, the Spark, the Blood, each distinguishable by contemporaries through subtle difference of costume.

To escape from these vulgar imitators the Quality must needs devise modes more exclusive. The gigantic turned-back cuff rendered the gentleman's arm a cumbersome ornament, while the ladies' hoop, an English invention, steadily expanded and 'serves to keep the men at a decent distance'.[3] But alas! exclusive modes are quickly

---

[1] *The Connoisseur*, 1756.
[2] *Universal Spectator*, 1734.
[3] *Whitehall Evening Post*, 1747.

copied by common folk, and a lady in 1722 lamented that her maidservant from the country 'had not liv'd with me three weeks before she sew'd three penny canes round the bottom of her shift instead of a hoop-petticoat'.[4]

Ladies and gentlemen of *ton* favoured expensive foreign imports as less easily copied, especially if the wearing of them was illegal; in 1749 French cambric and lawns were prohibited and therefore extremely fashionable. So, too, the wearing of buttons covered with textile materials (to help the metal-button trade of Birmingham). The con-

[4] *The Artifice*, Mrs Centlivre.

Fig. 1. The bridal couple: Joseph in a plain coat with round cuffs, Fanny in 'a white dimity nightgown ... a short round-eared cap under a little straw hat.' From an illustration by J. Hulett dated 1742 to *Joseph Andrews*.

stant lament that 'we take our fashions from the land we hate', and scorn for 'admirers of foreign gewgaws' had little effect. A character in *The Provok'd Husband* of 1728 protests that 'we have City wives here who will give £20 for a short apron', and a small provincial paper of 1739 advertised 'French, Mechlin, and other Flanders lace at £1 to £5 a yard'. Multiply these figures by ten for modern equivalents and we see that even the middle class was decidedly 'fashion conscious'.

There was of course the group of quiet gentlefolk, described by J. Macky in 1722: 'The dress of the English is like the French but not so gaudy; they generally go plain but in the best cloths and stuffs and wear the best linen of any Nation in the World; not but that they wear Embroideries and Laces on their Cloathes on Solemn Days but they do not make it their daily wear as the French do.'

From the mass of evidence, often conflicting, describing the dress of the period we, at this distance, can now detect the introduction of a new idea. Hitherto fashions had originated at the top of the social scale gradually percolating downwards; but about 1730 a reverse movement took place, and for the first time in our history the gentleman began to borrow actual garments from the 'common man' as being more comfortable than his own. 'There is at present a reigning ambition among our young gentlemen of degrading themselves in their apparel to the class of the servants they keep.'[5] The specific garments which thus changed hands and entered the gentleman's wardrobe were, as we learn from Soame Jenyns, in *The World*, 1756, the frock, the buckskin breeches, and the flapped hat. To sacrifice symbols of class for mere comfort was indeed an explosive idea, destined eventually to shatter for ever aristocratic distinctions in dress, and resembling that other event of fifty years later. '*C'est une révolte? Non, Sire, c'est une révolution.*' It is significant that this English innovation was not copied by the French aristocrat until some thirty years later; while here the gesture began to smooth out a perilous diversity.

[5] *Universal Spectator*, 1739.

It seems, then, that an epoch, looking placid enough in a portrait gallery, had in reality disturbing fashions expressive of opposing impulses, with rank resisting the invasion of wealth and multiudes busy imitating both who in their turn imitate the multitude. So that by the middle of the century the social scene had conspicuously changed and 'thanks to the foolish vanity that prompts us to imitate our superiors ... every tradesman is a merchant, every merchant is a gentleman, and every gentleman one of the nobless. We are a nation of gentry'.[6] And the writer continues:

> 'We have no such thing as common people among us, the sons of our lowest mechanics acquiring the laudable ambition of becoming gentlefolks ... their girls are all milliners ... attorneys' clerks and city apprentices dress like cornets of dragoons. ... A kind of perpetual warfare between the *good* and *bad company* has subsisted for half a century last past in which the former have been perpetually pursued by the latter and fairly beaten out of all their resources for superior distinction; out of innumerable fashions in dress, every one of which they have been obliged to abandon as soon as occupied by their impertinent rivals. ...'

We have to look twice to see that the date is 1755 and not two centuries later.

Male fashions

The suit comprised coat or frock, waistcoat, and breeches. The coat, cut without a seam at the waist, was close-fitting and waisted, with flared skirts reaching to just below the knee, and with two pleated side vents and a centre one between two deep inverted pleats. There was no collar.

Until *c.* 1740 the front line was vertical, then becoming slightly curved away below waist-level, and by 1760 the flare was disappearing. Buttons were usually domed and covered with material (though illegal). At first buttons reached from neck to hem, but after about 1720 they ceased below waist level. The outside pockets had scalloped flaps. (There was no inside pocket.)

The turned-back cuff of the close-fitting sleeve, extended, in the 1730's to the elbow, either closed and round – known as a 'boot sleeve', or open at

[6] *The World*, 1755.

Fig. 2. Before the Justice: Fanny in a round gown with turned-back cuffs; the man in the doorway in a frock; the Justice, seated wearing old-fashioned shoes with square tongues. From an illustration by J. Hulett dated 1742 to *Joseph Andrews*.

the back. Sometimes without a cuff the 'slit sleeve' exposed the ruffled shirt sleeve. In the 1750's the round cuff was wide and 'winged' (i.e. falling away from the sleeve on the outer side).

The frock, borrowed from the working-man, began in 1730 to be worn by the gentleman as a form of 'undress', at first for country wear and riding, but soon for day wear in town, and by 1748 we hear of a gentleman at a ball 'dressed in a green frock'. It resembled an easy form of the coat, though shorter, and was distinguished by a small flat turned-down collar, known as a 'cape', generally of a different material. The sleeves ended in round closed cuffs usually deep and wide. The buttons were generally metal, often of Sheffield plate after 1750. Its attractions over those of its rival the coat were described by Arthur Murphy in 1752: 'I was so damned uneasy in a full dress coat with hellish long skirts ... I frequently sighed for my little loose Frock which I look upon as an emblem of our happy constitution; for it lays a man under no uneasy restraint but leaves it in his power to do as he pleases'.[7]

[7] *Gray's Inn Journal.*

Fig. 3. Parson Adams in the foreground 'in his half-cassock and flannel nightcap'; the beau by his side in a great-coat. Note heavy riding-boots on top shelf. From an illustration by J. Hulett dated 1742 to *Joseph Andrews.*

The waistcoat or vest was close-fitting to the waist; the flared skirts, stiffened with buckram like those of the coat, ending above the knee. It too had no collar, and after 1740 the front line began to be curved away and becoming shorter exposed more of the breeches. Sleeves without cuffs persisted until the 1750's. From the 1730's a few were double-breasted, but single-breasted was the rule. The waistcoat was fastened by buttons or hooks and eyes, the upper part being left open to display the ruffled shirt. There were two flapped pockets resembling those of the coat.

The knee-breeches, designed to hang on the haunches without braces, were made with a full seat gathered into a waistband with buckle at the back. The legs ended just below the knees in a band slit on the outer side and closed there by four buttons. Breeches were fastened either by buttons down the front without a fly, the buttons being concealed by the long waistcoat; or by a small or a whole fall, which method became general after 1750, when the fashionable garment was close-fitting and short, exposing the knees. Coat materials for 'undress' were cloth, camlet, plush, velvet, silk and satin with trimmings of lace braid and fur. For full dress, gold and silver stuffs, brocades, flowered velvet and embroidered cloths.

The frock, never embroidered, was of cloth, fustian, plush and serge. The waistcoat, for undress, was of cloth, serge, camlet and calimanco; while for full-dress brocades, damasks, heavily embroidered silks and satins; and fringed waistcoats were fashionable. Wedding waistcoats were white. The breeches, for undress, were of cloth, plush, and for riding, leather, especially buckskin. For full dress, silk, satin and velvet. All these garments were lined (for the upper classes). Prices were often staggering, in terms of modern money (i.e. multiplied by ten). 'Black velvet for breeches 26/ a yard' (1726). 'A frock suit of superfine broadcloth £8.15.' (1755).

The gentleman's negligée garments were a nightgown, resembling the modern dressing-gown, tied at the waist by a sash; the morning gown, similar but usually shorter and closer-fitting; and the banyan or Indian nightgown, a loose knee-length coat with a wrapping front. These three, worn informally at home, usually with a nightcap in place of a wig, could also be worn out of doors.

'Sometimes in slippers and a morning gown
He pays his early visits round the town.' [8]

They were often of brightly coloured materials, from chintz to flowered satin.

Neckwear

The cravat, worn until the 1740's, was a strip of linen, lawn or muslin wound round the neck and loosely knotted under the chin, the hanging ends edged with lace. The 'Steinkirk', a cravat with the ends twisted and threaded through a button-hole, ceased to be fashionable after *c.* 1730, when the cravat was replaced by the stock. This was a piece of linen or cambric folded to form a high neckband often stiffened with buckram and buckled behind. With it a solitaire or length of black ribbon was worn over the stock and loosely tied in a bow in front. The front of the shirt was ruffled, and likewise the sleeve-ends emerging from the coat-sleeves.

Outdoor garments

The surtout ('great coat' or 'cape coat') was also known, from the 1730's, as a 'wrap-rascal', as resembling a highwayman's, being large and loose, reaching below the knees, with a flared skirt and a broad flat collar or two. It was buttoned from neck to hem, and for riding might be double-breasted. This was made of cloth, duffle, frieze or kersey. The cloak, ceasing to be fashionable after 1750, was full and gathered at the neck under a flat turned-down collar, and reached below the knees. A *roquelaure*, a popular form of cloak, was ample, shaped to the neck, and with a back vent; often of coloured cloth; closed by brass buttons.

Footwear

The toe of the shoe became more rounded, and the tongue, worn high by the military and the beaux, was reduced in height, together with a lower heel, for the ordinary gentleman. Red heels

were the mode for 'dress' wear up to 1750. The buckle, a small square or oblong until 1725, then increased in size assuming baroque patterns, made of white metal, steel, pinchbeck, or silver according to the social position. Pumps with low heels and thin soles were worn even out of doors by the fop, whose 'Spanish leather pumps without heels and burnished toes and fine wrought buckles near as big as those of a coach-horse, covering his instep and half the foot' (*The London Magazine*) (1734) were in the extreme of fashion. Slippers, resembling modern mules, were worn indoors, while for riding jack-boots with bucket tops and reaching above the knees, or jockey-boots to below the knees and with turned-down tops, were in common use. Against wet weather spatterdashes (leather or canvas gaiters) were worn on horseback.

Day stockings, of worsted or thread, knitted by hand or machine, were often ribbed or chequered (after 1730), and of various colours, including scarlet. At a royal wedding 'white stockings were universally worn by the gentlemen as well as the ladies'.[9] For evening wear stockings were of silk, with clocks. Until the 1750's stockings (of the gentry only) were rolled up over the knees of the breeches, but already by 1735 the new fashion for gartering below the knee with the breeches buckled over the stocking was beginning to come in. The older style gave the name of 'roll-ups' or 'rollers' to stockings.

Headgear

Owing to the wearing of a wig the hat was no longer an important feature, and was often carried under the arm. Its usual shape was three-cornered (to which the next century gave the name 'tricorne'). The brim, bound with braid and fringed with ostrich feather, was turned up or 'cocked' on three sides, and worn with the point in front. The crown was fairly deep, flat or rounded on top. The 'Kevenhuller Cock', 'broad brimmed and staring', had the front peak given a 'smart pinch', while the 'Dettingen Cock', fashionable in the 1740's, had extra large cocks to it. Both styles had larger brims than those of the 1730's.

[8] Soame Jenyns *Poems*, 1748.

[9] *Read's Weekly Journal*, 1736.

The Round Hat, with round crown and un-cocked brim, was a form taken in the 1730's from the artisan, and was described as 'slouched' or 'flapped'. One reads, at a theatre, of 'a parcel of the strangest fellows, with gold-laced hats slouched',[10] and of gangs of disorderly youths comprising 'those who wore hats fiercely cocked and those who preferred the nab or trencher hat with the brim flapping over their eyes'.[11] Hats, trimmed with metallic braid ('laced'), were made of beaver or inferior imitations, and for country wear straw was sometimes used for round hats.

Another of those fashions taken from the lower classes in the 1730's was the Jockey Cap, round and black, with a flat peak in front and by no means only worn when riding. 'A set of Sparks who chuse rather to appear as Jockeys and it is seldom or never they are to be seen without Boots, Whips ... and black Caps ... in these they come into the boxes at the theatre'.[12]

Indoors for negligée in place of the wig a linen nightcap with round crown and rolled brim was commonly worn on the shaven head.

The wig

Worn by all classes and in many varieties, with or without a queue behind.

The principal ones without queues were:

1. The full-bottomed with a mass of curls falling on to the shoulders; ceasing to be fashionable after 1730.
2. The campaign, a bushy wig framing the face with a centre parting and having three tails; a short central curl fell on the nape of the neck. Worn especially when travelling; fashionable to the 1750's.
3. The bob, an 'undress' wig worn by all classes, the long bob covering the neck, the short bob exposing it.
4. The scratch, from about 1740, was of minimum size, convenient for travelling and sport.
5. The cut wig, also small and plain, was worn by artisans.

The two last merely covered the crown of the head.

Fig. 4. A man in a nightcap and banyan. After *The Rake's Progress*, Plate 2, 1735.

Fig. 5. A man in a bag-wig with solitaire. After *The Rake's Progress*, Plate 2, 1735.

[10] *The London Evening Post*, 1738.
[11] *Jonathan Wild*, H. Fielding, 1743.
[12] *The Universal Spectator*, 1739.

Fig. 6. A group of men: note campaign wigs, coats with large round cuffs
hanging away from the sleeves, roll-up stockings, and rounded toes of shoes.
From Bickham's *The Universal Penman*, 1742.

6. The physical wig, appearing about 1750, worn by the learned professions, was a larger version of the long bob without a centre parting and bushed out at the sides in horizontal rolls.

In wigs with queues the lock of hair behind was tied in a ribbon, and the front hair, until *c.* 1735, was parted in the centre. But from 1730 the toupee or foretop was introduced, the hair being brushed straight back from the forehead in a roll above the temples.

There were many varieties:

1. The tye wig, for 'undress', the hair drawn back and the curls bunched together to form a queue tied with black ribbon.
2. The bag wig, for 'dress', the queue enclosed in a square black bag.
3. The pig-tail wig, a smart kind for 'undress', the queue being very long and intertwined with black ribbon.
4. The Ramilies wig with a long, diminishing, plaited queue tied above and below.

5. The Major (known in France as the Brigadier) with a double queue; dating from the 1750's and primarily a military wig.

Wigs were made usually of hair, human or animal (such as horse, cow, or goat); but also of feathers (a drake's or mallard's) for the foretop, worn especially by the clergy and known as 'parson's feather tops'. Wigs of these materials were both inflammable and also damaged by rain, so in 1750 metal wigs were introduced. 'A certain peruke-maker has distanced all his brethren by a new invention of making a wig of copper wire which will resist all weathers and last for ever.' [13] And Horace Walpole (1751) reports: 'Brought from Paris an iron wig; you literally would not know it from hair'. But this fashion did not long survive.

Prices of wigs depended on the materials. A provincial advertisement of 1739 announces: 'Wigs, human hair 30/. Fine white horsehair 12/. It is ingenuously acknowledged that the Horse-

[13] *Ipswich Journal*, 1750.

K

hair Wiggs are rather for Sight than Service'. For better qualities prices were much higher, e.g. 'For a tied wig £7.1.0'.[14] The colours ranged from white, flaxen, brown, grizzle to black, usually powdered.

Gloves were plain, either wrist-length or 'high-topped' reaching beyond the wrist, and often fringed. Large muffs were carried and a sword, or from 1730 a long cane. The face was clean-shaven.

The Beau took as much pains as the Belle over his make-up, 'redning his lips and painting his nauseous phiz'.[15] The cheeks were embellished with patches and Exquisites 'have their toilette set out with washes, perfumes, and cosmetics; and will spend a whole morning in scenting their linen, dressing their hair, and arching their eyebrows'.[16] In addition 'a new pair of calves this morning I put on'.[17] An ounce of best carmine, costing £3 and 'a night mask to take away freckles £1.1.0' appear in a fop's bill of 1743.

[14] Essex Records, 1734.
[15] Tricks of the Town, 1735.
[16] The Connoisseur, 1754.
[17] The Gentleman's Magazine, 1732.

The task of dressing was for the beau an arduous business. 'A slovenly fellow might hustle into his clothes in an hour but a *Gentleman* could scarcely dress in less than two.'

Female fashions

The dress consisted of gown and petticoat (often called simply a 'coat'), the gown being formed of a bodice and skirt joined together. The skirt was either open in front to reveal the petticoat (the 'Open Robe') or was closed.

The open robe

The boned bodice, open in front, had its borders edged with sewn-down revers ('robings') which joined to form a V at the waist. The gap between was filled by an ornamental stomacher or by a corset with an embroidered front. The robings until *c.* 1750 ended at or just below the waist level and were usually plain, seldom embroidered before 1745, except for Court wear.

The stomacher was a panel, pointed, rounded or scalloped below, with a straight upper border, and was stiffened with pasteboard, padding or bones. Some were trimmed with a ladder of bows

Fig. 7. Lady in an open robe with furbelow trimmings to the hem, embroidered stomacher, the triple flounced elbow sleeves with triple ruffles, and flounced petticoat. The boy, in sleeveless waistcoat, dressed for cricket. After 'Mrs Matthew Michell and family' by Thomas Hudson, *c.* 1750–55. *Leicester Museum and Art Gallery.*

known as 'échelles'. The stomacher was pinned in place under the robings or if plain, laced across. The corset, laced behind, could have a plain or embroidered front if acting as a stomacher.

The closed bodice (of the open robe) had a round decolletage without robings and was buttoned down the front to the waist; mainly a fashion of the 1720's.

Sleeves ended above or just below the elbows and were finished with turned-up cuffs, which were small until 1740, when they became 'winged', i.e. stiffened and falling away from the sleeve on the outer side. From about the same date the cuff began to be replaced by two or three flounces ('ruffles') sewn on to the sleeve which had now become close-fitting so that the ruffled sleeve of the chemise could no longer protrude.

The overskirt and petticoat were adapted to the varying shapes of the hoop beneath, the former being pleated to the bodice in wide pleats, with – from 1730 – the back cut *en fourreau*. In this the back panels were each carried in one piece from neck to hem without a seam at the waist. The petticoat, usually of a different colour from that of the gown, was often embroidered (flounced for Court wear only, until the 1750's). The quilted petticoat was common in the '30's, '40's, and '50's.

The principal variations of the open robe were:

1. The mantua, fashionable to 1750. In this the bodice was not boned, and the skirt was trained. It might be of the richest materials, being worn on all social occasions and at Court.
2. The nightgown. This term came to indicate an ordinary open robe with robings, the decolletage covered with some kind of neckwear and worn as a form of 'undress'. 'Nightgowns are worn without hoops.' [18]
3. The Trollopee or Slammerkin, coming into fashion about 1750, appears to have been a loose sack not fastened at the waist; the bodice had no bones and was loose-fitting; the overskirt was trained and the petticoat

[18] *Mrs Delany*, 1756.

Fig. 8. Back view of a woman wearing a Petenlair. From a Chelsea porcelain figure, *c.* 1755, in the *Wernher Collection, Luton Hoo*.

short. Always a form of 'undress' it might be worn indoors without a hoop.

The closed robe or 'round gown'

1. The wrapping gown (1735–50). This had a close-fitting bodice without robings, with round decolletage. Its front, continuous with the skirt, wrapped across, secured at the waist by a brooch or clasp. The neck was finished with a tucker or modesty piece. The short sleeves had either turned-back cuffs or multiple ruffles.
2. The bodice with an edge-to-edge closure was popular in the 1730's and 1740's. The front of the skirt was made with a short 'fall' pleated above into a waistband with strings tied behind under the bodice.
3. The sack, worn in England from 1720 to about 1750 as a closed gown, afterwards becoming an open robe.

At first (to 1730) the gown was capacious and shapeless, falling from neck to hem like a bell tent. Behind, small box-pleats stitched down to the neckband spread out in ample folds to the ground. In front stitched-down flat pleats from the shoulders converged to a point at the waist, the gap filled by a stomacher. From 1730 the bodice was shaped to the figure by means of a tight lining and robings ending at the waist were added. The 'sack back' (miscalled later the 'Watteau pleat') comprised two double or treble box-pleats on each side of the centre back seam, their upper part stitched down, but flowing free from the shoulder level. The sleeves had cuffs, closed or winged.

The separate bodice and skirt style

1. The jacket bodice (the French *casaquin*), with a round or square decolletage, was close-fitting to the waist, whence it flared out over the petticoat to below the hips. The front was fastened by lacing or concealed hooks and eyes.
2. The petenlair, fashionable in the 1750's. This was a jacket bodice in the form of a sack shortened to above knee length.

'... thy skilful engineer
Lopp'd half the sack and form'd the pet-en-l'air.'[19]

These jacket bodices were worn with untrimmed petticoats, usually over domed hoops. It was essentially a morning style of dress commonly adopted by the housewife. (Although actual specimens of the petenlair do not seem to have survived, it is often well represented on Chelsea figures of the period where its various aspects can be examined.)
3. The riding habit. Consisting of jacket, waistcoat and petticoat. The jacket, without a collar before 1730 and afterwards with one, was cut, like the waistcoat, on masculine lines buttoning left over right. The petticoat was full and long. By the middle of the century the lady's riding habit, previously made of camlet, grogram or other silks, began to be made of superfine cloth (anticipating the 'tailor-made coat and skirt' of a hundred years later).

Silks, satins, tabby, brocade, damask, chintz and Indian cottons were used for gowns and petticoats, the two garments usually of contrasting colours. Velvet was reserved for Court wear. Yellow·was the fashionable colour for the quilted petticoat in the 1740's.

The wedding dress was usually white, and the material for mourning was black bombazine.

The neck was covered with a tucker or a modesty piece, and from 1730 a laced tippet frequently surrounded the shoulders.

The apron, long with a bib or short without, was a fashionable decoration.

An important feature of the dress of the 1750's was the excessive width and depth of the decolletage, which provoked much hostile criticism. 'The fashion is now to show as low as one possible can'.[20] 'The fashion came up among ladies of wearing their gowns off the shoulders.' [21]

'Let your stomacher stretch from shoulder to shoulder,
And your breast will appear much fairer and bolder.' [22]

The hoop

The dome-shape known as the cupula, expanded in size and 'after ages, who perhaps may see this contrivance only in the paintings of some great masters, shall with pain believe what the justness of the pencil presents'.[23]

In the 1740's and 1750's the more fashionable shape was pyramidal, the 'fan hoop'.

'The vast expanse of whose enormous size
And wide dimensions would provoke surprise,
Full nine long yards the stiff'ning whalebone bound
The circle's wide circumference around.' [24]

The oblong hoop, fashionable in the 1740's and 1750's, was flattened front and back and immensely wide; over it the skirt was carried out horizontally from the waist on each side to hang vertically down over the pair of 'false hips' or bag-like bustles which provided the excessive width. Hoops, worn by all classes, were even sometimes worn on horseback.

---

[19] *The Gentleman's Magazine*, 1751.

[20] *Gray's Inn Journal*, 1752.
[21] *The World*, 1753.
[22] *The Gentleman's Magazine*, 1754.
[23] *The Whitehall Evening Post*, 1747.
[24] *The Westminster Journal*, 1748.

Outdoor garments

Cloaks and large enveloping scarves, some with capes, were general. By the middle of the century the pelisse, a long cloak hanging straight, and a short hooded cloak were becoming fashionable, and the Joseph, a surtout usually green, was worn for riding. Over the hooped gown it would have been impossible to wear any sort of fitting overcoat.

Headgear

The cap tended to be inconspicuous; the pinner, circular and flat on the crown, with frilled border, might have long hanging lappets. This in the 1730's was being replaced by the round-eared cap, slightly bonnet-shaped and curving round the face to the level of the ears. Its frill increased and widened so that by 1746 it stood out from the face as 'vast winkers', which became still more emphasized in the 1750's. The round-eared cap is noteworthy both as a fashion borrowed by the upper from the lower class, and also as the first instance of a garment made fashionable by a work of fiction. Hence the allusion:

'Our thoughtless sons for round-ear'd caps may burn,
And curse Pamela, when they've serv'd a turn.' [25]

The mob cap, with a puffed-out crown high on the head, a deep flat border surrounding the face and dangling side pieces known as 'kissing strings', became fashionable for 'undress' wear from the 1730's on. All such caps (and ruffles) were usually starched and those of foreign laces were often extremely costly. 'Lace lappet heads from 10 to 50 guineas a pair.' [26] A curious 'relapse' of fashion occurred early in the 1750's. Just as younger gentlemen abandoned wigs, so the ladies' caps either shrank in size or vanished. 'Our caps have from the size of a china plate dwindled away to the breadth of a half crown and then entirely vanished'. [27] 'They wear no cap and only substitute a variety of trumpery ribbands.' [28]

However, the cap soon revived as a small lace affair wired in the shape of a butterfly and known

Fig. 9. Family at breakfast: the women in round-eared caps and round morning gowns with robings; the father in a coat; his son, opposite him, in a frock, the smaller children dressed like adults. From an illustration by J. Hulett dated 1742 to *Joseph Andrews.*

as the butterfly cap, the borders decorated with sparkling brilliants. With this cap, or sometimes by itself, there was worn the pompon, from 1748. This appears to have been 'a complication of shreds and rags of velvet, feathers, and ribbands, stuck with false stones of a thousand colours', [29] and worn in the centre above the forehead.

Outdoor headgear

Hats were usually worn over day caps, though often the latter was worn without a hat. Hats, of

[25] *The London Magazine & Monthly Chronologer,* June 1741.   [26] *Ipswich Journal,* 1749.
[27] *The World,* 1754.   [28] *loc. cit.,* 1854.

[29] *Lord Chesterfield,* 1753.

straw, silk, felt and chip, had various shapes and sizes.

1. Small with shallow crown and narrow brim and ribbon hat-band. Worn throughout the period.
2. The slouch, with shallow crown and wide flopping brim.
3. The *bergère*, a large flat straw hat with shallow flat crown and wide brim either rigidly flat or flexible, the curve secured by ribbons tied under the chin.
4. The witch's hat with pointed crown and flat brim had a brief spell in the 1740's.
5. For riding, either a three-cornered hat, usually worn with a wig, or the jockey cap, both similar to the men's.

Hair styles

The hair was waved back from the forehead and temples, with a cluster of ringlets at the back. From 1730 to 1750 the fashionable coiffure was the *tête de mouton*, composed of false curls arranged round the back of the head.

'... like their beauty put on
By the promising curls of the *tête de mouton*.' [30]

In the next decade simpler styles were in vogue, the hair combed straight back from the forehead and either turned up in a bun or flat plait, or, for riding, allowed to hang behind in a queue.

Footwear

The shoe with pointed toe had a massive waisted heel to 1730; the toe then became shorter

[30] *The Gentleman's Magazine*, 1745.

and blunter with lower tongue and a small buckle. In the 1750's the slender-waisted high French heel came into fashion.

Materials were kid decorated with metallic braid ('lace') or brocade. For muddy weather stout leather clogs were worn over the shoe; and clogs of brocade for the fashionable saunter.

Stockings

Knitted, of thread, worsted or silk, usually brightly coloured, though 'a lady's leg is a dangerous sight in whatever colour it appears but when it is encased in white it makes an irresistible attack upon us'. [31]

Accessories

Elbow-length gloves were universally worn out of doors and often in, or mittens.

Small muffs and folding fans were necessary accessories, the fan becoming 'wonderfully increased in size from three quarters of a foot to a foot and three quarters or two feet' in the 1740's. [32]

Patches, powder and paint were lavishly employed. 'Our modern belles are obliged to retouch their cheeks every day to keep them in repair ... our polite ladies have thought fit to dress their faces as well as their head à la mode de Paris'. [33]

SHORT BIBLIOGRAPHY.—*Historic Costume*, by Kelly and Schwabe (1929). *Histoire du Costume*, by M. Leloire (tomes X & XI, Paris). *Handbook of English Costume of the Eighteenth Century*, by C. Willett and Phillis Cunnington (1957).

[31] *The Universal Spectator*, 1737.
[32] *The London Magazine*, 1744.
[33] *The Connoisseur*, 1754.

Portrait Miniatures

JONATHAN MAYNE

Writing some fifty years later in his *Anecdotes of Painting*, Horace Walpole observed somewhat icily that 'the reign of Anne, so illustrated by heroes, poets, and authors, was not equally fortunate in artists. ... Lord Sunderland and Lord Oxford collected books; the Duke of Devonshire and Lord Pembroke pictures, medals, statues; the performers of the time had little pretensions to be admitted into such cabinets'. It must be allowed at once that posterity has continued to endorse Walpole's verdict, and further, that the art of the miniaturist, though unspecified by him in this context, offers no exception to his general criticism. The seventeenth-century tradition, which had flowered so gloriously at the hand of Samuel Cooper and his contemporaries and immediate followers, was losing its impetus. Flatman and Charles Beale were already dead; Nicholas Dixon and Lawrence Crosse had not many years of activity left to them.

If it is possible to isolate any one characteristic of this period, it is, in the words of Mr Reynolds,[1] 'a rather blank cosmopolitanism'. Large-scale portraiture in England was dominated by Dahl and Kneller; and so far as miniature-painting is concerned, the century starts also with a small group of foreign artists. Setting aside for a moment the enamellists, who will be considered later in this essay, we may start by devoting a little attention to the two most important of these – Christian Richter, a Swede, and the Swiss artist, Benjamin Arlaud.

[1] Graham Reynolds, *English Portrait Miniatures*, London 1952, p. 95.

Christian Richter and Benjamin Arlaud

Richter (1678–1732, Pl. 81A) came to England in 1702 and remained in this country until his death thirty years later. He had studied medal-engraving, and for three years had been apprenticed as a goldsmith – a type of training which many miniaturists, from Hilliard onwards, had received. Though Richter is said to have painted in enamel and in oil, it is on his water-colour miniatures that his reputation now exclusively rests. These were usually painted on vellum, and in technique they show a natural development of, rather than a marked break with, the seventeenth-century tradition, except for the fact that he gradually adopted a system of stippling instead of the generally linear style of his predecessors. Richter's miniatures are nearly all copies from full-scale portraits by other artists. This fact we know from Vertue – who added nevertheless that he could draw better from the life than any of his contemporaries. Perhaps it would be more exact to say that Richter's copies, or miniature reductions, were more in the nature of personal interpretations of his models, for they have a particular delicacy and gentleness of their own which establish them as self-consistent works of art. Richter's use of colour moreover shows a remarkable and individual subtlety.

Benjamin Arlaud (worked 1701–31?) also came to England in the early years of the century, perhaps as early as 1701, with which date is inscribed a miniature of his which seems to represent William III. Neither his dates of birth nor death are, however, recorded. He was certainly here until 1717, and may perhaps have remained longer. His brother, Jacques Antoine, was a fashionable miniaturist in Paris during the same period. Like Richter, Benjamin Arlaud reflects in his miniatures the accepted full-scale portraiture of his time – that of Kneller and Dahl; while the miniatures of his brother, Jacques Antoine, who paid a short visit to this country in 1721, express rather the French style of his friends Rigaud and Largillière. Though rarely met with, Benjamin Arlaud's miniatures (usually painted on vellum) are of high quality and often have a jewel-like intensity of colour. But like those of Richter, they are more properly to be considered as the final developments of the seventeenth century miniature-portrait, rather than as starting-points of the eighteenth century tradition.

Introduction of ivory, and the Lens family

The discovery which was to have the greatest effect on British, no less than on continental, miniature-painting of the eighteenth century is generally attributed to the Venetian artist, Rosalba Carriera (1675–1757). This was the use of ivory instead of vellum, which until this time had remained the normal painting-ground for miniaturists. Exact documentary evidence is lacking, but according to an anonymous memoir published two years before her death, Rosalba began to achieve fame for her small portraits on ivory as early as 1696; and at all events her diploma-work at the Galleria di San Luca in Rome, which is dated 1705, is painted on that substance. In England Rosalba's lead was followed (whether consciously or not it is uncertain) by Bernard Lens (1682–1740, Pl. 81B, C), the son of an engraver and drawing-master of the same name, who himself founded a dynasty of miniaturists which was to dominate in England for the first half of the century.

Although the full potentialities of ivory as a ground for miniature-paintings were not realized until towards the end of the century, when Meyer, and following him Cosway and Engleheart, adopted the consistent use of a more transparent water-colour, nevertheless we can already see a stylistic change coming over the miniature-portrait from the time when Bernard Lens and his followers took over the innovation. That this was due as much to the artistic personalities of the painters concerned as to the nature of the new medium is not to be denied. Technically speaking, Bernard Lens was no great original artist. Many of his pictorial conventions he took over almost ready-made from the Kneller school, and particularly is this true of the wide oval faces with which he, and even more his sons, were inclined to endow their sitters. But a certain stolid English quality is also characteristic of the works of the Lens family, a quality which seems to transform the mannerisms of Kneller into something like a Hogarthian literalness of vision. There is a kind of provincial honesty about these portraits, amounting sometimes to a naïve stiffness, which is English rather than baroque.

Bernard Lens' career was a successful one. As well as becoming miniature-painter to George I and George II, he had a fashionable practice as a drawing-master, numbering Horace Walpole among his pupils, and he made regular sketching-tours into the country in search of subjects for topographical drawings.[2] He also continued the earlier tradition of making miniature copies of classical figure-paintings, and although the best and most characteristic of his works are *ad vivum* portraits, he regularly made miniature copies, as had Richter, of portraits by other artists. A striking example of this type is the well-known 'Lens school' portrait of Mary Queen of Scots, originally copied, and 'amended', for the Duke of Hamilton by Lawrence Crosse from a doubtful original. Crosse's embellished copy was itself copied several times by Bernard Lens, as it was by his son A.B. Lens and by other artists too; examples are not infrequently met with. Presumably the eighteenth century amateur saw in these works authentic likenesses of the sitter; to us they provide little more than an amusing object-lesson in the temporal mutability of the portrait-painter's

---

[2] One of these is reproduced on Pl. XIV of I. A. Williams, *Early English Water-colours*, The Connoisseur, 1952.

vision. For in spite of a careful attempt to preserve the original pose and costume, the impression that one gains is of some noble guest at a fancy-dress ball, and the face has entirely altered its shape, becoming fashionably Hanoverian. If an ikon were sought effectively to destroy rather than to preserve the Stuart myth, one might imagine that this was it.

Two of Bernard Lens' sons followed their father's calling; these were Andrew Benjamin (1713?–after 1779?) and Peter Paul Lens (1714?–1750?), and in their earlier works at least they both showed such an exemplary degree of filial piety that, if they were not signed (which they regularly were), the miniatures of all three members of the family might often be indifferently attributed to any one of them. (All three artists in fact used an easily distinguishable form of signature, being a monogram, often in gold, of the initials B.L., A.B.L., or P.L.) Andrew Benjamin Lens (Pl. 81D) exhibited miniatures and other works at the Incorporated and Free Society of Artists from 1764 until 1779, shortly after which date he is presumed to have died. Works from the earlier period of his career are, however, more frequently met with, and in the maturer of these we can already see a gradual development in the direction of naturalness – the direction in which Bernard Lens himself had already set out.

Rather more is known of Peter Paul Lens, and he also seems to have been a more precocious and original miniaturist than his brother. The curiously attractive genre piece (Pl. 82A) by him which is reproduced here is in fact almost unique for its period in this country. But in spite of an outstandingly professional fluency, Peter Paul Lens could seldom rise above the naïvety of his vision – this constitutes, indeed, one of the striking charms of his work – and his circular-faced children are more satisfactorily realized images than his portraits of grown-up sitters, where his simplicity is often in danger of becoming over-simplification.

Peter Paul Lens' personal history is illuminated for us by at least one colourful incident. In 1737, while in Dublin, he became a member of a notorious hell-fire club called 'The Blasters'. In the fol-

lowing year a committee of the House of Lords, reporting on the state of affairs, remarked that 'Peter Lens, lately come into this kingdom, professes himself a Blaster and a votary of the devil, and that he hath offered up prayers to him and publicly drunk to the devil's health, and that he hath several times uttered the most daring and execrable blasphemies'. He left Ireland to avoid arrest, and continued his artistic career in London.

The enamel miniaturists

It is necessary at this point to return once more to the beginning of the century in order to consider briefly the closely allied art of miniature portraiture in enamel. Some artists in fact worked in both media – Richter, for example, as we have already seen. But, technically speaking, the two arts were quite distinct. Enamel miniature portraiture had already had a brief phase of popularity in England during the 1640's, when the French artist Jean Petitot was employed for a time at the court of Charles I. On his return to France, however, there was no native artist left to continue working in the medium, which fell into disuse until the last years of the century. Then again it was a foreign artist – the Swedish painter Charles Boit (1662–1727, Pl. 82B) – who introduced, or rather reintroduced, the use of enamel for miniature-portraiture in England. Boit first came here in 1687, five years after his compatriot Michael Dahl; much indeed of his work was concerned with making enamel miniature copies of oil-portraits by Dahl. On this occasion he remained for ten years or so, and then left to work for a time in Holland, Düsseldorf and Vienna. He returned to England in 1703 and remained until 1714, when he left finally.

Boit's period of activity thus ceases in the year in which our present concern begins. But he is nonetheless important to us, because, unlike Petitot, he founded a school which was to flourish after his departure. Boit's enamels are excellent, and he was a master of that difficult technique. His pupil, the German, Christian Friedrich Zincke (1684?–1767, Pl. 82c, D), proved a worthy follower – indeed it is necessary to look forward to the Court career of Richard Cosway, almost two generations ahead, to find a parallel to his spectacular worldly success.

Christian Friedrich Zincke

Zincke came to England in the early years of the century at the invitation of Boit. By about the time of the death of Queen Anne he had already set up in practice on his own, and we find him being promoted by Kneller as a rival to Boit, who was consistently, though not exclusively, employed by Dahl. Vertue, who has a considerable amount to tell us about Zincke, records that by 1726 he was 'so fully employed that for some years he has had more persons of distinction sitting to him than any Painter living'. And so his success continued and increased until failing eyesight (his vision had already started to give trouble in the 1720's) forced him to reduce his output. To this end in 1742 he raised his price from 20 to 30 guineas for a head, and during the next few years he seems more and more to have confined himself to working for his own pleasure rather than to increase his fortune. He had another twenty-five years of life ahead of him, but apart from the instruction that he was to give to his compatriot Jeremiah Meyer in the late 1760's, his professional work was already done.

As one would expect from a portrait-painter with such a wide and successful practice, Zincke's work varied very much in quality. Though he seldom fell below the high technical standards which he had inherited from Boit, nevertheless, artistically speaking, his portraits err only too often in the direction of the mechanical and perfunctory; and, as one recent writer has pointed out, his style was to a large extent dependent, though with a slight time-lag, on the fashionable oil-painters of his long career. Starting as a miniature reflection of Kneller, he ended by mirroring the style of such painters as Vanderbank and Highmore, adding but little of his own on the way. His work should not, however, be dismissed as historically unimportant for this reason. For Zincke, with his professional cosmopolitanism, kept alive a spark of pictorial sophistication which was largely lacking in the contemporary water-colour school of Bernard Lens and his sons, and

in this way he prepared the way not only for his successors in the art of enamel, such as Prewett (Pl. 84c) and Spencer, but, more important still, for the water-colour miniaturists of the next generation and the great *floraison* of the art towards the end of the century. As we have already noticed, late in his life he gave instruction to Jeremiah Meyer, and this in itself would give him an honoured place in the history of the eighteenth-century miniature.

The Modest School

The miniaturists working in England between 1740 and 1760, many of them both in water-colour and enamel, may be classified without doing damage to their delightful individualities, as forming an essential and unified link between the solid if somewhat wooden sincerity of the Lens school and the rococo brilliance of the age of Cosway, during the last decades of the century. Their virtues which are often those of a self-effacing delicacy and naturalness, have for long been insufficiently appreciated, and it is to be hoped that Mr Reynolds, by giving them a chapter to themselves in his *English Portrait Miniatures*, and still more by giving them a name of their own, 'The Modest School of Miniaturists', will have brought them to the notice of a wider body of collectors and amateurs. For in fact this group of miniaturists, which includes Gervase Spencer, Nathaniel Hone, Samuel Cotes, Penelope Carwardine, Luke Sullivan and Gustavus Hamilton, as well as many others of comparable talent, represents a charming field for exploration. Their most evident characteristic, as one would suppose from the name that has been given to them, is an unpretentiousness and gentleness of manner that is to be noticed in the scale on which they worked no less than in the more properly imaginative qualities of their portraits. Dramatic profundity of characterization they neither achieved nor sought. But a quiet and sympathetic naturalism, and a delicacy of perception, they achieved almost as a matter of course.

The first of this group to be considered here is Gervase Spencer (d. 1763, Pl. 83A, B), who was one of those who was equally at home in enamel and water-colour. Little is known of his biography, except that he had been a footman, and, according to Vertue, that he was self-taught. His miniatures and enamels are regularly signed with his initials (occasionally with his full name), and dated between 1740 and 1761. He exhibited at the Society of Artists in 1761 and 1762, and Reynolds painted his portrait. Spencer is a typical member of the 'Modest School'. His miniatures and enamels are usually small; and his execution, both in water-colour and enamel, is restrained and delicate. He was at his best with female sitters, and the portrait of Lady Mary Wortley Montagu in Turkish costume, reproduced here (Pl. 83A), is a dazzling example of the freshness that he could preserve in the laborious medium of enamel.

Considerably more is known of Nathaniel Hone, R.A. (1718–84, Pl. 83C), both as painter in oil and as miniaturist. Born in Dublin, he came to England as a young man and worked for a time as an itinerant portrait-painter. He married in 1742 'some Lord's cast off mistress for £200 a year', according to a contemporary diarist, and then settled in London. Later he went to Italy for a few years, and thereafter returned to London, where he remained, apart from visits to Dublin and Paris, until his death. Hone was a foundation-member of the Royal Academy, but he appears to have been elected for his work as a painter in oils rather than for his miniatures.

As a miniaturist Hone, like Spencer, worked both in enamel and water-colour; he was in fact more prolific in the former medium. His miniatures of both types are of a consistently high standard, being well and delicately drawn and of good colour. A comparison of his enamels with those of Spencer shows that his forms are drawn with a clearer outline, whereas Spencer had an attractive, slightly blurred touch. Hone's colour, especially in the draperies and accessories, is somewhat richer than that of Spencer. In his water-colour miniatures he often used opaque white in his rendering of lace; and in the faces of some of his male sitters there is a noticeable diagonal hatching which seems to look forward to Meyer. Hone regularly signed his miniatures with a monogram in which the last stroke of the N forms the first stroke of the H.

Luke Sullivan (1705–71, Pl. 84A) was also of Irish birth, and came early in his life to England, where his father was groom to the Duke of Beaufort. He was trained as an engraver, and worked in this capacity for Hogarth. He also painted water-colour landscapes, architectural views and miniatures. The latter are infrequently met with, but their high quality of execution and their general attractiveness suggest that he may have worked more in this medium than one would imagine from the rarity of his works. The particular characteristic of Sullivan's miniatures that sets them apart from those of his British confrères is a certain rhythmic, rococo quality which might imply an acquaintance with the contemporary Continental schools. J.T. Smith, writing many years later in his *Book for a Rainy Day*, said, 'Sullivan ... was, in my humble opinion, the most extraordinary of all miniature-painters. I have seen three or four of his productions, one of which was so particularly fine that I could almost say I have it on my retina at the moment. It was a portrait of a most lovely woman as to features, flesh and blood. She was dressed in a pale silk gown, lapelled with straw-coloured satin; and in order to keep up a sweetness of tone, the artist had placed primroses in her stomacher; the sky was of a warm green, which blended harmoniously with the carnations of her complexion; her hair was jet, and her necklace of pearls.'

Sullivan signed with a monogram, in which the S is entwined round the lower part of the stroke of the L.

Samuel Cotes (1734–1818, Pl. 84D), the younger brother of Francis Cotes, the well-known portrait-painter, was by some years the junior of the miniaturists whom we have so far considered, though in style his work is justly to be associated with the rest of the 'Modest School'. Study of this artist is to some extent complicated by the fact that there was a second contemporary miniaturist of the same initials – Samuel Collins (d. 1768), described by Nollekens as 'a very indifferent miniature-painter' – and it is possible that some works of the 1750's and 1760's signed S.C. may be by Collins rather than Cotes. There is, however, a sufficient body of work securely attributable to Cotes to give us a flattering picture of his accomplishment. His drawing was subtle and his modelling was often of unusual distinction. His colouring was generally fresh, although examples exist which might almost be described as in *grisaille*. Cotes formed his style in the 1750's, and although he lived through the period of Cosway and Engleheart, he hardly seems to have been affected by their innovations. Samuel Cotes painted miniatures in both water-colour and enamel. He exhibited at the R.A. from 1769 until 1789, and is said to have continued to work until the early years of the nineteenth century.

Miniatures signed 'P.C.', of which there appear to be a fair number in existence, were for some time held to be by a sister of Samuel and Francis Cotes, named Penelope. Examination of the facts by various recent scholars has revealed that there is no evidence even for the existence of such a person, and further research has shown that 'P.C.' was in all probability Penelope Carwardine (*c.* 1730–*c.* 1800, Pl. 84B), the eldest daughter of a landed family in Herefordshire who took to miniature-painting when her father ruined the family estates. The stylistic similarity of her work to certain examples of that of Samuel Cotes may have been responsible (though it can hardly be said to excuse) her invention as his sister. Penelope Carwardine was in fact the pupil of Ozias Humphry (who had himself been taught by Samuel Collins), and she is known to have been practising in 1754.

A final addition to this anthology of mid-eighteenth-century miniature-painting in the British Isles shows amongst other things that date-brackets are liable to be misleading if applied too strictly to an organism as complex as the history of art. Gustavus Hamilton (1739–75, Pl. 84E), a Dublin artist, does not seem to have started working until the terminal date of this essay, and the example of his work reproduced here belongs to 1768. And yet the miniatures which he painted from 1760 until his death in 1775 continue to be excellent and characteristic examples of the 'Modest School'. Others could be chosen to illustrate the same fact; even the early works of Cosway and Engleheart can hardly be said to foreshadow the remarkable developments of a decade ahead. It is sufficient perhaps to remark in closing that the exact moment for the birth of a new style is no easier to pinpoint in the history of the miniature than in any other art, and that just as the beginning of the period under discussion was marked by an overlap from the previous tradition, so its end cannot be made to coincide with any arbitrarily selected date.

SHORT BIBLIOGRAPHY

The essential source-book for the study of this subject is Basil S. Long's *British Miniaturists* (London 1929), which is a comprehensive dictionary of artists, arranged alphabetically. Graham Reynolds' *English Portrait Miniatures* (London 1952), provides by far the best connected account of the subject. Torben Holck Colding's *Aspects of Miniature Painting* (Copenhagen 1953: London 1954) relates the British school of miniaturists to its European context.

Jewellery

J. F. HAYWARD

The process of decline in the artistic status of jewellery, which began in the second half of the seventeenth century, was not interrupted in the early eighteenth century; it was, in fact, hastened through the increasing concentration on the beauties of precious stones at the expense of the fine settings made by the goldsmith. This decline was not due to any lack of skill on the part of the goldsmith, nor to a lack of appreciation of quality on the part of those who purchased and wore jewellery; it was the result rather of the fascination exercised by new discoveries in the field of technique.

The brilliant-cut

About the year 1700 the Venetian jeweller Vincenzo Peruzzi had invented the brilliant-cut with fifty-eight facets, a development which was as great an advance on the rose-cut as the latter had been on the sixteenth century table-cut. The result of this invention was that the precious stones became the most important, if not the only important, element in the jewel, and the setting was reduced to a mere framework for holding the stones in place. The skeleton-like character of most eighteenth century settings for jewels can be particularly well seen in Thomas Flach's designs for the use of jewellers, which were published in 1736 (Fig. 1). Another consequence of the introduction of the brilliant-cut was the recognition of the diamond as the pre-eminent stone; in the eighteenth century the finest jewels were composed entirely of brilliant-cut diamonds. Such was the predominance of the diamond that the far less

precious metal, silver, was used instead of gold in the settings, since, being colourless, it was less obtrusive than the brighter gold, and did not detract from the effect of the stones.

The invention of the brilliant-cut did not mean that rose-cut diamonds were no longer used. It was possible to re-cut a rose and turn it into a brilliant, but the great loss in weight and value that this process involved doubtless deterred jewellers from doing so, at any rate in the case of less important stones. Roses continued to be used for the less expensive jewellery; the difference in price between the two is well illustrated by the entries in the account-books of the jeweller George Wickes, whose business was later taken over by R. Garrard, the Crown Jeweller. These books are still in the possession of the latter firm. The cost of jewellery depends entirely on the importance of the stones used, and it is therefore difficult to make comparisons based on accounts which do not indicate the size of the stones. Jewels set with brilliants were as a rule far more expensive; thus a pair of rose diamond flower-de-luce earrings purchased by the Bishop of Norwich in January 1736 cost 9 guineas, whereas a pair of brilliant earrings cost 21 guineas in the preceding year.

The firm of George Wickes and his successors during the eighteenth century were more active as goldsmiths than as jewellers, and for this reason their accounts contain few references to important and valuable stones. They numbered amongst their clientèle persons of the highest rank, such as Frederick, Prince of Wales, the Princess of Wales, the Duchess of Norfolk, the Duchess of Gordon

L

Fig. 1. Title page from Thomas Flach's pattern book of jeweller's designs, London, 1736. *Victoria and Albert Museum.*

and the Chancellor of the Exchequer, Sir Robert Walpole, later Earl of Orford, but most of the jewellery they sold was purchased by their less distinguished customers. Only very rarely do the account books give any details as to the construction of a jewel. An exception is the reference to a 'brilliant solitaire with a red double middle stone and drop', which cost £90 in May 1740 – also the 'pair brilliant three drop rings ear-rings' purchased in June 1741 for £170.

Mourning jewellery

As in the seventeenth century, the provision of mourning or motto rings was a steady, though perhaps not particularly remunerative, side of the jeweller's business. The custom of presenting mourning rings of gold, engraved with some motto appropriate to the melancholy occasion or with the name of the deceased, to the chief mourners became general amongst the upper classes during the eighteenth century, and we find repeated references to them in the Garrard accounts. They cost a guinea apiece and were bought in considerable numbers. Thus in February 1735 the executors of Sir Brownlow Sherrard purchased forty-six motto rings, while in 1745 seventy-two rings were required for distribution at the funeral of the Earl of Orford.

Naturalism in jewellery design

During the early years of the eighteenth century the silver or gold setting was no more than a framework with little or no æsthetic significance, but as the century advanced the development of the rococo style was accompanied by an increasingly naturalistic character in the settings, which were rendered in the form of flowers and foliage, the centre of each leaf or petal being filled by a stone. On the whole the terms baroque or rococo are barely applicable to jewellery, the design of which was conditioned by factors that were little affected by changes in international art styles. Nevertheless this naturalistic trend together with a certain light and informal spirit characteristic of Rococo was reflected in eighteenth century jewellery design. A comparison of the jewels of the early eighteenth century (Pls. 85, 87D) and those

of fifty years later (Pls. 87A, B) will illustrate the change from formality to delicacy and freedom of design. A typical manifestation of the naturalistic trend in eighteenth century jewellery was the popularity of nosegays, which were worn on the body, in the hair or upon the hat in the form of brooches or pins. These nosegays are to be found in most of the eighteenth century pattern books, but, perhaps on account of their fragile construction, hardly any survive.

Disappearance of enamel from settings

Amongst the developments that helped to simplify eighteenth century jewellery in comparison with that of the previous century was the disappearance of enamel from the setting. Enamel, which had once constituted one of the main forms of enrichment, had already been banished to the back of the jewel during the second half of the seventeenth century. It was now entirely abandoned, and the backs were either engraved with foliage or left plain. That the jeweller was in the eighteenth century still capable of producing the finest enamel work is shown by the superb enamelled snuff-boxes which were fashionable during the latter three-quarters of the century. An earlier example of English eighteenth century enamelling may be seen in the Garter Jewel given to the Duke of Marlborough by Queen Anne (Pl. 86A). This superb jewel, profusely set with rose diamonds of great size, illustrates well the new methods of setting with the stones so close to each other that the setting itself is hardly noticeable. A second George of precisely the same period and design belongs to H.M. the Queen.

Another piece dating from the beginning of the eighteenth century and of undoubted English origin demonstrates the tendency of jewels to degenerate into mere arrangements of stones. This is the parure of necklace, corsage ornament, earrings and clip brooches (Pl. 85) from the effigy of Frances Stuart, Duchess of Richmond, in Westminster Abbey. The Duchess died in 1702, and the jewels presumably represent the fashion at the time of her death. They are, in fact, only of paste, but evidently copy the more valuable jewels, composed of precious stones, worn by the Duchess during her lifetime. The only part of the parure in which the setting has any pretensions to significance is the corsage ornament. Here we see a more or less geometrical arrangement of stones superimposed on a flowing foliate design of a type that remained the basis of most gem-set jewels until the last decades of the eighteenth century.

The influence of pattern books

While surviving jewels of the eighteenth century can rarely be dated with any exactness, it is possible to obtain precise dates from printed pattern-books and from dated jewellers' designs. An interesting light is thrown upon English eighteenth century jewellery by a book of water-colour drawings of jewellery by a certain Marcus Gunther, now preserved in the Gothenburg Museum (Fig. 2). Gunther, who was of English birth, was not a professional jeweller, but a designer who was prepared to produce designs for ornament for a variety of occasions. He spent many years travelling in Europe, and his book of drawings is particularly interesting, as most of the jewellery designs are not only dated, but also record the town in which they were executed. The fact that an English artist could travel about Europe in the eighteenth century and find a market for designs which show no particular stylistic variety is indicative of the completely international character of jewellery fashions, and explains the extreme difficulty of establishing the origin of a jewel. An interesting feature of his drawings is the early appearance of asymmetrical designs. Whereas, however, in other fields of applied art in the mid-

Fig. 2. Designs for stick knobs after drawings by Marcus Gunther, 1716.

eighteenth century asymmetrical designs of rococo character were alone acceptable, in jewellery asymmetry never became an exclusive fashion and symmetrical designs are found alongside the asymmetrical ones, as in Flach's pattern book of 1736 (Fig. 1). Though Gunther was not a practising jeweller, the tendency during the eighteenth century was for the jewellery trade to become more specialized and, as a result, for the pattern books to be the work of professional jewellers. As precious stones became an increasingly important feature of the jewel, only an artist possessed of a technical understanding of the character and possibilities of the various gem-stones could design jewellery.

The standard forms of jewel in the eighteenth century, which are to be seen in many portraits of the period, were the two types of brooch worn at the centre of the corsage. The first was of girandole design, consisting of a large central stone about which were grouped a number of smaller stones from which hung three large pendant pearls or drops (Pl. 87c). The second type was an openwork bow, from which hung a pendant with one or more intervening links, commonly known as a Sevigné; whether the name was borrowed from Madame de Sevigné has never been established (Pl. 87D). Both these jewels had an extraordinarily long run of popularity, from the third quarter of the seventeenth until well into the eighteenth century, though the bow tended to be replaced by a floral composition (Pl. 87A) towards the middle of the eighteenth century.

Another survival from the seventeenth century was the ornamentation of the bodice with a stomacher or with a series of graduated bows or frogs (Brandenburgs). One bow from a superb set of three, probably of five originally, is illustrated in Pl. 86B. The bows are composed entirely of brilliant-cut diamonds set in silver, and in view of the lightness of the design can be dated to about the middle of the eighteenth century. Few jewels set with brilliants of this size and quality have survived since the eighteenth century, but it is possible to find exactly similar designs executed in pastes, as for instance the parure preserved with the effigy of the Duchess of Richmond (Pl. 85).

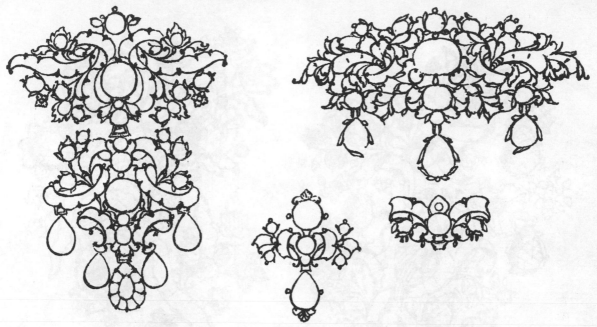

Fig. 3. Designs for brooches and pendants by Christian Taute, reproduced from pencil drawings.
Mid-eighteenth century. *Victoria and Albert Museum.*

The Garrard accounts contain many references to paste jewellery and show that the upper classes did not scorn its use (Pl. 87c). The most frequent references are to paste buckles or buttons intended for wear by gentlemen. In 1736 a pair of paste buckles cost two guineas. Paste jewels for ladies wear did not cost much more: 'a pair of fine paste three drop earrings and coloured drop' cost only four guineas in 1752.

Masculine jewellery

Masculine clothing in the eighteenth century provided little opportunity for the wearing of jewels, apart from the buckles and buttons already mentioned. The small-sword, which was an indispensable feature of masculine dress during the whole of the early Georgian period, might, however, be elaborately jewelled, though few such swords have survived outside the treasuries of the ruling or former ruling houses of Europe. An idea of the splendour of such swords can be gathered from the following item in the Garrard accounts for March 1759: 'Joseph Pickering, Debtor: A fine silver gilt sword set with 148 roses, 72 emer-

alds and 249 rubies £90.' The price seems moderate in view of the large number of jewels, but they may have been of small size and some, if not all, may have been supplied by the client.

During the seventeenth century a profuse display of jewellery was an invariable feature of the portrait of a lady of fashion. The gradual decline of formality in English costume during the eighteenth century swept away jewellery from all but the most official court portraits. Not only does the historian lose thereby an invaluable source of information as to the development of jewellery fashions, but its very absence symbolizes a decline in status of the jewel, from which it has never fully recovered.

SHORT BIBLIOGRAPHY

Joan Evans, *English Jewellery from the Fifth Century A.D. to 1800*, London, 1921.

Joan Evans, *A History of Jewellery 1100–1870*, London, 1953.

Garrard and Co., *Garrard's 1721–1911. Crown Jewellers and Goldsmiths*. London, 1912.

H. Clifford Smith, *Jewellery*, London, 1908.

Erich Steingraeber, *Alte Schmuck*, Munich, 1956.

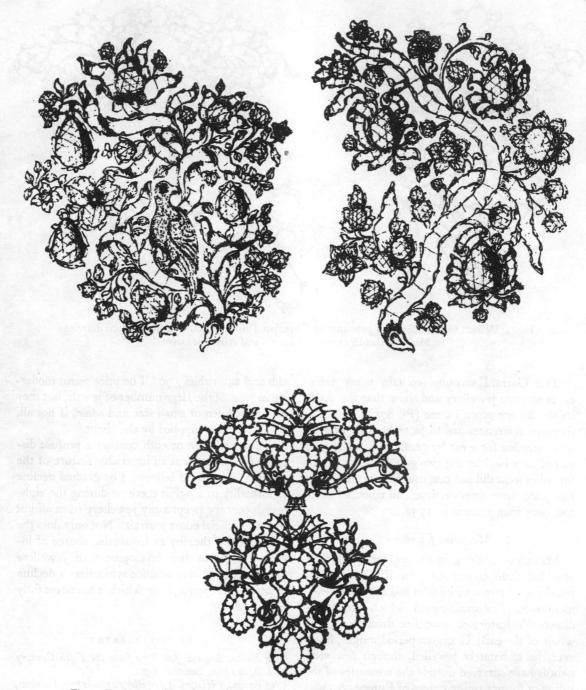

Fig. 4. Designs for brooches and a brooch and pendant by Christian Taute, mid-eighteenth century, reproduced from pencil drawings. *Victoria and Albert Museum.*

740

Music and Musical Instruments

ROBERT DONINGTON

In the history of every art there arise mysteries which seem set there with the very purpose of reminding historians that the Muses after all are women, and that no woman is ever to be more than partially understood. Just such a mystery lies behind the course of English music under the early Georges.

Our Tudor music is a by-word for transcendental counterpoint: Byrd and Tallis challenge comparison with the great Palestrina himself. The tenderness of Gibbons, the bravura of John Bull, the tranquillity of Jenkins and the audacity of William Lawes – all these in their different idioms carried our tradition of superb musicianship into Stuart England. The Puritan administration interrupted our church music, it is true, but had nothing but encouragement for the other branches (the first English opera was staged during the Commonwealth). There was no dearth of talent under the later Stuarts, and at the end of the century this talent burst forth in the glorious work of Purcell. There has never been a more English composer, nor a more individual genius. No one could possibly have imagined that there was anything wrong with English musical tradition at the time of Purcell's death, in 1695.

While Queen Anne reigned there still became visible no immediate cause for apprehension. Purcell's memory was still fresh indeed; he was not one of those who have to wait for recognition. Young though he died (he was only thirty-six), he was a prophet already honoured in his own country. Among those who most revered his memory was the very man who had once taught him com-

position: John Blow, who survived him by thirteen years, during which he went on writing excellent music in what we now think of as the Purcellian idiom. That, incidentally, is not quite fair to Blow, who was as influential in the development of this idiom as Purcell himself, while both men alike owed more to their immediate predecessors (such as Lawes and Jenkins) than has yet been fully recognized. However, excellent though Blow's music was and continued to be under Queen Anne, it has none of it the ultimate genius of Purcell. And perhaps for that reason, though it was greatly enjoyed at the time, and served to keep a genuinely English style in being, it had not the stamina to perpetuate this style into the ensuing period when the test came.

The test, when it came, took the severe form of George Frederick Handel. This mammoth of abounding invention, this tachyderm among composers, this inexhaustible provider of staple musical fare came to England on a visit in 1710; liked what he found; returned in 1712 ostensibly on leave of absence from George, Elector of Hanover; attracted the favourable attention of Anne by a *Te Deum* for the celebrations of the Peace of Utrecht; was granted the very substantial pension of £200 a year; and settled down undeterred by the indignation of his rightful employer. Two years later the death of Anne, and the succession of the Elector as George I of England, regularized the situation very neatly from Handel's point of view. He was speedily forgiven; and here he stayed as in outward effect (not, we shall suggest, in inward reality) the most prominent of English composers until his death in 1759, only a year before the death of George II. Almost to a year, the story of English music under the first two Georges is the story of our native reaction to the foreign stimulus of Handel's residence.

It would no doubt be an exaggeration to speak of our reaction as one of simple subservience. Yet the truth is not very greatly otherwise. After Blow, who died in 1708, the idiom we call Purcellian was quietly dropped. It is true that William Croft (1678–1727) was an avowed follower of Purcell, and in the Burial Service by which he is now most deservedly remembered, he tells us that he

'endeavoured as near as I could, to imitate that great Master and celebrated Composer, whose name will for ever stand high in the Rank of those who have laboured to improve the English style in his so happily adapting his Compositions to English words in that elegant and judicious manner as was unknown to many of his predecessors; but in this respect both *His* and *My* worthy and honoured Master, Dr Blow, was known likewise to excel.'

But no one followed Croft in his turn; he left little mark on later music. Maurice Green (1695–1755) was an inconsiderable and even sycophantic Handelian: he fawned on both Handel and his operatic rival Bononcini at the same time, until Handel found him out and set him at a distance – which did not unfortunately make his music any less pseudo-Handelian. Perhaps his most valuable undertaking was the collection of a large body of English Cathedral music, which he was prevented by failing health from carrying through to publication, but bequeathed to a friend and pupil of much greater stature, William Boyce. The edition which Boyce eventually produced is notable for including a proportion of works by Tallis, Byrd, Gibbons and other Tudor and early Stuart composers who might otherwise not have been so well remembered; its financial success was only moderate, but it had a most important influence. It could not keep the great English tradition in being; but it could and did keep it to some extent in memory.

As a composer, William Boyce (c. 1710–79) is one of the two best of the early Georgian period (the second being Arne, as we shall see). He had a most distinguished career, becoming Composer to the Chapel Royal and Master of the King's Music in addition to his great reputation as organist and conductor. He was prolific of church music and court odes; his trio sonatas for two violins and continuo are not entirely unworthy successors to those of Purcell, and had a particular success; he composed for the theatre and for the highly fashionable Gardens at Vauxhall and Ranelagh. Burney wrote of him later in the century:

'with all reverence for the abilities of Handel, [Boyce] was one of the few of our church composers who neither pillaged nor servilely imitated him. There is an original and sterling merit in his productions, founded as much on the study of our own old masters, as on the best models of other countries, that gives to all his works a peculiar stamp and character of his own. ...'

What makes this comment all the more interesting is that Handelian is just what, to a modern listener, Boyce's style appears to be: how much more so, then, those others whom Burney thought did 'servilely' imitate Handel! There is, however, as we have said, one other early Georgian composer to whom a degree of originality can be attributed – rather more so, in fact, than to Boyce. This is his exact contemporary, Thomas Augustine Arne (1710–78).

The career of Arne began in one romantic respect as Handel's did: he turned to music in face of initial parental opposition. He practised at night on a muffled spinet; he heard opera in borrowed livery from the gallery where the coachmen waited for their masters; he took violin lessons to such good effect that he was found one evening by his father playing first fiddle at an amateur concert – and finally permitted to follow his obvious destiny. He gained early success as a composer for the stage, wrote a great many songs for Vauxhall, Ranelagh and Marylebone Gardens, was appointed official composer at Vauxhall, and altogether hit off fashionable taste to a nicety. He essayed Italianate opera, and the opposite extreme of ballad opera: both attempts were well received. He revelled in glees and catches. He gave us 'Rule Britannia' – it is the final number of his Masque

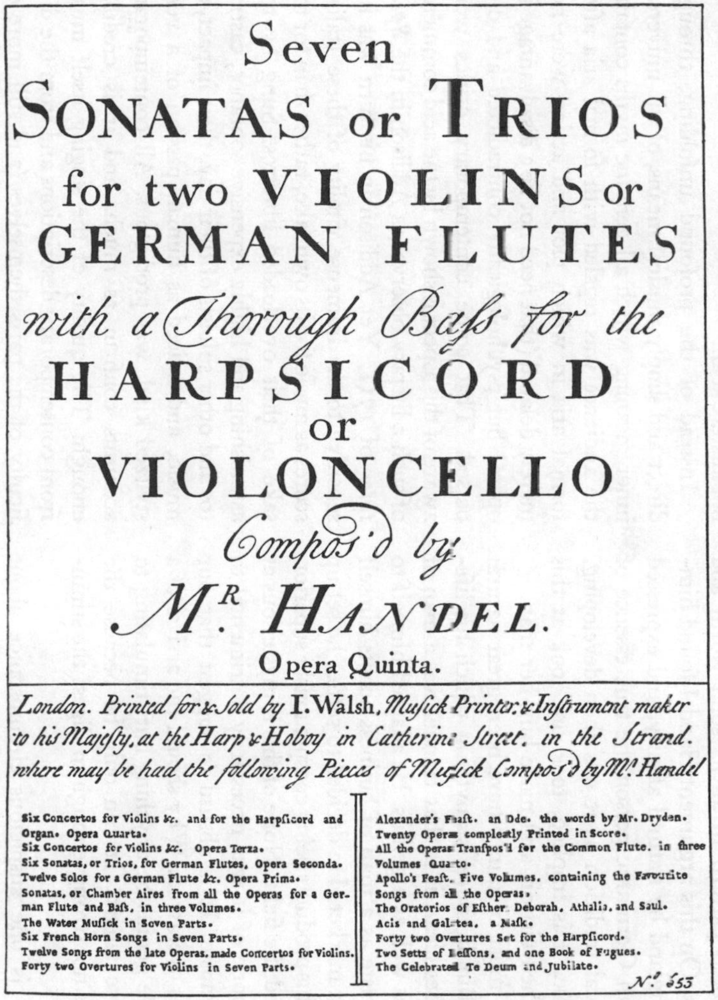

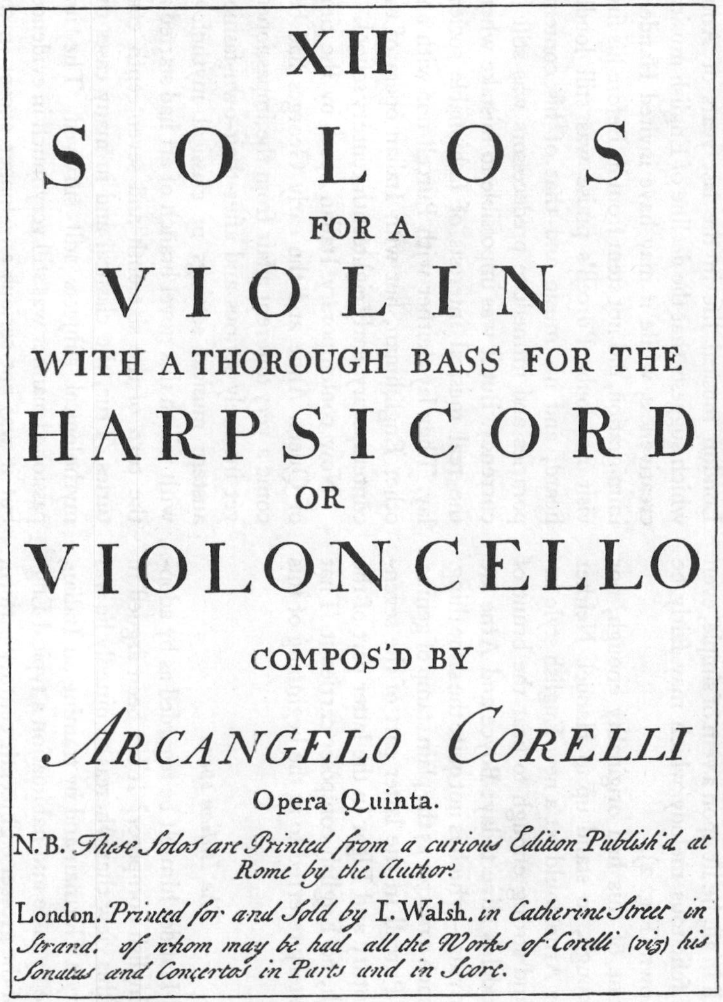

XII SOLOS FOR A VIOLIN WITH A THOROUGH BASS FOR THE HARPSICORD OR VIOLONCELLO

COMPOS'D BY

ARCANGELO CORELLI

Opera Quinta.

N.B. These Solos are Printed from a curious Edition Publish'd at Rome by the Author.

London. Printed for and Sold by I. Walsh, in Catherine-Street in ye Strand, of whom may be had all the Works of Corelli (viz) his Sonatas and Concerted in Parts and in Score.

N°. 555

(B) Title-page (engraved) to the parts of XII *Solos for a Violin* by Arcangelo Corelli, early eighteenth century. Reduced.

Seven SONATAS or TRIOS for two VIOLINS or GERMAN FLUTES with a Thorough Bass for the HARPSICORD or VIOLONCELLO

Compos'd by Mr HANDEL.

Opera Quinta.

London. Printed for & sold by I. Walsh, Musick Printer & Instrument maker to his Majesty, at the Harp & Hoboy in Catherine Street, in the Strand. where may be had the following Pieces of Musick Compos'd by Mr Handel

Six Concertos for Violins &c. and for the Harpsicord and Organ. Opera Quinta.
Six Concertos for Violins &c. Opera Terza.
Six Sonatas, or Trios, for German Flutes, Opera Seconda.
Twelve Solos for a German Flute &c. Opera Prima.
Sonatas, or Chamber Aires from all the Operas for a German Flute and Bass, in three Volumes.
The Water Musick in Seven Parts.
Six French Horn Songs in Seven Parts.
Twelve Songs from the late Operas, made Concertos for Violins.
Forty two Overtures for Violins in Seven Parts.

Alexander's Feast, an Ode, the words by Mr. Dryden.
Twenty Operas compleatly Printed in Score.
All the Operas Transpos'd for the Common Flute, in three Volumes. Quarto.
Apollo's Feast, Five Volumes, containing the Favourite Songs from all the Operas.
The Oratorios of Either Deborah, Athalia, and Saul.
Acis and Gal-tea, a Mask.
Forty two Overtures Set for the Harpsicord.
Two Setts of Lessons, and one Book of Fugues.
The Celebrated Te Deum and Jubilate.

Fig. 1. (A) Title-page (engraved) to the parts of *Seven Sonatas or Trios* by Handel, early eighteenth century. Reduced.

THE EARLY GEORGIAN PERIOD

Alfred. All in all, he lit upon a vein of simple, even naïve yet felicitous melody which may fairly be called his own (Fig. 2).

Yet none of this had originality enough, nor weight enough, to stand up to Handel. Neither Boyce nor Arne could set a new English style individual and strong enough to bear the brunt of time. Handel is alive today: Boyce and Arne are worth reviving—which is not quite the same thing. There is such a matter as the plain stamp of genius. Between Purcell in the latter part of the seventeenth century and Elgar in the latter part of the nineteenth, no English composer carried it. That is the mystery referred to at the beginning of this chapter.

The Italian opera

Should Handel himself be regarded as by adoption an English composer? It has been argued in favour of this view that whereas admittedly he was by heredity a German and by training an Italian, he became by taste and habituation a typical Englishman of the grosser eighteenth century pattern, and that his music came more and more to reflect this supposed pattern in all its solid worth and earthiness. On this argument Handel found himself in England by natural affinity, and expressed in his own Germanic person the true essence of our musical tradition as it was then developing. Our Muse, it is implied, took one look at this distinguished visitor, and made him her man.

There must certainly have been great natural affinity. But if there is anything which his life-story makes clear, it is that Handel was a man of business as well as a genius. He adapted himself to English taste as a man of business adapts himself to his best market. He decided to settle; he set up in trade; his products being conspicuously superior, he soon led the field. None of this is mysterious at all, and none of it was necessarily detrimental to English music. It is absurd to suggest that our Muse was overawed. Why should the arrival of a formidable genius be anything but stimulating to true native talent? It can only be because the talent was not strong enough to digest the stimulant.

There is one suspicious circumstance about London musical life in the last years of Anne which suggests that the decline of English musical creativeness, while it may have invited Handel's immigration, did not stem from it. Before his first visit no doubt Purcell's praise was still loudly heard, and his music and that of his contemporaries and immediate predecessors was still in currency. But it was impossible to mistake where the real musical interests of fashionable society lay. They lay neither with Purcell nor with any other Englishman, but with Italian opera of the contemporary, early eighteenth century school.

Now contemporary Italian opera by the time of Queen Anne and the early Georges had become a very different affair from the impassioned, yet intensely serious and after-their-own-fashion austere musical settings of classical mythology with which this novel branch of art had started at the turn of the sixteenth and seventeenth centuries. True, the classical and in many cases the mythological subjects still survived. The impassioned manner was still very much in evidence; but it was not serious any longer except in the sense of having grown extremely pompous. It was not austere at all.

Instead of the profound unfolding, through direct and simply musical means, of the universal inner meaning which all genuine myths contain, the audience was regaled with formal aria after formal aria in which plot and action were not merely delayed (that need not be a disadvantage in opera) but psychologically contradicted and dispersed. That some contemporary critics were aware of this aspect is shown by the acid comments of such a literary observer as Addison in the *Spectator* of 1711. Yet Addison in his turn was insensitive to the immense vitality of these Italian scores as music for its own sake, rather than for the sake of their overloaded librettos. Sung by the astonishing and highly expensive sopranos, castratos and other soloists of their day, their impact, as music, and indeed as human passion of a very stylized kind, was prodigious. All contemporary accounts confirm as much, and it is credible enough. The quality of the singing itself must, from contemporary descriptions and from the difficulty of the parts themselves (and still more of

Fig. 2. An engraved page from *Calliope or English Harmony*, 1739–46, with a song by
Arne, composer of *Rule, Britannia*.

the improvized ornamentation of which we have some written record), have been extraordinary.

It was this stylized and expensive art of Italian opera which was all the rage in London when Handel first paid us a visit, and which presumably suggested to him that there was profit and reputation to be won here by a man gifted and trained as he was to compose and produce that kind of opera in any quantities required. He did so; and with royal patronage to help him, he met with very considerable financial and honourable success. But there were great difficulties to contend with, not by any means all of them of a musical order.

To begin with, the rivalry in this field (though not in the field of native musical composition) was very acute. There was cut-throat competition both for the star performers imported at alarming cost, and for the audiences which were to hear, applaud, and pay for them to the producer's profit. Thus while the cost went up, the profit did not always materialize. Next, there were intrigues of astonishing virulence and complexity: and while Handel in the course of these had on the whole the advantage of the King's patronage behind him, his chief adversaries had that of the Prince of Wales. Hair-raising as this strange side of contemporary London musical life must have been, it had, of course, little directly to do with music. Yet even so its indirect influence was considerable. It undoubtedly contributed to forcing Handel partly out of the precarious field of Italian opera into another less over-tilled and potentially not only almost as lucrative, but as productive of artistic fruit. This fruit was the Handelian oratorio.

The Beggar's Opera

There is one more most pleasantly ironic fact to be recorded here. Torn though it was by commercial rivalries, professional jealousies, breaches of faith and malicious acts of every kind, the Italian opera continued to be the most prominent feature throughout early Georgian musical activity. There was no holding that fashion; yet it did take a shaking at the hands not of either of its chief contesting parties, but of a pair (in the view at least of these injured parties) of rank outsiders. They were the poet Gay, in the rôle of dialogue and lyric writer, and the learned musician Dr Pepusch (to add to the irony, he was himself a German immigrant and Handel's own predecessor as organist at Canons) in the rôle of arranger. Between them they concocted that most famous of all ballad operas, *The Beggar's Opera*. Its success when first produced in 1728 was instantaneous, and led to a number of imitations. Not only is *The Beggar's Opera* a diabolically effective parody of the more pompous aspects of the contemporary Italian opera; it also, with its subsequent imitations, displayed the yet more damaging faculty of drawing off a sizeable proportion of the operatic audience. The Italian opera ran into yet worse financial embarrassments. Neither Handel nor his rivals thought of giving up the struggle; but there is no doubt that Handel was yet further encouraged to develop what started as a promising sideline, but grew to be the branch of music by which he left his greatest impression on posterity: his oratorios.

The Handelian oratorio

Handel's Italian operas are excellent embodiments of their typically Latin models. His fine concertos, trio sonatas, violin, flute or oboe sonatas: all these are sound, splendidly constructed orchestral and chamber music of the normal baroque pattern of their day, not markedly distinct from that of Corelli or Vivaldi – perhaps a little less classically transparent than the former and a little less temperamental and poetic than the latter, but certainly showing nothing that can be called characteristically English as the melodic contours and the poignant harmony of Purcell can be called English. They are not even German in the sense that Bach is German; nor are they so highly individual. Insofar as they are not Italian, they are cosmopolitan. His harpsichord suites, with certain notable exceptions, are a little tame; but that is because in actual performance he enriched them with bold improvization, like the singers and other virtuoso performers of his time.

But the oratorios are another matter. Here he evolved a style which was neither German, Italian, nor cosmopolitan. Then was it somehow English? Is that peculiar solidarity, produced as it undoubtedly was in England and with English audiences in view, an English solidarity?

We must first offset a partial misunderstanding. Some part of the solid and almost priggish weightiness we associate with Handel's oratorio comes not from his music but from our habit of performing it with incongruous nineteenth century massiveness, and disappears in a stylistically appropriate rendering with small forces and a lively articulation. Not, however, all of it. Even when allowance has been made for this important matter of interpretation, the fact remains that the idiom is more strong than subtle. It accords well enough with the stolid John Bullishness (John Bull the eighteenth-century national caricature, by the way, not John Bull the seventeenth century virtuoso composer) which still passes in some quarters for the English character.

True it is that only the English have really taken oratorio to their hearts. Did we then actually grow somewhat pedestrian and unimaginative in the eighteenth century, and is this the reason for our musical impoverishment? If so, or in so far as it is so, it is an explanation which itself needs explaining. The Elizabethans were anything but stolid; Stuart England was far from tranquil; and in the eighteenth century there was plenty of enterprise in other fields than music. Even in music there was no slackening of activity other than the creative activity of genius. Our performers were eminent; our makers of musical instruments retained an enviable reputation. In the other arts, particularly in literature and in painting, we were conspicuously inspired. The Age of Reason had certainly an element of self-satisfaction, and this element may possibly be mirrored in the *Messiah*. We might then look to find, perhaps, some musical counterpart to Alexander Pope, with a dry wit and a controlled sentiment in keeping with that mood among the many moods our Muse has shown through her long history. But we do not find him; he does not exist.

John Bull is not a bad fellow. A certain imperturbability is among his specially valuable characteristics. But he has deeper feelings and is more susceptible to the finer emotions than his eighteenth century caricature suggests; and it is un-

fair to suppose that the limit of his musical capabilities consists in listening to oratorio. It was not so even under the Georges, when his powers of composition were at their lowest ebb. Essentially then the mystery remains.

The flow of amateur music

John Bull as an amateur performer of music was only a little less cultivated in the eighteenth century than he had been in the seventeenth. The direction in which there was most decline was that solemn chamber music of the viols which Roger North, writing his nostalgic memoirs as a very old man in 1728, recalled as among the profoundest delights of his own youthful upbringing. The viols, with their intimate tone and their highly contrapuntal and musically exacting repertoire, were rapidly becoming obsolete; the more assertive and extravert family of violins was already supreme even in England, where this transition occurred somewhat later than in other countries. The only viol which fully held its own for most of the eighteenth century was the bass viol, or viola da gamba – the instrument both then and now known familiarly and conveniently as the gamba. This is the real soloist of the viol family, its thin strings and light construction giving it a free vibration and a golden tone more related to the violin than to the violoncello. (The treble viol is also a soloist, and in that capacity it remained quite fashionable in France well into the eighteenth century; but in England it was never so favoured for solo purposes.) Some of the finest extant gambas are the work of the English maker Barak Norman, who was in active business in London down to 1740.

In chamber as opposed both to orchestral and to solo music, the eighteenth century form of chief importance was the trio sonata. This is not basically a contrapuntal form, though counterpoint can play a considerable incidental part in its construction. Basically it is so to speak a reduplicated or twin pair of treble melodies supported by a melodic bass line. That gives three melodies, whence the description trio sonata. Besides the three melodic instruments, however, a fourth partner is required: a harpsichord, or sometimes an organ or a lute, to fill in the harmonic texture and join the outer melodic parts across their intervening middle register. Not contributing any further essential melody, this harmonic partner was not included in the arithmetic, and we have thus the unusual spectacle of four partners adding up to three parts. At a pinch, however, either the melodic bass instrument, or the harmonic instrument doubling its line while adding harmonies and subsidiary melodies above it, could be dispersed with – but not, of course, both together.

Unlike the grave chamber music of the viols, the trio sonata is a form which encourages professional virtuosity and is as fitted for public as it is for private performance. Public concerts with a paying audience were becoming increasingly fashionable throughout the eighteenth century. Opera was essentially a professional province. The supremacy of the musical amateur was ending; and with this change the inward spirit of music was changing too, both gain and loss resulting. But under the first two Georges the cultivated amateur had not yet been altogether outshadowed by the regular professional, nor had the two branches been so decidedly separated as afterwards became the case. A great deal even of professional activity was conducted in private drawing-rooms, with the patron often associating on more or less equal terms with the musicians he engaged.

Singing was probably the most highly professionalized career in music; but even here the numerous publications of operatic excerpts testify to the popularity of amateur performance. Harpsichord reductions of opera were another favourite. Some of the most splendid eighteenth century harpsichords were made in London, particularly by Kirkman and Shudi; and there are some English tutors for this instrument. The number of proficient amateur performers was certainly large. The flute was a much-favoured instrument

largely subsisting on operatic excerpts, but also figuring extensively in the trio sonata, and rather less so in the solo literature (many parts are for violin, flute or oboe at the player's will). The violin was widely cultivated, the earliest full-scale tutor for this instrument, by the Italian immigrant Geminiani, being published in London, probably about 1741. Many houses still had a chamber organ as well as or in place of a harpsichord or spinet. But the clavichord, as in the seventeenth (though not the sixteenth) century, was for reasons unguessed a great rarity in England. Only one clavichord of English manufacture is known to survive (Pl. 91A). English pianos were made before 1760; but it was only after this date that this instrument was seriously undertaken by the English makers, though they then became some of the leaders in the field.

This is not, taken as a whole, the picture of a 'land without music', as an unsympathetic German once called us in the nineteenth century. Yet he had the excuse that until Elgar, rather late in his life, established an unchallengeable reputation (it is quite pleasant to note that he did so first in Germany), England did appear to be a land without major composers; and so it was in the period here under review. After so many generations of superlative achievement, why this disproportionate decline? Various answers have been suggested, and some of them have helped to clarify the issue; but only on a comparatively superficial level. It is no longer, perhaps, a very burning issue, now that Vaughan Williams has followed Elgar, and the younger generation of Tippett and Britten has put us back so conclusively among the leading musical nations. But it is a mystery, for all that; and at bottom there is nothing we can really say about it, except that our Muse, after her inscrutable fashion, would have it so.

Bookbinding

HOWARD M. NIXON

The history of English bookbinding during the reigns of the first two Georges is unexciting, and for much of the period the dead hand of tradition guided the finisher's tools. Apart from the mantling round the arms on the bindings produced for (or possibly by) Elkanah Settle, the City Poet, there is little sign of influence by, or awareness of, other contemporary applied arts. The 'cottage-roof' design, with its broken pediments, which had originated in the early years of the Restoration, persisted (growing more and more feeble) until after 1760. The only characteristic new mode – the Harleian style – had a wide border formed by rolls or repeated impressions of the same large (and mainly rather dull) tools. In the centre of the frame so formed, the more elaborate bindings had a diamond-shaped centrepiece built up of small tools, many of which had been familiar to binders since the reign of King Charles II. The style was probably introduced in the 1720's, in the library of Robert Harley, first Earl of Oxford, much of whose binding was carried out by Thomas Elliott. Despite, however, the constant nagging of his lordship's librarian, Humfrey Wanley, most of the bindings for that library are on leather of inferior quality. It was left to a provincial binder, Moore of Cambridge, to produce the most attractive examples of this style in the years 1745–55 (Pl. 93A).

The only Oxford craftsman of the period whose work is distinctive showed less taste, but more enterprise, in producing some lavishly tooled covers embellished with spidery mosaics in inlaid leather. (The best known example of his work covers Dr George Clarke's Prayer Book in the library of All Souls College, Oxford.) Another not altogether happy attempt to copy the great mosaic bindings being produced in Paris is to be found on the British Museum and Royal Library, Windsor, copies of the 1743 London edition of Gabriel Faerno's *Fabulae centum* (Pl. 93B). The binder of these books bound others for Frederick, Prince of Wales, and the second Earl Granville.

The binder of the period with the greatest reputation was Richard Montague, who was employed by Thomas Hollis in the 1750's to bind copies of works by English protagonists of liberty, which he sent to institutions in foreign countries observing his republican principles. A set of these bindings now in the Biblioteca Nazionale at Florence has covers and leather doublures of contrasting colours, but the only innovation in design is the substitution of a central figure of Britannia within a circle of small tools for the customary lozenge-shaped Harleian centre-piece.

No one could accuse Andreas Linde, a native of Germany, who held the appointment of bookbinder to George III when Prince of Wales, of insipidity, but the bindings by him which survive in the Royal Library at Windsor and in the British Museum are most charitably regarded as an expression of German taste quite uninfluenced by English domicile.

More pleasing, if less ambitious, is the work of John Brindley, who was binder to Frederick, Prince of Wales, and to Queen Caroline. Most of his bindings for the Royal Family have only a rather dull rectangular border with a coat of arms in the centre of the covers, but he seems to have specialized in the treatment of the edges of the leaves. He continued the practice of painting decorations under the gold on the fore-edge of his bindings, and on the sets of the leather-bound copies of his pocket editions of the classics he obtained charming results from marbling under gold. A more elaborate binding that is presumably his work is found on several copies of his 1737 edition of the Duke of Newcastle's *Méthode ... de dresser les chevaux.*

Printing

RUARI McLEAN

The ordinary book of the early and mid-eighteenth century in England showed very little improvement on its predecessors. A characteristic work published in 1719 was *The Life and Strange Surprizing Adventures of Robinson Crusoe, of York, Mariner*: the title, as was then the fashion, goes on for fifty-three further words before finishing '*Written by Himself*. LONDON: Printed for W. Taylor at the Ship in Paternoster Row, MDCCXIX'. (Taylor's business was later bought by Thomas Longman, and the firm he founded still uses the Ship as its sign.) *Robinson Crusoe* is an octavo volume, with a copper-plate illustration as frontispiece; on the title-page a plain double rule, not very straight, goes round outside the type. Perhaps it is rather better turned out than the average of its day; but the types are rough and not very well printed, the paper is coarse, the

production has a primitive air. Many surviving books of the period look much worse: the impression of the type is so grey as to be hardly legible, the paper is thick and varies greatly in colour.

Some early eighteenth century printers could, however, do better. It has been said that the place to find the best printing of the eighteenth century in Britain is in the editions of the ancient Greek and Roman authors, particularly Homer, Virgil and Horace, because 'the eighteenth century reading public believed the classics to be the most valuable source of polite learning available to it, and was prepared to pay a little extra to obtain them in a suitably dignified form'.[1]

[1] Philip Gaskell, 'Printing the Classics in the Eighteenth Century' in *The Book Collector*, Vol. I, 1952.

THE
LIFE
AND
STRANGE SURPRIZING
ADVENTURES
OF
ROBINSON CRUSOE,
Of YORK, MARINER:

Who lived Eight and Twenty Years,
all alone in an un-inhabited Island on the
Coast of AMERICA, near the Mouth of
the Great River of OROONOQUE;

Having been caſt on Shore by Shipwreck, wherein all the Men periſhed but himſelf.

WITH

An Account how he was at laſt as ſtrangely deliver'd by PYRATES.

Written by Himſelf.

LONDON:
Printed for W. TAYLOR at the *Ship* in *Pater-Noſter-
Row.* MDCCXIX.

Fig. 1. The title-page of the first edition of *Robinson Crusoe*, 1719.

This is in the main true, although one of the finest productions of the whole century was the first edition, in three folio volumes, of Clarendon's *History of the Rebellion*, 1702–4, printed at Oxford by the University Press; and several of Jacob Tonson's editions of Milton, Dryden, Addison and Pope were as well produced as any of the editions of the classics. Tonson, the leading London publisher of the period, produced his books as well as they could then be produced. Most of them were printed by William Bowyer the elder (1663–1737), and later by his son, the scholar-printer William Bowyer the younger (1699–1777). Tonson and Bowyer books have some style. The usual formats were quarto and folio, so the layout was not cramped, and the type was decently spaced and printed. Engraved or etched frontispieces (often portraits of the author, rarely illustrations of the work) were commonly used, and so were engraved head- and tail-pieces and initial letters in the text pages. The title-page was almost invariably typographical: the engraved title-page typical of the Stuart period had now gone out of favour. Woodcut ornaments of French inspiration and arrangements of printer's flowers were also used on text pages: sometimes the first volume of a work would have engravings and the second, presumably to save money, woodcuts.[2]

Illustration in serious books was nearly always by copperplate: woodcuts generally appeared only in the cheapest literature, children's books, ballads, pamphlets and news-sheets. Illustrations to literature were rare, but increased as the popularity of reading for entertainment increased, with the rise of the novel. The frontispiece to *Robinson Crusoe* (1719) was a true illustration: so were Hogarth's plates for *Hudibras* (1726) and *Tristram Shandy*, which, however, Hogarth did not engrave himself. Those were, practically speaking, the only book-illustrations made by England's first great artist-engraver, whose main business lay in prints, which were published by themselves. The chief English book-illustrator of the period was Hogarth's friend, Francis Hayman (1708–

76); but the great French illustrator and engraver Gravelot also worked in England for many years, and illustrated, among other books, *Pamela* and *Tom Jones*. Two other engravers of plates in early Georgian books were George Vertue (1684–1756) and Gerard Van der Gucht (1696–1776).

Type faces

The types used in England at the beginning of the eighteenth century were nearly all Dutch. In the Elizabethan period the best roman types came from France, in particular, the designs of Garamond, Le Bé and Granjon, which have never been surpassed to this day. In the seventeenth century the leadership in type design and production passed to Holland, especially to the foundries of Van Dyck and Voskens, although many of the types they made were really of French origin. At the end of the seventeenth century there were four type-foundries in London, but most of their punches and moulds, and certainly their better ones, were Dutch; and when efforts were made to improve the standards of English printing, it was to Holland that we find Fell of Oxford, Bentley of Cambridge and Tonson of London sending or going for new types.

The fact that this need for improvement of English printing was so obviously felt, and that the restrictions on the commercial development of printing in England had been lifted in 1695,[3] made it probable that English technical ability would soon assert itself in printing and type-founding. And in the 1720's, England produced her first great type-founder, William Caslon.

The manufacture of type by hand is perhaps one of the most complex and laborious skills in the world. Every letter has first to be cut in reverse and in relief on the end of a steel bar, called a punch, which is, after hardening, struck into softer metal to make a matrix. The matrix is then fitted into a mould in which the individual types are cast, the casting itself being a manual process of

---

[2] E.g. *The Genuine Works ... of George Granville Lord Landsdowne*, Tonson, 1732.

[3] The lapsing of the Licensing Act in 1695 (which among other things had limited printing to London, Oxford and Cambridge) did not free the Press, in the widest sense, but it restored normal commercial competition.

Two Lines Englifh.

Quoufque tandem abutere, Catilina, patientia noftra? quamdiu nos e-

Quoufque tandem abutere Catilina, patientia noftra?

Two Lines Pica.

Quoufque tandem abutere, Catilina, patientia noftra? qu

Quoufque tandem abutere, Catilina, patientia noftra? quam-

F L O W E R S.

Great Primer Flowers.

Fig. 2. Specimens of William Caslon's roman type, in two sizes, and ornaments.

considerable skill. The art of the type-founder lies in making letters which are beautiful, or right, not individually but in combination. It is the 'fit' of the letters – the exact position, to a fraction of a millimetre, of the type face on its body – that is the crux of the whole process. Masters of this art have always been rare.

William Caslon

William Caslon, born in Shropshire in 1692, was apprenticed to a London engraver of gun-locks and barrels, and afterwards set up in that trade himself. His skill made him increasingly well known, and his work began to include chasing silver and designing and engraving the tools of book-binders. This brought him into touch with book-sellers: and, according to the story, the printer John Watts (for some time a partner of Jacob Tonson II, and the employer of Benjamin Frank-lin) encouraged him to take up type-cutting. In 1720, Caslon set himself up as a type-founder, with £500 capital subscribed by John Watts and two other leading London printers, John Betten-ham and William Bowyer the elder.

In ten years Caslon had established his superior-ity over the other London type-founders. His first work was not roman type, but a fount of Arabic for the Society for Promoting Christian Know-ledge. This was followed by founts of Hebrew and Coptic. His first roman and italic was probably cut in the pica size and appeared about 1725.[4]

Gradually other sizes of roman and italic, and other foreign alphabets, were cut. Caslon's first Specimen sheet was issued in 1734. By the middle of the century his fame and his trade had extended across Europe. He died in 1766, leaving a flour-ishing business in the hands of his capable son.

Caslon's achievement has been variously as-sessed. Mr Stanley Morison, one of the greatest living authorities on type design, says: 'William Caslon was inspired to cut on the Dutch pattern, and, although his punches were better cut, his matrices better justified, than any English pre-decessor, the historic "Old Face" ... of Caslon is in no way superior to the finest founts of the Amsterdam houses; neither does it compare fav-ourably with the best of Garamond or of Gran-jon, nor, indeed, is it any advance upon the Aldine archetype of 1495. In the Pica some characters, e.g. the lower-case short s, are in fact amateur-ish. ...' [5] Caslon's types were superseded by the in-novations of Baskerville and Bell later in the cen-tury. Yet there is no question that in their day they represented an enormous improvement on what was previously available; and the recutting of Cas-lon by the Monotype Corporation in 1922 played a great part in the revival of printing during this century in Europe and America. Many typo-graphers today, on the Continent as well as in Britain, if faced with the necessity of throwing away all their type-faces except one, would prob-ably choose to keep Caslon. This book is set in Caslon. There is something humane about it which types with fewer imperfections do not share.

William Caslon's career did much to encourage and revive the art of printing in England, and was a prelude to the great period of English printing in the reign of George III.

Scottish Printing

In the middle of the eighteenth century the most interesting printing in the British Isles, and perhaps in Europe, was being done in Scotland.

Scottish printing had always had a style of its own. A growing awareness of the art is shown by the appearance in 1713, at Edinburgh, of *The History of the Art of Printing*, printed by James Watson and sold 'at his shop opposite the Lucken Booths' ... etc. It is not an original work, being mostly a translation of De la Caille's *Histoire de l'imprimerie* (1689); but the preface contains some useful information about contemporary Scottish printing; and it was the first work on the history of printing to appear in the British Isles.

The middle and later half of the eighteenth century was the great period of Scottish culture,

[4] See A.F.Johnson, *The Monotype Recorder*, Vol. 35, No. 4 (Winter 1936), and his Appendix on Caslon's first types in T.B.Reed, *A History of the Old English Letter Foundries*, 1952, p. 253.

[5] Introduction to Berry and Johnson's *Catalogue of Specimens of Printing Types*, 1935.

Fig. 3. Engraved heading from Bickham's *The Universal Penman*, 1742.

the time of David Hume and Adam Smith, Joseph Black and John Hunter, the brothers Adam, Allan Ramsay and Robert Burns. At the same time the brothers Foulis in Glasgow, and other printers in Glasgow, Edinburgh, St Andrews and Dunfermline, were establishing a tradition of fine and scholarly printing which has never been lost in Scotland.[6]

Robert Foulis[7] set up as a bookseller to Glasgow University in 1740, published and sold books in 1741, and printed, published and sold them in 1742. About 1748 Andrew Foulis joined his brother as a partner in the business. Until Robert's death in 1776 the press issued at least 608 known editions. Robert's son Andrew carried on the business until 1795, although few books were printed after 1787. The press became famous for the accuracy and excellence of its editions of the classics, mostly in small formats: many of these, being unpretentious and unillustrated, can still be obtained today very cheaply in second-hand bookshops (Pl. 96).

[6] See *Catalogue of an Exhibition of Eighteenth-Century Scottish Books*, Cambridge University Press, 1951.

[7] See Philip Gaskell, 'The Early Work of the Foulis Press and the Wilson Foundry', in the *Transactions of the Bibliographical Society*, June 1952.

Robert Foulis was a great printer and a powerful influence on later book designers: he showed what excellent results can be obtained by severely plain typography without any use of ornament. In title-page design he led the way to modern usage (followed by Baskerville and others) in using only letter-spaced capitals, in a few sizes; it was normal, at that time, to use roman and italic lower case, and italic caps, as well as two sizes of caps in the same line. Foulis was also the first to omit catchwords (the first word of the next page printed at the foot of the preceding one) – a habit later adopted by the rest of the trade.

Most of the Foulis Press types were supplied by Alexander Wilson, the distinguished Scottish type-founder who cut, in 1755, the best fount of Greek type yet made, and was then appointed the first Regius Professor of Practical Astronomy in the University of Glasgow, where he made important contributions to the theories of the nature of sun-spots and of the galactic systems.[8]

Writing-masters

Apart from the work of Foulis, no printing under the early Georges showed much art. The

[8] Philip Gaskell, op. cit.

most beautiful work to appear on book-pages during that period has not yet, however, been mentioned: it is the engraved calligraphy of the writing-masters. Their copy-books were not real books, but they produced isolated pages of entrancing charm. It is curious that no one of them appears to have thought of working for the booksellers or of engraving, for example, a calligraphic edition of Shakespeare's sonnets or even of some of Lord Chesterfield's Letters, rather than pages of moral precepts and Bills of Lading.[9] But significantly it was a writing-master turned printer, John Baskerville, who raised English book-design to a European level. The age of the writing-masters has, however, its own memorial in one curious and famous book, Bickham's *The Universal Penman*. The Bickhams were a family of pen-men and engravers, and they had the idea of producing what has aptly been called 'a writing-book to end all

writing-books'[10] with pages designed by twenty-five of the leading writing-masters of the day, but all engraved by John and George Bickham. They also had the less good idea of issuing it in weekly parts, which ended in failure. The first parts stumbled out in 1733; but the book did at last appear complete some nine years later. Its pages form an impressive record of early Georgian graphic art (see Figs. 3, 4, and the illustrations on pp. 592, 723, 734, 750, 755 and 756).

While *The Universal Penman* was in its birth-throes the young Birmingham writing-master John Baskerville (who had not contributed) turned to japanning to make his fortune; and in 1750 he began experiments in letter-founding and printing. In 1757 his first book, the *Virgil*, 'went forth to astonish all the librarians of Europe'. Baskerville's achievement is described in *The Late Georgian Period* in this Guide.

[9] John Pine's *Horace* (1733–37) was printed entirely on engraved plates, and is a remarkable book. But Pine was an engraver, not a writing-master; and the design of the book is that of the conventional printer.

[10] P.H.Muir, 'The Bickhams and their *Universal Penman*', in *The Library*, 4th Series, Vol. 25 (1945).

Fig. 4. Engraved heading from Bickham's *The Universal Penman*, 1742.

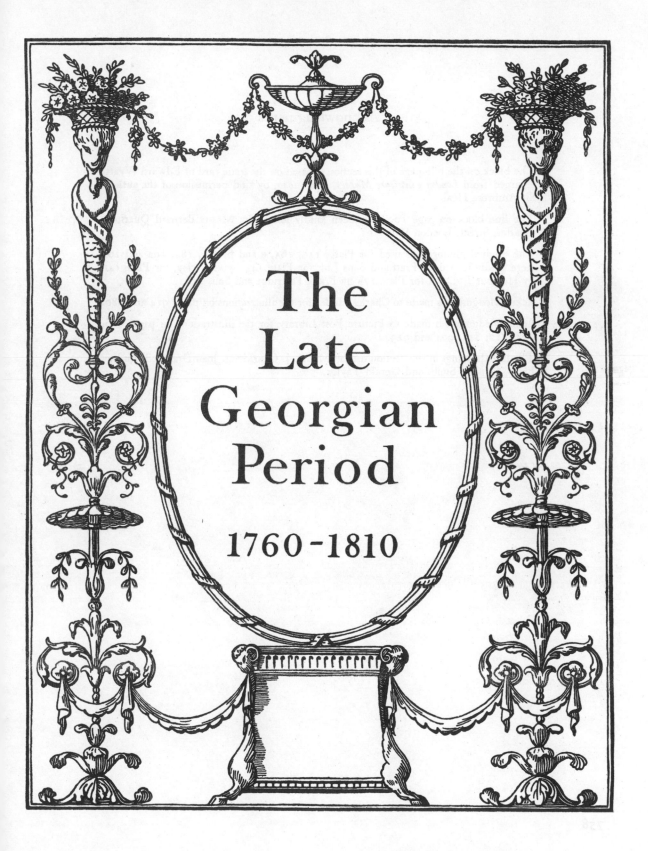

The
Late
Georgian
Period

1760-1810

Acknowledgments

The block on the title-page of this section is based on the trade card of Edward Wyatt, enlarged from *London Furniture Makers, 1660—1840,* by kind permission of the author, Sir Ambrose Heal.

The line block on page 1004 has been kindly loaned by Messrs Bernard Quaritch, Grafton Street, London W1.

The original photographs used for Plates 14C, 16A, B and D, 17A, 18A, 19B and 20B were kindly loaned by Pratt and Sons Ltd, for Plate 14A by G. Jetley, for Plate 14B by Hotspur Ltd, and for Plate 17B by Frank Partridge and Sons Ltd.

Acknowledgment is made to Charles Hasler for the illustrations on pages 914 and 980.

Acknowledgment is made to Picture Post Library for the illustrations on pages 806, 808, 812, 815, 904 and 923.

The line drawings in this section are by Mrs R. J. Charleston, Joan Drabwell, Audrey Frew, Daphne Smith and Gerald Taylor.

The Age of George III

IAN R. CHRISTIE

The year 1760, in which George III succeeded to the throne of his grandfather, marks no particular landmark in British history. A young, conservative-minded personality had become head of the state, a new factor in its politics: but the broad flood-tide of the nation's exuberant life swept on unchecked and undeflected. By this date Great Britain was firmly set, with slow but gathering momentum, on far-reaching lines of development and change. Signal progress was achieved in the next sixty years. Up to within a few years of George III's accession, the country was, internally, a land of stable population, predominantly agricultural in its economy though with an enterprising and gradually expanding industry; and, externally, one – and not clearly the strongest – of a group of west European states reaching out in competition with each other towards the heritage of world trade and empire. Very different was the scene at the close of the reign in 1820. By then, the mode of living and the resources of Britain's mounting population were being transformed by the great advances in transport and industry commonly described as the Industrial Revolution. And the successful conclusion of the wars against Revolutionary and Napoleonic France left her indisputable mistress of the seas with unrivalled opportunities for trade and imperial expansion.

The sinews of power

Its people is the heart of a nation's strength. When, soon after the turn of the century, the statistician, John Rickman, began to analyse the figures available in the early census returns and in other sources, contemporaries were amazed to find that the number of the people had increased by nearly half since the King's accession and was still increasing. During most of the first half of the eighteenth century the population of England and Wales had been fairly stable. But from about 1750 an upward trend began. In 1760, at the accession of George III, the people numbered some six million and a half. By the time of the first census in 1801, the figure was about nine million, and each decennial census thereafter disclosed a population mounting ever higher. In the period 1760–70 the rate of increase was about 7 per cent; for the last decade of the reign, after 1811, it rose to the remarkable level of over 16 per cent. Scotland showed a similar trend, and in Ireland the rate of increase was even higher.

No simple explanation can be given for this remarkable expansion in numbers. It may be attributed with varying degrees of certainty to several factors. Agricultural improvement – of which more below – probably played a considerable part, by making a better variety and quality of food available and by removing the check of periodic famine. Fresh vegetables were more abundant – the potato was the basis of Irish prolificity, and it formed an increasing part of the diet of the English peasantry though they never became so completely dependent upon it. Stock-rearing with the aid of root-crops for winter feed made it possible to vary diet with fresh meat in the winter months and may also have made more milk available. The development of regional economies, based upon better transport facilities and involving

759

as one consequence a greater mobility of labour, may have evened out the local disparities in the numbers of the sexes to be found from one village to the next, and so have increased the rate of marriage. The extent of the grants of poor relief was thought to encourage early marriages. Of more importance, perhaps, than any save the first of these factors, was the growing attention paid to health, with its startling effect upon the death rate and more especially on infant mortality. About the middle of the eighteenth century seventy-five out of every hundred children died at birth or before their sixth year: by its end the rate had fallen to 41 per cent. If medicine had made no startling technical advances during most of this period, at least its practitioners had grasped the all-importance of cleanliness and fresh air in combating disease; and their knowledge was used and spread abroad by the hospitals which had been founded both in London and the provinces during the earlier years of the century. At the century's end a great technical advance was at last achieved: Edward Jenner's discovery of vaccination, a powerful new weapon in the battle against smallpox – hitherto a terrible scourge, especially to children – was thought by contemporaries to have contributed greatly to the rapid increase in population. As each additional child saved was a potential parent, the effect on the rate of population increase was cumulative, until, at the very end of the reign, counteracting tendencies to check the marriage and birth rates began to make their appearance.

Some eighteenth-century writers had expressed fears lest Britain's power might fail for want of numbers. Such an idea, which had in any case never been widely accepted, was entirely dispelled by the first census taken in 1801. On the contrary, it was clear that the country's human resources were on the upgrade, and that youth, with its vigour, exuberance, enterprise and eager response to novelty and change, formed an increasing proportion of them. Measured in terms of the age of her population, Britain in the early nineteenth century was a country of youth: here lay part of the secret of her strength, in war and in peace.

Another part of this strength lay in her command of natural resources: to this advancements in agriculture, transport and industry all contributed in plenteous measure.

The demand of a growing population for more food was the main stimulus to agricultural improvement: indeed, from 1793, after the commencement of the great war against Revolutionary France, this became a matter of official concern, which led to the creation of the advisory Board of Agriculture. In the enclosure of waste and common land, the marling of light soils, the use of crop rotations, and the improvement of breeds of cattle and sheep, the men of George III's reign were less inventors or originators than followers of lines of advance already marked out by pioneers in the earlier part of the century, but their zeal and enterprise made an indispensable contribution to the nation's prosperity. To quote but one name: Thomas William Coke, of Holkham, pursued experiments which turned his native county of Norfolk into one of the granaries of England. Information about new farming methods was constantly circulated. Coke himself turned his annual sheep-shearings into agricultural conferences attended by farming enthusiasts from every part of the country: these meetings even achieved an international fame. By the medium of books and pamphlets Arthur Young won brilliant success as a popularizer of agricultural science, publicizing the latest results of observations and experiments which he culled on his journeys across the length and breadth of England. Through the enterprise of the landed aristocracy and gentry, agricultural production virtually kept pace with population throughout the reign.

Road and water transport were vastly improved. By the middle of the century much attention was being paid to the country's roads, and numerous turnpike trusts were established for this purpose. But better roads could not meet the needs of industry. They facilitated an increasing long distance traffic mainly of passengers and of goods of small bulk and high value, but for most purposes the cost of moving bulky and heavy goods, upon which tolls had to be paid every few miles, made this mode of conveyance unduly expensive. So, almost simultaneously with the beginning of the reign, the demands of commerce and industry for cheaper transport facilities set going the great canal boom of the later eighteenth century, of which the wealthy Duke of Bridgwater and his brilliant engineer, James Brindley, were the pioneers. Within a few years, cheaper, quicker transport by the new canals gave an enormous stimulus to industrial development.

The year 1760 is no longer considered as marking the commencement of an 'Industrial Revolution'. The developments in industry which took place in the reign of George III followed naturally from those which had occurred earlier in the century: at the most there was a quickening of pace, technical advances following more rapidly one upon another and reacting over wider spheres of industrial activity. Development was uneven, and some industries forged ahead far faster than others, cotton and iron making the most rapid advances. Like children captivated by a new toy, the industrial entrepreneurs were elated and enthralled at the new powers which inventions were bestowing upon them – witness, for instance, John Wilkinson, whose fanatical interest in the uses to which abundant supplies of iron might be put went so far as directing that he should be buried in an iron coffin, who built the first iron bridge in 1779, experimented with iron-built lighters for inland navigation, and supplied forty miles of cast iron piping for the water supply of Paris. The importance of James Watt's invention of the steam engine has always been singled out in popular imagination; and before the end of the reign the advantages of this revolutionary contrivance, both for pumping out mines and as a source of motive power for machines in factories, were clearly apparent over large sections of the field of industry. New machines and new processes quickened the pace of industrial output. Really dramatic results only began to show in the last quarter of the eighteenth century. In so far as what is meant by the 'Industrial Revolution' was a sudden quickening of the rate of production, the turning point came about 1780, towards the close of the American War of Independence. If the figures for imports and exports in the peace-decade 1764–73 are taken as a starting point, comparison shows

that trade fell off slightly in the next decennium, during most of which the American War was dislocating commerce and diverting the nation's energies. But in the next peace-decade, 1784–93, the value of imports and exports was between a fifth and a quarter higher than in the years 1764–73, and each year showed an upward movement, which continued through the war period after 1793.

Industrial development brought changes in the way of life of many of the common people, but generalization about whether these changes were for better or for worse is almost impossible. One feature of the period which greatly struck contemporaries was the crowding together of workpeople in factories. This was not a new phenomenon; nor, on the other hand, was it nearly so widespread as later in the nineteenth century: but with the expansion of industry it became more common. Conditions in factories were often undoubtedly bad, but it is questionable whether they were worse, or the hours of labour longer, than hours and conditions in domestic industry. Probably the most hateful feature of factory life was its compulsory uniformity and strict discipline: there was also social prejudice against it, grounded upon a terminological confusion of the poor-law workhouse with the factory and upon the fact that factory labour was recruited largely from among tramps and paupers, the least reputable flotsam and jetsam of society. Nevertheless, factory life offered the attraction of wages which, so far as one can generalize from the information available, seem to have been on the whole rather better than those obtainable in domestic industry and clearly higher than wages in agriculture. Apart from the disruptive effect of the business cycle, much of the social distress which was to be revealed by both private and public enquiry in the years after the close of the Napoleonic wars was due less to the new industrial developments than to the economic dislocation produced by war and then by readjustment to peace conditions.

As the population grew and was attracted to centres of factory industry, so its distribution within the country changed. Already, in the earlier part of the century, a tendency to become relatively

761

more populous was discernible in Lancashire and the central and west midlands. This trend continued after 1760, but it was now accompanied by a much more rapid growth of towns – Manchester, for instance, had in 1757 less than 20,000 inhabitants, but by 1790 they numbered 50,000 and were nearly double that figure by the turn of the century. Locally the consequences were over-crowding, cellar-dwellings, jerry-built tenements with inadequate sanitation or ventilation, squalid conditions: but as yet only a small minority of the nation was affected; the greater part of the English people still lived in the countryside, and only just over a fifth in towns with 10,000 or more inhabitants.

The oligarchs

Social and political leadership in this robust society still rested predominantly in the hands of the landed class. Within this social group the distinction between aristocracy and gentry was more artificial than real. Title had meaning in the court circle. But numbers of country gentlemen could boast a rent-roll and a local influence greater than that of many members of the peerage. From time to time, in the obituary notices of wealthy commoners, comes the phrase: 'reputed one of the richest men in the Kingdom'. Such outstanding individuals were of course exceptions: more common were those comfortably situated gentlemen with £2,000 to £5,000 a year, the placid domesticity of whose lives is portrayed for us in the novels of Jane Austen.[1]

The country houses of peer and gentleman were the nurseries of national culture and tradition. Gentry of the wealthier sort sent their sons to Westminster or to mix with the young lords at Eton· the future squire would learn the elements of his law at the inns of court: for some there followed a spell at Oxford or Cambridge, capped perhaps by the broadening experience of the Grand Tour. Till the long French wars broke the tradition after the turn of the century, the Grand Tour helped to widen the cultural horizon of the English ruling class. In the earlier years of the reign, Horace Walpole or George Augustus Selwyn moved as easily in the society of Paris as that of London. The end of a war, 1763, 1783, 1802, saw a rush of Englishmen to France, to renew old acquaintance and re-experience the well-appreciated stimulus of foreign contacts: a spirit of international fraternity outweighed all bitterness bred of national rivalries. Italy was more difficult of access – nevertheless numbers of young Englishmen on tour reached Florence, Venice, Rome, and absorbed some knowledge of their people and their style. Other parts of the Continent were perhaps less popular, but were by no means neglected.

Richard Arkwright, the cotton manufacturer, it is said, contemplated accumulating enough wealth to pay off the national debt! Josiah Wedgwood of pottery fame died reputedly worth over half a million. These men were exceptional, but they stand as reminders that trade and industry were increasingly the basis of fortunes which could compete on even terms with those derived from the land. Land and trade were interests which sometimes might, and did, clash in the sphere of politics. But Britain gained inestimably from the circumstance that no caste barrier divided landowner and merchant. The enterprising landed proprietor, like Coke of Holkham, was at heart a business-man: it might be pure chance whether the undertakings in which he interested himself were entirely agricultural, or whether he branched out, as did the Duke of Bridgwater, into investment in canals and the production of coal. Younger sons of the peerage and gentry went into commerce: and often enough their elder brothers, who took the land or the title, picked their wives from the wealthy merchant class. Snobbery there might be, but no caste division: thus in Staffordshire the leading landed magnates paid due personal attention to Josiah Wedgwood, treating him as one of the important figures in county life – as indeed he was.

Political power, the conduct of public affairs, lay in the hands of the landowners and, to some extent, of the commercial class. In the countryside, the squires ran the local administration and dispensed justice, in quarter and petty sessions, and

[1] About 1809 "all the country gentlemen of any note" in Kent were said to have £3,000–£4,000 a year (*British Public Characters*, Vol. X (1809–1810), p. 534).

through their membership of improvement boards and turnpike trusts. At the centre they brought their influence to bear on the national councils in parliament. To the men of the eighteenth century, parliament was primarily a meeting place of interests. The greatest of these was the landed interest, for those who held landed property had a stake in the country more distinct than that of any other class. By comparison the commercial interest was less important, though it was recognized that its claims must also be given due weight. And there were also others: for instance, attention – perhaps at times too much attention – was usually paid to the West Indian planters from whose ranks came a small, compact group of men in the House of Commons. Mere numbers having no place in the orthodox contemporary theory of representation, the astounding, antiquated anomalies of the representative system drew little fire except from a small radical minority. What matter that a green mound at Old Sarum returned two members, and by the *fiat* of a single individual who owned it? Pocket boroughs were even defended, as providing a way into parliament for representatives of the landed and commercial interest with the minimum of trouble and expense. The metropolitan area, as radicals were never weary of pointing out, had but eight members in parliament – two for Middlesex, two for Westminster, four for London – whereas by the proportion of land tax its inhabitants paid it could well claim fifty. But compensation was provided within the system, since thirty or forty London merchants would usually buy their way into parliament *via* the small rotten and pocket boroughs of the southern and western counties. Very populous constituencies appeared positively disadvantageous, at a time when the mass of the people was largely illiterate and entirely indifferent to political questions, and elections became competitions in the provision of bread and circuses – a number of such constituencies were to suffer a measure of disfranchisement at the hands of the propertied reformers of 1832. Except in the counties and a few leading city constituencies (and not always in these) politics played little or no part in the determination of contested parliamentary elections.

Party divisions of the modern type did not exist. The name 'Whig' was regarded as having a mystical aura of constitutionalism and virtue, and from time to time various political groups in opposition laid exclusive claim to it as part of a 'smear' campaign against their successful rivals in office. But its value as a political connotation was *nil*. It is impossible to maintain on the evidence, that the younger Pitt, for instance, was less 'whig' than Charles James Fox. Fox's associate, the Duke of Portland, once spoke of the value to the country of a 'whig' party, but this was only a few months before he carried his political following into Pitt's ministry in a war-coalition.

Limited monarchy

At the head of the government stood the King. In theory he was still the active leader of the executive, enjoying a right to employ the ministers of his personal choice which was sometimes challenged but very generally conceded. The constitution established by the Revolution of 1689 set, so it was assumed, King, Lords and Commons in mutual balance, each with power to keep the activities of the others within due bounds. In practice the King was obliged to carry on the government with close attention to the wishes of the House of Commons, from which, periodically, money or assent to legislation had to be obtained. Convenience dictated the selection of a leading minister in whom the House of Commons placed confidence: no government would last long if this rule were not observed. But the sovereign's choice was not determined, as now, by party, nor did party solely sustain the government in parliament. Political parties in the eighteenth century were no more than personal followings limited in size: the party numbering more than thirty or forty in the House of Commons was exceptional. The members of a government, while drawing part of their parliamentary support from their own factions, relied largely upon the votes of members of two perennial parliamentary groupings which the onset of democracy has since swept out of existence – these were the party of court and administration, composed of courtiers, government officials, contractors, pensioners and parasites, who gave political allegiance to the King's government whoever composed it, and the independents, for the most part country gentlemen, who scorned attachment either to the court or to a faction and voted as led by their conscience, or their judgment, or by their response to some brilliant piece of oratory. Parliament paid due deference to the King's government. But it stood apart, an independent authority, reserving the right to reject measures of which it disapproved: such a rejection was not, however, normally intended or construed to mean a withdrawal of confidence and did not entail the ministers' resignations.

This eighteenth-century parliamentary system allotted no logical or recognized role to an Opposition, although oppositions were almost always in the field, led by disgruntled politicians who found themselves excluded from office, and backed by the natural critics of authority, who may be encountered in any representative gathering of men. But since the phrase 'the King's government' then carried a more literal meaning than in our modern usage, signifying government by the King and his ministers, a systematic opposition, aimed at discrediting a group of ministers, could plausibly be considered an attack upon the King himself and was often looked upon as discreditable, if not disloyal. Also, as the electorate (such part of it as was politically conscious) did not regard itself as arbiter in the conflict between rival gangs of politicians contesting for office but thought that this should be decided by the King, opposition of this kind was hardly ever successful.

The operation of this system of 'limited monarchy' required good judgment and balance on the part of both the King and his leading minister, qualities not conspicuously present in the early years of the reign. George III, approaching twenty-three at the time of his accession, was particularly nervous and immature, of high ideals and virtue but narrow outlook, entirely without experience of the world, and frankly terrified of his new responsibilities. Brought up by his domineering mother in complete isolation from the youth of aristocratic society – contact with whom, she feared, would corrupt him – it was small wonder that at first he found it almost impossible to take people as they were. Far too conscious of other people's moral failings, he felt that practically all the politicians were worthless, and thought it hard that he must perforce employ them. Thus at first he clung in desperate dependence upon his friend, Lord Bute, a worthy, serious-minded, well-intentioned man, full of book-learning, but in politics as much a greenhorn as his master and not competent to occupy the leading place in government into which he was soon thrust by the King's insistence. Not for several years, and then, in part, only because he was bullied by George Grenville out of his habit of turning constantly to Bute, did George III begin to stand on his own feet. Thereafter he tried to cover up his lack of talent by incessant industry, and in time he acquired a very considerable experience and knowledge of affairs. But he can hardly be said to have had much aptitude or judgment. Little originality of mind is apparent in his voluminous correspondence with his ministers, and his opinions, once formed, were impervious to the best-marshalled arguments. In private life he had many estimable qualities, a sincere religious feeling, a strong sense of family responsibility, and wide cultural interests. But he had to force himself into his public role by conscious effort, and it was many years before he could play it with assurance. He was conscientious to a fault: but for all the close attention which he paid to the activities of his ministers, it cannot be said that he ever stepped outside his recognized constitutional position, and historians are now agreed that there was no real foundation for the charge that he attempted to resume a vanished royal authority and to pervert the constitution of 1689 – this bogey existed only in the fertile Irish imagination of Edmund Burke. A man of no more than average ability, he could not give a lead in statesmanship: rather he faithfully reflected the conservative opinions and prejudices of the great majority of his subjects on such major political issues as the American War of Independence, constitutional reform, the French Revolution, the emancipation of Roman Catholics.

The combined ineptitude of the King and the politicians at first produced a series of weak and short-lived governments. Consciousness of his own incapacity for the political game soon drove out Bute. His successor, George Grenville, had good abilities but little vision, and was overbearing and tactless. After two years his services were dispensed with to make way for the even briefer ministry of Lord Rockingham, an amiable amateur who hardly dared open his mouth in the House of Lords. When twelve months later this government dissolved away through internal weakness and the King turned to Chatham, faint hopes appeared of firm leadership and a more stable political order. But almost immediately Chatham was stricken by gout and manic depression, and his deputy and later successor, the Duke of Grafton, a youthful rake who later became a prim Unitarian, was a political nonentity. Not until 1770, after five ephemeral ministries in ten years, did government at last settle down to some sort of stability. Lord North, the new first minister, intelligent, witty, popular, imperturbably good-humoured, was a first-rate House of Commons man, though sadly lacking in driving force. He retained office for nearly twelve years, until irretrievable defeat in the American War of Independence finally discredited his ministry and obliged the King, greatly against his will, to part with it. From the subsequent two-year period of political confusion and short-lived ministries a new stable government at last emerged under the leadership of the younger Pitt. Though mistakes can be laid to his charge, Pitt was nevertheless the ablest first minister of George III's reign, active, clever, flexible of mind, as assured of support in the House of Commons as North, but commanding it quite differently, by force of character rather than popularity; far ahead of North in his grasp of economic and financial principles and in his willingness to promote advantageous policies and sound administration. Though out of office between 1801 and 1804, Pitt dominated the political scene from 1784 till his death in 1806 — and even afterwards, for his young followers provided the core of later ministries.

The problems of empire

Problems loomed before these successive governments, requiring far greater powers of statesmanship than lay at their disposal. Most constant of them was the consolidation and development of empire — empire conceived primarily as an area of trade relations with non-British peoples, Redskins, Asiatics, Africans, rather than as an area of settlement. The reign opened in the midst of a great struggle — the Seven Years War of 1756 to 1763 against France (latterly also against Spain) — which was primarily a war for empire. The successful conclusion of this conflict at the Peace of Paris of 1763 reaffirmed British naval superiority and transferred to British rule large tracts of the empires of her Bourbon rivals. In a spirit of heady self-confidence the nation set forth to exploit these advantages to the full. Hence disputes with Spain over the Falklands and Vancouver Island, a renewed outburst of oceanic exploration, and the search for the supposed wealthy and populous southern continent — a myth finally dispelled by the voyages of Cook, who pressed south with supreme intrepid daring to the forbidding frozen barriers of the Antarctic. To the East there were abortive attempts during the 'seventies to establish a commercial base in North Borneo, a stepping stone to the expansion of the China trade. For the same purpose Penang was purchased in 1786, and a little later Lord Macartney sent as envoy to Pekin: but China, as yet, kept the British at arm's length. During the great wars with France after 1793, the safety of the long trade route to the East was a primary concern of British statesmen, leading to the occupation, and eventual retention at the peace of 1815, of Dutch and French settlements at the Cape, Ceylon and Mauritius.

Ideally an empire of trade involved no more expense or responsibility than the upkeep of a few commercial posts. This was the initial assumption underlying British penetration into India, and it seems at times also to have coloured official views about relations with the native peoples of North America. But an empire of mere trading posts proved untenable in the face of European competition. The pressure from France left the British no choice between withdrawal or the assumption of new territorial commitments. Advance or retreat — these were the alternatives

765

posed during the Seven Years War, and the victorious peace of 1763 ensured that the advance would be sustained.

In India the war secured primacy for the British East India Company over its French competitors. But at the same time, the involvement of the Company's agents in native politics, partly to win commercial advantage, partly to counter the intrigues of the French, led inevitably to political domination. Step by step, the Company was brought to assume the administration of Bengal, to add to its territories in the presidencies of Bombay and Madras, and to form a network of protectorates and alliances covering the whole of south and central India. Meanwhile British ministries gradually progressed from regarding India merely as a milch cow to accepting responsibility for the good government of the native peoples which the course of events had brought under the Company's rule. Reform owed much to the generous humanitarianism of Edmund Burke, though its practical application owed more to one or two leading government officials and especially to that oft-maligned Scotsman, Henry Dundas. The India Act of 1784, with later amending legislation, subjected the Company's administration to some degree of government control, and under the great pro-consuls, Cornwallis, Wellesley, Minto, India began to receive the best that Britain could give. 'Unimpeachable character', declared Dundas, could be 'the only proper ground of recommendation to situations of importance'. Thus began the tradition of the 'White Man's burden', which was to inspire so much of British imperial enterprise in the following century.

Similarly, in North America, the close of the Seven Years War brought the British new responsibilities in an enormous area peopled by a few thousand French settlers and unnumbered Red Indians. The double task of grappling with this problem and with the financial disorder produced by the war, led to one great reverse in the onward march of empire which many contemporaries regarded as an irretrievable disaster – the loss of the thirteen 'old' North American colonies. For long afterwards the history of the British part in this great crisis was written from a 'Whig' tradi-

tion, of which the basic texts were the fulminations of Edmund Burke and the letters and memoirs of Horace Walpole – and the Americans were represented as the active champions and saviours of the constitutional liberties won in 1689, menaced after 1761 by the high monarchical pretensions of George III. This tradition was a travesty of the facts. Politically and economically the old colonies had grown to maturity, and the removal of the French from Canada relieved them of any sense of dependence upon Great Britain, giving free rein to the nascent sense of nationhood which almost every fibre of their existence had helped to foster. The root cause of the American Revolution was the determination of British governments to restrain within the old, traditional framework of colonial organization a great association of communities which had largely outgrown it. A series of administrative and legislative measures followed hard upon the peace of 1763 – the tightening up of the revenue services, the imposition of new restraints upon trade, direct taxation by the Stamp Act of 1765, indirect taxation by the Revenue Act of 1767, the establishment of a colonial board of Commissioners of Customs, the strengthening in 1768 of the system of vice-Admiralty courts in order to enforce observance of the laws made at Westminster. Vacillation in the application of this policy from time to time in face of spontaneous resistance – the repeal of the Stamp Act in 1766 and the modification of the Revenue Act in 1770 – were rightly construed by the colonists as signs of weakness, and encouraged resistance. For resistance was immediate and widespread. At bottom, the demand of the Americans was for free and equal association within the empire. In 1765 Governor Bernard of Massachusetts observed: 'In Britain the American governments are considered as corporations, empowered to make bye-laws, existing only during the pleasure of parliament. . . . In America, they claim . . . to be perfect states, no otherwise dependent upon Great Britain than by having the same king.' That most eminent of Americans, Benjamin Franklin, stated, in a letter to his son, the view that the British Empire was not a single state but comprehended many: 'The

King, with their respective parliaments, is their only legislator.' In our own days such a conception has become an accepted commonplace. But two centuries ago it was entirely unacceptable to British statesmen. For them the constitutional unity of the empire, manifested by the legislative supremacy of parliament throughout all its parts, had become an unquestioned axiom, alike for economic and for political reasons. The King reflected a general opinion when he declared in 1775: 'America must be a colony of England or treated as an enemy. Distant possessions standing upon an equality with the superior state is more ruinous than being deprived of such connections.' It is against this background of conflicting principles, clashing economic interests, and emotional reactions, that the detailed steps in the quarrel between Britain and America find their true context. Regulation provoked disobedience, attempts at enforcement provoked disorder; finally conflicting claims to legislative sovereignty were put to the arbitrament of war. A variety of factors decided the outcome in favour of the Americans: on the British side, a confusion of aim, wavering between suppression and conciliation; consistent under-estimation of the enemy, which halted the mobilization of resources at home and vitiated the conduct of operations in America; apathy and lack of enterprise among the commanders; and, at the last – and this was decisive – inability to keep command of the seas when France and Spain at last intervened to help the Americans: on the American side, their familiarity with local conditions, the extent of their territory, above all, ruthless purpose and superiority of morale, typified by the persecution of the empire loyalists and by the unswerving tenacity of Washington. Britain with a limited army of professionals and mercenaries could never hold down a nation in arms. The Franco-American victory at Yorktown in 1781 forced home this lesson, and by the treaty of Versailles of 1783 Great Britain conceded the independence which she no longer had the power to deny. But the growth of British communities overseas continued. The future dominion of Canada was to grow from the province taken from France in 1763 and from the older colony of Nova Scotia won from the French half a century before. Migrants flowed in both from Britain and – in the considerable numbers of the empire loyalists – from the territories of the newly-established United States. By the end of the Napoleonic Wars the population of British North America was already well over half a million. Australia, from 1788, played the humbler role of a home for convict settlements, though free settlers were beginning to arrive by 1815.

Ireland set another problem which was never satisfactorily solved. Economically it stood as the most important subordinate unit in the British Empire, regulated, like other parts of the Empire, for Britain's benefit. During the American War, encouraged by American example, an Irish national movement, led by the gentry, the merchants and the professional class, pressed for and largely secured the removal of commercial restrictions and the grant of equal constitutional status. But the Irish executive still remained responsible not to the Irish nation and parliament but to the British government. Still worse, the religious animosities which had been sunk during the early nationalist agitation of the 'seventies soon reappeared to embitter the political scene. In a country with an overwhelming Catholic majority a small episcopal Protestant minority continued to monopolize control of power and patronage. The demands of the Irish Catholics for full political enfranchisement were stubbornly resisted by a die-hard Protestant group in power at Dublin, and discontent, stimulated by the impact of the French Revolution, soon reached the verge of rebellion. In 1800 Pitt attempted a solution of legislative union, which was virtually condemned to failure from the start, owing to the veto pronounced by the King and many of Pitt's colleagues against Catholic emancipation and the conflicting interests and aspirations of the two nations thus yoked together.

Britain and the age of revolution

At times, during the 'sixties, the career of John Wilkes caused almost more noise in politics than did America. This squinting demagogue richly deserved his punishments. But he struck decisive blows for the freedom of the press. After 1771, journalists, printers, and publishers could neither be pursued by secretaries of state employing general warrants nor by the House of Commons arrogantly intent on preserving its privilege of secrecy of debate. Newspapers flourished on the growing appetite for political news, though the press was still, at the turn of the century, a puny stripling in comparison with the giant it was later to become.

Wilkes and America kindled the flame of political radicalism. Thinkers, historians, and doctors of divinity re-scrutinized theories of political obligation and the principles – and legends – of parliamentary representation in England. If the Americans were right in their claim that there should be 'no taxation without representation' – which so eminent a politician as Chatham was prepared to allow – what of the many humble subjects of the King at home who had no real voice, or no part at all, in the choice of representatives? There were not wanting extremists like John Cartwright, who followed this theme to its logical conclusion and plumped for universal male suffrage. Until the French Revolution, and the wide circulation of Tom Paine's *Rights of Man* with its slashing attack on the aristocratic system, radicalism remained the sport of an intellectual minority: it struck no popular roots. After 1789, it began to gather support among both the middle and the lower class. But moderate reformers in general (being propertied men) recoiled from 'mobocracy' and contented themselves with proposals aimed to diminish the supposedly excessive influence of the executive in parliament. In the search for a stick to beat the ministers, opposition politicians of whatever persuasion could be united in support of the traditional policy of an attack upon placemen: this was the theme of the much vaunted, and also much overrated, schemes of economical reform, elaborated by Burke and others, and enacted in 1782. A smaller proportion of the politicians were won over to the idea of minor changes in the representative system, but trial proved that such proposals had little chance of acceptance in parliament, and

after the outbreak of the French Revolution the governing class closed ranks almost unanimously in defence of the established order.

For over twenty years from 1793, the great wars against France absorbed Britain's attention and dominated her politics, damping down the response to pressure for reforms, giving birth to repressive legislation for security reasons, drawing most political groups into active support of the government, leaving only a factious minority in opposition. During the first part of the wars Pitt showed at his worst. He had judged France's strength by the disorder of her finances, expected the early collapse of her military efforts, never comprehended the dynamic violence of the French Revolution or the nationalist upsurge that placed Napoleon at the head of a nation in arms. British war councils were divided. To Pitt the war began as an operation to check French aggression in the Low Countries and maintain the balance of power – a task in which British naval supremacy would be employed to win colonies, some of which might be kept, others used as bargain counters at a peace. To the King, and to many of Pitt's colleagues, the war was a crusade in defence of the civilized order: Toulon and Vendée should be put before the West Indies. In consequence the country's resources were frittered away in various theatres of operations, in no one of which was decisive superiority achieved. Only at sea did Britain hold firm. The moral of the American War was not forgotten. In 1793 Britain at least had the ships, and it was not long before proof was given that she still had men who could direct and operate a fighting machine of superb efficiency. But not until after many years, and after Pitt was dead, did British ministers fully absorb the lesson, that Britain could not expect the continental enemies of France to do all the land fighting but must perfect a large and efficient army and achieve concentration at the opponent's weakest point. In the meantime the navy kept the country secure from invasion and the sea-lanes open, until at last Napoleon committed his fatal blunder, leading the *Grande Armée* to destruction in the Russian snows. England, as Pitt had foretold, had saved Europe by her example, holding

(A) The Earl of Bute, by Sir Joshua Reynolds. (B) Frederick North, 2nd Earl of Guildford by Nathaniel Dance. (C) King George III, Studio of Lawrence. (D) William Pitt, 1st Earl of Chatham, Studio of R. Brompton. (E) William Pitt the Younger, by J. Hoppner. *The National Portrait Gallery*.

PLATE 1

(A) Pitt addressing the House of Commons, 1793, by K. Anton Hickel. Members include Canning, Wilberforce, Sheridan, Erskine, Fox. *The National Portrait Gallery.*

(B) William Drake, M.P. for Amersham and his family, by J. H. Mortimer (1741–79). *Francis Tyrwhitt-Drake, Esq., and History Today.*

PLATE 2

(A) Coffee Room, by THOMAS ROWLANDSON.
Messrs Ellis and Smith, and The Avalon Press.

(B) Portsmouth Harbour, by THOMAS ROWLANDSON.
The British Museum and The Avalon Press.

PLATE 3

Bedlam Furnace. Water colour by JOHN SELL COTMAN, made after his visit to Coalbrook Valley in 1802.
Sir Edmund Bacon and the Courtauld Institute of Art.

PLATE 4

(A) ROBERT ADAM. Osterley (1761–80). The original Jacobean house given dignity by a raised entrance court and stately portico. *C. Musgrave*

(B) Kedleston Hall, Derbyshire (1765–70). Robert Adam's South front. The strong relief of the design illustrates his theory of 'movement'. *A. F. Kersting*

PLATE 5

(B) Syon (1762–69). The State Drawing-room. One of Adam's finest doorcases, with characteristic ornament.
C. Musgrave

(A) Syon. Robert Adam's magnificent ante-room (1762–69) with verd-antico marble columns dredged from the Tiber, and gilt plaster reliefs by Joseph Rose. *A. F. Kersting*

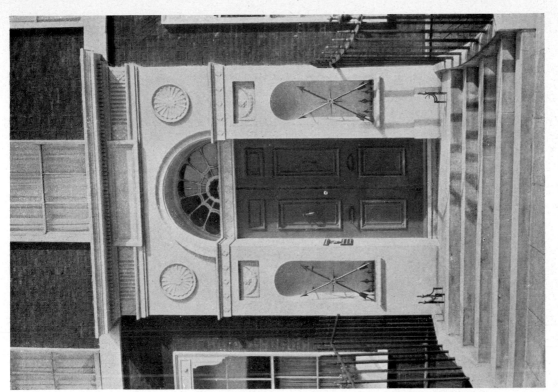

(B) THOMAS LEVERTON. No. 1 Bedford Square, London (c. 1775). An individual interpretation of the neo-classic manner. *C. Musgrave.*

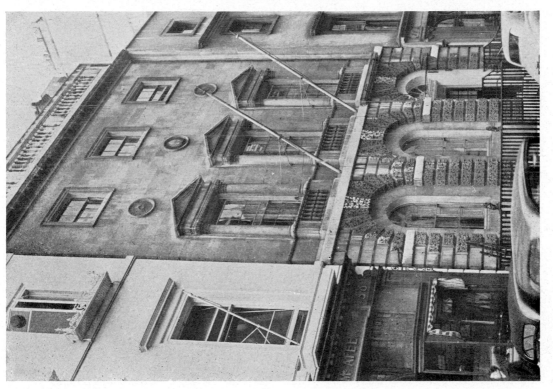

(A) SIR ROBERT TAYLOR. Ely House, 37 Dover Street, London (1772). Palladian order and Taylor's austere elegance. *C. Musgrave.*

PLATE 7

(A) Kedleston Hall, Derbyshire (1765–70). A fireplace in the Marble Hall. Adam's delicacy and refinement in the ornament. The plaster reliefs are by John Rose, the roundel painted by Zucchi. *A. F. Kersting*

(B) The Steine, Brighton (*c.* 1780). An elegant porch in a simple form of Roman Doric, for a small town house. *C. Musgrave*

776 PLATE 8

(B) JAMES WYATT. Heveningham Hall, Suffolk (c. 1782). The Entrance Hall. 'Fluted-shell' fan-vaulting, and ceiling ribs repeated in the floor design. *A. F. Kersting.*

(A) Kenwood, London (1767–9). The Library. One of Robert Adam's most superb rooms; its ornament in his richest and best-proportioned form. *By permission of the London County Council.*

PLATE 9

(A) Milton Manor, Berkshire (1764–72). Stephen Wright's delightful Gothic Library, deriving from Kent's simple early Gothic rather than from Strawberry Hill. *A. F. Kersting*.

(B) Heveningham Hall, Suffolk (*c.* 1782). The Wagon Room. A simplified coffered ceiling with *guilloche* border. James Wyatt's restraint in a small interior. *A. F. Kersting*

PLATE 10

(A) Attingham, Shropshire (1783–85). George Steuart's elegant but restrained façade. *A. F. Kersting*.

(B) Pitzhanger Manor, Ealing (1800–3). Sir John Soane's elaborate exterior treatment, based on the Roman triumphal arch. *A. F. Kersting*.

PLATE 11

(A) Osterley House, Middlesex (1761–80). The Library. The small-scale ornament of Robert Adam's middle period. *A. F. Kersting.*

(B) Mellerstain, Berwickshire (1770–?8). One of Adam's most beautiful libraries.
The restrained ceiling is of his best middle period (1770) and has painted panels
by Zucchi. *A. F. Kersting.*

PLATE 12

The Drawing Room, West Wycombe Park, Buckinghamshire, showing upholstered chairs in the French style, popular in the Adam period. *West Wycombe Park, National Trust.*

PLATE 13

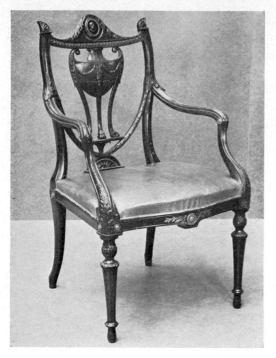

(A) Mahogany shield-back armchair, decorated with paterae and foliage in holly wood, *c.* 1870. *Earl of Yarborough Collection.*

(B) Mahogany armchair, with splat work of carved drapery, *c.* 1785.

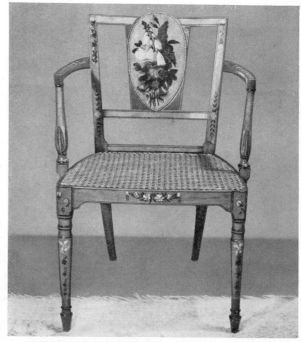

(C) Rosewood armchair, with turned front legs, stretchers, arm supports and cresting rail. Note the panel of cane in the back, *c.* 1800.

(D) Armchair with painted floral designs, turned legs and arm supports, and cane seat. *c.* 1795. *Col. J. M. Wadmore Collection.*

PLATE 14

(A) Commode, veneered and inlaid with various woods, *c.* 1765. *Formerly Earl of Shaftesbury Collection.*

(B) Regency bookcase inlaid with brass. Its low height is due to the fashion of leaving the walls free for pictures. *Metropolitan Museum, New York.*

PLATE 15 783

(B) Pembroke table with cross-banded top and reeded legs.

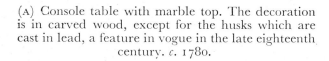

(A) Console table with marble top. The decoration is in carved wood, except for the husks which are cast in lead, a feature in vogue in the late eighteenth century. *c.* 1780.

(C) Bow-fronted mahogany sideboard, with satin-wood inlay, late eighteenth century.

(D) Pedestal and urn, with carved and inlaid neo-classic decoration. Part of a dining-room suite, *c.* 1775.

PLATE 16

(A) Regency rosewood sofa table with curved and reeded legs, brass feet and turned stretcher.

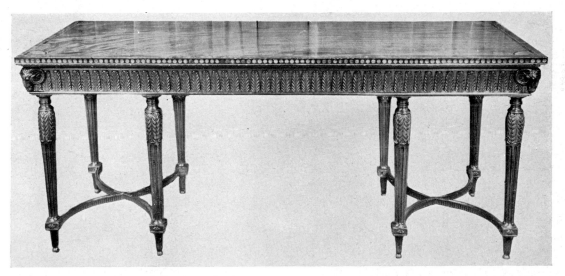

(B) Carved and inlaid mahogany side table, part of a dining-room suite, *c.* 1775.

PLATE 17

(A) Regency circular table inlaid with brass, showing the prevailing pillar and claw support.

(B) Painted tripod table with hinged top and curved feet, c. 1795. *Col. J. M. Wadmore Collection.*

(C) Cabinet, c. 1770, veneered on mahogany with West Indian satinwood inlaid with neo-classical designs. Attributed to Chippendale and Haig. *Viscount and Viscountess Gage Collection at Firle Place.*

PLATE 18

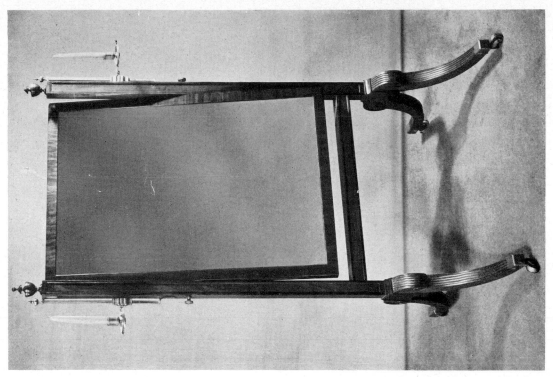

(B) Cheval glass with curved and reeded legs, brass feet and brass sconces, c. 1800.

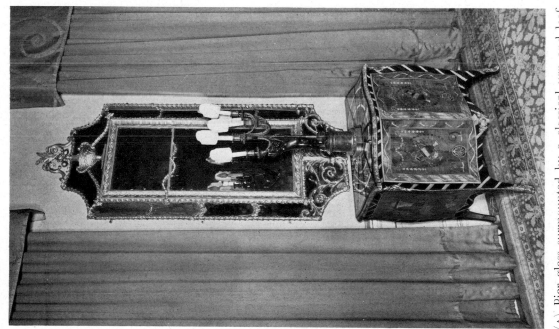

(A) Pier glass surmounted by a classical urn and leaf motif. Below, a commode, inlaid in neo-classic taste. *West Wycombe Park, National Trust.*

PLATE 19

(A) An example of portable furniture: a travelling chair
bed made by Thomas Butler, *c.*1790, and carrying his label.

(B) A sculptor's mahogany adjustable
modelling table, *c.* 1775.

(C) Mahogany library wheelbarrow with shaped sides
and curved arms, early nineteenth-century.
Lord Fairhaven Collection.

PLATE 20

(A) JOHANN ZOFFANY's 'Tribune of the Uffizi (1772–6) (*reproduced by gracious permission of H.M. the Queen*), sums up the sophisticated taste of the age which found expression in such works as: (B) JOSEPH NOLLEKENS' 'Castor and Pollux' (1767) (*Victoria and Albert Museum*), which is based on a Roman group, and (C) SIR JOSHUA REYNOLDS' 'Mrs Siddons as the Tragic Muse' (1784) (*The Governors of Dulwich College*), which is derived from a Sibyl by Michelangelo.

PLATE 21

THOMAS GAINSBOROUGH. 'John, 4th Duke of Argyll' (1767).
The National Galleries of Scotland.

PLATE 22

A

B

C

Water colour landscapes: (A) J. R. COZENS. 'Ariccia' (*c.* 1790), (B) FRANCIS TOWNE. 'The Vale of St John' (1786), and (C) THOMAS GIRTIN. 'Ripon Minster' (1800). *Leeds City Art Gallery*.

PLATE 27

B

The literary vogue for *sensibility* as expressed in (A) JOSEPH WRIGHT's 'Miravan opening the Tombs of his Ancestors' (1772) (*Derby City Art Gallery*); (B) THOMAS GAINSBOROUGH's 'The Girl with Pigs' (1782) (*Major George Howard*). (C) GEORGE MORLAND's 'Farmer Buying Sheep' (1794) (*Leicester City Art Gallery*).

A

C

(A) JULIUS CAESAR IBBETSON. 'A Phaeton in a Thunderstorm' (1798).
Leeds City Art Gallery.

(B) JOHN OPIE. 'A Peasant Family' (1783-5).
The Tate Gallery.

PLATE 29   797

(A) JAMES BARRY. 'The Foundation of the Royal Society of Arts' (1777–83).
Royal Society of Arts.

(B) The engraving by WILLIAM WOOLLETT (1776) of 'The Death of Wolfe', painted
in 1771 by Benjamin West. *Picture Post Library.*

PLATE 30

A

B

The contrast between the naturalistic and the neo-classical treatment of 'history' is shown by (A)
J. S. COPLEY's 'Death of Major
Pierson' (1783) (*The National Gallery*), and (B) JOHN DEARE's marble
relief, 'Edward and Eleanor'
(1788).

PLATE 31

A

(A) THOMAS BANKS. 'The Falling Titan' (1786), *The President and the Council of the Royal Academy*. (B) JOHN BACON. 'George III' (1775), *reproduced by gracious permission of H.M. the Queen*. (C) JOSEPH NOLLEKENS. 'Laurence Sterne' (1766), *The National Portrait Gallery*. (D) CHRISTOPHER HEWETSON. 'Gavin Hamilton' (1784), *by permission of the University of Glasgow*.

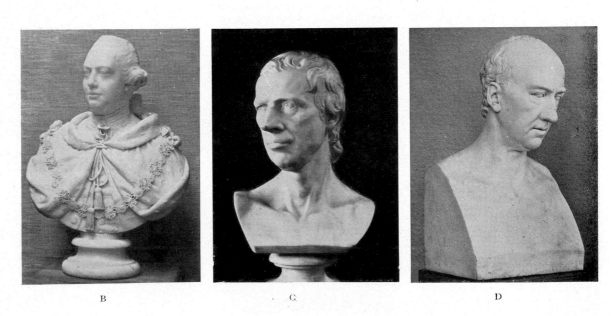

B   C   D

out hope and maintaining a centre of resistance against the most formidable military machine hitherto known.

The mind and spirit of the age

A survey so brief as this of an age so crowded with life and movement can do little more than outline the major themes: justice can hardly be done to the richness of its achievement or to the wealth of talent that treads the stage. The keynote was an exuberant vitality: not for nothing was there some conscious turning back to the Elizabethan past: and that same vitality at work in the growth of commerce and empire can be seen also in the nation's intellectual and cultural life. The work of craftsmen, artists and architects will receive mention in other sections of this work, but reference must be made here to advances in science and to the great literature of the early romantic period. Experiments by such men as Dr Priestley, Joseph Black, Henry Cavendish, John Dalton and Sir Humphrey Davy carried scientific knowledge forward with decisive strides. Dalton's development of the atomic theory placed chemistry at last on the basis of an exact science. Under the direct patronage of George III, Sir William Herschel became a pioneer of sidereal astronomy. On many fronts the work of enquiry went on, stimulating, and deriving advantage from the formation of numerous scientific societies and a growing output of scientific journals. Literary and kindred pursuits displayed, in their own fashion, the same vigorous independence and questing spirit. In prose and in poetry there was revolt against the formal style and artificiality of the earlier eighteenth century. With deliberate, conscious purpose, Wordsworth led the search for simple, natural expression of the deepest human emotions, producing much rubbish in the process, but in the true flights of his genius carrying English poetry forward to long unheard heights of achievement. The literary exuberance of the age appears again in Boswell's *Life of Johnson* and in Sheridan's plays; its robust intellectual confidence

in the works of history and economics from the pens of Edward Gibbon and Adam Smith.

Last, but not least, the Evangelical movement, of which the first springs lay earlier in the century, was broadening and deepening its influence, reaching rich and poor, giving a sense of purpose and Christian mission both to the Church of England and to the sects. Evangelicalism brought back into religious observance and the conduct of daily life the enthusiasm and fervour which the leaders of eighteenth century society had regarded as 'bad form'. In the 'nineties it drew increasing strength from the reaction against the pagan character of the French Revolution. Apart from its general evangelism, it gave a new impetus to the humanitarian movement and stimulated demands for social reforms. An active humanitarianism showed itself in many ways – for instance, in the demand for the reform of the ferocious penal code; and, above all, in the great crusade conducted by Wilberforce and others against slavery and the slave trade, a battle partly won, when, in 1807, the slave trade was made illegal. Another of the fruits of the movement was the establishment of Sunday schools which made more widely available at least the first elements of education: for many years the Sunday schools provided all the education, either religious or secular, which many children received. The legacies of the Evangelical movement were great and lasting. 'Methodism' had an influence far wider than that of the sect which took its name. It was a way of life devoted not only to religious observance but to self-discipline and work for others. As such it was a powerful instrument of social cohesion, impressing upon those who had wealth and power the need to observe their responsibilities no less than it reconciled the poor to the idea that suffering and poverty were part of the natural order. Finally here was to be found the great formative influence moulding the British character for the next three generations, implanting in it a sense of mission and devotion to a stern code of moral behaviour, a strength of fibre and a strength of will.

Coal being loaded on the Tyne. Tail-piece from Thomas Bewick's *A History of British Birds*, Vol. 2, 1804.

Architecture

CLIFFORD MUSGRAVE

The classical tradition

The reign of King George III saw developments in architecture no less momentous and even more swiftly varying in mood than those of the first half of the eighteenth century. Fashionable society, the *dilettanti*, the connoisseurs and amateurs of the arts were mercurial in their response to rapidly succeeding tendencies of style. Despite the rapid fluctuations of taste, throughout the period different schools or movements flourished independently at the same time, or even intermingled.

The impetus of the Palladian movement initiated by Inigo Jones, and promoted from about 1720 by 'that Apollo of the Arts', Lord Burlington, was to inform architecture to the end of the century and even beyond. By 1760, however, the leaders of the movement, William Kent, Giacomo Leoni, Colin Campbell, and Lord Burlington himself, were dead. For over a decade, architecture in the Burlingtonian tradition had tended increasingly to consist of uninspired applications of the Palladian formula. The perfection of classical form and proportion according to the rules laid down by the ancient Roman architect Vitruvius, and his sixteenth-century disciple Palladio, had been regarded more and more as having declined, in the works of the Burlingtonian followers, into mere 'correctness', purity of style into coldness and monotony.

Before long, fashionable patrons were to welcome the dazzling innovations of the brothers Adam, but the time of distinguished achievements by upholders of conservative tradition was not entirely past. The two leaders of this school at the middle of the century, Sir Robert Taylor and James Paine, 'nearly divided the practice of the profession between them, for they had little opposition till Robert Adam entered the lists'. So wrote Hardwick in his life of Sir William Chambers. Although their popularity waned somewhat during the meteoric rise of Adam, without departing from scholarly correctness, they rivalled him with the elegance of their interior designs, which derived frequently from sources that the Scottish architect had used.

Little of the work in our period of James Paine (1716–89), is accessible, save the central block and curved connecting corridors of the north front at Kedleston, Derbyshire (1757–61) (Pls. 5B, 8A), where Adam followed him, as he did also at Nostell Priory, Yorks, the building of which Paine had been 'entrusted to conduct' at the age of nineteen in 1735.

Paine's north front at Kedleston is very heavily Palladian, with niches instead of windows behind the columns of the portico. The individual charm and elegance of his style is expressed in the grouping in pairs of the columns and pilasters of the façade of Wardour Castle, Wiltshire (1770–6).

Sir Robert Taylor (1714–88) began his career as a sculptor. The carved pediment at the Mansion House was executed by him in 1744. He soon abandoned this profession for architecture, and before long was appointed Surveyor of the Bank of England, and to other official posts in which he was able to display his sound scholarly accomplishments.

Taylor's interiors at the Bank of England (now either demolished or reconstructed) were among his loveliest work. No. 37, Dover Street, London (1772) (Pl. 7A), which he built for the Bishop of Ely, shows his great elegance of style in the columns flanking the windows, while the pronounced rustication of the arched ground floor gives firmness of character to the façade. Rusticated arches are also used with impressive effect in Maidenhead Bridge (1772), and the engaged columns appear again on a more monumental scale in the end pavilions of the little known Stone Buildings at Lincoln's Inn (1775), which is truly but austerely Palladian, with the main block lacking a central feature, and unrelieved windows.

The most splendid of all his works was Heveningham in Suffolk, c. 1782 (Pls. 9B, 10B), where the interior was magnificently remodelled later by Wyatt. Here Taylor relieved the traditional Palladian severity by enriching the great central block of the north front with an imposing attic having four sculptured figures standing before pilasters, a theme of French origin which a fellow traditionalist, Sir William Chambers, was to use at Somerset House later. The tendency to increased decoration is shown in the heavy festoons and sculptured medallions of the centre block, and in the relief panels with which Taylor adjusted the size of the first floor windows to the scale of the frontage.

A provincial contemporary of Paine and Taylor, and like them a Palladian traditionalist, John Carr of York (1723–1807) achieved a very considerable reputation throughout the north of England. One of his earliest commissions was Harewood House, Yorkshire, but his work there was almost entirely altered by Adam, and later Barry. The whole of the village, however, is by Carr, and his cottages are simple, solid and admirably proportioned. Several houses in York are his, but his masterpiece is the austerely graceful Assize Court (1773–7). With its recessed Ionic portico, roof balustrade, the small attics carrying urns, and the sculptured figures, the building combined delicacy with monumental impressiveness. The

Female Debtors' Prison (1780) opposite the Court is also Carr's work, but enlarged by Atkinson in 1803. Carr built the stables at Castle Howard, the Town Halls at Chesterfield and Newark, Nottinghamshire (1776), and the graceful Royal Crescent at Buxton (1779–84).

The stupendous Palladian achievement of the Royal Crescent at Bath built from 1767 to 1775 by John Wood, the younger (1728–81), must be regarded as belonging to the school of traditional classicism. The great sweep of the Crescent contains 114 gigantic Ionic columns with the angular Roman volutes which Adam disliked. The Crescent is the culmination of the work of the Woods in Bath, and inspired the building of Royal Crescents in other towns such as Buxton and Brighton.

In domestic architecture the Palladian ideal found expression more easily in large houses, or in great monumental street compositions with a number of houses combined in a single palatial unit, than in the restricted scope of the small house.

Up to the time of Adam, the 'Wren' house, of red brick with a steep tiled roof and dormer windows, had remained the standard of vernacular building, with Palladian details of porch, pediment and modillion cornice applied according to the means of the owner. In the middle century, plaster walls had taken the place of pine panelling, but in small houses plaster decoration rarely approached the rococo elaboration of the great mansions, and was usually confined to a moulded cornice and possibly some enrichment in the shape of a 'tabernacle frame' above the chimneypiece. The lighter mouldings and stucco ornaments of the Adam brothers, and to some extent also of Taylor and Chambers, lent themselves more readily to use in small houses.

An invigorating influence in the development of traditional classical architecture was the growing conviction that the 'true style of the ancients' was to be found in the buildings of ancient Rome, rather than in the work of the fifteenth- and sixteenth-century Italian architects which inspired the Burlingtonians. Two books published by Robert Wood on the buildings of the Roman Empire, *The Ruins of Palmyra* in 1753 and *The*

Ruins of Balbec in 1757, were early contributions in this country to the neo-classical movement. They were followed in 1764 by the folio which recorded a visit to Spalato in Dalmatia by Robert Adam during his studies in Italy several years earlier, *The Ruins of the Palace of the Emperor Diocletian at Spalatro* (see Pl. 93A).

All through the years of Robert Adam's fashionable supremacy, an official architect, Sir William Chambers (1723–96), maintained his leadership of the traditional school. Surveyor-General (1782) and first Treasurer of the Royal Academy, he was Adam's greatest rival and critic. Two of his works lie at extremes of scale. One is the delightful Casino at Marino, Dublin (1761). Despite its smallness, there are monumental qualities in the beautifully balanced harmony of Doric columns, pedimented doors, and ornament of sculptured urns and figures. The other work, Chamber's masterpiece, is Somerset House (1776), one of the grandest compositions of its time. The Strand front, with its Corinthian façade and sculptured figures, displays the influence of French architecture. The great quadrangle is given impressiveness by the central Corinthian features upon each side. Upon the embankment side the extended composition is broken up by three principal features, the two on either side being the most beautiful of the whole work. They take the form of Palladian bridges built on water-gates over rusticated Doric archways. The river front was completed to the original design by Sir Robert Smirke in 1830, and the west façade was built by Sir James Pennethorne in 1856: a skilful addition which is not conspicuously out of harmony with the original composition.

As an official architect, Chambers built few houses, but Asgill House, Richmond, is a distinguished example of his style.

Chambers advocated purity of style and masculine qualities of design. His power of majestic composition was combined with a sense of grace and beauty in decorative detail, acquired during his studies in Italy and France, of a kind regarded in conservative circles as being less facile and evanescent than the frivolous style of the Adam brothers. His great treatise on *The Decorative*

Part of Civil Architecture, published in 1759, became the standard authority upon classical design, and was being republished even as late as 1862. It was probably due to the corrective influence of Chambers at the time of the Adam brothers that the work of the succeeding period developed in a sound and satisfying manner.

The Adam revolution

When Robert Adam returned in 1758 from four years' study in Italy it was to a world of fashionable patrons eager for the innovations in architecture and decoration which he offered them.

Robert Adam (1728–92) was the second of the four sons of a successful Scottish architect, William Adam (1689–1748). The most important of the houses he built was Hopetoun, which occupied him until his death, when it was completed by Robert.

The style which Robert Adam, and later his brother James, acquired in Rome was an eclectic one, compounded from various sources, from Roman and Greek buildings of the classical period, the Roman architecture of the Renaissance, the painted 'grotesque' decorations imitated by Raphael and his pupils from classical originals in the loggias of the Vatican and the Villa Madama, and the arabesque decorations of Herculaneum and Pompeii.

The innovations which they introduced lay not so much in the characteristic ornament of the Adam style, the festoons of husks, the swags, the garlands, the vases, urns, tripods and gryphons, the arabesques and scrolls – many of these motifs had been used by other architects – but in the highly personal refinement and delicacy which Robert Adam gave them, the lighter proportion of the elements of a design to the space containing them contrasting with the heavier treatment of earlier times. When in 1773 the brothers Adam published the designs of their principal achievements in *The Works in Architecture of Robert and James Adam, Esquires*, they spoke of the 'almost total change' they had effected. While they decried the 'ponderous compartment ceiling' of earlier times,

Fig. 1. Luton Hoo, Bedfordshire. Built by Robert Adam, *c.* 1768–75, the interior was entirely remodelled after a fire. It houses one of the most important collections of art treasures in the country. In 1816 Robert Smirke replaced Adam's delicate bow-shaped portico with a heavier rectangular pedimented entry. From Jones' *Views of the Seats of the Noblemen and Gentlemen of England, etc.,* 1829.

they did not abjure it entirely, but only those of the 'most enormous weight and depth' of the seventeenth and early eighteenth centuries. In the half-domed apses of Adam's entrance halls and dining-rooms, and in the drawing-rooms and saloons of Syon (Pl. 6), Kedleston (Pls. 5B, 8A) and Osterley (Pl. 12A), and other houses, are to be seen beautiful examples of these forms, with square, circular, lozenge and octagonal panels or *caissons*.

Robert Adam's fame is shared with his collaborators. Joseph Rose, the creator of his plaster ceilings, trophies of arms and other decorations, was one of the greatest artists in stucco of any country or age.

The painted panels, roundels and medallions depicting somewhat primly elegant scenes from an idealized world of classical mythology, which are found in Adam's interiors, are mostly from the hands of Angelica Kauffmann (1741–1807), an Academician at the age of twenty-six, and her husband Antonio Zucchi.

One of Adam's earliest works was the Admiralty archway (1759) which expressed that talent for monumental design which he always believed was his especial *métier*. With this screen of Doric columns, decorated with charming sculptures by Michael Spang, Adam successfully corrected the faulty composition of Thomas Ripley's dull Palladian Admiralty building of 1724, with its excessively projecting wings.

The interiors at Hopetoun, where Robert worked before visiting Rome, is in the prevailing rococo style of the mid-century, but in the acanthus scrolling of his gilded friezes there is to be seen the precursor, on a bolder scale, of the 'flowing rinceau' or branched ornament which is one of Adam's favourite motifs. The magnificent ballroom has a handsome Venetian window, but with the typically Palladian angular volutes to the Ionic capitals which he was later to abhor. This type of window, with arched central portion and two side-lights, appears in almost all of Adam's frontages, and is seen at its loveliest, with columns of pink alabaster, in the state dining room at Kedleston.

Adam's new style is shown in a robust and vigorous form at Hatchlands, Surrey (1758–61), especially in the dining-room ceiling and the sculptured fireplace, but the bay-leaf frieze and ceiling mouldings of the staircase hall still have a hint of early Georgian heaviness.

Harewood, where Adam worked from 1759 to 1769, completing and transforming the work of Thomas Carr of York, was the first of Adam's palatial houses. It is famous for his early collaboration, as at Nostell Priory, Kenwood, and other houses, with Thomas Chippendale, who provided the magnificent furniture almost certainly to Adam's designs.

An important aspect in Adam's system of design was the planning of rooms to obtain dramatic variety of scenic effect, with varying geometrical shapes in successive rooms, in the manner of the ancients. He preferred to make a room octagonal or circular rather than square, and oblong rooms were diversified by apses and recesses (exedrae). Relief was given also by changes of colour, tone and texture, in order to express the character and purpose of different rooms. Dining-rooms were usually given painted and stuccoed walls instead of textile hangings which might retain the smell of food.

Adam's conception of classical planning was intended in his great palatial houses to serve the 'parade, the convenience, and the social pleasures of life', and it is seen in its most majestic form at houses like Syon and Kedleston. But it applied also to the smaller houses built by himself and his followers, where each room was given its distinctive character.

At Syon the varying levels of the old house aided Adam's planning for scenic variety. The ante-room there is one of the most glorious rooms in England, with its twelve immense columns of verd-antico marble, dredged from the Tiber, surmounted by life-size gilded statues, and gilded trophies by Joseph Rose. The state dining-room is one of Adam's finest and most characteristic, with its arched recesses, apses and half-domes and columnar screens, a noble fireplace, and a ceiling of the best early flat type, with the famous 'flowing rinceau' in the frieze. The excessive length which Adam found in the Jacobean long gallery

807

Fig. 2. The British Coffee House, Cockspur Street, London S W 1. Built by Robert Adam 1770, demolished 1886. Decorative richness in a narrow town exterior. From *The Works in Architecture of Robert and James Adam*, 1773.

808

he remedied by dividing the room into five units of three doors and two fireplaces, and by leading the eye outwards towards the walls by the recessed geometrical figures of the ceiling ribs. With its soft pink and green colouring, and small scale of ornament, the gallery was intended to afford 'great variety and amusement' to the ladies of the household, and a contrast to the more vivid splendours of the state drawing-room.

Robert Adam's reputation survives chiefly as an interior architect, but at Kedleston, where he completed work begun by Paine in the most severe Burlingtonian manner, he created an impressive example of that baroque quality of 'movement' which he admired in the work of Vanbrugh, and strove to restore. By 'movement' he intended 'the rise and fall, the advance and recess within the diversity of form in different parts of the building'. This quality of depth, of three-dimensional architecture, Adam expressed in his splendid south front at Kedleston by his use of the Roman triumphal arch theme with projecting entablature and disengaged columns, and by contrasting the convex curve of the dome with the superb concave sweep of the double flight of entrance steps (Pl. 5B).

The marble hall at Kedleston, with its twenty immense monolithic Corinthian columns of Nottinghamshire alabaster, rivals the ante-room at Syon in splendour. The contrast between this hall and the great domed saloon is one of the most striking examples of Adam's dramatic planning. The saloon rises half as high again as the hall, with a dome coffered with octagonal panels.

At Osterley, Middlesex, Adam gave dignity to an existing Elizabethan house by adding a magnificent Ionic portico. Begun in 1761, but not finished until 1780, his early and middle styles are revealed in an enchanting succession of beautiful rooms. The entrance hall is of the customary Doric order, and has coffered apses in his early style. In the library the fireplace and bookcases have ornament of the small scale which, in his middle period, tended to fussiness, but here the effect is of a restful softness of texture as in the gallery at Syon. The drawing-room (1773), praised by Walpole, has a ceiling of early character coffered with octagons, and an astonishingly beautiful central oval with long radiating leaves, adapted from a ceiling in the Temple of the Sun at Palmyra. This ceiling design was used also at Woburn by Flitcroft, and in West Wycombe Church. The three following rooms are of later date, and looking through the vista from the gallery, the increasingly diminishing scale of Adam's ornament with the years is seen in the decoration of the successive doorcases.

Adam's planning for scenic variety and contrast in his rooms is seen on a smaller and more domestic scale in the beautiful tapestry room, dining-room and library at Newby, Yorkshire. Begun in 1767, though not completed until 1785, or even later, the spirit of the interior is of his early phase, and the house has many affinities with Osterley and Kenwood. The sculpture gallery, with its coffered domes and stucco ornament, reflects the influence of the Catacombs and of Herculaneum, but its beauty is cold and static, for unlike Adam's libraries and dining-rooms, it has not become part of the instinctive life of its users.

Kenwood (1767–9) marks the culmination of Adam's first period, and embodies in the Great Library one of his masterpieces (Pl. 9A). Here his use of apses is carried to a glorious climax, their semicircles joining with those of their half-domes, with the arches of the bookcase recesses, and with the vault of the ceiling. The entablature, carried across the apses upon the Corinthian columns and pilasters of the screens, forms the stable rectangle which holds these curves in tension.

The following decade, from 1770 to 1780, saw the creation of the famous London house interiors, such as Chandos House, Home House, Portman Square (now the Courtauld Institute), and 20, St James's Square. In the first of these Adam indulged on a small scale his genius for varied internal planning, but in the decoration began to depart from his early robust manner in favour of a more superficial and linear design. In the exteriors of these houses too, the treatment is lacking in relief.

Home House (built 1775–7) is one of the most elaborately superb town interiors in existence yet it marks the distinctive moment of change

in Adam's decorative work to a completely flat and geometrical scheme of ornament. The virtuosity of the decoration is breathtaking in its mathematical complexities, but after this date there will be little of his subtle judgment in the relationship of forms to space, and instead a tendency to fill every void with facile and meaningless ornament. It was such over-elaboration which caused Horace Walpole to speak of Adam's ornament as 'larded and embroidered and pompomed with shreds and remnants, and *clinquant* like all the harlequinades of Adam, which never let the eye repose a moment'.

At Nostell Priory, Yorkshire, Robert Adam made additions to the house built by James Paine between 1735 and 1750. Adam's interiors here are among the loveliest of his middle period, especially the salon and hall, the latter containing a skilfully conceived apse to give drama to an otherwise uninterestingly square room.

In his Scottish castles Robert Adam developed some of his youthful romantic imaginings. Mellerstain, Berwickshire (1770–8), is a romantic battlemented house, with enchanting interiors. The library, with its ceiling panels painted by Zucchi and its stucco relief panels, is one of his most superb rooms (Pl. 12B). The dining-room also has a beautiful ceiling of his best middle period. Culzean Castle, Ayrshire (1777–90), is Adam's most picturesque building, with battlemented towers, and an exceptionally fine oval staircase hall.

Bradwell Lodge, Essex, is a highly characteristic small house, with its delicate staircase, the marble mantelpiece with a frieze attributed to Angelica Kauffmann, and blue and white plaster reliefs.

In the years from 1780 to his death in 1792 Robert Adam turned to town-planning schemes and public buildings, striving to realize his ambition to create works of great monumental quality. In all these projects he was denied the fulfilment of seeing them completed, but all show a return to his early three-dimensional exterior design, and some of them, such as the National Register House (1774–92) of Edinburgh, and the University there (1789–91), serve as true memorials to the architect's greatness.

In his designs for Fitzroy Square and Portland Place, London, and Charlotte Square, Edinburgh, Robert Adam carried forward the Palladian ideal of unified town-planning embodied in the work of the Woods at Bath. James Adam was chiefly responsible for Portland Place, of which only a few houses remain, including Nos. 37, 46 and 48, distinguished by pairs of front doors combined under a single arch, anthemion decoration and sculptured plaques.

From the publication of the *Works* in 1773 onwards, the diffusion of the Adam brothers' distinctive style throughout the land became irresistible and limitless. The 'electric power of that revolution in art' which they effected, to use the words of Soane, ran through the whole field of design concerned with houses. A host of designbooks placed the Adam repertoire of ornament in the hands of architects, builders, decorators, merchants and craftsmen of every kind. In many towns of these islands, the brothers Adam or a follower of theirs created pleasing expressions of the new outlook, especially in the form of assemblyrooms and ballrooms like those of Crunden and Goulden at Brighton, of Baldwin at Bath, and at Shrewsbury and Bury St Edmunds, which reflected the new and gracious phase which had been reached in the evolution of social intercourse.

The Adam manner, with its light mouldings and delicacy of plaster decoration, was more readily modified to the needs of small houses and for cheapness than the heavier or more complicated rococo plaster ornament of the Palladian fashion, and the new style quickly penetrated throughout all classes of domestic building. Even the Venetian window could be used in the simplified and inexpensive form of a round-headed central window with two narrow lights at the side, without columns or pilasters, but within an arched recess.

Many of the criticisms of the Adam manner resulted from the use of patent stuccos and compositions which enabled his designs to be massproduced by innumerable imitators, with a consequent degradation of the style and a loss of its true character.

Of all the Adam followers, Thomas Leverton (1743–1824) was perhaps the greatest. His work is chiefly to be seen in Bedford Square, where each side has a pleasant central feature, and there are in some of the houses rooms of very great delicacy and charm. No. 1 has his characteristic shallow arches and a flat saucer-dome (Pl. 7B). No. 13 was the architect's own house.

Thomas Baldwin (1750–1820) was responsible for many of the most attractive buildings of the late eighteenth century in Bath. Great Pulteney Street, in particular, has the grace and dignity of Adam's finest street compositions, and his ballroom at the Guildhall (1775–6) is one of the most magnificent in the Adam manner.

John Crunden (1740–c.1828) is famous chiefly for Boodle's Club, St James's Street, London (1775), a charming design with a beautiful central feature of a Venetian window within a recess with a fluted tympanum. He also built the ballroom of the Castle Inn, Brighton (1776), which eventually became King George IV's Chapel Royal. This was afterwards demolished and re-erected as St Stephen's Church, Montpelier Street, Brighton, and is still worth visiting for the sake of the elegant details of its interior, such as Adam's favourite motif of a simple Corinthian capital from the Tower of the Winds at Athens.

Experiments in the picturesque

Aspirations towards classical purity were paralleled by the yearnings of romanticism. The cult of the Picturesque, which had brought about the revolution in landscape gardening effected by 'Capability' Brown and Humphrey Repton, created an interest in rural cottages, lodges, dairies, and farmhouses, which from about 1790 onwards became widespread through the publication of innumerable books of designs, by such architects as Charles Middleton, John Plaw, James Malton, and in his early years, by John Soane.

Blaise Hamlet, Gloucestershire, a village designed by the Regency architect John Nash, early in his career, in 1809, provides perfect examples of picturesque *cottages ornés*, with delightful variations of thatched and tiled roofs, gables, verandahs and porches.

Chinese pagodas, temples and summer-houses had been popular as picturesque features in the new 'irregular' park landscape since before the middle of the century. Sir William Chambers had travelled to China as a young man, and published his famous volume of *Designs for Chinese Buildings* in 1757, with the expressed intention of correcting the absurdities which had developed in the vogue for Chinese furniture, decoration, and garden buildings during the previous years. About the same time, while serving as architectural tutor to the Prince of Wales, who was in 1760 to become King George III, he was employed by the Dowager Princess Augusta to lay out the grounds at Kew Palace. Chambers embellished the gardens with pavilions, temples and other fantastic structures which are described in his book of 1763, *The Gardens and Buildings at Kew in Surrey.*

It is interesting to conjecture how much these buildings, several of them oriental, may have stirred the imagination of the new Prince of Wales, George Frederick, son of King George III, throughout the years of his childhood spent at Kew Palace, and inspired the oriental fantasies he was eventually himself to create.

The most important of the Kew buildings was the Chinese Pagoda, of ten stories, 160 feet high. Originally, on the angles of the roofing at each stage crouched guardian dragons holding bells in their mouths. They were covered with layers of multi-coloured glass, producing dazzling reflections in the sunlight. Eventually they disappeared, but the Pagoda still stands, brightly painted in red and blue, so impressive a landmark that Horace Walpole pretended that it could be seen from Yorkshire.

In 1784 the young Prince of Wales set up a marine residence at Brighton, in a 'respectable farmhouse', which Henry Holland was commissioned to rebuild in 1787 as a simple and elegant 'Graeco-Roman' villa, with a shallow domed rotunda and Ionic colonnade. Not long after, in 1801, Holland's assistant, P. F. Robinson, an architect of Picturesque country houses, made it more of a *cottage orné* with such typical features as verandahs, and shell-shaped canopies to the balconies, which from about that time came into fashion and are now regarded as charmingly distinctive of the smaller houses of the period, especially at the seaside.

The interior of this first 'Marine Pavilion' at Brighton was originally in the restrained classical manner of Henry Holland, though painted in gay colours of 'French-blue', bright yellow, maroon, and with ceilings of grey and white. At the time of Robinson's alterations the Prince of Wales had the whole of the rooms altered to a Chinese scheme of decoration, which the interior of the Pavilion, although later enlarged, has retained ever since. The rooms were decorated with Chinese wallpapers, porcelain, and furniture of bamboo and lacquer.

Unlike the reticent *chinoiserie* interiors of the 1750's and 'sixties, every detail, mouldings, fireplaces, doorways, was in the Chinese manner. Many reasons have been suggested for this revival in astonishing exuberance of the Chinese vogue, which had been in something of a decline, but it is possible that the Prince of Wales had found Henry Holland's rather primly simplified Adam style insufficiently gay for a holiday palace. Most of the State Apartments at the Royal Pavilion today have the magnificence which was given in later transformations of the building, but several rooms still retain the lively and barbarically colourful character of the first Chinese interior.

In 1803, William Porden (c.1755–1822), a pupil of James Wyatt, and who was then building Eaton Hall in Cheshire, with gothic tracery of cast-iron, was commissioned by the Prince to design a Royal Stables and Riding House at Brighton. They remain today, the Stables now a concert and conference hall called The Dome, the Riding House a banqueting and exhibition hall.

The exteriors are little changed, and form one of the most impressive architectural compositions in England. The style was not Chinese, but Indian, for the trend of romantic interest had switched away from China to that newly developed sub-continent, whose dazzling marble mosques and palaces seemed to offer rich new possibilities for Picturesque architecture.

The Indian interest was largely inspired by the drawings and aquatints of Indian buildings made

Fig. 3. Sezincote, Gloucestershire, by S. P. Cockerell, *c.* 1805. Indian architecture in an English setting, which inspired Humphrey Repton's designs (not executed) for rebuilding the Brighton Pavilion in Indian style. From Jones' *Views of the Seats of the Noblemen and Gentlemen of England, etc.,* 1829.

by Thomas and William Daniell in India a few years earlier. At that moment the Daniells were in fact working at Sezincote in Gloucestershire, which was then being built in the Indian style for a retired nabob by S. P. Cockerell (1754–1827) (Fig. 3). Humphrey Repton, the landscape architect, was also at Sezincote laying out the grounds, and in 1805 he was called from there to Brighton to design an extension for the pavilion in the Indian manner to accord with the new stables.

Repton's designs are reminiscent of Sezincote, with its single bulbous dome and scalloped Saracenic arches, but the Prince was overwhelmed by financial difficulties and the scheme was never carried out.

The final transformation of the Pavilion as an Indian palace by John Nash belongs to the flowering of the Picturesque movement in the time of the Regency, and must be left to the later volume dealing with that period.

Sezincote stands today, a dreamy Indian palace of honey-coloured stone, with a little Indian temple, fountain and bridge, in the wooded park which remains as Humphrey Repton planned it.

Graeco-Roman elegance

Robert Wood's two folios, *The Ruins of Palmyra* and *The Ruins of Balbec*, became prominent landmarks in the battle of the books which was waged over the relative merits of Roman and Greek architecture when the German scholar Winckelmann published his treatise on *The Imitation of Greek Works of Art* in 1755. The Roman architect Piranesi, in his earlier volumes, strove to demonstrate the unsurpassable glories of Roman architecture, but in his later works admitted the existence, and eventually the superiority, of the Greek.

The victory of the Greek style throughout Europe was consolidated by the publication over many years from 1762 onwards of the four volumes of *The Antiquities of Athens* by James Stuart and Nicholas Revett, 'painters and architects'. The first of these authors immediately became the recognized authority upon the pure Greek style. He was nicknamed 'Athenian' Stuart and received a number of important commissions. Eventually, however, his drunken habits and unreliable business methods caused his never very extensive practice to dwindle away.

His Doric Temple at Hagley Park, Worcestershire (1758), a copy of the Temple of Theseus at Athens, is the earliest neo-Greek building in this country.

Although Shugborough, Staffordshire (1764–88), is not frequently accessible, it must be cited for the important work of Stuart's it contains, both in the house and park. In the latter there are copies of the Tower of the Winds and the Choragic Monument of Lysikrates at Athens, and a Doric Temple similar to the one at Hagley. Few others of his important works survive, save 15, St James's Square, London, an early expression of Greek Ionic, with caryatids copied from the Temple of Minerva, and the interior of the Chapel at Greenwich Hospital (1779–88). If the design is wholly Stuart's, and not partly by his assistant William Newton, the Chapel is Stuart's masterpiece, a glorious achievement with a lovely organ gallery with Ionic columns, and a superb ceiling of shallow vaulting. The astonishing church at Newnham Courtenay, Oxfordshire, where Stuart 'corrected' his patron's design, has another very graceful Ionic portico (to a blind wall) and a remarkable dome.

Robert Adam was a close friend of Stuart's, and absorbed a great deal of Grecian detail from the *Antiquities* into his own work. Indeed, Adam derived more from Stuart's book than from his own *Spalatro*: for example, the very charming and graceful capital from the Tower of the Winds consisting of an inverted bell covered with long smooth leaves, and a single row of curling acanthus leaves round the base. This and many other details of the buildings of Athens informed not only the work of Adam, but of the Wyatts,

Holland, and later, Nash, and the host of architects of the Greek Revival of the first four decades of the nineteenth century.

Nicholas Revett (1720–1804) practised but little, and left even fewer architectural works. At West Wycombe Park, Buckinghamshire, Revett built the stately Ionic west portico (1771), and in the park a delightful version of the Tower of the Winds, a Temple of Flora, and a Temple of Music (1778–80).

Revett's famous church at Ayot St Lawrence is a somewhat coldly beautiful composition with flanking colonnades and small pavilions, recalling the Palladian fashion, but the details are Greek, and the Doric columns with recessed cap and base derive from the Temple of Apollo at Delos. The interior is most striking in an austere way, with large vaulted window openings, domed apse and ceiling, and simple recessed ornament, but its antecedents appear to be the Roman basilicas rather than the temples of Greece. It is an interior that anticipates the domed halls and arches of Soane.

The small number of surviving buildings by George Dance, junior (1741–1825), reveal little of the profound and far-reaching influence he exercised upon architecture, especially upon the work of his more famous pupil Soane, and eventually through him upon that of Smirke, Wilkins and Nash, and thus upon the great monuments of the later Greek revival.

One of his gifts was his ability to create dramatic effects without the use of columns, pilasters and other features of the classical orders, a characteristic which was later to become distinctive in the work of Soane, Henry Holland and James Wyatt. His style possessed a simple virile quality which derived from the Egyptian designs of Piranesi, and from neo-classical motifs which were predominant in French architecture at the time, such as pediments with acroteria, or corner ornaments.

His masterpiece, Newgate Prison, no longer exists, but the Bank of England Printing Works, Old Street, London, shows something of his dramatic power. In the houses on the north side of Finsbury Square, London (1777), can be seen the graceful shallow arches above windows that proclaim his work, and the south front of the Guildhall which he rebuilt (1785) is an essay of his in the playful unscholarly Gothic of the eighteenth century.

While the Adam brothers were at the height of their fame, James Wyatt (1747–1813), a young architect who had returned from his studies in Rome in 1768, astonished the world of taste with a sensational design for rebuilding the Pantheon assembly rooms (demolished in 1922) which he carried out in 1772 at the age of 25. Henceforth Wyatt never lacked fashionable and wealthy patrons. When Chambers died in 1796, Wyatt was appointed in his place as Surveyor-General and occupied it until his death in 1813.

In 1776 Wyatt was called to Oxford to complete the Radcliffe Observatory which was left unfinished at the death of its designer Henry Keene. Keene (1726–76) was a minor architect who did much work of Gothic character in Oxford and elsewhere. The Saloon at Arbury, Warwickshire (1762–90), is a charming example of his Gothic style, and ranks as a considerable work of Georgian Gothic with Strawberry Hill and Lacock. Wyatt gave the design for the Observatory 'a distinction and originality of treatment altogether beyond the powers' of his predecessor. The octagonal tower is based on the Tower of the Winds, but the whole structure, with its graceful Ionic pilasters, pedimented windows and porch, has a charm that is distinctively Wyatt's (Fig. 4).

The over-elaboration and tendency to fussiness of Adam's interior designs during his middle period caused many patrons to turn their attentions elsewhere. Wyatt, with his adaptability and command of a wide range of styles, was able to make a virtue of the simplicity, within the general spirit of Adam design, which clients were now seeking. In his later life, Wyatt confided to his master, King George III, that 'on returning from Rome, he found public taste corrupted by the Adams, and he was obliged to comply with it', but early in his career he was able to create a formula which offered a relief from the less pleasing aspects of their style.

James Wyatt opposed the Palladian tradition and expressed the growing impulse towards simplicity by making very restrained external use of the classical orders, and designing his porticos with the columns rising direct from a pavement at ground level or with a few steps only instead of from a high podium. Frequently he used a simple balustrade instead of an elaborate pediment and dispensed with an attic storey. He greatly reduced external ornament, but gave an effect of repose and stability by horizontal bands or string courses at the levels of the various floors. Wyatt also gave interest to the simplified mass of his buildings by the use of bow-fronted wings, sometimes crowned by domes, and by bowed window-bays rising through two or more stories.

Wyatt's south front at Heaton Hall, Manchester (1772), has a restrained severe beauty, with its semi-circular central bay flanked by recessed Venetian windows, and colonnaded loggias linking it with octagonal end pavilions. The rooms show the inspiration derived by Wyatt from the brothers Adam, who indeed in their *Works* accused him of plagiarism, but generally the interior has a chaste simplicity and refinement of character that is a rarification of the brothers' style.

Heveningham Hall, Suffolk (c.1772–4), is Wyatt's interior masterpiece, remarkable for the completeness and unity of the decorative scheme and for the superb quality of detail, equalling that of Syon and Kedleston. The rooms have an entrancing, serene loveliness; the Hall with exquisite fan-vaulting in the barrel ceiling ; the saloon with a shallow vault and domed apses with recesses in them. The Etruscan Room is one of the most engaging of the several ventures in this manner. These beautiful rooms, mostly with painted decorations by Biagio Rebecca, stand as the most glorious achievement of the modified Adam inspiration (Pl. 9B).

Whoever was the architect of Rudding Park, near Harrogate (1805), it is a most refined and beautiful example of the mature Wyatt manner, with its bowed windows rising through two stories, and its rich yet restrained interior. The lovely silk-hung yellow drawing-room illustrates his simplification of the Adam style in its ceiling of

Fig. 4. The Radcliffe Observatory, Oxford, by James Wyatt, 1776.

concentric circles without the Adamitic infilling of ornament. In the planning of the house, devised to admit the sun throughout the day, it anticipates the functional lay-out aimed at by Regency architects. The Doric portico and balustrade resembles the south front at Heaton, and repeats on a smaller scale elements in James Wyatt's entrance at Goodwood, Sussex (1780), where the portico is of superimposed orders of Doric and Ionic with a balustrade, and his bowed features appear now as angle towers.

Castlecoole, Fermanagh, Ireland (1790–97), and Buscot Park, Berkshire (1780), are also pleasant examples of his style.

The legendary medieval world which was recreated with delicate rococo fancy at Lacock and Strawberry Hill in the mid-century, increasingly enthralled the imagination of clients and architects. James Wyatt's Gothic creations embodied scholarship as well as charm, and were interposed between his periods of classical building.

Ashridge is the principal existing example of these Gothic exercises, but is rarely accessible. Fonthill Abbey, in Wiltshire, Wyatt's stupendous Gothic fantasy, has vanished. So, too, has the most exquisite of his Gothic creations, Lee Priory – the 'true child of Strawberry' – with its graceful fan vaulting, but the fittings from one room there have been saved for re-erection at the Victoria and Albert Museum.

James Wyatt was the greatest of a widely ranging family of architects of that name who mostly perpetuated the style he had developed. His significance is that he simplified the refined neoclassical system of design introduced by the Adam brothers, and established a distinctive style of unaffected grace in place of Palladin pompousness.

George Steuart (c. 1740–1806) was a minor architect (not to be confused with 'Athenian' Stuart) who left two buildings of note. Attingham, near Shrewsbury (1783) (Pl. 11A), is basically Palladian in design with its columned portico and curved flanking colonnades to side pavilions, but it illustrates the reaction from Palladian pomposity in the way the basement story has become lowered so that the pavement of the portico is only a few steps above the ground. This has the result of increasing the height of the portico, its tall Ionic columns giving an impression of great elegance. This effect, which is fully developed in the work of James and Samuel Wyatt, is to be found also in the buildings of Henry Holland and Sir John Soane of a later date. Steuart's interiors at Attingham bear a strong resemblance to those of Robert Adam's best period, with ceilings of well-proportioned design. The drawing-room fireplace is especially fine, with coupled Corinthian columns and a sculptured frieze.

The little Rotunda drawing-room is charming, with fluted Corinthian columns forming the walls into panels, which are decorated with restrained and graceful grotesques.

The church of St Chad, Shrewsbury (1790), is an astonishing creation. It has a circular nave and gallery in a rotunda behind a Doric portico and tower, the last feature superimposing the Choragic Monument from Athens upon the Tower of the Winds in a fashion which Regency architects were later to make popular.

The reaction against Adam found another champion in Henry Holland (1746–1806) who, like Wyatt, provided an antidote to the increasing effeminacy of the Adam manner in a restrained firmness and simplicity of design.

The two schools face each other across St James's Street, London: on the one hand is Boodle's Club (1775), by a disciple of Adam, John Crunden. On the other hand is Brooks's Club, remodelled by Henry Holland in 1776 as a severely elegant and somewhat simplified Palladian building.

Before long Holland had evolved the highly personal classical manner with a considerable admixture of Grecian ornament, which he called Graeco-Roman. This he adopted when re-building Carlton House for the Prince of Wales (1783–85). After making a visit here Horace Walpole wrote, 'How sick one shall be, after this chaste palace, of Mr Adam's gingerbread and sippets of embroidery!' Holland's new style was also apparent in the Marine Pavilion at Brighton which he built for the Prince in 1787, but which was later transformed by Nash. In the same year, Holland made alterations to Melbourne House (later Dover House and now the Scottish Office, Whitehall) where his pleasant little portico may be seen to be based on the drawings in *The Antiquities of Athens* of an Ionic temple on the Illisus at Athens. The simple version of the Ionic order used here shares with its richer and more sophisticated sister of the Erectheion the honours of a great deal of neo-Grecian architecture during the next fifty years. The same simple form of the Ionic appears in Holland's beautiful library at Althorp, one of the several lovely rooms remodelled by him in 1789, when he also gave the house its distinguished entrance front and casing of his favourite white brick.

At Woburn, Bedfordshire (1787), the most accessible portions of Holland's work are the sculpture gallery and the charming Chinese dairy, one of the few surviving examples in this country of that fashion. The Swan Hotel at Bedford was also designed by him (c. 1790).

Holland's outstanding surviving creation, though not frequently accessible, is Southill, Bedfordshire,[1] which he remodelled in 1795. The garden front, with its loggias of coupled columns, has the simple elegance typical of Holland. The interiors are among Holland's finest, and, as at Althorp, combine the Greek and Roman elements with French influences which derived from his study of French architectural works, and from his employment of French craftsmen.

Holland's interiors are extremely restrained in style. The ceilings sometimes have a shallow vault, but are frequently plain, relieved only by narrow ribs or bands of plaster with key-pattern, *guilloche* or other simple ornament. The foliated capital from Athens, of which Adam was so fond, Holland also used after simplifying it by omitting the row of acanthus leaves. Holland's rooms breathe a spirit of dignified grace that is the expression of his reserved and thoughtful nature.

[1] See *Southill: a Regency House* (various authors), Faber & Faber, London, 1951.

Among the most glorious interiors of the late eighteenth century, rivalling Heveningham and Southill, is Inveraray Castle, Argyllshire, where the little-known architect and engineer Robert Mylne (1734–1811) created the rooms (1772–82) in a castle built by Roger Morris in 1746. The beautiful ceilings, graceful gilded anthemion and foliage friezes, and painted decorations by Biagio Rebecca, are of extraordinary elegance and refined delicacy. The Wick, Richmond, Surrey (1775), is another house of Mylne's.

From 1770 onwards, the smaller houses had reflected increasingly the influence of the Adam brothers, but towards the end of the century the impress of Wyatt was seen in the use of bowed features or wings in country-houses, and very characteristically in the bow-windows of small villas or town-houses. Decoration rarely now extended beyond a classical porch or the ironwork balcony with a canopy which began to appear early in the 1780's. In small houses, the large proportion of window space to blank wall was often so naturally good as to make decoration superfluous. Brown and yellow bricks appeared now instead of red. Stucco was seen increasingly, especially with the rising costs and scarcity of building materials during the Napoleonic wars. In the south, as at Brighton, many houses were fronted with the cream coloured or black glazed 'mathematical' tiles from Hampshire which Holland used at Althorp and at the Prince of Wales's first Marine Pavilion.

In the small interiors of this time, although on a modest scale, architectural features displayed the characteristic Adamitic influences in the decoration of a fireplace or the frieze of a room with festoons of husks or a running acanthus scroll, or revealed the inspiration of Holland or Wyatt in the plainer neo-Greek recessed ornament of a key-pattern or incised lines, or in the restrained adornment of semi-circular or elliptical arches to recesses flanking a fireplace, even in the most unpretentious houses.

One of Holland's pupils, Sir John Soane (1753–1837) served him for six years, but it was his 'first revered master' George Dance, junior, who exercised the profoundest influence upon Soane throughout his career. After studying in Italy, at an early age he was appointed Surveyor to the Bank of England in succession to Sir Robert Taylor, and served in this capacity – 'the pride and boast' of his life – from 1788 to 1833. It was at the Bank that Soane executed the masterpieces of his highly individual style. In abandoning the use of classical orders – columns, pilasters, entablatures and pediments – especially for interiors, Soane continued the attempt of Dance years earlier to free architecture from the rules of Vitruvius and Palladio. By the simplification which Soane and Dance effected they anticipated much that is good in modern architecture, with its insistence that the beauty of the essential masses of a building should depend upon classical proportion and not upon ornament.

In Soane's interiors at the Bank he achieved an almost mystical effect in the abstract handling of space, with a counterpoint play of arches, vaults, and domes, and sparing ornament in the form of incised lines, sunken strips and panels, and areas of grooving.

Soane had been fascinated in Italy by the impedimenta of the Roman Empire, the tripods, urns, vases and sarcophagi with their pedimented lids and acroteria, which are piled up on Piranesi's engraved frontispieces. These elements Soane used with great prodigality on his exteriors, where he permitted himself greater richness and indulged in the use of orders.

The 'Tivoli' corner (1802) at the Lothbury angle of the Bank, with its rich Corinthian columns, heavily swagged frieze, and elaborate attic decorated with amphorae, derives from the beautiful Temple of the Sibyl at Tivoli.

At Aynho Park, Northamptonshire, where Soane made alterations (1800–2), he built the entrance in the form of an elaborate Roman triumphal arch, but his interiors in this delightful treasure-house have a contrasting cool simplicity. The rooms are almost devoid of ornament, but are given distinction and beauty by semi-circular and semi-elliptical arched recesses and curved apses, most notably in the drawing-room and the splendid library.

At Pitzhanger Manor (1800–3, now the Ealing

Public Library), which was for a time Soane's own house, the theme of the triumphal arch appears again in the gracious frontage of Ionic columns with projecting entablature carrying statues. The rooms here are in Soane's reticent interior manner, with shallow arches and plain, narrow ribbed mouldings, but there is also some restrained ornament of recessed ceiling panels with rosettes, and a charming sculptured plaque of dancing nymphs. Two of the rooms have Adam-like ceilings and scrolled friezes, and are the earlier work (1770) of George Dance, junior (Pl. 11B).

The mind of Soane is studied best of all in his own house at 12, Lincoln's Inn Fields, now Sir John Soane's Museum (1792–4), where he spent the latter part of his life, and housed his large collection of architectural casts, models and drawings, and paintings, sculpture and antiquities of many kinds, with the object of representing 'the union of architecture, sculpture and painting'. Here are displayed in the fabric itself the motifs of Soane's own designs, and in the collection an

epitome of the themes of classic architecture which were used both by the ancients and by the architects of his own day. In the picture cabinet, with its hanging Gothic arches, and the breakfast room, are found some of the elements of the Picturesque which for Soane went to make up the 'poetry of architecture'.

Soane's later work, at Dulwich Art Gallery and Mausoleum, in his churches, and elsewhere, belongs to a later volume in this series. His influence on contemporaries may be seen in the affinity of his work with that of Holland and Wyatt. Much of his significance rests in the invigorating effect his severe disciplined style had upon architecture when about 1790 it lacked direction for new developments. It is very largely through Soane that Grecian classicism became established as the language of the next cycle of architecture, and that this inspiration was carried forward in the work of his pupil Smirke, and of Wilkins and Nash in the triumphs of the Greek Revival of the Regency, and up to the opening of the Victorian age.

Fig. 5. The Tower of the Winds, Athens. From Stuart and Revett's *Antiquities of Athens*, 1762. Source of inspiration for James Wyatt's Radcliffe Observatory at Oxford, and other small buildings of the late eighteenth century.

Furniture

E. T. JOY

Few students of furniture history would quarrel with the statement that the half century or so after 1760 marked the zenith of English cabinet-making. During this period the closest harmony existed between the work of the architect and that of the furniture-maker, and the skill of the craftsman was at its highest. English furniture in the neo-classical style set a European fashion, and equalled in technique the best work of the great French cabinet-makers, two facts which give point to Hepplewhite's statement in 1788 that 'English taste and workmanship have, of late years, been much sought for by surrounding nations'.

For the whole of this period furniture-making was carried on by the traditional methods of the craftsman, although wood-working machinery had been patented by Sir Samuel Bentham in the 1790's. There was, however, no simple pattern in the organization of the industry; on the contrary, since early Georgian times almost every type of industrial organization had been developing, especially in the towns, and above all, in London. This diversity is explained by the growth of specialization and the extent of the market. The village craftsman represented the unspecialized workman because his market was so limited. 'A country carpenter', wrote Adam Smith in 1776, 'deals in every kind of work that is made of wood . . . (he) is not only a carpenter, but a joiner, a cabinet-maker and even a carver in wood.' This was in marked contrast with the specialization of the town craftsmen, among whom could be found minute sub-divisions of trades. In London a

cabinet-maker – to take only one class of craftsman as an example – might mean one of several things: a craftsman-shopkeeper who was responsible for the making on his own premises of the furniture which he sold to the public; or a capitalist-shopkeeper who was a dealer only, retailing furniture which he bought from outside craftsmen, and sometimes supplying it to other dealers for sale in different parts of the country and overseas; or a working master who was not a shopkeeper, but had his own workshop where he made furniture, or parts of it, for the shops and other craftsmen; or, finally, one of the numerous journeymen who either worked at home as outworkers by the piece for the shops and masters, or were wage-earners in other craftsmen's workshops. These divisions were subject to endless variations as one merged into the other.

The pre-eminence of London

It is well to emphasize the predominant position of London, not only in the size of the market and the physical output of furniture – the capital's population was a million at the census of 1811, when Manchester's, then the next largest city, was some 130,000 – but also in its leadership in styles and techniques. There were, of course, plenty of excellent craftsmen in the main provincial towns, but they looked to the capital for the latest furniture fashions, and one of the chief functions of the many design books which emanated from London in this period was to spread these new ideas (to quote Hepplewhite again) 'to many of our own Countrymen and Artizans whose distance from the Metropolis makes even an imperfect knowledge of its improvements acquired with much trouble and expense'. Ever since Defoe's day there had been a noticeable tendency for some London furniture shops to grow in size. In the second half of the eighteenth century St Paul's Churchyard began to lose some, but by no means all, of its reputation as the main centre for high-quality furniture, for many of the fashionable shops were now to be found in the Covent Garden, St Martin's Lane and Long Acre district, and in Soho, Old and New Bond Street, Oxford Street and Tottenham Court Road, where they were close to the newer residential areas. Some shops where the furniture was made on the premises under the control of a craftsman were of a large size and resembled in a way a departmental store. Such, for example, was the well-known shop of George Seddon in Aldersgate Street (not, it will be noted, in one of the fashionable areas just mentioned) which was described by a German visitor, Sophie von la Roche, in 1786 as a large building with six wings employing 'four hundred apprentices (i.e. journeymen) on any work connected with the making of furniture'.[1] The stock of the firm, including carpets, wood and mirrors (which were cast and cut in the basement) was valued at nearly £119,000 in 1789, shortly after the above description was written.

Even in the case of the smaller shops the nature of the work must have made the craftsmen in charge more business men than craftsmen. Chippendale, for instance, travelled so much about the country to attend to customer's requirements, which often included the fitting up of a whole house, that he could not possibly have had time to see personally to the work being carried out in his workshop. This means that much of the fine furniture which came from the better-known shops was made, not by the craftsman whose name appeared on the bill, but by the foreman and band of highly-skilled, unknown workmen – carvers, inlayers, chair-makers, upholsterers, etc. – to whom the real credit should go.

[1] *Sophie in London*, 1786 (trans. by C. Williams, 1933).

Little is known in detail of the other kinds of shops which were run by dealers, but it is clear that there were very many of them in London doing a considerable business. Mortimer's *Universal Director* of 1763, which was the first London directory to classify trades, stated that its list of cabinet-makers 'contains only such as either work themselves, or employ workmen under their direction; and that not one of those numerous Cabinet Warehouses which sell ready-made Furniture bought of the real artist, is to be met with in this work'. The general scope of the work of these dealers is illustrated by the handbill of Wilkinson & Sons who kept a 'Cabinet, Upholstery, Carpet and Looking-Glass Warehouse' in Cheapside. This bill (in the Guildhall Collection, dated 1779) advertises that the shop 'keeps ready made in the most genteel taste' a very wide range of goods which are given in detail, including such items as 'library, writing, ladies' dressing, Pembroke, dining, card and tea tables' and 'cabriole, japand, dyed and Windsor chairs'. The statement concludes: 'N.B. Merchants, Captains and others may be supplied with the above Goods at the most Reasonable Rates,' indicating that these shops were one of the channels through which furniture and upholstery were sent from London to distant parts of the country and overseas.

London cabinet-ware exports reached all parts of the world with which we had trading relations, foreign countries as well as British colonies. In 1800 the total value of British furniture exports (mainly from London) was well over £38,000 in the official Customs returns, even though we were then at war with France; and this figure was certainly an understatement, for the real value was probably well above that given, and did not include all the furniture taken out of the country by emigrants, or the goods traded privately to India by the officials of the East India Company. It was not, of course, only dealers who sent goods abroad, for furniture from good craftsmen's shops is known to have gone to the rich planter classes in the West Indies and to North America where it was imported by rich Americans or by the cabinet-makers to copy and re-sell. This trade continued to flourish well into the nineteenth century until it was curtailed by the increasingly heavy duties on imported timber. The English furniture industry in the Georgian period can never be divorced from its world-wide setting.

The Adam style

For a quarter of a century after 1760 the great name in furniture design was Robert Adam (1728–92). In place of the medley of styles of the early Chippendale period – the rococo, Gothic and Chinese, which were in reality variations on the same theme – he designed in the neo-classical style, and his furniture was an essential part of his scheme of treating the decoration of a house, inside and out, as a harmonious whole. In his own words in the preface to *The Works in Architecture* in 1773 he was greatly inspired by 'the grotesque . . . that beautiful light style of ornament used by the ancient Romans in the decoration of their palaces, baths and villas. . . . This classical style of ornament, by far the most perfect that has ever appeared for inside decorations . . . requires not only fancy and imagination in the composition, but taste and judgement in the application; and when these are happily combined, this gay and elegant mode is capable of inimitable beauties.' Adam's furniture in this style employed a variety of classical motifs carried out with great delicacy; among them were festoons of husks, paterae, the honeysuckle, ram's heads, vases, urns, the acanthus leaf, and medallions (Pls. 16D, 17B, 19A). These could be found carved in low relief in the solid, or, perhaps at their best, in the fine inlaid work, for which many choice coloured woods were used, particularly satinwood. Adam designed for rich patrons and the furniture was made by leading craftsmen, including Chippendale at Kenwood, Harewood House, Nostell Priory, Mersham Hatch and elsewhere, France and Beckwith at Kenwood, Linnell at Osterley, and Norman at Moor Park. Among the earliest furniture Adam is known to have designed was some for Queen Charlotte, and her beautiful bed, which originally stood in the Queen's House, now Buckingham Palace, can be seen today in the Public Dining Room at Hampton Court.

The new style did not completely sweep away the Chinese and Gothic modes, which still found a certain amount of favour; and French-style furniture continued to enjoy a vogue among the upper classes. Many cabinet-makers imported French pieces to sell to their clients or to copy – Chippendale was fined by the Customs in 1769 for alleged under-valuation of chairs which he had imported from France – and Adam complied with the demand by designing pieces, particularly upholstered chairs, with a distinctly French flavour. But his new classical style was catching on in the 1760's. 'The light and elegant ornaments,' wrote Sir John Soane in the early nineteenth century, '. . . were soon applied in designs for Chairs, Tables, Carpets, and in every other species of Furniture. To Mr Adam's taste in the Ornaments of his Buildings and Furniture we stand indebted, in-as-much as Manufacturers of every kind felt, as it were, the electric power of this Revolution in Art.' [2]

Holland and the Regency style

The inevitable reaction against the Adam style set in before the end of the century, and the changes were heralded by the work of the gifted architect and designer, Henry Holland (1745–1806). Unlike other architects, he did not make a tour of classical sites abroad, and this probably made him more receptive to new trends, especially from France, for he was also closely connected with the Whig coterie which surrounded the Prince of Wales (the future Regent and George IV), and he shared their enthusiasm for French ideas. At first he followed a modified Adam style, but later branched out into the English version of what came to be known as the French 'Directoire' style. He stressed the close adaptation of Graeco-Roman forms of decoration, and to obtain accuracy of detail he sent his draughtsman, C. H. Tatham, to Rome in 1794 to study antique classical ornament at first hand. Holland's best-known furniture designs were carried out for the Prince of Wales at Carlton House from 1784 (some of this furniture is now

[2] Sir J. Soane, *Lectures on Architecture*, 1809–36 (ed. A. T. Bolton, 1929).

at Buckingham Palace), and for Samuel Whit-bread at Southill from 1795. The strength of French influence is shown by the fact that Holland employed French craftsmen at both places.[3]

This new classic style has been given the general name of 'Regency'. So far as furniture is concerned, this must remain a somewhat vague and elastic term, by no means coinciding with the actual political limits of the Regency, for while the latter lasted from 1811 to 1820, the changes in design, as has been shown, were clearly evident before the close of the preceding century. In fact, it was in 1785 that Horace Walpole saw Holland's work at Carlton House and wrote his well-known comment: 'How sick one shall be after this chaste place, of Mr Adam's gingerbread and sippets of embroidery!' We must allow that Walpole was not a friendly critic of Adam's work, but his sentiments were shared by others after the turn of the century. In 1808, for instance, C. A. Busby described Adam as 'a mannerist' and wrote: 'This ebullition of a false taste having now subsided, the latter (i.e. Adam) is considered only as an Artist of enterprize and ability.' [4] Soane's appreciation of Adam, already quoted, was noteworthy at a time when the latter's style was considered outmoded.

Holland had a sure grasp of style, and however much he was influenced by French designs, he never fell into the habit of merely copying them, but gave them an unmistakable English twist. He favoured the use of rosewood with resplendent ormolu mounts, marble tops to chiffoniers, tapered, gilded and fluted pillars, lion's legs on smaller tables, and round tops for larger tables mounted on a massive pedestal or monopodium. He also designed chairs and settees at Southill in imitation bamboo, in the Chinese fashion, and at times used Egyptian motifs, such as the lotus leaf, another characteristic of the Regency style.

[3] For Holland's furniture see D. Stroud, *Henry Holland* (1950), and F. Watson's chapter in *Southill: a Regency House* (1951).

[4] C. A. Busby, *A Series of Designs for Villas & Country Houses* (1808).

After Holland

While Holland was alive this new treatment was kept under control, but after his death in 1806 it began to degenerate into a somewhat narrow archaeological approach which resulted in very close copies of classical furniture, Egyptian, Greek and Roman. The pioneer of this new interpretation, which was at first founded on sound scholarship, was Thomas Hope (1769–1831), a rich banker and collector of antiques, who had had some training as an architect. In 1807 he published his *Household Furniture and Interior Decoration* in which he aimed, as he wrote in the introduction, at 'that breadth and repose of surface, that distinctness and contrast of outline, that opposition of plain and enriched parts, that harmony and significance of accessories . . . which are calculated to afford to the eye and mind the most lively, most permanent and most unfading enjoyment'. He spoke of the 'association of all the elegancies of antique forms and ornaments with all the requisites of modern customs and habits'. It is not difficult to understand how designers of the time who lacked Hope's scholarly knowledge merely imitated ancient furniture, often in a lifeless way, and these results could be seen at the very end of the period under review.

The ideas behind all these changes in design after about 1785 were well expressed by Archibald Alison in his *Essays on the Nature and Principles of Taste*, which were first published in 1790 and reached their sixth edition in 1825. He stressed the importance of delicacy and straight lines: 'All Furniture . . . is Beautiful in proportion to its quantity of Matter, or the Fineness or Delicacy of it. Strong and Massy Furniture is everywhere vulgar and unpleasing . . . progress terminates in that last degree of Delicacy and even of Fragility, which is consistent either with the nature of the Workmanship or the preservation of the Subject.' The models should be 'the Forms of Grecian or Roman Furniture . . . in scarcely any of them is the winding or serpentine Form observed; . . . on the contrary, the lightest and most beautiful of them are almost universally distinguished by straight or angular Lines'. All this is typical of what we call Sheraton style furniture. Alison justified the Chinese and Gothic styles by the ideas with which they were associated. For example, Chinese furniture, 'however fantastic and uncouth the Forms in reality were ... brought to mind those images of Eastern magnificence and splendour of which we have heard so much'. Similarly, with regard to the Gothic taste, 'this slight association was sufficient to give Beauty to such Forms, because it led to ideas of Gothic manners and adventure'.

The design books

The architect-designers worked for a relatively small clientèle and designed furniture of high quality. The translation of their styles into general furniture, including quite humble pieces, was accomplished by the authors of design books which were intended, as Hepplewhite wrote, to be 'useful to the mechanic and serviceable to the gentleman'. Chippendale's *Director* of 1754 had been the first of such furniture catalogues to be published by a cabinet-maker and not by a builder, artist or architect, and it was followed by many others. At the end of the decade 1760–70 the neo-classical style began to appear in such publications. At first the mid-century fashions set by Chippendale, the third edition of whose *Director* appeared in 1762, were continued in Ince and Mayhew's *Universal System of Household Furniture* (1759–63) and in various works by Matthias Lock, Robert Manwaring (who specialized in chair designs) and others. But in 1769 Lock, who was a carver as well as designer, and had been the pioneer of the rococo in England, showed his versatility by publishing two works, the *New Book of Pier Frames* and the *New Book of Foliage* which contained the first engraved designs of furniture in the Adam style. What really popularized the new mode, however, was Hepplewhite's *Guide* of 1788, published two years after the author's death. With nearly 300 designs, covering all kinds of furniture, it illustrated admirably how the application of Adam's principles, 'the latest or most prevailing fashion', could 'unite elegance and utility, and blend the useful with the agreeable'. Designs similar to Hepplewhite's appeared in the *Cabinet-Makers' London Book of Prices*, also published in 1788; many of the plates for this had been designed by Thomas Shearer, who re-issued them under his own name as *Designs for Household Furniture* in the same year.

The changes at the end of the century were interpreted in Thomas Sheraton's famous *Drawing Book*, published in parts between 1791–4. It reflected the emphasis on light and delicate furniture, the making of which required a very high standard of skill from the craftsmen; in fact, the furniture of this particular period can properly be considered among the most technically perfect ever made in this country. Sheraton also published a *Cabinet Dictionary* in 1803, and the first volume of an unfinished *Encyclopaedia* in 1805. The latter, however, showed signs of the deterioration which was then beginning to mark furniture design. Hope's publication of 1807, already referred to, differed from the others in that it was not the work of a craftsman. His principles were generally applied to furniture in 1808 by George Smith, a cabinet-maker, in his *Household Furniture*. Smith did not possess Hope's scholarship, and he lost some of the spirit in which Hope's interpretations were made.

Leading cabinet-makers

Some of these designers were also craftsmen of great repute in their own day, but this by no means applied to all of them. Among the names in the above list, those of Chippendale, Hepplewhite and Sheraton are household words, and will remain so. Their fame, however, is due to their well-advertised skill as designers and to the very convenient way in which their names can label the furniture of their period, rather than to their supremacy as craftsmen. Chippendale was certainly responsible for fine pieces, but he had no royal appointment and it is a curious fact that his best work was done, not in the styles of his own *Director*, but in the quite different Adam style. Hepplewhite does not seem to have enjoyed any great reputation as a furniture-maker. As for Sheraton, who died in poverty, there is no evidence that he ever had a workshop of his own.

Many contemporary craftsmen of outstanding

worth have been unfairly overshadowed by these designers. In the 'sixties flourished the great partnership of William Vile and John Cobb; Vile, indeed, did work in the rococo style in its later phase here which surpassed that of Chippendale. When the neo-classical style took root, outstanding pieces, in addition to Chippendale's (already noted), were produced by William Gates and John Linnell. At the end of the century and just after, prominent names were those of William Marsh, Thomas Tatham (these last two were partners for a time), Thomas Chippendale the younger, and George Oakley. On the other hand, among those who published design books we find that the partners Ince and Mayhew ranked highly as craftsmen, and so did George Smith, who had royal appointments in the early nineteenth century. Two long-lived firms, those of Gillow and Seddon, were also widely known throughout this period.

Decoration

Several new forms of decoration, and revivals of older ones, appeared on furniture during this period. And one traditional decorative craft, that of the carver, though strongly evident for most of the period, was decaying in the early nineteenth century. In 1761 J. Collyer described carvers as 'ingenious men . . . never out of business', but in 1813, T. Martin, author of *The Circle of the Mechanical Arts*, wrote thus: 'Carving in wood has long been in the background, as a branch of the arts. . . . There are now only eleven master carvers in London, and about sixty journeymen (though at one time there were six hundred); many of the latter are now very old. They make no shew of their work, and live in private houses.'

One feature of the Adam style was the revival of marquetry in the form of fine inlaid work (Pl. 16D, 18c). This was similar in technique to the marquetry of the walnut period, but differed from it in emphasizing classical decoration. Towards 1800 this kind of decoration gradually gave way to the simpler form of 'stringing', by which a thin line of wood or, more particularly at the end of this period, brass, was inlaid on the furniture (Pl: 15B, 18A). This change, and the reasons for

it, was thus described by Sheraton in 1803: – 'Inlaying, in cabinet-making, was much in use between twenty and thirty years back; but was soon laid aside, as a very expensive mode of ornamenting furniture, as well as being subject to speedy decay. The present mode of inlaying with brass, is most durable and looks well let into black woods of any kind.' This brass work is a characteristic feature of furniture at the turn of the century, and set off the dark glossy and striped woods which became popular after the decay of carving and inlay.

There were new developments in metal mounts. When Matthew Boulton, the industrial pioneer and partner of James Watt, opened his famous factory at Soho, near Birmingham, in 1762, he began to manufacture ormolu mounts, finely chased, and of a rich, golden colour. Boulton always aimed at a high artistic standard in his products, and was influenced by Adam's work. Samuel Smiles, in his life of Boulton and Watt, quotes Lord Shelburne as writing to Adam that 'he (i.e. Boulton) is very desirous of cultivating Mr Adam's taste in his productions'. In the last quarter of the century a new method of manufacturing back-plates for drawer handles came into use. In 1777 two Birmingham brass-founders, John Marston and Samuel Bellamy, improved upon John Pickering's invention of 1769 by patenting a method of stamping ornaments on plated metal for cabinet furniture.[5] The plates of brass were moulded by dies, and were usually circular, oval or octagonal in shape (Pl. 16B). About 1800 another form of handle appeared: small brass knobs, many in the shape of a lion's head with a ring through the mouth. Turned mahogany knobs were also used (Pl. 17A).

The vogue for lighter and more delicate furniture led to a revival of three fashionable late seventeenth-century features which had undergone a more or less total eclipse: turning, cane work, and japanning. Turned legs on chairs and tables, of slender proportions and often fluted, were in great favour (Pl. 14C and D, 16B).

[5] Patent Office Library, Old Series of Abridgements of Specifications, Class 39, Furniture & Upholstery, 1620–1866 (1869).

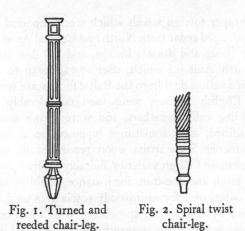

Fig. 1. Turned and reeded chair-leg.   Fig. 2. Spiral twist chair-leg.

Sheraton also shows turned and reeded legs (Fig. 1) on some of his pieces, and about 1800 spiral-twisted turning could be found on chair legs and backs (Fig. 2), and as columns at the corners of chests of drawers. As for cane work and japanning, these went together, as Sheraton himself pointed out: 'Caning cabinet work is now more in use than it was ever known to be at any former period. About thirty years since, it was quite gone out of fashion . . . But on the revival of japanning furniture it began to be gradually brought into use, and to a state of improvement.' This later method of japanning, however, was much inferior to the original process; it was merely paint and varnish, even in the case of the well-known bedroom suite for Garrick at Hampton. At the end of the century it was often used for brightly coloured patterns (Pl. 14D).

Woods: mahogany

The extensive character of British trade enabled the cabinet-makers of the later Georgian period to take their pick of the world's choicest furniture woods. The outstanding wood was mahogany from the West Indies and Central America, and the most important event in the history of the mahogany trade was the Act of 1721 (8 Geo. 1, c. 12) which freed timbers grown in the British plantations in America (including the West Indies) from their former heavy import duties. In 1750 the value of imported mahogany, which included wood smuggled from Spanish colonies via Jamaica to avoid the duties on foreign timbers, was nearly £30,000, compared with £221 in 1721. So important had the trade become that in 1770 the Government, at the instigation of Customs officials, passed another Act (11 Geo. III, c. 41) extending this freedom from duty to all American timbers, foreign and British alike, as mahogany – so ran the preamble of the Act – had 'become very useful and necessary to cabinet-makers' and further supplies would encourage increased exports of furniture from Britain. In 1792 the import value was £79,554, and in 1800, despite the war with France and the re-imposition of duties, £77,744. The quantity represented by these last two sums was in each case well over 7,000 tons. After about 1750 the Cuban variety of mahogany, easier to work, richly coloured, and often with a range of beautiful figures (among them 'fiddle-backs', 'roes', and 'curls') began to replace the earlier San Domingo variety, which was harder and denser, and had little figure. In the later part of the century mahogany from Honduras (often called 'baywood') was popular; it was lighter in both colour and weight, and was sometimes used as a carcase for Cuban veneers, though for this purpose red deal, imported from North America, was commonly employed. In the figures quoted for import values in 1792 Honduras mahogany accounted for nearly £46,000 of the total, and in Sheraton's day it was 'the principal kind of mahogany in use among cabinet-makers'.

Satinwood and rosewood

Towards the end of the century two other woods were in demand for the best quality furniture: satinwood and rosewood. Satinwood was imported from both the West and East Indies, and its light yellow colour and fine figure, which showed up beautifully under polish, made it ideal for the delicate pieces of the period. It was used mainly as a veneer on case furniture (Pl. 18c), though some work in the solid (chairs and tables) was evident about 1800. Rosewood was particularly important after 1800; heavy, dense, and marked with dark streaks, it set the current fashion for dark, glossy woods, and its use was

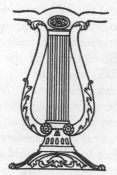

Fig. 3. Lyre back of chair.   Fig. 4. Prince of Wales' feather back of chair.

encouraged by the opening of direct trade with South America, where the chief source of supply was Brazil, during the Napoleonic Wars. It would be incorrect to assume that these woods supplanted each other in turn, as mahogany had supplanted walnut; it would be more accurate to say that one was more fashionable than the others at particular times, for fine furniture. In general terms it may be said that towards the end of this period mahogany was used for the best furniture in dining-rooms, bedrooms and libraries, and satinwood and rosewood in drawing-rooms and boudoirs. But it can be noted that in 1810 cabinet-makers were still defined in *Crosby's Pocket Dictionary* as 'workers in mahogany and other fine woods'.

Other woods

Many timbers besides those mentioned were in demand for their colour or figure. Fustic, long imported from the West Indies for dyeing, enjoyed a temporary popularity in cabinet work after about 1770 because of its yellow colour, but it fell into disuse when it was found to fade to a dead brownish hue. Various beautiful shades of brown and red, light and dark, were provided by exotic woods like calamander from Ceylon, coromandel from India, thuya from Africa, kingwood, partridge wood, purple wood, zebra wood and tulip wood all from Brazil, and amboyna from the West Indies. All these could be found as veneers or decorative bandings. It was the great demand for veneers with striped figure which explains the particular use of many of these woods after 1800.

Cheaper foreign woods which were imported included red cedar from North and Central America for boxes and drawer linings, and red deal from North America which, after 1750, began to replace yellow deal from the Baltic for carcase work.

English timbers were used considerably by leading cabinet-makers, and were by no means confined, as is sometimes supposed, to country craftsmen. Some native woods resembled the more expensive foreign varieties. Suitably figured pieces of birch and chestnut, for instance, could be used as substitutes for satinwood; acacia was used instead of tulip wood; and ebony, which had been imported since the sixteenth century for its black colour, was not now in such demand, since it could be imitated by staining close-grained woods like pear and willow for the 'ebonized' stringing on Regency pieces. Sycamore, stained to give a greenish-grey colour, and known as silver-wood or harewood, was often used as a veneer on late eighteenth-century work. Without such refinements, these and other native woods were found on the simple but attractive furniture made by country craftsmen or by cabinet-makers in the smaller towns, in imitation of better quality work. For painted furniture beech was usually employed, but plane was often substituted for this in country areas. And in the traditional craft of Windsor chair-making elm for the seat, beech or ash for the spindles, and yew for the frame continued to be frequently used.

Fashionable furniture: chairs

Under Adam's influence chairs were lighter and more graceful than those of the rococo period. Characteristic features were straight legs which tapered from knee blocks at the level of the seat rail to feet ending on small plinths, delicate classical motifs carved, inlaid, or painted, and a graceful outline for the backs. The latter had many variations; oval, shield and heart shapes became fashionable, but the rectilinear form was also in use, as, for example, on some early specimens of about 1775 which had lyre-shaped splats (Fig. 3). Where carving was employed it usually took the form of delicate channelling or fluting on the back frame, carved oval paterae on the knee blocks, fluting on the tapered legs, and continuous moulding along the seat edge. Adam's upholstered chairs closely followed French models, and he used beautiful materials like brocades and tapestries for upholstering both backs (which were oval in shape) and seats. The latter were overstuffed, but showed the lower part of the seat frames clear, and these were often decorated with gadrooning. Sometimes chairs of this kind had serpentine-curved front legs ending on scroll feet, the last version of the cabriole leg, and had arms with padded tops, covered with the same material as backs and seats (Pl. 13).

As can be expected, oval, shield and heart shapes figured prominently on the chair designs in Hepplewhite's *Guide*, and in many cases the splats were not connected with the back of the seats. Hepplewhite's name is particularly associated with the shield back and the familiar Prince of Wales' feathers (Fig. 4), but he designed many other fillings for his backs, including leaves, drapery, wheat-ears, vases and honeysuckle, and he by no means neglected rectilinear backs. The legs were generally of square section and tapered slightly to plinth feet. Many of the supports of the arms of both Adam and Hepplewhite chairs had a common feature in that they did not rise from the side rails of the seat, but continued from the front legs to just above the seat, and then swept backwards in a pronounced curve to straighten out at the arm-rests, which joined the back of the chair about half-way up. (For these details see Pl. 14A and B.)

A great variety of designs was found on chairs of the Sheraton style, but the emphasis was decidedly on backs of rectangular shape. Some cresting rails were turned; others were wide and flat and overran the uprights, and were curved for the sitter's back – this was a novel design very characteristic of chairs of about 1800. The backs were left as open as possible; the fillings took many forms – sometimes a single cross rail, or, when splats were used, trellis bars, pierced circles between pairs of bars, or a panel of cane set in a small frame. Painted chairs usually had bright designs on a black background, turned legs, and seats of cane. A feature of front legs was that they were often shaped in concave curves and tapered gradually to the floor without any special foot design. It was another characteristic of chairs of this time that their arms swept up in a pronounced S-curve to join the back uprights close to the cresting rail. Stringing, the delicate, thin lines of wood or brass, could be found on the broad types of cresting rails. In general, this period was distinguished for the delicacy of its chair design, but the lightness was soon to be lost in the heavier decoration of the Regency style. (Sheraton chairs, Pl. 14c and D.)

Settees followed the same main trends as chairs; they must, however, be carefully distinguished from sofas or couches which were popular at the time. Settees were extensions of armchairs, while couches were descendants of day-beds, and were used for reclining. The couch of classical design figured very prominently in the Regency period (Fig. 5).

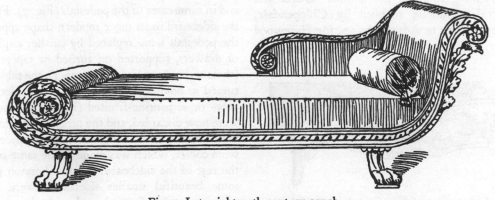

Fig. 5. Late eighteenth-century couch.

Chests of drawers, commodes, tallboys

Chests of drawers of the old plain rectangular form continued to be made after 1760, but often with five or six drawers, and thus somewhat taller than the earlier ones. Many were made of mahogany, either solid or veneered; in the latter case, it was usual to have a carcase of red deal and drawer linings of oak. A general feature of this type was the cock bead round the drawer edge; in fact, this form of moulding, which was introduced during the walnut period, was almost exclusively used throughout the century after about 1745. Some low chests of drawers had the top drawer hinged at the bottom so that it could be opened as a writing flap, and the drawer itself could be pulled forwards. This construction succeeded the writing slide which had been fitted above the top drawer of many chests in the earlier part of the century, and which was pulled out with small loop handles. After 1770 French influence could be seen on these plainer pieces in the form of a delicate outward curving of the feet, instead of the square bracket feet.

But it was in the development of commodes that the French taste was most marked. These pieces stood in reception rooms or the best bedrooms and were often elaborately decorated. Pl. 15A shows a remarkably fine specimen of this kind of about 1765. In the Adam period outstanding examples were made of satinwood inlaid with various woods and decorated with a variety of classical motifs, or with figures and scenes from classical mythology, all worked with the greatest skill. Among them is the famous 'Diana and Minerva' commode supplied by Chippendale, almost certainly to Adam's design, for Harewood House in November, 1773. The inlay work on

this piece is superb, particularly on the concave surface of the knee-hole, and the veneers, which are still in excellent condition, illustrate the extraordinary care with which cabinet-makers chose their woods for work of this kind.

After 1775 many chests of drawers were bow- or serpentine-fronted (Fig. 6). Reeded quarter columns were sometimes found on the front corners, and spirally turned feet were fashionable. Stringing in wood or brass was used as a decoration for drawer fronts in the Sheraton period, another distinctive feature of which was the exceptionally wide frieze above the top drawer.

Tallboys or chests-on-chests continued to follow the main developments of the plainer chests of drawers, but they were gradually going out of fashion in the later part of the eighteenth century owing to the inconvenient height of the upper drawers. In the final phase, some bow-fronted ones were made.

Sideboards

One interesting development in this period was the emergence of the sideboard, and credit for this new piece is now generally given to Robert Adam. 'A side Board table in the dining-room' appears among Adam's designs for Kenwood in the *Works in Architecture* of 1773. This shows the first stage in the arrangement of the sideboard – a side table flanked by two detached pedestal cupboards supporting urns (Pl. 16D). Later the two pedestals were joined directly to the table to form one complete unit. The urns were retained and were used as knife boxes, and drawers were fitted to the table and in some cases to the pedestals (Fig. 7). Finally, the sideboard in its more modern shape appeared; the pedestals were replaced by smaller cupboards or drawers, supported on turned or tapered legs (these were six or eight in number), the table continued to hold drawers, and the whole piece was bow- or serpentine-fronted (Pl. 16c). The urns were now discarded, and the central bay below the table top was often designed to allow space for a wine cooler, which was made in the same style as the rest of the sideboard. In the Sheraton period some beautiful smaller sideboards were made, often serpentine-fronted, and with characteristic

Fig. 6. Apron piece of bow-fronted chest of drawers.

Fig. 7. Adam sideboard, second half of eighteenth century.

turned and reeded legs. As a piece of furniture the sideboard quickly achieved popularity; 'the great utility of this piece,' wrote Hepplewhite, 'has procured it a very general reception.' Many were fitted at the back with a brass rail for displaying the family plate.

Early in the nineteenth century the sideboard lost its general lightness and there was a revival of the earlier type of pedestals and table. Urns were not used, but the pedestals were heavier in design than the earlier variety. The cupboards in all types were used for storing the various appurtenances of the dining-room, and sometimes they were lined with metal to keep plates hot, to hold wine bottles, or even to contain water for rinsing. A vivid light on the social habits of the time is thrown by the revelation that they also contained what a foreign visitor, Louis Simond, a Frenchman long domiciled in the United States, delicately described during his visit to England in 1810–11 as 'a certain convenient piece of furniture, to be used by anybody who wants it'. The reasons for its presence can best be left to Simond's own words: 'I once took the liberty to ask why this convenient article was not placed out of the room, in some adjoining closet; and was answered, that, in former times, when good fellowship was more strictly enforced than in these degenerate days, it had been found that men of weak heads or stomachs took advantage of the opportunity to make their escape shamefully, before they were quite drunk; and that it was to guard against such an enormity that this nice expedient had been invented. I have seen the article in question regularly provided in houses where there were no men, that is, no master of the house; the mistress, therefore, must have given the necessary orders to her servants.' [6]

Tables

Tables varied so much in size that they are best considered in three categories – small tables, dining tables and tripod tables. In addition to the side tables which were components of the early sideboards, the Adam period saw the development of variously shaped small tables – tops, semi-circular

[6] L. Simond, *Journal of a Tour & Residence in G. Britain, 1810–11* (1817).

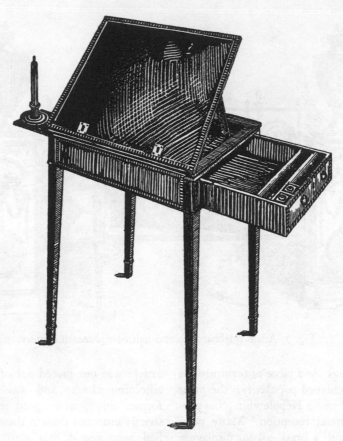

Fig. 8. Sheraton writing table.

when closed, were popular – for tea-drinking, card-playing, writing, dressing, or as pier and console (Pl. 16A) tables. On all the classical ornaments might be carved, inlaid, or painted. These tables usually had either square or turned tapering legs, often fluted, or slender French cabriole legs with knurl or scroll feet. Early in the Adam period the Pembroke table began its long vogue. This type had two flaps (usually semi-circular) and often a drawer (which might be at one end only, with a dummy drawer at the other) (Pl. 16B). The Sheraton period is distinguished for the number of very delicate tables which were made. The high standard of workmanship of the time meant that such tables could be very strong despite their fragile appearance. It was the custom to stand many of these tables about the living rooms of

large houses, and as some were expressly designed for ladies' use portability was an important consideration. Among them were little writing tables (Fig. 8) 'finished neat, in mahogany or satinwood', work tables with ingenious arrangements of drawers and sliding tops, and nests of tables. From the Pembroke table developed the sofa table, a longer version with small end flaps, standing (unlike the Pembroke, which almost always had four tapering legs) on a pedestal foot, or on two end supports linked by a stretcher (Pl. 17A). A very typical piece of the Regency period was the round topped table for writing or for use in libraries. This was mounted either on a turned column resting on curved (and often reeded) legs, or on a solid pedestal base with claw feet. The top had a frieze with drawers, or it might be left open for books.

For dining tables mahogany remained the favourite wood; its long planks gave both spaciousness and strength. Various forms of the gate leg were still made. One type consisted of a pair of tables each of which had a fifth leg which could be swung out to support a flap, the whole piece, when fitted up, forming a rectangle. In other examples three units were employed, two semi-circular side tables and a gate-leg table with rectangular flaps; and when a long table was needed for dining, the flaps were raised and the side tables stood at each end. When large single dining tables were used they did not look cumbersome, despite their size, for they often had tapered and fluted legs on plinth feet (Pl. 17B). Towards the end of the century some ingenious devices for extending tables were patented, among the best known of which was Gillow's 'telescopic' dining-table, with sliders that could be drawn out to hold flaps. About this time there were other distinct changes. It was usual for table tops to be supported on two or more columns each with four legs, of the kind known as 'pillar and claw'. The pillars were turned and the claws, which were at the end of curved and reeded legs, were often in the shape of lion paws and made of brass, with castors. Circular tables, similar to those described above, were also found in the dining-room, mounted on a pillar and claw (Pl. 18A).

Tripod tables were an important element in large houses after 1760, and were used for a variety of purposes, for tea, as occasional tables, and, in slightly modified forms, as candle stands and firescreens. As tea tables they were in great demand when tea-drinking in public gardens fell into disrepute among fashionable people and was carried on instead in private houses. The tops of these tables were sometimes hinged or, in some cases, could be lifted off their supports. In the neo-classic period the solid carved tops, cabriole legs, and ball-and-claw feet were gradually replaced by inlaid tops and modified forms of the cabriole. Later the tripod legs became very delicate and had clearly-defined concave or convex curves resting on dainty, pointed feet (Pl. 18B). In the case of the more elaborate firescreens and candle stands, the legs were longer and sprang from a small central platform for additional strength.

Bureaux, bookcases, cabinets, etc.

Bureaux followed closely the changes in fashion of the chest of drawers with regard to drawer fronts, feet, etc. Fronts and writing flaps, for instance, were often inlaid with classical designs under Adam's influence. Later in the century a curved apron piece often connected the legs beneath the plinth, and the legs themselves were slender and outward-pointing. About 1800 the writing flap was sometimes replaced by a sliding cylinder or tambour front. This treatment was favoured by Sheraton, who indeed claimed that he had found bureaux 'nearly obsolete in London; at least . . . among fashionable people', but that he had 'endeavoured to retrieve their obscurity by adding to them an open bookcase and modernizing the lower part'. Some of these later bureaux were made with slender legs and a single drawer under the writing section.

Where the bureau had a bookcase the latter often had a clear architectural character, as had larger bookcases, cabinets, and similar pieces. The tops were frequently decorated with a broken pediment – angular, swan-neck or curved – though this was by no means universal, for many cabinet-makers preferred a simple straight cornice. Glazing bars of mahogany were extensively used in the second half of the century, and some very graceful patterns were obtainable. In the Adam period cabinets were veneered with woods of contrasting colours (Pl. 18C). Larger pieces of this kind often had a break front, i.e. the central part was made to jut out a little. Shortly after 1800 the traditional design of the bookcase was modified; it was made to a low height so as to leave the walls above free for pictures (Pl. 15B).

Mirrors

There were considerable changes in the design of mirrors after 1760. In the middle of the century large mirrors, particularly the pier glasses which stood between windows, were perhaps the best examples of the rococo and Chinese styles in their most intricate and asymmetrical forms. The

Fig. 9. Circular mirror, about 1800. *Victoria and Albert Museum.*

classical revival swept these excesses away. Large glasses now usually had rectangular frames which were carved and gilt with decorations of paterae, honeysuckle and festoons surmounted by an urn, bird, etc. (Pl. 19A). Sometimes the more delicate decoration was carried out by mounting a specially prepared composition on metal threads. Smaller mirrors were oval and rectangular and had narrow frames with surrounds and crests of open work. Carving on frames, however, was soon to be largely replaced by painted decoration.

At the end of the century came another notable change – the general introduction of convex, circular mirrors which had been used in France since the 1750's (and had indeed been illustrated in Ince and Mayhew's *Universal System*). Their

frames, moulded and gilt, had a black (ebonized) fillet on the inside edge near the glass, and a reeded outer edge; the hollows of the moulding contained gilt balls. The favourite cresting above the frame was an eagle on a plinth with acanthus foliage (Fig. 9).

Dressing or toilet mirrors – little mirrors on stands fitted with drawers – provided delightful examples of fine craftsmanship. The frames, of rectangular, oval or shield shapes (Fig. 10) swung on two uprights fitted into the stand, which was often bow- or serpentine-fronted. Taller dressing glasses, known as cheval or, in Sheraton's words, 'horse dressing glasses', stood, as their name implies, on four legs. The uprights followed the prevailing modes of carving, turning or painting, and feet were reeded and curved outwards (Pl. 19B).

Long-case clocks

Though Sheraton described long-case clocks as almost obsolete in his day in London, they were still being made in the late eighteenth century, many of them with walnut veneers when this wood had become unfashionable. After 1760, however, mahogany was increasingly used, and the general tendency was to make the cases broader, the bodies shorter, and the bases heavier, and thus the slender proportions of the earlier japanned and walnut pieces tended to disappear. At first dark mahogany was in vogue, with carving and fretwork, but from about 1770 the emphasis was on finely-figured wood which was often veneered on a carcase of oak, with inlaid or painted classical designs. Small classical columns were also found at the sides of the head, and fluted and reeded pilasters at the front corners of the body. The hood was often surmounted by a broken

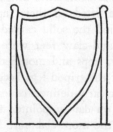

Fig. 10. Toilet mirror, shield shape.

finials (Fig. 11). At the very end of the century there was a distinct break with the traditional design, for some fine pieces had pedestal-shaped bodies, veneered with mahogany or satinwood and inlaid with various woods, and a plainer circular dial in a narrow frame, instead of a hood. An important feature of the period was the great improvement in provincial clock-making. Provincial clocks tended to be even broader than London ones, and many were made of oak.

Other furniture: country

Little enough is known about the furniture in cottages and smaller farmhouses in remoter areas of the country. In many cottages the contents must have been extremely primitive, like those seen in Devon by Louis Simond in 1810–11: 'the floors appear to be a pavement of round stones like the street, – a few seats, in the form of short benches, – a table or two, – a spinning wheel, – a few shelves.' But that cottage furniture of even a simple kind was regarded as a valuable possession is clear from the way it was put to as many uses as possible, and also handed down in the family for generations. Goldsmith, in his poem *The Deserted Village* (1770), wrote of the cottage chest which 'contrived a double debt to pay, a bed by night, a chest of drawers by day'. In the later eighteenth century furniture could be found in rural districts which dated back to early Stuart and Tudor times. In 1761, for example, Horace Walpole wrote: 'Dicky Bateman has picked up a whole cloister full of old chairs in Herefordshire – he bought them one by one, here and there in farmhouses for three and sixpence and a crown apiece. They are of wood, the seats triangular, the backs, arms and legs loaded with turnery. A thousand to one but there are plenty up and down Cheshire too.' Such chairs, collected by Georgian devotees of 'Gothic' furniture, were of a medieval pattern which rural craftsmen had continued to make well into the seventeenth century. It is clear, too, that much of the furniture in country places was made at home. This was true not only of the very poor, but also of people of more substantial station, even of the smaller gentry. At Townend, near Troutbeck, Westmorland, which for several centuries was

Fig. 11. Clock hood, about 1780. *Victoria and Albert Museum.*

the home of a well-to-do yeoman family, the furniture (now under the care of the National Trust) was largely the work of many generations of the family, down to the death of the last of the male line in 1914. It could also happen that some cottages contained furniture of distinctly good quality which was passed on to them from the local manor house where it had been discarded in favour of more fashionable pieces – just as the servants' quarters in large houses might have furniture formerly in the best rooms.

Provincial towns

Provincial towns had their reputable cabinet-makers who could supply all classes in the neighbourhood. Some of these craftsmen, indeed, achieved real distinction, like the Gillow family of Lancaster. Even when this firm opened a branch in London about 1760 the furniture was still made at Lancaster for a time and sent to London by sea. From their Lancaster workshop the family supplied furniture to local magnates in that part of the country – such as the Curwens at Workington Hall – where it would obviously be very difficult to get goods from London. In general, however, the upper classes obtained much of their furniture from the capital, whence, as has been seen, cheap furniture could also be supplied to the lower classes by middlemen. In the latter case, the chief consideration was geographical; most of these cheaper goods seem to have been

833

shipped from London as part of the coasting trade. Middle-class people in the provinces usually found local sources of supply sufficient. Parson Woodforde, in his famous diary, describes how he obtained some of the furniture for his parsonage at Weston, some ten miles from Norwich. 'Bought this day,' he wrote in November, 1789, 'of William Hart, Cabinet-Maker on Hog Hill, Norwich, 2 large second hand double-flapped Mohogany Tables, also one second hand Mohogany dressing Table with Drawers, also one new Mohogany Washing-Stand, for all which paid £4.14.6, that is, for the 2 Tables £2.12.6, Dressing Table £1.11.6, Mohogany Wash-stand £0.10.6.' Later, in April, 1793, he noted: 'About 2 o'clock this Afternoon two Men of Sudbury's at Norwich came with my Side-Board and a large New Mohogany Cellaret bought of Sudbury, brought on the Men's Shoulders all the way and very safe.' [7] This last entry is a comment on the state of the country roads at that time.

London

With regard to the furniture used by the lower and lower-middle classes in London, there are only scanty records. A pamphlet of 1767, however, gives the contents of a furnished room rented at half a crown a week by an unmarried clerk in a public office who, with a salary of £50 a year, is described as 'in a middling Station'. The room has 'a half tester bedstead, with brown linsey woolsey furniture, a bed and bolster, half flock, half feathers . . . a small wainscot table, two old chairs with cane bottoms, a small looking-glass six inches by four in a deal frame painted red and black, a red linsey woolsey window curtain'.[8] In considering furniture of this sort it is important to remember the cramped living conditions of many Londoners at that time. Lack of cheap transport kept most workers to the immediate vicinity of their places of work. Very many of them lived in furnished rooms as weekly ten-

ants, and even the comparatively small group who reached the superior status of householders normally lived in only part of their houses and let the rest to lodgers. Landlords stocked furnished rooms with much old-fashioned furniture, and those tenants who had to provide their own furniture often bought it by weekly instalments – an old practice which remained popular right through the century. Naturally, better-class tenants could count on improved conditions. C. Moritz, a foreigner who travelled in England in 1782, wrote with appreciation of the room he had rented in London: 'I now occupy a large room in front on the ground floor, which has a carpet and matts, and is very neatly furnished; the chairs are covered with leather, and the tables are of mahogany.' [9]

This crowded way of life explains the development of what Martin in 1813 called 'the fashion of the day, to resort to a number of contrivances for making one piece of furniture serve many purposes'. The cabinet-makers' design books, which came out after 1760, had many examples of ingeniously-contrived, space-saving furniture. Some pieces of this kind were patented, such as Eckhardt's portable table and chair (1771), and Gale's bedstead which could close to look like a bookcase or wardrobe (1772). Closely related to the making of this fitted-in furniture was that of invalid furniture, in which some cabinet-makers specialized. In the early nineteenth century, for instance, Pococks of Covent Garden advertized ten different sorts of invalid furniture, including 'Patent Sympathetic and Self-Acting Dining Tables, Patent Boethema or Rising Mattresses, Merlin's Reading and Gouty Chairs, and Patent Sofa Beds' [10] (Pl. 20A).

Ships' furniture

Another line of furniture-making which is often overlooked, but which was an important one in that period of naval and commercial activity and of emigration, was the fitting up of ships'

[7] *The Diary of a Country Parson* (ed. J. Beresford, 1924–31).
[8] Considerations on the Expediency of Raising . . . the Wages of Servants that are not Domestic, particularly Clerks in Public Offices (B.M.T. 152/4, 1767).

[9] C. Moritz, *Travels in England in 1782* (1924 reprint of trans. of 1795).
[10] This advertisement appears among Foreign Office archives for Spain, 1814 (Pub. Record Office, F.O. 185/50); some of the pieces may have been used by army officers.

cabins. Some ships were very handsomely furnished. In 1768 William Hickey described the cabin of the third mate of the *Plassey* at Gravesend as 'neatness itself and most elegantly fitted up. It was painted of light pea green, with gold beading, the bed and curtains of the richest Madras chintz, one of the most complete dressing tables I ever saw, having every useful article in it; a beautiful bureau and bookcase . . . and three neat mahogany chairs, formed the furniture.' [11] This was the cabin of an officer in the merchant navy. In the Royal Navy the chief officers had good, attractive furniture designed for hard wear. Mahogany furniture, once belonging to Captain Cook, Lord Nelson and other officers can still be seen at the National Maritime Museum, Greenwich. Nelson's cabin on board the *Victory* contained (as recounted by Miss Carola Oman) two black leather arm-chairs (lashed together, when necessary as a couch), an ottoman, folding bedstead, dining table, circular pedestal tables, other chairs, a sideboard, tallboy, washstand – all of mahogany.[12]

Cabin furniture was an important item for emigrants, for they normally hired only cabin space on board, and then bought furniture which they could take on shore with them. This was a regular practice with all emigrants to the colonies. In 1821 P. Cherry wrote from India to his three daughters who were intending to leave England for Madras: 'Your cabin furniture, if it has no other recommendation, is English, and will always have a value in proportion to your length of absence from England. I have now most of my cabin furniture which I bought in 1811.' He said the following were essential for the voyage: 'Two or three small bureaus with bookshelves on them, two or three sea couches with drawers to convert into sofas in the day-time, a wash-hand stand . . . a foot-tub and three chairs.' [13] The cabinet-maker's side of all this may be best summarized by quoting the trade card of Thomas Butler of the Strand, about 1800: 'Bed Furniture and Mattresses calculated for the East and West Indies. Ship Cabbins furnished. Articles particularly adapted and for Travelling and Exportation.' [14]

REFERENCES. Two indispensable works for a study of this period are the *Dictionary of English Furniture* by P. MacQuoid and R. Edwards (3 vols., revised edition by R. Edwards, 1954), and *Georgian Cabinet-Makers* by R. Edwards and M. Jourdain (revised edition 1955). The quotations from Hepplewhite and Sheraton in the text are taken from, respectively, the *Guide* (1788) and the *Cabinet Dictionary* (1803), except Sheraton's reference to writing tables (from the *Drawing Book*, 1791–4).

[13] Quoted by Sir M. Malcolm, *Annals of an Anglo-Indian Family* (undated).
[14] Sir A. Heal, *London Furniture Makers, 1660–1840* (1953).

[11] *Memoirs of William Hickey* (ed. A. Spencer, 1913).
[12] C. Oman, *Nelson* (1950).

Wood engraving by Richard Austin for Bell & Stephenson's Type Specimen, 1789.

JOHN LACEY,

Cabinet and Chair-Maker,

In Cheap-Street, Frome,

Makes in a neat Manner, and sells at a low Price,

All SORTS of

Cabinet Goods

ALSO

Sells common, round, and quartered Ash and Elder
Chairs, white and coloured, from eight to forty
Shillings per Dozen.

The printed handbill of a late eighteenth-century provincial craftsman. From R. W. Symonds' *Furniture Making
in seventeenth and eighteenth-century England.*

Painting and Sculpture

HUGH HONOUR

'Our eloquence and the glory of our arms have been carried to the highest pitch. The more peaceful arts have in other countries generally attended national glory. If there are any talents among us, this seems the crisis for their appearance: the Throne itself is now the altar of the graces, and whoever sacrifices to them becomingly, is sure that his offerings will be smiled upon by a Prince, who is at once the example and patron of accomplishments' (Horace Walpole in the preface to *The Anecdotes of Painting*, 1760).

It was with such high hopes that the artistic world of London greeted the accession of George III, and although royal patronage was to fall short of Horace Walpole's expectation, his prophecy was in the main fulfilled. It is sufficient to mention the names of the principal artists of the period to show that it was indeed the golden age of English painting and sculpture – Reynolds, Gainsborough, Wilson, Stubbs and Romney were all at the height of their powers, as were also the watercolourists J. R. Cozens and Thomas Girtin, and the sculptors Wilton, Banks and Nollekens. The first few years of the period were illuminated by the sunset of Hogarth, Thomas Hudson, Allan Ramsay and the trio of anglicized sculptors, Roubiliac, Rysbrack and Scheemakers. The first few years of the nineteenth century saw the rise of Lawrence, Raeburn, Constable, Blake, Turner and Flaxman, who had already begun to make their personalities felt. Indeed, it would not be too much to say that all but a handful of the greatest English artists worked during the long reign of George III.

For the history of English painting, no less than for the painters themselves, the most important event in the period was the foundation of the Royal Academy. Such an institution for the establishment of the 'rules' of high art is, of course, a necessary adjunct of any classical period; but the forces which brought about the foundation of the Academy in England were perhaps social as much as artistic, and it reflects the decline of aristocratic patronage and the rise of a much more diffuse and less homogeneous class of patrons. It is unnecessary to repeat here the tedious history of the jealousies and squabbles which marked the earliest years of the Royal Academy. '*Tantaene animis caelestibus irae?*' Suffice it to say that a group of artists who had exhibited works at the Foundling Hospital held a larger exhibition in the rooms of the Society for the Encouragement of the Arts in 1760. This exhibition was a resounding success and gave rise to three rival bodies: the Free Society of Artists of Great Britain which petered out in 1779, the Society of Artists which was incorporated by Royal charter in 1765 and lasted until 1791, and the Royal Academy itself which was founded in 1768 under the presidency of Reynolds. All three institutions held annual exhibitions but gradually the leading exhibitors deserted from the other societies to the Royal Academy where all the most important painters save Romney were to exhibit at some time. The Royal Academy was largely responsible for raising the status of artists above that of mere tradesmen or craftsmen; its banquets were attended by members of the Royal Family, by diplomatists and politicians – a far cry from the jovial carousings of the old artists' clubs. Its schools gave students a good academic grounding with the opportunity to draw from the nude or from a collection of casts such as had previously been available for study only to those with the *entrée* to houses of great collectors. But, above all, its annual exhibitions gave artists the opportunity of studying each others' works and provided them with a shop window in which to show their performances, thus helping to free them from the old system of patronage and the tyranny of the picture dealer. Whereas the majority of pictures had formerly been painted to fulfil commissions, the Academy, and the other societies, opened up a much wider market enabling artists to exhibit history pictures, fancy scenes or landscapes on the chance of finding a purchaser or attracting sufficient interest to justify the publication of engravings.

Much as the artists complained of lack of patronage, especially for large history pictures, the sheer quantity of paintings, particularly portraits and cabinet pieces, produced during this period, is witness to the demand from new and more modest patrons who sought pictures to complete the furnishing of a small town or country house. So widespread became this demand for 'art' that an unprecedented quantity of engravings were produced to satisfy the voracious appetites of those unable to afford the price of an original painting. Engravings had always been bought by collectors, indeed, as Strutt remarked, 'almost every man of taste is in some degree a collector of prints', but their importance in the history of English painting has never been justly appreciated. They served as advertisements for the painter, spreading his fame far beyond the country house to the trim villa of the provincial lawyer or prosperous tradesman. Mezzotints, stipple and line engravings of the famous beauties of the day, of notable politicians, of scenes from recent history or of fancy pictures found their way into all but the humblest of homes. Their vogue made the painting of modern histories a profitable business and Benjamin West is said to have made as much as £15,000 out of Woollett's engravings of his *Death of Wolfe*. Indeed, artists such as M. W. Peters and Francis Wheatley must frequently have

worked with one eye on the burin very much as novelists of today write with one eye on Hollywood. In this way engravings made it possible for painters to cater for a wider public than that represented by the purchasers of original pictures.

Taste and patronage

Nevertheless, the most eminent painters of the day were working for a clearly defined and limited market and their paintings reflect the taste of their wealthy patrons to the same extent as the great houses that were springing up throughout the country and the furniture that was produced for them. The size of rooms still made large pictures fashionable and whole length portraits, always favoured in England, were turned out in great quantity. But the chaster style of interior decoration introduced by the Adam brothers limited the art of the purely decorative painter to the small roundels of the ceiling, occasional panels in the wall and, more rarely, views of imaginary architecture, supplied by Biagio Rebecca, Angelica Kauffman and her prolific husband Antonio Zucchi. The titanic gods whose athletic amours had decorated many a wall and ceiling in the earlier part of the century gave place to simpering personifications and pretty prospects of ruins. The Adams were also responsible for the conception of a room as a whole with every part in concert from the ceiling to the carpet and from the chimney-piece to the door knob, and pictures must needs fit into this all-embracing scheme. Great portraits by Reynolds and Gainsborough were designed for the grand salon, fancy pieces for the boudoir, history pictures for the gallery; and it is pertinent to note that when these works are removed from their setting the pictures, no less than the rooms, lose much of their beauty and significance. Similarly, Reynolds' portraits of his literary friends, and Gainsborough's of his musical cronies, were intended for the more modest apartments of the town, and the provincial artist's style was adapted to the requirements of the minor country house, reflecting its greater solidity and less elegant refinement. The period is marked by the existence of a number of good provincial artists who, like Joseph Wright of Derby, worked mainly for the patronage of their district.

Although, as we have already observed, patronage was by no means confined to members of the upper class, their influence remained predominant none the less. This was the great age of the Grand Tour when every young man of good family was expected to have spent some months in Italy where, under the supervision of some bear-leader or guided by a seldom altruistic cicerone, he made a nodding acquaintance with the arts which stood him in good stead for conversation on his return. His more lowly contemporaries were inclined to ape his pronouncements until, as reported by an anonymous writer of 1775, 'even the lowest people tell familiarly of Hannibal Scratchi, Paul Varnish and Raphael Angelo'. Painters consequently emulated the styles of the most popular Italians of the sixteenth and seventeenth centuries in both portraits and history pieces, though they seldom impressed the newly returned *macaroni* who, like Sterne's critic, would remark of them that they contained 'nothing of the colouring of *Titian*, the expression of *Rubens*, the grace of *Raphael*, the purity of *Dominichino*, the *corregiescity* of *Corregio*, the learning of *Poussin*, the airs of *Guido*, the taste of the *Carrachis* or the grand contour of *Angelo*'. It was at such moments that Sir Joshua 'shifted his trumpet and only took snuff'; though no one was a more enthusiastic admirer of these artists, and the standard of taste in old masters is nowhere better expressed than in the *Discourses* he delivered each year to the students of the Royal Academy. The Italianized taste of the aristocracy, which was also, of course, the official policy of the Royal Academy throughout this period, is displayed to perfection in Zoffany's *Tribune of the Uffizi* (Pl. 21A) in to which he has crammed all those objects and paintings which the patron coveted and the artist emulated.

As the tourist admired only the classical sculptures and old master paintings in Italy, so did the painter. Contemporary foreign artists were generally considered of little account save for Pompeo Batoni, the most elegant and expensive portrait painter in Europe; Canaletto, who had nearly disgraced himself in the eyes of Taste by stepping on English soil; Zuccarelli, who came to England in this period but appears to have retained his Italian integrity, and A. R. Mengs who was more popular for his portraits than his history pictures. Batoni's influence may be discerned in the work of Ramsay, Nathaniel Dance and even to a slight degree in Reynolds himself, but the others made little impression on English painting in this period. The neo-classic style, which may owe as much to the Scottish Gavin Hamilton as to Mengs, found comparatively little favour in these isles. Hamilton did contrive to insinuate some of his vast canvasses into otherwise immaculate British houses but he had to make their purchase a condition of sale for classical sculptures and old masters. In sculpture, however, neo-classicism enjoyed uninhibited popularity because it emulated the style of the most admired statuary of the past, directly reflecting the taste of the collector.

Partly by his own inclination, and partly to cater for the taste of his patron, the English artist seeking the best market for his works modelled himself on the masters of the cinquecento and the seicento. He might also turn to seventeenth century Dutch painting which was ranked second only to Italian, and it seems likely that Gainsborough, Stubbs and, towards the end of his career, Reynolds, imbibed some inspiration from this quarter. As the reign of George III progressed, however, members of the untravelled middle classes began to grow in importance as patrons, desiring less of the grand manner but greater sentiment and truth to nature as they saw it; consequently small *genre* pieces and English landscapes became more popular. Whereas the great patron would demand grandiose portraits and, on rare occasions, such history pieces as might be mistaken for old masters in a bad light, the less wealthy wanted more intimate works; and, of course, the sporting pictures which were the particular joy of the squirearchy.

The price of pictures

In order to give some idea of the markets for which painters catered, and before proceeding to a more general account of the trends of taste in the period, a word should be said of the prices charged. When Romney was travelling round the north of England as an itinerant face painter, between 1757 and 1762, he is said to have received two guineas for a head and six for a whole length. At the same time Reynolds was charging 25 guineas for a head and 100 for a whole length and had doubled these prices by 1779 when he was the best paid portrait painter in England. Gainsborough's prices were slightly below those of Reynolds and in 1786 he was charging 40 guineas for a head and 160 for a whole length. Once he was established Romney charged 15 guineas for a head and 60 for a whole length and had doubled these prices by 1793, when Beechey was asking the same and the young Lawrence could already obtain as much as Gainsborough at the height of his power. The prices asked for subject pictures were more variable; Reynolds obtained 50 guineas each for the little *Shepherd Boy* and the *Strawberry Girl*, but got £200 for *The Death of Dido*, 700 guineas for a replica of *Mrs Siddons as the Tragic Muse* (Pl. 21c) and 1,500 guineas for *The Infant Hercules* which was sold to Catherine the Great – he bought Gainsborough's *Girl with Pigs* (Pl. 28B) in 1782 for 100 guineas. In 1770 West was charging £300 for a history painting 'not too large to hang over a chimney' and some twenty years later Opie received 100 guineas for his *Ruth*. These are not small figures and are some indication of the prosperity enjoyed by the most popular artists, though not all – towards the end of his life Wilson considered himself lucky if he could obtain 15 guineas for a landscape. By way of comparison, it is worth recording a few of the prices paid for old masters. At Sir Luke Schaub's sale in 1758 a Claude fetched £105 and a Raphael £703; forty years later at the sale of the Orleans collection the top price of 4,000 guineas was paid for Annibale Caracci's *Descent from the Cross*, 3,500 for the *Raising of Lazarus* by Sebastino del Piombo and 3,000 for a *Virgin* by Raphael.

Literary influences

It is not necessary to indulge in elaborate comparisons between the oratory of Burke and the grand portraits of Reynolds, or between Gibbons's attitude to history and the paintings of Copley, to see how the main tendencies in literature were paralleled in the painting of the period. White's *Natural History of Selborne* and Gray's diaries have in their scientific observation of nature an obvious parallel in the animal paintings of Stubbs. The spirit of nationalism, which was an important force in the Gothic Revival, was characterized by an increased interest in the earlier English writers and a growing preference for the native landscape adorned by gothic rather than classical ruins – tastes which are clearly expressed in the history pictures and the landscapes of the day. The popularity of Macpherson's *Ossian* was mainly based on the pleasing supposition that he supplied the want of a British Homer, and he was commemorated in painting and sculpture. Ossian's appeal was also due to a curiously remote cult of the simple life, the ideal, the unspoilt barbarian, the noble savage indeed, who was depicted in his own exotic surroundings by William Hodges and was personified in Omai whom Sir Joshua Reynolds painted on more than one occasion.

Above all, the cult of Sensibility pervaded a period in which Richardson's novels were read with tearful affection – not to mention Sterne's *Sentimental Journey* (1765), Goldsmith's *Vicar of Wakefield* (1766) and, most lachrymose of all, Henry Mackenzie's *Man of Feeling* (1771). Novelists and poets indulged a pleasing melancholy strain and invited the tear over descriptions of descents from greatness to misery, ruins (real or artificial), wild landscapes, children and the short and simple annals of the rustic poor. In an age when weeping was a mark of refinement and a young woman might die from excessive sensibility, it is hardly surprising that the dewy-eyed Magdalene of Guido Reni should have been among the most popular of pictures. The influence of sensibility on art is to be discerned in many a rugged, gloomy or mellifluously sweet landscape, in views of towering ivy-clad ruins, the resort of moping owls, and in scenes from recent history – the death of Wolfe (Pl. 30B) in the hour of triumph or of Chatham 'heart sick for his country's shame' – or in *genre* pictures of rustic groups which 'only nature could have supplied and taste and sensibility selected' (to quote the words of Martin Archer Shee on Gainsborough's *Girl with Pigs*). Even in a picture of a scientific experiment – *The Bird in the Air Pump* – Joseph Wright of Derby introduced figures of children to shed innocent tears. With the notable exception of Stubbs, no successful painters in this period failed to succumb at some time to a literary taste which they no doubt enjoyed as much as their patrons.

The trends of taste apparent in the paintings of the half century under consideration can receive only the most cursory treatment in a brief survey. It is a subject much complicated by the fact that most painters indulged in the expression of more than one artistic fashion and tried their hands at nearly every *genre*. Reynolds and Gainsborough painted both grand and informal portraits, landscapes and fancy pictures; Romney hankered after history painting and Barry, all too rarely, painted portraits. In an article which is devoted to the place of English paintings in the home rather than to criticism or biographies of artists, it seems most convenient to treat the subject by *genres* – portraits, fancy pictures, landscapes, animal paintings and histories.

Portraiture

Portraiture retained its popularity throughout this period, and although artists were prone to complain of its drudgery few were so high-minded as to despise its rewards. Considered as essential for the decoration of a great house by the aristocracy, and as the first emblems of gentility by the bourgeoisie, portraits might be found in practically every house that contained pictures; and the artists, from Reynolds in London to the now forgotten journeymen in the provinces, worked hard to satisfy an ever-increasing demand. As early as 1759 Reynolds is known to have had some 150 sitters, and Gainsborough painted more than 700 portraits in the course of his career. Much as Reynolds hankered after history, as Gainsborough longed to escape to some remote village where he could settle down to landscape, or as Romney wished to realize the grandiose projects he sketched, all three were most admired and are best remembered as portrait painters.

In 1760 Reynolds was well established in London where his only rival was Allan Ramsay who had recently returned from Rome with a brand-new style based on the French pastellists and Pompeo Batoni. But although Ramsay painted some of his best portraits during the first nine years of this period, most of his time was consumed by uncongenial, though no doubt remunerative, royal commissions, and in 1769 he retired altogether from the scene. The year 1760 is of singular importance in Reynolds' career, for with the portrait of *The Duchess of Hamilton as Venus* he marked his change from the intimate to the grand manner. In the fond hope of deflecting the taste of his patrons from portraiture to 'history' he dressed his female sitters in classical garments, placed them in the attitudes of Michelangelo or Albano and sought to draw the general out of the particular. In his use of 'timeless' costume he attracted few followers, though Francis Cotes once surpassed himself and nearly equalled Sir Joshua in this manner (Pl. 24B). After 1765, when Reynolds exhibited the most remorselessly classical of all his portraits – *Lady Bunbury Sacrificing to the Graces* – he seems to have realized that the British public would not be dictated to in such a fashion and he resorted to a less artificial but no less magniloquent style. But he never condescended to the ephemeral dictates of the *modiste* and he was consequently able to portray the fashionable hostess of the moment, like Lady Hertford (Pl. 24A), *en grande tenue* as a beauty of all time. In portraits of men he resorted to fewer devices for his sharp psychological penetration enabled him to paint into them such strength of character as would transcend the bounds of time (Pl. 23). The friend of *literati* rather than painters, he was ideally suited to depict the great men of his age, and he painted them with such force that we can now see them only through his eyes. But Reynolds could descend from his dais, dropping the grand manner and his tone of high seriousness when occasion offered: he could even laugh at his high-flown pretensions, as witness the charming parody of his own grand manner in the portrait of *Master Crewe as Henry VIII* or *Garrick between Tragedy and Comedy*. His range was

841

indeed enormous, much wider than has sometimes been supposed. He was very much more than the 'official' portrait painter of his age, and his success in his own day, no less than his enduring fascination, resided in his variety – 'Damn him,' said Gainsborough, 'how various he is.' He could adapt his style and composition to depict with equal felicity the robust and vigorous admiral or the elegant and diaphonous *belle*, tender and melting motherhood or hard and glittering urbanity.

In 1774 Thomas Gainsborough moved from Bath to London where he could more effectively challenge Reynolds' position as the leading portrait painter of the day. Never before or since has English society been served by two artists so great and so complementary. Whereas Reynolds was a painter of intellect, Gainsborough was of feeling; Reynolds the master of substance and pose, Gainsborough of fleeting effects of light. Gainsborough's more exquisite, more feminine talent, his delicious creamy paint, his fine draughtsmanship and his transformation scene effects will never lack admirers, especially among those who find it difficult to appreciate Reynolds' subtlety. Moreover, Gainsborough could be no less effective than Reynolds in the grand manner as is evinced by the magnificent state portrait of the Duke of Argyll (Pl. 22) in which he has firmly grasped the forceful character of his sitter, presenting an image or great power and solidity which is in no way weakened by his delight in the beauty and variety of the textures of his robes, painted, as always, with the utmost virtuosity, in a shimmering pattern of brilliant flicks and blobs of paint. The strength, weight and solidity of this portrait (dating from 1767) was not often to be recaptured for Gainsborough gradually succumbed to the fascination of textures and surface effects so that his figures became increasingly wraith-like and insubstantial. Enamoured as he was of silk and satins, Gainsborough rarely forewent the pleasure of painting his sitters' costumes himself; his canvasses are therefore seldom marred by the mechanical touch of the 'drapery painter' or studio assistant, and every part of his best portraits is from his own hand and of equal artistic merit.

Those who desired neither the elevation of Reynolds nor the shimmering evanescence of Gainsborough might, after 1773, employ George Romney, who was born to be the fashionable portrait painter *par excellence*. He could always be relied upon to produce a good likeness, and sometimes displayed a keen insight into character as in his capital portraits of the young Etonian, Lord Grey (Pl. 25), the disillusioned ageing statesman, Warren Hastings, or the elegant young couple setting out to inspect their estate (Pl. 63D). Eminently professional, his work generally smells too much of the studio, and even when painting his *femme fatale*, Emma Hart (later Lady Hamilton) he appears thin-blooded and coldly calculating. Despite his charm and accomplishment, it is difficult for us now to understand how the London of 1783 could be of two factions, Reynolds' and Romney's.

Towards the end of his career Romney was rivalled by John Hoppner and William Beechey, both of whom catered for more humdrum sitters and produced portraits which appeal to us now mainly as period pieces. They had a sharp eye for fashion in dress and *toilette* which endowed their female sitters with a certain charm, though they occasionally made them look as if they might at any moment fall prey to excessive sensibility. A more lively note was struck by the arch-realist J. S. Copley, who painted the sparkling rococo group of *The Three Princesses* (Pl. 24C).

Before leaving the subject of portraiture a word should be said of the pastellists who enjoyed a considerable vogue until the 'nineties, when the most notable, John Russell, who had in his heyday commanded prices as high as Reynolds, was forced to tour the provinces in search of sitters. He executed a vast number of portraits, some of which show a refined sensitivity and all of which are characterized by an admirable respect for his medium. Francis Cotes, William Hoare, Ozias Humphrey and Daniel Gardner were also prominent portraitists in pastel.

John Zoffany

The taste for conversation piece portraits, which was well established before the period began, was given new impetus by the arrival in

England of John Zoffany. With his almost photographic technique which enabled him to reproduce the minutiae of fashionable clothes and interior decoration as if seen through a quiz-glass, he won immediate popularity and went to Florence to paint the *Tribune of the Uffizi* (Pl. 21A). This picture delights us now as an amusing and authoritative epitome of the current taste in pictures no less than as an illustration of the Grand Tour, while his equally delightful painting of Charles Townley among his 'marbles' affords an intimate view of the *virtuoso* at home. Other artists who worked in this *genre* included Francis Wheatley and Arthur Devis.

Fancy pictures

Sir Joshua Reynolds found it hard to determine whether Gainsborough had 'most excelled in portraits, landscapes or Fancy pictures' but confessed himself to have been captivated by 'the interesting simplicity and elegance of his ordinary little beggar children'. The first of Gainsborough's fancy pictures to be exhibited appeared in the Academy of 1781 and, although it does not seem to have won the approval of the *cognoscenti*, it made a great impression on the artists. Reynolds later bought his *Girl with Pigs* (Pl. 28B) and essayed the same style in his *Strawberry Girl* and *Shepherd Boy*. Within a few years the exhibitions were abundantly supplied with little scenes of rustic innocence which made an immediate appeal to the urban middle classes. Of the many artists who worked in this *genre*, Francis Wheatley was probably the most successful but none was more ruthless than George Morland (Pl. 28c) in his exploitation of the nostalgia for a rural society that was already vanishing, for a poverty more picturesque, if no less miserable, than that of the town. The *genre* scenes of John Opie, the Cornish Wonder (Pl. 29B), are less densely clouded by the romantic attitude to rustic life, the harsh reality of which he had experienced in person.

Closely connected with fancy pictures, illustrations of scenes from contemporary literature also enjoyed a wide popularity. The most interesting artist in this vein was Joseph Wright of Derby, who extracted incidents from Sterne's *Sentimental Journey*, and from the poems of Hayley, Langhorne and Beattie, whose Edwin would sometimes emit 'a sigh, a tear so sweet, he wish'd not to controul'. Although Wright lived solely in Derby, he exhibited regularly in London and never appears to have lacked patronage for his pictures, or a market for prints after them. The source for one of his more remarkable works, *Miravan Opening the Tomb of his Ancestors* (Pl. 28A) has never been identified but it takes place in the vault of some neo-classical castle – of Otranto or Udolpho – and is a curious mixture of all the fashionable tendencies of the time. John Hamilton Mortimer also painted pictures of a literary character, but specialized in *banditti* which were thought to challenge comparison with Salvator Rosa. A less gloomy figure, the Rev. Mathew William Peters, painted little pictures of a faintly *risqué* nature, illustrated such passages from Shakespeare as could include simpering femininity; and finally, after he had taken orders, turned to religious paintings in the style of Mengs. He too was widely popularized by stipple engravings and mezzotints.

Landscape

Like fancy pictures, landscapes owed their patronage mainly to the rising middle class who seem to have appreciated them for their content rather than for their truth to nature. Consequently Gainsborough found that he could make his landscapes saleable only by the introduction of figures – on one occasion he copied his pig girl group into the middle distance. His landscapes of this period are characterized by a sweet lyricism, a feeling for gently undulating country and an appearance of naturalism, though many were painted from little arrangements of moss and pebbles in his studio. They are, in fact, subtle evocations of the English scene rather than accurate delineations of it, and it would frequently be hard to identify his trees, let alone his grasses. Nor was Richard Wilson a greater respecter of topography except when engaged in painting the 'portrait' of a country house in the Claudean setting of its landscaped park. Too much an artist to resort to a purely topographical technique and too stoical to indulge the tear of sensibility, he fell between the two stools of the accepted landscape tradition. It is significant that his most successful picture showed Niobe in a wild setting of rocks, and that it brought in £2,000 for Woollett the engraver. His views of the English or Welsh scene (Pl. 26A) are carefully composed, flooded with Italian light and exquisitely restrained; but they were hardly calculated to appeal to the man of feeling who wished to indulge sweet melancholy over a ruin or be chilled into a pleasing horror by a mountain. Wilson was too classical, and thus out of tune with his age which allowed him to die in poverty. It is remarkable and, indeed, un-accountable that his works should have been sought after within a decade of his death, since when his reputation has steadily increased until it reached its present height (a Wilson now fetches more in the London art market than a capital piece by his master Claude).

George Barrett, a man of sound common sense with an eye for the picturesque possibilities of a real scene, produced just what his patrons wanted, and succeeded as a prose Wilson. Artists like Michelangelo Rooker were able to extract the most from a crumbling ivy-clad ruin, and Thomas Patch could do the same for such an Italian scene as *The Falls of Terni*. The Smith brothers of Chichester adapted the Dutch style to the English landscape and achieved a considerable success, both through their paintings and the prints after them. Towards the end of our period Julius Caesar Ibbetson showed himself an adept of the sweet pastoral scene or the wild romantic land-scape, the ideals of which are clearly expressed in his picture of a *Phaeton in a Thunderstorm* (Pl. 29A) in which he has made use of every device to accentuate the melodrama — lowering clouds, beetling crags, savage country and a modish vehicle involved in a horrifying incident.

Watercolour

No outline of landscape painting in the late eighteenth century would be complete without some mention of those in watercolour, a medium particularly well suited to the delicate tonality of the English countryside. Watercolours enjoyed popularity first as topographical records and then as independent works of art. One of the leading practitioners of the medium, Paul Sandby, was employed by the equivalent of the Ordnance Survey Department. Francis Towne, who is a dis-covery of recent years, was known in his own time, if he was known at all, as a meticulous and uninspired painter of country house prospects in oils, but his delicate watercolours or tinted draw-ings, in which mountain scenes were reduced to a series of plane surfaces (Pl. 27B) were representa-tive of a trend in the attitude to landscape. His purely linear method is in contrast to the style of John Robert Cozens whose romantic approach, emphasized by smoky washes which endowed his works with a depth and mystery (Pl. 27A), made an appeal to such men of taste as William Beck-ford. In 1794 Cozens went out of his mind and was cared for by Dr Thomas Monro, an able amateur draughtsman, the friend of Gainsborough and the patron of Thomas Girtin, J. M. W. Turner and John Varley. Until his early death in 1802, Girtin may well have appeared the most promising of these young artists and his brilliant use of glowing transparent colours prepares us for the mature work of Turner in the nineteenth century, though his attitude to landscape was entirely of his age (Pl. 27C). John Varley occa-sionally came near him in his large views of Wales but clung more closely to the topographical tradition.

Animal painting

In the earlier part of the eighteenth century it is hard to separate landscape from sporting paint-ing, for until his death in 1756 John Wootton had been pre-eminent in both *genres*. His successor, George Stubbs, was primarily a painter of animals, and as such he was considered beyond the pale of the Royal Academy until 1780, when he had dis-tinguished himself by exhibiting history pictures and portrait groups. But although he was ne-glected by the grand theorists, he seems to have attracted a wide and, no doubt, profitable patron-age. By scientific investigation he came to a full understanding of the anatomy not only of the horse but of man, all domestic and some wild animals; his curiosity also led him to study flora and enabled him to paint trees and grasses with accuracy. But his painting was characterized by something more than truth to nature, as may be seen from the subtle pattern of curves he derived from a horse, a man and a dog (Pl. 26B). Moreover, one feels that he painted men and beasts to emphasize the greater magnificence and beauty of the animal. In the history of English art he is an isolated figure, for he founded no school of animal painting and his influence is most notable in the work of Constable and the French romantics.

The nineteenth-century school of sporting and animal painting derives from Sawrey Gilpin, a younger and less able painter than Stubbs, who was also forced to exhibit histories in order to win the recognition of the Academicians. Lacking Stubbs' anatomical knowledge and feeling for supple line, he had a great liveliness and was the formative influence on Ben Marshall and James Ward, whose work was begun before the end of this period but belongs stylistically to the next. Gilpin stands above the general run of sporting painters of the time, notably the Sartorius tribe, whose paintings of Derby and St Leger winners, reproduced in countless prints, graced the walls of the horsier country houses.

History painting

Mention of the history paintings of Stubbs and Gilpin bring us to the form of art which, at some time, seems to have excited the ambition of nearly every artist of importance in this period. The belief that History was a higher form of art than portraiture or landscape had been established earlier in the century, and Reynolds gave it further encouragement in his *Discourses*, though his own eclectic, not to say plagiaristic, works in this vein had little but prestige value. Without the patronage of great institutions or a church (religious paintings are relatively few though more numerous than is commonly supposed) for which they might work on the grand scale, painters set up a wail that the 'highest' art languished unappreciated. In fact, most of the histories hung at the Academy appear to have been sold; the more important were widely diffused by engrav-

ings and Benjamin West seems to have made a fortune out of painting them.

When West arrived in England in 1763 he settled down to paint portraits and 'Poussin size' histories, winning an almost immediate success which brought him to royal notice and patronage. These works were little more than exercises after Gavin Hamilton, whom he had met in Rome; but he created a furore in 1771, when it was still customary to represent the heroic in classical dress, by painting the *Death of Wolfe* (Pl. 30B) in modern costumes, though in no whit relaxing his previous grand manner. The great popular success of this picture marked a turning point in history painting; from thenceforth classical subjects gave way to events from English history represented in the costume of their time. However, except for his abandonment of classical costume, West clung steadfastly to the established rules of the *genre* – notably by his formal composition, his reliance on poses derived from the Old Masters and his utter disregard for the known facts of the historical scene depicted. The next, and more important, step in the development of history painting was taken by J. S. Copley whose *Brooke Watson and the Shark* of 1778 broke every known rule in the cause of Truth. Copley followed up the success of this picture by painting the *Death of Major Pierson* (Pl. 31A), the *Death of Chatham* and the *Repulse of the Floating Batteries off Gibraltar*; all of which drew crowds when they were exhibited and enjoyed popularity as engravings.

Whereas West and Copley made a financial success of history painting, James Barry was less ready to conform to the desires of the time and was consequently a failure. His *chef d'œuvre*, the decoration of the lecture hall in the Royal Society of Arts is, however, the most considerable achievement of any British artist in the grand style in the century, and the scene which represents the culmination of the *Progress of Culture* (Pl. 30A) – the foundation of the Society – contains so great a concourse of the notabilities of the day that it may find a place even in a book devoted to the art of the English home. He is now remembered chiefly because of his influence on William Blake who considered him the rival of Raphael and Michelangelo, in which judgment he would have concurred. Another history painter to influence Blake was the Swiss Fuseli, whose wildly romantic talent derived subjects from Shakespeare. As Professor of painting at the Royal Academy from 1799 to 1825, he exerted a strong influence on the young painters whose work will be considered in the next volume of this series. But Fuseli is here important as an illustrator of Shakespeare and was widely known by engravings after the vast canvases which he, together with several other artists, contributed to Alderman Boydell's ambitious scheme for a Shakespeare Gallery.

Rowlandson and Gillray

Prints after the most admired history pictures of the time must frequently have found their way into comparatively humble homes where they might be seen among their natural antitheses, the caricatures of Rowlandson, Gillray, the amateur Bunbury and a host of others. Thomas Rowlandson's rollicking rumbustious productions, which call to mind scenes from Smollett, are an effective antidote to any impression of overmastering sensibility in the conduct of life in this period. His drawing of the confused rabble visiting the Academy must be before any writer who deals with the high or the exquisite turns of eighteenth century taste. He was, however, a perceptive satirist by no means without delicacy of feeling and touch, as is shown by his watercolour landscapes. Less able as an artist, but more virulent as a satirist, James Gillray is a more important figure in the history of caricature. With the rival policies of Pitt and Fox, the French wars and the *amours* and eccentricities of the Prince Regent as targets, he had the perfect field for his abilities, and presented the political and social background of the period in its utmost squalor.

Sculpture

Although we may expect to find paintings or prints after paintings in all but the humblest homes during this period, original sculpture re-

mained the prerogative of the wealthy; and the middle-class family who might collect pictures in a small way would seldom encounter it outside the church. The wealthier institutions and the grander houses would usually contain a few marble chimney-pieces and, perhaps, a bust, but figures, groups and low reliefs were reserved for the galleries of the wealthy. Those who could not afford this expensive taste would have to content themselves with reproductions of original works in pottery, terra-cotta or artificial stone. It was the invention of Coade stone in 1769 which placed moulded sculpture within the reach of a wide public, and this substance, which was impervious to frost, quickly found its way into the houses and gardens of all the propertied classes. The Coade factory at Lambeth, which sent its wares to such distant places as Poland, Russia, the West Indies and North America, could provide anything from an Ionic capital (13s.) or a frieze of griffins (10s. a foot) to a bust of Queen Elizabeth (3 guineas), a 'Psyche fitted up with spring tubes for light' (5 guineas) or a 'River God 9 feet high with an Urn through which a stream of water may be carried' (100 guineas). Some of these works were designed by the first artists of the day, John Bacon, Flaxman and Banks among them, and brought sculpture into the homes which could not afford the marbles with which we are here primarily concerned. The Coade factory was also responsible for many of the capitals, friezes, low reliefs and even pediments which are such a notable feature of the urban architecture of the early nineteenth century.

Large sculptured marble chimney-pieces were going out of fashion at the beginning of this period and it is significant that one of the most notable, that carved between 1762 and 1764 at a cost of £325 for the gallery of Corsham Court, was by Scheemakers, an artist most of whose career belongs to the first half of the century. A more delicate style of interior decoration introduced by the Adam brothers demanded less pompous ornaments, and the groaning caryatids were replaced by trim frames lightly carved in low relief or prettily inlaid with scagliola. Although they were sometimes supplied by the leading practitioners,

The Sculptor

Rowlandson inv

Fig. 1. Nollekens carving a Venus, by Thomas Rowlandson.
British Museum.

847

such works can hardly be described as sculpture. Above the fireplace or elsewhere in the room a decorative feature was occasionally made of a low relief such as that carved by John Deare in 1788 (Pl. 31B).

Deare's relief stands mid-way between the decorative and what may be called history sculpture, reflecting the more absurd neo-classical tendencies of the period. It may be doubted, however, whether his contemporaries would have shared our delighted surprise on learning that these elegant Greeks were none other than our own King Edward I and Queen Eleanor. This exquisite relief is proof, if proof were needed, that neo-classicism was a stronger and more durable force in sculpture than in English painting.

Long before this period began sculptors were commissioned to copy the celebrated antique statues in Florence and Rome, and when they were asked to produce more original works they were expected to carve such figures as could barely be distinguished from the fragments ingeniously put together by the Roman dealers. The restriction was a hard one for an original genius, but a sculptor of ability, like Nollekens, could often obtain a good effect as in the group of *Castor and Pollux* (Pl. 21B) which he executed for Shugborough Hall in 1767. In low reliefs and small figures, moreover, Thomas Banks, the most notable history sculptor of the period, was able to draw a strong personal style out of the neo-classic mode. In his *Falling Titan* (Pl. 32A) he achieved an effect of such remarkable grandeur that anyone familiar with the photograph must be astonished to find that the marble itself measures no more than 33 inches in height. In *Thetis Dipping the Infant Achilles in the Styx* he was able to show a three-dimensional quality, rare indeed in English sculpture, and the flowing lines of the figure seek to leap out of the classical pattern, restrained only by the careful balance of the limbs.

Among men of taste the popularity of busts increased considerably during this period, no less for the depiction of the living than for the commemoration of the great dead. No 'gentleman's library' was complete without its poets and philosophers,

the natural genii of the place. Busts of Pope, Milton, Locke and Newton were produced throughout the period, nor were Homer and Plato forgotten. Wilton carved a bust of Alfred the Great for Lord Radnor (who presented it to University College, Oxford); Bacon began his career with a bust of Ossian and later carved those of Dean Collet for St Paul's School and Inigo Jones for the Carpenters' Hall. Busts of the contemporary great were frequently repeated by their carvers, and Nollekens sold 74 replicas of his bust of Pitt at £120 a piece. Furthermore, busts were often incorporated in church monuments, as every reader of Gray's *Elegy* knows.

Most of the notable sculptors of the period seem to have tried their hands at portraiture, one of the most successful being John Bacon who, according to Cowper,

> Gives more than female heart to stone
> And Chatham's eloquence to marble lips.

But, as in the bust of George III (Pl. 32B), it was a precise imitation of draperies rather than animation of features which distinguished his work. In contrast, Joseph Nollekens, unquestionably the best portrait sculptor of the period, dispensed with or formalized the drapery, did away with the wig where possible and was consequently able to work unhampered in the neo-classic spirit. In portraits of ladies – the most notable is that of the Countess of Yarborough – he managed to perpetuate the beauty and freshness of his models, despite a tendency to make them so prettily sensitive that one expects them to blush at an unmannerly remark. His singularly penetrating busts of men – Laurence Sterne (Pl. 32c), Sir George Savile, Dr Johnson, Charles James Fox – are worthy to stand among all but the very best painted portraits of the period. Many other sculptors executed busts of excellent quality, like those of Pope Clement XIV and Gavin Hamilton (Pl. 32D) by Christopher Hewetson, but the majority of these have survived only in funerary monuments.

In this period church monuments grew larger and more numerous than ever before and one has the feeling that his way was indeed obscure whose memory was not graced with a tablet bearing at

848

least an urn. A legion of sculptors and stone-masons laboured to fill our gothic churches with an assemblage of classical figures representing not only the deceased but the Virtues, the Muses, and whoever else might be introduced to lament his death or support his tomb. Nor did sculptors find this work unprofitable – Nollekens charged £100 for the sketch of a monument and Bacon received no less than £6,000 for the memorial to Lord Chatham in Westminster Abbey. Indeed, to satisfy an enormous demand the sculptors were forced to employ an army of assistants and some of them never laid hand to chisel once their success had been established.

Monumental sculpture was at this time, dominated by neo-classicism which permitted such delightful incongruities as the figure of Admiral Holmes, in breast-plate and toga, resting his hand upon an unmistakably eighteenth-century cannon, or Sir John and Lady Salusbury who appear to have strayed out of Addison's *Cato* or some long forgotten classical tragedy. There was, nevertheless, a strain of naturalism which found its most notable expression in low reliefs of land and sea fights and flourished towards the end of the period when modern dress began to make its return. Large monuments gave sculptors the chance to include whole concourses of figures bewailing the subject, but when they worked on a smaller scale they usually had to content themselves with a limited stock of symbols: urns, extinguished torches, wreaths and, if all else failed, what John Bacon called 'our old friend the pelican'.

In the early years of the nineteenth century no sculptor was more versatile in providing monuments for a wide market than John Flaxman, whose work ranges from the gigantic Nelson memorial in St Paul's Cathedral to numerous little tablets in country churches. Although his classicism had been more thoroughly assimilated than that of any other sculptor of the time, he permitted himself to depart from the strictest rules when the occasion offered. His heroic figure of Nelson is by no means without a touch of naturalism in the head and his charming relief of Dr Warton and his scholars, in Winchester cathe-dral, is as fresh and vivid as it is unsentimental. Moreover, he was far better equipped to treat the nude than any previous English sculptor, as may be seen from his figure of Death on Lord Mans-field's monument in St Paul's; but his technique is more of low relief than sculpture in the round. It is significant that he is the only English sculptor to win a measure of European fame, albeit this was due more to his linear illustrations to Homer and Dante than to his carvings.

The beginning of the nineteenth century

This brief survey of late Georgian painting and sculpture comes to its close in 1810, when the future of the arts was regarded with much less hope than it had been fifty years before. For more than a decade, Europe had been closed to the student and the collector, though the needs of the latter were amply supplied (as a result of the Revolutionary wars) by a greater importation of old master paintings than ever before. Martin Archer Shee complained that the country was 'glutted with pictures from the best that genius can boast to the worst that fraud can manufacture; until all the wealth of individuals disposable for objects of virtue has been diverted into channels from which our native arts can derive no benefit'. For lack of patronage alone, he argued, English art was sinking into a decline; yet it was from no want of employment that Flaxman and Lawrence were rising to occupy the places of leading sculptor and portrait painter; and, on the other hand, it was from no spectacular acts of munificence that Constable and Turner were to become our greatest landscape painters. As the attitude to art, to nature, to life, was changed by the French revolution and the subsequent wars, so new artists rose to reflect new tastes. Sensibility gave way to subjective romanticism: the real landscape took the place of the imaginative or improved; and in painting, no less than in poetry, the visionary was making his appearance.

Although he belongs to the nineteenth century, William Blake, who styled himself a visionary, had deep roots in the previous era. The contemporary artists who most influenced him were Fuseli, Flaxman and Barry, who derived much of their inspiration from Italy. He was one of the first to dispute the authority of Reynolds' academic precepts as laid down in the *Discourses*, but was none the less inspired to borrow postures from Scamozzi and Michelangelo. His poetry, no less than his painting, showed him to be the fieriest of spirits; and yet he illustrated Blair's *The Grave*, a poem redolent with the distant sensibility of the earlier eighteenth century. Furthermore, in his study of medieval sculpture and manuscript illumination he showed himself to be a child of the Gothic Revival. His illustration of the tomb in Blair's *The Grave* (Fig. 2) shows at once how much he was of the eighteenth century and yet how far he looked beyond it.

BIBLIOGRAPHY

The essential book for the study of painting in this period is *Painting in Britain 1530–1790* by E. K. Waterhouse (1953) which is provided with an invaluable bibliography. *A Century of Painters of the English School* by R. and S. Redgrave (ed. Ruthven Todd, 1949) is useful for the last two decades of this period.

The *Dictionary of British Sculptors* by Rupert Gunnis (1953), the fullest and best account of sculpture in the period, is well supplied with bibliographies for the individual sculptors.

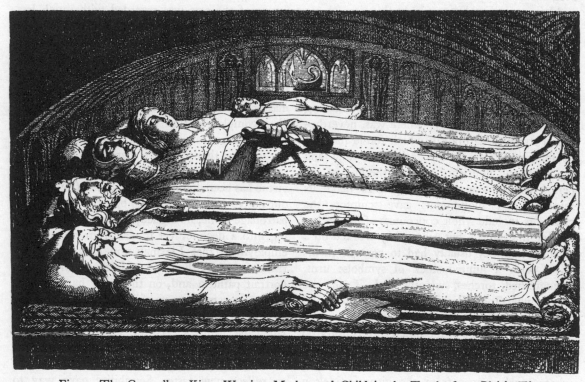

Fig. 2. The Counsellor, King, Warrior, Mother and Child in the Tomb, from Blair's *The Grave*, illustrated by William Blake. *British Museum*.

Silver and Plate

GERALD TAYLOR

Changes in style evolve slowly and to a great extent almost imperceptibly so that no sudden transformation in the forms of plate can be expected to coincide with the accession of George III in 1760 or with the year 1811 when the Prince of Wales became Prince Regent. It will, however, be shown that during the intervening half-century the Rococo style was outmoded by the Adam style (a discussion of the characteristics of which forms the chief part of the following contribution) and that the latter in its turn gave place to what is now known as the Regency style. The transition from Rococo to Adam, naturally later in plate than in architecture, began about 1765, and was, with few exceptions, completed before 1775. The emergence of the Regency style from that of Adam, perhaps more correctly described as an evolution, during the last quarter of the century, was accomplished by 1810. It must be understood that these generalizations apply only to the metropolitan silversmiths and do not relate to the work of provincial or American craftsmen.

As in its development the light Rococo style accumulated supplementary ornaments of naturalistic flowers (Pl. 33A), classical figures, or exotic *chinoiseries*, so the succeeding Adam style, likewise essentially light, assimilated Gothic, Chinese, Egyptian and emblematic motifs taken from nature, as well as more elaborate and massively conceived forms and ornaments selected from equally diverse and remote sources. An analogy may be made with the development, though it continued over a much longer period of time, of imperial Roman architecture from the purer styles preceding it.

The decline of so contrived and sophisticated a style as the Rococo was protracted by the adoption of foreign and quite unrelated motifs. With increasing momentum the inevitable reaction of 'taste' against the Rococo coincided with the introduction of a quite incompatible vocabulary of motifs, – neo-classical, positive, rational – which conformed with the underlying tradition of classical idealism that since the Renaissance had never been entirely submerged. The introduction of neo-classical motifs and forms into the silversmiths' repertoire can be noted in the capitals of western Europe shortly after the accession of George III and about ten years before Louis XVI came to the throne in France, where he gave his name to the new style. The designs of plate became strictly symmetrical, their proportions based on those of architecture, and their ornaments impersonal, regular, and stylized to a high degree.

The approach to and independent studies of classical remains by many intelligent and some brilliant men of the period, such as Winckelmann, Adam and Piranesi, were perhaps more informed and penetrating than those of their predecessors in the late fifteenth and the sixteenth centuries. Nevertheless even the best-informed contemporary students made some attributions of artifacts to centuries and civilizations, which might seem arbitrary to our eyes. The practical application to plate of their findings, however, at a time when a greater number of educated persons were more familiar with classical history, ideas and imagery, than ever before or even today, met with widespread understanding and approbation. The beginnings of analytical study of classical ornament at this period had produced a clearer conception of its principles and effected a wider application of its details to the arts.

Thence it was often possible for the designers of plate to apply much authentic ornament to vessels whose proportions were based on what were then accepted as the correct classical forms. Their task required more imagination than, for example, that of architects, not only because the principal hoards of classical plate had yet to be discovered, but also because nearly all of the classical artifacts illustrated in published works had been made for ceremonies and uses no longer current, and the forms of which were not readily adaptable to the requirements of the eighteenth century. Indeed 'Adam' plate was rather inspired by, if not deduced from, the better-known remains of architecture, sculpture and vessels of bronze or pottery only.

The introduction of the Adam style, its swift ascendancy and dominance for two decades, were followed by a gradual process of development and transformation culminating in the Regency style. Predominantly Graeco-Roman, it also included Gothic, Rococo and Egyptian terms so that by the beginning of the Regency period it may be said that no coherent and distinguishable style existed for plate, but rather an eclectic combination of forms and motifs suitable for each and any particular purpose.

At this time, British plate was being exported abroad and began to influence the wares of Scandinavia and the Iberian Peninsula. Considerable quantities were also shipped to the United States of America, whose independence, acknowledged in 1782, coincided with westward expansion and whose rich resources heralded the future of a flourishing silver industry which had roots in the British elements of Boston and Philadelphia, and among the Dutch immigrant craftsmen in New York. Moreover, by the Treaty of Commerce in 1786, imports of English silverware were again permitted into France and, finally, at the Revolution the work of the Parisian goldsmith whose standard of quality hitherto had command of the world's market – in which weight of metal, excellence of workmanship and well-proportioned designs were considered of greater importance than price – gave way to the productions of London.

In widespread ways commercial and industrial progress follows the fortunes of peace and war and both have direct repercussions on the craft of the silversmith. At the time in question, moreover, there were men of strong character and inventive mind who had no small influence on the developing industry; for the manufacture of plate, as of so many other products, was indeed becoming industrialized. Instead of being hammered, sheets of metal could be rolled from the ingot; stamping and piercing operations could be quickly performed by machinery and without the aid of skilled craftsmen.

Among the more enterprising figures in the rising industry was Matthew Boulton [1] (1728–1809), whose business relations with Watt, Adam and Wedgwood kept him in the forefront of industrial pioneering in many fields almost throughout the reign. He began to produce in mass roughly-finished component parts of plate to be sold for assembly by independent workers. Engineering and metallurgical advances not only improved production machinery but led to new fields for expansion. Bronze- or copper-gilt had been common in earlier centuries, and ormolu was in wide current use; but at this date a method of fusing a copper ingot between two thick silver plates and rolling out the whole into a thin composite sandwich, enabled objects to be made of this cheaper and lighter substitute which to all intents and purposes had the appearance of solid silver. Invented in Sheffield and first applied to the making of buttons about 1743, the idea was gradually applied to larger objects and finally industrialized on a large scale by the partners Boulton and Fothergill in Birmingham. Sheffield Plate, the name by which it came to be, and is still

[1] H. W. Dickinson, *Matthew Boulton*, 1937, pp. 51–3 and *passim*.

known, was made in increasing quantities by a number of other firms until the middle of the succeeding century.[2]

The rise of the factory presented a threat to the livelihood of small workers who followed traditional methods of production. Many of them were induced to specialize in a particular type of work, especially flat ware and candlesticks, while others, unable to hold their own, became employees of large concerns. The cleavage between the plate-worker and the retailing goldsmith grew wider. The large and prosperous firm was enabled to attract and employ the more outstanding designers and craftsmen and the fact, for example, that there is reason to believe Matthew Boulton had an interest in schools for designers in Birmingham is significant.

The growing threat of the Birmingham and Sheffield factories to the established quasi-monopoly of the London goldsmiths (as well as to the older provincial centres of the craft), as represented by Boulton's activities, was more than met by the rapid rise to prominence of Paul Storr (freeman 1792; d. 1834) and by the immense size of the Rundell–Bridge–Storr–Mortimer–Hunt and Roskell concern – which is reputed to have employed 1,500 hands at one time – as well as by the considerable productions of other large firms, the Batemans, the Hennells, or the Parker–Wakelin–Taylor–Garrard succession. London was never in danger of losing its lead either in the weight of plate produced, or, more importantly, in the quality of its design and execution.

Boulton's persistent efforts for the establishment of assay offices at Birmingham and Sheffield – the latter ironically was given as its mark a *crown* which Boulton has used on his own earlier plate and Sheffield Plate – were however justified by the distances of other provincial offices, notably of York, Chester (where Boulton used to take his wares), or Newcastle from the growing centres of production. At Exeter the craft had dwindled from the middle of the century. The evidence of

the assay-masters of these last four offices before a commission of 1773 shows a slackness in administration, which was as much due to lack of supervision from the Lord Chancellor's office and the Royal Mint as to the inadequacy of their own small establishments. Edinburgh remained the principal Scottish office although the importance of Glasgow increased considerably. In Dublin the craft flourished, as may be judged from the fact that 136 goldsmiths registered their names, if not all their marks, in compliance with the statute of 1783.

To satisfy the demands of the growing middle classes, goods of inferior weight and simple ornament, in silver, Sheffield plate [3] and Britannia metal [4] were produced in quantity, and throughout the reign the production of plate and with it of course, the number of plate-workers increased immensely. Nevertheless it was naturally the ruling class with its international connections which continued to order the largest quantities of the finest plate and in the newest fashion. The King himself patronized Thomas Heming (cf. Pl. 33A) but his preference for the quietness of domestic life reduced requirements for formal State plate to little or none.[5] Indeed, almost the only purchase of any consequence made by George III was of a set of French plate, by Henri Auguste. His heir, on the other hand, played a very active and even over-liberal role in setting the fashion in plate as he did in so many other aspects of fashionable life. It was a curiously prophetic circumstance that the Prince of Wales was offered the Freedom of the Goldsmiths' Company when only a boy of nine, but it was not until a separate establishment was set up for him in Carlton House, at the age of 18, in 1781, that he provided confirmation of his extravagant leanings. Perhaps the first piece of plate he acquired personally was the cup by

[2] Paul Storr's Galvanic Goblet (1814) heralded the electro-plating industry, developed especially by Messrs. Elkington. See C. C. Oman, and N. M. Penzer, *Country Life*, CXV (4 March 1954), p. 606.

[3] The most comprehensive work on the subject is F. Bradbury's *History of Old Sheffield Plate*, 1912.

[4] See G. B. Hughes, *Country Life*, CXIV (20 August 1953), p. 562.

[5] E. A. Jones, *The Gold and Silver of Windsor Castle*, 1911, *passim*. See also *Catalogue of the Exhibition of Royal Plate*, held in the Victoria and Albert Museum in 1954, and the *Small Picture Book* of the same title (No. 37), which illustrates it.

R. Salmon presented to him on his attaining his majority. Just after the turn of the century, three important royal services were ordered, the Jamaica, the Egyptian and the Grand. The first was commissioned by the Jamaica Assembly from Rundell's, and made by Digby Scott and Benjamin Smith in 1803–4 to be presented to the Duke of Clarence (later William IV); the service included four soup-tureens, eight sauce-tureens and six ice-pails, all decorated with panels of naval and military trophies. The Egyptian Service was assembled in the same years, but was the product of three workshops. It includes four soup-tureens by Paul Storr, eight salts and twelve sauce-boats by Scott and Smith, in which much of the ornament was derived from ancient Egypt, though intermingled with it were the prevalent Graeco-Roman motifs.

The assembling of the Grand Service, begun by the Prince of Wales in 1805, and continued for a quarter of a century until his death, was in keeping with the practice of most of the sovereigns of Europe, particularly of Denmark and Portugal, who at this period were amassing magnificent plate.

Commissions from wealthy private individuals and from institutions were on an extensive and almost as lavish a scale. A few examples, all of them manufactured by Paul Storr, will suffice to illustrate the fact: the gold font made (1797–8) for the christening of the eldest son of the fourth Duke of Portland; Lord Desborough's dinner service of eighty-two pieces (1797–8); and 125 plates for the Goldsmiths' Company (1808–11). Perhaps the most interesting and important group of commissions is that of plate for presentation to the heroes of the day, the victorious admirals and generals whose successes in battle came as such relief to the overwhelming campaigns conducted by Napoleon. Lloyd's, with their especial concern with war at sea, made presentations after Howe's victory of 1794 and again from their Patriotic Fund after the Battle of Trafalgar (1805) to some of the senior officers engaged. One of these vases (Pl. 35), made by Scott and Smith to the design of John Flaxman, ingeniously combines classical motifs with contemporary emblems: acanthus leaves round the surbase alternate with acorns rep-

resenting the ships of English oak; 'Britannia triumphant' is seated holding a figure of Victory in her right hand; on the pedestal, formed by the cover, stands a finely modelled lion, between two volute handles, in which the paterae have been replaced by Tudor roses, and round which are applied rope-mouldings. An equally eclectic approach is seen in a parcel-gilt sauce-tureen of the Deccan Service in the Wellington Museum at Apsley House [6] (Pl. 37B) presented to Sir Arthur Wellesley (later Duke of Wellington) by the officers of the Army of the Deccan. Ornamented with a band of interlacing laurel wreaths and with two realistic intertwined serpents for each handle, the bowl is raised up on four elephants, placed back to back on a circular base, which is also ornamented with a band of laurel in low relief; on the broad rayed pedestal sits an oriental figure beneath an umbrella. In spite of the introduction and realistic rendering of these exotic motifs, this set of tureens of 1806 retains a predominantly classical feeling. By contrast, however, a more romantic impression is produced by a parcel-gilt candelabrum in the same museum. At each corner of the heavy triangular plinth the concave sides of which are ornamented with battle scenes in low relief, sits a soldier in contemplative attitude; above them on a fluted tambour four other soldiers, also in contemporary uniform, stand reaching up to support a fasces, from which spring six curved leafy branches, each bearing a socket at its tip. In spite of its height of 31 inches, it lacks the monumental quality that is evident in the centre-piece commissioned from Paul Storr (Pl. 40) and presented to Wellesley a few years later by the field officers of the Army of Portugal; only a little taller, it is by contrast a restrained and monumental work. A massive but graceful two-handled vessel of low proportions, surmounted by a finial figure of Victory posed on a globe, is set on a large square plinth magnificently engraved, at the corners of which are piled muskets and flags; the remainder of the ornament is restricted to the neo-classical repertoire and is therefore without

[6] Victoria and Albert Museum, *Small Picture Book*, *No. 33, Regency Domestic Silver.*

special associations; it includes gadrooning, laurel leaves, both conventionally wreathed and more naturally rendered, lanceolate and acanthus leaves, and fleshy vine-tendrils for the handles.

Although the Duke of Wellington was not appointed Ambassador to the French Court until 1814, his issue of plate contained much of an earlier date; this he retained as a perquisite, as had other ambassadors, though he was one of the last to be allowed to do so. Among it is a gilt sugar-vase of 1810–11 by Benjamin and James Smith (Pl. 39) which closely resembles a set of eight of 1809–10 in the Royal Collection, and four others made five years earlier by Scott and Smith for Earl Howe. In their ornament it seems that Tatham's strictures (see below, p. 856) had already been heeded, or even anticipated, inasmuch as the luxurious profusion of Imperial Roman ornament is there represented to the full on a domestic vessel, no more than eight inches in height, the design of which would lose little of its monumentality if cut in stone many times as high. From the same issue and from the same year, but by Paul Storr to the order of Rundell's, is a centre-piece which serves as a fruit-bowl, one of a number of similar vessels, set in a circular basket supported by three caryatids, each standing on the arm of a triangular base raised on satyrs' masks with swags of fruit between. Here no extrinsic motif had to be introduced to dispel the purely classical impression imparted by the tripod form and the three caryatids, each with her two thyrsi crossed in saltire with those of her neighbours.

If William Kent (1684–1748) had shown the advantages of designing a house and its interior furnishings as a single entity, Robert Adam believed that an architect should be responsible for every detail, and accordingly produced designs for all kinds of furniture, among them articles of plate.[7] When in Rome in 1756, Adam found Allan Ramsay, a former acquaintance, who had just published his *Dialogue on Taste* in friendly rebuttal of Hogarth's *Analysis of Beauty* (1753).

Whereas the empirical and pugnacious Hogarth intended 'to fix the fluctuating ideas of taste', his book was rather in the nature of a belated apology of the Baroque and Rococo styles (indeed, the candlesticks he illustrated were those in fashion when he was still apprenticed as an engraver on silver) with continuous belittlements of classical art. Ramsay, on the other hand, spoke out for Gothic, and being drawn into the Graeco-Roman controversy, next preferred Greek to Roman. In spite both of occasional studies of Gothic remains (similar to, but less advanced than those of classical remains) and of some enthusiasts who built in imitation of the Gothic style, its motifs were much more widely used in furniture than in plate – even in church plate until A. W. N. Pugin's advocacy coincided with the rise of the Tractarians. Indeed it was only in repetitive pierced work that pointed or cusped tracery or quatrefoils were used, particularly on the sides of salt-cellars and sugar-bowls, and even then perhaps derivatively from the pierced galleries on tables of the Chippendale gothic vogue.

Objects from ancient Egypt had no English protagonist, though many were illustrated in de Caylus' *Receuil*. Opportunities were given for the use of Egyptian motifs in English plate when presentations were required for the victors in the Egyptian battles.[8] Thereafter Egyptian motifs were sometimes mingled with others of classical origin, though they were never popular.

From further East, naturalistic motifs were derived from the Indian scene (see above, Pl. 37B) and elsewhere, but with regard neither for their local significance nor indeed for the styles of indigenous art. *Chinoiseries* retained for a short time their old allure, appropriately on tea-caddies (Pl. 36A), tea-urns, tea-pots and epergnes until the discontinuance of the Rococo style. But for a short time Chinese symbols, scarcely studied and little understood, like the rest of Eastern art, were sometimes engraved on tea-caddies during the transition from the Rococo to the Adam style (Pl. 36A).

[7] Some of his designs are preserved in Sir John Soane's Museum, see Pl. 34.

[8] E.g. the Battle of the Nile Cup, in the National Maritime Museum, Greenwich; repr. N. M. Penzer, *Paul Storr*, 1954, p. 106, Pl. XIV.

c. 1790

c. 1800

Fig. 1. Tureens.

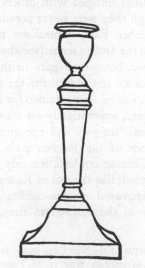

Fig. 2. Candlestick of a type common 1775–90.

Classical antiquities had never been without their devotees and students – even in the most anti-classical style of all, Rococo, some classical motifs were introduced. In addition to the predominantly classical basis of University studies, the illustrated publications of Winckelmann, Piranesi, Stuart and Revett, de Caylus, Adam and others during the latter half of the eighteenth century [9] prepared the way for its revival. In a narrower circle, the *Discourses* of the first President of the Royal Academy, and the writings of Fuseli, its Professor of Painting, helped to instil in students of design a high regard for the finest works of antiquity. It is significant that the best known designers of plate, John Flaxman (1755–1827), his intimate friend Thomas Stothard (1755–1844), Charles Catton (1756–1819) (until his emigration to the United States in 1806) and others should have studied there. Moreover, Flaxman, like the Adam brothers, spent several years in Italy, and, after working for Josiah Wedgwood, undertook designs for plate and attracted the attention of Philip Rundell and his partners. The neo-classical style was indeed deliberately fostered as a matter of business by a nucleus of influential employers, including Adam, Boulton, Wedgwood and Rundell. In particular, the perceptive and enterprising Boulton realized that even if his own education was deficient, taste played an important part in the lives of those with money, and he therefore set himself to ensure that it was evident in his plate, Sheffield plate, ormolu, cut-steel jewellery, and other fine products.

Another theorist, the architect Charles Heathcot Tatham (1772–1842), published the first book of English designs specially for plate [10] as opposed to those intended for more general purposes – in which he complained that 'instead of Massiveness, the principal characteristic of good Plate, light and insignificant forms have prevailed, to the utter exclusion of all good ornament whatever'. It is true that much plate of the later

[9] Their works are briefly discussed and their contemporary influence assessed by J. Lees-Milne, *The Age of Adam*, 1947, pp. 42–56.

[10] *Designs for Ornamental Plate*, 1806.

Hanoverian period was intended to appear light, and was indeed often very light in weight for its size, but it was by no means devoid of good ornament. Nevertheless as a champion of Roman architecture, Tatham's arguments may have helped to direct designers towards the Regency style.

More recently, J. Hambridge and L. D. Caskey [11] have convincingly demonstrated that Greek potters designed and made their wares, as the architects their public buildings, accurately in accordance with two systems of proportion which are capable of infinite variation and yet are easily delineated with the aid of dividers and a ruler. Geometrical proportions were much the more frequently employed, arithmetical proportions scarcely at all. One of the former recurs very frequently, namely that of the golden, or divine, section; it was revived during the Renaissance and used, to cite but one example, in a silver-gilt cup (belonging to Dr C. H. Josten) made in Nuremberg in the later sixteenth century. It is not surprising therefore that it was again applied to plate, as well as ceramics, during the neo-classical revival and an illustration is provided by Boileau's design of 1800 for the Doncaster Race Cup.[12] Nevertheless, these isolated examples are given here to emphasize the completeness of the return to ancient inspiration and should not be considered to reflect anything like a universal attention to these principles of design.

Much greater evidence is available about the ornament of neo-classical plate. Much of its permanent value and a strong reason for its repeated use and revival lie in the fact that for the most part the motifs represented, though in a style or on an object that can be meticulously dated, are themselves natural, and therefore timeless and impersonal.

The wide range of classical motifs were ultimately derived from vegetable, animal, geometrical and artificial forms. In the first and largest group are included the acanthus leaf and the lanceolate leaf, usually placed side by side as a calyx or surbase; the bay or laurel leaf, both braided as a garland and in a continuous band; the leaf as a sheath at the springing of handles or applied to them; vine leaves and tendrils and bunches of grapes; anthemion, honeysuckle, lotus, or palmette; the oak leaf and acorn, as a finial; and the husk, usually graduated, in swags or pendent; heads of rams, satyrs (Pl. 38), lions, etc.; skulls of oxen, small infants, often incorporated in rinceaux, and other human figures in low or full relief in imitation of antique sculpture, though often in contemporary attire. In the second group the fret (key-pattern or meander) appears in great variety, as well as fluting (spiral, or straight, deep or shallow, tapering or regular), gadrooning, guilloche, and beading (paralleled by the half-pearl borders of watches, brooches, rings, etc.). In the last group medallions, containing imitations of antique busts or figures, oval and circular paterae, festoons of drapery, and ribbons, and the wave-pattern.

These ornaments were carried out in all the techniques available to the goldsmith. Gilding or parcel-gilding of important pieces was frequent (Pl. 37B, 40); solid gold was rarely used. Enamelling was much used on watch-cases and other jewellery. The weight of metal employed, like the quality of workmanship, varies from the lavish and magnificent to the mean and skimped. Boulton once wrote to Fothergill, 'How can I expect the public to countenance rubbish from Soho, while they can secure sound and perfect work from any other quarter?' There are many large castings of finely modelled and finished figures; the standard of chasing and embossing had never been surpassed in London. Where the commission demanded, nothing was spared to produce the desired effect.

Better known by name and far more numerous than the designers or writers are the goldsmiths themselves who effected their ideas. The life and works of the greatest maker, the last great silversmith, Paul Storr, are the subject of a monograph.[13] He was apprenticed to the Swedish immigrant Andrew Fogelberg, whose London work dates from 1770 and is notable for applied silver

[11] L. D. Caskey, *Geometry of Greek Vases*, 1922.

[12] Victoria and Albert Museum, *Small Picture Book, No. 35, Adam Silver*, Pl. 30.

[13] N. M. Penzer, *Paul Storr, the last of the Goldsmiths*, 1954.

c. 1790

c. 1800

c. 1810

c. 1810

Fig. 3. Teapots of the period.

858

cameos, an idea perhaps derived from his neighbour James Tassie (1735–99), though it was not unknown in Tudor, early Stuart and Huguenot plate. When Storr obtained his freedom in 1792 his work resembled his master's, just as de Lamerie's had resembled that of Harache, but in the next five years during his Piccadilly partnership with Frisbee and perhaps through Tassie's introductions, he had established a reputation for himself as a craftsman of outstanding talent. The mastery displayed in the Portland font (see above, p. 854) was maintained in all his later work (Pl. 40). After that of Paul Storr, perhaps the reputation of Hester Bateman (cf. Pl. 37A) is next in public estimation. Yet there were many other equally original and distinguished individuals and many firms more productive of fine plate than that conducted by the Batemans between 1774 and 1840. Thomas Heming (cf. Pl. 33A) was given the Royal warrant and was responsible for much excellent plate in the Rococo and French Louis XV styles, and latterly in the neo-classical style. In this appointment his successors were the partners Rundell, Bridge and Rundell, with whom Storr was the principal plate worker; they not only had their individual and joint marks but engraved their names followed by AVRIFICES REGIS ET PRINCIPIS WALLIAE LONDINI FECERUNT. Other firms who put out work were Portal and Gearing, and later Green and Ward, both of Ludgate Hill.

Parallel, but not necessarily connected, developments were affecting not only the processes of manufacture and sale of plate, but also the vessels for which it was used. As some social practices were discontinued and others were introduced, so the manufacture of plate for the former purposes gradually ceased and the development of new forms for the latter was begun. A noticeable result of the search for homogeneous domestic interiors is the development of matching services, tea-services, dinner-services of considerable size with matching plates and dishes, matching tureens for soup and sauce, and huge sets of matching cutlery. An extreme example is the magnificent Howe double breakfast service of 1812–13 by Storr, of 16 pieces, weighing together nearly 800 ounces.

Other innovations were 'argyles' (small vessels with lid and spout for serving gravy), goblets, stirrup-cups, honey-pots, tea-urns, toasted-cheese dishes, toast-racks, egg-cups and stands, and cruet stands with glass bottles for several kinds of sauce in addition to wine and vinegar. Some vessels like the 'argyle' were experimental; others, like the tea-urn, stirrup-cup and toasted-cheese dish were in vogue for a comparatively short time; but most of them had come to stay.

Without reference to ecclesiastical and municipal plate, the variety of uses for which silver was found suitable at this time is very large when compared with any other material; tea-cups and saucers were exclusively made of ceramics which rivalled the previous metals or their baser substitutes for many other uses; glass was unchallenged in the service of wine; on decanters and sauce-bottles, silver played a subsidiary part in their embellishment but a superior role in salt-cellars, mustard-pots, sugar-pails and cream pails. Wood was a useful ancillary, as were ivory and cane, for handles of tea- and coffee-pots, or the base of coasters. A list of the principal items made of silver, entirely or partly, is set out at this point.

Tankards, mugs, goblets, stirrup-cups; punch-bowls and ladles; wine-coolers, ice-pails; wine-funnels; wine-labels; wine-coasters (decanter stands); epergnes; centre-pieces; baskets; toast-racks; soup-tureens, mazarine-dishes (fitted with a strainer, for fish, etc.), entrée-dishes; supper-dishes; toasted-cheese dishes; serving dishes, and covers, of various sizes; plates for soup, meat and other courses; sauce-tureens and sauce-boats; 'argyles'; dish-crosses; dish-rings; cruet-frames and fittings; sugar-castors; salt-cellars; pepper-castors or pots; mustard-pots; salt- and mustard-spoons; knives, forks and spoons; ladles for soup and gravy; fish-slices and trowels; asparagus-servers; grape-scissors; skewers; marrow-scoops; candlesticks; candelabra; chamber-sticks; taper-sticks; trays; tea-pots; tea-caddies and caddy-spoons; tea-urns; coffee-pots; milk-jugs; hot-water jugs with or without lamps; basins, baskets and bowls for sugar; sugar-nippers and tongs; tea-spoons; inkstands; waiters (salvers); hand-bells;

pap-boats; and a variety of indeterminate small wares which come near to being jewellery, such as snuff-boxes, mounts of walking-sticks, watch-cases and chatelaines.

The complex Rococo forms, with their irregular and asymmetrical shapes (Pl. 33A, B) gave place to simpler ones based on the circle, oval, square, hexagon and octagon. In their purest forms, they were found to provide suitable outlines for trays and salvers.

For some of the objects listed above it was possible to use the shape most characteristic of the period, notably for race-cups, large and small ornamental vases, tea-urns, jugs, hot-water jugs, pepper-castors and even 'argyles' (see Pl. 34).

A second shape with close affinities, suitable for vases, urns and tea-pots, offers an instructive comparison between plate and ceramics. In the Victoria and Albert Museum are a silver-gilt vase of 1775 by John Arnell (Pl. 38) and a vase of black basaltes ware, marked 'Wedgwood' [14] and made about a decade later. They differ a little in ornament and proportion (the cover of the latter is less exactly a hemisphere), yet the oviform shape, the handles, the striped effect and the swags of drapery offer striking parallels. Of about 1775 — and thus corresponding in date with the silver vase — is another marked 'Wedgwood and Bentley' of agate-ware, which has the same form of handles, though it is less remarkably similar in other respects.

For soup and sauce-tureens the former vase was compressed in both elevation and plan; the resulting form (Pl. 36B) was more pleasing when the urn was swept upwards towards each loop-handle (Fig. 1), one of many forms adapted for the salt-cellar.

For many vessels simple geometrical forms were introduced, the pure cube for tea-caddies (Pl. 36A), and the cylinder, less often round (for 'argyles') than oval (for tea-pots, tea-caddies and salts) (Pl. 37A). Although these basic shapes assumed varied accretions of superficial ornament and necessary components, such as handles, finials and spouts, during the next two decades, they

[14] W. B. Honey, *Wedgwood Ware*, 1948, Pl. 57, and also for the second comparison Pl. B.

themselves underwent more fundamental modifications by variation of their proportions and elaboration of their forms. Thus, an examination of this fundamental trend in relation to the tea-pot reveals that not only are there numerous variations in the oval plan, but also many elaborations of the superstructure with low domes and mouldings (Pl. 37A), of the sides and spout with curves, so that by the early years of the nineteenth century the only horizontal line left is often that around the base. The tureen, and with it the related forms of salt-cellar, was likewise the subject of many variations until the basic shape of both tureen and tea-pot became almost identical, that is to say of a complex bombé form on a rounded oblong plan. Efforts to design a matching tea-service perhaps influenced this trend strongly, in that the conflicting shapes of tea-pot, sugar-bowl and milk-jug found at the accession of George III were resolved by using the shape of the sugar-bowl as the master design, with its two like handles at opposite sides or at each end; on the milk jug, which was of a different size, one handle was replaced by an everted lip; on the tea-pot, the handle was suitably modified to afford insulation, while an opposed curving spout was added, usually tapering and of a compressed section; the shape of the coffee-pot was achieved either by erecting a tall concave neck on a body matching that of the tea-pot or by placing on a foot, or feet, a heightened body of similar form with handle and spout suitably heightened. However attractive these simplifications may appear, the diversity of designs made during this period, even within the limits of these four vessels, was such that a reference to the numerous exceptions will result in pointless confusions.

To other objects a variety of shapes derived more or less faithfully from antique remains were found suitable. One of the more straightforward adaptations, quite in harmony with the spirit of the neo-classical revival, was the stirrup-cup in the shape of a fox's head. The forms of the calyx-krater and volute-krater lent themselves with scarcely any alteration for wine coolers or presentation pieces respectively. Even small antique oil-lamps were copied from ceramic or bronze prototypes, perhaps more in a spirit of antiquarianism than for actual use.

From classical candelabra and altars, in stone and metal, were derived many tripod motifs. Classical architecture provided suitable designs for some objects, notably the candlestick to which Corinthian and composite columns were easily adapted. A term (inverted obelisk) surmounted by an urn for the socket was no less successfully and widely used (Fig. 2). The deep helmet-shaped jug, the four-legged salt-cellar or sugar-bowl, and tripod jugs bear further witness to the pervasive influence of ancient forms.

On the other hand it must be mentioned that many recent and traditional forms were retained for plate in constant domestic use, notably for sauce-boats, castors, salt-cellars or tankards.

The 'Hanoverian' form of spoons and forks gave way to the 'Old English' by a reversal of the curve on the tail of the handle and a lightening of the structure due to the use of machinery. The edges of the handles were often beaded, threaded or 'feathered', and their upper side ornamented with bright-cut engraving, the most typical decorative technique of the time. It was by no means confined to flat-ware, but is seldom found in conjunction with any other ornament except piercing. Its shallow curving facets enliven the patterns with sparkling reflections, in a manner impossible with the deep channels cut into the metal according to the traditional technique, still then used for lettering, coats of arms, and crests.

During the later years of the period form and ornament reveal other characteristics which foreshadow the full flowering of the Regency period, as well as combinations of Romanticism, further flung eclecticism and other influences that are not generally obvious until the nineteenth century was well advanced.

Pottery and Porcelain

PATRICK SYNGE-HUTCHINSON

The decade immediately following the first half of the eighteenth century may be regarded as a period at which the ceramic craft of England, having emerged from the pre-porcelain era, was about to establish itself on a basis that would enable it to play no small part in the movement which, during the next 50 years, was to effect the gradual transformation of this country from a rural into an industrial community.

The setting up of factories making soft-paste porcelain at Bow and Chelsea, from about 1745 onwards, was soon followed by undertakings at Bristol, Worcester, Derby, Longton Hall, Liverpool and Lowestoft, all of which, unlike their principal rivals at Meissen and Sèvres, relied on private enterprise rather than Royal patronage for their establishment.

In Staffordshire the coming of the china factories had imparted a fresh impetus to the making of earthenware figures and other wares, for, whereas the earlier potters had created a style whose charm lay in its native character and lack of sophistication, a new movement was now beginning which, gaining in scope and strength, was to bring Staffordshire, through the innovations of Josiah Wedgwood, an international market that has survived to the present day. It does not of course follow that the productions of the second half of the century were in an aesthetic sense superior to those of the first. In many respects quite the reverse is true. Names like those of Wedgwood, Thomas Whieldon, and the Wood family of Burslem, Ralph senior, his brother Aaron and their sons Ralph junior and Enoch,

are associated with the highest standards of craftsmanship, but it must be remembered that all these, with the exception of the two younger Woods, were born and reared in the traditions of the earlier potters. Wedgwood alone was responsible for the great changes that were soon to take place. The population of England and Wales was rising, due largely, as G. M. Trevelyan points out in his *English Social History*, to 'The Act of 1751' which placed a high tax on spirits and forbade their sale by distillers and shopkeepers. Not only did this do much to counteract the terrible ravages caused by the drinking of cheap gin, but also helped to popularize tea as a national beverage, which, after the middle years of the century, became a formidable rival to alcohol with all classes both in town and country. Porcelain was a costly material to produce and no doubt the potters of Staffordshire and elsewhere found an increasing demand for tea equipages which were within the means of the less well-to-do. Figures too, both human and animal, had greatly increased in popularity, principally as a result of importations from the Continent, especially Meissen, and imitations made by the English porcelain factories.

The makers of the traditional salt and lead-glazed wares had now to adapt their production to meet these new demands, and it was perhaps unfortunate that they found it necessary to seek inspiration from the more sophisticated styles of foreign Courts and Graeco-Roman art rather than pursuing their native craft within the sphere of its own limitations.

Salt-glazed stoneware had, since the beginning

861

of the century, been a staple product of the potteries, and the use of plaster-of-Paris moulds, introduced it is said by Ralph Daniel in 1740, made possible the casting of such pieces by means of pouring the liquid clay slip into the mould and allowing the porous surface of the plaster to absorb the moisture. The mould was then removed and the piece made ready for firing. Hollow vessels were cast in this way while dishes, lids, etc., were made by pressing a flat piece of clay into the surface of the mould. These methods greatly facilitated increased production and by the middle of the century salt-glazed ware had obtained a considerable market, some being exported to Holland. Two Dutchmen settling at Hot Lane, now Cobridge, are supposed to have introduced into this country the enamel painting with which, in a further attempt to emulate porcelain, much of it was decorated after 1750. This form of painting adopted by local artists was of various types and employed a strikingly contrasting palette including intense blues, pinks and greens. Besides Chinese themes, floral subjects and coloured grounds were used, presumably in imitation of Sevres. Commemorative pieces include teapots celebrating the wedding of George III in 1761 and portraits of popular figures such as Frederick the Great, at that time an ally of this country. Figures of various subjects, mostly inspired by Meissen originals, are known (on the evidence of his account book) to have been painted with enamel colours in the Kentish Town workshop of William Duesbury, later proprietor of the Derby Porcelain Factory. At Liverpool, transfer printing, generally of a brick-red colour, was applied with most pleasing effects by Saddler and Green. Two figures of Turks (Plate 41A) of about 1760 are illustrative of the influence of porcelain being more or less direct copies of models made by J. J. Kaendler at Meissen in 1745. William Read in his *Staffordshire Pottery Figures* states that the models in question were probably made at Longton Hall by William Littler. They are also known in Bow porcelain. Another method of decorating salt-glazed pieces was by filling incised patterns with blue colouring, a type known to collectors as 'Scratch blue'.

In spite of the fact that this ware continued to be made for more than twenty years after 1750, it is not really typical of the period. Its extreme hardness and slightly abrasive surface, which scratched silver, rendered it less agreeable to public taste by comparison with the cream-coloured wares perfected by Wedgwood, and by 1770 its manufacture had largely declined, ceasing altogether before 1790.

Although the importance of Staffordshire pottery makes it usual to discuss it quite separately from that made elsewhere, we may at this point make a brief digression in order to mention another class which, like salt-glaze, was to become outmoded by the use of new materials, namely the tin-glazed earthenware made principally at Lambeth, Bristol and Liverpool and known as English delftware. This type, largely derived from Italian and Dutch sources, was made in England as early as the sixteenth century. By the beginning of the eighteenth century the Chinese influence had become predominant in the style of decoration, and continued to some extent during the remaining period of its manufacture. In addition to the simple blue-and-white, palette painting in polychrome was used extensively on a great variety of articles; also transfer painting. Besides plates, dishes and bowls, characteristic examples of English delftware are to be found in the shape of puzzle jugs, drug jars, pill-slabs for apothecaries and the so-called bricks with perforated tops, intended either for flower holders or receptacles for ink and quill pens. A large number of tiles was also made (Pl. 42A), a typical feature of some eighteenth-century houses being a recess lined with such tiles and containing a ceremonial washbasin and water bottle. They were also used in the surrounds of fireplaces and for lining the walls of larders and shops.[1] Dated inscriptions occur frequently, also political slogans and the recording of events such as Lunardi's balloon ascent in 1783. In spite of the latter date delftware had largely gone out of fashion by the last quarter of the century, and like salt-glaze was not made after 1790.

[1] See 'An Introduction to Bristol Delftware Tiles', by Louis Lipski, *The Connoisseur*, May 1953.

As we have already seen, it is in many instances quite impossible to draw an arbitrary date line within which we may state what is characteristic of one half of a century and not of the other. Many types are transitional, and it is therefore only possible to note their production during the particular period with which we are dealing. In this category must be included the mottled or tortoiseshell wares chiefly associated with the name of the famous Staffordshire potter Thomas Whieldon (born 1719) whose factory was at Fenton Low and with whom the young Wedgwood was working from 1754–9. These mottled effects were brought about by the blending of metallic oxides in a clear lead-glaze which was applied over a cream earthenware body. Manganese produced the rich madder-brown of the tortoiseshell, while other colours were obtained by the use of oxides of copper, iron and cobalt which caused brown, green, yellow, blue, purple and grey tones to mingle in the fluid glaze with pleasantly harmonious effects. Glazes stained with either a single colour, or in the various combinations described above, were used on pieces with both applied and moulded reliefs. They include teapots, coffee-pots, tea-caddies and the whole range of table wares. Figures, both human and animal, were also coloured in this way. The teapots and similar pieces sometimes show evidence of the silversmith's influence (Pl. 41B), while the later figures were in many instances suggested by foreign originals. They are nevertheless, unmistakably the work of a native craftsman, and as such no doubt found their way on to the shelves and mantelpieces of the local homesteads. Under the present heading mention may also be made of the agate or marbled effects obtained by the blending of various coloured clays. In the 'solid agate' these clays were used to form the body, but marbling was also simulated by applying them over a plain surface. A brilliant black glaze on red earthenware is also typical. It is often seen on tea and coffee-pots ornamented with small reliefs. The same shapes, together with a similar glaze, were also used at Jackfield in Shropshire, though the latter type is without relief decoration.

During his partnership with Whieldon, Wedgwood was continually experimenting with both technical and material improvements made in order to stimulate an increased demand for their products, as in spite of reduced prices lack of public interest had already been reflected in a steadily declining market. Among these improvements was the perfecting of a green glaze which he used in combination with yellow on teapots and other vessels made in imitation of fruit and vegetable forms, known as 'Cauliflower' and 'Pineapple' wares. Although excavations on the site of his factory show that Whieldon made the whole range of Staffordshire pottery favoured in his day, his productions were not marked. His fame as a potter, however, has caused a whole class to be identified with his name. He was a man of great integrity, and before his death in 1795 became Sheriff of his county.

The name of the Wood family is to many only connected with the making of Toby Jugs. They were, in fact, extremely versatile in their output. Of the two elder brothers, Aaron (born 1717) was the most celebrated 'block cutter' of his time, that is, he prepared the first intaglio moulds in alabaster or other hard substance from which, after the taking of a master cast, the plaster moulds already described were eventually obtained. He worked for most of the leading Staffordshire potters, including Whieldon, and was probably at some time in partnership with his brother Ralph. He is also credited with the making of some of the most interesting figures of which the so-called 'Pew Groups' are notable examples. Aaron's brother, Ralph (born 1715), and his son, Ralph junior (born 1748), besides making useful wares were, from about 1765 onwards, responsible for a large output of figures coloured in the Whieldon style. It is generally agreed, however, that they themselves were principally concerned with the

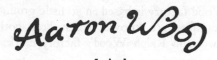

Incised

Fig. 1. On a 'block' in the British Museum.

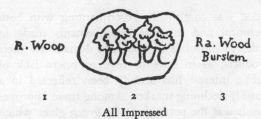

R. WOOD   Ra. Wood
Burslem

1   2   3

All Impressed

Fig. 2. 1 and 2 are believed to be the marks of R. Wood senior. 2 is supposed to be a rebus on the family name. About 1770. 3 is believed to be the mark of R. Wood junior. 1772–95.

I·VOYEZ
1788

Impressed

Fig. 3. Signature on a 'Fair Hebe' jug.

technicalities of manufacture rather than the creation of the types for which their name has become famous, and the best of the later models are confidently attributed to an itinerant artist of French extraction named Voyez. John Voyez was born about 1740 and was trained as a jeweller. On first coming to London he worked for a time at this trade and also as a carver for an artificial stone manufactury, exhibiting work in both wax and artificial stone at the Society of Artists in London, 1767–8. Josiah Wedgwood was originally responsible for bringing him to Staffordshire in 1768, but his habits were totally at variance with the former's high standards of moral rectitude, and after his disorderly conduct had led to a term of imprisonment their association terminated abruptly, though Wedgwood thought so highly of Voyez's abilities that he tried to deny his services to rival potters by bribing him not to work for them.[2] But Voyez was not to be tempted and is known on the evidence of signed pieces to have worked for both Humphrey Palmer of Hanley and T. Hales of Cobridge. His association with the Wood factory is based on stylistic grounds, as no examples are known which bear both his signature and Ralph Wood's factory mark. The

[2] See Herbert Read's *Staffordshire Pottery Figures*, London, 1924.

864

grotesque vessels known as Toby Jugs are perfect examples of rural English pottery of this period, adorning as they did the chimney pieces of farm houses and cottages. It is thought that their original form was inspired by engravings of 'Toby Philpot', the subject of a song called 'The Brown Jug' translated from the Latin by Francis Fawkes and published in 1761. The subjects are, however, considerably varied, names being applied to them such as 'The Thin Man', 'The Planter', 'Martha Gunn', 'Prince Hal', (Pl. 42c), etc. In the catalogue of the late Captain Price's collection it is suggested that the last named represents George IV, when Prince of Wales, masquerading at a Brighton ball as Bluff King Hal. Toby Jugs were made by other potters besides the Woods, and have continued to the present day, generally with steadily declining merit. Well known examples of Voyez's work are the rustic jugs moulded in the form of a tree trunk with figures in relief, and an inscription 'Fair Hebe' (Pl. 42B). These are often signed and dated 1788.[3] Other figures from the Ralph Wood factory include copies of originals by Paul Louis Cyfflé of Luneville, musicians, pastoral and classical subjects and satirical groups such as 'The Vicar and Moses' in a double-decked pulpit. In addition to colouring in the Whieldon style the Woods developed a method of laying the metallic oxides on under the glaze into which they were partly absorbed, a technique that produced beautiful and characteristic effects. The elder Ralph died in 1772, and his son in 1795.

Enoch (born 1759) was the son of the block-cutter Aaron. He was in partnership with his cousin from 1783–90, and James Caldwell from 1790–1818. Enoch was a modeller on his own account though his work lacks distinction. A number of busts such as those of George Washington and the preachers Whitfield and Wesley are the best known examples. The latter was modelled from life in 1781. He also made figures, some of which are of considerable size.

[3] The author had in his possession an example stamped with the mark ASTBURY, indicating that it was made by R. M. Astbury, who directed a factory at Fenton, 1785–1800.

(A) THOMAS HEMING. Gilt ewer, 1763. *Sir W. Williams Wynn.*

(B) WILLIAM PLUMMER. Basket, 1767. *Holburne of Menstrie Museum, Bath.*

PLATE 33

DANIEL SMITH and ROBERT SHARP, designed by Robert Adam. The Richmond Cup, gilt, 1770.
Height 19 in. *Marquess of Zetland.*

PLATE 34

DIGBY SCOTT and BENJAMIN SMITH, designed by John Flaxman. The Trafalgar Vase, 1805.
Height 17 in. *Victoria and Albert Museum.*

PLATE 35 867

(A) AUGUSTUS LE SAGE. Tea-caddy, 1767. Height 3½ in. *Ashmolean Museum.*

(B) RICHARD CARTER, DANIEL SMITH and ROBERT SHARP. Sauce-tureen, 1778. Height 5 in.
Ashmolean Museum.

(A) HESTER BATEMAN. Tea-pot, 1785. Height 5¾ in. *John Bell of Aberdeen Collection.*

(B) JOHN EDWARD. Sauce-tureen, parcel-gilt, 1806. Height 8 in. *Wellington Museum.*

PLATE 37

JOHN ARNELL. Gilt vase, 1772. Height 8¼ in. *Victoria and Albert Museum.*

PLATE 38

BENJAMIN and JAMES SMITH. Gilt sugar-vase, 1810. Height 8 in. *Wellington Museum*.

PLATE 39

PAUL STORR. Parcel-gilt centrepiece, 1810. Height 33 in. *Wellington Museum*.

PLATE 40

(A) A pair of figures of Turks, after models in Meissen porcelain by JOHANN JOACHIM KAENDLER. Salt-glazed stoneware, painted with enamel colours, *c.* 1760.
Victoria and Albert Museum.

(B) Coffee-pot, earthenware with mottled glaze ('tortoiseshell' ware). Staffordshire, *c.* 1760. Height 8½ in.
Victoria and Albert Museum.

PLATE 41

(A) Delftware tiles of the eighteenth century, *c.* 1765, in polychrome with *bianco-sopra-bianco* border. *The Bristol City Art Gallery.*

(B) Jug, modelled by JOHN VOYEZ, inscribed on the reverse side 'Fair Hebe', and signed and dated J. Voyez, 1788. *Victoria and Albert Museum.*

(C) 'Prince Hal' Toby jug by RALPH WOOD, Burslem, *c.* 1765. Height 14 in. *Lord Mackintosh of Halifax Collection.*

PLATE 42

(A) A plate from the Empress Catherine of Russia Service, cream-ware painted in blackish purple monochrome, the crest in green. Wedgwood, 1773–4. *Hanley Museum, Staffs.*

(B) A plate with lilac pink border and gold edging. Painted in the centre with a spray of poppies by William 'Quaker' Pegg. These poppies are similar to a spray in Pegg's own sketch book, which has survived and is now in the Derby Museum. Mark, a crown with crossed batons and D. in blue. Derby, *c.* 1800. *G. W. Capell Collection.*

PLATE 43   875

(A) Figure of Voltaire in black basaltes ware. Wedgwood, Etruria, c. 1777–80. *Victoria and Albert Museum.*

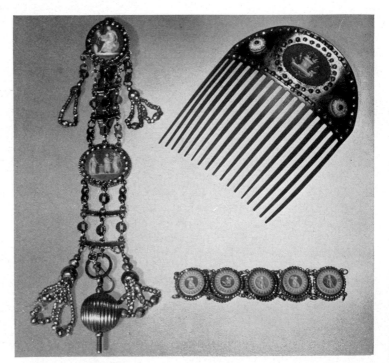

(B) Chatelaine, comb and bracelet, coloured jasper ware mounted in cutsteel. Wedgwood, Etruria, c.1786–90. *Josiah Wedgwood and Sons Ltd.*

PLATE 44

'The Music Lesson', adapted from a painting by François Boucher, entitled 'L'Agréable Leçon', porcelain painted in colours. Mark, an anchor in gold and 'R' impressed. Chelsea, *c.* 1765. *Victoria and Albert Museum.*

PLATE 45

(A) Pair of Chelsea figures, 'The Harvesters'. Height 10 in., mark, an anchor in gold, 1758–60. *Mrs H. Synge-Hutchinson Collection.*

(B) The épergne from the service given by King George III and Queen Charlotte to the Duke of Mecklenburg-Strelitz. 'Mazarine'-blue ground covered with insects in gold, enclosing panels painted with festoons of flowers. Mark, anchor in gold, Chelsea. *c.* 1763.
By gracious permission of H.M. Queen Elizabeth the Queen Mother.

(A) Bonbonnèries and scent bottles. Chelsea porcelain, *c.* 1755–65. *Victoria and Albert Museum.*

(B) Three grouped pieces, representing the Royal Family, after a painting by Zoffany, unglazed porcelain (biscuit), Derby, *c.* 1771. *By gracious permission of H.M. The Queen.*

PLATE 47

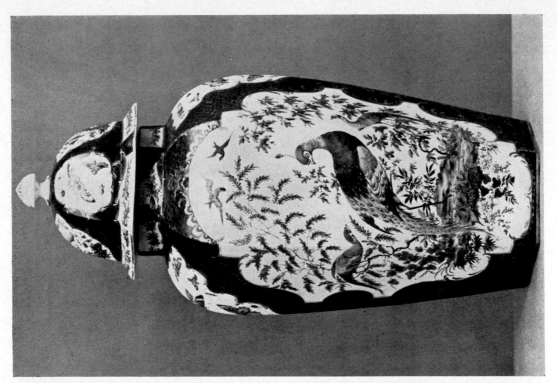

(A) A mug, transfer printed in black with a full length of Frederick the Great, and a battle scene in the background. On the reverse is a large trophy of arms and flags. Signed R. H. Worcester and dated. Worcester, *c.* 1757. *G. W. Capell Collection.*

(B) Vase and cover, with scale-blue ground and large shaped panels painted with exotic birds among trees and bushes. Mark, a fretted square in blue, Worcester, *c.* 1770. *Victoria and Albert Museum.*

PLATE 48

(A) Adam pine column mantelpiece with applied enrichment in lead composition. Steel grate with pierced apron, and pierced fender. *Mallett and Son Ltd.*

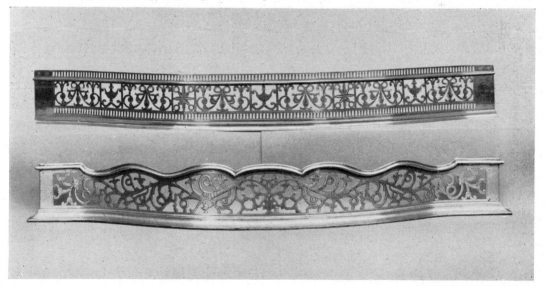

(B) Pierced and engraved fenders of the late eighteenth century: (*top*) in 'tutenag' (base metal alloy, whitish in colour); (*below*) in steel. *Victoria and Albert Museum.*

PLATE 49   881

(A) Brass candlesticks in which socket and stem were cast in a single hollow piece and attached to square hollow foot. Fashionable during late eighteenth century but made in a wide variety of stem patterns until mid-nineteenth century. *Victoria and Albert Museum.*

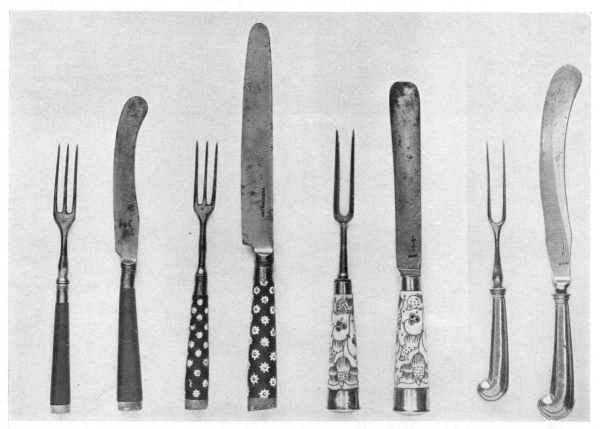

(B) Hand-forged steel knives and forks, silver mounted handles: 1st, green stained ivory, 2nd, South Staffordshire enamel, 4th, stamped Sheffield silver (all late eighteenth century); 3rd, late seventeenth century, engraved ivory inlaid with silver. *Victoria and Albert Museum.*

PLATE 50

(A) Japanned tray with hand grips, painted with an all-over sporting scene,
c. 1800. *A. E. Bastien, Esq.*

(B) Copper warming pans with stamped ember
pans and lids, cast brass ferrules, handles of
japanned beechwood. Late eighteenth century.
Author's Collection.

(C) Coffee urn in Pontypool japan, decorated
with rustic landscape with figures and sheep, by
Thomas Barker. *National Museum of Wales.*

PLATE 51

(A) A group of late Georgian Sheffield plate showing a pair of muffineers and a cream boat, a pair of pierced wine coasters, and a pair of salt cellars with blue glass liners. *Private Collection.*

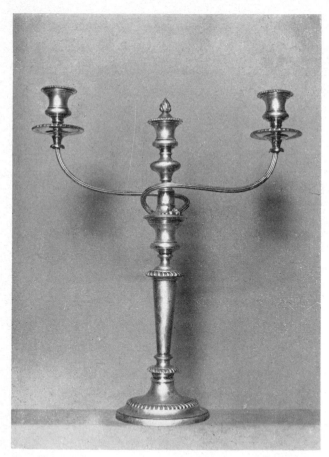

(C) Pewter tankard showing the bulbous body, massive recurved handle and perforated thumb-piece of the late Georgian period. *Victoria and Albert Museum.*

(B) Two-branch candelabrum with branches twisting around the central finial which is removable so that a third light may be used. About 1800. *Private Collection.*

(D) Teapot and stand of Vickers white metal, designed and engraved in the style of contemporary silver. Marked beneath I. Vickers. Late 1780s. *Private Collection.*

Tapestry Room at Osterley Park. The room designed by Robert Adam; the tapestry hangings and upholstery woven at the Gobelins 1775–6, by Jacques Neilson, after designs by François Boucher.

PLATE 53

Detail of coverlet of embroidered satin, designed by Robert Adam 1776, for the state bed at Osterley Park.

PLATE 54

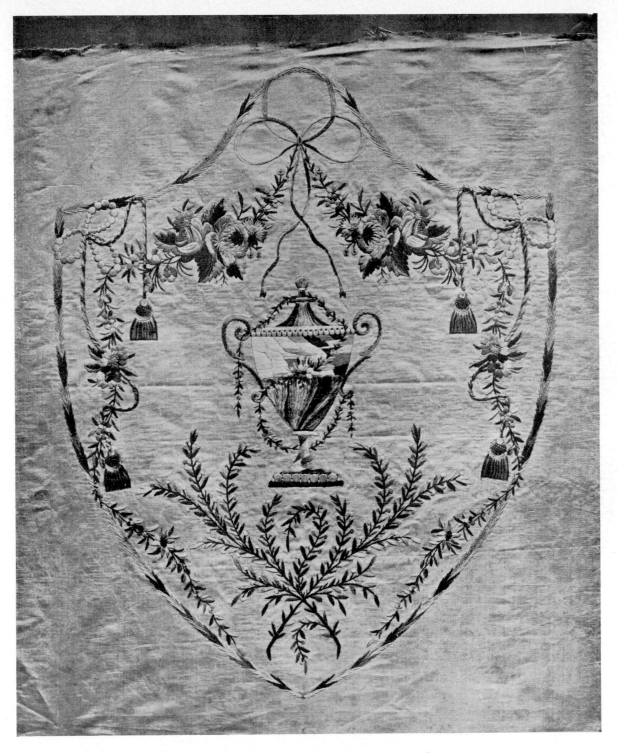

Embroidered panel for a pole screen, about 1790. *Victoria and Albert Museum.*

PLATE 55

Embroidered portrait of George III, after Zoffany, worked by Mrs Mary Knowles, *c.* 1771.
Victoria and Albert Museum.

PLATE 56

Furnishing print, by Robert Jones of Old Ford, 1769. *Victoria and Albert Museum.*

PLATE 57

Carpet in the red drawing-room at Syon House: by Thomas Moore of Moorfields, 1769, after a design by Robert Adam. *The Duke of Northumberland.*

PLATE 58

(A) Carpet in the tapestry room at Osterley Park; by Thomas Moore, about 1775, after a design by Robert Adam.

(B) Carpet in the drawing-room at Osterley Park; by Thomas Moore, about 1775, after a design by Robert Adam.

PLATE 59

Carpet, probably Axminster, 1780–90. *Victoria and Albert Museum.*

PLATE 60

(A)   Duke of Grafton, 1760. Country suit of cloth, the frock and waistcoat of same material.
Temple Newsam House, Leeds.

(B) Four men, by BATONI, 1766. Two wear coats, two frocks. Each shows considerable difference in details (cuffs, neckwear, embroidery, materials).

PLATE 61

Francis Fountayne-Whichcot and wife, 1768–70. The lady in open robe edged with robings, triple wrist ruffles and apron. The man in a suit (coat with small cuffs). Tie wig. *Temple Newsam House, Leeds.*

PLATE 62

(A) A Macaroni, 1772.
From 'The Macaroni Magazine'.

(B) The Caddick Family, 1785. Note a double-breasted waist-coat, another horizontally striped. The lady in bouffant dress and towering hat. *Walker Gallery, Liverpool.*

(c) 'Autumn', a print by R. SAYER, 1786. The woman's feathered hat, puffed-out bodice and flounced skirt of her gown are conspicuous. The man in double-breasted waistcoat with wide lapels and round hat.

(D) Sir Christopher and Lady Sykes, by ROMNEY, 1786. His frock with high standfall collar and skirts sloping away; she in open robe and pointed bodice. *Temple Newsam House, Leeds.*

PLATE 63

(A) A 'Jessamy' caricature, 1790, wearing a bicorne hat, a huge catogan wig, short coat and high stand-fall collar.

(B) John Jackson, by B. MARSHALL, 1810. A double-breasted frock coat with wide rolled collar, tight breeches. The high stepped collar of the waistcoat is just visible.

ENOCH WOOD & CO   E WOOD

ENOCH WOOD   WOOD & CALDWELL
   SCULPSIT

All Impressed

Fig. 4. Marks used by Enoch Wood. His partnership
with Caldwell was from 1790 to 1818.

During this later period the practice already
used by the china factories of painting in opaque
enamel colours over the glaze was adopted. This
lacked the charm of the earlier methods and has
not proved practical, as the colours usually flake
off with the passing of time. Enoch, who did not
die until 1840, came to be known as the 'Father
of the Potteries'.

Some critics have accused Wedgwood of spoiling a native art by turning it into a manufacture
and urging his employees to desert nature and seek
inspiration in examples created by an archaic civilization; but these criticisms, although undoubtedly
merited in some respects, do less than justice if
they cause us to ignore his mighty achievements
both in the field of technical improvement and in
the setting up of a great industry demanding the
highest standards, not only in the materials used
but in the craftsmanship applied to them. Even
the most individual spirits cannot remain uninfluenced by the tastes and fashions of their times,
and in this respect Wedgwood was not the creator
of the neo-classical movement, though he found
himself in complete harmony with the aims and
ideals of its devotees. Although as a potter he may
not have been a great creative artist, he was undoubtedly an extremely competent one; and it is
surely remarkable that a man who had received
only an elementary education should have been
able to engage successfully in experiments that
today would be regarded as the work of highly
skilled experts.

A man of strong social and moral convictions,
his sympathies lay with the American Colonies
in their fight for independence. He also joined the
campaign for the abolition of slavery. A medallion
of a slave in black and white Jasper ware, modelled
at the factory by William Hackwood, and inscribed 'Am I not a man and a brother' was

adopted as the seal of the Slave Emancipation
Society, of which Wedgwood was a keen supporter. Yet in spite of these activities his achievements secured for him the highest social contacts,
including the frequent patronage of Royalty. The
London Ledger, 1793–1806 shows an order placed
by Queen Charlotte in 1795, listed [4] as follows:

'12 Milkpans Sundries	6 Dog Pans
18 Plates Green Ivy	3 Dog Pans
	Silver Spout Teapot
2 Teapots	Jasper Vases and Gerandoles
6 Plates Green Ivy	2 Toy Tea Sets Sandwich Set'

Born in 1730 at Burslem in Staffordshire,
Josiah Wedgwood was, at the age of 14, apprenticed to his brother Thomas who had inherited
the family business known as the Churchyard
Pottery. His apprenticeship lasted for five years,
but it seems unlikely that he left the Churchyard
before 1752, when he went to Stoke and entered
into a partnership with John Harrison at the factory of Thomas Alders. This does not appear to
have been of long duration and was followed, as
we have seen, by his association with Whieldon
from 1754–9. During this time he accumulated
sufficient capital and experience to set up on his
own account at the Ivy House, Burslem, where
he continued to produce the Whieldon types with
improvements in the shapes and glazes. Being a
man of great foresight and business acumen, he
was quick to realize that these were already declining in popularity, and to see before him the
possibility of capturing a large market if he could
offer to the public something which should be
without the practical disadvantages of salt-glaze
and at the same time of a sufficiently stable body
and colour to be produced in large quantities at a
price that would make it available to all classes.
To this end he set about a further refining of the
cream-coloured earthenware body used by Whieldon and the earlier potters. His business premises

[4] *Catalogue of Early Wedgwood Pottery Exhibition*, Josiah
Wedgwood & Sons, 1951.

were extended in 1764 to include the neighbouring Brick House Works, later known as The Bell House, and by 1765 he had so far progressed in the making of cream ware as to obtain the patronage of Queen Charlotte and the right to name his new product Queensware, a type which with continued improvements was to capture a world market. The early factory decoration of Queensware is of a simple classical style, but much was sold in the white to be painted elsewhere, as well as being sent to Liverpool for transfer printing by Saddler and Green. It was readily adaptable to every kind of use and Wedgwood made from it articles ranging from dairy and culinary equipment to the Imperial Russian Service, consisting of 952 pieces, made in 1773 to the order of the Empress Catherine II and known as the 'Frog Service', owing to the fact that it was to be placed in the Palace of La Grenouille near St Petersburg and has the device of a green frog in a shield painted on the border of each piece (Pl. 43A). It is further decorated with English views in dark purple monochrome. The eventual cost of this service was about £3,500, on which only a small profit was made.

While visiting Liverpool in 1762 Wedgwood first met the merchant Thomas Bentley, who, it is said, inspired him with his love for the antique. The friendship and mutual interest between the two men grew steadily, and in 1768 a partnership was decided upon and Wedgwood commenced the building of the great manufactory just outside Burslem which he named 'Etruria', Greek vases at that time being thought Etruscan. In the same year he opened a large London showroom in Newport Street.

The partnership with Bentley was for the making of ornamental pieces only, the ordinary wares continuing for a few more years to be made at the Bell House. By 1769 the premises at 'Etruria' were completed and opened, and Wedgwood was now fairly launched on his projects to emulate the examples of antiquity.

In his search for materials other than the cream and marble bodies suitable for this purpose, he had once again made use of a local product, namely the black unglazed pottery known as 'Egyptian

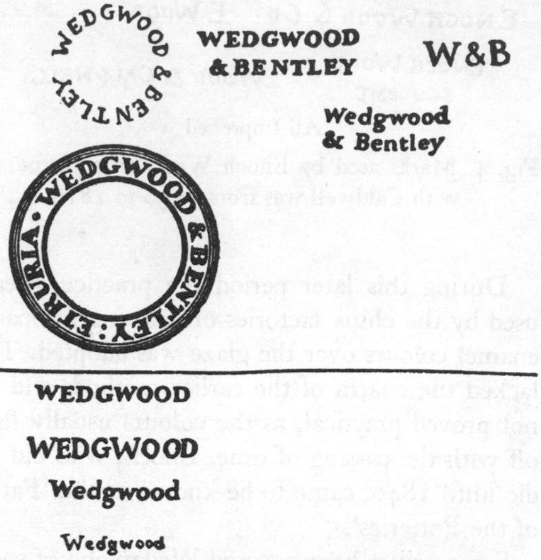

Fig. 5. Specimens of the marks generally used by Wedgwood. Those above the line are of the Wedgwood and Bentley period, 1769–80; those below are later marks, from 1771 on useful wares, and from 1780 onwards on all classes. The mark was of various sizes, the letters being sometimes in upper and sometimes lower case. All impressed.

Black'. This he improved and refined to obtain a fine quality black stoneware of extreme hardness from which he made many vases and other pieces, naming them 'Black Basaltes'. Some of these vases, in addition to being decorated with engine turning, were 'bronzed with light gilding, and others painted with 'encaustic' enamel in imitation of Greek vases. The latter work was probably done at an enamelling establishment opened in Chelsea in 1769 under the supervision of Thomas Bentley. The Frog Service was certainly painted there. Besides the usual domestic articles a series of busts for library decoration were made in black basaltes, also figures; that of Voltaire (Pl. 44A) made about 1777 is a well-known example. It was also used for the making of small relief medallions to meet the current vogue for collecting cameos in cabinets; the originals being too costly for the ordinary purse, most people had to be contented with imitations made in inexpensive materials. Among other unglazed bodies were the buff-coloured 'cane ware' and a red stoneware called by Wedgwood 'rosso antico'. It is interesting to note that, at the beginning of the nineteenth century, the scarcity of flour was so acute that imitation pie-crusts made of cane ware were used instead of the real thing.

Best known of all Wedgwood's creations are the coloured ground or 'jasper' wares, and one has only to think of a room designed by Robert Adam to realize how admirably suited they were to the surroundings in which they were so often incorporated.

Once again the problems of composition arose and were solved by patient research and experiment. A pure white stoneware capable of tinting throughout with oxides was the basic requirement for the making of the coloured bodies and white reliefs. Barium sulphate obtained in a mineral form from Derbyshire, where it was called 'cawk', was found to be the necessary ingredient, and by the end of 1775 jasper was being made in two or three shades. The range was soon increased and instead of being tinted throughout the pieces were immersed in a solution that coloured the outer surface only, referred to as 'jasper dip'. The most usual colour is light blue; a darker blue, two shades of green, lavender, lilac, black and rarely yellow were also used; while for the famous copies of the 'Barbarini' or 'Portland Vase', started in 1786, the body was of a blue-black 'solid jasper' in imitation of the glass from which the original was made.

Many of the forms in jasper repeat those of the black basaltes and are too well known to warrant description. It was however put to innumerable uses. Wedgwood himself lists 38 different items in a single order made by a merchant in Manchester for supply to the King of Naples,[5] from which the following examples are taken:

Rings.	Coach Panels.
Snuff Boxes.	Swords.
Window Shutters.	Chairs.
Metal Boxes.	Cabinets.
Door Handles.	Watches.

Buffets.	Desks.
Chest of Drawers.	Metal Lamps.
Chatelaines.	Buckles.
Etui Cases.	Daggers.
Bell Pulls.	Opera Glasses.
Smelling Bottles, etc.	Coat Buttons.

The metal work on pieces mounted in ormolu and cut steel jewellery (Pl. 44B) was carried out by the Birmingham metal workers Boulton & Watt, with whom Wedgwood was constantly in touch.

About 1780 a white semi-porcellaneous version of the Queensware was perfected and named 'Pearl Ware'. This was used largely for services made in competition with the china makers. Silver and coloured lustres also came into use in the late eighteenth and early nineteenth century. A well-known example is the pink variety often found on services made in the shape of shells. Enamel painting in the Chinese style on the black basaltes was also done, though the combination appears entirely incongruous.

Wedgwood was tireless in his efforts to obtain not only the highest standards of workmanship but also to seek out the best examples of antiquity which could be adapted to his uses. To this end he employed many well-known artists and craftsmen, as well as gaining access to famous collections such as that of the Duke of Marlborough. James Tassie, well known for his casts of antique gems, worked for him, also John Flaxman the famous sculptor, who, together with Henry Webber, spent some time in Rome supervising the making of reductions and adaptations from the antique for use at the factory. The wax modellers Mathew and Isaac Gosset are known to have worked on a series of contemporary celebrities known as the 'Illustrious Moderns', with William Hackwood, for many years principal modeller at the factory. Besides the work of professionals, some charming designs in relief of women and children are attributed to Lady Templetown, Lady Diana Beauclerke and a Miss Crewe. George Stubbs, the celebrated animal and portrait painter, who was a friend of Wedgwood's, also designed a number of relief medallions of equestrian subjects. Many

[5] See Wolf Mankowitz, *Wedgwood*, London, 1953, p. 108.

other names are known, but space forbids their inclusion here. All work was subject to Wedgwood's supervision, being altered or adapted at his discretion, and this, together with the fact that names of individual artists were rarely allowed to appear, sometimes makes personal attributions largely conjectural.

Thomas Bentley died in 1780 and in 1790 Wedgwood's three surviving sons, John, Josiah and Thomas and his nephew, Thomas Byerley, were taken into partnership. Within three years however Wedgwood senior, Josiah II and Byerley alone remained. In 1795 the founder himself died and Byerley in 1810.

It was inevitable that, as the creator of new materials and forms of ceramic expression, Wedgwood should have a host of followers. The Queensware was copied by most of the potters of his time, and even rivalled in quality, notably by that made at Leeds in Yorkshire; while the jaspers, besides inspiring local imitators such as William Adams, John Turner and Samuel Hollins, compelled even the great continental factories of Sevres and Meissen to follow the English example.

The pottery industry from the Midlands to north of the Border was now well on the way to complete industrialization and therefore largely stereotyped in its products. The figures of John Walton, with their clumsy tree-stump supports and vivid green foliage, are obvious copies of Chelsea Derby porcelain, but a certain degree of originality is shown in the blue, green and orange palette of the so-called Pratt wares, while the firm of J. Neale & Co., later Neale & Wilson, made figures and table wares of good quality, often tastefully painted with bright enamel colours. Fresh inspiration was, however, lacking, and the nineteenth century produced no innovators capable of leading a new revival.

Fig. 6. Impressed on a scroll. Late eighteenth and early nineteenth century.

Fig. 7. The marks of Neale & Co. and Neale & Wilson. Late eighteenth and early nineteenth century. All impressed.

Porcelain

Unlike earthenware English porcelain had no roots in the national tradition. It was a new and untried medium with high costs and hazards of production that caused its makers to cater essentially for the tastes of the fashionable and monied classes rather than the humbler sections of the community.

The first porcelain seen in Europe was imported from China and was so highly prized that attempts were continually made to discover the secrets of its composition, the great distinction being its whiteness and translucency compared to the dense opacity of earthenware.

In the sixteenth and late seventeenth centuries soft paste or artificial bodies were achieved in Italy and France, but true porcelain in the Chinese sense was not made in Europe until Johann Friedrich Böttger, working at Meissen in 1709, discovered the secret of compounding china clay (kaolin) with china stone (petuntse). These, when fired at a high temperature, combine to form the hard vitrified material known as hard paste or true porcelain. This discovery, which was of immense financial value, was jealously guarded, Böttger being kept a virtual prisoner by Augustus the Strong, Elector of Saxony, under whose patronage the great German factory near Dresden was established in 1710.

In England no such discovery was forthcoming and, with the exception of that made by William Cookworthy at Plymouth 1768–70, and later by Champion of Bristol, who sold the patent to New Hall, all English porcelain was of the soft paste variety. In the foregoing circumstances it was inevitable that Meissen, or Dresden china as it is better known, should become the model on which the first English styles were based, the majority being close imitations; though silver was also copied, particularly at Chelsea. Early English porcelain is, by reason of its paste, glaze and re-strained decoration, of a quality equal to anything made elsewhere. It does not, however, come with-in the scope of this survey as by 1760 the baroque force of Meissen had given way to the rococo extravagances of the royal factory at Sèvres. Nowhere was this change more apparent than at the Chelsea factory, where the proprietor, Nicholas Sprimont, had inaugurated the final phase of production known, from the mark used, as the 'gold anchor' period (1758–70). Previously figures made in England had, like their German counterparts, been designed for use principally as table decorations and therefore could be viewed from any angle. Now, however, they had become popular as garnitures for mantelpieces and china cabinets, and the simple mound bases gave way to rococo scroll work mounted on feet, a design more suggestive of ormolu than porcelain. These bases were picked out in bright colours and gilding, while trees with branching foliage and flowers (bocage) often formed the background against which the figures were set, either singly, or as groups, the largest and most famous of the latter being the 'Music Lesson' (Pl. 45) taken from a painting by Boucher. Other groups of unusual size are a 'Roman Charity' and a pieta, while the best of the single figures include two finely

Fig. 10. Marks used on Chelsea porcelain during the 'gold anchor' period, 1758–69. 1 and 2 are in gold. 3 is impressed and is the mark of a 'repairer' (one who moulds and assembles the model) and not that of Roubiliac the sculptor as is sometimes supposed.

modelled Harvesters (Pl. 46A), a set of Apollo and the Muses and another set known as the Ranelagh Masqueraders.

The diarist [6] Mrs Philip Lybbe Powys, who wrote during the years 1756 to 1808, and who gives a glimpse of the domestic activities of the upper classes of those days, does not fail to men-tion china collections. 'Lady Dashwood's china-room,' she observed after a visit in 1778 to Kirklington Park, 'is the most elegant I ever saw. 'Tis under the flight of stairs going into the gar-den; it's ornamented with the finest pieces of the oldest china, and the recesses and shelves painted pea-green and white, the edges being green in a mosaic pattern. Her Ladyship said she must try my judgement in china, as she ever did all the visitors of that closet, as there was one piece there so much superior to the others. I thought myself fortunate that a prodigious fine old Japan dish almost at once struck my eye.'

A larger and more splendid collection was at Blenheim. It delighted the Duchess of Northum-berland when she saw it in 1752: 'We were also shown a little China Room, very prettily fitted up in wᶜʰ is the China presented by the K. of Poland to the present Duke.' This china closet was not the one which the indefatigable Mrs Lybbe Powys saw at Blenheim in 1799: 'I went in the post-chaise to Blenheim, to see the new china-rooms. They are not in the house, but built just after you enter the park, four little rooms fill'd with all sorts of old china fix'd to the walls by three screws, one of which takes out to let them be removed, others are placed on pedestals or shelves. The whole has a pretty effect, but to

[6] Quoted in 'The China Case and China Closet', by R. W. Symonds – *The Connoisseur*, June 1952, p. 11.

in blue, red or gold   incised   in blue

Fig. 8. Marks on Plymouth porcelain, 1768–70.

All in blue

Fig. 9. Marks on Bristol porcelain (Champion's factory), c, 1770–81.

others might be more amusing than to Lady Hardy and myself, as each of us has most of the same sort.' The Blenheim 'China Gallery' was fitted up in 1796, 'an additional attraction to the visitors of Blenheim, who delight in the antique, rich, and curious specimens of the porcelain, delf, and japan manufacture'.[7]

The ground colours of Sèvres were also imitated, such as the 'gros bleu' (called 'mazarine' blue), a rich claret (contemporarily 'crimson'), also green, turquoise and yellow. Typical examples of these ground colours are seen on the sets of elaborate rococo vases lavishly gilded and painted with figure subjects after Rubens, Boucher and Teniers. Chinoiseries in the style of Watteau and Pillement were also popular, together with birds, flowers and fruit. Famous among the vases is the claret-ground set of seven, once in the possession of Lord Dudley and now in Lord Bearsted's collection.[8] They are painted with mythological subjects and birds in the manner of Hondecoeter. The Huntington Art Gallery in California also possesses a fine pair and they are well represented in the British and Victoria and Albert Museums.

The table wares were no less magnificent in their ground colours and painting; a superb example is a tea and coffee service, the bequest of Emily Thompson, which may be seen at the Victoria and Albert Museum. Even more elaborate is the enormous equipage given in 1763 by George III and Queen Charlotte to the latter's brother, the Duke of Mecklenburg-Strelitz. It is

mentioned by Horace Walpole as consisting of 'dishes, plates without number, an epergne, (Pl. 46B) candlesticks, salt-cellars, sauceboats and tea and coffee equipages costing £1,200'. He adds, however, 'I cannot boast of our taste; the forms are neither new, beautiful, nor various. Yet Sprimont the manufacturer is a Frenchman. It seems their taste will not bear transplanting.' This service, which is decorated with exotic birds and flowers within mazarine-blue and gilt borders, is now in the private collection of H.M. Queen Elizabeth, the Queen Mother; but a damaged pair of candelabra was sold by the steward of the Duke's household and is in the Schreiber collection at South Kensington. In the private collection of Her Majesty the Queen are two remarkable clocks with claret grounds, gilt scroll work and pastoral figures in the style of Boucher.

A charming feature of this period, although they were also made earlier, are the miniature objects known as 'Chelsea toys'. They are of a great variety, including tiny figures, in which seals were set, thimbles, étuis, scent-bottles, bonbonnières, etc. (Pl. 47A). These last were often mounted in gold, the bonbonnières having painted enamel lids. The scent-bottles were contained in shagreen cases and were often carried by ladies on coach journeys.[9] Chelsea toys almost invariably bear inscriptions in French which are, however, frequently misspelt.

In 1769 Sprimont sold the factory to James Cox who, in the following year, re-sold it to William Duesbury and John Heath of Derby. Duesbury continued for a number of years to use the premises, the productions of this period being known as Chelsea-Derby. They are in most cases somewhat insipid in character and not typical of the best of either factory. The table wares usually follow the style of decoration favoured by the neoclassical revival, while the figures are pale echoes of their predecessors. In 1784 the factory was finally closed and the moulds and workmen removed to Derby.

Although Bow ranks with Chelsea as the first

---

[7] It seems obvious that the above cannot refer to English porcelain. In the first paragraph Mrs Lybbe Powys is speaking of a visit to a porcelain-room which she made in 1778, and states that it is 'ornamented with the finest pieces of the oldest china': this could hardly apply to English porcelain made only twenty or thirty years previously, and the 'fine old Japan dish' was probably oriental. In the second paragraph the Duchess of Northumberland's visit to Blenheim was in 1752, and the 'K of Poland' was the Elector of Saxony, owner of the Meissen factory: it would seem, therefore, that whatever porcelain he gave to the Duke of Marlborough most likely came from that establishment. The 'delf' is presumably Delft, and would be tin-glazed earthenware, while that of 'Japan manufacture' would, again, be oriental.

[8] On loan to the Victoria and Albert Museum.

[9] See G. E. Bryant, *The Chelsea Porcelain Toys*, London, 1925.

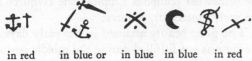

in red   in blue or   in blue   in blue   in red
          red

Fig. 11. Marks found on Bow porcelain from 1760 onwards.

of the great factories very little of any consequence or originality was made there after 1760. The rococo style prevailed in the forms, which were similar to those of Chelsea, while much of the bright colouring was probably applied outside the factory. One of the owners, Wetherby, died in 1762, and his partner John Crowther went bankrupt in the following year. After this the history becomes obscure. Like Chelsea, it was probably financed by Duesbury and removed to Derby about 1775. A valuable contribution to the making of porcelain which originated at Bow was the use of bone ash in the paste. This made production less hazardous as it stabilized the body and helped to prevent collapsing in the kiln.

Of the early factories, Longton Hall closed in 1760, and only three, Worcester, Derby and Lowestoft, survived into the nineteenth century. The two former are still flourishing, but Lowestoft closed in 1802. This Suffolk factory could lay claim to few of the pretensions of its rivals. Its wares were for the most part of a utilitarian character and catered for a less opulent market. Many pieces bear scenes and inscriptions relating to the locality, typical examples being the well-known inkwells, mugs, etc., inscribed 'a Trifle from Lowestoft'. No recognized marks were used, and owing to the publication of a notorious mistake much Chinese export porcelain has been wrongly attributed to this source.

Worcester during its best period (1751–83) was under the direction of Dr Wall, the founder, and William Davis a partner and manager. The figures made there were negligible both in quantity and quality, but in the sphere of table wares, vases, etc., their work was unsurpassed.

One invention, which, although it did not originate at the factory, was more widely prac-

tised there than elsewhere, was transfer printing, chiefly in black, over the glaze. This method, of which Robert Hancock the engraver was the chief exponent, may be claimed as an original English contribution to ceramic art. It was used at Worcester from about 1757 onwards and forms an interesting group, mainly depicting the scenes and customs of the time. Armorial and commemorative pieces were also made, the best known of the latter being the signed and dated mugs with portraits of the King of Prussia (Pl. 48A). Chinoiseries in the manner of Pillement were another feature.

In 1769 there was a migration of workers from Chelsea to Worcester, after which the rich ground colours and gilding of the former factory predominated in the more ambitious productions. Coloured fish-scale grounds, ultimately derived from Meissen, were also a great feature, blue being the most usual. They are often seen in combination with exotic birds (the 'fantasie vögel' of Meissen) painted in panels (Pl. 48B). Oriental influences appear in the so-called 'Japan patterns' and various chinoiseries, the neo-classical style coming later.

A number of celebrated services were made, to which the name of distinguished patrons have been attached. One of the best known is supposed to have been made for William Henry, Duke of Gloucester. It is painted in the centre with large clusters of fruit within gilt and green borders intersected by compartments with sprays of fruit and insects.

The best known painters of Worcester porcelain are John Donaldson, the miniaturist, and Jeffrey Hamet O'Neale. Much outside decoration was also done in the London workshop of James Giles.

After the death of Dr Wall in 1776 and William Davis in 1783, various changes in ownership and partners caused the firm to come successively under the management of Thomas Flight, Flight and Barr, and Barr Flight & Barr, the last partnership ending in 1813. Robert Chamberlain, another member of the firm, having seceded in 1789, set up first as a decorator and later a manufacturer in opposition. The last phase is characterized by

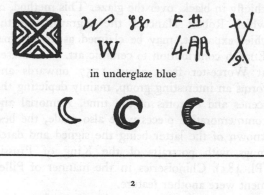

in underglaze blue

All in black

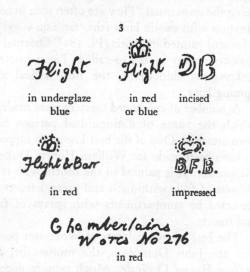

Rd. Worcester   R. H.f

R. Hancock fecit Worcester

All in black

in underglaze blue   in red or blue   incised

in red   impressed

in red

Fig. 12. Marks on Worcester porcelain. 1 and 2 were used during the Dr Wall period, 1752–83. The pseudo-Oriental characters occur on pieces of the 'Japan patterns', about 1760–75, and the crossed swords are in imitation of Meissen; the number is sometimes 91. The fretted square is of Chinese origin. 2 shows the marks of Robert Hancock found on transfer printed pieces. The anchor is thought to be a rebus on the name of Richard Holdship, who was in charge of the printing department: it also occurs on pieces signed in full by Hancock. 3 shows the marks of the late eighteenth and early nineteenth century.

the somewhat pompous Empire style favoured in the early nineteenth century.

The great beauty attained in the early days at Derby was not fulfilled during the middle period. Many figures were made, some depicting contemporary notabilities; that of David Garrick in the character of King Richard III is a familiar example. This was modelled from an engraving by J. Dixon, published in 1772, after the painting by Nathaniel Dance, exhibited in the Royal Academy in 1771. In most instances, however, Meissen was once again the source of inspiration. The colours are generally bright, a dry turquoise blue which tended to discolour and become brown, being particularly characteristic. The Continental

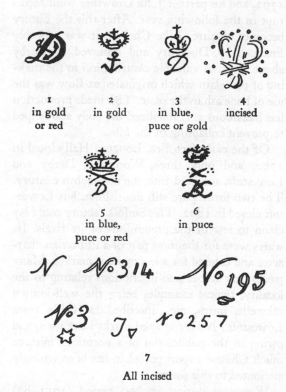

1   2   3   4
in gold   in gold   in blue,   incised
or red   puce or gold

5   6
in blue,   in puce
puce or red

7

All incised

Fig. 13. Derby factory marks. 1 is usual on Chelsea-Derby porcelain, 1770–84. 2 is about 1770–80. 3 is about 1780–4. 4 is incised on figures 1770–80. 5 is about 1784–1810, the red mark is late. 6 is the mark of Duesbury and Kean, about 1795. 7 shows marks incised on figures 1770–1800, they are the catalogue numbers of the model. The symbols are those of 'repairers'.

influence is further seen in a class of white, un-glazed biscuit groups intended to imitate marble, which were a speciality of the factory. One of the first and most important works in this medium is grouped as three figures representing the Royal Family after a painting by Zoffany (Pl. 47B). The only complete set known is in the possession of Her Majesty the Queen. Some of the later models are by J. J. Spengler, son of the director of the Zurich Porcelain factory, who was at Derby from 1790–5.

Decoration on the later table wares, vases, etc., was of a very high standard and many talented artists were at work. Zachariah Boreman painted landscapes, James Banford and John and Robert Brewer figures, landscapes and other subjects, while the naturalistic flowers of William Billingsley and William Pegg (Pl. 43B) are notable, as are the pink monochromes in the Sèvres style by Richard Askew, and the birds of Complin.

Others were Fidèle Duvivier, Lawton and Hill.

William Duesbury died in 1786 and was succeeded by his son of the same name, who, in 1795 took a miniature painter, Michael Kean, into partnership. The second Duesbury died in the following year and Kean carried on the factory until 1811.

Outside the larger establishments porcelain was also being made at Coalport in Shropshire and Pinxton in Derbyshire, as well as at Liverpool. But by the end of the eighteenth century the greater part of the industry was concentrated in Staffordshire, the chief makers being New Hall, Spode, Minton, Davenport and Ridgeway. Josiah Spode had introduced the bone porcelain which henceforth became the standard English body, and everywhere the advance of industrialization brought with it a degree of similarity that makes individual descriptions largely superfluous.

Fig. 14. Staffordshire pottery cock and hen, late eighteenth century. 8¼″ and 7¾″. *Schreiber Collection in Victoria and Albert Museum.*

Figs. 41. Staffordshire pottery cock and hen, late eighteenth century.
41 and 41. Derby(?) China hen in Victoria and Albert Museum.

Domestic Metalwork

G. BERNARD HUGHES

Late Georgians took a lively pleasure in the metalwork that graced their homes. Never had its quality been so fine nor lent itself to such varied treatment; never had there been such a range of wares to ensure the requisite air of elegance, and never again, perhaps, would there be such a solid basis of traditional good craftsmanship to ensure lastingly beautiful, satisfying design and execution.

Sheffield plate brought, to more modest homes, much of the gracious loveliness of silver; brass shone with a newly-won golden brilliance; heart-warming copper wares enriched living rooms as well as kitchen quarters, but were rivalled by the rainbow brilliance of japanned iron. The cool sheen of burnished steel was never more perfectly displayed, and the fading beauties of pewter were superseded in the home by the tougher, more lastingly clear-toned Britannia metal. And behind every one of these developments, as behind many other associated refinements, was an English invention.

Sheffield plate had been invented by Thomas Bolsover in 1742. It was an inestimable boon to the less-than-wealthy home: almost everything made in silver was repeated in what, until about 1770, was known as copper rolled plate. Sheffield plate domestic ware dates no earlier than 1758 when Joseph Hancock established the trade in Sheffield, having devised the lapped edge which hid the streak of copper beneath the silver that had declared itself wherever a cut edge was visible. By the early 1760's his range of domestic hollow-ware was considerable, all heavily lined with tin until the invention of double-sided plate in the early 1770's.

Chronology of Sheffield plate

Edgings and mounts on pieces of Sheffield plate display a chronology of improvements by which late Georgian examples may be grouped into six classes. These are: (1) single lapped edge, 1758–80; (2) double lapped copper mounts, 1768–early nineteenth century; (3) silver lapped mounts, 1775–1815; (4) solid silver mounts, 1780–1830; (5) drawn silver wire mounts, 1785–1820; (6) silver stamped mounts from the early 1790's. Much of the work was hand-raised but stamped lids and spouts were introduced in the 1780's, and flat and plain work was shaped by stamping from the early 1790's; the spinning of hollow-ware dates from the beginning of the nineteenth century.

Domestic table ware in production by 1790 might be listed to the number of one hundred and fifty different articles, some of which, such as candlesticks and cruets, were issued in hundreds of different patterns. Dinner and dessert services were selling at the factory for from fifty to three hundred guineas and breakfast sets for as much as two hundred guineas. At this time Sheffield plate was selling at about one-third the price of silver plate, which from 1782 was taxed to the extent of sixpence an ounce.

Proof of success was the devastating effect on the craft of silversmithing despite efforts at price-cutting factory methods. In 1797 the Goldsmiths' Company, on behalf of the Birmingham silversmiths, petitioned the government complaining that 'plated ware manufacturers have produced articles of the highest elegance and fashion, many of which are now made with solid silver borders, shields, ornaments, finished in exact resemblance of real plate'. A request was made that an excise duty of threepence an ounce should be placed on plated ware and that platers should be compelled to strike name or initials and the word 'plated' on each piece. It had been optional since 1784 to strike these, together with a registered trade mark or device. The plate varied in quality, ten to twelve ounces of sterling silver to eight pounds of copper being the standard proportions. When deep-cut engraving was required the thickness of the silver was doubled.

Candlesticks and candelabra

Candles of wax and tallow were still the most usual source of domestic illumination when George III was crowned. Chandeliers of brass and latten had been replaced for the most part by gilded wood and glass lustres. With these, in drawing- and dining-rooms, appeared shapely Sheffield plate table candlesticks and candelabra, their bold designs rendered adequately stable by fillings of melted resin and sand.

The classic ornament that swept through English industrial design during the 1760's revolutionized candlestick styles. Traditional baluster forms were outmoded by shouldered stems with vertical outlines. In Sheffield plate the stem was usually circular, tapering towards a round foot. Until the late 1770's it was without ornament: then stem and socket might be gadrooned and the lower stem fluted. The four-sided shouldered stem was also made, tapering to a square foot. There were architectural columns too, until the 1780's, capital and base usually matching their order. Less costly were the cylindrical stems, with trumpet-shaped feet at first and with square feet from about 1790. The variety of candlestick designs is beyond computation, but they follow definite fashion styles.

Branches were fitted to Sheffield plate candlesticks from the 1760's: from about 1780 it was customary for these to twist around a central finial rising from the pillar. To strengthen them and to assist stability, their arms were filled with soft solder.

Brass candlesticks were made in ever-increasing numbers during this period, price reductions and increased prosperity taking them into new homes. A new process applied to casting made it possible for stem and socket to be made in a single hollow piece, thus obviating the disfiguring hair-line marks of the vertical joins (Pl. 50A). The foot was cast separately and attached.

The major feature of brass history of this period, however, was the new brass composed of copper and zinc patented by James Emerson in 1770. This brass was described by R. Watson in *Chemical Essays*, 1786, as being 'more malleable, more beautiful, and of a colour more resembling gold than brass containing calamine'. It produced clear-cut modelling of a quality formerly attainable only by the costly use of princes metal and pinchbecks and the surface was rarely disfigured by pitting. The demand for table candlesticks in the new brass became enormous and by 1780 was responsible for the establishment of a new specialist trade.

Brass candlesticks of the early 1760's were for the most part square-footed with plain edges; moulded edges appeared by 1765 and the now rare gadrooned edge by 1770. Stems varied between the plain, attenuated baluster rising from one or two knops, and the plain or fluted column rising from the flat platform of a stepped plinth. From about 1780 to the end of the period the most popular stem was in the form of an elongated cone, round or square in section, and generally fluted, with a high pyramid or domed foot. The telescopic candlestick, found also in Sheffield plate, was patented in 1796 and had a considerable vogue.

Numerous other domestic accessories were cast in Emerson's brass and double gilded, such as pastille burners, girandoles, inkstands, paperweights, thermometer stands, watch stands, busts and figures of animals.

Crusie lamps in brass and copper

Open-flame crusie lamps in brass or copper plate came into widespread use from the early

1760's and continued into the Regency period. Such lamps might hang as chandeliers; others were table lamps, the design usually including a hollow stem rising from a spreading foot, pedestal and foot being weighted with sand.

Improvements in oil refining, wick manufacture and lamp designing at this time increased efficiency and resulted in almost smokeless and non-odorous illumination. For the first time the cylindrical reservoir was provided with a hinged lid, the straight tubular burner was fully enclosed, and oil dripping was prevented. Each burner – there might be as many as thirty – gave a yellowish flame equal to about two ordinary modern candles.

The Argand lamp in Sheffield plate and in brass appeared on the domestic scene in the 1780's, burning a tubular wick that provided an air passage in a ring flame which was made steady by a glass chimney. James Watt, the English licencee of the Argand lamp, recorded that 'they gave a light surpassing in steadiness anything known hitherto'. Liverpool lamps, also in Sheffield plate and brass, were evolved in about 1800. The principle was the same, but an adjustable disc set above the wick increased illumination by expanding the flame, the lower part of the chimney therefore being made globular. By about 1800 oil lamps were made for suspending from the ceiling and from wall brackets, catalogues referring to them in Grecian and Etruscan designs.

Emerson's brass rolled into sheet was shaped into domestic hollow-ware by stamping, a process patented in 1769 by Richard Ford of Birmingham. Compared with hand-raising this lessened the weight of metal required by more than two-thirds, with labour comparably reduced. Kitchenware was the chief production until 1780 when stamped brasswork, gilded and lacquered, was made for interior decoration. This included mouldings for wall panelling, sconces, and looking-glass frames. In 1783 Gee and Eginton advertised 'gilt metal or burnished gold frames, borderings and ornaments for rooms in stamped gilt metal'. The Birmingham firm of Yates, Hamper and Company issued a pattern book illustrating such ornament of the 1790's and examples

inspected by Aitkin in 1862 were reported as showing 'that sharp, shallow dies were used and so richly were they gilt that they pass with very good judges for burnished gold'.

Heyday of copper wares

Copper domestic ware continued to be made as formerly. The town coppersmith could show burnished coffee pots with ebony-stained boxwood handles; saucepans of all sizes with uprising handles in hardwood, often the yellow sapwood of *lignum vitae*; slow-burning charcoal braziers for warming foods; ladles and perforated skimmers; chestnut roasters; coach, foot and stomach warmers; cheese toasters; egg poachers and coddlers; wine strainers; flour and pepper boxes; washhand basins and jugs; knife, spoon and cheese trays; card racks, and a hundred other articles of domestic use. Frying-pans were made in great quantities, the half-hoop handle fitted with a swivel eye for hanging from a pot-hook. Ale warmers were in common use, the early form in the shape of a boot now superseded by the conical type for pushing down vertically into the heart of a grate fire.

Hollow-ware intended to contain food or water had to be tinned inside to combat poisoning hazards associated with copper and brass. Re-tinning was needed very frequently until 1774 when John Bootie patented the long-wearing method of tinning with hot sal-ammoniac and pure molten tin. Even this was far from permanent.

The stamp was brought into use for shallow, light-weight hollow-ware such as warming-pans, plate covers and ladles. Curves were now introduced into warming-pan design and from 1780 handles were usually black japanned. The Earl of Carlisle's household papers show that a copper warming-pan cost him fourteen shillings in 1741 but in 1780 only three shillings and tenpence. By 1780 the wooden handle might be made to unscrew from its socket, enabling the pan to remain fully enclosed by the bedclothes. The hot-water warming-pan, at first in pewter, gradually superseded the charcoal-heated variety from the 1770's and, according to Edward Thomason, a maker of warming-pans, few of the charcoal-heated type were sold after about 1810. The hot-water warming-pan had a brass cap in the centre for filling (Pl. 51B).

Bottle roasting jacks operating by clockwork mechanism of brass within cases of brass or copper date from the 1760's onwards, and within twenty years their manufacture had become a considerable trade. John Linwood, in the late 1790's, made mechanical improvements that enabled them to twist and untwist for from two to four hours according to the weight of the load. Such a roasting jack was suspended from a jack-rack clamped to the extending centre of the mantelshelf, or hung within the tall, niche-shaped enclosure of tinned sheet iron known as a Dutch oven. This measured about five feet in height and enabled roasting to be done in front of a coal-fire grate. Its curved sides and top reflected heat upon the rotating joint from which fat and gravy fell into a deep pan below.

Urns for tea and coffee

Tea and coffee urns came into use early in the 1760's, silver styles quickly being reflected in Sheffield plate, copper and japanned iron. They were evolved from the 'tea fountain', a hot-water kettle with a tap fitted immediately above the kettle's flat base, a type that continued throughout the period.

The first tea urns contained a quart and were heated with charcoal. In this design the vessel could be lifted from its stem, which supported a perforated cylinder containing burning charcoal. These were outmoded by 1774 when John Wadham patented an urn in which heat was maintained by a cylindrical box iron. This was made red-hot in the kitchen fire and inserted into a close-fitting heater case, rising centrally from the base within the urn so that the water circulated around it. This type of heater became widespread after expiration of the patent in 1788. At about this time some urns were heated with spirit lamps, these vessels tending to be of fine quality for the smokeless spirits of wine was a costly fuel. Mortar candles might also be used from the late 1790's

910

Three standard sizes of urn were in regular production in the eighteenth century – quart, three pints and gallon. Giant urns of five to eight quarts date from about 1805. Late Georgian hardware catalogues illustrated them indiscriminately as tea and coffee urns, with the exception of three-pint sizes which were almost invariably captioned as 'Coffee Urn to hold 3 pints' (Pl. 51C).

The dating of japanned wares

Colourful japanned urns and other articles contributed a delightful radiance to late Georgian homes. Vermilion, rich green, chocolate, yellow, tortoiseshell or black formed the background to pictures of considerable merit painted by clever artists and efficient but less persuasive work by capable artisan copyists. Japanned iron took on a new brilliance in the 1760's when new japanning factories opened at Wolverhampton, Birmingham and elsewhere, striving their utmost to emulate Pontypool japan ware, even to the extent of naming their productions 'Pontipool japan'. The scope was wide and included urns, kettles and smokers' brazier sets, chestnut servers, cheese cradles, toilet boxes, coasters, tea canisters, letter racks, trays and waiters (Pl. 51).

Oriental figures and landscapes in shaded gold formed the predominant type of decoration until the mid-1760's when colour was introduced to the gold, creating rich effects. Large areas might be painted with landscapes or architectural designs, such an article as a tray being covered to the edge of the rim. Flower painting dates from about 1780 with flowers and foliage in dull bronze shades. By the 1800's there was a vogue for huge chrysanthemums or asters: stalks were in gold and leaves in shades of yellow. In early work as many as fifteen stovings were given to background colours, the final coating remaining in the oven for between three and four weeks.

A japanned tea-tray, known as a 'hand tea table' was used for the tea equipage, being set out with a tea urn and porcelain. At first it was square or oblong with corners folded and riveted; by 1770 corners were cut and brazed; and from the 1790's hammered turn-over rims were frequent. A circular or oval tray hammered from thinly rolled plate – tinned for fine work – might be encircled with a border of pierced pales, and narrow handle holes might be cut.

Pewter and its rivals

The introduction of liquid lead glaze on ceramics immensely widened the scope of enamelled earthenwares in the average home, as it did the porcelains of the wealthy, and one obvious result was a drastic reduction in demand for the pewterer's domestic ware. Candlesticks in shapes resembling those of brass continued to be made, however, along with a variety of kitchen ware such as salt cellars, casters, jugs, tea canisters, the newly-invented hot-water dishes, and so on.

Highly ornamental desserts of lavish proportions were fashionable at this period and pewterers were called upon to make capacious jelly and blancmange moulds designed to open piece by piece, so that undercut effects such as piles of luscious fruits could be removed without damage. In another design the top and base of the mould might be separate from the main section which was delicately fluted within.

Pewter had other competitors too. A soft tin alloy, so closely resembling silver in appearance that the casual observer would never differentiate between the two, was introduced in 1769 by John Vickers of Sheffield. In the 1780's he was advertising such domestic ware as teapots, sugar basins, cream jugs, beakers, tobacco boxes, caster frames, all following Sheffield plate designs in 'Vickers' White Ware' (Pl. 52D).

Pewter met with additional, and this time deadly, competition in the early 1790's when John Vickers introduced Britannia metal, an alloy of tin, antimony, copper and bismuth, rolled into plate or cast. Its toughness made it a distinct advance on pewter. When polished, this silvery-white metal, faintly tinged with blue, became highly lustrous and greatly enhanced the tables of those who could afford neither silver nor Sheffield plate. Standard quality Britannia metal, if struck with a wooden rod, emits a clear, ringing tone, similar to that of X-crown pewter.

Britannia metal domestic ware until about 1805 was made only in small sizes, constructed from hand-raised and stamped units. Early in the nineteenth century, however, hollow-ware was spun, and cast decoration might be added. Such ware was lighter in weight than pewter of comparable size. Earthenware and stoneware drinking vessels were made with Britannia metal rims and hinged lids. Spoons and ladles were cast and burnished.

The considerable mid-Georgian trade in tin plate domestic ware continued into the period under review. Table ware included heavily tinned and burnished venison dishes, salmon dishes, soup tureens and vegetable dishes, between the invention of the process of tinning and the development of Sheffield plate. Dish covers and teapots were hammer-shaped, but the seams prevented attractive outlines.

Iron 'kitchen furniture'

Iron plate could be shaped into pots, kettles and saucepans at this period for about one-third the cost of copper, but they were cumbersome objects until the 1760's when carbon iron made possible scale-free plate more suitable for tinning. The Cort patents of 1784 so vastly improved the puddling and rolling processes that almost every article of domestic ware could be made in tinned iron plate. Output soared: in 1788 there were 77 blast furnaces operating in England; by 1806 there were 222. Domestic ware continued to be hand-made for iron plate could not yet withstand the stamp without splitting: a patty-pan, for instance, consisted of several pieces of tin plate brazed or soldered together.

Domestic hollow-ware, catalogued as 'kitchen furniture', in long-wearing, light-weight tinned cast iron dates from 1779 when Jonathan Taylor, a workman at the Eagle Foundry, Birmingham, patented a method of casting oval-bellied and round cast iron pots 'nealing, turning, tinning and finishing the same'. These were attractive in appearance and much cheaper than hand-wrought plate, brass or copper. At first black lead was used as an outside coating: this was replaced by stove-dried varnish from about 1800. At about the same time umbrella stands, door-porters, door-knockers, shoe-scrapers, smoothing-irons, latches and handles were cast by the same process.

Malleable cast iron, in which small objects for the home could be sold at less than one-third the cost of wrought iron, was invented in 1804 by Samuel Lucas of Sheffield. Handles and latches made of malleable cast iron were, for their purpose, quite as strong as those of wrought iron.

Burnished steel around the fire

The focal point of a fashionably furnished room was the fireplate equipped with a portable grate, fender and fire-irons in burnished steel. John Byng in *The Torrington Diaries*, 1791, recorded that 'in summer the grates and fenders are polished up, the tongs, shovel and poker laid up for the summer'. He also observed that when a fire was lighted the brilliancy of the grate was spoiled. Architects designed mantelpiece, grate and fender; the pierced motifs in the steel were repeated in the carving (Pl. 49).

The pierced steel fender, bowed and often with an undulating upper edge, was costly but gave unlimited wear. The hand-sawn pierced design extended from end to end in a single over-all pattern composed of birds, animals, flowers, foliage and scrollwork, surface chased in a manner resembling ornament on silver, and edged with narrow wrought moulding. This style, continuing from early Georgian days, was followed by alternating classic motifs such as the anthemion and star, or urn and rosette, the upper edge bordered with a low, vertical fret-cut rim of repetitive motifs. The same theme might be repeated on the apron of the grate.

These were followed in the 1790's by press-cut steel in thinner gauge, factory made in short panels, wide and narrow, bordered top and bottom with narrow bands of vertical piercings. Many of these were made at Kirkstall Forge, Leeds, where there was an extensive mill for grinding and polishing steel units. Other pierced ornaments consisted of a central band of convex medallions enriched with bright cutting, with pierced backgrounds and borders, the top and bottom edges being strengthened with rows of beading. A panel displaying a large version of the predominating motif might be riveted in the centre. Complex trellis work is also found. Fenders in all these styles were made of

latten or battery brass sheet, too, and late in the period the grate and fender might be of heavily cast and chased brass.

Tongs, shovel and poker were made of burnished iron. At first handle ornament was wrought in the solid metal, but improvements in the quality of iron during the 1780's made it possible to do this by lapping, that is, by turning a piece of hot iron around the heated rod wherever a knop was required. The twisted shank dates from the 1790's, shaped by tools or hand-twisted. The shovels were cut from sheet iron.

Wolverhampton locks

Door locks in the main followed the early Georgian styles with Wolverhampton still leading the way. When George III equipped the Queen's House, now Buckingham Palace, he specified that every state-room lock should be made in Wolverhampton. A new style in mortice lock furniture for fitting into solid mahogany doors was sponsored in the mid-1760's by Robert Adam. Such a lock, which cost twelve guineas, consisted of an expansive back plate of chased and gilt cast brass, in scrollwork designs symmetrically arranged with festoons of husks, centring on the door knob and flanked with a keyhole escutcheon and a matching dummy escutcheon, or a small knob for operating a night bolt.

Lock cases stamped from rolled brass, weighing less than a third of the earlier hand-made type, date from the late 1770's. They were cast too in Emerson's brass with plain, square or moulded edges and surfaces were virtually unflawed by pitting. Brass locks continued to be finely engraved, and intricate damascening was revived from the seventeenth century.

Security emphasis was laid upon wards which had now become highly complicated, but were still not proof against skeleton keys. Robert Barron patented in 1778 a system of fixed wards in combination with levers. Only its own specially made key would open such a lock which within a few years had achieved world-wide renown. Joseph Bramah invented the first door lock with a small key in 1784, operating, not on a sliding bolt but through the medium of a rotating barrel –

thus anticipating Yale's cylindrical lock of 1848. The first cheap locks were made in 1796 when Isaac Mason of Willenhall first cut the cases from sheet iron and punched and bolstered them by the fly press.

Ornament in lead

Lead found a new purpose in the home during the late eighteenth century when interior decorators took it into use for making relief figure panels, garlands, vases and frets which were double gilt, or painted after washing eight times with 'gum lac, parchment and red lead'. The Somerset House accounts for 1780 record many payments for decorations of this nature such as lead pateras $2\frac{1}{2}d.$ to 10$d.$ each; 19 ornamental friezes to chimney pieces £10 17$s.$ 8$d.$; lead frieze to book cases, 2$s.$ 6$d.$ per foot. In 1778 John Cheere, lead figure maker, submitted a bill for 'moulding, casting and finishing four large

sphinxes, lead and block tin, at each, £31'. Lead figure making was an established craft of the period. Soft pure lead was used hardened by a process invented by William Storer in 1770 by which 'all sorts of girandoles, frames for pier glasses, tablets, friezes and brackets for chimney pieces and rooms could be chased to the full relief of the boldest and richest carving in wood'.

Front door fanlights were filled with gracefully designed windows outlined with lead castings made sturdy with a backing of iron. Staircase balustrades might also be cast in panels of hard lead lattice work fixed between iron standards a yard or more apart. To the late Georgian even homely lead was an artistic medium, confined within the limited scope of permissible neoclassic design, but playing its gracious part in an age that expected its metalwork to contribute ornamental refinement as well as enduring service to the elegant home.

Tail-piece from T. Bewick's *A History of British Birds*, Vol. 2, 1804.

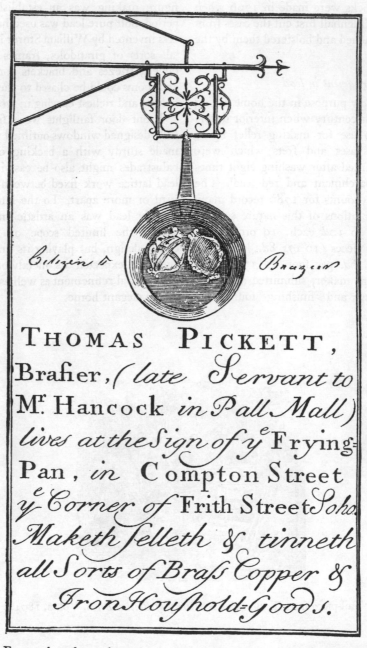

Citizen to Brazers

THOMAS PICKETT, Brafier, (late Servant to Mr. Hancock in Pall Mall) lives at the Sign of ye Frying-Pan, in Compton Street ye Corner of Frith Street Soho. Maketh selleth & tinneth all Sorts of Brass Copper & Iron Houshold-Goods.

Engraved tradesman's card of the late eighteenth century. From Sir Ambrose Heal's *London Tradesmen's Cards of the Eighteenth Century*, 1925.

914

Textiles

DONALD KING

In the overall effect of the late Georgian interior, the patterns of textiles played a less dominant role than they had done in earlier periods. This is not to say that the domestic use of textiles diminished or underwent any fundamental change. Textiles retained their practical and decorative value as coverings for floors, chairs, settees, cushions, tables and beds, and as hangings for beds, windows and walls. Quantitatively, the textile furnishings of a fashionable room tended to increase rather than decrease, so that at the end of the eighteenth century interiors such as those of Carlton House were muffled and shrouded in a plethora of draperies, curtains, festoons and fringes. But the taste of the age inclined mainly to plain, unpatterned stuffs, or to materials having designs in a single colour or discreetly powdered with small polychrome motifs. Moreover, it was to the advantage of the artist-decorator, who achieved a new prominence in this period, to exclude from his schemes strongly patterned textiles of variegated colour, in order that the subtlety of his own arrangements of line and form, colour and texture, might be the more apparent. As a result, the more boldly patterned woven stuffs tended to disappear, while tapestry and embroidery, techniques particularly adapted to large-scale polychrome designs, lost their former importance. Only carpet-design retained a bold scale, since the interior decorators found that it could be used to re-echo at floor level the design of the plasterwork of ceilings.

Woven textiles

Besides the non-textile material, leather, which was extensively used for upholstery, a very large proportion of the woven textiles used in the interior decoration of English houses consisted of plain, unpatterned stuffs. The sheen of satin was much appreciated, and white, cream and other pale-coloured satins were used in great quantities. Lady Mary Coke, visiting Lord Bute's house in 1774, gives a characteristic view of an interior in the contemporary style, when she writes that almost all the rooms were hung with light green plain papers, showing the pictures to great advantage, while the chairs, beds and so on were chiefly of satin, light green and white, which had a very good effect. In Mrs Fitzherbert's house in Pall Mall, Mary Frampton's journal records a room 'hung with puckered blue satin'. Hepplewhite's *Guide* (1788) observes, *à propos* bed-hangings, that 'they may be of almost every stuff which the loom produces' but that 'in state-rooms, where a high degree of elegance and grandeur are wanted beds are frequently made of silk or satin, figured or plain, also of velvet, with gold fringe, &c.' Plain velvets were frequently used for hangings and upholstery, generally in muted shades such as the drab green used by Adam for the gathered wall-hangings of the state bedchamber at Osterley.

Watered silks and silk mixtures were also favourite materials for upholstery, while in the second half of the period chairs and settees were often covered in materials having wide or narrow satin stripes. Silk and silk mixture damasks were extensively used for both upholstery and hangings, as may be seen for instance from their frequent occurrence in Chippendale's bills. These damasks had floral designs, often of a rather conventional character, in a single colour, generally red or blue, though yellow, green and other colours also occur. Damask was a favourite material for the hangings of state beds; the *Universal System* (1759–63) of Ince and Mayhew records a domed bed in blue damask, while a bed of about 1770 at Harewood has a valance of red damask. In the crimson drawing-room at Carlton House (about 1790) the wall-hangings and window curtains were, according to Pyne, of crimson 'satin damask of a beautiful figure and texture from the British loom'; similarly in the rose drawing-room the curtains and wall-hangings were of rose-coloured satin damask with gold fringes.

Among silks of more than one colour, that used by Adam for the wall-hangings, window curtains and upholstery of the red drawing-room (about 1770) at Syon, with a design of serpentine ribands and large semi-naturalistic flower sprays in white on a plum-red ground, makes an unusually bold effect. Normally more modest patterns were preferred, and fabrics such as the polychrome Genoa velvets with their large Baroque designs, so much used earlier in the eighteenth century, were no longer fashionable. Brocaded satins, with small polychrome flowers on white or pale-toned satin grounds, were much favoured.

Of woven stuffs in linen, wool and cotton, only the tablecloths and napkins of linen damask demand particular notice. Their designs, entirely in white, were generally floral or armorial; hunting scenes are also occasionally found.

Very little information is available regarding the origins of these various woven materials. The linen damasks seem to have been made in a number of places in England, Scotland and Ireland. Of the silks and velvets, some were no doubt imported from Lyons and other French and Italian centres of silk-weaving, but many were probably woven in England. The weaving of silk was carried on in various towns, among them Macclesfield, Manchester and Norwich, but the chief English centre of the craft remained the district of Spitalfields and Bethnal Green, where it seems to have been introduced by Huguenot refugees at the end of the seventeenth century.

Unfortunately, the detailed history of Spitalfields silk-weaving remains to be written and little is known at present of the designers and master-weavers of the late Georgian period. The decline in the vogue for patterned silks, for both dress and furnishing purposes, evidently caused some distress and unemployment (it was estimated in 1776 that one thousand seven hundred and sixty-eight silk looms were idle), but it is likely that production remained at a sufficiently high level to fulfil most of the domestic demand both for plain and for patterned stuffs.

Tapestry

In the second half of the eighteenth century, the demand for tapestry wall-hangings dwindled almost to vanishing point. The great Flemish workshops, which had supplied England and the rest of Europe with most of their tapestries ever since the middle ages, decayed and died. The production of the last notable tapestry-weaver of the eighteenth century in England, Paul Saunders (died 1770), belongs essentially to the preceding period. Only the French centres of the craft, possessing the best designs and the most skilful weavers of the day, and supported by state patronage, kept alive the traditions of fine tapestry-weaving.

It is characteristic of the taste of the time that some of the most fashionable of the French designs were not of an exclusively pictorial type, but consisted mainly of simulated silk damask with a floral pattern, while the nominal subject of the tapestry was rendered in the guise of a small framed painting, apparently hanging on a wall covered with the feigned silk stuff. Tapestries of this type, the well known *Tentures de François Boucher*, in which the pictorial panels with the loves of the gods and other subjects were designed by Boucher and the floral surrounds by Maurice Jacques, were woven several times by Jacques Neilson at the Gobelins for English patrons. They were not intended to be hung indiscriminately in any convenient room, but were woven to measure, often with furniture *en suite*, for special tapestry rooms, where they were hung edge to edge, so as to cover the entire wall-surface above the dado, in the same way as a silk wall-hanging; it is note-worthy that this method of hanging tapestries seems to have been peculiarly English and was unknown in France. The more important of the sets of the *Tentures de François Boucher* woven for English houses are the following: (1) three large and eight small hangings, with two settees and six chairs, on a rose damask ground, woven 1766–71 for the Earl of Coventry, formerly at Croome Court; (2) three large and six small hangings, with two settees, twelve chairs and a screen, on a mauve damask ground, woven 1766–71 for William Weddell, at Newby Hall, Yorks.; (3) three large and five small hangings on a rose damask ground, woven 1766–71 for Sir Henry Bridgeman, at Weston Park; (4) one large and eight small hangings, with eighteen pieces of furniture, on a grey damask ground, woven 1767–9 for Sir Lawrence Dundas, originally hung at Moor Park and subsequently removed to 19 Arlington Street, London; (5) five large and eleven small hangings, with a settee, eight chairs and a screen, on a crimson damask ground, woven 1775–6 for Robert Child, at Osterley Park, (Pl. 53); (6) three large and three small hangings, with a settee, twelve chairs and two screens, on a crimson damask ground, woven in 1783 for the Duke of Portland, at Welbeck. These hangings for Welbeck represent the last notable commission for tapestries in the Georgian period.

Bibliography: Maurice Fenaille, *État général des tapisseries de la manufacture des Gobelins*, Vol. IV, Paris, 1907.

Embroidery

Embroidery, like tapestry, was much less prominent in the later Georgian house than it had been in earlier periods. In particular, needlework in *gros point* and *petit point*, which had been extensively used hitherto for wall-hangings, carpets and upholstery, failed to harmonize with the lightness and elegance of the new furnishing styles. It persisted, still using the large polychrome floral designs of the preceding period, for carpets, chairs and firescreens, down to about 1765, but thereafter it became comparatively rare. The few carpets and chairs worked in this kind of needle-work during the late eighteenth century generally have insignificant geometrical diaper patterns in a restricted range of colour.

A technique more in harmony with prevailing taste was that of embroidering naturalistic flower-groups in flat stitches on a white or pale-coloured satin ground. This type of embroidery was principally used, as in the preceding period, for bed-furniture. The hangings of Queen Charlotte's bed (about 1775) at Hampton Court, of lilac and pale primrose satin, have attractive needlework of this kind worked by a Mrs Pawsey, who had a school of embroidery at Aylesbury. A cradle destined for one of Queen Charlotte's children, and now in the London Museum, has a white satin coverlet and curtains embroidered in a similar style. The green velvet and satin furniture of the domed state bed at Osterley, designed by Adam in 1776, also has flower garlands and classical motifs worked in this manner (Pl. 54). These provoked Horace Walpole's caustic observation that the bed was 'too like a modern head-dress, for round the outside of the dome are festoons of artificial flowers. What would Vitruvius think of a dome decorated by a milliner?' The same kind of embroidery, worked with coloured silks in flat stitches on a white satin or silk ground, continued in use down to the end of the century for the small oval, rectangular, or shield-shaped panels of pole-screens. In these panels the motifs most frequently seen are bouquets of naturalistic flowers, maps, or classical urns (Pl. 55); a pole-screen designed by Adam, in the Etruscan Room at Osterley, has an embroidered panel with an urn design.

Wall-hangings in needlework were extremely rare in this period, but Adam's work for Thomas Hogg at Newliston, near Edinburgh, included designs for twelve large embroideries inset into the panelling of the drawing room. These, worked by Lady Mary Hogg in wool appliqué, with the details partly stitched and partly painted in water colours, on a cream watered silk ground, show urns, sphinxes, acanthus scrolls and cameo panels. In humbler settings, the appliqué technique was utilized for coverlets, with floral motifs, cut from printed cottons, stitched to a cotton ground;

towards the end of the period floral panels were being specially printed to serve as centrepieces for such coverlets. A few examples of patchwork quilts, with geometrical designs built up from countless small regularly shaped pieces of silk or printed cotton, may also be attributed to this period.

There can be no doubt, however, that the type of domestic needlework most characteristic of the late eighteenth and early nineteenth century was the embroidered picture. The retreat of embroidery into the picture-frame, a process which had begun already in the seventeenth century, now reached its culmination in an attempt to reproduce the effects of painting. In this field a number of ladies achieved a fame and eminence which today seem vastly exaggerated, if not entirely misplaced. The embroidered copies after paintings by old and modern masters which these ladies produced, covering their canvas completely with coloured worsteds in long irregular stitches which sought to imitate the brushwork of the painter, are often, indeed, remarkable for their dexterity, but it is hard to take seriously the taste which rated them equal, if not superior, to the paintings which they copied, and set on them values running into hundreds, and sometimes into thousands, of pounds. Of Miss Grey, of Northamptonshire, a contemporary observer notes that she astonished 'the world of painters by her works in worsted'; in 1755, there is mention of 'a bunch of grapes of her doing that are equal to anything of Rubens'; and the Princess of Wales, on seeing another picture of hers, after Rubens, is said to have given her an honorarium of a hundred guineas. It may be that the vogue for these needle-paintings owed something to Queen Charlotte s taste. Mrs Mary Knowles (1733–1807), referred to in a letter from Dr Johnson to Mrs Thrale as 'the Quaker, that works the sutile pictures', was a frequent visitor at Buckingham Palace, and one of her principal works was a portrait of George III after Zoffany, worked in 1771 at the express command of the Queen (Pl. 56). Horace Walpole had at Strawberry Hill a landscape after van Uden by her hand. The most renowned of the workers in this style, however,

was Miss Mary Linwood (1755–1846) of Leicester. In 1776 and 1778 she showed specimens of her work at the exhibitions of the Royal Society of Artists, and in 1787, having first been received and complimented by the Queen, she opened a large exhibition of her embroidered pictures in London. This exhibition subsequently visited Edinburgh, Dublin and the chief provincial towns, and it was once more a feature of the London scene as late as 1831, when *The Times* commented enthusiastically on her last work, 'The Malediction of Cain', observing that 'the forms and expression of the figures discover the power of Michael Angelo, and the whole effect of the piece . . . is almost magical, and beyond the power of the pencil'. Her masterpiece, the 'Salvator Mundi' after Dolci, for which she is said to have refused an offer of three thousand guineas, she bequeathed to Queen Victoria; it still hangs at Windsor Castle. A collection of her work may be seen at the Leicester Museum.

The less skilful or ambitious needlewoman could emulate the productions of these virtuosi by buying panels of white silk on which pictorial designs had been drawn, chiefly in outline, but with the sky and flesh-parts carefully painted in water colours. The dresses, hair and landscape were then embroidered with coloured wools and silks in the characteristic long stitches, while the painted parts were left exposed. The subjects of these pictures are generally romantic scenes of a somewhat lugubrious cast – Charlotte at the tomb of Werther or Fame strewing flowers on the tomb of Shakespeare; mythological, Scriptural and Shakespearian subjects also occur. Another type of embroidered picture was worked in black silk only, on a white silk ground, in imitation of engravings; this style, essayed by Miss Linwood in 1782, was still being practised as late as the 1851 exhibition. Such pictures are generally topographical, though portraits and other subjects are also found.

The trend towards pictorialism in needlework also affected the embroidered sampler, which in this period almost entirely lost its original function as a practice and reference sheet for a variety of stitches and motifs and became a decorative exercise in cross stitch, incorporating a representation of a house, human figures and other pictorial elements, together with some pious verses. Samplers of this type were frequently framed and hung on the wall like the embroidered pictures. Maps, of England, Europe and other parts of the world, were also worked and treated in the same way.

Bibliography: M. Jourdain, *English Secular Embroidery*, London, 1910; A. F. Kendrick, *English Needlework*, London, 1933.

Painted and printed textiles

Painted and printed textiles, though not generally used in the state rooms of the grandest houses, were none the less of great importance in late Georgian furnishing. This was no new phenomenon. In one form or another they had played a significant role since the Middle Ages. But the lightness of their effects was especially congenial to the new furnishing styles and they were extensively used as bed-hangings, coverlets and window-curtains, and for the upholstery of chairs and settees.

Some of the painted silks were imported from China; these have polychrome floral patterns executed in body-colour, generally on a white satin ground. Others were made in England. The brothers Francis Frederick and George Eckhardt, whose factory was in King's Road, Chelsea, took out a variety of patents from 1780 onwards for painted and printed silks, linens and papers; among their specialities were varnished, washable furnishing fabrics printed in gold and silver. Sheraton, in his *Drawing Book* (1791–4) writes of the printed and painted silks of the Eckhardts as being 'adapted for the purpose of ornamenting panels and the walls of the most elegant and noble houses', but no surviving examples of this type are known. Both Hepplewhite's and Sheraton's books suggest the use of small panels of painted or printed silk for the decoration of chairs; this usage is exemplified by a settee of about 1785 at Kyre Park, which has three oval panels of silk, painted with figure subjects, inserted in the back. Similar small panels, with figure scenes painted in water colours, were

also employed for pole-screens, while a cabinet of about 1780 in the Lady Lever Art Gallery has its doors lined with satin panels painted with designs of urns and flowers. The Eckhardt factory is known to have closed in 1796, but others were no doubt active; as late as 1808, George Smith, in his *Household Furniture*, included painted satin among the materials suitable for expensively furnished rooms.

The import of chintz, the painted and dyed cotton material of India, had been banned since 1701, but it is clear that the prohibition was sometimes evaded. There is an amusing correspondence of 1775 between David Garrick and Sir Grey Cooper, in which the actor pleads for the release of some chintz bed-hangings, which, after being in his wife's possession for four years, had been seized by the Customs authorities. Garrick's wit was not wasted; the hangings, with their designs of slender trees, found their way back to his villa and, eventually, to the Victoria and Albert museum. Mrs Lybbe Powys, visiting Sir Walter Blount's house, Mawley, near Ludlow, in 1771, was moved to remark, 'I think Lady Blount has more chintz counterpanes than one house ever saw; not one bed without very fine ones.'

The work of the English printers of cotton and cotton mixture materials in the eighteenth century, to judge from the admiring comments of continental competitors, was second to none in both design and technique. Hepplewhite's *Guide* (1788) pays it a somewhat involved compliment in recommending for bed-hangings the employment of 'printed cotton or linen . . . the elegance and variety of which afford as much scope for taste, elegance and simplicity as the most lively fancy can wish'. Unfortunately, these materials were little valued by succeeding generations and surviving examples are rare. In particular the stuffs printed from wood-blocks, which formed the bulk of the production, have almost entirely disappeared. Their floral patterns, often of an Oriental character, were produced by the old Indian technique of madder-dyeing, in a colour range of blues, reds, and violets, with a little yellow and green, generally on a white ground;

dark, almost black, grounds were a special feature of the 1790's, and towards the end of the period the palette was enriched by advances in dye chemistry. Some of the best designs were produced in the old centres of the English cloth-printing industry, on the rivers Lea and Wandle near London, but these factories suffered heavily in this period from the competition of the rapidly developing Lancashire factories, which employed the technique of printing from rollers to introduce a new class of cheap, mass-produced goods.

Besides the block-prints, cloth printed from engraved copper plates in a single colour (red, blue, violet or sepia; additional colours were occasionally added by block-printing) on a white ground enjoyed a great vogue in this period. Such prints have come to be known as 'toiles de Jouy', with reference to the well-known examples produced at the Oberkampf factory at Jouy, near Versailles, but they had been an English speciality for fully a quarter of a century before Oberkampf first turned his attention to them. The earliest record of the process dates from 1752, when Mrs Delany visited at Drumcondra, in Ireland, 'a manufactory that is set up there of printed linens done by copper plates; they are excessive pretty'. This factory was that of Francis Nixon, who in 1757 transferred his activities to Phippsbridge, near Mitcham. In 1758, Benjamin Franklin, on a visit to London, sent home to his wife, for bed and window curtains '56 yards of cotton printed curiously from copper plates', and by the 1760's a considerable number of manufacturers had adopted the new technique. Some had the fortunate habit of signing their work. Without doubt the finest surviving specimens of the type are two signed by Robert Jones of Old Ford, whose factory and equipment (including two hundred copper plates and two thousand wood-blocks) were sold by auction in 1780. The first of these, dated 1761, and printed in red, has pastoral and other subjects derived from engravings by Berchem, Barlow and Sympson; the second, dated 1769 and printed in violet, with additional colours added from blocks, shows some elegantly drawn personages on shooting and fishing expeditions (Pl. 57). John Collins, of Woolmers in Hertfordshire, signed two prints

with rustic subjects in 1765, and a *chinoiserie* piece, based on Sir William Chambers' engravings of his buildings in Kew Gardens, in 1766. A print with fashionably dressed ladies and gentlemen in a garden is signed by the engraver D. Richards of Manchester and dates from about 1785. A design commemorative of George Washington, doubtless made for export to the United States, bears the signature of Henry Gardiner, who operated a factory at Wandsworth in the late eighteenth and early nineteenth century. There are also a number of anonymous examples with floral, rustic, classical, *chinoiserie*, sporting and topical designs. Our knowledge of this type of textile print has recently been greatly extended by the discovery of three books (one now in the Victoria and Albert Museum, London, two in the Musée de l'Impression at Mulhouse) containing paper impressions from several hundred copper plates of London textile printers of the late eighteenth century. The popularity of these engraved furnishing prints declined after about 1790 and the early nineteenth century examples, often printed from rollers, tend to be less sophisticated in design and comparatively coarse in execution.

Bibliography: Frank Lewis, *English Chintz* (2nd edition), Leigh-on-Sea, 1942; *Catalogue of an Exhibition of English Chintz*, Victoria and Albert Museum, 1955.

Carpets

Heavy, durable fabrics suitable for floor-coverings may be made in a variety of ways – by embroidering in wool on canvas, by weaving, and by pile-knotting as in Oriental rugs. All three methods were in use in the late Georgian period, though the first-named, as has been mentioned above, became comparatively rare.

The tapestry process does not seem to have been applied to carpet-making in England, although carpets woven by this method at Aubusson in France were imported and used in this country. There was, however, a flourishing English industry engaged in the production of various other types of woven carpets. Some were double cloths, i.e., they consisted of two plain cloths of different colour woven together in such a way that first one

Fig. 1. English late Georgian textile patterns: (A) Silk, *c.* 1770. (B) Brocaded silk, *c.* 1770. (C) Brocaded silk, *c.* 1780. (D) Printed cotton, *c.* 1790. *All in Victoria and Albert Museum.*

and then the other cloth appeared on the surface, thus producing a thick material with a two-colour design. Kidderminster gave its name to this type of fabric, which had been made there since the seventeenth century; the same method was also in use in the Scottish centres of the industry, such as Kilmarnock. Better wearing qualities and patterns, with up to six colours, could be obtained in Brussels carpets, which have a looped pile woven in the manner of an uncut or terry velvet. These were woven at both Wilton and Kidderminster; by 1807, the flourishing carpet industry of the latter place numbered as many as a thousand looms. In a refinement of the Brussels type, introduced at Wilton and subsequently known as Wilton carpet, the loops of the pile are cut, on the analogy of a cut-pile velvet, giving a richer, softer texture. Unfortunately, no English woven carpet of this period has yet been identified. Most of them were probably plain or with fairly simple patterns, and were woven in narrow widths which could be joined together to form a large carpet.

Of hand-knotted carpets, the great majority in use in England were imported, as in previous periods, from Turkey, Persia and India, and conformed to the Oriental traditions of carpet design. A few may also have been imported from continental factories, of which the most important was that of the Savonnerie, near Paris. It was the arrival in London in 1750 of some former workers of the Savonnerie that brought about a renewal of the craft of carpet-knotting in England, where, although it had been widely practised in late Tudor and Stuart times, it had since almost entirely disappeared. In 1756, 1757 and 1758, with a view to encouraging the nascent industry, the Royal Society of Arts offered premiums to makers of hand-knotted carpets. The awards were shared equally, in the first year of the competition, between Thomas Moore, of Chiswell Street, Moorfields, and Thomas Whitty of Axminster; Moore's carpet was considered to be the finer but was denied first place since it was nearly three times as expensive as Whitty's carpet, though of the same size. The next year, Whitty again shared the prize, this time with Claude Passavant, a native of Basle who had set up a factory at Exeter,

and in the third year he won the competition outright. These three firms, of Moore, Whitty and Passavant, were the principal English producers of hand-knotted carpets in the late Georgian period. Passavant's work, however, is known only from carpets made before 1760 and is therefore discussed in the preceding volume.

Moore evidently worked for the best houses. Horace Walpole ordered Moorfields carpets for the additions to Strawberry Hill which were completed in 1764. In 1768, Lady Mary Coke paid a visit to the factory and noted in her diary: 'They make several different kinds, and some remarkably fine: we saw one that was making for Ld. Coventry, that he had agreed to give a hundred and forty guineas for: it is indeed excessively fine. There are other kinds that are made like the persian, look quite as well.' Moore is best known for his collaboration with Adam. A carpet at Syon House, with a classical design by Adam carried out in numerous brilliant colours, is signed 'by . Thomas . Moore . 1769' (Pl. 58); an almost identical carpet belongs to the Earl of Shrewsbury. Some carpets with classical and floral motifs at Osterley Park, for which Adam's designs, two of them dated 1775 and 1778, are preserved in the Soane Museum, were probably made by Moore (Pl. 59A, B). Other carpets which probably resulted from this collaboration are two at Saltram, one in the Music Room at Harewood, and several formerly at 19 Arlington Street, which were probably removed, like the Boucher tapestries, from Moor Park. A notable feature of several of these Adam carpets is that they were designed to echo, without exactly reproducing, the designs of the ceilings beneath which they were placed.

Moore's principal competitor, Thomas Whitty, encouraged by seeing Parisot's factory at Fulham, began his first knotted carpet at Axminster in 1755; the factory flourished for many years and remained in his family until it closed down in 1835. Unfortunately, although a few documented pieces exist from the last period of the firm's activity, there is nothing that can be attributed with complete certainty to its first sixty years. One of the strongest candidates is a carpet

Fig. 2. Female workers 'pencilling' printed textiles, i.e. adding blues and yellows by
hand-painting. 1754.

with a heterogeneous collection of motifs in the Pompeian style which was made for the Throne Room at Carlton House (now lent by Her Majesty the Queen to the Victoria and Albert Museum). Closely related to this, and likewise probably Axminster work, are several carpets whose designs of classical and floral motifs are characterized by large central medallions and narrow rectangular panels at each end. Carpets of this group include examples in the Victoria and Albert Museum (Pl. 60) and at Rocklease Manor, near Exeter, and one formerly at Woodhall Park, Herts. Other carpets attributed to Axminster are two with floral patterns at Althorp and four with classical designs, belonging to the Duke of Devonshire.

Bibliography: C. E. C. Tattersall, *A History of British Carpets*, Benfleet, 1934; *A Dictionary of English Furniture* (Revised edition by Ralph Edwards, 1954), s.v. Carpets.

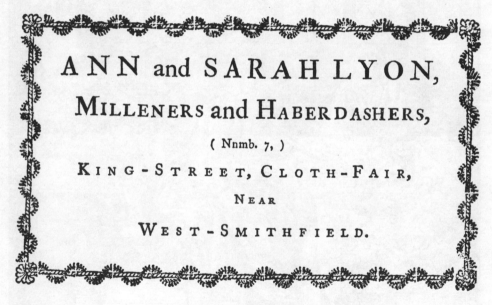

ANN and SARAH LYON,

MILLENERS and HABERDASHERS,

(Nnmb. 7,)

KING-STREET, CLOTH-FAIR,

NEAR

WEST-SMITHFIELD.

A late eighteenth-century printed handbill.

Costume

C. WILLETT CUNNINGTON

The fashions of an epoch, viewed from a certain distance, often seem to have been designed to suit a particular age-group. In the first half of the eighteenth century, for instance, male fashions imparted an air of dignity to a man of substance and assured position; one might say that those fashions had an 'optimum age' of about 35 to 40.

But in the second half of that century, and beyond, male fashions became more youthful in appearance, more slender and fitting the figure, less stiff and substantial; their optimum age was perhaps 20 to 30.

A similar, though less marked, change may be detected in the female fashions; a massive triangular shape became undulating with emphatic curves. But as there is always in them the desire – outspoken or whispered – of sex-attraction, the range of age-variation is narrower than in male fashions. Their optimum age sways to and fro from 17 to 30 but seldom beyond.

It is as though man's ideal woman varied at times from 'sweet seventeen' to *La Femme de trente ans.*

In the first half of the eighteenth century feminine fashions favoured the latter; in the second half there was a progressive movement towards the former, culminating in the virginal white frock of the Regency period displaying the charms of the youthful form.

This, then, was the essential feature in the fashions of the period 1760 to 1810, a phase of 'Youth knocking at the door'.

It was not unnatural that the fashions of England and France should have had much in com-mon; if the English gentleman provided the model for men, the young French queen Marie Antoinette was the ideal mannequin for women.

There was also a practical reason why this should have been so: from the beginning of the century the English gentleman had worn woollen textiles for his day suit and towards its close was using them also for evening, reserving silks and satins for ceremonial wear. And English woollen cloth had become the best in the world. On the other hand French silks were unrivalled and English women of fashion naturally favoured them. So that male fashions tended to come from England, female fashions from France.

The Revolution of 1789 was at first viewed with a good deal of sympathy from this country and there seemed nothing to interrupt the exchange of fashions until the Terror led in 1793 to the onset of a war lasting twenty years.

The event divided the period 1760–1810, and with it the trend of fashion in each country. Thanks to smuggling the interchange of textiles and costume designs did not cease during the long war, but in the exciting atmosphere of war, and without the check of foreign criticism, English taste was free to run riot.

It is convenient, then, to take the onset of war in 1793 as a division and to treat the fashions of each part separately.

The former was a phase of extravagant luxury with an abundance of imported silks from France; the latter a phase of wartime substitutes and imported cottons from India.

Whenever the pendulum of fashion swings in

this way towards younger forms of expression it coincides always with a phase of new and disturbing ideas floating in the social consciousness; ideas repugnant to the mature mind of the middle-aged, but attractive and exciting to the younger generation; whereupon fashion turns scornfully away from the one and casts its glamour on the other.

In France those new ideas, traced to the Encyclopedists, exploded in the Revolution of 1789; but they were germinating in England too. Social unrest, an upthrust from the lower classes against the upper, a breaking-down of forms of class-distinction, and a demand for a more democratic form of government, all these were disturbing the social structure in the opening years of George III's reign. In 1760 the heavy Hanoverian atmosphere of the Court disappeared; the new king was a young man of 22 with an English love of outdoor activities, and by the time George III had reached middle age the Prince of Wales had become the leader of fashion. Men's dress could hardly fail to be affected by the youthfulness of, first, sovereign, and then prince.

Feminine fashions tend always to follow man's lead; as he appears more youthful or more mature, so woman hastens to adjust her age to his taste. In the period following 1760 it was natural that her fashions should have started to become younger. Once this direction was taken the impetus swept on until, near the close of the century, the desire to discover modes still more youthful than the last produced the so-called 'classical dress'.

This doubtless had a resemblance to the garb of ancient Greece, but its more obvious appeal was that it was white. Being of cotton and cheap, any woman for a few shillings could assume the dress of a young girl. Being worn with a minimum of underclothing it had the further advantage of revealing the outlines of the whole body and for the first time the shape of the lower limbs became visible; a fashion which favoured only the youthful form and made the middle-aged look ridiculous.

Caricatures of the period perpetually satirized the spectacle of what the Prince Regent described as 'mutton dressed like lamb'. Never before had feminine fashions been so merciless to maturity.

The Macaroni

Fashions are not only sensitive to prevalent ideas which they attempt to express, but also to certain kinds of events. The reign of George II opened triumphantly; the victories of Clive and Coote had established the English hold on India, whence began to flow homeward a stream of Nabobs laden with spoils.

This new type of *nouveaux riches*, eager to exhibit their wealth, excited an orgy of extravagance in the fashions of the 'seventies, accompanied by a phase of delirious gambling; fortunes were won – or lost – by the turn of a dice-box.

The war with the American Colonies and its humiliating defeats passed almost unnoticed by the world of fashion; far more attention was being paid to that strange phenomenon the Macaroni. 'The Macaroni Club', wrote Horace Walpole in 1764, 'is composed of all the travelled young men who wear long curls and spying-glasses.' It had originated as a kind of protest against the crude fashions of the day, not unlike the Aesthetic Movement of a century later, and the members affected an extreme sensibility and an effeminate style of dress. This soon became yet another form of fantastic extravagance, spreading so widely that contemporaries detected the taint in the costume of the learned professions and there were Macaroni ladies clothed in Macaroni textiles. 'What is England now?' exclaimed Walpole in despair. 'A sink of Indian wealth filled with Nabobs and emptied by Macaronis.'

Beyond the charmed circle of fashion it is not surprising that there was a rising tide of discontent, together with complaints that those decent barriers which used to separate the social classes were disappearing. It was becoming difficult to distinguish the gentleman from his base imitators.

The fact that the tension did not, as in France, explode into revolution was perhaps partly due to this freedom to imitate the fashions and habits of the quality; it allowed a repressed force to dissipate its energy in vulgar mimicry. Our native gift of snobbery proved, as always, a steadying influence. Our fashions in the 1780's, so admired in France, seemed to have a freer air; men with a suggestion of the hunting field, and women, discarding the hoop, wearing even cloth 'tailor-mades' (which they called 'habits').

Sport, in many forms, captured the fancy of all classes; with hunting, horse-racing, prize-fighting, cock-fighting and cricket matches available, who would exchange these for the doubtful excitements of a revolution?

Male fashions, 1760–1793

The suit comprised coat or frock, waistcoat and breeches. The *coat*, now worn for full dress only, was close-fitting, the signs of waist and flaring of skirts disappearing after the 'sixties, the fronts being sloped away; from the 'seventies the curve away from the waist increased so as to expose the bottom of the waistcoat. The close-fitting sleeves had closed cuffs, usually small. From 1765 a narrow stand collar was added. The buttons were flat.

The *frock*, a garment originally adopted by the gentleman from his social inferiors and then somewhat loose, was now close-fitting and distinguished from the coat by its flat turned-down collar. At first worn for 'undress' it became from the 'seventies worn on all occasions except at Court, where a fully trimmed version, the 'French frock', was allowed. The English frock was always plain except for braid edging.

For riding and sport its length was reduced and the skirts often caught back on each side, leading to their being cut away into a 'tail coat' about 1790.

The collar (known as a 'cape') rose from 1785 into a 'stand-fall' for dressy occasions, becoming the 'frock-coat'.

It was single-breasted until 1780, then double-breasted with lapels, often angular and becoming wider in the 'nineties.

Its buttons, unlike those of the coat, were large, becoming enormous and plate-like in the 'seventies, and of metal.

An inside breast-pocket was introduced by the Macaronis in 1777.

The *waistcoat*, without sleeves, had the skirts

of the foreparts cut back at an angle and in the 'eighties gradually shortened, when the popular style was the square-cut 'Newmarket', becoming general in the 'nineties. At first single-breasted, the double-breasted form appeared occasionally in the 'sixties and 'seventies and was very common in the 'eighties and 'nineties.

It had two rectangular pockets; from the 'eighties without flaps.

The *breeches* were close-fitting, becoming excessively tight; closed by whole- or small-falls. The knee was covered over the stocking, with a knee-buckle, replaced by strings in the 'nineties. Braces buttons, one on each side in front, began to appear at the end of the 'eighties, and the garment was beginning to be known as 'smallclothes', from the 'seventies.

Materials

For *coats* and *frocks*, cloth for day wear; for 'dress', velvet, brocade, silks and satins.

Waistcoats: cassimere, fancy silks. *Breeches*, cashmere, buckskin, and stocking-net.

Other garments: The *nightgown* or *morning gown*, a wrapping negligee worn indoors in place of a frock.

The *banyan*, a loose short gown often worn out-of-doors in place of a frock; knee-length with a wrapping front.

The *surtout* or *great coat*, with two or three broad falling collars.

Neck and wrist wear

The cravat was a strip of lawn or muslin worn round the neck, loosely knotted under the chin and the ends hanging, a fashion favoured by the Macaronis.

The stock was a folded neckcloth round the neck, fastened behind by a buckle. Steadily increasing in height it became known as a 'cravat' from 1785 and was then usually made of muslin.

Lace ruffles were worn at the wrist, disappearing temporarily in 1790 as a 'democratic' gesture in sympathy with the French Revolution.

Footwear

Shoes had rounded toes until 1790; heels were

low and square. Red heels for Court wear were revived in the 'seventies.

The buckles, oblong and smooth, became enormous from 1775 to 1785. At the end of the 'eighties shoe-strings began to replace buckles.

Jockey boots, close-fitting, ending below the knee, the tops turned over, were fashionable for walking in from the 'seventies.

Stockings

A fashion for stripes was marked in the 'eighties and 'nineties.

Headgear

The three-cornered hat, the brim turned up or 'cocked' in a variety of forms (the 'Kevenhuller' with a high cock in front, in the 'sixties; the 'Fantail' with the brim turned up high behind, from the 'eighties); the bicorne hat with front and back brim turned up, from the 'eighties. The round hat, with flat-topped crown and flat brim, appearing first in the 'seventies for riding and destined gradually to develop into the gentleman's 'top hat'; commonly made of beaver.

The hair

Wigs were worn by all classes until the war-tax in 1795 on hair-powder. The many varieties fall into two groups:

(1) Wigs without queues: The bob with several rows of curls round the back of the head. Full dress bobs came into fashion in 1760. The scratch bob covered only the back of the head and simulated the natural hair. Cut wigs were short, without curls; worn by the working classes.

(2) Wigs with queues: These gradually became smaller.

The front ('toupee' or 'foretop') was brushed up, and in the 'seventies raised on pads, the natural hair blending with that of the wig by the use of pomatum, the whole powdered.

The sides of the wig had rigid tubular curls ('buckles') lying horizontally, replaced in the 1780's by bushy hair.

The queue had various forms:

(a) the tye, a short bunch of curls tied at the nape of the neck.

(b) the ramilies, the tail plaited and tied.

(c) the pigtail, very long and plaited with ribbons.

The queue became shorter from 1780.

The bag-wig: for full dress, the queue being concealed in a short black silk bag at the nape of the neck.

The Catogan or Club wig: the queue, broad and flat, was turned up on itself and tied to form a pendant loop of hair; very popular in the 'seventies, especially with the Macaronis.

The Major or Brigadier wig: military but often assumed by civilians, resembled a Bob with two corkscrew curls tied together to form a queue.

Wigs were made, not only of hair (human, horse's, cow's, goat's) but also textiles such as mohair and worsted; of copper and iron wire (in the 'sixties and 'seventies), and of feathers, usually drake's or mallard's, which were used to form the summit. Parson's 'feather tops' were very common, and feather wigs for sporting.

Hair powder, of starch, was white for dress wear but blue and other colours were also used; the powder being applied by a blower or dredger or powder puff, the face and clothing protected by a powdering jacket or gown.

The face was clean-shaven.

The beau carried a muff, a long cane, and in the 'seventies 'all the very fine men wear two watches'. A snuff-box was essential. The more extreme exquisites, with faces rouged and patched, in tight stays and false calves, and heavily scented:

'Soft silky coxcombs, full of nice punctilio,
  All paste, pomatum, essence and pulvilio,
  With huge bouquets, like beaupots, daily go,
  Tricked out like dolls, to pace the Rotten Row.'

Male fashions, 1794–1810

The war with France from 1793 and 'the era of Jacobinism and Equality' had a marked effect on male costume. 'It was then', wrote Wraxall, 'that pantaloons, cropped hair and shoe-strings, as well as the total abolition of buckles and ruffles and disuse of hair-powder characterized the men.'

To indicate democratic sympathies it was with some the fashion to look slovenly. 'Slouch is the word now, you know. That's the fashion; that's

(A) Fashion plate. Lady in dress of 1766.

A Lady in the Dress of the Year 1766.

A Lady in full Dress, and an other in the Riding Dress of 1778.

(B) A Lady in riding dress and another in Court dress of 1778. *From 'The Ladies' Pocket Book'.*

PLATE 65   929

(B) A duchess, 1770. The 'Dormeuse' Cap.

(A) Fashion plates of 1784. One lady wears an open robe and the other a closed gown with fichu scarf. *From 'The Ladies' Pocket Book'*.

(C) Fashion plate, 1789. Figure on left shows a towering hat, the shoulders draped in a scarf, and high-waisted dress. The other shows the back of a riding habit. *From 'The Ladies' Pocket Book'*.

PLATE 66

A

B

(A) Catherine, wife of John Lucas of Stouthall, 1788. The vandyke edging round the top of the bodice was the height of fashion.

(B) Two ladies in day dress, 1801. High-waisted white cotton dresses suitable for winter. Thin pointed slippers without heels. *From Heideloff's 'Gallery of Fashion'.*

(C) Two evening dresses 1801. Trained open robes over light-coloured dresses. Figure on the left wears a turban. *From Heideloff's 'Gallery of Fashion'.*

PLATE 67

(A) Two ladies in evening dress, 1807. Muslin frocks over coloured slips. Very high-waisted and trained; short shoulder sleeves, elbow gloves. *From 'Fashions of London and Paris'.*

(B) Three ladies in day dress, 1808. All wearing round dresses, high-waisted; the one on the left wears a Spencer of lilac sarcenet over a white muslin walking dress. The centre figure wears a white muslin dress, made with a 'waistcoat bosom'. The right-hand figure is in a cambric frock, buttoned behind, with a Spanish vest of blue sarcenet. *Fashion plate from 'La Belle Assemblée'.*

(c) Lady at her toilet, 1810, by GILLRAY.

PLATE 68

(A) JEREMIAH MEYER, R.A. (1735–89). An unknown Lady. *Victoria and Albert Museum.*
(B) JEREMIAH MEYER, R.A. Thomas Frankland, aged 24 in 1775. *Louis Clarke Collection.*
(C) RICHARD CROSSE (1742–1810). An Officer. *Victoria and Albert Museum.*
(D) RICHARD CROSSE. An unknown Lady. *Private Collection.*

A

B

C

(A) RICHARD COSWAY, R.A. (1742 ?–1821). Anne, Countess Winterton. *Bernard Falk Collection.*
(B) RICHARD COSWAY, R.A. The Duke of Wellington, dated 1808. *Victoria and Albert Museum.*
(C) RICHARD COSWAY, R.A. Mrs Lowther, in the lid of an ivory and gold snuffbox. *Victoria and Albert Museum.*

PLATE 70

(A) RICHARD COSWAY, R.A. Philip James de Loutherbourg, R.A. *Minto Wilson Collection.*
(B) JOHN SMART (1742 ?–1811). An unknown Lady, dated 1779. *Victoria and Albert Museum.*
(C) JOHN SMART. An unknown Girl, dated 1781. *Private Collection.*
(D) JOHN SMART. Self portrait, dated 1797. *Victoria and Albert Museum.*

PLATE 71   935

A

B

C

D

(A) GEORGE ENGLEHEART (1750–1829). An unknown Lady. *Victoria and Albert Museum.*
(B) GEORGE ENGLEHEART. Mrs Gillespie. *Victoria and Albert Museum.*
(C) GEORGE ENGLEHEART. Mr George P. Barclay, dated 1807. *Victoria and Albert Museum.*
(D) JOSEPH SAUNDERS (worked 1772–1808). An unknown Lady. *Victoria and Albert Museum.*

PLATE 72

(A) OZIAS HUMPHRY, R.A. (1742–1810). An unknown Lady. *H. E. Backer Collection.*
(B) OZIAS HUMPHRY, R.A. An unknown Lady. *H. E. Backer Collection.*
(C) WILLIAM WOOD (1768 ?–1809). An unknown Man. *H. E. Backer Collection.*
(D) JOHN BARRY (worked 1784–1827). An unknown Man. *Private Collection.*

PLATE 73

937

(A) ANDREW PLIMER (1763–1837). An unknown Man. *Victoria and Albert Museum.*
(B) ANDREW PLIMER. An unknown Lady. *Victoria and Albert Museum.*
(C) SAMUEL SHELLEY (1750 ?–1808). An unknown Lady and two Children. *H. E. Backer Collection.*

PLATE 74

GEORGE CHINNERY, R.H.A. (1774–1852). Mrs Robert Sherson,
dated 1803. *Victoria and Albert Museum.*

PLATE 75   939

A

B

C

D

(A) CHARLES ROBERTSON (1760–1821). The Hon. Thomas St Lawrence, D.D., Bishop of Cork and Ross. *Victoria and Albert Museum.*

(B) ANDREW ROBERTSON (1777–1845). The Duchess of Breadalbane, dated 1810. *Private Collection.*

(C) JOHN COX DILLMAN ENGLEHEART (1784–1862). An unknown Lady, dated 1809. *V. and A. Museum.*

(D) JOHN COMERFORD (1770 ?–1832). Possibly Mr Charles Farran, dated 1805. *V. and A. Museum.*

　　　　　　PLATE 76

Page from S. Dinglinger's book of designs for jewellery, published in London in 1751. It shows designs for a stomacher, a corsage ornament and six brooches.

PLATE 77

(A) Necklace with pendant, garnets set in silver-gilt, about 1760–80. (*left*) Pendant, gold set with garnets and diamonds, late eighteenth century. (*right*) Pendant, gold set with garnets and pearls and an enamelled miniature of Queen Charlotte, late eighteenth century.

Note: Fashion in eighteenth century jewellery was to such an extent international that it is extremely difficult to determine its country of origin. Not all the pieces illustrated are of English manufacture but they do nevertheless represent the types worn in England between 1760 and 1810. Those most likely to be of actual English manufacture are shown on Plates 78A and C, 79B and C, and 80A. All the pieces illustrated are in the Victoria and Albert Museum.

(B) Breast ornament in form of bouquet of flowers, enamelled gold set with diamonds, about 1770–80.

(C) Spray brooch, gold and enamelled silver set with rubies and diamonds, about 1760–70.

PLATE 78

(A) Necklace, silver set with emeralds, rubies, foiled crystals, and topazes,
about 1760–80.

(B) and (C) Two spray brooches, silver set with diamonds, early nineteenth century.

PLATE 79

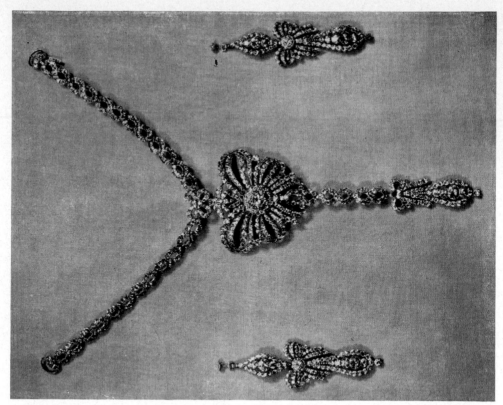

(c) Necklace with pendant and pair of earrings, silver set with pastes, end of eighteenth century.

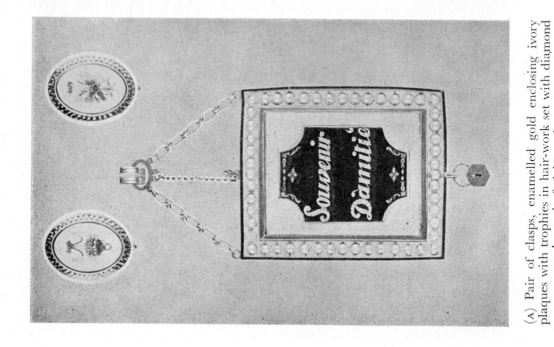

(A) Pair of clasps, enamelled gold enclosing ivory plaques with trophies in hair-work set with diamond sparks, end of eighteenth century.

(B) Frame for a miniature with chain for wearing as a pendant at the waist, early nineteenth century.

PLATE 80

Trade-card of Maydwell and Windle, glass-sellers in the Strand, *c.* 1770.
Sir Ambrose Heal.

PLATE 81

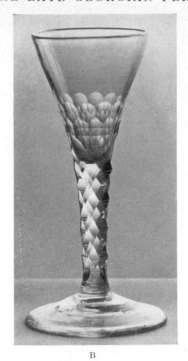

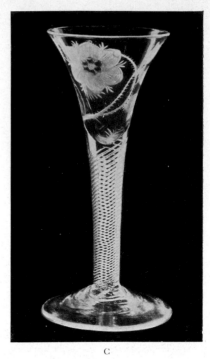

A

B

C

(A) Cordial-glass with opaque-white twist stem, the bowl enamelled in white. Probably Newcastle-upon-Tyne (Beilby), *c.* 1770. 5¼ in.   (B) Wine-glass with facet-cut stem, *c.* 1760. 7¼ in.   (C) Wine-glass with air-twist stem, engraved with Jacobite emblems, including the Stuart rose, *c.* 1750. 6½ in.

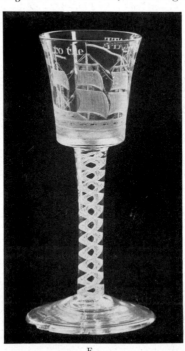

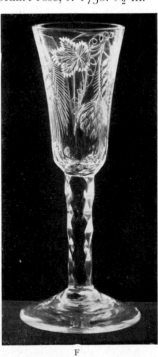

D

E

F

(D) Wine-glass engraved with *chinoiserie* subject, *c.* 1760. 9⅜ in.   (E) Wine-glass with opaque-white twist stem. Engraved with representation of a frigate and inscription: 'Success to the Eagle Frigate. John Knill, Commander', *c.* 1760. 6½ in.   (F) Ale-glass with faceted stem, the bowl engraved with hops and barley, *c.* 1760. 7½ in. *All Victoria and Albert Museum.*

PLATE 82

A   B   C

(A) Decanter for white wine, with engraved 'label' and faceted stopper, *c.* 1760. 11 in. (B) Spirit-decanter, blue glass with gilt decoration, *c.* 1780. 9¾ in. (C) Decanter and stopper, cut in facets, *c.* 1760. 12 in. *All Victoria and Albert Museum.*

(D) Cruet bottles with silver or plated mounts. That on the left has the London hall-mark for 1798; centre (7⅞ in.), *c.* 1765; right, *c.* 1790. *All Victoria and Albert Museum.*

PLATE 83

Cut-glass chandelier from Wroxton Abbey, Oxfordshire, *c.* 1810. 6 ft.
Victoria and Albert Museum.

PLATE 84

(A) Square Pianoforte by Johannes Zumpe, London, 1767. 4½ octaves, bicord, 2 hand stops (damper and sourdine). Trestle stand. One of the earliest surviving English pianos. *Victoria and Albert Museum.*

(B) Square Pianoforte, by John Broadwood, London, 1792. 5 octaves, bicord, no stops or pedals. French stand. Underdamper action. *Author's Collection.*

PLATE 85

Harpsichord, by Burkat Shudi, London, 1766. 5 hand stops, 'machine' and 'Venetian swell' pedals. Shudi patented the swell action in 1769. *W. R. Thomas.*

PLATE 86

Grand Pianoforte, by John Broadwood, London, 1798. 5½ octaves, tricord, 2 pedals.
Author's Collection.

PLATE 87

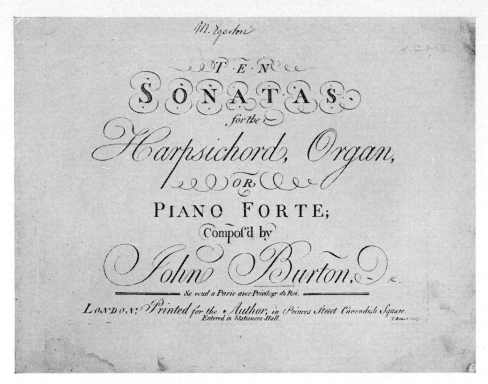

(A) Title page of the earliest English music to mention the pianoforte, 1766. *British Museum.*

(B) Opening page of Clementi's Sonata Opus 2, No. 1 (*c.* 1772) for Pianoforte. *British Museum.*

PLATE 88

Opening page of the full score of Handel's 'Fireworks' music, from Dr Samuel Arnold's collected edition, Part 24 (*c.* 1790).

PLATE 89

953

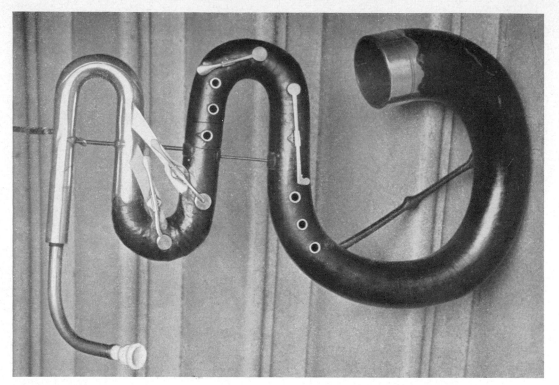

(B) Serpent, by T. Key, London, *c.* 1830. 7 keys. *Lancelot Vining.*

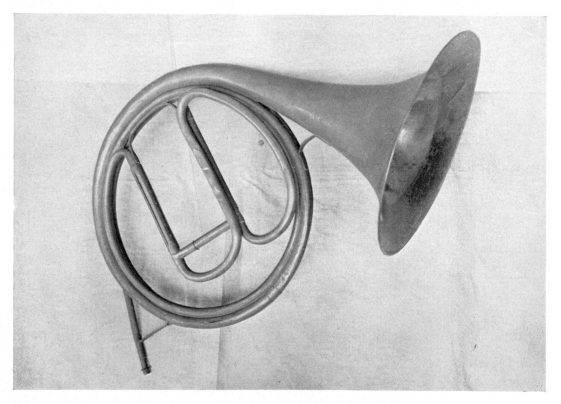

(A) Hand-horn, French, early nineteenth century. *The Galpin Society.*

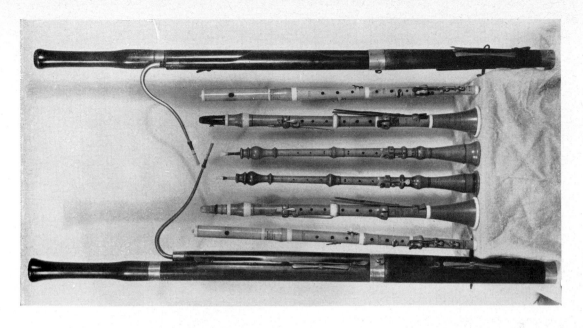

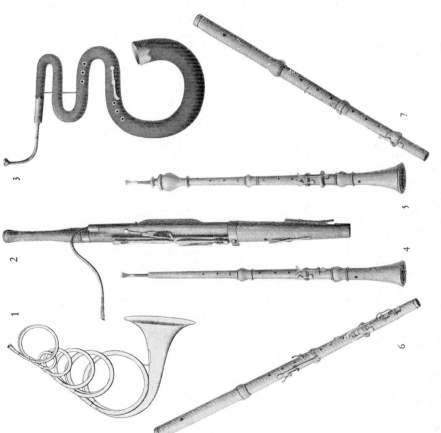

(A) Wind Instruments. (*After engravings dated 1807–11 from Rees' Encyclopaedia at the British Museum.*) 1. French Horn, with crooks; 2. 8-keyed Bassoon; 3. Serpent; 4 & 5. 2-keyed Oboes, straight and decorated types, showing the characteristic difference of length due to the rise in pitch; 6. 7-keyed Flute; 7. 1-keyed Flute.

(B) Woodwind Instruments. Pairs of 6-keyed Bassoons (by Parker and Milhouse), 6-keyed Flutes (by W. H. Potter), 6-keyed Clarinets (by Cramer and Simpson), and 2-keyed Oboes (by Milhouse and Goulding). *Author's Collections.*

PLATE 91

(A) Violin by James and Henry Banks, 1798
W. E. Hill & Sons.

(c) Double Bass, by William Forster, senior, 1789. Made for the private band of George III.
The Galpin Society.

(B) Violoncello, by William Forster, senior, 1782. Painted with Royal Arms and Prince of Wales' feathers and the inscription 'Liberty and Loyalty'. *W. E. Hill & Sons.*

PLATE 92

(B) A London binding in the rococo style, 1774. *Beattie on Truth*, 1774. Presentation copy to King George III. *British Museum.*

(A) Binding probably designed by Robert Adam on his *Ruins of the Palace of the Emperor Diocletian at Spalatro*, London, 1764. The dedication copy to King George III. Red morocco, gold-tooled. *British Museum.*

PLATE 93

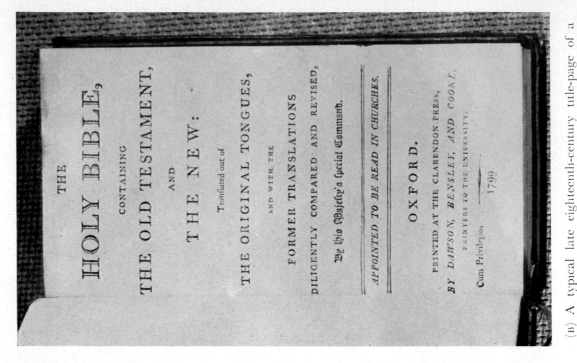

(B) A typical late eighteenth-century title-page of a pocket Bible, 1799, during Bensley's association with Oxford

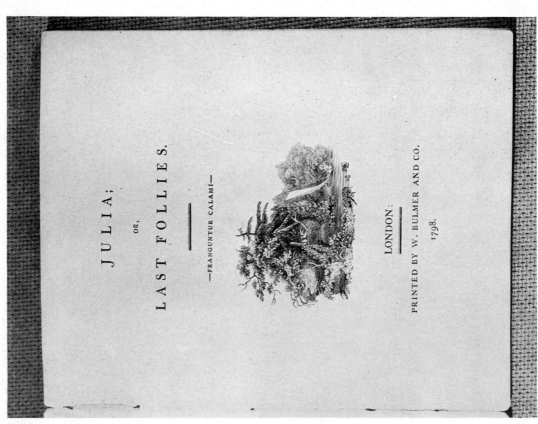

(A) A restrained Bulmer title-page, 1798

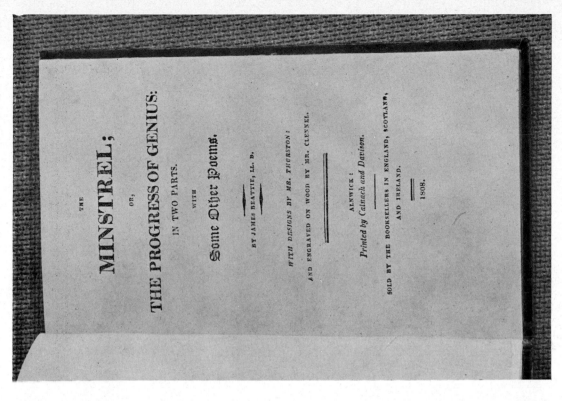

THE

MINSTREL;

OR,

THE PROGRESS OF GENIUS:

IN TWO PARTS.

WITH

Some Other Poems.

BY JAMES BEATTIE, LL. D.

WITH DESIGNS BY MR. THURSTON;

AND ENGRAVED ON WOOD BY MR. CLENNEL.

ALNWICK:
Printed by Catnach and Davison.

SOLD BY THE BOOKSELLERS IN ENGLAND, SCOTLAND,
AND IRELAND.

1808.

THE

SHIPWRECK,

A POEM,

BY

WILLIAM FALCONER,

A SAILOR.

WITH

A LIFE OF THE AUTHOR.

EDINBURGH:
Printed by J. Ballantyne and Co.

FOR ALEXANDER MACKAY, HIGH STREET, EDINBURGH;
AND JOHN MURRAY, NO. 32, FLEET STREET,
LONDON.

1807.

Two title-pages showing the simple elegance widespread in Britain at this period: (A) printed by Ballantyne at Edinburgh, 1807; (B) printed by Catnach and Davison at Alnwick, Northumberland, 1808.

PLATE 95

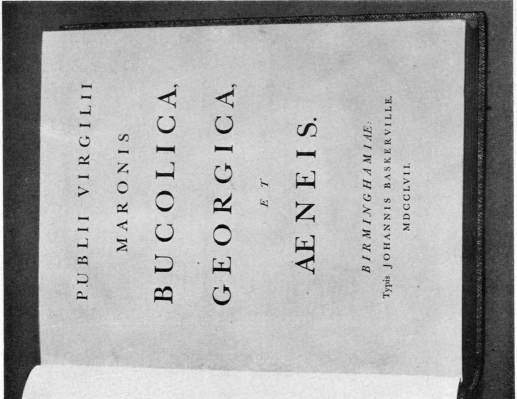

(B) Title-page of Baskerville's first book, the Virgil of 1757.
B. Quaritch.

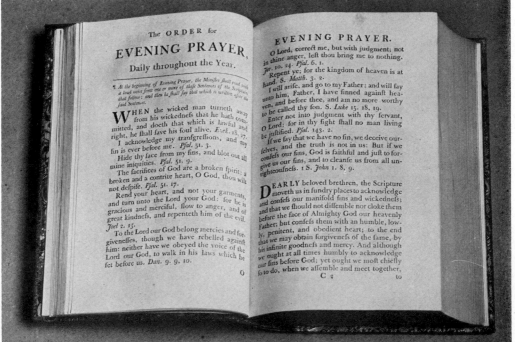

(A) An opening of Baskerville's Prayer Book, 1767.
B. Quaritch.

modern ease' (G. Colman, *The Heir at Law*, 1797).

And while gentlemen were affecting to look like ruffians 'the Lower Classes are invading the boundaries and privileges of the great and fashionable, aping the dress of persons of rank'. (*The Morning Chronicle*, 1800).

In the midst of this fashion ferment there appeared, soon after 1794, a sartorial Napoleon to restore order to chaos. It was the genius of George Brummel which introduced an entirely new idea into the art of male costume.

The Brummel 'Code Napoleon' ordained that henceforth the dress of a gentleman must be distinguished by an inconspicuous propriety, and that its design must no longer be pictorial but architectural; that is to say, it must express social superiority not by colours but by line and proportion, which meant high quality in tailoring and exquisite taste in the wearer.

Against the vulgar intrusions of democracy he set the subtle barrier of 'good taste'. Reform was necessary as the war was producing 'everything disgusting in the name of Fashion . . . slouched hats, jockey boots, half-boots, leather breeches, cropped heads, unpowdered hair . . . and the present race of Bucks without blood, Beaux without taste, and Gentlemen without manners' (*The Oracle*, 1804).

From 1794 the frock-coat developed an immensely high stand-fall collar cut back in front to allow for the high neckcloth swathed round the neck up to the chin. The fronts of the frock were cut away leaving little more than coat-tails at the back, reaching to the knee. The double-breasted style was general, worn buttoned up so that only the bottom of the waistcoat was seen. Wide lapels and large flat buttons gave a military air.

The sleeves, close-fitting, were slightly gathered at the shoulder seam, becoming padded up by 1800. The cuff was inconspicuous, often only a line of stitching or left unbuttoned.

The coat, for full dress, had a high stand collar; in other respects it resembled the frock-coat.

The old-fashioned style of frock with turned-over collar of no great height continued to be worn for sporting activities. It is noteworthy that never

before had the gentleman worn a buttoned-up coat concealing the waistcoat; the latter was losing its importance, being very short and square-cut, generally double-breasted and having a stepped stand-collar with wide angular lapels.

Near the close of the century the double-breasted waistcoat might have a rolled collar continuous with the shawl lapel, though this rolled collar was quite uncommon.

A feature of the 'nineties was the underwaistcoat, a shortened version of the over-waistcoat but protruding an inch or so above its upper border. The under-waistcoat seems to have declined in favour after 1800.

The aim of the short waistcoat and cut-away coat fronts was to expose as much as possible of the legs and thighs encased in tight breeches or pantaloons; a fashion clearly designed to be sex-attractive and favouring the slim figure of youth.

Breeches reached well below the knees where they were tied with strings. The opening was a small fall. As braces had become necessary with these skin-tight garments braces buttons came into use.

Pantaloons, appearing in the 'nineties, were equally tight and reached to the ankles where the sides were slit for the purpose of pulling on and then buttoned.

From 1800 male fashions tended to become somewhat modified; the day frock-coat becoming known as a 'morning coat,' often single-breasted though still buttoned up, developed a rolled collar and lapels shrank in size or disappeared.

The waistcoat, usually striped, with a lower stand-collar cut well back, and the neckcloth now no longer enveloping the chin but with a broad bow spread under it.

By 1806 the day and evening coat had acquired an inside breast pocket and pockets in the tails, the outside pockets having often disappeared (Figs. 1, 2).

For evening the white waistcoat and the coat of dark blue or green with light-coloured breeches and white silk stockings, were becoming the recognized garb of the gentleman. By 1807 the evening breeches were invariably black.

In 1810 nankeen trousers were becoming

Fig. 1. Full Dress, December 1806. *Le Beau Monde, or Literary and Fashionable Magazine.*

Fig. 2. Morning Walking Dress, 1806. *Le Beau Monde, or Literary and Fashionable Magazine.*

fashionable at seaside resorts for summer wear by day; this garment, borrowed from sailors, and destined eventually to obliterate the allurement of the male leg in an irrecoverably dark, total eclipse, had a social significance; a century before the gentleman had adopted the working-man's frock, and now the sailor's trousers, a plebeian garment to which ladies of refinement would allude as 'a gentleman's inexpressibles'.

There was, of course, the exquisite Dandy 'dressed for the morning in my Brutus wig, coatee, waist-coateen, boots, gilt spurs, Barcelona neck-cloth, my shape braced up in stays' (*The Morning Herald*, 1809) but such, who figure so largely in the caricatures of the period, scarcely represented the true fashions.

The tax on hair-powder in 1795 led to the general abandonment of wigs except by those who chose to pay the guinea tax; the rest wore their own hair somewhat long and dishevelled—the 'Brutus crop'; short whiskers imitating the military began to appear soon after 1800. Powder on the natural hair was still used for 'full dress'.

Out of doors the fashionable footwear was the Hessian boot, calf-length and decorated in front with a tassel, and jockey boots reaching nearly to the knee and having the tops turned over; indoors, long pointed shoes with low heels.

The overcoat or surtout had two or three cape-collars.

The round hat had replaced the angular, and the crown was tall and straight, the brim often very wide; but with the new century the shape began to approximate towards that of the Victorian 'top hat'.

Feminine fashions

In the half century from 1760 to 1810 the feminine shape passed through a striking sequence of changes. In 1760 the domed hoop had passed its maximum size and had begun to shrink, so that from a vast triangular outline woman's form became in the 'seventies undulating with small 'pocket hoops' and in 1775 a 'false rump' (or bustle). In the 'eighties the hoop vanished (except for Court wear) and exaggerated curves, with a bouffant figure resembling that of a pouter pigeon, became the mode.

At the onset of the great war in 1793 the artificial shape which woman had preserved for centuries was discarded and thin flowing 'Classical' robes, over a minimum of underclothing, revealed the outlines of the body to the astonished spectator.

As the new century opened a more tubular outline with stiff vertical lines completed the transformation of shape, from that of the Great Pyramid to Cleopatra's Needle.

The phase of artificial shapes, 1760 to 1793

The three structural types of dress were the *open robe*, exposing in front an ornamental petticoat, the *closed robe* or *gown*, and the separate *bodice* and *skirt*, each type with its varieties.

(1) *The open robe.*

(*a*) The sack with box-pleated back and the overskirt, trained or short, commonly hitched up to expose the flounced petticoat. A style going out of fashion by 1780.

(*b*) The English gown with close-fitting back continuous with the overskirt; sleeves to the wrist. A style lasting well into the 'eighties.

(*c*) The nightgown, a fashionable demi-toilette with the overskirt pleated all round to the bodice but open in front. This persisted into the 'eighties.

(*d*) The Polonese, the height of fashion from 1770 to 1785; the overskirt was bunched up into three puffed-out draperies at the back exaggerating the bustle shape. 'It is janty beyond expression.'

In the 'eighties the open robe acquired a high waist, the front of the bodice puffed out by a 'buffon'. With this a sash was worn and the trained overskirt no longer hitched up.

(2) *The closed robe*, developing in the 'eighties and being known as a 'gown'; the bodice closed by lacing, and the lower part by buttons or ties to the hem. Long tight sleeves to the wrist.

The 'great-coat dress', popular in the 'nineties, resembled a buttoned-up great-coat.

(3) *The separate bodice and skirt*, as a form of 'undress' or morning dishabille, comprising a jacket and petticoat, appeared in the 'seventies. A version was the 'Riding Habit', the jacket cut on masculine lines and worn with a waistcoat. Made of cloth, this forerunner of the 'tailormade' was worn not only for riding but also as a morning costume.

Neckwear

From the 'seventies on the neck was draped with a kerchief, very much puffed out in the 'eighties (the 'buffon') and often a ruff, while a tippet covered the shoulders.

Other accessories: Aprons long or short were worn on all occasions.

Outdoor garments were cloaks, long and short, with threequarter-length hooded cardinals, and pelisses, threequarter-length with armhole slits.

From the 'eighties, after the hoop had been discarded, great coats buttoned down the front.

Headgear

For indoors, butterfly-shaped 'fly caps' in the

Fig. 3. Ladies in the most fashionable headdresses, 1780.

'sixties; followed by mob caps and in the 'seventies the 'dormeuse' with side flaps concealing the cheeks. The cap increased in size in the 'seventies and 'eighties as the coiffure expanded. Turbans for 'dress' and 'undress' were worn from the 'sixties on.

For outdoor wear hoods and calashes from the 'seventies.

As the hair mounted in height in the 'seventies the hat was either very small or else large and worn tilted on one side or the coiffure covered with a towering beehive-shaped hat.

The brim expanded in the 'eighties, becoming the shape familiar in Gainsborough's portrait of the Duchess of Devonshire; or with a puffed soft crown (the 'balloon hat') or tall in the shape of a flower-pot.

Immense attention was devoted to the head and hair in the 'seventies with masses of artificial hair raised on pads and rolls, mixed with pomatum and covered with powder; the whole decorated, in the evening, with flowers, vegetables, etc., and crowned with a plume of ostrich feathers; the feathers surviving for Court wear down to modern times (Fig. 3).

Footwear

Pointed shoes with narrow heels and large buckles were the mode.

Feminine fashions, 1794–1810

The war, starting in 1793, appeared to originate a change in woman's dress which was, in fact, a stage further in that simplification which had already begun. Silk became extremely expensive and woollen cloth was needed for uniforms, whereas Indian cotton textiles were available and cheap.

Consequently white dresses of muslin, cambric and calico became the mode even in winter and

964

were worn by all classes. The signs of class distinction, at least by day, almost disappeared, and the cruder forms of sex-appeal became universal. The general aim was to look as naked as possible.

The open robe with petticoat still persisted but was being gradually displaced by the round gown (a closed dress later known as a 'frock').

The round gown was at first constructed with the upper part of its front made as a pinned-up flap which could be let down so that the gown could be put on over the head; after 1800 a simpler construction began to come into favour, with a back opening fastened by lacing or buttons.

For day wear the round gown was quite plain, but for evening a half-length 'open robe' or else a sleeveless 'vest' of richer material could be worn over the gown.

In 1806 the 'chemise dress', the neck closed by a draw-string and edged with a frill, closely resembled the undergarment of that name.

Throughout this period the very high waistline (Fig. 4) accentuated after 1800 by short corsets, emphasized the bosom, especially when the top of the dress was cut as low as possible. 'What delicate mind can view with unconcern the *nudes* we meet everywhere? . . . the bosom shamefully exposed, and far more, the ankle' (1806).

The classical form of dress with flowing train gradually abated; by 1803 a single flounce or tucks appeared round the hem, as the skirt, becoming tubular, was shortened to ankle-length.

By 1807 the hem was being embroidered or vandyked, and the skirt slightly gored so that its shape became a narrow isosceles triangle sustained over petticoats.

The classical features had practically disappeared, as in that year the Spanish slashed sleeve was in fact a symptom of gothic revival, coupled with vandyking and scalloping of borders and elaborate embroidery over the bodice.

The phase when 'all the necks, arms, shoulders and bosoms in the kingdom were thrown open to the eye of the gazer' was over; it had been found difficult to look distinguished when multitudes of bodies much alike were exhibited in dresses much alike.

By 1810 the ancient principle of illusion and

the subtle charm of class distinction recovered their sway as irresistible lures.

Accessory garments

The spencer was a short-waisted, skirtless jacket with long sleeves worn over the dress out of doors.

The shawl, originating in the 1780's, became highly fashionable in the 'nineties and beyond, the small Norwich silk shawls being especially so; the 'pine pattern' started its long career in the 'nineties. Large silk shawls with a deep fringe and square Scotch shawls of silk and cotton with printed patterns appeared by 1800.

The pelisse of cambric or muslin, with long sleeves, and the fronts hanging down to the knees, and Josephs (long tunics with loose sleeves) together with cloaks of various lengths were for

Fig. 4. London Dress, May 1799.

outdoor wear. Shoes were flat and pointed, with thin soles, the toe becoming rounded and a slight heel added by 1810.

The hair was 'dressed in the Grecian taste' with light curls in front becoming 'cropped in full curls' by 1808. In the early years of the century wigs were often worn over cropped hair by the 'dashers of the haut ton'.

Headgear

For day, mob caps of a large size covered the head. For evening, the half-handkerchief flat on the crown or the cornet cap with a cone-point behind; for more dressy occasions, the turban.

For outdoor wear an immense variety of hats and bonnets appeared, especially after 1800; all possible shapes and sizes of every implication except the demure, came and went, and small veils were often worn with them.

Both hair and hat attempted to reflect in spirit the events of the war; Egyptian modes in 1805 and 1806, military helmets, Spanish touches during the Peninsular campaign, a Trafalgar turban in 1806 . . .

Materials

Although simple muslins, cambrics and calico sufficed for a few years after war had broken out, smuggled silks soon re-asserted their appeal and Italian sarcenet, satins, velvet and lace became increasingly in demand, especially for evening wear, after 1800. As the dress had no pockets, handbags ('ridicules') were carried. All through the war facial make-up was lavish, especially in the years of classical 'simplicity' when artificial bosoms of wax or wool provoked *The Times* to exclaim, in 1799: 'The fashion of *false bosoms* has at least this utility; that it compels our fashionable fair to wear *something*.'

The most singular feature of the costume in these war years was that though we were fighting against revolutionary France, Englishwomen affected a 'democratic' simplicity of dress imitating more or less the French spirit of equality, of which the logical expression is nudity. Hence the lament of *The Chester Chronicle* in 1799: 'There is so little to be concealed at present that there is scarcely room for any fashion at all!'

Tail-piece from T. Bewick's *A History of British Birds*, Vol. 1, 1797.

Portrait Miniatures

JONATHAN MAYNE

IT is usual to regard the period of the maturity of Sir Joshua Reynolds as the golden age of British portraiture in oils, and until recently it was equally usual to consider the contemporary school of miniaturists as representing the highest peak of achievement which that art was to reach in this country. If a change of taste and an increase of knowledge during the last twenty years or so have between them done much to modify this somewhat naively 'progressive' view, it would be foolish to deny however that in the hands of its finest exponents – Meyer, Cosway, Smart, Engleheart, for example – the later Georgian miniature offers a dazzling spectacle. As Mr Carl Winter has pointed out in a lecture [1] on the subject, 'it must finally be said that, tempting as it is to generalize about the character and tendency of eighteenth-century miniature painting, no other period produced actual works of outstanding individual quality in such large numbers. If one could assemble all the excellent miniatures of the period, without regard to the names of their authors or their subjects, they would prove a difficult obstacle to belief in the theory of decline' (a theory which has sometimes been put forward in direct opposition to the previously held belief in the gradual and steady progress of the art from humble Tudor beginnings to its apogee in the Age of Cosway).

But it is better, no doubt, to cease from fruitless and invidious comparisons between one age and another, and to content oneself with saying that the Late Georgian period, which is the subject of the present essay, saw the last of several great flowerings of the British Miniaturist's art. It saw the full exploitation of the possibilities of the use of transparent water-colour on ivory, and, before its close, the onset of that attempt to rival oil-paint in a suggestion of permanence and solidity which, when a little later it was combined with the anti-linear influence of the first developments of photography, was responsible for the final debasement and virtual eclipse of the art.

Jeremiah Meyer

Our period may conveniently be held to start with an exhibition – that of the Society of Artists, which opened in London in April 1760 and was the first ever to be held in England at which the works of living artists were presented to the public. In the following year a secessionist group, The Free Society of Artists, initiated its series of annual exhibitions, and these were followed in 1769 by the first exhibition of the newly founded Royal Academy. The first miniaturist whom we have to consider here was in fact an exhibitor with the Society of Artists from the beginning, and furthermore he was the only miniaturist pure and simple among the foundation-members of the Royal Academy. This was Jeremiah Meyer, R.A. (Pl. 69A, B), who, though born at Tübingen in Germany in 1735, had lived in England since the age of about fourteen and later became a naturalized citizen. In his early twenties he received

[1] 'The British School of Miniature Portrait Painters', Annual Lecture on Aspects of Art, Henriette Hertz Trust of the British Academy, 1948 (London, Geoffrey Cumberlege), p. 16.

instruction in enamel portraiture from Christian Friedrich Zincke, who also was of German birth, though long since permanently settled in England. Meyer continued to paint enamels throughout his career – indeed his first exhibit with the Society of Artists was in this medium – but it is as a technical innovator in water-colour on ivory that his great accomplishment and historical importance lies. Although ivory, in distinction to vellum, had been adopted by miniaturists abroad and in this country from the early years of the eighteenth century (Rosalba Carriera is generally credited with its earliest use), it is nevertheless true to say that for a long time its possibilities had been neglected, or at least unexplored. That is to say that for the first sixty or so years of the century miniaturists had painted more or less thickly on the surface of the ivory, so that its characteristic glow and sparkle had been to a large extent obscured. Although in his earliest works Meyer followed the practice of his senior contemporaries, from the early 1770's, when his existing miniatures become more numerous, we begin to see emerging those qualities which, when further developed by Cosway and others, constitute the special glory of the late eighteenth-century miniature – qualities of freedom and elegance in drawing, delicacy in colour, and above all luminosity. To some extent these qualities are interdependent; a controlled freedom of drawing (helped by an increase in the physical size of the miniature which is noticeable in the 1770's), when combined with an evanescent delicacy of colour, allows the brilliance of the thin ivory to make its full effect. Meyer's mature style, as shown for example in his portrait of an unknown lady reproduced here, is essentially linear. If it is difficult to appreciate this satisfactorily in a reproduction, the treatment of the sitter's hair nevertheless betrays it to an evident degree; an original miniature by Meyer when studied under a glass reveals in fact a whole surface built up not of stippling but of an infinity of fine lines crossing and recrossing one another at more or less acute angles. A sketchbook in the Victoria and Albert Museum, which was previously attributed to Hoppner but has now been convincingly restored to Meyer by Mr

Graham Reynolds,[2] demonstrates this fact even more clearly.

Meyer's career was one of official as well as artistic distinction. Before his election to the Royal Academy he had already received a gold medal from the Society of Arts and had been appointed miniature painter to the Queen and painter in enamel and miniature to the King. He exhibited at the Royal Academy from 1769 until 1783, when he retired from practice. He died in 1789.

Richard Crosse

Richard Crosse (1742–1810), only a few years younger than Meyer, deserves to be considered next for stylistic no less than chronological reasons. As in the work of Meyer, there is a strong linear element in his painting, and like Meyer he enjoyed a new freedom of style which contrasts markedly with the work of his immediate forerunners. In his idiosyncratic system of colouring, however, the resemblance ends. Richard Crosse's miniatures have a tendency to be dominated by a bluish-green tone which, as Mr. Reynolds[3] has pointed out, suggests an affinity with the earlier portraits of Reynolds. While this particularity renders Crosse's miniatures comparatively easy to identify, it can sometimes become an unattractive trait, especially when it invades the complexions of his sitters. Apart however from this general stylistic criticism, and apart from an occasional hint of sentimentality in his work, Crosse was a miniaturist of consistent accomplishment. His drawing was distinguished, and his feeling for character, particularly in his male sitters, was perhaps more acute than that of Meyer.

Unlike the majority of artists working at this time, Richard Crosse (Pl. 69c, D) came from a family of landed gentry, living near Cullompton in Devonshire. It is not known with whom he studied – indeed he is said to have been largely self-taught – but by the end of the 1770's he is shown by his record-book (which is now in the library of the Victoria and Albert Museum) to

[2] In his *English Portrait Miniatures*, London, A. & C. Black, 1952, p. 136.
[3] Graham Reynolds, *op. cit.*, p. 142.

have been a prolific worker. A few years later his production began to decline, and, although he did not die until 1810, he seems to have given up practice entirely by the end of the century. Little of detail is recorded concerning his biography; he is known, however, to have been born a deaf-mute, and to have spent his last years in the care of a cousin who was a prebend of Wells. He remained a bachelor throughout his life, having in 1778 fallen deeply in love with his cousin's sister, a Miss Sarah Cobley, who was already at that time engaged to Benjamin Haydon. She married Haydon in 1782, and Benjamin Robert Haydon, a son of the marriage, relates in his *Memoirs* the affecting story of a last reunion between his mother and Crosse, the day before her death and three years before his. The account is too long to be quoted here, but it is to be recommended as bringing before us in a touchingly sympathetic manner the figure of a miniaturist who otherwise is hardly known to us except through his works.

Richard Cosway

The next two miniaturists to be considered – two indeed of the best-known in the history of the art – were born within a year or so of one another. The exact birth-date of neither is recorded, but available evidence suggests that Richard Cosway (Pls. 70A, B, C, 71A) was born in 1742 (at all events he was baptized in November of that year) and John Smart in 1742 or 1743 (probably not in 1741, as has often been maintained). About Cosway there is a considerable amount of biographical material. He was the son of the headmaster of Blundell's School, Tiverton, and showed early ability as a painter; indeed before he was twelve years old he was sent to London to study with Thomas Hudson, who had been Reynolds' master. Cosway's first ambitions were in fact in the direction of full-scale portraiture in oils, and his first exhibit, at the Society of Artists in 1760, was a portrait in that medium of the drawing-master Shipley. In the following year he began to exhibit miniatures, but he continued also to paint and to show oil-paintings throughout the greater part of his career. On the foundation of the Royal Academy Cosway enrolled as a

student (at the age of 27), becoming in 1770 an Associate, and in the following year a full, Academician. Ten years later he married a Miss Maria Hadfield, who, though of Irish parentage, had been born and brought up in Italy, where she had herself studied painting and had had (according to her own testimony) the advantage of associating with some of the leading artists of the time. It was in the years immediately succeeding his marriage that Cosway's real artistic and social fame began. Already well known for the foppishness of his appearance and behaviour, as is evidenced by two satirical prints published as early as 1772, it was about 1783 that he seems first to have attracted the favour and patronage of the Prince of Wales; very soon he became the centre of an almost notoriously gay social life. Living first in Berkeley Street, and then, from 1784 until 1791, in the central part of Schomberg House in Pall Mall, the Cosways entertained lavishly, holding a regular *salon* at which many of the social notabilities of the time were frequent visitors. The patronage of the Prince, which is said to have been bestowed as a result of a miniature-portrait which Cosway painted of Mrs Fitzherbert, furthered his professional success to a degree unreached by any of his contemporaries, and the nature of his particular talent was such that it flourished in the atmosphere of this success as at no other period of his life.

It was about this time that Cosway took to signing his miniatures, on the back, with the somewhat bombastic Latin inscription which is familiar to all students – and forgers – of his work: 'Rdus Cosway RA Primarius Pictor Serenissimi Walliae Principis Pinxit.' The earliest recorded example of this signature bears the date 1787, but there is evidence that he was already using some such form in the previous year, to which date should probably be referred his appointment (if he was ever officially appointed) as First Miniature Painter to the Prince.

In 1791 the Cosways moved to Stratford Place, Oxford Street, where they were to remain until 1821, the year of Cosway's death. During this last period of his life, Cosway's character and circumstances appear to have gradually altered. Like others of his contemporaries he became interested in the occult and the esoteric (Blake indeed was not alone in claiming to have had ghostly sitters in his studio); but, what was worse for his material prosperity, he became sympathetic towards the revolutionary ideals which were current at the time. According to the testimony of his cousin, quoted in Cunningham's *Life*, 'he was one of those sanguine men who perceived in the French Revolution the dawn of an empire of reason and taste in which genius and virtue alone would be worshipped'. It was only to be supposed that this would affect his relationship with the Prince, and we find in fact that little by little court patronage began to decline. Cosway retained a fashionable clientèle, however, and though his style became gradually less flamboyant and more austere, he does not seem to have lacked for sitters.

As a painter Cosway can trace his origins to the same tradition as Meyer, though, as we have seen, he was some seven years younger than that artist. Like Meyer, he is known to have studied the technique of enamel in his youth, and like Meyer's, his earliest work is not altogether unconventional for its time. Although there is a paucity of dated 'documents' for his development into the great Court miniaturist of the 'eighties and 'nineties, it seems likely that it was Meyer's example that pointed the way to his full understanding of the use of transparent water-colour. Such miniatures as can be referred to the 'seventies already show a partial realization of these possibilities (see, for example, Pl. 70A), but it was not until a little later that he came to make a regular practice of that elegant and dashing economy of pigment which is such a feature of his best Court work. Again like that of Meyer, Cosway's fully developed style was essentially linear, though whereas Meyer's use of line tended towards angularity, Cosway's was more gently rhythmic and on the whole somewhat broader. His palette was severely limited; a pale blue sometimes predominates, especially in the background which he often painted in the manner of a sky; apart from this, he virtually confined himself to greys, sepias, blacks, carnations and pale yellow, 'green', as Dr Williamson pointed out in his book on the artist, 'being an exceptional colour, very seldom made use of'. At the same time he began to adopt certain distortions in his drawing; enlarged eyes and gracefully lengthened necks become in fact a kind of hallmark of his middle period—mannerisms which were taken over by many of his followers and imitators.

Reference has already been made to an austerity which begins to be noticeable in Cosway's miniatures from about 1805. This coincides in time with the cessation of the Prince's patronage, and takes the form of a more penetrating, psychological type of portraiture, careless of artificial elegance and depending for its realization on colours which are almost muddy. Some of the artist's most telling works are the product of this period; one may reasonably regret the wonderfully controlled flamboyance of the earlier works, those perfect counterparts of the late eighteenth-century age of elegance, but it is at least arguable that many of these austerer works of the artist's old age, which have not unreasonably been compared to the last works of Frans Hals, have a peculiar merit of their own which is in its own way as valuable.

John Smart

John Smart (Pl. 71B, C, D), who was Cosway's almost exact contemporary, was in some ways his almost exact antithesis. Described in an eighteenth-century *Memoir* [4] as 'a man of the most vulgar manners, grossly sensual and greedy of money to an extreme', he nevertheless lived a quiet, industrious life, and painted a series of miniatures whose almost unwavering excellence of quality is perhaps only surprising for the fact that he nowhere shows the slightest awareness of the contemporary developments of the art at the hands of Meyer, Crosse or Cosway. If Meyer be held to mark the point in the history of the eighteenth-century miniature at which a decided innovation took place, Smart may with equal justice be regarded as the conservative follower of Luke Sullivan, Gervase Spencer, and other members of the mid eighteenth-century group which Mr Rey-

[4] *Memoirs of Thomas Jones,* published as the Walpole Society's Volume No. 32 (1946–8), p. 73.

nolds, in his book already cited, has named 'The Modest School'. Very little is known of Smart's early life; he must, however, have been a precocious child, for he won second prize (to Cosway's first) at the first competition of the Society of Arts, which was held in 1755 and was open to boys and girls under fourteen years of age; he continued to win prizes in succeeding years, and in 1758 was placed first, to Cosway's second.

The earliest extant miniature by Smart is signed and dated 1760, and already it exemplifies the fundamental characteristics of the artist's mature style to a degree unparalleled by the early works of any of the artists so far considered. The reason for this is fairly evident, and has already been implied above. For Smart had no stylistic conflicts, and but few stylistic developments ahead of him. The manner which he inherited from his predecessors and early made his own was to be the manner in which he worked throughout his life. It is possible to confirm this with considerable accuracy, for it was Smart's almost invariable habit to sign and date his miniatures from the very outset of his career, and thus a fairly complete index of his year-to-year achievement is available for study.

The most important episode in his life, perhaps, was his visit in 1785 to India, where he remained for ten years. There he met with considerable success, being appointed for the duration of his stay as miniature-painter to Muhammed Ali, Nawab of Arcot, and his family. Several of his miniatures of that native prince are known, as are other portraits of Indians. He also worked extensively for the English community in India. The miniatures of this period can be easily distinguished by the fact that Smart added a Roman I after the date which followed his signature.

On his return to London he began in 1797 to exhibit at the Royal Academy, having previously remained faithful to the Society of Artists, and indeed having borne office in that organization. Thereafter he continued to exhibit at Somerset House until his death in 1811, and his later works show little or no falling off in his powers.

Smart's style is one of the most easily recognizable of all the late eighteenth-century masters; his enamel-like finish is indeed all but unique in a period which saw a sudden loosening and broadening of brushwork and a development of calligraphy such as we have already noted in some of his predecessors and contemporaries. Nor did Smart adopt the exclusive use of transparent colour in the manner of Cosway or Meyer. His colour is bright and fairly thickly applied, and it is perhaps for this reason that his miniatures remain today to a remarkable degree unfaded. His imagination and vision were indeed limited; he seldom seems to have aspired beyond the immediately pretty, and where that prettiness does not already exist in his sitters, he tends to present us with a somewhat prosaic image. Much subtlety of characterization was beyond him, and even the faintly ironical smile in his self-portrait of 1797 (Pl. 71D) is an unusual feature of animation to be found in his work. When this much has been said in criticism, it is possible to endorse the generally held view of the outstanding attractiveness of his miniatures. Given a child or a pretty girl as his sitter, he is inimitable; his painting of costume and accessories is of the greatest delicacy; and even when the physical size of miniatures began further to increase in the 'eighties and 'nineties of the century, he still contrived to preserve that jewel-like quality of surface which, on a slightly smaller scale, had been his special prerogative from the outset of his career.

George Engleheart

George Engleheart (Pl. 72A, B, C), the third of the three artists who together seem to form a kind of triumvirate over the late Georgian miniature, was born in 1750, some eight years after Cosway and Smart. His father, a plaster modeller, was of German origin, and his early studies were carried out first with George Barret, RA, the landscape painter, and then in Reynolds' studio. It was not until 1775 that he set up in practice on his own as a miniaturist. From that date until 1813, when he retired to the country, he led a life of phenomenal industry; his record-books, like those of Crosse and of certain others of his contemporaries, have been preserved, and from these we can gain an idea of his activity. In the years between 1775 and

1813 he painted nearly five thousand miniatures – an average of well over a hundred a year. It is small wonder that his works are so frequently met with. Even after he retired from regular practice he continued to paint on occasions, his last work being dated 1829, the year of his death at the age of seventy-eight.

Engleheart's style followed the general pattern of his times. His earlier miniatures, belonging to his first five years or so of practice, are modest in scale and restrained in idiom. From about 1780 a greater assurance becomes evident, and certain characteristic mannerisms begin to be developed – for example, a brittle and crimped manner of drawing hair, a use of opaque white in the outlining of drapery which almost gives an impression of starch, and an enlargement and intensification of the eyes. Nevertheless, in spite of a certain automatic elegance which is sometimes to be held against them, the miniatures painted by Engleheart during this central part of his career contain a surprisingly high proportion of authentic masterpieces. If, as Mr Winter [5] has suggested, 'the animal that lurks in the breast even of civilized man seems to have been seen too often by Engleheart rather as a complacent tabby asleep in a milliner's box', it must nevertheless be conceded that the animal, even if unduly domestic, was regularly of the highest possible breeding and distinction.

Engleheart's final phase may be distinguished in his work from the mid-1790's until the end of his career. His miniatures of this period are frequently of larger size than before, and the scale of his forms is also correspondingly greater. Although it is hard to detect a diminution in his technical powers at this time, there does seem nevertheless to be a slight decrease of intensity, and this is perhaps to be attributed to a defect of imagination rather than to any other single cause. Engleheart's style had been formed under the influence of an aristocratic ideal; if it could effectively enough accommodate itself to the growing bourgeois ethos of the early nineteenth century, it could only do so at a certain sacrifice. Engleheart

[5] Carl Winter, *op. cit.*, p. 15.

was perfectly capable of providing the more prosaic and realistic images which the new patronage required; the problem however of bringing an equal emotional pressure to bear on this new type of work was perhaps more than he was able, or inclined, to solve, and thus there seems often a certain lack of vitality about the miniatures of this last period.

Some lesser miniaturists

In an essay of the present scope it is impossible to do more than draw the main outlines of the period, and when, as in the late Georgian epoch, there were probably more miniaturists at work than at any other time, before or since, in our history, it is inevitable that a considerable injustice will be done to some of the secondary figures. Some of these indeed it is already unjust to characterize in this way. Ozias Humphry, R.A. (1742–1810) (Pl. 73A, B), for example, was an artist of great distinction, and is often considered on the same level as Cosway, Smart and Engleheart. He is one of the exceptional artists of the period whose work in certain of its technical respects, provides a small-scale counterpart of the full-scale portraiture of the time – in this case, that of Reynolds. Andrew Plimer (1763–1837) (Pl. 74A, B) has also been greatly admired in modern times, but of recent years his popularity would seem to have been on the wane. He is said to have been a servant to Cosway in the early 1780's, and it is true that his style owes something to that master. But his mannered and repetitive elegance often tends to superficiality. Other artists, who though correctly described as 'minor', yet maintained a remarkably high standard of workmanship, were such men as Samuel Shelley (1750?–1808) (Pl. 74C), Joseph Saunders (exhibited 1772–1808) (Pl. 72D), Richard Collins (1755?–1831), Charles Robertson (1760–1821) (Pl. 76A), John Barry (worked 1784–1827) (Pl. 73D), George Chinnery (1774–1852) (Pl. 75), J. T. Barber Beaumont (1774–1841) – but the number could easily be doubled or trebled without admitting any perceptible lowering of standard.

We have already noticed, when discussing Engleheart, a slight change that began to characterize the patronage of the early nineteenth century, and in concluding this brief survey it is necessary to return for a moment to this point. For it was this cause above all, perhaps, that helped to bring about a perceptible modification in the miniature-portrait itself. The aristocratic ideal, as best realized by Cosway and Engleheart, was already losing its impetus, and a new bourgeois naturalism was beginning to take its place. At the same time the miniaturists, like the contemporary water-colourists, were seeking to enhance the status of their art; one can detect symptoms of this in the still increasing size of their works, and even more in an increased solidity of facture. Miniatures were ceasing to be elegant objects of adornment – pendants, bracelets or brooches – as in some sense they had been since Holbein's time, and were already becoming small pictures to be framed and hung on walls or stood on tables.

Andrew Robertson

It is usual to refer this development to the conscious innovations of the Scottish miniaturist, Andrew Robertson (Pl. 76B). Born in Aberdeen in 1777, Robertson came to London in 1801. He had already worked for some years in the North, but his real historical début occurred when shortly after his arrival in London he made a large miniature copy (measuring some 8 inches by 7) of Van Dyck's portrait of Cornelius van der Geest (then believed to represent Govartius). When this was shown to Cosway he could not at first believe that it was a water-colour miniature at all, it was so heavily painted in imitation of oil: and when Shee, the future P.R.A., saw it, he realized that here was the new type of miniature that he had been looking for; in the words of a contemporary

writer, 'Cosway and Shelley he [Shee] allowed had their merit, but a person is wanted ... to paint large miniatures in the style of that picture of Govartius'. The new style gained rapid favour, and Robertson was soon appointed miniature-painter to the Duke of Sussex; a year or two later he spent some time at Windsor painting portraits of the Royal princesses.

As befits a man who was deliberately seeking to make something that would challenge the oil-portrait on its own ground, Robertson was a slow and conscientious worker. We know, for example, that one portrait took him $22\frac{1}{2}$ hours of sittings, as well as half as much time again spent on background and accessories – 'a week's hard labour', as he described it. But in spite of this, Robertson's work at its best has a lively and sometimes even a spontaneous quality that comes as a surprise to us when we think only of his unusually painstaking methods. He had a strong gift for characterization and a sense of drama which together saved his portraits from being merely accurate inventories of faces. The revolution in style which he initiated was indeed made necessary by the general movement of events in the general world of taste; but he was something more than just a peg on which events hung themselves, and the same may be said of the best of his contemporaries and followers, such as A. E. Chalon (1780–1860) and Sir W. C. Ross, R.A. (1794–1860), who reacted to the same set of external stimuli and furthered the same development in the art. The fact that, wise after the event, we can see only too clearly that these developments were leading towards a not too distant degradation should not blind us to a real merit in the works of those artists who came to maturity in the early years of the nineteenth century.

Jewellery

JOHN HAYWARD

During the eighteenth century fashion in jewellery developed slowly. A jewel made in the early years of the century would not, for instance, have looked greatly out of place in the coronation year of George III. This conservatism in jewellery fashion persisted until the nineteenth century, when increasing use of cheaper materials and the larger number of persons wearing jewels gave rise to more frequent change of fashion. The earlier conservatism was doubtless due in part to the high cost of re-setting precious stones, but also to the fact that the wearing of jewellery was mainly confined to the most formal occasions, when novelties in fashion would have been out of place.

The period from 1760 to 1810 can, as far as jewellery is concerned, be divided conveniently at about 1790, the break being occasioned by the French Revolution. Though this event had no immediate large-scale social repercussions in England, the new fashions in dress which accompanied the Directoire, the First Consulate and the Empire régimes in Paris were soon transmitted to and eagerly adopted in London. These fashions called for types of jewellery more in keeping with the bourgeois background of the French Revolution and greatly different from those worn during the earlier part of the century.

Decline in the importance of setting

The year 1760, which, in other respects, marks the beginning of the transition from the carefree raptures of Rococo asymmetry to the elegant austerity of the neo-classical style, has no particular significance as regards the history of jewellery. The types of jewels worn in the second half of the eighteenth century had become standardized as long as a hundred years before. They had originally been devised for the ladies of the court of Louis XIV, but in the meantime a taste for lighter designs had developed. The tendency during the century had been for settings to become less obtrusive, and in fact to be suppressed as far as was technically possible. Many of the later eighteenth century jewels relied for their effect exclusively on the precious stones of which they were composed. This end was achieved by the introduction of the pavé setting, in which the precious stones were placed so close to each other that the surrounding metal, in which they were embedded, was hardly noticeable. The construction of such settings called for a degree of skill on the part of the jeweller that had not hitherto been attained. In dealing with the earlier part of our period, we are much less well served with sources of information than might be expected. Very little important jewellery of the eighteenth century survives in the condition in which it was originally made; nearly all was re-set in the nineteenth century. It is a peculiar fact that though the brilliant cut, which did so much to bring out the latent beauties of the diamond, was introduced early in the eighteenth century, the majority of surviving eighteenth century jewellery is set not with brilliant but with rose-cut stones. The reason for this apparent anomaly is that the more valuable brilliants were almost invariably reset later, while the old-fashioned rose-diamonds were not considered worth the trouble of resetting.

975

Cost of jewellery in the 1770's

In the ledgers of the Crown Jewellers, later known as Messrs. Garrards, for the second half of the eighteenth century, orders for resetting brilliants or roses are considerably more frequent than those for new pieces of jewellery. The only pieces which were purchased new by many of their clients, who included all the nobility and gentry of the country, were inexpensive objects such as finger or ear-rings. An exception is the brilliant necklace purchased by the Earl of Rosebery for £800 18s. 6d., or the 'double-row'd brilliant necklace' which cost £114 in 1775. Many of the prices seem quite moderate: thus two rose diamond pins cost twelve guineas; a brilliant cluster ring nine guineas; a fine brilliant diamond brooch with inside locket and gold back £17 10s.; a pair of pearl ear-rings three guineas; an amethyst motto ring set round with brilliants £8 10s. All these prices date from the 1770's but are valid for most of the century, as the value of money remained stable.

Apart from surviving jewels, the most likely source of information would seem to be contemporary portraits of ladies of fashion. It is, however, surprising how few of the English portraits of the second half of the eighteenth century, other than those of members of the Royal family, show the sitters wearing much jewellery. One sees an occasional brooch, more frequently a necklace of pearls, or of amber or coral beads, but no more. While portraits of ladies painted by artists at other European Courts show them wearing a great deal of jewellery, in England the enthusiasm for nature, which led to the destruction of nearly all the great formal gardens in the country, seems in portraiture to have banished jewellery from the feminine toilette. The throat and bosom of the sitter, although generously revealed to the on-looker, were customarily left unadorned and free of any adventitious aids to beauty. The contemporary attitude to the use of such accessories is reflected in Sir Joshua Reynold's *Discourses on Painting*. In his Fourth Discourse, he condemns excessive attention to details of materials, while in his Seventh Discourse he deprecates the use of

modern dress in portraiture on the grounds that its excessive familiarity detracted from the dignity of the sitter.

Jewellery in fashion plates

Another source of information as to jewellery fashions is to be found in the columns of the *Lady's Magazine*, which covers most of our period, the first volume having appeared in 1770. This magazine was, however, primarily concerned with fashions in dress and references to accessories such as jewellery are only incidental. The early years provide a meagre crop of information: in March 1774 we read that small drop ear-rings are worn, by July of the same year they seem to be out of fashion again, though 'fine blond lace in puffs drawn through diamond rings or fastened with a diamond buckle' is being worn. In August 1780 we read of 'pearls round the neck in falls' a feature often seen in contemporary portraits. It is not, unfortunately, until after the turn of the century that the *Lady's Magazine* is more explicit about jewellery fashions.

Pattern books of jewellery

It is not then to contemporary portraits, nor to fashion literature, nor to surviving examples that we must turn in order to get an idea of the capacities of the English jeweller in the second half of the eighteenth century. There remains to be mentioned the pattern books published by enterprising jewellers as guides to their less gifted colleagues in the trade. A comprehensive picture of the type of jewellery that was made at the beginning of our period can in fact be obtained from a work published in 1751 entitled *A new book of designs for Jewellers Work by Sebastian Henry Dinglinger. Jeweller. London*. Although his Christian names appear to have been anglicized, it is probable that this Dinglinger was related, perhaps a son or younger brother, to the famous Johann Melchior Dinglinger, Court Jeweller to Augustus the Strong, King of Poland and Elector of Saxony. Dinglinger's book illustrates the whole range of jewellery of the period. As would be expected at the time, the designs show a definite Rococo tendency, though applied to the familiar eighteenth century forms. They illustrate girandole ear-rings, Sevigné bows, large bouquets, corsage ornaments, stomachers, ornaments for sewing on the dress, little moths, flies and butterflies intended as hair ornaments, and finally chatelaines, buckles and fan-mounts. In spite of their rococo feeling, the designs are mainly symmetrical; what is mostly expressive of their period is the naturalistic treatment of the floral motifs that form the basis of so many of them. The earlier designs were considerably more formal in character: the girandole, consisting of a large circular stone above with three pear-shaped pendants, known as briolettes, below: the Sevigné, an openwork bow from which hung one or more pendants, often ending in a cross: the aigrette, a hair ornament of a design somewhat similar to an ear of barley. By the 1760's, though the same basic forms were still in use, the effect had been lightened, firstly by the predominantly floral designs, and secondly by the use of semi-precious stones to give more colour variety. The heavy Sevigné was quite transformed when it was composed of light leaf-like members set with many coloured stones. Not only did the jewellers of the third quarter of the century make increasing use of floral designs but they rendered them, as far as their material permitted, in a naturalistic manner. Their most pleasing achievements in this style were the bouquets intended for corsage ornaments. Examples are to be seen in Dinglinger's pattern book, but extremely few have survived: that shown in Pl. 77 is not of English origin, and is perhaps a little more magnificent than would usually have been found in England at the time. Such bouquets of coloured stones are referred to in Colman and Garrick's play *The Clandestine Marriage*, published in 1766, where the Bride remarks 'I have a bouquet to come home tomorrow, made up of diamonds and rubies and emeralds and topazes and amethysts – jewels of all colours, green, red, blue, yellow, intermixt – the prettiest thing you ever saw in your life.' While these bouquets were undoubtedly the most handsome productions in this *genre*, coloured stones in floral designs were also applied to rings and smaller brooches.

There are numerous descriptions of naturalistic floral ornaments composed of jeweller's work in the catalogue of James Cox's Museum, a collection of clocks, automata and ornaments advertised for sale by lottery in 1774. The first items in this collection were a clock and a pair of vases valued at £5,000 which, it was claimed in the characteristic puffing style of the eighteenth-century advertising copy writer, formed 'the richest set of imperial ornaments ever made, and well deserving a place in the finest palace of the earth'. One of the vases is described: 'In the centre of the rock (forming the base) is fixt a most splendid bunch of flowers, copied with the utmost exactness from nature, in all its infinite variety of tints and forms, with different colour'd gems. The flowers are all in motion, being fixed to springs of tempered gold, which gives them vibration, as if they were blown by the wind; innumerable flies and insects, all of jeweller's work, hover upon and amongst the flowers . . . the different flowers have their different leaves, made of the finest transparent green, and amidst the flowers and leaves, splendid stars, of various magnitudes, are introduced . . . The stars are of jeweller's work, adding greatly to the elegance and richness of these very capital ornaments and have been the labour of many years.'

Diamond floral sprays

Of all the types of jewellery of this period that which has most commonly survived is the brooch composed of a spray of flowers and leaves of diamonds set in silver. The reason for their survival is that they remained fashionable during the nineteenth century and escaped the usual fate of being broken up and reset. It is not at first sight easy to distinguish between eighteenth- and nineteenth-century floral sprays of this type; but the presence of a clear setting, that is with the backs of the stones left open so that light may be transmitted through them, signifies a date not earlier than the end of the eighteenth century. Previously stones had been set in collets that were closed at the back; this method had the advantage from the point of view of the jeweller that he could use stones of inferior colour, and strengthen their effect by providing them with a background of coloured foil which reflected the light, but was concealed from view by the closed collet at the back of the stone. When stones were set in open collets, it was no longer possible to conceal their deficiencies. For women of rank and great wealth a number of flower sprays were put together to compose a stomacher or corsage ornament. The most familiar example is to be seen in Allan Ramsay's well-known coronation portrait of Queen Charlotte, painted about 1762. The Queen is shown wearing a stomacher of almost triangular form which covers the whole front of her dress from the neck down to the low waist; it is composed entirely of floral motifs of silver set with diamonds. Queen Charlotte's diamonds were justly famous; the *Lady's Magazine* gives us a description of them in the issue of June 1800: 'Her Majesty was magnificently attired in a lilac crape petticoat . . . with five superb diamond bands, composed of collets, and fifteen large brilliant roses and stars, at equal distances on the bands; these bands were terminated at the bottom with four very magnificent bows and tassels of diamonds and large pearls, from which were also suspended festoons of beautiful pearls in wreaths; over the left side flowed two corners of lilac crape edged with diamond chains and pearls, with pearl tassels at the bottom, and fastened at the pocket holes with a superb diamond and pearl bow; all the diamond and pearl bands and chains being displayed to great advantage by being placed on wreaths of purple jessamine leaves. Her Majesty wore a superb diamond stomacher and necklace and a beautiful diamond bouquet; her head-dress was chiefly composed of a magnificent diamond bandeau, with brilliant drops of immense value; in short, her Majesty's whole dress was never decorated with such profusion of diamonds and pearls, and in point of value greatly surpassed anything of the sort ever displayed in this or any other country.' It is probable that Queen Charlotte, who could ignore the new fashions in jewellery that were coming over from Paris, was still wearing the same stomacher that may be seen in the Ramsay portrait of her. The impression given by this enthusiastic description is that of a lady dressed according to pre-Revolution fashion. The claim that the Queen had never before worn so many diamonds is not likely to be correct. It was the peculiar custom in the eighteenth century for the coronation robes and regalia to be adorned with as many diamonds as could be obtained on loan from the London jewellers. At the coronation of George III and Charlotte, the bill for the hire of diamonds from the Crown Jewellers, Messrs John Wakelin and Edward Parker, amounted to £15,024. The diamonds borrowed were valued at the immense sum of £375,600.

During the third quarter of the eighteenth century, elaborate towering head-dresses were worn which gave considerable scope for a display of jewellery. In English portraits, we rarely see anything more elaborate than a rope of pearls worked into the coiffure, sometimes accompanied by one or more pendants. The aigrette, worn at the side of the head, had a long period of popularity until it was replaced in the early nineteenth century by the tiara, a form that accorded better with the classical revival dress of the Empire. These aigrettes consisted of a delicately constructed bouquet of precious stones in a very light setting. The individual fronds or stalks were often mounted on springs so that the slightest move set them vibrating, thus bringing out the full brilliance of the diamonds with which they were mounted.

No mention has hitherto been made of paste jewels, but in fact, there was a considerable production of paste, and many of the most attractive jewels surviving from the earlier part of our period are of paste. The designs for paste jewels did not, however, differ in any way from those used for precious stones, and they do not, therefore, call for separate treatment.

The fashion columns in the *Lady's Magazine* of the last decade of the century give us several hints as to the changes that were taking place. Thus in June 1790 we read of a necklace of two rows of fine filigree work, the lower hanging below the waist; in April 1794 'the fashionable earrings were in double rings of fillagree gold mixed with brilliants, pearls and enamel, the necklaces to suit': in June 1798 enamelled chains and necklaces of diamonds set in collets and linked together were suitable for wear at Court, while strings of garnets were worn on ordinary occasions. In 1802, necklaces of pearl, amber and coral were still being worn, but we read the following somewhat astringent comment: 'Trinkets in the shape of harps fastened by gold chains round the neck; a diamond crescent is worn on the bosom, indicative, we imagine, of chastity; the horn of the lamp of Eve cannot be supposed to refer to the happy husbands of our modern belles.'

The Grecian Revival

The colour plates which accompany these issues of the *Lady's Magazine* show that the Grecian Revival fashions from Paris had been wholeheartedly adopted in London, and it is against such a background that the jewellery of the latter part of our period must be envisaged. It might even be said that the early nineteenth century saw the birth of what is now known as costume jewellery, for the cameo set tiaras, necklaces and bracelets that were worn at the time were consciously designed to match the fashions in dress that had been imported from Paris. A noticeable trend at the end of the century was the general use of less expensive materials, and not only by the bourgeoisie. Besides true cameos cut in hardstone, shell and even lava cameos were popular. Lowest of all in degree were the paste cameos of moulded glass, which were the invention of the Scot, James Tassie. Other alternatives to precious stones were the medallions with classical subjects turned out by Wedgwood at Burslem, and enamelled plaques from South Staffordshire.

Cheap jewellery in the form of pastes had, however, been known for centuries and the desire for less expensive jewellery was not the decisive factor in the introduction of the new fashions. The great archaeological discoveries of the second half of the eighteenth century profoundly influenced fashion; and the practice of wearing Roman intaglios or cameos or reproductions thereof on head, arms and neck was simply a manifestation of the fashion-consciousness of society at the beginning of the nineteenth century.

Besides the introduction of the tiara in place of the aigrette, the early nineteenth century saw one other important innovation in jewellery fashion. This was the adoption of the parure of matched pieces, consisting of necklace, ear-rings, pendant, bracelet and sometimes a tiara as well, all *en suite*. Such parures might be of immense value, composed of finely matched stones, but inexpensive versions were also produced in semi-precious stones mounted in stamped gold or even pinchbeck settings.

Mourning jewellery

A feature of the latter part of the eighteenth century was the fashion for mourning jewellery. The considerable quantity that survives, especially in the form of mourning rings, would seem to suggest that it must have been the most popular form of jewellery, but this high survival rate is due to the combination of sentimental appeal and a low intrinsic value. Mourning jewellery was by no means a new idea; it had long been the custom for a testator to leave money for the provision of mourning rings for the chief mourners at his funeral. That the expansion in the fashion for such jewellery dates from after 1760 is demonstrated by the neo-classical flavour of the subjects treated. As a rule oval frames were favoured, of varying size according to the ultimate destination of the jewel, i.e. ring, pendant, locket or bracelet slide. These frames were set with enamels or miniature paintings of funerary urns on plinths by which stood inconsolable widows under the shadow of weeping willow trees. The back of the frame was filled with an appropriate design, often a monogram of the deceased's initials executed in a lock of the latter's own hair. Such jewellery was usually inexpensive; a thin gold frame was set with, at the most, seed-pearl or diamond sparks. The extreme sentimentality of this jewellery was out of key with early nineteenth century taste, but to pursue the history of jewellery through the ever increasing tempo of early nineteenth-century changes of fashion would take us beyond the limits of the particular period which is the subject of this book.

PALL MALL

61

New Furniture Warehouse

Designer & **Manufacturer**

ALLEN

*Has the honor to acquaint the Nobility and Gentry,
that he has open'd private Ware rooms, for the express
purpose of supplying the most fashionable Furniture
Calicoes at such moderate charges that he shall have
no Competitor: And, in order to merit the patronage
of the Nobility, & Gentry, he undertakes to make up
every kind of furniture to which such goods are
adapted with an Elegance & taste not usually met with.*

*NB: Elegant Specimens of made up Drapery for
various purposes may be seen at the Warehouse as above*

Girtin sc. 3. Charles St. Midd. Hosp.

An early nineteenth-century engraved tradesman's card.

Glass

R. J. CHARLESTON

The history of glass is not limited by political boundaries, and the accession of George III was accompanied by no change in glass-style. 'About 1760', however, is a significant dating in eighteenth-century English glass, since it represents the apogee of the rococo phase of that art, as of others. But to see this climax in its true light, it is necessary to cast back and survey what went before.

George Ravenscroft's invention of glass-of-lead about 1675 was an epoch-making discovery. Before that date, lightness had been unhesitatingly accepted as the hallmark of the best glass. After that date, a fresh set of glass values supervened and gradually made themselves felt throughout the civilized world; until, by the end of the eighteenth century, 'English crystal' was synonymous with what was most desirable in glass, just as 'Venice glass' had been for the preceding century. The immediate consequence of Ravenscroft's revolutionary discovery, however, was that by the increasing use of lead-oxide, a glass-'metal' was produced which was unsuitable for working by the old Venetian-derived methods. The best results of this new English style are the so-called 'baluster' glasses of about 1700, in which simplicity and solidity are combined with a harmonious relationship of the parts to the whole. Thereafter the general movement of taste towards lighter forms led to a heightening of the stem and a thinning of its component knops and balusters. This general movement was in the case of glass accentuated by the imposition in 1745/6 of an Excise levied on the material by weight. It now behoved the glass-maker to be as sparing of his metal as he could. To compensate for loss of form, he turned to ornament.

Decoration of glass: stem-twists

Some writers on glass have inferred that the movement towards ornament during the second quarter of the eighteenth century was solely caused by the Excise of 1745/6. The truth is that glass followed in the wake of larger movements. The rococo, which began to win general acceptance in England about 1750, was primarily a decorative movement, in which surface embellishment was nearly everything. In this it contrasted with the baroque, which moved in depth, with massive sculptured forms and dramatic contrasts of light and shade – virtues, incidentally, of the best 'baluster' glasses.

The first of these adventitious forms of ornament was the air-twist stem, in which threads of air are twisted spirally to form a silvery coil within the thickness of the stem (Pl. 82c). Beginning tentatively in the first decades of the century, this technique reached its perfection in the 'thirties and 'forties, only to dwindle in significance after the mid-century.

From the air-twists, which are no more than drawn-out bubbles of air, it was but a short step to the enamel-twist, which is a series of opaque-white rods embedded in a clear matrix, drawn out thin and twisted. Although enamel-twists came in before 1750, their hey-day was the third quarter of the century; a further excise in 1777, which extended the tax to enamel-glass, giving the death-blow to what was already probably a dying fashion.

Towards the end of this period, glasses were occasionally made with twists incorporating coloured as well as opaque-white threads (Pl. 82A, E).

Engraving, enamelling and gilding

The forms of decoration already described were all carried out in the glass-house while the material was still hot and ductile. Of more significance was the ornamentation executed in various types of decorating-establishment on the blank glasses as received from the glass-house. Of these forms of ornament, cutting is by far the most important and will be dealt with at length later. Closely akin to it is the art of engraving. In both the surface of the glass is broken into by means of an abrasive suspended in a liquid and fed on to the point of contact between it and a rotating wheel. The engraver's wheel is usually made of copper, in a great variety of shapes and profiles. After the rough cuts have been made, they may be polished at will by a series of wheels of softer materials used with abrasives of a progressively finer texture. Engraving was introduced to England by German craftsmen, but never aspired in this country to the heights which it often attained in its German and Bohemian homelands. English engraving is usually restricted to simple borders, armorial devices and mottoes, artless sprays of flowers, and an occasional unambitious figure subject. Although they are seldom remarkable as works of art, English engraved glasses are often of considerable interest for their subject-matter. Particularly is this so where they are the vehicles for the propaganda of Jacobites and Hanoverians, at whose meetings the drinking of toasts from suitably engraved glasses played an important part (Pl. 82C). Perhaps the most charming of all the engraved English rococo glasses, however, are those which adapt the *chinoiseries* of Pillement or Boucher within the limitations of the executant's technique (Pl. 82D), or conjure up tiny vignettes of English rural life and scenery, much in the spirit of Bewick's tail-pieces.

This same spirit informs some of the best enamelling of the period. Nor is this altogether surprising, for Bewick himself was apprenticed in the family which was responsible for the best of it.

This was the Beilby family at Newcastle-on-Tyne, of whom William and Mary were entrusted with the work on glass. The best of their enamelling is done in monochrome white on drinking-glasses and decanters, although their ambitious armorial goblets in full heraldic colours are splendid things. Their simpler pieces are decorated with no more than a scroll of the fruiting vine or a flower-spray, but on the more elaborate glasses appear little vignettes of rural life and sport (Pl. 82A), classical ruins and obelisks in the taste of the time, or fictitious coats-of-arms painted in colours but enclosed in the most delicate of rococo scrollwork painted in white.

Enamelling of another sort, but often of comparable quality, was done on opaque-white glass made to imitate porcelain. Here, naturally enough, the ornamentation too simulated that of porcelain, mainly in sprays and sprigs of flowers, often accompanied by the little insects first familiarized on European porcelain by the factory at Meissen. This opaque-white glass, not being suitable for tea- or coffee-services, was employed mainly for ornamental vases and beakers, tea-caddies, candlesticks and the like. Contrary to popular belief, it was not made only, or even mainly, in Bristol; but also in London, Newcastle, Warrington and elsewhere. Some of it was almost certainly decorated in the South Staffordshire area, in which enamelling on metal had been practised since well before the middle of the eighteenth century. Here too were probably decorated the small facetted scent- and smelling-bottles, *étuis*, etc., of blue, green or purple glass, with their tiny scenes of birds, flying and swimming, or their inch-high shepherdesses with hay-rakes. These were usually enamelled and gilt, but sometimes gilt only, and this type of decoration became popular on blue glass in the same period which saw the 'mazarine blue' grounds on Chelsea porcelain decorated with birds in thick rich gold. The bases of candelabra were often decorated in this way, while some blue fingerbowls and stands with gilt key-fret borders are among the few examples of glass certainly attributable to Bristol, being signed by the maker (Fig. 1). Such finger-bowls, however, must have enjoyed a general vogue at the time, for a Ger-

Fig. 1. Blue glass finger-bowl with gilt decoration. Signed 'I. Jacobs Bristol'. Probably made at Jacobs' 'Non-Such Flint Glass Manufactory' in Bristol, about 1805. Ht. 3⅞ in. *Victoria and Albert Museum.*

man visitor remarks: 'The blue glass bowls used for rinsing hands and mouth in at the end are quite delightful' (1786). Smollett, however, writing in his *Travels* (1766), thought quite differently about this habit: 'I know of no custom more beastly than that of using water-glasses in which polite company spirt and squirt and spue the filthy scourings of their gums.' Colourless glass too was occasionally decorated with gilding. This work is usually unpretentious, and consists of no more than a stem of vine-leaves and grapes, or the like.

Cut-glass

Of all the methods of decorating glass used in the eighteenth century, however, cutting is by far the most important. The tools of cutting are large wheels of stone or iron, on to which a mixture of sand and water plays at the point of contact with the glass. The edge of the wheel may be flat, rounded or bevelled, producing cuts of different section; and the glass may be offered to the wheel in the plane of its rotation or obliquely, producing symmetrical or unsymmetrical cuts. From the varieties of cut offered by these different combinations is built up a geometrical tessellated pattern. Cut-glass was the supreme manifestation of English glass in the eighteenth century, for two reasons: first, because cutting was a decorative technique intimately related to the form of the vessel on which it was used; and secondly, because English lead-glass was ideally suited to it, both because it was soft and therefore easily worked, and because its high refractive index brought out the maximum play of light.

Cutting, like engraving, came to England from the German lands, where the stems of engraved wine-glasses were frequently facetted. The first cut glasses in England were certainly made during the first quarter of the eighteenth century, but it was the second quarter which saw its real development. Cutting was at first limited to parts of a glass which offered a thickness of metal to the wheel. Rims of bowl-forms (such as sweetmeat-glasses) were notched or scalloped, whilst cruet bottles and the stems of wine-glasses were cut into all-over patterns of flat or slightly hollowed hexagons or diamonds (Fig. 2), obtained by overlapping facets cut on the flat or rounded wheel. A more elaborate style of cutting was evolved during the third quarter of the century, when oblique cuts producing lunate forms were combined with the motifs already described in a variety of ways, resulting in remarkably rich effects (Fig. 3). Amongst the motifs thrown up by this style of cutting was a triangle or a diamond in low relief. When the neo-classical movement began to make itself felt in glass, it had the effect of sobering down the rich cutting-style of the 1760's and 1770's. Amongst the cut motives which remained in favour, however, were the vertical flute, with its elegant slimming effect, and the relief-diamond.

The course of development of cut-glass was affected within a very short span of years by the impact of two economic measures. The first of these was the severe increase in 1777 of the tax on glass by weight: the second was the freeing of Irish trade in 1780. Ireland was now free to export glass anywhere in the world, and her glass-makers were unhampered by the Excise. The effects were twofold. In the first place, many English glassmen migrated to Ireland: in the second, the development of style in cutting was unhampered in Ireland by considerations of economy. It was therefore naturally the Irish glass-houses which took up and developed those

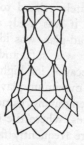

Fig. 2. Neck of a decanter showing fluting, scale-pattern and flat diamonds, about 1760–70 (after Thorpe).

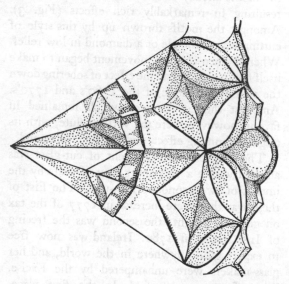

Fig. 3. Section of a dish showing the full development of English sliced cutting, about 1775.

Fig. 4. Field of strawberry diamonds, early nineteenth century (after Thorpe).

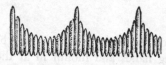

Fig. 5. 'Herring-bone' fringe, early nineteenth century (after Thorpe).

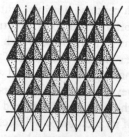

Fig. 6. Field of relief diamonds, late eighteenth and early nineteenth centuries (after Thorpe).

motifs which required the greatest thickness of metal – the pillared flute (in relief), the deep horizontal groove, and, most important, the relief-diamond (latterly made smaller and sharper), with its developments, the hob-nail diamond and the strawberry diamond. These, arranged overall in relatively large fields, and often combined with fluting, became the dominant motifs of late eighteenth- and early nineteenth-century cutting (Figs. 4, 5, 6). Their uniformity called for great precision in cutting, but led to aesthetic monotony and a boring profusion of decoration, seen at its worst towards 1850.

The uses of glass

Glass in our period was used in almost as many ways as it is today. Then as now, however, glass for drinking took pride of place, and among drinking-glasses the wine-glass was king (Pl. 82B–E). On it and its concomitant decanter were lavished the most up-to-date forms of decoration. There was not, however, with one or two insignificant exceptions, a differentiation between the shapes and sizes of glasses used for different types of wine. This was a product of nineteenth-century connoisseurship. The wine-glass was simply a glass of about one-third to one-half gill in capacity, of varying bowl-shape. Somewhat smaller than the wine-glasses, but often on a proportionately higher stem, was the glass used for drams or cordials (Pl. 82A) – and small wonder, when one reads some of the recipes of the time:

A very rich Cherry Cordial

'Take a Stone Pot that has a Broad Bottom and a narrow Top, and lay a layer of Black Cherries and a Layer of very fine powdered Sugar; do this 'till your pot is full: Measure your Pot and to every Gallon it holds, put a quarter of a pint of Spirit of Wine. You are to pick your Cherries clean from Soil and Stalks, but not wash them. When you have thus filled your Pot, stop it with a Cork, and tie first a Bladder, then a Leather over it; and if you fear it is not close enough, pitch it down close and bury it deep in the Earth six months or longer; then strain it out and keep it close stopped for your Use. 'Twill revive, when all other cordials fail.'

A further type of glass of small capacity, with a tallish narrow bowl, is usually termed a 'ratafia' glass, but ratafia was little different from other cordials, and a good case has been made out for these glasses being in fact champagne-glasses. Champagne, then as now, was an expensive drink (in 1762 it was offered at 8s. a bottle, as contrasted with 6s. for Burgundy or 5s. for Claret), and was apparently notable for its strength. Lady Mary Wortley Montagu, somewhat earlier, wrote:

They sigh not from their hearts, but from their brain Vapours of vanity and strong Champaign.

That the champagne-glass offered one of the exceptions to the rule of non-differentiation enunciated above is proved by the fact that, in bills rendered by the glass-cutter Thomas Betts in the 1750's, 'champagnes' are singled out by contrast with mere 'wines'. There is good reason why these champagne-glasses should have been small, and the almost cylindrical shape is, from the wine-taster's point of view, better for champagne-drinking than the modern shallow hemisphere – a form which probably did not come in before the second quarter of the nineteenth century. The eighteenth-century glasses of this general shape are certainly almost always sweetmeat-glasses.

Set apart from the form of the ordinary wine-glass was the 'firing-glass' or the toast-master's glass. The latter might be a trumpet-shaped glass on a slender stem, or a glass with a deceptive capacity obtained by the use of abnormally thick metal. The 'firing-glass' was usually trumpet-shaped, short-stemmed, and equipped with a thick disc-foot able to withstand hard banging on the table, in an age when drinking was of the order described in Dyott's *Diary*: 'The Prince (afterwards George IV) took the chair himself and ordered me to be his Vice. We had a very good dinner and he sent wine of his own, the very best Claret I ever tasted. We had the Grenadiers drawn up in front of the messroom windows to fire a volley in honour of the toasts. As soon as dinner was over he began. He did not drink himself: he always drinks Madeira. He took very good care to see everybody fill, and he gave 23 bumpers without a halt. In the course of my experience I never saw such fair drinking. When he had finished his list of bumpers, I begged leave as Vice to give the Superior, and recommended it to the Society to stand up on our chairs with three times three, taking their time from the Vice. I think it was the most laughable sight I ever beheld to see our Governor, our General and the Commodore all so drunk they could scarce stand on the floor, hoisted up on their chairs with each a bumper in his hand; and the three times three cheers was what they were afraid to attempt for fear of falling . . . There were twenty dined; we drank sixty-three bottles of wine.'

Ale was drunk from glasses with tall tapering bowls. In high-class specimens, the bowl is frequently decorated with a hops-and-barley motif engraved, enamelled or gilt (Pl. 82F). In taverns, the glasses were plain, or at best ornamented with a wrythen mould-blown rib-pattern.

The decanter, although a late-comer to the table, was well-established by 1760. It could vary in capacity from a pint (which must surely have stood at one man's elbow and not been passed round the table) to the equivalent of twenty bottles. In 1760 two forms of decanter were current. The first was broadest at the shoulder and was usually decorated with all-over diamond-cutting (Pl. 83C). The second had a sloping shoulder (Pl. 83A), and was more frequently decorated by engraving, enamelling or gilding (often with a cartouche enclosing the name of the wine). With the coming of neo-classicism these decanters were refined by a reduction in diameter and by a smooth unbroken transition in the curve from neck to body (Pl. 83B). These elegant decanters were usually only lightly decorated. From 1775 onwards an entirely new form takes the field – a decanter with barrel-shaped body and outsplayed lip. This shape was well-suited for decoration by cutting, and was taken over by the Irish glass-houses. Towards the end of our period the disc-stopper was replaced by a mushroom-stopper, and the neck of the decanter was equipped with three horizontal rings to facilitate a grip (Fig. 7).

Spirits too were kept in decanters, frequently of coloured glass with gilt labels showing their contents. These were often square in section and

986

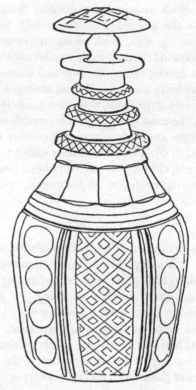

Fig. 7. Decanter and stopper, cut with panels of 'strawberry diamonds'. Early nineteenth century. Ht. 9⅛ in.

could therefore easily be carried about in travelling-cases. Thus in 1784 Fogg & Son, the noted London 'chinamen' and glass-sellers, supplied Sir John Griffin with '4 Square Glass Bottles Cut All Over – 10/–'. Such bottles were often simply referred to as 'Squares'.

Although the service of alcohol was the most important function of glass in the eighteenth century, its use spread far beyond this. At table, cruet-bottles and sugar-casters were frequently made of glass fitted with silver caps (Pl. 83D). When the dessert-course came on, glass had a particularly important part to play, for the centre of the table was frequently taken by an imposing 'pyramid' of glass. A broad salver on a low foot formed the bottom tier of this pyramid, and on it was set another of narrower diameter but with a taller stem: and on this sometimes a third. Each tier was set round with jellies (Fig. 8) or wet and dry sweetmeats, in tall conical or low round glasses, whilst as the crown of the whole was set a large sweet-meat glass with hemispherical bowl on a tall stem (Pl. 81). Dishes, plates and pickle-trays of scalloped and sliced cutting might also adorn the table, whilst openwork baskets wrought from glass-threads whilst still plastic might serve to hold fruit. Tea-caddies, and more rarely teapots and cups and saucers; jugs and basins, patch-boxes, *étuis* and seals, were also occasionally made in glass.

Of all the uses to which English glass was put in the eighteenth century none was more suited to its peculiar character than its employment for lighting fittings. The high powers of light-refraction possessed by English lead-crystal have already been mentioned: when cut, a prismatic effect was added to it, and when wax candles were set in cut chandeliers and candelabra, the effect must have been brilliant indeed – but of a brilliance softened by the slight darkness of the glass-material itself. The candlesticks of our period were mostly plain-shafted, with a broad domed foot and a detachable grease-pan. The shaft was usually cut in diamond facets, the foot and grease-pan scalloped and cut in accordance with the changing modes of the time.

Far more elaborate were the great cut-glass chandeliers which blazed in the reception-rooms of great houses, or in the Assembly-rooms of such cities as Bath, York or Newcastle. The glass chandelier had evolved in the first half of the eighteenth century to a form where S-shaped arms radiated from a semi-spherical cup which was itself only one of a number of spherical ornaments, usually simply cut, strung on a tall vertical shaft. In the second half of the century this basic pattern was merely elaborated. To the shaft were added canopies, scalloped at the edges and pierced for hanging drops cut in a variety of patterns; cutting became more elaborate, the candle-arms themselves being notched to add to the prismatic effect, and cut spires, themselves often topped by cut canopies, being set on the branches (Pl. 84). This was the apogee of the rococo chandelier. The first effects of neo-classicism were to be seen in the appearance of an urn-shaped member on the vertical stem, and gradually the whole chandelier began to be stripped of its more frivolous trappings. Cutting became sparser, and the medley of hanging ornaments gave way to a uniform type of brilliant-cut, usually pear-shaped, drop. These drops were often strung in swags from branch to branch and round the canopies, and the multiplication of these festoons of drops began to obscure the basic design of the chandelier. Arms, no longer readily visible, became plain, while the ornamental parts of the stem, except the canopies, lost importance. The final stage of this evolutionary process, which culminated about 1810, saw the eighteenth-century chandelier completely transformed. Below a series of drop-hung canopies, ropes of drops formed a sparkling tent, the widest part of which was an ormolu hoop, in which were set numerous short, S-shaped arms, heavily notched and terminating in richly cut candle-holders and grease-pans (Pl. 84).

The chandelier, which must have formed so striking an adjunct of the eighteenth century salon, was not, however, without its disadvantages. Lady Mary Coke, writing in 1768, remarks: '. . . I went to the Ball at eight o'clock . . . I think 'tis one of the finest Houses for an entertainment that I know, and nobody does the honours better or more agreeably than Lady Holland, yet I cant say I thought it went off well.

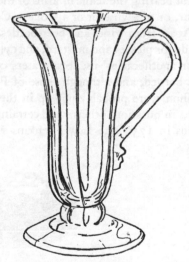

Fig. 8. Jelly-glass. Mid-eighteenth century. Ht. 4½ in.

The Dancers complained of the heat . . . A great branch Candle Stick fell down over Lady Holland, and very narrowly missed her head.'

Common glass

The glass so far described was for the most part of a luxurious character, and reserved to the houses of wealth and importance. It was made in glass-houses devoted solely to the manufacture of 'white' glass. Far more numerous, however, especially in the Bristol, Stourbridge and Newcastle areas, were the window- and bottle-houses. In the latter, enormous quantities of bottles were produced by hand, whilst in their spare time, using the fag-end of a pot of 'metal', the workmen might produce simple jugs, cream-pans and the like, to satisfy a local market (Fig. 9).

The wine-bottle in the period under consideration suffered very little mutation compared with that undergone in the previous hundred years. By the middle of the eighteenth century the previously sloping side of the wine-bottle had become vertical, and the modern bottle, capable of being binned on its side, had to all intents and purposes evolved. The eighteenth-century bottle was blown by hand and not moulded, and still bore round its neck the ribbon of glass which had originally served as an anchor for the wire fastenings of the cork. Occasionally a bottle is equipped with a seal bearing the name or arms of the owner of a cellar, or of a vintner or a College Common Room. Apart from wine- and beer-bottles, bottles were made for pickles and mustard, and cylindrical phials for apothecaries' use. Spa waters could be obtained bottled, and although those of Pyrmont and Pouhon were probably put up in the bottles of the Spa in question, others were certainly English. Thus in 1759 one Lewis Jenkins supplied,

Fig. 9. Green glass jug decorated with blobs and threads of opaque-white glass. Late eighteenth or early nineteenth century. Ht. 7¾ in.

in addition to Pyrmont and Pouhon waters, 'Bristol Hot Well Water, fill'd by Smith and Woodall, at 7s. per doz.'

The standard wine-bottle of this period contained a quart, although hand-making rendered it difficult to maintain exact uniformity—so much so that a Member of Parliament, suitably enough the Member for Cork, brought in a Private Member's Bill in 1802 'that a quart bottle should hold a quart'. There were, however, also half-bottles, and even quarter-bottles; while, on the opposite side of the scale, there were Jeroboams and Rehoboams accommodating 4 and 6 bottles respectively, Methuselahs for 8 and Salmanazars for 12, and even monsters which held 28 bottles.

Tail-piece from T. Bewick's *A History of British Birds*, Vol. 2, 1804.

Music and Musical Instruments

ERIC HALFPENNY

With the death of Handel in 1759, his Italianate Baroque influence, though still powerful, began to give place to the newer 'Galant' style of the early Classical symphonists, then infiltrating from the Continent. The new style reached its apotheosis later in the century in the mature symphonies of Haydn and Mozart, and its innovators belonged to countries other than England. England's expanding economy and growing commercial wealth made her a consumer rather than a producer of masterpieces. Her contribution to the art of music in late-Georgian times was perhaps material rather than spiritual; in the manufacture of instruments and in music-printing; above all, as a cosmopolitan asylum for composers, virtuosi and craftsmen from abroad, many of whom settled here, to the permanent enrichment of our musical scene.

Pianoforte and harpsichord

The English sponsorship and development of the pianoforte after 1760 was the most important and far-reaching single event of the period. Although the instrument was invented in 1709 by Cristofori of Florence, it did not come into much prominence until the second half of the century, by which time the initiative was being taken outside of Italy. The quite sudden appearance of the instrument in England dates almost exactly from 1760. The story has often been told, how a number of German craftsmen, driven here by the Seven Years War, brought with them the *métier* of piano-building from the workshop of Gottfried Silbermann of Dresden, whose early copies of Cristofori's instrument are said to have been criticized by J. S. Bach. The earliest English printed reference to the pianoforte is contained in a London directory for 1763, where Frederic Neubaur is listed as a maker, among other things, of 'Piano-fortes'. This entry is of particular interest since Neubaur seems to have been an associate of Roger Plenius, an English harpsichord maker of great inventive talent, said by Burney to have been the first maker of a piano in this country. Plenius became a bankrupt in 1756, having beggared himself in his attempts to popularize his Lyrichord (Fig. 1), an enormously complicated keyboard instrument which produced sustained sounds from strings by means of rotating wheels, after the manner of the hurdy-gurdy. This amazing instrument passed into Neubaur's possession, and was eventually sold at Christie's with the rest of his stock-in-trade, in 1772, for the sum of fifty guineas. Its subsequent fate is unknown.

The earliest surviving English-built piano is dated 1766. This instrument, curiously enough, is quite unorthodox in having seventeen notes to the octave for the greater part of its compass, instead of the normal twelve. This idea, though not then new, was probably directly inspired by the writings of Dr Robert Smith, of Trinity College, Cambridge, who a few years before had advocated a 24-note octave in order to secure purer tuning in all the major and minor scales. It is remarkable, however, that the new type of instrument should so soon have been used as the basis for such experiments.

Johannes Zumpe, whose work it is, was a

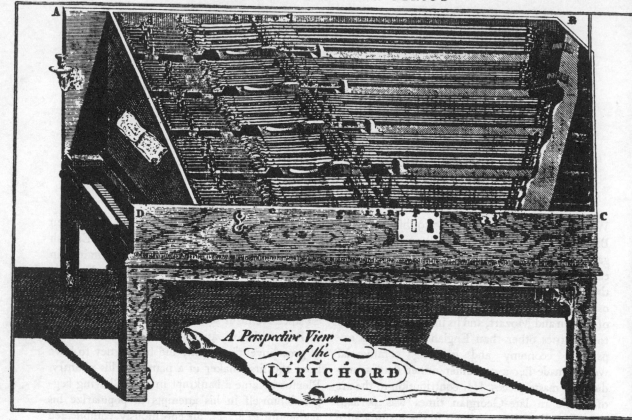

A Perspective View of the LYRICHORD

Fig. 1. The Lyrichord: from an engraving dated 1755. Invented by Roger Plenius about 1740 and subsequently exhibited many times in London. It was the most elaborate of many attempts to obtain sustained sounds from a stringed keyboard instrument. The strings were drawn down by the keys on to resined wheels, of which there were fifteen, rotated at different speeds by clockwork. Plenius was one of the English pioneers of the pianoforte.

German who occupied premises in Princes Street, Hanover Square, from 1761 onwards. There can be no doubt at all that Zumpe was entirely responsible for creating the early vogue for the pianoforte in England, and was the first to begin the systematic manufacture of such instruments (Pl. 85A). Zumpe's pianoforte made no pretence of competing with the concert harpsichord of the day. It was a small domestic instrument in the form of a shallow rectangular box on a trestle stand, and known from its shape as the 'square' piano. It is due entirely to the immediate popularity of the square that the pianoforte so rapidly gained a foothold in this country. The serious challenge to the harpsichord came later, when the larger pianos, significantly called 'grands' in contrast to the (by now) common squares, began to be developed by other makers. Nevertheless, the instrument had already begun to appear in public before 1770. It was first mentioned as an alternative to the harpsichord on an English music title-page in 1766 (Pl. 88A). In 1767 Mr Charles Dibdin demonstrated the new instrument between the acts of the *Beggar's Opera* at the Theatre Royal, Covent Garden, and in 1768 John Christian Bach (eleventh son of J. S. Bach) gave a public recital on a Zumpe for which he had paid fifty pounds. Bach's Opus 5 Sonatas, published in the following year, was the first of his compositions to cater specifically for the new instrument. These events would seem to mark the end of the experimental stage of the pianoforte in this country, and the beginning of its wider propagation. The polite letters of the *dilettanti* frequently leave us in no doubt as to the fashionable cult of the Zumpe piano. The trend of taste is also clearly shown by the title-pages of keyboard music published in England during this period. These begin to include the piano as an alternative instrument to the harpsichord about 1770. During the next twenty years the custom of catering for both instruments became almost universal, following which there was a steady decline in the number of times the harpsichord was mentioned, until by the end of the century it had practically disappeared from printed titles.

Zumpe's prototype was widely copied, and although improvements and modifications soon followed, it remained basically the same almost to the close of the century. The original action was of the simplest description (Fig. 2). The compass, at first $4\frac{1}{2}$ octaves, was soon extended to five, and this remained standard until 1795 or thereabouts, though it was exceptionally exceeded before that date. The stringing was 'bicord' (two strings per note), the upper strings being steel, the middle plain brass, and the lowest dozen or so overspun with an open spiral 'gimping' of finer wire. The strings passed diagonally across the case from hitchpins along the back, behind the keyboard, to tuning or wrestpins set in the small square soundboard at the right-hand end of the case. Dampers were provided for every note. These projected on arms from the back of the case, and rested on the strings just above the hammers. Each damper was raised when the key was pressed, by a little ivory push rod resting on the back or tail of the key. There were usually three hand stops, housed in the box-like end of the case beside the bass keys. Two of these raised the dampers in the same way as the modern 'loud' or sustaining pedal, but in two sections, treble and bass. The third pushed a strip of soft leather – the *sordino* or mute – against the underside of the strings for soft effects. There were occasional variations in the number and

arrangement of the stops, but the important and permanent feature which they served to establish was the independent damper-lifting mechanism of the pianoforte.

Space does not allow a full description of all the developments which took place prior to 1810, but a few may be touched upon. John Broadwood's partnership with the harpsichord maker, Shudi, dated from 1770, and very shortly afterwards the firm began making pianos. The earliest known Broadwood square was made in 1774. In 1783 he patented a slightly improved underdamper action for squares (Fig. 3). This enabled the wrestpins to be placed in a better position at the back of the case instead of on the soundboard, but although the patent provided for a damper pedal, neither this nor hand stops appear to have been fitted to surviving specimens, and the design must therefore be considered reactionary in this respect (Pl. 85B). In 1786, John Geib, a native of Leipsig, introduced into the square piano action an adjustable spring-loaded jack in imitation of Cristofori's original action (Fig. 4). In 1794, Southwell of Dublin devised a means of extending the compass of the square while retaining fairly compact proportions by placing the highest section of the action and keyboard on a separate frame which slid under the soundboard. He also reverted to an improved form of overdamper, associated with a somewhat clumsy pedal mechanism which took off the dampers by lifting all the key tails, consequently reducing the depth of touch of the keyboard when operated. This defect was subsequently rectified.

The square piano is often treated with scorn by modern writers, but technically it was one of the most difficult forms of stringed keyboard instrument to make. English and Anglo-German craftsmen reached a particularly high standard of excellence with this form of the instrument, and in doing so they created the domestic vogue for the piano which has lasted almost to our own day. In the formative years of the pianoforte, a great deal of pioneer work and experiment was carried out first on the square, the extensive demand for these instruments ensuring that any new device was adequately tested.

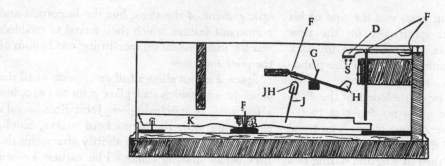

Fig. 2.

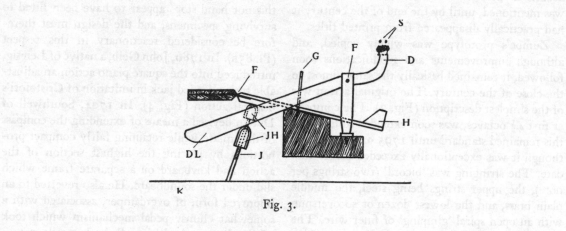

Fig. 3.

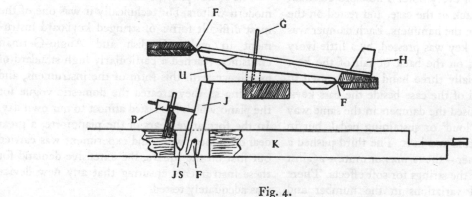

Fig. 4.

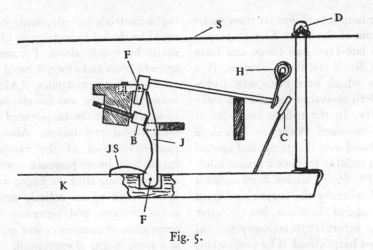

Fig. 5.

Fig. 2. Cross-Section of a Square Piano, c. 1760 (after Zumpe). Showing Action Unit. A wire jack rigidly fixed in the key merely pushes the hammer towards the strings. At the same time the damper is lifted from the strings by the key tail.

Fig. 3. Square Pianoforte Action (Broadwood, 1783), with gravity-return Underdamper. The hammer is operated as in Fig. 2, by a rigid jack, the lower head of which also lifts the weighted damper lever. The damper unit is made of brass.

Fig. 4. Square Pianoforte Action, with Spring Jack (after John Geib, 1786: from an instrument by Longman and Broderip, c. 1790). The principle of the moving jack enables it to drive the hammer towards the string until the last possible instant, when it clears, or 'escapes', thus letting the hammer fall away on

rebound though the key remains down. The Geib action also includes a separate 'underhammer' lever which allows the motion to be transferred very close to the hinge of the hammer proper, and improves velocity and touch. This action is a late adaptation of that used by Christofori, the inventor of the piano, c. 1709–20.

Fig. 5. The English Grand Pianoforte Action. Evolved after 1770 by the pioneer makers of the English grand, Backers, Broadwood and Stodart, this type of action was still in use at the end of the nineteenth century. The jack acts directly on the hammer butt. As it rises it is thrust aside by the set-off button, thus effecting 'escapement', and leaving the hammer free to fall. While the key remains down the hammer is held by the check to prevent a ricochet and aid quick repetition of the note if required.

KEY TO FIGS. 2–5.

B.	Set-off Button.	G.	Guide Pin.	K.	Key.
C.	Check.	H.	Hammer.		
D.	Damper.	J.	Jack.	S.	Strings.
DL.	Damper Lever.	JH.	Jack Heads.		
FF.	Fulcra or Pivot-Points.	JS.	Jack Spring.	UH.	Underhammer.

Meantime, the harpsichord was far from moribund. Indeed, some of the finest English harpsichords date from late-Georgian times, and from the workshops of Shudi and the Kirkmans. It is these instruments which have been most influential in the modern revival of harpsichord making in this country. In the 1760's Shudi introduced his much-discussed 'Venetian Swell', a louvred shutter placed over the strings and opened or closed by a foot pedal to produce a graded loudness or softness (Pl. 86). This has been called a 'last-ditch device' whereby the harpsichord tried to meet the challenge of the piano; but the latter was in no fit state before 1770 seriously to rival the well-established harpsichord. The swell seems rather to reflect the growing 'sensibility' which was infusing all musical activity at this time. It was the *grand* piano which, a few years later, gradually began to replace the harpsichord as the typical concert keyboard instrument. The last harpsichords were made in England about the year 1800.

The English grand is less-well documented than the square, but it is believed to have been developed by Broadwood, Stodart and Backers between 1770 and 1780. In its final pre-1800 form it had a compass of $5\frac{1}{2}$ octaves of tricord strings, steel in the treble and brass in the bass, none of the latter being overspun. The 'English' action, which has been attributed to Backers, was always used (Fig. 5). There were two pedals, as on the modern instrument, the right a damper-lifting or sustaining pedal, the other a soft pedal, shifting the keyboard and action bodily sideways to strike 3, 2 or 1 strings of the tricord (Pl. 87).

Musical effects of the piano

The influence of the pianoforte on the trend of musical taste was beginning to be felt in a number of ways by about 1780. It was increasingly realized that the instrument was capable of certain forms of musical treatment which were unsuitable for the harpsichord. By reason of the fact that both loudness and accentuation were directly under the control of the fingers, the piano even in its early state was potentially capable of 'sing-

ing' a cantabile melody, while its accompaniment could be shaded to any degree of relative softness, again by touch alone. Percussive full chords, spread chords and arpeggii, rapid repetitions of the same note, tremolandos, 'Alberti basses', all sounded effective and convincing on the pianoforte where on the harpsichord they would have been trivial and lifeless. Above all, the independent control of the damping – which the harpsichord never possessed – whereby the sound could continue after the finger was lifted from the key, opened up an entirely new range of keyboard textures and sonorities which the next generation of composers was quick to seize upon as a fresh means of expression.

One of the most influential pioneers in composing in the new keyboard style was Muzio Clementi (1752–1832), a native of Rome who had been brought to England as a youth by Peter Beckford, and who subsequently became famous as a player on, and composer for, the piano. Even in his early Opus 2 Sonatas (see Pl. 88B), written at the age of eighteen, he already showed an amazing grasp of the essential 'pianism' of the piano. They contain many passages which would have been unthinkable on the harpsichord, and made a profound impression on his hearers when he played them in London a year or two later. Clementi rose to great eminence as a composer for, and teacher of the piano, on which he must be considered the first virtuoso performer. He was also an excellent business man, and through his personal energies resuscitated the firm of Longman and Broderip, transforming it into an important publishing house and piano manufactory which survives to this day as Messrs Collard and Collard.

One other repercussion the advent of the pianoforte had on the musical scene must not be overlooked. In the last quarter of the century the general pitch of musical instruments rose sharply in England. So long as the harpsichord held sway, the pitch stayed close to the old chamber pitch which had been used since the late seventeenth century, for the harpsichord worked best with long, thin slack strings. The piano not only required shorter and thicker strings to withstand the

994

impact of the hammer action; it forced the general pitch up in its quest for a singing tone in the treble register. On the evidence of wind instruments, the orchestral pitch rose about a semitone between 1760 and 1800, by which time it was practically at the same level as it is today.

Changes in wind instruments

By 1760 the heyday of the recorder, or English flute, was at an end. True, it still survived in one form or another, but with the passing of the Baroque trio-sonata and the Baroque orchestral style it was no longer an instrument of the professional wind player. The transverse, or German flute, which had been gaining ground steadily since the beginning of the century, now assumed complete ascendancy. It is often said that the flute replaced the recorder because it was louder, but this is scarcely true of the contemporary instrument. The flute had the advantage of a tone-colour more directly under the player's control, a more extended compass and a more caressing and vocal type of articulation. These were musical qualities which were increasingly being sought in the newer styles of contemporary music. In many ways the differences between the two types of instrument resembled those of the harpsichord and piano, and the same trends in musical taste were responsible for the replacement of one by the other. Shortly after 1760 the simple 1-keyed flute underwent an important modification; additional keys were added to eliminate some of the 'cross-fingered' semitones. The scale of the simple flute did not agree very well with the preferred tonalities in which orchestral music was, for a number of reasons, being written, and it was brought into line by giving it this higher degree of mechanization. The flute was the first woodwind to be so treated, and it was in England that the lead was taken in the matter. The Frenchman, F. D. Castilon, writing in the Supplement to Diderot's *Encyclopédie* in 1777, reported the English 7-keyed flute, and examples made before 1770 are known (Pl. 91A(6) and B).

The oboe emerged from its highly-ornate Baroque form about 1760, when there was a reaction towards a plain-looking model much favoured by makers and players up till about 1775. These instruments were made in large quantities in England but apparently nowhere else. W. T. Parke, the oboist whose *Memoires* were published in 1830, disliked it and said that it looked and sounded like a post-horn (Pl. 91A(4)). About 1775, and coincident with the rise in pitch from the Baroque *Kammerton*, there was a reversion to the ornamented style prevalent on the Continent (Pl. 91A(5), and B), with the prominent 'onion' swelling at the top. This played a considerable part in forming the ideal tone of the early oboe, which was an instrument of far greater musical subtlety than is now suspected. The oboe was, in fact, the most useful and adaptable of the woodwind, capable of meeting the new demands for finer shades of expression without any essential modification of its Baroque form.

The most important addition to the woodwind after 1760 was the clarinet. This instrument, which was invented just before 1700, had taken about fifty years to develop, because the principle of the cylinder-bored tube coupled to a single-reed mouthpiece gave rise to technical problems which were not at first fully mastered. Much experiment was carried out, chiefly abroad, but by 1760 the instrument was available in this country and had begun to appear in opera scores. The first English instruments appeared a little later. They were made in four sections; the long, beak-like mouthpiece with its connecting socket (later separated as a short wooden sleeve, known as the 'barrel'); the upper and lower middle joints, each with three finger holes, and the stock and bell on which were mounted the three lowest keys. Towards the end of the century the stock was also separated from the bell as a matter of expediency in manufacture. These instruments had five keys, usually made of brass. With this equipment the clarinet was only barely on a parity with the two-keyed oboe, owing to the peculiarities of its scale. Even so, it was capable of playing safely in only two key signatures as against the six or seven of the simple oboe, and for this reason the custom arose, and persists to the present time, of building clarinets in different sizes or tonalities (Pl. 91B). Yet despite its technical disadvantages the clarinet was welcomed everywhere in cultivated music for its new and ingratiating tone. The recognition and assimilation of its qualities came fairly early in England. It was probably here in 1763 that the infant Mozart first heard the clarinet, for which he was later destined to do so much.

The bassoon remained much the same through the greater part of the eighteenth century. It had always been a capable soloist and the most useful and flexible bass voice amongst wind instruments. But, after 1760, as it gradually became dissociated from the old style of 'general bass' and was required to stand alone as the bass to a steadily expanding wind ensemble, steps were taken to increase its sonority. Although the key mechanism was added to (from four keys in 1760 the number rose to eight in 1800) this was relatively unimportant beside the change in its tone, which was achieved by alterations in the bore and the size and disposition of the note holes (Pl. 91A(2), and B).

The French horn remained a 'natural' instrument, playing only the harmonics proper to its tube length, although this could be varied by the addition of interchangeable 'crooks' to put it in the key of the music being played. Such horns were known in England as 'chromatic French horns' (Pl. 91A(1)). A great advance in its musical possibilities had been introduced about the beginning of this period by a horn player named Hampel, of the Dresden Court. Hampel played with his hand in the bell of his instrument, and by this means was able to control the pitch of the natural sounds sufficiently to obtain a complete scale from that part of the compass where this did not nominally exist. Gradually a regular technique was worked out which supplied all the missing notes in the natural harmonic scale by skilful changes of the hand position. With the growth of this custom, however, the whole character of the instrument changed, for the stopped notes were veiled, dreamy and 'romantic', quite unlike the bright open sonority of the instrument as formerly played. The universal adoption of the hand-horn belongs to the early nineteenth century, but travelling virtuosi did much to popularize it before then,

and to influence the way in which horn parts were being written in the new Classical orchestra (Pl. 90A).

The natural trumpet, also played with crooks, was supplemented near the end of the eighteenth century by the reappearance of the slide-trumpet, an instrument well-known in Purcell's time. It had a telescopic U-tube at the upper end, which could be extended, as in the trombone but in the reverse direction, towards the player. The object was again to supply missing notes and to correct others. Early in the nineteenth century there was brought out the keyed bugle, with note-holes cut in the sides after the manner of a woodwind instrument – again with the idea of giving it a complete scale.

Finally we must mention the serpent, in the construction of which the English excelled from the late eighteenth century onwards. This instrument first appeared in France towards the end of the sixteenth century, and was described in an English manuscript about a hundred years later. But most surviving instruments date from the late-eighteenth and early-nineteenth centuries. The serpent is a bass wind instrument, played with a cup mouthpiece like the brass, yet having fingerholes like the woodwind. Its peculiarity is the shape that gives it its name (Pls. 90B and 91A(3)). It is made of wood laboriously built up into a wide, expanding tube, in thin curved sections, the whole being bound together with leather and canvas for strength. Its immense popularity was due to the lack of any other bass wind instruments at this time having a full-bodied and substantial tone.

The Wind Band and its music

Music for wind instruments received considerable attention during the second half of the eighteenth century, when wars and rumours of wars led to the creation of so many military bands. In writing for an all-wind combination, composers were forced to consider more closely the nature of the medium and to invent ways of blending the different species of instruments effectively according to their several tone qualities and technical idiosyncrasies. This was a new problem, for though wind music had always existed in association with Royal and military pomp, there had never before been so great a variety of instruments from which to make up a balanced effect. Most composers of the period were caught up in this occupation at one time or another, and it brought beneficial results to the art of music as a whole and the orchestra in particular.

The standard minimum wind band was probably evolved in Germany, where it became known as the *Harmoniemusik*, a name which itself suggests chorus effects. This consisted at first of pairs each of oboes, clarinets, horns and bassoons, to which were later added flutes and perhaps a trumpet and serpent. At the same time, a number of Oriental percussion instruments was taken over, such as bass drums, triangles, cymbals and bells, to add to the prestige and the din. These instruments, known collectively as 'the Turkish Music', are the direct ancestors of the modern orchestral 'kitchen'.

The Classical orchestra, which is the basis of all modern orchestras, came into being when the self-complete *Harmoniemusik* was grafted on to a string section, and the old ensemble organization centred on the 'basso continuo' with its accompanying keyboard instrument was finally discarded. Composers now learned to fill-out and complete the harmony by careful disposition of the available instrumental voices, instead of relying on the improvisation of the continuo player. They found that horns added more to the fulness of the sound when given unassuming middle parts in the harmony, instead of being made to play melodies in their highest register; and for the same reason, that trumpets, when used, had greater weight and portent the nearer they kept to the traditional outline of their field calls.

All in all, the proper blending together of wind instruments profoundly influenced the development of the orchestra, and although the finest results belong to the symphonists of the Viennese school, the English contribution was by no means negligible inasmuch as we, as a military nation, developed wind bands and wind playing to a high degree.

Stringed instruments

In late Georgian times the English school of violin making rose to greater eminence, and if it never quite reached that superlative class of the greatest Italian masters, at least it maintained a supply of native-built instruments, many of which were of considerable distinction. It was now that English makers began to desert the high-modelled Stainer pattern of the violin for the shallower and more elegant contours of the Amatis and Stradivarius (Pl. 92). The most eminent pioneers in reviving Cremonese models were Benjamin Banks of Salisbury (1727–1795) and William Forster ('Old Forster', 1739–1808). It seems to have been realized that while the Stainer model worked well at the Baroque low pitch, and with the smaller-toned and more incisive attack of the older bow, it tended to become nasal and thin under a higher string tension and with the heavier and longer negative-curved bows then coming into use. England did not produce a bow maker of the genius of the Parisian, Tourte (1747–1838), but it contributed in no small measure to the transition from the short, straight, pointed bow of Baroque times. This transition is epitomized in the surviving work of John Dodd (1752–1839) in which the gradual evolution of the 'hatchet' head and the rationalization of the curvature and taper of the stick may clearly be seen.

Music publishing

The publishing of music was greatly encouraged and expanded throughout this period by the potential market which the growing middle classes presented, with their ever-increasing curiosity about all cultural matters. The pleasure gardens and the theatres provided ready platforms for the public performance of every kind of music, from which the amateurs of the day could carry off their favourite airs to play on the new pianoforte at home. Many firms sprang into existence to meet this demand. Music became a lucrative commodity with its own warehouses, selling instruments, music and accessories. Many of these warehouses had their own workshops for the manufacture of instruments, while others put their names to instruments made by the leading craftsmen of the day. Even the instrument makers dabbled in music publishing.

Home tutors for instruments, usually containing a good proportion of the popular tunes of the time, which had been a feature of English music publishing since the Commonwealth, now became a spate; while orchestral music – symphonies, overtures (the terms were practically synonymous) and other pieces, besides the band parts of whole oratorios and operas were now printed, and thus facilitated the wider dissemination of these larger forms. Some full scores had appeared. The mammoth Handel Festivals, held in Westminster Abbey in 1784 and subsequently, inspired the first 'collected edition' of any great composer's works, Dr Samuel Arnold's (1740–1802) *Works of Handel in Score*, published between 1787 and 1797 in 180 parts and containing the bulk of Handel's output including many works never before printed (Pl. 89).

Tail-piece from T. Bewick's *A History of British Birds*, Vol. 1, 1797.

Bookbinding

HOWARD M. NIXON

Throughout the reign of George III the stock of a bookseller would normally be bound either in plain leather (calf or sheepskin) or in paper-covered boards. The library of a nobleman, however, or even that of many a mere gentleman, would largely be clothed in full morocco, often with elaborate gold tooling, and the consequent boom in the 'West End' trade attracted a number of German binders, many of whom quickly rose to positions of eminence in their profession. The first to arrive was probably John Baumgarten. He was evidently an established figure in the West End trade by 1771 and when he died in 1782 he was described in the *Gentleman's Magazine* as 'a man of uncommon excellence in his profession'. Two other Germans who worked for him, C. S. Kalthoeber and Henry Walther, became figures of importance in the 1790's, while others who made their mark at this period included Charles Hering, Charles Meyer and the partners Staggemeier & Welcher. The Germans did not, however, have everything their own way, and two of the most famous of English binders flourished in the last quarter of the eighteenth century – Edwards of Halifax and Roger Payne.

Stylistically the most remarkable feature of the period is that some neo-classical bindings preceded any examples in the rococo manner. Bindings are known from several different shops with characteristic rococo 'C' scrolls, figures and animals, often accompanied by decorative elements in the Chinese taste, but these are unlikely to be earlier than 1770 and illustrate a common tendency of English fine binding design to lag behind the current mode in other arts. The bindings of the presentation copies of the first volume of Stuart and Revett's *Antiquities of Athens*, 1762, and Robert Adam's *Ruins of the Temple of the Emperor Diocletian at Spalatro*, 1764, are in the vanguard of fashion, however, for they were evidently designed by their authors and they are decorated with typical classical ornament. Adam's binding is illustrated in Pl. 93A; the binding of the *Antiquities of Athens* has a central gilt medallion depicting Athene with her owl and serpent within a laurel wreath and an outer anthemion border. The Edwards family, booksellers and binders in Halifax, who subsequently opened a shop in London, specialized in novelties, the most famous being their painted vellum bindings, which had the designs painted on the under-surface of vellum rendered transparent and placed over boards covered with white paper. Roger Payne, notorious for allegedly drunken habits and quaintly-worded bills, was little influenced by current artistic fashions but produced admirable pieces of craftsmanship beautifully tooled to simple but effective designs. The typical 'gold-studded work' on the spines of his bindings was copied not only by most of the German binders in London, but also by the binders of Paris. But while the French were for once imitating their English rivals, the opposite, and more normal, procedure was also in operation, both Walther and Staggemeier & Welcher copying in the 1790's the inlaid bindings with *à répétition* tooling which had been produced in Paris in the first half of the century. Classical designs did not become firmly established in England until the first decade of the nineteenth century, and it is surprising to note that there is hardly a trace of Gothic until the very end of our period, when 'cathedral' bindings with motifs of Gothic tracery were introduced.

Printing

RUARI MCLEAN

In 1760 the Press was not yet free; but facilities for publication in England were easier than they had been for the previous two hundred years.

The time when an author required wealthy private patronage was over; the days of his bargaining with publishers were just beginning. Printing and publishing were not yet big business, as they were to become when the population began its steep rise at the end of the century. But publishing was evolving as a separate profession. Foundations were laid in this century of firms whose names are still familiar: Rivington in 1711, Longman in 1724, John Murray in 1768, and Constable and Thomas Nelson in Edinburgh before 1800.

It was Johnson who said that the best writing was done for money. His *Dictionary* was published in 1755 at the risk of a group of publishers, including Murray, and he said they treated him very fairly. Hume said of his *History* (1761) that it made him 'not only independent but opulent'. Smollett's *History of England* (1757/8) yielded £10,000. The circumstances of the publication of Gibbon's *Decline and Fall*, as described in his *Memoir*, have a modern ring. The first impression of the first volume, in 1776, was to have been 500 copies, but this was increased to 1000 at the last moment by the optimism of Strahan, the printer and co-publisher. The book was immedi-

ately successful and ran through further impressions of 1500 and 1000. The accounts between author and publisher for the third impression survive and show that Gibbon took two-thirds of the profit, which on 1000 copies was £326 13s. 4d., and the publishers, Strahan and Cadell, took only one-third, so the author had every reason to be satisfied.

But much was being produced in the book trade besides literature. In this period of expanding economy and industrial revolution, publication was of more and more importance to engineers, inventors, designers and manufacturers. Other chapters in this volume show the large part played by books in the history of architecture and furniture design, for example, during this period. What state had the technique of printing reached in 1760?

It had altered in no important detail since Elizabethan days. All type had still to be set up by hand, letter by letter. All paper was hand-made, and therefore limited in size to the dimensions of a tray that a man could lift in his two hands. In 1772 James Whatman, the leading paper-maker in England, did not make paper larger than 40″ × 26½″, and doubted if any larger sheet was made in Europe; however, at the instigation of the Royal Antiquarian Society he proceeded to make special equipment for turning out a sheet for them, for a special engraving, measuring

52" × 31", and found a profitable new market.[1] Whatman – his name is still synonymous with fine hand-made paper – was also probably the inventor and first manufacturer of wove paper in Europe, first used for Baskerville's *Virgil* in 1757.

That paper was thus limited in size did not in any case matter at this time, since the letterpress printer could not have worked a larger sheet. To obtain one impression, the series of motions – the laying-on of the paper, the running in of the bed, the pulling down of the platen by a lever, and then the previous movements in reverse – was the same as it had always been. Good workmen, whether in Aldus' office in Venice in 1500, or Strahan's in London in 1760, could not exceed about 200 impressions an hour. In 1798 Earl Stanhope patented the first all-iron hand press, and in the nineteenth century expert workmen on iron presses could produce 250 impressions an hour. The first real step in the mechanization of printing was not taken until competition between newspapers to get news on to the streets made it vital to increase the speed of printing. In 1814 *The Times* was printed on a cylinder press driven by steam. This machine was capable of 1800 impressions an hour – a speed not often exceeded today for book printing—but the size of the sheet could now be greatly extended, so that more and more pages could be printed together. And the Fourdrinier invention (*c.* 1804) of making paper by machine, on a roll, provided paper in any size of sheet required.

The problem of casting and composing type by machine took the whole of the nineteenth century to solve.

Of greater importance to the men of the Industrial Revolution, in 1760, were the processes available for the reproduction of plans and drawings. Here, technical facility was probably in advance of what was required of it: engraving on steel could give a fineness of line and clarity in detail that no other process has ever given, and the engraved plans of this period were probably often drawn to a greater degree of accuracy than their subjects attained in construction. Today, our maps and charts of land and sea, our plans for buildings and machines, printed lithographically, are ignoble affairs, compared with the engravings of the eighteenth century.

As well as engravings on steel or copper, etchings and woodcuts were also used for book illustration. Only the woodcut could be printed with type. Until the end of the eighteenth century, engraving was the predominant illustrative process. Lithography was not invented until 1796.

There was no multi-colour printing; but labour was cheap and engraved prints could be coloured by hand, giving effects that no colour printing has ever achieved.

This, then, was the general position of printing in England at the accession of George III. The following sixty years of his reign were a golden period of book design in Great Britain. Among the men then at work were the printers Baskerville, Bulmer, Bensley, Ballantyne, the brothers Foulis and Whittingham the elder; the typefounders Thorne, Joseph and Edmund Fry, William Martin and Figgins; the artists Bewick, Stothard and Rowlandson; the publishers Dodsley, Boydell and Ackermann; and the paper-maker Whatman. These are only a few of the greater names; there were many other fine craftsmen. It is actually more difficult to find an ill-printed book of this period than a good one.

In mid-eighteenth century England even some authors were aware of the difference between good and bad printing. Sterne, for example, when he decided to print the first edition of *Tristram Shandy* at his own expense, wrote to Robert Dodsley (who had declined to pay £50 for the copyright): 'The book shall be printed here, and the impression sent up to you; for as I live at York, and shall correct every proof myself, it shall go perfect into the world, and be printed in so creditable a way, as to paper, type etc., as to do no dishonour to you, who, I know, never choose to print a book meanly. Will you patronize my book upon these terms, and be as kind a friend to it as if you had bought the copyright?'[2] (Sterne got £480 for the next edition).

[1] See J. Wardrop, 'Mr. Whatman, Papermaker', *Signature*, 9, London, 1938.

[2] R. Straus, *Robert Dodsley*, London, 1910.

Robert Dodsley, publisher and playwright, indeed never chose to print a book meanly. He was Baskerville's publisher.

John Baskerville was born in Worcestershire in 1706, at a time when the printing trade in Britain was at a low ebb, but had just become freed of the government restrictions that had been throttling it for 150 years. During Baskerville's young manhood William Caslon became the first English type designer and founder to achieve international fame.

Baskerville became a writing master in Birmingham, and then turned to japanning, a decorative art and manufacture in which his enterprise and skill made a fortune in five years. He then became interested in printing and set himself to print books better than they had ever been printed before. When he died in 1775 he had printed over fifty books, including Prayer Books and a Bible; and he had become the first English printer since Caxton whose books are known by their printer's name before their author's.

Baskerville was never a commercial printer. Like William Morris, a century later, he was a wealthy experimenter, but he was more of a technician, more of a pure typographer, and very much more of a calligrapher, than Morris. He designed his own types: it is a matter of opinion whether they were better artistically than Caslon's, but they were certainly better for the smoother papers that Baskerville also helped to introduce. As far as the design of the letter forms themselves is concerned, it has been shown,[3] from comparison with English engraved writing books of 1715 onwards, that 'Baskerville was only the first to admit into the type foundry a [design of] letter which had been clamouring outside its door for at least half a century'. Baskerville did not cut his own punches but they were cut under his close supervision in his own house. He made his own black ink and had paper specially made for him; and after printing he placed the newly-printed wet sheets [4] between hot copper plates. The gloss

thus imparted to the sheets does not strike our eyes today – partly because it has probably worn off, and partly because in any case we are accustomed to so many kinds of shiny paper – but it was a great novelty to his contemporaries.

The first book Baskerville produced, after years of experimenting, was a Virgil in 1757 (Pl. 96B), which was sold by Dodsley and established his reputation. His great Folio Bible was published in 1763: to obtain the right to print it he had to get himself appointed as Printer to the University of Cambridge.

Despite support and admiration from the discerning bookmen of his day – including Benjamin Franklin, with whom his relations were long, fruitful and cordial – Baskerville's efforts did not meet with financial success, a fact possibly not surprising when we read in a contemporary letter that 'the expence of printing a sheet . . . at a common press is eighteen shillings, and at Baskerville's about three pounds ten shillings'.[5]

His books are still much to be admired today; they are severe and classical and do not rely on ornament or illustration of any kind, as did most books of his day. Yet in this he was no innovator: Tonson and Bowyer had printed books like this years before. Baskerville died in 1775, directing in his will, as a last gesture of rationalism against superstition, that he should be buried upright in non-consecrated ground in his garden at Easy Hill, outside Birmingham. 'He was not among the world's greatest printers,' wrote the great American printer D. B. Updike. 'When we look at his books we think of Baskerville; while to look at the work of Jenson is to think but of its beauty and almost to forget that it was made with hands!'[6] Yet his type, in the excellent version of it cut by the Monotype Corporation in 1923, is one of the most popular type faces for the English language today.

William Bulmer (1757–1830) and Thomas Bensley (c. 1760–1824) were two printers who applied some of Baskerville's lessons to commercial book production. Their books are distin-

[3] *The Monotype Recorder*, Vol. XXVI, No. 221, Sept. 1927.

[4] Hand-made paper always requires to be dampened before printing.

[5] Quoted in Straus & Dent, *John Baskerville*, London, 1907.

[6] D. B. Updike, *Printing Types*, Vol. II, p. 116, Cambridge, Mass., 1922.

guished by plain typography and careful printing on good paper, rather than by elaborate adornment, either typographical or engraved.

Bulmer was a native of Newcastle, and as a young apprentice proofed Bewick's wood-cuts; later, as a master-printer in London, he was able to give Bewick's blocks the sort of printing they deserved but had not previously received. About 1787 he set up the 'Shakespeare Press' for George Nicol, the King's bookseller who was then projecting his great edition of Shakespeare with the publisher and art dealer Boydell. The Boydell Shakespeare started appearing in January 1791, and was completed in nine folio volumes. A new type was cut for the edition by William Martin, a brother of Baskerville's foreman, developing Baskerville's ideas in type design a long way towards the not-yet-born 'modern' face. The volumes were illustrated with engravings after paintings by Westall, Hamilton, Smirke, Stothard, etc. It was a noble eighteenth-century monument; and a set still commands a fair price in antiquarian bookshops.

Numerous other fine works were issued by Bulmer from the Shakespeare Press, which are now much collected.

Although Bensley's life was shorter than Bulmer's, his imprint extends over a considerably larger period. His typography was more delicate and subtle than Bulmer's, and his books for that reason perhaps more attractive. In Bensley's workshop the German inventor Koenig developed his steam cylinder press, to which *The Times* went over for its printing in 1814.

The efforts of all the printers so far mentioned were consciously directed towards fine, but also large and expensive, book production, requiring wealthy patronage. At this time also, and for this sort of market, another fashion began: that of the colour-plate book. It had always been possible to print in colour from wood blocks in register, but the technique was difficult and no artist had exploited it. It was also possible to hand-colour prints from either wood blocks or copper plates. Now a new process, that of aquatint, was

Fig. 1. (*right*) The title-page of the first edition of *Tristram Shandy*, 1760. (See page 1000.)

developed, which led to a series of books which must rank as among the most beautiful things ever made in Britain, and which no subsequent kind of colour printing has ever surpassed.

Aquatint is a kind of etching. A grain is laid on a copper plate which, when printed, gives the effect of a water-colour wash; hence 'aqua-tinta'. It was most useful for reproducing, in books, the scenes from nature being newly discovered by the romantic revivalists and amateurs of the picturesque. The first book of aquatints published in England was Paul Sandby's *Twelve Views in South Wales*, 1775, which very quickly had its successors and imitators. At first the aquatint engravings were printed in black or sepia only, then in a second colour; then the plates, printed in

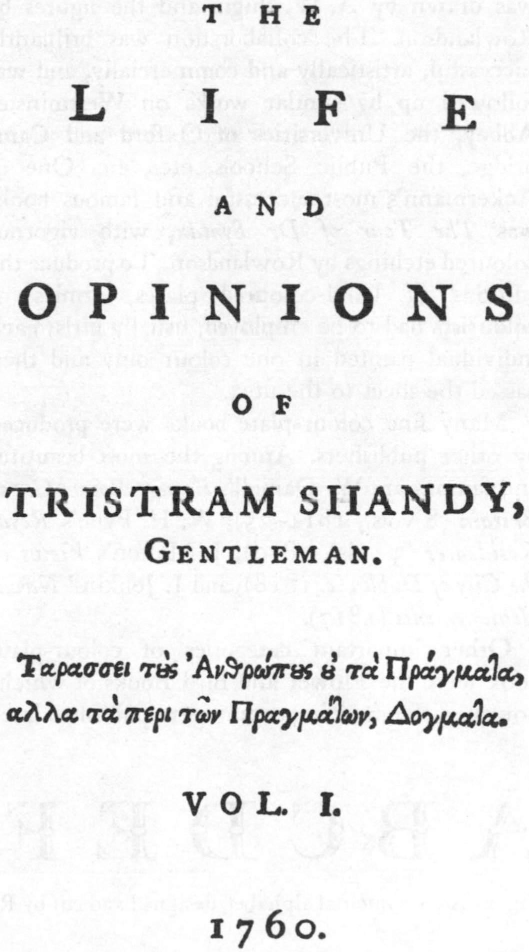

T H E

L I F E

A N D

O P I N I O N S

O F

TRISTRAM SHANDY,

G E N T L E M A N.

Ταρασσει τὺς Ἀνθρώπυς ἐ τὰ Πράγμαλα,
αλλα τὰ περι τῶν Πραγμάλων, Δογμαλα.

V O L. I.

1760.

either one or two colours, were coloured in water-colour by hand. What is known to collectors today as a colour-plate book of this period is a book containing plates, either etched, engraved, or aquatinted, and subsequently coloured by hand.

The publisher whose name is chiefly associated with colour-plate books is the versatile Rudolph Ackermann (1764–1834). Born in Germany, he came to England to seek his fortune as a coach painter and designer, and in 1795 he opened a print shop. As a designer and painter of coaches he must have reached the top of his profession, for he prepared the heraldic designs for Lord Nelson's funeral car. But it is as a publisher that he is better known. In 1808 he began to issue, in monthly parts, *The Microcosm of London*, with coloured aquatint plates in which the architecture was drawn by A. W. Pugin and the figures by Rowlandson. The collaboration was brilliantly successful, artistically and commercially, and was followed up by similar works on Westminster Abbey, the Universities of Oxford and Cambridge, the Public Schools, etc., etc. One of Ackermann's most successful and famous books was *The Tour of Dr Syntax*, with vigorous coloured etchings by Rowlandson. To produce the editions of hand-coloured plates, armies of colourists had to be employed, usually girls; each individual painted in one colour only and then passed the sheet to the next.

Many fine colour-plate books were produced by other publishers. Among the most beautiful and famous are W. Daniell's *Voyage Round Great Britain* (8 vols., 1814–25); W. H. Pyne's *Royal Residences* (3 vols., 1819); J. Malton's *Views in the City of Dublin* (c. 1818); and J. Jenkins' *Naval Achievements* (1817).

Other important categories of colour-plate book were the Flower and Bird Books of which, however, the most important were published later than our period. In these books were published and illustrated the discoveries of scientific exploration sponsored by wealthy collectors, societies and Governments.

The great period of the aquatint was roughly between 1800 and 1830. It was killed by lithographic colour-printing, made inevitable by the needs of mass-production.

The colour-plate books, although many of them were issued in monthly parts, were destined then as now for collectors and people of wealth. They were mostly large quartos, usually prefaced with a List of Subscribers headed by royalty. And the taste for bulk in books persisted even among the reading public. It is interesting to note that the Waverley novels, which began publication in 1814, and were extremely successful, were all first issued in 2 or 3 volume editions.

But not all people want large books and not all people can afford them. Charles Whittingham (1767–1840) was one of the first printers to feel in this way and to print small, inexpensive books well. From 1790 he concentrated on small books and was soon publishing as well as printing them. 'Whittingham's Cabinet Library', a series of miniature books which first began appearing about 1814, are the forerunners of innumerable series catering for the massive new reading public which was just being born. Whittingham did not print colour-plate books but he excelled at printing wood-engravings: notable examples of this kind are his Northcote's *Fables*, 1829, and *The Tower Menagerie*, 1829.

In 1810 all type was still being cast by hand and set by hand; and although newspapers were soon to be printed on cylinder presses, all books were printed then, and for many years to come, on hand presses, on hand-made paper. But wholesale mechanization and technical development in every branch of the printing trade were in the air.

A B C D E F G H J K L M

Fig. 2. An ornamental alphabet, designed and cut by Richard Austin in 1796, now known as 'Fry's Ornamented'.

THE
REGENCY
PERIOD

1810–1830

Acknowledgments

The typographical border on the title-page of this section is adapted from that used on the wrapper of *The Beauties of Brighton*, printed by and for R. Sickelmore Jun., Brighton, *c.* 1830, and reproduced on page 49 of J. R. Abbey's *Scenery of Great Britain and Ireland*, 1952.

For the illustrations on pages 1072, 1120, 1249, 1250, 1251 and 1252 acknowledgment is made to St Bride Printing Library for the loan of Vincent Figgins' specimen books of 1821 and 1835.

For the loan of various books, including the one illustrated on Plate 94, grateful acknowledgment is made to Berthold Wolpe.

The photograph used for Plate 95 was taken by Jarrold & Sons Ltd, Norwich, for Plates 8A, 13, 17B, 19A and 20 by A. F. Kersting, for Plates 5A, B, 6A, B, 7, 8B, 9A, B, 10A, B, 11B, 12B, 14B, 15A, B, 16A, B and 17A by Clifford Musgrove, and for Plate 12A by J. F. Smith.

For the following plates acknowledgment is made to the Victoria and Albert Museum, who hold the copyright in the photographs: 69B, 71B, 72B and 73B.

Acknowledgment is made to Temple Williams for Plates 21A, D, 28A, 29B and 31, Pratt and Sons for Plates 21C, 22B, 23A, B, 24A, B and 25B, Hotspur Ltd for Plates 25A and 28B, Christie, Manson and Woods for Plates 57D, 58A and 61A, and Delomosne & Sons Ltd for Plates 62A and C.

For the following illustrations acknowledgment is made to Hulton Picture Library: Plates 3A, 4, 89A, 90A, D, 91A and B, and the line illustration on page 1243.

The line drawings in this section are by Betty Bradford, Audrey Frew, Diana Holmes and Carol Oblath.

The Age of the Prince Regent

IAN R. CHRISTIE

The Rulers

When, at the end of 1810, the mind of George III lapsed finally into the twilight of insanity, the kingly role passed to the member of the Hanoverian house least fitted to bear it – George Augustus, Prince of Wales, who in 1820 succeeded his father as George IV. At no period in modern times has the British throne been so dragged into disrepute as by the Regent and his six brothers, 'the dull dregs of their race, who flow through public scorn'; men seeming, in the view of one worthy county member of parliament, 'to be the only persons in the country who were wholly regardless of their own welfare and respectability'. They were, according to Wellington, 'the damnest millstones about the neck of any government'; and the Whig, Brougham, when asked why he prayed so hard for the Regent's health, declared that if he died the Tory Ministry would then be released from all its embarrassments.

The Prince Regent inherited the exuberant vitality but not the steadiness of character of his father. Married, in the eyes of Rome, but not by the law of England, to Maria Fitzherbert, and separated both from her and from his legal wife, Caroline of Brunswick, his swerving devotion to one elderly mistress after another outraged the increasingly stern moral outlook of a great part of the nation. His patronage of the arts revealed a reckless generosity – with the taxpayers' money – which his ministers had constantly to resist. Cultured and affable, he had to the full the royal gift of personal attraction: 'You lose', wrote Sir Walter Scott, 'the thoughts of the Prince, in admiring the well-bred accomplished gentleman.' For a short time after his accession his efforts to cultivate popularity were not unsuccessful, and he scored a triumph with his visit to Dublin – the only one ever made by a Hanoverian monarch. He was not without shrewdness, and he displayed a genuine affection for his family, especially for his only child, the ill-fated Charlotte, whose death in childbed, less than a year after her supremely happy marriage to Leopold of Saxe-Coburg, deeply affected him. But these good qualities were betrayed by his instability of temperament. Those who were in constant contact with him saw another side. Obese, self-indulgent, vain, wayward, deceitful, supremely egotistic – to Greville, 'a spoiled, selfish, odious beast' – pursuing with undignified rancour the wife whom he had married unwillingly and under pressure, and whose conduct, if equivocal, was not a tithe so disreputable as his own, no figure could be more calculated to bring monarchy into the gravest discredit: it was as well, perhaps, that a generation of conflict with revolution had so sharpened British attachment to the monarchy as to other existing institutions, that for the time being much might be forgiven its representative.

Government in this age rested in the hands of the pupils and associates of William Pitt. If none of them, save perhaps Canning, showed a spark of Pitt's genius, nevertheless their leaders had gifts of a high order, a capacity for sound administration, and a determination to do what they thought right regardless of the Regent's whims. For most of these years the highest place was held by one man,

Lord Liverpool, Prime Minister from 1812 to 1827, frank, amiable, sensitive, 'the honestest man that could be dealt with', an able manager of men, dexterous at reconciling the conflicting views of his colleagues, soothing and pliable, but capable of a firm stand at times of crisis. The tremendous respect accorded to his high moral character was one of the greatest assets of his ministry; and in parliament his sound but sober, even pedestrian, explanations of policy carried more weight than the glancing brilliance of a Canning. For the first ten years of his ministry his chief lieutenant was the Foreign Secretary, Castlereagh, stubborn, reserved, cautious, laborious, but withal a man of vision and resource; and after him, Canning, in so many ways the opposite of both, brilliant, epigrammatic, volatile, flamboyant, and impetuous. Alongside these statesmen brooded the aloof personality of Wellington, lonely, sensitive, punctilious, realistic, a master of the strategic retreat in politics as in his own profession of war, and after his victory at Waterloo a figure of European fame. In their train were the professional administrators of humbler rank but no less ability, Herries and Huskisson, the exponents of the new economic teaching to which Liverpool himself also subscribed.

These men and their colleagues in government have gone down in the history books as 'Tories'; but they thought of themselves more as 'the friends of Mr Pitt', from whom they inherited a medley of liberal and conservative traditions; and the 'Toryism' which embraced Huskisson's political economy, the pro-Catholic sentiment and Liberal trends in foreign policy of Canning, and the enlightened administration at the Home Office of Robert Peel, was an elastic concept, if indeed it had much meaning at all. In the first years after the war an understandable fear of revolution led them into policies of repression, and the same fear made them obstinately opposed to constitutional change; but they were by no means entirely reactionaries, and, especially in the 'twenties, after these fears had subsided, they made many creative contributions to British advancement. The men who came to dominate the administration in these later years were well aware of the dangers of blind reaction: 'those', said Canning, 'who resist indis-criminately all improvements as innovations may find themselves compelled at last to submit to innovations although they are not improvements'. Law, fiscal administration, and economic life all benefited greatly at their hands.

Opposition, conducted by the heirs of Fox and Shelburne, initially with the support of Pitt's old associate, Lord Grenville, was spasmodic, and its inspiration was at times more personal than political. Bitterly disappointed at the Regent's refusal to give them power when the right to do so passed into his hands, they laboured to embarrass him and his ministers, digging still deeper the pit which separated them from office. They despaired of victory against Napoleon, would have withdrawn Wellington's army from Portugal and acquiesced in a stalemate – one at least of the reasons which, initially, kept the Prince from turning to them. Later they exploited the undignified wrangles between the Regent and his wife, and raised against the administration traditional eighteenth-century cries of extravagance, corruption and threats to liberty. But they shaped policies out of immediate circumstances which might embarrass the ministers, not on sound principles; and they had no solution for the social and economic dislocation that were the real problems of the age. They made Catholic Emancipation one of their causes, but on this they were divided from a part only of the Tories. On parliamentary reform their aristocratic wing was for long lukewarm. The more strident demands of such radicals as Whitbread, Romilly, Burdett, or Brougham grated on the ears of a Lansdowne or a Grey; and in the 'twenties, divided on this ground, and also by personal antipathies, they ceased for a time to act as a party at all. More and more, contemporaries were aware of the artificiality of faction fights between two ghosts: 'Whig and Tory, Foxite and Pittite, Minister and Opposition have ceased to be distinctions, but the divisions of classes and great interests are arrayed against each other,' Fox's nephew, Holland, wrote in 1826. The last years of the Regency saw a growing tendency towards coalitions and a shifting of loyalties.

There had been little change since the eighteenth century in the working of the constitution or in the distribution of political power. Power remained in the hands of the wealthy landed class, who controlled local government in the shires and dominated the Houses of Parliament. The oligarchs had even risen in wealth and influence. Agriculture had so prospered through war demands and the increase of population, that rents in many parts were five times what they had been a generation before. In Cheshire alone, about 1814, there were fifty landed estates of from £3,000 to £10,000 a year, an income worth six or seven times as much in modern currency. Rents fell heavily after 1814, but still remained substantially higher than before the French Revolution; and there were many peers and gentlemen who found their estates appreciate to fantastic levels, through the exploitation of mineral deposits previously unknown, or for which there had been no market until the coming of steam power and the canal. From these classes came five-sixths of the House of Commons, and nearly two-thirds of the seats, in pocket boroughs like Calne or depopulated Old Sarum, were at the disposal of some two hundred peers and commoners. Political parties were still loose and indeterminate; they could provide an element of the support for the King's Government, but never the whole. As in the previous reign, the ministry depended on parliamentary support from independent members and from those who belonged to the Court and administration group. This last was a dwindling force. Suppressions of sinecures in response to parliamentary demands for economy, and deliberate attempts to improve the professional character of the revenue services — Liverpool sacrificed political advantage by removing from the sphere of political patronage the appointments to the higher offices of the customs department — were reducing the traditional methods which drew a parliamentary phalanx in the train of the Government. In another respect, too, administration was more weak in the face of Parliament and more responsive to opinion within and outside it than had been the case a generation before. Public opinion, roused and directed by an expanding Press, was increasing in political importance. It played a decisive part in securing the abolition of income tax in 1816 and the return to a Gold Standard after 1819. In the 'twenties the ministers consciously sought the support of the commercial interests for their economic policy and Canning broke all precedents by his publication of despatches intended to secure public approbation of his diplomacy.

Britain and the world

In the opening years of the Regency the minds and energies of the nation's leaders were absorbed by the great war against Napoleon — a struggle in which as yet only the eye of faith could descry a path to victory. Britain at sea, Napoleon on land, each seemed supreme, and impervious to attack; and, in default of other means, each sought the other's ruin by economic war — Britain by the blockade, Napoleon by his 'Continental System' designed in vain to strangle British trade with Europe. The year 1812 brought further embarrassment. The blockade provoked a declaration of hostilities by the United States — the beginning of the two-years war ended in 1814 by the Treaty of Ghent — and, although the American naval and military threat was not very formidable, the consequent interruption of trade had severe effects upon British industry. Among the Government's critics there were not lacking counsellors of despair, to whom a continuation of the war seemed futile: better to make trial once more if one might trust the Corsican. But this was not the view of the King's ministers. They knew the deadly dangers of appeasement. So long as the slightest weak spot appeared in Napoleon's Fortress of Europe they were prepared to sap and mine, in hopes of an internal explosion which might shatter the dictator of the Continent and all his works. Spanish guerilla resistance to French domination proved their opportunity, and they had faith in Wellington's appraisal: 'If we can maintain ourselves in Portugal, the war will not cease in the Peninsula, and, if the war lasts in the Peninsula, Europe will be saved.' 'If', indeed: but this general of sepoys was proving himself a genius in war. The brilliant military prologue to the Regency was the scorched earth of northern Portugal and the lines of Torres Vedras; and a month after power passed into the Prince's hands, the last French attempt to drive the British out of Portugal ended with the withdrawal of Massena's armies, reduced nearly to half by starvation and disease.

British tenacity in the Peninsula soon reaped its reward. Others observed that France was not invincible. Russia grew recalcitrant in her role of satellite, and Napoleon, gambling with failing judgement for ever higher stakes, flung the flower of his army against Moscow, only to lose both army and reputation in the Russian snows. While Wellington bestrode Spain to the Pyrenees, central Europe rose once more against the French, and Britain became again pay-mistress of a European coalition, strong enough this time to beat Napoleon down.

Rarely have British statesmen shown more awareness of the interdependence of Britain and the Continent than did Castlereagh and his colleagues in the years of peace-making from 1813 to 1815. The war had left Britain the great oceanic Power: the opportunities for imperial development were incalculable and the temptation to isolation strong; but at the same time it had emphasized her dependence on events in Europe. British policy in Europe had two essential aims, defined by Castlereagh as the reduction of the French state to its former limits and the guarantee of this limitation by the other Powers: 'it is the fear of our union that will keep France down'. To these ends there must be territorial adjustments to establish a cordon on France's frontiers, conflicting ambitions in Central Europe must be checked to prevent a fatal breach between the Great Powers, and the war-time alliance must be extended to guarantee the peace. All these things Castlereagh successfully accomplished by 1815. He hoped for more. Two years of constant personal contact with the rulers of Europe had convinced him that nothing could so greatly conduce to the peace and prosperity of the Continent. It seemed to him 'a new discovery in the European government, at once extinguishing the cobwebs with which diplomacy obscures the horizon, bringing the whole bearing of the system into its true light, and giving to the councils of the Great Powers the efficiency, and almost the simplicity of a single state'. Here was a noble vision, that Europe might be kept at peace by congresses. But the dream soon faded. When the Tsar sought to turn the Concert of Europe into an instrument for the suppression of revolution, with a right to interfere in the internal affairs of any state, British participation became impossible. As Castlereagh pointed out, Britain's form of government was itself founded on a revolution. She could not, her people would not, subscribe to a doctrine which sanctified absolutism and proscribed the right of revolt: 'The House of Hanover could not well maintain the principles upon which the House of Stuart forfeited the throne.'

By Castlereagh's death in 1822, Britain's association with the Congress system was plainly foundering. Reluctantly he had been driven towards a breach. But his successor was an isolationist by conviction. Canning, defending purely national interests, broke with the Congress completely over Latin America and with pleasure saw it drive to destruction on the Eastern Question. Spanish America, asserting its freedom during the upheaval of the Napoleonic Wars, had become a vast free-trade area open to British commerce. Spain sought the re-establishment of her imperial authority. But to permit the restoration of a protectionist Spanish imperial system was unthinkable; and when Spain turned for aid to France, to let France gain exclusive commercial advantages was also unthinkable; and so, forestalling both France and the United States, came Canning's recognition of the Latin American republics, swinging them decisively into the commercial and diplomatic orbit of Great Britain, offsetting French influence in the Peninsula, calling, as he put it, 'the New World into existence to redress the balance of the Old'. The Congress Powers were rudely informed they had no ground for interference: 'it was a maritime and commercial question of concern to England ... the influence of the Continental Powers ceased with the bounds of Europe'. Faced in the Near East with the Greek struggle for independence, Canning stirred not a finger to keep united the Russian and Austrian keys of the Congress arch: over the ruins of the Congress system rose his alliance with Russia and France, to impose a settlement in Greece which would spare Britain any danger from an advance of Russian power.

A land of promise and a land of grief

So great was the increase of Britain's wealth that her economy rode buoyantly through the long war against France. Despite vicissitudes, its expansion was sustained after the peace. This prosperity owed much to the oceanic supremacy and the expansion of Empire assured at Trafalgar. Many conquests were, it is true, returned at the peace. Britain was comparatively moderate in her territorial demands, and retentions of conquests—notably the Cape Colony and Ceylon—were determined mainly by strategic considerations. More important, older parts of the Empire could be held and extended. In India needs of defence advanced British territories and protectorates over the greater part of the Maratha states and led to annexations from Nepal; and a little later Burmese advances into the Brahmaputra valley provoked the British annexation of Aracan and Tenasserim and the establishment of a protectorate over Assam. British colonization within the Empire was as yet mainly confined to the Canadas and the colonies of the St Lawrence estuary, where the population nearly doubled in the fifteen years after the peace of 1815, and this area was of growing though still relatively minor commercial importance. Other lands suitable for settlement were relatively remote or offered little opportunity. A trickle of British settlers was added to the Dutch population at the Cape. New South Wales and Tasmania were in 1811 still convict settlements with very few free settlers. By 1830 the population of New South Wales was still only about 50,000, more or less equally divided between free settlers and those who had come as convicts; that of Tasmania was about half this figure. The potential wealth of the southern continent was becoming evident, and a small flourishing export trade in wool to Great Britain had been established. But only in 1829, when the French threatened to forestall us, was Western Australia annexed and the whole land thus opened to British exploitation.

At the heart of Britain's mounting prosperity were the increase in her population and the native vigour and ingenuity of her people. In 1811 the population of England and Wales was just over ten million. In twenty years it increased to nearly fourteen million. In the same period Scotland's population of one and three-quarter million increased by half a million and Ireland's of some six million by over a million and a half. In 1811 already rather more than half the people of England and Wales were employed in commerce, navigation, and manufacture, less than half in agriculture and mining. In the next twenty years, although agricultural production practically kept pace with demand, the numbers employed in it rose very little: practically all the increase in population was absorbed in industry and allied pursuits. Urbanization was proceeding apace, especially in Lancashire, Durham, the Midlands and South Wales, while greater London grew at an unprecedented rate, adding in twenty years half a million souls to the million within its confines in 1811.

Great as was the increase of the population, Britain's mounting industrial power more than kept pace. The key to the future lay in the sources of energy locked away in her coal-seams, and the exploitation of these was assured by various new techniques, particularly improved winding gear and the use of pit-props. The statue to Sir Humphry Davy in Helston churchyard pays tribute to the protection to life brought by the invention of his safety lamp; but the nation also owed to him a greatly increased command of its most valuable natural resources, for the safety lamp removed one of the most serious obstacles to deeper working: about 1830 it was described as operating 'as a complete renovation to many of the collieries which were then in a state of exhaustion'. Iron production, which might otherwise have been curtailed for lack of fuel, was also advancing, finding, as war requirements came to an end, new uses in the manufacture of machines, bridges, gas and water piping and countless other requirements. The Scottish iron industry benefited greatly from Neilson's discovery in 1829 of the use of the hot air blast in smelting, which brought substantial economies in the consumption of coal of the types mainly produced by the Scottish pits. The most spectacular advance was made by the cotton industry, which by 1831 was consuming three times as much raw cotton as in 1811 and had secured a lucrative and unlimited market in India, where it undercut native domestic manufacture. About 1811 water was still the main source of motive power for the factories, but by 1830 steam power was well on the way to supplanting it. Power-loom weaving in factories was steadily ousting the handloom weaver. The number of power-looms in the country doubled and redoubled in the ten years before 1830; about 1826 it was calculated that a youth in charge of steam-driven machinery could produce six times the output of a skilled handloom weaver in the prime of life, and costs of production were so reduced that by 1830 the prices of cottons had fallen to a fifth of their level about 1815. The cotton handloom weavers became an impoverished and declining class. They could no longer command high wages, and, except in the fancy lines, were sure of employment only in boom periods, when demand exceeded factory capacity. But there were estimated to be still over 200,000 of them about 1830, the worst-hit victims of industrialization, constituting a grave social problem to which no government of the day could see any ready solution. The railway age was yet to come. These last decades before the railway began to revolutionize transport were the heyday of highways and canals, with no important centre of population more than fifteen miles from a waterway and coach services at ten miles an hour on McAdam's roads. But the essential pioneer work on the railways had been done by 1830. By the 'twenties, Trevithick, George Stephenson and others had proved the practical possibilities of steam traction. The business partnership of Stephenson and Edward Pease led to the opening of the Stockton–Darlington line in 1825, with results which, if not regarded as decisive, at least commanded attention. The rate of carriage per ton of merchandise to Darlington was cut from fivepence to a fifth of a penny per mile, carriage of minerals from sevenpence to three halfpence, and the cost of coal at Darlington was more than halved. In 1830 followed the Liverpool–Manchester line, for which Stephenson was the construction engineer, and its success overcame all doubts of the usefulness of extensive railway networks throughout the country: in 1829, at the trials at Rainhill

near Liverpool, Stephenson's *Rocket*, which secured him the contract for locomotives, attained the then phenomenal speed of thirty miles an hour. There were other portents. A few small steam-driven vessels were coming into use on inland waterways before 1820; and a little later services across the Channel and the Irish Sea began. Oceanic steamships still lay in the future, and the iron-built ship was as yet a curiosity. But at sea, as on land, the way had been prepared for the tremendous advances in transport of the early Victorian age.

Changes of such magnitude in trade and industry, though they added greatly to the nation's general wealth and prosperity, were not achieved without much hardship and social dislocation. In the early years, dislocation due to war – especially interruption of trade with the United States – and later alternate boom and depression, created grave problems of unemployment, aggravated particularly after 1815 by the ending of war contracts and the demobilization of nearly a quarter of a million men. Slump and boom alike gave rise to industrial unrest, as workmen resisted attempts to lower wages and turned to the destruction of the machines to which they attributed their loss of work, or else sought their share of rising profits in higher pay. Certain skills, like that of the handloom weavers, were becoming redundant, and those who practised them had the hardest time of all, as the market for their labour narrowed inexorably, squeezing them gradually out of economic existence. Distress also stalked the agricultural south. Much of the rural area of southern England was suffering from over-population. If the widespread Speenhamland system of subsidizing agricultural wages out of rates had not encouraged the birth-rate, it was nevertheless a major cause of this state of affairs by keeping in their villages on a pittance men who might otherwise have migrated to the towns in search of work. With labour plentiful no part of the profits made by landlords and farmers was passed on to the labourer. Enclosures, which rose sharply during the war, made matters worse by depriving the peasant of the chance to eke out his living from the common, and those who turned in desperation to poaching their landlord's hares or pheasants ran the risk of transportation under the ferocious laws for the preservation of game. If bread prices rose from a sudden scarcity, the men who grew the wheat found themselves facing actual starvation: the labourers who rioted in Suffolk in 1816 followed a flag inscribed with the words 'Bread or Blood'. A Bedfordshire labourer declared before a committee on wages in 1824 that he and his family lived mainly on bread and cheese and water, and that sometimes for a month together he never tasted meat: in the 'twenties wages and poor relief together did not provide subsistence.

Government and the people

Those who controlled the country's destinies were only too aware of the stresses imposed by economic development, and were not without a will to solve them. But they were hampered by at least two major circumstances – their conviction of the correctness of the doctrines of *laissez-faire* preached by the leading thinkers on political economy, and the oligarchical character of the State, which gave predominance to certain group interests and caused any stirring of the masses to be regarded as dangerous. Also the situations which faced them were unprecedented. No society in human experience had undergone such radical transformations, and it was small wonder that the policies adopted by governments were sometimes sectional and appeared to be unfeeling and harsh. Not least, politicians were dogged by memories of the disasters which had befallen France and Europe after the revolutionary outbreak of 1789.

In a parliament composed mainly of landowners a protectionist policy for agriculture seemed essential, and the slump of 1815 was hastily met by a Corn Law excluding foreign wheat till the home price touched 80 shillings per quarter. Rightly or wrongly, this was regarded as inflicting dear bread upon the people, and aroused much popular discontent; and in 1825 the farmers had to see the Government take power to admit warehoused corn for consumption in time of dearth at a reduced duty and to admit more foreign corn at a low duty at discretion, while three years later the level of protection was reduced. More dangerous to the landowning interests than the agitation of the common people was the challenge from the rising class of merchants and manufacturers. During the last twenty years of the unreformed Parliament there were usually well over a hundred representatives of these groups in the Commons, and government was becoming increasingly responsive to their pressure. More plausibly than the land-owners, they could plead that their panacea – free trade – would benefit not just themselves but the country as a whole. Free interchange of commodities between nations would benefit all and reduce the tensions between them; while for Britain in particular it was necessary to secure cheap food and enable foreign countries to pay for British goods in return. In the 'twenties the increasing attention paid to commerce by the ministers aroused the jealousy of representatives of the landed interest, convincing them that in face of this rivalry old party animosities were of no account. Coke of Holkham told the Commons in 1822 that 'unless there should be a union of both Whigs and Tories, unless the country gentlemen on both sides of the House should combine their efforts the total destruction of the agricultural interest must ensue'. The battle was joined that would lead more than twenty years later to the repeal of the Corn Laws and the end of Protection.

Up till the 'thirties the industrialists' demands for cheaper corn for the workmen were not loud enough to flutter the nerves of the landed interest; but their pressure was subverting the old foundations of commercial policy and opening the way to the age of *laissez-faire*. In Huskisson, Liverpool and Herries they found after 1820 a trio of ministers whose views on commercial matters were sufficiently forward-looking to meet some at least of their demands, and who struck decisive blows at the restrictive commercial and navigational system of the eighteenth-century Empire. Up till 1822 the old system, mercantilist in character, still predominated. With some exceptions, overseas dependencies could trade only with the mother country or between each other. Traffic with foreign territories was restricted. The Empire formed a system of closed monopolies, and tariff barriers protected from foreign competition the industries of the homeland. Tariffs were attacked by the industrialists, who held the now quite justified belief that they could outsell the rest of the world if only they were given a free hand by access to markets without the penalties of duties charged either by their own or foreign governments. They hoped that a lowering of duties at home would be answered by similar action on the part of the foreigner. And from 1822 they got their way with the throwing open of the colonies to direct trade with Europe, the passage of a Reciprocity of Duties Act, and a series of further measures reducing British tariffs.

Also they attacked the shipping restrictions maintained under the Navigation Acts, by which the carrying trade between Great Britain and the dependencies was reserved to the ships of the mother country or of the dependencies themselves. The main defence for this monopoly of the Empire's carrying trade was still, as it had been in the eighteenth century, the provision of seamen for the Navy in time of war. On purely economic grounds it was much less defensible. The commercial interests blamed it for keeping artificially high the cost of freight. And though the ship-owners defended themselves hotly against this charge, they had no answer to the attack from a different quarter, when foreign governments insisted that their ships must be admitted to a share of the trade with the British colonies, otherwise British ships bringing colonial produce would be excluded from their ports. In the eighteen-twenties radical changes in the Navigation Laws were enacted in response to this combination of foreign and domestic pressure.

This enlightened policy had already gone far by 1828, and Huskisson and Herries were ready to take it further, by means not at all to the taste of the landed interest. At the moment when office was snatched from them in 1828 they were prepared to introduce some form of income tax or property tax which would have financed still more sweeping reductions of the revenue duties, which they regarded as 'most obstructive' to the industry of the country, 'most detrimental to it in its growing rivalry with the manufacturers of the Continent, and ... obnoxious to the public feeling'. Had they remained in office the work of Peel in the 'forties might have been anticipated by over a decade.

Material benefits were a major object of these commercial reforms. But to Huskisson at the Board of Trade, the minister chiefly concerned, the new policy had also another and more important object. He thought also in terms of political advantage. He argued that the American Revolution had been due more to British regulation of colonial trade than to any other single cause, and he wished to prevent repetitions of this disaster. *Laissez-faire* meant the abrogation of commercial control. By steering clear of action damaging to the interests of the colonies, their loyalty, he thought, might be kept at least for a time; and even afterwards, if they insisted upon their ultimate independence, the ties of friendly intercourse might be maintained. In 1825 he appealed to the House of Commons: 'Let us, as the parent state, fulfil our duties with all proper kindness and liberality. This is true wisdom: affording us on the one hand, the best chance of perpetuating a solid and useful connection, and on the other the best hope if ... that connection is ever to be dissolved, that separation may not be embittered by acrimony and bloodshed; and the certain consolation that, however brought about, it will not have been hastened or provoked by vexatious interference or oppressive pretensions on our part.'

Government response to the half-articulate mutterings of the masses was varied and by no means entirely negative. At first, indeed, it saw the problem of internal policy as one of order and little else, grappling with it by suspensions of Habeas Corpus, by strong backing for magistrates who called in the military, and by suppression and restriction of public meetings and the radical press. Such a policy was not entirely without justification. There was a lunatic fringe among the discontented inclined to appeal to force: in 1820 the Thistlewood group conspired to murder the Cabinet and proclaim a revolutionary régime. But repression for its own sake was no part of the Government's intentions, and with the more prosperous 'twenties these measures were soon relaxed. Prevention of crime was pursued both by the introduction of a more humane and therefore more effective criminal code and by the institution, in 1829, of the Metropolitan Police. On a different level were the Government's grants of money for the building of churches – a million pounds in 1817 – designed partly to counter the spread of Methodism, but of importance in bringing to the rootless immigrant populations of the unparished industrial towns an element of social cohesion and moral guidance. Yet another step in 1824 and 1825 was the legalization of limited trade-union activity, through which, it was hoped, labour might find and understand – and so accept – the role allotted to it by the political economists.

With radicalism Government would have nothing to do. It dismissed as chimerical the pleas of Cartwright, Orator Hunt, or William Cobbett, that Britain's welfare depended on a reform of Parliament, to make it truly representative of the people's views. But the pressure of middle-class radicalism for economy and improvements in administration could not be wholly withstood. It led to the abolition of sinecures and patronage and a growing professionalization of the revenue services. Under Peel's ægis the legal system was overhauled, stripped of medieval anomalies and obstructive technical processes, made less expensive and more accessible for the public. The Court of Chancery had become a by-word for inefficiency and was years in arrears: one critic observed that its work was divided into two parts – one, under the Chancellor, was *oyer sans terminer*, the other, under the Vice-Chancellor, *terminer sans oyer*. Peel's committee of inquiry into its operations was an indispensible preliminary to essential reforms.

Towards the close of the period, reforms of a different order began, when the political monopoly of the Church of England, a corner-stone of English polity since the Restoration, was destroyed by the two Emancipation Acts of 1828 and 1829.

The Protestant Dissenters were at law still excluded from public life. In practice they had for long been virtually admitted within the pale of the Constitution, and were sheltered from most of the consequences of their anomalous legal position by the operation of the annual indemnity acts. Practically the only sphere of public life barred to them was the borough corporation, and this was more because of the oligarchical structure which there obtained than because of the law. The legal situation of the Dissenters was illogical and quite indefensible, and when their demand for justice was raised in Parliament in 1828, hardly anyone was prepared seriously to resist it.

A year later the partisans of the Established Church had to swallow the admission of Roman Catholics also to full political rights. Catholic Emancipation in 1829 was the sequel to over thirty years of agitation. Throughout this period the Catholic question was, in effect, the Irish question. The English Roman Catholics were few and unimportant, and in the main reconciled to exclusion from public life. But the Roman Catholics in Ireland were an overwhelming majority of the population. They were, however, still victims of political discrimination, for Pitt had found it impossible to carry emancipation as he had wished to do in 1800, when the Union between Great Britain and Ireland was enacted. Catholics in Ireland could vote in elections, but they could not enter Parliament, and they were debarred from the higher civil and military offices. They were taxed to maintain an alien Church, of which only about a tenth of the inhabitants of Ireland were communicants. The success of the campaign for their emancipation was due to two circumstances: the emergence of a born leader and an effective organization. The leader was Daniel O'Connell, the organization was the Catholic Association. Many outstanding qualities brought O'Connell to the forefront of the Catholic movement: his integrity in the pursuit of Irish interests, his enthusiasm and zeal, his power of oratory, and his exceptional legal skill and knowledge. His ability as a lawyer was of particular importance to a cause always facing the necessity of evading legislation intended to crush it altogether, and to followers who were inevitably in conflict with those who administered the law. These gifts, employed with all the exuberant energy of which he was capable, soon made O'Connell a national hero.

In 1823 O'Connell re-created the Catholic Association, as an instrument to awaken political consciousness among the Irish Catholic peasantry – not the first or last time that a Church has contributed to the development of a national consciousness – and as a means of putting pressure on the British Government. Held together by the Catholic priesthood and hierarchy, the Association soon became a state within a state, administering its own equitable jurisdiction without reference to, and in defiance of, the central authority at Dublin which represented British rule. From 1826 it began to intervene effectively in parliamentary elections, protecting the humble voters from the consequences of defying the instructions of their Protestant landlords, and securing the return of champions of Emancipation. The climax of these demonstrations of power was the return of O'Connell himself for County Clare in 1829, although he was a Catholic and not legally eligible. This gesture of strength made it clear that the power of Protestant ascendancy over Irish elections was completely broken, and that the events in Clare would be repeated at the next general election in nearly every county in Ireland. The British Government had no choice but to give way or to take police action, which Peel thought would lead straight to civil war. Catholic emancipation was conceded to a nationalist demand which few in their consciences were prepared to resist by the only means possible – by force.

Mental horizons

The virility displayed by the British people of this age in their international relationships and their development of commerce and industrial resources was paralleled by the vigour of their intellectual life; and while much of the cultural efflorescence of the Regency is a subject for other writers in this volume, its literature, science, and spiritual life require mention here.

The literature of the Regency afforded a wonderful diversity of riches. In these years the younger Romantic poets flowered and died – Byron, the 'Titan', lonely and passionate rebel, the lyric and prophetic Shelley, and Keats, with his sensual love of natural beauty. Scott's romantic novels had captured the public and were bringing him a European reputation. On a different scale, Jane Austen was writing her exquisite miniatures of country-house life, and a little later Miss Mitford's sketches of 'Our Village' illustrated the less sophisticated delights and wonders of rural society. Among the essayists, Charles Lamb was launching into his best work after 1808 – the *Essays of Elia* were

written during the 'twenties. New opportunities for this *genre* were opened by the expansion of the periodical press – the *Quarterly Review* was founded in 1809, followed within the next few years by *Blackwood's* and the *Westminster Review* – and were exploited by (among others) Hazlitt, de Quincey, Jeffrey, John Gibson Lockhart, and the Mills, father and son. Travel literature was increasing in popularity: Cobbett's *Rural Rides* appeared during the 'twenties. In the reviews literature touched – often more than touched – on the fringe of politics. Otherwise literary art in this period was on the whole devoid of conscious social purpose, although Shelley and one or two others foreshadowed the trend of the following generation, in which it became more nearly associated with great public questions. Philosophic thought provoked both a revolutionary and a reactionary current. On the one hand stood the gospel of universal love preached by Shelley, evolved from rationalist assumptions of human perfectibility. On the other might be traced a movement, earlier visible in the last writings of Burke, and given expression in the work of the Lake Poets, of recoil from the bare reason back to the emotions as a truer guide to the inner meaning of things, basing upon them an innately conservative attitude to problems of political obligation and social structure.

Meanwhile the scientific mind enlarged its horizons. In pure science there was no great name at this period. The best work of Dalton and of Davy had already been done, and though Faraday was serving his apprenticeship to scientific inquiry, his greatness was revealed only in the next generation. It was in practical applications of scientific knowledge that advances were made in many and varied fields. Civil and mechanical engineering were emerging as professions. By 1830 George Stephenson had established himself as a railway engineer. McAdam, whose name gave a new word to the language, reached the height of his reputation as a constructor of highways. In 1819 he published his *Practical Essay on the Scientific Repair and Preservation of Roads*; and though his techniques were at first derided by scoffers who quipped about 'quack-adamizing', they were soon accorded general recognition: in 1827 he was appointed Surveyor-General of Roads. Other great achievements in the construction of roads, bridges and canals were due to Telford, under whose supervision the work on the Caledonian Canal was completed in 1822. In 1818 Telford was one of the founders of the society which a few years later became the Institution of Civil Engineers. A marked advance was made by the medical profession when, in 1815, the Society of Apothecaries secured an Act giving it power to examine all entrants into the profession. A regular training for apprentice doctors was thus assured. Also, the Regency coincided with the most fruitful period in the career of Charles Bell, whose discoveries concerning human and animal physiology rank in importance in medical science with Harvey's demonstration of the circulation of the blood nearly two centuries before. Bell published in 1811 his *Idea of a New Anatomy of the Brain*, and in 1830 gathered together the fruits of twenty years of research in his volume *The Nervous System of the Human Body*. In the same period Marshall Hall had begun his distinguished career as a medical researcher, teacher, and physician, though his most important contributions to medical knowledge were not made till after 1830.

The structure and the problems of society were also made the subject of scientific inquiry. John Rickman applied statistical methods to the analysis of the census returns, and the habit of gathering statistics about various aspects of economic life made rapid headway. Economic dislocation, and the currency problems produced by war-time inflation, stimulated economic thinking – David Ricardo began his career as a pamphleteer on the bullion question in 1809 – but the political economists also turned their attention to more general problems, such as distribution and the theory of value. James Mill, Malthus, and others were also writing on economic questions, but Ricardo, who in 1817 published his main work, *Principles of Political Economy and Taxation*, was the principal founder of what has been called the classical school of political economy. Mill, one of his close associates and a fellow founder in 1820 of the Political Economy Club, was better known for his exposition of Bentham's philosophy of Utilitarianism, and in his *Essay on Government*, published in 1820, setting forth the logical necessity for an adult male franchise if government and people were to be kept in step, he preached the beliefs and objects of political radicalism based upon Benthamite principles.

If Mill, Bentham, and some of their associates were sceptics, nevertheless the great clash between religion and science still lay in the future. Not till later was the controversy over *The Origin of Species* to set priest and scientist at odds. Men of culture still combined their knowledge of material things with a faith resting on literal acceptance of the Scriptures. But there were already vague rumblings of the impending battle in clerical dislike of the 'march of mind'. Purely secular pursuit of knowledge was condemned by some, as in the words of Dr Howley: 'The diffusion of knowledge, disjoined from religious instruction, stands in the same relation to ignorance as positive evil to the absence of good'. Churchmen looked askance at the Mechanics' Institutes popularized by Brougham, and at his society for the Diffusion of Useful Knowledge, which published informative literature at cheap rates. Towards the close of the period, their reaction was immediate to the foundation of the University of London, shortly to become University College, as a University for non-sectarian education: King's College, London, followed quickly as a Church foundation. But the Church's monopoly through the two older universities was now for the first time broken.

The end of the eighteenth century had seen a religious revival in full tide, and the impetus of this was not yet spent. Methodism was still spreading, especially in the industrial districts, and within the Church of England itself Evangelicalism now began to take a firmer hold. In some ways the Church was becoming more alive to its responsibilities. Much was done after 1809 to augment and endow benefices in the new growing towns, and up to 1824 Parliament voted two and a half million towards this work. But sectarian squabbles hampered the effort to provide elementary education, and for many reasons the Church of England laboured under difficulties during the later years of George IV's reign. As magistrates its clergy came into conflict with the labouring poor. As collectors of tithe they alienated the farmer and discouraged agricultural enterprise. And the Church remained a haunt of privilege and abuses. Plurality and non-residence were still widespread: for instance, Bishop Sharpe of Ely, his son, and his son-in-law, drew more than £30,000 yearly from church endowments, whilst at the other end of the scale, too

many parishes were still left to the ministrations of penniless curates. Evangelicalism did little to break down these abuses, and its hostility towards secular learning contributed in these years to that intellectual isolation of the Church which in the next generation was to prove disastrous.

George Stephenson's *Rocket*.

Architecture and Interior Design

CLIFFORD MUSGRAVE

By the opening of the Regency in 1811 architecture in Britain had been given its main directions for the next twenty to thirty years. The classical inspiration had gained new impetus from two influences. One was the vitalizing force of Greek architecture, sensationally revealed in the series of folios *The Antiquities of Athens*, published by James Stuart and Nicholas Revett, in the years from 1762 onwards. Another invigorating impulse was the impact of the cult of the Picturesque, which during the eighteenth century had confined itself mostly to landscape gardening and rural buildings, upon the planning of town architecture, imparting to it new variety and individuality.

The play of these forces, both independently and upon each other, brought into being the fascinating and at times bewildering range of Regency styles. Running through this rich diversity, two main trends of taste are discernible. One phase is that of the restrained, elegant classical tradition evolved after Adam by Dance, Soane, Holland and Wyatt, of simplicity and good proportion in form and decoration. This mood, though most prevalent in the earlier part of the Regency, up to 1815, nevertheless persisted to the end of the period.

After Waterloo the second phase becomes more strongly apparent. It is the time of a more sumptuous, florid and amply proportioned richness in classical decoration, especially of palatial interiors. It is an age of the growing Picturesque transformation of houses, of the full tide of the Grecian Revival, and the rich flood of Regency medieval romanticism.

The picturesque

Ideas of the Picturesque had been developing ever since, early in the eighteenth century, William Kent revolted against the symmetrical formal gardening favoured until then, and in the words of Horace Walpole 'leap'd the fence and found that all Nature was a garden'.

Controversy over the picturesque methods of Lancelot ('Capability') Brown caused several important works to be published during the years 1794–5, which established the 'Principles of the Picturesque'. The most important of these was *The Landscape, a Didactic Poem* by Richard Payne Knight, a wealthy and eccentric but highly capable scholar and connoisseur. Another work, *Sketches and Hints on Landscape*, 1785, was that of the professional landscape gardener, Humphrey Repton. He claimed in fact to be the first to use the title.

Knight also made a sound practical contribution to the newly rationalized science of the Picturesque. This was Downton Castle, the house he built for himself near Ludlow in 1774, the precursor of all the castellated mansions, both large and small, which became such distinguishing landmarks of the Regency scene, the movement culminating eventually in the rebuilding of Windsor Castle for King George IV from 1824 to 1836.

About 1796 Repton took into partnership John Nash (1752–1835). He had been an assistant in the office of Sir Robert Taylor, and after an early bankruptcy, had moved to Wales, where, during some twelve years, he built up a good practice as an architect of country houses. While with Repton

Fig. 1. Luscombe Castle, Devon, by John Nash, 1804. From *Jones' Views of the Seats of Noblemen and Gentlemen in England, etc.*, 1829

One of Nash's most charming small domestic castles.

Nash undertook all the architectural work involved in the improvement of country estates.

A natural flair for the element of drama in architecture combined with the experience of six years' partnership with Repton caused Nash virtually to inherit the leadership of the Picturesque movement, and he was soon well advanced on the path that was to lead him to fame as the designer who more than any other sums up in his work the architectural achievement of the Regency age.

Nash's early work included many designs for castellated mansions, but none survive of his larger examples, like his own at East Cowes, Caerhayes in Cornwall, and Ravensworth in Co. Durham; but his castellated style still exists on a delightful small scale at Luscombe, near Dawlish, in South Devon, where the house he finished in 1804 lies at the head of a long valley, flanked by cedars that Repton planted (Fig. 1). The delightful Kentchurch Court, Hereford,* is one of Nash's earliest domestic castles (*c.* 1795). Two of his smaller castles were built near each other in Sussex for the sons of Walter Burrell the historian. One, Knepp Castle (1806), is happily still preserved as a home by the same family (Pl. 5A). West Grinstead Park is derelict and almost certain to be demolished. All of them, with their large drum towers, tall narrow watch-towers, and square entrance towers, and their battlements and machicolations, derive from Downton.

The architect P. F. Robinson observed 'a passion for dwelling in cottages has been apparent',

* Indicates that the house is open to the public.

and in books of designs that appeared year by year he and other architects, like J. B. Papworth, excelled themselves and each other in producing notions for cottages, summer-houses, dairies, cowsheds, and conservatories that became more and more romantically extravagant as the years of classical restraint receded. Nash's interpretation of the *cottage orné* (Pl. 5B) is seen in perfection at the model village of Blaise Hamlet,* near Bristol, built in 1812, where he gathered together a collected edition of cottage designs he had executed in various places. Here his rustic fantasy may be seen in a delightful combination of dove-cot gables, clustered chimneys of brickwork moulded in lozenge, spiral and chequered designs, broad-eaved thatched roofs, arbours and porches and leaded windows.

Two of Nash's most notable early designs for private houses embody features that were to become distinctive contributions to the Regency commonwealth of styles. Southgate Grove, now Grovelands Hospital (1797), set the type of his later classical villas, and has a quality of gaiety and robustness that was welcome after the excessive delicacy of the Adam school. More refreshingly unfamiliar to the English scene were his houses like Cronkhill, Shropshire (1802), and Sandridge, Devon (1805), which established the type of the Italian villa, having the round towers with flattish conical roofs, the arched loggias and round-headed windows of the houses seen in such paintings of the Roman countryside as Claude Lorrain's *Landscape with a View of the Ponte Molle* at Birmingham Art Gallery.

One of the strongest influences pervading the architecture of the Regency, and one of the most subtle in bringing about the fusion of classical and Picturesque, was the intensely individual style of Sir John Soane (1753–1837), whose early career has been discussed in a previous volume. In his domestic interiors Soane brought to a new pitch the severity favoured by Dance, Holland and Wyatt, giving his rooms their characteristic dignity and simple beauty by means of semi-circular or semi-elliptical arched recesses with curved apses, and ceilings of shallow, flattened vaults as at Aynhoe, Northants (1800–2).* His ornament was confined to narrow ribbed mouldings, Greek key pattern decoration, and incised groovings, with occasionally recessed ceiling panels with rosettes, or small sculptured plaques with figures in relief, as at Pitzhanger Manor (1800–3),* at one time his own house, and now Ealing Public Library.

Soane's genius was for the handling of masses in a broad yet dramatic fashion with severe subordination of decorative detail. The Mausoleum and Picture Gallery * that he built for Sir Francis Bourgeois at Dulwich, now restored after damage during the war, is among the supreme examples of this quality in his work.

Soane gave similar treatment to his own house at No. 13 Lincoln's Inn Fields, which with No. 14 he added in 1812 to No. 12, where he had lived since 1792. Against the reticent brick façade of the three houses, Soane built a projecting frontispiece of stucco which he gave his characteristic pilaster-like treatment with recessed lines and key-pattern ornament. It was intended to form one of the side wings of an extended design across Nos. 13, 14 and 15, with a colonnade of coupled Ionic columns forming the centre, but the whole magnificent project was never completed. No. 13, now Sir John Soane's Museum,* was created to serve as dwelling-house, office, museum and gallery, to illustrate 'the union of architecture, sculpture and painting', and in the immense collection of casts, models, drawings, paintings, pottery, sculpture and antiques, the house embraces all the motifs of ancient architecture which were the inspiration of his time.

The rooms of the house have a multiplicity of shallow domes and vaults, lantern lights and clear-storys, arched openings and mirror-friezes, all creating those endless indeterminate vistas and recessions with which even in this circumscribed space, as in his earlier arched, domed and vaulted halls at the Bank of England, Soane strove to create the sense of infinity.

The Regency house

The Regency age was not, like the eighteenth century, one to favour the building of great country houses. The number of immense aristocratic fortunes was smaller, and the Napoleonic

Wars caused restrictions of material. The Regency was pre-eminently the age of the smaller house, and in it Picturesque ideas inspired the individuality and charm which are so characteristic of the time.

The diversity of styles consisted in a wide range of variations upon a few basic themes. The underlying tradition was classical, flowing smoothly on from the restrained neo-classical phase of the late eighteenth century. The curved window bays and low roof parapets favoured by Wyatt became some of the most distinctive features of Regency building. These bays, of semi-circular or sometimes shallower segmental form, with sash windows shaped to the curve, rose to differing levels, sometimes through one or two storeys only, at times to roof level. In the early Regency this point was marked by a slender cornice with brick dentils; later a more heavily modelled and deeper cornice gave emphasis to the upper walls, and became characteristic. Frequently instead of the shallow roof, almost concealed behind the parapet, the Italian type of roof with overhanging eaves came to be favoured. Angular bays usually belong to the later Regency years, although of mid-eighteenth century and earlier origin.

Early in the period the brown brick of former years gave place increasingly to yellow stock bricks, which add gaiety to so many of the Regency houses of London and the seaside, but bricks of deep red continued to be used. The plain square or rectangular brick house of the eighteenth-century tradition, with its simple classical porch as the only adornment, persisted to defy the fevers of the Picturesque right through the Regency period up to the 'thirties and 'forties till its evolution into the square Victorian villa.

An excellent example of the Regency brick villa is Clissold House, Stoke Newington,* built by J. Woods about 1820-30, and now a tea-house. The central block has a projecting Doric portico of six columns, with balcony above a stone parapet and flat roof, and is flanked by single-storey wings with bowed ends.

In flat-fronted houses the severity of the plain façade was sometimes modified by recessed relieving arches of semi-circular or flattened curves above the window, as at Keats' House, Hampstead.*

The adornment of even the severest type of house by window-balconies (Pl. 6A) with delicate cast or wrought-iron railings was customary, and as Picturesque influence became more pervasive the window-canopy which now seems inseparable from the idea of the Regency house, especially at the seaside, became generally adopted. These delightful appendages of sheet metal of tented or Chinese pagoda form, sometimes fluted, did not come widely into use until after their introduction, together with verandas and trellis (Pl. 6B), by P. F. Robinson at Brighton Pavilion* in 1802, as part of the transformation of Henry Holland's building from its original prim severity to the gaiety and friendliness of a rural *cottage orné*. Many Brighton houses had balconies at an early date, but were not given canopies or verandas until about 1815 or later. The later canopies, of about 1820 onwards, were like ladies' bonnets, having a bulbous upper part and a skirt-like rim, separated by a broad ribbon (Pl. 7).

The covering of the ground-floor walls by stucco, which had been popularized by Adam, continued generally into the early Regency, the surface frequently being rusticated with deep horizontal joints emphasizing the long, reposeful proportions of a façade, especially that of a street terrace. The use of painted stucco for covering entire house fronts became more common from 1810 onwards, and was to form another of the celebrated characteristics of Regency building, culminating in its use for John Nash's great palatial terraces of Regent's Park. The hackneyed jibe against Nash from the *Quarterly Review* of 1826 is quoted again, if only that the use of the material may to some extent be vindicated.

Augustus of Rome was for building renown'd,
And of marble he left what of brick he had found;
But is not our Nash, too, a very great master?
He finds us all brick and he leaves us all plaster.

Aesthetically, at least, Nash was justified in using painted stucco, for with it he was able to give the terraces the gaiety and brilliance which are among their chief beauties, when seen flashing

Fig. 2. Grange Park, Hampshire, by William Wilkins, 1810. From *Jones' Views of the Seats of Noblemen and Gentlemen in England, etc.*, 1829.

A country house in the severest manner of the Greek revival.

in the sunshine across the green of Regent's Park on a summer's day, or in the clear evening light of spring or autumn. The Regency terraces of sea-side towns like Brighton and Hastings would lose much of their quality of shining elegance without stucco. It was at the seaside, as Humphrey Repton explained, that the two virtues of the material first appeared. One, to obtain the utmost play of light and shadow upon buildings; the other, to seal brickwork against driving rain and winds heavily laden with salt spray.

Kent Grange, Hampstead (*c.* 1810), is a stucco house of unusually charming character, with its interplay of curves in double window bays, iron-work balconies and upper windows set within arched wall-recesses. For the moderate-sized country house of stucco may be cited Bignor Park, Sussex, built in restrained neo-classical style be-

tween 1826 and 1831, by Henry Harrison, an architect of whom little work is recorded.

Characteristic of the more informal and inti-mate tendencies of the Regency was the change in the conception of the villa, a term which no longer signified the imposing Palladian villa of Burlingtonian days, but now indicated almost every type of separate house of individual design between the cottage and the mansion.

The standard for those of medium or larger size was set by the villas of Regent's Park, which ranged from the severest manner of the Greek Revival (Fig. 2), as in the Doric Villa by York Terrace, to freer exercises in the Grecian taste, like The Holme, which Decimus Burton built for his father, and villas embodying strong Italian in-fluence in round-headed windows and deeply over-hanging eaves. No. 1 Gloucester Gate, by J. J.

Scoles, and many other villas of the Park, displayed the imaginative handling of the Classical tradition inspired by Picturesque ideas, in the way the masses of a building, while embodying Grecian detail, were broken up or detached to form a varied composition of dramatic and interesting outlines.

One of the most original domestic designs of the early Greek Revival is the Doric House, Sion Hill, Bath, built about 1810 with a Doric colonnade of two storeys, as a house and picture-gallery for the painter Thomas Barker by J. M. Gandy, A.R.A. (1771–1843), the friend and disciple of Soane.

For the expression of romantic moods in villa and cottage, however, the Gothic style was supreme, but less in the elaborate rococo manner of Strawberry Hill than in the playful style of Stephen Wright's Milton Manor, Abingdon.* Shelley's House at Great Marlow displays this gay spirit in its charming flattened ogival pointed windows. Extremes of Picturesque medieval fantasy are reached at Belsize Lane, Hampstead, where Hunter's Lodge (c. 1825) shows round towers with conical roofs, and again, ogival windows.

But the type of villa that breathes the Regency spirit more than any other is that which combines with the utmost freedom, frequently in a single building, the various elements of brickwork or stucco, curved window-bays, verandas, balconies, ironwork railings, trellis-work, classical porch, and either deep cornices with a parapet or broad eaves. Examples are found in every town possessing a Regency phase of building, but outstanding instances are Claremont Villa, Cheltenham; Kent Grange, Hampstead (already mentioned); and Rheola, Glamorgan, a house which John Nash built for his friend John Edwards, M.P., and now sympathetically used as a factory guest-house and offices. Halnaker Lodge, Coldharbour Lane, Brixton, and houses in Dulwich Village; at Twickenham, Strand-on-the-Green, Chiswick and Hampstead, at The Terrace, Barnes; Richmond Hill and the Park Villages East and West, Regent's Park, also finely represent the type.

The seaside town of Southwold in Suffolk deserves special mention for its medium-sized Regency houses of excellent quality, grouped mostly around the Gun Green and built about 1828. They form a delightful anthology of the favourite Regency styles from the severely non-columnar Grecian of Soane's inspiration (Pl. 9B) to stucco villas and houses with bows, balconies and verandas, while in the villages around are found plainer yellow-brick houses with porches of Doric and Tuscan and even, occasionally, Egyptian design.

The unconventional form of many Regency houses is not always due to fantasy, or the demands of the informal landscape, but to originality and experiment in planning to secure convenience in living, and the maximum admission of light and air. An early manifestation of this aspect of Regency thought is the astonishing Clare House at East Malling, Kent (1793), built by Michael Searles, architect of the Blackheath Paragon. In this house the intriguing circular form was determined by the planning of all living-rooms round a central hall. A similar house of a few years later is the charming villa at Havering-atte-Bower in Essex, where again the circular form ensured the procession of the sun through all the rooms of the house during the day. 'La Ronde'* near Exmouth is another example of a circular house, and contains astonishing decoration of shell-work.

The reticent manner of the post-Adam period which Holland showed in his houses at Sloane Street and Hans Place in the 1790's, persisted in the town terraces of the early Regency, as on the north side of Brunswick Square, London, where the houses, built about 1802, have a simple stucco ground floor, round-headed front-doorways, iron balconies, a flat stucco cornice, and first-floor windows within shallow arched recesses, flanking a central Wyatt-like segmental window bay rising through all floors to relieve the long facade. This terrace was part of the development of the Foundling Estate by James Burton, the remarkably capable London builder whose fame has been overshadowed by his more well-known son Decimus.

A transitional phase between this reserved early style and the more spectacularly palatial stucco Regency terrace of the years from 1815 onwards is marked by the terrace on the east side of Mecklenburgh Square, London, built in 1812 (Pl. 8A).

(A) The Duke of Wellington, by T. Phillips. *Courtesy the Earl of Shrewsbury*. (B) Robert Banks Jenkinson 2nd Earl of Liverpool, by Sir Thomas Lawrence. *National Portrait Gallery*. (C) George IV, Regent 1811–20, reigned 1820–30, by Sir Thomas Lawrence. *National Portrait Gallery*. (D) Robert Stewart, 2nd Marquess of Londonderry (Lord Castlereagh), by Sir Thomas Lawrence. *National Portrait Gallery*. (E) George Canning, by Sir Thomas Lawrence. *National Portrait Gallery*.

PLATE 1   1025

(A) Politics for popular consumption: the radical, Samuel Whitbread, is worsted by Castlereagh. A print published by S. Knight of Sweeting Alley, 1815. *British Museum.*

(B) The 'lunatic fringe' among the discontented. Members of the Thistlewood group resisted arrest with fatal results for one of the police officers concerned. Coloured etching by George Cruikshank, 1820. *St Marylebone Public Library.*

PLATE 2.

(A) The Royal Cockpit, Birdcage Walk, 1808. An aquatint by Rowlandson and Pugin from
The Microcosm of London, 1808.

(B) A Cricket Match in the 1820's. North-east view of the cricket-fields at Darnall, near
Sheffield. Coloured aquatint by Robert Cruikshank, 1827. *Marylebone Cricket Club.*

PLATE 3   1027

In the heart of London's commercial world: the Customs House from the River Thames. From
The Microcosm of London, 1808.

PLATE 4

(A) JOHN NASH. Castellated Mansion. Knepp Castle, Sussex. 1806.

(B) Cottage Orné, Suffolk, in the manner of John Nash. *c.* 1815.

PLATE 5

(A) Verandah, with cast-iron railing, at Richmond, Surrey. *c.* 1815.

(B) Trellis verandah, with cast-iron railing, at Brighton. *c.* 1815.

PLATE 6

Villa at Brighton with bowed front, stuccoed, cast iron railings and canopy. *c.* 1820.

PLATE 7

(A) JOSEPH KAY. Town Terrace. Mecklenburgh Square, London. 1812–21.

(B) A small town-terrace. Montpelier Square, London. *c.* 1818.

PLATE 8

(A) House in Sidmouth, with an especially original quality of fantasy in trellis work balconies and Gothic windows.

(B) Villa at Southwold, in the manner of Sir John Soane. *c.* 1815.

PLATE 9

(A) Balcony railing of cast-iron with a Grecian Doric porch at Brighton.
c. 1820.

(B) Balcony railings of cast-iron, at Brunswick Square, Hove. *c.* 1826.

(A) Drawing-room with segmental window-bay and ceiling with shallow arches and groining in the manner of Sir John Soane. Sarsgrove House, Glos. *c.* 1815.

(B) JOHN NASH. Knepp Castle, Sussex. 'Gothic' decoration in the form of miniature vaulting. *c.* 1806.

PLATE 11

(B) DECIMUS BURTON. Doorcase, painted and gilt, and enriched modillion cornice, at The Holme, Regent's Park, London. c. 1818.

(A) Double staircase with cast-iron balusters, at Eastern Terrace, Brighton. c. 1824.

Cranbury Park, Hampshire. The Tent Room, formed when J. B. Papworth made additions.
c. 1829–31.

PLATE 13

(A) JOHN NASH. The Royal Pavilion, Brighton. The East Front. 1815–22.
Brighton Corporation.

(B) JOHN NASH. Cumberland Terrace, London. 1826.

PLATE 14

(A) The Tower House, Park Village West, with villas of Park Village East in the distance, probably by James Pennethorne, under Nash. *c.* 1824 28.

(B) Italian Villa, at Park Village West. *c.* 1824–28.

PLATE 15

(A) C. A. Busby. Brunswick Square, Hove, Sussex. 1825.

(B) Decimus Burton. Adelaide Crescent, Hove. 1830–34.

PLATE 16

(A) C. A. Busby. Brunswick Terrace, Hove. 1824.

(B) George Basevi. Pelham Crescent, London. c. 1829.

PLATE 17

(A) Belvoir Castle, Leics. The East Front by Thoroton, imitating James Wyatt's theme of deeply embrasured 'Norman' windows. *English Life Publications*.

(B) BENJAMIN WYATT. The Elizabeth Saloon, Belvoir Castle, Leics., using doorcases and wall-panels from a French *château*, and marking the origin of the Louis XV revival of the early 19th century. The ceiling was painted by Matthew Wyatt. *English Life Publications*.

　　　　　　　PLATE 18

(A) GEORGE BASEVI. Belgrave Square, London. 1825–40.

(B) JOHN NASH. The Royal Pavilion Salon. 1815–22.
Brighton Corporation.

PLATE 19

BENJAMIN WYATT. The Waterloo Chamber, Apsley House, London, 1828.

PLATE 20

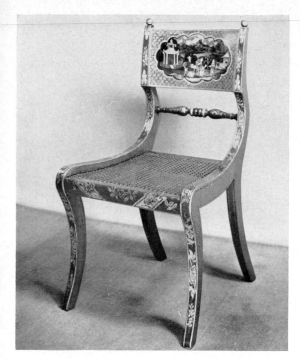

(A) Chair japanned in black and gold in the Chinese taste, *c.* 1810.

(B) Mahogany chair with lyre-shaped splat, *c.* 1800.

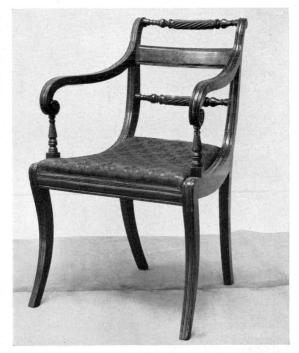

(C) Mahogany armchair with spiral reeding on the rails in back, *c.* 1810.

(D) Japanned chair with panel painted in the Chinese taste, *c.* 1810.

PLATE 21   1045

(A) Mahogany sofa table inlaid with brass; pedestal supported by a platform on splayed feet, *c.* 1815. *J. W. Evill Collection.*

(B) Mahogany pedestal library table, with ebonised stringing on the drawer fronts, *c.* 1815.

(A) Mahogany extending dining table, on a central pillar-and-claw; two of the reeded end legs swing
out to give space for extra leaves, *c.* 1820.

(B) Rosewood architect's table, inlaid with brass. The miniature table folds up and shuts away as a
drawer, *c.* 1810.

PLATE 23

(A) Mahogany circular pillar-and-claw dining table, showing method of adding leaves, *c.* 1815–20.

(B) Mahogany side table inlaid with brass, supported by lion monopodia, in the Egyptian taste, *c.* 1810.

PLATE 24

(A) Rosewood side table, with ormolu mounts, marble top, and supports in the Egyptian taste, *c.* 1810.

(B) Mahogany side table with carved paw feet, ormolu mounts and brass gallery, *c.* 1810.

PLATE 25

1050

PLATE 26

The Chinese taste: two stands, painted ivory, with mounts of ormolu and carved wood, gilt, and white marble tops. Made for the Saloon at the Royal Pavilion, Brighton, about 1822. (*On permanent loan to the Royal Pavilion from H.M. the Queen*).

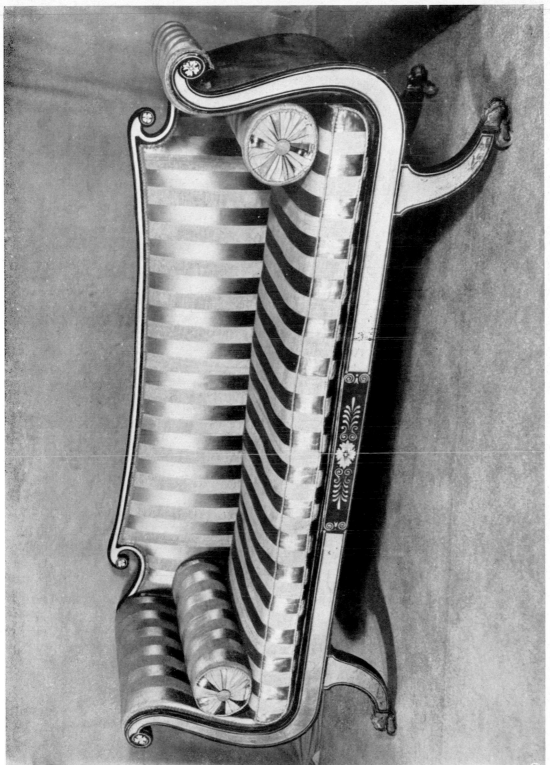

Painted and gilt sofa, with brass paw feet on the outward-curving legs, *c.* 1810. *Victoria and Albert Museum.*

PLATE 27

(A) Rosewood cabinet with marble top, lion masks and feet and brass trellis doors and sides, *c.* 1810.

(B) Mahogany music stand ('Canterbury'), *c.* 1810.

PLATE 28

(A) Chiffonier, ('used chiefly for such books as are in constant use', G. Smith, 1808). Lotus and anthemion decoration, paw feet and brass trellis door, *c.* 1810.

(B) Small rosewood bookcase on stand, showing characteristic turning and brass decoration, *c.* 1810.

PLATE 29   1053

English commode with marked French influence; boulle work panels, c. 1800–10.

PLATE 30

Mahogany side table with imitation bamboo decoration in the Chinese taste,
c. 1810.

PLATE 31

1055

One of a set of four painted satinwood armchairs with panels of flowers and cupids and with cane
seats, *c.* 1810. *In the collection of Mr and Mrs Frederick Poke.*

PLATE 32

This delightful design was the work of Joseph Kay, architect for the Mecklenburgh Square development in the Foundling Estate scheme with his master, Charles R. Cockerell, as consultant. A similar note on a more domestic level is struck by Trevor Square, Knightsbridge, London (1818), where again stuccoed ground storeys combine with severe brickwork, plain window-openings, and simple iron balconies to give a touch of smartness and gaiety.

The tradition of discreet design in the smaller house terrace (Pl. 8B) persisted right through to the end of the Regency period, and is seen in all its qualities of charm and reserve in Alexander Place, South Kensington, probably built about 1827–31, under the direction of George Basevi, who was responsible for Pelham Crescent and the Thurloe Square development. Here again are the shallow window bows, cast-iron balconies without hoods at the first-floor windows, and round-arched front doors. The ground storey is stuccoed and there is a moulded stucco cornice. A little-known, but enchanting *enclave* of simple Regency terrace houses is Edwardes Square, with Earl's Terrace, off Kensington High Street, London. This square was built between 1811 and 1819 by an unknown architect for a French speculative builder named Changeur. The long terrace of brick houses with stucco ground floors, where at No. 32 Leigh Hunt once lived, is approached past a tiny pedimented Doric gardener's lodge called The Temple.

From the middle of the eighteenth century onwards, as the popularity of sea-bathing developed, the idea of an annual holiday by the sea became more and more a national institution, and the demand for summer lodgings was enormous. At Brighton from 1795 onwards many new houses were being erected. Regency Square, begun in 1818, was the first of the Brighton squares on a larger scale, but still in the early tradition of yellow brick with rusticated stucco ground floors, bow fronts, and balconies with ironwork railings. These last owe much to the designs of the architect Busby and to the foundries for Sussex iron at Lewes nearby (Pl. 10A, B). The Brighton railings are almost invariably cast, not wrought, and ex-

hibit a delightful variety of classical designs. One of outstanding fineness and delicacy, incorporating the honeysuckle motif, is seen not only throughout Brighton but in London, Cheltenham, Worthing and elsewhere.

Worthing, Hastings, Ramsgate, Margate, Weymouth and a host of other towns provide delightful examples in the earlier Regency seaside idiom of brick and stucco, bow windows and ironwork balconies, as well as important instances of the later phases of style. At Sidmouth the houses have an especially original quality of fantasy in trellis-work balconies and Gothic windows (Pl. 9A).

At Cheltenham, the pre-eminent Regency inland town, the first phase of its architectural development lasted until the advent of Papworth and Forbes about 1825. To this earlier period belong the stone-faced, bow-fronted houses Hygeia (once Vittoria) Lodge, *c.* 1813, and Claremont Lodge. This time saw also the creation of several works of monumental quality, favoured greatly by the existence of Cotswold stone, as well as many smaller buildings of high merit and individual character.

Royal Crescent, *c.* 1805–9, was the first of the large-scale groups, and still contains good interior work such as curved doors, fine plaster ceilings, and fanlights. An outstanding contribution is made to the quality of Cheltenham's Regency architecture by the remarkable beauty of its ironwork, based frequently upon generally available designs like those in Cottingham's *Directory*, but owing much to the fineness and delicacy with which the graceful linear Grecian detail has been executed by local craftsmen.

At Bath the Paragon (*c.* 1809–14) offers a striking example of individuality in terrace design, with its projecting semi-circular Grecian porches and double front-doors shaped to the curve. The great days of Bath were not in the Regency, but as well as having many pleasant domestic examples of the period, it provides a rather *triste* epilogue to the romantic adventure of Fonthill, in the shape of the classical Lansdowne Tower (1825),* built by Henry Edmond Goodridge (1800–63), where William Beckford ended his days.

Interior design

Just as the varied styles of Regency building resolved themselves into three or four basic types, so also interior architectural decoration ran in a few main currents. In the Picturesque house the spirit of interior design frequently bore no relation to the style adopted for the exterior. At Downton Castle, Richard Payne Knight deliberately retained a classical scheme as embodying 'the greatest convenience and progress' in interior arrangement. The Gothic Luscombe has classical rooms. Sezincote, the Gloucestershire villa in the Indian style, had a restrained classical interior. The Indian exterior of the Brighton Pavilion cloaks a *chinoiserie* decorative scheme.

The predominant trend in small and medium houses was towards greater simplicity, in whatever style was adopted. The style of Robert Adam, strictly modified in this direction, retained its popularity right through the period, from the latter half of the eighteenth century to the 1840's. In the smaller houses such decoration would be confined to a single circular garland of husks upon the ceiling with a small central ornament of leaves, a narrow frieze of delicate swags around the walls, and a similar frieze, or reticent decoration of an urn, vase or medallion gracing the chimney-piece, which might be of painted wood, composition or marble.

The decorative style of George Basevi as expressed in the houses of Belgrave Square at the end of the Regency was modelled closely upon the manner of Adam and Wyatt, especially in the design of the chimney-pieces. His ceilings there are frequently plain, but with rich palmated coving and cornices. As at Bignor Park, Sussex, ceilings might be portioned out into squares or rectangles, with fine bead mouldings, another form of treatment, highly simplified, deriving from the Adam school of design. Frequently, cornices were of straight classical mouldings, sometimes called architrave mouldings, from their similarity to those used for the door-cases. Chimney-pieces were also designed in this way, with no other ornament except perhaps a fluted frieze or sculptured panel. This mode of interior design, restrained to the

Fig. 3. The entrance to the Royal Pavilion, Brighton, from John Nash, *The Royal Pavilion*, 1826

point of plainness, is frequently found in the houses of Nash, in the villas and terraces of Regent's Park and elsewhere, even in some of the private apartments of the Royal Pavilion at Brighton.

Nash delighted in the use of arched openings in doorways and corridors, usually of a flattish curve, with a simple torus moulding on the edge. It is a tendency he may have absorbed from Soane, who made the contribution of his distinctive Grecian style to interiors in a similar fashion to that he had employed at Aynhoe in 1804. There, and at Sarsgrove House, Oxfordshire (*c.* 1810), which was built, if not by him, then under his influence, a severely plain interior is relieved by shallow arched recesses in the walls, by arched door openings, and by ceilings of shallow vaulting, sometimes divided into four parts by blunt-angled groining (Pl. 11A). The chimney-pieces of Soane's style were of marble or fine stone, with plain jambs, and bearing his restrained incised Grecian ornament, the frieze probably incised with a full Greek key pattern design. Soane's interior method seems rarely to have been imitated other than by Nash, except occasionally in the provinces as by Foulston. at Plymouth.

Despite stylistic divergencies, the integration of interior with exterior was frequently expressed in the endowment of rooms with beautiful curved shapes created by the rounded bays at the front or end of a house. These bays were often associated with the long French or, as they were sometimes called, 'Italian' windows, reaching down to ground level. The Romantic pre-occupation with nature, as well as the growing informality of manners, among women no less than men, may have stimulated the fondness for such windows, which enabled the occupants to move out upon the lawn at a single step, and filled the rooms with light and air. The windows of angular bays served the same growing aspiration. Malton wrote: 'In consequence of the inclined lights, the sides of the room ... are better lit than they possibly can be through square openings in the wall.' Even though, as at 'Northanger Abbey', the Gothic form of window was preserved, nevertheless 'every pane was so large, so clear, so light!'

The desire for informal living among the family or household continued the development of the open planning of rooms favoured by Adam, and just as the French windows broke down the barrier between house and garden, large folding doors abolished the distinction between one room and another.

A phase of severe archæological exactitude in the interpretation of Greek ideas was introduced by the wealthy banker and antiquary, Thomas Hope, at his house Deepdene, near Dorking, where he arranged a series of interiors not only in the Greek, but also in the Egyptian style, which the campaign of Napoleon in Egypt and Nelson's victory of the Nile had made fashionable. His work

on *Household Furniture and Interior Decoration* was published in 1807, but his influence was limited. The Egyptian vogue manifested itself more in furniture and objects of art than in architectural decoration, though in a few interiors there were chimney-pieces with the tapering jambs of Egyptian pylons, and ornament of lotus design.

For the Gothic interiors of John Nash's domestic castles, such as Knepp Castle, and West Grinstead Park, Sussex, he evolved a Gothic decorative style of great delicacy, gaiety and charm, consisting of ceilings with light plaster ribs in the interlacing curvilinear or geometrical designs of the sixteenth century. The ornament of cornices or ceiling coves is especially charming, being in the form of Gothic arcading on a small scale with intersecting arches, or resembling miniature vaulting (Pl. 11B). Nash's assistant, George Stanley Repton, son of the landscape gardener, might have been responsible for the designing of this ornament, for his sketch-books indicate an interest in Gothic not possessed by Nash, who would complain that the designing of a single Gothic window took up more time than a whole house. But even in these Gothic interiors there were lapses into the classical, especially in the design of fireplaces, which were sometimes of simple architrave mouldings with a classical plaque in marble, or, if Gothic motifs were used, it was in the form of a Gothic arch, sketchily indicated on the fireplace jambs in the incised grooving of Soane's style.

Throughout the houses of the Regency, from the simplest to the most palatial, the tendency was for ceilings to be plain in the main portion. The sides were frequently coved, but although decorated centres are found in some of the great state apartments of the Regency palaces, even in these the plain expanse of ceiling is not unusual. Where chandeliers were used they frequently depended from a central ornament of leaves, sometimes composed in a swirling design (Fig. 4).

This kind of foliated ceiling ornament, which is found in every type of house from the smallest to the most elaborate, and which in a shrunken, enfeebled form survived all through the nineteenth century up to Edwardian days, descends from the magnificent central ornament of leaves in that

Fig. 4. A classical interior, from *Designs for Ornamental Villas* by P. F. Robinson, F.S.A., 1827.

An 'enriched' cornice and ceiling mouldings, but with a plain coving and ceiling, with small central ornament.

ceiling of the Temple of the Sun at Palmyra, which Flitcroft imitated at Woburn,* and Robert Adam paraphrased so gloriously in the ceiling of the Drawing-room at Osterley.*

If not plain, the ceiling might be given a compartmented form, but with plain shallow panels instead of the deep coffers containing rosettes as in the preceding years.

The fully Grecian villas of the Revival, such as those at Pittville and Bayshill, Cheltenham, or of Regent's Park, often had ceilings with flat borders or friezes of Greek key pattern, or of *guilloche* design resembling flat interlacing ribbon. The

door-cases (Pl. 12B) frequently were given fluted architraves, with corner blocks carrying floral rosettes, a lion's mask, or a plain knob-like roundel. The frieze might be adorned with the *anthemion* design, in which the lotus flower alternates with palm leaves, the latter being frequently confused with honeysuckle, an equally popular motif. Other decoration might take the form of plaques of classical subjects on the walls of entrance hall or staircase. In wealthy houses, mouldings of doors, of skirtings and cornices were frequently 'enriched' with dentils – small block-shaped ornaments with narrow spacing – or with widely spaced modillions either of simple block-form or, in the richer examples, in the shape of a scrolled bracket carved with an acanthus leaf. In some of the smaller interiors, as at Luscombe, classical mouldings were frequently used of delicate and slender proportion, using tongue-and-dart, acanthus-tip, palm or bay leaf designs, often gilded (figs., pp. 1072, 1120).

During the later Regency years interior ornament in some of the palatial houses, especially that of cornices, coves and friezes embodying scrolling of acanthus and other foliated or flower design, assumed a more sumptuous character, as in the work of Benjamin Wyatt described later, that was to become distinctive of this phase. The extreme delicacy which Adam had given this ornament, creating with it such eloquent shapes within the open voids of his borders, or the nervous vitality of James Wyatt's decoration as seen at Heveningham, was lost, and stalk, flower and leaf now assumed a luxuriant bold fulness, expanding to fill, almost to burst beyond, the confines of the frieze or coving it occupied.

The delicacy initiated by Robert Adam, refined and simplified by Henry Holland and James Wyatt, was, as in so many other features, the predominant influence in the design of staircases. The gracefully soaring curves, or elegant articulated angles of mounting treads, and the delicate line of handrail which they developed are the familiar marks of the Regency staircase (Pl. 12A). Much individuality was expressed in the patterning of iron balusters, in which the familiar classical motifs of acanthus and honeysuckle played restrained or florid parts, or in which pure linear designs of exquisite grace and subtlety were used, as by Soane in his staircases at Moggerhanger.

The lessened importance attached to the chimney-piece in Regency times was deplored by Papworth, who observed that greater decorative value had been transferred to immense gilt mirrors, which, as Britten remarked, were adopted 'to extend the apparent dimensions of our rooms', as in the dining-room at Uppark, Sussex,* remodelled by Humphrey Repton, and to create perspectives, as in his unfulfilled design for a flower corridor with mirrors at the ends at the Brighton Pavilion. John Nash used the same device in the mirror-

faced doors at the ends of the Long Gallery in his own transformation of the Pavilion. It was a development again expressive of the Regency aspiration towards light and space.

The fondness for tents as part of the Picturesque equipment of park and garden in Regency times caused many designs for tented rooms indoors to be produced. One perfect room of this type was created at Cranbury Park, Hampshire,* designed in Adamesque style by George Dance (c. 1780–90), where J. B. Papworth formed the Library about 1831 (Pl. 13).

The Regency designers in their interiors, as well as externally, endowed their houses with gracious individuality, seemliness, and sunny charm, and reached a condition in architecture from which a sensible and agreeable modern style might well have emerged a century earlier than the Victorian obscurity allowed. It was the Brighton architect, Charles Busby, who remarked with justifiable complacency that 'the true impressions of cheerfulness, elegance and refinement are so well understood and so happily united in our modern domestic dwellings that I hesistate not to say we are rapidly advancing to a state of perfection'.

The Oriental episode

Towards the end of the eighteenth century the place which China had occupied for nearly a hundred years as a land of romantic nostalgia had been taken by India, largely through the interest in Indian art and culture awakened by Warren Hastings when Governor of Bengal. Engravings made by William Hodges and by Thomas Daniell and his nephew of the buildings and scenery of India enthralled the English imagination with 'the splendour of the minarets and pagodas that shone out from the depths of its woods', and the Prince Regent's biographer Croly wrote of the mosques and palaces of Hindostan as the inspiration for 'a new poetic architecture'.

Thomas Daniell collaborated at Sezincote in Gloucestershire (1806), with the architect Samuel Pepys Cockerell, Surveyor to the East India Company, in rebuilding it as an India villa for a retired nabob. William Porden, who had been a pupil of

Cockerell, had built at the same time the Royal Stables and Riding House at Brighton for the Prince of Wales, and Humphrey Repton, who had been laying out the grounds at Sezincote, was summoned from there by the Prince to advise upon rebuilding the Pavilion in the Indian style, but his designs, which closely resembled Sezincote and seem to have been based on one of William Hodges' *Views*, were never carried out. It was not until 1815 that the Prince, then four years Regent, decided to go on with the project for rebuilding the Brighton Pavilion, but now with John Nash as his architect (Pl. 14A and Fig. 3).

Nash skilfully incorporated the original classical villa into the fabric of the new building, adding two great new State apartments to the ends, one a Banqueting Room, the other a Music Room, and gave unity to the whole by linking old and new parts with a long battlemented cornice, and rows of Indian columns along the eastern façade. Those outside the two great new rooms formed a screen linked by pierced stone-work lattice screens like Indian *jalis*, that give a delightful effect by casting dappled patterns of sunlight and shadow on the stucco walls. The roofs were crowned with Indian domes of exquisitely subtle contour, but remembering the essential character of a pavilion as a tent, Nash placed above the two large rooms not domes but spires, like the concave roofs of Crusaders' tents in a novel of Walter Scott's. Nash has wrongly been accused of plagiarizing Repton's designs, for there are no details which correspond.

The theme of the tent appears again in the interior, where Nash, with consummate skill, used drooping tented ceilings – in one room of black and gold and in another of bamboo – to form the transition from the low domestic scale of Holland's small rooms to the palatial height of the new great State Apartments. The palm-tree motif also persists throughout the Pavilion, in the design of the columns in the window-bays of the drawing-rooms, sometimes naturalistic, sometimes formalized. Even the cast-iron columns of the Great Kitchen become palm trees with fronds of sheet copper at the summit. And cast-iron is the stuff of the imitation bamboo staircases, exquisitely

gay and light. The cast-iron of Functionalism underlies the fantasy of Romanticism, and makes the Pavilion doubly a monument of its age. Cast-iron forms the framework of the domes, and the tubular, bolted cores of the towering chimneys, minarets and pinnacles. With its long, reposeful, harmonious proportions, its classical symmetry, for all its oriental character, and the subordination of the small details to the main masses of the building, and in the graceful curves of dome and arch, the Pavilion embodies some of Nash's most brilliant work, and has been invested by him with more poetic beauty than any other of his designs.

Later Regency houses and terraces

The principal factor which determined the character of the later Regency houses and terraces was the increased permeation of domestic architecture by the Greek Revival. It was a style having qualities of simplicity and sincerity that made it adaptable to the smallest private buildings, and provided inspiration for multitudes of villas and smaller town houses, from the Grecian villas of Regent's Park to those of Pittville Spa at Cheltenham.

The excitement of a mounting tide of victory in the wars against Napoleon and the sense of the beginning of a new historical epoch when George, Prince of Wales, was proclaimed Regent in 1811, found expression in the gigantic programme of public works carried out in London – the Metropolitan Improvements – between 1812 and 1828, the purpose of which was to provide much needed new housing in the north of London beyond what became Oxford Street, and to link this district by broad processional streets in place of squalid, mean alleys to the centre of government in Whitehall, and a great new Royal Palace to be built near St James's Park. It was a gigantic enterprise, which provided a city that had become the capital of Europe with many of the great monuments and landmarks that are the glory of London.

The scheme began in 1812 with the transformation of Marylebone Park from a tract of marshy farmland, with 'paltry cabins and monotonous cow-lairs' into a landscaped park with lakes, islands, villas and with the long ranges of palatial terraces that are its great glory. The designer was John Nash, who had been appointed as an architect to the Commissioners of Woods and Forests in 1806. On the death of Wyatt in 1813 Nash was given his place as Surveyor-General, though he had to share the post with Sir John Soane and Sir Robert Smirke. However, Nash was henceforth responsible for most of the Royal building programmes.

The planning of the terraces was based upon the principle of designing a row of houses to form a single magnificent palatial unit, usually with a central pedimented portico and flanking pavilions on the Palladian model. It was the principle, giving dignity and scale to a town area, that was first used in Grosvenor Square, London, by Edward Stephen in 1727, and which had inspired the Woods of Bath in the planning of their great unified street and square compositions.

In many of the terraces, so as not to mar the broad unity of design by a row of separate front-doors, the main entrances to the houses were at the back of the terrace. Further behind were stables and mews and rows of lesser houses, for tradesmen and artisans, devoid of ornament but nevertheless designed with seemliness and good proportions.

The terraces are not all of the same order of magnificence, and vary also in quality of design and execution. Nash's genius was for the dramatic, spectacular and picturesque in architecture and planning, but this gift was combined with impatience over detail, which caused him to be criticised for 'carelessness, sometimes degenerating to littleness, with a deficiency of elegance in the details' by James Elmes, who described the great schemes of the time in his volume on the *Metropolitan Improvements* in 1828.

The two chief entrances to the Park are on the south, and consist of two fine compositions: York Gate with Philip Hardwick's Church of St Mary-le-bone facing the Park between the two halves of York Terrace, and the entrance from Portland Place through the two curving wings of Park Crescent, with its beautiful ranges of coupled Ionic columns.

York Terrace (1822) stretching in two sections across York Gate is one of the most magnificent of the larger groups, having as Elmes said 'the semblance of the residence of a sovereign prince'. Like many of the Park compositions, the terrace is Palladian in conception, but with Grecian detail. Although on a smaller scale, Cornwall Terrace (1821), the first of the terraces to be built, has the richness of the Corinthian order, and is prettily detailed. Clarence Terrace (1823) is probably due to Decimus Burton. Sussex Place (1822), designed by Nash with ten melon-shaped cupolas, was condemned by contemporary critics, but is an exhilarating design, with the grand sweep of the two curving wings. Hanover Terrace (1822–3) is again on a splendid scale, but was regarded as 'more grammatical' in its rather dry Doric manner. Northernmost on the eastern side is Gloucester Gate, one of the most elegant of the terraces, with an Ionic façade, begun in 1827. Cumberland Terrace (1827) is the stupendous centre-piece of the great architectural panorama of the Park (Pl. 14B). The immense block of the central portico is crowned by a pediment containing a group of terracotta figures by J. B. Bubb, representing Britannia attended by the arts and sciences. On either side range the deeply recessed wings of the main building, with gigantic porticoes linked to those of further separate wings by triumphal arches leading into courtyards where cobbled ramps lead down to stables. The order is Ionic, and the balustrades and pediment carry statues. This brilliantly composed piece of dramatic scenery must be reckoned Nash's finest single classical work. The grandeur of Cumberland Terrace was difficult to challenge, but Chester Terrace (1825) next to it achieves its effect of splendour by the original device of triumphal arches forming the entrances at either end of the long façade.

Of the twenty-six villas originally intended, eight were built, so as not to spoil the rural character of the Park. Several, such as Hanover Lodge, St John's Lodge (now the Institute of Archæology), and Lord Hertford's Villa (now the American Ambassador's house) have been much rebuilt. The Doric Villa near York Terrace is severely Grecian. The Holme (1818), now part of Bedford

College for Women, was designed by Burton for his father, and is the prettiest villa in the Park, containing one of the most enchanting Regency rooms in existence (Pl. 12B). Behind the grand terraces are a number of smaller terraces of stucco designed with great simplicity, such as Munster Square (once York Square) built in the late 1820's, as houses for the lower clerical and artisan classes. Provision was made for middle-class families in a kind of garden suburb, Park Village East and Park Village West, which Nash conceived as a picturesque village similar to Blaise Hamlet, but the building was carried out by other architects. The delightful little houses display all the familiar devices of Picturesque Regency domestic architecture, fretted eaves-boards, trellised verandas, and canopied balconies. The Tower House in Park Village West is the most striking, with its charming octagonal tower and sculptured panel, a domesticated version of the familiar Temple of the Winds from Athens (Pl. 15A).

The new street leading to the West End was linked to the Park by Portland Place at York Gate, where Nash 'joined his bold style to the finicking finish of the Messrs Adams with good effect'. Of Regent Street itself nothing remains of Nash's except its noble sweeping curves, which, alas! no longer open up successive vistas of its varied original buildings, but only the drab façades which replaced Nash's work when it was demolished in 1922. Carlton House, which Holland had built for King George IV when Prince of Wales in 1783, was found to be in need of repair and was demolished in 1827. At the same time St James's Park, which had become a muddy swamp since its hey-day in the time of Charles II, was laid out by Nash as a landscaped park, much as it is to-day. Buckingham Palace was begun in 1825, but it was the least successful work of the ageing and heavily pressed architect. The death of the King in 1830 prevented its completion by Nash, who thus lost the baronetcy that was to have been his reward. It was finished in 1831–7 by Sir Edward Blore, but the present familiar east front was built in 1913 by Sir Aston Webb. Where Carlton House had stood the Duke of York's Steps were built to form an opening into the Mall, flanked on either side by the two massive ranges of Carlton House Terrace which make the broad avenue leading to Buckingham Palace one of the grandest processional ways in Europe.

A pupil of Soane, Sir Robert Smirke (1781–1867), whose Covent Garden Theatre of 1809 was the first Grecian building in London, designed one of the noblest works of the Metropolitan Improvements, the British Museum (1823–47), the dramatic Ionic colonnades of which have little of his usual pedantic dulness. It is doubly a monument of the Regency, since the eastern wing was built to house the King's Library, the collection of books once possessed by his father, that was given to the nation in 1821 by King George IV. William Wilkins (1751–1815), whose new buildings at Downing College, Cambridge (1807–20) * were the first major work of the Greek Revival, gave University College, London (1827–8) * what Professor Sir Albert Richardson has called the 'finest classic portico in England'. The National Gallery * was built (1832–8) on the site of William Kent's old Royal Mews, to house Julius Angerstein's great collection of paintings, which had been bought for the nation at the King's suggestion. Here, again, Wilkins created a magnificent portico, with an impressive arrangement of steps, using the entrance columns from Carlton House. In sentiment, and historically, no other use could have been more fitting. At Hyde Park Corner St George's Hospital (1827–8), designed by Wilkins, gives stolid support to two much-loved works nearby, the Ionic Screen and the Triumphal Arch at the top of Constitution Hill, both designed by Decimus Burton. Burton's greatest work was his superb contribution to the great club-building movement of the Regency, which came into being through the growth of the professional and learned classes. His Athenæum Club (1829–30) in Waterloo Place consists of a single block, of such eminently satisfying proportions that even the later addition of an attic did not spoil it. In deference to the Roman character of Nash's United Services Club opposite (now much rebuilt), Burton adopted the Roman Doric order for the coupled columns of the beautiful porch, which is surmounted by a gilded statue of

Pallas Athenae. This delightful adornment, and the sculptured frieze of the Pan-Athenaic procession, relieve the simple façade. In his massive treatment of buildings Burton seems to have absorbed some influence from Smirke, but in the Italian trend of his detail, as in such features as his deep cornices with console supports, he anticipates here the Italian phase of the years following the Regency era which was established by Sir Charles Barry.

Edinburgh

In Edinburgh, the 'Modern Athens', the Greek Revival established itself naturally where great works by Robert Adam and Sir William Chambers and others had been fostered by the classical trend of the city's culture during the later years of the previous century. With the ending of the Napoleonic struggle the building of the New Town was resumed, and a group of Scottish architects of great distinction came into prominence. Their work, however, took on some of the grimness of the Scottish stone even when the northern gravity of mind did not overwhelm the Regency sense of gaiety and elegance.

Archibald Elliott (1764–1823) carried out one of the earlier works of this phase, Waterloo Place, Edinburgh, begun in 1815. Eastwards, the vista of Waterloo Place is filled by the Acropolis-like eminence of Calton Hill, where it was intended should stand monuments to Scotland's greatness in war and in the arts, but the site was only a visual and not an organic social focus, and as interest waned, the erection of the buildings was delayed, curtailed, and eventually abandoned. But the unfinished portico of the National Monument (1812), which was designed by W. H. Playfair (1789–1857) with C. R. Cockerell, has a dramatic stark dignity that makes it a not unworthy memorial.

Playfair's plans of 1819 to re-organize the schemes for developing the New Town of Calton Hill resulted in little more than the building of one vast block, Royal Terrace, consisting of a single façade nearly a quarter-mile long. Regent Terrace, south of the hill, is less overwhelming, but St Bernard's Crescent, built in 1828 on land be-longing to Sir Henry Raeburn, across the Water of Leith, plumbs the depths of portentous gloom. Playfair built also, in 1823, the severely plain Royal Circus. But in Ann Street, also on Raeburn's land, the houses are fronted by gardens and have intimate charm. Less scholarly, but dignified and pleasing in the Tuscan order, are Moray Place and Albyn Place, laid out in 1822 by James Gillespie Graham.

Brighton

The splendour and success of Nash's dazzling town-planning schemes in the Metropolis inspired great landowners, like Thomas Read Kemp in Brighton, and Pearson Thompson and Joseph Pitt in Cheltenham, to promote large speculative estate developments that would transform their towns with a similar grandeur.

In Brighton hitherto building had been on the modest domestic scale of the early Regency terraces and small squares like Regency Square. This was designed by the architect Amon Wilds, probably in conjunction with his son Amon Henry Wilds. From 1821 onwards they carried out extensive work with the architect Busby. These three men, frequently in partnership, but sometimes also separately, were to be responsible for the creation of the greater part of the squares, crescents and terraces of Regency Brighton.

Charles Augustus Busby was born in 1788. He studied at the Royal Academy and published two books of designs, *A series of designs for villas and country houses*, etc., 1808, and *A collection of designs for modern embellishments*, etc., c. 1810. This last included cast-iron balcony railings, and he is believed to have been responsible for designing most of the ironwork around Euston Square.

The first of the great Brighton architectural groups was Kemp Town in East Brighton, named after the landowner, who was M.P. for Brighton and Lewes. With Busby as architect, work began in 1823. The scale of Kemp's project was monumental, and although only half the number of houses originally intended were built, it is only exceeded in magnitude by Nash's scheme of

Regent's Park, and unlike this, which is broken up into separate units, Kemp Town is a single, immense closely-knit entity. It consists of Sussex Square opening on its seaward south side into the great sweep of Lewes Crescent with a span of 840 feet, 200 feet wider than the Royal Crescent at Bath. The Crescent is then flanked upon the sea-front by two great terraces, Chichester and Arundel Terrace. Despite sometimes ungainly modern additions, the whole architectural composition retains the impressiveness and beauty that are given by the lovely sweep of Lewes Crescent and the array of painted stucco fronts, shining in the brilliance of sea-coast sunshine against the background of deep blue sky.

From Kemp Town to Royal Crescent range the long groups of the stately terraces and smaller groups of enchantingly varied Regency styles that help to make the Brighton sea-front one of the most impressive in the world.

The second of the great monumental architectural compositions that distinguish the sea-front of Brighton and Hove is Brunswick Square and Terrace (Pl. 17A), built from 1825 to 1828 by the Wilds-Busby partnership. Although the square is smaller than Sussex Square, the architectural detail is more pronounced, and the two great flanking ranges of Brunswick Terrace are of impressive magnificence (Pl. 16A).

The third great architectural unit, which gives the western end of the sea-front such superb richness, is Adelaide Crescent, begun in 1830 but not finished till 1850. The architect was Decimus Burton, who was then working with his father, James Burton, upon the development of St Leonards-on-Sea. Only ten houses were built to Burton's design, but the Crescent retains the glorious double curve which gives it an extreme elegance and grace of line (Pl. 16B).

Right up to the opening of the Victorian period innumerable squares, terraces and streets of houses were built in Brighton, mostly by Busby and the Wilds, working either jointly or independently. They embody a multitude of delightful combinations of Regency features, and make that town one of the most fascinating architectural centres in the whole country.

Cheltenham

The combination of landlord and architect that had been so fruitful at Kemp Town, Brighton, was to bring about no less interesting developments of later Regency architecture at Cheltenham. These have for long been, and always will be, indissolubly associated with the name of Papworth, but as Bryan Little has revealed, the influence of this most interesting architect upon Cheltenham is due less to the few buildings which it is certain he designed than to 'the ideas ... the philosophy, of development and town planning' that he inspired and which were carried into monumental effect not only by himself, but by other designers and builders who worked upon these lines.

John Buonarotti Papworth (1775–1847) had been trained in the office of William Plaw, the famous designer of picturesque cottages and farm-buildings. It was no doubt this experience that laid the foundation of his *Rural Residences* published in 1818. At Cheltenham Papworth was commissioned in 1825 to carry out developments upon the Montpellier and Lansdowne Estates, which belonged to the landowner Pearson Thompson.

The central improvement was the redesigning with a domed Rotunda of the Montpellier Pump Room, a charming early work (1817) of the local architect John Forbes. Although the banking crisis of 1825 prevented Thompson's magnificent ideas from being fully realized, the schemes that Papworth devised may very well have inspired the excellent work that was eventually carried out by others, especially the local architects R. W. and C. Jearrad. Outstanding among these works are Lansdowne Terrace and Crescent, built about 1828. The first is a noble composition in stone with elaborate pedimented porticos of coupled Ionic columns framing the first floor windows. The other is a restrained facade in plain stucco on a long graceful curve broken by simple projecting Doric porches. Each admirably expresses the character and proper potentialities of its own material.

It is perhaps in the villas of Bayshill Road that it is most difficult to deny the hand of Papworth, and one of them corresponds closely to a design he made of 'Montpellier Lodge' for Pearson Thompson himself. Each embodying some variation on the Grecian theme, all of considerable graciousness and beauty, these houses stand with those of Regent's Park in representing the Regency villa of the Greek Revival at the summit of its development.

At Pittville, Cheltenham, Joseph Pitt, a wealthy banker, aimed at an architectural and picturesque garden lay-out as the setting for a grand Pump Room surrounded by squares, terraces and villas. Pitt's architect was John Forbes, who created what was not only one of the grandest Assembly Rooms in the Kingdom, but one of the most beautiful monuments of the Greek Revival. The interior of the Pittville Pump Room has something of the splendour of one of Adam's great halls, but possesses the restraint in ornamentation and the subtlety in the handling of interior space that had been learned from Holland and Soane. Although the assemblies of the Regency were never held in a lovelier room, the Pittville Spa was just too far from the centre of the town to become part of its organic life. Mercifully it has been preserved, though its fate until recently was in the balance.

Around the Spa lie the Grecian villas of Pittville, smaller in scale than those of Bayshill Road, and less formal in their picturesque modelling. Arundel Lodge is the most individual of these. Thirlstaine House (1823), now one of the buildings of Cheltenham College, was one of the earliest and most accomplished manifestations in the provinces of the Grecian movement. It was almost certainly designed by the owner himself, J. R. Scott, a friend of Wilkins, Smirke and W. H. Inwood. The Entrance Hall has great dignity and serenity, modelled, as Bryan Little has perceived, upon the Great Hall at Kedleston, and containing twelve Ionic columns deriving from the Temple of Dionysos at Teos.

Other provincial towns

Other notable examples of later Regency terraces are Pelham Crescent, Hastings, flanking the astonishing circular Regency church of St Mary in the Castle; Camden Crescent at Bath; Wellington Crescent, Ramsgate (1819–24), with its long Doric colonnade, and Spencer Square (1820), retaining the severer early tradition; and one of the most Nash-like of the provincial terraces, the delightful Crescent at Alverstoke, c. 1826.

At Tunbridge Wells Decimus Burton emulated the Regent's Park development by laying out the Calverley Estate on Mount Pleasant (1828–52). The Crescent has a severe classical elegance, but in the villas of the Park the ponderousness of Burton's Italianate manner is emphasized by the grey local stone.

The years following Waterloo saw accelerated progress in the development of great estates in London, chiefly through the immense undertakings of the great firm of Thomas Cubitt and his brothers, who introduced more highly organized methods of work into the building industry, and brought new standards of quality into material and construction. Their undertakings were scattered all over the metropolis, and later extended to provincial towns such as Brighton, where the firm completed the Kemp Town development, and Thomas Cubitt himself had a house. Polesden Lacey * near Dorking was rebuilt by him in 1824 and though altered since then retains its original beautiful Ionic colonnade.

In Tavistock and Gordon Squares the Cubitts built delightful houses of semi-Grecian design, linked by low screen walls. In Woburn Place this restrained treatment gave place to the use of the richer Roman orders for the columned façades. Their greatest enterprises in London, however, were the developments of Belgravia and Pimlico from about 1824 onwards, following the improvement in the character of the district caused by the building of Buckingham Palace.

The architect George Basevi (1794–1845) designed the houses of Belgrave Square (Pl. 19A), except for the large separate mansions at the corners. Basevi gave the main blocks of the square a palatial treatment of sumptuous richness presaging the ultimate floridity of classicism that was to appear later at the Fitzwilliam Museum, Cambridge. In 1829 Basevi became architect to the

Fig. 5. Eastnor Castle, Herefordshire, by Sir Robert Smirke, 1810–15. From *Jones' Views of the Seats of Noblemen and Gentlemen in England, etc.*, 1829.

A monumental example of Smirke's 'square' style.

Smith's Charity Estate and that of Mr Alexander adjoining, in South Kensington. Here he designed Alexander Place in the charming and simple early tradition, and Pelham Crescent which has a more sophisticated elegance (Pl. 17B).

In the final phases of Regency town house design there was a new reaching out on the part of architects like George Stanley Repton, once Nash's assistant, towards the regularity and re-straint of the Palladian, possibly in reaction from the more absurd excesses of the Grecian and Pic-turesque. Through this impulse a number of ter-races were built in London, Brighton and else-where from the late 1820's and into the 1840's, of severely classical character with porches of simple square columns, windows with moulded architraves surmounted by the segmental and tri-angular pediments that derive from Palladio and

Inigo Jones, and flat, reticent façades with scrolled modillion cornices. But the instinct for the Pic-turesque had developed too strongly to be sup-pressed by this puritanical classicism, and the Italian characteristics displayed in so many villas of the time, like those designed by Decimus Burton at Tunbridge Wells, and even in his more formal Athenæum Club and his Hyde Park Lodges, became increasingly cultivated until the style at-tained full stature in the design of the Travellers' Club by Sir Charles Barry in 1829, and the Italian villa built by him at Queen's Park, Brighton in the same year. It was this kind of plain square house, with broad eaves and sometimes round-arched windows, somewhat simplified in the smaller ex-amples, which became one of the standard types of English house from the end of the Regency right through the Victorian period (Pl. 15B).

Fig. 6. Lowther Castle, Westmorland, by Sir Robert Smirke, 1806–11. From *Jones' Views of the Seats of Noblemen and Gentlemen in England, etc.*, 1829

Smirke's medieval romanticism.

Regency medievalism

The romantic antiquarian nostalgia which had been fed by James Wyatt's graceful and refined Gothic creations such as Lee Priory in the later years of the eighteenth century had grown by the Regency to a thirst for more elaborate medieval pageantry. Wyatt's overwhelming fantasy of Fonthill, built for William Beckford, collapsed just before the opening of our period, in 1807.

Wyatt's Gothic designs for Plas Newydd, Anglesey, were not completed till 1826, long after his death, by his pupil Joseph Potter. Some of the original Gothic detail has been lost, and the house has reverted partly to the classical character of the 1790's that it already possessed in the Staircase Hall, the Drawing-room, Dining-room and Library, but the Gothic remains in the Entrance

Front, charmingly fenestrated with large windows containing Wyatt's pleasant geometrical tracery. The Entrance Vestibule and Hall are also Gothic, with simple, graceful vaulting. The whole house breathes the unpretentious elegance and fine proportions that distinguish Wyatt's work, heightened by the dramatic beauty of the house's setting upon a wooded slope above the Menai Straits.

Like Wyatt, the other principal practitioners of Regency Gothic, William Wilkins and Sir Robert Smirke, were equally adept in the Grecian mode. The Battle of the Styles, which was waged with such bitterness in the field of religious and public architecture after the close of the Regency period, resulting eventually in the victory of the Gothic on moralist grounds, seemed in the realm of domestic architecture to become instead a gay, unwarlike pageant in which the contestants cheerfully mingled, and donned each others' clothes.

The 'square style' of Smirke's Grecian Doric was not required to change its nature for his Gothic Eastnor Castle, Herefordshire,* which has a central block rising out of the main rectangular mass (Fig. 5). The Gothic rooms are sombre, but there is a pleasant classical Octagon saloon. Lowther Castle, Westmorland (1806–11) (Fig. 6), is of similar design, but survives today only as a picturesque, empty shell. Panshanger, Hertfordshire (1806–22), for all its Grecian interior, was built on the rambling unsymmetrical lay-out of the medieval house. Its architect, William Atkinson (1776–1839), a pupil of James Wyatt, designed Thomas Hope's museum of frigid archæological eclecticism at Deepdene, Surrey (1806–22), and a house that is more truly a monument of Regency romanticism, Abbotsford, Roxburghshire (1822–3),* the home of Sir Walter Scott.

Eaton Hall, Cheshire (1804–12), was built by William Porden, architect of the Prince Regent's Royal Stables (The Dome) at Brighton. Some of his drawings for the rooms at Eaton remain at the Royal Pavilion. With its innumerable crocketed pinnacles and towers in 'Cathedral Gothic', the mounting ranges of terraced buildings, and the richly fan-vaulted ceilings of its rooms, it exceeded Fonthill in romanticism, and in its construction, including window-tracery of cast iron, surpassed Beckford's folly in durability. Eaton survives as a school, but was much altered in the 1870's by Waterhouse.

Arundel Castle, Sussex,* the home of the Earl Marshal of England, possesses as well as its truly Norman Keep and Barbican, and its convincing medieval stone scenery of the late nineteenth and early twentieth centuries, a 'Baron's Hall' remodelled in 1806 by J. Teasdale, and a Gothic Library also rebuilt in the Regency period.

The Regency castellated tradition attained its overwhelming climax at the end of the period in Penrhyn Castle, Caernarvonshire,* designed in 1827 by Thomas Hopper (1776–1856), who built the famous cast-iron Gothic conservatory at Carlton House for the Prince of Wales in 1807.

The Great Keep has the severe Norman dignity of Castle Hedingham in Norfolk, from which it is copied. The round tower at the angle is reminiscent of Downton, but there is great character and beauty in the design of the round-headed windows. The interior carries the Romanesque style to a development never attained in the Norman era. The complexity and elaboration of the deeply cut mouldings of round arches, and heavy ribs of groined vaults, the small patterning of arcading round the gallery of the Great Hall, the writhing, interlaced ornament of the flat library ceiling, constitute as it were a 'rococo' phase of the Norman style far exceeding in exaggerated invention the mature richness of the Romanesque in the west towers of Ely, or the delicate fancy of the Galilee chapel at Durham.

As a background for the sophisticated life of nineteenth-century people, with their highly civilized and delicate clothes, manners and furnishings, this staggering phantasmagoria of Romanesque forms is incongruous, but it is redeemed as a successful artistic creation by the overwhelming vitality and robustness with which it has been carried out. It has its significance if only in expressing the overpowering force of the Romantic imagination in the Regency age.

Four great establishments

The height of magnificence in Regency exoticism was reached in the Royal Pavilion at Brighton (Pl. 19B). The culmination of splendour in the classical style of the period may be studied in such great palatial establishments as Belvoir Castle, Windsor Castle, Apsley House and Londonderry House.

Belvoir Castle, Leicestershire,* is the fourth to occupy the site since its founding soon after the Norman conquest. Its present form is due partly to James Wyatt, who began rebuilding in 1800, and to the Rev. Sir John Thoroton, chaplain and friend of the 5th Duke of Rutland, and an amateur of architecture, who carried out his own designs after a fire in 1816. Wyatt had died in 1813. Towering high upon a wooded hill, Belvoir is one of the most beautifully and romantically sited of all castles. The south-eastern and south-western ranges are the surviving work of James Wyatt. The northern and eastern ranges are Thoroton's (Pl. 18A). His interior work is derived from Early English details at Lincoln Cathedral, and is in severer mood than Wyatt's more poetic interpretation of Gothic. The decorative work of the magnificent State Apartments was mostly designed by James Wyatt's own sons, Benjamin Dean Wyatt and Matthew Cotes Wyatt the sculptor. The most splendid room is the Elizabeth Saloon (Pl. 18B), so named after the 5th Duchess, herself a connoisseur of architecture, who decreed the adoption of the Louis xv style by having panelling brought from a French château of the period. The decoration of the ceiling, painted by Matthew Cotes Wyatt, makes the room one of the most sumptuous in the whole of the country, and displays for the first time that florid exuberance that is to be seen later at Apsley House, York House (now Lancaster House), and Londonderry House, all of which are Benjamin Wyatt's work. It is a manner representing the final opulence of the Regency outlook and is, as Summerson shows, the origin of that revival of French eighteenth-century decorative design that persisted throughout the nineteenth century and into the years of the Edwardian reign in the more lavish interiors of London.

Windsor Castle,* despite improvements in the direction of greater domestic convenience carried out by King George III, was at the opening of our period little more than a primitive, comfortless and straggling ruin. Transformed by Sir Jeffrey Wyatville (1766–1840) for his master King George IV, Windsor today is one of the most glorious monuments of the Regency age, a building nobly composed, with a skyline perhaps the most famous in the world, a symbol of the medieval romanticism that was among the invigorating influences of the period, and a palace worthy of the ancient lineage of our sovereigns. Under the direction of Wyatville the Castle was given unity and coherence of design. The principal improvements were the raising of the Round Tower by doubling its height, adding variety and interest to the skyline by the addition of lesser towers, and the construction of a broad corridor

of two storeys round the inner side of the Quadrangle. By this means separate access was created to a large number of private rooms which previously could only be entered by passing successively through each. More than the building was transformed by the work. The architect was born Jeffrey Wyatt, but adopted his new name, more in keeping with the medieval atmosphere of the Castle, upon the laying of the foundation stone of the new King George IV Gate in 1824. He was knighted at the completion of the Royal quarters in 1828.

The Grand Reception Room, originally the King's Guard Chamber, was decorated for King George IV in the French taste of Louis xv, but with gilt ornament surpassing that of Belvoir in liveliness and delicacy. Wyatville gave St Stephen's Hall its present character, with a flat-arched timber-panelled ceiling of Tudor design. The most notable Regency apartment of the Castle is the Waterloo Chamber. This was built within an open space called Horn Court to contain the magnificent series of portraits which King George IV commissioned Sir Thomas Lawrence to paint of the sovereigns and leaders of the European nations which had been united with England against Napoleon. It is here that State Banquets are held in commemoration of the Battle of Waterloo.

Londonderry House, Park Lane, London (1825), represents consistently throughout its interior Benjamin Wyatt's sumptuously ornate mode of late Regency classicism, the Banqueting Room being an exceptionally fine example of his revival of the rococo manner. The Grand Staircase and Ballroom are richly palatial, the latter reminiscent of the Gallery at Belvoir, their magnificent coved ceilings coffered with rosettes, the friezes and pilasters of extreme florid splendour.

Apsley House, Piccadilly,* once the residence of the 1st Duke of Wellington, together with the magnificent collections it contains of paintings, silver, porcelain, furniture and other works of art, has been presented to the nation by the present Duke. As the Wellington Museum, administered by the Victoria and Albert Museum, it forms a national memorial to the life, achievements and taste in the arts of the Iron Duke, conqueror of

Napoleon. The house, originally built in the 1770's by Robert Adam for Lord Bathurst, was given its present Grecian exterior of Bath stone with a Corinthian portico when remodelled by Benjamin Wyatt in 1828–9 for the 1st Duke. Although the external appearance is severely plain and even pedestrian, the interior has an atmosphere of light, dignity and spaciousness. Adam's decoration of the 1770's survives in the Green Portico Room, and the delightful Piccadilly Drawing-room with its characteristic half-domed apse and barrel-vaulted ceiling. The striped Drawing-room and the Dining-room are of Regency character, with coved ceilings, that of the latter with a fine palmette frieze. Overlooking Hyde Park from the Western side of the house is the great Waterloo Chamber, which is rivalled in magnificence only by John Nash's State Apart-

ments at Buckingham Palace, and in which Benjamin Wyatt displays his re-interpretation of the Louis xv style in its finest form (Pl. 20). It is in such monumental interiors that the decorative art of the Regency period attained its zenith of·richness at its moment of historical triumph.

SHORT BIBLIOGRAPHY

John Summerson, *Architecture in Britain, 1530–1830*, Penguin History of Art, 1953.

John Summerson, *Georgian London*, 1945; *John Nash*, 1949.

Christopher Hussey, *English Country Houses*, Vol. 3, *Late Georgian*.

Donald Pilcher, *The Regency Style*, 1947.

H. M. Colvin, *Biographical Dictionary of English Architects*, 1954.

Bryan Little, *Cheltenham*, 1951.

Typographical borders from the 1821 Specimen Book of Vincent Figgins. These neo-classical motifs are similar to those found in friezes of classical Regency buildings and derive from the same sources. The anthemion (honeysuckle) motif occurs in the first two.

Furniture

E. T. JOY

The furniture of any given period is a reflection of what Horace Walpole called 'the history of the manners of the age', and this is particularly true of the two decades 1810–30 which saw the important social and economic changes occasioned by the upheaval of the long wars with France (1793–1815) and the increasing tempo of industrialization. The wars had 'doubled the cost and trebled the difficulty of genteel living',[1] with the result that the long and salutary domination of good taste in furniture by the upper classes was now drawing to a close. Their place was gradually being taken by the new middle classes, who owed their wealth and position to industry; they lacked the high standards, based on many generations of classical learning, of their predecessors, and they sought fresh styles in the belief that experience and knowledge were no longer necessary to judge decorative forms. Thus the Regency period (which in furniture overlapped the nine years – 1811–20 – when the Prince of Wales was Regent) saw the last phase of the classical development in furniture design which had begun in the seventeenth century. The transition to new forms was made easier through the gradual abandonment of traditional decorative methods like carving and inlay, and through the growing influence of machinery on furniture-making. Wood-working machines, able to carry out almost all the processes which are known today, had been patented by Sir Samuel Bentham between 1791 and 1793, and already in 1807 Thomas Hope in his *Household Furniture* was

warning his readers against the debasement of furniture design 'through the entire substitution of machinery to manual labour'.

It was symptomatic of the changing ideas of the time that much of the formal grace which had distinguished the interiors of great houses in the eighteenth century was disappearing. Louis Simond, visiting Osterley House in 1811, wrote that 'Tables, sofas and chairs were studiously *dérangés* about the fire places, and in the middle of the rooms, as if the family had just left them ... Such is the modern fashion of placing furniture, carried to an extreme ... that the apartments of a fashionable house look like an upholsterer's or cabinet-maker's shop.'[2]

The best furniture of the period was still, of course, of a high standard in both design and workmanship, and it should always be related to its setting, which conformed to a carefully-thought-out scheme of decoration. But while this is true of the finest pieces, in others the deterioration in standards is all too evident, heralding the decline of the early Victorian era.

The Regency Style

In general terms the Regency style in furniture may be described as a close reproduction or adaptation, carried out in a strong antiquarian spirit, of Græco-Roman types of furniture and forms of decoration. It was inspired by (but was not a close version of) the contemporary French Directoire and Empire styles, and for that reason was for long

[1] *The Lady's Keepsake and Maternal Monitor*, 1835.

[2] L. Simond, *Journal of a Tour and Residence in Great Britain 1810–11*. (1817).

known as 'English Empire'. In view of the war period it may seem surprising that English designers should have been influenced by artistic movements in France. This, however, is to look at wars through modern spectacles. France had been too long the arbiter of Europe's taste for war to destroy her prestige, and in any case the connexion of ideas was maintained through the many French craftsmen who took refuge in England from the revolution in their own country. When peace came in 1815 an English writer acknowledged the relationship in these words: 'The interchange of feeling between this country and France, as it relates to matters of taste, has not been wholly suspended during the long and awful conflicts which have so greatly abridged the intercourse of the two nations, and as usual the taste of both has been improved.'[3]

The chief spokesmen for the style in France were Charles Percier and Pierre Fontaine, whose *Recueil de Décorations Intérieures*, 1812, coinciding with Napoleon's widespread conquests, had a great influence throughout Europe. They regarded the study of the decoration of antiquity, with its 'simple lines, pure contours and correct forms', as the most fruitful source of inspiration for architects, designers and craftsmen, whose work, they considered, had an essential unity. 'Furniture', they wrote, 'is too closely allied to interior decoration for the architect to remain indifferent to it. Decoration separated from construction will lead to all sorts of absurdities and misinterpretations.' They were at pains, however, to warn against too slavish an imitation of the models of antiquity; these should be 'followed, not blindly, but with the discernment allowed by modern manners, customs and materials'. Such, then, were to be the principles to be observed: inspiration and admiration tempered with discrimination; the avoidance of mere imitation; the unity of all forms of decoration; and due acknowledgement of modern processes and habits.

In this country the origins of the Regency style in furniture can be clearly seen at the end of the eighteenth century in the work of the talented architect and designer, Henry Holland (1745–1806).

[3] R. Ackermann, *The Repository of the Arts*, Feb. 1815.

With delicacy and a sure touch, he adapted ancient forms into a unified system of decoration without losing the spirit of antiquity or falling into the error of copying contemporary French work. The furniture which he designed for the Prince of Wales at Carlton House (1784) and for Samuel Whitbread at Southill (1795) established his reputation and encouraged imitation. The new style is foreshadowed in Sheraton's *Drawing Book*, 1791–4, and *Cabinet Dictionary*, 1803. But after Holland's death in 1806 the designing of furniture was soon to become an antiquarian pursuit, missing the spirit of antiquity, and seeking to reproduce the actual forms of ancient furniture.

Holland's immediate successor in the field of furniture design was Thomas Hope (1768–1831), whose *Household Furniture and Interior Decoration* was published in 1807. Hope, a man of wide interests and sound scholarship, had been trained as an architect and had travelled extensively throughout the eastern Mediterranean, where he had spent some eight years studying architectural remains. He was a friend of Percier and an admirer of his work. With this background Hope aimed to give the public a range of furniture designs which would 'cultivate a new description of art, so urgently wanted and hitherto so rarely possessed'. At Deepdene, his house in Surrey, furniture of his own design had been made for the rooms where he kept his collection of antiquities, 'forming', he wrote, 'the entire assemblage of productions of ancient art and modern handicraft, thus intermixed, into a more harmonious, more consistent and more instructive whole'.

These words echoed the sentiments of Percier and Fontaine, but it was too much to expect Hope's and Holland's scholarly approach to be shared or understood by the many craftsmen and designers who now took up the new mode wholeheartedly. Hope was well aware of the dangers of imitation, for he could already see them at work: 'extravagant caricatures, such as of late have begun to start up in every corner of the capital, seem calculated for the sole purpose of bringing this new style into disrepute'.

The main features of Regency classical furniture were extreme simplicity of outline, large uninterrupted surfaces emphasizing horizontal and vertical lines, subordination of ornament to a minor role, and a stress on solidity – characteristics which Brown summarized in 1820 as 'bold in outline, rich and chaste in the ornaments, and durable from the rejection of little parts'. The favourite methods of decoration were metal inlay and reeding. At first Greek, Roman and Egyptian antiquities were the models, but as time went on 'Grecian severity' became the rule. Interest in Greece was intensified when the Parthenon sculptures were bought by public subscription in 1816, and when the Greeks revolted against the Turks in 1821. Wherever possible, from vase-paintings and similar sources classical Greek furniture was copied, as in the fashionable Grecian sofa and chair; when this could not be done, antique forms were adapted to modern usage. Simple straight lines and bold curves marked this quest for severity. 'Grecian' now became a much-favoured word among furniture craftsmen and designers; and in 1836 Loudon's *Encyclopædia* could still describe the 'Grecian or modern style' as 'by far the most prevalent'.[4]

The design books

As in the eighteenth century, the current furniture trends were set out in several design books intended for the trade and the general reader. George Smith's *A Collection of Designs for Household Furniture and Interior Decoration* appeared in 1808 and popularized the new style. Smith was a cabinetmaker who described himself as 'Upholsterer Extraordinary to His Royal Highness The Prince of Wales', and his book contained 158 plates in colour 'studied from the best antique examples of the Egyptian, Greek and Roman styles' with some Gothic and Chinese designs added. Many of the plates showed a somewhat extravagant treatment of the new fashions. In 1820 Richard Brown published *The Rudiments of Drawing Cabinet and Upholstery Furniture*, which had a second and revised edition in 1822. He claimed to be giving craftsmen not only designs for furniture but also the principles which lay behind them (which, he said, the

'trivial compositions' of men like Chippendale and Sheraton had omitted to do). His book was a version of the designs of Hope, Percier and Smith, to whom he paid full acknowledgement. In 1826 many coloured designs, with much Greek detail, appeared in *The Practical Cabinet Maker, Upholsterer and Complete Decorator* by Peter and Michael Angelo Nicholson. In the same year George Smith, now styling himself 'Upholsterer and Furniture Draughtsman to His Majesty', issued *The Cabinet Maker's and Upholsterer's Guide, Drawing Book and Repository*. He stressed the 'perfection of Greek ornament', but included plates of Egyptian, Etruscan, Roman, Gothic and French interiors. He seemed to sense the growing poverty of ideas. About chairs he wrote that 'the necessity for economy urged by many at the present day is in itself sufficient to check and weaken the spirit for design, and thus we see nothing but a monotony of character in this article of furniture'. Of a different nature from the above books was R. Ackermann's *The Repository of the Arts*, published in monthly parts between 1809 and 1828. Each issue had a section devoted to fashionable furniture illustrated by coloured plates, providing an interesting record of contemporary taste.

Other styles: *Gothic*

The Regency period was marked by a restless search for new forms. So rapid were the changes in design that we find Thomas Martin in 1820 suggesting 'were it practicable, it would be necessary that cabinet, like female fashions, should be published monthly'.[5] Smith in his *Guide* of 1826 confessed that the designs which he had submitted in his *Household Furniture* of 1808 had become wholly obsolete and inapplicable owing to the changes in taste during the last twenty years. It was thus natural that the search for novelty did not stop at Græco-Roman furniture; other styles were attempted, including the Gothic, Chinese and Egyptian.

There was, of course, nothing new in the application of Gothic motifs to furniture. The 'Strawberry Hill' Gothic of Horace Walpole extended

[4] J. C. Loudon, *An Encyclopædia of Cottage, Farm and Villa Architecture and Furniture*, 1836.

[5] T. Martin, *The Circle of the Mechanical Arts*, 1820.

its influence long after the rococo period of the mid-eighteenth century which gave it birth. The Romantic Revival in literature added to the strong interest in medieval antiquities, with its stress on the picturesque. But both these trends had been aristocratic in origin and remained subordinate to the classical tradition of the upper classes. Now two new tendencies were at work: one was the growing partiality of the middle classes, shortly to be the final arbiters of taste, for the Gothic; the other was the belief that the Gothic was an essentially English style, with a robust vigour which had a strong emotional appeal. Furniture with Gothic motifs, often in the form of window tracery and pinnacles, was increasingly made for the now fashionable villas and 'cottages ornés'. In 1836, when Loudon was noting the predominance of the Grecian style, Sir Samuel Meyrick voiced the opinion that Grecian forms were no longer suitable for English residences, and that support for the Gothic was growing.[6]

At this time the Gothic was divided into the Tudor (or Perpendicular) and the Elizabethan. The former was held to be the improved style introduced by Henry VII and Henry VIII, and the latter was the English version of the Renaissance. 'Elizabethan' furniture was to have a growing appeal to the popular imagination, despite criticisms of its spurious character.

Chinese

The revival of the Chinese taste was partly due to the Prince of Wales. Carlton House, his London residence, had a Chinese drawing-room which is illustrated in Sheraton's *Drawing Book* and for which Henry Holland designed some furniture in 1790. In 1802 the Prince had a Chinese gallery made at Brighton Pavilion to show some beautiful Chinese wall-paper which had been presented to him. But the most important work of this kind at Brighton took place between 1815 and 1821, when extensive improvements were made to the Pavilion under the direction of John Nash, and the interior was decorated in the Chinese

manner, mainly by Frederick Crace and Robert Jones.[7]

Chinese furniture of this period made free use of dragons, pagodas, mandarins, and other oriental motifs. Much of it was japanned, especially the cheaper sort intended for the general public. Another characteristic was the use of imitation bamboo on chairs and small tables. Like the Gothic, the Chinese taste can be considered as part of the cult of the Picturesque; the justification for such styles was said to lie in the train of romantic and agreeable ideas which they produce (Pls. 21A, 21D, 26, 31).

Egyptian

Unlike the Gothic and Chinese revivals, the Egyptian revival was a novel development of this period, and one that will always be associated with Regency furniture. Egyptian antiquities had already been attracting some attention among European artists in the later eighteenth century, and this interest was considerably quickened in England and France after 1798, the year in which Napoleon began his Egyptian campaign and in which the French fleet was destroyed by Nelson at the Battle of the Nile. Napoleon took with him a team of French scholars, one of whom, Dominique Vivant Denon, later Director-General of the Museums of France under the First Empire, published in 1802 *Voyage dans la Basse et la Haute Egypte*. This book, with its many illustrations of Egyptian ornament, was soon available in an English translation, and was destined to have an important influence on furniture design. Egyptian motifs were used by Thomas Chippendale the younger in some of the furniture which he made for Sir Richard Colt Hoare at Stourhead, Wiltshire, in 1804–5. The new style was taken up by Thomas Hope, and his *Household Furniture* contains an engraving of the Egyptian decoration and furniture which he had designed for the room containing his collection of Egyptian antiquities at Deepdene. He had many imitators, despite his warnings against indiscriminate use of the style. The vogue was per-

[6] Sir S. Meyrick, *Specimens of Ancient Furniture*, 1836.

[7] C. Musgrave, *The Royal Pavilion*, 1948, and p. 1061, above.

haps at its height about 1810, encouraged by the incorporation of Egyptian motifs in Smith's design book of 1808; but it by no means died out rapidly. Ackermann's *Repository* of May 1812, for example, illustrates a library table with supports in the form of sphinxes, although an earlier issue, that of August 1809, had declared that 'the barbarous Egyptian style' was already on the wane. Brown's *Rudiments* of 1820 shows examples of decoration with the 'Egyptian lotus, or water-lily of the Nile', and similar Egyptian ornament was still being advocated by the Nicholsons and Smith in 1826.

Among the Egyptian motifs found on furniture were the lotus leaf, sphinx heads, lion supports, and, in the more extravagant examples, crocodiles and serpents (Pls. 24B, 25A, 28A). The style could easily get out of hand, especially when it was injudiciously mingled with the Gothic and Chinese. The resulting confusion is satirized by Miss Mitford in her account of a visit to Rosedale Cottage:

> 'Every room is in masquerade: the saloon Chinese, full of jars and mandarins and pagodas; the library Egyptian, all covered with hieroglyphics, and swarming with furniture crocodiles and sphinxes. Only think of a crocodile couch and a sphinx sofa! They sleep in Turkish tents, and dine in a Gothic chapel.... The properties are apt to get shifted from one scene to another, and all manner of anomalies are the consequence. The mitred chairs and screens of the chapel, for instance, were mixed up oddly enough with the squat Chinese bronzes, whilst by some strange transposition a pair of nodding mandarins figured amongst the Egyptian monsters.'[8]

Woods and decoration

The emphasis on plain lines and unbroken surfaces led to the use of dark and glossy woods, such as mahogany and rosewood, and of woods with boldly striped figure, such as amboyna, calamander and zebra-wood. These gradually replaced the lighter-coloured woods which had been fashionable in the Adam period.

Mahogany remained the established favourite in the library and dining-room. Rosewood, zebra-

[8] M. R. Mitford, *Our Village*, 1824-32.

wood and kingwood all came from Brazil, whence direct trade with Britain had been opened during the Napoleonic Wars. Rosewood, which was also imported from the East Indies, was in great demand; it was a hard, heavy wood marked with dark streaks. Kingwood was finer in the grain than rosewood and generally lighter in tone. Zebrawood took its name from the streaks of deep brown and white; it could be highly polished and was very fashionable until supplies began to run short after about 1815. Calamander, imported from India, Ceylon and the East Indies, had a hard and fine grain and was of a light brown colour mottled with dark brown and black. Amboyna from the East and West Indies was distinguished by a figure of small knots and curls, resembling bird's-eye maple, on a warm brown ground. It was the practice of the time to obtain some of these fashionable colours and figures by staining other woods, and this was done even in the case of good furniture. Rosewood, for instance, could be closely simulated by staining wood with logwood and marking the streaks with vitriol. Much furniture was also japanned to accord with the Chinese taste.

At the end of the war with France, French polish was introduced into this country and quickly became popular. It was described by Loudon as by far the best polish 'for bringing out the beauties of the wood and giving it a brightness and richness of colour which nothing else hitherto invented can produce'. Much old furniture was stripped and the polish, consisting of shellac disolved in spirit, was then applied. The grain had first to be filled and the substances used for this purpose have subsequently bleached, thus spoiling the furniture.

Both the economic effects of the war period and the changes in taste caused the gradual abandonment of the two decorative processes of inlaying and carving which had been used in the late eighteenth century. The former was found to be too expensive and the latter was fast becoming a decaying craft. According to Martin in *The Circle of the Mechanical Arts*, 1820, only eleven master carvers were then at work in London, and though the old title of 'Carvers and Gilders' appeared over the doors of many shopkeepers, it could be 'proved that hundreds of the latter never saw a carving tool in their lives'. In 1835 the architect C. R. Cockerell asserted that a very great dearth of carvers had existed for fifty years.[9]

The principal new decorative medium was brass, which was both cheaper and more durable than the former methods, and also showed up handsomely against dark woods. It was used in a variety of ways on almost all types of furniture: inlays of delicate lines or of more ornamental scrolls and floral and classical motifs; galleries on the tops of sideboards and similar pieces; colonnettes to support galleries and shelves; ornamental beading; wire trellis in the doors or sides of cabinets, bookcases, cupboards, etc.; lion feet on tables; castors on chairs and tables; and ringed, lion mask handles on drawers (Pls. 22A, 23B, 24B, 25B, 28A, 29A and B and p. 52). Brass inlay was a specialized craft centred in London in the area of St Martin's Lane, and good work of this character found on furniture of the period is a sure indication of its London origin. Chased ormolu work, on the other hand, was a French speciality, and when it is found on English furniture it is most likely that it was done by immigrant craftsmen. A certain amount of the furniture of this time was also decorated with boulle work – inlay of metal and tortoiseshell – at the 'Buhl factory' established by the Frenchman, Louis le Gaigneur, in the Edgware Road about 1815, and at other workshops where English craftsmen carried out this traditional French decoration (Plate 30).

At its best, metal ornament was used in a restrained and delicate fashion, but there was inevitably a tendency to extravagance. In 1820 Brown warned cabinet-makers that a very important part of their skill lay in 'harmonizing metals with woods, so as not to overload the articles with buhl, bronze or ormolu, which is too frequently to be seen'.

Fashionable furniture: chairs and other seat furniture

There was so much variety in chair design during this period that Brown declared that it baffled 'the most skilful artist to produce any new forms'.

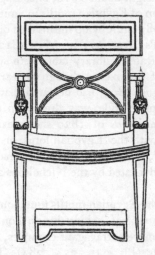

Fig. 1. Armchair from Hope's *Household Furniture*, 1807.

Typical of Hope's influence was the fashionable Grecian chair, which figures prominently in the interior scenes of Henry Moses' *Designs of Modern Costume* (1823). On this kind of chair the rear legs and the back formed a bold continuous curve, balanced by a forward curve of the front legs. The cresting rail, following the fashion of the beginning of the century, was a wide board set at shoulder height, generally over-running the uprights. In the case of armchairs, the arms, which usually had supports coming straight up from the front legs, often swept upwards to join the back uprights near the top, though in some examples, favoured by Hope and Smith, the arms were straight and joined the back about half way up (Figs. 1, 2, 3).

By about 1830 something of this form was still preserved in the backs and rear legs; the cresting rail, however, was now to be found slightly curved in shape and resting on the uprights; while a more noticeable change was in the front legs, which were straight and turned, often ornately.

The bergère continued to enjoy favour; the best examples were made of mahogany and had the

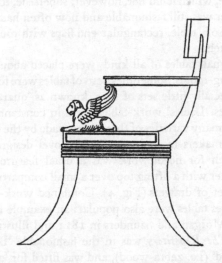

Fig. 2. Armchair from Hope's *Household Furniture*, 1807.

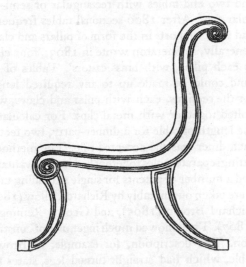

Fig. 3. Chair from Hope's *Household Furniture*, 1807.

seat, back and sides of cane-work. Among other decorative features of the chairs of this period were spiral reeding (Pl. 21c), lion feet and lyre-shaped splats, the latter being a revival of a fashionable motif of the later eighteenth century (Pl. 21B). What were termed 'fancy' chairs were often made of beech and painted or japanned (Pls. 21A, 21D), or had turned framework to imitate bamboo. Gothic chairs had their backs carved and fretted to represent tracery, and sometimes had small pinnacles on the back uprights.

The sofa or couch was a prominent piece which now became more fashionable than the settee. The Grecian sofa is described in Ackermann's *Repository* (1811) as 'adapted for the library, boudoir or any fashionable apartment'. Where the couch form was employed, based on classical models, there was usually a boldly curved head-piece and a similarly scrolled end, and as the couch was intended for reclining, there was normally a short arm-rest on one side of the larger end. The legs were of various shapes: lion feet, or outward curving, or turned in the form of tops. Other kinds of sofas had uphol-

stered backs, curved end-pieces of the same height, and usually short feet which curved outwards (Pl. 27). Ottomans (or 'Turkey sofas') were also in fashion. They had no backs or sides and were chiefly intended, according to Brown, 'for music rooms and picture galleries', though he presented some modified designs for boudoirs and cabinets. The circular ottoman, on which the sitters were back to back, was a novelty, and was used in rooms which had bow windows or circular ends.

Stools were a familiar part of Regency interiors, for window recesses, or to accompany elegant sets of chairs. The X-shape cross frame was in vogue, often with lion feet.

Tables

It was customary in the larger houses to have large dining-tables made up of sections which could be fastened together as required, and several varieties of these were to be found (Pls. 23A, 24A). In the later eighteenth century what was known as a 'set of dining-tables' had three units — a centre table with rectangular flaps supported on gate-legs, and two end tables with rectangular or semi-circular tops. After 1800 sectional tables frequently had their supports in the form of pillars and claws, generally, as Sheraton wrote in 1803, 'four claws to each pillar, with brass castors'. Tables of this kind could be made up to any required length, for the sections, each with pillar and claws, were bolted together with metal clips. For calculating the length of table for a dinner-party, two feet for each diner was the accepted rule. The method of fitting separate tables together had its disadvantages, and a number of patents for single extending tables were taken out, notably by Richard Gillow (1800), Richard Brown (1805), and George Remington (1807). They showed much ingenuity of construction. The description, for example, of Brown's table, which had straight turned legs, states that 'the end rails of the table frame are connected by pieces of wood so jointed together as to form what are commonly called lazy-tongs'.

Though pillars and claws were so fashionable, they seem to have caused a certain amount of inconvenience. *The Repository* in 1810 illustrates a patent sideboard and dining-table (given the name 'Trafalgar' because one was supplied, it is claimed, to Nelson) in which the table could be pushed into the sideboard and extra flaps kept in the drawers; the advantage being that the 'feet of this table are completely out of the way ... in this particular they far excel the claw tables'. It was for this same reason that Smith in 1808 recommended the use of the circular dining-table supported on a pedestal or circular base, and this type came into wide use, especially as it had the additional advantage of avoiding invidious distinctions among guests when seated at dinner.

The sofa table was also in general demand after 1800. The table-top, when its two small end-flaps were extended, was some five to six feet long, and about two feet wide, and it was supported either by two end supports linked by a stretcher, or by a pedestal on a small platform with splayed feet (Pl. 22A). This attractive and useful table was often fitted with two drawers in the frieze and was intended for the library, drawing-room, boudoir or any ladies' apartment, for reading, writing or drawing. It was a development of the smaller Pembroke

table, which it did not, however, supersede, for the latter was still fashionable and now often had, like the sofa table, rectangular end flaps with rounded corners.

Small tables of all kinds were placed about the living-rooms. Sometimes nests of tables were found, expecially little sets of four, known as 'quartetto' tables. Ladies' work-tables were in constant use, and many varieties of these were made by the cabinet-makers in their search for novel designs. A pouch for needlework was a usual feature, together with a lifting top over a small compartment or set of drawers (Fig. 4). Combined work-and-games tables were also popular; an example made by Morgan and Saunders in 1811 and illustrated in *The Repository* was in the fashionable 'Brazil wood' (i.e. zebra-wood), and was fitted for 'seven different accommodations', including reading, writing, needlework, chess and backgammon. Tables of this kind, and other sorts of combined games-and-card tables, tended to oust the old-established card-tables, for fewer of these were now made; one does find, however, 'loo tables' specially made for the popular card game of the period.

Fig. 4. Work Table, from Ackermann's *Repository*, 1811.

In libraries the pedestal table with knee-hole and flanking drawers or cupboards followed the traditional form (Pl. 22B), except for the addition of details like lion feet and Egyptian figures to accord with changing fashions. A more novel type was the Carlton House writing-table, which made its appearance at the end of the eighteenth century. This had a superstructure of small cupboards and drawers running round the back and sides of the top, and drawers in the frieze. The reason for its name is a mystery, as there is no evidence to connect it with Carlton House.

Side or pier tables continued in use in dining-rooms, often supported by lion monopodia or Egyptian figures. Some examples had a low platform at the base and were occasionally fitted with silvered glass on the inside and back, 'to produce', in Smith's words (1826), 'a reflecting effect from the china objects which are usually placed in such situations'. The tops of some of these tables were of solid marble (Pls. 25A, 28A, 29A).

Bookcases

For larger libraries cabinet-makers continued to make the traditional type of bookcase in two stages, in which the lower stage of cupboards was surmounted by rows of shelves enclosed by glazed doors. Classical proportions were maintained, with some concessions to prevailing decorative changes. Thomas Hope, for instance, designed a bookcase of this kind for Deepdene which had carved sphinx heads on the pilasters separating the four glass doors, and four lion monopodia on the lower stage.

A distinctly new piece in fashion in the early nineteenth century was the dwarf bookcase, the doors of which were either glazed or fitted with a trellis of brass wire. It was made purposely low to leave 'an ample space on the wall above for the placing of pictures' (Smith, 1826). Several varieties were found, in use in the sitting-room and boudoir as well as in the library. One type shown by Brown in 1820 was a lady's bookcase with cabinet, the object of the latter being 'to contain ladies' jewels, ancient medals and precious stones, with other valuable curiosities' – an interesting reminder that the hobby of collecting curios, which had stimulated the production of cabinets in the late seven-

teenth century, was still very much alive among richer people.

The revolving circular bookcase was an innovation of this period. One kind was patented by Benjamin Crosby in 1808 and was described as 'a machine or stand for books, which may be made either circular, square or any other convenient shape, and which may be turned or moved at pleasure, with cases to receive books, as well as various other articles and things'. This type and others of the same kind followed the general principles of a central shaft to which cylinders holding the shelves were screwed.

The trend towards lightness in bookcases produced one of the most attractive of the smaller Regency pieces, the little set of portable open shelves which could be carried by ladies about the room, or from one room to another. The sides of the shelves were often made of brass wire. There were many other kinds of small bookcases (Pl. 29B).

In large libraries, for reaching the books on the upper shelves, library steps were indispensable, and some of these were in the form of folding steps ingeniously fitted into chairs, stools and tables; the back of a library chair, for example, could be swung over to the ground, disclosing a small set of steps (Figs. 5, 6).

Sideboards and other dining-room furniture

In the early years of the nineteenth century the lighter kind of sideboard associated with Hepplewhite and Sheraton went out of favour, and there was a revival of the sideboard table fitted with pedestal cupboards which had been developed from the designs of Robert Adam. This was the type favoured by Smith in 1808. It soon became a commodious piece of furniture and lost its former graceful proportions. The pedestal cupboards, which often tapered slightly almost to floor level, were used as cellarets and plate-warmers, and on them often stood knife-boxes of similar tapering shape, in place of the urns which had been found in the Adam period. All these fittings were necessary, as the servants still washed the glasses and cutlery in the dining-room between courses. A characteristic feature of the later sideboards of this type

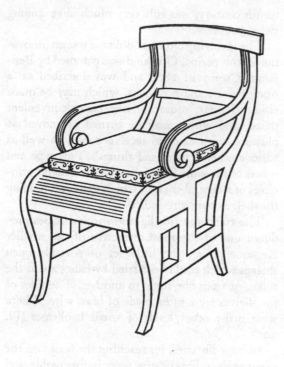

Figs. 5 and 6. Combined library chair and steps, from Ackermann's *Repository*, 1811.

was the high back-piece rising above the table-top (Fig. 7).

Sideboard tables, without the pedestal cupboards, were also in use. These tables were large, and sometimes had animal supports which stood on a plinth. A cellaret or wine-cooler, commonly of sarcophagus form at this time, stood in a central position beneath the table, and drawers with brass lion-mask handles were often found in the frieze. An elaborate brass gallery usually ran along the back of the table.

Several other accessories were necessary in the fashionable dining-room. Dumb waiters continued in use, but with rectangular tiers and supports of pillars and claws instead of the circular tiers and tripod bases of the earlier varieties. One of the two pieces called a 'Canterbury' (the other was a music-stand) was a plate-and-cutlery stand described by Sheraton as 'a supper tray, made to stand by a table at supper, with a circular end and three partitions cross wise, to hold knives, forks and plates at that end, which is made circular on purpose'.

Chiffoniers, chests of drawers, etc.

The French-inspired commode of the later eighteenth century, with its curved surfaces and decoration of fine inlay and painting, did not lend itself to the bold outlines which were now in favour, and its place was taken by the chiffonier. This was not a new name, for it had been in use in Chippendale's time, but the chiffonier of the eighteenth century seems to have been modelled on the French chiffonière, which was a small case of drawers on legs, whereas the Regency chiffonier was a low open cupboard with shelves for books (Pl. 29A). It held the books which were in constant use, and was found in both the drawing-room and the library. Sometimes a small set of shelves stood on the top.

The chest of drawers retained its traditional form, and continued to be straight- or bow-fronted. Since the end of the eighteenth century, however, new features were spirally reeded columns at the front corners (about 1810 spiral reeding began to replace the plainer vertical reeding), and a deep frieze above the top drawer. Also characteristic of the period were lion-mask handles. The old-established tallboy or chest-on-chest was only occasionally made at this period, owing to the inconvenient height of the upper drawers.

Other small pieces

Among the newer pieces of the period were the what-not, a portable open stand with four uprights enclosing shelves for books and ornaments, and the music Canterbury, a small stand usually mounted on castors, with partitions for music books, and sometimes small drawers for sheets of music (Pl. 28B). The fire- or pole-screen, necessary to give protection from the intense heat of open fires, was not, of course, a novelty, but it now underwent two distinct changes: the former tripod base gave way to a solid base, and the screen took the form of a banner hung from a bar on the upright. The teapoy, a small three- or four-legged table or stand which was not originally associated with tea, was also in use in drawing-rooms at this time (Fig. 8).

Mirrors

Shortly after 1800 the circular convex mirror, made in varying sizes from a foot to perhaps three feet in diameter, became very popular in this country after a vogue of half a century in France. The gilt frame had a hollow moulding for which a filling of evenly-spaced gilt balls was a common form of decoration; the outer edge was usually reeded, with a reeded ebonized fillet on the inner edge next to the glass. This type of mirror, surmounted by a carved eagle with outstretched wings, or by acanthus foliage, and sometimes fitted with candle branches, was a prominent feature of Regency interiors.

In the living-rooms of the wealthier houses large mirrors continued to be fashionable. The chimney-glass, set over the chimney-shelf and extending for most of its length, was in a gilt frame which normally had a pilaster at each end and a straight cornice above. Beneath the cornice a hollow moulding was often found, decorated, like the frame of the circular mirror, with a row of balls. The glass did not always extend over the whole area of the frame, for sometimes there was a deep frieze below the cornice, and this was decorated with classical

figures in low relief, or with a painting. Large pier-glasses were also found, extending in some cases up to the ceiling.

Mirrors were deliberately placed to catch the reflections within a room or between rooms. 'A pier-glass', wrote Loudon, 'placed opposite the chimney glass always has an agreeable effect, as they reflect one another; so that the size of the room is doubled, from whichever end the spectator directs his view.' And at night time mirrors gave added attraction to the much-improved illumination provided by the large cut-glass chandeliers suspended from the ceiling. The angularity of the many small pieces of faceted glass in the great lustres was noted by Archibald Alison, whose *Essays on the Nature and Principles of Taste* ran into six editions between 1790 and 1825, in the following words:

> 'In a Lustre, one of the most beautiful productions of this manufacture, all is angular. The Form of the Prism, one of the most regular and angular of all Forms, obtains everywhere, the Festoons even are angular, and instead of any winding or waving Line the whole surface is broken into a thousand little Triangles.'

One of the favourite kinds of smaller mirrors was the cheval or horse dressing-glass, a toilet mirror in an upright rectangular frame on four legs. The glass frame pivoted on screws set in the uprights, or could be moved up and down by means of a weight within the frame ('the same as a sash-window': Sheraton).

Other furniture

The search for novelty was reflected in the number of patents which were taken out in this period for furniture, fittings and upholstery. Whereas between 1620 and 1799 thirty-three patents altogether were registered under these headings, no less than sixty-eight were taken out between 1800 and 1830, fifty-three during the years 1810–30.[10] They included invalid furniture, extending tables (to which reference has been made) and chairs, adjustable screens and bed-frames, and

[10] Patent Office, Old Series of Abridgements of Specifications relating to Furniture and Upholstery 1620–1866 (1869).

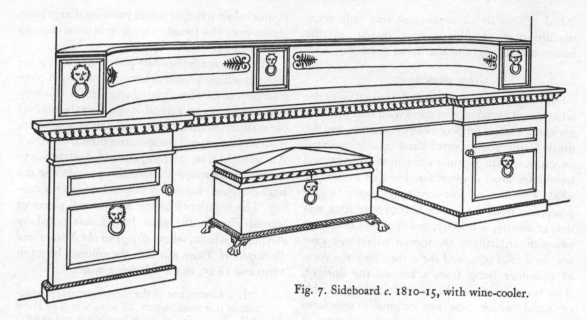

Fig. 7. Sideboard *c*. 1810–15, with wine-cooler.

several kinds of castors. These last were an indication of the growing massiveness of furniture.

It was at this time that High Wycombe in Buckinghamshire became an important manufacturing centre of Windsor chairs. For at least a century previously these chairs had been made in the woods around the town. 'Bodgers' turned the legs, stretchers and sticks on their pole lathes; benchmen made the seats, bows and splats; and framers saw to the assembling and finishing. Local woods were used, mainly elm for the 'dished' seats, ash, yew and willow for the bows, and beech and ash for the legs and sticks. In 1805, according to local tradition, Samuel Treacher, a farmer, started chairmaking as a winter occupation for his hands on Marlow Hill. Thomas Widginton came to High Wycombe to teach these men how to assemble the chairs from parts supplied by the rural craftsmen, and about 1810 he set up the first furniture factory in the town. It is known that by 1837 Widginton was a substantial property-owner with his own Chair Manufactory.[11] Windsor chair-making was

[11] F. Roe, *Windsor Chairs* (1953).

not, of course, confined to High Wycombe or to Buckinghamshire; it was an old rural craft which continued in other parts of the country. In fact Loudon referred to Windsors as 'one of the best kitchen chairs in general use in the midland counties of England'.

Other cottage furniture varied considerably both in quantity and quality. In poor homes in out-of-the-way areas such as Devonshire and Cornwall only the most rudimentary kind might be found. But more comfortable furniture could be seen in those places where it could be supplied cheaply from London (perhaps by sea) or from other convenient sources of supply; or else the cottage might occasionally have pieces from the local manor house which had got rid of them to make way for a re-furnishing.

Where the farm-house had profited from the rising food prices of the war period the opportunity was often taken to replace the old furniture with something more up-to-date. This excited the indignation of William Cobbett, who regarded the change as aping one's betters. He described a Surrey farmhouse in 1825 in these terms:

'Everything about this farmhouse was formerly the scene of plain manners and plentiful living. Oak clothes-chests, oak bedsteads, oak tables to eat on, long, strong and well supplied with joint stools.... One end of this once plain and substantial house had been moulded into a 'parlour': and there was a mahogany table, and the fine chairs, and the fine glass, and all as bare-faced upstart as any stock-jobber in the kingdom can boast of.'[12]

It was an interior of this kind which Gillray showed in his etching of 1809, 'Farmer Giles and his wife showing off their daughter Betty to their

[12] W. Cobbett, *Rural Rides*, 1821–32.

Neighbours' (shown as Plate 27 in Trevelyan's *Illustrated English Social History*).

SHORT BIBLIOGRAPHY

For general study, the best work is *The Dictionary of English Furniture* by P. MacQuoid and R. Edwards (3 vols., revised edition by R. Edwards, 1954). For more detailed study of the period, M. Jourdain's *Regency Furniture* (revised edition, 1948) is indispensable. See also Brian Reade's *Regency Antiques*, 1953, which contains records of some 340 London cabinet-makers and furniture firms of the period. Among the contemporary sources quoted in the text, the works of Smith, Hope, Sheraton, the Nicholsons, Brown, Loudon and Ackermann all contain interesting illustrative material. The quotations from Sheraton in the text are from his *Cabinet Dictionary*, 1803.

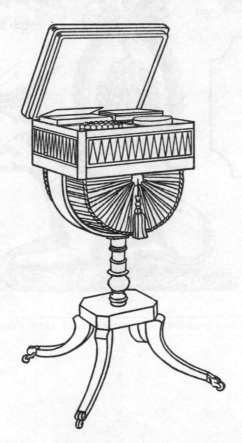

Fig. 8. Teapoy, rosewood with parquetry decoration, *c.* 1820
Victoria and Albert Museum.

Chair Ornaments *with Spikes to drive*

Brass chair ornaments, from a brass-founder's pattern book *c.* 1820. *Victoria and Albert Museum.*

1086

Painting and Sculpture

BERNARD DENVIR

A few days after the publication of the Order in Council appointing him Prince Regent, the future George IV attended a banquet given by the Royal Academy at its headquarters in Somerset House. He behaved with noticeable affability, proposing the toast, 'Prosperity to the Fine Arts and the Royal Academy'. The remaining ninety years of the century were to see the ample fulfilment of this wish, a fact which must be attributed in part at least to the efforts of the extraordinary person who so felicitously voiced it. The Prince Regent, however much he differed from his father, resembled him at least in his warm feeling for the visual arts. Constantly attending exhibitions, a collector of works by old masters – and in this he relied on the advice of several *virtuosi* including Sir Charles Long (later Lord Farnborough) – the younger George was an enthusiastic, kindly patron of contemporary artists. His commissioning of Lawrence to paint the series of portraits which now adorn the Waterloo Chamber at Windsor Castle was prompted no doubt by that sense of England's historic grandeur which warmed many imaginations after the defeat of Napoleon, but he had well-defined, less official, more personal inclinations. From Wilkie he bought and commissioned on a scale which was almost lavish. He was one of the main supporters of that distinguished animal painter Ben Marshall (1767–1835), who rivalled, if he did not excel, the masterpieces of the great George Stubbs (1724–1806); and in the very Academy banquet speech referred to above, he paid 'high compliments' to J. M. W. Turner's *Mercury and Herse*, a fact which, according to an account in the contemporary press, 'became the source of much embarrassment to the ingenious artist, as two of his earliest and warmest patrons have been so eager to possess it, that rather than disoblige one of them, he has resolved not to part with it at all'.

On the walls of Carlton House there hung, beside the old masters, works by Stubbs, Ben Marshall, and Sawrey Gilpin (1733–1807), whose main contribution to the art of the *animalier* was the addition of wild, romantic landscapes. There were also: Gainsborough's *Diana and Actæon*, which had been bought for the Prince in 1797; six or seven Spanish and Italian scenes by Wilkie, as well as the famous *Blind Man's Buff* and *The Penny Wedding*, both of which had been commissioned by the Prince in 1813; Mulready's *Interior of an English Cottage*, and Sir Joshua Reynolds' *The Death of Dido*, which had been bought on his behalf by David Seguier, a dealer and restorer whose brother William became Keeper of the National Gallery.

The very diversity of these paintings suggests the curious fact that, although in the social and decorative arts there is a distinct and recognizable 'Regency style', the painting and sculpture of the period are not marked by the same well-defined characteristics. It is perhaps illogical to expect that it should have been so, for the evolution of style is in the 'fine arts' a slower and more involved process than in the sphere of the decorative arts, where the pressure of social and economic factors compels speedier adaptation to the dictates of that nexus of influences which we call 'fashion'. Even more

1087

baffling to the historian, however, is the refusal of English art during the period between 1810 and 1830 to allow itself to be coaxed into the category of 'romantic'. Between the works of Lord Byron and Coleridge there are stylistic affinities which cannot, by any stretch of the imagination, be detected as linking the works of Mulready with those of Constable. The dominant type of portraiture was still founded on the formulæ perfected by Lely and Kneller and polished up by reference to that international 'grand style' which had found its popular exemplar in the Roman Pompeo Battoni. It is significant, however, of the underlying 'romantic' temper of the time that Lawrence, its most successful portraitist, offered, as his diploma piece on election to the Royal Academy, an immense and horrific image of Lucifer. This was not only influenced by Fuseli, but was virtually cribbed from that impressive Swiss, who for most of this period was Professor of Painting at the Royal Academy schools, a position from which he exercised a great influence on the outlook, if not on the style, of many of the younger generation.

Although it is difficult to impose a stylistic label on the works of those painters and sculptors who flourished during the period of the Regency, a list of the works at Carlton House alone suggests the emergence of the pattern which was to characterize English art throughout the nineteenth century. The popularity of animal paintings, the overwhelming vogue for *genre* pictures,[1] a tendency to pay lip-service to the iconography of classical art, and a penchant for exotic and picturesque scenery, wherever it was to be found, provided the main themes upon which exhibitors at the Royal Academy's Summer Exhibitions were to supply variations until well into the twentieth century. When John Hoppner (born 1758) died in January 1810 the vacancy created in the Royal Academy was filled by Augustus Wall Callcott (1779–1844), who had been his pupil. Hoppner had been thought of as the peer and the rival to Reynolds; Callcott's name suggests the Victorian era.

In the decorative arts the period between 1810

---

[1] This subject is treated by John Woodward in the chapter on Early Victorian painting and sculpture.

and 1830 saw the last great statement of the ideals of the eighteenth century. In the fine arts it saw the establishment of those relationships between art and society which have prevailed ever since. The artists of the twentieth century can look back to Turner, Constable, Blake, and to many others who were at the peak of their powers between 1810 and 1830, as their lineal ancestors. Those of the preceding century belong to the remoter branches of the family tree.

The artist and the public

Whether or not Turner's *Mercury and Herse* did place him in the awkward position suggested by the newspaper report quoted is, in a way, irrelevant. The interesting and suggestive fact is that it should have appeared at all. Artists had always been aware, to varying degrees, of the benefits to be obtained from 'puffs' and publicity, but the circumstances of the early part of the nineteenth century demanded of them a more extensive acquaintance with this kind of guile. The rapid increase in population, the diffusion of literacy, and the steady expansion of fluid wealth promoted an increase in the size, variety and quality of the periodical press. *The Times*, which had been erratic in the quantity of its art criticism, felt itself in 1818 driven to apologize for the fact that:

'If we have not been accustomed to notice in our journal the proceedings of the Royal Academy, and especially its periodical displays of the works of genius, it is not because we are indifferent to the welfare of the Royal Academy, or insensible to its claims, but because our observations have been chiefly directed to objects yet higher in respect to National Importance, the great concerns of civil society, of legislation, trade and commerce.'

In other daily or weekly papers there was throughout the period a great increase in the amount of space devoted to the visual arts.

Still more important was the influence of the less frequently issued periodicals, the editors of which must often have been hard pressed for material. William Hazlitt, himself a painter, wrote extensively and inspiringly on art in the *Morning Chronicle*, the *Champion*, the *Examiner*, the *Edinburgh Review*, the *Encyclopædia Britannica*, and other publications. He also produced guides to various art collections and other miscellaneous writings about art. He was one of many, and in addition to this ephemeral literature, each year more books about art and about artists were published. Many of these were written by artists and were biographical or autobiographical; others expounded theories of aesthetics or revealed.unknown aspects of the art of the past, or of other cultures. The Napoleonic campaigns had focused on Egypt an attention which was largely tinctured with æsthetic preoccupations, and from Italy, Greece, Asia Minor, as well as from Egypt itself, there came a constant flow of antiquities. The most spectacular of these were the Elgin Marbles (removed to the British Museum in 1813) and the sarcophagus of Seti I which was bought by Sir John Soane the architect from Giovanni Battista Belzoni in 1824 for £2,000.

Art was 'news' to an extent unknown in Britain before, and the æsthetic experience of the nation was sharpened by the increasing ease of foreign travel. The poetry of Byron and Samuel Rogers, no less than the prose of countless others who rushed into print to record their experiences before the Acropolis or the Colosseum, did more than anything else to lift art out of the category of a craft, and establish it as a branch of polite learning.[2] Even more important perhaps was the fact that actual visual experience of works of art was being brought within the reach of thousands. For every single person in Great Britain who had seen a 'real' painting in 1720, there must have been at least ten thousand in 1820.[3] A growing sense of national pride had led in 1824 to the opening of the National Gallery, after a long and painful period of gestation. Ten years earlier the Dulwich Gallery had been made accessible to the public, and

though the Soane Museum did not become one, in the formal sense, until the death of its founder in 1837, access to its treasures had never been difficult. The popularity of the British Museum was increased by the disputes about the aesthetic value of the Elgin Marbles, and its importance in the world of art was considerable, since art students were permitted to draw from the antique in its galleries. An interesting record of the new role which was played in the world of culture by museums and galleries is provided by John Scarlett Davis (1804–44), whose style was closely allied to that of Bonington. He became a specialist in the painting of the interiors of the Louvre, the Uffizi, and other famous art galleries (Pl. 33A).

Of even greater importance, as far as artists themselves were concerned, was the attitude of great collectors, who not only made their treasures available, but were prepared, from time to time, to lend artists certain works for study. Between 1810 and 1830 men such as Sir George Beaumont, the Marquis of Stafford, Dr Monro, Sir John Leicester and many others took a positive view of the functions of patronage, helping and advising their protégés, and offering them support on levels other than the merely economic.

Nor should it be forgotten that during the period immediately following the Napoleonic wars, London was rapidly becoming one of the more important centres of the art-selling world. The political and economic turmoil which followed the French Revolution broke up many of the great collections of France, Italy and Spain. In England a generation of art dealers, more alert, more adventurous, and more discriminating than any this country had known, scoured the Continent whenever opportunity offered. Men such as Buchanan, Fagan

---

[2] By the 1820's the guide-books of John Murray, with their fairly exhaustive treatment of the fine arts, had begun to flood the market.

[3] In 1720 the only public exhibitions of pictures were those which took place at auctions and sales. By 1820 there were at least four annual exhibitions of pictures in London, one at the Royal Academy, two at the British Institution (one of contemporary paintings in the winter, one of old masters in the summer) and two of water-colours. Various dealers, such as the enter-

prising Bullock, not only showed paintings in London, but toured them (e.g., Géricault's *Wreck of the Medusa*) around the British Isles. Large collections brought to the London market for sale (e.g., those of Orléans, de Calonne, Truchsess) were put on public exhibition before being disposed of, and many artists (e.g., Wilkie and Haydon) held what we would now call 'one-man exhibitions' of their works. There were also regular public art exhibitions in towns outside London, including Edinburgh, Liverpool, Glasgow, Norwich and Bristol.

and the Woodburn brothers brought to London works of art which are still among our most important national assets. At the same time too, the reputation of the auctioneers, led by James Christie, ensured that several important collections, notably those of the Duc d'Orléans and of the French politician de Calonne, were sold here. The influence of these movements in the art market was considerable; it is doubtful, for instance, whether Constable would have developed as he did, had it not been for the influx of a great number of works by Claude and many other European landscape painters between 1800 and 1820.

The machinery of buying and selling had improved beyond all expectation. Contemporary artists could now sell their pictures, at open auctions, at their own galleries, or exhibitions (as Turner did), at any of the large mixed exhibitions, or at the premises of the ever-increasing number of dealers who were prepared to traffic in the work of the living. Above all, the Royal Academy had become so firmly entrenched that it was now, to mix a few metaphors, a shop-window, a sounding-board and a market. It was now difficult to succeed without its support and impossible to maintain success without becoming an academician.

Portraiture

Throughout most of the eighteenth century, artists had been complaining about the necessity of painting portraits when they should have been devoting themselves to the claims of 'high art'. By 1820 it was becoming apparent that their agitations had succeeded. Portraiture was never to lose its popularity, nor to be displaced as one of the most certain ways of making a large income; but it was never again to hold the near-monopoly of the art market which it had enjoyed in England between 1680 and 1780.

Yet by a curious irony England had produced in Thomas Lawrence, who died in 1830, a portrait painter who reached a European eminence which was only to be rivalled by that of Winterhalter half a century later. A biography of Lawrence by Douglas Goldring is entitled *Regency Portrait Painter*, and of all the artists who flourished during this period he is the one who has been most closely identified with it. The son of an innkeeper, his is one of the most baffling personalities in the history of British art. A superb, though occasionally a meretricious technician, handsome, a courtier to his finger-tips, fêted from one end of Europe to the other, he was able to charge for his services prices which even now seem very high. A scholar, and the owner of one of the finest collections of old master drawings ever known, he was harassed by the most atrocious, and largely inexplicable financial difficulties, and his habit of accepting half-fees on commissioning led him to undertake far more works than he could ever finish. Many of these uncompleted portraits have a charm and beauty of their own, and it is a tribute to Lawrence's exacting artistic conscience that he never scamped a work, preferring to leave it unfinished. If a portrait painter's success is to be measured by the degree to which he satisfies the needs and demands of his clientèle, Lawrence was pre-eminently successful.

His technical innovations were so slight that it is difficult to describe any of the many artists whose works were similar in some ways to his own as followers. The word may justly perhaps be applied to William Owen (1769–1825) and to Richard Rothwell (1800–68). The point was of course that few others were able to contact such influential clients. Sir William Beechey (1753–1839) had owed his success to the support of George III and Queen Charlotte, and his work seems to us now sufficiently embedded in that period to excuse our thinking of him rather as looking back towards Reynolds than forward to Millais and Leighton.

Of the other portraitists of the period Richard Cosway (1742–1821) is the one who, after Lawence, is most typical of the spirit of the Regency. This was due rather to his personal friendship with the Prince of Wales, and to his extravert, even eccentric, social behaviour than to any qualities peculiar to his art. He was indeed essentially a miniature painter, and his style reflects the brittle elegance which that kind of work implies.

By far the most interesting portraitist of the period apart from Lawrence is the Edinburgh-born Andrew Geddes (1783–1844) who had much to do with the revival of interest in etching, and whose works in every medium which he used are marked by strong personal characteristics. He was one of the many artists of the period who asserted the prominence of Scotland in the artistic history of the period (the Regent himself was partial to tartans and had an ambivalent passion for the Stuarts). More famous than Geddes, and usually described as the rival of Lawrence, was Sir Henry Raeburn (1756–1832), whose work, at first sight anyway, more rugged than that of his English contemporaries, suggests at times the influence of Hogarth. On the whole, artists from north of the Border tended to look towards Flanders rather than towards Italy for their exemplars, and the troubled history of the Netherlands was directing towards Britain an increasing number of works from those countries.

The subdued richness of colour which marked the works of John Jackson (1778–1831), whose career reflected the patterns of the eighteenth century in that it was based on the patronage of such north-country aristocrats as Lord Mulgrave and the Earl of Carlisle, suggested the influence of Rembrandt, and there were similar features to be detected in the work and career of Henry Howard (1769–1847), who was also known for his historical and classical subjects. Few artists confined themselves to the exclusive practise of portraiture; Wilkie, Haydon, and Etty,[4] for instance, all produced important portraits, and achieved varying degrees of fame in that genre. Among the less exalted, the idea of having one's portrait painted was widely accepted as a social necessity. Certain artists specialized in certain types of sitter. Thomas Phillips (1770–1845), who was born at Dudley and trained as a glass painter, changed to portraits and tended to specialize in those of members of the literary world, whilst Samuel de Wilde (1748–1832) dealt with personalities of the stage.

The success of Henry Edridge (1769–1821), who produced successful tinted portrait drawings, was symptomatic of the wide demand for portrait painters, who by now counted among their ranks

[4]William Etty is dealt with in detail in the Early Victorian section of this Guide.

such female professionals as Margaret Carpenter (1793–1872).

During the years 1810–30 it became evident that there would be no dearth of efficient portrait painters for some time to come, and it would be outside the scope of this work to discuss them all. One may note, however, the names of George Richmond (1809–96), David Scott (1806–49), George Henry Harlow (1787–1819) and Sir William Allan (1782–1850).

The *réclame* of men such as Beau Brummell, with their insistence on sartorial uniformity, ensured that the general tone of portraiture would be a good deal more restrained than it had been in the past. Ideals were domestic rather than official; the parlour table was succeeding the Roman arch; the dress-coat, the toga. Wealth had come to be considered more important than station. As we look at it in retrospect, it is not surprising that the Prince Regent, who was by way of being a sponsor of lost causes, should have preferred himself to be painted in rather spurious armour. Nor is it unforgivable that he should have detailed a sergeant in the Scots Guards to pose to artists for those portions of his own Royal anatomy below the neck-line.

Landscape and water-colours

The major hypothesis of all romantic art is that it should be engendered by emotion and feeling. In the late eighteenth century the attempt often resulted in a note of false theatricality, a fact largely due to the absence of a suitable vocabulary and of a suitable medium. Feeling and emotion become stale when they are over-polished. The phenomenal development of water-colour provided for painters a solution to this problem.

Between 1810 and 1830 there were still living and flourishing representatives of the older style of water-colour. John Smith (1749–1831) had been on the Grand Tour with the Earl of Warwick, and his topographical drawings and paintings were always slightly redolent of Hadrian's Villa, but he lived to become, between 1814 and 1817, President of the Old Water-Colour Society. This had been formed to combat the neglect, real or imagined, which the Royal Academy showed of the medium. John White Abbott (1763–1851) was so entrenched in the older practise of the art that in his copying of paintings and drawings by the old masters he might have been emulating the earlier activities of a Vertue or a Mrs Beale.

Men such as these were, however, exceptional. The new attitude towards water-colour was voiced early in the nineteenth century by Edward Dayes (1763–1804), the teacher of Girtin: 'The nearer a drawing (i.e. a water-colour drawing) can be brought to a picture (i.e. an oil painting) the better.' Water-colour made possible an immediacy of expression and spontaneity of feeling impossible before. It permitted of open-air painting; it cleared from the palette those 'chiaroscuro' effects which had led Sir George Beaumont (1753–1827), himself a respectable amateur practitioner in the older styles of landscape art, to suggest that a good painting should be as brown as an old violin. It permitted a new devotion to those topographical and landscape subjects which fascinated the age, and having set off with the desire to emulate the grandeur of oil painting, it had come, by 1830, to impose its own standards on that more viscous medium.

So closely had landscape art become interlinked with the discoveries of water-colour painting, that it is almost impossible to consider them apart. Our current sensitivity to the charm of Constable's sketches derives very largely from the fact that they are, as it were, water-colours in oil. Less expensive than oils, more readily adaptable to the decorative schemes of the medium-sized 'villa', water-colours introduced a feeling for art into new social regions. There were many less famous than John Ruskin, who discovered the ease of execution and satisfaction of accomplishment which the actual exercise of the art entailed. Foreign scenes, hitherto accessible only to the accomplished traveller, were revealed to those whose previous experience of them had been limited to monochrome engravings. The facile art of Samuel Prout (1783–1852) made the inhabitants of Denmark Hill or Putney as familiar with the Gothic façades of Rouen or Chartres as they were with those of their own parish churches. Prout's vast, widely disseminated output would have been impossible in oils. The necessity to 'feel'

opened up new fields of observation for artists, and though some followed the tradition of Fuseli and Martin in exploring the realms of the horrific, others achieved this end by more familiar means. The sea appeared for the first time as an important subject, igniting the genius of Turner, and stirring the imaginations of Francia, Bonington, Copley Fielding and George Chambers, to name but a few.

The experience of water-colour, whether it was visual or practical, endowed the eye with that kind of artistic honesty which Wordsworth and his literary peers valued so highly. It gave the final blow to the persistence in landscape art of those classical accessories which may be thought of as the graphic equivalents of the Latinised metaphors and similes of Pope and Dryden. It destroyed that sense of theatricality so obvious in the work of an artist such as Philip James de Loutherbourg (1740–1812), who in 1767 had become a member of the French *Académie*. He indeed had some excuse, for, settling in London in 1777, he devoted much of his time and attention to devising elaborate theatrical exhibitions and devices, which influenced his work even when he came to devote his attention to the industrial landscapes of the north.

The development of topographical art gave landscape painters an inclination towards regional fidelities. The Norwich School was one of the main nurseries of genius, and the variable talent of John Varley (1778–1842), whose activities as a teacher forced him into exorbitant mannerisms, was at its best when it contemplated the mountains of Wales. Art clubs flourished in Liverpool, Birmingham and elsewhere. Artists frequently became associated with some particular spot. In 1820, 1821 and 1823 Constable stayed with the Fishers at Salisbury, producing that cycle of views of the great cathedral which forms a contrast to his usual preoccupation with the part of Suffolk which has now come to be known as 'Constable's country'.

Such allegiances were noticeable in the work of lesser men. Luke Clennell (1781–1840), a farmer's son, born near Morpeth, became an apprentice of the famous Bewick,[5] and though he came

[5] See the chapter on Late Georgian painting and sculpture by Hugh Honour.

to London in 1805 and eleven years later won a prize for a sketch of *The Life Guards charging at Waterloo*, the roots of his art were, in the best sense of the word, provincial. The only pity is that his frequent attacks of insanity make it difficult to evaluate his full potentialities. John Glover (1767–1849), also a farmer's son, from Leicestershire, moved in 1794 to Lichfield, where he taught painting and drawing and made his first essays in oil. He did not reach London till eleven years later, and after some time there, during which he helped to found the Royal Society of British Artists, migrated to Tasmania, where he managed to combine being a successful *rentier* with the exercise of his profession.

Glover's Tasmanian paintings did not make any impact on the English art world, though they were admired by Louis Philippe. Many of his contemporaries did, however, base their reputations on a skilful exploitation of the exotic. George Chinnery (1774–1852) claims our attention if only because he was the first English artist known to fame whose dislike of his wife drove him to migrate, first in 1802 to Madras, then, being followed by his spouse, to Calcutta in 1807; finally to Canton and Macao in 1827. A facile yet distinguished painter, his delightful paintings and drawings of oriental scenes and subjects are among the more fascinating by-products of English art.

Although men like Frederick Catherwood were prepared to endure endless discomfort depicting the landscape of remote Mexico, most artists found the exotic nearer home. David Roberts (1796–1864) and William James Müller (1812–45) shared a penchant for Spain and the Near East; and it is impossible to enumerate the artists whose views of France, Germany, Switzerland and Italy perpetuated for those who had visited the places the memory of one of the highlights of their lives. The Grand Tour had become a mass-produced pleasure, and whereas a century earlier the aristocracy had been accompanied by their tame painters who recorded their experiences for them, in the nineteenth such relics were purchased subsequently.

France was in a special position, and it was during this period that the artistic relations between the two countries were at their most cordial. England had come to be looked upon as one of the main progenitors of romanticism, and the *Salon* of 1824 was known as the *Salon des Anglais* because of the impression created by the works of Constable, Bonington and Copley Fielding. The precocious Richard Parkes Bonington (1802–28), born at Arnold near Nottingham, was the son of a local portrait painter who had been Governor of Nottingham Gaol. He accompanied his father to France in 1817, and studied for some time at Calais under Louis Francia (1772–1839), who had spent much of his life in England, and who was to be largely responsible for introducing into French art the lessons of the English water-colour tradition. Later Bonington worked at the Louvre and the Institut de France under Baron Gros. His work, brilliantly lucid, clear, and spontaneous, was produced almost entirely in France and dealt with French subjects. He also worked in lithography and, after 1824, in oils. After his early death his paintings were much publicized by his father. Anthony Vandyke Copley Fielding (1787–1855) was also, as his names might suggest, the son of an artist, and though he achieved great popularity in his own lifetime, he is now less highly esteemed.

The main developments of water-colour painting had been made possible by the work of men who almost entirely specialized in that medium. Peter de Wint (1784–1849), who was of Dutch extraction, is mainly responsible for an immense widening of the visual and technical horizons of water-colour, for a startling vindication of its powers of expressing mass and volume, and for his expressionist freedom of handling and technique.

John Sell Cotman (1782–1842) was born in Norwich, and was for some time an employee of Ackermann (cf. *Engraving and Illustration*, passim). He was one of those employed, if that is not too ponderous a word, by Dr Monro, the far-seeing patron of many artists. His greatest works were connected with the landscapes of Wales, Yorkshire and Norfolk. From 1810 to 1824 he was much preoccupied with the exhibitions and activities of the Norwich Society of Artists, producing illustrations for various archaeological books. After various tours in France, he was appointed in

1834 Professor of Drawing at King's College. Throughout his life he was much afflicted with nervous and economic troubles.

John Crome, known as 'Old Crome' (1768–1821), was also a native and resident of Norwich. Like many of his eighteenth-century predecessors, he had been apprenticed to a coach-painter, but through the good offices of a local collector, Thomas Harvey of Catton, he became acquainted with the works of Hobbema and Gainsborough, which, with those of Richard Wilson, were to be the main influences on his subsequent development. He was the guiding spirit of the Norwich School, and painted in both oil and water-colour, bringing to the delineation of landscape and architectural subjects a bold simplicity of handling and a sensitivity to atmosphere which foreshadow many of the attitudes of later artists.

It seems absurd to think of Turner and Constable as 'artists of the Regency', yet that fact alone suggests how remote from the accepted pattern of the times painting in effect was. Between 1810 and 1830 both these artists produced some of their greatest works. But though we think of them in the same breath, their contemporaries did not. In 1810 Turner, who was thirty-five, was a popular and well-established artist, and on 17 August of that year he held £7,216 16s. 2d. in the funds. The critics and the general public saw nothing difficult in his works, and Hazlitt's earlier description of them as 'containing the very elements' was a formula which won fairly widespread acceptance. During this period he was consolidating his gains, establishing his reputation, and making possible those post-1830 forays into fields of expression where few of his contemporaries could follow him.

Constable, a year younger than Turner, at the beginning of the period, had yet to become an Associate of the Royal Academy, and at the end of it had just managed to attain that full membership which he was to enjoy only for seven years more. The French critic Charles Nodier had hailed *The Haywain* (1821) as a painting which could compare with the finest of the works of the old masters, but Constable's English contemporaries were obsessed with the 'coarseness' of his handling and saw him merely as a minor landscape artist, precluded from greater successes by a lack of technical expertise. Yet during these twenty years he produced, among other works, *Dedham Vale* (1811), *Boat Building* (1815), *Hampstead Heath* (1827), *The Leaping Horse* (1825), and the Salisbury Cathedral cycle (1821–4).

In style David Cox (1783–1859), though not of the same stature, merits comparison with Constable. Although he worked his way up the social and artistic ladder, having spent some time in the profession of scene-painter, he was an articulate and sophisticated artist, who published a book on water-colour painting, and for some time taught drawing to the senior officers of the Military College near Farnham, a knowledge of the rudiments of landscape art being then considered essential for warfare. Cox greatly enriched the technique of water-colour painting, producing by means of wet colours and broken tints a richness and complexity which allowed the medium to assume the textural intricacy of oil-painting in the expressionist tradition.

Engraving and illustration

The period of the Regency may be looked upon, as far as the arts of illustration and engraving are concerned, as a golden age. Hand-processes and mechanical processes were in a state of equipoise, and a greater number of first-rate artists applied their talents to these arts than was ever the case before or since. It was a honeymoon period in the chequered history of the matrimony of art and industry.

Originally the outlook had not been propitious. The wars of the Napoleonic period had dealt a serious blow to English engravers who had dominated the European market. In 1787 it had been asserted that 'the export of our engravings to France far exceeds the trade at home, and of the more costly works, the French exceed by three to one the buyers in England'. The cessation of this trade forced into bankruptcy men such as Alderman Boydell, who had been responsible for its existence.[6]

[6]See the chapter on Late Georgian painting and sculpture by Hugh Honour.

This position, however, was only temporary. By the second decade of the century other factors were coming into operation which stimulated trade in the home market, and opened up new fields of exploitation in places as far away as Mexico and China. Aquatint had first been used in 1775,[7] and the cheap use of colour which it facilitated produced a revolution in taste and in the art-buying habits of the public, the effects of which became increasingly obvious during the next half-century.

Close on the heels of aquatint, with its variations in tone and texture, and its influence on both book-publishing and print-production, came lithography. This was introduced into Britain in 1808 by Philip André, and extended still further the fields in which artists and printers could co-operate.

The potentialities of lithography were brought to the attention of Rudolph Ackermann (1764–1834), who in 1817 published in that medium *Albert Dürer's Designs of the Prayer Book*. In so doing he discovered weaknesses in the process as it then stood, and two years later crossed over to his native Germany to meet the actual inventor, Senefelder. As a result he published Senefelder's *A Complete History of Lithography* (1819), and presented a portable lithographic press to the Royal Society of Arts. The implications of lithography were not at the moment fully realized, and Ackermann used it mainly for the many text-books on the art of drawing and painting which he published. These, of course, in themselves, promoted an active and a fruitful interest in art.

Had it not been for Ackermann, who did for English art in the first half of the nineteenth century what Boydell had done in the eighteenth century, it is doubtful whether either aquatint or lithography would have produced such startling results in so short a time. Ackermann was born in Germany: his father was a coachbuilder, one of the aristocrats of the craft tradition, and he himself was concerned with the design of Nelson's funeral car. But he was primarily interested in publishing and bookselling, and established in the Strand the *Library of the Fine Arts*, which was at once a bookshop, a print shop, a library, a place for the

sale of artist's materials and a social centre. *Conversazioni* were held there on Wednesday evenings, and the place served as a kind of *salon* for the 'middling and mercantile classes', where they could hear about art, meet artists and buy, in a reasonably cheap form, their productions.

The inventive and enterprising Ackermann represented the best type of artistic impresario, and the appearance of his name on a print or title-page indicates artistic excellence. Perhaps the most spectacular of his publications was the *Microcosm of London*, published between January 1808 and May 1810, with letterpress by William Combe, author of the famous 'Dr Syntax' tours; and hand-tinted plates, the joint work of Rowlandson (see previous volume) and Augustus Charles Pugin (see below). It was a perfect combination; the neat, laborious accuracy of the Frenchman complementing the vital social reportage of the great caricaturist, and the *Microcosm* was one of the most magnificent publications of its kind ever to appear, its immediate success being no less than the approbation subsequently accorded to it by posterity. It propounded for the first time a theme which the illustrators of the period were to make popular, the pictorial possibilities of the urban scene. Similar publications, especially those dealing with Oxford and Cambridge, appeared and very soon other publishers adventured into the same field.

The success of these publications emphasized a revolution which had been taking place in the respective positions of artist and engraver. The increased demand for works of a certain kind meant that the artist was now the dominant partner, for he had become not merely a commentator and a provider of visual beauties, but an illustrator of current events. That chain of causation had begun which was to lead to the *Illustrated London News* and the pictorial journalism of the nineteenth century.

Sir Charles Eastlake (1793–1865), later to become President of the Royal Academy, Director of the National Gallery, and one of the most impressive cultural tycoons of the century, achieved his first success by hiring a boat to row out to the *Bellerophon*, when it anchored off Plymouth.

[7]See below, p. 1248, note.

There he did a painting of Napoleon, and so brought his name before the public in the most advantageous way.[8] Turner was equally aware of 'news value'. This is evident not only in the *Battle of Trafalgar*, but in the work with the now innocuous title of *Ships Dropping Anchor* which was in fact a record of the arrival in home waters of two captured Danish frigates. He changed the title because of the outcry aroused by this hostile act against a neutral nation. Artists had begun to realize that if they could record an interesting event, the completed work would first of all be exhibited in London, then, possibly, in the provinces, and that some publisher or engraver would probably buy the reproduction rights.

There were few artists who did not, at some time or another, come into contact with Ackermann, for in addition to his publishing activities, he maintained a circulating library of prints and drawings for the use of artists and 'amateurs'. In 1809 he also started publication of the famous *Repository of the Fine Arts*, a monthly journal which created new standards of presentation and production in the world of periodicals. Finely printed, with a wealth of illustrations and with such novelties as insets of new dress materials, it was intended to appeal to the tastes of both sexes and all classes, adding the sugar of fashion to the pill of art. Exhibitions, books, cattle prices and social gossip jostled each other in the lively pages of a magazine which employed, even for its fashion plates, artists of distinction. Chief among these was Thomas Uwins (1782–1857), who, having commenced his career as an engraver, attended the Royal Academy Schools, and by 1813 was secretary of the Old Water-Colour Society. As a result of the employment given to him by Ackermann he was able to embark on a series of foreign tours from which he derived the material for his popular and picturesque water-colours of Spain and elsewhere.

Ackermann catered for the middle classes, but the higher ideals of Regency sartorial culture were expressed by the drawings of Niklaus Wilhelm von Heideloff (1761–1839), whose *Gallery of Fashion* is an outstanding achievement of its species.

The Repository of the Fine Arts, with its wide range of interests, indicated the way in which the work of the illustrators tended to give a unity to all the various art manifestations of the age, encouraging the application to decorative and architectural uses of themes and motifs evolved in the realm of the graphic arts. A great step had been taken towards the standardization of taste, for the middle classes, with their rising incomes and their empirical tastes, untouched by traditions of patronage, could now be kept abreast of the latest trends. The wives of Birmingham and Liverpool business men could have their clothes cut to the latest Parisian styles, and their husbands could exhort their architects to follow the latest innovations of Mr Nash or Mr Papworth.

The magazine was also used to publicize Ackermann's productions and artists, thus establishing a closed circuit of patronage and interest. When John Martin (1789–1854) first came to London from his native Newcastle, where he had been apprenticed to a coach-painter, he took three of his drawings along to Ackermann, who bought them for 12s. 6d. Twenty years later, however, when he came to add up his accounts, he recorded that between June 1826 and December 1827 he had received £691 18s. from Ackermann, £476 from Moon, £87 from Colnaghi, and £259 2s. 3d. from Agnew and Zanetti of Manchester. Martin, who in 1816 won the British Institution's prize and secured a great reputation in 1821 with his apocalyptic *Belshazzar's Feast*, had a talent which was especially inclined towards literary illustration, but the sums which he received from these four printsellers may be taken as presenting a reasonable picture of the extent to which an artist of his calibre depended on reproductions (cf. Thomas Balston, *John Martin*, London 1947, p. 91). Significant too is the appearance of Manchester as a point of sale. Ackermann indeed told Martin on one occasion that the small engravings of his works which he published were very popular in China.

There was a growing awareness of the new forms of beauty produced by the industrial Revolu-

---

[8] Eastlake procured a signed statement from one of the officers in the *Bellerophon* that he had produced a good likeness of Napoleon.

tion: in 1831 Ackermann published what has come to be considered a classic of railway art, Thomas Talbot Bury's *Coloured Views on the Manchester and Liverpool Railway*. Visual standards of beauty were now applied to objects which had hitherto been judged by purely functional considerations. The taste of the nineteenth century was to be dominated by pictorial sensibility, and the foundations of this sensibility were laid by the printmakers and illustrators of the Regency period.

That feeling for the 'Picturesque' which had been evolving throughout the eighteenth century received a powerful stimulus from the literature of the early nineteenth. Improvements in transport and means of communication, both at home and abroad, fostered the spread of sensitivity among those sections of the population who had hitherto had little opportunity of venturing beyond their own immediate neighbourhood. The *Tours of Dr Syntax* (including one *In Search of the Picturesque*) were half-serious parodies of a craze for books of this nature. One of the finest was *A Voyage round Great Britain* (1814–25), with exquisite coloured aquatints by William Daniell (1769–1837), who is also known for his fine Indian views, executed there when he was working in collaboration with his uncle, Thomas Daniell (1749–1840). A taste for the Oriental was yet another aspect of the picturesque which was to be popularized during this period.

Even though these luxurious publications were produced in instalments, their price necessarily restricted their circulation, and in 1823 Ackermann produced his *Forget-me-not*, a stout little volume, $5\frac{1}{2}'' \times 3\frac{1}{2}''$, which was destined to release an avalanche of similar publications. These were to dominate the artistic habits of an entire generation, and give employment to a multitude of artists, ranging from Turner to gifted female amateurs. To be found on every dressing-table and in every parlour, they brought a taste for art within the range of many whose outlook would in an earlier age have been uninfluenced by such matters. The mere fact that their titles were so overtly æsthetic as *The Landscape Annual* gives some indication of the extent to which interest in them gradually shifted from the letterpress to the illustrations.

Single proof impressions of particular plates were soon fetching higher prices than those of the original volumes.

The predominant public interest in landscape was fostered still further by publications such as Cooke's *Picturesque Views on the Southern Coast of England*, the first four parts of which were published in 1814. William Bernard Cooke, who undertook the series with the assistance of a syndicate of publishers, including John Murray, was a professional engraver. Turner, who had been commissioned to provide twenty-four drawings for the book, eventually produced thirty-nine, for which he was paid ten guineas each. Each part contained, in addition to the letterpress, three full-page engravings and two vignettes. This was Turner's first experience of this kind of work, and it was to be for some considerable time one of his main occupations, and an incentive to many of his major landscapes.

It may well be that the extent to which artists came to rely on the engraver had a cumulative influence on their style, making for that clear definition of colour and form which was to be a characteristic of 'high Victorian' painting. Normally, however, it was considered to be supplementary to an artist's activities, and there were few who specialized in work for the engravers. One who, however, is chiefly remembered for his work in this field is the architectural draughtsman, Augustus Charles Pugin (1762–1832), a refugee from the French Revolution, who was much employed by Ackermann and others, and whose most characteristic work was carried out in conjunction with John Nash. The folio *The Royal Pavilion at Brighton* was prepared at the command of the Prince Regent. A drawing and a water-colour were needed for each plate, and Pugin exhibited these at the Old Water-Colour Society's exhibitions.

Several artists directed their attention to the production of flower paintings for reproduction, and Francis Bauer (1758–1840), who settled at Kew in 1790 and remained there for the rest of his life, has been described by Mr Wilfrid Blunt (*Flower Books, an Exhibition at the National Book League*, 1951) as 'perhaps the most brilliant horticultural draughtsman of all times'. An outstanding compilation of floral prints was *The Temple of Flora*, edited by Dr Robert John Thornton (1768–1837), which contained reproductions of works by all the finest practitioners of the time, and resulted in the editor's financial ruin.

Another remarkable development of the time, and one which is hard to associate with our usual preconceptions of the period, is the development of wood-engraving in the hands of the group of of artists associated with William Blake (1757–1827).[9] In 1820 Blake cut seventeen remarkable woodcuts for a new edition of Ambrose Philips' *Pastorals*. These had a great influence on the work of Edward Calvert (1803–83), whose pastoral and poetic subjects, produced in the period 1827–9, have an extraordinary charm and fascination. Equally remarkable was the work of Samuel Palmer (1805–81), who in the period 1826–33 was producing at Shoreham paintings, water-colours and engravings of one kind or another the reassess-

ment of which during the last twenty-five years has been one of the more fruitful artistic experiences of our time.

NOTE: It is clearly impossible in a work of this kind to enumerate all the artists whose work in the fields of engraving and illustration are of value or importance. In addition to those mentioned above the following are notable.

Etching: J. M. W. Turner, John Crome, John Sell Cotman, Edward Thomas Daniell, Andrew Geddes.

Line-engraving: William Miller, J. T. Willmore, W. Radclyffe, Robert Brandard, John Pye, R. Wallis, J. B. Allen, E. Goodall.

Mezzotint-engraving: John Raphael Smith, William and James Ward, S. W. Reynolds, Charles Turner, George Dawe, R.A.

Stipple-engraving: Peltro William Tomkins, Thomas Cheesman, John Ogborne, Robert S. Marcuard, Luigi Schiavonetti, Giovanni Vendramini.

Aquatint: J. C. Stadler, Thomas Sutherland, J. Bluck, Daniel Havell, C. V. Fielding.

[9]See the chapter on Late Georgian painting and sculpture by Hugh Honour.

Sculpture

'Of all the arts', said Théophile Gautier, 'the one which least lends itself to the expression of the romantic ideal is sculpture, which seems to have recieved its definitive form from antiquity'. The history of that art in England bears witness to his words. At one point in the nineteenth century there were few forms of life, from 'what-nots' to prayer-book covers, untouched by the Gothic Revival. Architects were prepared to cut each others' throats over the respective merits of the round and pointed arch; painters grew agitated as to whether Raphael marked the beginning or the end of artistic excellence. The major problem which exercised sculptors, however, was whether trousers were to be preferred to togas. Works of art in stone and marble enjoyed a comparative freedom

from the social exigencies of the time, and though the nude was looked upon as a medium for the indulgence of the baser passions, young men and women frozen into permanent poses exposed their chiselled forms to view in the most public places, without exciting anything but æsthetic comment.

Sculpture, indeed, retained many of the characteristics of the eighteenth century. By its very nature the profession tended to exclude amateurs, demanding of its practitioners an almost menial skill. Men such as Gibson and Chantrey came from lower-class backgrounds; they began their careers as apprentices, and it was not unusual for a sculptor such as John Bacon to 'inherit' his father's practice.

Patronage was ample, finding its fullest deployment in the commemoration of political and military achievements, in funerary monuments, and, of course, in portraiture. The practitioners of sculpture ranged from wax-modellers such as the famous Catherine Andras, who modelled the funeral effigy of Nelson, to national figures of the stature of Chantrey. One may note, as typical of the general run, the names of Matthew Cotes Wyatt (1777–1862) and George Garrard (1760–1826). More successful than either of these was William Behnes (1795–1864), the son of a Hanoverian piano-tuner, and the unlikely preceptor of G. F. Watts. Commanding the ability to display a Roman verism in his portraiture, Behnes, who received much patronage from the royal family, fell on evil days, and died suddenly in the streets, of a stroke. He was also a draughtsman of very considerable powers, and there is a large and impressive collection of his work in the Department of Prints and Drawings at the British Museum.

John Bacon (1777–1850) began as a precocious youth, winning the Royal Academy's silver medal at the age of sixteen and its gold medal a year later, but his subsequent career did not quite live up to this promising beginning. A more interesting figure is that of Samuel Joseph (1795–1850), whose seated figure of Samuel Whitbread is a remarkable creation.

By constant application to the demands of those who indulged in the current passion for the trappings of death, Richard Westmacott (1775–1856) did better for himself than his father had done as a painter, and won a knighthood in the process. One of his main claims to our attention, however, was that it was he who was responsible for the almost embarrassingly unadorned statue of Achilles in Hyde Park, made out of French guns captured at Waterloo, and commissioned in 1826 by the Women of Britain to commemorate the achievements of the Duke of Wellington.

Sir Francis Legatt Chantrey (1781–1841) first achieved fame by his portrait bust of Horne Tooke, the famous radical and scholar, and by an emotionally expressive monument in Lichfield Cathedral based on a design by Stothard. Starting off as a jack-of-all-trades, prepared to turn his hand to anything from portrait painting to woodwork, Chantrey, who died worth £105,000, foreshadowed in his career the ideals which were later to be enunciated with such compelling force by Samuel Smiles. Running his own foundry at Pimlico, and employing many assistants, Chantrey applied to his art many of the principles which were winning acceptance in the fields of industry and commerce. Our own romanticized conception of the artist's role has often allowed these facts to blind us to the real merits of his work. In the history of sculpture he represents a period marked by the dependence of all the arts on the graphic ones. He was the supreme exponent of the pictorial.

When, in the discussion of any of the art forms of early nineteenth-century England, one refers to classical ideals, it must be understood that these ideals are derived from Italianate prototypes, and that it was to the studios of Canova and Thorwaldsen rather than to the workshops of ancient Greece that most sculptors directed their attention. There were always sculptors of Italian birth or descent working in England as assistants or independent artists, among whom were Pietro Cingolnelli (1760–1825), one of Flaxman's assistants, and John Charles Felix Rossi (1762–1839), the son of an Italian doctor who practised in Nottingham. Rossi was apprenticed to G. B. Locatelli in London, and became an R.A. in 1802.

The peak of the Romanizing tendencies – and one must not forget that in the background hovered the slightly sententious figures of Mengs and Winckelmann – was John Gibson (1790–1866), the son of a market-gardener of Conway, who was apprenticed to a monumental mason in Liverpool. He attracted the attention of that fascinating banker, collector and scholar William Roscoe (1753–1831), and eventually made his way to Rome, where he worked with Canova and Thorwaldsen, and built up an almost mystic reputation for himself. Although Gibson, whose work is to be seen in abundance in the gallery devoted to it at the Royal Academy, was mostly known for his 'high art', posterity tends to look with a more favourable eye at his portraits.

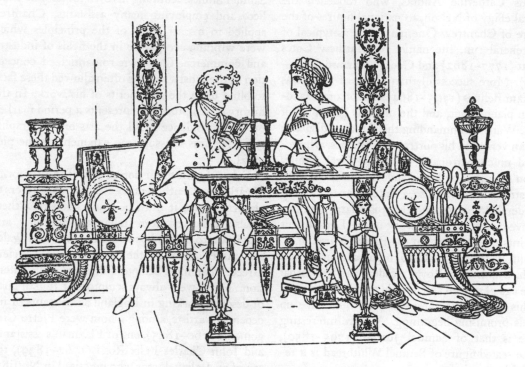

The poet reads his Works. From a drawing
by Henry Moses, *Modern Costume*, 1823

Miniatures

JONATHAN MAYNE

In 1801, as readers of the chapter on Late Georgian miniatures may remember, the Scottish miniaturist Andrew Robertson (1777–1845) (Pl. 41A) surprised and delighted the *cognoscenti* of London with a large, elaborately-wrought copy which he had made after a portrait by Van Dyck. Painted solidly, as though in imitation of oil (so that Cosway, when he saw it, could not at first believe that it was a water-colour miniature at all), Robertson's copy seemed at that time to point the way towards an enhanced seriousness in the status of the art; and today it may conveniently be considered as marking an important stage in the transition between the elegant, aristocratic style of the late Georgian age and the heavier, more bourgeois climate of the succeeding period. Although it would be a mistake to suppose that the transition was a sudden one – indeed, at the turn of the century Cosway and Engleheart had still many years of activity ahead of them – it is with the 'new style', consciously initiated by Robertson and adopted by the majority of his contemporaries and pupils, that we shall be primarily concerned in our consideration of the Regency and Early Victorian miniature.

Andrew Robertson

Andrew Robertson was born in Aberdeen in 1777. When about sixteen he went to Edinburgh to study landscape and scene-painting under Nasmyth; but far more influential for his future career was his meeting at this time with Raeburn. According to Robertson's own account, Raeburn received him kindly and gave him permission to copy one of his portraits; he also allowed him to be present on occasions during his portrait-sittings. The result was a stylistic influence that can be discerned in Robertson's work throughout his career. His system of lighting and modelling, his feeling for three-dimensional structure, and above all his concentration on characterization may all be attributed in some degree to his study and admiration of Raeburn. From the outset of his career in London, in 1801, Robertson showed an almost puritanical conscientiousness: 'I *shall* draw well', he wrote in a letter to his brother, 'and go more to the bone than any other artist – shall study anatomy, the driest part, many say it is a bugbear. Miniature painters study no more than the head. *I must do much more*' And again, of the miniatures of Cosway he wrote, 'They are pretty things, but not pictures. No nature, colouring, or force. They are too much like each other to be like the originals.'

This second remark throws additional light on Robertson's aims. The miniature, hitherto regarded as, in some sense, an article of adornment, was to become a picture in its own right. Already in the last years of the eighteenth century, as has often been observed, miniaturists had begun to explore the possibilities of larger sheets of ivory. Robertson and his contemporaries were consciously to exploit this tendency, and to combine with it a seriousness of craftsmanship, amounting almost to a moral earnestness, which may seem to be an implied criticism of the style of their predecessors. 'I have done some things lately in Cosway's style', wrote Robertson in 1802, 'and I see it does not require a conjurer to succeed in it – a *little* genius

– knowledge of the figure and drapery is all that is necessary.'

From all this it might be expected that Robertson's finished works would be estimable but academic, and it comes perhaps as a surprise to find him capable of such a degree of sympathetic understanding and charm of colouring in his best portraits. The seal was set on his early success by his appointment in 1805 as miniature-painter to the Duke of Sussex; and in 1807 he was at Windsor, engaged in painting portraits of the Royal princesses. By this time his style was fully formed, and he was launched on a lifelong career of official distinction.

Sir William Charles Ross

Robertson's most eminent pupil was undoubtedly Sir William Charles Ross, R.A. (1794–1860) (Pl. 43), who today seems to represent his age as completely as did Cosway the late Georgian or Hilliard the Elizabethan periods. After a precocious youth, during which he won a succession of prizes at the Society of Arts, Ross entered the studio of Robertson in 1814 as assistant, and as a result of this employment his original desire to make a name for himself as a history-painter became deflected into another channel – though it is interesting to note that as late as 1825 he was exhibiting at the Royal Academy a large oil-painting, with life-size figures, of 'Christ casting out the Devils from the Maniacs of the Tombs'. Ross's status as a leading miniaturist of his time was confirmed by his appointment as miniature-painter to the Queen in the year of her accession, and in the following year he was elected an Associate of the Royal Academy; in 1842 he became a full Academician, and was knighted. He continued to work until he suffered a stroke in 1857, three years after which he died.

Ross's style represents a consolidation of the developments initiated by Robertson. The Redgraves, in their *Century of Painters*, point to indications of his study of Reynolds, but to the twentieth-century eye this is discernible no more than would be expected in the work of any portrait painter of his generation. Rather we would tend to think of Lawrence or even of Winterhalter

when examining a series of miniatures by Ross; Reynolds' epic distinction is already giving way to a type of good-natured, domestic elegance, and in spirit, if not in style, we are at a long distance from the great portrait-machines of the eighteenth century. The Redgraves go on to observe that Ross 'possessed the great power of combining a faithful resemblance and individuality of character and expression with art of a high class', and with this praise one would not quarrel. 'His drawing was refined and accurate', they continue, 'his composition and grouping agreeable, his colouring of the complexion, hands and arms of his female sitters admirable, and the draperies, accessories and background painted and arranged with great taste and skill.' Ross was capable both of a high degree of finish and of a bolder, sketchier manner, either of which he employed at will. In composition his works are sometimes of a telling simplicity, and at others strikingly intricate. In one important respect Ross showed a marked difference from his master, Robertson; this was in his fluency and speed of execution. As may be remembered, Robertson records that an early miniature-portrait took him well over thirty hours – 'a week's hard labour' – to complete; and although he was doubtless able to improve on this time-table as his skill developed, he can have come within no distance of rivalling the total of over 2,200 miniatures, many of which were on a large scale and of great elaboration, with which Ross is credited. In the recent past Ross's work has been insufficiently appreciated; already, however, in 1929 Basil Long, in his *British Miniaturists*, was looking forward to a juster estimation of his powers, and today it is already possible to regard him as among the great artists of our school of miniaturists.

Newton and Cruickshank

If Robertson and Ross represent as it were the mainstream of miniature-painting during the first half of the nineteenth century, a number of lesser artists may be considered as roughly grouped around them and as sharing to some extent their stylistic atmosphere. In his time probably the best-known of these was Sir William John Newton (1785–1869), who enjoyed a career of considerable success. While good miniatures by Newton are not infrequently met with, they can seldom provoke comparison with the works of his two greater contemporaries, and today he is perhaps best remembered as the author of two of the largest miniatures ever painted – each about 27 by 37 inches in size – representing the marriage of Queen Victoria and Prince Albert, and the Christening of the Prince of Wales. A more interesting artist, who painted both miniatures and water-colour portraits, was Frederick Cruickshank (1800–68) (Pl. 41B), a pupil and fellow-countryman of Andrew Robertson. He exhibited regularly from 1822 until within a few years of his death, and as a rule his work reflects the influence of his master. The example reproduced here, which is a sketch rather than a finished work and which is executed almost entirely in tones of grey and brown, with a little pink in the face, is particularly interesting for its controlled freedom of brushwork. Very little is recorded concerning the biography of Cruickshank, but it appears that he was able to build up a successful professional connexion in London, and he also lived – and presumably worked – in Manchester. According to family tradition he was unstable and erratic of temperament, and towards the end of his life he suddenly packed up and left his wife and family, 'in very much the same way, and for the same reason, that caused him to "down tools" when the spirit moved him'.

Others who may be said to come within the Robertson–Ross orbit were such artists as Henry Collen (worked 1820–72) (Pl. 42B), G. L. Saunders (1807–63), Alfred Tidey (1808–92), Annie Dixon (exh. from 1844), Reginald Easton (1807–93), and Robert Thorburn, A.R.A. (1818–85). John Linnell (1792–1882) (Pl. 42A), the friend and disciple of William Blake, who is far better known as a landscape-painter, nevertheless executed a number of interesting miniature-portraits during the early part of his career, and two examples in the Victoria and Albert Museum give a flattering impression of his powers in this medium. He developed a strongly personal manner, in which an emphatically linear definition of forms is combined with a type of free stippling which is familiar from his water-colour landscapes.

A. E. Chalon

In spite of the dominant influence exerted by Robertson and his 'new style' during the first decades of the nineteenth century, one other small, and to some extent independent succession of miniaturists remains for consideration. The leader of this succession – if something so loosely organized can be so described – was Alfred Edward Chalon, R.A. (1781–1860) (Pl. 42c), an artist of French descent, whose family came to settle in England in 1789. Chalon received instruction in miniature-painting from the Genevan artist L. A. Arlaud, who was in London in the 1790's, and began to exhibit water-colour portraits and miniatures in 1801. Thus, professionally speaking, he was an almost exact contemporary of Andrew Robertson. But stylistically the two artists had little in common beyond a fondness for painting on a fairly large scale. Chalon's particular gifts led him to specialize in the portraiture of elegantly dressed women, and in this he achieved a brilliant, fashionable success. Writing some years later, a friend observed that Chalon was 'so fond of painting ladies in flowing silks and airy laces that some of the artists published an advertisement in one of the morning papers to the effect that "muslins and laces would be done up equal to new at 19 Berners Street" ' – which was his address at that time. And towards the end of his life, when Queen Victoria remarked to him that she feared that photography would ruin his profession, Chalon is said to have replied, 'Ah non, Madame, photographie can't flattère'. But it would be a mistake to suppose from anecdotes of this kind that Chalon was a mere 'society painter' – a kind of Laszlo of his time. Quite apart from an acute and delightful sensitivity to the vagaries of fashion and a Gallic appreciation of female beauty, his work shows a firmness of drawing and a vivacity of colour which themselves would entitle him to serious consideration. Chalon is also well known today for his entertaining caricatures of opera singers.

The Rochards

The arrival in London in 1816 of the French miniaturist Simon Jacques Rochard (1788–1872)

(Pl. 44) and, a year or two later, of his younger brother, François Théodore Rochard (1798–1858) is a further indication that the Robertson school was not alone in the field. The Rochards, whose individual styles it is often difficult to distinguish one from the other, worked in a manner not far removed from that of Chalon, though the general influence of Lawrence's bravura is sometimes more noticeable in their work. Like Chalon, they were masters of a brilliant, flickering brushwork, and were particularly skilled in the depiction of elegant female beauty. S. J. Rochard is said to have been a pupil of Isabey, and though nothing is recorded of his younger brother's training, it is reasonable to suppose that he was brought up in the same tradition. Between them the Rochards established a successful practice, which lasted until 1846, when the elder brother left London to settle in Brussels; four years later François Théodore retired.

With the working lives of Chalon, the Rochards, and the pupils of Robertson we have already been taken beyond the Regency period and into the reign of Victoria. But while it is a fact that good miniatures continued to be painted at least until the death of Ross in 1860, it is also true that the last significant developments in the art occurred during the first three decades of the century; and because of this it has seemed natural to include in our survey some artists whose training and formation took place in the earlier period, but many of whose best-known works belong to the later. The precise reasons for the decline and exhaustion of the art of miniature-portraiture about the middle of the nineteenth century are difficult to define; but the invention of photography and the substitution of a diffused, tonal vision for one more properly linear must be held to a large degree responsible. Although miniatures were still to be painted, in dwindling quantities, throughout the century, and although more recently attempts have been made to infuse new life into the art by a conscious return to earlier traditions, the recorded death-bed lament of Ross that 'it is all up with future miniature-painting' must seem to most students today to have been only too accurate a prophecy.

Mr and Miss Wilkinson, a cut-paper silhouette by Augustin Edouart, 1829. Reduced from 12 ins. wide. *Victoria and Albert Museum.*

Silver and Plate

N. M. PENZER

Regency silver

In the present section the term Regency Period is used to cover the years 1810-30, but such dates are clearly employed more as a designation of convenience than as covering the entire period to which such a term can reasonably be applied. The previous section – the Late Georgian Period 1760-1810 – will make this appear obvious. There the silver section will be found to include much that is Regency, for the dates cover not only the Nelson victories, but also the Indian and Portuguese campaigns of Wellington. Thus though George, Prince of Wales, did not become Regent until 1811, by then the Regency Period, as the term is popularly understood, had practically reached its peak, a fact we must realize in the present section. We may, however, consider for a moment the difficulties which arise in attempting to date the so-called Regency Period. A term which has to cover, apart from its historical significance, not only architecture, painting, sculpture, furniture, plate, textiles and ceramics, but all the minor arts and crafts as well, is bound to receive many interpretations so far as its duration is concerned. Thus some writers, such as Margaret Jourdain in her *Regency Furniture*, begin at 1795, the date of the marriage of the Prince of Wales to Caroline of Brunswick, and end in 1820 with the death of George III. The Victoria and Albert Museum, in their excellent series of 'Small Picture Books', prompted by the fact that by 1800 the Adam style had lost its original vigour and those who sought to guide public taste were looking out for fresh sources of inspiration, place the commencement of the Regency as 1800, and its end as 1830 with the death of George IV.

Writing on the architecture in his *Regency Style*, Donald Pilcher also chooses 1800-30 in order to include the 'formative period' which dates roughly from the beginning of the century.

In one point alone everybody appears to be agreed – that the Regency Period in art in no way coincides with the political Regency, which extended only from February 1811 to January 1820. It refers, rather, to the period affected by the personal tastes of George Augustus Frederick as Prince, Regent and King. Whether such tastes are regarded as beginning in 1783, when the Prince became of age and paid his first visit to Brighton; about 1790, when his father introduced him to the firm of Rundell and Bridge; or in 1800, when the Adam style had greatly declined in popularity, seems to be largely a matter of opinion. We must leave it at that.

It is by no means easy to determine when one style ends and another begins. Styles often overlap and the gradual change is almost imperceptible. Yet a new style is sometimes occasioned by a reaction to the existing one – as with neo-classic following Rococo – and a period of temporary vacillation, a kind of art interregnum, may exist before some definite 'movement' shows the way. Such a lead may be afforded by some trenchant utterance of the sovereign, some political or military crisis at home or abroad, or some important archæological discovery which, by its very innovation, fires the imagination of the public. Any or all of these things may contribute to a new style, but more often it is the publication of a work by an architect, goldsmith, furniture-maker or designer that is of far greater importance. As the Classical Revival is equally manifest in both the Adam and Regency styles, it can be claimed that the latter was but a culmination of the former. It must not be supposed, however, that when a style changes such a change is complete and absolute. Far from it, as the repeated occurence of the Rococo in both the above styles proves. Politically, the Regency covers a period of glory, triumph and progress which, save for the Elizabethan age, stands alone in English history. As far as the goldsmiths' craft is concerned, the glory and triumph showed itself chiefly in the imposing and massive presentation plate made to celebrate the long series of victories, both naval and military, which started with that of Lord Howe on the 'Glorious First of June' in 1794, and ended with Waterloo in 1815.

The 'progress' appeared in the rise of the factory, the commercial and industrial activities of men like Matthew Boulton, the ever-increasing output of machine-made component parts of plate – especially in Birmingham and Sheffield, and the consequent speed with which the growing middle classes could be supplied with silver articles which their prosperity now permitted them to enjoy. The retail goldsmith was taking the place of the individual plate-worker, and it was now possible to see the finished article in the shop windows of the leading firms before an order was given. Even the finest plate, such as that required for the royal services, or by the ruling noble families, was usually ordered from one of the great retail houses.

In studying Regency plate it is necessary to consider to what extent the Regent himself was responsible for the style implied by that term, to what degree the royal collections benefited during the period in question, and the debt, if any, that English art as a whole owes to his personal taste and patronage. It will be generally agreed that Regency art is largely neo-classical in concept, although Chinese, Egyptian, Gothic and especially Rococo styles are also found. Such eclectic features may make the study of the period difficult and somewhat confusing, but at least by their variety of form and decoration they contribute to what has, with good reason, been called the Age of Elegance.[1]

The first opportunity the Prince had of satisfying his personal taste was when in 1783, the year of his coming of age, he was presented with Carlton House as his separate establishment. It was sadly in need of renovation and enlargement, and so offered ample opportunity for self-expression and the releasing of those inhibitions which the restrictions of life at Buckingham House had imposed. In choosing Henry Holland (1745–1806) as his architect, the Prince had selected a man who, shunning the Adam school, followed the contemporary Whig taste of French neo-classicism. The Louis XVI style was selected as having the necessary dignity and restraint, and Frenchmen were employed for the decoration and furnishing. J. P. T. Trécourt was Holland's leading assistant, Guillaume Gaubert his foreman who supervised the architectural ornament of the rooms, and Dominique Daguerre, late 'marchand privilége de la Cour' of Louis XVI, the art dealer who supplied most of the furniture. It was, however, not in the stately rooms that we find any trace of the Prince's love of the fantastic, the bizarre and the exotic. For this we must turn to the Gothic additions to the lower storey and the Chinese drawing-room of yellow silk filled with Chinese furniture and porcelain.

There is no need to give further details of this strange house with its varying styles embodying the luxury of East and West. It was merely a sample of the eclectic tastes of the Prince which were to be developed further in that Oriental fantasy at Brighton, the Pavilion.

Before considering the plate in detail, it is necessary to appreciate the situation at the time when the Prince moved into Carlton House. As every-

[1] There is no better way of coming to appreciate the Age of Elegance than looking through the forty volumes of Rudolph Ackermann's *Repository of Arts, Literature, Commerce, Manufactures, Fashions and Politics*, published in monthly parts from 1809–29. The coloured plates are of remarkable quality. Brian Reade (*Regency Antiques*, p. 22) rightly calls the *Repository* the 'Key to the life and works of the Regency period'. Both the British Museum and Victoria and Albert Libraries have complete sets.

body knows, at the Restoration the royal collection of plate was non-existent, or very nearly so, and even the coronation of Charles II had to be postponed partly because there was no regalia to complete the ceremony. Gradually the collection was built up and the palaces supplied with ample plate, so that by the time of Anne it was necessary only to supplement the domestic items. In 1721 George I ordered an inventory to be taken, and this MS is now at the Public Record Office (Treasury Board Papers (T.I.) bundle 235, No. 25). From its 266 items, which include plate at all the palaces as well as at the Tower, we note, especially, a generous supply of sconces and andirons in nearly every room at St James's, Kensington and Windsor – the very type or article which was soon to become 'old fashioned', and so doomed to extinction. Records exist at Windsor, however, which show that a considerable number of these discarded pieces were sent to Hanover. The ewry, spicery, scullery, kitchen, confectionery, pantry, etc., were well supplied with all that was necessary, and we find the usual salts, bowls, cups, dishes, ice-pails, and an 'Aparn' recorded. But what we do *not* find is any mention of important ceremonial pieces with which Tudor inventories abound. We can only conclude that they had never been replaced, owing chiefly to the fact that the first two Georges hardly ever entertained. So, too, the retiring disposition of George III left matters very much as they were. Such plate as he did buy was for ordinary domestic use, although after he had transferred his patronage from Thomas Heming to the goldsmiths Rundell and Bridge of Ludgate Hill, his interest in plate considerably increased, and had it not been for his repeated illnesses it seems probable that substantial additions to the royal collections would have been made. But as things turned out this was reserved for the Prince Regent. What plate was sent to Carlton House in 1783 we do not know, but it would never have been sufficient in quantity or importance to cope with the receptions and banquets held there. As was usual on such occasions, it was doubtless hired for the evening and often left on display for several days after. The Prince's interest in plate dates from about 1789, when George III returned to Windsor

from Weymouth, where he had gone to recuperate after his first serious illness. True to his nickname, Farmer George, in discussing local agricultural matters, decided to visit a farmer named John Bridge who lived near Bridport. The meeting was highly successful, and a mutual respect and understanding followed. At one of their many meetings Bridge mentioned that his cousin, of the same name, was a partner in a firm of goldsmiths on Ludgate Hill and begged of the King his gracious support and recommendation. On his return to London, George III sent for Bridge, and was so pleased with him that he not only appointed Messrs Rundell and Bridge to the office of Jewellers, Gold and Silversmiths to the Crown, but obtained a similar warrant from the Prince of Wales and the entire royal family. It appears to have been from this time that the Prince of Wales began to show an interest in plate, a taste which John Bridge took every opportunity to cultivate. With the enormously increased orders from both royalty and the nobility which his firm was now receiving, it was found necessary for Rundell and Bridge to improve their stock very considerably. A great opportunity to do this was afforded by refugees from the French Revolution, whose sole remaining wealth lay in what jewellery and plate they were able to bring with them. The renewal of the war with France in 1803 caused rents to rise, and the landed gentry put their unexpected profits into plate. It was about this time that the Prince of Wales discussed with Bridge the manufacturing of a service of silver-gilt plate of sufficient size and importance for use on State occasions. There was now adequate stock for the Prince to select the styles which most appealed to him – not only the neo-classical vases, centre-pieces, and candelabra, but also the Rococo of Meissonier and his school, the table-services of Thomas Germain and his son Francois, Jacques Roettiers, Henri Auguste and many others. According to a MS account of the history of Rundell, Bridge and Rundell by one of their former employees,[2] sufficient pieces of the royal

---

[2] This MS is in the Baker Library of the Graduate School of Business Administration, Harvard University. A photostat copy can be seen at the Victoria and Albert

service were finished by 1806 – the date of the building of a new show-room to the premises – for an exhibition of them to be held for three days of every week during the spring of 1807. Invitation was by ticket only, and 'all the Rich, the great and Noble of the Land' flocked to see the wonderful display, while Ludgate Hill became blocked by their carriages until seven o'clock each evening. Thus the fashionable world was able to see the personal taste of the Prince, and the Regency style was about to be established.

With one exception, all the plate exhibited in 1807 was made either by Digby Scott and Benjamin Smith, by Benjamin Smith alone, or with James Smith.[3] The one exception was the four large soup tureens of Egyptian design made by Paul Storr[4] in 1803 and 1805.[5] This apparently formed the first item of the 'Grand Service' to which George IV was to add continually for the rest of his life. Between 1802 and 1807 Storr was fully occupied with the 'Nelson Plate'. No wonder other work had to be put out to associated firms such as Scott and the Smiths. After 1807, however, Storr was able to devote himself to the Grand Service, and his production, especially in 1809–15, was enormous.

Reverting to the soup tureens, they are of interest for several reasons. The use of Egyptian motifs at this particular time – the Battle of Alexandria and the surrender of the city having occurred in 1801 – had a special significance. Storr had already (1799) made the Nile Cup presented to Nelson by the Governor and Company of Merchants

of England trading in the Levant Seas, and cornucopia handles had been used in both cases, although it must be admitted that the sphinxes issuant from those of the Nile Cup are much more 'Egyptian' than the winged Ephesian Dianas (Artemis) of the tureens.[6] Digby Scott and Benjamin Smith also used Egyptian motifs for their two dozen round chased salts made for the Grand Service in 1802 (another dozen was added later), and twelve helmet-shaped sauce-boats made in 1804. The use of Egyptian motifs at this time[7] was only sporadic and never became popular. It should be noted that the large circular stands for the tureens were French in design, having been copied by Storr from a pair made by Henri Auguste in 1787 and subsequently purchased by George III at the sale of the effects of a Neapolitan Ambassador.[8] Turning to some of the other pieces shown at the 1807 exhibition, we find several examples with classical motifs, which were later to be used much more generously. Thus the twelve bottle-stands, made in 1805, are richly chased with boys, tigers and vine-leaves; a bread-basket is ornamented with grapes, vines and tendrils with goats' heads at the hinges of the handles and a lion's mask at the centre.

In some of the candelabra the tapering shafts encase the attenuated bodies of Greek maidens, Korai, whose heads with long tresses falling over their bosoms appear as capitals, while their bare feet and edges of their plaited garments protrude below to rest on a plain circular base.[9]

Of considerable interest and beauty is a set of

Museum library (86.DD.27). The writer was a man named George Fox, who was with the firm from 1806 to 1833.

[3] Digby Scott and Benjamin Smith entered their joint mark on 4 October 1802, and Ben. and James Smith on 23 February 1810.

[4] Storr did not join Rundell, Bridge and Rundell (which it had become in 1805) until 1807. Previously he had worked for the firm from his own place in Air Street, Piccadilly. The Royal Inventory, prepared by Garrard and Co. in 1914, includes articles by Storr from 1794 to 1802, but several of these dates need checking.

[5] This dating is according to Jones, Gold and Silver of Windsor Castle, p. 166. Garrard gives the dates as 1802 to 1803.

[6] For the Nile Cup see N. M. Penzer, Paul Storr, Pl. XIV; and for the tureens see Jones, Gold and Silver of Windsor Castle, Pl. LXXXIV.

[7] This was no introduction of Egyptian motifs. Such elements had been used in European Arts, from time to time, since the Renaissance, and both Piranesi in Rome and Tatham on his return to England had published Egyptian designs. See further Hugh Honour, 'The Egyptian Taste', Connoisseur May, 1955 pp. 242–6.

[8] See E. Alfred Jones, op. cit. Pl. XLVIII, and No. 15 of the Victoria and Albert Royal Plate 'Small Picture Book', No. 37, 1954.

[9] See E. Alfred Jones op. cit. Pls. LXIV and LXXX, and Storr's seven-light candelabrum from the Londonderry collection here reproduced (Fig. 1).

double-lipped wine-glass coolers, described as 'Verriers'[10] in the inventory of William IV prepared by Rundell, Bridge & Co. (as it was then) in 1832 (Pl. 45A). They are embossed on either side with a classical subject in relief on a matted ground framed by a narrow acanthus border. One shows a muscular youth (*not* Hebe, daughter of Zeus, as Rundell's inventory says!) seated on a tree-trunk feeding an eagle, while the other represents a Naiad feeding a long-tailed sea-horse. The projecting lateral lips of the vessels are supported by double-tailed mermen. An egg-and-dart moulding runs round the edge. They were made by Digby Scott and Benjamin Smith in 1805–6. In the years 1809–12 many additions were made to the 'Grand Service', most of which were in a strictly classical style, for Rundell had employed Flaxman to make the designs. We shall return to him later.

On the other hand, we find highly rococo pieces, such as the soup-tureen and stand shown on Pl. 45B, being added to the royal collection at this time. The tureen, one of a pair, was made by Paul Storr in 1812 and clearly betrays its French inspiration. It may, indeed, have been inspired by similar *soupières* acquired by Rundell from the French refugees. The massed fish and vegetables on the lid, the extravagant use of the foliated acanthus for both handles and legs, the tortoise feet to the stand, and the rich effect obtained by the introduction of lobing, fluting and gadrooning — all can be found on French pieces of the eighteenth century by such designers and goldsmiths as François Germain, Juste Aurèle Meissonier, Edme-Pierre Balzac, Jacques Duguay, Jean-Baptiste Chéret, and François Joubert.[11] The

[10] This word is not English, but represents the French *verrière* which means both a monteith and, as here, an individual wine-glass cooler. Double-lipped coolers usually accommodated glasses for champagne and hock, those for red wines being placed on the table.

[11] For these see Henry Nocq *Le Poinçon de Paris*. As some of the finest examples are in Russian and Portuguese collections reference should be made to A. de Foelkersam *Inv. de l'Argenterie ... des Palais Impériaux*, St-Petersburg, 1907, Vol. 1, Pls. 24–8 (particularly for Louis Lenhendrick) and C. G. Bapst, *L'Orfèvrerie français à la Cour de Portugal au XVIIIᵉ*.

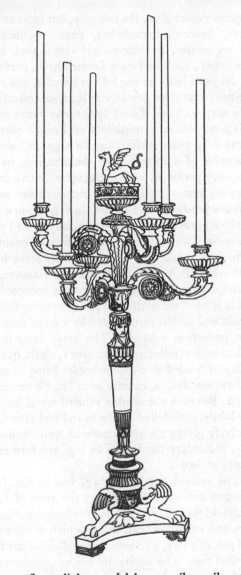

Fig. 1. Seven-light candelabrum, silver-gilt, the tapering shaft encasing three Greek maidens whose feet protrude on a plain circular base. The base is in the form of a tripod of three lions' feet with acanthus decoration. The central light socket is surmounted with the Londonderry crest. Height 34½ ins. Paul Storr, 1814–15. *From the collection of the Marquis of Londonderry.*

siècle, 1892, Pl. V, fig. 19, and Pl. VI, fig. 27, elaborate centre-piece by F.-T. Germain, and Pls. VII, VIII and IX for rococo soup-tureens.

objects depicted on the lids vary, but include lobsters, broccoli, artichokes, peas, cauliflowers, pomegranates, mushrooms and vine-leaves. Some craftsmen, such as Louis Lenhendrick, preferred to use *putti* both for the lid and handles, and magnificent examples are in the Russian collections. We may well ask if such sumptuous pieces as the 1812 tureen, so reminiscent of French plate of some fifty years earlier, can be regarded as true examples of a rococo type characteristic of the Regency period, or are merely copies. Such a doubt is by no means lessened if we consider some of the tureens produced in England during the first half of the eighteenth century – especially those by De Lamerie. We may take two by way of example. The first, made in 1736, was in the Swaythling collection (P.A.S. Phillips, *Paul de Lamerie*, Pl. CVIII), and can be described as wildly rococo. The cover is overlaid with dead birds, flowers, foliage, weeds and scrolls surmounted by a large crowned lion passant as a handle. The fluted body is enriched with scroll- and basket-work, shells, quatrefoils and beaded shields, the border being of reed-and-ribbon design, exactly as in Storr's tureen of 1812. Beneath the double voluted scroll handles are lobsters modelled in the round and free from the body giving the appearance of, quite unnecessary, secondary handles. The legs are formed as dolphins' heads.

The second, made in 1747, was in the J. P. Morgan collection,[12] and bears the arms of Lord Lichfield[13] enclosed within spreading floral branches and ears of wheat, below which is the mask and pelt of a ewe, a conceit repeated above the four scrolled feet. The distinctive feature, however, is the finely wrought spread eagle, with its talons embedded in dead game, which forms the finial to the highly decorated cover. It has a silver liner which was made by Storr in 1806. Many examples of less ornate mid-eighteenth-century tureens could be quoted, but sufficient has been said to show that

those which appeared in Regency days were but a revival of French and English types which had been popular in the reigns of Louis XV and George II.

The extravagant and exotic tastes of the Prince Regent clearly found satisfaction in such rococo pieces which suited the French and Chinese decoration of Carlton House better than those of the more austere neo-classical type, and they again became fashionable with the upper classes. All kinds of plate, besides soup- and sauce-tureens, were affected, including candlesticks, ice-pails, coasters, tea equipage, salvers, dishes, épergnes and centre-pieces. Usually the work was pure rococo, but *rococo chinoiserie* is also found, especially on tea-caddies and occasionally on borders of salvers. Mention should also be made of what we might call the marine Rococo, possibly inspired by Nicholas Sprimont of Liège, silversmith and manager of the Chelsea porcelain factory from 1750 to 1770. The chief object used was, of course, the shell, which varied in shape and size according to whether it was for mere decoration, when it mingled with coral, seaweed, lobster claws, etc., or was for use as a container – as a salt-cellar, sauce-boat or soup tureen. In this case large decorative bivalves, such as the giant clams, were more suitable (Pl. 46A). In the latter years of George IV's reign John Bridge made several such pieces, including the great wine-cooler of 1829.

In view of all this evidence, it is clear that we must regard the continuance of Rococo into the early nineteenth century as an important part of the eclectic whole which we call Regency.

To return to the subject of classical *motifs* in Regency plate, a most necessary piece for the dining-hall, chiefly for purposes of display, was what the royal inventory lists under the heading 'Sideboard Dishes'. A prominent maker of such dishes in the early nineteenth century was William Pitts,[14] who executed several orders for the Prince of Wales and members of the nobility between 1810 and 1812. He also made eighteen dishes as

---

[12] See E. Alfred Jones, *Old Plate of J. Pierpont Morgan*, pl. XLV, and the Parke-Bernet Galleries sale catalogue, 1947, lot 474.
[13] i.e. George Anson (1697–1762), admiral, circumnavigator and reformer of the Navy.

[14] What relation he was, if any, to Thomas Pitts whose premises at 20, Air Street, Piccadilly, were taken over by Paul Storr in 1796, appears to be unknown.

his share in the enormous silver-gilt service ordered in 1814 by the Duke of Wellington on his appointment as Ambassador to Paris. He usually enriched the centre of his dishes with some familiar classical scene in high relief, such as the Feast of the Gods, the Battle of the Giants, the Rape of the Sabines, etc., and surrounded it with a broad border either of marine monsters and grotesque masks; or else, inappropriately enough, with a peaceful scene of swans and bulrushes (Pl. 46B). In one instance [15] he used small plaques bearing hall-marks of the time of Charles II depicting the tale of Daphne and Apollo, and enclosed them with wide scalloped borders divided into panels filled with various flowers embossed and frosted on a matted ground. In other cases, as with two pairs of dishes made for the Marquess of Londonderry in 1810 and 1817, the centre was embossed with a Tudor rose surrounded by sprays of flowers and foliage in straight or curved panels, the edges in all cases being scalloped. It is clear, then, that the dishes of William Pitts were not contemporary in design or feeling and tended to hark back to Caroline times (Pl. 46c). Such classical *motifs* as the Adam brothers had introduced obviously did not appeal to him, and he would have applauded the remark of George III recorded by Joseph Farington (*Diary*, 16 January 1800) to the effect that he considered that the Old School was not enough attended to and that the Adams had introduced too much of neatness and prettiness.

Moreover, it must be remembered that at the time there was very little Græco-Roman plate from which to copy, and the great classical hoards were yet to be discovered. Any delving undertaken was not into the hidden recesses of a cache, but rather into the pages of Ovid's *Metamorphoses*. In 1814 another sideboard circular dish appeared. It had a design by Thomas Stothard, R.A. In the centre is the 'Triumph of Bacchus and Ariadne', (Pl. 46D). The happy couple stand side by side in a chariot drawn by four prancing centaurs who are playing on musical instruments or wielding

the cone-tipped *thyrsus*, which is also seen in the hands of both Bacchus and Ariadne. But it is the broad, flat rim that concerns us particularly, for here we see a strange assortment of Bacchic emblems of all kinds – the syrinx, *thyrsus*, *pedum*, tambourine, and over a dozen masks arranged both singly and in pairs. Some of them seem familiar, and are, in fact, taken from the famous Warwick Vase. Owing to persistent misconceptions regarding its age, history and facsimiles, a brief statement of facts concerning this vase may be of interest. It was found in 1770 with many other marbles, in a very bad state of repair, in the stagnant lake of Pantanello on that great site, fifteen miles east of Rome and two miles south-west of Tivoli (Tibur), known as the Villa Adriana, or Hadrian's Villa. The excavator was the Scottish painter Gavin Hamilton (1730–97), who with his partners, the unprincipled Thomas Jenkins, and Joseph Nollekens, an equally strange character, was buying and digging up statues, busts, vases, etc., to sell to British collectors after they had been restored by such men as Cavaceppi, Pacetti and Piranesi. Sir William Hamilton came from Naples to inspect the great vase and agreed to pay for its restoration, which was immediately put in hand. The work was done chiefly by Nollekens and Piranesi, and included the addition of several new heads – or masks, as they are usually called – and when completed Sir William tried in vain to sell it to the British Museum. He was, however, more successful with his nephew, George Greville, Earl of Warwick, and after a pedestal had been made for it with a pompous inscription explaining the large part Sir William had played in its restoration, it reached Warwick Castle in 1774 (Pl. 47A).

Four years later Piranesi published his important *Vasi, candelabri, cippi* ... , which included three excellent engravings of the Warwick Vase,[16] and in due course a copy of the large oblong folio found its way to Paul Storr's workshop, where it was discovered among his papers just prior to the last war, when it was destroyed with everything

---

[15] See E. Alfred Jones, *op. cit.*, p. 194 and Pl. XCVIII, and for other dishes by Pitts see p. 114, Pl. LVIII, and the two (unillustrated) pairs on p. 219.

[16] Among others it had two engravings of the Lante Vase, also found on the site of Hadrian's Villa, and having masks very similar to those on the Warwick Vase.

else. Storr at once realised how suitable was its shape for cups, soup-tureens and ice-pails, while the bearded heads, the lion's skin hanging from the projecting 'shelf', and the Bacchic emblems would provide classical *motifs* of which endless use could be made. The Prince Regent showed particular interest in the Warwick Vase and ordered a set of eight silver-gilt ice-pails of two sizes, the larger having basins for iced fruit. They were finished in 1812, and four concave fluted pedestals were added for the larger set in 1813 and 1816. In 1814 another four of smaller size were added, bringing the complete set up to the dozen.[17] Edward Lascelles, created Earl of Harewood in 1812, also ordered a pair with fruit dishes in that same year (see Pl. 47B).

Meanwhile in 1813 Lord Lonsdale (3rd Earl, 1787–1872) gave an order to Rundell, Bridge and Rundell to make a full-size facsimile of the vase in solid silver. The necessary set of wax models was duly made, but disagreement over the price caused the project to be abandoned. Some seven years later the firm decided to use these models in making a facsimile of the vase in bronze. Accordingly, they searched for an eminent bronze-founder and, failing to find one in England, entrusted the work to Charles Crozatier of Paris. Two copies were cast, and the work was excellently done. As soon as George IV saw them he purchased one for Windsor, where it is still to be seen on the steps leading from the Castle into the East Terrace garden. It is of interest to note that Crozatier also cast the large statue of *Hercules* for Windsor Castle which graces the same garden only a few yards from the Warwick Vase. The King seems to have had a particular liking for the vase, for in 1827 he had a reduced copy made which is now entered in the furniture inventory at the Palace as an 'indoor article'.

The other bronze facsimile found its way to the lawn outside the Senate House at Cambridge, to which university it was presented in 1842 by the Duke of Northumberland on his election as Chancellor. The only other facsimile of the Warwick Vase ever made was one cast in iron with a metallic 'finish' invented by its maker, Edward Thomason of Birmingham. Although many years were spent in perfecting the process, its success was only temporary, and after the 'bronze' had worn away it began to rust badly and is now in a sorry plight in the grounds of Aston Hall.

Copies of the Warwick Vase in varying sizes were made by firms other than Rundell's.

In some cases while the original shape was retained the heads were replaced by other ornamentation. Thus on the cup belonging to the Goldsmiths' Company oak foliage has been substituted. In other cases the central body has been left plain, sometimes to receive a crest or coat of arms. When used as a racing cup, horses' heads replace the Bacchic masks, as in the example at the Art Insitute of Chicago.

As to the date of the original marble vase, evidence, into which we cannot enter here, proves conclusively that those portions of the vase that are genuine are of Hadrianic age and must be assigned to the second century A.D. It should be realized that in concept and decoration the vase is Greek, not Roman, and was very possibly made by Greeks employed by Hadrian in Rome. His object was to demonstrate the importance of Greek idealism in art as a valuable possession for the Roman world. It was, in fact, an example of classical revival in Roman times. How strange that it was destined to play a similar role again – but this time in the nineteenth century.

As already mentioned, Philip Rundell had employed John Flaxman (1755–1826) as a designer for much of his neo-classical plate. In 1794 he had returned from his seven years' residence in Italy a famous man. He had not only made reductions and adaptations from the antique and executed numerous commissions for classical and emblematic groups, but had achieved an enormous success with his outline illustrations to the poems of Homer, Aeschylus and Dante, based on drawings on Greek vases.

One of the first commissions Flaxman received from Rundell was to design the Trafalgar Vases, of which sixty-six were made between 1804 and

---

[17] For further details see E. Alfred Jones, *op. cit.*, p. 208, and the 1914 Royal Inventory, pp. 22–3, where the dates differ in some details.

1809. He also executed several important orders for George IV, as Prince of Wales, Prince Regent and King. In 1809 he designed the pair of massive candelabra, five feet in height, one representing the Three Graces gathering the apples of the Hesperides (Pl. 48A), the other Mercury presenting Bacchus to the Nymphs. Each candelabrum has three double and six single branches for candles, and it is between these two tiers that the classical subjects are modelled. Below the lower tier three piping fauns sit on the projecting base of a truncated column which forms part of the central support. According to the royal copy of the 1914 inventory a total sum of £4,003 15s. was paid for the pair in 1811. An interesting item, formerly in the possession of the Prince Regent and now in the collection of Charles Oman, is a pair of jugs, said to have been designed by Flaxman from Roman vases, to which spouts, handles and lids were added. They are quite plain, except for bearded heads affixed beneath the spouts and handles. They were made by Paul Storr in 1810–11 (Pl. 48B). One of the most notable Flaxman pieces, made in 1812, is the so-called Theocritus Cup, the subjects on which are taken from his first Idyll. One side shows two youths contending for the favour of a maiden (Pl. 49B); the other depicts an aged fisherman dragging his net, while above a boy squats on a rock intent on making a cricket-cage [?] to the advantage of a fox who sniffs at his wallet placed on the rock behind him (Pl. 49A). Both subjects are framed above and laterally by vine-branches and grapes. Although the cup is formed in the shape of a Greek Krater, Theocritus' original description clearly refers to a rustic bowl of Kylix shape. Another two-handled Krater, based by Flaxman on the Theocritus cup, was commissioned in 1817 by Mrs Saltren, sister of Lady Manvers, as a memorial of Charles, 1st Earl Manvers[18] who had left her a legacy in his will. Its chief interest lies in the fact that the scenes are not taken direct from Greek mythology, but were

apparently designed by Flaxman to represent in Homeric idiom the Fields of Elysium to which favoured heroes are translated by the Gods (see Pls. 46C and D).

Of interest in the history of goldsmiths' work is the little gilt cup on a slender stem made in 1814 and decorated from designs by Flaxman with three floating figures of the hours, linked by a floral garland, with a chaste ivy scroll on the foot. It bears the badge of the Prince of Wales, and underneath are the words 'Galvanic Goblet' (Pl. 56A). Thus we have here a very early example of electro-gilding, for the introduction of electro-plating is usually attributed to Arthut Smee in 1840, when it was immediately taken up by Elkington & Co. It is not known if the experiment was suggested by Storr, who made the cup, but this appears to be the only article produced by the process. Of considerable beauty is a Krater-shaped two-handled vase at Windsor made by John Bridge in 1826–7 from a design by Flaxman[19] based on Hesiod's description of the Gold and Silver Ages in his *Works and Days* (lines 110–39). One side is in white silver, the other in gilt. The subjects of the two Ages are in rectangular panels, slightly tapering with the lines of the vase. The lower portion is engraved with a Greek running scroll pattern, while at the base, and also on each side below the handles, is a shell ornament. It is engraved with the Garter and motto. Height, $5\frac{1}{2}$ in.; 7 in. at mouth and $3\frac{3}{4}$ in. at base. Perhaps the most famous creation of Flaxman was the Shield of Achilles designed in 1818 to the order of Rundell, Bridge and Rundell. The subject was taken from the XVIIIth book of the *Iliad*, where from line 478 to the end is a detailed description of the great shield made for Achilles by Hephaestus. After the general design had been modelled it was then cast in plaster, and finished by cutting away. The silver-gilt shields were made from this model, the first of which was purchased

---

[18] Major-General Lord Charles Wellesley, second son of the Great Duke, married the only daughter of the third son of Earl Manvers, and so the cup has become the property of the present Duke of Wellington.

[19] See E. Alfred Jones, *op. cit.*, p. 108 and Pl. LV. Plaques of the two designs are in the John Soane Museum. They were given by Flaxman's sister-in-law Maria Denman in 1836–7. There is also a plaque, with the figures reversed, at University College, London. See *A New Description of Sir John Soane's Museum*, 1955, p. 11.

G

by the Prince Regent and displayed at the Coronation banquet in 1821. Other copies went to the Duke of York, Lord Lonsdale and the Duke of Northumberland. Bronze versions were also cast, and Rundell presented one to each university. In 1834 the firm gave the cast to Sir John Soane. The diameter of the shield is 37 in. and the weight 660 oz. It bears the maker's mark of Philip Rundell and the date-letter for 1821–2. In his work on Flaxman, W. G. Constable describes the shield as undoubtedly a most skilful piece of work, exhibiting all Flaxman's powers of combining many figures into a harmonious, smoothly flowing design which served Wedgwood so well. But, he adds, like the illustrations to the *Iliad* and *Odyssey*, it expresses nothing of the full-bodied, heroic quality of the Homeric warriors (Pl. 50A).

With it we can compare the 28-in. silver-gilt salver designed by Benedetto Pistrucci, the famous gem-engraver and medallist, also for Philip Rundell. In 1820–1 he had engraved the coronation medal for George IV, as well as the coins of the early part of his reign. In the centre of the salver is a fine relief of St George and the dragon, such as had appeared on the sovereigns. The border is adapted from the frieze of the Parthenon – the famous Elgin marbles. The rim is a design of anthemions and ovolos. It bears the date-letter for 1822–3, and is in the Victoria and Albert Museum (Pl. 50B).

Each year a Regency Exhibition is held at the Royal Pavilion, Brighton. One of the chief attractions is always the wonderful display of Regency plate in the Banqueting Room, where the table is laid for twenty-four guests, reproducing the well-known painting in Nash's *The Royal Pavilion*, 1826. In past years H.R.H. the Princess Royal and the Earl of Harewood have lent a large portion of plate, with loans from many other famous collections, including that of the Marquess of Londonderry. The 1957 Exhibition, however, displayed all the Londonderry plate of the Regency period, which includes many magnificent pieces, as well as the famous gold inkstand with its great historical associations – to be described in detail shortly.

Much of the silver was purchased by Charles, 3rd Marquis of Londonderry (1778–1854), who, as General Sir Charles Stewart, served with the Duke of Wellington in the Peninsular campaign. In 1814, as Ambassador to the Emperor of Austria, he was in Vienna during the Congresses. Britain was represented by Lord Stewart's half-brother, the famous Viscount Castlereagh. Several pieces of his plate are shown here. Of the non-Ambassadorial plate, many fine examples were purchased by the second wife of Lord Stewart, Francis Anne (1800–65), daughter of Sir Henry Vane-Tempest, Bart.

One of the earliest pieces to fall within our period is the toasted-cheese dish made by William Eley in 1798–9 (Pl. 51). Its beauty lies chiefly in its plainness, the only decoration being the gadrooned edge to the dish and the horizontal reeded handles. The cushioned cover, hinged to the body, but removable, is surmounted by a baron's coronet and cap upon a cushion, and is engraved with the arms and crest of Lord Stewart. It is $12\frac{1}{2}$ in. wide. The interior is fitted with six small square dishes. With this type we can compare that at Brasenose College, Oxford, made by Storr in 1815–16, which has a small reeded handle on the cover and a pear-wood handle fitting into a protruding socket at the back. In this case there are twelve cheese containers. The humble wine-label is well represented in a fine set of nine in silver-gilt made by Benjamin and James

Fig. 2. Wine label, modelled with a design of grapes and vine leaves and a lion's mask. Paul Storr, 1811–12. *Victoria and Albert Museum.*

Smith in 1809–10, with a design of grapes and vine-leaves (cf. also Fig. 2). The same design was also made by Digby Scott and Benjamin Smith. There is an example of 1806–7 in the Cropper collection in the Victoria and Albert Museum, and another in a private collection.[20] We pass on now to a typical example of a Regency tea-urn (Pl. 52). It stands on a plain-square plinth, the lower part of the body being gadrooned, as is also the domed cover surmounted by a floral and reeded finial of acorn shape. Reeded handles each side spring from pairs of lions' heads. The reeded spigot has an ivory tap. It is 17 in. high, and was made by Richard Cooke in 1809–10.[21] Of light and graceful appearance is the pair of silver-gilt fruit-baskets and stands made by J. W. Story and W. Elliott in 1811–12. Both body and stand are of wire-work through which vine tendrils meander, bunches of grapes and vine-leaves completing the decoration. The edge is in the form of twisted rope-work, showing plain and striated sections alternately. The solid central bases are engraved with a marquis's coronet and Londonderry monogram. The base of the stand is formed of rococo volutes (Fig. 3).

We turn now to a fine pair of silver-gilt tureens, covers and stands made by Storr in 1813–14. They are decorated with the anthemion and lotus design, a great favourite of the period. The plain domed covers are surmounted by a winged dragon *statant*, the Stewart crest, while applied plaques each side bear the royal and Stewart arms respectively. The stands have small handles and lion-pad feet with water-leaves above (Fig. 4). A pair of matching ice-pails were made at the same time, with the anthemion and lotus design round the upper part of the bodies. Reeded handles spring from lions' masks. The rim and bases are gadrooned. Another typical Storr piece, made in 1814–15, is a hot-water jug, 10 in. high, with gadrooning on

Fig. 3. Silver-gilt fruit basket with stand. Of wire work decorated with grapes and vines, twisted rim showing plain and twisted sections alternately. The solid central base is engraved with the Londonderry coronet and monogram. Diameter 7½ ins. J. W. Story and W. Elliott, 1811–12. *From the collection of the Marquis of Londonderry.*

Fig. 4. Silver-gilt tureen with cover and stand. Enriched with palmettes and lotus ornament and gadrooning. Applied plaques bear the royal arms one side and those of Stewart on the other. The covers are surmounted by handles in the form of the Stewart crest, *a winged dragon statant.* Height of tureen 13 ins. Width of dishes 19½ ins. Paul Storr, 1813–14. *From the collection of the Marquis of Londonderry.*

[20] See *Journal Wine-Label Circle*, No. 3, December 1952, pp. 27 and 28.

[21] The earlier type of tea-urn, which had succeeded the tea-kettle about 1760, was pear-shaped, followed by the classical vase-shape of the Adam period. The type shown here was greatly favoured in the Regency period, many examples being made by Paul Storr.

the lower part of the body and a guilloche band round the neck (Pl. 53). An ivory handle, twisted near the middle, springs from the bodies of two serpents rising to a single winged head which rests against the neck. The broad spout is enriched with an anthemion on the under side. Of interest is the silver-gilt tea, coffee and breakfast service made in 1818–19 by an unidentified goldsmith whose initials are SH in an incurved oblong (Pl. 54A). The set is chased with an all-over floral pattern. The knobs surmounting the larger covered pieces are in the form of the bust of a Chinaman. The set comprises a kettle with stand and spirit lamp, a coffee-pot, two sizes of teapots, a sugar basin, milk jug, egg-stand, toast-rack and two small salts.

Quite apart from its value and rarity, the solid gold inkstand made out of twenty-two gold diamond-studded portrait snuff-boxes is of historical significance. It was presented to Lord Castlereagh after the signing of the various treaties both before and after the Congress of Vienna. As can be seen from the illustration (Pl. 54B), the inkstand is oblong in shape with rounded corners, and supported on four acanthus scrolled legs with lateral volutes to which bunches of grapes and a central shell ornament have been added. The rim is enriched with a shell and foliage design, while the handles at either end are formed of acanthus leaves in two sections, the voluted terminals of which meet in the middle. Below, the plain sides are covered with arms which will be noted further when we discuss the engraving. From the centre of the stand, and of the same oblong form with rounded corners, rises a plain platform with slightly concave sides, while each side is a round-ended channel for writing accessories. On the platform is the quill-cleaner in the centre, with the ink-pot one side and the sand caster [22] the other. The quill cleaner,

filled with small lead shot, and also used as a pen-holder, is in the form of a bunch of lanceolate leaves, interspersed here and there with some campanulate plant like the Canterbury Bell. This bunch of foliage, which spreads out and hangs down at the top, is secured below by a calyx of acanthus leaves, while others are spread out on the platform as a base, the ends curling upwards. The two containers, which match exactly, have plain lobed surfaces and rest on four scroll feet surmounted by sprays of oak-leaves which spread out over most of the lower part of the bodies. The plain domed covers are edged with a shell and foliage design similar to that round the rim of the main body of the stand. A Viscount's coronet and cap acts as a finial, below which is engraved Lord Castlereagh's crest within the Garter motto – he had been invested on 28 June 1814. Along the front concave side of the central platform is an inscription which reads as follows:

This Inkstand is Composed of the Gold taken from the Portrait Snuff Boxes which were presented by the SOVEREIGNS whose Arms are engraven hereon. To Viscount Castlereagh upon the Signature of the Several Treaties concluded in the Years 1813, 1814 & 1815.

On the plain surface near each handle are engraved within laurel wreaths the arms of Russia, France, Austria and Prussia. Round the sides are twelve

---

[22] This is a more correct expression than *pounce-box*, for the use of pounce, powered gum sandarac (*callitris quadrivalvis*), or shells of cuttle-fish, was succeeded by that of sand, as being more easily obtainable. *Pounce*, derived from *pumex*, pumice-stone, was originally used to prepare the surface of parchment for writing. Its absorbent nature also prevented the spreading of ink over an erasure or on unsized paper. Thus *pounce*, first applied to powdered pumice-stone, was also used for any

absorbent powder, and even for powder used on a lady's hair. Several writers on silver say that the pounce-box or sand-caster were used prior to the introduction of blotting-paper. This is certainly not true. Blotting-paper was invented at least as early as the fifteenth century and has actually been found in account books of that date. We may well ask, then, why the sand-caster has persisted to quite modern times, and no use appears to have been made of blotting-paper. One can only guess the reason, but it may be because large pieces of coarse grey unsized paper appeared more suitable to the pages of a ledger, than to the sophisticated elegance of a silver inkstand, or standish – a word the etymology of which has never been satisfactorily explained. Whether the pouncet-box of *Henry IV, Part I*, Act 1, Sc. iii, 38 means a box for pounce or a pierced (i.e. pounced) box is still undecided.

other coats of arms, also within laurel wreaths. Those in front, reading from left to right, are Papal States, Bavaria, Portugal, Saxony, Sardinia and Hanover. Those at the back are Sweden, Wurtemberg, Naples, Spain, Denmark and Netherlands. At each end between the two sets are, respectively, the royal arms and the Castlereagh arms. Applied Tudor roses decorate the rounded corners. The inkstand was made by Rundell, Bridge and Rundell, but, as its various parts contain two sets of makers' mark, some explanation is needed. On unscrewing the wooden base which is fitted underneath, we find Rundell's Latin inscription with a full set of marks, including that of Philip Rundell and the date-letter for 1819–20. His mark also appears on the top of the stand without date, and on the inner lids of both inkpot and sand-caster with the date-letter for 1818–19. But the quill-cleaner, ink-pot and sand-caster, with the outer lids of the two latter objects are all stamped with Paul Storr's mark for 1818–19. The explanation of this seems to be as follows. We may take it that the whole inkstand was made by Storr, and it was perhaps the last thing made for Rundell, as he left the firm in 1819. This fact led Rundell to take out a mark for himself, which he did on 4 March 1819. There was just time for him to use it on the inkstand, a thing he must have made up his mind to do, because the goldsmiths' year starts on 29 May and as the 'c' for 1818–19 did not end until 28 May 1819, he was able to stamp those parts already done with his own new mark and the 1818–19 date-letter. The rest of the inkstand was finished the following year and naturally was stamped with the 'd' for 1819–20 – again with Rundell's mark. It should be realized that Rundell was not a working goldsmith at all, but a diamond merchant and jeweller. Storr never worked for the firm again until after Rundell's death in 1827.

In the MS. account of the firm by George Fox, one of their employees, there is an interesting and amusing section (cols. 85–8) about the inkstand. He tells us that when the snuff-boxes were broken up the diamonds 'were employed partly for Her Ladyship's jewels and partly for His Lordship's Star Badge, etc. etc.' The average value of the boxes was put at £1,000, and some of the gold therefrom was used on his sword, the rest went to the inkstand. He relates that the breaking up of gold presentation snuff-boxes became such a regular practice that Joseph Hume raised the whole question in the House. Fox then explains that when a snuff-box, supplied by their firm, was presented to a Foreign Ambassador it was immediately sold back to them, and was thus ready to be sold to Downing Street again. In some cases the same box was sold six times over. 'This was no bad means of making money!' concludes the sly Fox!

Another inkstand worth noting, if only to demonstrate the persistence of a type familiar from the days of Queen Anne, is one of the so-called 'Treasury' pattern, the characteristic feature of which is its division into two equal rectangular sections, each with a flat lid operating from a central joint. One of these divisions held the inkpot and sand-caster, often with additional partitions for wafers, etc. The other division was to hold quills, lead pens (pencils), sealing-wax, knives and so forth. In the offices of the Privy Council there are eight inkstands of this type, three being by Charles Shelley, 1685, one by 'M' of the same date, and four of 1702 by Philip Rollos. They have central hinged handles and four solid cast feet of foliage. In the Treasury are three more of 1685, one by Shelley and the other two by Francis Garthorne.[23] Reference should also be made to the beautiful one by de Lamerie originally belonging to Sir Robert Walpole,[24] and a very handsome plain one formerly the property of Lord Chesterfield of *Letters* fame.[25] The type is also known as the 'ambassador' inkstand, owing to the convenience with which such a flat object could be carried about. The Londonderry example (Pl. 55B) was made by Hannah Northcote in 1805–6. It is quite plain except for reed-and-tie borders, which also appear on the four feet. There is a

[23] See the pamphlet by E. Alfred Jones, *Catalogue of the Silver Plate in the Offices of the Privy Council and H.M. Treasury*, 1932.

[24] E. Alfred Jones, *Connoisseur*, September 1936, pp. 140–1.

[25] Helen Comstock, *Connoisseur*, April 1940, p. 165.

hinged central handle. One of the divisions contains a cut-glass inkpot and sand-caster. One lid is engraved with the royal arms, and the other with those of Lord Stewart. The breadth is 12 in.

Although a very large proportion of the plate which we have been discussing comes from royal or noble collections, much of it being gilt and of a ceremonial and official massiveness and grandeur, we must not forget that the amount of 'ordinary' plate being bought by the prosperous landed and mercantile classes – both in London and the provinces – was enormous.

The outstanding name in the history of factory-made plate, for either completed articles or component parts, is undoubtedly that of Matthew Boulton of Birmingham. After his success in the manufacturing of Sheffield plate, and adopting the use of the stirling 'silver thread' edge, he decided to turn his attention to silver plate. It was merely a change of material; the same machines, designs and workmen could be used as with Sheffield plate. The screw- or fly-press was capable of cutting out thin metal with great rapidity and forcing it into any required shape. Repetitive patterns in the flat could assume a circular or oval form when bent to the required shape and soldered, thus providing the carcasses for salts, mustard-pots, coasters, the lids of casters and many other objects. At first Boulton was faced with the trouble and risk of sending all his silver articles to Chester, York or London to be hall-marked. With Sheffield the distances were not quite so far, but both Sheffield and Manchester applied for separate Assay offices, which, owing largely to the tireless efforts of Boulton, they obtained in 1773. After this the industry increased immensely, as the lists of goldsmiths entered at both Assay offices testify.

Apart from salts, peppers, mustard-pots and casters, the types of plate most in demand included tureens, vegetable dishes, entrée dishes, coasters, sauce-boats, cruets, toast-racks, wine funnels, cake-baskets, tea and coffee services, salvers, waiters, candelabra, candlesticks, inkstands and all kinds of flat plate, including fish-slices, marrow scoops, etc. To a lesser extent can be added large centre-pieces, épergnes, complete dinner services, punch-bowls, wine-coolers, argyles, tea-urns and lamps. Of small articles we may mention skewers, caddy-spoons, wine-labels, strainers, vinaigrettes, snuff-boxes, table-bells, tobacco-stoppers, etc. Many of these display the most exquisite workmanship. Take, for instance, that charming trifle – the vinaigrette,[26] the very symbol of the Age of Elegance. A later development of the pomander, the dry-spice container, the vinaigrette, as the name clearly indicates, is a container for aromatic vinegar 'to correct the bad Quality of the Air'. The specially fine compact little sponge, which soaked up the aromatic liquid, was covered by a pierced grill on which the goldsmith lavished all his skill, producing charming designs of birds, flowers, musical instruments and even noble country houses.

As a separate entity, the vinaigrette dates from sometime between 1775 and 1790, and we find earlier specimens chased with typical classic motifs, such as the floral swag, the urn, etc. But every technique of the craftsmen was employed on these little objects – different colours of gold, sometimes severely plain and solid, at other times inlaid with precious stones, or fashioned from agate, bloodstone, cornelian or topaz. The designs tended to persist with little change, but if it were necessary to say which typified the Regency, one would indicate the plain engine-turned specimens. As to the makers, we find that the great majority are Birmingham craftsmen, thus indicating that after the Assay office had been established there in 1773, the vinaigrette was one of those miniature pieces which especially appealed to them. Such names as John Bettridge, Francis Clark, John Lawrence and Co., Matthew Linwood, Samuel Pemberton, John Shaw and John Turner may be mentioned. Several London goldsmiths, such as William Abdy, Robert Burton, Samuel Massey, T. Phipps and E. Robinson, are known as makers of both vinaigrettes and wine-labels. As so many of the articles mentioned above are of a type in constant use at the time, we must not expect their designs to conform to a single contemporary style, but to reflect

26 See L. G. G. Ramsey, *Connoisseur*, October 1956, pp. 95–9, and Eileen Ellenbogen, *English Vinaigrettes*, Cambridge, 1956.

rather the personal taste of the owner. We have seen how both rococo and neo-classic designs were popular in Regency times, and it is no easy matter to recognize a typical Regency piece – whatever that is – among ordinary family plate.

There are cases, however, when the 'latest fashion' in silverware declares itself clearly, as for instance when an order is given for an 'up-to-date' set of spoons and forks, or, on the other hand, for something rather unusual in, say, tea-urns or lamps. Just as the age of the lovely Queen Anne tea-pot had long since passed, so, too, the beautiful Old English pattern[27] of spoons and forks had given place to what Jackson calls 'that type of nineteenth-century florid vulgarity known as the King's Pattern'. Its chief characteristic was, of course, the shouldered stem, which had first appeared somewhat unnoticed on double-drop and bright-cut spoons in the middle of the eighteenth century, to which the name of 'fiddle-pattern' was given. If quite plain, the type was simply called 'fiddle-pattern'; if it had reeded borders it was known as the 'Queen's pattern'; but with the additional ornamentation of shells and anthemions it became the 'King's pattern'. Occasionally, as in the two great sets by Paul Storr at Windsor, further embossing was added down the stems. The first of these sets, consisting of over 1,300 pieces, was made between 1811 and 1814, and is known as the 'Boar Hunt and Mask' pattern, while the second set, of slightly earlier date, runs to nearly 2,500 pieces and is known as the 'Honeysuckle' pattern. The line drawings in Fig. 5, taken from a photograph in the special royal inventory at Windsor, shows some of this latter pattern.

The only remaining piece of plate we need mention is the lamp. As we should expect, the neo-classical lamp was based on the Roman lamps such as we find reproduced in the works of Piranesi, Tatham and Hope. There is, however, a most original pair at Windsor made by Storr in 1817. They represent a phœnix rising from the ashes, on rocky plinths, and were intended to burn naphtha,

[27] Oman describes this pattern as more attractive and more usable than any other type produced since 1660.

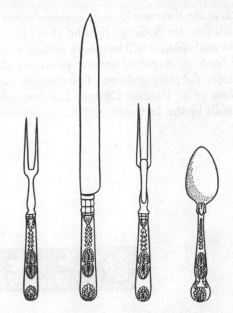

Fig. 5. Examples of the 'Honeysuckle' type of flat plate made by Paul Storr between 1808 and 1812 for the future George IV. *From the Royal Collection at Windsor Castle. Reproduced by gracious permission of Her Majesty the Queen.*

Fig. 6. One of a pair of phoenix lamps intended to burn naphtha. Paul Storr, 1817. *From the Royal Collection at Windsor Castle. Reproduced by gracious permission of Her Majesty the Queen.*

which at the time was an early example of the use of such fuel for domestic lighting (Fig. 6).

In conclusion, it will have been noticed that we have confined ourselves entirely to secular plate. Ecclesiastical plate undergoes few changes, but in the case of St Pancras Church, London, which was built by the Inwoods on Athenian models, it

was necessary to have plate to match. This was made possible through the generosity of H.R.H. Frederick, Duke of York, who commissioned Paul Storr, the greatest figure in Regency gold-smithing, to make a set of fifteen pieces, which he executed with his usual artistry, as our Pl. 55A testifies.

Typographical borders from the 1821 Specimen Book of Vincent Figgins. The top one shows an acanthus, the bottom a lotus flower design.

(A) JOHN SCARLETT DAVIS. The Interior of the British Institution Gallery.
Courtesy Lt.-Col. A. Heywood-Lonsdale. (Canvas $43\frac{3}{4}'' \times 55''$).

(B) C. R. LESLIE. The Grosvenor Family. *Courtesy the Duke of Westminster.*
(Canvas $46'' \times 64''$).

PLATE 33

(A) THOMAS PHILLIPS, R.A. Lady Caroline Lamb. *The Trustees, the Chatsworth Settlement.*
(*Canvas* 36″ × 27½″.)
(B) RICHARD WESTALL. Lord Byron. *National Portrait Gallery.* (*Canvas* 29½″ × 24½″).
(C) SIR HENRY RAEBURN. Self-Portrait. *National Gallery of Scotland.* (*Canvas* 34½″ × 26½″).
(D) ANDREW GEDDES. The Artist's Mother. *National Gallery of Scotland.* (*Canvas* 28¼″ × 23½″).

PLATE 34

(A) JOHN CONSTABLE, R.A. Malvern Hall, Warwickshire, from the Garden Side. *National Gallery.* (*Canvas* $20\frac{1}{4}'' \times 30''$).

(B) JOHN CROME. Moonrise on the Yare. *National Gallery.* (*Canvas* $28'' \times 43\frac{3}{4}''$).

(C) J. M. W. TURNER. Somer Hill, Tonbridge. *National Gallery of Scotland.* (*Canvas* $25'' \times 47''$).

PLATE 35

1123

(B) WILLIAM ETTY. Self-Portrait. *The Ashmolean Museum, Oxford. (Pen and brown ink).*

(A) HENRY EDRIDGE. Robert Southey. *National Portrait Gallery. (Pencil and chalk, 11″ × 8¾″).*

PLATE 36

JOHN CROME. Castle Eden Dean.
National Gallery of Scotland.
(Water-colour on buff paper, 16⅝″ × 14¾″.)

PLATE 37

(A) AUGUSTUS CHARLES PUGIN. A Room in the Royal Pavilion.
Courtesy C. Musgrave, Esq. (Water-colour).

(B) DENIS DIGHTON. The Third and Last Challenge by the Champion during King George IV's Coronation Banquet in Westminster Hall. *Royal Collection, Windsor Castle. Reproduced by gracious permission of Her Majesty the Queen. (Water-colour $16\frac{3}{4}'' \times 21\frac{1}{2}''$).*

PLATE 38

Sir Francis Legatt Chantrey, r.a. Mrs Jordan and her family. *Courtesy the Earl of Munster. (Marble 72″ high).*

PLATE 39

(B) Samuel Joseph. Lady de L'Isle and Dudley.
Courtesy Viscount de L'Isle. (Marble 31" high).

(A) William Behnes. Samuel Woodburn.
Ashmolean Museum, Oxford.

1128

PLATE 40

(A) ANDREW ROBERTSON (1777–1845). An unknown lady.
Victoria and Albert Museum.

(B) FREDERICK CRUICKSHANK (1800–68).
Mr W. H. E. Pattisson. Sketch for a miniature
portrait. *Victoria and Albert Museum.*

PLATE 41

(B) HENRY COLLEN (worked 1820–72) Captain Octavius Vernon-Harcourt, signed, and dated 1838. *Victoria and Albert Museum.*

(A) JOHN LINNELL (1792–1882). An unknown man, signed. *Victoria and Museum.*

(C) ALFRED EDWARD CHALON, R.A. (1781–1860). An unknown lady, signed, and dated 1828. *Victoria and Albert Museum.*

PLATE 42

SIR WILLIAM CHARLES ROSS, R.A. (1794–1860). Mrs Bacon, signed, and dated 1841. *Victoria and Albert Museum.*

PLATE 43

1131

SIMON JACQUES ROCHARD (1788–1872). Miss Mary and Master Patrick Stirling, signed, and dated 1826. *Victoria and Albert Museum.*

PLATE 44

(A) DIGBY SCOTT and BENJAMIN SMITH, 1805 6. Pair of double-lipped wine-glass coolers, embossed each side with classical subjects on a matted ground. *From the Royal collection at Windsor Castle, by gracious permission of H.M. the Queen.*

(B) PAUL STORR, 1812–13. One of a pair of highly rococo silver-gilt soup-tureens and stands resting on the backs of tortoises. The arms of George III are applied each side of the body. Weight 1,073 oz. (the pair). *From the Royal collection at Vindsor Castle, by gracious permission of H.M. the Queen.*

PLATE 45

1133

(A) JOHN BRIDGE. Silver-gilt tureen. One of a set of four made for George IV in 1826. Height 15¼ in. *From the Royal Collection at Windsor Castle, by gracious permission of H.M. the Queen.*

(B) WILLIAM PITTS, 1809. One of a pair of silver-gilt dishes, with shaped edges, the centre panel embossed with a scene of Jupiter in the clouds taking vengeance on the earth, the panel surrounded by swans and bulrushes. *Courtesy the Marquess of Londonderry.*

(C) WILLIAM PITTS, 1810. One of a pair of silver-gilt dishes, with escalloped edges, the broad rim embossed with sprays of different flowers in panels. In the centre is a Tudor rose encircled by a wreath of husk design, with an outer floral border. Diam. 15¼ in. *Courtesy the Marquess of Londonderry.*

(D) PAUL STORR, 1814–15. Circular dish of silver-gilt depicting the Triumph of Dionysus (Bacchus) and Ariadne. The Bacchic emblems seen on the broad rim are largely taken from the Warwick Vase. The royal arms of George IV were added later. Designed by T. Stothard, R.A. Diam. 31 in. Weight 374 oz. 15 dwt. *From the Royal Collection at Windsor Castle, by gracious permission of H.M. the Queen.*

PLATE 46

(A) The Warwick Vase, in its restored state, with a Latin inscription on the pedestal recounting its history and the part played by Sir William Hamilton in its restoration. *Warwick Castle.*

(B) PAUL STORR, 1812–13. One of a pair of silver-gilt wine-coolers in the form of the Warwick Vase, the rims chased with vines on a matter ground. The Harewood coat of arms is applied to the square plinth. Fitted with fruit dishes to match. Height 18 in. *Collection of H.R.H. The Princess Royal and the Earl of Harewood.*

(c) Details of one side of the Warwick Vase showing the eighteenth-century female head on a modern background. The head to the left is original, and that to the right is also eighteenth-century work. *Warwick Castle.*

PLATE 47

(A) PAUL STORR, 1809–10. Candelabrum—silver-gilt—designed by John Flaxman, R.A., depicting the Three Graces gathering the apples of the Hesperides. Height 60 in. Weight 1,386 oz. *From the Royal Collection at Windsor Castle, by gracious permission of H.M. the Queen.*
(B) and (C) PAUL STORR, 1810–11. Pair of silver jugs, based on Roman originals by John Flaxman, R.A. to which spouts, handles and lids have been added. Height 7 in. Greatest circ. 16½ in.
Courtesy Charles Oman, Esq.

PLATE 48

(A) and (B) PAUL STORR, 1812–13. The silver-gilt Theocritus Cup, designed by John Flaxman, R.A. Side showing two youths contending for the favour of a maiden. Height 9½ in. Weight 90 oz. 15 dwt. *From the Royal Collection at Windsor Castle, by gracious permission of H.M. the Queen.* (C) and (D) PAUL STORR, 1817–18. Memorial two-handled cup depicting scenes from the Fields of Elysium, designed by John Flaxman, R.A. Height 9⁵⁄₁₆ in. Width 9⁷⁄₈ in. Weight 82 oz. 9 dwt. *Courtesy the Duke of Wellington, K.G.*

(A) PETER RUNDELL, 1821–2. The Achilles Shield, designed by John Flaxman. *From the Royal Collection at Windsor Castle, by gracious permission of H.M. the Queen.*

(B) PETER RUNDELL, 1822–3. Silver-gilt Salver designed by Benedetto Pistrucci, with a central plaque of St George and the Dragon, and a border adapted from the procession of cavalry on the frieze of the Parthenon. Diam. 28 in. *Victoria and Albert Museum.*

(A) and (B) WILLIAM ELEY, 1798–9. Toasted-cheese dish. The hinged and removable cover is surmounted by a finial in the form of a viscount's coronet and cap. The interior is fitted with six small square dishes. The edge of the dish is gadrooned, and the reeded handles project horizontally. Engraved with the arms and crest of Lord Stewart. Width 12½ in. *Courtesy the Marquess of Londonderry.*

RICHARD COOKE, 1809–10. Tea-urn, with the lower part of the body and the lid gadrooned. Ovolo mouldings to the rims and circular base, reeded handles springing from lion-masks. Reeded spigot with ivory tap. On a square pedestal with scroll feet. Height 17 in. *Courtesy the Marquess of Londonderry.*

PLATE 52

PAUL STORR, 1814–15. Hot-water jug, with gadroon, leaf and shell ornament, vertical reeding on the base. The ivory handle springs from two serpents and rises to a single winged head. Engraved with the royal arms and those of Lord Stewart. Height 10 in. *Courtesy the Marquess of Londonderry.*

PLATE 53

(A) Tea and coffee service in silver-gilt. Chased with an all-over floral pattern. The knops surmounting the larger covered pieces are in the form of the bust of a Chinaman. Mark: SH in an incurved oblong. London 1818–19. *Courtesy the Marquess of Londonderry.*

(B) PAUL STORR and PHILIP RUNDELL, 1818–19 and 1819–20. The Congress of Vienna gold inkstand, made from snuff-boxes presented by the various European countries to Lord Castlereagh. Length 17 in. Width 9⅝ in. Weight 145 oz. *Courtesy the Marquess of Londonderry.*

PLATE 54

(A) PAUL STORR, 1821–22. A selection of the silver-gilt altar plate presented by H.R.H. Frederick, Duke of York, to St Pancras Church, London.

(B) HANNAH NORTHCOTE, 1805–06. Inkstand of 'Treasury' pattern, with borders of reed-and-tie design. The top hinged, with a central handle, and the interior divided, one half fitted with two cut-glass containers for ink and sand. Engraved with the arms of Lord Stewart. Length 12 in. *Courtesy the Marquess of Londonderry.*

PLATE 55   1143

(B) HANNAH NORTHCOTE, 1805–06. Two-handled Vase and cover; reed-and-tie ornamentation on the handle, rim, base and edge of the cover which is surmounted by a Viscount's coronet and cap. Engraved with the royal arms and those of Lord Stewart. *Courtesy the Marquess of Londonderry.*

(A) The Galvanic Goblet. This shows the first electro-gilding in England. *From the Royal Collection at Windsor Castle, by gracious permission of H.M. the Queen.*

(B) Stone china dish with the well-known 'Peacock & Peony' pattern: transfer printed outline over-painted with enamels. Marked SPODE STONE CHINA printed in black. c. 1815. *Spode-Copeland Museum, Stoke-on-Trent.*

(D) Pair of square bulb pots in Swansea porcelain. The covers marked SWANSEA in red. 1814–17.

(A) Dessert plate of felspar porcelain bearing the arms of the Goldsmiths' Company in colours and gold within a rim of apple green, its gadroon edge etched with gold. c. 1820. *Spode-Copeland Museum, Stoke-on-Trent.*

(C) Earthenware vegetable dish and cover in blue and white showing 'Hog-Hunters meeting by surprise a Tigress' taken from Samuel Howett's book *Oriental Field Sports.* c. 1820. *Courtesy Gresham Copeland, Esq.*

PLATE 57

(A) Part of a 33-piece Derby (Bloor) dessert service in bone china, painted in colours with named views.

(B) Part of a teaset in bone china with English scenes hand-painted in colours. Wedgwood, 1815.
Wedgwood Museum, Stoke-on-Trent.

PLATE 58

(A) Blue and white transfer-printed earthenware: 'The Bridge of Lucano' set in a border of corn, vine and olive motifs. Spode. *c.* 1820. *Spode-Copeland Museum, Stoke-on-Trent.*

(B) Bone china plate painted with a country scene. The buff-coloured rim is ornamented with gold spots and brown bell-shaped drops. Marked SPODE impressed. From 1819. *Spode-Copeland Museum, Stoke-on-Trent.*

(C) Sunderland pottery ewer and basin in mottled pink lustre with transfers of the Wearmouth Bridge and the sailing ship 'Northumberland'. Marked DIXON & CO. 1813–19. *Lent by Dr J. Dixon Johnson to the Sunderland Museum.*

(D) Swansea porcelain tea warmer heated by spirit lamp or scented mortar candle. 1814–17. *Victoria and Albert Museum.*

PLATE 59
1147

(A) Ice cream pail with cover and lining. The body and cover are painted with flower groups in natural colours and the crimson ground is ornamented with arabesque embossments in gold. Marked SPODE *967* in red. *c.* 1825. *Spode-Copeland Museum, Stoke-on-Trent.*

(B) Earthenware jug painted with 'The Prince of Wales' stage coach which operated between London and Swansea. Inscribed 'Jacob Goodwin 1810.' Rim and base decorations are in silver lustre. *Brighton Art Gallery and Museum.*

(C) Bone china teapot decorated in the Imari style in deep blues, bold patches of brick red, and green enamels, with gilding. Marked SPODE *967. c.* 1820. *Spode-Copeland Museum, Stoke-on-Trent*

(D) Loving cup in cream coloured earthenware, inscribed 'George Barlow, Ecclesfield, 1822'. *Courtesy Clifford Chubb, Esq.*

PLATE 60

(A) A pair of Derby flower bouquets, the green stalks tied with blue ribands, the flowers modelled in relief and decorated in natural colours; late 1820's.

(B) Rockingham toby jug in bone china; early 1820's. Formerly in the Penrose collection. *Trust Houses Ltd.*

(C) Rockingham china figure ornaments in the form of a dog with puppies and a cat with kittens in baskets. Early 1820's.
Wernher Collection, Luton Hoo.

(D) Staffordshire earthenware figures: a baker's errand boy and a pair of deer with trees, all in painted enamels. *c.* 1825.
Wernher Collection, Luton Hoo

(E) Pearlware figures: Mars in the centre $10\frac{1}{4}$ in. high, flanked by symbolic figures of Spring and Autumn and two figures of musicians. All marked LEEDS POTTERY. Before 1820. *Leeds City Art Gallery.*

PLATE 61

1149

(A) Heavy flint-glass hollow-ware lavishly cut, the forms of cutting being variously combined. 1820's.

(B) Cylindrical decanters with mushroom stoppers. Lavishly decorated with deep cutting in a wide variety of motifs.

(C) Jug, honey-pot and toilet table bottle decorated with large relief diamonds and prismatic cutting.

(D) Finger bowls cut with bands of plain sharp diamonds and fluted bases, and, *below*, wine glass coolers star-cut beneath and with bands of plain sharp diamonds. 1820's. *Courtesy R. Holland, Esq.*

PLATE 62

(A) *Crystallo ceramie* cup with portraits of George III and the Prince Regent between panels of fine diamond-cutting: made by Apsley Pellat. Early 1820's.
By gracious permission of Her Majesty the Queen.

(B) Rummer for serving toddy engraved with scenes in the life of a butcher. This view shows him on his way to deliver meat to a country house. *c.* 1810.
Courtesy O. N. Norris, Esq.

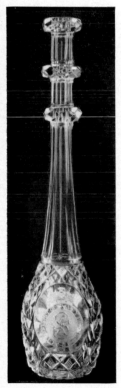

(C) Flint-glass toddy lifter made for the Duke of Sussex. *c.*1820.
Victoria and Albert Museum.

(D) Pair of girandole candlesticks in flint-glass with revolving canopies, gilded metal stem units, and round feet radially cut beneath. Late 1820's. *Corning Museum of Glass, U.S.A.*

PLATE 63   1151

(B) Ormolu and glass chandelier. In the drawing room at Gadebridge Park, Hemel Hempstead, Hertfordshire. c. 1810.

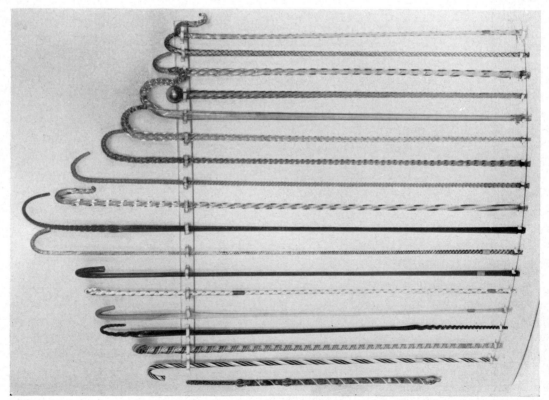

(A) Glass walking sticks: the majority are solid with coloured twist decoration, others are hollow and filled with 'hundreds and thousands' in bands of alternating colours. 1810–30. *Courtesy the Rt. Hon. Alan Lennox-Boyd, M.P.*

PLATE 64

Earthenware, China and Glass

G. BERNARD HUGHES

The Countess of Granville in the autumn of 1810 wrote: 'Dinner [for the earl and herself] consisted of soup, fish, fricassée of chicken, cutlets, veal, hare, vegetables of all kinds, tart, melon, pineapple, grapes, peaches, nectarines with wine in proportion. Six servants wait upon us, a gentleman-in-waiting and a fat old housekeeper hovering round the door. Four hours later the door opens and in is pushed a supper of the same proportion.'

Silver, plate, china and cut-glass for such a meal was equally profuse: when guests were present the amount tabled was prodigious. Butlers now stored their silver in strong rooms, although in old-fashioned establishments the plate was returned to chests deposited in the trunk room adjoining the master's bedroom.

China and glass not in daily use was stored in the china closet. Tiers of shelves to the ceiling displayed gleaming surfaces of glaze painted with rich, lustrous enamels. Many of these treasures were, of course, inherited: soft paste porcelains potted at Bow, Chelsea, Derby and Worcester, and fine earthenwares from Wedgwood and Spode. By 1810 these had been joined by bone china and the so-called semi-porcelains such as stone china (Pl. 57B) and felspar porcelain (Pl. 57A). These were fashionably enamelled with the family coat-of-arms in full colours, or might display fantastic birds with long tails and crested top-knots, among flowers of impossible colour and form; fierce dragons with knobbly claws and rolling eyes; rivers thickly sprinkled with tiny, fairy boats; English scenes and mansions among homely meadows and heavy trees. Every room in the house, too, was garnished with china, ranging from vestibule vases, capacious fish globes, and pastille burners to toilet sets in the dressing rooms.

It has become customary to decry English ceramics of the early nineteenth century. Those who do so fail to appreciate their technical excellence. Improved methods produced stronger and more colourful ware capable of giving enduring service yet within purse reach of the general public. The pottery industry was revolutionized and Britain dominated world markets for the next hundred years.

Bone china (Pls. 58A, B, and 59B) was the most important of the new ceramics, replacing as it did the soft porcelains. It was brought to perfection by Josiah Spode in the early 1790's, and ledgers still in existence prove it to have been on sale in 1794 under the name of British Cornish china. The term china was eventually deemed unsatisfactory, as for almost half a century it had been associated in the public mind with the more fragile soft porcelains. Josiah Spode II, then, in 1810, under pressure from his partner William Copeland, renamed their British Cornish china, calling it Stoke porcelain. When in 1814 Spode (Pls. 57B; 59A, B; 60A, C) was appointed potter to the Prince of Wales he was cited as 'Potter and Manufacturer of Stoke Porcelain'. Bone china is a late Victorian trade name.

Domestic ware in bone china gave enduring service, and its glaze was such that overglaze colours sank into it permanently and did not flake. Enamelling became a less hazardous process and the intense fusion produced a less painted-looking finish.

1153

Greater brilliance in the hue of the enamel was possible after 1812 when Samuel Walker's high temperature enamelling kiln replaced the small box muffle in which ware had been baked without exposing it to direct contact with the flames. Hitherto it had been customary for purchasers to select their patterns from the china-seller's sheets of hand-painted designs. The dealer then commissioned an independent enameller to decorate the service, which had been bought from the potter in the white. The introduction of the enamelling kiln now meant that much more domestic ware was painted in the factory than formerly.

Oriental designs adapted to the English taste were ornamenting bone china table services by 1805 and had become the height of fashion by 1810. If analysed such patterns may appear more essentially Chinese than Japanese, although a superficial resemblance to Imari porcelain has led to their classification as Japanese. Less numerous on table services were decorations of the Kakiemon type. The Shanghai pattern by Spode was of Chinese inspiration and copied by other Staffordshire potters using the old muffle enamelling process on bone china badly flawed with specks. Although the Chinese influence on table services declined during the 1820's there was a distinct vogue for patterns in the Imari style, with flowers and shrubbery in vivid colours surrounded by gilt tracery.

Hard, translucent felspar porcelain, again a Spode invention, enriched many a nobleman's table in the form of magnificent dinner services in which the centre of each piece expansively displayed in full colours the owner's coat of arms (Pl. 57A) and the rims were radiant with heavily gilded ornament. Sometimes an old gold colour replaced gilding, its effect being considered more in harmony with the enamelled armorial design. Dessert services in felspar porcelain might bear painted landscapes with titles, and borders of conventional flowers. Stone china (Pl. 57B), a felspathic earthenware of delicate grey-blue body which emitted a clear ring when lightly tapped, was ornamented with old Chinese designs. Extensive table services in this ware were in great demand.

Families at this time were large and entertainment lavish. Dinner services were standardized to

twelve covers, but frequently extended to thirty-six, with thirty serving dishes for game and meat. Plates for the three main courses were of the same size and the service also included soup plates. Dinner and dessert services combined became fashionable, the pieces matching. These ranged from soup and vegetable tureens to shell-shaped dessert dishes and dessert plates. The old practice of serving dessert on ware of a different type and pattern continued, however. A typical family service contained a pair of tazze, four dishes and twelve plates.

Special services were evolved for supper and from about 1815 were made up of about 130 separate pieces: four fan-shaped dishes and covers, four square dishes and covers, one octagonal dish, liner and cover, two sauce tureens and stands, with ladles, two oval egg-stands each with twelve egg cups, six octagonal meat dishes, four oval dishes, a salad bowl, twenty-four each of soup, dinner and dessert plates. The combined tea and coffee set with but a single set of saucers now gave way to one with a full complement of saucers.

The late Georgian period was the heyday of blue-and-white transfer-printed domestic ware (Pls. 57C and 59A), from table services to toilet accessories, in bone china and in earthenware. The majority were made in Staffordshire, many at Leeds and on Tyneside. Fine tone gradations were achieved by 1810 by combining line and stipple engraving on a single copper-plate. Skilful use of light and shade resulted for the first time in well-balanced pictures, clear in detail, yet covering every part of the ware, thus concealing surface flaws in the fabric which in consequence was of a cheaper quality than that needed for enamel painted decoration.

Blues became more brilliant from about 1816 when the close of the Napoleonic wars made it possible once more to import fine Saxon cobalt. Shades of blue were now given such trade names as Canton, zaffres, glowing blue, willow blue, mazarine, and flower-blue. The war-time English cobalt blues and synthetic blues continued in use but only on the cheapest earthenwares. In 1828 it was discovered that certain crushed enamel colours mixed with barbados tar would, like cobalt, print direct to the fired but unglazed ware known as the biscuit, without distorting during glazing. These were various tints of green, red and yellow, but although they had a few years of popularity they failed to oust Staffordshire blue.

Transferred subjects had been derived formerly from Chinese blue and white. These gave way from about 1810 in favour of purely English subjects. Dinner and tea services presented the English scene with imaginative enthusiasm – the beauty spots, cathedrals, cities and resorts then considered to qualify as picturesque views. Staffordshire blue was not intended for use on formal occasions, but for daily service in the home, its pattern being protected by the glaze.

Each flat piece in a Staffordshire blue table service, every dish, plate, sauce-boat and gravy-tray displayed a picture. Each piece of hollow-ware, whether jug, vegetable dish or sugar-bowl, carried three or four differing scenes on its inner and outer surfaces. At least twelve pictures belonging to a series would decorate a table service, but as many as seventy-two have been noted on a dinner service illustrating the travels of Dr Syntax. Between 1816 and 1830 the list of potters specializing in blue-printed ware exceeded fifty, in addition to the transfer-print departments operated by several of the great potters.

A glimpse of the large amount of miscellaneous ware that might be stored in the china closet was extracted from the Spode ledgers of this period by Arthur Hayden. Included were artichoke cups, asparagus trays, broth bowls, butter tubs and stands, card racks, chamber candlesticks with extinguishers, cheese dishes, cheese toasters, chestnut vases, chicken tureens, custard cups, cylinder pin-cases to screw, ice-pails, inkstands and pen-trays, match-pots, mugs, radish trays, roll-trays, root-dishes, rouge-pots, salad bowls, sandwich sets, scent-jars, snuff-boxes, snuffer trays, steak-dishes with compartments, strawberry baskets, sugar boxes, supper plates, syrup pots, toast-racks, turtle pans, violet baskets and wafer boxes. Punch and toddy bowls ranging from two gallon to quart capacity were bought in matching sets. It was customary for these drinks to be served hot, hence the tall foot rim for protecting the table surface from heat.

Ironstone china, patented by Charles James Mason in 1813, was a hard earthenware capable of development far beyond the range of tableware, for which it was eminently suitable. Sets of bedposts, enormous vases for drawing-rooms and vestibules, huge wine cooling cisterns and goldfish globes were made as well as fireplaces in full- and half-size. Fireplaces, typically, were finished with a white-glazed ground enriched with trailing leaf-patterns in gold and panels of flower and foliage sprays in pink, puce, pale green, apple green, vermilion, blue. Panel ornament differed in each; flowers included peonies, full blown roses, hawthorn sprigs and daisies, all with their foliage, as well as dragonflies, butterflies and other flying creatures. It was Mason who evolved the celebrated jugs which bear his name and appear to have been in unceasing production since. These octagonal jugs with snake handles and colours of sparkling brilliance were issued in sets of a dozen sizes. Their low price precluded high quality in decoration and finish.

The Napoleonic style in ornamental ceramics is recorded in pattern books of 1810, with such features as the plinth base with lion-paw feet. Details were sumptuously gilded, often with scroll-work in low relief, as evolved in 1802 by Henry Daniel. Solid grounds in burnished or matt gold, and grounds of gold scale on blue and of stippled gold were fashionable. Increased domestic illumination from oil-lamp and gas-chandelier made the most of this brilliance. The revived Rococo style of the silversmiths was adopted by Coalport and Rockingham and within five years every leading potter had followed their example.

Pictorial reserves (Pls. 58A and B; 59A and B), from about 1815, tended towards the English rural style with such border *motifs* as birds, landscapes, flowers, fruit, shells and feathers. These were usually painted on the white against such ground colours as dark and scale blues, apple green, yellowish green, deep yellow, canary yellow, greyish turquoise, marbled brown, marbled blue, crimson, salmon, lavender and cane colour. Designs favoured half a century earlier by Chelsea and Worcester were revived, and much of this bone china now masquerades as soft porcelain in the cabinets of collectors. The claret ground with bird decoration in gold, a Chelsea style, was widely copied, the finest coming from Spode, but even his ground colour failed to reach Chelsea's full splendour until the 1830's. Spode did succeed, however, in reproducing the *gros bleu* of Dr Wall's Worcester, although in the salmon-scale ground his blue was livelier than the original.

George IV as Regent and as King was an extravagant collector of pre-Revolution Sèvres porcelain. He established a vogue that made the French ware so scarce that by 1815 it was almost unobtainable. The trade in Sèvres for decorating the home became so profitable that any expedient was used for acquiring supplies. These was a demand, long in vain, for an English potter capable of reproducing old-style Sèvres complete with the famous double-L monogram. In 1825 Thomas Randall established a pottery for this purpose at Madeley in Shropshire, but refused to forge the Sèvres mark. His productions were virtually indistinguishable from Sèvres, and many china cabinets of the period and today preserve old Madeley instead of Sèvres. Consignments of Madeley porcelain are known to have been sent to Dover and from there despatched to London as fresh arrivals from Parisian dealers.

The finely modelled figures in soft porcelain that had formerly decorated pier tables and wall brackets and had been grouped at the centre of dining and dessert tables, were now superseded by ostentatious vases, singly, in pairs or in garnitures of three or five. Three tall urns flanked by a pair of pot-pourri vases decorated in a matching design constituted a drawing-room vogue of the period and in the late 1820's these might be centred by a clock set in a flamboyant flower-encrusted case of bone china.

For drawing-rooms, entrance halls and passages there were massive covered vases in bone china, sometimes exceeding a yard in height, supported on separate pedestals rimmed with pierced galleries of ormolu. Oval *jardinières* might have a dark blue ground with rims encircled in non-repeating flower patterns and mounted with elaborate ormolu work. Some vases early in the period displayed Moorish characteristics in their richly gilt arabesque patterns. Later vases with a *bleu de roi* ground were enriched with reserves containing meticulously painted pictorial scenes or copies of French paintings.

Ceramic figures (Pls. 61 D and E) were made in vast quantities, but these were mainly in earthenware and found no place in the fashionable home unless in kitchen or servants' quarters. The Derby factory continued making the figures that had brought wealth to Duesbury in the eighteenth century, but now in bone china. These were more lively and of greater charm than any competing figures until the 1830's. There was little enough to recommend them, however, beyond a general gaudy splendour.

The general public, nevertheless, clamoured for the crudely formed, garishly coloured earthenware figures issued in many tens of thousands each year and sold in the streets from a tray of twenty or thirty specimens balanced upon the hawker's head. A prolific maker of these was John Walton of Burslem, using a cheap, brittle earthenware capable of high-speed moulding. Almost every small home in the country possessed a few of these colourful trifles costing only a few pence each. Ralph Salt of Hanley specialized in the rather more costly *bocage* pieces, sporting dogs, and sheep with hand-raised wool: these had a country-wide sale. Among the twenty other potters producing figures at this time was Obadiah Sherratt of Hot Lane, who made some popular large chimney-piece ornaments; his 'Politos Menagerie' of about 1816 was considered a triumph of casting and firing.

Any home of pretension, no matter what its size, ensured that every room was sweet-smelling in those days of perfunctory sanitation by using pastille burners. Such a burner from about 1820 might be in the form of a bone-china or earthenware cottage containing a slowly smouldering perfumed cone composed of powdered willow-wood charcoal, benzoin, perfumed oils and gum arabic. These cottages represented old-world dwellings surrounded by gay flower-beds, minute coloured flowers encrusting the walls and edging the roof, with gilt chimneys from which curled the pastille's scented fumes. There were also turreted castle gateways, circular toll houses with conical roofs, clock towers, thatched farmhouses with flowery arbours, and many another rustic building.

Night-light shelters in the form of cottages immediately followed the invention of the self-consuming candle-wick in 1825. Faint, unflickering light from a short, thick mortar candle that did not require periodic snuffing glowed from the cut-out windows. The tiny flame was well-protected against draughts, too, and was a source of flame in those days of laborious flint-striking.

Lithophane night-light shelters date from 1828. These pictorial transparencies were made from a thin, glassy hard porcelain and gave the effect of detailed mezzotints by precise variations in the thickness and consequent opacity of the material. Lithophanes were also used as firescreens and panels for hall lanterns. Even teacups with enamelled decoration on their sides might surprise the visiting users with lithophanes in their bases, the pictures becoming visible as the cups were tilted against the light.

Food warmers, catalogued as pap-warmers, performed the duties of night-light shelter as well as keeping hot liquids warm enough to drink during the night. These vessels were in three parts: pedestal, loose cup and cover. The pedestal was an open-sided cylinder fitted with a mortar which acted as a source of heat and a night-light. Fitting loosely into its open top was a round-based covered cup. The pedestal top from about 1825 might be made in a piece with a deep inner bowl for containing boiling water. Into this fitted the covered drinking cup. This was still heated by a mortar. At about the same time appeared tea warmers in bone china and porcelain (Pl. 59D). The fully enclosed pedestal held a teapot, the whole being enamelled to match the tea service.

The scintillating glints of lustre ware began to enliven the living-rooms and kitchens of lesser homes during this period and even tea services were decorated with films of lustrous metal. Silver lustre, obtained from platinum oxide, was introduced by the Wedgwood firm in 1805, but the all-over form which made earthenware resemble sterling silver plate or plated ware began its astonishing vogue in 1823.

Stencilled effects were evolved by John Davenport in 1806, but little was made until 1810, when it met with the competition of silver resist lustre. In the same years Peter Warburton of New Hall patented a method of transfer-printing in gold and silver lustre. Moonlight effects, now known as marbling, were introduced in the same year. Later came the mottled pink lustre of Sunderland (Pl. 59C).

Mocha ware, so named because of its resemblance to the quartz mocha stone, was in demand for kitchen jugs and mugs and large cups and saucers after its invention about 1780. Its base was of cream-coloured earthenware. The shaped clay was covered with chestnut brown, green or yellow slip: over this was applied a slip in contrasting colour – usually brown, but green, blue and black might be used – mixed with tobacco and hops. This spread into patterns suggestive of trees, feathers and moss. From about 1830 a stronger base was used, either white earthenware or cane-coloured stoneware.

Dipped ware was also a favoured decoration for inexpensive but colourful kitchen earthenware. This consisted of hollow-ware in which slips of three colours – blue, brown and yellow – were applied to the biscuit. Skilful workers could produce attractive bands, stripes, spots, curves and spirals at great speed. The ware was fitted into a lathe and, when revolving, slips were poured into a three-sectioned funnel, emerging from adjoining openings and held in such a way that a fine stream of tri-coloured slip flowed upon it.

A list of major potters is given on page 103.

Glass

Flint-glass was never more splendid than in the days of the Regency and George IV. Lavish cutting gave it a spectacular prismatic fire, as innumerable diamond shapes were cut deeply and expertly over the entire surface of table ware or ornament. But equally notable in its way was this period's accomplishment in providing a reasonably effective substitute for this craftsman-created glitter, so that middle-class homes could enjoy less costly decorative glassware shaped by blowing in open-and-shut moulds and only finished by hand. Glass-cutters from about 1810 were installing steam-driven cutting wheels, the speed of production enabling more complex patterns to be cut at no extra cost. The high excise duty, however, ensured that finely cut flint-glass remained in the luxury class of domestic refinements. The size of the diamonds was gradually lessened, the tendency being to reduce cross-cut diamonds to small plain diamonds and the latter to even smaller dimensions from about 1820, when prismatic- or step-cutting was also used with scintillating effect.

Armorial table services were a source of pride to those who could afford them at this period. A combined wine and dessert service would consist of more than five hundred matching pieces, blown from the finest piling pot glass and each engraved with an expansive coat of arms cut on a shield against a plain ground reserved in the cutting design. Some of these coats of arms were superb examples of the glass engraver's craft, the Lambton arms, for instance, possessing a shield with twenty-five quarterings. The Marquess of Londonderry's service made by the Wear Flint Glass Company in 1824 cost two thousand guineas. This was designed for twenty-four covers and consisted of more than five hundred pieces, including wine-glasses in four sizes, ship's decanters and other quart-size decanters (Pl. 62B), claret jugs, water jugs (Pl. 62A), finger bowls (Pl. 62D), wine-glass coolers (Pl. 62D), tumblers, dry sweetmeat jars (Pl. 62C), dessert dishes and plates.

The shapes of table ware during the period were based on geometric forms (Pl. 62B). Decanters, for instance, were cylindrical, at first with deep relief cutting on the shoulders and from 1820 with prismatic cutting, and by the mid-1820's with horizontal shoulders. These vessels were of thick section and much heavier to lift than formerly. The body was fashionably encircled with two or three bands of contrasting cut motifs separated by flat polished rings. These were produced in endless variations. Some of the most complex designs in diamond-cutting are to be found on cylindrical decanters from about 1820. Mushroom stoppers continued in use until about 1820 when heavy pinnacles became the fashionable stopper finials.

Mouths flared widely and gracefully outward from immediately above the neck rings. At the coronation of William IV in 1831 Apsley Pellat introduced the 'royal shape' nearly cylindrical decanter with sides slanting outward from the shoulder to base and these cut with twelve or fourteen bold vertical flutes. Fancy decanters date from the same year.

The fashion for drinking hot toddy increased during the late Regency years, and many a home possessed a pair of giant rummers in which the toddy was prepared. A bucket or ovoid (Pl. 63B) bowl was usual on such a rummer, and this might be lavishly engraved with personal emblems or cut in a stock pattern with a cartouche left for engraving crest or cypher. Such a rummer was accompanied by a toddy lifter (Pl. 63C) – a pipette with a long slender tubular neck terminating in a bulbous container, drilled with a hole in its flat base. Among other glassware that now found a place in the home were such pieces as beehives and covers for honey, butter boats with handles, and egg-cups.

Table glass might be blown within a two-piece open-and-shut mould which had come into general use by 1810. By this means the form of the vessel and elaborate all-over designs in relief could be made in a few simple hand operations. By 1820 three-piece moulds were in use. This process brought flint-glass to the everyday tables of the middle-classes and into general use on formal occasions among the not-so-rich.

Almost every vessel made by free-blowing and hand-cutting was reproduced in the open-and-shut mould, such as celery vases, sugar basins, *compote* bowls, salt cellars, hats for tooth-picks, jugs, casters. Some hollow-ware vessels, such as cordial decanters, salad bowls, rummers and so on, were given pinched square feet, made separately and welded into position. Until the early 1820's the patterns on blown-moulded glass were geometrical; then baroque ornament was made possible by the three-piece mould and designs included fanciful curves in high relief with the addition of honeysuckle flowers, hearts, shells, fans, trefoils and the guilloche motif specifically designed to suit the new method.

Heavy tumblers were made in both fine quality

and tale flint-glass by this method. Tumblers in tale glass, a second quality glass taken from the top and bottom of the melting pot, now toughly annealed, replaced pewter mugs in taverns and other places of public resort. Tumblers at this time were short, broad and heavy-based. In best flint-glass the sharpness and fine detail of the cutting gave to the metal in certain lights a brilliance akin to that of silver. Serving jugs in great variety were moulded for pattern and body shape in open-and-shut decanter moulds and finished by hand manipulation.

Wax candles, faintly perfumed, burning in cut-glass fixtures were considered the ultimate in Regency illumination. The crystal arms to such fixtures were festooned with ropes of carefully faceted lustres and often the candles rose from flower-calyx sockets. The chandelier of the mansion state-room now became a vast canopy of pendant lustres closely spaced and entirely enclosing the central shaft, now of metal; from concentric rings fixed to the base sprang several short branches fitted with sockets. These were entirely of glass, except for the rings. Less lavishly there was a central ornamental shaft of glass constructed from blown units, with six, eight, or twelve branches extending from an urn-shaped member near the base. Canopies and base were hung with lustres. Sets of wall lights were entirely of glass, except for the back-plates of gilded brass: there might be as many as a dozen matching lights on the walls of a drawing-room in addition to a single magnificent chandelier. These were festooned with strings of lustres. In the 1820's joints in the shaft and the socket holders might also be in gilded brass.

By 1810 candelabra for pier table and mantel-shelf had lost their attractive light reflecting finials: instead, every part of the glass surface was diamond-cut, and by 1820 foot, pillar and canopy might be step-cut, the prisms cut at angles best suited for reflecting the light. Lustre drops were now elongated into a drooping slenderness: these were used in association with festoons of smaller lustres. They were succeeded by flat-surfaced hanging prisms more adequately reflecting the greater illumination provided.

The girandole-candlestick was now made with an inverted saucer foot of the same diameter as the canopy, its edges either plain or encircled with short, narrow flutes. Then, in about 1815, came the umbrella canopy and from a heavy, facet-cut knop rose an expansive saucer-shaped socket with a spreading horizontal rim. The entire surface was diamond-cut in relief. This was followed by the double-cascade girandole-candlestick. In the early 1820's the flat, disc foot was preferred and long lustres resembling thin, pear-shaped icicles, each extending almost the length of the body (Pl. 63D).

Desks, dressing-tables and dining-tables during the 1820's might be enriched with glass accessories containing profile portraits, coats of arms and other ornaments emitting a silvery brilliance within the glass. These were invented in 1819 by Apsley Pellat and marketed as *crystallo ceramie* (Pl. 63C). Late Georgians were fascinated by the wide range of glass in which these trifles were embedded: decanters and stoppers, goblets, tumblers, mugs, sugar-basins in tea-caddy sets, ice plates, knife-rests, scent and aromatic vinegar bottles, and wall plaques of celebrities.

Coloured glass in quantity began to enrich the English home from about 1815, its cost being one penny per pound more than clear flint-glass. Bristol blue had been harshly purple in hue because of war-time withdrawal of supplies of Saxon zaffre and smalt, synthetic ultramarine being used as an alternative from about 1805. By about 1820 the use of Saxon smalt was producing a royal-purple tinge. This became known as king's blue when George IV expressed his admiration of a coronation gift of a gilded blue glass spirit set—three labelled decanters, a dozen glasses and a large oval tray of blue glass. It thereupon became a fashionable conceit to make finger-bowls and wine-glass coolers in this metal, the remainder of the table equipage being in fine-quality cut flint-glass. King's blue was costly and found only in blown ware. Pot metal coloured with zaffre was used for cheaper glass. Pale green hock glasses with wide hollow stems were also fashionable, a style revived from the late seventeenth century. They were catalogued as 'Hock Glasses, threaded and prunted, 1/- per pound more than wines'.

H

Christmas lights – they were of course used for other occasions – were blown in open and shut moulds from transparent pot metals of blue, purple, green, ruby red and amber, the surface decorated with a close diamond-quilted pattern. The little oil-burning bowl, without stem or foot, was rimmed to take a wire for hanging.

The colourful trifles in glass associated with the name of Nailsea, but made also at other glass centres such as Tyneside and Stourbridge, gave a touch of luxury to many otherwise austere homes. A pale-green bottle glass blown into flasks and decorated with loops, mottles and flecks in white had been evolved to avoid the high tax payable on flint-glass. By 1815 this low-taxed glass was coloured with metallic oxides to give shades of blue, green, amber and red. These flasks in flattened baluster forms were produced in large numbers: for the most part they were sold as containers of toilet waters. For toilet water too was the gimmel flask – a twin flask with two containers and spouts. Some were given a crimped or petal foot for standing upright on the toilet table.

Flasks in the form of hand-bellows were made in flint-glass enriched with notches, loops and trailed work, and in coloured glass such as blue or red with loops and trailed work in white enamel. Giant bellows flasks, a foot or more in height, for mantelshelf or dressing-table, were made, their nozzles expanded into deep saucer shapes and crimped. These were filled with perfumed water, which pleasantly scented the room.

Coloured glass bells with clappers in clear flint-glass had a delightful resonant tone and were used on the table to summon a servant or in the hall to summon the family at meal-times. These were made in pot-metals, handle and bell in contrasting colours.

Among the larger ornaments intended to hang on parlour walls during the 1820's were slender poignards and dress swords; coaching horns, measuring forty to forty-five inches in length and often containing three loops; giant tobacco pipes; riding-crops. There were walking sticks (Pl. 64A), too, and canes and shepherds' crooks, red, white and blue spirals being particularly popular. These were tapered at the ends and might be enriched with spiral threads in red, blue, green, amber or white opaque glass. Hollow canes of clear flint-glass were filled with comfits and the ferrules plugged with cork.

Rolling-pins in bottle-glass continued their traditional use as salt containers until about 1820, hanging in the kitchen fireplace to keep dry the expensive salt then burdened with a tax of thirty times its cost of manufacture. Some were sold filled with tea or sugar. By 1815, made in clear flint-glass, rolling-pins might be filled with colourful comfits, and became attractive gifts for sweethearts. Soon they were being gilded, painted and engraved with mottoes and good wishes. Such rolling-pins were regarded as lucky charms and were not removed from the wall until pastry was being prepared ceremoniously for a wedding breakfast. They were also advertised as 'sailors' charms'.

Glass spheres, known as watch-balls, in which a whole room was mirrored in miniature, continued to be made, but with some distortion in the reflections. Nailsea also made balls in coloured glass intended as jug-covers to prevent the entry of insects and dust. From 1820 these might be spotted, looped or spiralled in opaque white.

The principal products of the leading Regency potters

NAME OF POTTERY	DATE OF ESTAB.	CERAMICS POTTED 1810–1830
Adams (Stoke-upon-Trent)	1790's	cream-coloured earthenware; basalt; stoneware; bone china from 1816
Coalport	1795	bone china; felspar porcelain from 1822
Davenport	1795	earthenware; cream-coloured earthenware; bone china; stone china; lustre ware from c. 1820
Derby (Bloor from 1815)	1749	bone china
Herculaneum (Liverpool)	1800	bone china; earthenware
Madeley	1825	soft paste porcelain
Mason	1797	earthenware; bone china; stone china; ironstone china from 1813
Minton	1793	earthenware; bone china
Nantgarw & Swansea	1813	soft paste porcelain and soapstone porcelain until 1823
New Hall	1781	hard paste porcelain to about 1810; bone china from 1810
Ridgway	1802	fine earthenware; stone china; bone china
Rockingham (Brameld)	1807	cream-coloured earthenware; stone ware; bone china from 1820
Spode	1776	earthenware; bone china; felspar porcelain; stone china; new stone china from 1810
Swansea (Cambrian Pottery)	1769	earthenware; cream-coloured earthenware; stone china; lustre ware from early 1820's (see Nantgarw)
Wedgwood	1759	earthenware; cream-coloured earthenware; basalt; unglazed earthenware; bone china 1812–1822
Worcester	1751	bone china

With the exception of Madeley and Nantgarw, all the above issued blue and white transfer printed ware. There were also twenty other makers of bone china in Staffordshire listed in 1818. Earthenware potters in 1820 numbered at least a hundred, established in Staffordshire, Yorkshire, Sunderland, London, Derbyshire and elsewhere. Some of the more important of these were Joseph Stubbs, Enoch Wood, Clews, Rogers, of Staffordshire; Joseph Bourne of Denby; Doulton at Lambeth.

Spode's 'Grasshopper' pattern: the transfer for
a six-inch tea plate taken from the original engraved copper plates. *Spode-Copeland Museum.*

Architectural and Domestic Metalwork

BRIAN READE

Cast iron

By 1810 the Industrial Revolution had transformed the character of the metal industries to a point where differences between metropolitan and regional craftsmanship scarcely existed. For all but the very rich, who could still afford to commission anything, it was the beginning of a ready-made age. An industrial hierarchy similar to the one we know had emerged, from manager to workman; and the products of the iron industry originated not from blacksmiths' fancies, out of tradition, but in the heads of designers, materializing at the hands of skilled, but largely dependent, artisans.

The art of casting from moulds goes back a long way. It was the scale that was new. And the scale of a cast-iron factory had to be fairly large to work economically. In other words, multiple production paid only when a large enough market was foreseen to justify the expense of equipment. Since moulds were not scrapped until they wore out, consumers had to accustom themselves to a degree of inflexibility in designs that was altogether novel. Some of the iron moulds made in 1810 are known to have been in use in 1830, and grates and railings designed in 1830 were still to be had new, without any modification of form or detail, in 1850. Moreover, while it was possible for someone in the depths of the country to order a stove of the best quality in the latest fashion, it was equally possible for someone in London to order a new stove in the style of many years back – and such things often took place. So that the age and generation of the consumer became more significant than his locality, and his tastes could be restricted within limits by

the iron trade just as long as those limits were profitable. In this context, therefore, conservatism became the new provincialism, and the time factor became more important than the geographical one.

The English metal industries had taken a considerable lead in these developments during the late eighteenth century, and at the end of the Napoleonic War there were even better opportunities for cast iron. Household and architectural fittings were produced in it more and more, leaving the blacksmith with little else than his horse-shoes and pothooks. An anonymous writer in Ackermann's *Repository* number of 1st December 1816, reflects some of the optimism that the iron-founders must have felt then.

> 'The manufacture of iron [he reports] has been greatly benefited by improvements in the art of casting it, by which the embossed parts are relieved from the moulds with so much purity, that little labour is afterwards required to complete the richest ornamental work in this metal, which is therefore performed at a small expense compared with the execution of such work a short time since, and as iron itself is now at a very reduced price, it may be expected that richly embossed works will come into frequent use.'

He adds that cast iron was by that date 'so generally substituted for several other materials, that the century may not improperly be called another *iron* age' ... and even less improperly perhaps a cast-iron age.

Although some of the great foundries were situated in London, many more were in Birmingham and Sheffield, and in other towns near to the coalfields: indeed, one of the biggest of them was the Carron Company, in the village of Carron in Stirlingshire. These foundries sometimes issued pattern-books of their products for the use of retailers; and what was probably the most ambitious book of cast-iron patterns issued during the Regency, with designs for grates, railings and other constructions, was published in 1811 by M. and G. Skidmore, founders, of High Holborn and Clerkenwell. 'The great Utility of this Work', says the preface, 'will appear ... to those whose Premises or Capital will not permit them to keep a Stock in Hand, and who are not willing to risk the Fluctuations of Patterns.' By and large, the patterns may be said to show the pervading influence of Soane. The motifs are mainly neo-classical, with reeding and lattice decoration to the fore; but Egyptian details abound, and there are quite a number of neo-Gothic designs. It was possible, as the preface explains, to vary the cast-iron members: frets, grate fronts and fire-pieces, for instance, could be transposed. But there is evidence too of the way in which these patterns survived the 'fluctuations' of twenty years in the fact that J. S. Mor-

ris, a stove manufacturer of Devonport, reproduced one for a Gothic grate in an advertisement in the Plymouth directory of 1830 (Fig. 1).

The Skidmore engravings show the hob grate, with cheeks and back in one piece; the vase grate in the new shape of a sarcophagus; the open grate in the late eighteenth-century style; and, most typical of the period, the register grate inspired by Count von Rumford's heating improvements of 1796. This type of grate was closed at the back, with a little hinged lid opening into the chimney, which arrangement not only concentrated the draught, but reduced gusts of smoke. In later designs, such as those issued in the 1820's by Longden, Walker & Company, of the Phœnix Foundry, Sheffield, the ornaments have become — as the Ackermann writer foretold — more richly embossed. (Pl. 65B). They have acquired a stolid kind of elegance to match the architecture of Basevi and furniture in the style of the Nicholsons. Apart from the older anthemion, water-leaf and acanthus ornaments of the Grecian taste (treated more naturalistically, however), the Longden patterns show a good many spiral

Fig. 1. Engraved advertisement from Robert Brindley's *Plymouth, Devonport and Stonehouse Directory*, 1830.

colonettes and beadings, a few wreaths and roses, and motifs of an indigenous character based on ivy- and oak-leaves. Some of the fire-bars are turned in baluster fashion, with large knops: some of the pedestals are decorated with acanthus leaves on consoles. Cast brass details are indicated more plentifully than in the Skidmore designs, making it clear that whereas in the eighteenth century the contrast of brass and steel or iron in a grate was a contrast of parts, by 1820 it had become a contrast of background and applied ornaments.

Closed stoves in the Continental style were also used, but mainly in public rooms. They were generally of the urn-and-pedestal shape, like the Empyreal Stove made by Izons, Whitehurst & Izon of Birmingham. At the end of our period the London firm of Rippon and Burton, established in 1820, patented the Chunk Stove, which was doorless, in the shape of a fluted half-column, with a pipe-flue to run under the floor.

It was the age, too, of the kitchen range (Fig. 1). Like the register stove and grate, this contrivance appeared on the market at the end of the eighteenth century, in the wake of Count von Rumford's researches. Describing a range in 1807 in his *Letters from England by Don Manuel Espriella*, Robert Southey tells us that 'the top of the fire is covered with an iron plate, so that the flame and smoke, instead of ascending, pass through bars on the one side, and there heat an iron front, against which food may be roasted as well as by the fire itself; it passes on heating stoves and boilers as it goes, and the smoke is not suffered to pass up the chimney till it can no longer be of any use. On the other side is an oven heated by the same fire, and vessels for boiling may be placed on the plate over the fire. The smoke finally sets a kind of wheel in motion in the chimney, which turns the spit.' With little modification, and not much improvement, this type of kitchen range survived until the middle of the nineteenth century.

In 1811 the Skidmores gave designs for six ranges, the most interesting of which is one with what they called a 'Rumfordized Inside', wind-up cheeks, caps on the cheeks that wind under the hobs, fall-down top-bar, swing trivet, sliding spit racks, and a fret underneath that drew out to form a dripping pan, stand or footman. One of the other designs shows a range with a stewing and ironing stove on one side, and a copper boiler on the other.

The factories which made stoves sometimes made fenders and fire-irons as well. Twenty-seven of these are listed in the Sheffield directory of 1828, including those that specialized in fenders. But there were only eight fender and fire-iron specialists in London in 1823, or, anyhow, eight who were important enough to be recorded. Of the ten fender-makers recorded in Birmingham in 1818, Nicklin & Son were in business throughout the Regency, and were evidently leading manuturers of wire fenders, together with bird-cages and other things in brass and iron wire. At its simplest this kind of fender consisted of wire lattices, or intersecting hoops (giving it a neo-Gothic air) between brass top-rails and bases. Other types incorporating bands of fret-cut brass or steel, with brass top-rails and bases and lion-paw feet, continued the forms evolved during the Adam period, without the apparent fragility of late eighteenth-century examples. The most conspicuous changes were changes of outlines. Serpentine fronts, which had been common until 1800, went out of fashion, to be superseded by straight, or slightly convex, fronts with rounded corners. Some fenders of the finest quality were embellished with cast brass figures of lions or sphinxes on pedestals at the corners: simple ones in solid cast iron were sometimes decorated with reeding or wavy flutes. Soon after 1820 a style of fender came into fashion which was made up of two tiers of openwork friezes between convex and reeded bands of metal, generally brass or steel.

The pierced designs decorating fire-shovels remained very formal. Though fire-iron handles were still being made with urn-shaped finials in the 1820's, many followed the baluster fashion in being emphatically knopped. In 1827 Ackermann's *Repository* published an engraving with some designs for neo-Gothic fire-irons by Augustus Charles (the Elder) Pugin (Fig. 2), and the influence of English on French taste at this time, when the *Style Cathédrale* was being fostered by the Duchesse de Berry, is suggested by the appearance of a copy of Pugin's designs in Mésangère's *Meubles et Objets de Gout*, issued, it seems, a year or so later.

With the development of landscape gardening came the need for iron seats and benches to rest on, during what the writers of the period called 'rambles'. In the first half of the nineteenth century much of this garden furniture was made of rods and strips of iron wrought into the skeleton forms of ordinary chairs and sofas (Pl. 66D). *Jardinières*, for example, were made usually on the principle of a dumb waiter with circular shelves diminishing in size upwards, but carried out in bent rods and strips; and here of course the blacksmith, as a unit in a factory, came into his own again. If we are to judge by Thomas Upfill & Son of Birmingham, a firm with a great reputation for garden furniture,

the industry was a conservative one. Some of the designs in the Upfill advertisements of the 1850's are exactly similar to those of the 1830's.

Cast-iron embellishments were probably not common in this field until well into the Victorian age, when seats composed of fern and other leaf forms came into vogue. In the issue of the *Repository* dated 1st September 1816, however, there is an article on garden furniture with two illustrations of recent inventions. The ironwork of these would have been mainly cast. One consisted of a garden seat protected by an umbrella structure with a roof of copper sheeting, inspired, so the author remarks, by 'those buildings in India that were frequently erected for monumental or devotional purposes'. The other seat is shown in the form of a bench with console-shaped feet involving the anthemion motif. A marquee covering of cloth painted with neo-classical motifs protected the bench, and this covering was supported on an iron trunk, or shaft, and roped and pegged to the ground.

As for the railings and balconies of cast iron manufactured during the Regency, many of these are still in use, or at least in place, as evidence of the outburst of activity in each grade of building at that period (Fig. 4). Before 1810 nearly all the neo-classic features in architectural iron were traceable directly to the Adelphi and other designs of Robert Adam, who was keen to take advantage of improvements in casting as a means to revive the ornamental use of this material. The firm of J. Collinge, in the Lambeth Road, came forward soon afterwards with the greater use of lead as a substitute for wood in ornaments and dripping-eaves. Certain motifs began to appear more prolifically among the older palmettes and Greek keys, such as the fleur-de-lys and the spear-head, which by the 1820's had become a pike with a tassel (Fig. 3), as in the gates to John Nash's house in Waterloo Place put up in 1822, and in much of the exterior ironwork in the Regent's Park neighbourhood. In the advertisement of a gatemaker, William Neville of Great Brooke Street, Birmingham, published in 1818, lyre-shaped finials are shown on the tops of a pair of gate piers, and another pair is shown with thin trellises of intersecting arcs in marked contrast to the heavier

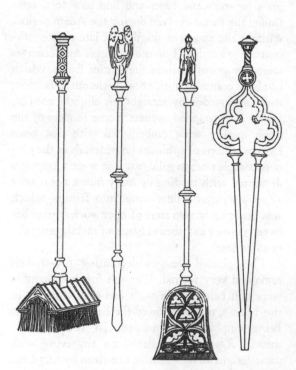

Fig. 2. Designs for fire-irons by Augustus Charles Pugin. From Ackermann's *Repository of Arts*, 1st September, 1827.

ironwork at the tops and bottoms. At Brighton, Cheltenham, Clifton and Plymouth, where building proceeded apace after the Napoleonic War, many of the stock motifs of the French Empire period were adopted in architectural iron. The outlines of these Hellenistic attributes, of which the commonest were perhaps arrows (Fig. 4D), wings, thyrsi and wreaths, were somewhat relaxed in English hands. At the same time crowded designs and fullness of forms were qualities typical of all the important outside cast ironwork of the 1820's: together they produced the sumptuousness seen in L. N. Cottingham's *Smith and Founder's Director* of 1823–4 (Figs. 3, 4) – or, better still, in the gates at Constitution Hill, cast by Bramah from the designs of Decimus Burton. By 1820 Chinese lattice patterns were no longer much favoured for railings and balconies, and the English taste for the Romantic was gratified more than ever by neo-Gothic designs. After 1830 the shells and scrolls of the neo-Rococo style began to appear in window guards, following a fashion which had declared itself in English silver twenty years previously.

Japanned iron

The town of Pontypool in Monmouthshire had great renown in the eighteenth century for its productions of japanned iron: so much so that the word 'Pontypool' was used generically at one time in Europe for all wares of this kind. But in 1813 the Cambrian Travellers' Guide noticed that the Pontypool works, founded by a member of the Allgood family nearly one hundred years before, had 'declined exceedingly'. This was shortly after the business had passed into the hands of Mary Allgood; and at her death in 1822 it became extinct.

Meanwhile the art of japanning metal had been carried on also at Usk in the same county, where a workshop had been founded by another of the Allgoods in 1763. The last owner of this name at Usk was Edward Allgood, who died at the end of the eighteenth century, the works then passing to John Hughes, and from him in 1814 to John Pyrke, and in 1826 to Evan Jones By 1835 the business had dwindled to a point at which it could be described by the Commissioners of Corporations as 'a small manufacture'. It succumbed finally in 1860 to

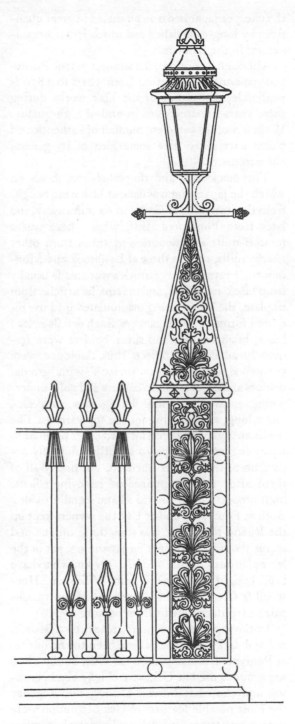

Fig. 3. Design for lamp, pier and railings of cast iron. From *The Smith and Founder's Director* by L. N. Cottingham, London, 1823–4.

the cheaper japanned iron produced in great quantities by long-established and much larger organizations in the Midlands.

Although, therefore, the amount of true Pontypool japanned iron dating from 1810 to 1830 is negligible, the output of the Usk works during these years remained steady, and of high quality. What is more, a sufficient number of authenticated pieces survive to give some idea of its general characteristics.

The black-iron and tin-plated-iron sheets on which the japanning was done at Usk were bought from the iron mills at Caerleon six miles away, and later from Pontypool itself, where there was a famous mill; and doubtless at times from other nearby mills, such as those at Lydbrook and Monmouth. Trays and large articles were made usually from black-iron plate, and the smaller articles from tinplate, the sheets being manipulated into the required forms by the japanners. Such details as lead bases, brass handles and silver borders were frequently added. All objects thus fashioned were enamelled on the clean surfaces with ground colours and decorations in colours and gold, undergoing repeated 'stovings' during these processes, and a long, slow stoving for the top varnish. The media that gave the brilliant hard effect peculiar to japanning were composed slightly differently according to the colours intended, but nearly all of them after 1750 contained as basic ingredients high proportions of linseed oil and metallic oxides. Both at Pontypool and at Usk the owners kept up the legend that there was something unique and secret about their recipes for japanning, yet in the later phase at Usk the varnishes are known to have been bought ready-made from Wilkinson, Heywood & Clark, Ltd, of London, and from various paint-manufacturers in Birmingham.

In the eighteenth century, black, tortoiseshell, red and dark blue grounds had been the favourites at Pontypool, and apparently at Usk; but by 1810 the grounds used at Usk were chiefly black, crimson and chocolate-brown. During the Regency the most notable features of Usk decoration were floral sprays treated in a delicate linear style, reminiscent of certain contemporary chintzes: in these star-shaped flowers occurred repeatedly (Pl. 66A).

Formal patterns included spaced stars, circuits of intersecting arcs, and the kind of vermicular ornament seen on Worcester porcelain of the same date, and known as the Stormont pattern. A letter of 1807 in the National Library of Wales describes a visit to the Usk japan works in that year, and records that 'any person wishing for a particular pattern – to have his Arms emblazoned – or a view of his house or grounds painted and japanned upon a tray or other article, upon sending a drawing, may have it executed to his wishes'. Examples of private commissions of this sort still exist.

On the whole, however, pictorial decoration, such as the landscape vignettes on French and Dutch *tôle peinte*, was not a common feature of Usk, or of English, japanning, although many oblong and oval trays were made with decorations copied from prints of hunting scenes and battles in the Napoleonic War. Most of the smaller metal articles japanned at Usk were either made there, or sent there from London and other towns for japanning. Brass and pewter as well as iron objects are known to have received this treatment. But chestnut-urns and knife-boxes, like those for which Pontypool had once been celebrated, had gone out of fashion by 1810 and were no longer manufactured at Usk during the Regency period.

Perfunctory stoving, less durable varnishes, less resistance to heat, less careful workmanship all round, and a greater range of colours were characteristics brought to the japanned-iron trade by the japanners of Birmingham, Bilston and Wolverhampton. The earliest factories of note in Birmingham were those of John Taylor (who had a reputation for snuff-boxes), and his rival John Baskerville, better known as a type-founder. Then, at the close of the eighteenth century, came Henry Clay, who moved to London in 1802, having for some time concentrated more on *papier-mâché* than on japanned iron. The Clay business passed in 1816 to Jennens & Bettridge, and these partners continued to produce articles in iron, although the bulk of their trade was in *papier-mâché*. One of the staple industries of the city remained in the production of japanned-iron snuff-boxes and other small objects, for which there was still a large export

Fig. 4. (A) and (B), patterns for balcony panels, from *Designs of Stoves, Ranges, Virandas, Railings, Belconets, etc.* by M. and G. Skidmore, London 1811. (C) and (D), designs for window-guards executed in London, (E) and (F), patterns for balcony panels, all from *The Smith and Founder's Director*, by L. N. Cottingham, London 1823-4.

market in the first half of the nineteenth century. Oddly enough, there was also a countervailing trade in the importation of similar objects from the japanned-iron factories of Holland, France and Germany, which makes for confusion.

At Bilston fifteen japanners were recorded in 1818. The export of tea-caddies, cash-boxes and useful articles like coal-scuttles and trays from there to North and South America was evidently considerable, but it is no longer a simple matter to distinguish its products from those of other Midland towns. The oldest Wolverhampton japanners were Ryton & Sons, founded in 1775; equally famous was the factory of Benjamin Mander, later known under the name of his son Charles Mander, and later still under that of William Shoolbred, to become then Shoolbred, Loveridge & Shoolbred, and from the 1840's until 1918, the well-remembered firm of Henry Loveridge & Company. Wolverhampton trays were produced in enormous quantities (50,000 in 1850), and were as a rule more interestingly pictorial than the ones made at Usk. The favourite early-nineteenth-century decorations were tigers, Chinoiseries, and landscapes in North Wales; but to identify the makers is seldom possible. Green and Naples yellow seem to have come into regular use as ground colours by the cheaper japanners slightly before 1830: indeed, the fashion for Naples yellow ran parallel with the use of the same shade in simulated bamboo woodwork, which was itself imitated in japanned iron. Black, however, was the commonest ground shade (Pl. 66c). Dark blue had been used at Pontypool in its heyday, but a lot of the blue, green and yellow grounds in existence are, in fact, on *tôle* of continental origin.

Pewter and Britannia Metal

From the middle of the eighteenth century the history of pewter is the history of a trade in decline. Two factors contributed to this state of things: the complacency of the Pewterers' Company in London, and the growth of the trade in fine pottery, such as that of Wedgwood and his imitators. The invention of bone-china in Staffordshire and the rise of the tax-free glass industries in Ireland reduced the market for pewter even more. By comparison with such materials as these pewter had three disadvantages: it was dearer; it was more sombre; it gave off a slightly metallic scent which affected the taste of food and drink. None the less it was still in regular use until well into the nineteenth century for the tankards, cutlery and cruets of taverns, and for the ink-wells of counting-houses and offices. At the end of the reign of George IV the Pewterers' Company, with its Hall in Lime Street, was still a circumstantial body, governed by a master, two wardens and twenty-eight assistants; but its statutory powers of interfering in the trade to maintain high standards were no longer put to the test, and in 1863 the Pewterers' Bill was repealed. Originally the Company had been empowered to make regulations whereby each pewterer had to put his name on large articles and his registered mark on small ones. This practice of marking with 'touches' died out in the nineteenth century. The last touch recorded on the plates at Pewterers' Hall is dated 1824.

Writing in 1823 the anonymous author of a tale called 'The Rookery', published in *La Belle Assemblée*, describes a farmhouse kitchen of the period in which the servants took their meals. And for this purpose, he says, 'there was a large white dresser, surmounted by a variety of pewter dishes and plates ... whose chief merit consisted in the brightness of their polish'. The passage gives a hint of the surroundings with which pewter was associated, and had been associated for quite a long time. From a factor's list in the Victoria and Albert Museum (E.I.D. Dept: M63a) we know that the prices of pewter dishes fluctuated very much at that date, suggesting the weakness of the market because of uncertainty in the trade.

Meanwhile the pewter relics from this last phase in the history of an alloy once treated with great respect imply that the profitable lines of production, apart from those already indicated, were on a small scale: salts, hot-water dishes, scale-plates, measures, jugs, pot-lids, bleeding-basins, ladles and kitchen spoons, candlesticks and snuff-boxes. Not many of these articles were made in the highest grade of pewter known to the seventeenth century. Indeed, the proportion of lead in them was often decidedly more than it ought to have been. For some reason the majority of tobacco-boxes were made in lead, not of pewter (Pl. 65G). With the exception of these leaden boxes, which had styles of their own, objects of pewter took shape from the current forms in Sheffield plate and silver, in which threads and gadroons were the routine enrichments. Even the better lathes that had been invented in the eighteenth century cannot be said to have affected the standard of turning in Regency pewter, which on the whole was rather rough.

Yet another, though minor, set-back in the pewter trade appeared when a new alloy was invented in 1770, composed of tin, antimony and copper, in the proportions of 50:3:1. This material was called White Metal from 1769 until 1797, and was first sold under that name by the earliest large-scale producers of it, Messrs Hancock & Jessop, of Sheffield. From 1797 it was generally referred to as Britannia Metal, and among the leading Regency manufacturers advertising it under that name were James Dixon & Sons, of Cornish Place, Sheffield (still making it today), and John Vickers, of Britannia Place, Sheffield, who was succeeded in the business before the beginning of Victoria's reign by Rutherford, Stacey, West & Company. Both firms stamped their wares plainly with their names. In Birmingham the most prominent Britannia Metal smiths seem to have been Brown & Hardman of Paradise Street, and William Thompson & Company of Ashted. Soap-boxes and ink-stands were specialities of James Whitworth of Aston Road, Birmingham, and Dixon of Sheffield was noted for teapots on pedestals, though these were made by other firms too. It is interesting to recall that Sir Walter Scott possessed a set of Britannia tea equipment, which was reproduced in Hudson Moore's *Old Pewter* (New York, 1905). Otherwise the range of Britannia Metal production was rather similar to that of Sheffield plate. The commonest application of the alloy, it appears, was in the manufacture of cheap spoons. These were cast from iron or brass moulds in the popular fiddle-pattern style, and were distinguishable by long ridges along the backs of the stems, which helped to strengthen them.

Spoons were also made in a white metal alloy

called Tutania, patented by William Tutin in 1770. This consisted of brass, antimony and tin in proportions of 8 : 32 : 7. For a time in the late eighteenth century, before they went out of fashion, buckles as well as spoons were produced in Tutania by the firm of Tutin & Haycraft of Coleshill Street, Birmingham.

Brass, bronze and small iron articles

When the first directory of Birmingham was published in 1777 it gave the names of thirty brass-founders in the city. Forty years afterwards the number had risen to seventy-nine, which gives some idea of the rate of expansion in the hardware industries, out of all proportion to the growth of population in Britain at that time. The products of this expansion were absorbed by a greatly increased middle class, whose mounting prosperity brought even more prosperity to the rich. Even so, that class alone cannot be held entirely responsible for such a huge trade, this being due in part to an export drive that was one of the remarkable features of the period 1770–1870. After the battle of Waterloo, the chief markets of the Birmingham brass-founders seem to have been in North America, Portugal, Spain, the Low Countries and Central Europe; also in the colonies, and for a time in Latin America. Surviving pattern-books sent by the founders to retailers during the first quarter of the nineteenth century show such things as wafer- and waffle-irons, intended clearly for North American customers. In the designs of these books, portraits of Washington and of the Polish patriot Thadeus Kosciusko appear alongside representations of Louis XVI's tomb, for Royalists, or later, of Napoleon in a pensive attitude, for Buonapartists: all of which indicates how far the tastes and feelings of foreign patrons were considered.

Brass articles were both cast from moulds and stamped from dies, most foundries using both processes. While in the technique of stamping metal the English led the way, it seems that finishing with a chaser was not carried out to any marked degree, except in ormolu. Brass was often lacquered and sometimes bronzed, but the standard of finish in ormolu was generally lower than in France:

on the other hand, French ormolu of the *Empire* and *Restauration* periods had a hard, finical quality that was never present in English metal-work. It is quite likely that in some cases the furniture fittings exported to France were chased by French cabinet-makers before being attached. There was, however, at this time an increase in the English use of rose engines with elliptical chucks for turned decoration. Henry Maudsley in the 1800's, and Holtzapffel in the second decade of the century, both invented improvements in the ornamental turning lathe, so that the mechanistic look of the formal enrichments on highly decorated brass and bronze objects of the period can be seen as the natural outcome of the desire to exploit these developments.

In cast or stamped brass the notable products were door-fittings, door-knockers, door-stops (or door-porters), curtain-bands, bell-handles, furniture-fittings (including castors, feet, mounts (p. 1086) and beadings), fender-footmen and candle-sticks. After 1825 the repertory began to be extended more to pastille-burners, paper-weights, letter-racks, watch-holders, spill-vases and other small articles, often made of bronzed brass (Pls. 68E–L). The increase in the number of motifs with Romantic

rather than Classical associations, such as representations of ivy- and clover-leaves, roses and even fuchsias, was very marked from 1820 to 1840, and went hand in hand with the revival of rococo ornament. Some factories concentrated on purely functional products, like hinges, bolts and stair-rods. Birmingham screws were world-famous, Maudsley's improved screw-cutting lathe invented in 1800 having facilitated the production of screws of better quality than were made anywhere else. Other factories specialized in the higher ranges of craftsmanship, in lamp- or fender-making, for instance. Tall objects in bronze, like the *guéridons* and lamp-stands fashionable on the Continent since the *Directoire*, seem to have been made very little in England at first, although it is known that things of this kind were produced in Italy to the specifications of English designers. It is true that in 1807 Thomas Hope published designs for Grecian-looking candle-stands of gilded bronze, and possibly some actual examples of these stands existed at Deepdene, his house in Surrey; but it is doubtful if more than a very few were ever made of bronze in the 1800's outside his circle. In 1823–4 appeared the third edition of Lewis Nockalls Cottingham's *Smith and Founder's Director*, with designs for large- and small-scale bronze objects modelled on Classical and French prototypes (Fig. 5); and by that time the larger sort of bronze furniture was evidently made in England (Pl. 66B). Brass too was being used more in furniture. A history of Birmingham published by Jabet and Moore about 1817 records that B. Cook & Company of Broad Street in that city were already making bedsteads of hollow brass pieces. Rods of brass had been used since the eighteenth century for sideboard railings, and by 1810 similar, if stouter, rods were incorporated in music-stands and other slender types of furniture (Fig. 6).

The evolution of the candlestick after 1805 was somewhat influenced by the introduction of the tall glass open globe or shade (often painted or wheelcut), which kept the flame from flickering, but which required the candlestick itself to be slightly shorter in proportion and heavier at the bottom, otherwise it would have overbalanced (Pl.

Fig. 5. Design for a vase in brass or bronze in the form of a Rhyton. From *The Smith and Founder's Director* by L. N. Cottingham, London 1823–4.

67D, E). From about 1805 to 1835 the vogue for short candlesticks, cast in brass and partly bronzed, was strongly maintained. The earlier ones were enriched with all the current neo-classical motifs that were appropriate, from Greek frets on the plinth bases to acanthus leaves on the shafts. Sometimes there would be a corona of leaves below the nozzle, or a circle of branches or 'showers', as they were called, for holding cut-glass 'icicles' (Pl. 66E). This kind of candlestick went on the chimney-piece. Eagles, putti, sphinxes and women in Hellenistic garments were used frequently for supports, either on columnar pedestals, or on triangular plinths with concave sides. About 1815 less classical forms came into fashion for the supporting figures, such as elephants bearing castles, and reclining hounds at the tail-ends of which stems, or sometimes the tails themselves, curled upwards to hold the nozzles off-centre. In large candelabra, figures of Atlas (Pl. 67B) and of Egyptian slaves were favoured; in fact the popularity of this type of supporter began to decline only when neo-rococo scrolls became the rage in the 1830's.

All this time the manufacture of plain brass candlesticks went on, some being short, like the fashionable ones, others being as tall as they had ever been. Probably the most characteristic base was oblong in plan (Pl. 68B): by 1830 the bases were usually oblong with chamfered corners, and the shafts had bold knops, often decorated with facets or with turned reeding. But the candlestick industry was without question reduced in scope by the new oil-lamps and finally by the arrival of gas.

Much of the best workmanship of the period went into the making of these lamps in either brass or bronze, which was chiefly undertaken by specialists. In comparison with candlelight, there was something very romantic about the moon-like glow of a lamp through a 'French-roughed', or ground-glass, globe. Such globes were occasionally referred to as 'moons'. There was, no doubt, another reason why so much attention was given to lamps in the Regency, and that was the presence in England of Aimé Argand, the Swiss physicist, who died here in 1803, having given his name to a business at 37 Bruton Street, for the production of the kind of lamp he had patented, with

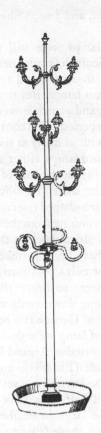

Fig. 6. Umbrella and hat-stand. From a brass-founder's pattern-book, c. 1820. *Victoria and Albert Museum.*

an air-burner and a cylindrical wick. In the early years of the century the Bruton Street business went under the names of Argand and Elgar, but at the end of our period the family of Bright, who were Sheffield-platers established at the same address, took over the business, and it became known in the 1830's as 'Bright, late Argand & Company'. Another famous lamp-maker of the time was J. Smethurst of 138, New Bond Street, a patentee of the lamp with a spiral burner. In Birmingham the two leading lamp manufacturers seem to have been W. Blakeway & Son of

I

Edgbaston Street, and Joseph Shelton of Bradford Street.

Open-wick lamps were still made, from the crusie type for Scottish farmhouses and the American backwoods, to ornamental types in the forms of ancient Roman lamps. But those with air-burners on the Argand principle were the most characteristic of the period. This contrivance was used in chandeliers with as many as six burners, and in table and sideboard lamps, either with one burner, or with two burners at the ends of arms set slightly forward from the shaft (Pl. 68c). The oil was poured into an urn-shaped reservoir or tank at the top of the lamp, running from there along the arm and into the cylindrical wick in the burner. Until 1840 it would have been spermaceti oil (from the sperm whale) or colza oil (from the colza seed), both of which were so heavy that they worked best when draining downwards to the wick.

In the course of George IV's reign, apparently, two new kinds of lamp were devised: the reading lamp with an adjustable Argand burner and a japanned-iron shade (Pl. 68A); and the Sinumbra lamp, wherein the burner was set below a hollow ring which acted both as a tank for the oil and as a rest for the large hemispherical, or sometimes flask-shaped, shade (Pl. 67A). The poisoner, Thomas Griffiths Wainewright, in one of his essays, describes the apartment of a London dandy, that is to say his own apartment in 1821, as being illuminated by what he calls a 'new elegantly gilt French lamp, having a ground glass globe painted with gay flowers and gaudy butterflies'. It is probable that the term 'French lamp' was generic; but in the advertisement of C. F. Younge in the Sheffield directory of 1828 it was clearly applied to the Sinumbra lamp, and this type of lamp, though doubtless invented in France, became very popular in England. As the name tells us, it cast no shadows. Quantities of Sinumbras, probably of English origin and dating from the 1830's, survive, rather green from disuse, in the palace of Mafra in Portugal.

The principle of the Argand burner was retained well into the Victorian age for gaslighting. In this form of illumination the English had been pioneers since the day in 1798, when it was first used experimentally at Boulton & Watt's foundry in Birmingham. Although relatively few have lasted to the present time, brass chandeliers and wall-brackets for gas, with prominent anthemion and acanthus features, were in production well before 1830. Cottingham, too, in his *Director*, gives some designs for gaslight stands which follow the conventions of oil-lamp stands and candelabra in the same book.

One of the accomplishments of Bucks and Corinthians under George IV was that of tearing off knockers from doors. They must have found out there was a kind of knocker in which the larger part consisted of the rapper secured to the door by a single pin, the other part being a mere bolt for the rapper to strike upon. Such was the wreath-and-hand knocker, very popular in the 1820's (Pl. 65c). Other knockers of the period seem to have been designed mainly on the following lines: those with ring-shaped rappers of bronzed iron on shields with brass centres (Pl. 65F); lyre-shaped rappers suspended from heads; semicircular or elliptical rappers suspended from urn forms. But the variations of detail were countless. Ring rappers in lions' mouths continued to be made as in the eighteenth century, but with small differences. More characteristic were the eagle-and-palmette knocker (Pl. 65E), and the kind with an acanthus leaf pointing downwards and a loop-shaped rapper.

The firms that made door-knockers were mostly in Birmingham, and the same firms generally made door-stops as well. These objects, then known as door-porters, were to be had in iron or brass, like the knockers, or with iron bases and brass handles. A conservative design going back to the late eighteenth century consisted of a base shaped like a bell cut in half longitudinally, with perhaps ball or lion-paw feet and a long, thin shaft topped by a lifting ring. Around 1820 the designs of door-porters became more fanciful, involving shell, acanthus, anthemion and lotus forms; and a favourite under George IV was that of a big lion's paw from which grew a long leaf ending in a handle simulating rope (Pl. 65D).

It is surprising how some of the patterns conceived in the first thirty years of the nineteenth century for functional articles survived as proto-

Fig. 7. Design for a bell-pull by Augustus Charles Pugin. From Ackermann's *Repository of Arts*, 1st September, 1827.

types. The old kind of coffee-mill, for instance (Fig. 8), still to be seen in Edwardian kitchens, with its bowl and pedestal outlines, is essentially a Regency invention, and was clearly thought out at the time when sloping Egyptian jambs began to fascinate designers and architects. Izons, Whitehurst & Izon of Birmingham showed one of these mills in an advertisement of 1818. A pattern-book of about 1820 shows a four-ale beer-pump with brass fittings, not very different from the ones we know. The Gillott steel pen, patented around 1820 by Joseph Gillott of Birmingham, is still with us, almost unchanged; and so, too, is corrugated-iron sheeting, which (in spite of the Oxford Dictionary) dates back certainly to the early 1830's, and probably before then. Regency designs were taken for granted only a generation ago. There is about them a curious mixture of the classical, the romantic and the whimsical. Whether ornate or severe, whether in coffee-mills or in lamps, the styles thus evolved passed with the political and commercial influence of England into the material culture of almost the entire civilized world of the nineteenth century.

SHORT BIBLIOGRAPHY

On most of the subjects discussed above no monographs exist, and little is to be gained by referring to general works on the history of brass and iron manufactures. In this connexion the Victoria and Albert Museum catalogue of *Old English Pattern Books of the Metal Trades* (1913), by W. A. Young, is of interest.

I am, however, much indebted to *Pontypool and Usk Japanned Wares* by W. D. John, Newport (Mon.), 1953; to *Tutenag and Paktong* by Alfred Bonnin, O.U.P. 1924 (for white metal alloys); and to *The Story of Cutlery* by J. B. Himsworth, London, 1953. *Old Pewter, its Makers and Marks* by H. H. Cotterell, London, 1929, is a standard book on the subject of pewter generally, to which may be added *Chats on Old Pewter* by H. J. L. J. Massé, London, 2nd edition, 1949. See also J. Seymour Lindsay's *Iron and Brass Implements of the English House*, London, 1927.

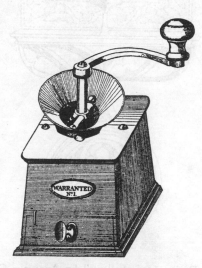

Fig. 8. Coffee-mill of iron and brass. From a brass-founder's pattern-book, *c.* 1820. *Victoria and Albert Museum.*

Textiles

BARBARA MORRIS

General introduction

Nothing could be further from the truth than the general assumption of the chaste and elegant *Regency-stripe* as the dominant style in textiles throughout the period 1810–30. Stripes do appear, in printed fabrics, but not until 1824, when the Regency proper had already ended, and their introduction is an anticipation of styles which became increasingly popular in the 1830's and 1840's. In the field of printed textiles the patterns had never been more exuberant or the colours more brilliant than during the Regency. In woven fabrics, however, the English manufacturers do not appear to have imitated the elaborate Empire designs of the Lyons silk weavers; and where such designs have been found on English upholstered furniture, the silk is almost certainly of French manufacture, for in spite of parliamentary legislation forbidding the import of French fabrics, a certain amount undoubtedly reached this country. Modified eighteenth-century floral damask patterns, or plain coloured silks and worsteds were most favoured, but the restraint in pattern was more than compensated by the lavish use of fringes and braids, and by the elaboration and complexity of the draperies.

Silk, wool or cotton damasks, or plain woven fabrics, including velvet and horsehair, were used for the furnishing of dining-rooms and libraries. Silk was also used extensively in drawing-rooms, bedrooms and boudoirs, but in these rooms chintz was a close competitor. At the beginning of the Regency, chintz was in high fashion among Royal circles and the nobility. In 1811 the Prince of Wales commissioned a 'rich furniture chintz' from Abraham Allen, a leading linen-draper in Pall Mall, for his bedroom at Carlton House. Allen was also patronized by H.R.H. Princess Elizabeth, and in 1813 the Duchess of Bedford selected 'an olive chintz for furniture' (with a small design of roses) for her new 'cottage' in Devonshire. At the end of the period, however, chintz was not in such high fashion, and in 1826 George Smith in his *Cabinet Maker's and Upholsterer's Guide* decrees that 'printed calicos may answer extremely well for secondary apartments, or for those in houses of persons of small fortune; but they are not at all suitable for those of persons of rank and splendid income'. These furniture chintzes were used for window and bed draperies, usually with a plain-coloured contrasting lining, and edged with variegated fringes. Chintz, particularly when patterned in imitation of damask, was also used extensively for upholstery. The Gillow account books at Lancaster for the years 1812–14 give considerable details of the use of chintz for furniture. Couches and sofas and the head- and foot-boards of French beds were covered with chintz as well as the loose cushions for both sofas and curricle chairs. Hassocks and footstools also had chintz covers. Chintz was also used extensively for 'throw-overs', that is dust-covers for the protection of furniture.

It is worth noting that the furnishings of the period were produced not so much for the great houses as for the terraces and squares of Brighton, Cheltenham and Regent's Park, and for the villas and '*cottages ornés*' scattered throughout the country. Few Regency interiors have remained intact, and since very few actual textiles appear to have survived, our information has therefore to be gathered almost exclusively from contemporary illustrations or written sources.

Drapery

Throughout the period the elaborate draperies, for both windows and bed-hangings, tended to be copied from the French and were often acknowledged as such in being described as 'French window curtains'. The Greek or classic style continued in favour throughout the period, but from 1825 onwards draperies in the Gothic taste were the recognized alternative to harmonize with the Gothic furniture popularized by the elder Pugin and others.

Whatever the individual modifications, the general scheme, whether symmetrical or asymetrical, consisted of an upper drapery or pelmet at the top of the window, behind which were floor-length curtains of the same or contrasting colour, and against the window itself sub-curtains of muslin or other transparent materials which served 'to break the strength of the light, without entirely secluding [sic] the cheering effect produced from the solar rays' (Geo. Smith, *Cabinet Maker's and Upholsterer's Guide*, 1826).

Until about 1818 fairly heavy styles were most favoured. The upper drapery was usually fringed and looped up at intervals, and from these points tassels were often suspended. Laurel wreaths, or other classical devices, were often embroidered on the upper drapery (Fig. 1). The main curtains were generally edged with a bullion or ball fringe, and the borders embroidered (or painted if of a heavy woollen material) with Greek designs of anthemion or similar motifs. Heavy wool or damask curtains were unlined, but chintz or light-weight silk curtains were usually lined with a contrasting colour. The muslin sub-curtains were often embroidered at the edge with a running floral or classical design, and edged with a vandyked or scalloped border, or with chenille fringe (Pl. 69A).

For single windows the simplest type of drapery consisted of a single curtain which was slung over a pole so that the shorter part in front formed the upper drapery or valance, and the longer part be-

hind the main curtain. The curtain was then looped to one side by means of a curtain-pin attached to the wall, revealing the muslin sub-curtain beneath. Circular-topped windows were often filled in at the top with drapery pleated fanwise to a central ornament. When there were several windows in one wall, it was usual to unite them by a continuous upper-drapery.

In 1819 a more fanciful type of drapery came into fashion which, although if anything more elaborate than the preceding styles, was of a lighter appearance, and had been fashionable in France some years earlier. In the description of a suite of draperies for drawing-room windows, published in March, 1820, Ackermann remarks on the 'playful external swags' which are formed by a continuous drapery looped over and under the curtain pole on either side of a central ornament to form a series of festoons. The central ornament often took the form of a bird, usually an eagle or a peacock (Pl. 69B), and the festoons were suspended from elaborate devices of carved and gilded wood in the form of clusters of grapes and leaves, pineapples or scrolling acanthus foliage, which were attached to the cornice pole at intervals by strong wire. The naturalism of the ornaments, although still basically classical in form, gave a more fanciful appearance to the whole scheme, and the curtains in this type of drapery were usually of light-coloured silks rather than of heavy velvet or wool (Fig. 2).

'Curtain cornices', a kind of rigid pelmet of carved and gilded wood, first introduced by Chippendale about 1775, appear again in 1819, and by 1820 Ackermann remarks that they 'are now adopted in a great variety and will probably very soon supersede the late fashion of suspending draperies by poles and detached ornaments'. These cornices were particularly suited to 'Gothic' styles of decoration and became increasingly popular after 1825, often being carved in imitation of architectural crocketting (Pl. 69C). With this style of drapery, the upper festoons were replaced by a more rigid valance made of buckram covered with velvet and cut into fancy shapes at the lower edge. Fleur-de-lys or other Gothic devices were applied in a contrasting colour, and the edge might be further embellished with tassels. Another type

Fig. 1. Drawing-room window curtain first published by Ackermann, 1st February 1813. The cabinet was designed by George Bullock.

of upper-drapery used with the cornice was termed 'hammercloth' or 'petticoat' drapery, in which the material was gathered into simple flutes from each of which a tassel was suspended.

An example of yet another type of pelmet, used mainly for libraries or dining-rooms, is illustrated by Ackermann in September 1819. The material, either moreen (a coarse fabric of woollen and worsted mixture) or velvet, was pleated into vertical pipes, stuffed with wool and mounted on to a stiff canvas, giving the appearance of much-enlarged corrugated cardboard. The centre portion of the pelmet was usually left flat and ornamented with a painted or embroidered figure.

Bed-drapery falls into three main types. The first type, the heavily-curtained four-poster bed, remained in favour throughout the period. The curtains and valances were made of chintz, silk or merino damask, ornamented with fringes and tassels. The draperies round the top of the bed sometimes reached an amazing degree of complexity, but the lower valance was kept fairly simple.

The lighter 'tent' or 'field' bed was found more suitable for small rooms or for the fashionable 'cottages' and villas. The posts, which were lower than those on the four posters, were masked by draped curtains and were united by curved rods, covered by drapery to form a tent or canopy.

The third type, the 'French bed', was in fact a kind of couch, which was placed against the wall, the drapery being suspended from a pole at right-angles to the wall about ten feet from the floor, or, alternatively, from a small canopy at the head.

Woven fabrics

In the field of woven fabrics, the introduction of new types of materials assumes more importance than superficial changes of pattern. In the manufacture of printed fabrics it was necessary to produce new and novel designs in rapid succession, for what was fashionable in one season was already out of favour in the next. With woven fabrics, however, because of the complexities of manufacture and the fact that the fabrics were intended to last for a longer period, the same considerations did not apply, and there are no very marked stylistic changes in design throughout the period. Towards the end of the period, however, the gradual introduction of the Jacquard loom made possible the production of more elaborately figured textiles at lower cost and paved the way to the more complex patterns of the Victorian era.

In contrast to the eighteenth century, when the costly hand-woven figured silks dominated the scene, during the Regency period plain fabrics in silk and wool, Manchester or cotton velvets, worsted and cotton damask, merinos and moreens, came to the fore as a result of the increasing mechanization of the textile industry. The evidence given to the Select Committee on Arts and Manufacture in 1835 makes it clear that the Spitalfields silk industry was not in a very flourishing condition throughout the period. There were no outstanding designers employed in the drawing of patterns and the weavers were engaged in producing plain silks or velvets or small figured patterns which showed very little originality, and the chair seat shown on Plate 70B must be regarded as something of a rarity. In spite of the fact that the import of French silks was forbidden, most of the designs seem to have been copied from the French, and the lifting of the ban in 1826 seems to have effected an improvement in inspiring the Spitalfields manufacturers to meet increasing competition by raising the standard of both design and colouring. In this year we read that 'our fair countrywomen have resolved to make silk of the Spitalfields manufactory a considerable portion of their dress (to relieve a distressed industry). His Majesty has given orders that the rooms of his palace at Windsor shall be hung round with silk of Spitalfields manufacture.' Presumably this latter was part of the extensive alterations and redecorations which were begun at Windsor in 1825, and the Windsor archives contain a detailed invoice for nearly £15,000 worth of silk from a Wm. Edward King, Silk Mercer.

While the Spitalfields industry was obviously in a state of decline, it is clear that other centres of weaving in the Manchester area, in Yorkshire and in Norwich, were rapidly advancing. In Ackermann's *Repository* for February 1821, it is stated that the 'loom of our country is now in that state of advanced perfection that damasks of the most magnificent kind in point of intensity of colour and richness of pattern are manufactured at prices that permit their free use in well-furnished apartments'. The introduction of power, and of the Jacquard apparatus, which did not necessarily go hand in hand, enabled woven fabrics to be produced in far greater quantities and at considerably lower cost. Power-weaving, which had developed particularly in Lancashire, was nearly always confined to the production of plain fabrics other than silks, such as calico and twills, and was wholly and necessarily conducted on the factory system. The Jacquard machinery, however, could be applied to almost any loom and was at first introduced in Yorkshire in places where the weaving industry was still on a cottage basis. The evidence of M. Claude Guillotte, a manufacturer of Jacquard machinery, given before the 1835 Select Committee on Design, affords details of its introduction into England. The first Jacquard looms were installed in Halifax, Huddersfield and the surrounding country in 1824. The earliest looms seem to have been used for producing small patterns, principally for waistcoats, but their use soon spread to the production of merinos and woollen damasks and by 1835 there were about 8,000 Jacquard looms in operation. The merinos (a thin woollen twilled cloth, sometimes a mixture of silk and wool) and woollen damasks, which were made in Norwich as well as in Yorkshire, were much in demand for curtains and bed hangings, for as George Smith put it in his *Cabinet Maker's and Upholsterer's Guide* they 'make up very beautifully, not requiring a lining'. The *Repository* includes in its 'Pattern of British Manufacture' for November 1812 'an entirely new article (a white cotton damask with a traditional pattern of formalized leaves and flowers) for white beds and other furniture. It has a beautiful effect in the piece and produces a rich appearance when made up. This handsome manufacture will be found desirable to persons who have large establishments to furnish, for it wants no lining.' It is not surprising that this last consideration was an important one, for an enormous yardage must

Fig. 2. Draperies for circular windows, designed by Stafford of Bath, and first published by Ackermann, 1st February 1820.

have been taken up by the complexities of the festoons and draperies then in fashion.

Similarly, on grounds of economy, the 'Manchester velvets', of cotton instead of silk, found a ready market. The Report of the Select Committee on the Duties Payable on Printed Cotton Goods, 1818, quotes the evidence of Thomas Hargreaves, a leading calico-printer, on woven cotton goods. He mentions that 'there is a good deal of dyed cottons which are embossed with machine, which are used as furniture'. These fabrics, which were stamped with small diaper patterns, seem to have been used mainly for upholstery and were presumably cheaper than the woven figured stuffs.

Considerable advances were made during this period in the production of linen damasks in the Yorkshire area, particularly in Barnsley. The linen and flax industry had been established at Barnsley about 1790, but until 1810 production had been confined to heavy linens such as sheetings, ducks and dowlas (a coarse, half-unbleached linen cloth). In 1810, however, production was extended to 'finer goods embracing huckabacks, diapers, damasks, fine broad sheetings ... rivalling in beauty the handsomest productions of Scotland and Ireland, and possessing great superiority in the quality of the material' (William White, *History, Gazeteer and Directory of the West-Riding of Yorkshire*, 1837). Although power was introduced for the weaving of some of the plain cloths, the production of damasks was organized on a cottage basis, the flax-yarn being purchased by the 'manufacturers' from the spinners and given out to handloom weavers who wove it in their own homes returning the finished goods to the 'manufacturer'. The Victoria and Albert Museum has several

English damask tablecloths of this period, including one with an all-over check and herringbone pattern dated 1818, the one illustrated (Pl. 70A) and an elaborate pictorial design dated 1830.

Printed textiles

The high standard which printed furnishing fabrics reached during this period has not generally been realized. Attention has been almost exclusively directed to the pictorial *toiles* printed from copper-plates, and since the few Regency examples that have survived are manifestly inferior to both eighteenth-century English examples and the contemporary French 'classical' *toiles*, English printed textiles after 1800 have been dismissed as of little interest. It has not been appreciated that by the turn of the century, the earlier copper-plate designs had been replaced in public favour by polychrome floral chintzes printed from wood-blocks. Recently discovered records have shown that these, far from declining in merit or interest after 1800, were immensely popular during the first decades of the century, and showed no deterioration of standards. Similarly, the high standard which roller prints achieved during the 1820's has also been ignored. Many of the finely-engraved designs were printed in fugitive colours, and since those pieces which have survived tend to be badly faded, it is only an examination of unexposed pieces in pattern-books that enables a true assessment of their merits to be made.

Although Thomas Bell's initial invention of rotary printing by engraved metal-rollers was patented in 1783, it was not until about 1820 that furnishing fabrics began to be printed by machine and until then the polychrome wood-block printed chintzes dominated the scene. Whereas in the eighteenth century most of the important calico-printing factories were situated near London, by 1810 most of these had closed down, or turned over to silk-printing, and the centre of production had shifted to the Lancashire area. Hundreds of different patterns were brought out each year by the leading factories such as Bannister Hall, near Preston; Peel and Co., Church, near Accrington; Samuel Matley of Hodge, Cheshire; and Hargreaves and Dugdale of Broad Oak, Accrington.

The Bannister Hall pattern-books (now in the possession of Stead, McAlpin Ltd) and others in the possession of the Calico Printers' Association provide a firm reference in plotting the various styles, month by month, throughout this period, and changes of style are so frequent and so marked that most of the surviving textiles can be pinpointed to a particular year.

The various patterns were in the main 'engaged' to the leading London linen-drapers and reserved exclusively for their use, although the designs were frequently pirated by other firms. The Copyright Act of 1787 (27 Geo. III c. 38) gave two months' protection to a design, and this was extended to three months in 1789 (29 Geo. III c. 19). However, the period was too short for the protection to be effective, and it was not until 1842, when registration of a design with the Patent Office gave three years' protection, that the copyrighting had any real meaning. It was usually the linen-draper who commissioned the design and sent it to one of the Lancashire firms for printing. The anonymity of the designer was in the main preserved, but the names of a few of the leading designers are known through extant signed designs, among them Daniel Goddard, who was active during the first ten years of the nineteenth century, and Vaughan, who is known to have been working between 1806 and 1826. The Bannister Hall records contain a separate series of original designs carried out for Richard Ovey, of Tavistock Street, Covent Garden, who was one of the leading suppliers of 'furniture prints' from 1790 to 1831. The fact that Ovey, and other leading linen-drapers such as Abraham Allen of Pall Mall; E. B. Dudding of Bond Street; Liddiards of Friday Street, and Miles and Edwards of Oxford Street, all called themselves 'furniture printers' has led to some confusion, for none of these merchants were in any sense manufacturers but merely retailers who used the big Lancashire firms as commission printers.

For the first ten years of the century the most fashionable 'furniture prints' had been in the 'drab style', that is, printed in shades of dull brown with some yellow and green but no red. By 1810, however, this style had in the main given way to polychrome chintzes which exploited the full palette available with the madder dyes and enabled the floral designs to be realisitically treated in natural colours. Plain blotch grounds, of which the beige 'tea-ground' and a sky-blue ground were the commonest, were widely used throughout the period.

From 1812 to 1816 architectural motifs were introduced into the floral designs which were usually arranged in a half-drop repeat (Pl. 71A). Both the Classic and Gothic tastes were represented by the introduction of appropriate ruins, but there is rarely any sense of scale or pictorial reality, the architectural motifs being introduced extraneously into a conventional floral chintz. From 1814 to 1816, game birds, particularly partridges, grouse and pheasants, were a popular subject, usually depicted singly or in pairs under a blossoming tree or an exotic palm (Pl. 71B). From 1810 to 1815 specially printed panels with matching borders were made for the centres of patchwork quilts, which achieved great popularity during the Regency. These were similar to the panels printed earlier in the century for chair-backs and chair-seats. The patchwork quilt panels are all polychrome, and all the surviving panels have such close stylistic affinities that they may have been the speciality of one printer. Some of the designs are commemorative, such as that made on the occasion of the wedding of Princess Charlotte in 1816; others depict baskets or bunches of flowers, birds, deer and *chinoiserie* subjects.

Patterns imitating damask, usually printed in shades of one colour, are found throughout the period, particularly between the years 1812 and 1814. Some of the designs are traditional damask patterns of formalized flowers and leaves, others are elaborate patterns of coiling acanthus foliage, and some are simple diapers of stars or other classical motifs. Many of these chintzes have an elaborate border, modelled on a classical frieze, with a simple filling in the ground of the chintz. A number of the designs are similar to plates in George Smith's *Collection of Ornamental Designs after the Manner of the Antique* (1812), which was intended for the use of the calico-printer no less than other manufacturers. A curious feature of these 'damask' chintzes is that the whole ground is often covered by fine diagonal parallel lines,

printed by machine after the main design had been printed by wood-blocks, usually in dark purple or blue. The purpose was, presumably, to imitate the effect of a twill weave, as the diagonal lines are rarely found except in those patterns which imitate a woven silk.

It was not until 1824 that any form of striped chintz, usually presumed to be characteristic of the Regency, appears in the pattern-books. The striped designs usually consisted of alternating vertical stripes and floral sprigs (Pl. 73B), but in some cases the vertical stripe was formed of overlapping lozenges placed one over the other in a continuous band. This latter variety remained in fashion for about two years and, as with the damask designs, there was often a broad border at each side of the chintz, and the pattern was so organized that it could be used vertically for curtains or horizontally for valances.

Chintz blinds, which were semi-transparent and intended to be hung flat without any folds, first appeared in 1825. Most of the designs were Gothic, with architectural tracery and imitation stained-glass panels of an heraldic character, but a number of chinoiserie designs have also been found. The fashion for Gothic chintz blinds lasted well into the 1850's, but by that time the designs had become extremely crude.

In 1829 there arose a fashion for large flowers, accurately drawn in the manner of a botanical plate. The pattern-books show that many of these designs were produced between 1829 and 1836, but very few of the actual fabrics appear to have survived. The same year, 1829, also saw the introduction of long-tailed birds and butterflies into the design. A favourite subject was the bird of paradise, and several chintzes, including one with the stamp of Miles and Edwards, have been found with life-size representations of the species.

The earliest furniture chintzes printed entirely by machine that have survived date from 1818 (Pl. 72A), and it is not until 1820 that they are found in any quantity. The majority of the designs are floral, but a number of pictorial designs, of the type printed from copper-plates in the eighteenth century, have also been found, including a group of rustic scenes from the printworks of John

Marshall of Manchester, which operated for six years from 1818–24 (Pl. 73A).

The styles found in the roller-prints do not exactly parallel those found in the wood-block printed chintzes, for much finer detail was possible with the engraved rollers. A number of what may for convenience be termed 'traditional' floral chintzes were produced with the red printed by engraved roller and the blue and yellow added by block, or surface-rollers, but more interesting are an entirely new range of furniture chintzes in which the whole basis of the design was finely engraved on a metal roller. The design was printed either in a monochrome version, or with additional colours added by block or surface roller (Pl. 72B). The standard of draughtsmanship of these early roller-designs was often extremely high, but the effect was often marred by the indiscriminate use of the new mineral and chemical dyes such as John Mercer's antimony orange (1817), Prussian blue and cochineal pink.

The fashions in the roller-prints were even more ephemeral than those in the wood-block field, and shipping-order books in the possession of the Calico Printers' Association show an almost unbelievable turnover of patterns. An account of the printworks of Hargreaves and Dugdale of Broad Oak, Accrington, reprinted in the 1850 *Journal of Design*, lists the different styles produced by that factory, which were also adopted by other Lancashire printworks. The standard of engraving at Broad Oak was high owing to their employment in 1822 of John Potts, a painter by profession, who was regarded as the 'foremost engraver of his generation', but the development of engraved rollers probably owes even more to Joseph Lockett, whose firm was famed throughout Europe as engravers of 'cover-rollers', from which were printed the fancy machine grounds popular in the late 1820's and 1830's.

Potts' first designs consisted of 'single columns of flowers in trails and stripes with stippled grounds'. A method of printing graduated stripes in 'rainbow' colours, was first introduced at Broad Oak in 1824, and this garish style was rapidly copied by other printers. The 'rainbow' ground was over-printed, or discharged, with vari-ous mossy patterns, and also with abstract designs of stars, concentric circles and 'Catherine-wheel' patterns giving the effect of bursting fireworks.

The year 1826 saw the revival of the pillar-print, popular in wood-block chintzes at the beginning of the century. Corinthian or Ionic columns, with elaborate capitals, entwined with finely engraved flowers, were printed on stippled grounds of graduated stripes or marbled effects (Pl. 72B). In the same years 'feather' patterns were introduced, and also designs of dancing cherubs.

Perhaps the most interesting of all the roller-prints, however, are a series of designs of birds and flowers, found in the Calico Printers' Association pattern-books, copied directly from Audubon's *Birds of America*, of which the first plates appeared in 1827. Six designs after Audubon were produced between 1830 and 1834, four of them in as many as twenty-five different colour-ways.

Carpets

There are few extant carpets of the Regency period, and our knowledge of them derives mainly from written sources and contemporary illustrations. Although in this period the main bulk of production was of carpets in which the pattern was woven on the loom, it is the more expensive hand-knotted carpets that have in fact survived.

A few documented pieces, made at the Axminster factory founded by Thomas Whitty in 1755, are extant. Two of these are fragments of the large hand-knotted carpets made for the Royal Pavilion, Brighton, in 1817. The carpet illustrated (Pl. 74) has been reassembled from pieces of the Saloon carpet which originally measured thirty-six feet in diameter and cost £620. The design of this carpet shows a mixture of oriental and floral motifs, but the carpet for the Music Room, a portion of which also survives, was of purely Chinese inspiration with a pattern of pairs of confronting dragons and Chinese sacred symbols in shades of gold on a blue ground. A similar carpet was also made at Axminster for the Banqueting Room. The pattern consisted of 'a dragon, three serpents coiled around and involving it, form the central ornament; this is surrounded by circles

(A) Marble chimney-piece and cast-iron grate with fender and fire-irons of brass, in Sir John Soane's house, Lincoln's Inn Fields, *c.* 1812. *Sir John Soane's Museum.*

(B) Design for a cast-iron grate published by Longden, Walker & Co., of the Phoenix Foundry, Sheffield. *c.* 1820–30. *Victoria and Albert Museum.*

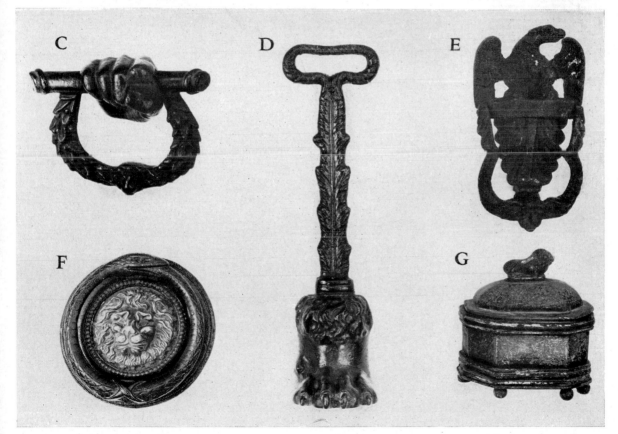

(c) Cast-iron door-knocker, *c.* 1820–30. (D) Cast-iron door-porter, *c.* 1820–30. (E) Cast-iron door-knocker, *c.* 1820–30. (F) Door-knocker of cast-iron with brass centre, *c.* 1810–20. (G) Lead Tobacco-box, *c.* 1820. *Edmund Ware, Esq., Messrs Pratt & Sons Ltd., and author.*

PLATE 65

A

B

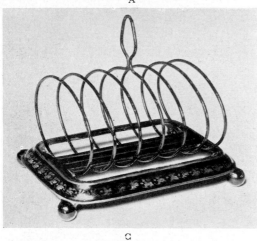

C

D

(A) Usk tea-pot of japanned iron: chocolate ground with decoration in gold; *c.* 1810–20. *National Museum of Wales.*

(B) Table with bronze base and shaft (in the style of a Herculaneum lamp-stand) and rosewood top inlaid with brass. *c.* 1820. *Woburn Abbey.*

(C) Toast-rack of japanned iron: black ground with decoration in gold. Probably by Shoolbred, Loveridge & Shoolbred, Wolverhampton, *c.* 1830. *National Museum of Wales.*

(D) Garden chairs of wrought iron, *c.* 1810–1820. *Courtesy John Fowler, Esq.*

(E) Three pairs of candlesticks, the middle pair lettered: 'PUBLISHED DEC 1 1809 CHENEY LONDON'. Brass, partly bronzed and partly gilt; *c.* 1810. *Courtesy W. G. T. Burne, Esq.*

(A) Sinumbra lamp of brass partly bronzed, with glass shade ground on the inside. Labelled: 'BRIGHT & CO. LATE ARGAND & CO. BRUTON ST'; *c.* 1830. *Woburn Abbey.*

A

B

(B) Candelabrum of bronze, partly gilt (one of a pair), *c.* 1820.
Victoria and Albert Museum.

(C) Pot-pourri vase of marble and ormolu, *c.* 1810–20. Showing Nysa receiving Dionysus from Hermes, etc. Similar vase-designs appear in the Tatham letters of 1795 (V. & A. M.), T. Hope's *Household Furniture*, 1807, and H. Moses's *Antique Vases*, 1814. Cf. also krater by Salpion in Naples Museum.
(D) and (E) Candlesticks with painted ground-glass shades: brass, gilt and partly bronzed, *c.* 1810–20.
Courtesy Raymond Barnett, Esq.

C

D

E

PLATE 67

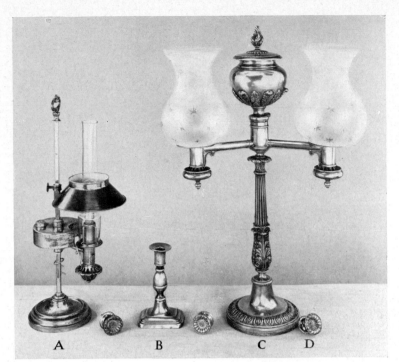

(A) Brass reading-lamp with green japanned - iron shade. Labelled 'BRIGHT & CO. LATE ARGAND & CO. BRUTON ST'; c. 1830–40. (B) Brass candlestick, c. 1820. (C) Brass Argand lamp for table or sideboard, c. 1820. (D) Drawer-handles of stamped brass, gilt; c. 1820–30. *Courtesy Raymond Barnett, Esq., Edmund Ware, Esq. and author.*

Articles of bronzed brass, (J) excepted. (E) Bust of Sir Walter Scott, c. 1830. (F) Egg-timer, c. 1830–40. (G) Table-lamp with lid, partly gilt, c. 1810–20. (H) Wax-Taper holder, mainly stamped and partly gilt. c. 1830–40. (I) Watch-holder, c. 1830–40. (J) Pastille-burner of bronze, partly gilt, c. 1820. (K) Box in the shape of a lavacrum, c. 1820. (L) Pastille-burner, c. 1820–30. *Courtesy Raymond Barnett, Esq., and author.*

PLATE 68

(A) *left:* Drawing room window curtain from Ackermann's *Repository*, March, 1815. The drapery is of azure blue silk edged with bullion fringe, the curtains held back by silk cords. The muslin sub-curtain has an embroidered border. *Victoria and Albert Museum.*

(B) *right:* Roller-printed cotton (in the possession of Messrs. G. P. & J. Baker) showing a draped window of about 1820.

(C) Curtains for a Gothic room from George Smith's *Cabinet Maker's and Upholsterer's Guide*, 1826. 'The cornice is supposed to be of oak, in which case, it will require to be wholly carved; but . . . it may be made of deal, and the ornamental parts made of composition . . . the arrangement would answer equally well for the drawing room, dining room, or library'. *Victoria and Albert Museum.*

PLATE 69   1189

(A) Damask table-cloth signed and dated
'F. & C. Smith 1828'. *Victoria and Albert
Museum.*

(B) Chair seat of silk brocade
probably woven at Spital-
fields for the Saloon of the
Royal Pavilion, Brighton,
about 1817.
*By gracious permission of
H. M. The Queen.*

PLATE 70

(A) Polychrome wood-block chintz, printed by Peel & Co., Church, near Accrington, in 1812. Another piece of the same design is stamped with Peel's mark and the excise stamp for 1812. *Victoria and Albert Museum.*

(B) Panel for a patchwork quilt, wood-block printed in polychrome, about 1815. Property of the Musée de l'Impression of the Société Industrielle de Mulhouse, Alsace.

PLATE 71   1191

(A) Cotton, roller-printed in blue and green. This is one of the earliest roller-printed furnishing fabrics known to have survived and was printed in 1818, probably by Samuel Matley of Hodge, Cheshire. *Victoria and Albert Museum.*

(B) Pillar print, roller-printed in sepia with yellow added by surface roller. Printed by Samuel Matley & Son at Hodge, Cheshire in 1826. Collection of Messrs. G. P. & J. Baker.

PLATE 72

(B) Striped chintz, printed from wood-blocks with 'tea-ground', c. 1824. Property of Miss Josephine Howell, New York.

(A) The British Isles. Cotton, roller-printed in red, probably by John Marshall & Sons, Manchester, between 1818 and 1824. *Victoria and Albert Museum.*

PLATE 73

Axminster hand-knotted carpet re-assembled from fragments of the
carpet made for the Saloon of the Royal Pavilion, Brighton, in 1817.
Reproduced by gracious permission of H.M. the Queen.

PLATE 74

(A) Two designs for carpets from George Smith's *Collection of Ornamental Designs after the Manner of the Antique*, London, 1812. *Victoria and Albert Museum.*

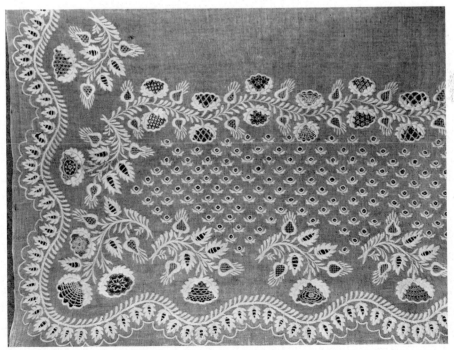

(B) Part of the skirt of a muslin dress (not made up) embroidered with cotton thread and further decorated with cut-work filled in with needlepoint stitches. Worked by Lady Mary Finch, daughter of the 4th Earl of Aylesford, probably shortly before her death in 1823. *Victoria and Albert Museum.*

PLATE 75   1195

(A) Sampler. Silk on linen; cross-stitch, tent, satin and encroaching stitches. Signed and dated 'Mary Ann Cook 1813'. *Victoria and Albert Museum.*

(B) 'The Setting Sun', after Gaspard Pousin. Fabric collage of tailors' cuttings worked by Mrs Dickson about 1825–30 and exhibited in Brighton and London about 1831. *Victoria and Albert Museum.*

Day dress of printed cotton, 1805–10. This dress is made with the bodice front fastening on the shoulders and shows the open neckline filled with white muslin. Chintzes with dark grounds, though much less common than white, are found amongst the plain morning dresses of these years. *Manchester City Art Galleries.*

PLATE 77

(B) Hat trimmed with ribbon and branches of 'Peruvian browallia'; bonnet with arbutus and satin bands, with curtain veil of blond lace; a cap with a beret crown in white crape and blue satin; and a half-dress cap of gauze and lace. From Ackermann's *Repository*, 1826.

(A) Mrs Catherine Morey, 1817, by MICHAEL KEELING. Her dress has the open bodice of 1815–20 and the portrait shows the skirt front meeting this at the waist. The muslin frill at the neck, the frilled cuffs and the cap, show an actual, personal expression of the growing elaboration of this date. *Walker Art Gallery, Liverpool.*

PLATE 78

The Cloakroom, Clifton Assembly Rooms, Bristol, by ROLINDA SHARPLES, 1816–20. The short low bodices and the fuller skirts of ball dress, 1816–20, show vividly against the growing darkness of men's dress. The difference in headdress of the younger and older women also appears in this contemporary record of an evening festivity. *City Art Gallery, Bristol.*

PLATE 79 1199

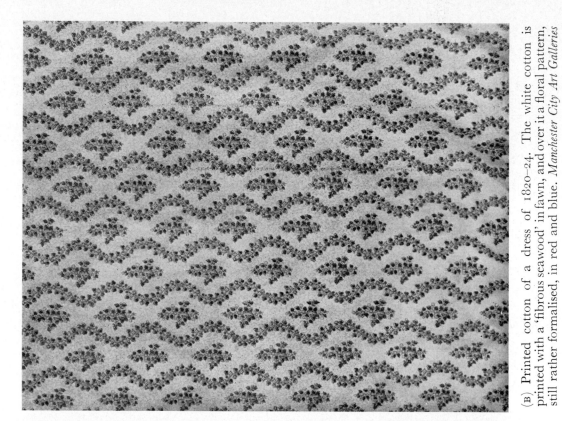

(B) Printed cotton of a dress of 1820–24. The white cotton is printed with a 'fibrous seaweed' in fawn, and over it a floral pattern, still rather formalised, in red and blue. *Manchester City Art Galleries*

(A) Ball dress of embroidered net over cream satin, 1821–23 *Manchester City Art Galleries.*

PLATE 80

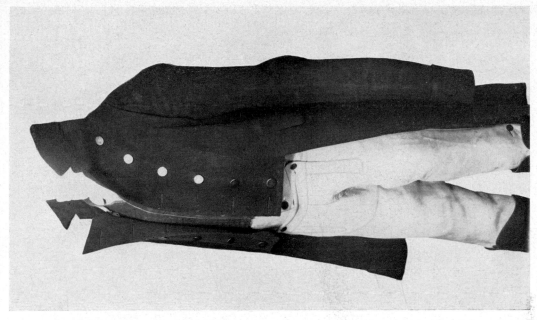

(B) Coat of green cloth, of the type worn by Lord Grantham (*left*), double-breasted, with brass buttons; leather breeches; 1810–20. *The London Museum.*

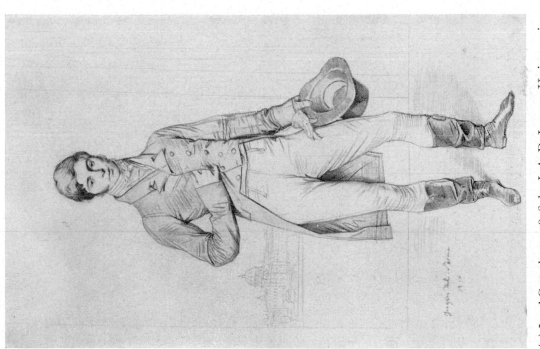

(A) Lord Grantham, 1816, by J. A. D. INGRES. He is wearing pantaloons with hessians. His coat has the double-notched lapel which appears mainly 1800–25, though remaining later on evening coats, and is worn with the waistcoat just visible at the waistline. *Courtesy Major Edward Compton.*

PLATE 81

Pelisse of green silk, figured, levantine with puffed over-sleeves; white satin bonnet, made on a framework of cane; cream silk scarf-shawl with ends and borders of woven pattern, 1818–20. *Manchester City Art Galleries.*

Evening dress of white muslin, with trimmings of satin and embroidery in many-coloured chain stitch, 1827–28. The satin bands at the hem are wadded. The gathering of the bodice under satin bands gives a stomacher form, which is enclosed in the pointed lapels which make one of the bodice styles, 1826–29. The point, here extending below the waistline, foreshadows the later development of the bodice. *Victoria and Albert Museum.*

PLATE 83

Beriah Botfield, aged 21, 1828, by THOMAS PHILLIPS. The coat is dark brown; the waistcoat and cravat black, the cloak dark purple, with a deep, black velvet collar. The fawn trousers show a very long, loose cut of this garment at a time when it was worn with a great deal of variety of form. *Courtesy The Marquess of Bath.*

PLATE 84

(A) Necklace and pair of ear-rings, gold filigree set with emeralds, rubies, pearls and other stones. About 1820–30. *Victoria and Albert Museum.*

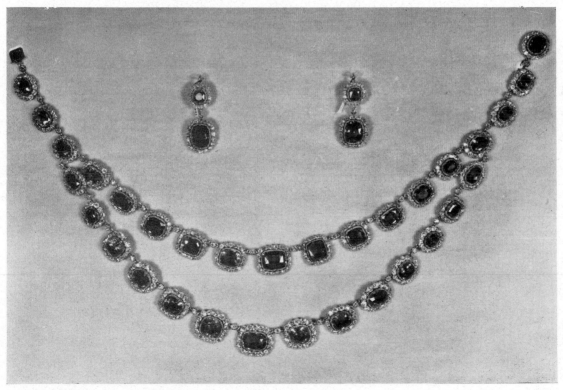

(B) Necklace and pair of ear-rings, composed of large sapphires set in gold and diamonds set in silver. Early 19th century. *Victoria and Albert Museum.*

PLATE 85

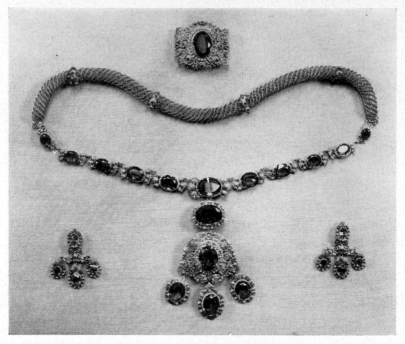

(A) Parure of necklace, ear-rings and clasp, filigree gold with tinted
gold flowers, set with glass pastes imitating rubies. About 1820–30.
Victoria and Albert Museum.

(B) Bracelet, gold filigree with tinted gold enrichments, set with amethysts and semi-precious gemstones.
About 1830. *Victoria and Albert Museum.*

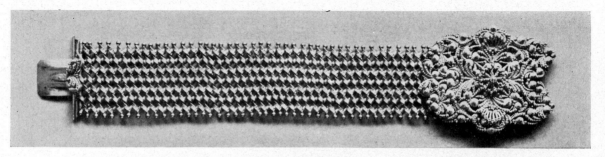

(C) Bracelet of interlaced gold wire, the clasp of gold filigree. About 1830.
Victoria and Albert Museum.

PLATE 86

(A) Tiara in two pieces, gilt metal set with imitation classical cameos of agate and onyx. About 1820. *Victoria and Albert Museum.*

(B) and (C) Bracelet of plaited human hair, the clasp set with a shell cameo, mounted in gold filigree. About 1820. Necklace of gilt metal set with roundels of cornelian, about 1810–20.
Victoria and Albert Museum.

PLATE 87

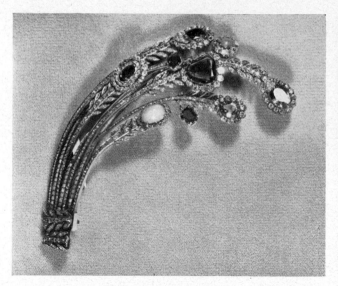

(A) Aigrette in the form of wheat-ears set with amethyst, emerald, turquoises, and diamonds. About 1820–30. *Victoria and Albert Museum.*

(B) Large floral spray brooch set with diamonds, early 19th century. *Victoria and Albert Museum.*

(C) Miniature portrait of a young woman, wearing a triple necklace of pearls, seed-pearl ear-rings, bracelets and belt-clasp *en suite* set with cameos. About 1820. *Victoria and Albert Museum.*

(D) Miniature portrait of Mrs de Wint, wearing ear-rings and necklace of coral. Probably painted about 1807. *Victoria and Albert Museum.*

PLATE 88

(B) Samuel Wesley, 1766–1837, by J. Jackson. *National Portrait Gallery.*

(A) Thomas Attwood, 1765–1838. *Royal College of Music.*

PLATE 89

(A) John Field, 1782–1837.

(B) Sir Henry Rowley Bishop, 1786–1855.
National Portrait Gallery.

(C) William Crotch as an infant prodigy, aged 3, by
I. SANDERS, 1778. *British Museum.*

(D) Charles Dibdin, engraving from a miniature
by R. W. SATCHWELL, 1819.

PLATE 90

(A) Covent Garden Theatre, by Pugin and Rowlandson, from *The Microcosm of London*, 1808.

(B) Humming-birds, or a Dandy Trio. Drawn by 'J. S.' and etched by G. CRUIKSHANK, 1819.

PLATE 91

(A) Piano. William Stodart. Early nineteenth century. *Victoria and Albert Museum.*

(B) Portable Pianino. Chappell. Early nineteenth century. *Victoria and Albert Museum.*

PLATE 92

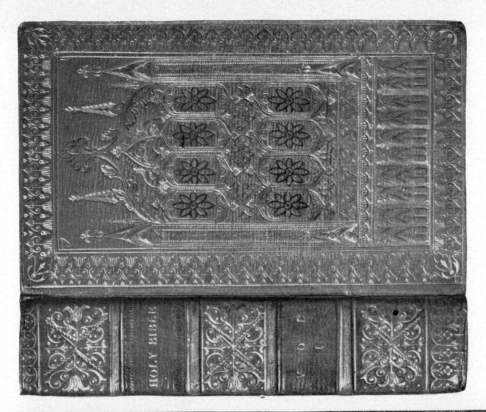

PLATE 93

(A) Binding by Charles Lewis, c. 1830. Longinus, *De sublimi genere dicendi*, Venice 1555. Brown morocco, gold-tooled. (Reduced.) *British Museum (Grenville Library).*

(B) 'Cathedral' Binding by William Lubbock of Newcastle-upon-Tyne, c. 1812. *Holy Bible*, Edinburgh, 1811. Red morocco, gold-tooled. (Reduced.) *Courtesy Mr and Mrs A. Ehrman.*

1213

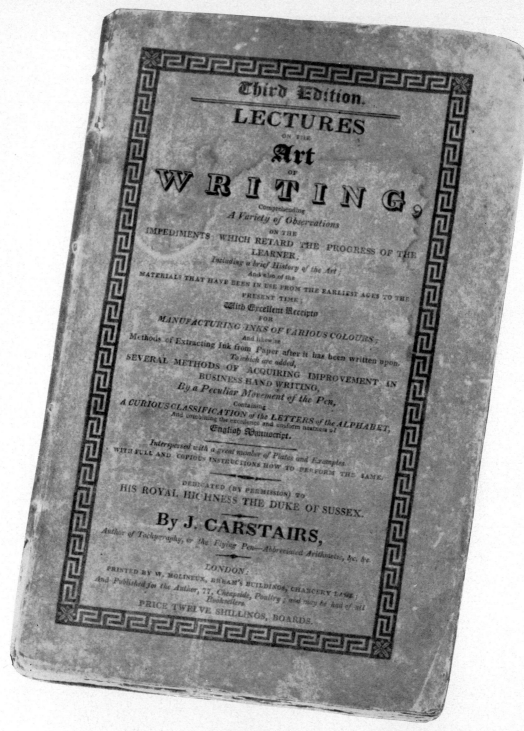

Dated 1816, this book (slightly reduced) shows the printed paper boards in which many books were issued before the introduction of cloth in about 1825. The 'shaded' type used for WRITING and the border are both Regency inventions. *Courtesy B. L. Wolpe.*

PLATE 94

The copper-engraved title-page (slightly reduced) of a three-volume bird
book published in Norwich 1815–22. The decoration of the engraved
letters indicates a new trend also being followed by the typefounders.
Norwich Public Library.

PLATE 95

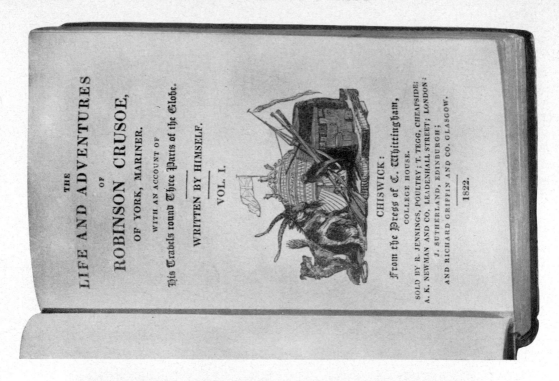

An example of Whittingham's Cabinet Library. The binding, contemporary, is in red morocco, gold-tooled. The title page is actual size. The illustrations were engraved on wood by S. Williams.

PLATE 96

diversely wrought, and increasing in diameter towards the border'. No portion of this carpet appears to have survived. All three carpets were designed by Robert Jones, and a fairly good estimate of the original appearance of them can be made from the plates of Brayley's *Illustrations of Her Majesty's Palace at Brighton* (1838).

Fragments of another Axminster carpet, woven in 1823, are in the Soane Museum, but the design is of less interest, being of an Oriental type based on Turkish *Ushak* carpets. The Victoria and Albert Museum has a hand-knotted carpet with a naturalistic floral design on a green ground which was probably made at Axminster during the last years of the factory which closed down in 1835. The Rev. Thomas Moore in his *History of Devonshire* (1829–31) regarded the factory as a flourishing concern and wrote that the 'carpets were never in higher repute than at present. His Majesty's Palaces at Brighton and Windsor are graced by the labours of the women of Axminster, as are also the mansions and country seats of the nobility.' At that time about a hundred people, mainly women, were employed in the manufacture, but since at least five women were employed on each loom, there must have been less than twenty looms in operation. The Axminster carpets were naturally luxury productions, for, as Moore says, 'the thickness of these fabrics being greater than any others of the kind, and the quantity of raw materials used in the manufacture of them being consequently large, – the labour, as the work is done by the fingers, being minute and tedious, – and considerable sums, occasionally thirty or forty pounds being spent on the pattern, the price of them is necessarily high'. Axminster was ultimately unable to compete with the increasing production of cheaper, woven carpets, and in 1835 the factory was closed down, and the equipment transferred to Wilton.

The carpets with the pattern woven on the loom were of the types known by their contemporary names of Brussels, Wilton, Kidderminster, Scotch and Venetian. In the Brussels type the worsted woollen warp was brought to the surface in raised loops to produce the pattern, the binding weft, of fine linen or hemp thread, being hidden by the pile. The Brussels loom was a draw-boy [1] loom which necessitated the weaver having an assistant. The Wilton type was a modification of Brussels in which the looped pile was cut after weaving to give a velvet effect. The Kidderminster and Scotch carpets were both of the ingrain variety. They were non-pile carpets, were usually reversible, with the warp and weft both contributing to the pattern. These carpets were normally of double-cloth or two-ply weaving, but in 1824 a stronger three-ply version was perfected at Kilmarnock and afterwards made elsewhere. The Venetian carpeting was an even cheaper variety, woven in a simple check pattern, with the weft covered by the heavy woollen warp.

A number of Brussels carpets were made for the Royal Pavilion, but no fragments appear to have survived, and their appearance can be judged only from contemporary illustrations. In the King's New Bedroom and the Library the same design was used, a geometric diaper of flattened hexagons arranged horizontally and vertically at right angles to each other. Patterns of this type are found in Ackermann's plates of *Fashionable Furniture* and the two carpet designs from George Smith's *Collection of Ornamental Designs after the Manner of the Antique* (1812), illustrated on Plate 75A are also similar. In the North and South Galleries of the Pavilion, Brussels carpeting in a trailing floral pattern on a cream ground was used, and in the Banqueting Room Gallery a Persian pattern in crimson and drab. The Brussels carpet was woven in strips and joined together and cost approximately £2 12s. a square yard.

Carpets were also made for Gothic interiors. Buckler's *Views of Eaton Hall* (1826) show both hand-knotted and woven carpets in Gothic patterns. William Porden embarked on the rebuilding of Eaton Hall in 1804, but the work was not completed until 1825. The drawing-room was equipped with a large hand-knotted carpet the central motif of which echoed the Gothic architectural detail of

---

[1] Draw-boy. The boy who pulls the cords of the harness in figure-weaving; hence, the piece of mechanism by which this is now done.—*Shorter Oxford English Dictionary*.

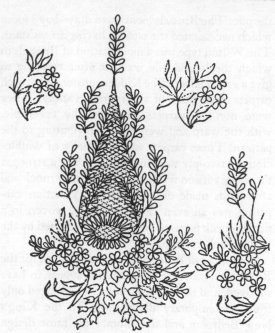

Fig. 3. Needlework pattern for muslin embroidery from Ackermann's *Repository* for August 1815.

Fig. 4. Muslin pattern from Ackermann's *Repository* for May 1828.

the elaborately vaulted ceiling. The dining-room carpet appears to have been of the Brussels or Wilton type, woven in strips, with a border imitating Gothic tracery and bosses, and the Library carpet had an all-over diaper of a quatrefoil design. The Gothic furniture in Ackermann's *Repository* is shown standing on carpets of similar design.

Brussels carpets were woven at Wilton, Kidderminster and in the West Riding of Yorkshire. The Wilton factory was established in about 1740 for the production of Brussels carpets, and the Wilton type, with the cut-pile, was first introduced there. Hand-knotted carpets were not made at Wilton until the Axminster equipment was transferred there in 1835.

Considerable advances were made at Kidderminster during the Regency period. In 1807, 1,000 carpet looms were in operation, and by 1838 there were 2,020, but in spite of the increase in the number of looms, the shuttle was still thrown by hand. Most of the carpets woven at Kidderminster appear to have been of the Brussels type, although the two-ply non-pile carpets, to which Kidderminster gave the name, were also woven there. The Jacquard apparatus was first introduced at Kidderminster in 1825, and was used for the weaving of the two-ply carpets. Among the leading Kidderminster firms were William Grosvenor and Co. (now Woodward, Grosvenor and Co. Ltd), and Brintons, established by Henry Brinton in 1819.

The English carpet-weaving industry also flourished in the West Riding of Yorkshire, particularly in the towns and villages of Leeds, Halifax, Dewsbury and Heckmondwike, and to some extent in Sheffield, where, in 1822, in addition to the weaving of carpets, some 100 looms were employed in the weaving of horsehair for upholstery. Although some of the larger establishments were organized on a factory basis, in many of the towns and villages the industry was still on a cottage basis, with the weaver producing the carpets on looms situated in their own homes. Edward Baines' *History, Directory and Gazeteer of the County of York* (1822) lists seven carpet manufacturers in the village of Heckmondwike. One of the largest concerns appears to be that of John Hanbury, whose family also wove carpets at Dewsbury. Another Heckmondwike factory was that of William Cooke, which was concerned mainly with the production of rugs. Cooke's son Samuel later established the firm of Cooke and Sons at Liversedge, a neighbouring village. Five carpet-weaving establishments, mainly producing Brussels carpets, are listed at Dewsbury, and four at Halifax. The factory of Crossley and Sons, now one of the largest in the country, was begun in a very small way in 1803 by John Crossley, a hand-loom weaver.

In addition to the hand-knotted and woven carpets, which were made on a commercial basis, a number of embroidered carpets made by individuals for their own use have been preserved. Some of these were purely floral, others copied the Empire designs of the French Savonerie carpets on a more modest scale, and a few the geometric designs of the Brussels and Wilton carpets. An interesting needlework carpet, now in the possession of Lady Leconfield, was worked by Mary Hutton Gooch, who died in 1836. The general scheme of the design, with the repeating pattern of hexagons and leaf border, is close to the designs of George Smith, but the floral sprays in the hexagons are of a type which seems to have been confined to needlework carpets. Each of the hexagons were worked separately and joined together to form the carpet which took fifteen years to complete.

Needlework and embroidery

The Regency period was not outstanding for its embroidery, and most of it that has survived is in the form of white-work embroidery for costume. Although the earliest embroidery patterns issued month by month in Ackermann's *Repository of the Arts* were for embroidery in coloured silks, chenille and worsteds, as well as in white thread, from 1815 onwards they were exclusively *muslin patterns*, that is patterns for embroidery on fine cambric in white thread with needlepoint fillings, and insertions of net and cutwork with buttonholing at the edges. The Victoria and Albert Museum has five sketch-books (from different hands) of designs for muslin patterns. These sketch-books contain

thousands of different designs dating from 1809 to the 1840's, and provide additional evidence of the immense popularity of this type of work during the Regency period.

This type of embroidery, or *Moravian work*, to give it its contemporary name, was extensively used on the fashionable 'jaconet muslin' round dresses and open robes (Pl. 75B), on petticoats, aprons, handkerchiefs, collars and on baby clothes. The earlier patterns, which were fine and delicate, were mainly floral in character (Fig. 3), although there were a number of running borders of formal decorative patterns. By 1825 the patterns were generally larger in scale, and somewhat coarser, with eyelet holes and stylized flowers and leaves in the manner of *broderie anglaise*. The borders normally had a regular vandyked or scalloped edge (Fig. 4), but in 1828 there was a fashion for asymmetrically scalloped edges.

The 'muslin patterns' were also used for embroidery on the new machine-made net, which had been patented by Heathcoat in 1809, and was made into veils and scarves in imitation of expensive, hand-made bobbin laces. The embroidery, which was worked in white thread mostly in running or tambour stitch, normally consisted of a border of sprays of flowers and leaves with a filling of tiny detached sprigs. Muslin or net curtains were also embroidered in white thread, sometimes with vandyked borders, or a running classical border, or with small detached sprigs scattered over the ground. Muslin bed-covers for daytime use were similarly embroidered.

Embroidery in satin stitch in coloured silks, or gold and silver thread, was used on upholstered furniture and on the borders of curtains and pelmets. The backs of sofas, and the loose cushions, were often covered with velvet, or plain silk, and embroidered with laurel wreaths, or other classical devices. These were probably made in imitation of the Lyons silks of the period, as woven silks of Empire design of English manufacture do not appear to have survived, and probably were not even made in this country. Appliqué embroidery in silk or velvet was used for curtain borders and pelmets, in designs appropriate to either the *Greek* or *Gothic* taste. Most of the embroidery for furnishings was in the classical style, but from 1825 onwards embroidery in coloured silks in designs of an architectural or heraldic character are found on upholstered furniture in the Gothic taste.

The beginning of the century saw a revival of tent-stitch embroidery on canvas. The year 1810 is that normally given for the introduction of 'Berlin wool-work', and although it is true that the Berlin patterns were not imported in any considerable quantity until about 1830, there is firm evidence that the designs, which were printed on squared paper so that they could be copied stitch by stitch on to square-meshed canvas, were in fact known in England as early as 1805. There are a number of original designs in the Bannister Hall pattern-books (see Section on Printed Textiles) and a corresponding textile in the Victoria and Albert Museum, which are called 'Needlework chintzes' and show a square mesh with vases of flowers and other floral motifs filled in by tiny squares of colour in exact imitation of the Berlin patterns. The 'Berlin wool-work' of the Regency period is more restrained than during the hey-day of the fashion in the 1850's and 1860's. The flowers, although drawn with a marked degree of naturalism, are not yet so elaborately shaded as to appear to stand out from the ground. The colouring is also more subdued, for the aniline dyes producing the characteristic magenta and vivid greens were as yet unknown. This tent- and cross-stitch embroidery was used for upholstery and for smaller household articles such as pole-screens. An impressive example of Regency needlework is a set of two sofas, six armchairs and a footstool, now at Buckingham Palace, worked by Frederica, Duchess of York, in 1815. The back and seat of the sofas have a design of a spreading basket of mixed flowers, drawn with the precision of a Dutch flower-piece, enclosed in a running border of curling leaves and flowers. The chairs, although worked at approximately the same time, show a design that has more in common with the later Berlin wool-work with a heavy wreath of elaborately shaded ivy-leaves on the back and oak-leaves on the seat. The bedroom chairs at Eaton Hall, Cheshire, had seats embroidered in tent-stitch in Gothic designs, but have not survived.

Samplers were as popular during the Regency period as in the preceding era, and show little change in either design or execution, being worked in either silk, or, less frequently, wool, in cross-stitch on fine canvas or 'tammy-cloth'. The sampler had firmly established itself as a child's exercise, and the general format was a squarish oblong with a running-floral border enclosing a variety of symmetrically arranged motifs, a religious or moral verse, and the child's name, age and date of working (Pl. 76A).

Embroidered pictures, in coloured silks and chenille on satin, known at the time as 'satin-sketches', continued in favour throughout the period, with subjects copied from popular engravings and the faces and other details painted in water-colours. Mary Linwood's (1755–1845) copies of oil-paintings in coloured worsteds, which she had first exhibited as early as 1776, received continued admiration, and her permanent exhibition in Leicester Square, opened in 1798, was still one of the sights of London in the 1830's. During this period, however, a type of embroidered picture, which may be regarded as the ancestor of the modern 'fabric-collage', came into being. Instead of laboriously imitating a painting with thousands of stitches in coloured worsteds, small pieces of fabric were cut out and roughly sewn to a fine canvas ground. As the pieces of fabric were overlaid one on the other, the surface of the picture was slightly uneven, and had the effect of a thick impasto. The foremost exponent, and apparently the originator, of this type of craft was a Mrs Dickson, who produced copies of oil-paintings using scraps of fabric from tailors' cuttings (Pl. 76B). Her work was exhibited at Brighton under Royal Patronage, and at Soho Square in London in 1831, shortly after her death. The London exhibition consisted of eleven copies of oil-paintings, after old masters such as Rembrandt and Titian and contemporary painters such as Angelica Kauffman. Five of Mrs Dickson's pictures are now in the Victoria and Albert Museum.

Costume

ANNE M. BUCK

WOMEN'S COSTUME

The changing style

In the battle of classical and Gothic taste at the beginning of the nineteenth century, women's dress was a field of minor skirmish. So when Thomas Hope published his *Costume of the Ancients* in 1809, this was welcomed not only for its historical interest but as a practical manual of dress for the discerning woman of fashion, 'To Mr Thomas Hope's recent publication on Ancient Costume is the latest change in dress principally to be attributed ... it is to be hoped that the publication ... will become the vade-mecum and toilet companion of every lady distinguished in circles of fashion.'[1] Henry Moses' volume of drawings of about the same time, *Modern Costume*, showed women's dress almost as antique in style and detail as that of Thomas Hope's book (Fig. 1). In turn some of the fashion journals 1807–10 gave plates and description which might be transcriptions of the designs in *Modern Costume*. And some women did turn to Thomas Hope for inspiration in their dress: 'Her dress was white satin trimmed with white velvet cut in a formal pattern then quite the rage, a copy from some of the Grecian borders in Mr Hope's book.'[2]

But the battle here was already lost. Judging from the dresses which have survived and from the

portraits of Englishwomen painted at this time, this last wave of Grecian taste washed only lightly over English dress. In 1810 women's dress was basically the same as it had been for the past ten years, a plain brief bodice, a narrow skirt falling straight and close to the figure from the high waistline in flowing, clinging lines of white muslin. The draped lines of soft white fabrics gave this style of the early nineteenth century an affinity with the sculptured forms of Greece and Rome, but its inspiration was romantic. The change from the eighteenth-century style to the nineteenth-century style was a movement from the formal, the restrained – the real classical temper – to the natural, the free – the romantic temper. And this romantic temper turned dress consciously back to the past. The inconstancy of its inspiration by the classical movement shows even in the first unfolding of the style, when between 1800 and 1810 such unclassical details as vandyked ornament, an 'antique stomacher', and 'Elizabethan' ruff appear within the classical form. And in 1811, when there were new offerings for Grecian taste, and while the word 'Gothic' was still the most severe censure for erring taste in dress or detail, the real direction of fashion is revealing itself. 'I fear the monstrous forms, discordant colours and ostentatious display of ornament, which distinguishes the dresses of the fourteenth and fifteenth centuries, are really more admired by ladies in their hearts than the pure taste and modest elegance of the Grecian costume.'[3]

[1] Ackermann's *Repository*, June 1809.
[2] Grant, E. *Memoirs of a Highland Lady*, p. 36, 1950.

[3] Ackermann's *Repository* ... March 1811.

Romantic extravagance turned not only to the past, 'All nations are ransacked to equip a fine lady.'[4] New forms were gathered from all parts of the world, particularly the more remote and exotic, in Moorish turbans, Circassian sleeves and laced peasant bodices. The campaigns of the long war with France also brought their fashions, the 'Vittoria cloak' or Pyrenean mantle, the Cossack mantle, and the Prussian helmet cap, carried out in canary-coloured silk. All these become naturalised into the dress of the years before 1814. The war brought another influence, in the penetration of trimmings from military uniforms into women's dress. Frogs, epaulettes and braided and corded trimmings appear on spencers and pelisses: 'I walked out like a hussar in a dark cloth pelisse trimmed with fur, and braided like the coat of a staff officer.'[5]

At first the plainness of line and surface was still unbroken by ornament. The muslin, continuing the fashion of the previous years, was embroidered with small sprigs over the surface, or with outlining borders, and with 'lettings-in' of lace, ornament which was part of the surface of the fabric and did not disturb the line of the dress. Some of the embroidered borders of dresses, worked perhaps from the patterns for dress embroideries inserted in the fashion journals, are the chief witness of the Grecian influence of these years.

From 1810 the draped, clinging lines of the dress began to harden. In 1813, when the fashion writers were still speaking of dresses of real 'Grecian design',[6] the line itself began to change. Frills appeared at the hem: 'She had double flounces to her gown. You really must get some flounces.'[7] At first they were few, small and plain, but gradually they grew more elaborate, increasing in number and depth until, by 1816, they had spread half-way up the skirt, and the hem, widened by them, swung out gently from the body and lifted slightly from

the ground. Embroidery was then concentrated on these flounces in 'a profusion of work', that is a profusion of white open-work embroidery, in vandykes and scallops, alternating with puffings, pipings, and tuckings of muslin and insertions of lace, which soften and break the line of the dress (Fig. 2). On silk, net and lace dresses the flounces are lace-trimmed and the hem made more elaborate by interlacing ornament and weighted by padded satin bands. Detail from the 'Gothic' past, military braiding, laced peasant bodices, met in the ornament which encrusted the bodice, although between 1815 and 1820 there was so little left of this part of the dress that it settled mainly on the sleeve, particularly on the full, short sleeve of evening dress. The dress of the early nineteenth century had moved into its decorated period.

This richness of ornament was changing its character, but to contemporary eyes the touchstone of classical or Gothic taste was the position of the waist. The English waistline had between 1808 and 1814 shown a Gothic tendency to lengthen, 'I can easily suppose that your six weeks here will be fully occupied, were it only in the lengthening the waist of your gowns.'[8] But in 1815, when English fashion was no longer cut off from France, it returned to a higher line. Ackermann's *Repository* was deceived into describing this as 'perfectly Grecian' in March 1817, but others were more aware of change: 'Waists are worn very short, but not in the foolish Grecian style we were once so pleased with, no, it is now a pretty little waist, very tight at the bottom, with the bust well marked out.'[9] The long flow of the skirt from its high waist-line kept up the illusion of a classical form until 1820. Then, as the waist at last began to move downwards, slowly but with certainty, the new character and form of dress began to appear clearly. As the waist line fell the skirt spread out more widely at the hem. And here the ornament, which had acted as a camouflage of change, became less lavish, gradually disappearing from the hem, until by 1830 the skirt was showing its new wide form in sharp, clear outline. Orna-

[4] *Mirror of the Graces*, 1811, p. 25.
[5] Grant, E., *Memoirs of a Highland Lady*, p. 214, 1950.
[6] *Lady's Magazine*, July 1813.
[7] Austen, J., *Letters*, Vol. 2, 14 October 1813.

[8] Austen, J., *Letters*, Vol. 1, 17 January 1809.
[9] *La Belle Assemblée*, July 1817.

Fig. 1. Drawings of costume, showing styles of dress with Grecian influence, which also appear in fashion plates 1807–10. From a drawing by Henry Moses in *Modern Costume*, 1823.

ment on the bodice was also smoothed out into flat, pleated bands, and on the sleeve was absorbed into a new spreading form. For from 1825 the sleeve became the dominant feature of the dress, and by 1830 was almost at its climax of fullness. Large balloon-like forms now billowed over the upper part of the body, where the longer bodice tightened to the figure. And below the falling, tightening line of the waist was the billowing spread of the skirt. This repetition of inflated forms gave to the whole dress its new character of exuberance and extravagance.

Fabric and colour

White muslin had from the end of the eighteenth century been the main fabric used for women's dress. To this fabric the evolving style owed much of its form and character and also its evocation of the sculptured garments of classical antiquity. It was still the general and correct wear for dresses of all kinds in 1810. Jane Austen, who is revealed in her letters as a very fashion-conscious woman, gave, in Edmund Bertram's sober compliment to his diffident young cousin, the conservative, masculine approval of a long-accepted fashion: 'A woman can never be too fine while she is all in white.'[10] It was for the whole period preeminent for morning wear: 'Nothing but white can be worn in the morning', stated *La Belle Assemblée* in 1810, and ten years later it was still 'white dresses are universal, either for morning costume or half dress, in the former cambric, for the latter of India muslin'. Only in the months of mid-winter did the hardy Englishwoman abandon it for silk, poplin or wool: 'Late as it is in the season, morning dresses continue to be still made of

[10] *Mansfield Park*, 1811–13.

muslin.'[11] The number of surviving dress of this period and the proportion of white muslin ones among them give still visible support to the assertions of the fashion writers.

Although muslin was worn less for evening dress after 1810, it still continued to appear, especially for informal summer occasions: 'Muslin gowns are worn by many of an evening, chiefly with coloured borders', Jane Oglander told her niece Fanny, in 1820.[12] These coloured borders were embroidered or painted, and during the next few years they change from borders of one, to borders of many colours (Pl. 83). Satin was much worn for evening dress, but the most popular fabrics for evening wear, between 1815 and 1830, were the light, delicate textures of net, gauze or lace, transparent cream or white worn over a slip of white or coloured satin, pale pink, blue or yellow. The gauze was often woven or embroidered with sprays in bright colour, and the satin appliqué trimmings and bands matched the colour of the pattern. Or thin crape with pale colour revealed the lustre of a white satin slip beneath. The lace was often bobbin or needlepoint, but the development of a machine-made net, 1810-15, which was then embroidered with silk sprays, was a cheaper, but still fashionable substitute, with the interest of novelty (Pl. 80A). Blonde, a silk bobbin lace, was much worn for trimmings throughout the period.

The day-time silks were still light in texture. Sometimes they showed a small covering pattern in the weave or were striped, usually on a cream or white ground, or checked, particularly after 1815. Levantine, a soft, twilled silk, was a characteristic material of these years, used both for dresses and pelisses and spencers (Pl. 82).

In 1825 the fashion writer of *La Belle Assemblée* wrote: 'It is rather more than three years since our modish fair ones patronized even to excess the British chintzes, preferring them for the greater part of the year to the finest cambric for morning dress.' Later in the same year this writer described the chintzes: 'On the pale modest straw colour we behold in delicate mosaic the red fibrous seaweed ... or on a ground of yet deeper though not dark yellow or of green every flower that can be named.' Such designs appear on many surviving dresses – the fibrous seaweed and coral pattern, often as a background in pale colour for another printed design in deeper, brighter colour over it (Pl. 80B). Floral patterns, flowing in many colours over the surface of the fabric, were replacing the small formalised sprays – worked, woven or printed, in one or two colours on a white ground – of the beginning of the period. The flowers and other natural forms were delicately and gracefully drawn, with increasing realism. But the really elegant were always cautious about the flowering muslins: 'though many of them are really beautiful they never appear upon any female however dignified by nature, like the attire of a gentlewoman'.[13]

The colours of the beginning of the period, clear yellow, pale blue or pink, soft green, were worn always against a background of white, appearing in cloaks, mantles, spencers and pelisses over white dresses. Colour was used sparingly and always relieved by white. No other dress than a white one is ever shown with a coloured pelisse or spencer. Then, with the growing elaboration of dress, came a less controlled use of colour. The individual colour took deeper tones, and colour mingled with colour with less and less restraint; a change which added to the character of exuberance in the dress of 1825–30.

Forms and construction

Three types of dress were in general use in 1810. In one the front of the skirt, open half-way down the side seams, was lifted to fasten round the waist like an apron, meeting a bodice, fastening down the centre front; in the second, a development of this, the front of the bodice was joined to the front of the skirt, and after the skirt had been lifted and fastened, the bodice front was lifted to fasten with pins or buttons on the shoulders; beneath it linen flaps, extending from the bodice lining, were pinned over each other to keep the back

[11] Ackermann's *Repository*, November 1816.
[12] Oglander, C. A., *Nunwell Symphony*, 1945.

[13] *La Belle Assemblée*, 1827.

Lady's Magazine   July. 1815.

Nº 7

Pattern for the bottom of a Dress.

Fig. 2. One of the patterns of 'the profusion of work' which was appearing at the hems of dresses. From the *Lady's Magazine*, 1815.

of the dress in position (Pl. 77); the third had a centre back fastening to just below the waist, with a drawstring across the back of the neck and waist. The first form is the oldest, a survival from the end of the eighteenth century, and was not much used after 1810. The second form was very common 1800–10 and was still very general until about 1820. The last form was used throughout the period, and became the normal after 1820. Other forms of dress were the pelisse robe with a fastening down the centre front, which appeared as a formal dress, 1820–30. There were also dresses of separate bodice and slip; and a coloured bodice over a white 'petticoat' was a popular fashion for many years; in 1813 it was 'so general that it can no longer be considered genteel',[14] but the fashion continued until 1820.

Between 1810 and 1825 a wrap-over form of bodice, and between 1815 and 1820 an open bodice, that is one with a deep V-neckline, meeting the high waist, were worn (Pl. 78A), but the normal and characteristic neckline was low and square, with a straight line across the bosom, meeting the narrow shoulder sections. After 1825 the new fullness of the sleeve drew the dress off the shoulder, the neckline and shoulder forming a single horizontal line across the top of the body.

Day dresses of 1810–25, as well as evening dresses, show this low neckline, but they were not so worn; the opening was filled with a tucker, habit shirt, or 'antique ruff' of white muslin: 'In the morning the arms and bosom must be completely covered to the throat and wrist'[15] (Pls. 77 and 78A). Many of the day dresses, particularly between 1820 and 1830, have a high, close neckline. As a contemporary writer pointed out, undress meant a closed neck and covered arms; half dress was rather more exposed and open; but full dress meant scarcely any covering for the upper part of the body at all[16] (Pl. 79).

Although day dresses usually had long sleeves and evening dresses short sleeves, there were years between 1810 and 1820 when long sleeves appeared with full evening dress. 'Mrs Tilson had long sleeves, she assured me they are worn in the evening by many.'[17] Transparent long sleeves depending from, or over, short sleeves, are very characteristic of evening dresses, 1820–30. At the beginning of the century sleeves were set far back into the back of the dress, making this very narrow across the shoulders, and giving a wide front to the bodice. This construction reveals the carriage of the body with the shoulders well back and the bosom prominent. It was changing by 1810, and the back of the dress became wider: 'backs are very broad and in slight materials usually full'.[18]

Trains had almost disappeared from day dresses by 1810, but they remained, though rather short, on evening but not on ball dresses, until about 1815. Widening gores at the sides of the skirt swept the new fullness to the back. Hems of silk dresses were padded, 1823–8, giving weight and swing as the skirt widened. The padding spread higher, but more thinly as ornament left the hem, 1829–30.

In 1810 cloaks and mantles, varying slightly in shape but bearing many different names, were worn folded loosely about the figure. But there were also the spencer and pelisse which fitted more closely, and these became the outer garments most characteristic of 1810–30. The early forms of spencer, before 1810, had extended below the waist, and the short form ending at the line of the waist was then referred to as the military spencer. After 1810 this form became general, although the high waist-line, 1816–19, meant it was then very short indeed. It remained fashionable until about 1827. The full-length companion to the spencer was the pelisse. This too was generally worn as an outdoor garment after 1810: 'Pelisses are higher than ever in estimation.'[19] Its waistline, sleeves and ornament followed the same changes as the dress. After 1827, when the large sleeves of dresses made a fitting form of outer gar-

[14] Ackermann's *Repository*, July 1813.
[15] *Mirror of the Graces*, 1811, p. 95.
[16] Ackermann's *Repository*, March 1812.

[17] Austen, J., *Letters*, Vol. 2, 9 March 1814.
[18] Ackermann's *Repository*, February 1816.
[19] Ackermann's *Repository*, April, May 1816.

ment impractical, cloaks, mantles and shawls replace the spencer and pelisse. Wadded, fur-lined and fur-trimmed cloaks and mantles were worn over a pelisse in carriages in the coldest weather. And a scarf or shawl was often worn over it. The scarfs and shawls were of all fabrics from gauze to cachemire, silk crape and silk twill with embroidered or woven borders being particularly popular (Pl. 82). In 1810 the usual form was a long scarf shawl, but by 1820 the square shawl, growing large and more enveloping, became a much used garment. Small squares folded, or a small triangle, were worn over the shoulders over a pelisse or spencer. Swansdown tippets, long ropes of swansdown, which had been a fashion in 1800–10, were worn again in 1829–30.

Nothing sets the dress of 1800–20 so much apart from the style before and the style which followed as the scarcity of the underwear beneath it. Although it was probably not usually so scarce as in the accusation that 'some of our fair dames appear summer and winter, with no other shelter from sun or frost, than one single garment of muslin or silk over their chemise – if they wear one, but that is often dubious',[20] it was scarce enough; a chemise of linen, long, reaching well below the knee; light flexible stays; a petticoat, cotton in warm weather, fine flannel in winter; and then the gown or slip. Many of the muslin gowns were worn over a silk slip. There is little evidence that the wearing of drawers was yet usual among Englishwomen. As the waist began to lower and tighten, the dominance of stays, which Englishwomen had felt only lightly for a quarter of a century, began to return. But as early as 1810 their wearing is beginning to influence the wearing of the dress: 'stiff stays have been creeping in upon us gradually and almost imperceptibly till at length concealment is no longer affected'.[21]

Hats and head-dresses

In the different and changing styles of hats and head-dresses, 1810–30, one aspect is constant: their steadily increasing size. In 1810 hats were varied in shape, but all, except the flat-crowned 'gipsy' hat, which after a long life was just going out of fashion, were rather small. A soft crown with a stiff, turned-back brim was the basis of many styles; or a stiff, helmet-like crown with a small brim. Bonnets had a brim in line with the crown, jutting over the face. They were of silk and velvet or straw, and were trimmed with ribbon or feathers, but not a great deal with flowers.

By 1815 the tall-crowned French bonnet with its brim spreading round the face was being worn; the crown grew wider and the brim curved out round the face (1815–20): 'I do recollect when a lady did not think it necessary to wear a bushel measure on her head ... when a face was sufficiently pretty without the foil of a coal scuttle, or when a chimney pot with the sweep's brush sticking out at the top of it was not thought the most graceful of all models of a fashionable bonnet.' Such was a harsh, but fairly accurate, contemporary comment on the new bonnets of 1815.[22] Silk and velvet were often gathered over a framework of cane or wire.

Straw bonnets were worn during the summer months for walking, Leghorn or fine Dunstable straw, usually plainly trimmed. Fashionable for all the summers of 1815–30, they remained comparatively plain even in the years of excessive trimming: 'Leghorn and Dunstable bonnets in cottage form ... the plainer the more genteel.' In winter black velvet replaced them. Bonnet veils were worn with bonnets of all kinds.

By 1825 the crown was worn higher on the head, the wide brim was released, and the ribbons floated over the shoulders, giving a hat rather than a bonnet as the fashion of the next few years (Pl. 78B). Crowns and brims grew large, 1826–8: 'Hats and bonnets are monstrous.'[23] Then by 1830 the crown dropped to the back of the head, became smaller and less important, and the spreading brim met it at an acute angle with the crown.

As hats grew larger trimmings grew more profuse. Plumes of feathers appeared year after year, but after 1825 flowers appear as much as feathers:

[20] *Mirror of the Graces*, 1811, p. 77.
[21] Ackermann's *Repository*, February 1810.

[22] Ackermann's *Repository*, May 1815.
[23] *La Belle Assemblée*, August 1829.
  ibid. August 1827.

'Branches of the tulip tree in blossom surmount the hat.'[24] For the next three or four years the fashionable hat was a tangle of loops and bows of ribbon. Lace and muslin caps were worn beneath the bonnets, 1830–20.

Indoors, caps of lace or muslin, usually fastening under the chin, were worn throughout the period; these, too, became more elaborate with bows and floating ribbons, when they were also, like the hat, worn on the top of the head, 1825–30. Caps were less worn at the beginning of the period, and young women did not generally wear them. Evening-dress caps and hats were also less worn about 1810 and seldom by the really young, whose head-dresses were flowers or bands of gauze. Turbans and berets, although 'confined to matronly ladies', were a characteristic fashion of these years, particularly 1825–30; and all head-dresses grew larger and more elaborate after 1820.

Boots and shoes

For walking there were half-boots, just covering the ankle and laced down the front, of leather, cloth, cotton or silk, and shoes, usually of kid. The colour of spencer, pelisse or hat or the trimmings of the dress was often repeated in the shoes, though less after 1825, and shoes in neutral shades and of printed kid were also worn. For evening white satin slippers were the general wear. Both boots and shoes had small, very low heels or no heels at all. The toes curved to a point in 1810, but later became rounded and narrow, and then squared by 1830. The fashionable stockings were of silk.

Gloves, bags and fans

For evening wear gloves were of white kid, to the elbow, or short of the elbow. For daytime wear they were of kid or suede, usually in yellow, buff or white. Small bags, called reticules or ridicules, were carried throughout the period, a necessity at the beginning with dresses which allowed no place for a pocket. They appeared in many shapes, and were made of fabric, often matching a part of the dress, or, less often, leather. They were drawn up with cords, or mounted on a frame. Fans which were used mainly for evening occasions were small. They had carved ivory sticks, or leaves of white crape, net or gauze often ornamented with spangles, and sometimes painted.

Jewellery

Jewellery was worn sparingly at the beginning of the period, but after 1820, and particularly after 1825, in much greater quantity, 'Trinkets of all sorts too prevalent and redundant in every style of dress.'[25] The most characteristic use of jewellery in the period is the wearing, 1826–30, of three or four bracelets over the long full sleeve like a cuff.

MEN'S COSTUME

The years 1810–30 are a period of particular significance in the history of men's dress, a period in which a change which had begun in the last quarter of the eighteenth century was, with lasting effect, completed.

In 1810 this dress was a coat, with high collar, double-breasted, the front cut away in a horizontal line at a high waist-level, leaving the thighs free (Pl. 81B). Its material was cloth, olive-green, claret colour, dark blue or black. Beneath it was a waistcoat of white marcella, and with it cream or light sage cloth breeches, white silk stockings and black slippers. At the neck the lawn or muslin frill of the linen shirt flowed out over the waistcoat, and the cropped head was held high by the deep white neckcloth, folded round the neck and knotted in front.

This, the formal dress for evening, shows that the penetration of cloth into men's dress had already been completed; the fabric of informal, out-of-doors or country wear had become the fabric of formal wear also, and the varying richness of colour and texture of silks and velvets, of woven and embroidered pattern, had departed from men's dress.

[24] *Lady's Magazine*, July 1827.

[25] *La Belle Assemblée*, October 1826.

In morning dress the general form and fabric of the coat was the same, but the waistcoat might be buff kerseymere or striped silk, and the breeches leather instead of cloth. The breeches were the remaining link with the eighteenth-century style, but by 1810 this part of men's costume was changing. Breeches were worn long and well below the knee – 'the knee band extends almost to the calf'[26] – and gradually this form merged with the pantaloons which had been worn with high boots and the half-length hessians from the end of the eighteenth century (Pl. 81A). Pantaloons were now worn long and tight down the calf, with half-boots and slippers as well. They were often of knitted silk for the tightest effect, as well as of cloth or leather. 'Be so good as to buy for William [Wordsworth] 2 pairs of pantaloons of the knit kind, such as you got him before when he was in Town, one grey and the other drab.'[27] Pantaloons appeared in a variety of lengths and degrees of tightness by 1820 – 'my husband has bought ... a pair of loose pantaloons, puffed out like a hoop petticoat'[28] – and then they merged gradually into the full-length, straight-legged form of trousers, which for some years had been worn by young boys. By 1830 this new garment had become established in men's dress, long over the instep and strapped beneath the boot or shoe (Pl. 84). But the long, tight pantaloons were still worn for evening, and loose forms for day. Trousers had the centre front fastening, the return of an old fashion, in place of the flap front of breeches and pantaloons.

In 1810 there was still some richness of colour left in the cloth of the coat, and the contrast of the dark tone of the coat with the light-coloured breeches or pantaloons. But gradually blue and black, favoured by Beau Brummell, became the most general wear for the coat. Black silk breeches had been worn for evening in 1810, and black for this part of evening dress became more fashionable, so that by 1825 darkness, except for the waistcoat, the shirt-front and the cravat, had settled on for-

[26] Ackermann's *Repository*, January 1809.
[27] Hutchinson, S., *Letters*, 16 May 1813.
[28] *La Belle Assemblée*, July 1817.

NECKCLOTHITANIA

Oriental — Mathematical — Osbaldeston

Napoleon — American — Mail Coach

Throne d'Amour — Irish — Ball Room

Horse Collar — Hunting — Maharatta

Gordian Knot — Barrel Knot

Way of Folding

Pub^d by I.I. Stockdale. 41 Pall Mall. 1st Septr 1818.

Fig. 3. The frontispiece of an essay on the neckcloth, showing some of the different ways of tying the cravat. Those with loose ends were held in place with tapes under the arms. 1818.

mal evening wear. 'As black has been long the favourite dress of men of fashion, this together with the negligent kind of home costume of the ladies gave a look of gloom to the audience.'[29] For day wear light, neutral colour remained a little longer in the pantaloons and trousers.

The black or dark blue coat of evening wear kept the cut-away front and narrow skirts at the back; this was now the almost static style of a particular occasion. But there was change in the coat of daytime wear. The horizontal cut-away disappeared as the skirts curved over the thighs to meet in a point at the centre front, a style that was being worn, as well as the cut-away form, by 1820. The skirts then widened and closed in front, and by 1830 this new skirted form had replaced the cut-away style for daytime wear, although this remained in riding dress.

Men's dress was still sensitive to the movement of fashion, sharing with women's dress the changing line. The high cut-away line of the coat matched the high waist-line on women's dress, and in 1809, when this was lengthening, the fashion notes of men's dress make the same comment, that coats are long in the waist;[30] and it moved, slightly, towards the new higher level 1816–19. The skirted coat of 1830 had a marked and lower waistline, and swung out at the hips, 'the last button not buttoned, to make the coat sit more out at the hips'.[31]

During the 1820's the lapels of the coat curved open to display the waistcoat, shirt and cravat. The waistcoat it revealed had the same long curving lapels to the short waist, and by 1830 was showing the same flowering in its silk as the fabrics of women's dress.

For men the neck has always been the point, which, by expense of work, elegance or discomfort, has given the blazon of gentility, and for the whole of this period the cravat and its tying was an important part of dress (Fig. 3). The neckcloth was a large triangle of white muslin, which was folded into a band, placed round the neck or twisted in front. At the beginning of the period white could be worn on all occasions, and white only in the ballroom; for evening white was still the only wear in 1830, although black silk, a fashion previously military, and some coloured silks were being worn for less formal occasions.

Out of doors, single-breasted greatcoats were worn. Fur was fashionable for collars, cuffs and lapels in 1810. For travelling one, two, three or four capes were worn on the coat. Cloaks were worn for evening occasions.

Hats were of beaver or silk, black, grey or fawn; the crown grew higher after 1815, and by 1830 its sides, at first slightly concave, had straightened, and the brim had become flatter and narrower.

[29] *La Belle Assemblée*, July 1825.
[30] Ackermann's *Repository*, January, March, July 1809.

[31] *Whole Art of Dress*, 1830.

From Figgins' Type Specimen Book of 1821.

Jewellery

J. F. HAYWARD

A complete transformation took place in jewellery fashions in Europe at the end of the eighteenth century; the early stages of this transformation were discussed in the jewellery chapter of the preceding section of this Guide. Its causes were rooted in the social changes which had followed on the French Revolution and the ensuing period of European war. The new jewellery was devised to meet the needs and satisfy the tastes of the bourgeoisie, a class which had already emerged as an increasingly influential element in Western European society before the Regency period proper had begun. In discussing Regency jewellery we are therefore concerned not with the recognition of a new style, but with the development of a style that was already approaching maturity.

The process of democratization which is so marked a feature of early nineteenth-century society is strongly reflected in the jewellery of the time. Economic and political uncertainties and the changing balance of society led to the temporary suppression of the more valuable stones. The aristocracy followed the bourgeoisie in wearing jewels of modest intrinsic value. The fact that less expensive materials were acceptable for jewellery led, of course, to a great extension of demand. This change-over of demand from a small aristocratic clientèle to a far more extensive middle-class one was followed in a timely manner by technical improvements that made possible the production of expensive-looking jewellery at much lower cost.

It cannot be denied that in comparison with the better-quality eighteenth-century jewellery, Regency jewellery shows a certain tendency towards vulgarity. The settings which in the eighteenth century had been so finely and delicately made that they were almost imperceptible, broadened out and became heavier, more decorative in appearance. In spite of their apparent massiveness, nineteenth-century settings often contained a smaller amount of precious metal than those of the preceding century. The extravagant-looking settings of the 1820's, sometimes composed of gold alloyed with other metals to produce contrasting tints and, incidentally, to reduce cost, were in many cases stamped by machine instead of being constructed with painstaking craftsmanship by the goldsmith.

The delight in colourfulness, of which the use of vari-coloured golds is one manifestation, is a typical feature of Regency jewellery, but it cannot be claimed that the colour combinations were always harmonious. Whereas in the past the majority of jewels had been set with diamonds, rubies and emeralds only, or with cheaper substitutes, such as crystal, garnet and chrysolite, which gave similar colour combinations, now the use of semi-precious stones was greatly extended. Among the gems that were now added to the former range were amethyst, aquamarine, topaz, peridot and even the strident turquoise.

By restoring the importance of the setting, the new style brought more opportunity to the goldsmith, at any rate so far as the better-quality jewellery is concerned. Though the new mechanical techniques robbed him of one opportunity to show his skill, settings were now enriched with elaborate and often extremely delicate filigree work to which was soon added another decorative process, that of granulation.

Filigree was exploited at this time to a hitherto unprecedented degree. In addition to the usual technique of twisted wire soldered to the surface of the area to be decorated, we find the wire wound into whorls and built up in relief with minute leaves stamped from tinted gold sheets (Pls. 85A, 86A, B, C, 87B).

The process of granulation which was based upon that found on ancient Etruscan jewellery, was first introduced about 1815 in Paris and came over to England somewhat later. It consisted of depositing a large number of minute grains of gold on a prepared gold surface, and had the effect of giving a matt finish to the gold, thus providing a further alternative to the tinted gold already mentioned. Although Regency fashion as a whole took the lead from Paris, English manufacturing technique, particularly in the production of cheaper jewellery, was so renowned that no less an artist than Jean Baptiste Odiot, one of the creators of the French Empire style in jewellery and goldsmiths' work, sent his son to London in 1815 to study production methods.

During the eighteenth century jewellers had shown a most determined conservatism, and changes in fashion in costume had not necessarily been accompanied or followed by marked changes in jewellery design. In the nineteenth century the tempo of change was speeded up and fashions in dress began to exercise a greater influence on jewellery, which became more of a costume adjunct. The tendency to employ less expensive materials helped to make such changes possible, for the passing out of fashion of jewels made of shell or lava cameos, of amethyst or of seed-pearl, caused no financial embarrassment to a lady of fashion. As a special section of this work is devoted to costume, it will suffice here to refer quite briefly to the changes introduced in the first decade of the nineteenth century. The new Grecian fashion was fundamentally austere; in seeking to reveal as effectively as possible the form of the female body, it left little place, at any rate logically, for extraneous decoration in the form of jewellery. The Empire style in France, however, while adhering to the Grecian fashions of the Directoire, required a display of jewellery appropriate to the splendour of an Imperial Court. In fact, in spite of its apparent severity, early nineteenth-century costume provided a by no means unsatisfactory background for jewellery, though of a different kind from that worn in the preceding century. The high waists and simple bodices with square décolletage (Pl. 88D) provided an admirable setting for a rich necklace or a brooch in the middle of the corsage. The short sleeves called for a lavish display of bracelets. Contemporary portraits of fashionable women show them wearing ear-rings, a necklace, or a sautoir chain (of which more later) reaching down to the waist, one or more pairs of bracelets and, of course, the inevitable rings. Finally, the girdle which encircled the waist was often held by a large jewelled clasp. (Pl. 88c).

The parure, or set of jewellery designed en suite, though it had been known long before the Regency period, became very popular at this time, and quite a number still survive in the leather cases in which they were originally supplied. It usually comprised a necklace, brooch, ear-rings, and sometimes tiara and bracelets as well (Pl. 86A).

Most of the standard types of jewel were given a different form during the early nineteenth century. The necklace of the period usually consisted of a series of large coloured gemstones with wide settings (Pl. 85A) and, in the case of the more expensive pieces, diamond or half-pearl borders, with links set with smaller stones of similar type (Pl. 85B). Radiating outwards from the links between the larger stones were often pear-shaped pearls or pendants composed of stones of the same colour as those of the necklace. Such necklaces were worn low down on the neck and shoulders, and their width was sufficient to balance the wide expanse of the square décolletage. While the necklaces intended for daily wear were composed of inexpensive materials, some of those for evening wear were of great splendour (Pl. 85B). An imposing effect could also be achieved with semi-precious stones in die-stamped gold or gilt settings, but these cheaper and rather meretricious necklaces were often bulky and coarse in design (Pl. 86A).

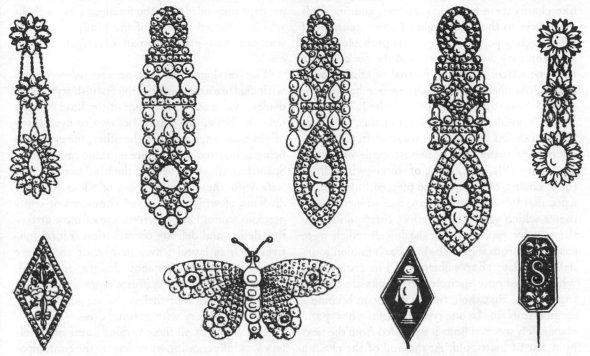

Fig. 1. Designs for ear-rings and a butterfly brooch set with pearls and pin-heads of enamelled gold. From an early nineteenth-century drawing. *Victoria and Albert Museum.*

Regency ear-rings also differed from those of the preceding century. Whereas the earlier ear-rings branched outwards and were almost as wide as they were long, the nineteenth-century type consisted of a single elongated pendant, shaped like a stalactite (Fig. 1). As the century advanced the length of ear-rings gradually increased; in 1817 a fashion journal already refers to 'Ear pendants of a prodigious length', and by 1830 they measured as much as two inches in length. Ear-rings formed an indispensible part of the parure and were worn *en suite* with necklace and pendant. For daily wear, however, the familiar pear-shaped pearl ear-ring, of the type that had been worn since the first half of the seventeenth century, was acceptable.

The bracelets of the late eighteenth and early nineteenth century had been lightly constructed of a series of plaques or cameos linked by slender gold chains, but towards the end of our period they also became much heavier in appearance, though the technique of stamping made it possible to pro-duce them of quite light metal (Pl. 86B, c). During the Regency period bracelets enjoyed a popularity which they had never had before and never enjoyed again. The new fashion of wearing the arms bare gave hitherto unprecedented scope for their display. As many as three were worn on each arm – at the shoulder, elbow and wrist respectively. A cameo or some large semi-precious stone usually formed their central feature (Pls. 87B, 88c).

Along with bracelets, chains came into fashion, having been neglected since the seventeenth century. They were often of great length and passed several times around the neck, even so leaving a loop which reached down to the high waist. Like all other kinds of jewellery, they tended to become coarser, being composed of heavy links, interspersed with the inevitable cameos or plaques.

A peculiar fashion existed in France in the early nineteenth century for wearing a long chain over one shoulder reaching down to the waist, where it ended in a large locket or pendant. These baldriclike chains were known as *sautoirs*, and one finds references to them in English fashion journals of the Regency period, though it is probable that in England they were worn around the neck like the usual necklace. A fashion journal of 1828 records that 'Gold chains with small essence bottles suspended from them are much admired'.

The considerable demand for chains, for necklaces, bracelets and *sautoirs* resulted in the introduction of many new varieties; made of plaited gold wire (Pls. 86c, 87c), of inter-twined links (curb chain), of stamped and pierced links, and in a peculiar tubular form of up to half an inch in diameter which gave a heavy effect corresponding to the massive appearance of the jewels which were suspended from it (Pl. 86A). A Paris fashion journal of the late 1820's observes: 'The chains with which ladies now encircle their necks are becoming so large that their weight will soon become a serious problem. In one type each of the heavy and elaborately worked links is separated from the next by a star of matt gold. At the end of the chain a heavy cross, rings *à la chevalière* or other jewels of a Gothic character are suspended'.

The simpler hair style of the period no longer offered the same space for chains, pearls and pendants as had the monstrous coiffures of the late eighteenth century. It did, however, provide an admirable setting for the tiara which now became an indispensable item of court dress (Fig. 2). Few of the more splendid tiaras of the Regency period have survived, but even a lady of title did not consider it beneath her to wear one of gilt metal set with copies of Classical cameos, such as that illustrated in Plate 87A. This particular tiara is of unusually solid appearance even for a period which accepted massiveness as a fundamental principle of design in applied arts.

Another hair ornament which made its appearance towards the end of this period was, in fact, a revival of a fashion of the first half of the sixteenth century. This was the *ferronière*, so called because a similar jewel is shown in Leonardo da Vinci's portrait of a lady, known as 'La belle Ferronière' and formerly believed to represent the wife of a blacksmith who became the mistress of the king of France. The jewel took the form of a pendant suspended over the forehead from a chain which encircled the top of the head; in 1825 it was said that every woman of elegance wore one.

The catalogue of hair ornaments continues with diadems and combs in the Spanish style. The diadem was worn at the front of the head straight over the brow, and sometimes two or even three might be worn, one above the other, the ensemble being completed in the more extreme cases with a Spanish comb at the back of the head decorated *en suite* with the diadems. Some of these Regency diadems, of which only those composed of semi-precious stones have survived, are of most attractive design and delicate construction. Floral motives such as laurel leaves or ears of corn were among the most frequent designs for them. Though the Regency coiffures were simple, they were required nevertheless to support a profusion of jewellery with evening dress.

The design of all these various forms of jewellery was influenced more or less by the contemporary interest in the arts of Classical Greece and Rome. Cameos or intaglios, in some cases antique, but usually contemporary copies from Italy, were introduced wherever possible as prominent features of all kinds of jewellery from finger-rings to tiaras (Pls. 87A, B). So highly were such cameos regarded that they were mounted alongside gems of very great value without arousing any feeling of incongruity. In France the enthusiasm for cameos as jewellery reached such a pitch that in 1808 the Emperor Napoleon required the Director of the Bibliothèque Nationale to hand over 82 classical cameos and intaglios from the ancient Cabinet du Roi for mounting as jewellery.

It was partly in order to accommodate the cameos, which were of larger proportions than precious stones, that early nineteenth-century settings were broadened out till in some cases they became clumsy. Authentic antique cameos and intaglios had always been rare; reproductions in hardstone had been produced in Italy ever since the Renaissance, often for sale as antique, but now the great increase in demand made it unneccessary to pass off modern pieces as classical cameos. Many of these reproductions were of notable quality and of high

Fig. 2. Design for tiara and floral brooches set with brilliants. From a drawing,
early nineteenth century. *Victoria and Albert Museum.*

cost, but the demand for less expensive cameos led
to the development of a large industry in shell cameos in Naples and the surrounding country. As
an even cheaper alternative cameos cut in lava
from Vesuvius were made and mounted in bracelets or necklaces while cheaper still were those of
moulded glass. The Staffordshire firm of Wedgwood had also been producing cameos of stoneware since the 1770's, and these continued in favour
during the early nineteenth century, though they
were not likely to satisfy the more archæologically minded ladies. The finest cameos were cut in
cornelian, jasper or agate, and for those who could
not afford to buy cameos in these materials necklaces and bracelets were produced set with plain
medallions of hardstone, mounted in pinchbeck, a
gilt base-metal, instead of gold (Pl. 87c). The
most popular hardstones were, of course, those

that had been used in classical times – namely, sardonyx, cornelian, onyx and agate.

The Empire style which dominated the early
years of our period placed no exaggerated value on
archæological exactness; it was sufficient that the
jewels should be set with classical or pseudo-classical gems and that their design be appropriate to
contemporary costume. Apart indeed from elements of obvious classical derivation such as the
cameos, some of the main features of the Empire
style had no particular relevance to antique jewellery. Among these may be numbered the emphasis placed upon harmony between brightly coloured
stones and settings of variegated gold, and the preference for shining and contrasting unbroken surfaces.

The end of the Napoleonic epoch in 1815 did
not lead in England to any drastic changes in

jewellery style. But in France the sudden change of fortune found many persons of importance without the substance to support their position, and there was for a while a strengthening of the fashion for jewellery of small intrinsic value. In general, a revival of interest in styles less remote than that of Classical Greece and Rome manifested itself. By the 1820's we find the first results of the blossoming of the Romantic taste, the pseudo-medieval *style cathédrale*, the revived Renaissance beginning with the *ferronière*, and even a trend towards orientalism, this last encouraged by Byron's activities in Greece. The post-Empire interpretation of the classical style was far more serious in attitude and was much concerned with questions of archæological exactness. In the 1820's the Roman jeweller Fortunato Pio Castellani began manufacturing reproductions of Etruscan and Classical Roman jewels based on examples in his own collection, and continued to do so until his death in 1865. He was particularly famed for his skill in reproducing the extremely fine granulated surface characteristic of Etruscan jewellery.

Romantic Gothic jewellery followed much the same course as the revived classical jewellery, that is to say, in its earlier phases it was merely fashionable and popular in spirit with no pretence at accuracy, but later it became consciously and painfully academic in its effort to reproduce faithfully its medieval prototypes. Among the revivals of the post-Empire period were the diamond sprays and bouquet brooches that had been so popular during the latter half of the eighteenth century. So closely (Fig. 2 and Pl. 88B) do they follow the naturalistic designs of the preceding century that it is often difficult to distinguish with certainty between the Regency and the eighteenth-century examples – with the exception of those set in collets closed at the back, a type of setting which was abandoned in favour of open collets about the end of the eighteenth century.

The aigrette, which had been crowded out by tiara, diadem and Spanish comb, also returned to favour in the 1820's; a particularly attractive example set with the fashionable gemstones of the time, turquoise, topaz, amethyst, emerald and diamond, is illustrated in Plate 88A. The design is based upon an ear of barley, a form which is frequently encountered in jewellery of this period. A Paris fashion note of 1822 refers to the popularity of the wheat-ear in jewellery: 'Are you going to a new play at the theatre? Twenty, thirty, fifty, even a hundred coiffures will display ears of corn, some of gold, the majority imitating the real thing'.

As in previous periods, jewellery fashions continued to be international; jewellers still neglected to sign their work, and the problem of determining the nationality of a given jewel is no easier to solve. One can say that the popular 'Berlin' cast-iron jewellery was probably not of English manufacture but imported, as were the hard-stone and the shell cameos and the Florentine miniature mosaics with views of Italy or sentimental dogs that garnished so many brooches and bracelets. Jet, on the other hand, which was much used for mourning jewellery, was produced in England at Whitby and can usually be recognized as of English origin. Mourning rings remained in great demand during the whole period, though their designs were less imaginative than those of the preceding century. The charming little sentimental devices of the late eighteenth-century mourning ring gave way to massive gold hoops inscribed only with the name of the deceased in enamel, black for married persons and white for the unmarried. Another type of mourning wear was the hair jewellery which became more popular in the 1820's. In the late eighteenth century lockets and rings with the initials of the deceased worked in a lock of the hair had been worn, but now the scale became larger and we find whole bracelets formed of intertwined hair (Pl. 87B).

The various styles which have been referred to above, Roman, Etruscan, Egyptian and Gothic, eventually passed out of fashion in the course of the later nineteenth century, but the new materials which had been introduced in order to cheapen jewellery and make it accessible to a wider public, had come to stay. The jewellery of the second half of the century was dominated by semi-precious stones such as amethyst, topaz and turquoise, and settings continued to be constructed of stamped scrollwork, filigree and granulated gold work.

Music and Musical Instruments

ROBERT DONINGTON

Diluted Handel, Haydn and Mozart

The glory of English music, so bright in the six-teenth and seventeenth centuries, yet so inexpli-cably diminished in the eighteenth, sank perhaps to its quietest state under the later Georges. No one really knows why; the period was by no means an uncreative one in England for the other arts. The fact remains that in musical composition we produced no men of undoubted genius at about this time, and very few of outstanding talent. As a natural consequence, such talent as did make its appearance was unduly influenced by models which were not indigenous. There were, it is true, a few exceptions; but their work, as we shall see, was either in too lightly popular a vein to carry much weight in the history of music, or too limited in scope.

This verdict is accepted by the general consent of historians. All the same, there is one sense in which it is too harsh. That the judgement of time has proved retrospectively unfavourable to most late Georgian music is not to be denied. But this judgement does not, perhaps, give an altogether fair impression of the state of that music as it affec-ted its own contemporaries.

In the first place, whatever it may have lacked in quality it undoubtedly made up for in quantity. And as we read through its numerous contempo-rary editions and its still more numerous manu-scripts, we are impressed by a certain impetus and vitality even in the least musically inspired regions of this imposing output. We are impressed by an unavoidable conviction that whatever monotony all these volumes of glees and ballad operas, an-thems and oratorios, may hold for us today, they represent a tremendous amount of uninhibited en-joyment both in the writing and in the perfor-mance of them for the musicians and the general public of their own day.

That is one important consideration. A second of more lasting interest is that in spite of the amount of sheer paltry Handelian imitation that had been going on ever since his sojourn and death (1759) in England, in spite of the equally paltry imitation of Haydn and Mozart that later added itself to the medley, and in spite of the con-sequent insignificance of most of our late Georgian music in the main current of European musical development, there were nevertheless one or two features of English musical life at the time which were not foreign imitations but had a truly indigen-ous zest and reality. They were, in fact, not in the main current at all. They drew little from it and they contributed little to it. But they were alive in their own right, they were genuinely English, and they are genuine musical achievements.

The so-called 'Ballad Operas'

One of these indigenous achievements was that form of entertainment which throughout its long history continued to go under the name of 'Ballad Opera', though in its later forms this name was no longer strictly appropriate. However, it was accu-rate enough when the species began. That was under the first George of England, in 1728, when the famous *Beggar's Opera* of Gay and Pepusch first took the stage. It is said on no lesser authority than that of Pope that Gay took his idea from a suggestion made by Swift to the effect that a 'Newgate pastoral', replete with jail-birds and their female appurtenances, might do very well for an operatic libretto. The suggestion was presumably meant satirically, and a fine satire Gay made of it: a satire at once of the Whig party with their leader Walpole, and of the ultra-fashionable Italian opera of the period with its leading exponents Bononcini and the great Handel himself. 'I hope I may be forgiven', says the prologue, 'that I have not made my Opera throughout unnatural, like those in vogue.' He had not indeed; it is all delightfully spontaneous, to (but not beyond) the point of enjoyable coarseness; and it is impossible not to see in this splendidly flippant and irresponsible affair the natural Englishman's answer to the excess of Mediterranean artificiality which, with all its undoubted musical excellencies, the Italian opera of the eighteenth century had come to represent.

Because it was natural and because it was English, the Ballad Opera took firm root. It has, indeed, the rare distinction of being one of the few English musical forms since the great harpsichordists of the early seventeenth century to have had any appreciable effect, though scarcely a weighty one, on continental music: it was one of the many starting-points of the German *Singspiel*. It had spoken dialogue (like the so-called '*opéra comique*'), not sung recitative (like 'grand opera'); and its airs were sung to tunes borrowed from the general stock of the ballad-mongers (itself often borrowed from folk sources), but as those were exhausted they were more and more commonly adapted from sophisticated sources which included Handel and the grand operatic composers themselves. Then, rather before the middle of the eighteenth century, the original craze for Ballad Operas petered out for a decade or two, and only a few were written.

Shortly before the period here under consideration, the Ballad Opera took on a second lease of life, at least as energetic and productive as its first. In this second phase, the borrowed ballad tunes were no longer a characteristic feature; yet the music composed for the airs in place of them kept a great deal of their easy-going popularity and directness. Among its most successful composers at this

stage were Charles Dibdin (1745–1814), James Hook (1746–1827), William Shield (1748–1829), William Reeve (1757–1815), the short-lived Stephen Storace (1763–96), his exact contemporary John Davy (1763–1824), and the remarkable tenor John Braham (1774–1856), whose imperious habit it was to compose all the music of his own part (but not of the unimportant other parts!) of most of the operas in which he appeared. With these men should perhaps be named Henry Rowley Bishop (1786–1855), a most prominent and prolific composer of opera and theatre music in great variety, from grand to popular, but not a Ballad Opera composer in the same sense as was Dibdin, Hook, Shield or Storace.

The late Georgian output of Ballad Operas reached a remarkable total, and very largely maintained that forthright and robust vitality which is its chief recommendation. Perhaps of all this music the most enduring is that to which Dibdin set his justly celebrated songs of the sea. But many good tunes, genuinely rousing in their extraverted way, can be found; and the whole episode is one of which English musicians (incurable snobs excepted) can rightly be proud.

Towards the end of our period, it must be admitted that the Ballad Opera was beginning to wear a little thin. The robustness grew less convincing; the tunes more threadbare; the manliness a trifle forced. Yet the form itself was by no means finished with. It remained in being until the Victorians Gilbert and Sullivan fastened on it with something in no way short of genius; crossed it with Italian opera, not of the heavy Handelian, but of the sparkling Rossini strain; and produced a yet more enduring English operatic achievement, the Savoy Operas.

The Glees and the Glee Clubs

A second late Georgian musical activity of an equally indigenous, and not far from equally popular, character was the fashion for what are generically known as 'glees'.

A glee is primarily an unaccompanied partsong. Some works known as glees for want of another name have instrumental accompaniments; the great majority do not. Many glees have a certain amount of contrapuntal workmanship in their construction; scarcely any have any elaborate artifices of this kind. Yet the workmanship is generally craftsmanlike; the parts are contrived neatly to give everybody a tuneful if not very independent melody to sing; the harmony flows skilfully if unsensationally; the rhythm is alive if not greatly varied.

In comparison with the finesse and subtlety of the best Elizabethan madrigals, a late Georgian glee is a somewhat obvious affair, and no doubt reflects a decline in the prevailing standards of amateur taste and musicianship. But not of musical enthusiasm; glee clubs founded specially for the enjoyment of such active music-making were numerous and well attended. As with the best Ballad Operas, the glees are attractive in proportion to their vitality. Unpretentious as they generally are, they make uncommonly good singing. Some of them, moreover, rise to genuinely poetic feeling, occasionally of extraordinary force.

Of the glee composers active within the years 1810–30, the following were among the more prominent; Samuel Webbe (1740–1816); William Shield (1748–1829); John Stafford Smith (1750–1836); John Samuel Stevens (1757–1837); Thomas Attwood (1765–1838); John Wall Callcott (1766–1821); Samuel Wesley (1766–1837); Reginald Spofforth (1770–1827); Mendelssohn's admired friend William Horsley (1774–1858); William Beale (1784–1854), some of whose glees are real madrigals; and the ubiquitous Henry Rowley Bishop (1786–1855). Quite an imposing list, and one that could readily be extended. Some of those mentioned in it were distinguished composers in other directions as well; some, such as Webbe and Stafford Smith, were not. It will be noticed that there is a certain overlapping with the list of Ballad Opera composers. Attwood, it may be mentioned, was a pupil of Mozart, and one of those who introduced a Mozartian style as a change from the perennial Handelian into the more serious forms of English music then prevailing. But unfortunately he was less successful as what was then an instrumental modernist than he was in the less ambitious indigenous form of the vocal glee.

In addition to its own musical value, the glee formed an indispensible link in that long tradition of unaccompanied vocal part-singing which has never been broken in England since the great madrigalians themselves, and indeed since far earlier. If our late Georgian forefathers had not been so fond of singing glees, our own generation might not so easily have taken to singing madrigals now that the Golden Age of English music has been brought out of the history books and into practical life again. The late Georgian composers were certainly unenterprising to a defect; but in so far as their lack of enterprise went with a healthy conservation, it had its corresponding virtues.

Interest in past music: Wesley and the Bach revival

This conservatism, on its healthy side, is pleasantly evident in an institution which would not evoke any particular comment in our own generation, when interest in music of earlier periods has become a commonplace, but which was certainly unusual in the early nineteenth century. I have in mind the series of 'Ancient Concerts' founded in 1776 and continued until 1848, the rule at which was that no music was to be included of less than twenty years' standing at the time of the performance. In theory, therefore, the rule was a sliding rule, bringing in an interesting succession of music from perhaps a generation ago. In practice, the exaggerated reverence for Handel made itself felt here as elsewhere. The proportion of the programmes handed over to his music was not healthy at all.

It was typical of our English conservatism, once again on its healthy side, that a new edition of nearly two hundred older pieces, mainly English, appeared in 1812 under the decidedly slapdash editorship of Stafford Smith. Good editing of early music was hardly to be expected in an age so patronizing towards pre-Handelian music; but in view of that, it is striking enough to meet with so much practical enthusiasm. Stafford Smith had already published a quantity of early Tudor music in 1779; he had greatly assisted Hawkins in the preparation of the latter's famous *History of Music*; and he died possessed of an astonishing collection of early manuscripts, which were unfortunately dispersed at the sale of his effects.

Another example of creative conservatism which it is pleasant to record is the part played by distinguished English musicians in the revival of J. S. Bach. It is well known that Bach, though a greater and more profound composer than Handel in every way, and in the long run actually possessed of a wider popular appeal, yet passed through a period of substantial neglect while Handel's fashion came to its peak. It is perhaps less well known that Mendelssohn, whose championship secured the first performance of the *St Matthew Passion* since its composer's death, found an early and powerful ally in Samuel Wesley the elder (1766–1837).

In many ways Wesley is the most noteworthy of the late Georgian composers. His enthusiasm for Bach began very early in his career, and remained one of its guiding influences. He was evidently a most formidable exponent of the organ works both of Bach and Handel, and an indefatigable propagandist for the former's claims; he shared with C. F. Horn (1786–1849) the credit of first editing a portion of Bach's music for the English market.

Some of the excitement which Wesley found in rediscovering this supreme genius of the past made its way into his own composition. Remarkably enough for an Englishman of that generation, he avoided oratorio after two exceedingly precocious and by no means unsuccessful attempts, the second of them at the age of eleven years. Less surprisingly, perhaps, in view of his serious if somewhat erratic personality (the erratic side was plausibly, but not necessarily with truth, attributed to a serious fall at the age of twenty-one), he avoided the stage: he was not one of the fashionable Ballad Opera men. Neither, however, did he essay grand opera. He did write glees, but here he was capable, as only few of his contemporaries were, of truly madrigalian workmanship. His Church music ranges from brilliant passage-work in the Mozartian idiom, to soberly wrought and profoundly felt counterpoint almost in the old Tudor vein. As an instrumental composer he was prolific, and at times inspired. He had an excellent chamber

vein, while as a symphonist of considerable structural abilities he was ahead of his English contemporaries. Altogether, he was both the solidest and the liveliest figure late Georgian musicianship could boast.

Two lesser church composers with some claim at least to solidity, if not to liveliness, were John Clarke-Whitfield (1770–1836) and William Crotch (1775–1847). The latter is the more substantial personage; he was a Handelian of Handelians, but in that line he was the best of his school, particularly in oratorio. What these two chiefly lack, however, is the quality of excitement which makes much of the elder Samuel Wesley so worthwhile.

A great Irish pianist-composer and others

There was an exciting enough school of pianist-composers more or less in or of Late Georgian England, of whom the three best representatives were not any of them strictly Englishmen. One was an Irishman who worked much and eventually died abroad; the others were continentals who worked much and died in England. The Irishman was John Field (1782–1837); the continentals were Muzio Clementi (1752–1832) and John Baptist Cramer (1771–1858).

Of the two continentals, Clementi was the more talented as a composer, though it is only his masterly studies for the piano which still survive. The same is true of his pupil Cramer. But the Irishman holds a more important place in the history of music. He was not only, like the other two, a brilliant pianist; he was a composer of so poetic an imagination that only its extremely limited scope prevents our calling him a genius. Perhaps, indeed, we should admit that genius can show itself in miniature, and call him one outright.

Field's contribution to the history of music is that slight but deeply felt form of piano music known as the Nocturne. It is a form upon which a composer to whom nobody would deny the name of genius set his stamp: that is to say, Chopin. But it seems certain that Chopin based his conception of the Nocturne upon Field's, and that Field's conception of it was his own. It was the one late Georgian creative achievement in music which did pass into the main stream, and deservedly. Most of Field's music is strung to too slack a tension to be of enduring value; but his Nocturnes place him, however inconspicuously, among the immortals.

Apart from Field, we seem to have imported rather than exported our top performers at this period. Even in the seventeenth century, a foreign name was already a commercial asset for a performer, though at that time English virtuosi stood in the front rank. In the eighteenth century, the foreign fashion grew, particularly for Italian singers – and with some good reason in that respect. By the early nineteenth century, continentals had the preference in many fields, particularly that of violin playing, where the Italian school had been in the lead for many generations, though the German and Franco-Belgian schools were soon to dispute this lead with them. Later in the nineteenth century, it is the German names that are most conspicuous here; in the period now under discussion, it is Italian names.

Viotti, who was the last great Italian violinist of the classical school, though by no means the last great Italian violinist, aroused remarkable enthusiasm in England where he spent intermittent periods between 1792 and his death in London in 1824. He was among the active founders of the Royal Philharmonic Society in 1813; his pupil Nicolas Mori was made the first professor of the violin at the foundation of the Royal Academy of Music in 1822 – Mori being the son of an Italian, but born in London.

Both these foundations were of lasting musical importance. As usual in the nineteenth century, we find no lack of intense musical activity in this country; but we do find a lack of confidence in our own indigenous powers. Could it be that we exercised a baleful species of auto-suggestion upon ourselves, to the effect that only wild looks and a continental name seemed compatible with true musicianship? Is that how the Italian, and later the German, spell held our home products at such a tacitly admitted disadvantage?

A thriving trade in instruments

Our makers of musical instruments, at any rate, as opposed to our performers, were at no such disadvantage. English keyboard instruments had a particularly high reputation not only in this country but abroad. English harpsichords were among the most favoured in the eighteenth century; and in the latter part of that century, the new art of piano-making received some of its most notable improvements at the hands of Englishmen. Indeed, at the time of which we now write only two piano actions were regarded as worth taking seriously, out of a multitude of less successful attempts. One was the 'Viennese action', with a supreme delicacy of touch and swiftness of repetition; the other was the 'English action', somewhat heavier and less volatile, but compensating for that drawback by an unrivalled sonority and depth of tone. Eventually the advantages of both were combined in the famous Erard 'repetition action' on which the double escapement actions of most grand pianos of the present time are based. It is not without interest that the great Sebastian Erard's son Pierre (his father being then too old to follow up his own invention) immediately patented it in England. The year was 1821.

Within the brief twenty years from 1810 to 1830 here under review, a number of English improvements to the piano were made, particularly with regard to the then novel principle of a metal-braced frame, the forerunner of the modern metal frames. The invention patented by Thorn and Allen in 1820 actually used metal tubes in an ingenious system by which their expansion and contraction at different temperatures compensated for similar changes in the strings, thus keeping the instrument in tune under varying conditions. This refinement was eventually abandoned; but the work done on it, together with other work carried out during this period by the firm of Broadwood, was of pioneering value in developing a frame capable of piano stringing.

The period was one during which a fairly rapid change was occurring in the nature and function of the piano, and the English contribution to this change was most important. The late eighteenth-century piano, the 'fortepiano' of Mozart's period, has thin strings and a light frame comparable to the harpsichord. It differs, of course, in having a percussive hammer action giving a continuous gradation of volume controlled by touch, in place of a plucked jack action giving little direct control of volume. But in the quality and colouring of its tone, the 'fortepiano' is very like a harpsichord indeed.

Not so the grand piano of 1810–30. By now the strings are thicker and tenser, yielding a more massive but less highly coloured tone. For as the thickness and tension of the strings increases, so does the proportion of energy sent into the lowest few harmonies of the natural harmonic series, while the proportion sent into the colourful high harmonies decreases. During the second half of the nineteenth century, this tendency was carried to extreme lengths, and the instruments of that time, though mechanically admirable, are tonally very different from those of the period here under discussion, and it is by no means certain that the difference is entirely for the better. The volume, however, is substantially greater. The English experiments in strengthening the frame were a necessary preliminary, especially since the period 1810–30 saw a disposition to enlarge the compass of the piano by adding further octaves, with a very considerable increase in total tension as a consequence.

In the year 1818, the firm of Broadwood sent a fine specimen of their newest grand pianos as a gift to Beethoven. This instrument made an extremely favourable impression both on the composer and on a number of distinguished continental pianists whom he caused to make a careful trial of it; on his death it came into the hands of Liszt. An instrument such as this, with its powerful and reliable English action and its strong yet resonant frame, represents one of the highest points in the history of the piano, being in its way quite the equal of any subsequent instrument, though dissimilar in the purposes for which it is most suitable. The modern piano is of a comparatively neutral, though big and beautiful, tone; but the Beethoven piano of this type, though already quite different from the harpsichord in tone, retains a stronger colouring and a more individual character, albeit less loud. There is no doubt that to hear a Beethoven concerto played on it, with the volume of the orchestra suitably adapted where necessary, can be a memorable and revealing experience.

In 1816 William Simmons took out a patent for a barrel mechanism to play piano, harpsichord, or organ automatically. In 1827, James Stewart patented an improved method of attaching the strings which effected a minor revolution in tuning technique and has not since been replaced. A more conspicuous innovation so far as appearances are concerned was Robert Wornum's introduction of the still popular cottage piano in 1811.

Wind and string makers, though not so markedly in the forefront, were very active. John Shaw's patent of 1824 for transverse Spring Slides on brass instruments may have inspired some important German improvements shortly afterwards. Boehm's famous systematization of the holes and keywork of the flute was influenced by the large holes of an instrument played to him by Nicholson in London, and it was the London makers Gerock and Wolf who in 1831 made an experimental prototype to his specification. The holes of the flute had previously been cut less large than is acoustically desirable, in order to be convenient for the normal size of finger-end; they had, moreover, been placed in positions other than those acoustically desirable, in order to be conveniently within the reach of normal fingers. Acoustically, in short, the entire system was a compromise. Boehm's plan was to reorganize the system on sounder acoustic principles, while overcoming the practical difficulty by using a set of padded stoppers worked through levers. These levers or keys were placed conveniently for the fingers; the holes could then be placed as widely apart and cut as large as the acoustic requirements suggest.

It is believed, though it is not at all certain, that this novel approach to the problem of the flute (which was later extended to some other woodwind instruments) had already been anticipated in England by Captain Gordon, an amateur maker. In most directions, however, the English makers of wind instruments were conservatives rather than innovators at this period. As such, they enjoyed an excellent reputation.

With the violin family, there was no longer a question of improvements at so late a date. The number of reputable English makers at work is surprisingly large: it included the younger Benjamin Banks and his brothers James and Henry; William Forster II and III; Henry Lockey Hill and his son Joseph III; and at least four of the Dodd family. These are all makers whose work is much in demand today, but there were plenty of others whose businesses were thriving at the time.

A pedestrian but not contemptible musical activity

So substantial a trade in musical instruments argues a plentiful supply of amateur buyers; even a flourishing profession could not have kept so many makers busy by itself. The piano trade in particular was clearly providing for great numbers of amateur performers, a majority of them content with the compact and economical 'square' (actually oblong) pianos so common under the misleading title of 'spinet' in the modern saleroom. Though pleasant enough when in good condition, they are not altogether satisfactory instruments, being neither incisive like a good harpsichord nor full-bodied like a good piano. Still, they served their purpose in very many music-loving households, both for solos and as instruments of accompaniment.

Glees must have been sung in household circles as well as in more formal glee clubs. On the other hand, nothing had arisen to replace the profound amateur chamber music of the viols, now forgotten for the best part of a century. The love of amateur string quartet playing which became so striking a feature of nineteenth-century Germany had scarcely yet reached England, nor did it ever strike root so deeply here. It was, indeed, an age of big orchestras and romantic virtuosos; the amateur came second where in Stuart England he had been very much to the front. All the same, countries do to some extent take turns in musical prominence. With the nineteenth century, Germany came to the top of the wheel, England to the bottom.

Yet even in this low trough of our musical fortunes, we made a better showing than the foreshortened view of history quite gives us credit for at this distance of time. We were not creative of any great benefits for posterity; but in addition to doing good trade, there is not the slightest doubt that we enjoyed ourselves. That may not be the only purpose of music; but it is one of them, and not the least.

Grand Piano with vertical stringing, by George Wilkinson, *c.* 1829.
From *The Pianoforte* by Dr Rosamund E. M. Harding, 1933.

Bookbinding

HOWARD M. NIXON

The years 1810–30 saw a revolution in the English binding trade, for it was during this period that the publisher's binding as we know it today was evolved. In 1810 the ordinary book was sold in stiffened paper wrappers or (sometimes printed) paper boards (Pl. 94), with the edges of the leaves untrimmed. A paper label on the spine, bearing the author's name and the title of the book, tacitly acknowledged that some buyers of the book might keep it on their shelves in this state, but this 'boards-and-label' style was essentially ephemeral: it had originally been conceived as a temporary covering for the sheets until they were more suitably bound in full or half-leather at the expense of the owner of the volume. By 1830 cloth, hitherto used only for chapbooks and school grammars, had achieved respectability, thanks to the efforts of the publisher William Pickering and the binder Archibald Leighton.[1] It was probably first introduced in 1822 or 1823 on one of Pickering's *Diamond Classics*, and the first examples have been claimed as the work of one Charles Sully. It is clear, however, that the development of bookcloth as a practical binding medium was the work of Archibald Leighton, who produced in 1825 a dyed glazed calico specially finished so as to be impervious to the adhesive. It was another seven years, however, before blocking in blind or gold was used on cloth-bound books, and up to 1830 decoration was limited to silk-bound annuals or to leather work.

[1] Cf. John Carter, *Binding Variants in English Publishing 1820–1900*, London 1932.

The leading figure in the 'West End' trade – the binders specializing in the best class of leather work – during the Regency period was undoubtedly Charles Lewis. His father, Johann Ludwig, had been one of the numerous German immigrants attracted to this country in the late eighteenth century by the passionate desire of the English collectors of the day to have all their books re-bound in full morocco. Once established in stylish premises on the ground floor in Duke Street, St James's, Charles Lewis secured the patronage of almost all the owners of great libraries of the day, including the Duke of Devonshire, Lord Spencer, Sir Richard Colt Hoare, Thomas Grenville, and Richard Heber. His style – doubtless in accordance with his patron's tastes – shows a steady deterioration from an early readiness to experiment, through a period of successful consolidation with linear designs and 'Aldine leaf' tools, to the skilful but insipid pastiches of 'Grolier' and other earlier styles which was to be the typical product of almost all European binderies from 1830 to 1880. Pl. 93A shows his characteristic linear style in the outer border and on the spine, combined with an interlacing lozenge and rectangle and a set of tools which are both copied directly from Grolier bindings of the 1540's.

Apart from Charles Lewis's ancestry and the continued existence of the firm of Hering, whose founder (another Charles) died right at the beginning of our period, the German influence of the previous thirty years faded completely. English binders were not entirely uninfluenced by events outside England, however, and the fashionable enthusiasm for all things Pompeian produced one or two interesting bindings by the firm of Dawson & Lewis, on which motifs based on decorations found at Pompeii were reproduced. The same firm was also among those who made use of Gothic decoration. The English 'Cathedral' bindings precede the French examples of the Romantic period and (except for late examples to be found on Prayer Books and Bibles of the 1830's) are normally built up of small tools, and not blocked from an engraved plaque. Sometimes the design depicts the west front of a church, as on Smith's *Antiquities of Westminster* in the Broxbourne Library bound by J. Mackenzie. More frequently the centre piece portrayed a rose window, while three or five lights from the window formed a type of fan decoration in the angles. Bindings in this style with heavily sunk panels were produced in George III's private bindery for the more important incunabula in his library, and are common on such books as Neale's *Westminster Abbey*, 1818–23.

Gothic binding was not the sole prerogative of London binders, however. Not only was it produced in Scotland and in Dublin, but also in English provincial centres, and Pl. 93B shows an adaptation of the style produced by William Lubbock of Newcastle-upon-Tyne. This was indeed the heyday of the provincial binder when, as Mr

Charles Ramsden's collection shows, they often vied successfully with their London rivals. The proximity of Sir Mark Masterman Sykes's seat at Syston Park justified the existence in Grantham of two rival binders, S. Ridge and R. Storr, both of whom could produce gold-tooled work of competence, if not of taste. And the Earl of Leicester and Dawson Turner evidently provided enough work to keep John Shalders at work in various Norfolk towns.

One other London binder worthy of mention was Thomas Gosden, who combined the trade with that of bookseller and print-seller at the Sportsman's Repository in Bedford Street, Covent Garden. His sporting propensities confined his work largely (but not exclusively) to books concerned with angling and the chase, while his antiquarian interests are reflected in the heavy boards and bevelled edges, derived from the fifteenth century, which he deemed suitable for binding nineteenth-century editions of a seventeenth-century angling classic. He executed some excellent blocked work, however, using the design found on the title-page of the first edition of Walton's *Compleat Angler* in gold and portraits of Walton and Cotton in blind; his introduction of bronze medals of the same authors was original, if cumbersome; and many of his small sporting tools are charming.

Printing

RUARI McLEAN

Thackeray (b. 1811) has described how, in his youth, children used to go on their holidays to look at the print-sellers' shops in Fleet Street, 'bright, enchanted palaces, which George Cruikshank [and Isaac Cruikshank, and Gillray, and Rowlandson, and Dighton, and Bunbury] used to people with grinning, fantastical imps. ... There used to be a

crowd round the window in those days of grinning, good-natured mechanics, who spelt the songs, and spoke them out for the benefit of the company, and who received the points of humour with a general sympathizing roar. ... '[1]

[1] W. Thackeray, 'An Essay on the Genius of George Cruikshank', in the *Westminster Review*, 1840.

Fig. 1. Mrs Humphrey's print-shop in St James's Street, from a print by
Gillray dated 1808.

We have a picture of such a print-seller's window, with a print in every pane, in Fig. 1 by Gillray (it is actually Mrs Humphrey's shop in St James's); and the publisher Tilt's window was drawn by Cruikshank. These windows supplied much of the public intelligence and news, for at that time many people still could not read, and the days of pictorial journalism did not start at least till the *Penny Magazine* of 1832. The prints were 'a penny plain, twopence coloured'. If coloured, it was by hand, by armies of girls and children, for colour-printing, by chromo-lithography, did not come in till about 1835. The prints were etched on copper, a process which the artist carried out himself, and could do almost with the speed of drawing on paper. Lithography, which had been invented by Senefelder in Bavaria in 1798, presented no advantages over etching until large editions (of, say, 1,000 copies or more) were required.

James Gillray (1757–1815), one of the greatest political cartoonists who ever lived, spent his life savaging politicians and the royal family, and died of drink; his successor George Cruikshank mirrored in his early prints the debauchery of the Regency, but lived on to throw his wildness into teetotalism and the illustration of fairy stories. The work of these two artists provides the most graphic pictures of the whole period, as future generations will recapture aspects of our own, not inaccurately, from the drawings of Giles.

Newspapers

On the 28th November 1814 the London *Times*, first of any newspaper in the world, was printed on a steam-driven machine instead of on a hand-press. The machine was a German invention, but Koenig, its inventor, could not develop it in Germany and brought it to England, the leading country for industrial production, where he found a patron in Thomas Bensley, the great book-printer. The first machine to work was sold to *The Times*, as speed in printing was then of greater commercial interest to newspaper proprietors than to book publishers. Machine printing for books was not widely adopted till much later in the century.

Newspaper at that time was heavily taxed and every inch of paper had to be used, resulting in solid walls of type which appear formidable to modern eyes. Illustrations were few and cut on wood: the editor's difficulties are shown by the cut of Nelson's Funeral Car for *The Times* of 10th January 1806, which was made in advance and turned out to be inaccurate.

During the editorship of Thomas Barnes from 1817 to 1841 *The Times* rose to a position of great power and prestige and became known as 'The Thunderer'.

Books

The most beautiful books published in Britain during the Regency were those illustrated by aquatint. Aquatinting was probably a French invention, but it was developed as a method of book-illustration in England by Paul Sandby and others from 1775 [2] and reached its greatest perfection during the 1820's and 1830's.

Aquatinting was a method of etching a copper-plate to produce tints which looked like washes of water-colour, and came just at the time of the discovery of the Picturesque – of scenery, in fact – and the desire to paint and record it, exemplified particularly in the books of travel in Great Britain by the Reverend William Gilpin, illustrated with his own aquatints. If it is true that Gilpin 'discovered' the beauty of mountains (which, for example, were not at all appreciated by Johnson and Boswell in their tour of the Highlands), it is interesting to note that Gilpin took no pleasure in the flowering horse-chestnut tree, which in 1794 he described as 'a glaring object, totally unharmonious and unpicturesque'; it was Samuel Palmer who first painted and Tennyson who first described its beauties.[3]

The first aquatints were printed in one or two colours, but soon they were combined with hand-tinting in water-colour; and some of the hand-coloured aquatint books so issued were of great

[2] The first dated aquatints in England were produced by P. P. Burdett in Liverpool in 1771, but the full possibilities of the process were developed by Sandby. See J. R. Abbey's *Travel*, vol. 1, London, 1956, p. 142.

[3] G. Grigson, *Samuel Palmer*, London, 1947.

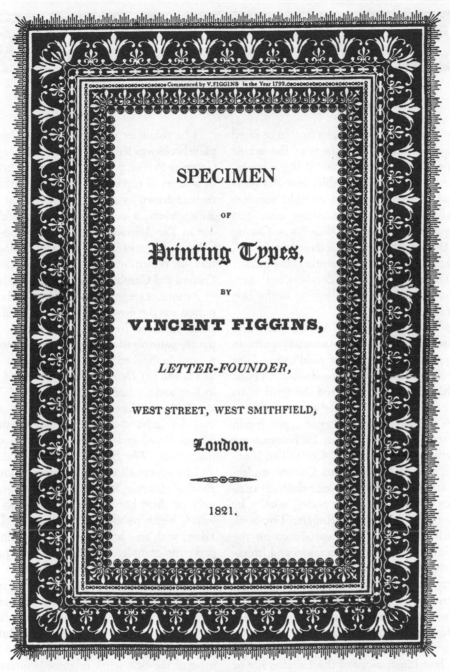

Commenced by V. FIGGINS in the Year 1792.

SPECIMEN

OF

𝕻𝖗𝖎𝖓𝖙𝖎𝖓𝖌 𝕿𝖞𝖕𝖊𝖘,

BY

VINCENT FIGGINS,

LETTER-FOUNDER,

WEST STREET, WEST SMITHFIELD,

𝕷𝖔𝖓𝖉𝖔𝖓.

1821.

Fig. 2. The title-page of Figgins' specimen book of 1821, showing a border made up of type-ornaments which were then new. Actual size. *St Bride Printing Library, London.*

Fig. 3. The typographic borders here and on p. 1252 are from Figgins'
specimen book of 1821. Actual size. *St Bride Printing Library, London.*

delicacy and beauty and deserve, in fact, to be rated among the most beautiful artifacts of the whole period. One of the most famous of these books, and now one of the most valuable, was *A Voyage round Great Britain*, published in eight volumes between 1814 and 1825, containing over 300 coloured aquatints by William Daniell, R.A. Owing to the fact that aquatinting was a hand process and that the plates deteriorated in printing, the quality of individual prints varies considerably: but there is a softness and subtlety of colouring in the best that is entrancing.

Some of the colour-plate books, including Daniell's, were first issued in monthly parts in paper wrappers – a method of publication later adopted for the novels of Dickens and others. A book issued in this way which captured the spirit of its period more than any other printed work was Pierce Egan's *Life in London*, which began appearing in monthly parts in October 1820. Its heroes were Jerry Hawthorn (a gentleman), Corinthian Tom (a pugilist), and Bob Logic (an Oxford undergraduate), and each part (price one shilling) contained three coloured aquatint plates, usually by George Cruikshank's brother Robert. The book was instantly successful, was reproduced on the stage, and initiated a host of successors and imitators. The characters gave their names to the age, so that thirty years later Surtees wrote about 'The old Tom-and-Jerry days, when fisticuffs were the fashion', and added that 'Tom and Jerry had a great deal to answer for in the way of leading soft-headed young men astray'. The plates are still among the best illustrations of the London life of the period.

The publisher who specialized in large colour-plate books was Rudolph Ackermann (see *The Late Georgian Period*, p. 1004): he had the brilliant idea of a series of topographical books with the architecture drawn by A. C. Pugin and the figures by Rowlandson, a collaboration successfully carried out in *The Microcosm of London*, 1808–10. Later volumes portrayed, in equal magnificence, the history of Westminster Abbey, the Universities of Oxford and Cambridge and the Public Schools.

Another category of colour-plate book of this period was the flower book. Perhaps the greatest of these appeared in France, where the great Redouté, patronized by Marie Antoinette and Napoleon, published his *Lilies* between 1802 and 1816, and his *Roses* between 1817 and 1824; but in England we had Samuel Curtis's *A Monograph on the Genus Camellia*, published in 1819 with magnificent hand-coloured aquatint plates by Clara Maria Pope, and the same author's even more magnificent *The Beauties of Flora* of 1820.

There were also the bird books. Audubon's *The Birds of America*, largest and most magnificent not only of these but almost of all books ever published, began publication in parts in London in 1827, with five hand-coloured aquatints in each part: the complete work contains 435 plates in four volumes, double elephant folio.

In the great colour-plate books, the typography of the letterpress did not usually achieve the same degree of magnificence as the colour-plates, unless it happened to be printed either by Bulmer, who died in 1830, or Bensley, who died in 1824; most of the best work of those printers was done earlier and is described in *The Late Georgian*

Period. They printed fine and expensive books worthy of the aristocracy and the wealthy merchants who were their principal patrons: the sort of books that were, perhaps, more often looked at than read.

The Chiswick Press

Charles Whittingham (1767–1840) was a very different printer. He rarely printed anything larger than an octavo, but everything he produced was carefully and usually beautifully designed and printed. He foresaw the expansion of the reading-public and the coming increased demand for books that could be carried in pockets, and pioneered both in printing and publishing them. From the beginning of the century he was printing cheap and elegant duodecimos, which greatly annoyed other publishers, whose octavos and quartos were so much more expensive. In 1805 he was printing the British Poets in duodecimo, and in about 1814 came Whittingham's Cabinet Library, a series of tiny books measuring about 5″ × 3″ and selling at from 1s. to 7s. each, depending on extent and binding (Pl. 96).

Whittingham was one of the first printers to use iron hand-presses, machine-made paper, overlays for printing wood-engravings (in which he was a master), and steam-driven machinery (for pulping paper). He also pioneered in the use of gas for lighting his factory.

The 'Chiswick Press' imprint was first used by Whittingham when in 1811 he moved his press from London to Chiswick. Whittingham's nephew Charles, who became as great a printer as his uncle, was indentured to the Press in 1810, be-

came a partner in 1824, set up on his own in 1828 and resumed control of the Chiswick Press in 1838, two years before his uncle died. The books produced by Whittingham the nephew and the publisher William Pickering will be described in *The Victorian Period*.

One of the most beautiful books printed by Charles Whittingham the uncle was Northcote's *Fables*, 1829, with wood-engravings after drawings by James Northcote, R.A. Of the same date was *The Tower Menagerie*, illustrated with wood-engravings by Branston and Wright. Both are octavos and show the art of printing from the wood at its best.

Thomas Bewick (1753–1828), who had published his *General History of Quadrupeds* in 1790, his *History of British Birds* in two volumes in 1797 and 1804, and his *Fables of Aesop* in 1818, was still working in his native Northumberland. In London, the most eminent engravers were Bewick's pupils, Luke Clennell and William Harvey, Robert Branston and his pupil John Thompson, W. J. Linton, and Samuel and Thomas Williams. Most of these men were artists in their own right, but most of their work was to interpret the drawings of others, which they did with a delicacy and fineness that make the best wood-engraving of the 'sixties look coarse. Many of George Cruikshank's drawings were engraved on wood by these men; for example, in *Points of Humour*, 1823; *Mornings at Bow Street*, 1824; *Three Courses and a Dessert*, 1830; and *Robinson Crusoe*, 1831. Cruikshank was the greatest illustrator of the Regency period; perhaps his best-known works of that time were his etchings for the first English translation

V. FIGGINS.

Fig. 4. The 'Egyptian' type-face, introduced by Figgins in 1815 in various sizes and in lower case as well as caps.

of Grimm's *Fairy Tales*, and *Peter Schlemihl*, both in 1823. His famous illustrations for Dickens, Ainsworth and other novelists were made in the reign of Queen Victoria.

The Type-founders

The last aspect of printing during the Regency that can be mentioned in this short account is the output of the type-founders, an activity that merits a book to itself.[4] There was a great outburst of invention in the design of type-faces and type-ornaments, which resulted in a permanent enrichment of the printer's and decorative artist's equipment. The spate of invention did indeed continue far into the Victorian period, when it sadly degenerated: but the Regency saw the emergence of Sans Serif, Egyptian (which one critic has described as 'the most brilliant typographical invention of the century, and perhaps the most complete and concise expression of the dominant culture of its brief period; more inspired than contemporary paintings, combining the elegance of the furniture, and the weight of the architecture, and the colour and precise romance of Bulwer Lytton'),[5] Fat Face, shadowed letters, and the earliest and best of the long line of nineteenth-century ornamented types, magnificently rich, theatrical and English.

These rich borders and bold types (which included many new varieties of black-letter, with gothic ornaments) were a conspicuous part of the movement in search of the picturesque; and they were first used on the labels and printed paper covers of books issued in parts, many of which were themselves catering for that movement. They quickly came into use also for tradesmen's announcements, but such advertisements were still, during the Regency, small, discreet, and in good taste.

Names of individual designers cannot now be established: in many cases the designs were probably originated by the founders themselves, men such as Vincent Figgins, Edmund Fry, Robert Thorne, and William Thorowgood. Theirs was among the most notable artistic achievement of the whole century, and it is not a mere whim of fashion, but because their designs were sound and are now being justly appreciated, that so many of their types have been recently revived and used not only in Britain, but all over Europe and the United States.

SHORT BIBLIOGRAPHY

G. Everitt, *English Caricaturists of the Nineteenth Century*, 1893. A. M. Cohn, *George Cruikshank, a Catalogue Raisonné*, 1924. J. Jackson, *A Treatise on Wood Engraving*, 1839. M. Weekley, *Thomas Bewick*, 1953. *The History of The Times*, 5 vols., 1935–52. S. T. Prideaux, *Aquatint Engravings*, 1909. A. Warren, *The Charles Whittinghams, Printers*, 1896. T. B. Reed and A. F. Johnson, *A History of the Old English Letter Foundries*, 1952. N. Gray, *XIXth Century Ornamented Types*, 1938. Sitwell, Buchanan & Fisher, *Fine Bird Boooks 1700–1900*, 1953. Sitwell, Blunt & Synge, *Great Flower Books 1700–1900*, 1956.

[4] See Nicolette Gray, *Nineteenth Century Ornamented Types and Title Pages*, London, 1938.
[5] N. Gray, *op. cit.*

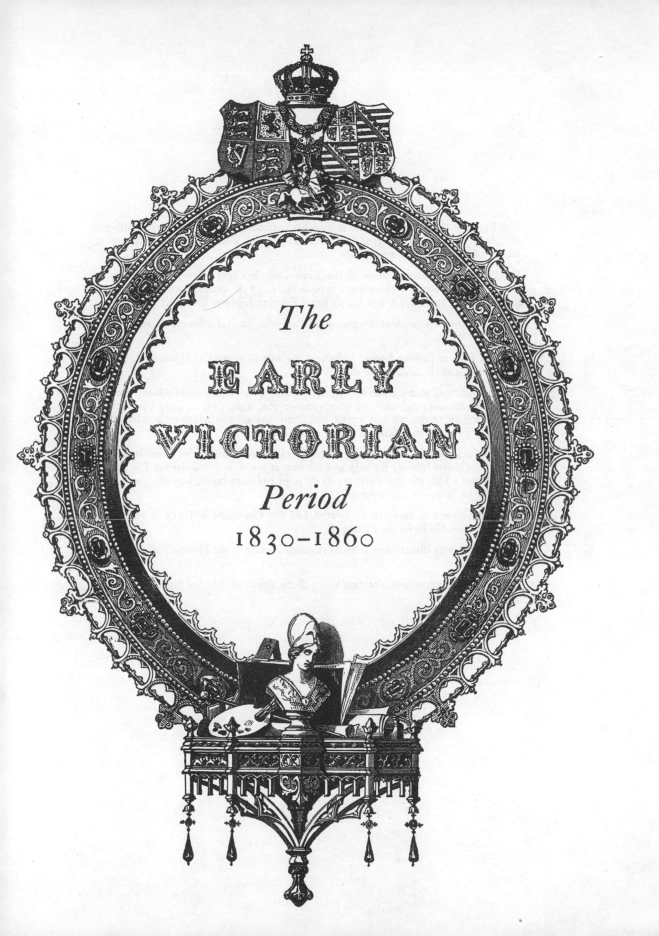

The
EARLY
VICTORIAN
Period
1830–1860

Acknowledgments

The block on the title-page of this section has been adapted from that on the title-page of *The Art-Journal Illustrated Catalogue*, 1851. The Coats of Arms at the top are those of Queen Victoria and Prince Albert.

For the loan of three volumes of the *Illustrated Catalogue of the Great Exhibition*, 1851, and the Wood & Sharwood type book, *c.* 1838, grateful acknowledgment is made to W. Turner Berry and the St Bride Printing Library, London.

For the loan of the original illustrated on Plate 96D grateful acknowledgment is made to James Mosley.

For the loan of various books, including the one illustrated in Plate 96C, grateful acknowledgment is made to Berthold Wolpe.

For the following plates acknowledgment is made to the Victoria and Albert Museum, who hold the copyright in the photographs: 26B, 49B, 53A, B, 54A, 55B, 57-61A, 62A, 63B, 64B, 69-76, 78 and 85-88. For Plate 39A acknowledgment is made to the Board of Trustees, the National Galleries of Scotland.

Grateful acknowledgment is made to the Librarian and staff of the Royal Institute of British Architects Library for help and the loan of books, in particular for *The Builder*, 1843, from which the line illustrations on page 1316 are taken, and also for the loan of Plates 5A, B, 10-13 and 19-20.

Acknowledgment is made to P. Levene Ltd for Plates 50B and 51A, B, and to the Knightsbridge Galleries for Plate 55A.

For the following illustrations acknowledgment is made to the Hulton Picture Library: Plates 2 and 3.

The line illustrations in this section are by Betty Bradford, Morley Bury, Audrey Frew and Jenefer Peter.

The Age of Progress

A. J. TAYLOR

'I believe a year never opened with less cheerful prospects to a country than the present for old England; distress attending all classes of the community'. – General William Dyott's Diary: Entry for 1 January 1830.

'Never was there a year ... in which so much has been done, and such vast progress made'. – *The Times*, 1 January 1861.

Europe in 1830 was a continent in ferment. From the Netherlands to Greece, from Poland to Portugal, the fires of revolution burned or smouldered. France dethroned the last of the Bourbons; Belgians and Poles rose against their alien rulers; in Brunswick, Saxony and Hesse-Cassel, German princes conceded constitutional reform in face of imminent revolution; insurrection threatened in the Papal States; and much-troubled Portugal and Greece knew the uneasy quiet which precedes the returning storm.

Britain's troubles were small beside these; but they were not to be lightly endured. Distress drove the agricultural labourers of the southern counties to actions unprecedented since the days of Cade and Ket: ricks burned, threshing-machines were destroyed, and in some villages the tricolour was raised. In the industrial districts of the north and on the coalfields cotton-spinners and miners struck against their employers; while in the Midlands Thomas Attwood of Birmingham, in initiating the Political Union movement, expressed a discontent whose roots lay deeper than immediate distress. Nor did 1831 promise any lightening of the gloom. Trade and industry, reviving slowly in 1830, relapsed into renewed depression; a long and bitter conflict convulsed the north-eastern coalfield; riots in favour of political reform broke out at Nottingham, Derby and Bristol; and in the southern counties the agrarian revolt collapsed only in face of vindictive intimidation and repression. Nature also was playing a hostile hand. The harvests of 1830 and 1831 were the worst for a decade, and in October 1831 the cholera, already forewarned from the Continent, reached Sunderland.

Not all the omens of these years were unpropitious, however. If profits and wages were low and unemployment high, British industry in 1830 was more productive than at any previous time in its history. In that year Henry Parnell published his influential and prophetic tract *On Financial Reform* and the first railway to be wholly served by steam locomotives was opened between Liverpool and Manchester; while at Westminster the long reign of the Tories, now led by the obdurate Duke of Wellington, ended, and the Whigs, committed in letter if not in spirit to radical reform, came to power. If the forces making for distress and revolution seemed all-powerful in the black autumn of 1830, not they but economic advance and reform – the railway, Free Trade and political liberalism – were in the long run to dominate the history of the British people in the ensuing thirty years.

The Railway Age

The middle decades of the nineteenth century have been variously and paradoxically described. It was the age of reform – but also of *laissez-faire*; of Chartism – and Free Trade; a Bleak Age, yet at the last an age of prosperity. In an era of change different men and different classes had varying fortunes: yet, with all this diversity of experience, few in 1860 could deny the enormous material progress which Britain had made in three decades. As early as 1846 G.R.Porter in his aptly titled *Progress of the Nation* had written of the surging tide of advance 'working with incessant and increasing energy'. He could see before him a time 'in which the most zealous advocates of progress may see their hopes outstripped, and their most sanguine wishes brought within the reach of accomplishment'.

Nothing had done more to promote this advance than the coming of the railway. In the late 1820's the prosperity of British industry was failing not for want of capital, labour or inventiveness, but through insufficiency of markets. The railway transformed this situation. With every mile of track the opportunities of merchant and industrialist expanded as goods were conveyed greater distances and at cheaper cost, to the benefit of buyer and seller alike. The length of public railway in Britain was increased from less than 100 miles in 1830 to almost 2,000 miles by 1843, and to five times that amount seventeen years later; and the conveyance of passengers and goods multiplied even more rapidly. By the middle of the century both the stage-coach and the canal-barge had virtually given up the struggle with the locomotive. Transport by sea as well as by land was revolutionized by the twin forces of steam and iron, but the victory of steam over sail and of iron over wood was less quickly accomplished than that of rail over road and canal. Not until after 1860, when the fuel economies effected by the compound engine became apparent, did the steam-vessel finally win its way; but already in 1858 the *Great Eastern* had been launched as a brave if ill-starred prophet of the coming new era of oceanic transport.

The supreme beneficiaries of the railway age were the basic industries of coal and iron. Between 1830 and 1860 coal output expanded threefold and pig-iron production five-fold, mounting to 80 million and 10 million tons respectively by 1860. The railway itself, in construction and operation, was a voracious consumer both of coal and iron. Not only this, by the ease and cheapness with which they transported heavy goods and by their quickening influence on the whole economy, the railways of Britain and Europe increased enormously the market for the basic raw materials of industry. Iron, symbolized as much by the humble drainage-pipe as by the liner, became the raw material of the age, and was put to use with equal effectiveness in the iron-girt Crystal Palace and in the steam-engine itself. By 1860, however, iron in its turn was giving way to steel, and an era which had been ushered in by Neilson's discovery of the hot-blast method of iron-smelting moved into its successor with the patenting of the Bessemer process for the large-scale manufacture of steel.

Hand in hand with the advance of basic industry went the growth of the activities of the engineer. In the first half of the nineteenth century engineering was rich in invention and innovation. The achievement of a succession of able and resourceful pioneers like Maudslay, Whitworth and Nasmyth, together with the demands of expanding industry, had not only enhanced the status of the engineer's craft but enlarged its scale. Where £50 had sufficed to equip a modest workshop in 1825, twenty times that sum might be required to establish a business less than a quarter century later; and as the engineer's tools were transformed, so was the organization of his craft. Nowhere in these years of growth is the mounting tempo of change more apparent than at this nodal point of Britain's industrial economy.

But if the changes of these years are most readily discernible in coal, iron and engineering, the developments in manufacturing industry were little less significant. With the stimulus of an expanding market, British manufacturers were enabled to carry on the work of innovation and enterprise to which the Watts and Arkwrights of the previous century had given such vitality. The steam-engine and the factory system had already established their place in the British economy even before 1800, but as late as 1830 large areas of the industrial world were still unaffected by them. In the next thirty years the steam-engine gained ground rapidly. Although important sections of British industry – tailoring and shoe-making among them – still lay wholly outside the orbit of the factory system in 1860, the days of domestic industry were clearly numbered.

Cotton, always in the van of technical progress, had already travelled far along the road of techno-logical and organizational change by 1830; yet it still numbered some 200,000 hand-loom weavers among its company of less than half a million workers. In the next twenty years the privations of these survivors of an older order frequently attracted the attention of Parliament. But by 1850 time had worked its own solution: the power-loom had won its victory and domestic employ-ment had virtually disappeared from the English cotton industry. Where cotton led, other textiles followed, some, like the worsted industry, with a rapidity no less than that of cotton itself; others, like wool, at a slower but no less certain pace. With increasing mechanization came heightened productivity: in a quarter of a century the cotton industry achieved a fourfold expansion in output with a negligible increase in its labour force. Out-side the textile industries, the steam-engine and the machine were also making rapid conquests. The domestic nailmakers of the Black Country were fighting their final rearguard action against factory industry in the 1850's, while a host of smaller industries likewise felt the impact of steam-power and the organizational revolution which it implied.

As significant as the transformation of old in-dustries, however, was the advent of new products and processes. None among these was more por-tentous than the advance of the rubber industry, which, originating in the earlier years of the cen-tury, came to maturity in the railway age. *Macin-tosh* entered the English language in 1836, and a decade later the vulcanization process and the pneumatic tyre were patented. With the striking of Pennsylvanian oil in 1859, the door was already being opened on a world where coal and the steam-engine itself would find their new-won supremacy strongly challenged.

More highly mechanized industries catering for bigger markets meant larger firms and greater de-mands for capital. Here, as in other things, the railway pointed the way. In its ultimate penetra-tion of the economic life of the nation the joint-stock company with limited liability derives its example and impetus from the needs of the railway promoters. No boom did more than the railway mania of 1844–6 to extend the investing habit and increase the numbers of the shareholding public, a development for which even the speculative machinations of George Hudson, 'the Railway King', were not too high a price to pay. In 1855 general legislative sanction was finally given to the limited liability company, in advance perhaps of the immediate demands of manufacturing indus-try, but to its lasting benefit. Eleven years earlier, in 1844, Parliament had passed the Bank Charter Act. This, with the legislation of the previous decade, had established English banking on the twin foundation of the central Bank of England and the joint-stock banks; and thereby given to it a structure which, for all its undoubted defects of detail, was to conserve and increase the nation's financial resources and prestige in the expansionist years which lay ahead.

The corollary to industrial growth was the ex-pansion of the export trade. Already in 1830, by accident rather than design, Britain had aban-doned the form, if not the pretence, of a balanced economy. Though in good harvest years the coun-try might still achieve a bare self-sufficiency in essential foodstuffs, she imported food and raw materials on an increasingly lavish scale in ex-change for the products of her mills and work-shops. Exports of British goods doubled in value between 1830 and 1850, and almost doubled again in the succeeding decade. In volume the overall increase was even greater. With the repeal of the protective Corn Laws in 1846 all pretence of maintaining balance in the economy dis-appeared; not only Britain's prosperity but her very existence was henceforth committed into the hands of her industrialists and merchants.

The fate of agriculture amid these changes and chances wore some of the marks of paradox. In 1830 farming had been more depressed than any other industry. Its sickness was of long standing, going back in the memories of some to the end of the French Wars. Yet opportunity for advancement was not lacking. A rapidly growing urban population made increasing demands for food; transport was improving; and tariff protection minimized the effects of foreign competition. Yet it was not till after 1850, with the Corn Laws repealed, that full revival came – a revival made possible by the removal of financial burdens, radical readjustment to new conditions, the advent of the railway, and a rapid improvement in urban living standards. The progress thus achieved, and measurable alike in terms of higher profits, rents and wages, should not, however, be misinterpreted. In their rate of expansion agricultural profits lagged far behind those of industry; and while the working population as a whole rose by over 1 million in the single decade 1851–61, employment in agriculture fell by almost 100,000. Agriculture, prosperous though it might be, had declined in status; and its decline had implications not only for the British economy, but for the country's social and political structure.

The mounting tide of industrial productivity brought with it a great increase in the nation's wealth. Before 1850, except in years of war, the State itself made little demand upon these growing riches, but much of the product of industry was reinvested to provide the capital assets for later generations. In the second quarter of the nineteenth century the railway was perhaps the finest outcome of this spirit of thrift, but in industry itself the constant pursuit of innovation reflects the same desire to live for tomorrow as well as today. The emphasis on long-term investment rather than on immediate consumption may explain in part the seeming poverty in the midst of plenty which clouds even the years of greatest prosperity in the two decades after 1830. Merchants and manufacturers might know increased wealth and display it not only in their expanded businesses, but also in the bricks and mortar of their town and country houses; but the economic progress of the industrial worker was less clearly marked. For the skilled craftsman, be he millwright or coal-hewer, cotton-spinner or carpenter, the rewards of an expanding economy could be measured in terms of a swelling pay-packet and an increasing command of goods and services, many of them cheapened by the cost-reductions of factory-industry. But for the less skilled, and for those employed in decaying domestic crafts – handloom-weavers, framework knitters, nailers and the like – the note of economic progress had a hollow ring. If the demand for labour was increasing, so too were the means of supply; for to the rapid natural increase of population was added the outpouring of an over-populated and famine-threatened Ireland. The high price of necessities, induced in part by the protective system, and the effects of slump following upon boom, served only further to depress the living standards of the still large numbers of the industrious poor.

To the problems which low wages, short-time and unemployment brought in their train were added those of life in the rapidly growing industrial towns. In the decades after 1830 house-building more than kept pace with population growth, but the continued low quality of construction and the neglect of earlier years laid a heavy burden on Victorian England. So rapidly had the new towns been called into being – Oldham, for example, increased its population from 12,000 to 53,000 in the first half of the nineteenth century and Manchester swelled from 77,000 to 316,000 in the same fifty years – that local authorities both before and after the Municipal Corporation Act of 1835 were unable to keep pace with the need for increased water-supply and improved sanitation. Not every town-dweller lived in a back-to-back house, devoid of running water and rudimentary sanitary provision, but such conditions were the rule rather than the exception in many of the urban areas of the new England of the North and Midlands.

From the middle of the century the life of the working-classes slowly took on a less sombre appearance. The wealth of the nation, if not more diffused, was at least so augmented as to raise the living standards of all but the poorest and least adaptable of the community. Even the farm-labourer, hitherto the most distressed member of a depressed economic group, felt the benefit of a buoyant economy. Corn, its price held firm in the midst of slow yet perceptible inflation, became of increasingly less account in working-class budgets; and rising living-standards were reflected not only in an expanding consumption of such working-class luxuries as rice, tobacco and tea, but also in the growth of the number of institutions for working-class thrift. Legislation had removed the worst of the evils attending the employment of women and children, and in the towns the new councils, increasing in strength and authority, not only built civic halls and reservoirs, but, equally significantly, appointed Medical Officers charged with the oversight of the manifold health problems of the growing urban communities. By 1860, though poverty, like disease, was far from conquered, the working man with his family could look to a future richer in wealth, leisure and the means of its enjoyment than his father could have dared to hope for thirty years earlier.

The age of reform

The spirit of reform was not born in the dark days of 1830, though economic depression in that year, as in 1842 and 1848, served to sharpen the fine edge of militant radicalism. Nor did it owe its existence wholly to the Industrial Revolution, even if the strong tide of industrialization and urbanization served to emphasize old problems and create new ones. The demand for reform was deeply rooted and sprang as much from the world of ideas as of material circumstance. There were those who, basing their views on principles of liberty developed in the seventeenth century by John Locke, sought primarily the emancipation of man's economic life. Such were the followers of Adam Smith, who extolled the virtues of international free trade and the benefits of an unfettered economic society – the Classical Economists, the Manchester School, the advocates of *laissez-faire*. Close to them in sympathy, if not in fundamental doctrine, stood the Utilitarian followers of Jeremy Bentham, believers in the principle of 'the

greatest happiness of the greatest number' as the yardstick of social behaviour and of the efficacy of social institutions. To them, unlike the extreme advocates of *laissez-faire*, the State had a limited right of intervention in the affairs of men, but its intervention must conform to the 'greatest-happiness' principle, and above all things be efficient. Both these groups approached economic and social problems with a scientific purpose and method. In others the heart seemed sometimes to speak louder than the head, a broad humanitarianism finding its rallying point in the reforming zeal of the Evangelicals, and its leader in the seventh Earl of Shaftesbury. All these movements found favourable soil for growth in mid-nineteenth-century England. Others, no less significant, were more alien to the temper of the times. The egalitarianism which in varied forms expressed itself in the writings and activities of Owen and Kingsley, of Ruskin and Marx, was in advance of its time. Similarly, that radicalism which nostalgically invited a return to a pre-industrial society ran counter to the prevailing spirit of an age exulting in the benefits which bourgeois capitalism and industrialization were bestowing. But, however much their origins and purposes might differ, the varied movements of reform shared a common dissatisfaction with men and institutions as they were, and an inquiring spirit far removed from the complacency which had characterized so much English thinking in the previous century.

When men spoke of reform in 1830, they meant the reform of Parliament. A radical revision of the system of parliamentary representation was looked upon as the key to all other reforms in society. In the eyes of utilitarians and working-class radicals alike the prevailing system of representation, with its grossly unequal electoral districts and unrepresented towns, its rotten boroughs and irrational franchises, stood condemned on grounds both of natural justice and governmental efficiency. Members of Parliament were less convinced of the validity of these strictures, but they could not resist their consequence. The Whigs were led to carry Reform in 1832 as much from motives of expediency as of principle: reform was for them a lesser evil than revolution. But it was the results, not the motives of reform which were to have lasting significance.

The Great Reform Act of 1832, the culmination of months of bitter struggle inside and outside Parliament, gave representation to large towns like Birmingham and Manchester and the vote to the wealthier sections of the middle classes in country and town alike. By design it tied the vote to property, enfranchizing those, and only those, who had a 'stake in the country'. The electorate was thereby increased by about 50 per cent, but, despite this significant numerical expansion, neither the methods of electioneering nor the personnel of the House of Commons were changed overnight. Dickens' Eatanswill belongs to the decade after the Reform Act and Trollope's House of Commons still had a strongly aristocratic flavour in the 1860's. Such a limited measure of reform could not satisfy either the more extreme among the radical thinkers or the politically-conscious sections of the working-class. Hence it brought quickly in its train the People's Charter of 1838, in which pride of place was given to the demand for universal male suffrage. But in Chartism, even more than in the reform movement of 1830–2, the demand for the vote soon became merely a means to an end – the social and economic regeneration of society. Every proletarian discontent found its rallying point in Chartism – the call for factory legislation, opposition to the new Poor Law, and, particularly in 1842, blind reaction to unemployment and distress – until in 1848, that *annus mirabilis* of revolutionary activity, the movement reached its culmination with the presentation of the Great Petition. By 1851, as a potent force, it was dead, killed by ridicule and prosperity.

The combined effect of rapid industrialization and population growth – the population of England and Wales alone rose from 9 to 14 million between 1801 and 1831, and to 20 million by 1861 – had produced a variety of urgent social problems, among them those of conditions in the new factories and in the new – and older – towns; of poverty, seemingly chronic in the rural south and deep, if spasmodic, in the industrial north; and of ignorance and illiteracy among the growing numbers of the working-class. To the resolution of these problems the reformers bent their best endeavours, though by no means always with common policy or intent. Evangelicals and humanitarians like the Tory Richard Oastler welcomed any and every limitation which the legislature might impose on the working hours of factory children; the more radical disciples of Adam Smith and Ricardo, on the other hand, could not countenance the infringement of *laissez-faire* which such limitation implied; while the Benthamite Edwin Chadwick advocated a middle course which combined a clearly defined and restricted intervention with the supervisory power of an efficient inspectorate. Likewise in the Poor Law reform of 1834, while, on the one hand, Malthusians might reject all attempts at relief as interference with the operation of the laws of nature, and, on the other, a Disraeli or a Dickens assert that to restrict relief was to cheat the poor of their rightful inheritance, it was Chadwick who, again pursuing the middle way, devised the 'Workhouse Test' and the centralizing organization of the Poor Law Board.

In brief, the Evangelicals and Utilitarians were the heart and head of the movement for social reform, even if at times heart spoke against head in no uncertain fashion. The greatest single triumph of the Evangelicals was perhaps the Abolition of Slavery in 1833, that of the Utilitarians the amendment of the Poor Law a year later; but, while the humanitarianism of the Evangelicals represents an ongoing tradition in British life and thought, the methods and achievements of the Utilitarians were in their day sufficiently novel to merit further examination here. The followers of Bentham, and first among them Chadwick, made the Royal Commission the instrument of their inquiries and the parliamentary Blue Book the vehicle of their propaganda. Inquiry and propaganda paved the way to reform, and here the Benthamite weapon was the parliamentary act and the administrative Board or Inspectorate. Factory Inspectors were first appointed in 1833 and Mines Inspectors in the following decade: the permanent Poor Law Commission was established in 1834, and the Central Board of

Health in 1848. In these two last Chadwick himself played a leading part. Thus over a wide field of social policy the influence of the Benthamites ran strong and deep. The followers of Bentham were to the nineteenth century what the Fabians were to become to the twentieth – agents of purposeful and scientific inquiry and protagonists of social reform through administrative centralization – and, like the Fabians, they were assailed for allowing the precepts of social theory to overrule the deeper promptings of humanity. In so far as the charge may have substance, it can perhaps be more justly levied at the results than the motives of their policies.

Posterity, however, owes an even fuller debt to the Utilitarians and those who kept close company with them. To men like G.R.Porter at the Board of Trade, Leonard Horner in the Factory Inspectorate, and, perhaps above all, to Chadwick himself, in his manifold public administrative duties, is owed that new conception of the functions of the public official which has been one of the great legacies of early Victorian England to later generations. Patronage, nepotism and the idea of the sinecure were slow in dying in the British Civil Service. Chadwick and those like him, by their example of tireless and efficient service, paved the way for that thorough-going reform of public administration which followed from the legislation of 1855, and the acceptance of the principle of open competition which it involved.

The industrial and commercial sections of the middle class, whom the Reform Act of 1832 had enfranchized, were more concerned with economic than with social reform. For them, after 1832, reform meant the reduction of the tariff and the repeal of the Corn Laws. Their earliest and best hopes lay with the party that had given them the franchise, the party not only of Grey and Russell, the architects of '1832', but of Henry Parnell and Poulett Thomson, of Villiers, Bright and Cobden, all unequivocal advocates of Free Trade. In the event, however, it was not the Whigs but the Tory Peel and his lieutenant Gladstone who liberalized the tariff. The decisive battle may be said to have begun with the foundation of the Manchester-inspired Anti-Corn Law League

in 1838. The movement for tariff reform derived impetus from the proceedings of the Select Committee on Import Duties of 1840, before which the Free Traders deployed their arguments with such adroitness as to discomfort thoroughly the protagonists of protection; it profited from a swing of the trade cycle, which, out of depression in 1842, imposed upon the Tory administration the necessity of adopting radical measures to meet the nation's economic difficulties and, in the prosperity of 1845, gave it the opportunity to justify and consolidate them; and it gained speedy realization of its best hopes from finding in Peel a minister of flexible outlook, who drew his inspiration not only from Harrow and Christ Church, which educated him, but also from industrial Lancashire, where his deeper roots lay. Peel attempted to restore the Government's credit and to revive the nation's trade by a temporary restoration of the income-tax and a reduction of prohibitory and protective tariffs. If of his work only the income-tax now remains, this is no measure of his immediate or ultimate achievement. On his work, at least in part, rested the prosperity that was to be Britain's for a generation and more.

Peel's crowning achievement was the repeal of the Corn Laws, an action enforced upon him prematurely by the Irish Potato Famine of 1845. It ended his ministerial career, broke the party which he had re-established little more than a decade earlier, and brought down upon him the execrations of many whom he had hitherto counted as his supporters and friends; but his reward was the reputation for high statesmanship which posterity has accorded him. In the next generation the work which he had begun so experimentally in 1842 was carried boldly and logically to its conclusion. The Navigation Laws, designed initially to protect the British carrying trade, were repealed in 1849; and in the two great budgets of 1853 and 1860 Gladstone completed the structure of Free Trade, adding to the last for good measure a commercial treaty with France.

The triumph of the middle class

The repeal of the Corn Laws was a political triumph for the middle class, won in part as a result of the most sustained and powerfully financed campaign in British parliamentary history. It was a victory for the interests of commerce and industry over those of the land and agriculture, gained in a parliament in which the landed interest still held a clear numerical ascendency. Such is not merely the verdict of the historian: it was the opinion of contemporaries on both sides of the argument, protectionists like Disraeli as well as Free Traders like Cobden. Where, then, one may ask, did political power reside in early Victorian England; in what institution and with what class? The question admits of no simple answer. The legalist might assert the supremacy of 'the King in Parliament' and interpret this in practical terms as the rule of the King's ministers. But whereas a century earlier the royal will had determined the fate of ministries, that authority had now passed to Parliament, and within Parliament to the House of Commons. In the thirty years between 1830 and 1860 no less than eleven distinct ministries were formed. Of these only a minority lived out their natural term of office: the rest died in parliamentary conflict, destroyed by the adverse votes of the Lower House. This was the outcome of an age where parliamentary majorities were generally small, and where party organization and party loyalty were conspicuously weak. At times, as in the crises over Reform and the Corn Law and during the Crimean War, the need for strong government asserted itself, but more often the Commons held the whip hand and made and unmade ministries almost at their pleasure, restrained only by the occupational risks – and costs – which a dissolution could bring to every member.

As within the body politic, so among classes the exact balance of power and influence is difficult to determine. Mere appearances would suggest the continuing ascendency of the aristocracy. Every administration between 1830 and 1860 drew at least half its members from the titled classes and none – Whig or Tory, Liberal or Conservative – counted less than a third of its members in the House of Lords. Palmerston's second Liberal Cabinet, formed in 1859, had three dukes, two earls, three lesser peers and three knights in its complement of fifteen. But although the road to political office might continue to lie, as Trollope's Phineas Finn discovered, through the doors of the houses of the aristocracy – and of their ladies – and though the patronage flowing from landed wealth still acted powerfully in determining the personnel of the House of Commons, the middle classes, when their vital interests were affected in the Corn Law struggle of 1846, were able to exert an influence out of all proportion to their representation in Parliament or Cabinet. The inheritance of power was seemingly theirs whenever they should choose to claim it, but for the present they were content to busy themselves about their own affairs, and to leave politics in the hands of those whose economic primacy they had usurped, well satisfied so long as industry and commerce were allowed to go their own ways unhindered and unmolested.

The Reform Act was a turning point in the history of parties as well as of the constitution. The old names of Whig and Tory – and by 1832 they had become little more than names – had outlived their usefulness as rallying points of opinion and interest. The Tories, beaten in 1830 and again in 1832, were the first to recognize this, and in 1834 attempted to regroup their forces under the banner of Peelite Conservatism, adopting as their principle the 'careful review of institutions, civil and ecclesiastical, undertaken in a friendly temper, combining, with the firm maintenance of established rights, the correction of proved abuses and the redress of real grievances'. But parties are founded on interest as much as principle, and when in 1846 interest and principle came into conflict, it was interest – the economic interest of the landowning classes – which triumphed, and Peelite Conservatism was doomed. It was left to Derby and Disraeli to attempt a second reconstruction. They recreated the party on the basis of an appeal to the disaffected and underprivileged, to the farm-labourer as much as the landowner, the factory-worker as the agriculturalist. The fruits of such a reconstruction, however, could not be garnered until a second Reform Act in 1867 had enfranchised the urban working-class. The Whigs knew no such extreme crisis as that which beset the Tories both in 1832 and 1846; but Whiggism, with its essentially aristocratic roots, was too narrowly based for the needs of a middle-class electorate in an industrial age. By 1860 the name of Whig had been exchanged for Liberal, and the party had broadened its ranks to include, not only a considerable and varied Radical element, but also the rejected of the Tory Party of 1846. The Liberals had thereby become predominantly the party of industrial England and of the middle class: Lancashire and Manchester would have none other, and Manchester's voice was prophetic of England's. But, like its opponent, the Liberal Party needed the stimulus of a widened electorate to find itself – and its organization – in fullest measure.

If parties counted for little in mid-nineteenth-century Britain, men counted for much. Grey and Wellington, Peel and Cobden, Palmerston and Bright, Russell and Derby, Gladstone and Disraeli – this roll of honour, already long, is still incomplete. It omits two prime ministers and a host of others who were rightly honoured in their generation. Grey and Wellington, the one Whig, the other Tory, represented in 1830 a dying order: for if Grey played the midwife at the birth of the new régime, he quickly retired from political life when this office was completed, and Wellington, though active in politics almost until his death in 1852, was content to tread the side-lines save when duty called him to placate a turbulent House of Lords in 1832 and 1846. If Grey and Wellington represented the past, Gladstone and Disraeli were the heralds of the future. By 1860 the star of both was clearly in the ascendent, but for neither was it fully risen. Gladstone had come a long way from his Tory beginnings in Eton and Christ Church. As a Peelite he finally crossed his Rubicon into the Liberal Party in 1859, but already under Peel's inspiration in the 'forties his deeper mercantile origins had asserted themselves, and joined Liverpool to Oxford in his mental and spiritual make-up. In two as yet brief but glorious periods at the Exchequer – between 1852 and 1855 and latterly from 1859 – the spirit of Liverpool had made itself manifest. The days of Ireland and the Midlothian Campaign – and the higher office

which they carried with them – still lay in the future, but in the emphasis on public economy which he added to that on Free Trade the heir of Peel had already made his firm mark upon the Victorian political scene. Palmerston and Russell still stood between Gladstone and the highest ministerial office in 1860. In like manner Derby barred the upward path of the ambitious Disraeli. Disraeli had prospered not by responding to the spirit of the age but by opposing it. From the wreck of Tory fortunes in 1846 he had survived as an almost lone eminence in a party deprived not only of numbers but of men of intellect by the defection of the Peelites. But in 1860, although already twice Chancellor of the Exchequer, his hour had not yet struck; nor would it until a changed electorate and a changing economic climate made possible an invocation of the spirit of empire out of place in the bourgeois England of the young Victoria.

If we seek to personify the spirit of this great age of parliamentary government, therefore, we must look neither to Grey or Wellington nor to Gladstone or Disraeli. In an era of change no other single name suggests itself. If choice be made, it must rather rest on the representatives of two conflicting traditions – the manufacturer, Richard Cobden, and the aristocrat, Viscount Palmerston. Cobden, the greatest back-bencher of the age, spoke, for all his Sussex birth, with the authentic voice of the industrial north. A whole-hearted believer in Britain's economic supremacy, he was yet an internationalist seeing in Free Trade a means to the greater end of universal understanding and peace. In him were conjoined the hard-headed realism of the business-man and the utopianism of the idealist – both ingredients in the make-up of the nineteenth-century Liberal. Palmerston has a more timeless quality. His parliamentary career (from 1807 to 1865) spans the old and the new in British politics. Secretary at War under four prime ministers before 1832, he survived to die in harness as Prime Minister – and the people's darling – in 1865. He was truly 'John Bull incarnate', pugnacious, firmly convinced of Britain's central position in the world, and willing to threaten a war to protect the life and honour of a British subject – the focal point of a nation's pride in an age when prosperity and power went hand in hand, and a Cincinnatus waiting recall when disaster threatened in the Crimean War. It was on the justice of the war with Russia that Cobden and Palmerston clashed, not for the first or last time; but, differ as they might in outlook and policy, each in his mounting confidence and vigorous optimism expressed the spirit and temper of the age. Palmerston, himself, felt the kinship and in 1859, only three years after the ending of the war, offered Cobden an honoured place in his last great administration; but Cobden, an unbending Radical to the last, refused.

Britain since the Revolution of 1688 had been but indifferently blessed in her kings and queens; and in none less than George IV, who went to an unhonoured grave in 1830. That the monarchy should have seen its power decline was perhaps inevitable, but that it should have lost a nation's respect was as unnecessary as it was unfortunate. Indeed, had republicanism been in the air in 1830 – had France preferred a President to the Orleanist Louis-Philippe – revolution, not reform, might have been the nation's choice. William IV, and still more the young Victoria, retrieved the monarchy's prestige, but they could not stem the ebbing tide of its political authority. Though both were able on occasion to use their limited powers – 'to be consulted, to encourage, to warn', in Bagehot's well-known phrase – to good effect, their capacity as creators of ministries or initiators of policy was waning and by 1860 had largely disappeared. William IV dismissed Melbourne in 1834 and five years later, in the comic opera episode of the Bedchamber Crisis, Victoria rebuffed Peel, but neither experiment was repeated. Thereafter the instances of effective royal intervention, as in the dismissal of Palmerston from the Foreign Office in 1851, are few and in sum of little importance, and when party organization strengthened, the opportunity for royal action would decline still further. Although the monarch might remain the supreme umpire in the parliamentary game, her verdict was rarely required or requested. Yet if the monarchy's political power continued to diminish, its prestige was enhanced with every

year of the young Queen's reign. The first phase of recovery was completed with the death of the Prince Consort in 1861. The Queen had then reigned for twenty-four years, and the example of her family life, her attention to her religious and political duties, her rigid moral code, high seriousness and industry, commended themselves to a nation which had grown weary of laxer standards. 'Middle-class morality' was not merely the reflected manners of a reformed Court – it grew out of the values which nonconformity and industrial growth engendered – but it responded in full measure to the changed behaviour of royalty. Looking back in 1861 to the reign of George IV, Thackeray could write: 'He is dead but thirty years, and one asks how a great society could have tolerated him? Would we bear him now? In the quarter of a century, what a silent revolution has been working! How it has separated us from old times and manners! How it has changed men themselves!' In a dynamic society in which, as the young Disraeli perceived, forces of social disintegration were threatening disaster, the reformed monarchy was a powerful binding force, reconciling in itself the institutions of the old order and the social needs of the new.

Britain and the world

A nation so busy about its own affairs had little time to look out on to a wider world. Though her citizens travelled abroad no less, Britain in the mid-nineteenth century was becoming increasingly insular in thought, culture and in foreign policy. In the troubles of the 1830's Palmerston had spoken powerfully and purposefully on the side of the liberal angels, but the exercise was not allowed to cost the life of a single British soldier; and after 1848 even the voice became less certain and effective. So long as no continental Power threatened to dominate Europe, Britain was content to stand aside. France and Russia at different times seemed likely to upset the European balance, and on each occasion the resources of Palmerstonian diplomacy were stretched to the uttermost in the attempt to contain the threatened advance. Thus France was checked first in the Netherlands, then in Spain and finally — though not with complete success — in Italy. Russia occasioned a deeper and more continuing anxiety. Here the threat was not only to the European balance, but to the United Kingdom's commercial interests in the eastern Mediterranean and beyond. In face of suspected Russian predatoriness in the Balkans, British foreign secretaries attempted to bolster up a disintegrating Ottoman Empire. As a result, in 1854 Britain tumbled into war with Russia in the Crimea, a war with but one heroine, Florence Nightingale, and one hero, the Light Brigade, and with little else to commend it to a nation disappointed by the news of military stalemates and the winter miseries of the British forces, and dismayed by the mounting evidence of bureaucratic maladministration and incompetence. But the appetite of the British public for foreign adventure, reawakened after long years of peace, survived the disenchantment of the Russian War to become the jingoism of Palmerston's declining years.

If Europe often seemed far away, the colonial empire was even more remote. This has sometimes been called an age of anti-imperialism. But perhaps these should rather be called years of imperial neglect, or more precisely of public apathy. The period of disillusionment which followed the loss of the American Colonies had passed — though memories of it were awakened when Canada flared up into rebellion in 1837; but if, as was widely believed, Free Trade and the repeal of the Navigation Laws were severing the final links of empire, few at home were disposed to wish it otherwise. The colonies, for their part, flourished on neglect. Canada, Australia and New Zealand moved forward towards self-government and dominion status; and their settlers, increased in number by the prospect of gold and the activities of Gibbon Wakefield and the Land and Emigration Board, grew not only in prosperity, but also in loyalty to the Crown. Out of apathy was born a Commonwealth: it was one of the richest if the most fortuitous of the legacies of early Victorian England to later generations.

Britain's 'other empire' — of trading-posts and commercial settlements, and less formally of economic concessions — could not be retained without conflict and expense. Between 1839 and 1842 British forces were engaged in unwanted and disastrous operations in Afghanistan to protect India's North-West Frontier. Over the same period a war, more successful in its conduct and outcome, was waged against the Chinese Empire. As a result the Chinese ceded Hong Kong, and the 'treaty ports' were opened to British trade. In 1858 the unequal struggle was renewed and by 1860 Britain had again asserted her authority in the China Seas. But the British public, diverted by happenings nearer home, could only enthuse ephemerally over such adventures.

By 1860, however, new comets were in the sky, though their portent was not yet understood. During the early years of Victoria's reign the British hold on the sub-continent of India had been gradually strengthened in part by force, in part by peaceful annexation, but always with little more than the passive acquiescence of the home Government. In 1858, however, following the Mutiny, the Crown assumed those responsibilities for the government of India which had hitherto been vested in the East India Company. Meanwhile, in Africa, David Livingstone, watched with increasing eagerness from Britain, was penetrating the heart of the unexplored continent. The stage was beginning to be set for the heady imperialism of the nineteenth century's closing years.

Though Britain might neglect her colonial empire, she was never allowed to forget Ireland. If Catholic Emancipation had assuaged a grievance, it had done nothing to feed a single Irishman; and so long as the land system remained unreformed there could be no true prospect of lasting peace in Ireland. The Potato Famine brought misery, depopulation, and, more tardily, land reform in its train. But already in the 'forties a deeper discontent had revealed itself. The Young Ireland movement paved the way not only for the fury of Fenian outrage in the 'sixties, but also for the broader political demands of the century's later decades. Ireland lay like a sullen volcano off the shores of England, never wholly quiescent, always seemingly on the point of violent eruption.

Change and tradition

No age lives by bread and politics alone; but, in the pursuit of both, men frequently reveal their deeper attitudes and values. In questions of religion the early Victorians showed that combination of adventurous advance and respect for established institutions which was so characteristic of their political life and thought. The early Victorian Age was in the broadest, if not necessarily the deepest, sense a religious age: it was certainly, by twentieth-century standards, an age of church-going. Five out of every twelve persons – young and old – in England and Wales are estimated to have attended a place of worship on 'Census Sunday' in 1851 – some on more than one occasion in the day. Only half of these worshippers were members of the Established Church. Dissent, which claimed the majority of the remainder, had won a powerful and numerous following in the industrial towns and on the coalfields; and among the sects none had achieved a larger body of adherents than the Methodists. Methodism had won its converts by the simple, evangelical appeal of Pauline Christianity, but the social and political implications of its achievement were complex. While the Wesleyan 'orthodoxy' of Jabez Bunting, for forty years 'the Premier of Methodism', enjoined an almost Tory respect for the powers-that-be within the State, the dissident Primitive wing of the movement was more radical in its social and political outlook and nurtured within itself the leaders of working-class revolt. The Established Church had been slow to respond to the needs of a growing industrial and urban society, but by 1850, under the powerful influence of the Evangelicals and the Tractarians, the work of church-building was going rapidly forward. The Tractarians, however, for all their evangelical and reforming zeal, were essentially a conservative force, attempting to revitalize the Church by recalling it to its ancient Orders and discipline. And in a wider sense the entire Christian Church in England, Catholic as well as Protestant, Nonconformist as well as Anglican, displayed a conservatism which belied the inquiring spirit of the age. Though divided in all else, Christians of different denominations were virtually united in taking their stand upon the Bible. A narrow literalism, which only a few dared to question, was accepted by every sect. Yet this rock was soon to prove shifting sand. With the publication of Darwin's *Origin of Species* in 1859, Christian orthodoxy found itself faced by revolutionary forces no less potentially solvent than those which had disrupted the Church of Rome three centuries before.

As in religion, so in education, the forces of change and tradition went hand in hand. The established connection between religion and education was one which few Victorians would lightly challenge. In 1860 the State still held aloof from direct involvement in the provision of elementary education, preferring to give financial aid to the competing sectarian bodies already in the field; and, despite its timidity, this policy had over a quarter of a century sufficed to bring almost every working-class child within the orbit of the educational system. At the same time, under the influence of the reforming Arnold at Rugby, provision for the educational needs of the expanding middle class was being made by a growing number of public and grammar schools; and even in the field of university education, with the advent of London and Durham and an incipient Manchester, the facilities for higher learning were being slowly increased. But to extend the bounds of opportunity in education was not necessarily to deepen its content. The three 'Rs' might be considered diet enough for the new working-class, but, as the Newcastle Commission reported in 1861, many – perhaps most – children left school 'without the power of reading, writing and cyphering in an intelligent manner'. Where teaching thus failed in its most elementary objective, it is not surprising that a sight of wider intellectual horizons was denied to the children of the labouring classes. The failings in the education of their social betters lay in other directions. Notwithstanding a modest widening of the curriculum at Rugby, the reform of the public schools had touched the spirit and temper rather than the content of education. The discipline of the classics might nurture a Peel or a Gladstone, but its adequacy in face of the changing social conditions of the nineteenth century was none the less open to question. More serious for individual and community alike was the failure to provide for the developing educational needs of the lower middle class. A society changing rapidly under the impact of the forces of science and technology was strangely blind both to the place of scientific and technical study in its schools and to the need for facilitating the further education of its leaders in industry and commerce. Well might the percipient Kay-Shuttleworth declare in 1866 that 'the education of the middle class is generally in a chaotic state. ... While a large part of Europe has been successfully preparing its entire peoples to meet the great crisis of their history with intelligence, we have refused to learn from their example and experience.' The bitter fruits of that refusal are not wholly ungathered today.[1]

Science, thus excluded from the schools, was compelled to find other channels of development. It was in societies like the British Association for the Advancement of Science and the London Statistical Society (both established in the 1830's) that a lively interest in scientific subjects was fostered and sustained; and it is against such a background that the high achievement of men of genius like Faraday, Thomson (the later Lord Kelvin), Darwin and Huxley is to be measured. Thomson was compelled to cross the Channel in 1845 to get the laboratory experience which Britain failed to give him. Twenty years later such a journey would have been unnecessary. The completion of the first laboratories at Oxford in 1861 is as momentous and pregnant an event in educational history as the opening of that university's doors to dissenters in the following decade.

The learned society was but one of the many forms of association to which the principle and practice of 'self-help' gave birth. That principle had its roots alike in resurgent puritanism and in economic liberalism; it was to be seen as much in the development of trade unions as in the lives of the entrepreneurs, as much in the emergent co-operative movement as in professional organizations like the newly-established British Medical Association. Yet though self-help might know no class frontiers, its ethos was predominantly that of the middle class. Thus by the 1850's both trade unions and co-operative societies had surrendered their earlier revolutionary positions and had reconciled themselves to the values and judgements of an essentially bourgeois society: in less than two decades Robert Owen's militant Grand National Consolidated Trades Union had given place to the respectability of the Associated Society of Engineers and of the Rochdale Pioneers.

The emergence of a powerful urban middle class also gave new significance to provincialism as a force in British social life. In the seventeenth and eighteenth centuries the increasing power of commerce had brought London to a position of overwhelming dominance both in the political and in the economic and cultural life of England; but with the growth of new industry the balance in terms of population and of wealth was readjusted. Although London continued to grow prodigiously, its rate of expansion was matched and surpassed by that of Manchester, Birmingham and a host of smaller towns; just as in Scotland, Glasgow came to outpace Edinburgh in its capacity for increase. With growth went vitality, and the provincial cities, though merely imitative in some respects — Manchester had its Piccadilly and its Athenæum — gave their own colour to the thought and culture of the age. Under the stimulus of the Municipal Corporations Act of 1835 town government was revitalized and civic pride enhanced, not the least of the fruits of this awakening being the advent of the public library and art gallery. Likewise, encouraged in part by the repeal of the Stamp Duty in 1855, but still more by the growing numbers of the literate working-class, the provincial Press entered upon its greatest age. Where in 1846 there had been 200 local newspapers, in 1865 there were 750, many of them 'dailies' like the Manchester *Guardian* and the Liverpool *Post*, exerting in the provinces an influence in politics as great as that of Delane's *Times* in the capital itself.

---

[1] These strictures do not wholly apply to Scotland where education up to University level was more readily obtained and more broadly based than in England.

The vigorous culture of the Manchester Man, however, carried within itself the defects of its own high qualities. No one would deny the creative power of this new provincial society; but its capacity for creative imagination or contemplation is more open to question. This was the age of the technologist rather than the scientist, the evangelist rather than the mystic. Even in literature, the crowning glory of the age, the distinction is to be sensed. The high noon of the Romantic period was passed, and notwithstanding the work of Tennyson and the Brownings, of Matthew Arnold and Swinburne, this is an age of prose rather than of poetry. In prose these are indeed years of plenty – the years of Carlyle and John Stuart Mill, of Macaulay and Froude, of Dickens and Thackeray – and in the novel, above all, years not only of abundance, but also of the highest achievement. Yet even in the novel the full depths of human experience are rarely sounded. The Brontës alone provide an outstanding exception to this generalization. With them, living out their timeless existence on the Yorkshire moors, we catch again the unreined imaginative power of a Shelley or a Keats. But in general, for the novelist at least, this was the age of the extrovert. Only at the last, with the advent of George Eliot and Meredith, does a new note of fundamental questioning and soul-searching emerge.

To say this is not to suggest that this was an uncritical age. Dickens, Mrs Gaskell, Disraeli and even Trollope explored the social and political tensions of their day and set their face against the evils of industrialism and of political jobbery which they saw around them. Outside the novel the accent of criticism is sharper and often deeper. In the essays and sermons of Carlyle and Ruskin, of Newman and Arnold, the spirit of the age – its materialism, self-satisfaction and insensitivity – is put to question and found wanting. But the abiding impression of the literature of these years remains one of assurance rather than of scepticism, of creative exuberance rather than of inward wrestling.

The Age of Progress

Wherein, then, lies the unity of this age of change? Perhaps to seek a unity deeper than

change itself is to pursue a shadow. By 1860 the idea of progress firmly held the field – the progress not only of the statistician and the Manchester merchant, but also of Macaulay's *History* and the *Origin of Species*. But this mood had been of slow growth. If it had captured the middle class by 1846 or earlier, as Porter suggests, its hold upon the proletariat was still precarious. Of a previous age – the mid-sixteenth century – it has been said that in it England turned a 'dangerous corner' in her history: such was now her experience once again. In 1848, as in 1830, Europe was torn by revolution and afflicted with cholera. In Britain, as industry languished and distress increased, the Chartists were preparing to march on London. To the mind of the comfortable there may have come at this time pictures of children dragging coal in narrow seams, of disease-ridden alleys in smoke-begrimed towns, of demoralized men in dreary workhouses. Reform had already removed the more tractable of these evils, but the Blue Books of a decade had imprinted them upon a nation's conscience. To the pessimist revolution may have seemed imminent.

But by 1851 the corner was being turned. All over Europe the tide of revolution had receded; in Britain it had never reached the full. Out of the struggles of the 'forties the nation had at last come to the high ranges of Victorian prosperity. If there had been no miraculous transformation of sickness into health, of poverty into riches, despair at least had been swallowed up in optimism. Throughout the summer of 1851 men and women of every class thronged into the great Crystal Palace. Each day Britain's new railways carried their trainloads of excursionists to the capital. Rich and poor alike were made to feel their pride and place in the story of a nation's progress. The Great Exhibition symbolized the conquering spirit of the age – brashly self-confident, blatantly materialist, yet imbued with a high seriousness of purpose and a sense of mission.

By 1860, in spite of the Crimean War, the Indian Mutiny and the economic crisis of 1857, nothing had shaken this fundamental confidence or sense of destiny. A stormy decade of war in Europe and America, and of agitation for reform at home lay ahead, but as yet these were the merest clouds upon a bright horizon. As the year closed, only a troubled Italy, striving for her unity, disturbed a continent's tranquillity. Britain, happy in her sovereign and prosperous as never before, was at peace with herself and the world. This was the age of progress, and there was no reason why it should not go on for ever.

Girders employed in the building of the Crystal Palace being tested, weighed and erected by a modification of Bramah's hydraulic press. *Illustrated Catalogue of the Great Exhibition*, 1851.

Obverse design of the Council, the Prize, and the
Jurors' medals, struck by the Royal Mint in commemoration of the Great Exhibition of 1851. Engraved
by William Wyon.

Architecture and Interior Decoration

DENYS HINTON

Most respectable guides and histories of architecture end at or about 1830. There may be many reasons for this. Architecture before the Romantic Movement falls easily into classified groups and is therefore more popular with those who write: and those who read desire, for the most part, guides to periods which they already know. But beyond these prejudices lurks an uneasy notion, that there is something disreputable about Victorian Architecture, that in the 1830's the virtue went out of it and never came back.

The irony of this notion is that what really distinguishes Victorian architecture is its high moral purpose and what Matthew Arnold called 'excellent high seriousness'. To Pugin it appeared that virtue had been absent from architecture since the Reformation and that he was restoring it. Fifty years later William Morris prepared for a golden age of socialism by turning back the clock: and throughout both of their lifetimes their contemporaries thought, talked and wrote about beauty, goodness and progress. There was never an age that was so serious about architecture and never an architecture so earnestly repudiated by its heirs.

This wholesale rejection of the work of three-quarters of a century has been an obstacle to serious study, and accounts for the fact that Victorian architecture has become the province of a few devoted specialists. Outside the work of this select band interest has centred largely on the superficial aspects of Victorian design and decoration – those, for instance, which have lent themselves to reproduction on the stage, where the literary and dramatic – not to say melodramatic –

associations of the period have gained them a steady popularity not for several generations enjoyed by the real architecture which they represent. More recently this theatrical taste has overflowed into the stream of contemporary decoration, mixing with the counter-flood to the severe functionalism of the 1930's to create a rather precious style in which interiors are, once again, filled with *objets d'art* and where diversity, even incongruity, is preferred to unity and restraint.

All this, however, owes more to the turning of the wheel of fashion than to the advance of historical knowledge: and the cult of Victoriana reflects no more understanding of the nineteenth century than Horace Walpole's Gothick did of the Middle Ages.

The absence of serious study has furthermore obscured the fact that between 1830 and 1900 English architecture moved from the era of John Nash to that of Charles Rennie Mackintosh – a period of change, the scope and rapidity of which are probably unequalled in its history. The first thirty years of this period, forming the subject of this guide, are a transition between the last great phase of Georgian architecture and town-planning and the High Victorian period of the 'sixties and 'seventies.

In 1830, Nash and Soane were both alive and active. Although each was a great individualist, each worked in an idiom that had its roots in the use of classical orders and proportions. The stuccoed Regency villa with its low-pitched roof and elegant detailing or, on a larger scale, the terrace, crescent or Town square, are not only the typical buildings of the nineteenth century's first decade, but also the continued expression of unquestionable confidence in the Georgian view of life. The story of Early Victorian architecture is a series of questions – mostly rhetorical – to which the whole fabric of architectural thought is subjected.

This is not the place to analyse in detail the causes, which lie outside the province of architecture itself. Yet all architecture is to some extent a reflection of contemporary events, thought and habits; and nothing would have been stranger than the survival of the eighteenth-century ideal after two such cataclysmic events as the Napoleonic wars and the Industrial Revolution. Parallel to the effect of these powerful political, technical and economic forces, the Romantic Movement in literature, the Oxford Movement in religion and the growth of a social conscience all exerted a powerful influence on architectural thought.

The London club houses

Yet to the architects of the first part of the century the problem must have appeared in simpler terms. They were at the end of a great period and were conscious that the rich seam was nearly worked out. In the 1820's there were manifestations of restlessness even among the Georgians. No less than in Soane's work at the Bank of England and in his own house in Lincoln's Inn, the younger men were looking for precedents outside the English Georgian tradition. Perhaps no building illustrates this more clearly than the evolution of the London club, which, from being in the eighteenth century a conversion from a coffee-house or a private residence, acquired a new status as a building type in its own right. One of the earliest buildings designed expressly as a club house was the United Service Club of John Nash, built in Waterloo Place in 1827.[1] It was essentially a Roman building with pedimented windows, deep cornice and richly relieved frieze. A portico through two storeys with twin Doric columns be-

[1] The name had formerly belonged to Smirke's building (1816) on the corner of Regent Street and Charles II Street, subsequently the Junior United Service Club and largely rebuilt in the 1850's by Nelson and Innes.

low and Corinthian above supports a pediment whose heavy detailing recalls the robustness of the Regent's Park terraces.

The Athenæum, by Decimus Burton, on the other hand, also built on an old Carlton House site, was distinctly Greek and must have appeared even more Greek before the addition of its present attic storey. Refined, detached and crowned with a panathenaic frieze, it is the stylistic heir to a score of other large classical buildings of the eighteenth century.

To resolve the contrast came the Travellers Club, founded by Lord Castlereagh before the end of the Napoleonic wars, but without a permanent home until 1831, in which year Charles (afterwards Sir Charles) Barry's building was completed. The inspiration for this club house and for that of the Reform Club which followed it, also by Barry, was the palazzo of the Italian Renaissance; and that to which it bears the strongest resemblance is Raphael's Pandolfini in Florence. The choice of precedent is an interesting one, and Barry's dexterous handling of it set a new pattern for Victorian secular buildings. The palace built round a courtyard provides an appropriate plan for the corporate home of a new ruling class. The site is small and the building, by comparison with its neighbour the Athenæum, is modest: the plan is asymmetrical and comparatively unpretentious, but the rooms are beautifully organized and the external features and decorations are articulated in a way quite foreign to those classical buildings which rely on the use of orders.

Almost ten years later than the Travellers', Barry produced on the site adjoining it in Pall Mall the Reform Club house – a commission won in a limited competition against the formidable field of Blore, Burton, Smirke, Basevi and Cockerell. Joined to the Travellers' by a link containing an entrance to the upper floors, the Reform building is conceived on a more generous scale than its neighbour and carries an attic storey. With minor variations, however, the elements of the façade are identical in detail and handling. The plan again centres on a cortile, adapted to the London climate by the use of iron beams supporting a glass roof. The staircase is again subordinated but, having a less restricted site than the Travellers', an almost symmetrical arrangement of rooms was possible. Their character, like that of the astylar exterior, and the careful study of kitchen planning to which Barry, rather surprisingly, gave great attention, became one of the models for London club houses of the next three decades.

Other prototypes followed in the 1840's, of which those of the Conservative Club (1844) and the Carlton (begun 1847) were the most significant. Like Arthur's Club, also in James Street, the Conservative was the joint work of Sidney Smirke and George Basevi. Its importance lies more in its scale than anything else, for the planning is much less coherent than Barry's and the exterior, with its vocabulary of rustication, Corinthian order and balustrade make it a rather ordinary late Georgian building.

The remodelling of the Carlton Club house, on the other hand, was very much an architectural event and in this case the commission was won by Smirke in competition with most of the leading club architects of the day – including Barry. The winning design took as its model Sansovino's Venetian Library of St Mark, introducing a few modifications to relate it to Pall Mall, the climate and taste of the English, but generally marking a movement towards a plastic, arcaded style which, with its elaborate moulding and carving, exercised a profound influence on later Victorian commercial architecture.

These clubmen's palaces in Pall Mall and elsewhere are the Early Victorian equivalents of the great houses of the eighteenth century and the last survivors of an epoch in which style was concerned with manners and architectural character was disciplined by a distinctive grammar. A new ruling class with new sources of wealth was moulding a new patriarchal society: its leaders, the kind of men who carried the Reform Bill (and named their club after it), were seldom given the chance to do anything similar in their private houses. Two exceptions, however, are worth quoting; one is Barry's Bridgewater House, and the other, Lewis Vulliamy's attempt to outshine Barry at Dorchester House, Park Lane. The planning of Bridgewater House is almost indistinguishable in principle from that of the Italianate club houses and the large central court is its main feature. Externally, the dominant elements are the windows of the first floor, lighting the principal rooms, their heavy segmental pediments filled with elaborate carving, and the rustication of the ground floor and corners. As in the Travellers' and Reform Clubs, Barry's interior decorations are outstanding, and indicate a growing taste for elaborate surface decoration.

On the more open site of Dorchester House, Vulliamy also used a rusticated ground floor. This was emphasized on the entrance side by a large projecting porch, while on the Park front a dramatic effect was achieved by omitting the centre section of the second floor.

In domestic architecture other signs of restlessness had appeared long before the end of the eighteenth century. The cult of the Gothic, beginning as a harmless affectation with buildings like Walpole's Strawberry Hill, had gathered momentum with Beckford's Fonthill, and during the Regency drew into its wake the cult of the picturesque, the *cottage orné*, Hinduism and chinoiserie. These little essays in sophistication led nowhere. Gothic was not yet a style, but only a decoration; but the change was not far off and was due to work itself out largely in the field of ecclesiastical architecture.

'Commissioners' Gothic'

In 1818, the Church Commissioners allotted a million pounds to the building of 214 new churches; of these 174 were Gothic. During the 1820's the youthful Barry was among the architects of the Gothic school which included not only those whose reputation rested entirely on neo-Medieval churches, but others who, like Barry himself, were versatile in both styles. Of these, one of the most competent was Thomas Rickman, an antiquarian who in 1817 produced *An attempt to Discriminate the Styles of Architecture in England* ..., thereby bringing into usage the classifications Early English, Decorated and Perpendicular. Rickman produced some scholarly churches in Birmingham and other provincial cities and added the new buildings at St John's College, Cambridge (1826–30).

Barry at Westminster

Barry's Gothic work included the King Edward VI School, Birmingham, now destroyed, but his great *tour de force* was his prize-winning design for the new Houses of Parliament following the Great Fire of 1834. The conditions of the competition make interesting study. Yevele's Westminster Hall survived the fire and had to be incorporated in the new scheme, which was, according to the select committee, 'to be either Gothic or Elizabethan'. For a Parliamentary committee so to endorse the Gothic style for Westminster, shows how well established and respectable it had now become. Furthermore, a patriotic note is sounded, even though many contemporary critics questioned whether 'Elizabethan' signified any real architectural style at all.

Barry's design was, as Hitchcock puts it, 'comprehensive and logical'. His building was planned as no building before the Renaissance could have been, for both the organization of internal spaces and the composition of the halls and towers possess a degree of sophistication unknown in English Medieval architecture – or even Elizabethan. Superficially, however, the design resembled a perpendicular palace, and for the detailing of the exterior Barry was indebted to Augustus Welby Northmore Pugin. (Ironically the style in which Pugin worked at Westminster was that which he was later to call 'debased'.) Not least among the many controversies aroused by the competition and its result was the dispute as to the true authorship of the winning design. In fact there is little doubt that the credit belongs principally to Barry: yet the building and the collaboration are both significant. Designed just before Queen Victoria's accession, the Houses of Parliament were not completed until the 1850's. By virtue of its size and the time taken to bring it to fruition, it occupies a central and dominant position in the period under review. Yet it is not a typically Early Victorian building nor even an influential one. It is more properly the last of a group of buildings conceived by detached and non-moralizing architects capable of turning their hands to any style.

What Barry achieved at Westminster he also essayed in the remodelling of Highclere Castle in Hampshire, where a plain Georgian block was converted, between 1840 and 1844, into another neo-Jacobethan palace. Here is picturesqueness without irregularity, the horizontal string-courses combining with the vertical pilasters to give a uniform reticulated exterior. At each corner Barry placed a tower with another in the centre dominating the composition and repeating the fretted and pinnacled silhouette of the main building.

Barry's work at Shrubland Park near Ipswich in the late 1840's is in quite a different category and also shows him at his best as a landscape architect. Shrubland, it is true, has a dominant tower, but it is Italian in character, with an open loggia top and linked to an elaborate Italianate garden. At Cliveden, rebuilt for the Duke of Sutherland in the 1850's, corner towers were included in Barry's first scheme, but gave way to a more economical design, regular, unromantic and combining many of his palazzo details with an Ionic order reminiscent of the early Palladians.

None of Barry's contemporaries possessed his extraordinary coherence as a designer: but coherence had almost ceased to be a virtue and was rapidly being overtaken by the enthusiastic exploitation of Gothic, Tudor and other revivalist styles.

Of Barry's contemporaries in the domestic field, Anthony Salvin was one who achieved a remarkable degree of authenticity in his neo-Jacobethan houses. This is especially true of Harlaxton, an enormous and very complex house near Grantham, whose erection was almost continuous between 1837 and 1860.

Harlaxton has a typical Elizabethan plan, a profusion of gables, bays and chimneys, and detailing of a kind not easily distinguishable from that of the early seventeenth century. Indeed, it has been suggested that this is actually a better Elizabethan house than many built in the reign of Queen Elizabeth I – a comment which raises the whole question of whether any kind of reproduction architecture can ever be satisfactory and the nicer issue of whether it is a virtue in an architect successfully to adapt the architecture of another period to the needs of his own. From this point of view Barry and Pugin may be regarded as successful architects, for their buildings, in spite of their borrowed details, have something to say which could only have been said in the first half of the nineteenth century. This is, indeed, the essence of the Early Victorian period and the reason why architects such as Salvin, whose work is archæologically interesting, cannot be regarded as typical. At Peckforton Castle in Cheshire, for instance, Salvin produced a fake castle which in siting, planning and massing, and every other quality expected of a castle, except that of falling into a state of picturesque decay, must be allowed to stand comparison with the best castles of the fourteenth century. At Scotney Castle, on the other hand, Salvin appears to have been caught between the genuine Elizabethan tradition and the Regency conception of a castle. Since the latter was a branch of the 'picturesque' cult it must therefore be regarded more as an example of survival than of revival and more allied to James Wyatt's work at Belvoir and Windsor and the castellated villas of John Nash.

Much the same can be said of Ramsey Abbey in Huntingdonshire, the work of Salvin's chief competitor in this field, Edward Blore, who enjoyed the double distinction of succeeding Nash at Buckingham Palace and Wyatt at Windsor. Ramsey Abbey is a tall building, three full storeys and a semi-basement, and the effect of height is increased by the strong vertical lines of buttresses and mullions on the face and by the pinnacles, turrets and chimneys which rise above the balustraded roof.

Built at the end of the 1830's, Ramsey Abbey was closely followed by Blore's large house at Worsley, near Manchester, for Lord Francis Egerton. Here again the planning is symmetrical and Elizabethan motifs are used only decoratively. Where the building differs essentially from those designed fifty years earlier to a similar formula is in the coarseness of detailing, the limited sophistication which could now be passed off as picturesque, and a total absence of charm.

What Blore achieved in decorative stonework at Worsley, P.C.Hardwick (son of the Philip Hardwick who was architect to the London and Birmingham Railway and his collaborator in the hotels at Euston and Paddington) attempted in the early 'fifties at Aldermaston Court, near Newbury, in a mixture of red brick and bath stone. This combination of materials, together with diaper patterning in the brickwork, was to become as familiar a feature of Victorian design as the restless outline and untidy profusion of forms for which Aldermaston is also remarkable.

Oddly enough, both these features were handled more successfully by the better church architects, who were, on the whole, inclined to avoid them when they turned their hands to secular building. Such discrimination was as rare as the really successful adaptation, but it is evident in the work of S.S.Teulon, particularly in his bold handling of Tortworth Court in Gloucestershire, which has the same firmness and confidence that make his later churches more than essays in copying. It also possesses the characteristic Victorian virtue of seriousness, which eventually displaced the picturesque, in the employment of towers, gables and turrets; not, as in the work of Salvin and Blore, merely for decoration, but each in order to express some distinctive element in the plan.

A. W. N. Pugin

Far more influential than Teulon, however, though his exact contemporary and also active in both ecclesiastical and domestic fields, was A.W.N.Pugin. Indeed, with the possible exception of Barry, there was not an architect in the whole of this period who exercised such an influence as this remarkable man.

Pugin's share in the new Palace of Westminster was, as we have seen, untypical, and his most important work was between 1835 and 1850. Both didactic and intolerant in his writing, Pugin observed consistently in his buildings the rules he laid down for others. He was the son of a French *émigré*, Auguste Charles Pugin, an authority and a prodigious publisher of works on Medieval architecture. Pugin was something of a prodigy as a draughtsman and an early convert to Roman Catholicism. Having 'ghosted' for Barry (and probably for Gillespie Graham as well) in the Westminster competition, Pugin published in 1836 *Contrasts or a Parallel between the Architecture of the 14th and 15th centuries and similar buildings of the Present Day.*

This was more than an affirmation of neo-Gothic. Gothic could be appropriate or 'debased' and what Pugin decided was appropriate was the Decorated or Middle Pointed Style. Moreover, he claimed that architecture was better or worse according to the morality and the religion of its creator – thereby ruling out all 'pagan' art, including that of the Georgian period. Nothing could equal his scorn for the frivolities of the Regency; and his adherence to truth, as he conceived it, included fidelity to purpose, place and time.

The arguments in his *True Principles of the Pointed or Christian Architecture* (1841) go further in their execration of 'shams' and anticipate many of the truisms of twentieth-century functionalism. But above all Pugin was a traditionalist and believed that truth was embodied exclusively in English architecture of the fourteenth century.

In a brief working life Pugin designed a large number of churches, including St Mary's, Derby, and St Chad's, Birmingham. At Ramsgate he designed and paid for St Augustine's (1846) and his own house, the Grange. This house, completed in 1843, seems a modest structure when compared with the palatial *tours de force* of the 'thirties and 'forties designed by the recognized architects of great houses. It is certainly one of the least pretentious of Pugin's own works, and although larger than his first house at Salisbury, built in 1835, has none of its eccentricity. Planned round a large hall rising the full height of the building and containing a gallery landing, the Grange owes to the basic form of a medieval house as much as, if not more than, it does to the superficial aspects of style. Externally the house almost achieves a look of crispness, with large areas of unadorned brickwork, simple bays with widely-spaced mullions, sharp gables and broad uncarved barge-boards. A simple brick tower adjoins the house on the east side.

Something of the same aversion to the purely picturesque may be seen at Bilton Grange, near Rugby, built by Pugin between 1841 and 1846. Here, as at Teulon's Tortworth, a strong sense of composition prevails, and instead of the irregular, almost fortuitous outline of houses whose plans are generated by the process of addition, we see bays and gables used as a series and reflecting the rhythmic pattern of rooms all more or less equal in size. Again, the crisp detailing of stonework is consistent with the firm outline of the timber structure where exposed in the interior and with the unadorned panelling of the main rooms.

At Scarisbrick Hall, near Manchester, Pugin enjoyed the patronage of an eccentric Catholic landowner, Charles Scarisbrick, whose father and grandfather had already commissioned Gothic extensions to an Elizabethan building. Pugin's commission began in 1837 and was unfinished at his death in 1852. Charles Scarisbrick was succeeded by his sister Anne in 1860, and she in turn commissioned Pugin's son, E.W.Pugin, to continue the work. It is therefore not easy to discern the contribution made by the elder Pugin: but it seems certain that he remodelled the west wing, completed the great hall, and added a clock-tower. The younger Pugin added an east wing in the 'sixties and increased the height of the tower so that it is no longer possible to say whether it resembles, as contemporary commentators declared, the tower of Big Ben. Scarisbrick thus achieved the romantic irregularity which so many early Victorians sought, but achieved it by a process very like that of the medieval buildings from which it claimed to draw its inspiration – from piecemeal growth and the attentions of many different owners and builders. Nevertheless, it is the heart of the building, A.W.Pugin's great hall and his richly carved interiors in the west wing, which are chiefly memorable – interiors more reminiscent of Pugin's churches than of the comparatively simple decorations of his other houses. Wall-panelling is used in profusion and is everywhere elaborately carved, painted and gilded, while on the upper walls and ceilings appear canopies and vaults in even brighter colour. In a Pugin church these things were at least an echo of reality: in a house they now strike us as magnificent, but slightly absurd scenery for an imaginary drama.

Just as Pugin's contribution to domestic architecture was coloured by his experience as an ecclesiastical designer, so other church architects of the 'forties and 'fifties bequeathed to the houses of the middle and late Victorian periods a number of novel ideas concerned with the use of materials.

The Tractarian or Oxford Movement in the early 'thirties was followed in Cambridge by the formation of the Camden Society in 1839 – known after 1845 as the Ecclesiological Society. Through its organ *The Ecclesiologist* this body continued to propagate Pugin's ideas and found a willing interpreter in William Butterfield.

William Butterfield

Butterfield was strictly a 'High Victorian'. His early works included a Perpendicular Dissenting Chapel at Bristol (1842), St Saviour's, Coalpitheath (1845) and St Augustine's College, Canterbury (1845–8). His most significant work is All Saints', Margaret Street – a model Ecclesiologists' Church. Designed in 1850, this was far more than a throw-back to English Decorated: it embodied many ideas quite foreign to English architecture, the most novel of which was the principle of 'Constructional Polychromy', which meant the incorporation of decorative courses of coloured brickwork and tiles, a feature which was widely imitated in High Victorian architecture and which gives a great deal of it such a restless appearance. The interior was equally colourful: as well as the novelty of red brickwork, Butterfield used mosaic tiles, red Peterhead granite, alabaster and gilding.

Second only to Butterfield as the darling of the Ecclesiologists was Richard Cromwell Carpenter, a perfectionist and devoted follower of Pugin. Apart from an erratic start in Georgian Tudor at Lonsdale Square, Islington (1838), Carpenter's work, largely on churches, is correct and dull. It includes St Magdalene's, Thurston Square (1849–52), St Paul's, West Street, Brighton (1840–8), All Saints', Hove (1848–52), and a thirteenth-century design for the Anglican Cathedral in Colombo. He also designed St John's College, Hurstpierpoint, built in 1851–3, and the college of Saints Mary and Nicholas at Lancing (1854–5) – finished in 1872 by Slater.

Scottish Baronial

Hardly less influential than the example of the Church was that of the State, and particularly of the Crown. Stimulated by the enthusiasm of Queen Victoria for travelling and living in Scotland, a new phase emerged in country-house design which is well described as Scottish Baronial. When analysed, this style proves to consist of little more than a mixture of the early fourteenth and seventeenth centuries, in which castellated details are juxtaposed with Jacobethan bays and gables while robust battlemented towers are conjoined with sharp pitches and clusters of chimneys: planning is additive and often functional but possesses little sense of modulation.

What commended the Scottish Baronial to the young Victoria and her subjects, however, was its romantic association with the novels of Sir Walter Scott. The archetype, Balmoral – which closely resembled Scott's Abbotsford – was acquired by the Crown in 1848 and extended by William Smith of Aberdeen, who had built the original house for Sir Robert Gordon. Thereafter the style became widely popular for houses of all sizes on both sides of the border.

The foremost specialists in Scottish Baronial were William Burn and David Bryce, who built Fettes College, Edinburgh, in the 'sixties. Before this Burn moved to London, and his largest work is at Fonthill, Wiltshire, where, in the late 'forties, he built a great house for the Marquess of Westminster. Sited auspiciously near to Beckford's Folly, Fonthill House has a romantic silhouette, but is coarse in detailing and dull in composition. It is nevertheless compactly planned (Burn enjoyed a reputation for being a 'convenient' planner), and only the obligation of the style makes the house look more complicated than it really is.

At home in London, the Queen dismissed from her mind the sentimental associations of Scotland

and set about the serious task of proving that the monarchy was respectable. One of her ways of doing this was to alter the face of that scandalous reminder of Regency depravity – Buckingham Palace. Whereas Nash's east front had been a tolerable Georgian, Blore's new elevation managed to look both conventional and vulgar at the same time. The Prince Consort, however, priding himself on his taste, ensured that in the interior of the new south wing added by James Pennethorne in the 'fifties the decorations should be neo-Raphaelite. Set in spandrels or rectangular panels, the fresco figures and cupids shared the walls with mirrors and patterned silks. In this respect too the Royal example was widely copied in homes and rooms very much more modest in scale.

Town houses

Almost every town possessed a neighbourhood which middle-class house building was to convert into a fashionable suburb. Eschewing what they regarded as the 'monotony' of Georgian and Regency street architecture, many developers offered the same plan with a variety of alternative elevations. Nevertheless, these houses were usually well sited and well built with large gardens often linked to the houses by conservatories or flower-rooms.

On a genuine town-planning scale, and highly prized by the London *bourgeoisie*, were the residential developments of districts on the north and south sides of Hyde Park. In Belgravia, as is normal in speculative development, the pace of building was uneven and work begun in the 1820's continued for many years after Queen Victoria's accession. This was essentially late Georgian planning, and the designs which George Basevi produced for the builder-developer Thomas Cubitt bear comparison with the best of Nash. They were followed by less happy examples in Bayswater and other suburbs, houses which, lacking the adaptability to survive the metamorphosis into apartments and boarding-houses, must, where they have not done so already, soon make way for twentieth-century planning.

The interiors of the better town houses retained much of the charm of their eighteenth-century counterparts, from which the basic planning differed only in detail. Certain changes in materials, finishes and equipment, however, were to change fundamentally the traditional idea of how the inside of a gentleman's house should be decorated. Of these, the invention of plate glass was one; and the consequent increase in the size of windows and the omission of glazing bars not only resulted, in the short period before the introduction of very heavy curtaining, in a marked increase in the degree of daylighting, but also changed the character of elevations by introducing large unbroken black rectangles and, of course, affecting the view of the outside world from within.

Equally significant was the introduction of gas for artificial lighting, which became available for most towns by the 1840's. Gas was usually brought to brackets on each side of the chimney-breast and to an ornate brass chandelier in the centre of the ceiling. The quality of light was more uniform and certainly no less pleasant than that of candles, and the equipment itself became a characteristic Victorian accessory.

Whereas rooms in the 1830's had a light rococo flavour combining gilt, rosewood and papier-mâché furniture with muslin and silk draperies, mirrors and light-flowered wallpapers and carpets, the 1840's saw the introduction of heavy materials and darker colours. Velvet and rep replaced the diaphanous curtains, falling in ponderous folds of crimson and dark green. Furniture increased in size and crowded into the centre of rooms, leaving less space to be enjoyed as space. Walls, also, ceased to be significant as walls and became surfaces on which to hang pictures, often so close together that hardly any of the wall itself was visible.

The fireplace remained the focal point of most rooms and marble the most popular material for its surround. Hard shiny and often dark marbles were preferred, and the shelf, in order to accommodate the accumulation of clocks, vases and other ornaments, became deeper. Cast-iron grates also became a standard feature, frequently with brass ornaments and usually restless and contorted in design. This was the sort of object for which industry had created a new kind of taste which the

Victorians, because the evidence of its commercial origin was so carefully disguised, regarded as artistic and which filled the pavilions of the Great Exhibition of 1851.

This remarkable building was regarded by its contemporaries as a novelty: its contents as significant 'designs'. Yet although we now claim to think the building more significant than its contents, reading the Exhibition Catalogues for amusement and tracing the evolution of the modern prefabricated framed building from Paxton's Crystal Palace, there are many, including architects, who have never really accepted the implications of the Industrial Revolution. For this failure to make contact with reality the architects of the Victorian era must take a fair share of the blame.

Public buildings

Almost equal with the spate of Early Victorian church building was that of Town Halls and similar public and semi-public buildings. This remained a sphere into which the Gothic Revival was slow to penetrate, and the best examples of the period are either very literal examples of Classical Greek buildings or ingenious and scholarly variations on the same theme.

Of the literal character, Birmingham Town Hall by J.A.Hansom, built in 1832, is a complete copy of a Corinthian Temple. Dramatically sited on sloping ground, the building stands on a rusticated podium above which fluted columns stand out against a wall, to which successive decades of grime have given an appearance not unlike that of an ancient naos seen in dark Ægean shadow.

More impressive in scale, and still one of the most imaginative designs for a public building in any period, is the even blacker silhouette of St George's Hall, Liverpool. Actually a combination of Hall and Assize Courts, this very Grecian building was the result of a competition held in 1839 and won by Harvey Lonsdale Elmes. The handling of the Corinthian order is confident and strict and there is a marked freedom from affected ornament and a willingness, as in certain French buildings of the same genre, to rely entirely on the powerful rhythm of columns and entablatures.

By contrast there is a restless character to the Fitzwilliam Museum at Cambridge, the work of George Basevi, in which a two-storey building is also faced with a massive Corinthian order. The Fitzwilliam was completed by Charles Robert Cockerell, who also designed the Ashmolean Museum at Oxford (1841–5) of which the incoherent plan is likewise concealed behind an unusual Greek order based on one studied by Cockerell at Bassae.

Cockerell was professorial by disposition and a great admirer of Wren. The son of S.P.Cockerell, with whom he was associated in the surveyorship of the East India Company, he was also the nephew of the nabob for whom Humphrey Repton designed the strange villa at Sezincote. In 1833 he succeeded Soane as Architect to the Bank of England, and introduced there a stricter and more trabeated style. Some of his most scholarly and, at the same time, most attractive work is in the interior of St George's Hall, where he worked after Elmes' tragic death, from 1851 to 1856. Of special charm is Cockerell's decoration to the elliptical hall, where his low relief, delicate cast-iron balconies, and graceful caryatids have all the grace of an early Georgian interior.

James Pennethorne, a late Georgian like Cockerell, who succeeded to Nash's practice, added a wing to Somerset House and designed the former Geological Museum in Piccadilly (1837) which is a derivative of the Doge's Palace in Venice.

The engineers

Sir Gilbert Scott said that it was the function of an architect to decorate structure. Many critics would now say that the structures which were architecturally most successful in the nineteenth century were the ones which the architects did not get their hands on.

Before the end of the eighteenth century, engineers had produced designs of real quality, such as the cast-iron bridge at Coalbrookdale (1779) and the Jones' Malting Building in Shrewsbury. John Rennie and Thomas Telford produced a number of bridges in the first thirty years of the century; Rennie's chief contribution being in London at Waterloo, Vauxhall and Southwark –

all now replaced – while Telford is best known for his road suspension bridge across the Menai Straits, built in 1819–24 and still the longest in the British Isles. Nearby is the Britannia Bridge, built in 1850 by Richard Stephenson and Francis Thompson for the Chester and Holyhead railway, in which tubular wrought iron succeeded the cast-iron technique of constructions.

The designing of bridges and aqueducts was stimulated by the growth firstly of canals and secondly of the railways. 1830 saw the building of the earliest important railway station at Crown Street, Liverpool, followed by the first of the Lime Street complex in 1836 (the work of John Cunningham), both using wooden queenpost trusses on cast-iron columns. Lime Street Station was built in 1846 to the design of Richard Turner, a contracting engineer whose inventiveness and imagination in creating a structure 360 feet long and $153\frac{1}{2}$ feet in span far outran that of the architect William Tite, who designed the brick and stone façade.

A more striking and also more familiar piece of railway architecture is the great doric arch or propylæum at Euston designed by Philip Hardwick. When the London, Midland and Scottish Railway extended its line to central London, Robert Stephenson (son of George Stephenson) designed the large 200-foot shed at Euston with metal trusses and elegantly detailed cast-iron supports. A similar shed and arch terminated the line at Curzon Street, Birmingham.

The Great Western Railway had as their engineer the brilliant I.K.Brunel, designer of the Clifton Suspension Bridge and of numerous stations between Paddington and Bristol. At the latter terminus Temple Mead Station (1839–40) was an essay in Tudor Stylism, using a wooden hammerbeam roof spanning 72 feet. By contrast the work of Lewis Cubitt at the Bricklayers Arms Station off the Old Kent Road (1842–4) and that of Sancton Wood at Cambridge (1844–5) was markedly Italianate. Cubitt was also the designer of the great twin-arched station which the Great Northern built for its London Terminus at King's Cross in 1852.

Among the Early Victorian iron constructions which merit serious consideration as architecture are the covered markets and the great conservatories. As a designer of markets, Charles Fowler was outstanding. He was responsible for Covent Garden and Hungerford Market and also for the interesting lower market at Exeter (1836). Smithfield was built in 1845 to the design of Boulnois, and Billingsgate and the Metropolitan Cattle Market, both in the early 'fifties, by the architect James Bunning and his successor Sir Horace Jones.

James Bunstone Bunning also used cast-iron extensively in the Coal Exchange, Lower Thames Street, London, where the delicate sections of the dome ribs show a real sympathy for a material which was in danger of becoming more widely used merely as a reinforcement to traditional constructions when enlarged to the scale required in Victorian building.

The great conservatories brought together glass and iron and created 'ferrovitreous' construction. Decimus Burton, designer of the Athenæum, was the architect for the conservatory built at Chatsworth (1837–40) for the sixth Duke of Devonshire, but it was the Duke's head gardener – Joseph Paxton – who was really responsible for the daring plan of an iron-framed building measuring 277 feet by 173 feet and roofed entirely with glass. Burton was also the architect for the beautiful conservatory at Kew – in a happy collaboration with Richard Turner, the engineer of the second Lime Street Station at Liverpool. Only the design of its chimney – disguised as an Italian Campanile – reveals the as yet inadequate vocabulary of architects working in these new materials.

The Crystal Palace

By far the most famous 'ferrovitreous' building of the nineteenth century was the Crystal Palace, erected in Hyde Park to house the Great Exhibition of 1851. Paxton, whose design was finally selected, had carried his experiments beyond the great conservatory at Chatsworth with an ingenious lily-house. The Crystal Palace was remarkable in many ways. It was enormous, with a cubic content of thirty-three million cubic feet

(A) Charles Grey, 2nd Earl,
by SIR THOMAS LAWRENCE.
(*detail*)

(B) Sir Robert Peel, 2nd Baronet,
by HENRY WILLIAM PICKERSGILL.
(*detail*)

(C) Richard Cobden,
by L. DICKINSON.
(*detail*)

(D) Lord Palmerston, 3rd Viscount,
by F. CRUICKSHANK.

All these portraits are from the *National Portrait Gallery*.

PLATE 1   1281

(A) The Crystal Palace, the Great Exhibition of 1851.

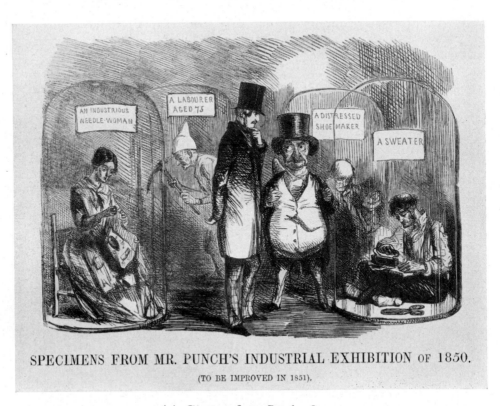

SPECIMENS FROM MR. PUNCH'S INDUSTRIAL EXHIBITION OF 1850.
(TO BE IMPROVED IN 1851).

(B) Cartoon from *Punch*, 1851.

PLATE 2

(A) An engraving of Lymington Iron Works on the Tyne,
by J. SANDS after Thomas Allom, 1835.

(B) A woman and child in a coal mine, 1842.

PLATE 3 1283

The first meeting of the reformed House of Commons, 1833. *National Portrait Gallery.*

PLATE 4

(A) SIR CHARLES BARRY. Front elevation of Reform Club House, Pall Mall, London, 1838–40.
Royal Institute of British Architects.

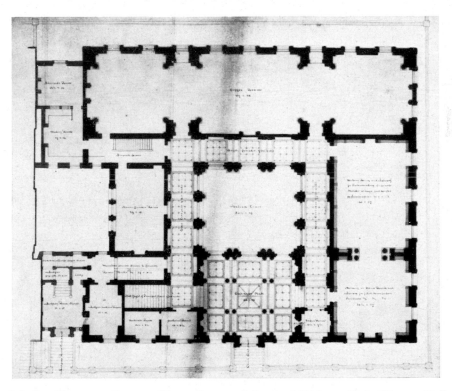

(B) SIR CHARLES BARRY. Plan of ground floor of Reform Club House, Pall
Mall, London, 1838–40. *Royal Institute of British Architects.*

PLATE 5   1285

SIR CHARLES BARRY. Travellers Club House, 1832, and Reform Club, 1838–40, Pall Mall, London.
National Buildings Record.

PLATE 6

(A) SIR CHARLES BARRY. Garden elevation of Travellers Club, Pall Mall, London, 1832.
National Buildings Record.

(B) SIR CHARLES BARRY. Entrance Hall of the Reform Club, Pall Mall, London, 1838–40.
Warburg Institute.

PLATE 7

SIR CHARLES BARRY. Bridgewater House, Westminster, 1847. *Warburg Institute.*

PLATE 8

SIR CHARLES BARRY. Gallery of Hall of Bridgewater House, Westminster, 1847. *National Buildings Record.*

PLATE 9 1289

(A) SIR CHARLES BARRY. Drawings for alterations to Clumber House, 1857.
Royal Institute of British Architects.

(B) WILLIAM BURN. Drawing for Fonthill, Wiltshire, 1849. *Royal Institute of British Architects.*

PLATE 10

(A) ANTHONY SALVIN. Drawing for Harlaxton Hall, Lincolnshire, 1837–60.
Royal Institute of British Architects.

(B) ANTHONY SALVIN. Scotney Castle, 1837. *Royal Institute of British Architects.*

PLATE 11

SIR CHARLES BARRY'S and A. W. N. PUGIN'S original design for the Westminster New Palace, 1836.
Royal Institute of British Architects.

PLATE 12

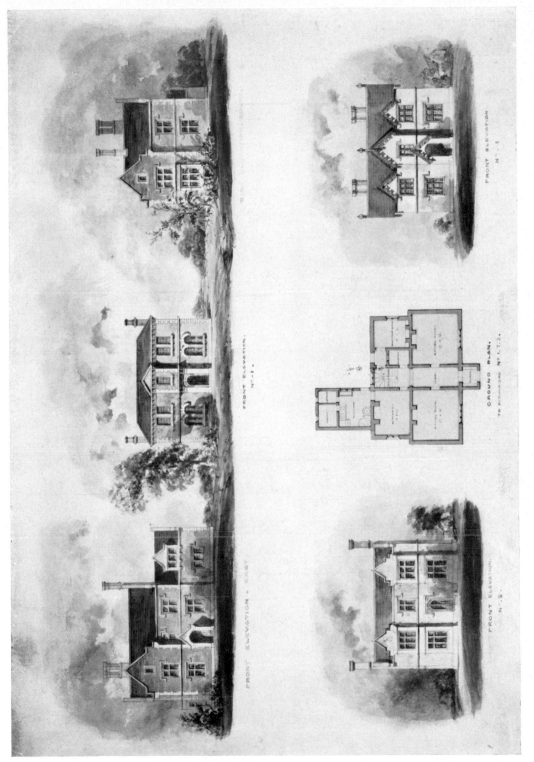

Plan with alternative elevations for Early Victorian villas, c. 1840. *Royal Institute of British Architects*

PLATE 13

A. W. N. Pugin, 1837–52, and E. W. Pugin's, 1860–8, remodelled Scarisbrick Hall, Lancashire.
P. Fleetwood-Hesketh, Murray's Lancashire Architectural Guide.

PLATE 14

(A) *Above left*, A. W. N. PUGIN. The King's Room at Scarisbrick Hall, Lancashire, 1836–9. *P. Fleetwood-Hesketh, Murray's Lancashire Architectural Guide.*

(B) *Above right*, A. W. N. PUGIN. The red and gold wall paper in the Red Drawing Room, hand-printed with blocks, designed for Charles Scarisbrick by A. W. Pugin, at Scarisbrick Hall, Lancashire, *c.* 1837. *P. Fleetwood-Hesketh, Murray's Lancashire Architectural Guide.*

(C) *Left*, A. W. N. PUGIN. View from the King's Room to the Red Drawing Room at Scarisbrick Hall, Lancashire, 1836–9. *P. Fleetwood-Hesketh, Murray's Lancashire Architectural Guide.*

PLATE 15   1295

WILLIAM BUTTERFIELD. All Saints', Margaret Street, London, 1859. *National Buildings Record.*

PLATE 16

WILLIAM BUTTERFIELD. Interior of All Saints', Margaret Street, London, 1859.
National Buildings Record.

PLATE 17

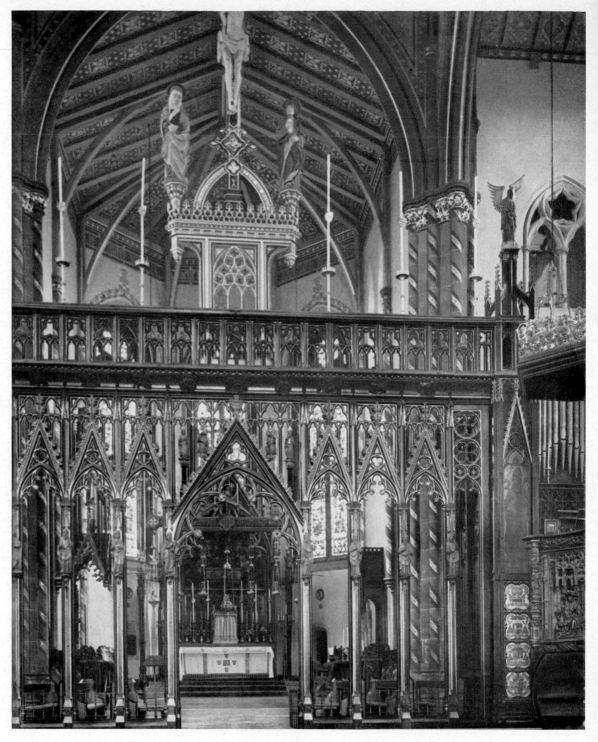

A. W. N. Pugin. Birmingham Roman Catholic Cathedral (St Chad's), 1839–41.
National Buildings Record.

PLATE 18

PHILIP and P. C. HARDWICK. The Great Hall at Euston Station, London.
Royal Institute of British Architects.

PLATE 19

1299

P. C. HARDWICK. The Coffee Room at Paddington Station, London. *Royal Institute of British Architects.*

PLATE 20

Carved and gilt couch and sofa in the Louis XIV style. Made by W. and C. Wilkinson, under the supervision of Philip Hardwick, for the Court Drawing-room, Goldsmiths' Hall, 1834.

PLATE 21

1301

(A) Carved and padded chair, made by W. and C. Wilkinson, under the supervision of Philip Hardwick, for the Court Dining-room, Goldsmiths' Hall, 1834.

(B) Carved and padded arm-chair, designed by A. W. N. Pugin for Scarisbrick Hall, 1835.

PLATE 22

(A) Side-table, made by W. and C. Wilkinson, under the supervision of Philip Hardwick, for the Court Room, Goldsmiths' Hall, 1834.

(B) Sideboard designed by Henry Whitaker for the Conservative Club (now the Bath Club), 1844.

PLATE 23

Table with inlaid amboyna top, designed by Henry Whitaker for the Conservative Club (now the Bath Club), 1844.

PLATE 24

(A) Originál design for carved and painted 'Gothic' sofa for Snelston Hall, Derbyshire, by Lewis Nockalls Cottingham, 1844.

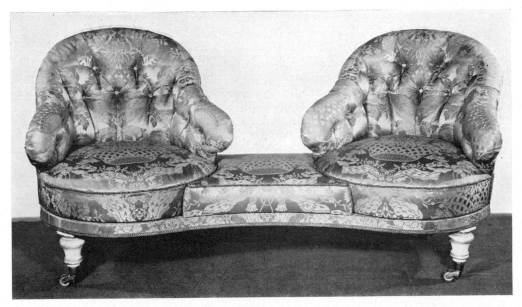

(B) Sofa ('Sociable') with double swivel ends, covered in silk damask woven by Baily and Jackson of Spitalfields. *Stoneleigh Abbey, Warwickshire, c.* 1844.

PLATE 25

(A) Turned 'prie-dieu' chair, with tent-stitch embroidery on wool. *Charlecote Park, Warwickshire, c.* 1845.

(B) 'Elizabethan' chair, with tent-stitch embroidery on wool, *c.* 1845.

(A) Carved and gilt chair, made by W. and C. Wilkinson, under the supervision of Philip Hardwick, for the Court Drawing-room, Goldsmiths' Hall, 1834.

(B) Carved and inlaid chair, with inset porcelain plaque depicting Queen Victoria. Designed and made by Henry Eyles of Bath for the Great Exhibition, 1851. *Victoria and Albert Museum.*

PLATE 27

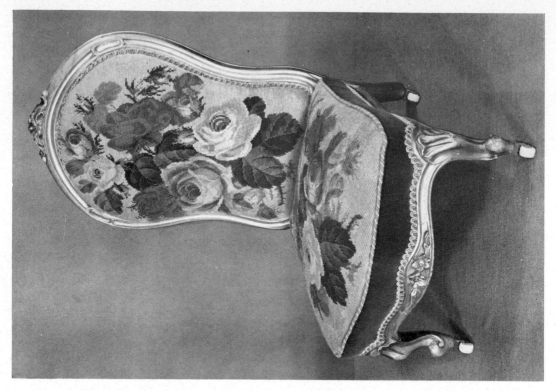

(B) Carved and gilt chair, with back and seat of Berlin wool-work.

(A) 'Elizabethan' fire-screen with panel of Berlin wool-work. c. 1855. *Charlecote Park, Warwickshire, c.* 1855.

Sideboard, designed by Hugues Protat and made by William Cookes of Warwick for Alscot Park, Warwickshire, 1853.
Courtesy Mrs Alston-Roberts-West.

PLATE 29

1309

(A) Carved and gilt music-stool in the 'naturalistic style', with seat in Berlin wool-work. *Charlecote Park, Warwickshire, c. 1855.*

(B) Fire-screen designed and carved in the 'naturalistic style', by William Kendall of Warwick. *Stoneleigh Abbey, Warwickshire, 1858.*

PLATE 30

Sideboard designed and carved in the 'naturalistic style', by William Kendall of Warwick.
Stoneleigh Abbey, Warwickshire, 1858.

PLATE 31

1311

Sideboard, designed and carved by James Morris Willcox of Warwick. *Charlecote Park*, *Warwickshire*, 1858.

PLATE 32

and contained 900,000 square feet of glass in a three-tiered building crossed by a gigantic dome 'transept' in which several elm-trees were preserved. It was not only a feat of engineering, but one of organization, for the cast-iron structure was entirely prefabricated and the working drawings were begun only nine months before the exhibition opened.

The story of the exhibition itself is well known and its financial success is embodied in the museum buildings of Kensington, whose architecture pays no homage whatever to Paxton's brilliant invention. Modern architects, however, are almost unanimous in expressing their acknowledgement. The Crystal Palace buildings were re-erected with towers at Sydenham in South London in 1854 and perished in a great fire in 1936.

Scott

Of all Victorian architects the best known is probably Sir George Gilbert Scott (1811–78). His personality has coloured our view of Victorian architecture as a whole and tended to obscure the qualities of some of his humbler contemporaries. Most of his important work (although in his own opinion he had no other kind) was done in the High Victorian phase: among Early Victorian architects he takes a place subordinate to that of Butterfield and Carpenter.

Scott's practice was founded on workhouses, of which, in partnership with William Moffat, he designed, in the 'thirties and 'forties, more than fifty. Of his early churches, St Mark's, Swindon (1843–5), received the approval of the Ecclesiologists, and St Andrew's, Leeds (1844–5), is of a simple Early English character which compares favourably with his later eclecticism.

Scott achieved international celebrity in 1845 by winning the competition for the Nikolaikirche in Hamburg. Since his German clients were Lutherans, his success lost him the support of the Camdenians, but his future was assured. He was a ubiquitous 'restorer' of old buildings, including several major cathedrals, and is famous for two memorials, one of which, the Martyrs' Memorial at Oxford (1841), falls within the Early Victorian period.

Built after 1860, but argued about continuously from 1856 onwards, the Foreign Office in Whitehall was Scott's sole essay in monumental Italian style. This was the subject of a protracted battle between Scott and Palmerston which ended in a rare act of submission by Scott.

If Scott was the High Victorian counterpart of Pugin in practice, John Ruskin (1814–1900) was his counterpart in literature. His main works *Modern Painters* (1843–60), the *Seven Lamps of Architecture* (1849) and the *Stones of Venice* (1851–3), all fall within our period, but it is doubtful if their full effect was felt until much later. Like Pugin, he hated everything Greek or Roman and proposed four styles for universal acceptance: Pisan Romanesque, Florentine Gothic, Venetian Gothic and English Early Decorated. How such suggestions and how his moralizing on Art in general were interpreted by a generation already greedily eclectic is a story which belongs to the years after 1860.

A LIST OF THE CHIEF ARCHITECTS MENTIONED
with their principal works dating from between 1830 and 1860.

BARRY, Sir Charles 1795–1860.

Traveller's Club, Pall Mall	1832	Clumber House, Notts.	1857
Reform Club, Pall Mall	1838–40	Bridgewater House	1847
St Peter's, Brighton	1824–28	Highclere Castle	1842–44
Houses of Parliament	1840	Cliveden House, Bucks	1850
		Shrubland Park, Suffolk	1848

BASEVI, George 1795–1845. Cousin of Disraeli and pupil of Sir J. Soane. Cubitt's architect in Belgrave Square.

Fitzwilliam Museum, Cambridge	1837
Conservative Club (with Sidney Smirke)	1843–44

BLORE, Edward 1789–1879.

Canford Manor, near Wimborne, Dorset	1826–36
Ramsey Abbey, Hunts	1838–39
Worsley Hall near Manchester	1840–45
East front at Buckingham Palace	1847
Architect to Westminster Abbey	

BRYCE, David 1803–76. Partner of Wm Burn.

British Linen Bank, Edinburgh	1850
Fettes College	1860
Numerous Scottish mansions	

BUNNING, James B. 1802–63. Architect to City of London 1843–63.

Billingsgate Market, London	1850
Islington Cattle Market	1852
Holloway Prison	1851–52
Coal Exchange, lower Thames St, London	1849

BURN, William 1789–1870. Specialist in 'Scottish Baronial', pupil of Sir R. Smirke, partner of David Bryce.

Montague House, Whitehall	1860
Beaufort Castle, Inverness	1834
Buchanan House, nr Glasgow	1849
Fonthill, Wilts.	1849

BURTON, Decimus 1800–81.

Athenæum Club, Pall Mall	1827
Hyde Park Screen	1828
Club Chambers, Regent St	1839
Conservatories at Chatsworth (with Paxton)	1837–40
and at Kew	1845–47

BUTTERFIELD, Wm. 1814–1900.

St Augustine's College, Canterbury	1845–48
All Saints', Margaret St	1859
Merton College Chapel	1849–50
St Matthias, Stoke Newington	1850
St Thomas, Leeds	1852
Restored Dorchester Abbey	

CARPENTER, R. C. 1812–55.

St Paul's, West St, Brighton	1840–48
All Saints, Hove	1848–52
St Magdelene's, Munster Square, London	1849–52

St John's College, Hurstpierpoint	1851–53
College of SS Mary and Nicholas, Lancing, Sussex	1854–55
Architect to Chichester Cathedral	

COCKERELL, Professor C. R. 1788–1863. Royal Academician 1836. Son of late Georgian architect S. P. Cockerell and assistant to Sir R. Smirke.

Taylorian Museum, Oxford	1841–45
Finished Fitzwilliam Museum Cambridge	1845
Finished St George's Hall, Liverpool	1851–56
Additions to Bank of England after	1833
Westminster Insurance Office, Strand	1833
St David's College, Lampeter	1828
Sun Assurance Offices	1839–42
University Library, Cambridge	1837

ELMES, Harvey Lonsdale 1813–47.

St George's Hall, Liverpool	1836
Collegiate Institution	1843
County Asylum, W. Derby, Liverpool	1840–47

FOWLER, Charles 1791–1867.

Charing Cross Market	
Exeter Town Market	1836

JONES, Owen 1809–74. Author of: *Polychromatic Ornament of Italy*, 1846 ; *Grammar of Ornament*, 1856.

Superintended Great Exhibition 1851 and Director of its interior decoration.

HANSOM, Jos. A. 1803–1852. Inventor of Hansom cab. Established *The Builder*, 1842.

Birmingham Town Hall	1832
Belvoir St Baptist Chapel, Leicester	1845

HARDWICK, Philip 1792–1870. Architect to London and Birmingham Railway.

Corner House, Belgrave Square	1841
Christchurch, Marylebone	1825
Doric Arch at Euston Station	1835–37
Great Hall at Euston Station	1846–47
Curzon St Terminus, Birmingham	1838
Euston Hotel	1839
Paddington Hotel	1852
Buildings at Lincolns Inn	1843–45

HARDWICK, Philip Charles 1822–92. Son and partner of Philip Hardwick and collaborator in most of his works.

PAXTON, Sir Joseph 1801–65. Gardener to Duke of Devonshire.

Conservatory at Chatsworth (with Decimus Burton)	1837–40
Lily House at Chatsworth	1849–50
Crystal Palace	1851
Mentmore, Bucks (with G. H. Stokes)	1852–54

PENNETHORNE, Sir Jas. 1801–71. Assistant to John Nash and pupil of Pugin the Elder.

W. Wing, Somerset House	1842
Record Office, Chancery Lane	1851
Geological Museum, Piccadilly	1837
Duchy of Cornwall office, Buckingham Gate	1854
Interior at Buckingham Palace	1852–55

PUGIN, Augustus Welby Northmore 1812–52. Author of: *Contrasts*, 1836; *Examples of Gothic Architecture*, 1836; *True Principles of Pointed or Christian Architecture*, 1841; *Apology for the Revival of Christian Architecture*, 1843; *Present state of Ecclesiastical Architecture in England*, 1843; *Glossary of Ecclesiastical ornament and costume*, 1844; *Floriated Ornament*, 1849; *Treatise on Chancel Screens and Rood Lofts*, 1851.

Details for Houses of Parliament	1835–36
St Mary's, Derby	1838–39
St Chad's, Birmingham	1839–41
Oscott College	1837
Killarney Cathedral	1846
St Giles, Cheadle, Staffs	1841–46
Alton Towers	1849
Scarisbrick Hall, Lancs	1837–52
The Grange, Ramsgate	1841–43
Bilton Grange, Rugby	1841–46

RICKMAN, Thomas 1776–1841. Author of: *Attempt to discriminate the styles of Architecture in England*, 1817.

St George's Church, Birmingham	1822

New Court, St John's College, Cambridge and numerous churches in the Midlands

SALVIN, Anthony 1799–1881. Pupil of John Nash.

Harlaxton	1837–60
Scotney Castle	1837
Restored Tower of London and Peterborough Cathedral	

SCOTT, Sir George Gilbert R.A. 1810–77.

Numerous churches and cathedral restorations

SMIRKE, Sir Robert 1780–1867.

British Museum	1823
Post Office, St Martins-le-Grand, London	1825–29
Oxford and Cambridge Club, London (with S. Smirke)	1835–37

SMIRKE, Sidney 1798–1877. Brother of Sir Robert Smirke.

Conservative Club (with G. Basevi)	1843–44
Carlton Club	1847–55
Athenæum Club, Bury	1850
Sorting Office, G.P.O., London	1845

TEULON, S. S. 1812–73

Tortworth Court, Glos.	1849–53
Enbrook, near Folkestone	1853–55
St Stephen's Church, Hampstead	
St Andrew's Church, Stamford St, E.C.	

TITE, Sir Wm. M.P. 1798–1873

Royal Exchange, London	1844
Westminster Bank, London, E.C.	1836
numerous Railway Stations	

VULLIAMY, Lewis 1791–1871

Dorchester House, Park Lane, London	1848–63

DESIGN FOR A NORMAN COTTAGE.

Ground Storey. (A), hall. (B), drawing-room; at the end is an arched recess, having on each side a lobby, one leading into the conservatory (C), and the other into the parlour (D); there is also a window on each side of the fire-place looking into the conservatory, which would have a pleasant and cheerful effect. (E), principal staircase, with water-closet under part, and steps to the offices in the basement story. (F), dining-room, with doorway to back entrance, and staircase to kitchen, for the purpose of serving the dinner quickly. (G), study. (H), bed-room for man-servant, with doorway to back entrance (K), which would be a protection to same in the night-time. (<), areas to admit light to the basement. On the one-pair would be five or six bedrooms and water-closet, and one bed-room in the tower, making in all seven or eight, with the one on the ground storey. In the basement storey are the domestic offices.

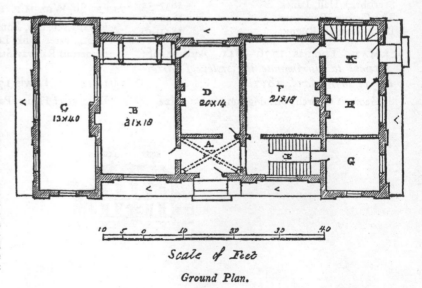

Scale of Feet

Ground Plan.

A cottage design from *The Builder*, December 1843.

Furniture

PETER FLOUD

The thirty years from 1830 to 1860 are the most neglected in the whole history of English furniture. There is hardly a book or even an article devoted to early Victorian furniture, and no systematic public or private collections of it. Those few students who venture beyond 1830 usually leap straight on to William Morris and the 1860's, with nothing more than a cursory glance at the Great Exhibition of 1851 to cover the intervening years. Indeed, the total neglect of the period is best epitomized by the fact that of the ten names listed by Matthew Digby Wyatt in 1856 (*Report on the Furniture at the Paris Exhibition of 1855*) as representing the most prominent furniture designers during the previous thirty years, only one – A.W.N.Pugin – is now remembered; three – Bridgens, Whitaker and Dwyer – though entirely forgotten, can still be identified because they published surviving pattern-books, while the remaining six have sunk into total oblivion.

During all other periods since 1700, furniture design has owed much to the inspiration of architects. During the early Victorian period this was not so. With the exception of Pugin, the only architects who seem to have designed furniture were Philip Hardwick and C.J.Richardson. Moreover, even the leading general designers did little in the field of furniture. The two best – Alfred Stevens and Owen Jones – turned to furniture design only at the end of their careers, after 1860, and we have to drop down to secondary figures such as W.B.Scott, L.N.Cottingham any J.K.Collings, before we find any consistent furniture designing.

Documentary evidence

In face of these difficulties, any serious study of the subject must start from an analysis of the surviving *documentary* evidence, and not from an inspection of the increasing quantities of so-called early Victorian furniture now being handled by furniture dealers. This surviving furniture is often quite untypical, and a survey based on it would only perpetuate that process of selective survival which over-emphasizes what is quaint but freakish, at the expense of what is dull but typical.

The available documentary evidence can be listed under seven heads. First, and most valuable of all, are the working records of the leading manufacturers. Unfortunately only one such series – the copious records of Messrs Gillow of Lancaster – appears to have survived intact. In view of the fact that, of all the great early Victorian cabinet-making firms, only two others – Messrs Trollope and Messrs Holland – still survive, and that both have lost all their earlier records, it seems doubtful whether others will come to light. Certainly there can now be little hope of discovering those of long-defunct firms such as Arrowsmith, Banting, Dalziel, Dowbiggin or Wilkinson, whose work was most typical of the period.

Second in importance are illustrated trade catalogues. Very few have so far been traced, and most relate to the single firm of William Smee of Finsbury Pavement. Although their plates are especially valuable as providing irrefutable testimony to actual production, they are almost always undated, and must therefore be used with great circumspection.

Third are the cheaper pattern-books with lithographed plates and no text, put together with no pretence of originality by hack designers for the use of firms too small or unenterprising to employ their own designer. They provide a record of the average taste of the times. They are best represented by the many volumes put out by Thomas King for the 1830's, and by Henry Wood for the 1840's and Henry Lawford for the 1850's. Requiring a different interpretation is the fourth category, namely the more expensive volumes, usually with engraved plates and some text, put out by designers with some claim to creative ability – such as Bridgens, Whitaker or Peter Thomson – and consequently including a high proportion of more fanciful 'prestige' designs. Although many of these designs were probably never executed, and although they cannot therefore be taken as a safe guide to general production, they are often useful as illustrating the beginnings of stylistic changes which only later became fashionable.

A fifth source of information is existing furniture which can be dated and attributed by the evidence of surviving accounts or similar records. Further research would no doubt disclose much more of this than the few examples investigated and illustrated for this article. It is perhaps unfortunate that for obvious reasons, some of the most readily available evidence of this kind is provided by furniture associated with the Royal family – as, for example, the library-furniture commissioned for Windsor by William IV, the furniture at Kensington Palace, the furniture designed by Henry Whitaker for Osborne, or the furniture in bedrooms occupied by Queen Victoria during visits to places such as Woburn Abbey or Stoneleigh Abbey. Such furniture is liable to give a distorted picture if used as an index to the dating of stylistic changes, for throughout the early Victorian period (and indeed from the death of George IV onwards) the taste of the Court tended to be some ten years or so behind that of London society generally; apart also from the untypical influence of Prince Albert's German associations.

The sixth category consists of the records of furniture designs registered for copyright purposes with the Patent Office from 1839 onwards. These are meagre for every category except papier-mâché and cast-iron. The last category consists of the copious records and illustrations, both official and unofficial, of the furniture displayed at the various exhibitions of the period, namely at Manchester in 1846, the four Society of Arts exhibitions in London from 1847 to 1850, Birmingham 1849, the Crystal Palace 1851, Dublin and New York 1853, and Paris 1855.

Exhibition furniture

These records have been deliberately placed last because they give an entirely misleading picture of the average production of the times. The illustrated catalogue of the Great Exhibition of 1851, being far more readily accessible than any of the other documentary sources just listed, has too often been used as exclusive evidence of early Victorian taste, without allowance for the fact that the furniture displayed in the Crystal Palace – in common with all the other exhibits – was mainly shown for its novelty and inventiveness. Richard Redgrave, R.A., was certainly not exaggerating when he criticized the whole principle of international exhibitions, and wrote that: 'Each manufacturer is striving his utmost to attain notice and reward ... by an endeavour to catch the consumers by startling novelty or meretricious decoration, leading, in most cases, to an extreme redundancy of ornament. The goods are like the gilded cakes in the booths of our country fairs, no longer for use, but to attract customers.' (*Report on the Present State of Design as Applied to Manufactures*, 1857.)

Where – as with Gillows' – it is possible to compare their exhibits with their everyday production, it is clear that the former were in no way typical of the latter, and the same was no doubt equally true of the other leading firms such as Jackson and Graham, Johnstone and Jeanes, and Snell. Moreover, the exhibition catalogues (especially the illustrations, which were paid for by the exhibitors) give a false impression of the relative importance of the various manufacturers, and in particular greatly exaggerate the real weight of the West End luxury firms such as Morant, John Webb, Levien, and Toms and Luscombe, who staged elaborate special displays of their wares. Indeed, so distorting are the conclusions usually drawn from these exhibitions, that it is advisable to dismiss the two principal ones before passing to a positive analysis of early Victorian styles.

The first misconception is that early Victorian furniture is fussy and elaborate, and generally covered with carving. This was certainly true of almost all the Crystal Palace exhibits. Few were quite so preposterous as the much-publicized bog-oak examples of Arthur J. Jones and Co. of Dublin, with carving so elaborate that a description of its symbolic significance required several pages, but even respectable firms such as Howard and Sons, and George Trollope and Sons, placed their main emphasis on pieces 'enriched by carved floriated ornament of cunning workmanship', to quote a contemporary account. The same preoccupation is shown by the way in which leading firms such as Snell and Co. and the Coalbrookdale Iron Company, when they wished to improve their standing by some specially-commissioned prestige pieces, turned for designs not to leading architects, as would have been normal in other periods, but to popular sculptors such as Baron Marochetti and John Bell.

This emphasis on decorative carving was no doubt the inevitable result of the competitive ostentation fostered by the spirit of the Exhibition, but it can also be partly explained by the influence of the propaganda and prizes of the Society of Arts in their preparations for the Exhibition, in which the personal enthusiasm of Prince Albert – with his memories of German peasant wood-carving – was a strong ingredient. It cannot, however, be said to have had any influence on the general run of furniture production. Indeed, its only noticeable effect, outside the Exhibition, was to encourage skilful wood-carvers such as W.G. Rogers – often referred to by contemporary commentators as the 'Victorian Grinling Gibbons' – and Thomas Wallis of Louth, and to stimulate noble patronage for the curious school of Warwick wood-carving represented by the firms of William Cookes and James Morris Willcox. Both these firms, and later the firm of William Kendall, who had originally been apprenticed to Willcox, pro-

duced between 1848 and 1860 a considerable quantity of carved furniture in a highly elaborate 'naturalistic' style, in which every article was enriched with carving with a narrative or symbolic significance, executed with the attention to detail of a *trompe l'œil* (Pls. 29–32). Their work is seen at its worst in such over-carved monstrosities as the 'Kenilworth Buffet' (1851) now at Warwick Castle, and at its best in Cookes's Alscot Park buffet (designed by Hugues Protat for the Great Exhibition of 1851 but actually shown at the Manchester Art Treasures Exhibition, 1857, Pl. 29), or Willcox's splendid sideboard (1858) now at Charlecote Park (Pl. 32).

Early Victorian conservatism

The second misconception for which the Great Exhibition catalogues have been mainly responsible is that early Victorian furniture was subject to a constantly shifting succession of stylistic revivals in which it is impossible to discern any consistent thread. A close examination of contemporary pattern-books – and particularly of the Gillow records – shows on the contrary that furniture fashions changed remarkably little between 1835 and 1860, and that the Early Victorian period was in this respect far more conservative than either the Regency or the mid-Victorian. One of the clearest testimonies to this conservatism is the fact that Thomas King's pattern-book *The Modern Style of Cabinet Work Exemplified* (1829) was reissued without alteration in 1862, while the furniture sections of J.C. Loudon's compendious *Encyclopædia of Cottage, Farm, and Villa Architecture* (1833) were incorporated with nothing omitted and very little added in all the later editions (1842, 1846, 1857). By comparison it would be quite impossible to imagine a pattern-book of 1810 being issued unchanged in 1840, or one of 1850 being reissued in 1880.

This Early Victorian conservatism may well have been the direct result of that rise of the *nouveau riche* patron, which is usually held to have upset all traditional standards of taste. Their lack of independent æsthetic standards, and their conformist social aspirations, would seem as likely to

D

have counselled a prudent acceptance of established conventions as to have led these new patrons into any stylistic adventures. Moreover, this tendency would have been reinforced by the fact that, as the demand for furniture increased, so did the proportion that was produced by firms without their own designers, and which were therefore compelled to keep to the repetition of stock patterns with no pretence of originality – a trend which was strengthened by the detailed price-schedules set out in successive editions of the *London Cabinet-Makers' Union Book of Rules* (1811, 1824, 1836), which gave the small employer every incentive to keep to the accepted patterns, rather than to launch out on new designs and thus risk pricing troubles with his workmen.

Before passing to an analysis of the consistent style which subsisted throughout most of the Early Victorian period, we must first glance at the very rapid and radical stylistic changes which were its prelude, over the years 1827 to 1835. Fortunately their documentation is made relatively easy by the survival of a wide variety of pattern-books covering these crucial years. The key to the changes was, of course, the breakdown of that long hegemony of the various styles based on the antique – whether Greek, Roman, Pompeian or Egyptian – which until 1827 had been challenged only by the Gothic – and then in only a very limited field. By 1830, however, they were faced with two new competitors – the revived Louis XIV style, and the revived Elizabethan.

The 'Louis XIV' revival

The reintroduction of Louis XIV furniture and furnishings can be dated precisely to 1827, when Crockford's new club-house was decorated by Philip and Benjamin Dean Wyatt. This was interpreted by the London decorators as authority to abandon the austerities of the 'Modern Grecian', and to revert to the opulent splendours of the *ancien régime*, whether in their baroque or rococo forms. Already by 1828 the change is visible in patterns for mirrors, frames, window cornices and the like, with scrolls and shells replacing the hitherto ubiquitous anthemion. By 1830 it had spread to movable furniture, and particularly to drawing-room chair-backs. Although evidently welcomed by the trade, this change was unanimously condemned by architects and designers who saw it as opening the gates to any hack furniture-maker who could now throw together an assortment of botched-up scrolls, cover them with gilding, and label them 'in the old French style'.

A critical attitude to the new style had already been voiced by George Smith (*Cabinet-Maker's and Upholsterer's Guide, Drawing-Book and Repository*) immediately after the opening of Crockford's Club, with the comment that 'As this mansion is solely appropriated to nightly purposes of pleasure, perhaps such a taste may be in unison with the wasteful transfer of property made in such establishments.' Similar views were presented before the Select Committee on Arts and Manufactures (1835), by witnesses such as J.B.Papworth and C.R.Cockerell, who not only deplored the licence provided to inferior designers by the new style, but also pointed out how what had started as a revival of the baroque splendours of Louis XIV very rapidly degenerated by its own internal momentum into indiscriminate borrowing from the rococo trivialities of Louis XV. Despite this almost universal condemnation by serious architects, however, the spread of these 'old French' styles was very rapid, especially for drawing-rooms and boudoirs. The extent to which the change was limited to these more feminine rooms, while leaving the furnishings of more masculine quarters relatively untouched, is very clearly shown by the suites of furniture supplied in 1833–4 by Messrs. W. and C. Wilkinsons to Goldsmiths' Hall, under the supervision of the architect, Philip Hardwick (Pls. 21–3, 27). It will be seen that, whereas the furniture for the Court Drawing-Room is entirely in the new style, that for the Court Dining-Room and for the Court Room itself shows little variation from the standard patterns of the 1820's. Indeed, for the more traditionalist institutions, these 'Modern Greek' designs remained in vogue for at least ten years longer, as witness the furniture designed by Henry Whitaker for the Conservative Club in 1844 (Pls. 23, 24).

The 'Elizabethan' revival

The Elizabethan revival was, by contrast, a conscious creation of the more sophisticated architects and designers such as C.J.Richardson. It first appears in furniture pattern-books just after 1830, directly inspired no doubt by the plates in T.F. Hunt's *Exemplars of Tudor Architecture and Furniture* (1829–30), closely followed by Henry Shaw's *Specimens of Ancient Furniture* (1832–6). In the early 1830's it was mainly limited to the making up of pseudo-Elizabethan cupboards and coffers out of old fragments, by firms such as Samuel Hanson, and James Nixon (see Loudon's *Encyclopædia* and Georges Fildes' *Elizabethan Furniture* (1844)). After about 1838 it takes its place in all the pattern-books in the form of strap-work carving applied to mirror-frames, sideboard-backs and the like. This Elizabethan revival was supported by the same arguments which were used to condemn the revival of the French styles. It was indisputably British; it was rich without being vulgar; and its coarse vigour did not overtax the somewhat limited finesse of the average British carver. Moreover, its romantic and baronial associations were, of course, entirely in keeping with current literary preoccupations.

By about 1835 both the Louis XIV and the Elizabethan styles had clearly established their right to equal respectability with the Gothic and the 'Grecian', and the long hegemony of the latter had finally ended. The change is summed up by the distinction between two of Thomas King's titles: in 1829 he published *The Modern Style of Cabinet Work Exemplified*, whereas in 1834 his *Designs for Carving and Gilding* bore the subtitle *in a variety of styles*. With four quite different styles legitimate, there was now no obstacle to an even more catholic eclecticism, and during the later 1830's we find an astonishing proliferation of titles, including the *Arabesque, the French Renaissance, the Cinque-Cento*, and so on. Indeed, the most noticeable feature of the pattern-books of the years 1835 to 1850 – best exemplified by Henry Whitaker's *Practical Cabinet-Maker* (1847) – is the determination that no design should be presented without an attribution to some historic style, and that the greatest possible variety of stylistic titles should be devised for this purpose.

It would be quite wrong, however, to take this eclecticism at its face value, for, oddly enough, it was just when it first became all-embracing – around 1835 – that we can first discern the emergence of a consistent and distinguishable Early Victorian style. We may, in fact, claim that it was only when the rigid classical hegemony had been finally broken, and when designers could at last give form to their personal fantasies in a now unfettered eclecticism, that the real spirit of the period begins to achieve spontaneous expression in its furniture. Moreover, so strong was the appeal of historicism at this time that even the most individual inventions had to be designated as in some earlier style, and we should not be surprised, therefore, to find designs which bear the unmistakable Early Victorian stamp, and which could not possibly have been produced at any other time, being solemnly described as 'in the purest François Premier taste'. One of the fascinations of Early Victorian furniture is the way in which its original quality is often clearest in just those cases where the designer evidently believed himself to have been most faithfully following historical precedent. This is particularly clearly seen in those frequent cases where the same designer has worked in a different style for each room – Gothic for the hall, Elizabethan for the library, Louis XIV for the drawing-room, and so on – but has nevertheless left a consistent Early Victorian stamp on each in turn.

Emphasis on comfort

It must be admitted that it is easier to refer to this Early Victorian style in general terms than to list its distinguishing characteristics in detail. They can be more readily illustrated than described. Paradoxically, in an age that was so obsessed with problems of stylistic purity, its keynote was the subordination of all stylistic considerations to the over-riding consideration of comfort. In this it contrasts sharply not only with the 1820's (as witness the primacy of stylistic criteria in the designs of Richard Brown, George Smith and the Nicholsons), but equally with the mid-Victorian period, in which – contrary to general belief – comfort once more took second place to various stylistic mannerisms, whether derived from the Middle Ages, from Sheraton or from Japan. A similar contrast also differentiates this early Victorian style from developments in France, and makes it possible to claim it as the first English style which marked a clear-cut divergence from contemporary French trends. It is perhaps no accident, therefore, that one of the earliest recognitions of its emergence, with a clear analysis of its revolutionary emphasis on comfort, should be found in a French discussion of the difference between French and English furniture as demonstrated by the Paris Exhibition of 1834. (Stéphane Flachat, *L'Industrie: Exposition de 1834.*)

Increased use of upholstery

An obvious corollary to this concentration on comfort was the increased use of padding and upholstery of all kinds, and in particular the evolution for the first time of articles of furniture in which the shape is determined much more by the upholstery than by the framework which it covers. It is sometimes suggested that this development can be related to technical advances in spring construction. In fact, however, these had already been made in the first decade of the century, and a more plausible explanation of these Early Victorian changes was the great improvement in cheap worsted covering-materials resulting from the expansion of Yorkshire power-loom weaving during the 1830's. Although these upholstery changes directly affected only chairs, sofas, ottomans and the like, they influenced, by association, the shapes of all furniture, and it is precisely the rounding-off of all corners and the elimination of all angularities and surface irregularities which is the main distinguishing characteristic of the Early Victorian style. All sharp outlines are smoothed down, rectangular frameworks become oval or semi-circular, edges are bevelled, and projecting pediments or finials are removed. At the same time all crispness or spring disappears from members such as table-supports or chair-backs, and is replaced by a uniform, flabby, unadventurous, heavy-handed curve – a curve which almost gives the wood the appearance of having been squeezed from a tube, and which is contrasted not only with the taut and basically rectilinear outlines of the Regency, but equally with the elegant twistings of the 'old French' styles.

Parallel with these developments went a tendency to merge the separate parts of each piece of furniture into a unified, undifferentiated whole. Arms and backs of sofas are joined together in a single enclosing sweep. Front and sides of chiffoniers are likewise embraced in a single enveloping semi-circle. The distinction between pedestal and base in the standard Regency loo-table is obliterated. Moreover, this process was visually accentuated by the virtual elimination of all the many processes by which cabinet-makers have traditionally varied the colour and texture of their surfaces. Inlay, marquetry and boulle-work, and the use of gilding and ormolu, went out of fashion for all normal domestic furniture soon after 1830, and it was not until about 1855 that there was any sign of their revival. The same tendency affected all knobs and handles, which were now usually made of plain wood rather than of metal. Even the use of contrasted woods was frowned on, and the various exotic timbers so favoured during the Regency – such as zebra-wood, satinwood and amboyna – were discarded in favour of plain mahogany, rosewood or walnut, and oak for furniture in the Gothic or Elizabethan taste. It should perhaps be emphasized that this preference for solid unadorned wood did not necessarily involve an increase in weight, for it is often possible to reduce both the size and weight by using solid timber in place of veneered surfaces on a separate core.

When we contrast this use of plain undecorated wood with the metal inlays and zoomorphic carving of the Regency, or with the inset porcelain medallions and embossed leather panels, which were so popular in the 1860's, we can see how wide of the mark is the belief that typical Early Victorian furniture must be over-ornamented and fussy. It may therefore be as well to confirm the point by a quotation from the most perceptive contemporary comment on Early Victorian furniture in general, namely Matthew Digby Wyatt's already mentioned *Report on the Furniture at the Paris Exhibition of 1855*. In his report he laments the conservative habits of the English cabinet-makers, who, for over a generation, had been content with 'good joinery, glueing up, and mitering, smooth, plain, veneering, and clean but not intricate turning', and criticizes them severely for having deliberately turned their backs on more elaborate surface treatments with carving or marquetry.

The use of wood substitutes

Reference should perhaps be made here to the use of wood-substitutes. Perusal of the catalogue of the Great Exhibition, and even more of the catalogues of the four Society of Arts Exhibitions which preceded it, might lead to the conclusion that a great deal of Early Victorian furniture made use of patent materials such as gutta-percha, stamped leather, carton-pierre, Albano's canabic composition, and so on. The evidence of the Gillow records, however, supported by accounts of current trade methods such as the comprehensive report incorporated in Blackie's *Cabinet-Maker's Assistant* (1853), show that, with the exception of papier-mâché, which is in rather a different category, these substitutes never had much currency. Perhaps the only decisive change in materials during this period arose from the universal introduction of Italian marble tops for washstands, and also to some extent for sideboards and chiffoniers, during the 1840's, as a result of price-reductions consequent on the perfection of steam-driven marble-cutting machines in the 1830's. The parallel efforts in the 1840's to popularize British substitutes such as the Derbyshire and Limerick near-marbles, and Magnus' patent painted slate, made no permanent impact, and ambitious projects like the fantastic slate-furniture at Penrhyn Castle must have been quite exceptional.

The use of machinery

A similar false impression results from assuming that the various wood-working machines, especially the patent carving machines of Irving, and of Taylor, Williams and Jordan, as demonstrated at these same exhibitions, were already in regular

commercial use during this period and influenced in some way the design of Early Victorian furniture. There is very little evidence to support this view. It is true that Henry Cole, in the guise of *Felix Summerly's Art Manufactures*, attempted, as one would expect, to exploit Jordan's patent, with a fantastic arm-chair called 'The Repose', which incorporated numerous figures designed by J.C. Horsley, the painter. It is also known that C.J. Richardson, the Elizabethan enthusiast, made designs especially for it. Neither the Gillow records nor the Blackie account, however, include any evidence of these mechanical developments. Moreover, the most authoritative contemporary report on the whole subject (a paper by G.L. Molesworth *On the Conversion of Wood by Machinery* to the Institute of Civil Engineers, 17 November 1857) implies that regularly used machinery at that date was limited to circular- and band-saws, and planing and mortising machines, which could have had little influence on design. There is, however, some reason to believe that the increased use of fret-cutting in the 1850's may have been connected with the perfecting of Sandy and Powell's fret-cutting machinery.

Stylistic changes from 1850–60

These generalizations about the 'Early Victorian style', are intended to apply to the whole period from 1835 to 1860. It must be admitted, however, that they require some slight qualifications when applied to new furniture designs produced after 1850. The most marked change thereafter was a tendency away from the completely upholstered chairs and sofas of the 1840's. Shapes remained unchanged, but the wooden framework was now usually visible rather than completely concealed as hitherto, and the incorporation of a little openwork carving, and especially fret-cutting, as just mentioned, became acceptable. Half-padded arms took their place beside the earlier fully-padded sides for easy-chairs. Visible legs were substituted for the solid box-upholstery of ottomans. These changes were not pronounced enough to invalidate the continued vitality of the Early Victorian style down to, and even beyond, 1860, but they anticipated further

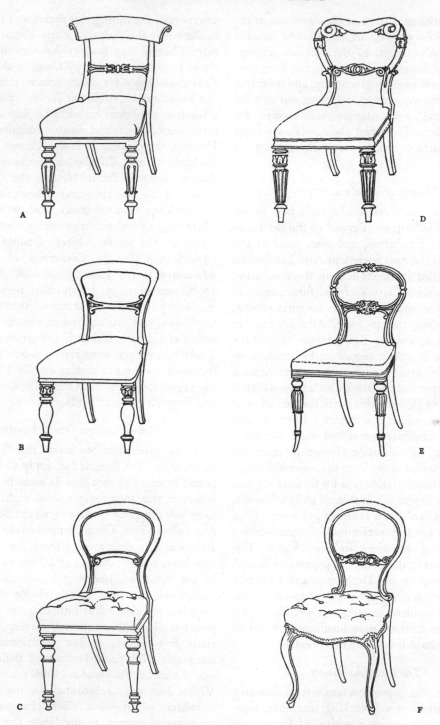

Fig. 1. The development of the Balloon back chair. (A), (B) and (C) are typical dining-room chairs, c. 1830, 1835 and 1850 respectively. (D), (E) and (F) are typical drawing-room chairs, c. 1830, 1835 and 1850 respectively.

changes which began to gather momentum in the very last years of our period, and which ultimately affected a radical transformation of English furniture styles in the late 1860's.

All that can be said here is that the basis of this later transformation was a reversal to straight lines in reaction against the Early Victorian curve, and a revival of interest in every type of polychromatic surface-treatment after the long reign of undecorated French polish. Only one facet of this complex transformation was already becoming visible before 1860, namely the revival of Louis XVI styles. This revival was inaugurated at the Paris Exhibition of 1855, and was signalized for English cabinet-makers in particular by a remarkable cabinet exhibited by Jackson and Graham, which gained them a 'Medal of Honour'. This splendid piece – it has unfortunately not proved possible to discover its present whereabouts – broke right away from early Victorian tradition. In the employment of French designers and modellers, in the use of satinwood and tulipwood in place of mahogany and rosewood, in the revival of marquetry and ormolu, and the incorporation of porcelain plaques, it fully anticipated all the characteristics of that elegant, elaborate style – sometimes thought of as a Sheraton revival – usually associated with the work of firms such as Wright and Mansfield or Holland and Sons in the 1860's and 1870's. Indeed, although one or two pattern-books published between 1855 and 1860 already incorporate a few 'Louis XVI designs', and although percipient contemporary commentators such as Richard Redgrave (who curiously called it the 'Gauthier' – though he presumably meant 'Gouthière' – style) noticed the change; its general impact was hardly yet discernible, and the fully-fledged revival of this style can be legitimately placed beyond the limits of the Early Victorian period.

These conclusions about the Early Victorian style in general must now be applied in turn to the main categories of furniture.

Chairs

The Early Victorian period was responsible for two significant contributions to chair design. The first, and most important, was the development of the balloon-back chair. In 1830 this was entirely unknown; by 1860 it had become by far the commonest type both for dining- and drawing-rooms. The stages by which it developed during the intervening years can be traced fairly accurately, but it is very difficult to offer any satisfactory explanation as to why it appeared just when it did. Strangely enough, contemporary writers on furniture seem to have been completely unaware of this basic change, and it has not proved possible to trace even a single contemporary reference to it. All that can be said with confidence is that it was an indigenous English development, not taken over from France.

In 1830 almost all chairs were still of a uniform sub-classical pattern, with a broad horizontal yoke-rail extending well beyond the plain uprights (which merely continued upwards the line of the back legs), a much narrower carved horizontal splat, a padded seat, and straight front legs. In the case of dining-room or parlour chairs, variations of this standard pattern were limited to the carving of the splat and to the slight enrichment of the ends of the yoke-rail with volutes and the like. In the case of drawing-room chairs the basic classical type was being increasingly challenged by the recently revived Louis XIV style, which at the least involved carving the yoke-rail and splat with baroque scrolls, and at the most replacing them by an elaborately carved back entirely made up of contrasting scrolls. In either case the front seat-rail and legs remained straight, and there was as yet no return to the cabriole leg.

The balloon-back seems to have developed from the simultaneous modification after 1830 of both the yoke-rail dining-room type and the scroll-back drawing-room type. By 1835 we find dining-room versions in which the yoke-rail has been rounded-off and made continuous with the uprights, and at the same time a simplified drawing-room chair in which the scroll-carving has been almost eliminated, leaving a plain curved top. The step from these two types to the fully-fledged balloon-back was easily made in the next ten years.

Once established, the balloon-back rapidly

became predominant, until by 1850 almost all trace of the classical yoke-rail had disappeared. It remained the standard pattern until the late 1860's, in a more austere form for the dining-room or library, and with carved enrichments within the basic rounded top for the drawing-room or boudoir. After 1850 cabriole legs usually replaced the earlier straight legs for the drawing-room versions.

Throughout this period bedroom or 'fancy' chairs followed the same changes, but with a lighter build – mahogany being replaced by japanned or stained birch or maple, the padded seat being replaced by cane, and the flimsier legs being strengthened by double side-stretchers.

The second original contribution to chair-design was the tall-backed, short-legged, low-seated, entirely upholstered chair, sometimes called a 'devotional', 'prie-dieu' or 'vesper' chair (Pl. 26A). This typical example of attention to the functional requirements of comfort at the expense of appearance seems to have been derived from the cane-backed Charles II chair, which, owing to a curious and incomprehensible confusion, was thought by the early Elizabethan enthusiasts to be a typical sixteenth-century design. By 1840 it had developed in two different directions. On the one hand, the more ambitious designers, such as Bridgens and Whitaker, elaborated a whole series of tall-backed chairs with turned legs and uprights, and incorporating heavy strap-work carving – a type which was carried into the 1850's by Blackie's already-quoted *Cabinet-Makers' Assistant*. On the other hand, the humbler men such as Henry Wood transformed it into the typical Early Victorian drawing-room chair, covered in Berlin wool-work, and decorated with tassels and fringes. The earliest of these date from about 1835 and they remained in favour until after 1860 (Pl. 26B). The specifically 'devotional' version, as found for example in Henry Lawford's design-books (1855), had a T-shaped tall back with a padded top-rest for use during family prayers.

The only other specifically Early Victorian chair style was the child's chair with straight tall back, tall legs and double-stretchers, called after Sir Astley Cooper (1768–1841), the anatomist on whose principles it was designed.

Sofas, couches, ottomans and easy-chairs

The Early Victorian emphasis on comfort rather than 'style' can be traced very clearly in the design of sofas, couches and ottomans. In 1830 the standard sofa had a rectangular plan, with straight back, front-rail and ends, all at right-angles to each other. Moreover, although the back might be slightly canted and the ends might curve over, all the horizontal lines were also straight. The only relief to the austere impression was provided by slight carved or inlaid enrichments – usually in the form of the anthemion – to the front-rail and the front surface of the arms, and by the two cylindrical bolster-cushions.

For more opulent interiors this standard neo-classical form had, from 1827 onwards, to meet the competition of the more heavily ornamented revived Louis XIV sofa, which usually took the form of a basically classical shape with the addition of carved and gilt cresting. For more normal domestic use the neo-classic remained in favour until the late 1830's, and was then superseded not by the baroque or rococo scrolls of the French eighteenth century, but by a styleless Early Victorian compromise. This had a straight front rail and plain legs, but a back which was rounded in both elevation and plan and was structurally continuous with the ends or arms. The typical version of the 1840's, as seen in the Smee pattern-books for example, was padded all over, with no wood visible except in the diminutive legs, and variations in design were therefore limited to the outline of the back, which was sometimes humped up in the centre and sometimes at each end.

In the 1850's the basic shape remained unchanged, but there was now a tendency to reintroduce a visible wooden framework to the back and arms, and the single-, twin- or even triple-humped back often incorporated elaborately carved or fretworked open panels. The variant known as the 'sociable', 'conversation sofa', or 'tête-à-tête', with the two ends facing each other on the lines of the French 'causeuse' (Pl. 25B), was popular for a short time during the 1840's, but seems to have already gone out of favour by the mid-1850's. It provided the hack designers with opportunities for some of their most fanciful inventions.

Single-ended couches followed the same changes as sofas, with an emphasis during the 1830's on an entirely plain type with a slightly canted end, designed to support the back while reading. This seems first to have been evolved by Thomas King, but it was immediately taken over by the trade generally as an 'Adelaide' couch.

Ottomans provided a more informal companion to the sofa throughout this period. Up to about 1845 the normal form was extremely simple, consisting merely of a plain free-standing upholstered box with a back and cushions, and with seats either on two or all four sides. By 1850 it had generally become more elaborate, with a visible wooden framework round the upholstery and with short legs in place of the previous box-base. A common pattern had the seat divided into compartments by arms, and sometimes the compartments formed individual segments which could be placed together or separately, as convenient. In the more pretentious examples the central back was surmounted by a *jardinière*.

Easy, or 'lounging' chairs, as they were usually called, tended to follow the same lines of development as sofas, and may therefore conveniently be considered with them. The basic transformation from the rectangular version of the 1830's to the tubby and rounded style of the 1850's can more readily be illustrated than described. For a short time in the early 1850's there was a vogue for a particularly clumsy-looking type in which the back, although separated from the arms, was joined to them by a separate member running from the cresting down to the arm-rest. The only other type deserving mention was the library-chair with the normal back and arms replaced by a heavily padded continuous horizontal semi-circle. This first appears in the 1840's with the semi-circle supported only in the centre, but by 1860 it had been modified so that the padded semi-circle was supported by turned balusters round its whole length, and as such remained a standard type until well into the twentieth century.

Tables

By comparison with other articles of furniture, tables afford little evidence of changes in Early Victorian taste. The standard extending dining-room table, the various types of occasional table, the ingenious rising side-tables operated with pulley and weights on the principle of the sash-window, and even the drawing-room work-table with pouch, altered comparatively little during the thirty years under review. Only the circular loo-table showed significant changes, which took two forms. In the first place, there was a tendency in the 1850's to enrich the top, which from 1830 to 1850 had normally been completely plain, either with a gadrooned moulding or with a scalloped outline. In the second place, the standard 1830 type with a clearly differentiated supporting pedestal – usually pyramidical – resting on a flat triangular block, itself often standing on claw or paw feet, slowly evolved over the next twenty years, until by 1850 it was normal for the three legs to flow directly from the central column in loose and relaxed curves which typify the more spineless qualities of the Early Victorian style. In the 1850's a more elaborate support, with a central column supplemented by three or four thinner ones, was introduced, and is found not only in the designs of men like Peter Thomson and John Dwyer, but even in the cheaper pattern-books. There seems little doubt that this is a case where a design originally evolved as suitable for cast iron, was later taken over and translated into wood.

In considering all Early Victorian tables, it must never be forgotten that, as A. J. Downing put it in 1850, 'they depend for this good effect mainly on the drapery or cover of handsome cloth or stuff usually spread upon their top and concealing all but the lower part of the legs' (*The Architecture of Country Houses*).

Sideboards and chiffoniers

The development of the sideboard during this period gives us the clearest evidence of that tendency to round off all angularities which we have claimed as one of the most typical manifestations of the Early Victorian style. Throughout the whole period the pedestal type of sideboard was the

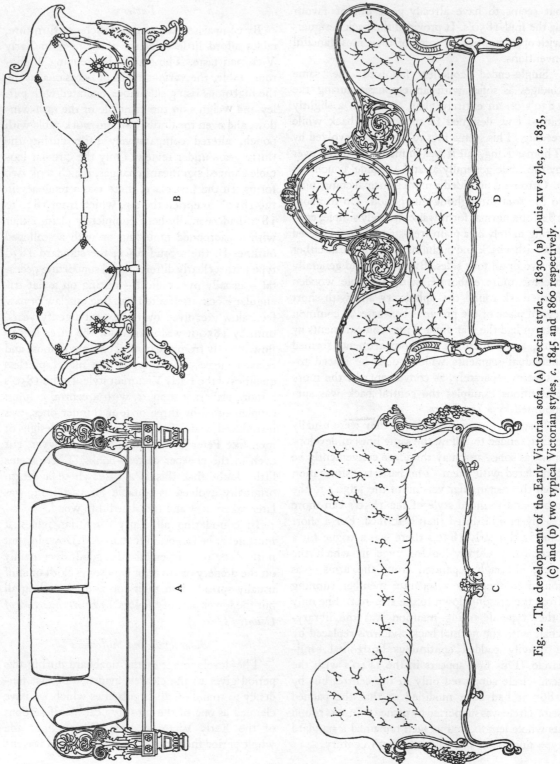

Fig. 2. The development of the Early Victorian sofa. (A) Grecian style, *c.* 1830, (B) Louis XIV style, *c.* 1835, (C) and (D) two typical Victorian styles, *c.* 1845 and 1860 respectively.

standard pattern for normal domestic purposes, with open-legged types rarely used. In 1830 the shape was rigidly rectangular, with a low wooden rectangular backboard. By 1840 backs were being made higher and were beginning to incorporate mirrors, which usually followed the three-fold division of the base, with a larger mirror in the centre, flanked by two smaller ones over the pedestals – still with rectangular outlines. By 1850 backs were higher still, and it became customary to raise the centre mirror above the flanking ones and to give all three semi-circular rather than rectangular crestings. By 1860 it was more common for the whole back to be merged into a single semi-circular mirror. Precisely the same development affected the pedestals, though with a time-lag, and it was not until after 1850 that the change towards a semi-circular elevation for the sideboard was paralleled by a semi-circular plan also, with the outer angles of the pedestals rounded-off.

The same changes can be traced even more clearly in the more modest chiffonier, which was regarded as the appropriate article for a dining-room which was too small or unpretentious for a full-scale sideboard. As an anonymous domestic manual of 1851 (*How to Furnish a House and Make it a Home*), points out, a sideboard with pedestals looks ridiculous if less than about 4 ft. wide, whereas a chiffonier, with its solid front, could reasonably be as small as 3 ft. wide. The standard type in the 1830's had a small shelf projecting from the wooden backboard, and supported on turned balusters or Louis XIV trusses, according to taste. There were usually two cupboards in front, with wire-grille doors backed with pleated silk. More elaborate examples incorporated a set of small bookshelves. As with the sideboards, the wooden backboard was gradually replaced by a mirror-back, the pleated silk was replaced by wooden or glass doors, the plan became semicircular, and curved open shelves were fitted on either side of the central cupboards.

When we turn to the more pretentious designs, either for sideboards or chiffoniers, we find a particularly rich crop of 'Elizabethan' examples. Whereas the first enthusiasm for the re-vived Louis XIV and XV styles during the years 1827–35 found its most natural expression in upholstered drawing-room furniture, the 'Elizabethan', with its emphasis on heavily carved solid oak, was thought to be especially well adapted to the more manly articles such as sideboards or buffets. The first examples, in the early 1830's, were merely reproductions of original Jacobean pieces. By 1838, however, we find men like Bridgens designing original 'Elizabethan' sideboards covered with carved strapwork for their rich clients (such as James Watt, the then owner of Aston Hall), and even the conservative firm of Gillow produced in 1841 a whole suite of most elaborately carved furniture in the Elizabethan style for the Richmond-Gale-Braddyll family of Conishead Priory. Every pattern-book of the 1840's, such as those of Henry Wood, automatically contained some elaborately carved Elizabethan sideboards, and these were continued into the 1850's also by Peter Thomson and others. The only slight change after 1850 – no doubt stimulated by the Great Exhibition – was for plain strapwork to be enlivened by the incorporation of naturalistic carved ornament usually with a 'literary-functionalist' flavour. In the case of sideboards this required the introduction of dead game, fishing-tackle, grapes and the like, as the appropriate symbols. Apart from the few first-class examples, which have already been referred to in connection with the Warwick school, this trend produced little of merit, for the carving is almost always perfunctory and mechanical.

Miscellaneous furniture

Of the many miscellaneous articles of furniture which made up the typical Victorian home, not much need be said. Certain types which were in regular use up to the 1830's, then virtually disappeared – such as the semi-circular wine-table, the ubiquitous Regency tripod-stand, the commode and (after about 1840) the classical hall-couch. Other types, such as footstools, fire-screens (Pls. 28A, 30B), work-tables and flower-stands, continued in use and faithfully reflected the changes of taste already mentioned for the more important items. Still others, such as

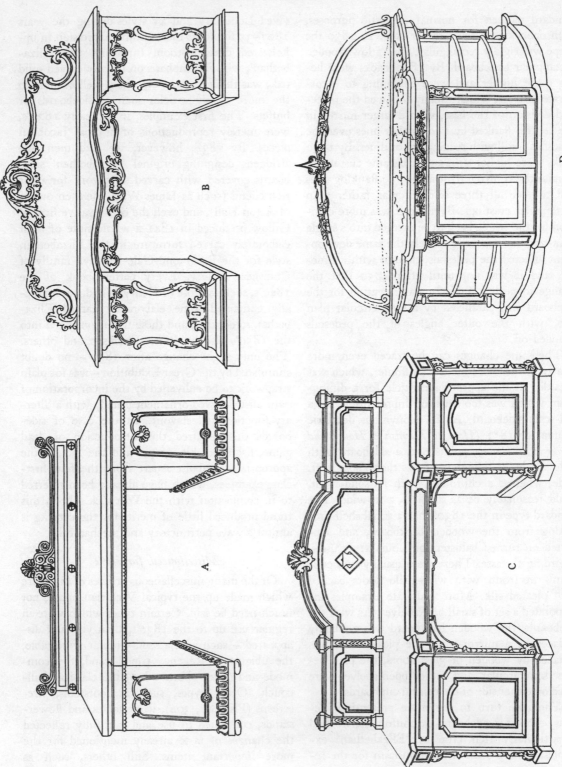

Fig. 3. The development of the Early Victorian sideboard. (A) Grecian style, c. 1830, (B) Louis XIV style, c. 1835, (C) Elizabethan style, c. 1845, and (D) a typical Victorian style, c. 1860.

davenports, table-flap cases, canterburies, music-stools and portfolio-stands, changed little throughout the period.

Almost the only article of furniture which first sprang into regular use during this period was the whatnot. Although known earlier, it only became a standard article after about 1840. The only change worth mentioning is that after about 1855 the earlier free-standing type takes second place to the later corner variety.

Gothic furniture

Gothic furniture requires separate mention, for throughout this period it remained rather isolated from normal furniture fashions. It was rarely regarded as appropriate for rooms other than the hall or library, or exceptionally for panelled rooms in old houses. The production of a whole range of Gothic furniture, such as that designed for Snelston Hall, Derbyshire, by L.N.Cottingham, the antiquarian, in 1844 (Pl. 25A), was quite exceptional. Normally speaking, the term merely implied a superficial tracery-pattern on the back of a hall-seat, or the incorporation of linen-fold panelling into a library settle. For obvious reasons the Elizabethan revival in the 1830's led to a good deal of confusion with the Gothic, and in many pattern-books of the 1840's it would be quite impossible, were it not for the captions, to know which style was intended.

It does not seem that the publication of A.W.N.Pugin's *Gothic Furniture* in 1835, and his many other efforts to propagate a true understanding of Gothic principles, had any marked effect on general furniture production; presumably because his admonitions appeared to be addressed mainly to architects and because the excellent and chaste Gothic furniture (Pl. 22B) which he himself designed for several of his clients was never illustrated. The only sign of his influence was the elaborate Gothic furniture which J.G.Crace – who had previously worked in entirely different styles – began to produce at the end of the 1840's, and which is typified by the well-known bookcase, supposedly to Pugin's own design, exhibited in the Medieval Court of the 1851 Exhibition, and now in the Victoria and Albert Museum, a remarkable range of pieces which he produced for Sir James Watts of Abney Hall near Stockport, in 1847, and an imposing piece which earned him an award at the Paris Exhibition of 1855.

Metal furniture

Metal furniture also requires separate mention. It falls into two categories. The first comprises cast-iron garden-furniture and hall-furniture, such as hat and umbrella stands and flower stands. This was made as a by-product of their normal industrial work by iron foundries such as Coalbrookdale, Shropshire, the Carron Company, Stirlingshire, and various smaller foundries in the area round Birmingham, such as Archibald Kendrick of Walsall, and Thomas Marsh of Dudley. It was already in production before 1830, but had a particular vogue between 1845 and 1855. During this period Coalbrookdale especially made great efforts to produce a full range of indoor cast-iron furniture, including pieces for living-rooms upholstered in damask or velvet. The majority were designed by Charles Crooke, but they also called in outside artists. Judging from contemporary illustrations of examples such as the 'hall stand for hats, cloaks, umbrellas, with looking glass, lamp, letter and brush box, and inkstand all combined', designed 'after a suggestion by Felix Summerly', which won a Gold Isis medal from the Society of Arts in 1849, and the 'deer-hound table' designed by John Bell, the popular sculptor, for the Paris Exhibition of 1855, one may hope that these ludicrous and impractical examples have all long since disappeared. The present-day habit of painting surviving pieces white may help to conceal their inherent ugliness, but at the cost of falsifying their original appearance, for they were normally produced in only three finishes: 'Berlin-black, bronzed, or japanned in imitation of oak'.

The second category consisted of brass furniture, produced by a different section of the Birmingham trade, namely the brass-foundries, who added beds to their traditional output of cornice-poles, fenders and the like. Although brass beds were being manufactured by 1825, they made so little impact at first that as late as 1844 the 'Art Union' reported the French metal furniture shown at the Paris Exhibition of that year as a great novelty. After about 1845, however, there was a spurt in Birmingham production, mainly as a result of Peyton and Harlow's patent (1841) for taper tubing. Their main competitor was R.W. Winfield, who produced some very attractive ornamental brass beds in the late 1840's.

In addition to these two main categories, there was also during this period a certain amount of experimental metal furniture, ranging from Mallet's preposterous chairs made of riveted gas-tubing, sponsored by J.C.Loudon in the 1830's, to elegant and practical pieces in square-section or strip brass.

Papier-mâché furniture

Although it is papier-mâché furniture which most readily comes to mind when the Early Victorian period is in question, it would be quite wrong to suppose that it was as frequently found in the average Early Victorian home as it now is in second-hand shops or in 'period rooms' in museums. The fact that the bulk of papier-mâché furniture can safely be assumed to be early Victorian, that marked pieces are fairly common, and that its pictorial decoration makes it susceptible to classification into various sub-groupings, has contributed to invest it with an exaggerated importance. If allowance is made for the fact that almost all the more attractive examples were made by the single firm of Jennens and Bettridge, and that both they and the other leading firms such as Loveridge, Thomas Farmer, Dean and Benson, and Footherape, Showell and Shenton of Birmingham, and Walton of Wolverhampton, were mainly occupied in making trays and boxes rather than movable furniture as such, it is statistically obvious that the total output of papier-mâché furniture must always have formed a very small fraction of the wood furniture turned out by cabinet-makers in every large town in the country. It is, indeed, symptomatic that none of the half-dozen or so domestic and house-keeping manuals in general circulation before 1860 mention papier-mâché furniture at all.

There is only space here to mention the two main technical developments which influenced the appearance of the furniture. Both are to the credit of Jennens and Bettridge. In 1825 they patented the use of pearl-shell in papier-mâché decoration, and in 1847 of so-called 'gem-inlaying'. Both processes are found applied not only to papier-mâché proper, but also to the stained and painted wooden furniture which is often confused with it.

Coat of Arms of H.M. Queen Victoria from a printer's Specimen Book of 1850.

Painting and Sculpture

JOHN WOODWARD

Portraiture

King George IV died in 1830, surviving by only a few months the painter who had served him so well as Regent and King. Sir Thomas Lawrence had created not only a splendid visual image of his master, but had brought to a superb and fitting climax the lifelong passion of George IV for surrounding himself with the portraits of the men of action of his day. The journeys undertaken in Europe to paint the portraits of those persons who had helped to bring about the ultimate overthrow of Napoleon, and destined for the Waterloo Chamber at Windsor, had not only added to the reputation of Lawrence himself, but had also brought about an entirely new respect for English Art. Although the influence of Lawrence continued to be noticeable for some years, taste was changing towards a more solid and domestic type of portraiture, more consistent with the changing style of costume and the return to a more domestic way of life. The sparkle, 'chic', and soulful sensitivity of Lawrence's men and women were alien to the Victorian drawing-room, bearing as they did something of the lightness of behaviour of their times.

The new King, William IV, turned wisely to Sir David Wilkie for his first official likeness, and the result was one of the most imposing, but neglected, portraits produced by an artist in the nineteenth century (Pl. 33). Wilkie's earliest portraits, such as the *Mr Morrison and Miss Bethune* 1805), were painted very much in the Raeburn tradition of solidarity and truth of character, but

they lacked subtlety. His fellow Scotsman Andrew Geddes in his early *Self-portrait*, or in the portraits of his mother, is far more arresting and sympathetic. Wilkie, however, found his true *métier* in small cabinet portraits which were among his greatest achievements, and which come as a welcome relief among the acres of canvas used for vapid and stiff full-lengths which the less-gifted fashionable painters have left us. These small paintings vary from crowded conversation pieces such as the *Neave Family* of 1810 to his undoubted masterpiece of *The Duke of York* (1823, National Portrait Gallery). His only competitor in this genre is perhaps Geddes, who painted the exquisite small portrait of Wilkie himself leaning on a chair. By 1830 Wilkie had abandoned these small-scale portraits and embarked on the grand full lengths inspired by his continental travels. They were thought to be Spanish, but were, in fact, much more in the style of Lawrence worked with the palette of Rembrandt and with reminiscences of the swirl and dash of Rubens. Unfortunately, many of these have been eaten away by bitumen, but those that remain – *George IV* (Apsley House), *Duke of Sussex* (Buckingham Palace), and *The Earl of Kellie* (Cupar Town Hall, Fifeshire) – are extremely impressive in colour and pose and with a solidarity of stance and cast of countenance that is reminiscent of the full-length figures in Holbein's Whitehall fresco. The full-length of William IV is the most remarkable achievement of Wilkie as a portrait painter. He has chosen to represent the Sailor King in the uniform of the Grenadier Guards using his

'Rembrandt–Rubens' manner with strong lighting contrasts and thick creamy paint. The painting of the cock's feathers of the hat is in itself a fine passage of still-life. It is hard now to understand why one critic found it 'stiff and starched as any drill Sergeant, glittering with varnish'. It is stark, and curiously still, in comparison with the sumptuous, restless, Coronation portrait of George IV by Lawrence, but it matches it in dignity, never allowing the pale face of the old King to be swamped by the scarlet of his uniform. Sir Martin Archer Shee, who succeeded Lawrence as President of the Royal Academy, was a far better man of affairs than he was portrait painter; and his work is consistent but seldom inspiring, and never reached the efficiency and breadth of his successor, Sir Francis Grant.

Younger painters, trained abroad and influenced more by continental Academic portraits than by Lawrence, dominated the early years of Queen Victoria's reign, and she herself had no doubts, as she confided to her diary, that George Hayter was the best portrait painter living. Hayter had gone to Italy to study when a very young man, and had produced while there some sensitive drawings of his family and of Italian life, as well as harbouring ambitions to be a history painter. On his return to England he quickly built up a lucrative practice, but his matrimonial troubles, although known and condoned by the Queen, kept him outside the Royal Academy. He was never a very gifted painter, alternating between lyrical but rather insubstantial full-length portraits and rather sombre and solemn half-lengths. None the less, he rose far higher than could reasonably be expected in his State portrait of Queen Victoria, seated crowned and holding the sceptre (National Portrait Gallery), a portrait so well known that its merits are sometimes overlooked and which is perhaps the most endearing State portrait of an English monarch that we have. Youth, dignity and ease are all suggested, and it blazes out, with its powerful colouring, among the portraits of black-coated statesmen who surround it in the Portrait Gallery. The extent of Hayter's achievement can be seen in the abysmal failures of Wilkie and Archer Shee to rise to the occasion in

their own portraits of the Queen. It is not without significance that the Queen commissioned a portrait of Lord Melbourne from Hayter, as she so strongly disliked the 'daub' by Lawrence. Melbourne himself, so the Queen records in her diary, had no doubt that C.R.Leslie was the best portrait painter of the day. In the 'forties Hayter, after a railway accident and a disagreement with the Prince Consort, gradually began to fall from favour, and as his star waned, royal patronage fell on F.X.Winterhalter, a painter of charm, from the Black Forest, whose earliest work in England is attractive but somewhat spoiled by some coarse painting; but he left a series of paintings without which our understanding of the Queen, her family and her Court would be considerably less than it is. Winterhalter worked at all the principal European capitals, and it is to his credit that all his sitters so completely belong to their own country. There is no attempt to place a Tuileries Second Empire gloss over Buckingham Palace or the Hofburg. His grandest English portraits are those of *The Duchess of Sutherland* (Pl. 36B), and *The Duke of Beaufort* (Badminton, Gloucestershire). Hayter had spent much of his time in the composition of vast group assemblages which are, despite their overwhelming mass portraiture, extremely able. The first of these, *The Trial of Queen Caroline* (1823, National Portrait Gallery), contained 186 portraits, and his last, *The House of Commons* (1833, National Portrait Gallery), had 375 portraits. This labour, seemingly of love, made enormous demands on his time and energy, but the portrait sketch-heads made for these finished works are among his best work, free in handling and clear in colouring (Pl. 34A). There was a demand for such assembly pieces during the whole century, and many of the commissions came from the Queen. C.R.Leslie, John Phillip, E.M.Ward, and W.P.Frith were all employed in this way; but although their standard was high, none of them excelled Hayter. The style was to deteriorate into what may be called 'Guildhall Processional'.

The taste of the Court reflected that of the nation as a whole; and there were painters, such as John Lucas, J.C.Horsley and Sir John Watson

Gordon, who could be relied on to give a solid performance and to produce portraits to be added to the family gallery or adorn public institutions. John Partridge, who had studied in Italy, was, perhaps, rather more talented, and had a gift for finding a correct and uncommon pose for his sitter and also experimented with the horizontal half-length, as in the portrait of Lord Aberdeen (National Portrait Gallery), which allowed him to paint more of the sitter's surroundings. An album of sketches of artists working in Italy in 1825 has recently been purchased by the Portrait Gallery and includes a portrait of *Charles Lock Eastlake* (Pl. 34B).

Some of the most pleasing portraits were those emanating from painters whose main work was not primarily concerned with portraiture. Sir Edwin Landseer must be considered first both for his charming conversation pieces, with or without animals, and for his single figure portraits. Queen Victoria made constant use of his brush for depicting herself, her Consort, the royal children, and the royal pets. When the painter died, she recorded in her diary that she had 'thirty-nine oil paintings of his, sixteen chalk drawings (framed), two frescoes, and many sketches'. These works include the well-known conversation piece with dead game, which depicts the Queen, Prince and their eldest child in a room at Windsor, while visible through the window is the old Duchess of Kent being propelled through the gardens in her bath chair; the sketch for this is at Kensington Palace. That the painter had a nice sense of humour is evident from the small portrait of *Princess Victoire de Nemours*, the Queen's Coburg cousin, where the juxtaposition of the lady's hair and the dog's ears cannot be entirely accidental (Pl. 35B). A perfect gift for the painter was *Van Ambrugh and his Animals*, which allowed him one human and a great variety of animal life (Pl. 38A). The collection of family portraits belonging to the Duke of Abercorn and the unfinished *John Gibson* (Royal Academy) show him at his best as a straightforward recorder of the human face. Sir Charles Eastlake painted a few portraits, and among these, one, of great charm and brilliance of colour, of Mrs Bellenden Kerr as an Italian

Contadina (Pl. 34C); but as Lady Eastlake remarked: 'These "fancy portraits" as they were called were greatly admired, and would have filled his hands with this class of occupation, had he not pertinaciously refused to devote himself to portraiture'. William Etty also produced several portraits of his family and friends of great strength of perception, an example being *James Atkinson* (Pl. 34D). Daniel Maclise rose to dramatic heights in at least two portraits, *Macready as Werner* (Victoria and Albert Museum) and *Lord Lytton* (Knebworth). John Linnell painted on a smaller scale some portraits of extreme delicacy, which are sometimes marred by a rather woolly application of paint; but his portrait drawings of Blake (Fitzwilliam Museum, Cambridge) are masterpieces. George Richmond was a competent craftsman, but his more delicate painting and drawing (often in silver-point) tend to be overweighted, in any assessment of his work, by his full-size competent, historically important, but deadly dull drawings of heads done in black chalk heightened with white. His self-portraits in the Birmingham Art Gallery and the Uffizi seem to have been influenced by Raphael and the German Nazarene painters. One of the most splendid portrait drawings of the period is the *Self-portrait* by Samuel Palmer (Ashmolean Museum, Oxford), where the painter has boldly projected his features and managed to convey the short-sightedness of his natural vision.

Those artists who formed or are connected with the Pre-Raphaelite Brotherhood between 1848 and 1862 all painted remarkable portraits, but thereafter their taste and skill deteriorated in a marked fashion, degenerating into either extreme affectation or into the realms of 'pot-boiling'. J.E. Millais is the most obvious case in point if one compares the sparkling jewel-like portraits of *James Wyatt and his Grand-daughter* (1849) and its companion, or the stern authority of *Ruskin at Glenfinlas* (1854) with the weakly painted academical likenesses of his later years. D.G.Rossetti left a touching and perpetual record of Elizabeth Siddal in the hundreds of delicate studies he made of her during their life together (Pl. 35A). Her death in 1862 – a date which makes such a convenient dividing line in the study of the Brotherhood's work – caused the features of Jane Morris and professional models to dominate his later work, which is on a larger and coarser scale. Holman Hunt also in his youthful self-portraits and in his *Canon Jenkins* (Jesus College, Oxford) showed an intimacy and spontaneity which later left him entirely, though his Portrait of *Wentworth Monk* (Ottawa) has a direct and rather alarming impact. Madox Brown painted few portraits but his *Self-portrait*, which so exactly mirrors his character as it is known to us, and his studies of his wife Emma make one regret that he did not turn his talents in this direction more often. One of the most hauntingly romantic portraits of this period is that of *Swinburne* by William Bell Scott (Balliol College, Oxford), where the small red-haired poet is posed against a part of the Northumbrian coast.

Lord Leighton in 1853 painted oval companion portraits of himself and his sister, Mrs Sutherland Orr, which clearly mirror his continental training and his knowledge of the Nazarenes in Germany. G.F.Watts, whose main work lies outside the boundary of 1860, painted some of his best portraiture when he was in Florence as the guest of Lord Holland in the 'forties and in his first years at Little Holland House. These include the studies of *Lady Holland* (Buckingham Palace and Compton), the full lengths of *Augusta, Lady Castletown* (1846, Tate Gallery) (Pl. 36A), an immature but ambitious attempt at grand portraiture, and the *Sir Anthony Panizzi* and *Princess Lieven* (both in the collection of the Earl of Ilchester). One of his most remarkable portraits dates from 1862, of *Lady Margaret Beaumont and her Daughter*, a work redolent of the era and strangely 'Gothick' in its pose and treatment.

The portrait painter had a constant patronage through the early nineteenth century not only from the Court and the aristocracy but also from the middle classes, whose wealth and social standing were being steadily consolidated. Many portraits were painted as deliberate bait for the visitors to the Royal Academy, and there was a steady flow of orders from civic authorities, institutions and colleges for the likenesses of their distinguished members and alumni. The sombre and solid worth of the majority of these likenesses is intensified by the dark clothes of the men, usually posed against dark backgrounds, and later by the fashion for wearing a beard, which was no less of a handicap to a painter than the wig had been to those of the later seventeenth century. Occasionally a painter could enliven his dark palette by a glittering fob or watch-chain. With women and with children it was easier to achieve a gayer colour scheme and a lighter background, but first the spaniel-ear arrangement of ringlets followed by the very severe arrangement of the hair smoothly across the head made the painter's task a heavy one. This severity of dress and hairdressing for both men and women has had a corresponding effect on the judgement of posterity on portraits painted between 1830 and 1860.

Historical painting

Thackeray had some wise remarks to make on the state of historical painting in England when, under the name of Michelangelo Titmarsh, in 1842 he wrote of the painters:

'They wisely, I think, avoid those great historical "parades" which cover so much space in the Louvre. A young man has sometimes a fit of what is called "historical painting"; comes out with a great canvas, disposed in the regular six-feet heroical order; and having probably half ruined himself in the painting of his piece, which nobody (let us be thankful for it!) buys, curses the decayed state of taste in the country, and falls to portrait-painting, or takes small natural subjects, in which the world can sympathise, and with which he is best able to grapple.'

In the following year he said much the same thing:

'They do not aim at such great subjects as heretofore, or at subjects which the world is pleased to call great, viz., tales from Hume or Gibbon or royal personages under various circumstances of battle, murder, and sudden death. Lemprière too is justly neglected, and Milton has quite given place to *Gil Blas* and *The Vicar of Wakefield*. The heroic, and peace be with it! has been deposed; and our artists, in place, cultivate the pathetic and the familiar.'

Certainly the old historical themes were dying out and the proud titles such as *Edward the Con-*

fessor Spoiling his Mother or *Scenes from the Life of Elizabeth Woodville*, which figure so frequently in the earlier catalogues of the Royal Academy, were no longer tempting painters. Vanishing too were the heroic allegorical subjects summed up again by Thackeray as *Britannia, Guarded by Religion and Neptune, Welcoming General Tomkins in the Temple of Glory*. The majority of visitors to the Royal Academy were intelligent and well-read families, who indeed spent a good deal of their quiet domestic evenings reading aloud to each other from history and from fiction. They therefore studied critically the attempts of painters to bring to life the people and scenes familiar to them from the written word. It was not a coincidence that the *Vicar of Wakefield* found so many painters eager to render the ever-popular episodes.

History painting during the period 1830–60 can roughly be divided into five main groups.

1. *The Grand Style.* This had fewer devotees than in the previous fifty years, but the teaching and inspiration of Reynolds lingered on in a few minds; and the irrepressible Benjamin Robert Haydon was always at hand to preach the cause of grand art and to cover acres of canvas, inspired by those 'perpetual urgings to future greatness' with what must be admitted were rather arid results. His most engaging works are the *Cassandra* and *Venus and Anchises* (S.A.Oliver Esq.), which have recently reappeared. It could be argued that Haydon has done a great disservice to the study of history paintings by being such an essential and key figure in its structure. We know so much of his hopes and failures and 'the hum of mighty workings' from his own writings that in assessing first the tragedy and then his disappointing canvases there is a tendency to ignore all the other painters who were working in the same vein.

The decoration of the New Palace of Westminster, which arose after the disastrous fire of 1834, led to grandiose schemes which were to engage many painters between 1841 and 1863. There were those who admired the frescoes of the German painter Peter Von Cornelius, but rather deplored the system of the 'master mind' and pupils which it entailed. Eastlake urged that the frescoes of Raphael should be followed rather than German Christian art. Lady Eastlake, his remarkable and intelligent consort, had found Cornelius' work extremely boring: 'He is the great gun of German Art, and a mere pop-gun in reality: covers miles of cartoon with what are called grand historical compositions, and which consist of an endless repetition of ill-drawn figures of the largest size and the smallest interest.' Prince Albert was made President of a commission to study the scheme for decoration, and Eastlake was the secretary. A competition was announced for cartoon drawings illustrating subjects from British History, or from the works of Spenser, Shakespeare or Milton. Haydon, to whom the whole idea was so dear, failed to gain one of the premiums. The final decorations are disappointing, but the work of William Dyce, A.C.Cope and Daniel Maclise merits more attention than it is usually allotted. The two major works of this scheme are the great frescoes by Daniel Maclise in the Royal Gallery, *The Death of Nelson* (detail, Pl. 38B) and *The Meeting of Wellington and Blücher*. Time and central heating have blackened these works, but the scenes of carnage which surround his central groups are indicative of his ability to draw and compose. The end of the commission saw the end of the desire for a national school of history painting, and the new generation of painters moved out of the Medieval or Early Christian world into the sumptuous marble surroundings of Greece and Rome as conjured up from the brushes of Lord Leighton, Sir Lawrence Alma Tadema and Albert Moore.

One or two painters of the Grand Style deserve a passing reference, and in particular David Scott, from Edinburgh, who worked on a gigantic scale and studied the Old Masters. Unlike Haydon, he travelled abroad and assimilated something of Delacroix and Géricault from France, as can be seen in his *Philoctetes Left on the Island of Lemnos* (Pl. 39A) and the German Nazarene style in his *Vintager*. On a smaller scale he painted one of the best Victorian history pictures, *The Traitors' Gate*. All of these are in the National Gallery of Scotland in Edinburgh.

Another neglected but historically important figure is Edward Armitage, a student under Paul

Delaroche in Paris, and who was the winner of one of the Premiums for the Palace of Westminster decoration. After visiting Rome he began to exhibit battle-scenes and history pieces. But it is his Biblical subjects, many admittedly painted after 1860, which are his chief monument. Rather statuesque in quality, but filled with glowing rich colour, they make an imposing impact on the spectator. The best of these are *Samson, But the Philistines Took Him* (1851, whereabouts unknown) (Pl. 39B) and *Esther's Banquet* (R.A. Diploma work, 1865). Paul Falconer Poole was another ambitious composer of historical groups, but at times he almost caricatures the style and shows all the dangers that lay in wait for a painter of mediocre talents. His *Solomon Eagle* is an excellent example of history getting out of hand and verging on the ridiculous. *The Visitation of Syon Nunnery* is a better venture in this vein, but his best work is probably *The Death of Cordelia* (Victoria and Albert Museum).

2. *The Medieval Style.* This term is only a very general one to cover the Early Victorian interest in the period of English history stretching from Harold to the death of Edward III. It is sometimes called *style troubadour.* This same interest can be seen in the vast tournament which was held in the grounds of the Earl of Eglington's castle in Ayrshire in 1839, a magnificent spectacle, somewhat spoilt by rain, and there are commemorative portraits by Francis Grant and Edwin Landseer of participants wearing armour. Later, a Court fancy-dress ball was held at Buckingham Palace with the Queen as Queen Philippa and Prince Albert as Edward III, and Landseer painted a double portrait to commemorate this (Buckingham Palace). Eastlake made several sorties, from his beloved Italy, into this period of history, and one of his most remarkable achievements is a painting full of his knowledge of the Venetian School, *The Champion* (Birmingham), which shows a knight wearing armour and a helmet having a favour tied to his arm by a lady who might have been painted by Paris Bordone. Maclise was also a successful exponent of a style which was to reach its climax in Landseer's *Chevy Chase* (Birmingham) and *Scene in the Olden Time at*

Bolton Abbey. Henry Perronet Briggs is remembered now mainly as a portrait painter, but his historical works should give him a more solid position if such works as *First Conference between the Spaniards and Peruvians* (Tate, Pl. 40B) and *The Challenge of Rodomont to Ruggiero* (Birmingham) are taken into consideration. This medieval style has dug deeply into the visual impressions of history not only because of the engravings which appeared in innumerable nineteenth- or early twentieth-century history books, but also for the influence it has had on the stage and on film companies.

3. *Biblical.* Apart from essays of Haydon, Maclise and Armitage, and, later in the century, Solomon J. Solomon, in grand Biblical painting, a new attitude was apparent. Wilkie, on the eve of his journey to the Holy Land, explained to his nephew his enthusiasm for the immense advantage he might derive from painting upon holy land, on the very ground on which the event he was to embody had actually occurred. One of his last works was a small painting of *Christ before Pilate*, and it may well be indicative of the work he would have done if he had lived longer. This doctrine of geographical accuracy was taken to its furthest point by Holman Hunt. William Dyce, inspired both by Raphael and the German Nazarene painters, produced his small Biblical works, which are beautiful in form and colour and strike an ideal middle course between sentiment and cold purity as in *Joash drawing the Bow* (Hamburg, Pl. 40A). His style was to change under Pre-Raphaelite influence. The indignant outcry of Charles Dickens against Millais' *Carpenter's Shop* shows how even an intelligent mind could react to a change in accepted fashions. It is not perhaps surprising that the Pre-Raphaelites should have found their main patrons among the new rich manufacturers from industrial cities, whose minds were less encumbered by knowledge of earlier styles and fashions in painting.

4. *Literary and Historical.* The eighteenth-century habit of depicting scenes from literature in a markedly theatrical manner, and with the characters wearing clothes reminiscent more of the prop. basket than of the period of history por-

trayed, dissolved into two streams. The influence of Charles Robert Leslie is very apparent in both trends. One of these was pure illustration born of the painter's imagination and inspired by his readings. Illustrations to novels and plays were increasingly popular during this period and reflect the current trends in domestic reading and family playgoing. Shakespeare was still popular, but the other authors so much favoured by the earlier generation gave way to Cervantes, Molière, Sterne and Addison. The greatest favourites were the ever-popular *Vicar of Wakefield* and, more strangely, *Gil Blas*. Thackeray became so tired of scenes from the last two that he threatened never to notice any of them again. However, his good resolution was shattered when he saw and greatly admired William Mulready's two scenes from Goldsmith in the Academies of 1844 and 1847. *The Whistonian Controversy* and *Burchell and Sophia in the Fields* (Pl. 41A) (both in the collection of Lord Northbrook), two of his best works, fine in colour and capturing the spirit of the novel. *Choosing the Wedding Gown* (Victoria and Albert Museum, London), a scene from the same book, is an equally charming and affectionate rendering. Leslie's *Autolycus* (1836, Bethnal Green Museum, London), is one of the best of all nineteenth-century attempts to illustrate Shakespeare on a modest scale. The pictures in this stream, although by the very nature of things somewhat dated, have none the less a timeless quality that best serves an author or a reader at the hands of an illustrator.

The next group to be noticed were more theatrical, or perhaps it would be clearer to describe them as charades taking place in the painter's studio. The men and women are clearly models dressed up and have the marked self-conscious air of dancers at a fancy-dress ball. W.P. Frith was a bad offender in this respect, and even the quality of his painting will not efface this conclusion. Towards the end of his long life this feeling of dressing-up became more marked and was the parent of academy period pieces which one associates with children in mob caps and Marcus Stone and E.A. Abbey. E.M. Ward is never at ease in the world of the French Revolution,

which he loved to depict, and one can never feel the tragedy of the *Family in the Temple*; but infinitely preferable is his portrait of *Lord Lytton* (Knebworth, Pl. 42A). Augustus Egg, however, in *Queen Elizabeth Discovers that She is no longer Young* (Pl. 42B), has achieved a more timeless and truly historical illustration.

5. *Academic.* The main exponent of academic historical painting was William Etty. He was born in York in 1787, and was to remain devoted to his native city for the whole of his life. His painting life was built around the life-class of the Royal Academy, where he devoted himself to 'God's most glorious work, Woman'. A visit to Italy instilled into him a love of Venetian colouring, and his subsequent work was to unite this rich colouring to academic forms. His grand compositions were to reflect overmuch the conscious posing of his models and, therefore, to rob them of spontaneity. His appeal was more to the senses than to the intellect. But his work is far more romantic than coldly classical and his paint is juicy, glowing and fluent. His greatest works are his *Judgement of Paris* (Port Sunlight, Cheshire), *Pandora* (Leeds) and *Judith* (Edinburgh); but one of his most memorable canvases is the *Hero and Leander* (Mrs E.J. Britten) (Pl. 43A), which is both romantic and dramatic and yet academically posed. His many male and female nude studies, often left unfinished and then tidied up by lesser hands, have flooded the dealers in recent times and caused his reputation to be engulfed. His landscape and still-life painting has been neglected and his portraiture has only recently been re-valued. In a work such as *The Repentant Prodigal's Return to his Father* (Ashmolean Museum, Oxford), which relies on no academic nudes, we can appreciate his gift for straightforward narrative in the simplest terms, and his rich handling of paint. Etty must always remain an isolated figure, and yet in his knowledge and application he remains essentially an artist of his own time.

Genre Painting

The painting of scenes from English everyday life did not really become popular until the early years of the nineteenth century. This new demand was probably inspired by Dutch cabinet pictures of the seventeenth century which were being collected by certain discerning connoisseurs led by the Regent. In 1812, Edward Bird painted *Choristers Rehearsing*, which was bought by the Regent; a companion was commissioned but never finished. Bird, in fact, preferred painting scenes from Shakespeare and from history. The most important English genre artist, David Wilkie, was born in the manse at Cults, Fife, in 1785. His earliest work was influenced by engravings after Teniers and Ostade. *Pitlessie Fair*, painted when he was only nineteen, is an astonishingly able composition, but the colour range shows clearly that he knew Teniers only through the engraver. In London, where he settled in 1804, he quickly established his reputation and found patrons eager to buy or commission his scenes from Scottish peasant life. His treatment was free from the rustic sweetness and 'Petit Trianon-like' make-believe of the previous century; but they are filled with anecdote and humour, bordering sometimes on caricature, to make them completely palatable. They were never to startle or dismay in the way that Courbet was to startle Paris when he painted the inhabitants of Ornans. Courbet depicted his peasants in a strictly realistic way, without subsidiary anecdote, and on a scale usually associated with history painting. George IV purchased Wilkie's *Penny Wedding* and *Blind Man's Buff* for the royal collection, and he was the first artist of his generation to be hung in the National Gallery. His early works are tightly painted, and the amount of thought that went into their composition can be gauged from the innumerable pen-and-chalk drawings and oil studies which he did as preliminary workings. Wilkie, in fact, almost equals Rubens in the amount of preparatory work that went towards the finished composition. His style broadened after a visit to Spain and Italy, and still found favour with George IV who purchased several examples. It was held in his lifetime, and by many today, that his style deteriorated. Thackeray, as he surveyed Wilkie's later work, sighed for the earlier genre and found his looser brush work, muddier colour and Rembrandtesque lighting a sad tumble from the incident-packed

earlier canvases. His middle and later works are in fact, very fine, and one of them, *Peep O' Day Boy's Cabin* (1836, Tate Gallery) (Pl. 43B) has some claims to be his masterpiece. His last rich colourful sketches and drawings were not seen by the public and critics until the posthumous sale of his works a year after his death and burial at sea, in 1841. His wash drawings (Pl. 44A) have deservedly come to be much sought after and revalued today.

William Mulready, an Irishman, worked at first in a style directed by Wilkie's earlier phase. He was, in fact, to change his method of painting several times, but always, after some initial stumbling, to master it. He worked on a small scale with no further ambition than to depict a scene with sympathy and clarity. His scenes from contemporary life had no social message and are painted with a glowing sense of colour and with perfect underlying drawing. His soundness as an academic draughtsman gives a greater solidarity to his work and raises him above his imitators. He was not only the perfect illustrator to Goldsmith (Pl. 41A), but could render in *The Sonnet* (Victoria and Albert Museum) all the tenderness and embarrassment of young love, as well as the expectation and shyness of reading and showing a self-revelatory poem. He was also fond of depicting the joys and squabbles of children as in *A dog of two minds* (Liverpool, Pl. 41B). Redgrave found violence and a lack of social consciousness in his work and complained that his peasants were too refined. To some extent this point of view is perhaps true and is indicative of his own uneasy temperament, but his pictures give, today, the same pleasure that they gave to his contemporaries. Apart from his anecdotal work, his *Interior of an English Cottage*, purchased by George IV, remains one of his most hauntingly lovely pictures, with its still serenity and soft pink light.

Thomas Webster was another faithful recorder of village life, and his *Village Choir* (Victoria and Albert Museum) or *The Playground* (Christopher Loyd) continue to remain popular favourites. B.R.Haydon in *Punch* or *Chairing the Member* moved from the grand style into London Life. Edwin Landseer painted shepherds in their natural surroundings in the Highlands as well as royal sporting occasions. His animals often hovered on the wrong side of sentimentality, but were lovingly and beautifully rendered. Richard Redgrave was far more direct in his appeal to sentiment, finding his heroines among mournful widows and depressed governesses. Augustus Leopold Egg was to become the friend and patron of the early Pre-Raphaelites, and his own style altered under their impact. In his new style he painted *The Travelling Companions* (Birmingham), two young ladies in their carriage passing the Mentone coast oblivious of the scenery and his dramatic *Past and Present* (Tate), a commentary in three canvases on the sadness of children when their parents fail to keep sacred the marriage vow. R.B.Martineau also pursued a similar subject in *The Last Day in the Old Home* (Tate), but his more pleasing works are *Picciola* (Tate, Pl. 44c) and *Kit's Writing Lesson* (Tate). The sincerity and skill of these works were almost buried by the social documentaries and moralizing sermons exhibited by many of their brother artists in the annual Academy.

William Collins, the father of Wilkie and Charles Alston, is of an earlier generation, but his peaceful scenes of country and seashore are a happy blend of genre and landscape and are some of the most pleasant and unassuming works of their time.

One artist has enjoyed an almost continual popularity for his popular scenes from Victorian life. W.P.Frith has left in his *Autobiography* a vivid account of his life's work from his early days and fame to the end of his long life, when he had somewhat outlived his earlier esteem with the critics. *Ramsgate Sands* (Buckingham Palace); *Derby Day* (Tate); and *The Railway Station* (Royal Holloway College, London) are always assured of an affectionate place in any anthology of Victorian painting. Nor must this sentiment for his work make one blind to his ability to compose and paint.

The Pre-Raphaelite painters and Ford Madox Brown were all fascinated by scenes from contemporary life. Rossetti dragged himself from his Arthurian and Dante studies to work on the moral picture *Found* (Bancroft Foundation, Wilmington, Delaware, U.S.A.), which was partly based on a poem by William Bell Scott. Holman Hunt went even further in preaching his moral in *The Awakening Conscience* (Sir Colin Anderson, London); but the great masterpiece in this vein to be produced by any member of the brotherhood is *The Blind Girl* (City Art Gallery, Birmingham), by J.E.Millais, a touching and yet unsentimental rendering of two tired figures seated in a landscape bathed in the light of a rainbow.

The Pre-Raphaelites

The term Pre-Raphaelite has been used, for far too long, as a convenient label attached to an untidy parcel of artists, flourishing between 1848 and 1880, many of whom had, in fact, nothing in common and whose painting sprang from different roots. The appellation Pre-Raphaelite should, in fact, belong only to the original Brotherhood, and not to Morris and Burne-Jones and their followers. The original Brotherhood was formed in 1848 and consisted of W.Holman Hunt, J.E. Millais, D.G.Rossetti, Thomas Woolner, F.G. Stephens, James Collinson and W.M.Rossetti. In 1850 their literary organ *The Germ* ceased to be produced and the Brotherhood was fast dissolving and by 1852 was extinct. 'So now,' as D.G.Rossetti wrote, 'the whole Round Table is dissolved.' The limited aims of these seven men have been stretched far further than the facts warrant, and the secret letters P.R.B., which occur on only three of their paintings, have, once revealed, been taken into the bosom of art history and used in a way that would have amazed them in later life; they all, with the exception of Hunt, believed that it was only a boyish enthusiasm. The original members of 1848 looked with disfavour at the annual exhibitions of the Royal Academy and in fact at all the damage that had been done to art since the time of Raphael. They floundered into a vague idea of early Christian art which was crystalized when they found a book of indifferent engravings by Lasinio, after the mural paintings in the Campo Santo at Pisa. These were Pre-Raphael, and so the name was born. The inevitable sad aftermath of the Brotherhood, men of such varied temperaments and ambitions, has been recorded by W.M.Rossetti:

'It is a sad and indeed a humiliating reflection that, after the early days of *camaraderie* and of genuine brotherliness had run their course, followed by a less brief period of amity and goodwill, keen antipathies severed the quondam P.R.B.s ... Woolner became hostile to Hunt, Dante Rossetti and Millais. Hunt became hostile to Woolner and Stephens, and in a minor degree to Dante Rossetti. Stephens became hostile to Hunt. Dante Rossetti became hostile to Woolner and in a minor degree to Hunt and Millais. Millais, being an enormously successful man while others were only commonly successful, did not perhaps become strictly hostile to anyone; he kept aloof however, from Dante Rossetti and I infer from Woolner.'

J.E.Millais was almost an infant prodigy. At sixteen he painted *Pizarro Seizing the Inca of Peru*, a remarkable performance perhaps influenced by Henry Perronet Briggs' *First Conference between the Spaniards and Peruvians*, 1826. (Pl. 40B). His early paintings and his masterly angular drawings are truly 'Pre-Raphael' (Pl. 46B) in spirit and touched with the lyrical beauty of Keats and Tennyson, his favourite poets, and their names conjure up the glowing jewel-like medieval world of his imagination – *Lorenzo and Isabella*; *Mariana*; *Ophelia*; and *The Return of the Dove to the Ark*. The furore caused by *The Carpenter's Shop* died down and was followed by his election to the Royal Academy in 1853. His marriage to Mrs Ruskin, and perhaps the new-found cares of family life, caused him to follow the amazing fluency of his brush and to become an over prolific painter of subject pieces and portraits. Sadder still was the extinction of his earlier gifts of poetry and imagination, which gave way, after 1857, to some unforgivable sentiment, and the voice of Keats was muffled by Tupper. Not all his later painting is bad; his technical ability never left him. He is reported to have said to Lady Constance Leslie, as he left, in tears, the retrospective exhibition of his work in 1886, 'In looking at my earliest pictures I have been overcome with chagrin that I so far failed in my maturity to fulfil the forecast of my youth.'

William Holman Hunt pursued to the end of his life what he believed to be the original aims of the Brotherhood. Like Millais, he studied nature closely, accepting and depicting everything seen, selecting and rejecting nothing, and firmly believing in the hard toil of obtaining verisimilitude of fact. His early work is ambitious and his composition and grouping in *Rienzi* (Pl. 45A) and *The Converted British Family* is remarkably effective. His imagination was on a higher level than any other member of the Brotherhood, but his work was overladen by the very painstaking method he chose to adopt, and the lyrical moments which he achieved in *The Hireling Shepherd* were soon swamped by his exact reportage from the Holy Land. He saw colour 'without eyelids', and the resulting harshness detracts from his merit as a painter. In addition, the woollen garments worn by his figures have the quality and appearance of having been knitted from wire mesh and detract from his ability to paint the human face.

Dante Gabriel Rossetti was both painter and poet, and his enthusiasm soon overcame his early stumblings. To both Hunt and Millais, overawed by his infectious but suspicious temperament, he must have seemed only an amateur. He was deeply read in Dante and the Arthurian legends; and in the beauty of his future wife, Elizabeth Siddal, he found his ideal Beatrice and Guenevere. The glowing colours of his watercolours found many admirers, including Ruskin, though the latter failed to mould the character of his protegé in the way he would have liked. *Dante Drawing an Angel*, *Leah and Rachel* and *Sir Galahad* are among the finest of these works, far surpassing the *Girlhood of the Virgin Mary* or *Ecce Ancilla Domini*, which were his first major works before he met Miss Siddal. The many studies of his wife are among his best drawings; 'Drawers and drawers of lovely Guggums,' as Madox Brown observed. The long illness of Elizabeth Siddal, which ended in her death in 1862, witnessed a change in Rossetti's style, and the face and dark hair of Jane Morris came to dominate his work. His later style was coarser, and the early medieval vision was buried under the large-scale portraits of his favourite models, who were labelled with exotic-sounding names.

Of the rest of the Pre-Raphaelite Brotherhood little need be said; Collinson and Stephens painted only a few pictures; Woolner was a sculptor and

W.M.Rossetti never painted, but was to be the faithful friend and chronicler of the whole movement.

Two other painters were on the fringe of the movement, Walter Deverell who died young, and Arthur Hughes (Fig. 1). Hughes was one of the most delightful artists, and his early work is full of a poetic beauty which was to leave him towards the close of his long life. His early lyrical works are never too obvious in sentiment or lacking in craftsmanship. How nearly he bordered disaster is apparent in his titles, *Home from Sea*, *The Tryst*, and *April Love*; but his triumphant handling of his subject matter gives him an assured place in the group.

Ford Madox Brown was never a Pre-Raphaelite, thought often classed as one. His training had been in Belgium, and his work reflects the current continental theories closely: his *Chaucer* is a very German picture. Much emphasis has been laid on the influence of German painters, such as Cornelius and Overbeck, on the Brotherhood, but their aims, apart from a sort of cousinly resemblance, are not really apparent except in Brown. Brown was the lifelong friend of Rossetti, but to the end of his days he refrained from identifying himself with any section of the art world. His greatest contribution lies perhaps in his landscape painting (Pl. 45B), which is redolent of his great clarity of vision; though it is sometimes marred by violent use of colour. His scenes from everyday life and from history are well drawn and composed, but rather spoiled by the toothy grimaces of his figures. Brown's influence was negligible, but, none the less, he remains the most considerable figure of the period.

The sight of Millais' *Return of the Dove to the Ark* in an Oxford shop caused two Oxford undergraduates, Edward Burne-Jones and William Morris, to devote the rest of their lives to art. Burne-Jones was influenced in his early work by Rossetti, whom he admired as an artist and loved as a man, but his roots were entirely different from the Pre-Raphaelites and sprang from his visit to Italy and his admiration for Botticelli and Mantegna. His pale, elongated and wide-eyed beauties have often, mistakenly, been held up as the ideal Pre-Raphaelite type. Subtle as a draughtsman, it was his misfortune to drive his talents towards compositions which were far too large in scale to house his imagination comfortably. His subject-matter was set in a timeless age and he was content, unlike the Brotherhood, to tell a story as a story-book picture and not as a projection of probability. His attainments lie outside the period and his influence was to continue for many years.

Landscape

The landscapes shown each year at the Royal Academy were dominated by those of the veteran J.M.W. Turner until he ceased to exhibit in 1850. His later works clearly demonstrate, year by year, his attempts to render light at the expense of form. Such famous works as *The Fighting Téméraire*, *Rain, Steam and Speed*, and the interiors at *Petworth* were done at this time. John Constable died suddenly in 1837, and the rising generation could not be thought the equal of two such undoubted masters. The Early Victorians demanded landscapes, with or without figures and animals, which had a straightforward rendering of nature and the elements and the simple rustic life for the adornment of their rooms. The atmospheric effects of Constable or the frenzy of light in a Turner were not nearly so comprehensible as the mediocre landscapes of Augustus Callcott. Callcott was knighted in 1837, and it is not at all easy now to understand his popularity or reputation. His wife, Maria Graham, better known as the author of *Little Arthur's History of England*, was an important influence on young artists whom she asked to her home and whose careers she encouraged. Thomas Creswick and F.R.Lee were other popular but commonplace artists. So many painters added to the vast output of landscape painting during these thirty years that it is impossible to chronicle their work. Reference must, however, be made to the Romantic vision of Francis Danby as well as to his depiction of the sea in both its gentle calm and its rock-grazing fierceness. His *Upas Tree* (Victoria and Albert Museum) is a sad wreck but *Disappointed Love* in the same collection will serve as an example of his vein of romantic sensibility. In *The Sixth Seal* (Dublin) he essayed a John Martin-like biblical explosion, the full effect of which is now obscured by grime. E.W.Cooke painted the calm of a shore liberally strewn with lobster-pots, and T. Sidney Cooper was to spend the ninety-nine years of his life recording the placid existence of cows in the English landscape. Cooper's 'Cowscapes', as they are so often termed, have been too easily despised. He is vastly superior to the hoard of Highland-cattle painters who arose to decorate the English dining-room. Painters not always associated with landscape also made their considerable contribution. Landseer, the painter of domestic and wild animals, also produced some exquisite landscapes; and Eastlake varied his rather bookish historical style with views of the monuments of his much-loved Rome (Pl. 37). Richard Redgrave also occasionally left his over-sentimentalized interior scenes to paint the landscape outside. This he did feelingly as in *Valleys Thick with Corn* (Birmingham), though his hand lacked the necessary breadth of touch.

Certain painters travelled extensively abroad. James Holland found his inspiration by the canals of Venice, where he painted with a richly loaded palette, making an interesting comparison with the effervescent effects of Turner. W.J.Muller varied his style between passable attempts in the manner of Constable and reportage of life in the Near East. A composition with a Bedouin encampment, an oasis and a palm-tree was almost certain of an immediate sale.

The Romantic artists of the previous twenty years outlived the poetry of their early work. John Linnell lived until 1882, and his work is less spontaneous, but seldom dull. His son-in-law, Samuel Palmer, died a year earlier, and although he is rightly most esteemed for the work he did under deep inspiration and religious intensity of feeling at Shoreham in the 'twenties and 'thirties, his later work in both Italy and England shows a grasp of medium which should not be undervalued. His water-colours done in Rome are especially skilful and mirror the feelings of English artists for the monuments and people of the eternal city, the mecca of so many artists. His illustrations to Milton are over-hot in colour, with a pre-

ponderance of purple, and far the least pleasing of his work.

The importance of landscape in the work of the Pre-Raphaelites is discussed under that heading, but it can be stressed that Madox Brown is probably the best landscape painter of the period, even if the intensity of his colour is at first inspection rather too rich and raw. *Walton-on-the-Naze* (Birmingham), *The Hayfield* (S.J.Gillum, Esq.) and above all *An English Autumn Afternoon* (Pl. 45B) are remarkable achievements. They show all the necessary 'truth to nature', and because there is no breaking down into irritating and scientific detail they preserve the largeness of a sympathetic and loving vision. John Brett is the exact opposite, following slavishly the teachings of Ruskin and demonstrating a painstaking understanding of the underlying geology. William Dyce in *Pegwell Bay* (Tate) also shows an acute feeling for landscape but with a shade too much precision of touch at the expense of atmospheric effect. Madox Brown wrote of his *An English Afternoon* 'a literal transcript of the scenery round London, as looked at from Hampstead. The smoke is seen rising halfway above the fantastic shaped, small distant Armule, which accompany particularly fine weather. The upper portion of the sky would be blue, as seen reflected in the youth's hat, the grey mist of Autumn only rising a certain height. The Time is 3 p.m., when late in October the shadows already lie long, and the sun's rays (coming from behind us in this work) are preternaturally glowing, as in rivalry of the foliage. The figures are peculiarly English – they are hardly lovers – mere boy and girl neighbours and friends.'

If it is hard to list the landscape painters it is certainly harder to enumerate the countless artists who found a ready market for their water-colours. There was a demand for framed water-colours, with their gilt surrounds, to decorate the walls of houses great and small. The older generation had tended to keep water-colours with drawings and prints in portfolios. Now they were full-dress exhibits, and it could be argued that the decline in the English Water-colour School can be measured from the time the painter began to think more in

SIR DAVID WILKIE. King William IV, 1833. *Wellington Museum, London.*

PLATE 33

(A) SIR GEORGE HAYTER. Princess Augusta, 1837.
Courtesy John Quilter, Esq.

(B) JOHN PARTRIDGE. Sir Charles Eastlake.
c. 1825. *The National Portrait Gallery.*

(C) SIR CHARLES EASTLAKE. Mrs Bellenden
Kerr, 1835. *The Tate Gallery.*

(D) WILLIAM ETTY. James Atkinson, 1832.
Yorkshire Philosophical Society, York.

PLATE 34

(B) SIR EDWIN LANDSEER, Princess Victoire de Nemours, 1839.
Kensington Palace, London.
Reproduced by gracious permission of H.M. The Queen.

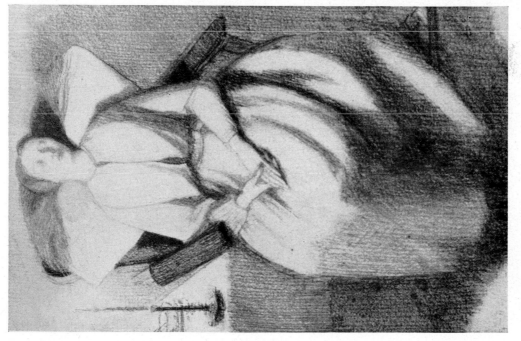

(A) D. G. ROSSETTI. Pencil drawing of Elizabeth Siddal,
c. 1860. Courtesy Sir Kenneth Clark.

PLATE 35

(B) F. X. WINTERHALTER. Harriet, Duchess of Sutherland, 1849. *Courtesy the Duke of Sutherland.*

(A) G. F. WATTS. Augusta, Lady Castletown, 1846. *The Tate Gallery.*

Sir Charles Eastlake. Pilgrims arriving in Sight of Rome, 1828. *Woburn Abbey, Courtesy the Duke of Bedford.*

PLATE 37

(A) Sir Edwin Landseer. Van Ambrugh and his Animals, 1839. *Buckingham Palace.*
Reproduced by gracious permission of H.M. The Queen.

(B) Daniel Maclise. *Detail from* Death of Nelson, 1865. *House of Lords, London.*

PLATE 38

(A) DAVID SCOTT. Philoctetes left by the Greek Fleet, 1840.
The National Gallery, Scotland.

(B) EDWARD ARMITAGE. Samson 'But the Philistines took him', 1851. *Whereabouts unknown.*

PLATE 39

(A) WILLIAM DYCE. King Joash Shooting the Arrow of Deliverance, 1844.
Kunsthalle, Hamburg.

(B) H. P. BRIGGS. First Conference between the Spaniards and Peruvians, 1531, *c.* 1826.
The Tate Gallery.

PLATE 40

(B) WILLIAM MULREADY. A Dog of Two Minds, 1830.
Walker Art Gallery, Liverpool.

(A) WILLIAM MULREADY. Burchell and Sophia in the Fields, 1847.
Courtesy Lord Northbrook.

PLATE 41

(A) E. M. WARD. Lord Lytton in his Study, 1851.
Courtesy Lady Hermione Cobbold.

(B) AUGUSTUS EGG. Queen Elizabeth discovers that she is no longer Young, 1848.
Whereabouts unknown.

(A) William Etty. Hero and Leander, 1829.
Courtesy Mrs E. J. Britten.

(B) Sir David Wilkie. The Peep O'Day Boy's Cabin, 1836. *The Tate Gallery.*

PLATE 43

(A) SIR DAVID WILKIE. Study for Mary Queen of Scots Escaping from Loch Leven, 1837. *City Art Gallery, Birmingham*

(B) SIR DAVID WILKIE. Mehemet Ali, wash drawing, 1841. *The Tate Gallery.*

(C) R. B. MARTINEAU. Picciola, 1853. *The Tate Gallery.*

PLATE 44

(A) W. Holman Hunt. Rienzi, 1849. *Courtesy Mrs E. M. Clarke*.

(B) Ford Madox Brown. An English Autumn Afternoon, 1854. *City Art Gallery, Birmingham*.

PLATE 45

(A) D. G. ROSSETTI. Sir Galahad at the Ruined Chapel, 1859.
City Art Gallery, Birmingham.

(B) SIR JOHN MILLAIS. The Disentombment of Queen Matilda, 1849. *The Tate Gallery.*

PLATE 46

(A) JOHN E. CAREW. Henry Wyndham, 1831.
Courtesy John Wyndham, Esq.

(B) WILLIAM BEHNES. Prince George of Cumberland, 1828. *Windsor Castle, by gracious permission of H.M. The Queen.*

(C) THOMAS WOOLNER. Alfred, Lord Tennyson, 1857.
Trinity College, Cambridge.

(D) JOHN GIBSON. Queen Victoria, 1848.
Corporation of Liverpool.

PLATE 47

(A) Joseph Durham. Waiting his Innings, 1866.
Corporation of London, City of London School.

(B) William Theed the Younger. Narcissus,
*c. 1847. Buckingham Palace. Reproduced by gracious
permission of H.M. The Queen.*

(C) John E. Carew. Adonis and
the Boar, 1826. *Courtesy John
Wyndham, Esq.*

PLATE 48

(A) Teapot (height 6¾ in.), Britannia metal, *c*. 1830. Maker's mark of James Dixon and Son, Sheffield, and a cream jug (height 3¾ in.), Britannia metal, *c*. 1840. Maker's mark of Joseph Wolstenholme, Sheffield. *Sheffield City Museum.*

(B) Teapot (height 6⅜ in.), silver, London, 1833–4. Maker's mark E. F. (Edward Feline?). *Victoria and Albert Museum.*

PLATE 49

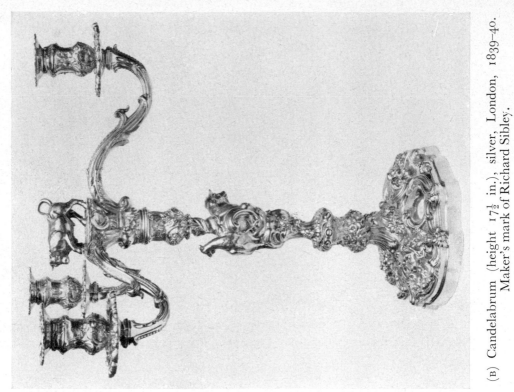

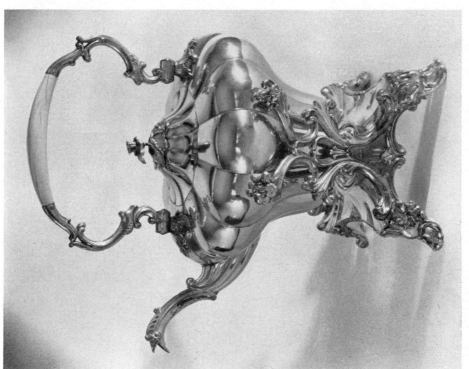

(A) Kettle and Stand (height 16 in.), Sheffield plate, c. 1838. Maker's mark of Henry Wilkinson and Co. *Sheffield City Museum.*

(B) Candelabrum (height 17½ in.), silver, London, 1839–40. Maker's mark of Richard Sibley.

PLATE 50

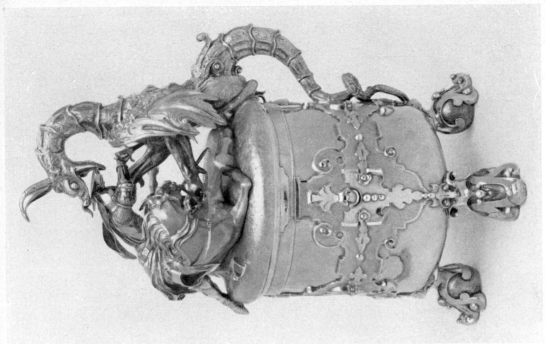

(B) Tankard (height 18½ in.), silver, parcel-gilt, London, 1846–7. Maker's mark of Robert Garrard. Inscribed on base: R & S GARRARD PANTON STREET LONDON.

(A) Wine cooler (height 13¼ in.), silver, London, 1844–5. Maker's mark of Benjamin Smith.

PLATE 51

Tea and Coffee set (heights: sugar basin 5 in., jug 6 in., coffee pot 11 in., teapot 8¼ in.), silver, London, 1848–9. Maker's mark of Edward Barnard and Sons. Part of a service in the Tudor style presented to William Chadwick, Esq., the chairman of the Richmond Railway, in February 1849.
Courtesy Lady Lenanton.

PLATE 52

(A) Mug (height 4 in.), silver, parcel-gilt, London, 1834–5. Maker's mark of Paul Storr. Inscribed: STORR AND MORTIMER NO. 356. *Victoria and Albert Museum.*

(B) Christening mug (height 4 in.), silver; designed by Richard Redgrave for the Summerly Art Manufactures, *c.* 1849. Exhibited by S. H. and D. Gass at the Great Exhibition, 1851. Reissued later by H. Emmanuel, London. 1865–6. *Victoria and Albert Museum.*

(c) Teapot (height 7½ in.), Britannia metal, electro-plated, *c.* 1850. Maker's mark of James Dixon and Sons, Sheffield. *Private Collection.*

PLATE 53

(A) Teapot (height 7¾ in.), silver, designed by A. W. N. Pugin *c.* 1848, Birmingham, 1861–2. Maker's mark of John Hardman and Co. Exhibited by Hardmans at the International Exhibition, London, 1862. *Victoria and Albert Museum.*

(B) Cake basket (diameter 10¾ in.), silver, Sheffield, 1853–4. Maker's mark of Henry Wilkinson and Co. *Private Collection.*

PLATE 54

(A) Jug (height 12½ in.), silver, parcel-gilt, designed by Pierre-Emile Jeannest c. 1853. Exhibited by Elkington and Co. at the Universal Exhibition, Paris, 1855. Reissued later by Elkingtons, Birmingham, 1884–5

(B) Tray (length 18 in.), nickel silver electro-plated, designed by Alfred Stevens, 1856. Maker's mark of Thomas Bradbury and Sons, Sheffield. *Victoria and Albert Museum.*

PLATE 55   1367

Group (height 26 in.), silver, London, 1854–5. Maker's mark of J. S. Hunt (Hunt and Roskell). One of a pair commissioned by the Goldsmiths' Company to illustrate the business duties and the benevolence of the Company. Exhibited at the International Exhibition of 1862. *The Worshipful Company of Goldsmiths*

PLATE 56

(A) Two examples of white stoneware made by the firm of Charles Meigh, Hanley.
The jug is dated 1842; the mug was the subject of a Society of Arts award in 1847.
Heights 6¼ in. and 7¼ in. *Victoria and Albert Museum.*

(B) Blue-printed dish with a fanciful view of Venice, made by Copelands, *c.* 1840.
Length 18⅞ in. *Victoria and Albert Museum.*

PLATE 57

(A) Coalport vase of porcelain, painted and with applied flower-work; *c.* 1830. Height 11 in. *Victoria and Albert Museum.*

(B) Parian porcelain vase with applied flower-work on a drab coloured ground, made by Mintons, *c.* 1854. Height 13⅝ in. *Victoria and Albert Museum.*

(A) Two of Copelands' parian porcelain statuettes. *Left,* 'Innocence' dated 1847 after an original by J. H. Foley; *right,* 'Musidora' dated 1857 after William Theed junior. Heights 16¾ in. and 16¼ in. *Victoria and Albert Museum* and *W. T. Copeland and Sons.*

(B) Staffordshire flat-back figure of Dick Turpin, *c.* 1850. Height 11½ in. *Victoria and Albert Museum.*

PLATE 59

1371

(A) 'Majolica' chestnut dish with spoon, made by Mintons, *c.* 1855. Diam. 9⅞ in. *Victoria and Albert Museum.*

(B) Part of an earthenware tea service designed by Henry Cole and made by Mintons. The service gained a Society of Arts award in 1846. Height of teapot 6 in. *Victoria and Albert Museum.*

PLATE 60

(A) 'Limoges ware', made by Kerr and Binns (from 1862 the Worcester Royal Porcelain Company) with white enamel painting by Thomas Bott. Cup and saucer dated 1859; plate dated 1867, with a pattern originally used on this ware in the middle 'fifties. Diameter of plate 10⅜ in. *Victoria and Albert Museum* and *Worcester Royal Porcelain Company.*

(B) Porcelain standing dish with parian figures representing 'Bottom and the Tinker', from the Shakespeare service shown by Kerr and Binns, Worcester, at the Dublin Exhibition, 1853. Height 15¾ in. *Worcester Royal Porcelain Company.*

PLATE 61

(A) Painted water-carafe, designed by Richard Redgrave for Henry Cole's 'Summerly's Art Manufactures' and made by J. F. Christy, Lambeth, *c.* 1847. Height 10¼ in. *Victoria and Albert Museum.*

(B) Painted opal vase, made by W. H.; B. and J. Richardson, Stourbridge, *c.* 1851. Height 17⅜ in. *Borough of Stourbridge Glass Collection.*

PLATE 62

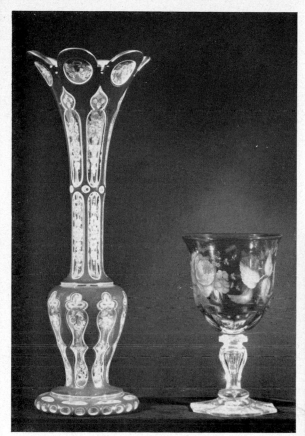

(A) A cased-glass vase with painted decoration, about 1848; and a goblet with cased bowl and with engraving designed by W. J. Muckley, said to have been shown in the 1851 Exhibition. Both made by W. H., B. and J. Richardson. Heights 16 in. and 7¾ in. *Borough of Stourbridge Glass Collection.*

(B) Engraved jug, shown at the 1851 Exhibition by J. G. Green, London. Height 13¼ in. *Victoria and Albert Museum.*

PLATE 63   1375

(A) Comport, dish and decanter of cut crystal, made by W. H., B. and J. Richardson and said to have been shown at the 1851 Exhibition. Heights 5¾ in., 2⅛ in. and 14¾ in. *Borough of Stourbridge Glass Collection (comport) and Mrs. E. Worrall.*

(B) Engraved wine glasses, with plain stem and with colour-threaded and convoluted stem, made by George Bacchus and Sons, Birmingham, about the early fifties. Heights 4½ in. and 5 in. *Victoria and Albert Museum.*

PLATE 64

terms of framed exhibition-pieces, and less in terms of a more intimate vision. The greatest, and perhaps the least understood in his lifetime, was J.S. Cotman, who felt deeply all that he saw in the silhouette of buildings and trees and the freshness of the landscape. David Cox was an uneven painter varying between a clogging heaviness of colour and sentiment and light brilliance which recalls the French eighteenth century. Redgrave said of him that 'the sparkle and shimmer of foliage and weedage, in the fitful breeze that rolls away the clouds from the watery sun, when the shower and the sunshine chase each other over the land, have never been given with greater truth than by David Cox'. The high standard of watercolour painting was not only to be found in the acknowledged masters but also in many amateur hands whose names have long since evaporated. Drawing masters, like the hero of *The Woman in White*, passed on their gifts to many a young lady or gentleman they were called upon to teach.

Travellers abroad

During the first thirty years of the nineteenth century many English artists made the pilgrimage to Rome, and several stayed there for long periods. They painted scenes from peasant life, sketched in the Campagna, and searched for models on the Spanish Steps. Several published letters and memoirs testify to their life there. Eastlake, indeed, seems to have been inspired to paint *The Spartan Isadas* (Chatsworth) after a rather similar incident had happened in a fire at Joseph Severn's house, but his best works are taken from the life around him. *Pilgrims in First Sight of Rome* (Woburn, Pl. 37) and *Peasant Woman Fainting from the Bite of a Snake* (Victoria and Albert Museum) are two of his most attractive canvases, which mirror the life he and his fellow artists sought and which inspired their subject-matter. Thomas Unwins is now a neglected and forgotten artist, but his *A Neapolitan Boy Decorating the Head of his Inamorata* and *An Italian Mother Teaching her Child the Tarantella*, both in the Victoria and Albert Museum, testify to his gaiety and sense of colour. Severn, forgetting Keats for a moment, produced a hauntingly romantic *Shelley*

in Rome (Keats–Shelley House, Rome). The inspiration they found in Rome was to be taken up by American artists, who were also drawn there and formed a similar colony. Later in the century Spain and the Near East was to draw John Frederick Lewis. Wilkie records in his letters his meeting with this artist, who had been absent from England so long. His works glow with a richer colour than those of any other artist, and today tend to be difficult to hang in other company for that reason. In fact, he achieved and recorded much more than Holman Hunt on the same territory. *The Doubtful Coin* (Birmingham) and *The Siesta* (Tate) are two excellent examples of his virtuosity. John Phillip, a Scotsman, spent most of his days in Spain, but his work is more *mouvmente* and fussy in grouping. His scenes are more studied from a picturesque angle of the ceremonies he witnessed, while Lewis preferred anecdotal reportage.

Sculpture

Four sculptors were to continue their craftsmanship into the period 1830–60 – years, in fact, which saw some of their finest works. Sir Francis Chantrey died in 1841 and his masterpiece *Mrs Jordan* (Earl of Munster) was completed ten years earlier, and his delicate bust of *Robert Southey* (National Portrait Gallery, London) dates from 1831. William Behnes lived until 1864, his busts and statues sometimes showing the delicacy of his earlier years, but at others demonstrating the dangers of over-productivity in a rather insensitive lumpiness. His bust of *Prince George of Cumberland* (Windsor, Pl. 47B) shows his skill with children. Samuel Joseph's two finest statues date from 1833 and 1842 respectively, namely his *William Wilberforce* (Westminster Abbey) and *David Wilkie* (Tate). A recent acquisition by the Victoria and Albert Museum is his bust of *George IV* (1831), a swagger piece which is almost a Lawrence done over in marble. John Gibson continued to be the doyen of English artists in Rome until 1866. His American pupil Harriet Hosmer described him as 'A God in his Studio but Heaven help him out of it.' His inability to cope with everyday life caused a railway porter in Italy to inquire if he was a foreigner. 'No,' replied Gibson, 'I am not a foreigner, I am a sculptor.' Twice he returned to England to make statues of Queen Victoria (Pl. 47D), the earlier of which he 'tinted' in the same way as his *Venus*. His great *Hunter and his Dog* dates from 1843.

The new generation produced no men as remarkable as these, though there was a continual demand for memorials, statues, busts and decorative works. The plethora of commissions seems almost to have deadened ingenuity, and the weight of white marble left in the churches and houses of England was to cause the best work to be unjustly neglected in a too-sweeping condemnation of the bulk.

E.H.Bailey was both a decorative and monumental sculptor. His work is uneven, but at its best comes close in quality to Chantrey. He made the statue of Nelson in Trafalgar Square. An excellent example of his wall monuments is that to the *Earl of Pomfret* (1830, Easton Neston). Joseph Durham trained under Bailey, and executed some worthy work, and is best known for his statue of the Prince Consort in front of the Albert Hall. *Waiting his Innings* (City of London School, Pl. 48A) is a charming rendering of youth, free of the sentiment that was soon to overwhelm nearly all sculpture of children, and his accuracy of detail ensures that even the studs in the boots are carefully sculpted. Resurrected for exhibition in Holland Park in 1957, it showed a surprising solidarity and perfection. On the other side of the Albert Hall towers the Albert Memorial, and John Foley was responsible for the statue of the *Prince Consort*, which was finished after his death, and which falls below his statue of *Charles Barry* in the Houses of Parliament. Much of his work is of the historical fancy-dress variety and fails to be convincing. A posthumous statue looks far more of an artificial fabrication than most painted historical scenes, and it would be a great boon to the world if worthy Societies would not attempt to commemorate the famous but long-dead by commissioning posthumous monuments and persuading deans to erect them. It may make good the neglect of an earlier age, but is seldom an ornament or a pleasure. The decoration of the new Houses of Parliament with statues of famous fighters for liberty, for two of which Foley is responsible, was a dismal error. His statues of *Outram* and *Hardinge* are in Calcutta. Patrick Macdowell is best known for his *Flora* (Royal Academy), and although his brother artist, Henry Weekes (Fig. 2), considered that he 'makes his appeal to our best and noblest feelings', this claim appears to be excessive. Weekes himself produced one of the best memorial busts of the period, *Robert Southey* (Westminster Abbey).

William Theed the younger was another pupil of Bailey, but who increased his knowledge of the neo-classical School by studying under Thorwalsden and Gibson. The influence of this School can be seen in his *Narcissus* (Buckingham Palace, Pl. 48B). He later left the neo-classical School and his *Queen Victoria and Prince Albert* in Anglo-Saxon costume, now in the Frogmore Mausoleum, Windsor, is one of his most startling works in this new manner. Richard Wyatt also studied in Rome, under Canova and Thorwalsden, and, like Gibson, settled there. He achieved fame late, but his *Glysera* and *Penelope* were both purchased by the Queen. Of the latter, the Hon. Georgiana Lidell wrote: 'Such a beautiful statue arrived here yesterday from Rome, a full length statue of Penelope by Wyatt, standing in a pensive attitude, with one hand on her heart and the other holding a crook, with a fine dog looking up in her face, the drapery is exceedingly graceful, and the expression of her beautiful countenance very lovely but sad. The Queen is much pleased with it and it is considered Wyatt's *chef d'œuvre*.'

John Lough was a controversial figure in his lifetime, either praised or execrated to excess by sections of the Press. His work could certainly be ludicrous and fussily flamboyant at times. *Milo* (Blagdon) is a fine work of great power and now shown magnificently in a setting by Lutyens, and his finest monument is that to *Bishop Middleton* (St Paul's Cathedral, London,) the first Protestant Bishop of India, blessing two members of his great diocese. This, although somewhat cumbersome, has strength and proves the sculptural possibilities of lawn sleeves. John Edward Carew was befriended by the Earl of Egremont up to the latter's death in 1837. Unfortunately, he made a consummate fool of himself in trying to extract money from the Earl's executors. He was a sculptor of originality and charm as can be seen by his *Adonis and the Boar* (1826, Petworth, Sussex, Pl. 48c) and the bust of *Henry Wyndham* (1831, Petworth, Pl. 47A).

The tastes for neo-classic and Renaissance ran side by side and never really resolved itself during this period. Royal taste turned towards Baron Marochetti and Jacob Boehme, worthy but pedestrian men. The one talent to span the time between the older generation and the appearance of Alfred Stevens was that of Thomas Woolner, an original member of the Pre-Raphaelite brotherhood. In 1852 he set sail to make his fortune in the Australian gold-fields. When this failed to be the lucrative adventure he had supposed, he returned to England and sculpture. His work rightly still enjoys a considerable reputation, and his busts, on their characteristic socles, are always rewarding to study. *Tennyson* (Trinity College, Cambridge, Pl. 47c); *Newman* (Keble College, Oxford) and *Gladstone* (Ashmolean) on his splendid pedestal, ornamented with bas-reliefs from the *Iliad*, are perhaps his deepest character studies. His monuments are less pleasing. The minor Pre-Raphaelite Sculptor Alexander Munro made the charming fountain in Berkeley Square, and among his other work is the bust of his wife (Mrs Munro, Oxford) which has a fresh spontaneity rare at this time.

Fig. 1. An illustration by Arthur Hughes from *Enoch Arden* by Alfred Tennyson.
Published by Edward Moxon, London, 1866.

Fig. 2. Weekes' Sleeping Child and Dog. *Illustrated Catalogue of the Great Exhibition*, Vol. II.
(*formerly coll. Sir Archibald Weigall*)

Silver and Silver Plate

SHIRLEY BURY

A great epoch in English silversmithing came to an end with the death of George IV in 1830. A few months afterwards, advancing age caused John Bridge, the senior partner of Rundell, Bridge and Company, the royal goldsmiths, to give up personal attendance on George's successor, William IV. The association between George IV and John Bridge, which began even before the Regency, was responsible for the revival or development of many styles as well as the accepted neo-classicism of the day; some of the most remarkable additions to the Royal Collections were made at this period. Royal patronage had also largely contributed, directly or indirectly, to the enormous wealth of Rundells, whose premises at Ludgate Hill were the resort of the world of fashion.

William IV showed little concern for plate, although he might perhaps have been induced to develop an interest if John Bridge had not retired. Bridge died in 1834, and the decline of the firm, which had begun in the late 1820's, continued steadily, partly as a result of bad management by the remaining partners. Rundells no longer went to the expense of commissioning designs from fashionable academicians, for in past years they had suffered badly from cheap pirated copies of work on which they had spent a great deal of money. Nevertheless, one member of the firm retained his interest in the patronage of artists. John Gawler Bridge, the nephew of John Bridge, gave two prizes for silver designs by students of the Government School of Design in 1841. Rundells were disbanded in 1843 and their

stock sold, but their effect on the organization of the trade was lasting. Most of the important work of the early Victorian era was carried out by large firms with extensive workshops in the tradition of Rundells, while the small family concerns often failed to survive.

Two firms competed for predominance in the 1840's. One, R. and S.Garrard and Company, the royal goldsmiths, were eighteenth century in origin, while the other, Hunt and Roskell, were the successors of Storr and Mortimer, the firm founded by Paul Storr after he relinquished the direction of Rundells' Dean Street workshops in 1819. These two firms, and other well-known London establishments such as that of Edward Barnard and Sons, had large workshops, although they also sold work by provincial makers. The Birmingham firm of Elkingtons appointed a London manager soon after 1840, and one of his first duties was to sell their productions to London firms with retail premises, while from 1843 onwards Hunt and Roskell purchased small batches of silver designed by Pugin from the makers, Hardmans of Birmingham.

Although London retained her importance as a centre for fashionable silverware during the thirty years under consideration, most of the major technical innovations belong to the provinces. The only contribution to which London silversmiths could lay claim was the revival of embossed work in silver. During the Regency period ornamental detail was generally cast, and this method of working continued well into the 1840's. An embossed silver table ornament shown by Benjamin Smith at the Society of Arts exhibition of 1847 was considered unusual enough to warrant a detailed catalogue note explaining the process of manufacture.

At the outset of the period manufacturers in Sheffield were still mainly concerned with the production of articles in Sheffield plate, although many makers also offered a small selection of their designs in silver. Sheffield plate had long since ceased to be made in Sheffield alone, and the term was used merely to describe goods made of copper plated with silver by fusion. With a few outstanding exceptions, however, the most important firms were to be found in Sheffield. A manuscript account of the industry, compiled between 1820 and 1832 by R.M.Hirst,[1] who was associated with the Sheffield plating trade, is an invaluable source of information about contemporary methods of production. Hirst begins with a description of the process of preparing the plated metal. Ingots of copper, slightly alloyed with brass, formed the basis, and to these sheets of silver were fused, generally on two sides of each ingot. After the fusing had been effected in a furnace, the ingots were sent to the rolling mills, where they were gradually rolled into the required thickness for working. Hirst makes no mention of a new foundation material, 'German silver' (now known as nickel-silver), consisting of copper, zinc and nickel, which had by that time reached Sheffield. As its name implies, it came to England from Germany. Samuel Roberts, Junior, of the firm of Roberts, Smith and Company, took out a patent in 1830 (No. 5963) for the introduction of a 'layer of German silver between the silver and copper (or copper and brass) usually constituting plated metal. By this means [he submitted], whenever the silver is partially or wholly worn off the defect will scarcely be perceptible'. This alloy was at first too brittle for general use, but its composition was varied by later experimentation and by 1845, then sometimes known as 'Argentine silver', it had largely replaced copper as the foundation metal for plate.

[1] R.M.Hirst: *A Short Account of the Founders of the Silver and Plated Establishments in Sheffield.* Bradbury Records, No. 299, Sheffield City Library.

The manufacture of articles from the prepared plate remained much the same as in the earlier part of the century, with one important departure from tradition. This was the general use of spinning for the shaping of articles. Small pieces, such as candlestick nozzles, were sometimes spun on a foot-operated lathe in the late eighteenth century, but it was not until about 1820 that steam-powered machinery made it possible for larger articles to be spun. Hirst explains how the flat metal was forced round the wooden 'chuck', or form, while being revolved at high speed, so that it gradually took the exact form of the chuck itself. Teapots, cream jugs and shallow wares were frequently produced by the process of spinning, as were also plain feet, spouts and covers. Very large pieces (Hirst instances tea-urns and ice-pails) had still to be cut out in parts, which were soldered together, the achievement of the shape being 'partially assisted' by the use of mallet and stakes.

Spinning was also used in the manufacture of articles from 'Britannia metal', a soft and easily worked mixture of tin, antimony and copper, which since the late eighteenth century had been used as a cheap alternative to Sheffield plate. The principal makers included Joseph Wolstenholme and James Dixon and Sons, both of Sheffield (Pl. 49A).

There were few Birmingham manufactories in 1830 which were comparable to the Sheffield firms. Matthew Boulton's factory, then known as the Soho Plate Company and administered by his son, Matthew Robinson Boulton, was still producing reputable work, although its days of real distinction were over. Second to Soho was the firm started in 1793 by Edward (later Sir Edward) Thomason, who had trained with Boulton. Both these manufactories included in their production domestic articles in silver and Sheffield plate. In general, however, Birmingham silversmiths and platers were concerned with the 'toy' trade (i.e. the manufacture of buttons, rings, beads for necklaces, and other very small objects exempted from licence and hall-marking). Some toy-makers produced their wares in Sheffield plate, others, although increasingly few, used the old system of close plating, which was suitable only for small articles. The object to be plated was dipped first into sal ammoniac, which acted as a flux, and then into melted tin, after which a shaped foil of silver was placed on top and made to adhere by the application of a soldering iron.

In 1840 the situation in Birmingham was radically altered by the introduction of electro-plating. The successful application of this process to commercial production was made by George Richards Elkington and his cousin, Henry Elkington, who took out the decisive patent in March 1840 (No. 8447). The two Elkingtons had been experimenting with the possibilities of electro-plating for some years, both separately and together, and G.R.Elkington, in collaboration with O.W.Barratt, had obtained a patent in 1838 for a process involving what was in fact, to judge from the specification, a primitive form of single-cell battery.

All the early attempts at electro-plating stemmed from Alessandro Volta's invention of an electric battery in 1799/1800. Volta's electric cell consisted essentially of two plates of different metals connected by an electrolytic solution, by means of which a sustained current could be produced. From 1801 to 1804 various experiments were made by William Hyde Wollaston, William Cruikshank, W.Hisinger and J.J.Berzelius on the decomposition of chlorides and other salts by the action of electricity, establishing the fact that metal was freed from the solutions and deposited on the negative pole. Brugnatelli was probably the first to achieve a practical piece of electro-gilding. In 1805 he coated two silver medals with gold by the action of electricity. The process, however, continued imperfect for some years; the metallic coating often failed to adhere through oxidation, and the electrical action was erratic.

Michael Faraday made an intensive study of electrolytic phenomena from 1821 onwards, basing his experiments on the work of Wollaston, Davy, H.C.Oersted, Ampère and others. His discoveries relating to electro-magnetism were later used by J.S.Woolrich of Birmingham, who in August 1842 obtained a patent for the first plating dynamo (No. 9431). It is recorded that in 1845, when the British Association met in

Birmingham, Faraday visited the workshops of Thomas Prime, where he was delighted to see the machine in action.

Between 1830 and 1840 there was a renewed spate of experimentation in electro-deposition; J.F.Daniell devised his constant voltage battery in 1836, and this became the standard equipment for research. A number of people, including M.H.Jacobi of St Petersburg, Thomas Spencer of Liverpool, and C.J.Jordan of London, were engaged in investigating a curious phenomenon noted in the *Philosophical Magazine* of 1836 by W. de la Rue, who described how the metal deposited on the negative pole of a battery 'has the counterpart of every scratch of the plate on which it was deposited'. In 1839, within a few months of each other, Jacobi, Spencer and Jordan announced similar findings, which had apparently been made quite independently of each other. In September of that year Spencer delivered a lecture to the Liverpool Polytechnic Society, in which he explained how he had made copies of medals by electro-deposition, using a wax preparation to enable him to separate the medals from the copper deposited on them. The process was later called electrotyping. None of the people concerned attempted to patent their discoveries, which were afterwards used by Elkingtons.

The patent specification submitted by Elkingtons incorporated an improved electrolyte which ensured continuous action by the battery and a firm deposit of metal. The credit for this is usually given to John Wright, a surgeon, who had made a series of successful experiments after coming across a passage in Scheele's *Chemical Essays*, where the solubility of the cyanides of gold and silver in cyanide of potassium is mentioned. Wright sold his discovery to G.R.Elkington, who undertook to pay him royalties for every ounce of gold or silver deposited. The surgeon's right to the discovery was disputed at the time; it was suggested that he owed less to Scheele than he did to Dr Sherman (or Shearman) of Rotherham, whose pupil he had been.

In 1840 the Elkingtons were established in their newly completed premises in Newhall Street, Birmingham, and there followed a period of rapid expansion. In 1842 they were joined by Josiah Mason, and the firm became known as Elkington, Mason and Company. Their employees were encouraged to suggest improvements in manufacture and were rewarded accordingly. Alexander Parkes, one of the firm's most expert metallurgists, invented a process for making electrotypes from non-metallic moulds, which he patented on behalf of Elkingtons in March 1841 (No. 8905). William Millward, another employee, evolved a method of producing bright deposits of metal that needed little burnishing, which he similarly patented in March 1847 (No. 11,632). It was also the firm's policy to buy up all other relevant patents, perhaps partly because their 1840 patent was being continually challenged as being vague and indefinite. Woolrich's patent for his plating dynamo was acquired in 1845, Thomas Prime undertaking shortly afterwards to operate the machines on Elkingtons' behalf.

In 1845 trade opposition to the process, which at first was intense, had begun to give way. The first licence to manufacture electro-plate was granted by Elkingtons to J.Dismore of Liverpool in about 1844. The next was acquired shortly afterwards by John Harrison of Sheffield, who sent one of his employees to Elkingtons to study the process. By 1855 there was hardly a manufacturer of plated goods in England who had not at least partly gone over to electro-plating, although it was still some years before Sheffield plate ceased to be made in small quantities.

The methods of manufacture employed in the electro-plating process were almost the complete reverse of those used for Sheffield plate, and often resulted in a loss of precision and clarity in the final appearance of the articles. This was due to the fact that articles were finished and cleaned before plating. Most works were cast, and the time, money and labour which were expended on the original model were fully justified by the innumerable casts that could be made from it. The design could therefore include modelled figures, relief work and chasing, techniques which were particularly suited to the French artists and craftsmen recruited for the firm by Henry Elkington. The casts were made from sand moulds taken from the model, and were usually of German silver. The simpler objects were made in one piece, and the more complicated or ornate in a number of separate parts. Another form of decoration, often used for mass-produced goods, was the simulation of engraved work by etching, which was first practised in the early 1840's. Spinning seems not to have been used in the new manufacturing process until the late 1840's, when it became possible to electro-plate Britannia metal and other soft alloys.

The electrotype technique was normally used for copying examples of metalwork, usually pieces of historic interest. In about 1844 the process invented by Alexander Parkes for the production of electrotypes from non-metallic moulds was considerably improved by the introduction of un-vulcanized rubber. This was used to make moulds from the works to be reproduced. The procedure then varied, but it was basically as follows: wax, mixed with a conductible material, was poured into the moulds, which were sufficiently elastic to be removed when it had set; the metal was then deposited on the wax. Parkes' method was also employed in the production of facsimiles of natural objects such as plants and flowers, and even small animals, which were coated with a conductible material and then immersed in a plating bath.

These innovations undoubtedly influenced the stylistic development of Victorian silversmithing, and in addition were the means of abolishing the gap that had previously existed between the design of silver and of plated articles. It became a frequent practice to produce articles in both silver and electro-plate. An example of this is the wine-cooler, dated 1844, by Benjamin Smith (Pl. 51 A). Smith, who was a relation, presumably the son, of the Regency silversmith of the same name, had a business arrangement with Elkingtons that lasted from 1839 until his retirement ten years later. The same wine-cooler appears in an Elkingtons' catalogue of electro-plated articles issued in 1847.

Despite the anxious discussion of æsthetic questions that continued throughout the early Victorian era, styles were somewhat slow to evolve. Manufacturers always made a prestige showing at exhibitions, yet this did not preclude

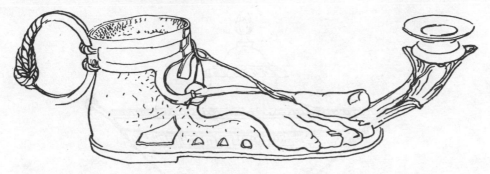

Fig. 1. Taperstick manufactured by Elkingtons. The design was supplied by
Benjamin Schlick and registered in October 1844.

the display of works which were in fact several years old. A vase and shield executed by Antoine Vechte was shown by Hunt and Roskell at the Great Exhibition, at the Paris Exhibition of 1855, and again in London in 1862, gaining high praise from the Juries on all three occasions. The vase (Fig. 7) actually dates from 1847, and the shield, begun in about 1850, was finally completed in 1855. These were admittedly virtuoso pieces, but more modest work also enjoyed a lasting vogue. The teapot made by John Hardman and Company from a design by A.W.N.Pugin (Pl. 54A) was made in 1861 and shown in the 1862 exhibition, but the existence of the original annotated drawing proves that it was designed well before Pugin's death in 1852, and that a prototype had been executed in about 1848.

The classic style of the Regency continued in a modified form throughout the 1830's and 1840's. Its adulteration with naturalistic ornament had begun in the 1820's, and the process was accelerated during the following decade. After 1840 it survived only as a very minor tradition. A few firms, such as that of Sir Edward Thomason, which was taken over in 1835 by G.R.Collis, continued to devote part of their output to straightforward reissues or copies of Regency pieces until quite late in the period, even including them in exhibition displays. Until his retirement in 1839, the great Regency silversmith, Paul Storr, still occasionally worked in the classic manner (Pl.

53A). Versions of classic designs remained among the staple productions of manufacturers in London and the provinces, but the recognizable Regency motifs of acanthus, vine leaves, masks and gadrooned ornament became markedly less conventional and symmetrical in character. It is possible to plot from the pattern-books of the 1830's the development of such details as the insertion of star-shaped flowers and posies into acanthus leaves and the progressive unfurling and irregular placing of the leaves themselves, resulting in a blurred and often unbalanced shape.

Soon after 1840 a style of more definitely antiquarian character began to emerge. This again stemmed from the Regency period, for Paul Storr and other silversmiths had occasionally made direct copies of Roman metalwork. A bronze reproduction of the Warwick vase, carried out in 1820 by Sir Edward Thomason, remained one of the show-pieces of G.R.Collis and Company, and is mentioned as late as 1855 in a guide to Birmingham. Elkingtons, however, were able to cater for public demand on a wide scale with their electrotype facsimiles of antique pieces. In 1844 they engaged for this purpose the Chevalier Benjamin Schlick, a Danish architect who had access to many European collections of Greek, Roman and Etruscan antiquities, both public and private. Schlick was responsible for making the moulds, and he also made good any deficiencies in the original, rearranging the parts if he felt it to be

Fig. 2. Tureen in the Greek manner manufactured by
Dixons. Shown at the Great Exhibition 1851.

necessary. The taperstick (Fig. 1) is an early
example of his work for the firm. A group of his
pieces was shown at the Birmingham Exhibition
of 1849, and again at the Great Exhibition. He
ended his connection with Elkingtons in about
1849 and was replaced by Dr Emil Braun, of Rome.

Elkingtons, and other manufacturers, also
adapted Greek and Roman forms to domestic
articles. A cream ewer, 'copied from the antique',
was shown by J.Dismore of Liverpool at the
Manchester Exhibition of 1845–6, and similar
pieces were included in the display of several firms
at the Great Exhibition. The current interest in
the antique was possibly responsible for the appearance of a specifically early Victorian shape for
jugs and coffee-pots, characterized by a tall, thin
neck, high lip and rounded, flat-based body which
is reminiscent of the Portland Vase. This shape
emerged in about 1849 and was widespread at the
time of the Great Exhibition. It is perhaps significant that copies of the Portland Vase were made
in the 1840's by a number of silversmiths, including Dismore and Hunt and Roskell.

From about 1846 onwards there was a con-
current use of classic motifs in a much freer, in-

spirational sense, and by 1850 this had become
canalized in the Greek style. James Dixon and
Sons included a 'plain but truly elegant' Grecian
dish and tureen in the firm's contribution to the
Great Exhibition. The shapes of these pieces were
simple and controlled, owing more to the Adam
period than to the Regency; the ornament was
confined to bands of engraved key pattern, with
beaded and gadrooned borders (Fig. 2). Throughout the 1850's many similar designs were patented
by manufacturers under the Copyright of Designs
Act of 1839. Some were rather more exuberantly
ornamented than the early Dixon pieces, others
were directly derived from Greek vase shapes, but
they were usually distinguished by a common discipline of shape and decoration. The principal
patentees of work in this manner (in addition to
Dixons) were Edward Barnard and Sons, Elkingtons; and Henry Wilkinson and Company,
Thomas Bradbury and Sons, and John Harrison,
all of Sheffield. Towards the end of the decade the
Greek style had become of major importance.

The Victorian rococo manner is characterized
by a heavy use of naturalistic motifs. Until late in
the 1840's the rococo was generally known as the

'Louis XIV' style, a term which led to a good deal of contemporary confusion on the part of designers and manufacturers, and often resulted in an admixture of the baroque and rococo. J.B.Papworth, the architect, giving evidence to the Select Committee on Arts and Manufactures in 1835, said that the style was not properly that of Louis XIV, but was 'the debased manner of the reign of his successor, in which grotesque varieties are substituted for design'. The style was never popular with the intelligentsia, but fifteen years after Papworth had condemned it, the *Journal of Design* had still regretfully to remind manufacturers that 'the detail of the age of Louis XV we would rather forget than perpetuate'.

In 1830 rococo shapes were widely used for small domestic articles in both silver and Sheffield plate. Teapots, cream jugs and so on, were often made in the rather flattened spherical or oval form, lobed like a cantaloupe melon, which was popular in the previous decade. Pear-shaped bodies, inverted and otherwise, were also produced at this time, although they became much more general in the late 1830's. The lobed ornament, known as 'melon pattern', was frequently used in the decoration of these pear-shaped articles (Pl. 50A), although this was not invariable, as is shown by the teapot illustrated (Pl. 49B). The decoration of this piece with scenes of debauch, and with four shell feet terminating in the busts of pirates, seems somewhat inappropriate to its function, but genre subjects of this kind appear intermittently on silver and plate throughout the period, and a similar teapot was shown at the 1862 Exhibition. A more common ornamental device was a stylized posy of flowers and leaves, used in conjunction with rococo scrolls and shells.

The larger pieces were usually more ambitious, in that the scroll and shell ornament was combined with a profusion of foliage and flowers, and with animals and figures, free-standing or in high relief. All these elements of design appear in *Knight's Vases and Ornaments*, one of a series of pattern-books issued by this publisher. The 'Vases' was published in January 1833; the list of subscribers includes many well-known firms in London and the provinces, such as Storr and Mor-

timer, Benjamin Smith and Dixons. An analysis of the plates shows a marked preponderance of rococo motifs, not only in the original designs for Racing and other presentation cups, but in the decoration of objects based on historic examples, which are frequently perverted into a more fashionable form. The floral decoration, though plentiful, remains fairly conventional, consisting either of acanthus arranged in an asymmetrical fashion, or of scattered bunches of roses or other flowers. The candelabrum illustrated (Pl. 50B) is typical of the elaborate rococo ornament of the 1830's, although the choice of animals appears to indicate that it might have been specially made for presentation to someone with agricultural interests.

The rococo tradition was continued throughout the 1840's. Spherical and pear-shaped tea- and coffee-pots, both plain and melon-patterned, were predominant, although the pear shape was now sometimes modified by wide facets round the neck of the body. The first innovation, which seems to date from about 1845, was the introduction of a multiple-footed body whose shape can best be

Fig. 3. Teapot from a tea and coffee set modelled on the pitcher plant, manufactured by Dixons. The design was registered in April 1851 and the set shown at the Great Exhibition.

compared to eighteenth-century rococo tea-caddies. The new shape was perhaps evolved from the early practice of casting electro-plated goods (Pl. 53c). Flowers and foliage, either in high relief or chased, as in the 1830's, were still often used in decoration, and occasionally showed signs of having been taken more directly from nature. Handles and feet were frequently entwined with foliage, or were themselves made in the form of plants. In addition, chinoiserie, arabesque, Gothic, Elizabethan (or Tudor: see Pl. 52), and seventeenth-century motifs were used, sometimes in combination with rustic elements. From about 1846 numerous pieces were made which were almost entirely covered with foliated or floral ornament, although the standard rococo shapes were still discernible. In 1850 Dixons patented an electroplated tea set in which the body and feet were overlaid with a simple leaf form. The *Journal of Design* for that year complimented the firm on the 'appropriate design'. Rococo pieces were still produced in some quantity in the following decade. Several manufacturers, including Broadhead and Atkin, Roberts and Hall, and Hawkesworth and Eyre, showed work in this manner at the Great Exhibition. There were few stylistic changes after this date. The cake basket illustrated (Pl. 54B), is an adaptation of a design registered by Henry Wilkinson and Company in 1849; the form is identical, but vine leaves have been substituted for the original ears of corn. The multiple-footed shape appears to have largely died out in the early 1850's, and to have been replaced by an upright oval form, often widening at the base.

The design of some small pieces, and of many of the larger articles produced in the 1840's, was so strongly affected by contemporary interest in naturalism that they must be regarded primarily as belonging to the naturalistic style, although a certain affinity with rococo is still often evident. The formative influences (apart from the character of Victorian rococo itself) which led to the development of naturalism in silversmithing are difficult to assess. One was probably the invention of the electrotype and its application to natural objects, another was contemporary French metalwork design, some examples of which were purchased from the Paris Exposition of 1844 by the Director of the Government School of Design at Somerset House. These, together with work in other media, were circulated round the principal manufacturing towns in England. Nevertheless, it is unlikely that this touring exhibition had as marked an effect on English manufacturers as their employment of French artists and craftsmen and their long-standing practice of purchasing designs from the Continent. From 1845 onwards, for the benefit of manufacturers, the *Art Union* published a series of illustrations of French pottery and metalwork, which included, together with examples of work in the Renaissance style, pieces such as a metal boudoir candlestick shaped as a leaf, with the candle-holder and handle in the form of a flower and stalk. English manufacturers took up this particular design with enthusiasm, and two rival versions of it, one of which was patented by the firm concerned, were the subject of the first case relating to infringement of the Copyright of Designs Act. The same principle was applied to other articles. Benjamin Smith showed thistle and convolvulus cups, made in the shapes of the plants, at the Manchester Exhibition of 1845–6.

It can be argued that this development is implicit in Knight's designs of 1833, in which figures, animals and natural objects are used with obviously allusive purpose on a fairly recognizable foundation of rococo or, more rarely, classical shapes. A pair of Dianas form the handles of one of his cups, the body of which is covered with huntsmen and dogs, partly in high relief, and partly, it appears from the design, free-standing, while foxes spring from acanthus leaves round the base. The classical vase shape has been treated in a similar way by Benjamin Smith in the wine-cooler, dated 1844, which is illustrated (Pl. 51A). The handles, stem and base are completely rustic, while the lip has dissolved under pressure of vine and foam ornament.

The most striking manifestation of the style was in Testimonial or Presentation plate, a category which includes Racing plate, decorative centrepieces, and table services whose primary function was adornment. Dickens described a typical set of such plate in *Our Mutual Friend*, in which 'a caravan of camels take charge of the fruit and flowers and candles, and kneel down to be loaded with the salt'. Broadly speaking, there were two kinds of naturalistic Presentation plate. One, which was the first to emerge, was concerned mainly with the sculptural and allegorical, and the figures rarely had to serve a structural purpose, while the other, which dates from about 1845, aimed at the closest possible reproduction of forms in nature, which were used as both structure and decoration.

The demand for sculptural plate gave manufacturers their greatest incentive to employ artists and modellers of repute. Edmund Cotterill, the sculptor, was already working for R. & S. Garrard in 1840. He produced the group of St George and the Dragon on the Garrards tankard illustrated (Pl. 51B) which was the Ascot Queen's Vase for 1844. Hunt and Roskell's modeller, Alfred Brown, was responsible for one of the most ambitious suites of sculptural plate of the 1840's, the Ellenborough Testimonial, which included a grand centrepiece, a pair of table ornaments and candelabra, and four ice pails (one of which is illustrated: Fig. 4). Most of the major firms had permanent designers, but in addition, following the Regency tradition, frequently commissioned work from independent artists such as Daniel Maclise, R.A., and Sir George Hayter, R.A.

In 1850 the *Journal of Design* made some severe criticisms of the sculptural treatment of silver, which were taken up and amplified by Richard Redgrave, R.A., in his report on design at the Great Exhibition. After remarking that the worst features of the naturalistic style were particularly apparent in silver and plate, he went on to deplore the 'imitations of textures, chain and plate mail' characteristic of the style, asking further what in these pieces 'could justify the employment of the precious metals, and what ought to be the more precious labours of artists?' Redgrave regretted that, on the evidence of the exhibits, the English were more culpable in this respect than any other nation. There were in fact few prominent manufacturers in this country who failed to show work of this kind at the Great Ex-

Fig. 4. Ice pail formed as lotus leaves and other plants, with figures of Indians grouped round. Part of the service of plate manufactured in 1848 by Hunt and Roskell for presentation to Lord Ellenborough by 'his friends and admirers in India'. Shown at the Great Exhibition, 1851.

hibition. In some of these Presentation pieces an architectural construction was used on which the figures were placed, but in others the groups were commingled arbitrarily with scroll ornament or with natural forms. Five years later, Redgrave, reporting on the design of British manufactures at the Paris Exhibition of 1855, found a marked improvement in the taste of English silver and plate, which he attributed in part to the influence of the French artists and craftsmen working in this country. The group illustrated (Pl. 56) was completed in 1854, and bears out Redgrave's comments regarding the higher standard of design in the 1850's. The ornament, although still lavish, has been kept subordinate to the finely modelled figures. This piece is one of a pair which were commissioned by the Goldsmiths' Company from Hunt and Roskell to illustrate respectively the business duties and the benevolence of the Company. They were shown at the 1862 Exhibition.

The fashion for Presentation plate made in direct imitation of natural forms reached its climax at the Great Exhibition, where a good deal of attention was aroused by the 'silver dessert service, of new design' modelled from water-plants in Kew Gardens and shown by S.H. and D.Gass, of London. The Exhibition catalogue gives an exact botanical description of each plant represented. Dixons exhibited a tray shaped as a leaf of the Victoria Regia lily, acknowledging their debt to Joseph Paxton, who had supplied the original leaf for copying, and a tea and coffee set modelled on the pitcher plant (Fig. 3). After the Great Exhibition the style lost favour to a certain extent, and was more generally found in electroplate than in silver.

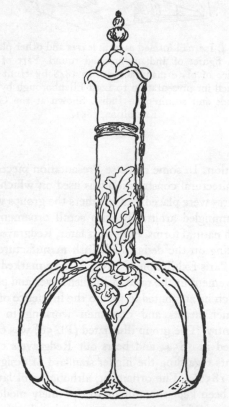

Fig. 5. Gothic wine flagon manufactured by Lambert and Rawlings. Shown at the Great Exhibition.
Victoria and Albert Museum

One of the earliest intellectual reactions against the extravagancies of the rococo and naturalistic styles was led by Henry Cole, who later became a member of the executive committee of the Great Exhibition. Using the pseudonym 'Felix Summerly', he submitted an earthenware tea set, made to his design by Mintons, to the first competition for Arts and Manufactures organized by the Society of Arts, and was awarded a silver medal. This was in 1846. His success encouraged him in his conviction that 'an alliance between fine art and manufactures would promote public taste', and in the following year he issued the first notice of the formation of 'Summerly's Art Manufactures'. The preliminary announcement stated that a number of well-known artists had agreed to design 'familiar articles in everyday use' for execution by the 'most eminent British manufacturers'. As far as works in metal are concerned, these manufacturers included Benjamin Smith (from 1848, B. and H.Smith), Hunt and Roskell, S.H. and D.Gass, Dixons, and Broadhead and Atkin. The organization lasted for about three years; Cole abandoned the project in 1850 because of his preoccupation with the Great Exhibition.

The whole scheme was based on the assumption, widely held at the time, that painters and sculptors, usually without knowledge of manufacturing processes, were the most suitable persons to design for the industrial arts, and that, moreover, these designs could equally well be rendered in several completely different media. The milk-jug from Cole's own prize-winning tea set was executed in porcelain and glass, and also in silver by Hunt and Roskell. The designs themselves were sometimes liable to suffer from an over-literal interpretation of the Summerly principle that decoration should consist of 'appropriate' motifs drawn from nature and relating to the use of the article. This led to a repetition of some of the faults of the naturalistic style and a consequent lessening of functional qualities. The *Journal of Design* pointed out this weakness in Richard Redgrave's 'Guardian Angel' christening mug (Pl. 53B) in 1850. The *Journal* approved of the 'perfect propriety' of the ornament, but found it disproportionate to the whole, and suggested that the rim would be better raised and widened so that the cup could be drunk from more easily.

There was widespread and bitter contemporary criticism of the Summerly Art Manufactures, which arose partly as a result of the generous showing afforded them at the second and fourth annual exhibitions of British Manufactures held at the Society of Arts in 1848 and 1850. Their influence, however, was probably greater than was suspected at the time by many indignant designers and manufacturers not in the scheme.

The Gothic style was primarily a religious manifestation during this period. Its chief protagonist was Augustus Welby Northmore Pugin, the architect, who as a boy of fifteen was briefly employed by Rundell, Bridge and Rundell to design church plate in the Gothic manner. He never lost his interest in silver, and continued designing on his own account. In 1836, by then a convinced Catholic, he published a collection of his drawings, begun in 1833, as *Designs for Gold and Silversmiths*. He met John Hardman the younger, a fellow Catholic, in the course of his architectural duties in 1837 and within a year had a business arrangement with him for the production of ecclesiastical metalwork. Hardman advertised in 1840 that he was now producing metalwork exclusively from Pugin's designs or from 'ancient examples' under Pugin's supervision. Hardman's early difficulties in finding suitable workmen for the enterprise were frequently referred to by contemporary writers; one of his particular problems was the recruitment of enamellers, for from about 1842 onwards much of the work was designed for enamelled decoration.

Although the greater part of the firm's production was devoted to ecclesiastical metalwork, a certain number of domestic pieces were also made. Pugin's house at Ramsgate was furnished with a silver service made for him by Hardmans, and examples of domestic silver and brassware were included in the firm's display at the Birmingham Exhibition of 1849, at the Great Exhibition and at the 1862 Exhibition. After his death in 1852 Hardmans continued to work from Pugin's designs. The teapot illustrated (Pl. 54A) is an example of such posthumous production. Pugin was

Fig. 6. Kettle from a Gothic tea and coffee set manufactured by Elkingtons. The design was registered in April 1851 and the set shown at the Great Exhibition.

of course unable to find Gothic models for such latter-day inventions as teapots, and he had to be content with the use of decorative detail. For other domestic pieces he was usually able to adapt a medieval form. The popularity of his designs led to a good deal of imitation by other manufacturers specializing in ecclesiastical metalwork. The closest rival to the Hardman firm was that of Francis Skidmore, who began making metalwork in the same manner in about 1847.

The use of Gothic motifs, or, more rarely, Gothic forms for domestic wares occurs on a minor scale throughout the period, although rarely inspired, even during the 1840's, by Pugin's antiquarian interests. Dixons had a few Gothic tea-sets among their stock styles from 1846 onwards, but the medievalism was confined to the ornament, for the shapes were rococo. Lambert and Rawlings of London contributed a remarkable pair of silver and gilt Gothic wine-flagons, each twenty-four inches high and holding twelve quarts, to the Great Exhibition (Fig. 5), while other manufacturers, including T. Wilkinson and Company and William Gough and Company, both of Birmingham, showed small electro-plated articles, such as cruet frames and butter coolers, which were pierced with perpendicular tracery. Elkingtons exhibited a Gothic tea and coffee set (Fig. 6), whose designer had obviously shared Pugin's difficulty in finding suitable shapes, and had solved the problem by using architectural features. In the 1850's several manufacturers, including John Harrison, registered a number of designs for articles with engraved Gothic decoration.

There were styles other than the Gothic which presented difficulties in the adaptation of decoration to nineteenth-century domestic silver and plate. The compromises involved often make it impossible to distinguish clearly between styles. The Victorians found it equally difficult, particularly where work in the manner of the fifteenth, sixteenth and seventeenth centuries was concerned, for here the problem was intensified by an uncertain historical knowledge. The *Art-Journal* of 1850 used the term 'Renaissance' to describe a sugar basket by Broadhead and Atkin decorated with Gothic tracery, and this mistake was not uncommon. In the 1851 exhibition Garrards showed ewers and cups variously listed as in the style of the sixteenth century and in the style of Cellini; C.F. Hancock and J.V. Morel, both of London, contributed respectively a tea set and a casket in the Florentine style, while many manufacturers included work in the cinquecento, Venetian and Italian styles. Many of these works, to judge from surviving illustrations, are very similar.

Only one sixteenth-century style, the Elizabethan, sometimes called the Tudor style, is consistently different from the rest. Its characteristic features are bold strapwork and scrolling cartouches which, in common with other styles of the period, were as frequently applied to rococo

and other shapes as to sixteenth-century forms (Pl. 52). The style was already popular by about 1840. From 1843 onwards some dozens of designs for Elizabethan soup tureens, candelabra and so on were registered by manufacturers, including Henry Wilkinson, who appears to have made a speciality of the style. Garrards often used it as an ornamental background to their Presentation pieces, as on the tankard illustrated (Pl. 51B). In 1851 a florid version of the Elizabethan manner was employed in the decoration of one of Elkingtons' special display pieces, the Vase representing the triumph of Science and the Industrial Arts at the Great Exhibition, while a number of other firms, including Gass, Henry Wilkinson, John Harrison and William Gough, showed more modest interpretations of it for domestic use. In the four years that intervened between the Great Exhibition and the Paris Exhibition of 1855 the style lost favour, and few new designs were produced after the latter date.

The term 'Cellini style' appears to refer, in particular, to the ewers of sixteenth- or early seventeenth-century form decorated with embossed or engraved figure groups. These were nearly always exhibition pieces made for prestige purposes. Antoine Vechte, the greatest exponent of this style, was probably in part responsible for the adoption of a form of ewer which was a much closer approximation of the true Renaissance shape than the pyriform version of the 1830's. Several firms, including Martin, Baskett and Martin of Cheltenham, showed ewers of this kind at the Great Exhibition. A curious variant on the pyriform ewer was the elongated jug or coffee-pot shape, with narrow curving body, which first made its appearance in the late 1840's and which was fairly widespread by 1851. Joseph Angell, of London, showed a coffee-pot of this shape at the Great Exhibition.

The Renaissance style, in the accepted sense, was current throughout the period, although it was not of major importance until the 1840's. Much of the work in this manner was executed from French designs or by French artists and craftsmen employed in this country. After the

1848 Revolution the number of French people in England was considerably augmented by the arrival of silversmiths who had lost their patrons, and Vechte and Paul-Emile Jeannest apparently came at this time. Vechte almost immediately started working for Hunt and Roskell, for whom he had already carried out a number of commissions while still in France. Jeannest spent some two years in London, contributing regularly during this time to the *Art-Journal*'s series of 'Original Designs for Manufactures'. Jeannest's designs were frequently illustrated with the qualification that their 'essentially French' character was not entirely suited to British taste. He nevertheless made few modifications to his style when he began working for Elkingtons, as is shown by the jug illustrated (Pl. 55A), whose design is very characteristic of his work. The decoration of acanthus foliage and cherubs is based on the work of the French seventeenth-century engraver, Jean le Pautre. The jug was shown at the Paris Exhibition of 1855 and again at the Crystal Palace in 1856. Another French immigrant was J.V.Morel, who entered his mark at Goldsmiths' Hall in 1849. The *Art-Journal* published an article on his work in 1850, commenting that it represented a compromise between the Renaissance and Louis XIV styles. His silver, which was usually richly jewelled and enamelled, appears to have had a great effect on other makers. Before Morel's arrival in this country, enamelled decoration was largely confined to work in the Gothic style. In the 1851 exhibition Morel's own display was closely rivalled by that of Joseph Angell, who showed pieces in gold and silver-gilt, heavily engraved and enamelled.

One of the great English designers in the Renaissance manner was Alfred Stevens, who had studied at the Academy in Florence for eight years, and whose designs were always based on the sculpture and architecture of that city. In 1851 he went to Sheffield to design grates and stoves for Henry Hoole and Company, and while working there he made a series of drawings and models for a set of so-called 'hunting knives', which were specially executed by George Wostenholme and Son for the Great Exhibition. After his return to London in 1852 he continued to design silver, sending up models to Sheffield from time to time. One of his pieces, a tray made by Thomas Bradbury and Sons is illustrated (Pl. 55B). Stevens was one of the few English artists to have a thorough working knowledge of manufacturing processes, and his instructions for the execution of the tray, contained in a letter to Joseph Bradbury, are still in existence. The tray was patented by the firm in October 1856, and produced in a number of sizes in both silver and electro-plate. It is, unfortunately, the only remaining example of Stevens' designs for these makers, although he is known to have supplied them with a number of models, including a dessert stand and an epergne, between 1856 and 1859.

The arabesque style, which late in the 1830's represented work in the style of the painted and stucco decoration carried out by the studio of Raphael in the Villa Madama, was completely changed in character by the time of the Great Exhibition. One of Elkingtons' exhibits was a tea and coffee service, listed in the catalogue as in the arabesque style. Its engraved decoration is, however, reminiscent of the Alhambresque manner which was popularized by the publication between 1842 and 1845 of Owen Jones' work on the Alhambra. There were numerous other styles of Eastern character, including the Turkish, the Persian and the Egyptian. Of these, by far the most defined was the Egyptian, whose ornamental motifs were invariably distinctive. This style was another inheritance from the Regency, although its only manifestation during the 1830's and early 1840's seems to have been in the use of the lotus leaf as decoration. In 1849 S.H. and D.Gass included an Egyptian centre-piece in their display at the Society of Arts exhibition, while Hunt and Roskell showed a large work in the same style, the testimonial to Sir Moses Montefiore, which was executed from the design of Sir George Hayter. Henry Wilkinson, and Hawkesworth and Eyre of Sheffield, showed small domestic articles decorated in the Egyptian style in the Great Exhibition, and later in the 1850's Wilkinson attempted direct reproductions of Egyptian pieces. In general, however, the Oriental affinities were vague.

Fig. 7. A vase by Antoine Vechte of Hunt and Roskell.
Inscribed: ANTOINE VECHTE FECIT 1847.
The Worshipful Company of Goldsmiths.

Pottery, Porcelain and Glass

HUGH WAKEFIELD

POTTERY AND PORCELAIN

Among the multiplicity of wares which poured from the British potteries during the three decades 1830–60 a broad distinction can be made between those of a popular nature which tended to persist in traditional forms and those of a more sophisticated appeal which readily reflected the complexities of contemporary fashions. The conservatism of the popular wares can be seen especially in the slipware of the country potteries, the 'mocha' and other more industrialized slipwares, the saltglazed stoneware, the lustre ware and the 'ironstone china' with derived oriental patterns. Such wares continued into or through the Early Victorian period, but their manufacture was mainly associated with styles which had been defined and popularized at an earlier date.

Printed and painted earthenwares

The transfer-printed earthenware, which was at the height of its popularity in the years around 1830, showed largely the same conservatism in an established popular style. A great part of its manufacture was designed for export, and through the 'thirties and 'forties it was made by almost every factory of importance in Staffordshire, and by several elsewhere. The use of fanciful scenes, and of actual scenes in this country, in America and elsewhere, continued as central motifs in the printed patterns. In the border decorations rococo foliage and scrollwork tended to become increasingly common, and this is particularly noticeable in the printed ware from Copelands (the Spode factory, known as 'Copeland and Garrett' from

1833 to 1847, and then 'W.T.Copeland, late Spode') (Pl. 57B). From Wedgwoods came some excellent over-all floral patterns.

Blue remained the most popular colour for underglaze transfer-printing; but from the mid-'twenties other colours were frequently used, and in the 'thirties and 'forties these included black and varying shades of red, green, yellow, brown and purple. The more expensive method of overglaze printing, by transfer from gelatine 'bats' instead o paper, was used where fine detail was required; and this proved especially useful for the delineation of the multitudinous girders of the 1851 Crystal Palace on souvenir ware of that year. Multi-coloured underglaze printing appeared in the later 'forties. Some particularly successful work of this nature was produced by Jesse Austin for the firm of F. and R.Pratt of Fenton. Colour-printing was much used by this firm for the decoration of jar lids, and it was used also on tablewares such as those which were shown at the 1851 Exhibition and which earned the firm a prize medal. The colour-printed tablewares were made chiefly for export to America, where they were still being sold in the 'nineties.

Painted decoration on earthenware tended increasingly to follow the styles of porcelain painting; and this was particularly true of painting on the new hard earthenwares which were being developed as imitations of porcelain. Some notable work, although largely in a porcelain style of painting, was being carried out during the 'thirties and 'forties, and later, by William Fifield junior on the cream-coloured ware of Rings of

Bristol. At Wedgwoods bold over-all patterns were produced in a more appropriately earthen-ware style, which are reminiscent of the same firm's printed floral patterns; and the earlier Wedgwood mode of painting in opaque colours on a black ground was taken up in the harshly coloured productions of the Lowesby pottery in Leicestershire about 1835.

Pottery figures

Pottery figures were made in great quantities during the period, and like most of the popular wares their styles show relatively slight changes from those which were in vogue earlier in the century. It is noticeable, however, that pottery figures tended increasingly to diverge in style and subject-matter from those made in porcelain (which will be described later). Made mostly by back-street potters in the Staffordshire pottery towns, the early Victorian pottery figures were destined for the most unsophisticated market and show to a surprising degree the simple vigour and ingenu-ousness of a 'peasant' art. Among the work of this nature produced in the years around 1830 two main types are prominent. One is that of John Walton and his followers, whose figure groups are mainly characterized by the use of 'bocage' back-grounds of trees or foliage. John Walton's own work seems to belong most typically to the 'twen-ties. Of his followers working in the following decade or so the best known is Ralph Salt who used lustre decoration as well as enamel colours. The second prominent type of figure-work is one which is thought to be associated with Obadiah Sherratt. It is characterized by a curious table base with bracket feet on which are placed groups depicting bullbaiting or else crudely humorous scenes. Much of this work is probably of the 'twenties, but that it continued at least into the middle 'thirties is shown by the use of the new word 'teetotal' in the title of a group illustrating the advantages of sobriety.[1] A later development was the 'flat-back' type of figures, which were mostly left white with a sparing decoration in colours and gilding (Pl. 59 B). These developed

around the middle of the century and achieved great popularity in the 'fifties. Among the makers of these figures in Staffordshire the firm with which they have been mainly associated is that of Sampson Smith of Longton, which continued over a long period to make wares of this nature including pottery dogs for mantelpiece decoration. Flat-backs and other sorts of simple coloured figures were also made in Scotland at Prestonpans and elsewhere.

Other manifestations of Early Victorian work in a broad-based popular spirit were the small models of buildings, such as cottages and churches, and the spirit flasks formed into the shapes of human figures. Many of the model buildings were decorated with roughened patches of vegetation, which also appear on certain dog figures as patches of fur; such work is often described as 'Rocking-ham', although most of it was probably made in Staffordshire.[2] The spirit flasks shaped into amus-ing or topical figures were intended for use in inns. They were greatly in vogue in the years around the passing of the Reform Act of 1832 with representations of the leading political figures of the time. In saltglazed stoneware they were made with other fancy wares by the firm of Bournes of Denby, by several small potteries in the Chesterfield district, and by firms in London, including Doultons of Lambeth. Elsewhere simi-lar flasks were made also in earthenware covered with a brown so-called 'Rockingham' glaze.

Fashionable wares

The wares described so far have been mainly popular wares, and most of them were made in styles which were comparatively long-lived. In contrast, the styles of the more fashionable wares are seen in this period to multiply rapidly and to affect different ceramic materials in differing de-grees, so that the general pattern of stylistic changes becomes one of great complexity. The ceramic arts were closely affected by the new spirit of self-consciousness which was characteris-tic of the Victorian approach to the decorative

[1] R.G.Haggar, *Apollo*, L., 1949, p. 146.

[2] W. B. Honey, *English Pottery and Porcelain*, 1947, p. 231.

arts and was expressed by the appearance of the Government Schools of Design in the late 'thirties and 'forties, by the beginning of circulating collections about 1844 from which the Victoria and Albert Museum was to develop, by the appearance of magazines such as the *Art-Union* and the *Journal of Design and Manufactures*, and, in 1851, by the first of the great international exhibitions. Perhaps the extreme instance of this new self-consciousness was Henry Cole's project of 'Summerly's Art Manufactures', which was being worked out in 1847 and 1848. Inspired by his success in winning a Society of Arts award for a simple well-designed tea service made by Mintons (Pl. 60B), he tried the experiment of commissioning designs for useful objects, including pottery and glass, from well-known painters and sculptors, such as Richard Redgrave, H.J.Townsend and John Bell. That such an experiment was made, and was received with initial enthusiasm, is of greater significance than that the artists themselves were unable to rise to the occasion.

The Revived Rococo

In 1830, and during the following decade, the most significant style in English porcelain was that of the Revived Rococo. It had come as a reaction against the formal heavily-gilded French Empire style of the early years of the century and by the 'thirties was at the height of its development. It was scarcely a directly imitative style in the sense of copying precise examples of eighteenth-century porcelain. In effect it used motifs from the general resources of the eighteenth-century rococo style as a medium for expressing a sense of freedom and of a certain extravagant prettiness. Into this category came much of the more pretentious work of the Rockingham factory at Swinton, Yorkshire (which was closed in 1842). It appeared in the work of the Derby factory (closed in 1848) and of the Davenport factory at Longport; but probably the most significant work in this style was that carried out at the factory of John Rose at Coalport (often referred to at the time, and today, as 'Coalbrookdale') (Pl. 58A).

Besides the use of scrollwork and the tendency towards asymmetrical forms which are implied by the title 'rococo', the revived rococo made an extensive and characteristic use of applied flowerwork. The great care and skill which was lavished on irregular groupings of flowers on the bodies of vessels, and on elaborate bouquets perched on lids, was in accordance with the Early Victorian respect for naturalism and greatly exceeded in botanical accuracy their eighteenth-century prototypes. In the 'forties the revived rococo style as such was on the wane, but the use of applied flowers continued, and the appearance of the new parian porcelain body in the later 'forties, with its marble-like qualities, led several manufacturers to use applied flower-work in the new body, unpainted and virtually unglazed. At the firm of Pountneys in Bristol Edward Raby was a notable specialist in applied flower-work who turned to parian in this way. The firm of Samuel Alcock of Burslem produced similar work; and at the 1851 Exhibition parian pieces with applied flower-work were shown by T. and R.Boote and T., J. and J. Mayer, both of Burslem. Such work in parian was clearly impractical for normal purposes, if only because of the difficulty of cleaning it, and comparatively little is heard of applied flower-work after the early 'fifties.

Relief decoration

One of the most characteristic products of the 'forties and early 'fifties was a group of wares with cast relief decoration. These were mainly jugs, but sometimes included also mugs and other similar objects. Many of the earlier examples of the jugs stand upon clearly differentiated feet; but in general they have loose sagging bodies with the weight well towards the base and wide upward-curving lips. The looseness of form was often accentuated by the great depth of the relief decoration, and this is in contrast to the comparatively shallow relief of Castleford and other earlier analogous wares. A number of different materials were used, varying from a putty-coloured earthenware to brown saltglazed stoneware and parian porcelain, but most frequently and characteristically the material was some form of hard vitreous white ware which can usually be described as a fine stoneware. Sometimes the jugs were coloured throughout or were painted; sometimes, as in the case of many of those produced by the Samuel Alcock factory, the ground was coloured, leaving the relief decoration in white, or vice versa, to give somewhat the effect of jasper ware. On some of the jugs, particularly in the early 'forties, the decoration was in the Gothic taste, as on examples made by W.Ridgway and Son of Hanley in 1840 and Charles Meigh of Shelton, Hanley, in 1842 (Pl. 57A). Bacchanalian themes were popular, as in an example with which Charles Meigh won in 1847 a medal offered by the Society of Arts for a relief-ornamented mug (Pl. 57A). Others were of gente subjects, such as the jug depicting a boy bird's-nesting shown by T., J. and J.Mayer in the 1851 exhibition, or subjects of contemporary commemorative interest, such as the 'Distin' jug made by Samuel Alcock and by Cork and Edge of Burslem depicting a family of saxhorn players who had given popular concerts in the Potteries.

Probably the most significant relief decorations, however, were the running plant patterns, consisting of long sprays or branches of a plant disposed about the surface of a vessel and originating usually from a rusticated handle. The use of these patterns was an expression of the same feeling for asymmetrical looseness and for naturalism as had inspired the revived rococo shapes and the use of applied flowers in porcelain; but with the important difference that whereas the applied flower decoration on elaborate revived rococo shapes tended to take the form of local embellishment, the running plant patterns were conceived in relation to the whole area to be decorated. A contemporary parallel to this treatment of plant patterns, and perhaps a source of inspiration, was the relief decoration on some of the French 'Beauvais' stoneware, which was shown at the Paris Exhibition of 1844 and was publicized by the Art-Union of that year. The free and highly naturalistic early-Victorian style of running plant patterns seems to have developed about the middle 'forties, when it can be seen for instance in the 1846 Art-Union in illustrations of the work of the firm of John Ridgway of Cauldon Place, Shelton (Fig. 1). Besides the stoneware jugs and similar wares it is noteworthy that this style appears also in re-lief decorated silverware and in engraved glass-ware. In parian porcelain the running patterns were used, particularly by Mintons, as cast relief decoration on a variety of objects, including even cups and saucers. It is interesting to notice that in the early 'fifties Mintons were also rendering these loose over-all patterns in applied flower-work on parian vases (Pl. 58B); and the style even appeared in jasper ware among Wedgwoods' collection at the Paris exhibition of 1855.

A similar, and more extreme, expression of the Early Victorian passion for naturalism was the use of plant forms for the whole shape of ceramic objects. The whole form and surface of a vase, for instance, might be shaped to represent the leaves of a lily-of-the-valley plant with the flowers protruding from the sides. Such conceptions were by no means new in ceramic history; but the mid-nineteenth-century versions were not normally designed in an imitative spirit, and together with the running plant patterns the plant forms can be regarded as an original expression of the æsthetic ideas of the period. This again was a style which ceramics shared with work in silver and other media. In the years around 1849–51 a great deal of interesting and often beautiful work of this nature was produced in parian porcelain and other materials by such firms as Copelands, Mintons, Samuel Alcock and G.Grainger of Worcester.

'Majolica'

Plant forms and heavy relief plant motifs of various sorts were also found to be appropriate in the Victorian version of 'majolica', which was produced by Mintons just in time for the 1851 Exhibition. In the 1856 Art-Journal (the successor of the Art-Union) the Minton majolica is described as 'one of the most successful revivals of modern pottery'. It is said that Herbert Minton was inspired by green-glazed flower-pots which he had seen in Rouen in 1849; and the durable coloured-glaze ware which resulted was mainly developed by Léon Arnoux, a young French potter who was later to be art director of the factory. The ware was regarded at the time as an imitation of Italian 'majolica', and in consequence the term (spelled with a 'j') came to be attached to this type of pottery which has little connection with the true tin-glazed and painted 'maiolica' of art history. Sometimes the Victorian majolica was painted, but usually the term was used merely to imply earthenware with coloured glaze or glazes. The heavy majolica, particularly with green glazes, was much used in forms incorporating large leaf shapes, as in the instance of a chestnut dish by Mintons (Pl 60A); and this fashion led Wedgwoods to revive their own eighteenth-century use of green glaze in the production of dishes covered entirely with large-scale naturalistic foliage in relief. Majolica in this sense became the common medium for the innumerable Victorian jardinières with plant-form or other decoration in bold relief, which were made in Staffordshire potteries throughout the rest of the century and beyond.

Sèvres imitations

Alongside these stylistic developments in the free use of rococo motifs and natural forms, much imitative work was being carried out in porcelain in the manner of the eighteenth-century wares of Sèvres, Dresden and Chelsea. Of these the work in the manner of Sèvres was by far the most important and became one of the strongest elements in the later porcelain tradition of this country. Victorian imitations of this sort differed from the 'revived rococo' in so far as the makers were serving an informed taste for the originals, and considerable efforts were therefore made to reproduce the original styles as exactly as possible. Admiration for Sèvres porcelain and the imitation of it had been virtually continuous in this country since the eighteenth century. In the 1830's much work in a distinctively Sèvres style was being carried out at Derby. During the 'forties it became the most fashionable style for the better class of porcelain at nearly all the leading factories, including particularly Roses of Coalport, Copelands and Mintons. The Coalport factory was the one which, under the influence of W.F.Rose from 1841, devoted the greatest amount of attention to the exact reproduction of the eighteenth-century Sèvres colours and decorations. In this the firm was also guided and encouraged by the important London

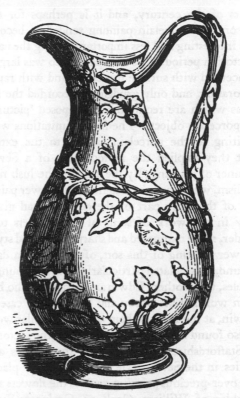

Fig. 1. Jug with painted relief decoration from the firm of John Ridgway, Shelton, about 1845. *Art-Union* (1846, 318).

dealers, Daniell and Co., whose name often appears on the wares. Great efforts were made to match the coloured grounds of the old Sèvres, and the Coalport versions of such grounds as 'bleu de roi', 'rose Pompadour' (mistakenly known at the time as 'rose du Barry') and turquoise were regarded as triumphs of imitation. Some of the imitations made at Coalport, and elsewhere, were so exact as to include old Sèvres marks: a refinement which can scarcely have been carried out without any intention to defraud.

Porcelain painting

Porcelain painting naturally tended to follow the porcelain styles. It is noteworthy, however, that neither the revived rococo nor the Sèvres style offered such wide opportunities to the porcelain painter as had the French Empire style of the early years of the century, and it is perhaps for this reason that porcelain painting tended to become less interesting and less important during the early Victorian period. The revived rococo was largely concerned with surface modelling and with raised decoration, and only grudgingly accorded the flat areas which are required for composed 'pictures' on porcelain objects. The Sèvres imitations were limiting to the porcelain painter to the extent that they implied the reproduction of a Sèvres manner of painting. By the 'thirties the lush naturalism, which had characterized the flower painting of the early part of the century, had given way in the work of some of the painters to a harder, more mannered and sharply coloured style. Flower painting of this sort, often against a dark ground, is associated particularly with the younger Steeles, the brothers Edwin and Horatio, who had been working at Derby and also, in the case of Edwin, at the Rockingham factory.[3] Similar work is also found from Coalport and from the factories in Staffordshire. The work of the 'forties and 'fifties in the Sèvres style led to carefully placed and over-precious painting, such as the flowers and trophies of William Cook of Coalport. Some interesting bird painting was also produced at Coalport in the eighteenth-century Chelsea manner. One of the more outstanding figure painters was Thomas Kirkby, whose finely painted amorini appeared on some of Mintons' porcelain at the 1851 Exhibition. Much of this artist's later work was carried out on the Minton majolica. Another accomplished figure painter was Thomas Bott of Worcester who became widely known in the later 'fifties and 'sixties for his white enamel painting on the 'Limoges ware' of Kerr and Binns (the Worcester firm which succeeded to the Chamberlain factory in 1852 and was known as the Worcester Royal Porcelain Comdany from 1862) (Pl. 61A).

Classical and other influences

The mid-century Sèvres imitations in porcelain represented in some degree a bridge between rococo and classical sources of inspiration. The Victorian interest in classical work was not, however, derived from this source. To some extent the direct imitation of classical shape and decoration seems to have continued since the days of the first Josiah Wedgwood; but the greatly increased interest in this sort of work in the 'forties has something of the appearance of an intellectually-inspired movement which had little in common with the general æsthetic outlook of the period. In the mid-'forties writers in the *Art-Union* were repeatedly stressing the importance of Greek inspiration, which in the idiom of the time was described as 'Etruscan' or 'Etrurian'. In the years around 1845 Copelands were producing a quantity of wares in direct imitation of Greek shapes and decorations, and were extending these ideas to such utilitarian objects as ewers and basins. In this phase the high-handled Greek 'oenochoe' jug shape was especially favoured (Fig. 2). During the late 'forties L. L. Dillwyn's Swansea factory was producing its 'Etruscan ware'; and Wedgwoods were reviving their eighteenth-century designs in jasper ware and black basaltes. In the same period, and in the 'fifties, the London firm of Thomas Battam made a speciality of imitative Greek wares, and at the 1851 Exhibition their display took the form of an artificial grotto meant to represent an 'Etruscan tomb' overspilling with appropriate pottery.

Another aspect of the revival of classical ideas can be seen in the widespread fashion in the 'fifties for work in terracotta; that is, in highly-fired unglazed earthenware. Attention had been drawn to French work in this medium at the Paris Exhibition of 1849. The material was considered to be particularly suited to garden ornaments, and at the 1851 Exhibition an amount of large work of this nature, mostly in classical shapes and with classical architectural detail, was shown by firms such as J. and M.P.Bell of Glasgow, Ferguson and Miller, also of Glasgow, and Blanchard of Lambeth.

Classical shapes and classical decorative motifs became part of the general repertoire of ceramic ideas; but so far as directly imitative work was concerned the main influence of classical ideas was naturally on decorative earthenware or stoneware rather than on porcelain. In the 'fifties this

[3] W.B.Honey, *Old English Porcelain*, 1948, p. 129.

museum-inspired interest tended to shift from classical Greek work to that of the Renaissance, and particularly of the French Renaissance. During the years following the 1851 Exhibition Mintons were producing their 'Palissy ware', which was allied to their majolica of the same period and included pieces made in direct imitation of the work of the French sixteenth-century potter and his followers with high-relief decoration covered by coloured glazes. The elaborately inlaid Saint-Porchaire ware, normally known to the Victorians as 'Henri Deux', was another French sixteenth-century source of inspiration for imitative work. The 'Limoges ware' of Kerr and Binns, which attracted much attention at the Paris Exhibition of 1855, had little but a vague technical similarity with the Limoges enamels, but much of the distinctive white enamel painting was based on Renaissance arabesques and figure-work (Pl. 61A). It is noteworthy that versions of Palissy, Henri Deux and Limoges wares can all be found among the work of French factories of the period. Part of this French influence was undoubtedly due to the number of French artists who were employed in Staffordshire, and particularly by Mintons, during the 'fifties. Besides the art director Léon Arnoux, Mintons employed a series of French sculptors primarily in modelling for majolica and parian work. During the 'fifties Emile Jeannest, Albert Carrier de Belleuse and Hugues Protat were employed in succession, and all of them were also instructors at the newly founded Potteries' Schools of Design.

Two other sources of inspiration need to be mentioned – the Gothic and the Moorish – which in the early Victorian context were largely architectural in origin. The use of Gothic patterns on stoneware jugs in the early 'forties has already been noted. In the middle 'forties Copelands were producing porcelain in a 'pierced Gothic' pattern; and in the later part of the decade A.W.N.Pugin, the chief protagonist of the Gothic style, designed decorations for Mintons which were printed and painted on a number of tablewares in the Minton 'New Stone' body and in porcelain, some of which were shown at the 1851 Exhibition. The Moorish decorations were used less frequently, but in a

similar manner to the Gothic. They were most often known as 'Alhambresque' and were derived from published illustrations of the stucco work in the Alhambra at Granada. They appear, for instance, on a jug and a flower-pot by Ridgway and Abington of Hanley which were illustrated in the *Art-Union* in 1845 and 1846: and at the Paris Exhibition of 1855 Copelands' chief exhibit was a three-feet-high Alhambresque vase which was said to be the largest vessel ever made of parian.

After the many imitative and derivative styles which have been mentioned, it is as well to point out that one of the most obvious sources of ceramic ideas, the pottery of the Far East, was largely ignored during this period. It was the period of reaction against the 'Japan' patterns which had been prevalent earlier in the century and which in

Fig. 2. A classical jug by Copelands, from the Manchester Exhibition of 1845–6. *Art-Union* (1846, 32).

early Victorian times were only being produced at a low level of fashion. In a review of the work of the John Ridgway factory in the 1846 *Art-Union* a solitary vase in the 'Chinese' style evokes the acid comment that it is 'not of a class we desire to see multiplied'. The Victorian revival of Far Eastern styles lay well beyond 1860. It should also be pointed out that whilst the modern eye is immediately struck by the elements of plagiarism in Victorian pottery and porcelain, it is rare to find that imitation has been so exact as not to leave scope for the expression of a contemporary Early Victorian spirit. Bemused as they were by the many examples of earlier work which were brought before their eyes, the early Victorian potters did nevertheless often combine these elements to produce work of original quality. Besides the free use of rococo and plant motifs, a number of distinctive styles emerged which were associated with particular factories. An example which has not so far been mentioned is the highly personal style of pierced porcelain made by Chamberlains of Worcester which attracted considerable interest in the years between 1846 and 1851 (Fig. 3). In general, the most publicized pieces tended to be the most imitative. Even around the middle of the century, when the Sèvres influence was at its strongest, Sèvres motifs appeared among the everyday table-services as only one element among a vast range of patterns most of which were in their interpretation entirely characteristic of their own period.

Fig. 3. Stemmed bowl of pierced porcelain, made by Chamberlains of Worcester in the later 'forties. *Journal of Design and Manufactures* (11, 95).

Porcelain figures

The earthenware figures of the time have already been described as wares of a 'peasant' quality. Porcelain figures were naturally more susceptible to fashion, and during this period came to diverge markedly from the earthenware figures not only in style but also in the nature of their conception. Some of the new porcelain figures of the years around the 'thirties, as seen particularly in the work of the Derby and Rockingham factories, were characterized by the use of strong contrasting colours applied flatly over large areas. The Derby biscuit figures were no longer made, apparently for technical reasons connected with the

factory's organization of firings. A quantity of new porcelain figures, both glazed and painted and in biscuit, were being made at Mintons in the later 'thirties and in the 'forties, and some at least of these were in eighteenth-century costume.

A notable change of attitude towards porcelain figure-work came with the introduction of the parian porcelain body. This new body was used for many different purposes and for many different styles of hollow wares, but it was originally produced for making figures and it was for this purpose that it was considered ideally suitable. It is said that experiments were being made concurrently at both Copelands and Mintons towards the production of a material of this nature. At Copelands the parian body seems to have been produced in the course of attempts to rediscover with the help of an ex-employee of the Derby factory the formula of the old Derby biscuit body. The potentialities of the new body, and the manner in which it was mainly to be used, were expressed in the first group of parian figures from Copelands which were shown at the Manchester Exhibition of 1845–6. The same body, with slight variations, was soon being made by many factories. Copelands called it 'statuary porcelain', Coalport and Wedgwoods called it 'Carrara', but it was the Minton term 'Parian' which eventually passed into the language. It was a comparatively hard form of porcelain, and as such was markedly different from the bone china which was otherwise in universal use as the standard British porcelain body. A writer in the 1846 *Art-Union* was already praising the 'lustrous transparency' of the surface of the parian figures in comparison with the excess of reflected light in glazed figures and the complete lack of it in the older biscuit figures. Although not immediately apparent, parian was normally given a slight 'smear' glaze, which imparted to it the dull smoothness of polished marble.

Modern taste is not easily reconciled to the use of one material in imitation of another. To the Early Victorians, who were inclined to emphasize imitative rather than original elements in the decorative arts, the resemblance of parian to marble justified the immediate and extensive use of the material for making figures in the style of marble statuary. The traditional rococo base, and the use of colour, suddenly became relatively unfashionable. Porcelain figures came to be called 'statuettes', and contemporary publicists were delighted at the elevating effect of copies of fine sculpture being within the reach of every home. The *Art-Union* of London prided itself upon its early recognition of the medium, and in 1846 commissioned reduced copies of John Gibson's 'Narcissus' and J.H.Foley's 'Innocence' (Pl. 59A) to be made by Copelands as prizes for its subscribers. In 1847 Mintons were producing two parian figures, both after John Bell, which were commissioned by Henry Cole for his 'Summerly's Art Manufactures'. Versions of Hiram Power's muchadmired statue 'The Greek Slave' appeared from 1849 onwards from Mintons, Copelands, and Pountneys of Bristol. R.J.Wyatt, William Theed junior (Pl. 59A), Carlo Marochetti, Richard

Westmacott and W.Calder Marshall were among the other contemporary sculptors whose work was represented in parian. Many of the Copeland reductions from large-size statues were effected by the reducing machine of Benjamin Cheverton, and the name of Cheverton on the base of a figure has often been misinterpreted to imply that he was the modeller in the normal sense of the word. Statuary was not, however, the only source for derivative designs. A Minton group of about 1849 was taken from a picture of Ruth and Naomi by Henry O'Neil; and Mintons' Prince of Wales in a sailor-boy's costume, of about the same time, was an adaptation of Winterhalter's picture.

Following the example of the great dessert service made by Mintons for the 1851 Exhibition the use of parian figures in combination with normal glazed porcelain became a recognized mode for factory prestige work. Probably the most distinguished of this sort was the 'Shakespeare service' made by Kerr and Binns for the Dublin Exhibition of 1853, in which Shakespearean figures, modelled by W.B.Kirk, were applied to porcelain pieces decorated with Renaissance motifs (Pl. 61B). Work of such virtuosity could not be considered typical, but the use of parian figures on great occasions was a measure of their popularity and of the extent to which the new medium was adapted to contemporary taste.

GLASS

During the eighteen-thirties and early 'forties clear lead crystal with cut decoration continued to be the characteristic product of the British glass factories. This was largely due to the international success of the English and Irish cut crystal of the earlier part of the century; but it can also be attributed in some degree to the heavy excise duty on glass and the restrictive methods used in its collection which tended to limit experiments in new methods of colouring glass and of decorating it.

The early nineteenth-century version of mitre cutting, with its diaper patterns of deeply cut diamonds arranged predominantly in horizontal motifs, became traditional to British cut crystal work and has survived in its essentials to the present day. In the more fashionable work of the 'thirties and early 'forties, however, a distinctive stylistic development was based upon the use of flat or curved surface cutting, implying the removal of slices from the surface of a vessel, rather than upon the criss-cross of mitre grooves. In this phase straight vertical motifs were preferred, and these were achieved most frequently by broadly hollowed or pillared flutes or more simply by flat vertical facets. The use of such motifs affected not merely the decoration of objects but also their shapes. Perhaps because it was easier to cut the broad flutes or facets on surfaces which curved only in one direction, the shapes tended to be ones with angular profiles. The barrel-shaped decanters of the earlier part of the century became basically cylindrical in shape; whilst the neck rings of the older type tended to disappear, probably because they interfered with a sense of simple vertical pattern. These characteristics can already be seen in the pattern drawings of about 1830 which belonged to Samuel Miller, foreman cutter at the Waterford factory,[4] and their development in the 'thirties and 'forties can be noticed in surviving pattern-books in English factories.

The angular broad-fluted work represented in glassware the last phase of the heavy formal Empire style which had affected all the decorative arts of the early nineteenth century. As such it stood in sharp contrast to the revived rococo style which had already developed by the 'twenties in British porcelain and silverwork as a reaction against the Empire formality. Rococo motifs could scarcely be used directly in cut crystal work, but the accompanying feeling for curving shapes and for curved and often asymmetrical motifs was a minor element in British glasswork during the 'thirties and was to become predominant during the later 'forties and 'fifties. Decanters or water-carafes with globular bodies were beginning to appear in the 'thirties alongside the many straight-sided cylindrical examples. The decanter with a globular body and tall slender neck was a natural glass shape which had appeared at many different times in the history of blown glass; and although the Early Victorian version of it was often decorated with facet or mitre cutting, it was best produced in comparatively thin glass with decoration of shallow-cut hollows or else of engraving. It is interesting to notice that of the six clear glass decanters which happen to be illustrated in the *Journal of Design and Manufactures* from the display at the Birmingham Exhibition of 1849, five are globular or squat-globular in shape. One of these, by George Bacchus and Sons of Birmingham, has engraved decoration, another by W.H., B. and J.Richardson of Stourbridge is mainly decorated by a pattern of cut hollows, and the others, by Lloyd and Summerfield of Birmingham and by Bacchus, are decorated by cutting over their whole surface. An analogous curvilinear shape was that of the champagne glass with hemispherical bowl, which was in fashion by the early 'thirties.[5] By the middle of the century wineglasses of all sorts were being made in a variety of curved, and often ogee-curved, forms.

The removal of the excise duty on glass in 1845 was followed by an enthusiastic development of deep mitre cutting on objects suitable for making in thick glass, and the more ambitious of this work included the use of curvilinear motifs such as that produced by Richardsons for the 1851 Exhibition (Pl. 64A). On the other hand, almost immediately after the 1851 Exhibition cut crystal work began to lose its fashionable standing, and during the remainder of the 'fifties, and beyond, new designs of this nature tended to be somewhat unobtrusive, such for instance as over-all patterns of small widely-spaced stars. The profiles of vessels made in the middle and later 'fifties were predominantly globular or curvilinear; and twisted work was beginning to be common, especially as a means of forming the handles of vessels.

Engraving

Throughout the Early Victorian period decoration by engraving was becoming increasingly popular. In the 'thirties engraving was being carried out in Dudley by the Herbert family, and

---

[4] M.S.Dudley Westropp, *Irish Glass*, 1920, p. 56, etc.

[5] W.A.Thorpe, *History of English and Irish Glass*, Vol. I, 1929, p. 314.

particularly by William Herbert, for the firm of Thomas Hawkes of Dudley. Around the 'forties the Wood family of engravers were working in Stourbridge, and Thomas Wood was among the independent exhibitors at the 1851 Exhibition. Of more specialized and local interest was the engraved work, mostly representing Sunderland Bridge, which was carried out in Sunderland on local glass in the 'thirties and 'forties by Robert Haddock and Robert Pyle. Probably the most outstanding engraved pieces shown at the 1851 Exhibition were the goblets with deep floral motifs designed (and perhaps engraved) by W.J.Muckley for Richardsons (Pl. 63A), and the engraved versions of Greek 'oenochoe' jug shapes which were commissioned and shown by the London firm of dealers J.G.Green and were perhaps made by Bacchus of Birmingham. The latter included a rare example of finely engraved figure-work (Pl. 63B). Flower and plant motifs varied from tight bunches in a style borrowed from porcelain painting to loose over-all running patterns which appeared equally in the late 'forties on pottery and silverwork. Probably in reaction against the excessively deep mitre cutting of the years around the middle of the century and against the cheap pressed-glass imitations of cutting, engraving became by far the most fashionable method of decoration during a long period following the 1851 Exhibition. In the 'fifties engraving was used for a wide range of wares from services with simple patterned edgings to elaborate prestige pieces closely decorated with Renaissance arabesques. The great vogue for engraving began to attract emigrant craftsmen from Central Europe. Prominent among these was J.H.B.Millar, a Bohemian, who towards the end of the 'fifties established in Edinburgh an important firm of engravers which was staffed initially by fellow Bohemian craftsmen.

Engraving by acid etching was used commercially in the 'thirties by Thomas Hawkes of Dudley. It was being used by at least one firm in Stourbridge about the early 'forties, and in the 'fifties further experiments were made by Benjamin Richardson (of the Richardson firm which in the later 'fifties was being operated under his

name alone). It was not, however, until the 'sixties that extensive use came to be made of the process in this country.

Colour

The styles of cut and engraved glassware which have been described so far were mostly made in the fine clear lead glass for which the glassmakers of this country had already achieved an international reputation. Contemporary British accounts of the glass in international exhibitions never failed to remark upon the superior quality of the British glass material, and the material was naturally seen to its best advantage when it was used clear and uncoloured. In the Central European glassmaking areas of Bohemia and south-east Germany a reaction against British cut crystal had resulted during the 'twenties and 'thirties in a remarkable development in the use of coloured glasses. The techniques and styles associated with the Central European coloured glasswork, of this so-called 'Biedermeier' period, were taken up by glass factories in western European countries and particularly by those of France. About the later 'thirties coloured glass was being used in British factories for simple cased, or layered, work and as an alternative material for pieces normally made in uncoloured glass. The firm of Thomas Hawkes were producing semi-opaque white glassware with gilt decoration in the mid-'thirties, and glasses engraved through silver stain were being made in Stourbridge about the early 'forties. But it was not until the removal of the excise in 1845 that the British glassmakers suddenly found themselves free to participate fully in the international coloured-glass styles. The leading spirit in this movement seems to have been Benjamin Richardson, and already in the Manchester Exhibition at the end of 1845 the main interest of the big display by the Richardson firm was in coloured, opal, cased and painted glasses.

Other firms followed rapidly to exploit this field of glasswork. Even the Birmingham firm of F. and C.Osler, mainly known for large-scale work in crystal glass, was found showing opal flower vases with relief painted decoration at the Royal Polytechnic Institution Exhibition of 1848.

At the Birmingham Exhibition of 1849 the great majority of the glasses of the Birmingham firms George Bacchus and Sons and Rice Harris and Son, as well as those of Richardsons of Stourbridge, showed the use of colour in one form or another. The fashion reached its culmination at the 1851 Exhibition where almost all the important glass manufacturers in the country were seen to be making plain coloured, cased or opal glassware. In the Exhibition catalogue the longest list of colours is that of Rice Harris, which is given as 'opal, alabaster, turquoise, amber, canary, topaz, chryso-prase, pink, blue, light and dark ruby, black, brown, green, purple, etc.'

Coloured glasses might be used for work in any of the current styles of uncoloured glasswork. Perhaps the most characteristic use of plain coloured glass was for comparatively small objects, toilet bottles and the like, in the sharply angular shapes with broad vertical facet cutting which were associated with the contemporary Bohemian coloured glass. The most dramatic use of coloured glasses, however, was in the cased glass of the period, which was also used largely in styles derived from the Biedermeier glass of Central Europe. In cased glass a semi-opaque white was frequently used as the outer layer, or else as an intermediate layer to give emphasis to the change of colour be-tween, say, clear blue glass on the outside and un-coloured glass on the inside. Such glasses were always decorated by cutting through the outer layer or layers of glass. The cuttings were usually spaced to leave between them undisturbed areas of the outer layer, and cut hollows and hollow flutes were often contrived in a manner which was sug-gestive of the lights of a Gothic traceried window and which accorded well with the neo-Gothic taste of the period (Pl. 63A). The richness of effect might be further enhanced by painting or engrav-ing on the glass exposed in the cut-away areas, or by gilding on the undisturbed areas of an outer white layer. Another use of cased glass was to give emphasis to engraving. A thin outer layer of clear coloured glass was used as a field through which a pattern was engraved on to the uncoloured body beneath. For this purpose casing had much the same effect as staining, but the depth of the colour

made it more suitable for use with comparatively deep engraving. A notable use of this technique was in some at least of the Richardson engraved work associated with W.J.Muckley, which has already been mentioned (Pl. 63A).

The opalines, or vessels made throughout of semi-opaque glass, appeared mostly in styles which were distinct from those of plain coloured or cased glass. Since this material was both coloured and obscured, there was little to gain by cutting it, and makers tended therefore to use it in natural flow-ing shapes. A current Central European style of two-colour opalines was represented in the work of Richardsons and probably of other Midland factories. White and green opal glasses were com-bined in the same vessels, the green being used in shapes suggestive of leaves for overhanging rims and other extruding parts. On the other hand, when the British glassmakers were concerned in producing painted and gilt opal glasses, their atten-tion was attracted by the work of the French fac-tories rather than by those of Central Europe. Large white opal vases with floral painting made by Richardsons around 1851 are scarcely distin-guishable in general style from the more ambitious French painted vases of the period (Pl. 62B). Most of the painted opalines were of white opal or of alabaster glass; and some of the most attractive of this work appeared on jugs and vases with low-bellied forms which are reminiscent of contem-porary jug shapes in pottery. Richardson examples were often painted with friezes of classical figures or with monochrome scenes; and also printed decoration was often used on opalines of this sort.

The fashion for enamel painting did not neces-sarily imply the use of semi-opaque glasses. The Richardson firm in particular was responsible for a considerable amount of painting on objects of clear transparent glass; and this was the most favoured medium for the glass designs commis-sioned by Henry Cole around 1847 for his 'Sum-merly's Art Manufactures'. The latter included glasses painted with a much-imitated motif of water-plants, which were designed by the painter Richard Redgrave and made by the firm of J.F. Christy of Lambeth (Pl. 62A).

The belated British participation in the coloured-glass styles of the mid-century was momentous in its time, but it was also short-lived. Two other influences upon British glasswork of the period need to be considered – those of Greek pottery and of Venetian glass. Neither of these influences was dramatic in its immediate effects, but both were to be of lasting significance in the developing tradition of modern British glassware.

Greek forms

The somewhat academic Victorian revival of Greek pottery forms was reflected in many of the details of glass shapes and decorations after the removal of the excise duty in 1845. The Greek pinched mouth, for instance, became a common feature of the opal and alabaster glass jugs. About 1847 a London dealer, a Mr Giller of Holborn, was producing (through Thomas Webb of Stourbridge and the London decorating firm of Thomas Battam) painted glassware which was deliberately shaped and decorated in the manner of Greek pottery. Other painted glass versions of Greek pottery were shown at the 1851 Exhibition by Davis, Greathead and Green of Stourbridge. The use of Greek jug shapes in clear glass with engraved decoration has already been mentioned in the instance of the display of the dealers J.G. Green at the 1851 Exhibition (Pl. 63B), and it was from sources such as this that the high-shouldered decanters and claret jugs of the later part of the century were derived.

Venetian influence

The Venetian influence is less easily defined. The word 'Venetian' occurs in the 1851 Exhibition catalogue in descriptions of the work of the Richardson firm, of Davis, Greathead and Green, of Rice Harris, and of Apsley Pellat; but it is difficult to find any common denominator among this work other than a certain freedom or eccentricity of style. Glasses made by Apsley Pellat were described as Venetian in the 1847 *Art-Union* with apparently little reason other than that they were engraved with Renaissance arabesque patterns; whilst the Venetian element in the same firm's 'Anglo-Venetian' glasses at the 1851 Exhibition consisted in their being frosted and gilt.

An important feature in the work of the Bacchus firm about the middle of the century was the use of multicoloured threading in the stems of wine-glasses, and these were often also convoluted (Pl. 64B). At the 1851 Exhibition threaded glass was also shown by Rice Harris, and elaborately convoluted stems were a feature of wine-glasses shown by Lloyd and Summerfield. The style of Venetian glass in the sense of a style using rapidly formed plastic shapes, was strongly advocated by Ruskin in the second volume of his *Stones of Venice* (1853); and this concept was applied by the architect Philip Webb when, around 1860, he was designing table-glasses to be made for William Morris by James Powell and Sons of London.

Novelties

A feature of early Victorian glasswork was the appearance of various sorts of glass novelties, which in effect meant the use of glass for unexpected purposes or the use of unusual glass techniques for the sake of their interest as curiosities. Apsley Pellat's 'cameo incrustations', or small white paste images enclosed within clear glass, were, in this country, a novelty of the early 'twenties, although the knowledge of them survived sufficiently for them to be included in the firm's display at the 1851 Exhibition. Around the middle of the century glass busts were being made by two of the Birmingham firms, F. and C.Osler and Lloyd and Summerfield. These were produced in moulds; and those by Osler, at least, were given a frosted surface by abrading. A novelty of the same period was the double-walled vessels with silvering on the interior surfaces, which gave an opportunity for interesting effects of reflection and colour. The patent for this method of manufacture was taken out in 1849 by F.Hale Thomson and Edward Varnish, and the vessels were apparently made at the factory of James Powell and Sons.

The most striking of the Early Victorian novelties, however, were the glass paper-weights enclosing ingenious coloured patterns. The vogue for paper-weights came to this country from France, where they had been made in great numbers since 1845. A writer in the first volume of the

Journal of Design and Manufactures in 1849 gives a clear indication of the extent of the popular fancy for paper-weights and of the firm which was responsible for developing their manufacture in this country: 'It were to be wished that Messrs Bacchus had been a little earlier in the manufacture of their Glass Paper Weights, for the specimens we have recently seen at their works are quite equal in transparency, colour, skilful arrangement of parts, and ingenuity of make, to the foreign works with which stationers' and fancy shops have been and are so crowded.' Most of the paper-weights which can be presumed to have been made in this country during the mid-century years are of the 'millefiori' variety, whereby an internal pattern was built up by arranging small coloured glass canes in concentric circles; and once acquired, the millefiori technique was used in the same manner for other objects, such as standing inkwells and door-knobs, which offered similar opportunities for the use of thick glass as a means of magnifying the internal pattern.

Pressed glass

Most of the fine glasswork of the period was made, as it is today, by the traditional methods of hand-craftsmanship; although some, such as opaline glasses with relief decoration, would be produced by blowing into moulds. This was a period in which the methods of moulding were greatly extended for the making of cheap glassware, and in particular it was the period in which the process of press-moulding was first developed for the production of dishes and other open shapes. The method of pressing glass between a mould and a plunger appears to have been mainly an American invention. In this country it was being extensively used from the early 'thirties onwards by a number of Midland firms, notably Thomas Hawkes, Bacchus (known during most of the 'thirties as Bacchus and Green), and Rice Harris; it was also presumably used by Apsley Pellat, who patented a small modification to the process in 1831. In America the pressed glass of the 'thirties and 'forties was mostly decorated in the 'lacy' style with elaborate relief patterns on finely stippled grounds, and a somewhat similar free style of relief decoration was used on pressed glass in France. Some of the early British patterns for pressed glass were no doubt of this sort; but it seems probable that the majority were in imitation of cut crystal styles, and this was perhaps natural in the country to which cut crystal was native (Fig. 4). Identifiable pieces of British pressed glass in 'lacy' and similar styles are usually found to belong to a later phase about the 'seventies and 'eighties when much of the British pressed-glass industry was concentrated in the north-east of England.

Fig. 4. Pressed-glass fruit dish made Birmingham, 1850. *Journal of* by George Bacchus & Sons of *Design and Manufactures* (IV, 94).

A gilt-brass three-light chandelier for burning oil, *c.* 1830.
Saltram Park, Devon. National Trust.

PLATE 65

(A) Chimneypiece and grate exhibited in 1851. The figures of gilt cast-iron, and the mouldings painted to imitate marble; the grate of burnished steel and the rococo ornaments of electro-gilt bronze by Coalbrooke dale Company. *Art-Journal Illustrated Catalogue*, 1851.

(B) A group of candelabra, lamps and a chandelier shown in 1851 by Messrs Salt and Lloyd of Birmingham. *Art-Journal Illustrated Catalogue*, 1851.

PLATE 66

'A four-post brass bedstead clothed in green silk, the metalwork in the Renaissance style, with figures, foliage, and scrollwork introduced.' Exhibited in 1851 by R. W. Winfield of Birmingham and London.

PLATE 67

(A) Japanned iron coal-box,
c. 1850.

(B) Gilt brass paperweight with black silk
tassel, 1855.

(C) An ornamental gas bracket shown
in 1851 by William Potts of Birmingham.

(D) Cast-iron table with white marble
top.

PLATE 68

(A) 'Elizabethan Window Curtains.' Plate 27 from *Furniture with Candelabra and Interior Decoration designed by R. Bridgens*, London, 1838.

(B) Window curtain in the 'François Ier' style. Plate VII from *A Series of Designs of Furniture & Decoration in the Style of Louis XIVth, Francis Ist, Elizabeth & Gothic*, designed and drawn by Henry Wood, London, n.d., *c.* 1845.

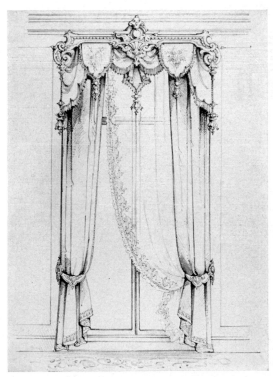

(C) A window curtain in the 'Louis Quatorze' style from *The Upholsterer's Sketch Book of Original Designs for Fashionable Draperies &c.*, by T. King, London, 1839.

(D) Window curtain. Plate 28 from *Select Designs for 1852. Window-cornices, Valances &c. Devised, Drawn on Stone & Published by Laugher, Dwyer & Greenberry, 17, Poland St., London.*

PLATE 69   1413

(A) Silk and linen damask with watered ground (tabbinet) woven by J. Stillwell & Co., White Lion Square, Norton Falgate, London, in 1843. *Property of the Patent Office.*

(B) Brocatelle woven by Daniel Walters & Son, New Mills, Braintree, Essex, in 1850. *Property of the Patent Office.*

(C) 'The Queen's Pattern.' Silk brocade designed and woven by pupils of the Spitalfields School of Design for the Great Exhibition of 1851. *Victoria and Albert Museum.*

(D) Silk brocade, purchased by the Victoria and Albert Museum in 1859. *Victoria and Albert Museum.*

(A) Wool and cotton damask, manufactured by McCrea & Shepherd, Halifax, 1847. *Property of the Patent Office.*

(B) Wool damask designed by A. W. N. Pugin for F. Crace & Son, 1850. *Property of the Patent Office.*

(C) Cotton and wool damask manufactured by John Shepherd & Co., Halifax, 1852. *Property of the Patent Office.*

(D) Wool and silk damask manufactured by James Akroyd & Son, Halifax, 1855. *Property of the Patent Office.*

PLATE 71

(A) Block-printed cotton with machine 'cover'. Printed by Charles Swainson at Bannister Hall, near Preston, 1837. *Property of Stead, McAlpin, Ltd.*

(B) Cotton, roller-printed in two colours, with additional colours printed by surface roller, 1834. The birds and flowers copied from J. J. Audubon's *Birds of America*, Plates 20, 123, 131 and 134. *Victoria and Albert Museum.*

(C) Cotton, roller-printed by Kershaw, Leese & Sidebottom, Ardwick Print Works, Manchester, 1847. The design shows the young Prince of Wales. A Berlin wool-work picture of the same subject is in the Victoria and Albert Museum. *Property of the Patent Office.*

PLATE 72

(A) Cotton block-printed for John Watson & Co., London, 1846.
Property of the Patent Office.

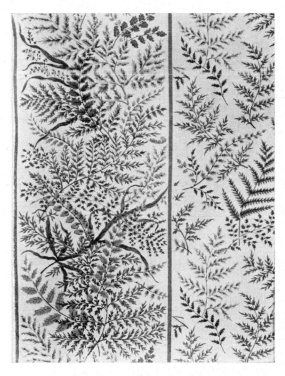

(B) Cotton, block-printed at Bannister Hall for Swainson & Dennys, 1848. Awarded the Silver Medal of the Royal Society of Arts in March, 1849. *Property of the Patent Office.*

(C) Cotton, block-printed by McAlpin, Stead & Co., Cummersdale, 1858. *Property of the Patent Office.*

PLATE 73

1417

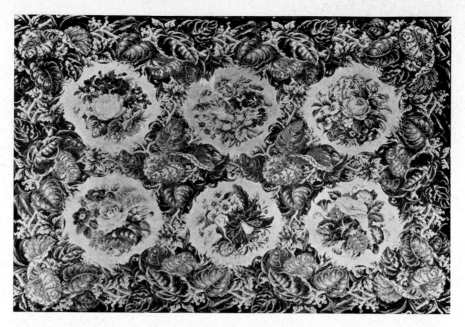

(A) Needlework carpet. Wool on canvas; cross-stitch, *c.* 1840–50.
Victoria and Albert Museum.

(B) Hand-knotted carpet; woollen pile on flax warps. Probably made at
Axminster. *c.* 1835. *Victoria and Albert Museum.*

PLATE 74

Hand-knotted Axminster carpet made by Jackson and Graham, Oxford Street, London, 1851 (Plate 132 of *The Industrial Arts of the Nineteenth Century* by M. Digby Wyatt, 1853).

PLATE 75

(A) Cushion. Silk on canvas; cross-stitch. Worked by Mary Anne Redfern (Mrs Hall) c. 1848. *Victoria and Albert Museum.*

(B) Stool cover. Wool on woollen cloth; tent-stitch. Worked by Caroline Davies (Mrs Boileau) c. 1850. *Victoria and Albert Museum.*

(C) Band of satin, machine-embroidered in ombré silks. Made by Houldsworth & Co., Manchester, and purchased by the Victoria and Albert Museum from the Dublin Exhibition of 1853. *Victoria and Albert Museum.*

(D) Panel. Silk on serge. Designed by William Morris for his own house, Red House, in 1860. *Property of George Howard, Esq., on loan to the Victoria and Albert Museum.*

PLATE 76

Detail of The Grosvenor Family, 1832 (exhibited). By C. R. LESLIE.

This shows women's dress just before change came to the sleeve. The standing figure is in outdoor dress, pelisse robe with wide lapels, wide-brimmed bonnet, with a spray of flowers beneath the brim, and parasol. The seated figure at the piano wears an elaborate dress cap and a muslin pelerine. The younger woman at the harp, who does not wear a cap, has 'jockeys' over the top of her full sleeves. The men, who have dark coats over light trousers, show three styles of neckwear, a white cravat, a black cravat, and a black cravat with long ends, filling the opening of the low-fastening waistcoat of figured silk. *The Executors of the late Duke of Westminster.*

PLATE 77   1421

Pelisse robe, purple silk, figured in blue, 1830–3.
The sleeves, very full at the shoulders, tapering slightly to the lower arm, remain the dominating feature of dress until 1835. The figured silk shows the growing fashion for fabrics resembling those of the eighteenth century. *Victoria and Albert Museum.*

Portrait Group, 1844. By FORD MADOX BROWN.

The dress and hairdressing of the older woman is still in the fashion of the late 1830s. She wears a sleeve still retaining part of its fullness in the lower arm and an elaborate cap of the 1830s shape. The younger women wear their hair in the smooth style of the 1840s, and all have the low neckline with the deep collar of lace which had just become fashionable. The bodice shaping of the 1840s and its deep-pointed waist-line can be seen in the dress on the extreme right, which also shows the sleeve beginning to open over white muslin undersleeves. The men both wear dark cravats, one black, the other dark blue spotted in white, above a shirt with plain front and button fastening. Their coat sleeves are open at the wrist, fastening with one or two buttons, a detail of the 1830s and 1840s. *Manchester City Art Galleries.*

PLATE 79   1423

Evening dress, blue and white striped silk, 1841–3.
This dress, which has an alternative, long-sleeved bodice for day wear,
shows the short, tight sleeve set low on the arm. The trimming at the neck,
flat folds of material, draped with a point at the centre, called 'à la
Sevigné', appeared on bodices throughout the 1830s and 1840s. The hair
is dressed in the ringlet style of the 1840s with a headdress of Honiton lace
and flowers. *Manchester City Art Galleries.*

PLATE 80

James Ramsay, Marquess of Dalhousie, 1847. By J. Watson Gordon. The double-breasted coat buttons high and the full skirts cover the upper part of the legs. The trousers show the narrow-legged form fashionable in the 1840s and 1850s. The black cravat makes a wide band covering the neck and is tied low, in a neat bow. *National Portrait Gallery.*

PLATE 81   1425

Family Group. Photograph.

The younger woman shows the style of bodice worn from about 1843 into the early 1850s, with draped fullness on the shoulders, gathered together at the centre waist. She wears a ribbon waist-band and a ribbon round her neck, crossed in front and fastened by a brooch, a favourite ornament, 1845–55. The older man keeps the earlier style of a white cravat; the younger shows the narrower band and large bow which had now developed; and in the wearing of his coat, follows a custom of the 1850s and 1860s of fastening the top button only. *Manchester City Art Galleries.*

PLATE 82

Three styles of bonnet, 1835–58.

(*Above*) A silk bonnet, over a stiff foundation, with cone-shaped crown, set at an angle to the wide brim, 1835–8.

(*Below*, *right*) A drawn bonnet of shot silk, gathered over a framework of cane, the brim in a straight line with the crown, the style of 1840–50.

(*Below*, *left*) A bonnet of split straw and horsehair plait, with the brim and crown in a line which slopes towards the back of the head, 1853–8.

All have the curtain, shading the neck at the back. *Manchester City Art Galleries*.

PLATE 83   1427

The Empty Purse, 1857. By JAMES COLLINSON.

She wears the fashionable bonnet of the mid-1850s, which slopes towards the back of the head leaving the front uncovered. The brim is trimmed inside and a small bonnet veil, now thrown back, is worn. On the stand at her side is a newly fashionable hat. The sleeve of the dress is in the 'pagoda' form, with lace-trimmed, ribbon-threaded undersleeves. The flounces of the skirt are woven with horizontal striping 'à la disposition'. The gloves are very short-wristed and the empty purse of the title is one of the netted, beaded purses which survive in large numbers from this period. *Tate Gallery, London.*

PLATE 84

(A) Bracelet of Berlin cast-iron work in Gothic Revival style, *c.* 1830.

(B) Bracelet of gold, ornamented with designs copied from an Assyrian relief in the British Museum. By John Brogden, London. Mid-19th century.

All the Jewellery illustrated on plates 85–88 is in the Victoria and Albert Museum.

(C) Enamelled gold pendant by François Froment-Meurice. Mid-19th century. (D) Pendant in revived Renaissance style, enamelled gold set with rubies, pearls, a diamond and a sapphire intaglio. By Castellani, *c.* 1860. (E) Brooch with locket, enamelled gold and diamonds, *c.* 1850/60.

PLATE 85   1429

(A) Brooch and pair of ear-rings. Peridots in stamped gold settings. Mid-19th century.

(B) Brooch, enamelled gold with glass paste. Mid-19th century. (C) Hair ornament, two-colour gold set with amethysts, turquoises and foiled crystals, c. 1840.

PLATE 86

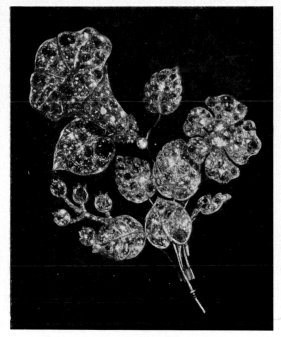

(A) Diamond spray brooch, *c.* 1830–40.

(B) Convolvulus brooch, gold set with turquoises and pearls. Mid-19th century.

(C) Brooch, gold set with diamonds, emeralds, and rubies, *c.* 1840.

(D) Spray brooch, turquoises and diamonds, set in silver with gold backing, *c.* 1860.

PLATE 87

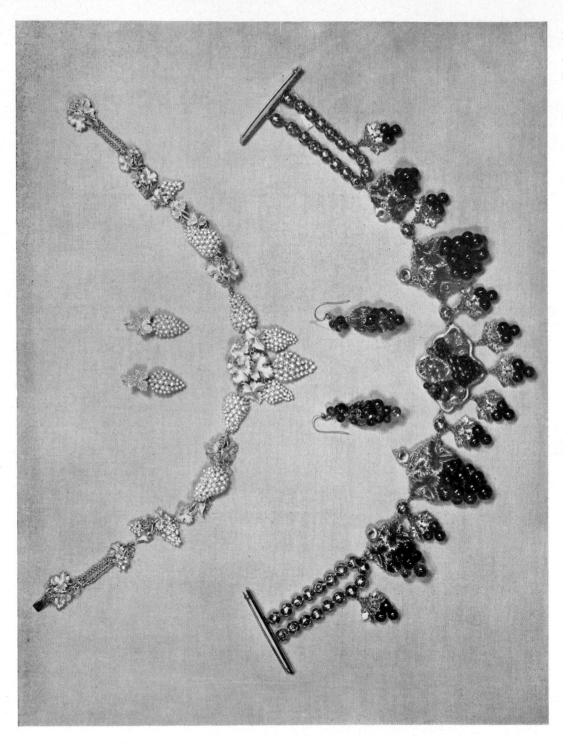

Above. Necklace and ear-rings. Two-colour gold and seed pearls, *c.* 1840. *Below.* Necklace and ear-rings. Enamelled gold and amethysts, *c.* 1840.

PLATE 88

Papier mâché upright Pianoforte by A. Dimoline, Bristol.

PLATE 89

Two artists' impressions of a grand Pianoforte with inlaid ebony decoration and ornamental gold relief work by Broadwood of London.

PLATE 90

(A) A square Pianoforte by Collard and Collard of London.

(B) A carved horizontal grand Pianoforte by Collard and Collard of London.
Art-Journal Illustrated Catalogue, 1851.

PLATE 91

1435

A grand Pianoforte and harps by Erard.

PLATE 92

(B) Mosaic binding by J. W. Zaehnsdorf, c. 1856. Kâlidâsa, *Sákoontalâ*, tr. M. Williams, Hertford, 1855. Brown gold tooled morocco, with a sunk panel of cream leather with onlays of various colours. Exhibited at the International Exhibition of 1862 in London. *British Museum*.

(A) A design blocked in blind on dark blue cloth (repeated front and back). Marryat, *The Pacha of Many Tales*, London, 1835.

PLATE 93

1437

(B) A 'Yellow back' binding, 1856. Maria Edgeworth, *Vivian*, London, 1856. Colour-printed yellow paper over paper boards. *British Museum.*

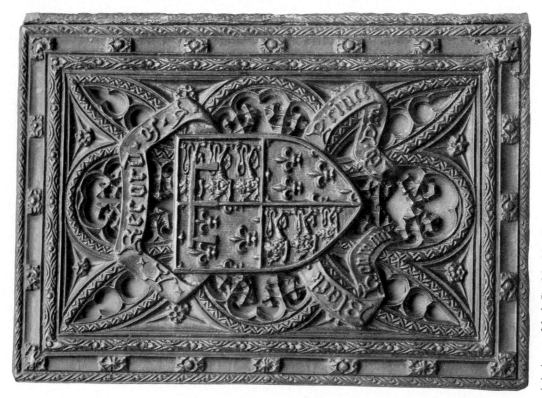

(A) A moulded Gothic binding, 1849. H. N. Humphreys, *A Record of the Black Prince*, London, 1849. Black moulded papier mâché covers ('in imitation of carved ebony') over a red ground, with a plain leather spine. The papier mâché covers were manufactured by Messrs Jackson & Son and the binding was the work of Jane & Robert Leighton, Harp Alley, both of London. *British Museum.*

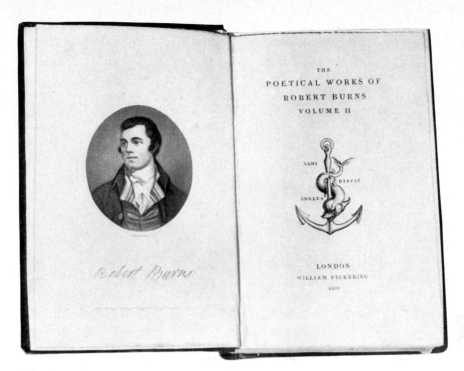

(A) The title-page opening are of Pickering's Aldine editions of the British Poets, 1830; page size 6½ × 4 in.

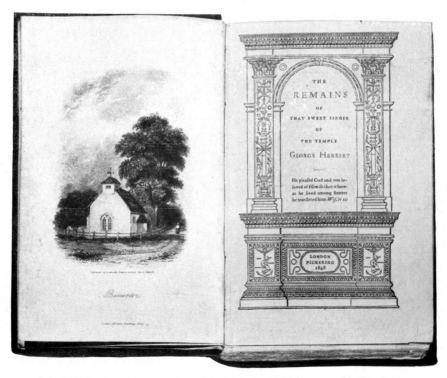

(B) A Pickering title-page in red and black of 1848; page size 6½ × 4 in.

PLATE 95

1439

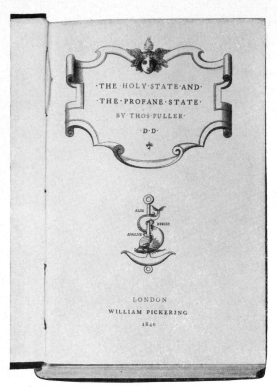

(A) A Pickering title-page in red and black of 1840, $6\frac{1}{2} \times 4$ in.

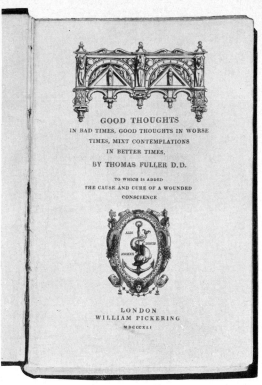

(B) A Pickering title-page in red and black of 1841, $6\frac{1}{2} \times 4$ in.

(C) An early chromolithograph title-page. *The Musical Bijou*, edited by F. H. Burney, London 1847.

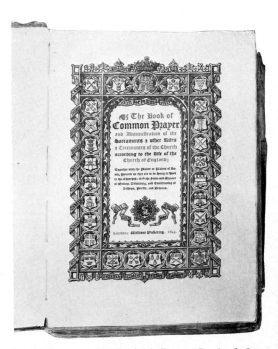

(D) Title-page of Pickering's Prayer-Book of 1844; page size $14 \times 9\frac{1}{4}$ in.

PLATE 96

Domestic Metalwork

JAMES MELTON

The period under review is notable for the wide incursions into the home made by metalwork of all kinds. The traditional hand methods of furniture-making were proving far too costly and slow to produce the increasing quantities of goods demanded by the rising population, and the opportunity to replace traditional wooden articles by those of cast-iron and brass was seized quickly by enterprising manufacturers.

Early in the 1830's John Claudius Loudon (1783–1843), editor of the *Architectural Magazine*, was foremost among those who advocated the greater use of metalwork in the home. In a monster volume, *An Encyclopædia of Cottage, Farm, and Villa Architecture and Furniture*, first issued in 1833, he wrote:

'The introduction of iron into the furniture of Farm houses would be attended with considerable economy, at least in the article of dining-tables, sideboards, bedsteads, and Hall, lobby or porch chairs. The sideboards may be formed of slabs of native marble in some districts, and slate in others, supported by enriched cast-iron feet, or by brackets of various kinds. Sideboards of this kind have a massive architectural effect, very suitable for all houses whatever, and especially for houses in the country, where room is not an object. For our own part, we should even prefer slabs of finely polished stone, as sideboards, to wood of any kind; but cast iron may be substituted; and where neither metal nor stone is approved of, wood of some kind is always to be obtained, and may be worked and polished at pleasure. The idea of having iron bedsteads will, we have no doubt, shock those who have been always accustomed to consider mahogany as essential for this piece of furni-

ture: but we can assure them that they are to be found in the houses of people of wealth and fashion in London; sometimes even for best beds.'

As in other instances, the new medium was introduced in the form of the material it intended to rival. The various articles of iron were moulded with bunches of flowers and fruit, rococo curves and other ornament in close imitation of the hand-carved woodwork they were to replace. Before long, an outcry arose and the pendulum of fashion was agitated violently in a reverse direction: away from the naturalistic and the curved line and backwards in time to the severe and medieval. This in turn was pounced upon by the contemporary critics, and their denunciations were in bitter terms. Augustus Welby Pugin (1812–52) wrote, in his *True Principles of Christian Architecture* (1841), of 'the inconsistencies of modern grates, which are not infrequently made to represent diminutive fronts of castellated or ecclesiastical buildings with turrets, loopholes, windows, and doorways, all in a space of forty inches. The fender is a sort of embattled parapet, with a lodge-gate at each end; the end of the poker is a sharp pointed finial; and at the summit of the tongs is a saint. It is impossible to enumerate half the absurdities of modern metal-workers; but all these proceed from the false notion of *disguising* instead of *beautifying* articles of utility. If a clock is required, it is not unusual to cast a Roman warrior in a flying chariot, round one of the wheels of which, on close inspection, the hours may be descried; or the whole front of a cathedral church reduced to a few inches in height, with the

1441

clock-face occupying the position of a magnificent rose window.'

Once launched, Pugin's pen sailed relentlessly onward. He attacked 'those inexhaustible mines of bad taste, Birmingham and Sheffield', and described 'staircase turrets for inkstands, monumental crosses for light-shades, gable ends hung on handles for door-porters, and four doorways and a cluster of pillars to support a French lamp; while a pair of *pinnacles* supporting an arch is called a Gothic-pattern scraper, and a wiry compound of quatrefoils and fan tracery an abbey garden seat. Neither relative scale, form, purpose, nor unity of style, is ever considered by those who design these abominations; if they only introduce a quatrefoil or an acute arch, be the outline and style of the article ever so modern and debased, it is at once denominated and sold as Gothic.'

Those who strove to draw attention to the many inconsistencies of contemporary design were themselves no less guilty in their striving after a pointless perfection. Their zeal embraced even the common door-hinge, and they deplored the fact that it was concealed in the jambs of doorways and cabinets, and was no longer the elaborate and decorative article of earlier centuries. Even the heads of bolts and rivets, they said, should not be left plain, but should be in the form of a rosette, quatrefoil or fleur-de-lys.

Altogether the attacks of Pugin and others had little effect on contemporary design. The mass of the people preferred and demanded plentiful ornamentation on everything they bought, and the manufacturers and the designers took care to supply it in quantity and variety. There were very few styles of the preceding centuries that were not incorporated, either singly or anachronistically and haphazardly with others, in the decoration of metal objects ranging from pokers to bedsteads, and from cradles to chandeliers.

Centres of manufacture

The manufacture of metal wares centred on Birmingham and Sheffield. At the latter were made principally articles of steel, but at Birmingham (which may be understood to include the nearby towns of Wolverhampton and Walsall and the numerous adjacent villages) was made a multiplicity of objects of all kinds, in both iron and brass, and of every quality – the latter, when at its lowest, having borrowed the name of its place of origin as a description, and the term 'Brummagem made' adheres to this day to anything of a trashy or counterfeit nature. In fairness, it must be mentioned that while a high proportion of goods from the Birmingham factories certainly were made for the cheaper markets, a considerable amount of high-quality work was done there. The standard set by the Soho Works of Matthew Boulton, who died in 1809, but whose manufactory was continued for a further period of nearly forty years, was not easily forgotten.

Between the years 1810 and 1850 the population of Birmingham increased by no less than 150 per cent, and at the same time the cost of goods made there was lowered by from 60 to 85 per cent. During the same period exported iron and steel wares rose from an annual figure of 5,800 tons to over 23,000 tons; the latter reaching a value of £2,200,000. Brass and copper goods exported in 1849 were worth nearly £2,000,000, and the majority of them went, incidentally, to India. The rapid rise in the population of the British Isles together with the lowering of the cost of manufactured goods continued until long after 1860, and were part and parcel of the competitive inventiveness that characterized the Victorian era.

Much of the manufacturing of metal wares in the Midlands was carried out in factories of a type similar to those universal today, but much was produced under a system peculiar to the district and the hardware trade. Single men, or groups of men, hired small workshops which were part of a large block where the power for turning and other mechanical processes was provided by the owner of the building; the rental paid for the use of the workshop including also the use of the power. The makers of goods under these conditions sold them each week to a merchant who was concerned with the marketing of them, and with the money received they purchased the materials with which to make their quota in the week to follow. The familiar factory slowly superseded this individualistic way of earning a livelihood, but in 1860 there were many 'power-hirers' still to be found.

Metal wares

The coming of the railway during the first decades of the period under review not only increased the speed of travel, but was the creator of an enormous demand for metal. Rails, engines, coaches, stations and every detail of the new means of communication called for increasing quantities of iron, steel, brass and copper. There was every inducement for manufacturers to improve and cheapen metals, and the ironmasters, especially, were striving eagerly to introduce any new method or appliance that would allow them to produce more metal for less money and at the same time increase their own profits. As a result, there was a plentiful supply of raw material available to the makers of domestic metal wares, who were enabled to reap the benefits of advances initiated by the Iron Horse.

The railways were responsible not only for calling forth abundant supplies of metal, but they played a further part by ensuring speedy delivery of the finished article. At the same time, with the increasing tempo of life and the greater rapidity of communications, the spread of ideas was facilitated. What was fashionable in London could be imitated in provincial centres in a matter of hours instead of days or weeks, and the opposite was doubtless similarly achieved.

Zinc, known and used from ancient times but not understood properly until the eighteenth century, came to the fore in the Victorian period. In 1833 Germany was producing about 6,000 tons annually, but then Russia commenced production and added a further 2,000 tons to the world supply. By 1855 England was herself producing some 3,000 tons a year. The metal was a valuable constituent of many alloys, of which brass is the best known. The process of 'galvanizing', by which iron articles are dipped in hot zinc and thereby rendered rust-proof, was patented by a Frenchman, M. Sorel, in the 1840's. Its use became widespread, and the familiar sheets of corrugated-iron for roofing were used by the Admiralty as early as 1850. Under the same authority galvanized iron was used for the lining of coal bunkers in the ships of the Royal Navy.

Britannia Metal, an alloy of antimony and tin with copper, lead and zinc or bismuth, and *German Silver*, an alloy of copper, nickel and zinc, were used in great quantities. Other imitations of silver were perfected, and ingenious methods of replacing the old manual processes were evolved.

These, however, lie outside the scope of this article, and the reader will find them described in detail in the chapter entitled *Silver and Silver Plate* (p. 1382).

Brass or bronze, gilded and known as *Ormolu*, had been widely popular since the eighteenth century. The gilding had been performed then by amalgamating pure gold with mercury, coating the article to be gilded with the amalgam, and driving off the unwanted mercury with heat. New processes which gave passably similar results, but without the use of gold itself, came into use, and the invention in 1832 by G.F.Muntz of *Muntz Metal* (known also as *Yellow Metal* or *Patent Metal*) resulted in the production of a material of a full golden-yellow colour that did not fracture too easily. Further, in the 1820's was discovered a method giving brass wares a 'rich dead gold-like colour'; one that was attained inexpensively by means of numerous baths in acid with a final application of lacquer to prevent tarnishing. Electroplating with gold was used also on occasions; it was found that variations in the strength of the current employed produced different shades of gilding, and that tints of green and red could be obtained by the addition of proportions of silver or copper respectively to the electrolytic solution.

Iron manufacture continued by methods that had been developed in earlier decades, but was being improved constantly in minor ways. It became possible, for instance, to make such things as bedposts in one single length; to make tapered tubes, and to cover tubing with a thin sheet of brass which was polished and lacquered to form the basis of the familiar 'brass' bedstead. Another advance was the joining of the tubes which comprised head and end rails by means of ornamented brackets. These were made in cast-iron moulds modelled with the required ornament in intaglio;

the tubes were placed carefully into the moulds in which entry-holes were left for the introduction of molten metal.

Bedsteads

Loudon, who is a reliable authority for the period 1830–40, states that cast-iron bedsteads made by William Mallet of Dublin were used in Irish farm-houses at that time. An illustration of one shows an uninviting trough-like contrivance with a pierced base which was 'well adapted for the ploughman's room'. Less Spartan in appearance, and doubtless more conducive to providing the average man with a night's rest, is an iron half-tester bedstead 'which, however, does not fold up, but which has the advantage of being remarkably cheap. It is manufactured by Messrs Cottam and Hallen, of two feet six inches in width, for 46s. 6d., and of five feet in width for 68s.; in both cases it is complete, with castors, head board, and curtain rods, and is thrice painted in oil' (Fig. 1).

In the years between 1850 and 1860 the metal bedstead competed seriously with that of wood, and the numerous examples shown at the 1851 Exhibition bear witness to the fact (Pl. 67). They were principally of traditional four-poster pattern, but half-tester, tent and folding-tent types also were exhibited. Their ornamentation generally was elaborate, and while the makers carefully designated their productions as being in some par-

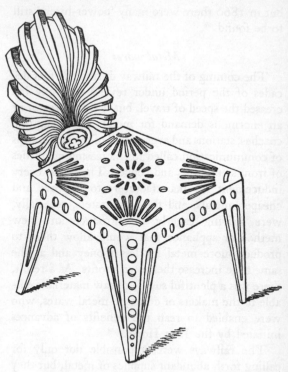

Fig. 2. Lobby chair of Etruscan design.

ticular style – English or Continental – students of the periods named would scarcely recognize any of the attributions. In addition to external embellishments, attempts were made to improve the comfort by using steel laths on which to rest the mattress, and various designs of this kind were registered. Apart from their low price and their appearance, the use of metal bedsteads was encouraged for their undoubted cleanliness when compared with those of wooden construction.

One field in which the metal-bedstead manufacturer was supreme was in the making of folding bedsteads for travelling; principally for the use of Army officers. One such article shown at the 1851 Exhibition was described as an 'officer's portable brass bedstead, to form sofa, with the exhibitor's patent spring mattress and musquito curtains'. The same maker, Henry Pratt, of 123 New Bond Street, showed a brass chaise-longue, and a 'travelling chair in brass, to form couch and bedstead'. Such pieces of furniture were contrived

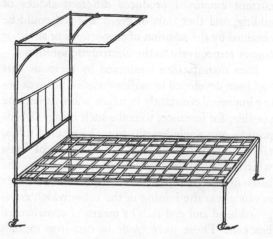

Fig. 1. Iron half-tester bedstead.

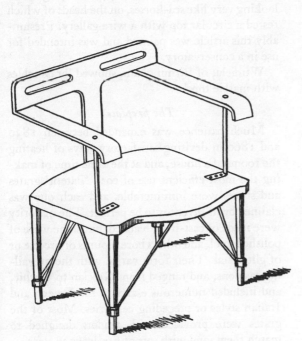

Fig. 3. Iron armchair, the seat of wood.

Fig. 4. Cast and wrought iron cottage chair. From Loudon's *Encyclopaedia*.

ingeniously to be packed for transit into wooden chests fitted with strong carrying-handles; while consideration was given to making the article occupy as small a space as possible, little thought was expended in lessening the weight.

Chairs

Loudon illustrates several examples of chairs, one of which is described as 'a lobby chair of cast iron, suitable for a porch (Fig. 2). The Design is Etruscan; and Mr Mallet, to whom we are indebted for it, says that it may be cast in two pieces. It would therefore, come cheap, and would look exceedingly well in the porch of a cottage in the Italian style. Mr Mallet observes that where carved work, or much ornament, is to be executed in furniture, cast iron will always be found cheaper than wood, even though a small number only of the article were wanting.' A further design from

the same source is of a more functional pattern: 'the back and elbows are cast in one piece; the supports for the elbows and also the legs are of gas tubing, screwed into a cross frame of iron, which proceeds from the back of the chair under the wooden seat' (Figs. 3, 4).

In spite of the enthusiasm of Mr Mallet of Dublin, metal chairs did not meet with wide approval, and very few were to be seen twenty years later at the 1851 Exhibition. One maker showed brass-framed rocking- and arm-chairs, upholstered in morocco, but on the whole such pieces do not seem to have been popular and the scarcity of surviving examples confirms the fact that very few were made.

Garden chairs and seats offered a more practical subject for the attention of manufacturers, and the heavy metals then in use were satisfactorily employed in making them in various patterns.

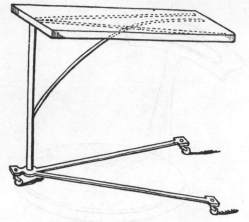

Fig. 5. Invalid's bedside table.

Articles for use outdoors were finished by the application of paints or lacquers, or by the newly-introduced process of galvanizing.

Tables

Loudon shows a circular-topped table, the top of wood and the base of cast-iron resting on ball-castors; and also a metal-based invalid's bedside table with a projecting wooden top (Fig. 5). In the next two decades the metal table would seem to have made little headway, and not a great number of them was to be seen at the Great Exhibition. The most enterprising display was that of the Coalbrookdale Company, of Shropshire, makers of the iron gates that remain in Hyde Park to this day, sited not far from where they were exhibited originally in 1851. This firm showed a number of metal tables, including: 'Cast-iron Chess-tables; Hall, or console-table, in cast-iron, painted in white and gold, marble top; Large table, with cast-iron legs, painted oak; Intricate iron casting, bronzed and marbled, of a hall-table, arranged with pedestals for hats, coats and umbrellas, containing also a pillar for a lamp and looking-glass, with boxes for letters and for brushes, and an inkstand.' (Pl. 68D.)

A table made entirely of wire was exhibited by John Reynolds, New Compton Street, under the description of an 'ornamental flower table'. It was in the form of three serpents, posed upright and looking very like sea-horses, on the heads of which rested a circular top with a wire gallery. Presumably this article was painted and was intended for use in a conservatory.

Winfield, of Birmingham, showed 'brass tables with marble tops'.

The fireplace

Much patience was expended between 1830 and 1860 in devising satisfactory ways of heating the rooms of a house, and at the same time of making the most efficient use of coal. 'Patent' grates and stoves were innumerable, and each one was claimed by its inventor to be perfect. The majority were made of cast-iron, blacked, but some were of polished steel, and others bore mounts of bronze or of gilt metal. Their form varied with the prevailing fashions, and ranged from Grecian to Gothic, and included numerous essays in the French and Italian styles of preceding centuries. Most of the grates were provided with fenders designed to match them, and with sets of fire-irons *en suite*.

A typical production of the 1850's was described by the makers, proudly and at length, in these words:

> 'Ornamental chimney-piece and grate, with decorations illustrative of deer-stalking, boar-hunting, and hawking. The figures are of cast-iron, electro-gilt, and the mouldings are marbled. The grate consists of a burnished steel front, and ornaments in bronze, electro-gilt. The decoration connects, in one design, the fender, ash-pan, and grate. The fire-brick for the back is in one piece, including the bottom of the grate, on which the fire rests. The fender, ash-pan and grate remove in one piece to afford greater convenience in cleaning the chimney.

This *tour-de-force* was modelled and designed by B.W. Hawkins, and is described as standing seven feet in height and four feet wide. It was referred to in a contemporary magazine as 'a beautiful example of manufactured Art' (Pl. 66A).

An important fireplace accessory of metal was the coal-scuttle, which was of brass, copper, or, sometimes, of zinc. It was of many shapes, and in the 1851 Exhibition Tyler and Sons, Warwick

Lane, showed their latest pattern (Fig. 6), in addition to 'copper coal scoops, exhibiting the changes in their patterns during the last 70 years'. The lidded coal-box, or purdonium, was made most often of japanned tinned-steel (see p. 1450), sometimes with a back-painted glass panel inset in the lid (see Pl. 68A).

Light-fittings

During the years between 1830 and 1860 changes in methods of lighting the homes of both rich and poor were taking place. In few preceding periods can there have been more time and thought devoted to the problem of obtaining a greater degree of illumination from a given quantity of illuminant. Experiment was ceaseless, and the foundations were laid for even more spectacular advances to be made in the lifetimes of coming generations. At the commencement of the period, gas-lighting for the home was slowly being introduced, but was still an expensive novelty that often produced no more than an intermittent flicker of light and an unpleasant smell, together with the twin threats of sudden explosion and asphyxiation. The use of the same agent for the cooking of foodstuffs was also little other than an interesting experiment that was more widely mooted than practised.

A company calling itself grandiloquently (and almost incredibly) 'The Patriotic Imperial and National Light and Heat Company' was promoted by a German, Frederick Albert Winsor, and, after Parliamentary opposition, was incorporated in 1810. In spite of Winsor's suggestion that subscribers to his enterprise would be assured of a profit of 10,000 per cent on a capital of £300,000, and the fact that Brougham sarcastically deflated the whole scheme in the House of Commons, the company did manage to prosper. It became later the Gas Light and Coke Company and is now merged in the Gas Board. Opposition to Winsor's company was led by William Murdoch, of Redruth, who had given demonstrations of gas-lighting as early as 1792, and who had commenced six years later to light Boulton and Watts' Soho, Birmingham, engine-works by the same means.

The use of the new illuminant was confined at first to the public highway, large buildings, and to the outdoor celebration of the Treaty of Amiens (1802). Such displays provoked great discussion and interest, but it was not until the decade of 1830–40 that the demand for gas grew large enough to merit the opening of works for its production up and down the country. Although it was not until shortly after the period under review that increased improvement in the efficiency of burners and in the quality of the gas ensured its universal adoption, minor innovations were being introduced continually and attention was paid to the design of wall-lights, chandeliers and other fittings.

While gas was the subject of general wonder, the humble candle continued in general use and was challenged strongly in the public favour by the oil-lamp. The latter, perhaps because of apprehension on behalf of interested parties that the competition of the newly introduced gas might prove disastrous, was constantly being improved. Thus, the *Moderator* lamp embodied a spring to raise the oil to the wick, while some employed clockwork for the same purpose and others increased their power of illumination by the admixture of oxygen or naphtha with the oil. Whale-oil, marketed under the name of *Train-oil*, was the most used,

Coal-scuttle, a pattern introduced in 1851.

1447

Fig. 7. Vine-pattern wall-light for gas.

but many others were tried and achieved a brief popularity. Lard-oil, benzene, camphene, turpentine and others had their devotees, and finally, in 1859, came the discovery of petroleum oil and the promise of ample supplies of paraffin to be realized in the years ahead.

The design of light-fittings during the years 1830–60 varied as widely as did the design of all types of metal wares. Functional efficiency was seldom the first consideration, and was usually disguised by every possible device of ornamentation, which was not always appropriate to the purpose. In the case of chandeliers and wall-lights, bronze chimeras were to be seen spouting flame from the tops of their heads, blameless lilies and cherubic infants were similarly involved, and the illuminant seemed to have been set an impossible task in finding a way through the mass of entwined metal tracery that encumbered the path to the final outlet (Pl. 68c and Fig. 7).

Probably the best-known metal articles of the period are reading-lamps, which have survived in large numbers to this day and seem assured of a further span of useful life when adapted for electricity. The lamps were made usually of bronze, ormolu or electro-plated nickel-silver, and often with base and capital of metal applied to a column of marble, coloured glass or some other suitably decorative material. Many of the columns were modelled on classical originals, and the most popular of all was the pure Corinthian Column, which was made in electro-plate or lacquered brass in great quantities. Other designs were entirely novel in conception; embodying *motifs* from several earlier styles, together with a generous sprinkling of contemporary vine-leaves complete with grapes and tendrils (Pl. 66B).

Kitchen wares

Metal wares continued to hold their place in the kitchen, and there were few notable changes during the period under review. Copper cooking-pans with tinned interiors were popular over the years, but in spite of the highly attractive appearance of a polished and gleaming *batterie-de-cuisine* of this metal, the 1850's saw the introduction and acceptance of the more hygienic and more easily-managed enamelled iron.

The greater number of households employed cooking utensils made from tinned steel, which, while it had neither the good looks nor the lengthy life of heavy-gauge copper, stood up to the rigours of daily usage in both skilled and unskilled hands. Articles made from this material included: basting ladles; coffee-boilers and coffee-pots; colanders; fish-kettles; saucepans; skimmers; slices; soup ladles and tureens; stewpans; and tea-kettles. The range of articles in sheet steel was even wider, and embraced: bed-airers; candlesticks; oval cheese steamers and toasters; chocolate pots and mills; coffee biggins; boilers, filterers and pots; allblaze (fireproof?) steak and fish dishes; covers for plates and dishes; egg-poachers, coddlers and ladles; Etnas, for boiling water; fish-knives; flour-boxes; graters; hot-water dishes and plates; inhalers; pepper-boxes; strainers for milk, gravy and gruel; moulds; 'tea-extractors' (infusers?), kettles and pots; warmers for carriage, for feet and for stomach; and wine mullers and strainers. Many of these things have long since passed out of use and have been discarded, and it needs a long memory to recall their exact appearance or, in some instances, their purpose. It would tax the resources of most to try to distinguish between, say, a strainer for gravy and one for gruel.

Pewter was in use throughout the period, although not by any means on as wide a scale as it had been a century earlier. It was employed, among other things, for the making of complicated moulds for the freezing of ice-puddings, and for the making of jellies and blancmanges. These moulds comprised a top and a base and a hinged central portion, each part being highly embossed with the design to appear in relief on the finished dessert. Although many moulds for these and other purposes were made of tin and copper, soft pewter was unsurpassed for the purpose, and managed to hold its own until the vogue for such edible extravagances grew less common. Ale-tankards of pewter were made and survive in large numbers.

The tea-pot was made often of metal, but it had long been standardized in form and function. Coffee, then as now, was the subject of many inventions designed to improve the flavour of the beverage and to extract the greatest good from the fewest beans. Percolators of various types were on the market, but more ingenious devices were made and used. One of these was *Beart's Patent Pot*, which was described in the 1850's in these words: 'The upper portion of the pot may be considered a cylinder, in which moves the coffee-holder, which consists of a piece of cloth strained over what may be called a piston, the action of raising which, produces a partial vacuum, and the coffee is strained through the sieve-like material of which the piston is composed, by atmospheric pressure.'

General decoration

In no department of metal wares was the demand keener than in that of the general fittings for the decoration of rooms. These included not only door-plates, knobs and escutcheons, decorative bell-handles and handles and mounts for pieces of furniture, but there was a large demand for the fashionable brass-cased cornice-poles with decorated end-pieces from which hung the curtains on large brass rings. Further, when drawn back in the daytime, curtains were held lightly but firmly in the grasp of a hold-back: a U-shaped bracket of metal screwed to the wall and with a decorated side facing into the room. These had been introduced in the early years of the century, and remained popular throughout the Victorian period.

Among the articles in this category that were included by various makers in the Great Exhibition were: 'brass window-cornices and ornaments; poles with ends, rings and brackets; curtains bands and pins; finger-plates for doors, brass and japanned; ornaments for watch hooks; frames for miniatures or pictures; specimens of door-handles, tea-bells, hat and coat hooks and castors, of new and ornamental construction; vases in various styles: bronze, electro-silvered, dead gold and relieved – also [vases] fitted with improved spring igniter for lighting the vesta matches.'

The writing-desk was also the repository of much metalwork, including such things as paper-clips, inkstands and paper-weights (Pl. 68B).

The metal used in making the majority of these objects was principally brass, treated to enhance its resemblance to gold and then lacquered to prevent tarnishing. Whenever possible, for reasons of economy, sheets of the metal were used and stamped with steel dies, in other instances casting was employed. Where extra strength was needed, as with cornice-poles, cast-iron was overlaid with brass. Hand-work was cut down to a minimum, and to produce the greatest quantity of goods to sell at the lowest price was the target; mass-production methods were brought quickly into use as the years proceeded, and hand processes were employed only for finishing. Designers gave full rein to their imaginations, and while many of the results may provoke a condescending smile or a gasp of horror, the majority do not fail to show considerable ingenuity on the parts of both artist and maker.

Mention must be made of the large numbers of bronze figures and groups that were made to adorn mantelpieces and sideboards. Many were the work of contemporary artists, but others were from classical or more recent sources; in the latter category is what is almost certainly the best-known of all – the *Marly Horses*, from the marble originals now in the Champs-Elysées, Paris, executed by Guillaume Coustou (1677–1746).

Japanned wares

Founded during the seventeenth century, the japanned metal industry centred on the Midlands reached its peak in the mid-nineteenth century. Wolverhampton gained a name for goods which showed a high quality of design and finish, while Birmingham and other places continued to supply articles for less discriminating tastes. The range of goods manufactured was very wide, and visitors to the 1851 Exhibition saw, among others, a comprehensive display comprising: 'Baths; bread and cake baskets; boiler fillers; bonnet boxes; botanical boxes; candle boxes and safes; candlesticks; canisters, round and square; cash-boxes; cheese trays; cigar trays; coal scoops, shovels, and vases; date cases; dressing cases; ewers and basins; fire baskets and screen; gunpowder canister; hearing trumpet; inkstands; jugs; knife trays; lamps; lanterns; leg bath; letter cages; music stand; nursery lamps; plate carriers and warmers; sandwich and spice boxes; spittoons; snuffer trays; sugar-boxes; tables; tea-caddies; toast racks; toilette sets; trays; umbrella stands; vegetable warmers; ventilators; waiters; water cans; wax boxes; and writing boxes.' While many of the articles were plainly japanned in black with no more than a line or two of gilding to relieve the surface, others were ambitiously painted with central coloured panels surrounded by elaborate gilt patterns. The better work was all painted and gilded by hand, but a transfer process was employed for cheap wares.

BOOKS FOR FURTHER READING

There are no books devoted specifically to the metalwork of the period as a whole, but most volumes published between the years 1830 and 1860 devoted to the Arts in general mention it, either at length or briefly. The designs current in the year 1851 are described (and, in many instances, illustrated) in the *Official Descriptive and Illustrated Catalogue of the Great Exhibition*, and in the *Illustrated Catalogue of the Exhibition of the Industry of All Nations* published by the *Art-Journal*.

Stamped and gilt brass cornice pole-end.

Textiles

BARBARA MORRIS

Introduction

'There is no general agreement in principles of taste. Every one elects his own style of art. ... Some few take refuge in a liking for "pure Greek", and are rigidly "classical", others find safety in the "antique", others believe only in "Pugin", others lean upon imitations of modern Germans and some extol the *Renaissance*. We all agree only in being imitators.'

This opening to 'Hints for the Decoration and Furnishing of Dwellings' (*Journal of Design*, 1849) sums up the eclecticism which is characteristic of the Victorian approach to the decorative arts, but it would be wrong to consider the Victorians as mere imitators. While borrowing heavily from the past, the leading designers imbued their work with a new spirit, recreating from their historic prototypes something that was essentially of their own age and could have been produced at no other time. In this way, although the source of inspiration is always apparent, whether 'Gothic', 'Arabesque', or 'Louis Quatorze', to mention only three, there is a certain affinity between all the styles.

The Victorian equation of elaboration with beauty is demonstrated by the use of pattern on all available surfaces – the walls, the carpets, the upholstery and the curtains. Carefully contrived schemes such as the 'Elizabethan' dining-room at Charlecote, where the pattern of the carpet echoes the strapwork design of the flock wallpaper, are exceptions, and a mixture of unrelated patterns was the general order.

Whereas during the Regency there was a pre-ponderance of plain fabrics for curtains and upholstery, during the period 1830–60 patterned materials were most favoured. Until about 1840 fairly light colours predominated, but thereafter darker colours, particularly crimson and bottle green, were most popular, which, when combined with the use of heavier fabrics, such as worsted damasks, velvet or brocatelle, gave a sombre but rich effect. These heavier fabrics were used extensively in drawing-rooms and dining-rooms, and chintz was more or less relegated to the bed-rooms, except when used to make 'throw-overs' or loose covers for upholstered furniture. Elaborately patterned machine-woven cotton lace or madras muslin replaced the plain or lightly sprigged muslin of the preceding era. An alternative was semi-transparent blinds, printed with imitations of stained-glass windows, or even with pictorial subjects, including representations of the Royal Family.

Draperies

Thomas King, writing in 1833 as 'an upholsterer of forty-five years experience', states that during this time 'has occurred the entire introduction of French Draperies and Curtains; then the extreme prevalence of massive brass Rods with Large Rings, and at a later period, the universal use of Piped Valances. Now the most modern style blends all three'.[1] (See Figs. 1–3.)

During the 1830's, in fact, very little that was absolutely new was introduced and generally

[1] *The Upholsterer's Accelerator*, 1833.

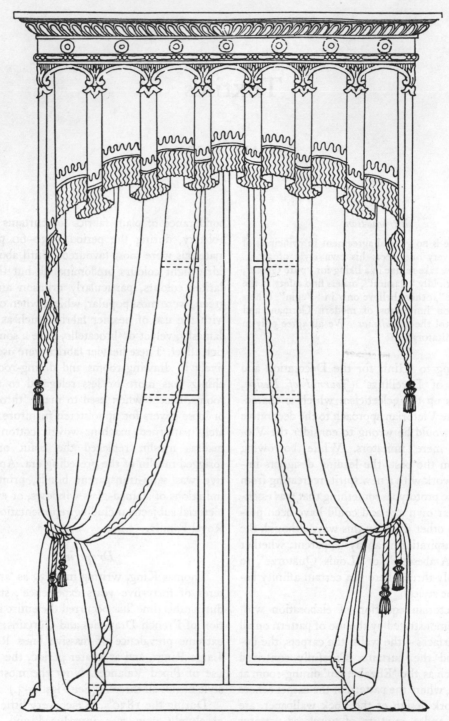

Fig. 1. Drawing-room window curtain from *An Encyclopaedia of Cottage, Farm, &*
Villa Architecture & Furniture by J.C.Loudon, London, 1833.

speaking most of the draperies were slight modifications of styles already in fashion in the 1820's. This was particularly true of draperies in the 'Grecian' or 'Gothic' style, although in both styles the carved and gilded cornices tended to be more elaborate. In the simplest styles, considered suitable for 'cottages in the Greek or Italian manner', the curtains were suspended by brass rings from a curtain-pole, and a simple fringed valance, gathered into pleats at intervals, was hung either in front or behind the long curtains. Muslin sub-curtains were often used, particularly in drawing-rooms and dining-rooms. More elaborate festoon draperies, with swags of material looped over the curtain-pole, were used with carved cornices in the classic style, particularly for drawing-rooms.

'Gothic' styles were more commonly employed in dining-rooms or libraries. For Gothic windows shaped valances or pelmets were most favoured, consisting either of a simple shape with deep corners which followed the general line of a Gothic arch, or a long straight piece cut into vandykes or other fancy shapes at the lower edge which was piped or edged with a contrasting colour and often further decorated with tassels. Both the valances and the borders of the curtains were often embellished with appliqué embroidery of Gothic ornaments such as oak leaves, fleur-de-lys or other heraldic devices.

By the late 1830's pure classicism had more or less disappeared and even more variety was apparent with elaborate draperies in the prevailing styles of 'Louis Quatorze', 'Elizabethan', 'François 1er', and 'Gothic', together with more fanciful expressions of the upholsterer's invention which bore little relation to any known historic style. By 1840 the elaboration and complexity of the draperies had reached a point where they were criticized not only on their æsthetic merits but also on utilitarian grounds. Pugin in his *Christian Architecture* (1841) writes that 'all the modern plans of suspending enormous folds of stuff over poles, as if for the purpose of sale or of being dried is [sic] quite contrary to the use and intentions of curtains and abominable in taste; and the only object that these endless festoons and bunchy tassels can answer is to swell the bills and profits of the upholsterers who are the inventors of these extravagant and ugly draperies, which are not only useless in protecting the chamber from cold, but are depositories of thick layers of dust, and in London not infrequently become the strongholds of vermin'.

Festoon draperies in the late 1830's and 1840's were especially prevalent in the so-called 'Louis Quatorze' style, having a natural affinity with the curves and scrolls of the elaborately carved 'rococo' cornices. This style was frequently adopted where formerly the 'Grecian' style was considered appropriate. Typical examples are included by Thomas King in his *Upholsterers' Sketch Book of Original Designs for Fashionable Draperies* (1839) (Pl. 69B). King includes not only festoon draperies made of a single piece, but also more complex types, with separate pieces hanging in deep oval swags, lavishly trimmed with fringe and tassels. Although examples of the 'Louis Quatorze' style are found considerably later, it appears to have reached its zenith as far as draperies were concerned in the 1840's; and Henry Whitaker, in his *Practical Cabinet Maker and Upholsterer's Treasury of Designs* (1847), seems to have some justification for his remark that the 'Louis-Quatorze style is going out very fast'.

The 'Elizabethan' style, although equally elaborate, presented a more formal appearance with flat valances cut at the lower edge into curved and angled shapes which echoed the strapwork and cartouches of the carved wooden cornices (Pl. 69A). The bottom of the valance was usually trimmed with a contrasting narrow band and tassels were suspended at regular intervals. These shaped valances were used equally for windows and for four-poster bedsteads in the Elizabethan style, with the curtains hung from poles, by large brass rings, set in front, or, less frequently behind, the valance.

It is not always easy to distinguish the 'François 1er' style from the 'Elizabethan', but generally speaking it was more elaborate and more curvilinear, with human figures and masks introduced into the carving. The window curtain (Pl. 69B) shown on Plate 7 of Henry Wood's *Designs for Furniture and Draperies in the Styles of Louis*

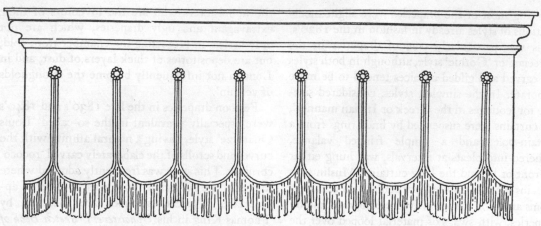

Fig. 2. Piped **valance** from *The Upholsterer's Accelerator* by Thomas King,
London, 1833.

XIVth, Francois Ier, Elizabeth and Gothic (London, n.d., *c.* 1845) is a typical expression of the style, particularly in the use of festoon drapery behind the flat-shaped valance.

In the 1850's the clear division into styles is often no longer apparent, and the leading upholsterers display an astonishing eclecticism in the selection of detail which includes 'Arabesque', 'Alhambresque', and 'Renaissance' ornament. For example, in the *Select Designs for 1852*, published by Laugher, Dwyer and Greenberry of 171 Poland Street, London, it is possible to attach an appropriate label to most of the cornices, but the draperies beneath them must be considered more or less interchangeable. The complex type of drapery, with looped swags and shaped embroidered panels shown in Pl. 69D with an 'Elizabethan' cornice, appears also, with only slight modifications, with a cornice of realistically carved vines. The same inconsistencies of style are also apparent in the draperies published by Henry Lawford in his *Cabinet of Practical, Useful and Decorative Furniture Designs* (1855) (Figs. 4, 5).

By the 1850's, instead of being held back by cords, curtains were generally fastened by curtain-bands, which were shaped pieces of material, stiffened by a canvas interlining, with a ring at either end which fitted over a hook on the wall.

The band was often decorated with a fringe, or embroidered to match the valance. Both valances and curtain-bands were supplied decorated by machine-embroidery in gold thread or coloured silks, ready to be made up by the upholsterer or housewife.

One of the most characteristic features of the period as a whole is the excessive use of fringes and tassels and fancy braid trimmings. Valances made entirely of cords and tassels were sometimes substituted for those made of stuff. Typical of these were examples exhibited at the Great Exhibition of 1851 by Mr R.Burgh of London (Fig. 6). Cheaper substitutes were made of printed cotton, with fringe and tassels imitated with printed shadows to give a three-dimensional effect. These printed valances seem to have been the speciality of James Burd, of Mount Zion Works, Radcliffe, near Manchester.

Although short muslin curtains were used in 'cottages', during the 1830's until about 1850, as during the Regency, the muslin sub-curtains were used full-length. After 1850, however, they were frequently used only at the lower half of the window, even in formal schemes of drapery. For a simple sash window, the muslin was stretched in taut folds by rings on small rods attached to the top and bottom of the lower half of the window. For

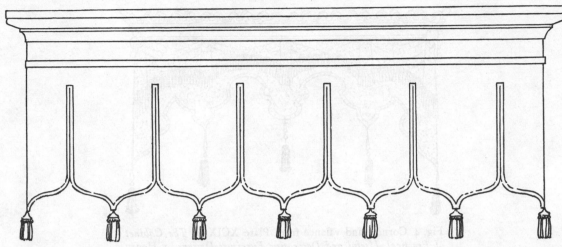

Fig. 3. Piped valance from *The Upholsterer's Accelerator* by Thomas King,
London, 1833.

French windows, two muslin curtains were used, one on each of the opening panes. By the 1840's elaborately patterned curtains of the type known as 'Madras muslins' or lenos were extensively used. These were mainly woven in Scotland by such firms as McLachlan & McLean of Glasgow and W.J. Lowndes & Co. of Paisley. Fancy machine net and lace curtains were also made by J.Heathcoat & Co. of Tiverton and Robert Scott of Leicester.

The styles of bed-draperies parallel those of the window-curtains. Beds for more formal apartments were usually of the four-poster variety, particularly in 'Elizabethan', 'Gothic', and 'Renaissance' styles, with shaped or pleated valances, decorated with fringe and tassels, and four curtains. Half-tester beds with canopies, called 'Arabian bedsteads', by Henry Lawford were also common. Tent beds and French beds are also found, particularly in the earlier part of the period.

Woven fabrics

In the field of woven furnishing fabrics the early Victorian period is characterized by the development of elaborate figured patterns, ranging from abstract designs of strapwork and Moorish arabesques to naturalistic designs of flowers and fruit. The complexity of the figured patterns was facilitated by the increased use, from 1830 onwards, of the Jacquard loom not only in the production of worsted fabrics in the Yorkshire area, but also in the production of silk fabrics in Macclesfield and Manchester and to a more limited extent in Spitalfields and East Anglia.

Immediately after 1826, when the embargo on the importation of French silks was lifted, the sale of English silks was 40 per cent below that of French goods. Contrary to expectations, however, the import of French goods gave an impetus to the English silk industry, and by 1832 the sale of English silks was only 20–25 per cent below the French figure, and English silks were even exported to France. The increase, however, was largely in the manufacture of dress fabrics from Macclesfield, and few English firms were producing furnishing silks that could compete with French articles.

As during the previous period, the main production of Spitalfields was of plain silks and velvets. For example, in 1849, when there were 8,000 to 9,000 weavers employed in the neighbourhood of Spitalfields, the proportion of plain to figured goods was in the relationship of ten to one. Patterned silks were, however, woven in Spitalfields, and their production was encouraged by the establishment about 1840 of the Spitalfields

Fig. 4. Cornice and valance from Plate XCIX of *The Cabinet of Practical, Useful and Decorative Furniture Designs* by Henry Lawford, London, 1855.

School of Design, which was set up by the Government to train designers for the industry. A typical example of the work produced by the students was the 'Queen's Pattern' (Pl. 70c), which was specially woven for the 1851 Exhibition. The leading producer of furniture silks in Spitalfields was the firm of Keith & Co. The *Journal of Design* instances their fabrics as 'conclusive proof that the present London weaver can do anything in silk weaving which the public would pay for'.

One of the most popular furnishing silks was a satin-striped silk known as 'tabaret', with broad alternating stripes of satin and watered material, differing from each other in colour. Originally woven in Spitalfields, the manufacture of silk tabaret was established in Manchester in 1830 by Louis Schwabe, who 'by his ability, ingenuity and excellent taste ... soon rivalled the manufacture of Spitalfields who had previously almost monopolised the manufacture of furniture damasks'. According to Cooke Taylor, writing in 1843, 'the flowers wrought in his silks and satins appear more like the work of the best painter than the weaver'. After the death of Louis Schwabe, the firm was taken over by Houldsworth & Sons (see also section on Embroidery).

Another popular furnishing fabric was 'tabbi-net', a heavy poplin with a silk warp and a woollen or linen weft, with figures woven on a watered ground. Tabbinets were extensively woven in Ireland by firms such as Pim of Dublin, Fry of Dublin and R. Atkinson & Co., but they were also made in the Norwich area and in Spitalfields, notably by the firm of J. Stillwell & Co., of Norton Falgate (Pl. 70A).

The leading producers of furnishing silks, Daniel Walters & Son, were situated not in Spitalfields but at Braintree in Essex. This firm received the Gold Medal of the Royal Society of Arts in 1849 and won prizes at the International Exhibitions of 1851 and 1862. The brocatelle shown on Pl. 70B, which helped to win the Gold Medal in 1849, was described by the *Journal of Design* as 'substantial enough to last as many centuries as the Bayeux tapestry'. The firm was established at Braintree about 1826 and expanded rapidly. By 1861 there were 150 Jacquard looms in operation with over 300 employees.

A type of textile, not hitherto manufactured in this country – a heavy, stamped Utrecht velvet – was introduced by the firm of Bennett and Co. of Manchester. A considerable quantity of this fabric was ordered from Bennett's in 1850 for Windsor Castle, where some of it still remains.

The furniture silks and velvets, however, can

Fig. 5. Cornice and valance from Plate XCIX of *The Cabinet of Practical, Useful and Decorative Furniture Designs* by Henry Lawford, London, 1855.

only be considered as luxury articles, and the most characteristic furnishing fabrics of the period are the elaborately patterned Jacquard and power-woven damasks in a mixture of cotton and worsted, or silk and worsted, that were produced in large quantities in the neighbourhood of Halifax and Bradford. Among the leading firms may be mentioned James Akroyd & Son of Bradford; John Priestley & Son, Wibsey, near Bradford; H.C.McCrea; Hoadley & Pridie; and Brown & Ward, all of Halifax. It is in the production of firms such as these, with their extensive output, that the successive changes in style and taste can be most clearly traced.

In 1830 most of the fabrics were in more or less traditional damask patterns of formalized flowers and leaves, usually woven in one colour, with fairly broad areas of warp and weft brought to the surface to form the pattern. A few designs with small figures, such as a sprig of lily-of-the-valley on broad alternating stripes, are found, and also designs in which vine ornament, trefoils and other Gothic motifs are introduced.

In the 1830's and early 1840's a number of designs of acanthus leaves or 'classical' motifs occur, but these become increasingly rare. The only ornamental style to find favour throughout

the period was the 'Gothic', and several distinct expressions of it are found. Formal patterns, of the type found on fifteenth- and sixteenth-century damasks or velvets, were introduced by designers such as Pugin, who designed fabrics for F.Crace and Son in the 1850's (Pl. 71B). Other designs were based on Gothic architectural details such as tracery, crocketing and cusping. A third type consisted of floral designs, with exaggerated spiky leaves, thistles and other naturalistic details, with a Germanic or Flemish Gothic flavour.

The first 'Elizabethan' designs appear about 1834 and become increasingly popular during the 'forties and early 'fifties. Some are purely abstract, with bands of strapwork, cartouches and bracket scrolls, but more common are patterns in which flowers are introduced. Another variant is designs suggestive of Elizabethan carved woodwork in which, by means of shading, the strapwork is given a three-dimensional effect.

Similarly, the 'Louis Quatorze' style was represented by designs with 'rococo' scrolls and cartouches filled with diaper ornament, combined with curling leaves and sprays of flowers. This style seems to have reached its peak in the mid-1840's, and by 1850 it had more or less disappeared.

Fig. 6. Valance composed of fringe and tassels exhibited by R.Burgh, London,
at the Great Exhibition of 1851.

Although Owen Jones published his *Plans, Elevations, Sections and Details of the Alhambra* in 1842, the 'Moorish' or 'Alhambresque' style does not appear in woven fabrics until about 1853; but by 1855 it had become the dominant ornamental style. Elaborate patterns of interlacing strapwork and asymmetrical scrolls cover the whole surface of the fabric or, alternatively, bands of Moorish ornament alternate with naturalistic floral cascades (Pl. 71 D). Purely geometric designs of interlocking tiles are also found.

Floral designs remained in favour throughout the period, but there are marked changes in both treatment and choice of subject-matter. During the 1840's turnover patterns of formalized flowers and scrolling leaves are most common, but about 1848 a fashion for exotic plants arose, a style which reached its culmination in the fabrics shown at the 1851 exhibition. Huge tropical plants, with luxuriant leaves and trumpet-like flowers, often over life-size, sprawled over the fabric. The repeat of the design was necessarily large, and the whole surface was covered with naturalistic detail. Not only exotic plants, but also vines and roses were similarly treated.

During the latter half of 1851, no doubt as a reaction against these sprawling designs, detached motifs of a single flower, or a single leaf, were widely spaced on a plain ground. This fashion

lasted throughout the 1850's. At the same time arborescent designs of blossoming trees were also popular and in 1852 designs of fruit were introduced. Throughout this year sprays of apple, pear, plum and currant remained the most popular subjects.

After 1855, purely floral furnishing damasks were less common, and the introduction of ornamental stripes became general. As with printed fabrics, the designs became increasingly eclectic, with motifs borrowed and adapted from every known historic style, and it is by no means rare to find a Moorish border combined with a naturalistic rose enclosed in a panel of Elizabethan strapwork.

Distinct fashions in colour, no less than in surface pattern, can be traced throughout the period. During the 1830's and 1840's bright, clear colours – scarlet, turquoise, yellow and light green – were used for the ground with the pattern in white or natural-coloured thread. In the early 'fifties the colours tended to become heavier, with crimson replacing scarlet, and a dark bottle green as the dominant colour. It was not until 1855, however, that the heavy sombre colours usually associated with the Victorian period were apparent. Hideous combinations of a dark maroon ground with flowers in bright tan and an ornamental stripe in a heavy green were all too common. Three or four colours were used in one design, where hitherto two had been the general rule.

Printed Textiles

The period 1830–60 saw a gradual decline in the level of design of both wood-block and roller-printed furnishing fabrics, although for the first few years the deterioration was hardly apparent and the high standard of engraving, which had persisted in the 1820's, was still maintained.

Generally speaking, the block-printed fabrics maintained a higher standard than the roller-prints, and the elaboration and naturalism of many of the floral designs have caused the Victorian era to be regarded as the high-water mark of the English floral chintz. These elaborate designs required the skilful cutting and careful registration of many blocks, and their production was virtually the monopoly of two firms, namely Bannister Hall, near Preston (under the successive management of Charles Swainson until 1856 and Thomas Clarkson 1856–93) and McAlpin, Stead & Co., the factory transferred from Wigton to Cummersdale, near Carlisle, in 1835. Since most of the designs printed by these firms were 'engaged' to leading London merchants and linen drapers describing themselves as 'Furniture Printers', the concentration of production is not generally realized. Among these the best known were Miles & Edwards of Oxford Street (taken over by Charles Hindley in 1847), John Watson & Co., Jackson & Graham (established 1836), and Clarkson & Turner, later known as Thomas Clarkson. Clarkson described himself as 'Furniture Printer to Her Majesty' and took over the Bannister Hall Printworks in 1856. In addition, between 1844 and 1856 Charles Swainson of Bannister Hall marketed his own productions in London under the name of Swainson and Dennys.

Large flowers, crisply drawn with the accuracy of a botanical plate and widely spaced on the fabric, were popular for the first five years. The ground was usually white, but a light green ground was also favoured. Machine-printed grounds, or 'covers', which were the speciality of Joseph Lockett (later Lockett, Crossland & Co.), were also employed (Pl. 72A). A simple, all-over pin design, known as a 'Stormont ground', or an all-over vermicular ground were the most popular, and some of the more elaborate grounds were reserved exclusively for the use of a particular firm.

By the 1840's the crisp drawing had been replaced by a looser technique, the petals being drawn without an outline and the shading achieved by the over-printing of light, transparent tones, giving the effect of a water-colour wash. The general use after 1835 of a solid green, which replaced the older method of the over-printing of blue and yellow, altered the appearance of the leaves and, in particular, the stems, which no longer had to have a dark outline to mask mis-registration.

In the 1840's scrolls and cartouches were often introduced into the floral designs with the pattern covering the whole surface of the fabric (Pl. 73A). A common variant was carefully drawn bunches of flowers set against an all-over background of more sketchily drawn flowers or leaves, often printed in drab shades, giving the effect of a design in two planes. This idea of two planes was also apparent in abstract designs where a design of scrolls, arabesques or Moorish-tile shapes were printed in strong, flat colours against a subsidiary but unrelated geometric background.

A characteristic style of the late 'forties was a continuous cascade of mixed flowers, usually over-life size, running down the middle or both sides of the chintz, with a filling of small detached sprays. This style was used with considerable effect on challet, which brought out the rich tones of the dyes with an increased brilliance that could not be achieved on cotton. Several of these 'cascade' designs were exhibited by Swainson and Dennys at the Royal Society of Arts Third Annual Exhibition of British Manufactures, March 1849, and won for them the Society's Silver Medal for printed fabrics (Pl. 73B).

Elaborate floral chintzes, with large bunches of flowers, printed in natural colours, were at the height of their popularity at the time of the Great Exhibition of 1851, but it is interesting to note that even at this time they were subjected to severe criticism on the grounds of naturalism by the 're-formers' of the day. Several of the chintzes that won prizes at the Great Exhibition were included only one year later in an exhibition entitled 'False Principles of Design' organized by Sir Henry Cole at Marlborough House, the 'false principle' in question being 'the direct imitation of nature'.

Roses were popular throughout the period, either on their own or combined with other flowers, and ranged from full-blown cabbage varieties to budding moss roses. Other flowers received less sustained attention and remained in fashion for a year or two at most. For example, in 1848 and 1849 convolvulus was much in vogue, also hydrangeas and striped tulips. Although large flowers remained popular throughout the 'fifties, smaller designs of violets, heather and hare-bells were popular about 1855. A fashion for delicate designs based on ferns is found from 1856 to 1860 (Pl. 73c). These years also saw a fashion for diamond trellis designs, with a border of related flowers or leaves. The end of the period saw the introduction of orchids and other exotics, already popular in woven fabrics, which, in the field of printed fabrics, appear to be the result of French influence.

Throughout the period 'Gothic' blinds, first introduced about 1825, remained popular. These blinds, which were intended to be hung flat, were usually printed with designs imitating stained glass in an architectural setting, often on semi-transparent materials so that the light glowed through them. Some of the earlier designs have a certain charm, but most of the later examples are crudely drawn and carelessly printed in harsh colours.

The enormous range and variety of the roller-printed fabrics make it possible to consider only the most significant of the successive styles. Undoubtedly some of the most bizarre and exotic were intended for foreign markets rather than for the home trade, and these must be discounted when dealing with the changes in English domestic taste.

Until about 1835 the standard of engraving remained high, and finely stippled designs, printed from one, two or even three engraved copper-rollers, with additional colours added by surface rollers or block, were produced by the Lancashire calico-printers. Outstanding among these are six

designs of birds and flowers copied from plates in Audubon's *Birds of America* (Pl. 72B). The six designs fall into three pairs, dated 1830, 1831 and 1834, and followed quickly upon the publication of Audubon's plates. The birds, and many of the flowers, are almost facsimile copies of his engravings, but no attention has been paid to their natural colouring. The new chemical dyes were exploited to the full, and each design was produced in over twenty-five different colour-ways, ranging from soft pastel schemes to brilliant reds and oranges on magenta grounds. In the same series of pattern-books (now in the possession of the Calico Printers' Association) are floral designs which show the same accurate drawing of large flowers that is found in the block-printed fabrics of the same date. By 1835, however, the standard is noticeably lower, and the introduction of inconsistent motifs, such as Paisley-shawl patterns, rococo scrolls and jewelled effects, combined with an indiscriminate use of colour, produced ill-organized and confused designs.

The last stage of the pictorial chintz, which finally died out about 1853, is manifest in the enormous variety of romantic, historical, commemorative and exotic designs produced mainly by the firm of Kershaw, Leese and Sidebottom of Ardwick Print Works, Manchester. The various scenes were usually vignetted in a floral wreath, and the design of the young Prince of Wales at Balmoral (Pl. 72c) is typical of their style. The subjects range from violent scenes of battles between Crusaders and Saracens to sentimental scenes of children and animals and parallel the subjects found in the contemporary Baxter prints and folios of engravings such as *The Drawing Room Scrap Book*. These Kershaw pictorials were invariably printed in the same colour range, a combination of subdued reddish-browns, purple and orange with a harsh, royal blue.

In the 1850's one of the most popular styles of cheap roller-prints was designs of flowers printed to imitate Berlin wool-work. Towards the end of the period the designers, confused and bewildered by the mass of 'historic ornament' presented to them both by such monumental works as Owen Jones' *Grammar of Ornament* (1856) and by cheaper, more ephemeral publications produced from the 1830's onwards, picked their motifs at random with an eclecticism that knew no bounds. Designs with 'Paisley' and Chinese motifs against a tartan background or naturalistic flowers set in ornamental panels with Renaissance jewels at the intersections are all too common. Although such travesties were severely criticized by the purists and reformers, this confusion of natural and formal details found general favour at the time, and fabrics of this type were awarded medals at the 1862 Exhibition.

Carpets

The carpet industry made great strides during the period 1830–60, particularly in the field of machine-woven carpets. A review of the Exhibition of Industrial Art at Manchester in the *Art-Union* of 1846 devotes considerable space to the industry. 'The carpet manufactory', says the reviewer, 'is in England carried to the ultimatum of excellence – the machine manufacture of carpets of all countries is incomparably inferior to ours. ... In France, those who purchase carpets are the wealthiest class of the community; but in this country every apartment is carpeted; the great consumption is, therefore, in the moderately priced article, for which in France there would be no demand.'

The main centres of the carpet industry were in Kidderminster, Halifax and other towns and villages in Yorkshire; Wilton, Axminster, Bridgnorth, Glasgow, Edinburgh, and Kilmarnock.

The most important centre was undoubtedly Kidderminster. In 1838 over 2,000 looms were in operation in the town and by 1850 the number had almost doubled. Fifteen large carpet factories, of which the leading firms were Henry Brinton (established 1819) and Pardoe & Hooman, were engaged in the production of all types of carpet. The simplest type, produced on an ordinary loom, was known as Venetian carpeting. It was woven in simple stripes or checks, with a woollen warp and the weft of hemp or cotton, and was used mainly for stairs or passages. The most important type of non-pile carpet was the Scotch or Kidderminster, an ingrain all-wool variety. These carpets were originally of double-cloth or two-ply weaving, with both warp and weft contributing to the pattern, and were usually reversible. In 1824 a stronger three-ply version was perfected at Kilmarnock, and the manufacture of this type soon spread to the other centres.

One of the basic types of machine-woven pile carpets was Brussels, with a looped, uncut pile. The Geneva carpet was a modification of Brussels in which parts of the pile were cut to give a velvety appearance. Wilton was a further modification of Brussels in which all the loops were cut to give a uniform pile. Saxony and Super-Saxony were both superior varieties of Wilton with the structure of a thick pile velvet.

The weaving methods of all these types of carpet necessarily imposed limits on the number of colours that could be introduced into the design, and two important innovations were the Patent Tapestry Carpets, originally patented by Richard Whytock of Edinburgh in 1832, and the Patent Axminster, a chenille carpet first introduced by James Templeton at Glasgow in 1839, which overcame this limitation. A full description of the method of manufacture of the Patent Tapestry Carpets can be found in the *Journal of Design*, April, 1850. The basic principle was that the yarn which was to form the pile was printed before weaving with an elongated version of the finished design, the extra length being taken up by the loops of the pile during weaving. The structure was essentially the same as that of the Brussels, and the pile could be cut or uncut.

In the Patent Axminster carpets the pile was formed by chenille thread, previously woven in the required colours. A strong warp and weft of hemp or linen formed the foundation of the carpet, with an extra warp to bind the chenille. Each row of chenille, with its different-coloured tufts, corresponded to one row of knots in a hand-woven carpet. The Patent Axminster made by Templeton's for the opening ceremony of the Great Exhibition of 1851 is now in the Smithsonian Museum, Washington (ill. Tattersall, *History of British Carpets*, Plate XCVII). It is a long, narrow carpet divided into three main panels by ornamental bands and garlands of flowers. The ground of the panels is covered with a damask-type pattern and there is a central cartouche with the date 1851 in Roman numerals.

Such methods, which imposed no limitations in either the number of colours or the complexity of design, led to the production of carpets which were unsuitable for their purpose and repudiated all canons of good taste. Contemporary critics deplored the use of 'shaded architectural ornament, often used very objectionably in carpets, and suggesting impediments and stumbling' and 'Louis Quatorze scrolls, gigantic tropical plants, shown in high relief and suggestive of anything but a level or plane'. A typical example of this type of carpet, with elaborate rococo scrolls and sprawling flowers, is that in the private apartments at Osborne, which have remained unaltered since the death of the Prince Consort in 1861.

Most of our information about the design of machine-woven carpets, however, must be taken from illustrations in contemporary periodicals and the Patent Office Design Registers.

At the beginning of the period most of the designs were 'classical' with acanthus-like leaves, scrolls and flowers. Carpets in the 'Gothic' taste with architectural motifs were produced throughout the 'thirties and 'forties. 'Louis Quatorze' designs first appeared about 1840 and large 'rococo' scrolls tended to replace the more formal classical ornament. A type of design also introduced about 1840 consisted of a diamond trellis of flowers or leaves which covered the whole ground of the carpet. Good examples of this type remain in the Wilton carpets at Charlecote and in the private apartments at Ickworth. The most exuberant designs belong to the 1850's, with huge exotic flowers, ferns and scrolls, elaborately shaded to give a three-dimensional effect. Patterns based on Persian and Turkish models are found throughout the period.

Hand-knotted carpets were made at Axminster until 1835, when the factory was closed down and the equipment transferred to Wilton. The most impressive hand-knotted carpet of the period to survive is that made in 1850 for the Green Drawing Room at Windsor by Blackmore Brothers of Burdensball, near Wilton, to the design of Lewis Gruner, the Prince Consort's German adviser. The carpet measures 52 ft. by 38 ft., with sixty-four knots to the square inch, and was one of the most admired pieces in the 1851 Exhibition. The design incorporated areas of naturalistic flowers with panels and bands of ornament in several styles. Several less ambitious hand-knotted carpets are in the Victoria and Albert Museum, including one made at Axminster shortly before 1835 (Pl. 74B). Hand-knotted carpets were also made in London by the firm of Jackson and Graham of Oxford Street (Pl. 75).

Needlework carpets were made throughout the period, mostly with floral designs with an affinity to the contemporary Berlin wool-work (Pl. 74A). More spectacular were co-operative efforts, worked in separate pieces and sewn together, such as the carpet (now in the U.S.A.) worked by ladies of the diocese and presented to the Bishop of Gloucester and Bristol in 1843, and that worked by '150 Ladies of Great Britain' from a design by John Woody Papworth for presentation to the Queen in 1851. The former carpet is a chequered design of seventy-seven alternating panels of bouquets and baskets of flowers and exotic and other birds. The Queen's carpet was composed of 150 squares of geometrical and floral ornament enclosed in a heraldic border containing the initials of all the executants.

Embroidery

During the period 1830–60 the craze for Berlin wool-work virtually eclipsed all other types of embroidery. It was in fact so ubiquitous that the terms 'embroidery' and 'Berlin wool-work' were regarded as synonymous. The preface to the *Illuminated Book of Needlework* (1847) by Mrs Henry Owen opens with the words 'Embroidery, or as it is more often called Berlin wool work, has been brought to such a high state of perfection ... the variety of patterns so great, and so well adapted to every purpose to which it can be applied ... that we do not hope here to be able to throw much new light on the subject'.

The first Berlin patterns were published in 1804, and although a number reached England as early as 1805, it was not until 1831, when Mr

Wilks of Regent Street began importing both the patterns themselves and the materials for working them direct from Berlin, that the fashion was fully established. By 1840 no less than 14,000 different patterns had been published and imported into England. The designs were coloured by hand on squared paper so that the design could be copied on to square-meshed canvas, each square of the design representing one stitch. Elaborate pictorial designs, with religious, historical and romantic subjects, were popular for framed pictures and firescreens. Floral designs, however, were even more popular, particularly for upholstery, and smaller domestic articles, such as hand-screens, bell-pulls, travelling bags and slippers. Bouquets and wreaths of flowers, naturalistically drawn, were worked in brilliant, harsh colours, and the height of attainment was reached when, by means of elaborate shading, the flowers appeared to stand out in high relief from the grounds. Birds, particularly parrots, were often introduced into the designs. At the beginning of the period the designs were rather more restrained and delicate, and were often worked in silk instead of wool. The designs were sometimes worked in the scale of petit-point embroidery on a white silk ground, particularly for small articles such as purses and pin-cushions. In the 1830's and early 1840's white or light-coloured grounds were often used, but by 1850 black backgrounds were almost universal, and served to emphasize the enormous flowers, worked in harsh colours of magenta and vivid primary colours, which, together with their veridian leaves, shone forth with all the brilliance of a stained-glass window. Many of the dyes used, however, were fugitive, and not many pieces survive unfaded.

The ubiquitous use of Berlin wool-work for all types of upholstery is apparent from even a cursory glance at the furniture pattern-books of the period. It is emphasized by publications such as that issued by Henry Wood about 1845 entitled *A Useful and Modern Work on Cheval and Pole Screens, Ottomans, Chairs and Settees, for Mounting Berlin Needlework*. The eighteen plates contain fifty designs for all types of furniture in the prevailing styles of Louis XIV, François 1er, Elizabethan and Gothic, but no attempt is made to adapt the needlework to the appropriate style, and the Berlin designs are, with two exceptions, exclusively floral, with the occasional introduction of rococo scrolls or cartouches.

The true Berlin wool-work was worked entirely in cross-stitch or tent-stitch, in coloured wools which were manufactured at Gotha and dyed in Berlin, but wools spun and dyed in this country were also used. A variety of the work in which beads, silk and chenille were introduced into parts of the design was known as German embroidery. Raised Berlin wool-work was also extremely popular. In this parts of the design, either individual flowers, a bird or an animal, were worked in loops, which were afterwards cut to give the effect of a thick velvet pile. In addition to the more usual cross stitch, other fancy canvas stitches were also used, particularly for geometric patterns. Mrs Henry Owen lists and describes thirty such stitches, including some with such ephemeral names as 'Hohenlinden' or 'Sutherland' stitch.

While most of the designs were worked from the squared Berlin patterns, by the mid-1840's patterns were sometimes printed or painted direct on the canvas, which made for speedier working. Instructions for Berlin wool-work were also issued in letters and numbers, and read like the instructions for a fair-isle knitting pattern.

Although the fashion for Berlin wool-work persisted well into the 1860's, from 1850 onwards it was subjected to increasing criticism, particularly in the 'art periodicals'. The general improvement in the standard of embroidery during the second half of the century was first noticeable in the ecclesiastical field, through the work and influence of leading architects and designers such as Pugin and Street. Some of the most devastating attacks on Berlin wool-work came from religious quarters. The broadside delivered by a clergyman named James in a paper on 'Church Work for Ladies', read to the Architectural Society of the Archdeaconry of Northampton in 1855, is worth quoting:

'They (that is the ladies) revolt at the continual slavery of basting and hemstitch and very properly allow their mind and their fingers to relax in fancy work. And what does it result in? Art must be invoked, the imagination of the worsted shop tasked and there grows under the needle something of this kind (here the Reverend Gentleman paused to hold up a coloured pattern for Berlin wool-work) or better still a Bandit in glowing coloured jacket, looking over a precipice, with a long gun in his hand – one clever dash of blue worsted gives the eye, at once so tender and so truculent, and the work is done. Or a less ambitious picture is a group of gigantic flowers, with pansies as big as pennies [sic], cabbage roses which deserve the name suggesting pickle rather than perfume; gracefully falling fuschia as big as a hand-bell. Is there any real beauty in this, any originality? – it is simply copy, copy, stitch by stitch. Fancy work without the slightest opportunity to exercise the fancy. Dull task work unenlightened by one spark of freedom and grace.'

Apart from Berlin wool-work, all other forms of domestic needlework took the form of 'Fancy-work' rather than true embroidery. An analysis of Victorian needlework books, such as *Treasures in Needlework* (1855) by Mrs Warren and Mrs Pullan, or of the current fashion periodicals, shows little evidence of a need for originality of design or skill in stitchery. Braiding, which required the couching down of ready-made braid in scrolls or arabesques, was the most popular adornment for table-covers, cushions and antimacassars. Another means of achieving effects with the minimum of skill was the use of *ombré* silks or wool, dyed in various shades of the same colour, whereby the effect of elaborate shading could be imitated with simple stitches. Simple appliqué embroidery was used to adorn small articles such as pocket-books, needle-cases, cigar-cases and smoking-caps. Patchwork was also favoured, often of silk and velvet rather than of cotton; but most of the surviving Victorian quilts are composed of simple hexagonal patches, with little originality or taste in the compilation of the design. Whitework embroidery, as in the preceding period, continued

in favour for costume, particularly for morning dress. The most general type was *broderie anglaise*, a heavy type of open-work with the pattern formed entirely of holes, variously arranged, and worked round in buttonhole stitch.

The period saw the introduction of machine-embroidered fabrics and trimmings. The leading firm in this field was Houldsworth & Sons of Manchester, who produced fabrics with embroidered figures worked by an adaptation of the pantograph (Pl. 76c).[2]

Whereas an improvement in the standard of ecclesiastical embroidery was apparent by the 1850's, as evinced at the 1751 Exhibition, it was not until the 1870's, as the result of the influence of William Morris and the foundation of bodies such as the Royal School of Needlework, that the same improvement was noticeable in the secular field. William Morris's first efforts at embroidery design do, however, just fall within the present period. These were made in 1860 to adorn Red House, the house built for Morris, by his friend Philip Webb, on his marriage in 1859. The Red House embroideries, which were worked by Jane Morris and her sister, were of two types. The most ambitious (Pl. 76D) were large figure panels, almost life size, representing 'illustrious women'. The figures, which were designed by Morris himself, are evocative of medieval stained glass, and are worked in wool and silk with fairly elaborate stitchery and fine detail. The other Red House embroideries were much simpler, and were worked with sprigs of flowers in coloured worsteds on a coarse serge ground. One of the patterns was of clumps of 'daisies', and foreshadows the 'Daisy wallpaper', the first paper produced by the Morris firm, established in 1862.

[2] For a detailed description of the process see W. Cooke Taylor, *Handbook of Silk, Cotton and Woollen Manufacture*, 1843, and Ure's *Dictionary of Manufacture*.

Costume

ANNE M. BUCK

WOMEN'S COSTUME

The changing style

Between 1830 and 1860 women's dress was dominated by the movement of its skirt which, for thirty years, without interruption or reversal, steadily grew larger. This increasing dome gave to the dress of the whole period a fixed, though constantly enlarging form.

The movement was already well begun in 1833, when 'skirts both of pelisses and robes, are of a still more extravagant width than last season'.[1] In the next year a rather sharp pen wrote, 'the diameter of the fashionable ladies at present is about three yards'.[2] Although in 1834 it was the circumference, not the diameter, which was between three and four yards, Mrs Carlyle's comment was almost prophetic of the size to come. Every year the spread of the skirt made a slightly larger circle, 'those skirts whose enormous and ungraceful width we had strong hopes would be at least partially curtailed ... their size is even a little augmented'.[3] Throughout the 1840's and 1850's it went on: 'amplitude of skirt still remains one of the leading features in dresses of all kinds',[4] until by 1860 a fashionable woman needed an area of twenty to twenty-five square feet in which to stand comfortably without compression.

The main feature of dress in 1830 was still its

[1] *Court Magazine*, Nov. 1833.
[2] Carlyle, *Jane Welsh, Letters*, 1834.
[3] *La Belle Assemblée*, Jan. 1836.
[4] *Ladies Treasury*, Jan. 1858.

enormous sleeves. They lost some of their fullness, 1831–3, in forms which, like those at the beginning of their growth, were tight in the lower arm; but there was no change in their billowing line until 1834, when a new line appeared at the shoulder, from the ornament of deep lapels which passed over the shoulder to the centre waist, and from the muslin pelerines, deep collars which spread over the shoulders, curved over the front of the bodice and ended in points or lappets at the waist (Pl. 77). These gave to the fullness at the shoulder a new declining curve, and by the following year the fullness of the sleeve was broken: 'They are not now one third of the extravagant size they were a year ago ... some are made to fit the arm and tight to it from a little below the elbow to the wrist, with the top disposed in two small bouffants ... there are also some tight at the top and bottom, but full in the middle.'[5]

This change pervaded the whole dress, changing its character and creating the early Victorian style. The dress of 1834 in fashion plate, portrait or surviving example clearly belongs to the years before; the dress of 1836 as clearly to the years which follow. The new downward curve at the shoulder into the tightening sleeve was repeated at the waist (Pls. 79, 80). The lapel trimming, which had helped to smooth down the fullness at the shoulder, and another bodice trimming — flat folds of material curving over the bust from shoulder to waist — both made a triangular shape on the bodice which foreshadowed its new shaping.

[5] *La Belle Assemblée*, May 1836.

Bodices with a pointed waistline had appeared on evening dresses by 1833, and within a few years were, for evening, the general form, 'pointed corsages decidedly the mode ... indeed no others are worn'.[6] This waistline, curving down to its centre point, continued to lengthen during the 1840's, 'now drawn down as low as possible',[7] and until 1855. The new tapering bodice, above the spreading curves of the skirt, remained the constant form of the next twenty years, showing elaboration and variation, but no major change.

Its line was loosened and softened in the 1850's by the development of the jacket bodice with basque (a continuation of the bodice) over the hips; and by the opening of the sleeves at the wrist over full, frilled undersleeves of muslin and lace. In evening dress the softening came at the neckline. This was worn low throughout the period, 'excessively low, far too much so for strict delicacy to approve'.[8] During the 1830's and 1840's it was trimmed with flat folds of material, horizontal or making a slight point at the centre (Pl. 80). By 1843 deep collars of lace, enclosing the arm and the short tight sleeve, fell straight from the low neckline, suggesting the style of 300 years before (Pl. 79). The drapery of flat folds disappeared by 1850, but the deep collar remained to be gathered up in a lighter drapery of lace, net and flowers, and the neckline rose a little on the shoulders to a wide shallow curve.

Double and triple skirts and flounces carried the skirt out to its ever-increasing width during the 1840's. In the 1850's the printing or weaving of flounces in their own patterns and their trimmed edges, which distinguish the flounces of this decade, add a more luxuriant character and a new horizontal emphasis to the widening curves of the skirt: an elaboration and emphasis repeated in the trimmings of the bodice.

Fabric and colour

In 1817 there had been a premature attempt to revive figured silks resembling those of the eighteenth century, 'The antique robes of our grandmothers, as far as relates to their texture, are again in revival; brocaded silks, small coloured sprigs on a white ground, have made their appearance.'[9] Neither the style of the dress nor the mood of fashion was then quite ready for a return to this more recent past, but after 1830, as the style drew nearer to that of a hundred years before, the revival came, 'In reviving the fashions of the seventeenth century (sic) we have also revived the superb silks and brocades that were then employed.'[10]

Silks now appeared in all their former richness. The light crapes and gauzes remained for ball dress, but for other evening wear there were rich brocades, 'that might vie with the stand-alone silks of our grandmothers and of very similar patterns'.[11] The brocades in dresses 1835–45 show fine examples of the silk-weaver's skill, and, as they often revived earlier patterns, are sometimes difficult to distinguish from those of the eighteenth century. The fashion for brocaded silks of eighteenth-century patterns was so strong that some eighteenth-century dresses which had been kept to this time were now remade: enough of these renovations survive in museum collections to show that this must have been a not uncommon practice. Printed satins, watered silks (plain or with satin stripes), velvet, and lighter silks (figured, checked, striped, plain or 'changeable'), were all worn. They were worn not only for evening and more formal day dress, but by 1840 were beginning to take the place of white cambric and printed muslin even in summer morning dress. 'Changeable' or shot silk, in delicate and subtle shadings, either plain or figured, is particularly characteristic of dresses of the 1840's. Silks *à disposition* – that is, woven with patterns as skirts or flounces, not as a continuous length of fabric – distinguish the dresses of 1851–60. This fashion was not limited to woven fabrics, but was carried out also in printed designs.

An increased use of wool, either alone or mixed with silk, appeared in dress fabrics of the 1830's, mixtures 'of silk and wool, quite as light as jaconot

[6] *World of Fashion*, March 1838.
[7] *Ladies Cabinet*, June 1844.   [8] *ibid.*, Feb. 1842.

[9] *La Belle Assemblée*, Feb. 1817.
[10] *World of Fashion*, Feb. 1839.
[11] *La Belle Assemblée*, Nov. 1835.

muslin'.[12] One of the most popular of these was chaly or challis, a fabric of silk warp and worsted weft, which in 1832 'has now retained its vogue for eighteen months',[13] and was to remain in fashion until 1840. It was usually printed, and sometimes woven with a silk stripe, and was used for all dresses except full evening wear. Very fine woollen fabrics appeared in the 1840's, like balzarine, 'of that exquisitely soft and fine cashmere wool ... and half transparent, is as light as muslin',[14] but there was also an increased use of the closer woollen fabrics, cashmere, and merino, 'certainly the material best calculated of all others for walking dress, and is also from the warmth of its texture, admirably fitted for winter costume in so variable a climate as ours'.[15]

The printed muslins which had been fashionable during the 1820's continued in fashion for morning dress in the summer months, 1830–40, but then lost their predominance, as silks, which now included washing silks, became more generally worn. Their patterns in the 1830's grew more complex in colour and design and the muslin was often woven with stripes or checks as a background for the printed pattern, 'quadrilled cambrics, muslins and ginghams are much in favour ... among the prettiest those with a small flower in the centre of each square'.[16]

Dresses of white cambric with embroidery also grew fewer in the 1830's, but much muslin and net, finely embroidered, appeared in the pelerines which fell over the shoulders, or canezous which covered the back and front of the bodice but not the sleeves. This embroidered muslin had its fullest display while the sleeve still spread widely at the shoulder, 'in truth a costly simplicity, for the lace and embroidery ... are much more expensive than the stiff brocades'.[17] (Fig. 1.) After 1845 the muslin lessened in area, and went beneath the dress in the chemisette worn with an open bodice, and in the undersleeves beneath the widening sleeve opening.

Fig. 1. Half-dress pelerine of worked muslin. *La Belle Assemblée*, May 1835.

In the 1830's the mingling of black with bright colours brought a new aspect to dress. Patterns in many colours were woven, printed or embroidered on a black ground, 'shawls of French cashmere, with black grounds, flowered in rich bouquets of very vivid colours',[18] and in the silks of the late 1850's, black made the pattern with a single deep colour. Flounces of black lace were worn over pale silks from 1840 to the end of the period, 'black lace will be as much worn as ever over the light silks'.[19] In the black gauze bonnet veils, which were popular during the 1830's, in the black gauze and lace shawls and black silk mantles, the contrast of black was replacing the ever-recurring white of the previous generation. The decorative aprons which were a fashionable addition to morning dress, 1830–50, were also often of black satin, embroidered in bright colours.

The black lace was a silk bobbin lace, black blonde, which, with the cream silk blonde, fashionable since about 1815, was worn during the 1830's and 1840's. After 1850 black lace is usually Chantilly or Maltese. About 1840 there was a revival of the point and bobbin laces of seventeenth-century pattern in the deep falling collars. Machine-made laces developed during the period and hand-made laces after 1850 lost much of their quality.

Apart from the flounces and collars of lace of

[12] *La Belle Assemblée*, May 1831.
[13] ibid., March 1832.   [14] *Ladies Cabinet*, July 1844.
[15] ibid., Jan. 1842.
[16] *La Belle Assemblée*, June 1835.
[17] ibid., July 1836.

[18] *Court Magazine*, Oct. 1836.
[19] *World of Fashion*, Jan. 1858.

K

the 1840's, the trimmings of the dress, 1830–50, were not elaborate. A contrast of texture only was characteristic of the restrained ornament of the 1840's, when silk dresses were often trimmed with velvet bands of the same colour. More elaborate trimming came after 1845 in silk fringes on dresses and outdoor garments, but by 1860 plain surfaces were again returning, and flat trimming, in bolder outline and contrasting colour, was being applied to them.

Towards 1860 colours deepened and were used in more striking contrasts than the subdued shadings of the 1840's, although pale colours still appeared in the heavier watered silks. Aniline dyes were being developed after 1857.

Forms and construction

From 1830 the skirt was usually lined in silk dresses and sometimes, though more rarely, in cotton dresses. It was set on to the bodice in pleats with gathers at the centre back, but as skirts grew wider a method of stiff gathering, in which the edge of the fold only was attached to the bodice, appeared in 1841, 'a new method of setting on the skirt by gauging it round the top as far as the points of the hips: by this means that excessive fullness which would be otherwise disposed in gathers or plaits, is formed exactly to the shape, but on the other hand this method lengthens the waist excessively and gives an air of stiffness to the figure'.[20] The lengthening of the waist, the stiffness of the 1840's style, were thus a technical consequence of the growth of the skirt. The lengthening continued until the spread of the skirt was supported by the crinoline frame. The earlier method of setting on the skirt with pleats, now double or triple box-pleating, was then resumed, with a raising of the waistline.

The growing width of the skirt was supported at first by petticoats, stiffly piped at the hem, then, as the spread became a matter of the whole skirt, not of the hem only, a series of waistlength petticoats accumulated beneath, over a stiff underpetticoat of horsehair, the crinoline petticoat.

Other devices gave the desired fullness to the

skirt in the 1830's, bustles, crescent- or bag-shaped, or of stiff frills, 'their bustles (false bottoms) are the size of an ordinary sheep's fleece, the very servant girls wear bustles'.[21] To support her fashionable skirt of 1842, Lady Aylesbury, who 'wears 48 yards of material in each of her gowns', wore a petticoat made of down instead of the usual horsehair one.[22] From 1855 the still-widening skirt was supported on a framework, as the skirt of the eighteenth century had been supported by hoop petticoats and the skirts of the late sixteenth century by a farthingale. This nineteenth-century hoop petticoat, at first hoops of whalebone in a petticoat, developed into light and flexible constructions of covered steel wire, taking from the stiff petticoat which it superseded the name of crinoline. Its lightness, compared with the weight of many petticoats, made it, in spite of its size, an advance in comfort and ease of movement. From this time drawers became an essential piece of underclothing, and these and the remaining petticoats were embroidered at the hem in white openwork embroidery, known as broderie anglaise. During the 1850's the stitching of the new sewing-machines begins to appear.

From 1836, bodices, which fastened at the back, were increasingly 'of the corset kind, cut in three pieces, sitting close to the shape' [23] (Pl. 79). Their corset quality was increased by their boned lining and by the corsets worn beneath them. During the 1840's this tight-fitting, back-fastening bodice was the usual form, 'the majority tight to the shape, but several are full in the shoulders, draped before and terminate somewhat in the fan form under the ceinture'.[24] This alternative form appears more often in photographs and in dresses surviving in English collections from the 1840's, than in fashion plates (Pl. 82). The pelisse robe, with a front fastening, was still worn, mainly as an outdoor style, in the 1830's (Pls. 77, 78), becoming less worn during the 1840's. After 1845 a

[20] *World of Fashion*, Feb. 1841.

[21] Carlyle, *Jane Welsh, Letters*, Nov. 1834.

[22] Clive, Caroline, Diary, 29 April 1842 (*Diary and Family Papers*, 1949).

[23] *Court Magazine*, Nov. 1836.

[24] *Ladies Cabinet*, June 1843

bodice open on the bosom over a chemisette was much worn. Small basques appear on bodices in the late 1840's, the beginning of the development of the separate jacket bodice which was the characteristic form of the 1850's. In 1859 a plain bodice was again appearing, and this became the form of the 1860's, retaining the front fastening of the jacket form.

Sleeves, while still at their climax of fullness, were supported by swansdown puffs. After the sleeve tightened to the arm it was set so low that it hampered the movement of the arm above the shoulder. The sleeve opened at the wrist from the mid-1840's, widening to the 'pagoda' sleeve of the 1850's, 'sleeves are worn of various forms, but pagoda is decidedly the most elegant with the beautiful engageantes below it' [25] (Pl. 84). The widening reached its climax in the wing-like sleeves of 1857–9, completely open, 'a squard of material pleated into the armhole',[26] but the open forms were then being superseded by the full bishop sleeve with a closed wrist which had appeared as an alternative form from 1855.

The fitted forms of outdoor garment, the full-length pelisse, and the spencer, the short jacket ending at the waist, were passing out of fashion in the 1830's, although the spencer had a brief revival, 1839–40.

The sleeves of the pelisse opened out to take the large sleeves of the dress, changing the pelisse into a fitted mantle with open sleeves. This and the cloak, often wadded and with a deep cape added to it, were, for most of the period, the wear for cold weather, 'neither novel nor dressy, but exceedingly comfortable and appropriate'.[27] In the late 1850's cloaks of wadded silk or the thinner woollen fabrics were joined by those of heavier materials, 'vecuna and those thick warm materials'.[28] Full length cloaks were more general in the 1830's, and three-quarter length or less after 1840, with still shorter versions from 1854.

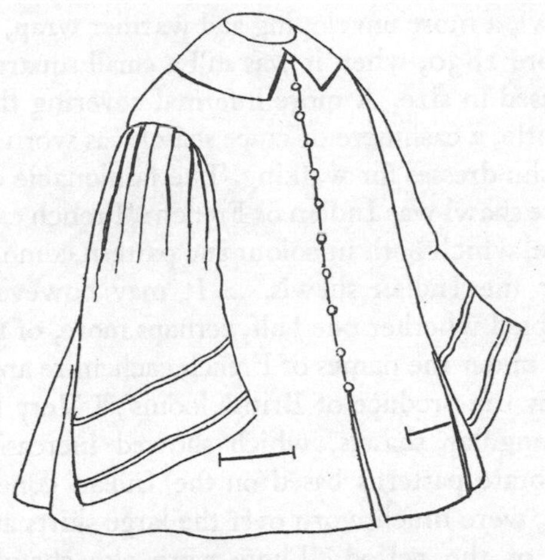

Fig. 2. Jacket mantle, for which a paper model was given in the *Ladies Gazette of Fashion*, April 1857.

The mantles bore a great variety of names and many slight differences of shaping, but most of them fell loosely over the upper part of the body so that the waist, so clearly defined in the dress, was, out of doors, obscured. The scarf mantelet was one of the most persistent forms. Shaped to fall as a cape or shawl over the shoulders, with long scarf ends to the knee in front, it appeared in white-embroidered muslin, 1830-45; in black silk from about 1835, sometimes lined with light silk and edged with black lace, resembling the black silk cloaks of the eighteenth century; and in the 1840's in 'changeable' silks, with ruched frills and fringed trimmings instead of lace. By the end of the period, jacket forms of outdoor garments, with sleeves, closed or open, were returning (Fig. 2).

Scarves were summer wear, 'they supersede for the moment both shawls and pelerines'.[29] They were of silk crape, of transparent gauze, of silk or silk and wool, of black lace or net. They were embroidered at the ends, 'cachemire de Thibet ... embroidered in palmettes',[30] or had woven borders. The scarf was worn less after 1845. The

[25] *World of Fashion*, May 1852.
[26] *ibid.*, Oct. 1857.
[27] *Ladies Cabinet*, Dec. 1843.
[28] *World of Fashion*, Jan. 1854.

[29] *La Belle Assemblée*, Aug. 1836.
[30] *ibid.*, June 1832.

shawl, a more enveloping and warmer wrap, even before 1830, when it was still a small square, increased in size. A more informal covering than a mantle, a cashmere or crape shawl was worn with muslin dresses for walking. The fashionable cashmere shawl was Indian or French: 'French cachemire, which both in colour and pattern come very near the Indian shawls. ... It may however be doubted whether one half, perhaps more, of those sold under the names of French cachemire are not really the produce of British looms'.[31] Very large rectangular shawls, which showed increasingly elaborate patterns based on the Indian cone design, were much worn over the large skirts at the end of the period. There were also shawls of printed satin, of plaid or shot silk, of damasked crape, and muslin, gauze, net, and lace.

Hats and headdresses

As the skirt of the dress grew larger, the bonnet, still large in 1830, grew smaller, diminishing rapidly after 1855. Soon after 1830 the crown became cone shaped – a cone with the top cut off – although the crown of drawn bonnets, those with the material gathered over a framework of cane or wire, had a horseshoe shape. The brim was still wide, encircling the face, but in 1832, 'bonnets of the small, close-fitting cottage shape ... coming more into favour with walking dress',[32] were a hint of the shape to come. By 1838 the new form, with brim and crown in a straight line, was established, and by 1841 no other shape was worn. It remained with little change for the next ten years, 'it is now a settled thing that the horizontal form will retain its vogue' [33] (Pl. 83). The only difference was between its close and open styles.

By 1850 the open form was appearing more often than the close, and from the open form came the new style of the 1850's. The brim spread more openly round the face and the crown grew lower and smaller, and was worn back on the head, revealing the face, 'it is the peculiar form of crown which gives this appearance, by

being made low and sloping towards the back' [34] (Pls. 83, 84). By 1858 the sides were receding a little further and the top of the crown tapered forward.

The hat, which had not been fashionable for a generation, returned in 1857. Hats were worn by children and had occasionally appeared as informal seaside or country wear (Fig. 6); they were now being worn by young women, 'of course they are not suited to elderly ladies' [35] (Pl. 84).

Winter bonnets were of velvet, in summer they were of watered silk, crape, straw, or the white rice straw, 'or as we call it in English chip'.[36] Fancy straws, openwork braids of split straw and horsehair, appeared in the 1830's, but were more popular after 1845 (Pl. 87). Felt appeared in 1849, but although it had been used in riding-hats, it did not come into fashionable use until the return of the hat.

Trimmings in the 1830's were of flowers, feathers and ribbon, with blonde lace and bows of ribbon inside the brim. The bird of paradise plume was the most fashionable 1835–45, but feathers were 'dressy or plain to suit the bonnet',[37] and trimmings generally became lighter after 1830. As the brim opened in the 1850's, trimming again appeared on the inside. Large veils were worn over bonnets in the 1830's, black gauze or lace being particularly fashionable for them, 1833–40, 'black veils are so generally adopted ... you see them upon nine ladies out of ten'.[38] Veils lessened in size and use after 1850. A small curtain frill was worn at the back of the bonnet, shading the neck.

In evening dress the turban and the beret were still worn, but these also were smaller by 1832, and by 1834 'berets so long in favour are now no longer seen in evening dress'.[39] Turbans continued to be worn for a few years longer, twisted into shapes from lace and gauze scarves. Probably many of the lighter scarves which survive from

[31] *La Belle Assemblée*, April 1832.
[32] *ibid.*, Jan. 1832.
[33] *Ladies Cabinet*, June 1845.

[34] *World of Fashion*, Nov. 1853.
[35] *ibid.*, June 1857.
[36] *Ladies Cabinet*, July 1844.
[37] *World of Fashion*, May 1841.
[38] *La Belle Assemblée*, Dec. 1834.
[39] *Court Magazine*, Feb. 1834.

Fig. 3. Fashions for January 1859, from the *London and Paris Ladies Magazine of Fashion.*

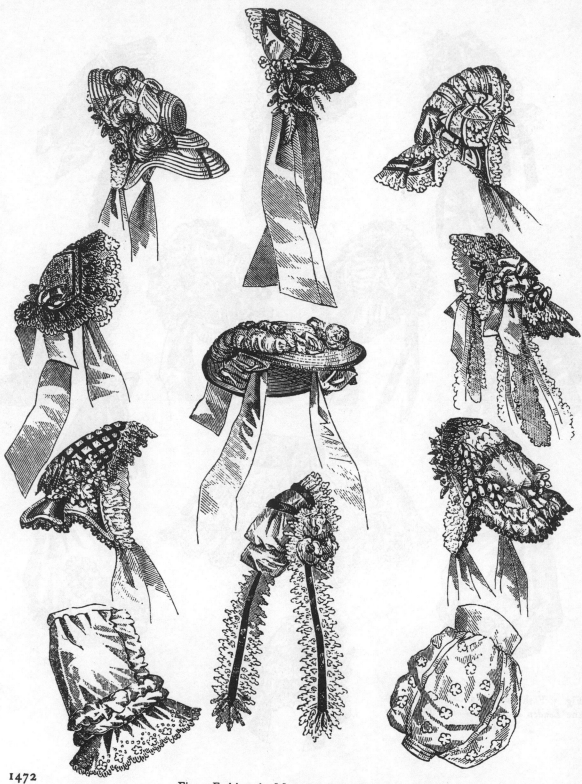

Fig. 4. Fashions for May 1859, from the *London and Paris Ladies Magazine of Fashion.*

these years were so used, but by 1836 'turbans have lost a little of their vogue',[40] and by the early 1840's they were little worn.

The cap of the 1830's was still round, its brim, like that of the bonnets, rising from the face (Pls. 77, 79), but by 1840 it followed the new bonnet line and lay close to the head. Morning caps were of net, muslin and lace, and evening caps of lace and gauze. The hair was generally worn uncovered with ball dress or ornamented with flowers. Although in 1838–40 there was 'a fashion of covering the head ... even by very young married ladies',[41] for evening, the wearing of caps by younger women was lessening.

Shoes and stockings

Shoes, which were invisible under the long, full skirts, were flat and heel-less, often with ribbons or elastic crossing over the instep. They were usually black or white, 'dark coloured shoes are in general to be preferred to bright',[42] in silk for evening wear, and silk, cloth or kid for day wear. Half boots, just covering the ankles and lacing on the inside, with a single thickness of leather for a heel, were worn for walking. These were usually of cloth in shades of fawn or drab, with a toecap of kid in matching or contrasting shade. Dress boots of silk were also worn. Elastic insets at the sides appeared instead of lacing from the 1840's and heels reappeared during the 1850's. All boots and shoes show a long, narrow shape with squared toes.

Silk stockings were worn, the silk usually ending in cotton tops, well below the knee, and cotton stockings. The cotton ones were usually white, but the silk ones sometimes pale pink or mauve. By 1860 colour began to appear in some stockings, matching the magenta woollen petticoats which were then being worn, 'stockings made in the same colour ... or striped with black'.[43]

Gloves and mittens

Evening gloves became shorter after 1830, and between 1835 and 1845 were ornamented at the

top with ruchings or flowers, 'gloves are worn so short in evening dress that there is space enough between the trimming which finished them at the top and the bend of the arm for three or four bracelets'.[44] By the middle of the 1840's they were wrist length. Evening gloves were usually of white kid, but when the mingling of black with colour was fashionable, black net gloves and mittens were also worn, embroidered in chenille, coloured silks and gold and silver thread, 'as to appear enriched with precious stones'.[45] Black and white mittens were also worn with day dress, and short, wrist-length gloves of pale kid were constant day-time wear (Pl. 84).

Bags, fans and parasols

Bags or reticules appeared in flat forms, hanging from the belt in the 1830's and early 1840's, but they became less used and necessary as the full folds of the skirt gave space for pockets in the seams. Tubular purses of knitted or netted silk, ornamented with steel beads, were made in large numbers and much used (Pl. 84).

Fans of the eighteenth-century style, with ivory sticks, carved and gilt, and painted, pictorial leaves, were carried in the 1840's and 1850's.

Parasols, like hats, grew smaller and shared the woven and watered silks, silks 'à disposition', and the fringed and lace trimmings of the dresses. There was a fashion for feather parasols in 1838. The handles were of wood, bone or ivory, often finely turned or carved; and usually hinged so that they could fold, on the small parasols carried from about 1838.

MEN'S COSTUME

As women's dress was dominated throughout this period by the increasing fullness of its skirt, a new character was given to men's dress by the skirted frock coat. The cut-away coat, which had been the style of the beginning of the century, disappeared only gradually, particularly for country wear, and remained as the style for evening dress, but for formal day-time wear its place was now

---

[40] *Court Magazine*, Feb. 1836.
[41] *World of Fashion*, Feb. 1839.
[42] *Art of Dress*, 1839, p. 45.
[43] *Englishwoman's Domestic Magazine*, Dec. 1860.

[44] *World of Fashion*, June 1837.
[45] *ibid.*, Oct. 1839.

taken by a full-skirted coat, which, single- or double-breasted, fastened over the front of the body and covered the legs to the knees or just above them (Pl. 81). The forms of men's dress were now as much influenced by the occasion of their wearing as by the period in which they were being worn. The relation between occasion and form, between the garment and its function, was, however, an arbitrary rather than a practical one; the form which had come into dress from the hunting-field and horseback remained for the ballroom, and the tendency was for new styles to pass from informal wear to general wear, and to end as the garments of formal ceremony.

The frock coat, with its full skirt, showed a long-waisted line a few years before the lengthening of the bodice gave the same emphasis to women's dress. In the 1840's, 'If a man be well made about the waist and hips ... a long-waisted frock or great coat which has the waist seam below the hips may be worn to advantage'.[46] The cut-away coat showed a similar lengthening of the waistline. The low fastening and the deep lapel of the coats of the late 1820's remained, but after 1840 the fastening rose higher and closed the coat over the chest in short lapels (Pl. 81). In the 1850's shorter coat-forms with narrower skirts, slightly curving away at the front, began to appear. Throughout the period coats were usually of dark cloth, particularly black or dark blue.

In contrast to the dark coat, trousers were light, drab fawn, grey or white cloth, although for evening wear they were black, matching the coat. For more informal wear during the 1840's trousers of checked cloth were popular, and plain ones often had a broad stripe down the outer leg in the 1850's. By 1860 dark trousers matching the coat were increasingly worn. The legs were very narrow during the 1840's and 1850's, and from 1850 the strapping under the foot was disappearing (Pl. 81).

Between the dark coat and the light neutral shades of the trousers was the last refuge of colour

in men's dress, the waistcoat. For evening this was usually white, but for day wear coloured silks figured in floral or formalized patterns were worn, and, less formally, fabrics in bright checks. At the beginning of the period it usually had an open front with low fastening and deep curved lapels. Here, as in the coat, the fastening rose and the low curved lapels were replaced by shorter pointed ones, but the two styles overlapped, the earlier line still remaining in the 1850's. The base of the waistcoat was already curving to a point at the centre in the 1830's, and this line generally appears throughout the period. In the 1850's the fronts were cut away slightly, making a small triangular gap at the centre front (Pl. 82). Between 1830 and 1850 the backs were laced, or still retained the earlier tape ties, but after 1850 lacing was generally replaced by a buckle fastening.

Shirts in 1830 still had a high collar and a frilled front opening. The frill remained on evening shirts until about 1850, when it was gradually replaced by a front section of vertical tucking or pleating, with button or stud fastening, which had been worn on day shirts from the 1830's (Pl. 79). A small frill sometimes remained round the vertical band containing the button-holes. The collar of the shirt still reached the ears and chin in 1830, but during the period became lower, and in the 1850's began to turn down over the cravat. Detachable collars which could be fastened to a narrow neckband were also worn. Shirts were of white linen, 'Gentlemen's shirts are usually made of fine Irish linen or lawn, and sometimes of longcloth. Some gentlemen wear striped calicoes, but seldom unless engaged in sporting, boating or fishing.'[47]

The cravat of 1830 was still a triangular piece of muslin, folded into a band, which was wrapped round the neck, and knotted in front. But during the 1830's black silk became increasingly worn for day-time and coloured silk cravats, striped or figured. These seem at times to have penetrated even into evening wear, where white still remained the main fashion, 'Already the young men of fashion have renounced black cravats for even-

[46] Good, T. and Barnett, G., *Scientific Cutting Simplified*, 1845, p. 109.

[47] *The Workwoman's Guide*, 1838, p. 142.

ing. The coloured are only used in the morning. At this I rejoice, never having been able to reconcile myself to them for dinner.' [48] The cravat was sometimes worn with long ends, crossed but not knotted, spread out into the space left by the opening of the waistcoat, and held in position by an ornamental pin. As the collars of the shirts grew lower, 1840–60, the cravat became a narrower band, tying in a wide bow; by 1860 the band had become still narrower and the bow smaller.

Out of doors, the cloak was, with varying length, still worn for evening. The frock-coat form was worn as an overcoat, and another overcoat was the Chesterfield, which was not seamed at the waist, although during this period it was shaped for the waist. This was sometimes worn not as an overcoat, but instead of a frock coat. The box coat – a much looser overcoat, a cloak with sleeves and cape – was also worn. Another cape with sleeves, 'much worn by London Fashionables for driving', was 'made of short milled cloth (either brown or drab) and has long been in wear as a "Macintosh" for driving, that is to say made of Macintosh's India Rubber cloth.' [49]

The tall cylindrical hat in silk, felt or straw, black or in pale shades of grey and fawn, was the only style worn except a low-crowned, broader-brimmed style for country and sporting wear.

Shoes and boots, which were now short, were of leather with long, narrow foot and square toe.

[48] Elizabeth, Lady Holland to her Son, 1821–45, (1946), 30 June 1840

[49] Good, T. and Barnett, G., *Scientific Cutting Simplified*, 1845, p. 55.

Fig. 5. The fashions for enormous crinolines, in *Punch*, November 22nd, 1856.

Fig. 6. The fashion for large hats, as observed by John Leech in
Punch, October 6th, 1855.

Jewellery

J. F. HAYWARD

The history of the applied arts in the nineteenth century presents a complex picture; fashions changed with such rapidity that it is difficult to trace any logical and continuous course of progress. In discussing the earlier periods dealt with in the preceding volumes of this work, it has always been possible to recognize some *leitmotiv* in taste; but in the nineteenth century style in the applied arts was at the mercy of an irresistible desire for novelty, a desire which involved an ever-increasing tempo of change. This constant search for something different was particularly strongly manifest in a minor art such as jewellery, which was affected not only by changes in the main stream of taste, but also by a host of minor fashions dictated by the course of feminine clothing fashion.

The effect of such changes in fashion was stressed in the Illustrated Catalogue to the Great Exhibition of 1851 published by the *Art-Journal*, a document of the greatest importance as a source of information concerning mid-nineteenth-century taste:

'The business of the manufacturing jeweller has undergone a great change during the last few years, for there is a fashion in the works of his hands, which, perpetually changing, compels him to seek new methods of exhibiting his taste and skill. We may instance, as an example, the manufacture of watch-seals, a branch of their art that is now rarely called into exercise. And again, in such objects as ladies' ear-rings which are almost wholly out of date, except as worn on what may be termed "state occasions". These alterations in the style of ornamental dress have compelled the manufac-

turer to devote his attention chiefly to bracelets ornaments for the head, and brooches. The last-mentioned objects, though of distant origin, have assumed a totally varied form and feature from even their more immediate predecessors. Here we have now imitations of flowers, either singly or in groups, in which not only their forms are closely followed, but oftentimes successful attempts are made to produce natural colours by the introduction of precious stones.'

Revivalism

The basic trend in jewellery fashion in the period 1830–60 was one of revivalism; revival not of one particular style or period, but of styles drawn from different periods and cultures. The interest in reviving earlier styles of jewellery had already been apparent in the earlier decades of the century, but no great importance had been attached to achieving exactness in their reproduction. The spirit which inspired the *style cathédrale* of the 1820's was not so far removed from that which had created the 'Gothick' fantasies of the mid-eighteenth century. Subsequently towards the middle of the century we find an attitude of almost excessive piety towards medieval art associated with the name of Augustus Pugin, and exact reproductions of earlier pieces were made – exact, that is, in design, but inevitably lacking the life and spirit of the original. In the case of the Gothic jewellery, which Pugin sought to re-create, the originals no longer survived, and his pastiches were based not on actual jewels but on representations in medieval manuscripts and paintings. The taste for romantic Gothic was not

1477

immediately banished by Pugin's purism, and even as late as the 1851 Exhibition the leading French jeweller, François Froment-Meurice, exhibited a number of frankly romantic Gothic jewels. Pugin was not the only protagonist of the purist movement in the first half of the nineteenth century, for the Roman goldsmith, Fortunato Pio Castellani, was until his death in 1865 producing the most careful copies of Etruscan jewellery, with its delicate granulated enrichment, the secret of whose manufacture he had himself re-discovered.

When considering the rapidity of fashion changes in the first half of the nineteenth century, it must be remembered that, in spite of ever-improved industrial techniques, costume jewellery was only in its infancy. Most jewellery was still composed of precious or of semi-precious materials and was, therefore, comparatively expensive, and could not be replaced, as can modern costume jewellery. Whereas fashion magazines announced new trends with regularity, it was not a practicable proposition to purchase new jewels to keep up with all the vagaries of taste. Types of jewellery which, according to the journals, were no longer fashionable continued, therefore, in use among all but the very rich. These same magazines do, however, give us much information concerning the details of the feminine *toilette*. As always, a distinction was made between jewellery suitable for daily and for evening wear. In her book entitled *Female Beauty*, published in 1837, Mrs Walker gives the following advice on suitable jewellery:

'In promenade or carriage dress jewels are out of place. Nothing should be worn round the neck but a plain or watered ribbon, about half an inch broad, or a chain of silver or gold, as a guard to suspend the watch, or eyeglass if the wearer be short-sighted, for wearing an eyeglass without occasion for it is a piece of impertinent affectation. ... The ball dress requires a union of beauty, elegance, lightness and magnificence. All the resources of the toilet must be lavished upon it. No trivial embroidery or ornaments of gold or silver must glitter there: their place is supplied with pearls, diamonds and other jewels.'

Among other points which are stressed in Mrs Walker's book is the fact that young ladies should prefer flowers to precious stones, leaving the latter to their elders: 'Flowers decorate the system of life which is exuberant only in the young; jewels decorate the system of mind, which excels in the old.' Again, 'Young ladies should never wear rings on their fingers, unless they desire to seem older.'

Fashions in the 1830's were dominated by the same trends as the preceding decade, that is, romantic Gothic and Renaissance. Alongside these fashions there was continuing production of the cheaper jewellery, composed of semi-precious stones with the elaborate filigree settings made of gold wire twisted in various forms known as *cannetille*. The later examples of this latter type of jewel became somewhat larger and coarser and were enriched with coloured enamel instead of having settings of tinted gold. The importance of the Gothic fashion is illustrated by the following extract from the *World of Fashion* for January 1839:

'The forms of our *bijous* are now entirely borrowed from the style of the Middle Ages; massive gold pins, with the heads richly chased, or composed of coloured gems set in small flowers, *couronnes* or *guirlandes* of gold and diamonds, or else of gold set with coloured gems. All our ornaments, in short, are *moyen age*.'

Gothic jewellery

The Gothic revival did not, however, exercise an influence on jewellery design comparable with the predominant role it played in the development of Victorian architecture. The most popular form of Gothic jewellery was that produced in cast iron, first made in Berlin, but subsequently in Paris and elsewhere (Pl. 85A). It was still to be seen in the 1851 Exhibition and, to judge by the numerous examples which are to be found in this country, it must have enjoyed considerable popularity here. Though the production of castings of such lace-like fineness was a considerable technical achievement, the poverty of the material renders them dry and uninteresting. Even the designs of Augustus Pugin, which were based on details copied from fifteenth-century Italian and Flemish paintings, lost most of their charm when they were

Fig. 1, Brooch, shown at the Great Exhibition by Messrs C.Rowlands. Enamelled gold with a carbuncle and diamonds.

made up through the inability of the nineteenth-century jewellers, in spite of their technical skill, to catch the spirit of the Middle Ages.

Renaissance jewellery

The revived Renaissance jewellery consisted for the most part of expensive pieces made by a small number of high-class jewellers, such as Froment-Meurice (Pl. 85c) or Castellani; some of it followed Renaissance prototypes very closely, to the extent even of being made after engraved designs by Renaissance artists. Like the Gothic jewellery, however, the cold precision of workmanship of these reproductions differentiates them completely from their Renaissance prototypes (Fig. 1, Pl. 85D).

The Rococo taste

More lasting in effect than either the Gothic or the Renaissance revivals was that of the 'rococo' taste, which enjoyed an almost uninterrupted run of popularity from the second quarter of the century onwards until its end. While silver plate had been made in the neo-rococo style as early as the second decade of the century, the typical nineteenth-century rococo jewellery appears somewhat later, though the fashion was certainly established by the 1830's. It cannot be claimed that much of the Victorian rococo jewellery bore any marked resemblance to what it was supposed to be emulating (Fig. 4). The Victorian taste for massive-looking settings and strong colours was fundamentally opposed to the light and frivolous spirit of eighteenth-century rococo, and only in one field – that of floral jewellery – can the revival be said to have been successful in producing anything more than a parody of the original. The complex settings which had been so carefully constructed by the eighteenth-century jeweller were now usually die-stamped by machine from thin metal. The play of delicate contrasting scrolls which is the basis of much eighteenth-century jewellery design could not be reproduced in the coarse and obese scrolls of which the Victorian versions were composed (Pl. 86A).

Floral jewellery

The revived rococo fashion gave a new impetus to the production of floral jewellery. The taste for diamond sprays had never ceased to be effective ever since the mid-eighteenth century, but in the 1840's the demand for them became stronger, and at the same time efforts were made to render such jewels even more naturalistic (Pl. 86B, c). Among the features which helped to give greater realism to the floral spray was the use of green enamel on the leaves (Pl. 86B, 88B) and the addition of butterflies or insects perching on the blossoms. This was commented on in the *Art-Journal* Catalogue of the 1851 Exhibition: 'the taste for floral ornament in jewellery has been very prevalent of late; and it is a good and happy taste, inasmuch as the brilliant colouring of an enamelled

Fig. 2. Brooch, shown at the Great Exhibition by Messrs C. Rowlands. It is set with diamonds.

Fig. 3. Brooch, shown at the Great Exhibition by Messrs Watherston and Brogden. Enamelled gold set with diamonds and pearls.

leaf or floret is an excellent foil to a sparkling stone.' An effective feature which seems to have appeared first in Paris during the 1840's was the application of falling cascades of diamonds which hung down from the sprays like brilliant rain. Examples of jewels with these cascades were shown in the 1851 Great Exhibition (Fig. 2), where indeed a large variety of jewels of naturalistic floral character was to be seen. Among them was a tiara of sapphires and diamonds, made for the Queen of Spain, the points being composed of diamond leaves, and having bands of diamonds falling in loops at the sides.

The most admired English jewel in the Exhibition was a diamond and ruby stomacher composed of naturalistic flowers by the firm of J. V. Morel. This jewel, which included a rose, a tulip and a morning glory, 'was originally intended and designed as a bouquet ... moreover, it was so constructed as to separate into several distinct pieces of jewellery, according to requirement. The setting was contrived with springs, resulting in a waving or slightly oscillating motion when in use, which displayed to the fullest extent the brilliant colours of the stones.' The most popular form of flower-spray in the mid-Victorian era was composed of wild roses in diamonds set in silver with a gold backing, or, after the middle of the century, in platinum.

In the eighteenth and early nineteenth cen-

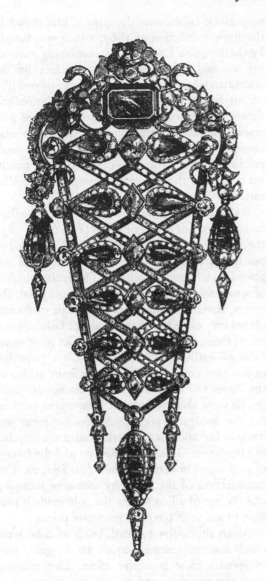

Fig. 4. Brooch, shown at the Great Exhibition by Messrs C.Rowlands. Gold set with rubies and diamonds, the design is based on an eighteenth-century stomacher.

Fig. 5. Brooch, shown at the Great Exhibition by Messrs Watherston and Brogden. Enamelled gold set with diamonds.

turies diamonds had always been set in silver, as it was considered that a coloured setting detracted from the effect of the stones. In the Victorian era silver was thought to be an insufficiently precious material in which to set valuable stones, and a laminated setting was used, the front being of silver and the back of gold (Pl. 87D). These laminated settings gave way in turn to platinum.

Two other floral details that were unfamiliar to the eighteenth-century jeweller, but were particularly favoured in the mid-nineteenth century, were ivy leaves (Fig. 3) and the convolvulus flower

Fig. 6. Breast ornament, shown at the Great Exhibition by Messrs Watherston and Brogden. Enamelled gold and pearls.

naturalistic fashion was the spray of lilac shown in the Paris Exhibition of 1867, which was bought by the Empress Eugènie. Its astonishing naturalism was said to have been due to the fact that the craftsman who produced it had a spray of real lilac on his bench while working on it. Naturalistic flower jewels were not necessarily made of precious materials. For the bourgeois taste there were brooches or necklaces composed of sprays of semi-precious stones set in two-colour gold or pinchbeck, such as the attractive example in the Victoria and Albert Museum (Pl. 86B).

As an alternative to flowers, we find jewellery based on fruit or even nut forms (Fig. 6). In 1837 the new brooches for evening were 'composed of pearls and turquoises; the pattern is a hazel nut placed on a branch of foliage. The fruit, which is of a tolerable size, is formed of a single pearl, the leaves, tastefully grouped, are of small turquoises placed very close together.' Another fashion journal of the same year informs us: 'The most novel form of setting diamond ear-rings is a grape between two vine leaves, the grape is in brilliants, the leaves and the stalk in small diamonds.' Such jewels were also produced in inexpensive versions for the bourgeois pocket. A popular form was made in imitation of grape-vines with the bunches of grapes of seed-pearl or amethyst and the foliage of gold tinted in various colours (Pl. 88A, B). The manufacture of the leaves by means of stamping and the use of alloys to tint the gold made it possible to sell such pieces at moderate prices.

As an alternative to pearl, beads of coral were much used to imitate berries; set in gold, they achieved a most attractive effect. Less pleasing were the brooches, and even tiaras, composed of coral branches in their natural state. Such was the importance of the fashion for coral jewellery in England that the London jeweller, Robert Phillips, who showed collections of carved coral at the various international exhibitions of the mid-nineteenth century, was decorated by the King of Italy for his work in developing the Naples coral trade. At the 1851 Exhibition Messrs Hunt and Roskell showed a coral branch tiara ornamented with leaves of enamel and gold enriched with diamonds.

and foliage. The great collection of nineteenth-century jewellery bequeathed to the Victoria and Albert Museum by Lady Cory contains examples both in diamonds (Pl. 87A) and in *pavé* set turquoises (Pl. 87B). The preference for turquoise, which had already manifested itself in the 1820's, became even stronger in the mid-Victorian period, and we find floral brooches and necklaces or bracelets made in the form of snakes profusely set with this stridently coloured semi-precious stone. The presence of the ivy or convolvulus can be accepted as fairly definite evidence of mid-nineteenth-century or later date.

Floral jewels were made in most of the European capitals, and it is not possible to determine their national origin. A typical expression of the

Enamelling

Enamelling returned to fashion as a form of enrichment for jewellery during the second quarter of the nineteenth century; the following quotation from the *World of Fashion* of September 1844, besides giving us full information about bracelet fashions, makes two references to their enamelled enrichment:

> 'Bracelets are now considered indispensable; they are worn in the following manner; on one arm is placed the sentimental bracelet, composed of hair, and fastened with some precious relic; the second is a silver enamelled one, having a cross, cassolette, or anchor and heart, as a sort of talisman; the other arm is decorated with a bracelet of gold net work fastened with a simple *noeud*, similar to one of narrow ribbon; the other composed of medallions of blue enamel, upon which are placed small bouquets of brilliants, the fastening being composed of a single one; lastly a very broad gold chain, each link separated with a ruby and opal alternate.'

A favourite combination in the mid-nineteenth century was to set small brilliants and half pearls against a ground of dark blue enamel; many gold pendants and lockets enriched in this way are still to be found (Pl. 85E). Lockets were the most popular form of mid-nineteenth-century sentimental jewellery; they were usually worn suspended around the neck by a chain or a ribbon, but were also hung from brooches, or even bracelets. The standard relic, as is indicated in the passage from the *World of Fashion* quoted above, was a lock of hair, plaited or arranged in the form of the dear one's initials. Memorial lockets were of similar form, but were enamelled black instead of blue. The recognition of the locket as the sentimental jewel *par excellence* drove out the mourning ring, which became obsolete during the 1840's. Hair-work, which was a natural corollary to sentimental jewellery, was still greatly in favour about the middle of the century, and among the more grotesque objects shown at the Great Exhibition was 'a large vase, most ingeniously composed of human hair, executed by J.Woolley'. Bracelets were also plaited from human hair, secured by a large and usually rather coarse gold clasp. Much ingenuity was shown in devising different ways of plaiting the hair, but the fashion for jewellery made entirely or almost entirely of human hair did not survive the period under review.

Cameos

Cameos had also retained their popularity until the middle of the century and later. Shell cameos, imported, like the carved corals, from Naples and the neighbouring towns along the coast, were much used for the cheaper jewellery, but cameos of onyx, agate or coral were recognized as suitable for wear by the socially ambitious, as is indicated by the following extract from a fashion note of 1857: 'A parure of these cameos (coral and onyx) is altogether aristocratic, and wholly unlike the cameos with which all the world is acquainted. They are pure works of art, modelled and cut by artist gravers, and mounted and ornamented by artists in bijouterie.' A number of cameos were exhibited at the Great Exhibition, mostly by Parisian jewellers, but a Mr Brett of London was amongst the exhibitors.

Minor fashions

Apart from the main course of fashion, there were many other minor fashions that were taken up for a while and dropped when the novelty had worn off. It would not be practicable to attempt to describe all the vagaries of fashion between 1830 and 1860, but the following are the most important. The excavations at Nineveh, an account of which was published in 1848, led to an Assyrian fashion (Pl. 85B), and in that year we read that flexible bracelets set with Assyrian rosettes or lotus flowers in precious stones were popular. Among the peculiarities exhibited at the Great Exhibition were the ear-rings of emeralds, diamonds, carbuncles, etc., based upon the sculptures from Nineveh, which were shown by Messrs Hunt and Roskell. The firm of Watherston and Brogden, who made the jewels shown in Figs. 3, 5 and 6, also showed examples of Assyrian jewellery at the Great Exhibition.

The campaigns fought by the French in

Algeria in the 1840's were followed by a fashion for elaborate knots and tassels copied from North African jewellery; and a Celtic phase was well represented at the 1851 Exhibition, where numerous reproductions of ancient Irish brooches were shown by Waterhouse of Dublin. Queen Victoria's pride in her Stuart ancestry led in turn to a fashion for traditional Scottish jewellery set with cairngorms and polished pebbles. Finally, after the Great Exhibition, increased interest was shown in Greek revival jewellery of the type that the firm of Castellani had been producing since the 1820's.

In considering Victorian jewellery as a whole, it has to be remembered that it was designed to be set against heavy fabrics of sombre colouring. The massiveness of the settings, now so apparent, must have been far less oppressive when seen in conjunction with contemporary clothing styles. The best of Victorian jewellery has been sacrificed to changes in taste and been broken up for re-setting. Unfortunately much of what remains is of the cheaper type, gaudy in colour and meretricious in design, with coarsely stamped settings of low-grade gold. Most of the Victorian reproduction jewellery failed in its purpose, owing to the impossibility of adapting the precise and altogether mechanical technique of Victorian craftsmanship to the spirit of earlier styles.

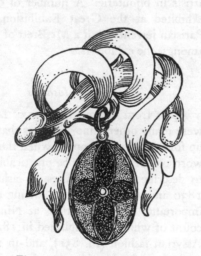

Fig. 7. Two water-colour designs for brooches with lockets. Mid-nineteenth century. *Victoria and Albert Museum.*

Figs. 1–6 have been reproduced from the 'Art-Journal Illustrated Catalogue', 1851.

Music and Musical Instruments

ROBERT DONINGTON

The old dominance of Handel

Music in eighteenth-century England had fallen under the spell of the great, but also very astute Handel to an extent which it is hard to credit now that his deserved reputation, as a genius of massive rather than ecstatic inspiration, has found its natural proportions.

In Early Victorian England the spell of Handel did not in the least diminish. He ruled undisputed, and there can have been few musically-inclined early Victorians who did not cherish the *Messiah* as the probable summit of musical achievement. A society known as the Handel Society 'for the production of a superior and standard edition' flourished from 1843 to 1848, and the publication was continued commercially until 1855, the year before the great German Handel Society was founded. In 1833 the Sacred Harmonic Society (founded the year before) was launched, with a programme almost entirely of Handel's music. Its criterion of a good Handelian performance included a considerable emphasis on volume, and by 1837 its combined orchestra and chorus numbered 500 – the chorus far outweighing the orchestra. North-country singers were brought to London to augment the ranks. They were amateurs, but they were found work in London for the purpose.

This emphasis on large forces, and on the grandiloquence of performing style inseparable from large forces, was somewhat typical of the period. It was not merely that the numbers were large, however; for that there were precedents, as in the commemoration of the centenary of his birth, that is to say in 1784 (actually a year early, since he was born in 1685). There was then a choir of 274 but an orchestra of 251, being both strong in the bass sections and with some chance of reasonable balance. The Early Victorian renderings started half a century later in 1834 with the balance quite upset in favour of the choir: 365 singers against 222 players. This was a mere beginning. For the centenary of his death in 1859 (there was a preliminary Festival in 1857) 2,396 performers were assembled in the only building large enough to contain them, the Crystal Palace, inherited from the Great Exhibition of 1851; and it seems almost unkind to relate that this apocalyptic array was subsequently outnumbered, the total rising to 3,500 in 1874 (in the proportion of six singers to each player) and to 4,000 in 1923.

This was a piece of musical ineptness and spiritual inflatedness, partly foreshadowed, it is true, before the Victorian Age, and continued long afterwards, that received its chief impetus from something in the times which we cannot help thinking of as characteristic of one of the many strains in that great, yet contradictory period. It argues a certain element of grossness and a certain ability to mistake the trappings for the reality. It was an inflation which collapsed with remarkable suddenness and appropriateness at the total destruction of the Crystal Palace by fire in 1936, by which time a movement was preparing to return, as many musicians are by now returning, to the small forces and crisp transparency of execution of Handel's own original performances.

Bad imitation Handel, mostly in the shape of

oratorio, came still more infelicitously from Early Victorian than from Regency imaginations; and the Victorian cantata was a new rival to the oratorio in weighty dullness. What partly saved this unfortunate situation, though at the price of a further servitude not much more wholesome than the old, was the fact that a rival was now found for Handel. He was not dethroned; there was still a majority to echo Stafford Smith's opinion of a short generation ago (in 1812) that 'the superior knowledge of instrumental effect possessed by Haydn, Mozart, Beethoven, and others, by no means compensates for the want of that manly, open, clear, vocal melody which characterised the work of Mr Handel'. But though not pushed from his throne, he had to share it as never previously in England, and share it with a visitor who was, like himself, a German and was, like himself, a man of sound business instincts as well as musicianship. This visitor was Mendelssohn.

The new influence of Mendelssohn

Mendelssohn came to London in 1829 on the first of a series of frequent visits throughout the remainder of his short life (he died in 1847, aged thirty-eight). As a young virtuoso of twenty he was welcomed as 'one of the finest piano-forte players in Europe ... supposed to be better acquainted with music than most professors of the art' (*Harmonicon*, 1829, p. 116). He was handsome and well-off (his father was a leading Hamburg banker); he had a precociously abundant talent and most winning manners; he was both artistically and socially more than acceptable. The friend of Goethe in Germany and later of Queen Victoria in England, he appeared to have every gift of fortune in his favour; but appearances were deceptive in one respect. He lacked one ingredient for lasting greatness: he knew very little about human suffering.

Mendelssohn's advance to popularity in England, at first as an executant but almost as rapidly as a composer, was little short of meteoric. He was soon worshipped almost to idolatry; and the influence of his genuinely inspired and readily attractive music swept the country. A new sect was formed that was not so very different from that of the Handel-worshippers. A new sect rather than a new religion, however; for in spite of their obvious differences of style and period, the two composers have an element in common which goes far to account for their common influence over Early Victorian musicianship. This element has to do with a certain unvarying optimism, imperturbable in the case of Handel, just perceptibly forced in the case of Mendelssohn, but in both of them unleavened by that sad wisdom which is an essential ingredient in every artist of the profoundest quality. Both composers had real greatness to substantiate their success; it was the uncritical reception of them which was its unhealthy aspect. They did not merely influence the Victorian musical scene; they imposed on it unnaturally. It is impossible to give any account of Early Victorian music which does not give these two foreigners pride of place.

Composers of talent but not of genius

We have first, paradoxically, to take one of those palpable exceptions which prove the rule concerning the dominant influences in early Victorian music. Robert Lucas Pearsall (1795–1856), a leisured amateur, worshipped neither Handel nor Mendelssohn; instead, his work reveals an intense interest in the one period least recognized by the average Handelian and Mendelssohnian, namely the golden age of the Jacobean madrigals. He wrote imitations of them which are so excellent that we are almost tempted to forget that they are in fact imitations, with the barest suspicion of Victorian sentiment to give the game away and to add at least a touch of originality. Unfortunately there is no law of nature and of art more inexorable than the law which prevents imitations, however excellent, from having the effect of originals.

Michael William Balfe (1808–70) was a composer of a very different stamp. An Irishman, the son of a dancing-master and brought up in a highly professional, not to say diversified environment, he was the very opposite of a cultured amateur, and the word leisure scarcely entered his vocabulary. He was playing the violin for a dancing-class at six and composing at seven. By eleven he had achieved public success in both directions. At fifteen he lost his energetic father, but earned his living without difficulty, including singing on the operatic stage among his professional successes – under the exacting Rossini, one of his patrons. By twenty he was an accepted Continental figure.

At a period when opera in London virtually spelt Italian opera, Balfe scored an immediate success with his first English opera, *The Siege of Rochelle*, first produced at Drury Lane in 1835. Others followed, but not all were successful. He lives now (and until quite recently lived very actively indeed) in his enormously popular *The Bohemian Girl* of 1843. His vein is tuneful, his style is catchy, his appeal is immediate – but indubitably shallow. Talent could hardly go farther, and very enjoyable talent it is in a certain mood. But genius, which is certainly not too strong a word for Gilbert and Sullivan in later Victorian England, is hardly in question with the facile Balfe. At least, however, he was not a post-Handelian, nor much of a Mendelssohnian; he shares these rather negative virtues with his fastidious opposite, Pearsall.

Samuel Sebastian Wesley (1810–1876) was the natural son of the great Samuel Wesley, and grew up in an equally professional atmosphere, though of a very different character. His background was ecclesiastical, and so is the bulk of his most important music. Though not quite a genius, he was more nearly so than any of his English contemporaries; he certainly seemed to be one to his own age, and it may be that the change in our tastes has been a little unfair to him. Spohr's testimony to him as candidate for the professorship of music at Edinburgh in 1844 is a fair and by no means unduly flattering description:

> His works show, without exception, that he is master of both style and form ... not only in sacred art, but also in glees and in music for the pianoforte. His sacred music is chiefly distinguished by a noble, often even an antique, style, and by rich harmonies as well as by surprisingly beautiful modulations.

In other words, he was Handel crossed with Mendelssohn: but that is not in itself an adequate summary of his achievement. In the first place, a further and valuable influence was the Tudor church music, with which he was more familiar than most Victorians. In the second place, like Pearsall he had a certain individuality of his own, and in a far more versatile and fluent form. His sentiment is decidedly Victorian, and the Mendelssohnian ingredient falls rather strangely on our modern ears in this religious context; but he kept on the right side of dignity. He was also evidently a most impressive executant on the organ. As a master of the rank just short of genius, he commands respect, and he might well for those in sympathy with his Victorian mood command affection too.

Sir George Alexander Macfarren (1813–87) had the force of character to overcome the handicap of a blindness which became total early in his career, and this force and the integrity which went with it are evident in his music. Handel and Mendelssohn are both hard at work in it, however, and the mixture in his sacred music is ponderous rather than explosive. But his secular works are far more lively; it is an unexpected coincidence that this very worthy man, like the volatile Balfe himself, had a dancing-master for a father, and we can only wish that this ingredient in his development had been a little more influential than it evidently was. He had the enterprise to edit Purcell's *Dido and Aeneas* for the Musical Antiquarian Society; but his editions of Handel Oratorio, as the Handel Society's secretary from 1843, are somehow more typical of the man. He wrote a number of operas, some, such as his *Robin Hood*, successful in their day; but that day is gone, while Balfe's more vulgar but robuster *The Bohemian Girl* may even yet be not quite finished.

Heinrich Hugo Pierson (1815–73) was born plain Henry Hugo Pearson, the son of an Oxford clergyman and don – an environment from which he appears to have reacted with little gratitude. He had some small success in England as a young man, and thereafter a very notable success in Germany, where he became increasingly acclimatized both in disposition and in composing style. Though on terms of quite close relationship with Mendelssohn, he never accepted him undiluted, as did most English musicians: he was more critical in his appreciation, and he was equally well acquainted with Spohr, Meyerbeer and above all Schumann, who took a favourable view of his talent. Indeed, German musical circles in general did so to an extent which it is difficult to justify today, since his music, though ambitious and by no means without the divine spark, was marred by incorrigible amateurishness of technique. The spark was there, and in a form more original, potentially, than in his English contemporaries; but it flickered too fitfully to survive the winds of time, and he is entirely neglected by now both in Germany and elsewhere.

There was another Englishman of much sounder talent who also aroused the high hopes of the most influential German musicians, Schumann and Mendelssohn among them. This was Sir William Sterndale Bennett (1816–75), the most substantial of the Early Victorian composers, and with no deficiency in his technical equipment to hamper him. The son and grandson of professional musicians, he had the thorough grounding which comes best from growing up in practical musical surroundings from the earliest age. He was something of a prodigy, but not an extreme one: he was accepted at the newly founded Royal Academy of Music, with a free place there, as a boy of ten. In 1832 he had his first public success as a composer, and this success was repeated a year later in the presence of Mendelssohn, who took him up at once and invited him to Germany. The influence was all too successful, and Bennett never really escaped from it.

That would not necessarily have been fatal – no contemporary influence is harmful to a strong talent, and at least Bennett did not seriously succumb to Handel and the lure of the glorious past. But for no obvious reasons, Bennett's talent, which really was strong at the start of his career, soon weakened, and at last dwindled to virtual impotence. His German friends could not conceal their disappointment – not excluding the generous Schumann. His case was one of those which cannot be accounted for by the musical historian, and which only a psychologist can understand. There is no question that the gift was there, and that it was by nature more substantial than that which any of his English colleagues showed. But there was an inner resistance to it in his own soul which slowed down the flow and eventually brought it to a standstill. His general influence as a teacher and administrator was wide and admirable.

Italian opera in London

If Mendelssohn's arrival in London aroused all too profound a response in the English musical world, there was another foreign body which the Victorians seemed to tolerate, and indeed enjoy, with no organic reaction of significance whatsoever. This was the Italian opera, which more than a century since its first advent was still the sacrosanct institution it had always been and was to go on being for a further half-century, when German opera, in the formidable person of Wagner, made some inroads.

The Haymarket, Drury Lane and Covent Garden competed for social and financial support with fluctuating fortunes. Mozart and Rossini provided the staple repertory; Weber, Donizetti, Meyerbeer and Bellini became scarcely less popular. Italian was the normal language, though German originals and English translations were not unknown. The English opera proper was so much lighter in style that it remained in a separate artistic class: which is presumably why it was so little susceptible to the influence of its more pretentious rival.

The history of internecine quarrels and financial crises which marked Italian opera from its early eighteenth-century acclimatization showed no sign of abating. In 1846 the conductor at Her Majesty's, Michel Costa, deserted to Covent Garden with most of his principals, to open there as the 'Royal Italian Opera House' in 1847. The singers presently assembled were of legendary variety and excellence; the opening night gave Rossini's *Semiramide* with Grisi, Alboni and Tamburini. A young and controversial addition to the list of composers was Guiseppe Verdi. In 1856 the building was for the second time destroyed by fire (1808 had been the first occasion); it was replaced by 1858 by the beautiful and acoustically admirable building which is still the main centre of London opera.

The Italian opera itself flourished in full vocal glory until the disruption of the first World War, after which the art of singing fell into a decline which has by now become catastrophic. The greatest German singers, like the Italians, were trained on Italian methods productive of feats of singing which can no longer be effected. The style passed with the glittering social order which supported it; but while it lasted, Covent Garden remained one of its greatest centres.

The contralto, a Victorian speciality

There was, indeed, one Early Victorian contribution to the art of singing of considerable, though not unreservedly beneficial, consequence. This was the popularization, by the phenomenal Madame Sainton (Charlotte Dolby), of the female contralto voice. There had always been traditional male altos, but the female of the species, though known, was something of a rarity. This is, however, a story which concerns oratorio rather than opera.

In opera, the second female line had traditionally been the mezzo-soprano, a tessitura much lighter than the contralto, much more ringing in quality and much more brilliant in execution. Only the very best contraltos avoid a certain fruity richness which may have been to the Early Victorian taste, but more because of its natural fitness to the heavier brands of oratorio than from any tonal charm. Since the purity of Madame Sainton's vocalization is the attribute most stressed in contemporary descriptions, there can be no doubt that she was one of the admirable exceptions; but her popularity opened the way for a lesser breed whose influence still helps to weight our performances of oratorio with that sense of leaden after-dinner discomfort peculiarly associated with this form of art.

The climax of Madame Sainton's career was also the climax of Mendelssohn's, and, in a sense, of Early Victorian music itself. This was the celebrated first performance, at Birmingham on 26 August 1846, of the only oratorio to have established itself in our English affections on an equality with the *Messiah*: namely Mendelssohn's *Elijah*. Mendelssohn wrote to his brother the same day that 'a young English tenor' – it was Charles Lockey– 'sang the last air with such wonderful sweetness that I was obliged to collect all my energies not to be affected and to continue beating time steadily'. The work was given next year in London, in four performances of which the third was attended by the Queen and the Prince Consort, to their great delight. Within a few months, Mendelssohn was dead, the news being received with particular grief in England.

Musical instruments

No major developments occurred in the manufacture of musical instruments at the hands of Early Victorian craftsmen, but a steady stream of small improvements continued, especially in the making of pianos. The most crucial English contributions to the latter had already been made in the previous generation, when the famous 'English action' had been evolved among other developments; but English pianos maintained their progress on an equality with those of continental design, and were indeed preferred by some distinguished continental performers.

The flourishing Regency school of violinmakers declined a little in the early years of Victoria, but there were still a number of good makers whose instruments are well regarded today – including a flourishing school in Aberdeen. Their work, however, was based on an excellent reproduction of the best Italian models rather than on original design. The English school continued to take its share in the evolution of wind instruments, with the same tendency to growing mechanization as is found on the Continent; but in some directions we were unusually conservative. The trumpet, for example, was in transition from Early Victorian times until the present century – possibly it is still; but at that period English players and makers held conservatively to the slide-trumpet, which had always been mainly an English variety, and for a time resisted the continental adoption of the valve trumpet. Kohler and Pace were both making valved F trumpets in England by the 1880's, but these were slow to take a hold. And on the whole the same obtains with other wind instruments. The century saw great changes, but not many of importance originated in England.

On the other hand, so far as quantity is concerned, the English makers held their own. The number of pianos produced by the leading firms was surprisingly large when their considerable cost is taken into account. Flutes were in quite astonishing demand, the more expensive having keys up to eight in number, the cheaper being less well provided in this respect: whole operas were transcribed for amateur performance on the flute. The harp was another instrument which flourished remarkably in Early Victorian England: it was the acknowledged adornment of ladies of good breeding, and graced many drawing-rooms with its romantic and by no means diminutive presence. But even the piano was thought in some circles to be a rather effeminate accomplishment, and a case is on record of a young male pianist being hissed off the platform on this account – by the undergraduates of Oxford, so the story runs.

The appearance of Victorian instruments

The mood of Victorian musicianship was closely reflected in the appearance given to those musical instruments whose appearance is in fact capable of considerable modification without interfering with their functions.

Of these, the organ and the piano are the most conspicuous. It is, of course, possible to show the working pipes of an organ, and when, as in the new Royal Festival Hall organ, this policy is adopted, the result can have genuine functional beauty. But that has never been usual with large organs, and we should not expect it in the Victorian age. It has always been, and was then, usual to set a screen of ornamental dummy pipes in front of those actually producing the sound. The screen fronts of Victorian organs tended to be neo-Gothic in style, and more than ordinarily ornate.

The shape of the piano is determined by the arrangement of its strings, which range from a few inches to perhaps seven feet in length; and there are only a few arrangements which are mechanically and acoustically satisfactory. The Victorian taste here made its appearance mainly in the decoration of the legs and sides. The legs, which must in any case be extremely robust to sustain the weight of a full grand piano, were ornamented with carving, often in very deep relief. Their main girth has to be in the upper portion where they meet the frame; their lower portion can be narrower without undue weakening. Hence where the harpsichord, and the earlier pianos of lighter weight, have no more than a slight tapering down from top to bottom, such as the universal principles of good design suggested, the very weighty Victorian pianos have a high degree of tapering, from wide top to narrow bottom. To avoid a clumsy appearance, the section, instead of being rectangular, normally became circular. The most popular materials were rosewood and ebony. The overall effect is rich and massive, but this effect is well in keeping with the structural and musical character of the instrument itself.

The musical character of the English pianos of the Victorian age, in common with those built on the Continent (to which the English makers had given the lead in certain respects since the last decades of the previous century), was determined by the use of very thick, heavy and tense strings, and by an action and a framework conditioned by this weight and tension (it might be well over two tons, a single string accounting for a pressure of perhaps 150 lb.). The resulting tone is somewhat deficient in the upper partials, but extremely powerful in the first six partials or so of the natural harmonic series. It is, therefore, of a less colourful quality than either harpsichord tone or early piano tone, but louder and more massive than either. It is this massiveness of tone which is so well conveyed visually by the weighty construction and heavy ornamentation which meet the eye in the illustrations to the present chapter.

The massiveness of tone in its turn corresponded, and was indeed produced in answer to a genuine musical demand. The music for which the harpsichord had been so well suited was largely contrapuntal, and even when not contrapuntal had been of a kind to need, above all other qualities, a certain clarity and transparency of tone at which the harpsichord excels. But the music of Mendelssohn, Schumann and other German favourites of

Fig. 1. A selection of Signor A.B.Ventura's string instruments exhibited at the Great Exhibition. *L. to r.*, the new British Ventura, the newly invented English Cetra, the Venturina, the Harp Ventura, and the Lyre Ventura. *Official Illustrated Catalogue of the Great Exhibition*, Vol. ι.

the Victorian musical salon and concert hall, together with the English piano music more weakly composed in imitation of these great romantics, does not require and would not tolerate the quality of clarity. The Victorian piano is capable of building up far more sonority than the early piano, and a totally different kind of sonority from the harpsichord. By the skilful use of the damper raising pedal, a surge of high partials is allowed to accumulate which adds to the tone that colourfulness and poetry which it is otherwise too neutral to possess. Cascades of arpeggios and runs intensify this colourful and atmospheric flow of sound — but at the almost total expense of clarity. This is precisely what piano music of the more romantic schools requires, and it was in this direction that the Victorian makers served their clients so well. The decorative exteriors, which were carried to their extreme development in the examples here shown from the Great Exhibition of 1851 (Pls. 89–91), have the undeniable merit of matching the musical idioms with which they were associated. Their artistic quality in itself, however, will probably be judged inferior to the best of the music, though their mechanical and acoustic virtues were on the highest level.

Most other instruments are so closely determined by their mechanical and acoustic necessities that even the Victorian taste for decorative exteriors could hardly affect them. The front pillar of the orchestral harp (then a fashionable instrument in the drawing-rooms of good society) took on an unmistakable neo-Gothic appearance, which it has never since lost. An occasional experiment was made in the outline even of the violin; but though such experiments have occurred before and since, they have never been permanently successful. A Victorian family settling down to play string quartets in its richly furnished drawing-room used instruments no different virtually from those of the classic period, or indeed of today. Yet the early nineteenth century had seen internal changes in the bass-bar of the violin, and an overall increase of tension, which somewhat changed the tone in the same direction (indeed for the same reasons) as that taken by the piano, though not to the same extent.

Such chamber-music playing was to become an increasing feature of domestic life. Neither in this period nor subsequently did it attain the range and popularity so conspicuous in nineteenth-century Germany, but it took a certain hold, and it did so in direct imitation of the German fashion. Here, as elsewhere, it is impossible not to detect and admire the influence of the Prince Consort. A genuine lover of music, and a most practical patron, Prince Albert left perhaps a clearer mark on the musical life of this country than on any other single activity.

The prominence taken by Victorian instruments of music at the Great Exhibition he did so much to further, paid a graceful tribute to his influence.

The spread of choral singing

But the most striking feature of early Victorian amateur musicianship was its enthusiasm for large-scale choral singing. The Georgian delight in glees and other part-songs diminished a little, though it by no means vanished. But the delight in great choirs grew beyond bound and reason. No glee or part-song could satisfy this mighty appetite: oratorio was its staple diet; cantata, as understood in those stalwart days, filled the gaps. The Sacred Harmonic Society of 1832 found speedy imitators. From 1840, recruits were trained in systematic classes pioneered by John Hullah and others. Hullah's 'Fixed Do' system of notation was one of the sources (for a time it attracted more attention as one of the rivals) of what

was to become a much more important system — John Curwen's famous 'Movable Do' tonic solfa system.

Although it was not immediately apparent, a movement had been launched in these developments which was to become one of the most influential in Early Victorian music, not, it is true, for the profession, but for the larger and less specialized body of those to whom music is important, and even necessary, without being a means of livelihood. When this did become apparent, a reaction followed which may seem ironical enough in the light of after events: for there were professional musicians who took genuine alarm at the prospect of thus bringing great music within the reach of so many whose understanding of it must inevitably be limited in extent, though not inevitably in depth of feeling. In fact, the consequences were certainly beneficial both to music and to the profession. There can be little doubt that it was this spread of musical enthusiasm which prepared the ground for the subsequent harvest which we are enjoying in the renaissance of English music begun by Elgar in later Victorian England. The German critic who dismissed England as 'the land without music' did not allow enough for the possibilities of new growth latent in this widening of the field under cultivation.

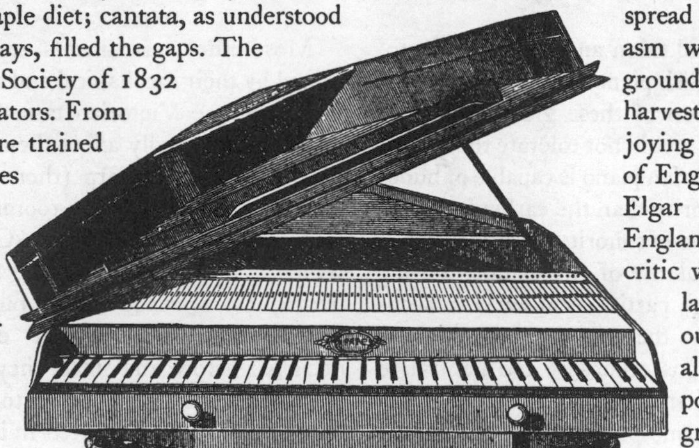

Fig. 2. A pianoforte by M.Pape of London which can also be used as a table when the top is shut down. *Art-Journal Illustrated Catalogue*, 1851

Bookbinding

HOWARD M. NIXON

By 1830 the 'extra' leather bindings produced by the 'West-end' section of the London bookbinding trade had begun to show a depressing lack of originality. For the next fifty years they tended to be beautifully tooled pastiches in the 'Grolier', 'Harleian', or 'Eve' styles – 'faultly faultless, icily regular, splendidly null'. Until his death at the age of fifty in 1836, Charles Lewis remained at the head of this branch of his profession. Francis Bedford, his foreman, carried on the business for five years for Mrs Lewis, then went into partnership with John Clarke, and finally set up on his own in 1850. He speedily succeeded to Lewis's former position and carried on his tradition of admirable technique and sad lack of invention. John Mac-Kenzie, 'bookbinder to their late Majesties, King George IVth and King William IVth', Wickwar and Hayday were other leading West End binders whose firms had a comparatively short life. Hayday produced some strikingly original bindings for J.W.K.Eyton in the 1840's. On the other hand, Robert Rivière and Joseph Zaehnsdorf (a native of Budapest) each founded a business which was to carry their name for over one hundred years. Both were capable of some originality. Pl. 93B shows a binding executed by Zaehnsdorf in the late 1850's which was ostensibly an imitation of the Oriental style, but is so far removed in both style and technique from the work of any Eastern craftsman that it may be appreciated as a new and imaginative design.

The developments that took place in commercial binding, as the publisher took over the responsibility of having his books bound, were far more interesting. The mechanization of the trade proceeded speedily, with Archibald Leighton, who had introduced book cloth in the middle of the 1820's, playing a leading part. By 1832 the problem of rapid commercial gold-blocking of book cloth had been overcome and blocking in blind was also mastered so successfully that five years later Saunders and Otley were able to commission the splendid binding shown on Pl. 93A for their illustrated editions of some of Captain Marryat's novels. Blocking was also revived on leather for such work as the 'illuminated bindings' of J.S.Evans. These were first blocked in blind, parts of the design were then coloured by hand, and finally the remainder was blocked in gold. Inferior leathers, such as skiver, generally maroon or black, were frequently used both on Bibles and prayer books and also on annuals such as *Friendship's Offering* in the 'thirties. The plates used for these skiver bindings were often very finely engraved. Some of the best are signed by De la Rue and Co. and other good examples come from the shops of Remnant & Edmonds and Westley & Clarke.

Binders such as these firms, together with Bone, Burn and the various Leightons, also did much cloth work, the most elaborate specimens of which were the table books, indispensable objects in the properly overcrowded Victorian drawing-room with their lavish gilding and colour. The printing of coloured inks on cloth was not mastered completely until after 1860, and on most of the earlier examples coloured paper onlays were ingeniously used to produce polychrome effects.

M

The decorative effect of early cloth bindings was by no means invariably the result of the lavish application of gold and colours, but was often inherent in the designs of the fabric itself. 'Watered' cloths were being produced by De la Rue at the suggestion of Archibald Leighton in 1831 and were followed by a particularly elegant series of 'ribbon-embossed' fabrics which unfortunately proved too expensive for general use. In addition, the passion for pictorial blocking in the 'forties encouraged the use of cloth with simple grainings, although about 1845 striped cloths flourished briefly and between 1851 and 1855 there was a vogue for marbled cloth.

As the distribution of novels was largely in the hands of wholesale booksellers, who supplied the circulating libraries of provincial towns and the larger country houses, and was not carried out by the publishers, cloth did not become the standard covering of novels for long after it was *de rigueur* for most other types of books. Even in the 'fifties novels were still being bound in paper-covered boards with printed paper title-labels. Another style in which many cheap novels were to be found was the 'Yellow-back' binding, developed about the middle of the century for display and sale on railway bookstalls. The essential features of the yellow back were the use of a glazed coloured paper (most frequently yellow, but sometimes pink, green, blue or grey) over thin strawboards, a pictorial design (often printed in several colours) on the upper cover, and advertisements on the lower cover (Pl. 94B).

The bindings of the period, however, which have most in common with other early Victorian applied art were neither of leather, cloth nor paper-covered boards. They cover a number of works written by H.N.Humphreys, or with illuminations by Owen Jones, all of which date from within two or three years of the Great Exhibition of 1851. Some have covers of carved wood, but several of the Humphreys books have most elaborate Gothic moulded designs usually built up in black papier mâché over a metal framework. One has six oval medallions in relief representing miracles of Christ; another has the Black Prince's arms, with titles and mottoes on a scroll, adapted from a panel on the prince's tomb at Canterbury (Pl. 94A); a third, covering *The Origin and Progress of the Art of Writing*, has a decorated Gothic T enclosing the rest of the short title. All have Gothic borders in high relief and were very clearly intended to lie on drawing-room tables rather than to jostle with other books on library shelves.

One interesting feature of the period is that quite a high percentage of the bindings are signed. Lewis, Mackenzie and the other West End binders usually used a name pallet impressed in gold or blind on the turn-ins of the leather, or in ink at the top of the fly leaf. In addition, the 'forties and 'fifties witnessed in cloth books a revival of the binder's ticket, which had been popular in leather work at the end of the eighteenth century. But whereas the earlier examples had generally been oblong and pasted on the verso of a fly-leaf at the beginning of the book, the new ones were customarily square (often printed lozenge-wise) and were pasted on to the pastedown at the end of the volume. One or two of the artists who designed the blocks also signed their work, and the initials of Luke Limner, the pseudonym of John Leighton, are frequently to be found on the best blocked work of the period.

HOUSES OF PARLIAMENT

Fig. 1. Elongated roman type, *c.* 1838.

Printing

RUARI MCLEAN

This period saw an enormous increase in Britain's population and a corresponding expansion of the printing and publishing trades. The average yearly number of new books (not including reprints and pamphlets) rose from about 850 between 1802 and 1827 to about 2,530 in 1853; [1] the sale of *The Times* rose from 6,000 copies daily in 1817 to about 65,000 copies in 1861. [2]

Among the many newspapers and magazines born during this period were *Punch* (1841), *The Illustrated London News* (1842), and *The News of the World* (1843).

It was the period of a new reading public, who devoured Dickens' and Thackeray's novels as they came out in parts, and the period of the first great popular illustrators, such as Cruikshank, 'Phiz', Leech, Tenniel and Doyle. The work of these artists was printed either by etching, lithography, or wood-engraving. The period also saw a proliferation of decorative type-faces for advertising, the displacement of leather balls for inking by composition rollers (patented by Cowper in 1818), and the commercial introduction of cloth for binding editions of books. Mechanical type-founding came in by about 1860, after much opposition from the type-founders, and by about the same time stereo plates for newspapers were in universal use; although Earl Stanhope had perfected the necessary process as early as 1802. During all these years attempts were being made to find a satisfactory method for setting up type mechanic-

ally, and for the photographic engraving of illustrations, but neither process was perfected till well after 1860.

During the whole of the nineteenth century the energies of nearly every progressive printer were directed to speeding and cheapening production, so that fine printing became increasingly rare; but our period includes the career of William Pickering, perhaps the first publisher to base a publishing policy consciously on design.

William Pickering

Pickering, said to have been the illegitimate son of 'a book-loving earl and a lady of title', was born in 1796, and started business as a bookseller in 1820. In the same year he began publishing, by launching a series of 'Diamond Classics', beginning with the works of Horace. Being set in 'diamond' type (equivalent to $4\frac{1}{2}$ point), they could not be read except with a magnifying glass; but the series was evidently successful, for it was continued and eventually included Shakespeare (1825), Milton (1828), and Homer (1831). The early titles were all printed by Corrall, of Charing Cross, but later titles were printed by other printers and were not all in diamond type. This series also made publishing history because it included the first books sold in cloth bindings. It is not certain which title was the first; but it is certain that the young Pickering was dissatisfied with paper boards, which were then the only alternative to morocco, and asked his binder to suggest 'some neater mode' (Pickering's own words): the binder showed him some music

[1] Marjorie Plant, *The English Book-Trade*, 1939.
[2] *The History of The Times*, vols. 1 & 2, 1935–9.

bound in light blue glazed calico which had been bought to line curtains; and some time, perhaps early in 1825, this revolutionary binding material was used for 500 copies of one of the 'Diamond Classics'.[3] By 1830 the idea had been widely adopted by other publishers. The description 'extra boards' in contemporary publishers' advertisements almost certainly meant 'cloth'.

After the 'Diamond Classics', Pickering published books in more normal formats, at the same time continuing to maintain a large antiquarian bookselling business. Most, but not all, of the books he published before 1830 were printed by Thomas White, whose work for Pickering is his chief claim to fame. In 1825 began the 'Oxford English Classics', a series published by Pickering in association with Talboys and Wheeler of Oxford, and printed at Oxford, but showing clearly Pickering's influence on the design. The whole series, which included Smollett's *History* and Gibbon's *Decline and Fall*, consisted of forty-four volumes, and fifty or seventy-five copies of each work were printed on large paper.

In 1825 came the first example of Pickering's well-known wreath ornament on a title-page, which became one of his characteristic and most charming styles, though not used for more than about thirteen books. It was not until 1828 that he first used the dolphin-and-anchor device of Aldus, the great Venetian sixteenth-century printer, combined with the motto 'Aldi Discipulus Anglus'. This was cut in various forms and became Pickering's most famous title-page device; it underlined his chief aim as a publisher, which was, like Aldus, to produce the classics in cheap and handy formats.

In 1828 he met Charles Whittingham, the printer and nephew of the founder of the Chiswick Press. A friendship began which lasted till Pickering's death in 1854. Whittingham the younger – born in 1795, the year before Pickering – had just separated from his uncle and set up on his own in Took's Court, Chancery Lane. The first book he printed for Pickering appears to have been *The Carcanet*, an anthology selected by Sir Nicolas Harris Nicolas (the editor of Nelson's Letters), dated 1828. From 1830 onwards nearly all Pickering's books were printed by Whittingham. The nephew, like his uncle, was a fine printer, but his typographic style before he met Pickering was undistinguished.

In 1830 Pickering began his 'Aldine Edition of the British Poets', a series of small volumes (6½ in. × 4 in.) which set a completely new standard in British book design, and which are still most agreeable books in which to read the included authors. The first poet was Burns (Pl. 95 A): the simplicity of the title-page was in contrast to the normal style of the time, which still tended to overburden title-pages with lengthy sentences. The series ran to over fifty volumes, all printed by Charles Whittingham the younger, and selling at 5s. each in cloth or 10s. 6d. in morocco. The cloth bindings were dark blue, with a paper label on the spine.

Pickering's friendship with Whittingham brought him into contact with Mary Byfield, the Chiswick Press wood-engraver, and it is probable that most of the decorations in Pickering's books after 1830 were cut by her. Elaborate frames and cartouches were designed for the title-pages of the works of George Herbert, Thomas Fuller, Francis Bacon, Jeremy Taylor and others (Pls. 95 B, 96 A, B), in a style of intelligent archaism.

Perhaps the most important books Pickering ever published were his series of liturgical histories and reprints of the Prayer Book. The first was William Maskell's *The Ancient Liturgy of the Church of England*, 1844. Seven further works of Maskell's were published by Pickering, of which the most important was *Monumenta Ritualia* (1846–7), 'the scientific value of which was confirmed nearly forty years later in 1882, when it was reprinted at the Clarendon Press. From Maskell ... English liturgical scholarship has gone from strength to strength.'[4] The reprints of the Prayer Book consisted of six magnificent folio volumes printed in black-letter, rubricated and

---

[3] John Carter, *Binding Variants in English Publishing 1820–1900*, 1932.

[4] S. Morison, *English Prayer Books* (3rd edition), 1949.

bound in vellum. Another fine piece of printing was Keeling's *Liturgiae Britannicae*, 1842, with complicated comparative settings and rubrication throughout. From a visual point of view, perhaps the most attractive book of all was the edition, in 1853, of Queen Elizabeth's Prayer Book of 1569. It was Mary Byfield's as well as Whittingham's and Pickering's masterpiece, for every page was ornamented with her wood-blocks. She cut over one hundred, based on those in the original edition, themselves based on designs of Holbein, Dürer, Tory and others. The blocks were designed in the style of the marginal borders of the old manuscript Books of Hours, and were in strip form. They could then be used again and again in different combinations, so that no two pages were identical.

Many of the designs for the decorative blocks cut by Mary Byfield were drawn by Whittingham's daughters Elizabeth and Charlotte. The Chiswick Press, which exists today, although no longer at Chiswick, still possesses, and shows in its specimen books, many of Mary Byfield's woodcut decorations and initial letters.

Pickering, it is sad to relate, died in bankruptcy, having backed a friend's venture which ended in failure. He was buried in the Whittingham family ground at Kensal Green Cemetery. His work, in his lifetime, was appreciated by the discriminating few, and then forgotten. Interest in him was not revived until the publication of Sir Geoffrey Keynes' admirable monograph, *William Pickering, Publisher*, in 1924.

Charles Whittingham the younger

Charles Whittingham, his printer friend and collaborator, was the finest printer in Britain and probably in Europe during the whole period. Whittingham became a partner with his uncle (also called Charles Whittingham) in the Chiswick Press in 1824, but set up on his own in 1828, and did not return to the Chiswick Press until, on his uncle's health failing in 1838, he resumed control of it. In 1840 his uncle died. Like his uncle, the nephew specialized in the printing of wood-engravings, and never installed presses for copper-plate printing or lithography. It is interesting to note that hand-presses only were used at the Chiswick Press until 1860, although the rotary steam press had been in use (for newspapers) since 1814, and for books since at least 1837.[5]

In 1833 Whittingham printed and Pickering published *Illuminated Ornaments selected from Manuscripts and early printed Books*, by Henry Shaw, F.S.A., which contained forty-nine colour plates of medieval lettering. These were drawn by Shaw in facsimile, printed from etched plates, and hand-coloured. The effect was superb, but such lavish use of colour could clearly not be economic. After producing one or two other books with a few coloured plates, Shaw issued in 1843 *Dresses and Decorations of the Middle Ages*, also printed (the letterpress pages only) by Whittingham and published by Pickering. This work in two volumes is illustrated on every page, nearly always in colour, either from hand-coloured etchings or wood-blocks printed in colour: the monochrome illustrations are wood-engravings probably by Mary Byfield. The effect is extremely rich and the work as a whole is one of the highlights of mid-Victorian book design and production. In *Alphabets Numerals and Devices of the Middle Ages*, which followed in 1845, and in *The Decorative Arts Ecclesiastical and Civil of the Middle Ages* (1851) Shaw introduced some colour-printing by lithography, as well as hand-colouring and printing in colour from wood blocks.

Shaw financed his own publications, and they were not, according to Warren (in *The Charles Whittinghams, Printers*), financially successful; but they represent a notable achievement in craftsmanship. Technically, their greatest interest lies in the use of colour-printing from wood blocks. This method, which dates back to the very earliest days of printing, had been demonstrated in 1822 by William Savage in his *Practical Hints on Decorative Printing*, in which one illustration was printed in thirty colours from twenty-nine blocks; in several others Savage successfully imitated hand-coloured aquatints or etchings with between three and ten printings from wood.

[5] Cf. J. Southwood, *Progress in Printing and the Graphic Arts during the Victorian Era*, 1897.

Henry Cole, one of the prime movers in the Great Exhibition, used Whittingham's skill in colour-printing from wood-blocks for his 'Felix Summerly' series of children's books, which from 1841 onwards were the most elegant and charming books of this kind that had yet appeared.

Whittingham's leading position in the printing trade was marked by his appointment as secretary of the jury in the section of printing and allied trades in the Great Exhibition of 1851. He died in 1876.

The Colour-printing of Edmund Evans

Colour-printing from wood-blocks at the Chiswick Press has been mentioned above. The development of this art is chiefly associated with the firm of Edmund Evans, and although his greatest artistic triumphs were the illustrations of Kate Greenaway, Doyle and Caldecott after 1860, his early work requires mention here.

Edmund Evans (1826–1905) was a wood-engraver who had been apprenticed to Ebenezer Landells, himself a pupil of Bewick and the chief originator of *Punch*. Evans set up on his own in 1847 and subsequently cut colour blocks for various Birket Foster illustrations. In 1853, after cutting pictorial colour blocks to be printed on the wrappers of Mayhew's *Letters Left at the Pastry Cook's* (itself a novelty), 'Evans had the [as it transpired] sensational idea of using yellow glazed paper and of mounting it on board. It is therefore certain that Evans was the first man to see the possibilities of coloured pictorial printing on coloured paper, and that to him more than to anyone else was due the establishment of the yellow-back in popular favour.'[6]

Yellow-backs, which became a tremendous industry and were a revolutionary new idea in publishing, were essentially books bound in printed paper-covered boards and sold at 2s., as against the 5s. or 6s. of the current and till then highly successful cloth-bound Standard Novels of Bentley, Colburn and Blackwood. The first series was the Parlour Library of Simms and McIntyre, which

began in 1847: it was followed by numerous imitators, of which the first and perhaps the most successful was Routledge's *Railway Library*, from 1849 onwards. In their heyday, during the 'fifties and 'sixties, yellow-backs were, as Sir Michael Sadleir points out in his essay quoted above, well-edited, well-printed, and adventurously and attractively designed. According to the same authority, 80 per cent of the yellow-back covers produced between 1855 and 1865 were the work of the firm of Edmund Evans: his early ones were signed in one of the bottom margins.

Pictorial yellow-back covers, from which the modern book-jacket is directly descended, were themselves anticipated by the cover designs of novels issued in parts, although these were not printed in colour. The publication of books in monthly parts was not a new idea in the nineteenth century, but it was not applied to fiction until the success of *Pickwick Papers* in 1836 pointed the way;[7] after that most of the major novels of Dickens, Thackeray, Marryat, Surtees, Trollope and many others were so issued. The parts were nearly always illustrated with etched plates and the covers (usually green, grey, red, blue or yellow cartridge paper) carried a pictorial design printed in black from a wood-block. Sometimes these designs were retained for the title-page of the book when it was later issued in bound form. Notable designs in this manner were made by George Cruikshank and 'Phiz'.

Another aspect of the same design problem was magazine covers, and indeed several magazines, such as *Bentley's Miscellany* and *Ainsworth's Magazine*, existed to publish novels in monthly parts. An example is provided by *Punch*, which started in 1841 with a cover designed by A.S.Henning and had four more covers until Richard Doyle, with his second attempt, produced in 1849 the famous design which survived so long. Doyle

---

[6] Michael Sadleir, 'Yellow-backs', in *New Paths in Book Collecting*, 1934.

[7] '*Pickwick* started slowly, sales of the first number (probably 1000) being so discouraging that only 500 of the second were printed. With the appearance of Sam Weller, popularity began and increased by leaps and bounds, so that first printings of the later parts ran well into five figures.' John Carter, *Victorian Fiction*, N.B.L. Catalogue, 1947.

FRANCE &

MUSIC

HUMBER

BRIGHTON

MARGATE

THE CONCERT

ROSE

Fig. 2. Early Victorian decorative type faces. All (except 'France &') are in *The Specimen Book of Types Cast at the Austin Foundry by Wood & Sharwoods, c. 1838*, but may have been cut earlier.

(1824–83) was an illustrator with a genuine, if highly individual, feeling for lettering, and in his title-pages for Ruskin's *The King of the Golden River*, 1851, and *The Scouring of the White Horse*, 1859 (and in his *Punch* cover), the lettering is completely, hauntingly, integrated with the illustrations.

Chromo-lithography

While experiments in colour-printing from wood-blocks were being made at the Chiswick Press in the 'forties, experiments were also being made by other printers in colour-printing by lithography. These soon led to success and to an immense new branch of the printing trade: many, if not most, colour posters today are still printed virtually by the same process.

Lithography had been discovered by the German, Senefelder, in 1798, and was soon introduced into England, but for some years its artistic potentialities were not understood, and it was despised as an inferior substitute for etching. The person who did most to pioneer and popularize lithography in Britain was Charles Joseph Hullmandel (1789–1850), an artist of German parentage born in London. He made several important technical innovations leading up to 'chromalithography', as it was then called, whereby the effect of a painting in oils, or water-colour, could be achieved by the superimposed printing of a number of lithographic plates. *Sketches at Home and Abroad*, by J.D.Harding, printed by Hullmandel and published in 1836 by Tilt, was one of the earliest books of tinted lithographs, with one tint only: Thomas Shotter Boys' *Picturesque Architecture in Paris Ghent Antwerp Rouen*, also printed by Hullmandel, and published by Boys in 1839, had four tints, and was perhaps the earliest masterpiece of colour lithography. *Original Views of London as it is*, 1842, also by Boys and printed by Hullmandel, was another early lithographic masterpiece in two colours, and an important record of London for this period.

Some magnificent colour-printing by lithography was also designed by the architect Owen Jones, who was responsible for the painting and interior decoration of the Crystal Palace in 1851.

Whereas Hullmandel and Boys were chiefly concerned to reproduce representational paintings, Jones used large numbers of flat colours usually in juxtaposition. Among his most interesting works are *Plans, Elevations, Sections and Details of the Alhambra*, 1841–5, *The Book of Common Prayer*, 1845, *The Illuminated Books of the Middle Ages*, 1849, and *The Grammar of Ornament*, 1856. They are triumphs of elaborate chromo-lithographic printing, but they do not make as pleasant books as Henry Shaw's collaborations with Whittingham and Pickering; and they certainly fathered much of the most tasteless decorative printing that followed.

Mention must also be made of the books designed and illustrated by Henry Noel Humphreys. *A Record of the Black Prince*, 1849, is an exquisite small book, printed by Vizetelly in black letter and illustrated with both wood-cuts and chromo-lithography. Another very pretty book of his is *The Gold, Silver, and Copper Coins of England etc*, 1846; with wood-cut borders and initials, and plates chromo-lithographed in gold, silver, copper and royal blue.

Baxter and Kronheim

George Baxter, whose first colour prints were made in 1834, did not use lithography, but 'used an engraved metal plate, usually aquatint, as a key-plate for the subsequent wood-engraved colour impressions'.[8]

J.M.Kronheim, a German who came to London in 1846, became a prolific colour-printer who used wood-blocks for the key and printed the colours from metal plates.

The primacy in cheap commercial colour lithography passed later in the century to Germany, with the result that the colour pages of many British books and magazines were imported from that country.

Type faces

During the Regency period the English typefounders had already invented fat faces, sans-serif

[8] See Michael Oliver's notes in J.R.Abbey's *Travel in Aquatint and Lithography*, 1956.

(sometimes confusingly called 'Egyptian', 'grotesque' or 'Doric'), 'Egyptian' (i.e. slab-serif, also known as 'Antique' or 'Ionic') and shadowed letters, both in roman and black-letter. The so-called 'Tuscan' had also already appeared, whose body and extremities were bifurcated and curled, forming types of great jollity which had their most appropriate use in circus and theatre printing, although they were by no means confined to that.

The way in which the types produced during the 'thirties, 'forties and 'fifties reflect the intellectual and spiritual moods of the period have been acutely described by Nicolette Gray in her *Nineteenth-Century Ornamental Types and Title-pages*, 1938. She traces a sudden change from Regency joviality to Victorian social conscience: a change also reflected in the difference between Dickens' first novel, *Pickwick Papers*, 1836, full of drinking and kissing, and his next book, *Oliver Twist*, 1837, devoted to reform of the Poor Laws. In the elongated romans (Fig. 1) which came in about 1838, Mrs Gray finds a face which has 'caught the symbolism of the Gothic spire'; and she points out that the sans-serif, although invented earlier, was in 1847 first produced in a normal form and was 'the letter *par excellence*, of the 'fifties' – the typographic counterpart of the architecture of the railways and the Crystal Palace.

Besides the types already mentioned, an increasing number of new decorated faces was being produced during the whole period, including outline letters, letters set on decorated backgrounds, and 'perspective' letters. These types were used in jobbing and commercial printing, not in books, except for labels and covers of part-issues.

The more startling aberrations of Victorian ingenuity in both type and book design fall, happily, outside our period.

A Select List of Contemporary Publications Mentioned

Index

Page numbers in italics indicate illustrations